B A S I C
P S Y C H O L O G Y

FOURTH EDITION

BASIC PSYCHOLOGY

FOURTH EDITION

HENRY GLEITMAN

W . W . NORTON & COMPANY . NEW YORK . LONDON

Printed in the United States of America

The text of this book is composed in Bembo, with the display set in Machine
Composition by TSI Graphics
Manufacturing by R. R. Donnelly
Book design by Antonina Krass
Cover illustration: *Tête blanch et rose* (*Pink and White Head*), 1914, by Henri Matisse, © 1995
Succession H. Matisse/Artists Rights Society (ARS), NY. Courtesy of the Musée National d'Art
Moderne, Paris; photograph by Phillipe Migeat, © Centre George Pompidou,

Library of Congress Cataloging-in-Publication Data

Gleitman, Henry.
Basic psychology / Henry Gleitman.—4th ed.
p. cm.
Includes bibliographical references and index.
1. Psychology. I. Title.
BF121.G57 1995
150—dc20 95-9311

ISBN 0-393-96916-9 (pbk.)

W. W. Norton & Company, Inc., 500 Fifth Avenue, New York, N.Y. 10110
W. W. Norton & Company Ltd., 10 Coptic Street, London WC1A 1PU

2 3 4 5 6 7 8 9 0

To Ellen and Zachary, Claire, David, and Philip

THE CONTENTS IN BRIEF

CONTENTS

PART TWO | COGNITION 121

PART FOUR | DEVELOPMENT 383

CHAPTER **13** | PHYSICAL AND COGNI-
TIVE DEVELOPMENT   385

PART FIVE | INDIVIDUAL DIFFERENCES 455

P R E F A C E

This is the fourth edition of my book *Basic Psychology.* One reason for this revision is the obvious fact that, like any other discipline, psychology advances and develops. When I began my graduate work fifty years ago, psychologists tended to be rather defensive about the status of the field and were perhaps a bit too loud in proclaiming that "Psychology is a science!" But by now there is no need for such defensive proclamations, for that assertion has become a simple statement of fact. In the last half a century psychology has assuredly become a "real" and vigorously progressive science.

As a field advances, so must all attempts to describe it. These advances, together with the suggestions by the many students and colleagues who have used this text, prompted a number of changes that I describe below.

THE OVERALL AIM: COHESION IN A DIVERSE FIELD

Before describing these changes, let me briefly review what has not changed: my original aims. In writing *Basic Psychology,* I sought to present the field in all its diversity while yet conveying the sense in which it is a coherent intellectual enterprise. In pursuit of this goal, I did the following:

1. To present the different sub-areas of psychology, I organized the book around five main questions: How do humans (and where relevant, animals) act, how do they know, how do they interact, how do they develop, and how do they differ from each other?

2. To provide some intellectual cohesion, I considered each topic against the backdrop of one or two major ideas that could serve as an organizing and unifying framework. Thus the chapter on the biological bases of behavior opens with Descartes' conception of the organism as a machine and the next chapter treats various aspects of motivated behavior as manifestations of negative feedback. To relate the material across chapters, I used several overarching themes. For example, the various chapters that deal with cognition ("Sensory Processes," "Perception," "Memory," "Thought and Knowledge," and "Language") all consider variations on the two controversies of nature versus nurture and psychological atomism versus organization.

3. In many cases, the attempt at integration required taking a step backward to look at psychology's intellectual history, for a number of the field's endeavors are hard to explain unless one points to the paths that led up to them. Why did Thorndike study cats in puzzle boxes? Why did his conclusions have such an important effect on American psychology? Why were they challenged by Köhler and Tolman? It still pays to take a serious look at the work of such pioneers before turning to the present. Much as a river's water is clearer when it is taken from its source, so issues that have become more and more complex as detail has been piled upon detail become plainer and more evident when traced back to their origin.

GENERAL ORGANIZATION

Several organizational changes distinguish this edition from the previous ones. One concerns the discussions of Freud, psychoanalysis, and current dynamic approaches to personality, which are now brought together. Toward this end I eliminated the separate chapter on psychoanalysis and dealt with that material within the general two-chapter discussion of personality (specifically, in Chapter 17). Another is a revision of the old chapter on thinking. This is now entitled "Thought and Knowledge" and deals with both the knowledge base of thought (that is, generic and semantic memory, which were formerly discussed in the chapter on memory) as well as the processes of thinking (that is, problem solving, reasoning, and decision making). As a result, the chapter on memory is primarily devoted to episodic memory. Further changes represent updatings (in some cases, major updatings) of the subject matter, which are best described within an outline of the overall structure of the book.

Another significant change is the addition of Focus Questions throughout and Questions for Critical Thinking at the ends of chapters. The Focus Questions have been added to help guide the students' reading, enabling them to attend more readily to the chapters' key points. The Questions for Critical Thinking have been added to help readers pull together the sometimes wide-ranging material covered within chapters. Both should help students think more clearly and more deeply about what they've read.

After an introductory chapter, the book is divided into five parts that reflect the perspectives from which most psychological phenomena can be regarded: Action, Cognition, Social Behavior, Development, and Individual Differences. In brief outline, they cover the following topics:

PART I: ACTION

This part focuses on overt behavior and its physiological basis. It begins by considering the biological underpinnings of human and animal action, leading to a discussion of the nervous system and its operation (Chapter 2) and some phenomena of motivation (Chapter 3). It then asks how organisms can modify their behavior to adapt to new circumstances, a topic that leads to a discussion of classical and instrumental conditioning, modern behavior theory, and more recent approaches that take a more cognitive slant (Chapter 4).

In Chapter 2 ("Biological Bases of Behavior") the discussion of cerebral structures is revised, with demonstrations of hierarchical organization integrated into the description of cerebral anatomy and a greater emphasis on evolutionary issues. Chapter 3 ("Motivation") uses the concept of potentiation as an overall organizational principle. It also includes a section on pain and endorphins, topics that were formerly dealt with mostly in Chapter 2. Chapter 4 ("Learning") stresses recent developments in animal learning, including work on contingency and modern cognitive approaches to classical and instrumental conditioning. It also explores the adaptive evolutionary perspective, as in a discussion of similarities and differences in the ways various animals learn.

PART II: COGNITION

This part deals with knowledge and how it is gained and used. It begins by asking how the senses provide us with information about the world outside (Chapter 5) and how this information is organized and interpreted to lead to the perception of objects and events (Chapter 6). Further questions concern the way this knowledge is stored in memory and retrieved when needed (Chapter 7), the way it is organized through thinking (Chapter 8), and the way knowledge is communicated to others through the medium of language (Chapter 9).

Many of the changes in this part reflect a greater concern with recent information-processing approaches and a greater stress on evolutionary adaptiveness. Chapter 5 ("Sensory Processes") contains a discussion of evolution and sensory equipment, as well as a new section on feature detectors (a topic formerly dealt with in Chapter 6). In Chapter 6 ("Perception"), the organization has been changed to give more prominence to modern approaches to pattern recognition. Chapter 7 ("Memory") focuses primarily on episodic memory, including the modern emphasis on encoding and retrieval, the role of schemas in memory, the issue of false memories, and the difference between explicit and implicit memory. Chapter 8 ("Thought and Knowledge") begins with the database on which thinking rests, including topics that were formerly dealt with in the previous chapter: analogical representations and symbolic or digital representations.

PART III: SOCIAL BEHAVIOR

This part concerns our interactions with others. It begins with a discussion of built-in social tendencies in humans and animals, a topic to which ethology and evolutionary theory have made major contributions (Chapter 10). It then turns to modern social psychology, considering how people try to understand the social situation in which they find themselves, how they interpret their own internal states and emotions, and how they interact with others (Chapters 11 and 12).

There have been several changes in this section. In Chapter 10 ("The Biological Basis of Social Behavior") the treatment of social cognition in primates has been expanded and now includes a discussion of whether monkeys and apes have a "theory of mind." The section on human mating patterns has also been revised. Chapter 11 ("Social Cognition and Emotion") continues to focus on the way individuals interpret social events, including discussions of attitudes, attribution, impressions of others, the interpretation of one's own internal states, and emotions and facial expression. Chapter 12 ("Social Interaction") continues to treat of the way individuals deal with others. In addition to discussions of social exchange, attraction and love, conformity, obedience, and crowd behavior, it has one new section on leadership and another on social dilemmas.

PART IV: DEVELOPMENT

■ This section contains two chapters on development. Chapter 13 ("Physical and Cognitive Development") continues to focus on recent, post-Piagetian approaches to mental growth and includes material on social cognition in infants and preschoolers, including studies of false beliefs and their bearing on the child's development of a "theory of mind." Chapter 14 ("Social Development") has been updated with expanded discussions of such topics as moral development, empathy, sex, and gender. Among topics treated in this chapter is the role of cultural factors in moral reasoning and recent discoveries about the physiological and genetic bases of homosexuality.

PART V: INDIVIDUAL DIFFERENCES

■ This part begins with a chapter on mental testing in general and intelligence testing in particular (Chapter 15), and then follows with two chapters on personality assessment and theory (Chapters 16 and 17). It continues by looking at several varieties of psychopathology and asking how they arise (Chapter 18), and concludes by examining various methods of treatment and therapy (Chapter 19).

Chapter 15 ("Intelligence") is updated in various ways, including the consideration of intelligence in a social and cultural context. As already noted, the two chapters on personality have been reorganized to include both early and more recent psychoanalytic conceptions, thus incorporating material that was formerly presented in a separate chapter on Freud and psychoanalysis. Chapter 16 ("Personality I") considers methods of personality assessment and discusses trait theory and behavioral-cognitive theory as two of five theoretical approaches to personality, with particular attention to the trait-situation controversy and to recent attempts to look for biological and genetic bases of personality differences. Chapter 17 ("Personality II") takes up three other theoretical approaches to personality—the psychodynamic, humanistic, and sociocultural. It includes a full treatment of psychoanalytic formulations, beginning with Freud's original theories and concluding with a discussion of early and later critiques. A completely new section describes some recent attempts to put the study of personality in a social and cultural context.

Both Chapter 18 ("Psychopathology") and Chapter 19 ("Treatment of Psychopathology") have been drastically updated to include modern developments, such as new pharmacological approaches to treatment and new approaches to the evaluation of treatment outcome.

THE READER AND THE BOOK

It is sometimes said that students in the introductory course want to learn about things that are relevant to themselves and to their own lives. But why should this be a problem? When you come right down to it, there is something odd about the idea that psychology is not relevant to anyone's particular life history—specialist and nonspecialist alike. Psychology deals with the nature of human experience and behavior, about the hows and whys of what we do, think, and feel. Everyone has perceived, learned, remembered, and forgotten, has been angry and afraid and in love, has given in to group pressure and stood up to it. In short, everyone has experienced most of the phenomena that psychology tries to explain. This being so, psychology cannot fail to be relevant.

I've tried to point out this relevance by a liberal use of examples from ordinary experience and a frequent resort to metaphors of one kind or another, in the hope that in so doing I would show the direct relation of many psychological phenomena to the reader's own life. In these attempts, the most important guide has been my own experience as a classroom teacher. There is little doubt that one of the best ways of learning something is to teach it, for in trying to explain something to others, you first have to clarify it for yourself. This holds for the subject matter of every course I have ever taught, but most especially for the introductory course. Students in an advanced course will come at you with tough and searching questions; they want to know about the evidence that bears on a theory of, say, color vision or language acquisition and about how that evidence was obtained. But students in an introductory course ask the toughest questions of all. They ask why anyone would ever want to know about color vision (or language acquisition or whatever) in the first place. And they also ask what any one topic has to do with any other. They ask such questions because they—unlike advanced students—have not as yet accepted the premises of the field. They wonder whether the emperor is really wearing any clothes. As a result, they make me ask myself afresh what the field of psychology is all about—what the emperor's clothes are really like when you look at them closely.

This book, as well as its predecessors, grew out of my attempts to answer such questions over the years in which I have taught the introductory course, to answer them not only to satisfy the students but also to satisfy myself.

SUPPLEMENTARY MATERIALS

To help serve the needs of students, instructors, and teaching assistants, several supplementary materials are available with this text.

1. For the student:

There is a complete study guide for students, prepared by two of my colleagues and collaborators, John Jonides of the University of Michigan and Paul Rozin of the University of Pennsylvania. This study guide, a revised version of the guide the same authors wrote for the four previous editions of *Psychology,* should prove very useful to students who want some help and guidance in mastering the material in the text. Moreover, for every chapter, it provides experiments and observational studies that students can carry out on their own to get some first-hand experience with psychology's subject matter.

2. For the instructor:

There is an instructor's resource manual, prepared by Kimberly Cassidy of Bryn Mawr College, Christine Massey of Swarthmore College, Hilary Schmidt of New Jersey Medical School, and myself, which offers specific suggestions for every textbook chapter, including discussion topics, a bibliography, an annotated film and media guide, and classroom demonstrations. Included in the demonstrations are materials necessary to perform some twenty-five in-class experiments covering a range of phenomena, from the speed of the nervous impulse, through the Stroop effect, to a demonstration of gender stereotypes. Transparencies, student worksheets, data summaries, and detailed instructions for the teacher are also included. These demonstrations are adapted from those that I and my collaborators, Paul Rozin and Lila Gleitman (both of the University of Pennsylvania), have used in our own teaching.

Paul Cornwell of Pennsylvania State University, Richard Day of McMaster University, and John Jonides of the University of Michigan, with the help of Tibor Palfai of Syracuse University, have prepared a test-item file, which includes questions for all chapters plus the statistical appendix. A proportion of these questions have been statistically analyzed at Syracuse and Pennsylvania State Universities; the resulting data are included in the printed test-item file. Of course, this test-item file is also available on diskette in MS-DOS and Macintosh formats.

ACKNOWLEDGMENTS

There remains the pleasant task of thanking the many friends and colleagues who helped so greatly in the various phases of writing this book and its predecessors. Some read parts of the manuscript and gave valuable advice and criticism. Others talked to me at length about various issues in the field, which I then saw more clearly. I am very grateful to them all. These many helpers, and the main areas in which they advised me, are as follows:

BIOLOGICAL FOUNDATIONS

Elizabeth Adkins-Regan, Cornell University; Dorothy Cheney, University of Pennsylvania; Steven Fluharty, University of Pennsylvania; Charles R. Gallistel, University of California, Los Angeles; Douglas G. Mook, University of Virginia; Thomas Parisi, St. Mary's College; Paul Rozin, University of Pennsylvania; Jonathan I. Schull, University of Rochester and Swarthmore College; Robert Seyfarth, University of Pennsylvania; Peter Shizgall, Concordia University; Edward M. Stricker, University of Pittsburgh.

LEARNING

Ruth Colwill, Brown University; Paula Durlach, McMaster University; Werner Honig, Dalhousie University; Robert Rescorla, University of Pennsylvania; Jonathan I. Schull, University of Rochester and Swarthmore College.

SENSATION AND PERCEPTION

Linda Bartoshuk, Yale University; Leo M. Hurvich, University of Pennsylvania; Dorothea Jameson, University of Pennsylvania; R. Duncan Luce, University of California, Irvine; Ricardo Morant, Brandeis University; Jacob Nachmias, University of Pennsylvania; Brian Wandell, Stanford University; Jeremy M. Wolfe, Massachussetts Institute of Technology.

COGNITION

Robert G. Crowder, Yale University; Linda Gerard, Michigan State University; Lila R. Gleitman, University of Pennsylvania; Douglas Hintzman, University of Oregon; John Jonides, University of Michigan; Michael

McCloskey, Johns Hopkins University; Douglas Medin, University of Illinois; Morris Moscovitch, University of Toronto; Daniel Reisberg, Reed College.

LANGUAGE

Barbara Landau, Columbia University; Anne Lederer, University of Pennsylvania; Elissa Newport, University of Rochester; Ruth Ostrin, Medical Research Council, Cambridge, England; Ted Suppala, University of Rochester.

SOCIAL PSYCHOLOGY

Phoebe C. Ellsworth, University of Michigan; Alan Fridlund, University of California, Santa Barbara; Clark R. McCauley, Jr., Bryn Mawr College; Dennis Regan, Cornell University; John Sabini, University of Pennsylvania; R. Lance Shotland, Pennsylvania State University.

DEVELOPMENT

Renée Baillargeon, University of Illinois; Adele Diamond, University of Pennsylvania; Susan Scanlon Jones, Indiana University; Ed Kako, University of Pennsylvania; Philip J. Kellman, Swarthmore College; Susan McFadden, University of Wisconsin, Oshkosh; Robert Schoenberg, University of Pennsylvania; Elizabeth Spelke, Cornell University.

INTELLIGENCE

Jonathan Baron, University of Pennsylvania.

PERSONALITY

Hal Bertilson, Saint Joseph's University; Nathan Brody, Wesleyan University; Peter Gay, Yale University; Lewis R. Goldberg, University of Oregon, Eugene.

PSYCHOPATHOLOGY

Lyn Y. Abramson, University of Wisconsin; Jeanne Albright, Loyola University; Lauren Alloy, Temple University; Sue Mineka, Northwestern University; Rena Repetti, New York University; Ingrid I. Waldron, University of Pennsylvania; Lisa Zorilla, University of Pennsylvania.

GENERAL ADVICE ON TOPIC COVERAGE

Thomas Critchfield, Illinois State University; Mark Fineman, Southern Connecticut State University; Murray Goddard, University of New Brunswick, St. John; Robert Stern, Pennsylvania State University; Toni Strand,

Ohio State University; David Thomas, Oklahoma State University; Lori Van Wallandael, University of North Carolina, Charlotte.

To state in detail how each of these people helped me is impossible. But I do want to express special thanks to a few whose comments helped me to see whole topics in a new light for this edition. I owe special thanks to Charles R. Gallistel of the University of California at Los Angeles, for enormously helpful comments on the entire book, especially the sensory and physiological chapters; to Doug Mook of the University of Virginia, who continued to give wise counsel on problems in the field of motivation; to Jeremy Wolfe of the Massachusetts Institute of Technology, who helped me to understand some important modern developments in the fields of sensation and perception; to Douglas L. Hintzman of the University of Oregon, whose sharp and incisive critique of my old chapter on memory forced me to see that entire area in a new light; to Ed Kako, who gave me some important insights into the nature of sexual orientation; and to Lisa Zorilla, who made me aware of some recent changes in the understanding of the biological basis of schizophrenia.

Yet another kind of thanks goes to Neil Macmillan, who wrote "Statistics: The Collection, Organization, and Interpretation of Data," an appendix for *Basic Psychology,* with a fine sense of balance between the demands of the subject matter and the demands of expositional clarity.

Three persons contributed in a special way: Alan Fridlund, Daniel Reisberg, and Paul Rozin. All three are distinguished scientists as well as dedicated teachers with considerable experience in the introductory course. They served as an editorial advisory group, counseling me on all aspects of this edition and sharing their knowledge of the subject matter as well as their experience in communicating it to beginning students. Alan Fridlund was particularly helpful in the areas of social processes, the emotions, and psychopathology. He also deserves warm thanks for writing all of the Focus Questions and Questions for Critical Thinking. Daniel Reisberg provided sharp criticisms and new perspectives, especially in the area of cognition. And as always, my old friend Paul Rozin helped me see many facets of the field in a new way, especially those that involve issues of evolutionary and cultural development.

In thanking all of these many people I take particular pleasure from the fact that a good number of them were once undergraduate or graduate students of mine. I find something reassuring in the reflection that those I once taught are now teaching me, though it's almost certain that I have learned much more from them than they ever learned from me.

To one person I owe a special debt: my wife, friend, and collaborator, Lila R. Gleitman. She not only wrote Chapter 9, "Language"; she also read virtually all chapters of this manuscript and did what she always does to the things I do and think and write about—she makes them better. Much better. I can't thank her enough.

Several people helped on this edition in still other ways. One is my secretary, Janet White, who helped to track down innumerable papers, references, illustrations, and God knows what else, and made sure that I hardly lost any of them. Further thanks go to many people at W. W. Norton: To Roy Tedoff, who managed the production of the book with his usual aplomb; to Antonina Krass, whose brilliance as a book designer continues to astound me; to Maura Conron and John McAusland, who executed some fine new drawings and illustrations; to Kate Brewster, who conducted the photo and art research; to Ruth Mandel, who gave so generously of her time in so many useful and pleasant discussions; to Roberta Flechner, for her remarkable efforts in arranging the layouts; and to Dan Saffer and Adam Dunn, who helped in many phases of the editorial aspects of the book, as they all worked together to fit the many pieces of the puzzle into a seamless whole.

I am especially indebted to two highly competent and indefatigable Norton editors. One is Cathy Wick, who provided invaluable advice, continual encouragement, and occasional psychotherapy, and whose personal contact with many psychology instructors throughout the country was of enormous benefit. The other is Jane Carter, who served as manuscript editor, a person of excellent taste and judgment, who combines the skills of a first-rate organizer with those of a fine literary critic. Authors need reinforcement no less (and probably more) than do rats and pigeons. Both Cathy and Jane provided it, making me feel they appreciated both me and what I tried to do. I hope they know how very much I appreciated them in my turn. It was a genuine pleasure to work with them both.

My final thanks go to Norton's chairman of the board, Donald Lamm. I met him over thirty years ago when he first gave me the idea to write this book. We have both aged (somewhat) in the interim, but he is still the same sharp-eyed critic that he was three decades earlier. Age has not withered nor custom staled his infinite variety. His ideas are as brilliant and outrageous as ever; his puns are as bad as ever. And my esteem and affection for him are as great as ever.

Merion, Pennsylvania

July 1995

BASIC PSYCHOLOGY

FOURTH EDITION

CHAPTER

1

INTRODUCTION

What is psychology? It is a field of inquiry that is sometimes defined as the science of mind, sometimes as the science of behavior. It concerns itself with how and why organisms do what they do: why wolves howl at the moon and children rebel against their parents; why birds sing and moths fly into the flame; why we remember how to ride a bicycle twenty years after the last try; why humans speak and make love and war. All of these are behaviors, and psychology is the science that studies them all.

THE SCOPE OF PSYCHOLOGY

The phenomena that psychology takes as its province cover an enormous range. Some border on biology; others touch on social sciences such as anthropology and sociology. Some concern behavior in animals; many others pertain to behavior in humans. Some are about conscious experience; others focus on what people do regardless of what they may think or feel inside. Some involve humans or animals in isolation; others concern what they do when they are in groups. A few examples will give an initial sense of the scope of the subject matter.

ELECTRICALLY TRIGGERED IMAGES

■ Consider the relation between biological mechanisms and psychological phenomena. Some investigators have developed a technique of electrically stimulating the brains of human patients who were about to undergo brain surgery. Such operations are generally conducted under local rather than general anesthesia. As a result, the patients are conscious, and their reports may guide the neurosurgeon in the course of the operation.

These and other procedures have shown that different parts of the brain have different psychological functions. For example, when stimulated in certain portions of the brain, patients have visual experiences—they see streaks of color or flickering lights. When stimulated in other regions, they hear clicks or buzzes. Stimulation in still other areas produces an involuntary movement of some part of the body (Penfield and Roberts, 1959; Penfield, 1975).

Related findings come from studies that look at the rate at which blood flows through different parts of the brain. When any part of the body is especially active, more blood will flow to it—to deliver oxygen and nutrients, and carry away waste products—and the brain is no exception. The question is whether the blood flow pattern depends on what the patient does. The answer is yes. When the patient reads silently, certain regions of the brain receive more blood (and are thus presumably more active) than others. A different blood flow pattern is found when the person reads aloud, yet another when he watches a moving light, and so on (Lassen, Ingvar, and Skinhoj, 1978).

AMBIGUOUS SIGHTS AND SOUNDS

Many psychological phenomena are much further removed from issues that might be settled by biological or medical investigations. To study these, one proceeds at the psychological level alone. An example is the perception of ambiguous visual patterns. Consider Figure 1.1, which is a photograph of a vase created for Queen Elizabeth on the occasion of her Silver Jubilee. It is usually seen as a vase, but it can also be seen as the profiles of the queen and her consort, Prince Philip.

The way ambiguous figures are perceived often depends on what we have seen just before. Take Figure 1.2, which can be seen as either a rat or an amiable gentleman with glasses. If we are first shown an unambiguous figure of a rat, the ambiguous picture will be seen as a rat. If we are first exposed to an unambiguous face, the ambiguous figure will be perceived as a face.

What holds for visual patterns also holds for language. Many utterances are ambiguous. If presented out of context, they can be understood in several different ways. Take the following sentence for example:

The mayor ordered the police to stop drinking.

This sentence may be a command to enforce sobriety among the population at large. It may also be a call to end drunkenness among members of the police force. Just how it is understood depends on the context. A prior discussion of panhandlers and skid row probably would lead to the first interpretation; a comment about alcoholism among city employees is likely to lead to the second.

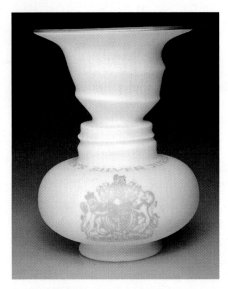

1.1 Reversible figure *Photograph of a vase celebrating the twenty-fifth year of the reign of Queen Elizabeth in 1977. Depending on how the picture is perceptually organized, we see either the vase or the profile of Queen Elizabeth and Prince Philip. (Courtesy of Kaiser Porcelain Ltd.)*

THE PERCEPTUAL WORLD OF INFANTS

Phenomena of the sort we've just discussed document the enormous effect of prior experience on what we see and do. But this does not mean that all psychological accomplishments are acquired by past experience. Some seem to be part of the innate equipment that all of us bring into the world when we are born. Take the infant's reaction to heights, for example.

Crawling infants seem to be remarkably successful in noticing the precipices of everyday life. A demonstration is provided by the *visual cliff*. This consists of a large glass table, which is divided in half by a wooden center board. On one side of the board, a checkerboard pattern is attached directly to the underside of

1.2 Perceptual bias *(A) An ambiguous form that can be seen either as (B) a rat or (C) a man with glasses. (After Bugelski and Alampay, 1961)*

A

B

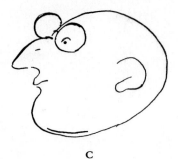

C

A

B

1.3 The visual cliff *(A) An infant is placed on the center board that is laid over a heavy sheet of glass, and his mother calls to him. If he is on the "deep" side, he will not crawl across the apparent cliff. (Courtesy of Richard D. Walk) (B) A similar reaction in a kitten. (Courtesy of William Vandivert)*

the glass; on the other side, the same pattern is placed on the floor three feet below. To adults, this arrangement looks like a sudden drop-off in the center of the table. Six-month-old infants seem to see it in much the same way. When the infant is placed on the center board and called by his mother, his response depends on where she is when she beckons. When she is on the shallow side, he quickly crawls to her. But when she calls from the apparent precipice, discretion wins out over valor and the infant stays where he is (see Figure 1.3).

This result suggests that, to some extent at least, the perception of depth is not learned through experience but is built into our system at the very start.

DISPLAYS

 Thus far, all our examples have dealt with individuals in isolation. But much of the subject matter of psychology is inherently social. This holds for animals no less than humans. For virtually all animals interact with others of their species, whether as mates, parents, offspring, or competitors.

In animals, many social interactions depend on largely innate forms of communication. An example is courtship in birds. Many species of birds have evolved elaborate rituals whereby one sex—usually the male—woos the other. Just what this wooing consists of depends on the species. Some males court by making themselves conspicuous. The peacock spreads his magnificent tail feathers, the blue bird of paradise displays his plumage while hanging upside down from a branch, and the red frigate bird inflates his red throat pouch. Other males take a more romantic approach: The bower bird builds a special cabin that he decorates with colored fruit and flowers. The males of other species offer gifts. In all cases, the fundamental message is the same: "I am a male, healthy, and willing peacock (or bird of paradise or frigate bird or whatever), and hope that your intentions are similar to mine" (see Figure 1.4).

Such social communications are based on built-in signals called *displays,* which are specific to a particular species. They are ways by which one individual informs another of his current intentions. Some are mating displays, as in the

1.4 Courting birds *Birds have evolved many diverse patterns of courtship behavior that are essentially built-in and characteristic of a particular species. (A) The peacock displays his tail feathers. (Photograph by Ed Reschke/Peter Arnold, Inc.) (B) The blue bird of paradise shows off his plumage while hanging upside down from a branch. (Photograph by David Gillison/Peter Arnold, Inc.) (C) The frigate bird puffs up his red throat pouch. (Photograph by Fred Bavendam/Peter Arnold, Inc.)*

A

B

C

A

B

1.5 Displays *(A) Threat display of the male mandrill, a large West African baboon. (Photograph by George H. Harrison/Grant Heilman) (B) The human smile. (Photograph by Peter Hendrie/The Image Bank)*

case of courtship rituals. Others are threats ("Back off or else!"; see Figure 1.5A). Still others are attempts at appeasement ("Don't hurt me. I am harmless!"). Some built-in displays form the foundation of emotional expression in humans. An example is the smile, a response found in all babies, even those born blind who couldn't have learned it by imitation. It is often considered a signal by which humans tell each other: "Be good to me. I wish you well" (see Figure 1.5B).

COMPLEX SOCIAL BEHAVIOR IN HUMANS

■ Human social interactions are generally much more subtle and flexible than those of animals. Male peacocks have just one way of going courting: They spread their tail feathers and hope for the best. Human males and females are much more complex, in courtship and many other social interactions. They try one approach, and if it fails, they try another and yet another. If these fail, too, the partners do their best to save the other's face. For much of human social life is based on one person's rational appraisal of how another person will respond to her actions: "If I do this . . . he will think this . . . then I will have to do this . . . ," and so on. Such subtleties are beyond the peacock. If his usual courtship ritual fails, he has no alternate strategy. He won't try to build bowers or offer flowers; all he can do is to display his tail feathers again and again.

While human social behavior has a strong element of rationality, there are some apparent exceptions in which we seem to act with little thought or reason. This is especially likely when we are in large groups. Under some circumstances, people in crowds behave differently than they do when alone. An example is panic (see Figure 1.6). When someone shouts "Fire" in a tightly packed auditorium, the resulting stampede may claim many more victims than the fire itself would have. At the turn of the century, a Chicago theater fire claimed over six hundred victims, many of whom were smothered or trampled to death by the frantic mass behind them. In the words of a survivor, "The heel prints on the dead faces mutely testified to the cruel fact that human animals stricken by terror are as mad and ruthless as stampeding cattle" (Brown, 1965). The task for psychology is to try to understand why the crowd acted differently from the way each of its members would have acted alone.

A SCIENCE OF MANY FACES

These illustrations document the enormous range of psychology, whose territory borders on the biological sciences at one end and touches on the social sciences at the other. This broad range makes psychology a field of multiple perspectives, a science of many faces.

Given the many-faceted character of psychology, it is not surprising that those who have contributed to it have come from many quarters. Some have had the proper title of psychologist with appropriate university appointments in that discipline, including two of its founding fathers, Wilhelm Wundt of Germany and William James of the United States. But psychology was not built by psychologists alone—far from it. Among its architects are philosophers, beginning with Plato and Aristotle and continuing to our own time. Physicists and physiologists have played important roles and still do. Physicians have contributed greatly, as have specialists in many other disciplines, including anthropology and, more recently, linguistics and computer science. Psychology, the field of many faces, is by its very nature a field of many origins.

In presenting the subject matter of psychology as it is today, we must try to do justice to this many-sidedness. In an attempt to achieve that, this book has been organized around five topics that emphasize somewhat different perspectives on the field as a whole: *action, cognition, social behavior, development,* and *individual differences.*

THE TASK OF PSYCHOLOGY

Psychology is sometimes popularly regarded as a field that concentrates on the secret inner lives of individual persons—why Mary hates her mother and why George is so shy with girls. But questions of this sort are really not psychology's main concern. To be sure, there is an applied branch of psychology that deals with various adjustment problems, but it is only a special part of the field. The primary questions psychology asks are of a more general sort. Its purpose is not to describe the distinctive characteristics of a particular individual. Its main goal is to get at the facts that are general for all of humankind.

The reason is simple. Psychology is a science and, like all other sciences, it looks for general principles—underlying uniformities that different events have in common. A single event as such means little; what counts is what any one event—or object or person—shares with others. Ultimately of course, psychology—again, like all other sciences—hopes to find a route back to understanding the individual event. It tries to discover, say, some general principles of adolescent conflict or parent-child relations to explain why George is so shy and why Mary is so bitter about her mother. Once such explanations are found, they may lead to practical applications: to help counsel and guide, and perhaps to effect desirable changes. But, at least initially, the science's main concern is with the discovery of the general principles.

Is there any field of endeavor whose primary interest is in individual persons, with the unique George and Mary who are like no other persons who ever lived or ever will live? One such field is literature. The great novelists and playwrights have given us portraits of living, breathing individuals who exist in a particular time and place. There is nothing abstract and general about the agonies of a Hamlet or the murderous ambition of a Macbeth. These are concrete, particular individuals, with special loves and fears that are peculiarly theirs. But from these particulars, Shakespeare gives us a glimpse of what is common to all humanity, what Hamlet and Macbeth share with all of us. Both science and art have something to say about human nature, but they come to it from different directions. Science tries to discover general principles and then to apply them to the individual case. Art focuses on the particular instance and then uses this to illuminate what is universal in us all.

Science and art are complementary. To gain insight into our own nature we need both. Consider Hamlet's description:

> What a piece of work is a man, how noble in reason, how infinite in faculties; in form and moving how express and admirable, in action like an angel, in apprehension like a god: the beauty of the world, the paragon of animals! (*Hamlet,* Act II, scene ii).

To understand and appreciate this "piece of work" is a task too huge for any one field of human endeavor, whether art, philosophy, or science. What we will try to do here is to sketch psychology's own attempts toward this end, to show what we have come to know and how we have come to know it—and perhaps even more important, how much we have not learned as yet.

Wilhelm Wundt (1832–1920) *(Courtesy of Stock Montage)*

William James (1842–1910) *(Courtesy of The Warder Collection)*

PART ONE

ACTION

CHAPTER

BIOLOGICAL BASES OF BEHAVIOR

The study of mind has many aspects. We may ask what human beings know, we may ask what they want, and we may ask what they do. Much of psychology is an attempt to answer the last question: What is it that humans do and why do they do it? In this section we will deal with the approach to mind that grows out of an interest in what all animals do, an approach that emphasizes behavior as the basic subject matter of psychology. We will focus on the particular version of this approach that is based on the notion that mind can be understood as a reflex machine. We shall see how the reflex notion has led to impressive achievements in our understanding of the structure and function of the nervous system and how this notion has been modified to encompass the phenomena of motivation and of learning in animals and humans.

hat are the biological foundations of mental life? The first steps toward an answer came from the study of human and animal action. The ancients, no less than we, wondered why humans and animals behave as they do. What is it that leads to animal movement, impels the crab to crawl, the tiger to spring? Prescientific folk could only answer *animistically*: There is some inner spirit in the creature that impels it to move, each creature in its own fashion. Today we know that any question about bodily movement must inevitably call for some reference to the nervous system, for to us it is quite clear that the nervous system is the apparatus that most directly determines and organizes an organism's reactions to the world in which it lives.

Modern advances in the study of this system have given us insights into its functioning that would have amazed the scientists who lived even a century ago, let alone the ancients. Some of the new techniques allow us to observe the operations of small components of individual nerve cells (see Figure 2.1). Others

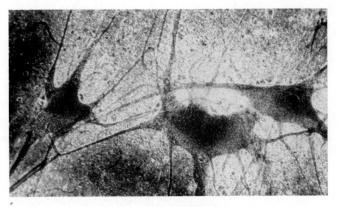

2.1   Observing the nervous system through a microscope   *A nerve cell in the spinal cord. (Photograph by Cabisco/Visuals Unlimited)*

2.2 Observing the living brain with PET scans *(A) Horizontal plane of brain used in taking the PET (Positron Emission Tomography) scan. (B) Four PET scans taken while the subject rests, listens to someone talk, listens to music, or both. These scans indicate the degree of metabolic activity in different parts of the brain, viewed in horizontal cross-section as shown in the diagram with the front of the head on top. Red indicates the most intense activity and blue the least. Listening to speech activates the left side of the brain, listening to music activates the right side, and listening to both activates both sides. (PET scans taken by Dr. John Mazziotta, UCLA School of Medicine, et al./Science Photo Library/Photo Researchers)*

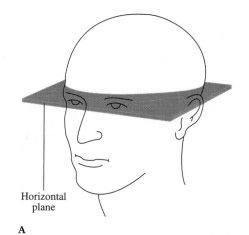

Horizontal
plane

A

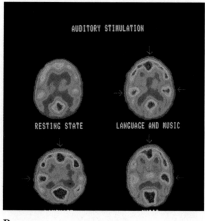

B

permit us to eavesdrop on the workings of living human brains without seriously disturbing their owners (see Figure 2.2A and B). Our advances have been considerable. But to put them in perspective, we must first look at some of the historical origins of our current conceptions.

We will soon ask many detailed questions about the structure and function of the nervous system—the apparatus that underlies human and animal action. But before we do so, we must address a more general question: Broadly speaking, what must this system accomplish?

THE ORGANISM AS MACHINE

FOCUS QUESTIONS

■ What is the machine metaphor that Descartes used to describe the actions of humans and animals?

■ What difficulties did Descartes encounter when he proposed his machine metaphor?

In modern times this question was first raised seriously by the French philosopher René Descartes (1596–1650), and his answer provides the broad outline within which we think about such matters even now. Descartes lived in a period that saw the beginning of the science of mechanics. Radically new views of humanity and its universe were being put forth. There were laws of nature that determined the fall of stones and the motions of planets: rigid, precise, and immutable. The universe was run by a system of pushes and pulls originally set in motion by God, the Great Watchmaker. At a more lowly level, these natural laws were mirrored in the workings of ingenious mechanical contrivances that were all the rage in the wealthy homes of Europe: cuckoo clocks that would call the hour, water-driven gargoyles with nodding heads, statues in the king's garden that would bow to the visitor who stepped on a hidden spring. The action of a lever, the release of a spring—these mechanisms could explain the operation of such primitive devices. Could human thought and action be explained in similar mechanical terms?

René Descartes *(Courtesy of the National Library of Medicine)*

DESCARTES AND THE REFLEX CONCEPT

To Descartes all action, whether human or animal, was essentially a response to some event in the outside world. His human machine would work as follows: Something from the outside excites one of the senses; this in turn excites a nerve that transmits the excitation upward to the brain, which then relays the excitation downward to a muscle; the excitation from the senses thus eventually leads to a contraction of a muscle and thereby to a reaction to the external event that started the whole sequence. In effect, the energy from the outside is *reflected back* by the nervous system to the animal's muscles—the term **reflex** finds its origin in this conception (see Figure 2.3).

Conceived thus, human doings could be regarded as the doings of a machine. But there was a problem. The same external event produces one reaction today and another tomorrow. The sight of food leads to reaching movements, but only when we are hungry. In short, the excitation from one of the senses will excite a nerve leading to one muscle on one occasion, but on another occasion it will excite a different nerve that may move an entirely different muscle. This suggests that Descartes' mechanism must have a central switching system, supervised by some operator who sits in the middle to decide what incoming pipe to connect with which pipe leading to the outside.

To explain these behavioral options mechanically was both difficult and dangerous. Descartes was deeply religious, and he was very much troubled by the theological implications of his argument should he bring it to its ultimate conclusion. In addition he was prudent—Galileo had difficulties with the Inquisition because his scientific beliefs threatened the doctrines of the Church. Descartes therefore shrank from taking the last step in his own argument, the reduction of human beings to the status of machines. Instead, he proposed that human mental processes were only semiautomatic. To handle the switching function he proposed that the soul, operating through a particular structure in the brain, determines the choice of possible nervous pathways.

Descartes asserted that, while animals were machines, humans were more than mere robots. But later thinkers went further. They felt that the laws of the physical universe could ultimately explain all action, whether human or animal, so that a scientific account required no further "ghost in the machine"—that is, no reference to the soul. They ruthlessly extended Descartes' logic to human beings, arguing that humans differ from animals only in being more finely constructed mechanisms.

Descartes' machine is an example of an influential scientific metaphor that affected the thought of many subsequent generations. Much of the history of science is the history of such metaphors. An illustration from physics is the description of the atom as a miniature solar system in which electrons circle the atomic nucleus just as the planets orbit the sun. Descartes' machine was similarly modeled on the water-driven machines of his day in which some motion was transformed into some other motion through a system of gears or levers until it finally led to the movement of the mechanism. Later theorists complicated the machine metaphor by borrowing from the technology of their time in likening the brain to a giant telephone switchboard. The details of the metaphor changed, but in some important regards the metaphor itself stayed the same: For the machinery that was thought to underlie psychological processes was always one in which some kind of energy (now electrical or chemical) was ultimately transformed into some bodily movement. The details changed, but the proposed machine was always one whose inputs come from the environment and whose ultimate product is action.★

★ In some later chapters we will turn to a rather different metaphor that likens mind and brain to a computer. (See Chapters 4 through 8.)

2.3 Reflex action as envisaged by Descartes *In this sketch by Descartes, the heat from the fire,* ***A****, starts a chain of processes that begins at the affected spot of the skin,* ***B****, and continues up the nerve tube until a pore of a cavity,* ***F****, is opened. Descartes believed that this opening allowed the animal spirits in the cavity to enter the nerve tube and eventually travel to the muscles that pull the foot from the fire. While the figure shows that Descartes anticipated the basic idea of reflex action, it also indicates that he did not realize the anatomical distinction between sensory and motor nerves. (From Descartes, 1662)*

THE BASIC NERVOUS FUNCTIONS:
RECEPTION, INTEGRATION, REACTION

■ Psychologists today still agree with Descartes that much of behavior can be understood as reactions to outside events: The environment poses a question and the organism answers it. This approach, like Descartes', leads to a tripartite classification of nervous functions: *reception* through the senses, *reaction* from the muscles and glands, and *conduction* and *integration* to mediate between these two functions.

The chain of events that leads to action typically begins outside of the organism. A particular physical energy impinges upon some part of the organism sensitive to it. This event we call a ***stimulus*** (a term that derives from the name of a wooden implement with a nail at one end used by Roman farmers some two thousand years ago to goad their sluggish oxen). The stimulus excites ***receptors,*** specialized structures capable of translating some physical energy into a nervous impulse. Once a receptor is stimulated, the excitation is conducted farther into the nervous system. Bundles of nerve fibers that conduct excitation toward the brain or spinal cord are called ***afferent nerves*** (from the Latin, *affere,* "to bring to"). These fibers transmit their message still farther; in the simplest case, to other fibers that go directly to the ***effectors,*** the muscles and glands that are the organs of action. Nerve fibers that lead to the effectors are called ***efferent nerves*** (from the Latin, *effere,* "to bring forth").

The transmission path from receptors to effectors is usually more circuitous than this, however. The afferent fibers often bring their messages to intermediate nerve cells, or ***interneurons,*** in the brain or spinal cord. These interneurons then either transmit the message to the efferent nerve cells or send it on to yet other interneurons. Typically, many thousands of such interneurons are "consulted" before the command to action is finally issued and sent down the path of the efferent nerve fibers. All this, in simple outline, is really a modern restatement of Descartes' reflex conception.

We now turn to a more detailed discussion of the nervous system. We will deal with progressively larger units of analysis, first discussing the smallest functional and structural units of nervous activity (the nerve impulse and the nerve cell), then the interaction among different nerve cells (at the synapse), and finally, the functional plan of the major structures of the nervous system.

NERVE CELL AND NERVE IMPULSE

FOCUS QUESTIONS

■ What basic structures are shared by all neurons?

■ What are some common types of neurons, and what functions do they serve?

■ How does a neuron's electrical potential change with stimulation, and how does that change travel along the neuron's axon?

Neuroscientists know that the basic unit of nervous function is the ***nerve impulse,*** the firing of an individual nerve cell, or ***neuron.*** Our discussion begins with a brief look at the anatomy of the neuron.

THE NEURON

The neuron is the simplest element of nervous action. It is a single cell with three subdivisions: the **dendrites,** the **cell body,** and the **axon** (see Figure 2.4). The dendrites are usually branched, sometimes enormously so. The axon may extend for a very long distance, and its end may fork out into several branches. Impulses from other cells are received by the dendrites; the axon transmits the impulse to yet other neurons or to effector organs such as muscles and glands. Thus, the dendrites are the receptive units of the neuron, while the axon endings may be regarded as its effector apparatus.

Many axons are surrounded by a **myelin sheath,** a tube mainly composed of fatty tissue, that insulates it from other axons. The tube is not continuous but consists of a number of elongated segments, with small uncoated gaps in the sheath, the **nodes of Ranvier,** which allow for a considerable increase in the speed of transmission (Figure 2.4).

A few details about neurons will give a feeling for their size and number. The diameter of an individual neuron is very small; cell bodies vary from 5 to about 100 microns in diameter (1 micron = 1/1,000 millimeter). Dendrites are typically short, say a few hundred microns. The axons of neurons can be very long: Some motor neuron axons extend from the head to the base of the spinal cord, others from the spinal cord to the fingers and toes. To get a sense of the cell body relative to the axon in a motor neuron, imagine a basketball attached to a garden hose that stretches the whole fourteen-mile length of Manhattan.

Different kinds of neurons are specialized for different tasks. We will mention only a few of the varieties. Some neurons are attached to specialized **receptor cells** that can respond to various external energies, such as pressure, chemical changes, light, and so on. These receptor cells translate (more technically, **transduce**) such physical stimuli into electrical changes, which then trigger a nervous impulse in other neurons. Receptor cells are like money changers, exchanging the various energies impinging from the outer world into the only currency acceptable within the nervous system—the nervous impulse.

Neurons that convey impulses from receptors toward the rest of the nervous system are called **sensory neurons.** Sometimes the receptor is a specialized part of the sensory neuron, as in the neurons that are responsible for sensing pressure on the skin. But in many cases, transduction and transmission are separate functions that are entrusted to different cells. In vision and hearing, receptor cells transduce optic stimulation and air pressures into electrical changes in the cell. These changes in the receptors trigger impulses in sensory neurons that then transmit their information to other neurons in the nervous system.

A

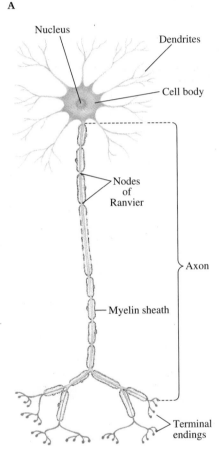

Nucleus

Dendrites

Cell body

Nodes of Ranvier

Axon

Myelin sheath

Terminal endings

2.4 The neuron *(A) A schematic diagram of the main parts of a "typical" neuron. Part of the cell is myelinated; that is, its axon is covered with a segmented, insulating sheath. (After Katz, 1952) (B) Highly magnified nerve cell in the human brain showing cell body and several dendrites. The long vertical bands are branches from other nerve cells. (Photograph by Manfred Kage/Peter Arnold, Inc.)*

B

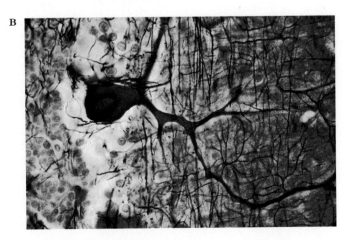

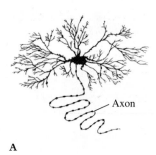

A

B   C

*2.5 Different kinds of neurons   (A) A
motor neuron of the human spinal cord. (B) A
neuron in the human cerebral cortex, the part
of the brain concerned with such higher mental
functions as perception and planning. (After
Kolb and Whishaw, 1990). (C) A specialized neuron in the cerebellum, a part of the
brain that controls motor coordination. This
kind of cell has been said to gather impulses
from as many as 80,000 other neurons. The
photomicrograph is from the cerebellum of a
twelve-month-old infant. It has been stained
by a special chemical that shows the extent of
the branching of the cell's dendrites. (©
Guigoz/Dr. A. Privat/Petit Format/Science
Source/Photo Researchers)*

Other neurons have axons that terminate in effector cells. An important
example is the *motor neurons* that activate the *skeletal musculature,* the muscles
that control the skeleton, such as those of the arms and legs. The cell bodies of
the motor neurons are in the spinal cord or brain, and their long axons have terminal branches whose final tips contact individual muscle cells. When a motor
neuron fires, a chemical event produced at its axon tips causes the muscle fibers
to contract.

In complex organisms, the vast majority of nerve cells are *interneurons,*
which have a functional position that is between sensory neurons and motor
neurons. Interneurons come in many shapes and forms. They usually show considerable branching, which produces an enormous number of synaptic contacts
(see Figure 2.5).

The total number of neurons in the human nervous system has been estimated to be as high as 1,000 billion (Nauta and Feirtag, 1986). Given that each
neuron may be connected to as many as 10,000 other neurons, it is no wonder
that the human brain is often said to be the most complex object in the known
universe.

THE ELECTRICAL ACTIVITY OF
THE NEURON

The biological function of neurons is to receive and transmit impulses.
But how do they perform these functions? How do they transmit signals,
influence each other, and cause muscles to contract? We now know that they do
so electrically. But the unraveling of this mystery required the development of
new scientific instruments to measure and depict not just anatomy, but electrical
activity—the movements of charged particles. Direct measurement of these
electrical currents in neurons only became possible with several key advances in
the twentieth century. One such advance was the development of ever finer
microelectrodes, some of which have tips tapered to a diameter of 1 micron.
Such electrodes can puncture a neuron without squashing it and detect weak
electrical currents without disrupting them. Equally important was the development of the oscilloscope, a device that amplifies and expands weak electrical signals and displays them as glowing lines on a fluorescent screen. The resulting
pattern then charts electrical changes that occur during a very short interval of
cellular activity. Another contribution came considerably earlier than the twentieth century; it was made by evolution, which provided the squid, an animal
endowed with several giant axons with diameters up to 1 millimeter—a great
convenience for electrophysiological work on the nervous impulse.

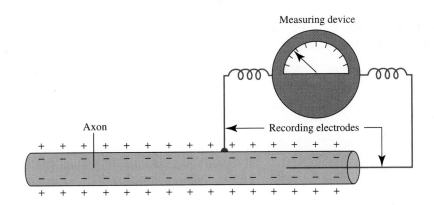

2.6 Recording the impulse *A schematic drawing of how the impulse is recorded. One electrode is inserted into the axon; the other records from the axon's outside. (After Carlson, 1986)*

THE RESTING POTENTIAL

Figure 2.6 shows one microelectrode inserted into an axon while another records from the surface of the fiber. In this manner one can record the electrical potential (the voltage) across the cell membrane. One fact emerges immediately. There is a difference in potential between the inside and the outside of the fiber when the cell is at "rest" (that is, not firing). The inside is electrically negative with respect to the outside. This *resting potential* is about −70 millivolts relative to the outside of the cell. This means that in its normal state the cell membrane is *polarized.* Its outside and inside are like the electrical poles of a miniature battery, with the outside positive and the inside negative.

THE ACTION POTENTIAL

What happens when the neuron is aroused from rest? To find out, neuroscientists stimulate the surface of the fiber by means of a third microelectrode, which applies a brief electrical pulse. This pulse reduces the potential across the membrane for an instant. If the pulse is weak, nothing further will happen. As the strength of the pulse slowly increases, the resting potential drops still more, but again with no further effect, until the pulse is strong enough to decrease the potential to a critical point, the *threshold* (about 55 millivolts in mammals).

Now a new phenomenon occurs. The potential suddenly collapses; in fact, it overshoots the zero mark, and for a brief moment the axon interior becomes positive relative to the outside. This flare lasts only about 1 millisecond and quickly subsides. The neuron then returns to the resting state. This entire sequence of electrical events is called the *action potential* (Figure 2.7).

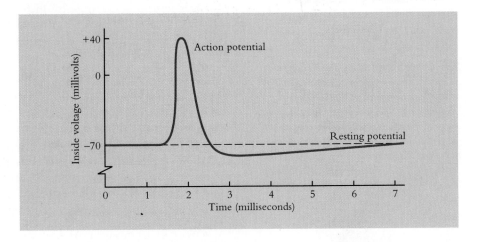

2.7 The action potential *Action potential recorded from the squid's giant axon. (After Hodgkin and Huxley, 1939)*

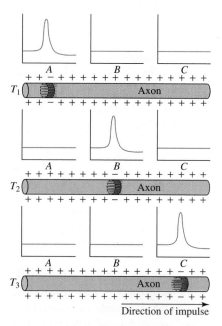

2.8   The action potential as it travels along the axon   *The axon is shown at three different moments in time—**T₁**, **T₂**, and **T₃**—after the application of a stimulus. The electrical potential is shown at three different points along the axon—**A**, **B**, and **C**. (After Carlson, 1986)*

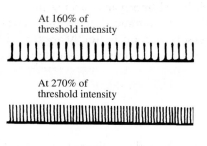

At 160% of
threshold intensity

At 270% of
threshold intensity

|← 500 msec →|

2.9   Stimulus intensity and firing frequency   *Responses of a crab axon to a continuous electric current at three levels of current intensity. The time scale is relatively slow. As a result, the action potentials show up as single vertical lines or "spikes." Note that while increasing the current intensity has no effect on the height of the spikes (the all-or-none law) it leads to a marked increase in the frequency of spikes per second. (After Eccles, 1973)*

The action potential is recorded from only one small region of the axon. What happens elsewhere in the fiber? Consider Figure 2.8 An *adequate stimulus*—that is, one that is above threshold—is applied to point *A,* and the potential is measured at *A,* as well as at other points along the axon, say at *B* and *C.* At first, an action potential is observed at *A,* while *B* and *C* are still at rest. A bit later, *A* returns to normal, while *B* shows the action potential. Still later, *B* returns to normal, but an action potential is found at *C.* (Of course, these time intervals are exceedingly brief.) The change in potential is evidently infectious, with each region quickly setting off its neighbor.

By now there is no doubt that the action potential is the physical event that corresponds to the nervous impulse. Consider the speed of the nervous impulse, which was measured in the middle of the nineteenth century, many years before anyone knew anything about the underlying electrophysiology of neural action. In humans, this was found to be about 50 meters per second. If action potentials and nerve impulses are one and the same, then the two should travel at the same speed. And in fact they do.

All-or-none law   One point should be stressed. The electrical response of the axon—that is, the action potential—is unaffected by the intensity of the stimulus, once the stimulus is at threshold level or above. Increasing the stimulus value above this level will neither increase the intensity of the action potential nor affect its speed of conduction to other points in the fiber. This phenomenon is sometimes referred to as the *all-or-none law* of axon reaction. The all-or-none law clearly implies that the stimulus does not provide the energy for the nervous impulse. It serves as a trigger and no more: Given that the trigger is pulled hard enough, pulling yet harder has no effect. Like a gun, a neuron either fires or does not fire. It knows no in-between.

Stimulus intensity   We have seen that the axon obeys the all-or-none law. But much of our everyday experience seems to deny it: We can obviously tell the difference between the buzz of a mosquito and the roar of a jet plane. How can we square such facts with the all-or-none law? In many cases what happens is that the more intense stimulus excites a *greater number of neurons.* Since different neurons vary enormously in their thresholds, a weak stimulus will stimulate all neurons whose thresholds are below a given level, while a strong stimulus will stimulate all of those, plus others whose threshold is higher.

While remaining strictly obedient to the all-or-none law, however, the individual neuron is nevertheless affected by stimulus intensity. This becomes apparent when we apply a continuous stimulus for somewhat longer intervals. Now we obtain not one impulse but a whole volley. We notice that the size of the action potentials remains the same whatever the stimulus intensity. What changes instead is the *impulse frequency.* The stronger the stimulus, the more *often* the axon will fire. This effect holds until we reach a maximum rate of firing, after which further increases in intensity have no effect (see Figure 2.9). Different neurons have different maximum rates; the highest in humans is of the order of 1,000 impulses per second.

I N T E R A C T I O N   A M O N G   N E R V E   C E L L S

F O C U S   Q U E S T I O N S

■ What is the simplest example of the interaction between neurons?

■ What basic structures make neurotransmission possible?

INTERACTION AMONG NERVE CELLS

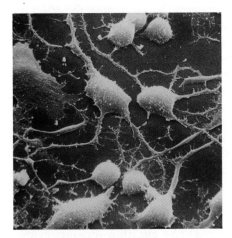

Interaction among nerve cells *An isolated nerve cell. The cell body is in contact with other cells through numerous extensions. The figure illustrates how nerve fibers cross each other to form an elaborate network. (Photograph by David M. Phillips / Visuals Unlimited)*

Sir Charles Sherrington *(Courtesy of the National Library of Medicine)*

- What findings suggested that the connections among neurons were interrupted by gaps or *synapses?*
- Why did researchers conclude that neurons interact via chemical transmission?
- What are some common neurotransmitters, and how can certain neurotransmitters help explain some drug effects and mental illness?

In a way, the neurons of our nervous system are like 1,000 billion speakers, endlessly prattling and chattering to one another. But each of them has only one word with which to tell its story, the one and only word it can utter. It can choose only whether to speak its word or keep silent, to speak it often or more rarely. Looked at in isolation, the individual speakers seem like imbeciles with a one-word vocabulary, babbling and being babbled at. But when taken as a whole, this gibbering becomes somehow harmonious. The trick is in the integration of the individual messages, the interplay of the separate components. The really interesting question for psychology, then, is not how a neuron manages to produce its word, but rather how it can talk to others and how it can listen.

THE REFLEX

To study the interactions among different neurons, we begin with the simplest illustration of such interactions—the *reflex.* Descartes pointed out that some of our actions are automatic, controlled by mechanical principles, not by the "will." Later progress in neuropsychology was made by studying animal motion that persists after the brain is gone. What farmer had not seen a chicken running around the barnyard without its head? Around 1750, the Scottish physician Robert Whytt showed that such movements are controlled by the spinal cord. He found that a decapitated frog will jerk its leg away from a pinprick, but when deprived of *both* brain and spinal cord, it no longer responded. Presumably, the frog's leg movement depended on the spinal cord.

Today we can list a host of reflexes, built-in response patterns executed automatically, without thought and without will and even without a functioning brain. Vomiting, the rhythmic contraction of the intestines (peristalsis), erection of the penis, blushing, limb flexion in withdrawal from pain, sucking in newborns—the catalog is very large. Some reflexes are produced by circuits (reflex arcs) composed of only two neurons, one sensory and one motor. More typically the chain is longer, with one or more interneurons interposed between the afferent and efferent ends.

INFERRING SYNAPTIC FUNCTION

Initially, many neurologists believed that the reflex pathway was across a long and essentially continuous strand of nervous tissue—in essence, along one neuron—but by the end of the nineteenth century most became convinced that there is a gap between neurons, the *synapse,* across which they must communicate. The critical studies establishing the role of the synapse and its place in nerve interaction were performed at the turn of the century by the English physiologist Sir Charles Sherrington (1857–1952). Sherrington's work was conducted at the level of behavior rather than that of electrophysiology. What he observed directly was reflex action in dogs, cats, and monkeys. How the synapse worked, he inferred. In this sense Sherrington acted more like a psychologist than a physiologist: He focused on behavior in order to gain insight into its underlying mechanisms.

Sherrington set out to study the *simple reflex,* that is, the reflex considered in splendid neurological isolation, unaffected by activities elsewhere in the nervous system. Of course, he was well aware that such simplicity does not really exist, for even the lowliest spinal reflex is modified by higher centers in the spinal cord or the brain. An itch in your side will initiate a scratch reflex, but if you are the catchman in a trapeze act, you will probably inhibit it. To remove the effect of higher centers, Sherrington used the **spinal animal,** usually a dog, whose spinal cord had been completely severed in the neck region. This cut all connections between the body (from the neck down) and the brain, so that spinal reflexes could be studied pure.

EXCITATION

Sherrington's method was simple. He applied mild electric shocks to some point on the spinal animal's skin and observed whether this stimulus evoked a particular reflex response (Figure 2.10). Sherrington asked whether conduction across neurons had the same characteristics as conduction within neurons. He discovered that it did not.

One line of evidence to support this conclusion came from **temporal summation** (see Figure 2.11). Sherrington showed that while one stimulus below threshold will not elicit the reflex, two or more of them (all equally subthreshold) may do so if presented in succession. The important point was that such temporal summation effects occurred even when the individual stimuli were spaced at intervals of up to half a second or thereabouts. How could this be? Sherrington argued that the most plausible interpretation is that some form of summation occurs at a crossover point between neurons. This crossover point soon came to be called the synapse.

Sherrington supposed that there is some kind of excitatory process (presumably caused by the liberation of a then still undiscovered chemical substance from the ends of the axon) that accumulates at the synapse and builds up until it reaches a level high enough (the threshold level) to trigger the next neuron into action. This hypothesis clearly accounts for temporal summation. Every time cell *A* fires, a tiny amount of the excitatory substance is liberated into the total synaptic gap between cell *A* and cell *B.* With enough repetitions of the stimulus, the total quantity of what Sherrington called the **central excitatory state** exceeds the threshold of cell *B,* which then fires.

INHIBITION

So far it would appear that neurons either vote "aye," thus adding to the central excitatory state at the synapse, or else abstain altogether. However, some neu-

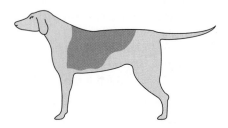

2.10   Saddle-shaped area of spinal dog
When a stimulus whose strength is above threshold is applied at any point in the "saddle," the animal will perform a scratching movement. (After Sherrington, 1906)

2.11   Temporal summation   *A subthreshold stimulus will not elicit the reflex, but two or more stimuli will if presented successively at intervals of up to half a second. This indicates that the effects of the first stimulus were somehow stored and added to the effects of the second.*

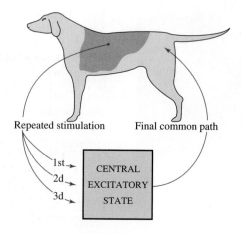

Repeated stimulation   Final common path

1st
2d
3d

CENTRAL EXCITATORY STATE

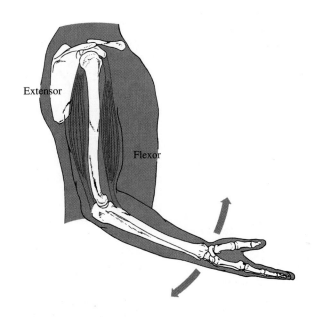

2.12 An example of muscle antagonists The figure shows how the members of an antagonistic muscle pair (biceps and triceps) oppose each other in flexing and extending the forearm.

rons may signal "nay" and set up an inhibitory effect, actively opposing and preventing excitation. One of the clearest demonstrations of such an effect is the phenomenon of *reciprocal inhibition.* Skeletal muscles typically come in antagonistic pairs—flexor and extensor (Figure 2.12). The antagonists must not both contract at the same time, like wrestlers straining against each other. For maximum mechanical efficiency, the force of the excited muscle should encounter little or no opposition from its antagonist.

Using a spinal animal, Sherrington found that stimulation of a sensory site that caused the flexor to contract had a further effect. It also caused the extensor to relax so that it actually became limp—limper in fact than it was in the normal resting state. Sherrington concluded that this unusually low level of muscular contraction could only be explained by assuming that a counteracting process nullifies the excitatory messages to the muscle fibers that maintain normal muscle tone—*inhibition.*

Whether a motor neuron fires (and thus activates a muscle fiber) depends upon the other neurons that send messages to it. Each of these cells gives a positive or negative signal or remains neutral and thereby determines whether the excitatory threshold of the motor neuron is reached and, therefore, whether it fires or does not.

THE SYNAPTIC MECHANISM

Sherrington could only guess at the specific physical mechanism that governs transmission at the synapse, but he did sketch some general guidelines. There had to be excitatory and inhibitory processes, accumulating over time, pooling effects from various neural inputs. But what was their nature?

SYNAPTIC TRANSMISSION

Sherrington and some of his contemporaries guessed that neurons communicate with their neighbors by means of some chemical substance that is released when the impulse reaches the end of the axon. The proof came in 1920 when Otto Loewi performed a crucial experiment. He dissected two frogs, removed their hearts, and placed each of the two hearts in separate, fluid-filled jars in which

2.13   Schematic illustration of Loewi's discovery of the action of neurotransmitters   The hearts in two jars, I and II, are beating. (A) The vagus nerve that is still attached to the heart in jar I is stimulated, thus inhibiting the muscle and slowing down the heartbeat. (B) After an interval, the fluid in jar II is replaced by the fluid from jar I. The heart in jar II will now slow down almost immediately. (After Groves and Rebec, 1988)

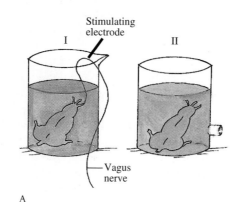
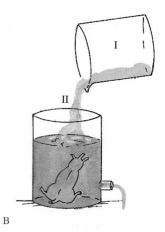

they kept on beating. One of the hearts still had the vagus nerve attached to it; this nerve inhibits the heart muscle and slows down the heartbeat. Loewi electrically stimulated the vagus nerve for half an hour or so. All this time the other heart stayed in its own jar and beat at its own, more rapid pace. After a while, Loewi took the fluid from the jar that held the first heart (whose beat had been slowed down by the vagus nerve) and poured it into the jar in which the second heart was kept. Almost immediately that second heart slowed down as well. The implication was clear. The stimulation of the vagus nerve liberated some substance whose effect on the heart muscle (a region that we now know acts just like a synapse) is to inhibit its function (see Figure 2.13). Loewi called that substance "vagus stuff." We now call it *acetylcholine* (usually abbreviated ACh), the first of a hundred or more chemical substances now identified as *neurotransmitters* (Loewi, 1960; Eccles, 1982).

Loewi's experiment had only shown that the transmission of the neural message involves a chemical substance. We now know quite a bit more about the way in which this transmission occurs in actual neurons. Let's begin by distinguishing between the *presynaptic neuron* and the *postsynaptic neuron.* The presynaptic neuron sends the neural message; the postsynaptic neuron receives it. The process begins in the tiny knobs of the axon terminals of the presynaptic neuron (see Figure 2.14). Within these swellings are numerous tiny sacs, or *vesicles* ("little vessels"), which contain neurotransmitters. When the presynaptic neuron fires, some of the vesicles in its axon knobs burst and release their

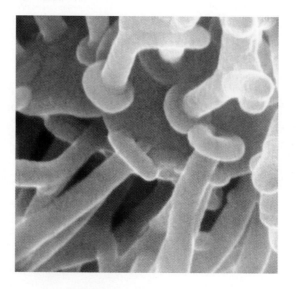

2.14   The synapse   Electron micrograph of synaptic knobs, the tiny swellings of the axon terminals that contain the vesicles. (Lewis et al., 1969)

INTERACTION AMONG NERVE CELLS

2.15 Schematic view of synaptic transmission *(A) Neuron A transmits a message through synaptic contact with Neuron B. (B) The events in the axon knob (the mitochondria shown in the figure are structures that help to produce the energy the neuron requires for its functioning). (C) The vesicle is released, and neurotransmitter molecules stream toward the postsynaptic membrane. (D) Transmitter molecules settle on the receptor site, an ion channel opens, and Na⁺ streams in. (After Bloom, Lazerson, and Hofstadter, 1988)*

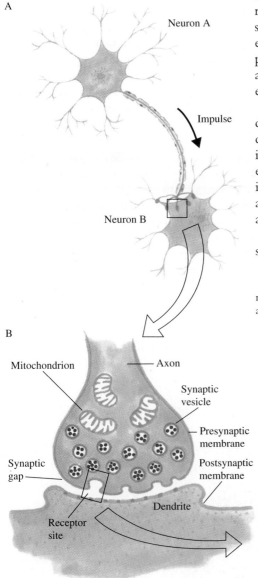

A

Neuron A

Impulse

Neuron B

B

Mitochondrion

Axon

Synaptic vesicle

Presynaptic membrane

Postsynaptic membrane

Synaptic gap

Dendrite

Receptor site

transmitter load into the **synaptic gap** that separates the two cells. The transmitter molecules diffuse across this gap and come to rest upon the dendrite or cell body of the postsynaptic cell (see Figure 2.15A and B).

Once across the synaptic gap, how do transmitters perform their transmitting function? They do so by activating specialized **receptor molecules** in the **postsynaptic membrane.** When one of these receptors is activated, it opens or closes certain ion gates in the membrane. For example, some neurotransmitters open the gates to sodium ions. As these sodium ions enter the postsynaptic cell, that cell's resting potential is *decreased* (see Figure 2.15C and D). (We'll consider inhibitory effects shortly.) As more and more transmitter molecules cross the synaptic bridge, they activate more and more receptors, which drop the resting potential of the postsynaptic cell further and further. These drops accumulate and spread along the membrane of the postsynaptic neuron. When the drop gets large enough, the threshold is reached, the action potential is triggered, and the impulse speeds down the postsynaptic cell's axon.

A similar mechanism accounts for inhibition. At some synapses, the presynaptic cell liberates transmitter substances that produce an *increase* in the resting potential of the postsynaptic neuron. This is in contrast to excitatory transmitter substances, which *decrease* the cell's resting potential.★ As a result, a larger drop in resting potential will now be necessary to set off the action potential in the postsynaptic cell. Since most neurons have synaptic connections with neurons that excite them as well as with others that inhibit them, the response of a given postsynaptic cell depends on a final tally of the excitatory and inhibitory "yeas" and "nays" that act upon it. If the net value is excitatory, and if this value exceeds the threshold, the cell will fire.

We can now see how these synaptic mechanisms account for Sherrington's discovery that conduction *within* neurons is governed by different principles than conduction *between* neurons. The ultimate reason is that the changes in potential in the dendrites and cell body produced by the neurotransmitters are quite different from the action potential in the axon. For unlike the action potential (which is all or none), these changes are **graded.** They add up over time: Small changes accumulate to create larger changes as more and more transmitter molecules affect the postsynaptic cell (thus accounting for temporal summation).

What happens to the transmitter molecules after they have affected the postsynaptic neuron? It wouldn't do just to leave them where they are, for they

★ Whether a transmitter is excitatory or inhibitory depends on its relation to the postsynaptic membrane. The same transmitter can be excitatory at some synapses and inhibitory at others. Thus acetylcholine excites the muscle fibers of the skeleton while inhibiting those of the heart.

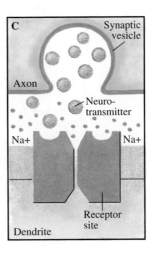

C

Synaptic vesicle

Axon

Neurotransmitter

Na+   Na+

Receptor site

Dendrite

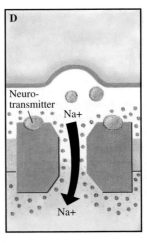

D

Neurotransmitter

Na+

Na+

might continue to exert their effects long after the presynaptic neuron had stopped firing. There are two mechanisms that prevent such false messages from being sent. Some transmitters are inactivated shortly after they've been discharged by a special "cleanup" enzyme that breaks them up into their chemical components. Others are removed from the synapse and recycled back into the presynaptic neuron.

NEUROTRANSMITTERS

On the face of it, one might think that the nervous system only needs two transmitters: one excitatory and the other inhibitory. But nature, as so often, turns out to be exceedingly generous, for in actual fact there are a great number of different transmitter substances. About a hundred or so have been isolated thus far, and many more are sure to be discovered within the next decade.

We will mention just a few of these neurotransmitters here. *Acetylcholine (ACh)* is released at many synapses and at the junction between motor neurons and muscle fibers (a junction that is a kind of synapse) and makes the fibers contract. Others include *serotonin (5HT)*, a transmitter that is involved in many of the mechanisms of sleep and emotional arousal, and *GABA* (or to give its full name, gamma-amino butyric acid), the most widely distributed inhibitory transmitter of the central nervous system. Yet others are *norepinephrine (NE)* and *dopamine (DA)* to which we will refer in later discussions of drug effects and certain mental disorders. For now, we only want to note that neurons differ in the transmitters they release as well as the transmitters that affect them. Thus neurons sensitive to dopamine will not respond to serotonin or to GABA, and vice versa. It is as if different neurons speak different languages. Some speak "Dopaminese," others speak "Serotonese," and so on.

One attempt to understand the differences in chemical responsiveness is the *lock-and-key model* of transmitter action. This theory proposes that transmitter molecules will only affect the postsynaptic membrane if their shape fits into certain synaptic receptor molecules much as a key must fit into a lock (see Figure 2.16). But the mere fact that a given molecule fits into the receptor is not enough to qualify it as a transmitter. The key must not just fit into the lock; it must also turn it. In the language of neurophysiology, the transmitter molecule must produce the changes in membrane potential that correspond to excitatory and inhibitory processes.

POISONS, DRUGS, AND NEUROTRANSMITTER ACTIVITY

The fact that communication between neurons depends on different neurotransmitter substances has wide implications for both psychology and pharma-

2.16 Lock-and-key model of synaptic transmission *Transmitter molecules will only affect the postsynaptic membrane if their shape fits the shape of certain receptor molecules in that membrane, much as a key has to fit into a lock. The diagram shows two kinds of transmitters and their appropriate receptors. (From Rosenzweig and Leiman, 1989)*

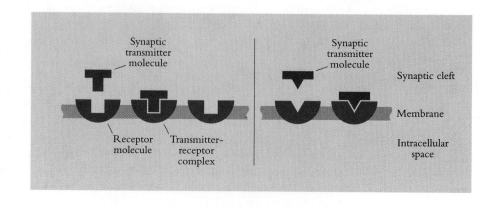

INTERACTION AMONG NERVE CELLS

A   B

Curare, the black widow's venom, and paralysis   *(A) This Cofan man from Colombia is using a curare-tipped dart to hunt. The curare acts as an acetylcholine antagonist: It inhibits this neurotransmitter's action, which leads to paralysis and death. (Photograph by B. Malkin/Anthro-Photo File) (B) The venom of the black widow spider also affects its victim's acetylcholine supply, but instead of inhibiting acetylcholine action, it acts as an acetylcholine agonist, quickly exhausting the victim's supply of this neurotransmitter. The end, however, is the same: paralysis and death. (Photograph © 1992, Comstock)*

cology. Drugs that enhance a transmitter's activity are technically called **agonists,** a term borrowed from Greek drama in which the agonist is the name for the hero. Drugs that impede such action are **antagonists,** a term that refers to whoever opposes the hero (so to speak, the villain).

Many such drugs operate by increasing or decreasing the amount of available transmitter substance. Some agonists enhance a transmitter's effect by blocking its **reuptake,** a process by which the transmitter molecules are more or less sucked back into the presynaptic neuron, thus terminating their effect on the postsynaptic membrane. Other agonists act by counteracting the cleanup enzyme, or by increasing the availability of some **precursor** (a substance required for the transmitter's chemical manufacture). Antagonists impede transmitter action through the same mechanisms operating in reverse: They speed reuptake, augment cleanup enzymes, and decrease available precursors. Still other drugs affect the synaptic receptors. Some are agonists that activate the receptors by mimicking the transmitter's action, much as a passkey opens a lock. Others are antagonists that prevent the transmitter effect by binding themselves to the synaptic receptor and blocking off the transmitter, thus serving as a kind of putty in the synaptic lock.

Acetylcholine, curare, and the black widow's venom   An example of an antagonist that works by blocking receptors is **curare,** a substance discovered by certain South American Indians who dipped their arrows in a plant extract that contained it, with deadly effect on animal prey and human enemies. Curare blocks the action of acetylcholine at the synaptic junctions between motor neurons and muscle fibers. The result is total paralysis and eventual death by suffocation, since the victim is unable to breathe.

The venom of the black widow spider, while actually an agonist, achieves a similar result. This substance initially enhances the production of acetylcholine at the neuromuscular junction, but it does so at such an accelerated pace that the neuron's currently available supply of the transmitter is quickly exhausted. The ultimate result is the same muscular paralysis produced by a direct antagonist such as curare.

Norepinephrine and amphetamine   **Amphetamines** act as agonists. These drugs enhance the release of norepinephrine from the presynaptic neurons and also inhibit its reuptake. Norepinephrine is the transmitter for neurons that have to do with general bodily and psychological arousal. The greater the activity of such neurons, the more active and excited the individual is likely to be. It is therefore understandable that amphetamine ("speed") acts as a powerful stimulant. In moderate doses, it leads to restlessness, insomnia, and loss of appetite; larger doses and continued use may lead to frenetic hyperactivity and delusions. Certain other stimulants, cocaine in particular, have similar effects.

Dopamine, schizophrenia, and Parkinson's disease   Some transmitter blockades, like that produced by curare, lead to catastrophic results. But other blockades may be beneficial. An example is the effect of various **antipsychotic drugs,** such as **Thorazine,** on the symptoms of schizophrenia, a serious mental disorder that afflicts about 1 percent of the population. In its more extreme forms, schizophrenia is characterized by delusions (believing what isn't so, such as conspiracies and persecution), hallucinations (perceiving what isn't there, such as hearing voices), or bizarre mannerisms and unusual postures that may be maintained for many hours. According to one hypothesis, schizophrenia is produced by an oversensitivity to the transmitter dopamine. Neurons that liberate dopamine have an arousing function in many parts of the brain. Adherents of the dopamine hypothesis believe that people who are overly responsive to this transmitter will be continually overaroused, which may ultimately lead to the symptoms of schizophrenia. One of the arguments for this theory comes from the fact that Thorazine, which blocks the effects of dopamine, has a pronounced effect in alleviating schizophrenic symptoms. While the dopamine hypothesis of schizophrenia is still a matter of dispute, many investigators do agree that disturbances in transmitter function play a role in the production of this and other mental disorders (see Chapter 18 for further discussion).

If the dopamine theory of schizophrenia is correct, the problem is an excess of (or an oversensitivity to) a certain transmitter, specifically dopamine. In other disorders, the problem is the very opposite. An important example is **Parkinson's disease,** which mostly afflicts people in their later years. It is characterized by tremors, rigidity, and serious difficulties in initiating voluntary movements. Here, too, the cause is related to dopamine, but now as a case of too little rather than of too much, for in Parkinson's disease there is a gradual degeneration of dopamine-releasing neurons in a pathway of the brain that is crucial for movement. Some of the symptoms of Parkinson's disease are counteracted by the administration of L-DOPA, a dopamine precursor that increases the supply of dopamine in the brain and allows the patient's surviving dopamine-releasing neurons to function more effectively. While this therapy alleviates many patients' symptoms, it does not constitute a real cure, for the progressive destruction of the dopamine-releasing neurons continues (Marsden, 1985).

INTERACTION THROUGH THE BLOODSTREAM: THE ENDOCRINE SYSTEM

FOCUS QUESTION

■ What is the endocrine system, and how does the role of the substances it releases resemble that of neurotransmitters?

Thus far, we have considered the primary instrument of communication within the body: the nervous system. But there is another organ system that serves a similar function: the **endocrine system** (see Figure 2.17 and Table 2.1). Various endocrine glands (such as the pancreas, adrenal glands, and pituitary) release their **hormone** secretions directly into the bloodstream and thus exert effects

Hypothalamus
Pituitary

Thyroid

Stomach

Pancreas
Adrenal
Kidney

Ovary
(female)

Testis
(male)

2.17   Location of major endocrine glands and hypothalamus

TABLE 2.1 THE MAIN ENDOCRINE GLANDS AND THEIR FUNCTIONS

Gland	Functions of the released hormones
Anterior pituitary	Often called the body's master gland because it triggers hormone secretion in many of the other endocrine glands.
Posterior pituitary	Prevents loss of water through the kidneys.
Thyroid	Affects metabolic rate.
Islet cells in pancreas	Affects utilization of glucose.
Adrenal cortex	Various effects on metabolism; some effects on sexual behavior.
Adrenal medulla	Increases sugar output of the liver; stimulates various internal organs in the same direction as the sympathetic branch of the ANS (e.g., accelerates heart rate).
Ovaries	One set of hormones (estrogen) produces female sex characteristics and is relevant to sexual behavior. Another hormone (progesterone) prepares the uterus for implantation of an embryo.
Testes	Produces male sex characteristics; relevant to sexual arousal.

upon structures often far removed from their biochemical birthplace. As an example, take the **pituitary gland.** One of its components secretes a hormone that tells the kidneys to decrease the amount of water excreted in the urine, a useful mechanism when the body is short of water (see Chapter 3).

On the face of it, the integration that the endocrine glands give us seems to be very different from that provided by the nervous system. In the nervous system, neurotransmitters are sent to particular addresses through highly specific channels. In contrast, the chemical messengers employed by the endocrine system travel indiscriminately to all parts of the body until they finally reach the one organ that is their destination. There is also an enormous difference in the distance these messengers have to travel. While neurotransmitters must only cross the synaptic cleft, which is less than 1/10,000 mm wide, the endocrine messengers may have to traverse half the length of the entire body. But at bottom the two communication systems have a good deal in common, for both systems deliver their messages by the release of chemical substances. In the nervous system, neurotransmitters excite or inhibit the postsynaptic cell; in the endocrine system, hormones affect specially sensitive cells in the target organ.

Several substances turn out to serve both as hormones and as neurotransmitters. For example, norepinephrine (also known as **noradrenaline**) is the transmitter released by certain neurons that make blood vessels constrict; it is also one of the hormones secreted by the adrenal gland with similar results. The adrenal gland's release of norepinephrine, and its close relative adrenaline, is controlled by pituitary hormones, and adrenaline (as we all know) increases psychological as well as physiological arousal through its effects on the brain and body.

THE MAIN STRUCTURES OF THE NERVOUS SYSTEM

FOCUS QUESTIONS

■ What are the major divisions of the human nervous system?

■ What structures comprise, and what functions are served by, the three major subdivisions of the brain?

Our general approach has been to move from the simple to the increasingly complex. We first looked at the operation of the smallest functional unit of the nervous system, the neuron, and then considered the ways in which two or more neurons may interact. We now turn to a still more complex level of analysis as we discuss the function of large aggregates of neurons. What can we say about the function of those clumps of nervous tissue, each made up of many millions of neurons, which comprise the gross structures of the brain and spinal cord?

THE EVOLUTION OF CENTRAL CONTROL

The nervous system is analogous to a government, and its evolution can be understood as the gradual imposition of central control over local autonomy. A first step was the establishment of regional rule. Early in evolutionary history the cell bodies of many interneurons began to clump together to form *ganglia* (singular, *ganglion*). At first, these ganglia served primarily as relay stations that passed on sensory messages from the receptors to the muscles. But eventually the closeness of the cells within these clumps of neural tissue led to the development of an ever-increasing number and complexity of synaptic interconnections. As a result, the ganglia became local control centers that integrated messages from different receptor cells and coordinated the activity of different muscle fibers. These regional centers were usually located close to the sites where important sensory information is gathered or where vital activity takes place.

As evolution progressed, the initial loose federation of ganglia gradually became increasingly centralized; some ganglia began to control others, and the ganglia located in the head became dominant. The various structures of the brain itself also tend to function hierarchically; as we will see, there are higher centers that command lower centers, that in turn command still lower centers, and so on.

DISINHIBITION

Another demonstration of the hierarchical principle comes from some cases of **disinhibition.** Higher centers often exert an inhibitory effect upon lower ones. The inhibitory effect of such brain centers is often discovered indirectly, by noting an *increase* in the strength of a reflex after the influence of this higher center is removed, an effect called disinhibition. A classic example is spinal reflexes in frogs, which are more vigorous when all brain structures have been removed.

A rather ghoulish instance of disinhibition is provided by the love life of the praying mantis (see Figure 2.18). The female mantis is a rapacious killer. She seizes and devours any small creature unfortunate enough to move across her

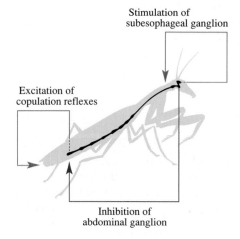

Stimulation of
subesophageal ganglion

Excitation of
copulation reflexes

Inhibition of
abdominal ganglion

2.18   The disinhibitory mechanism in the praying mantis   *Excitation of the abdominal ganglion leads to copulatory movements in the male. But the sight of the moving female stimulates the subesophageal ganglion in the male's head. This in turn inhibits the abdominal ganglion so that copulation stops. Decapitation severs the subesophageal ganglion. The result is disinhibition and copulation resumes. Here, dark green indicates excitation and dark red inhibition. (Roeder, 1967)*

field of vision. Since the male mantis is considerably smaller than the female, he too may qualify as food. This cannibalism is quite puzzling. How can the mantis survive as a species given a behavioral tendency that counteracts successful fertilization?

According to one hypothesis, the female's predatory pattern is triggered almost exclusively by moving visual stimuli. The courting male's behavior is delicately attuned to this fact. As soon as he sees her he becomes absolutely immobile. Whenever she looks away for a moment he stalks her ever so slowly, but freezes immediately when her eyes wheel back toward him—an inhibitory effect upon overall reflex activity. When close enough to her, he suddenly leaps upon her back and begins to copulate. Once squarely upon the female's back he is reasonably safe (her normal killer reflexes are elicited only by moving visual stimuli, and he is mostly out of sight). But the dangers he must surmount to reach this place of safety are enormous. He must not miss her when he jumps; he must not slip while upon her. Should he fall, he will surely be grasped and eaten. Fairly often he does lose his balance, but even then all love's labor is not lost—for his genes, if not for him. The female commences to eat her fallen mate from the head on down. In almost all instances, the abdomen of the male now starts vigorous copulatory movements that are often successfully completed. Clearly, the male performs his evolutionary duty whatever his own private fate. But what is the mechanism?

It appears that the intact male's copulatory reflexes are inhibited by the subesophageal ganglion, located in his head. When this nerve cluster is removed, the animal will engage in endless copulatory movements even when no female is present. The same thing happens if the female chances to seize her mate and eat him. She first chews off his head and with it the subesophageal ganglion, thus disinhibiting the male's copulatory pattern, which now resumes in full force (Roeder, 1935). Poets may appreciate this finding as further proof that true love can survive the grave. But for our present purposes it is a demonstration of the principle of hierarchical organization. As we will see, this principle is even more important in vertebrate nervous systems than in the less developed neural structures of invertebrates such as the mantis.

THE PERIPHERAL AND CENTRAL NERVOUS SYSTEMS

Taken as a whole, the human nervous system consists of a fine network of fibers that gradually merge into larger and larger branches which converge upon a central trunk line, like the tributaries of a stream. This system is composed of the central and peripheral nervous systems. The ***central nervous system*** (usually abbreviated *CNS*) is made up of the brain and spinal cord. The ***peripheral system***, as its name implies, comprises all nervous structures that are outside of the CNS (see Figure 2.19).

Anatomists distinguish between two divisions of the peripheral nervous system—the ***somatic*** and the ***autonomic.*** The somatic division is primarily concerned with the control of the skeletal musculature and the transmission of information from the sense organs. It consists of various nerves that branch off from the CNS—efferent fibers to the muscles and afferent fibers from the skin, the joints, and the special senses. The autonomic nervous system (ANS) serves the many visceral structures that are concerned with the basic life processes, such as the heart, the blood vessels, the digestive systems, the genital organs, and so on.

The central nervous system can be described as a long tube whose front end is much thickened and has a number of structures attached to it. The portion of

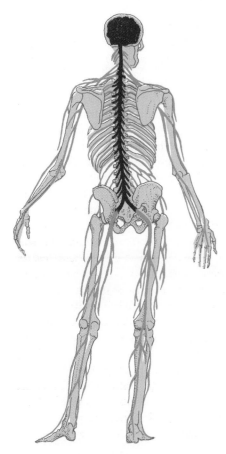

2.19 Central and peripheral nervous system *The central nervous system (in dark red) and the peripheral nervous system (in orange). (After Bloom, Lazerson, and Hofstadter, 1988)*

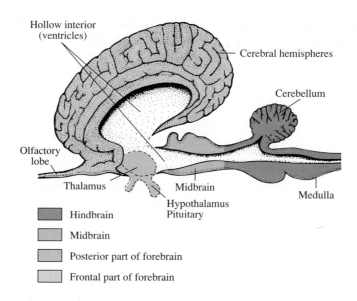

2.20 The central nervous system *This diagram is a highly schematic representation of the main parts of the brain. (After Lickley, 1919)*

the tube below the skull is the **spinal cord,** while the portion located in the skull is the **brain.** Two structures are attached to the **brain stem.** One is the pair of **cerebral hemispheres,** which are very large and envelop the central tube completely; the other is the **cerebellum** (literally, "little brain"), which is located lower down and is much smaller (see Figure 2.20).

Neuroanatomists find it convenient to consider the brain in terms of three major subdivisions: the **hindbrain,** the **midbrain,** and the **forebrain** (see Figure 2.21).

THE HINDBRAIN

The hindbrain includes the **medulla** and the **cerebellum.** The medulla, the part of the brain stem closest to the spinal cord, controls vital bodily functions such as heartbeat, circulation, and respiration. The cerebellum, a deeply convoluted structure that controls bodily balance and muscular coordination, functions as a specialized computer whose 30 billion or more neurons integrate the information from the muscles, joints, and tendons of the body that are required both for ordinary walking and for the skilled, automatic movements of athletes and piano players.

2.21 The human brain *(A) A photograph of the brain cut lengthwise. (Photograph by Biophoto Associates, Photo Researchers) (B) A diagram of the brain, cut lengthwise. The colors are analogous to those used in Figure 2.20 to indicate hindbrain (dark blue), midbrain (aqua), and forebrain (light green). (After Keeton, 1980)*

A

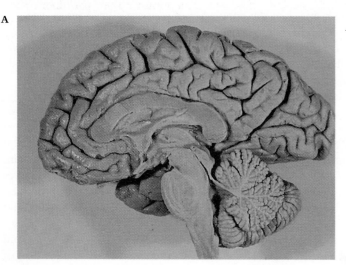

B

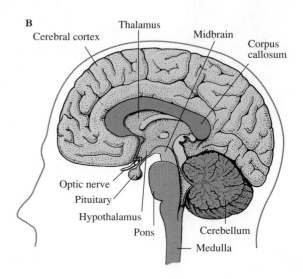

The hindbrain is on a fairly low rung of the nervous system's hierarchical ladder. This is shown by the behavior of cats whose brain has been cut at a point just above the hindbrain, severing the parts of the nervous system below the cut (that is, the hindbrain and the spinal cord) from all control by the portion above. The question is what the part below the cut can do now that it is on its own.

The answer is that the resulting hindbrain animal can still make the various limb and trunk movements that are required for standing, crouching, or walking. But it can't put them together. As a result, it is unable to stand or make walking movements unless supported by straps. Without support, a hindbrain cat will collapse, unable to come up with more than disorganized reflex twitches if stimulated. Reduced to a hindbrain, the animal has become a mere biological marionette without a puppet master: "It can move, but it cannot act" (Gallistel, 1980).

THE MIDBRAIN

The midbrain contains several neural centers that control some motor reactions and that also have some limited auditory and visual functions (such as controlling eye movements). True to its name, the midbrain can be regarded as a form of neural middle management that knits together the simple movements organized by the hindbrain to form larger wholes. An animal with only a hindbrain and a midbrain can stand, walk, crouch, and so on, but it can't organize these actions to achieve a goal, like stalking prey. The midbrain contains the circuitry that coordinates lower-level building blocks, such as reflexes, and forms them into the most basic acts of the organism. But the orchestration of these basic acts into patterns of purposeful behavior is conducted at a higher level still.

FOREBRAIN: THALAMUS, HYPOTHALAMUS, AND LIMBIC SYSTEM

The forebrain is made up of the two *cerebral hemispheres,* the *thalamus,* the *hypothalamus,* and the *limbic system.* Anatomists usually distinguish several large sections within each hemisphere, called *lobes.* There are four such lobes, each named for the cranial bone nearest to it: the *frontal, parietal, occipital,* and *temporal* (see Figure 2.22). The thin outer layer of the cerebral hemispheres is called the *cerebral cortex* (see below).

Nestled under the cortex are several forebrain structures that represent the topmost regions of the brain stem. One is the *thalamus,* a large system of various centers that serves as a kind of reception area for the cerebral hemispheres. Fibers from the eyes, the ears, the skin, and some motor centers pass their information to the thalamus, which then forwards it upward to the cerebral cortex. Another major structure in this region is the *hypothalamus,* which is intimately

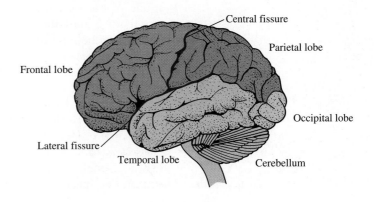

2.22   The cerebral hemispheres, side view

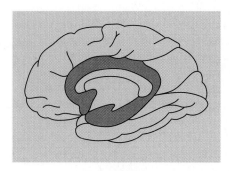

2.23 The limbic system *A schematic diagram of the limbic system (in blue) shown in side view. (After Russell, 1961)*

involved in the control of behavior patterns that stem from the basic biological urges (e.g., feeding, drinking, maintaining an appropriate temperature, engaging in sexual activity, and so forth; see Chapter 3). Finally, the third set of structures in the subcortical forebrain is located near the center of the cerebral hemispheres in a region that borders on the brain stem (see Figures 2.21 and 2.23). These are often grouped together under the term ***limbic system*** (from the French *limbique,* "bordering"). Many elements of the limbic system are part of what (in evolutionary terms) is an older unit, sometimes called the "old cortex." The limbic system has close anatomical ties with the hypothalamus and is involved in the control of emotional and motivational activities, and some aspects of learning and memory (see the discussion of the hypothalamus in Chapter 3).

An animal with a hindbrain, a midbrain, and all the structures of a forebrain but that of a cortex can organize its separate acts toward some purpose, but its performance is inept. When attacked by another cat, it strikes back, but quite ineffectively. Its blows are poorly directed and easily avoided by its enemy. The limbic animal can coordinate its acts into a sequence that has an aim. But that sequence and the environment in which it is enacted must be very simple. If it is at all complex, the animal will fail. The limbic animal can act, and its acts have some purpose. But lacking a cortex, it is stupid (Bard and Rioch, 1937; Wetzel and Stuart, 1976; Gallistel, 1980).

THE CEREBRAL CORTEX

FOCUS QUESTIONS

■ What are the major areas found in the cerebral cortex, and what general functions do they serve?

■ How are the areas devoted to specific movements and sensations organized in the cerebral cortex?

■ What techniques can be used to discover where particular functions are localized in the brain?

■ Which kinds of neurological disorders are commonly associated with damage to which regions in the cerebral cortex?

We finally turn to the structure that has traditionally been regarded as the functional summit of the behaving organism (or at least, of the thinking organism): the ***cerebral cortex.*** The cells in the cortex are so densely packed that they are capable of the most complex synaptic interconnections. While the cortex is only about 3 mm thick, it comprises a substantial proportion of the entire human brain because the cerebral hemispheres are deeply folded and convoluted. Thus crumpled up, the cerebral surface that can be packed into the cranial cavity is very much increased (see Figure 2.24).

The cortex is the most recent structure of the brain to emerge in the course of evolution. Fish have none at all, reptiles and birds have but a poor beginning, while in mammals there is considerable enlargement, especially in the primates. The cerebral cortex is that part of the nervous system that allows us to be intelligent, and its absence is catastrophic. For without a cortex there can be no planning, no complex sequence of motor movements, no perception of organized form, and no speech—in short, no semblance of anything that we call human.

2.24 Important structures of the brain
Thalamus, hypothalamus, and other structures as if seen through a transparent hemisphere. (After Bloom, Lazerson, and Hofstadter, 1988)

PROJECTION AREAS

Among the first discoveries in the study of cortical function was the existence of the *projection areas.* These serve as receiving stations for sensory information or as dispatching centers for motor commands. *Sensory projection areas* are those regions of the cortex where the messages that come from the various senses (usually through some other relay stations) are first received. *Motor projection areas* are those from which directives that ultimately go to the muscles are issued. The term *projection* is here used in a geometrical sense: Motor and sensory areas of the body are projected (mapped) onto particular regions of the cortex, resulting in a rough topographical correspondence between the location in the body and the location of the receiving or dispatching center in the cortex.

MOTOR AREAS

The discovery of the cortical motor areas began over a hundred years ago, when several physiologists opened the skull of a lightly anesthetized dog and then applied mild electric currents to various portions of its cerebral cortex. They discovered a region in the frontal lobe in which stimulating a given point led to motion of the forelimb, stimulating another point led to motion of the trunk, and so forth. Stimulating the left hemisphere led to movements on the right side of the body; stimulating the right hemisphere caused movements on the left. This made good anatomical sense because most of the major efferent pathways from the brain cross over to the opposite side just as they leave the hindbrain.

Some sixty years later, similar studies were conducted on human subjects by the Canadian neurosurgeon, Wilder Penfield. The stimulation was administered in the course of a brain operation. Penfield's studies showed that the cortical motor area in humans is in a region of the frontal lobe that is quite similar to that found in dogs. Stimulation there led to movement of some parts of the body, much to the surprise of patients who had no sense of "willing" the action or of "performing it themselves." Systematic exploration showed that for each portion of the motor cortex, there was a corresponding part of the body that moved when its cortical counterpart was stimulated, with each hemisphere con-

3 1

A

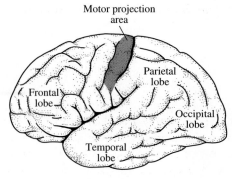

Motor projection area

Frontal lobe
Parietal lobe
Occipital lobe
Temporal lobe

B

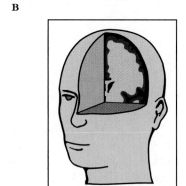

C

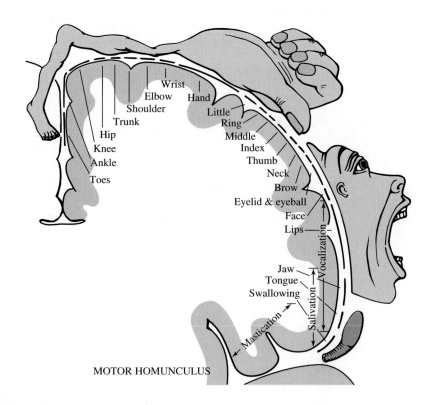

Wrist
Elbow
Hand
Shoulder
Trunk
Little
Ring
Hip
Middle
Knee
Index
Ankle
Thumb
Toes
Neck
Brow
Eyelid & eyeball
Face
Lips

Jaw
Tongue
Swallowing

Mastication
Salivation
Vocalization

MOTOR HOMUNCULUS

2.25   The motor projection area of the human cortex   *(A) The location of the motor projection area in a side view of the brain. (B) The head shows the plane of the cross section of the figure. (C) The motor projection area of one hemisphere shown in a cross section of the brain. The location and relative amount of cortical space allotted to each region of the body is graphically expressed as a motor homunculus. (After Penfield and Rasmussen, 1950)*

trolling the side of the body opposite to it. The results are sometimes expressed graphically by drawing a "motor homunculus," a schematic picture of the body with each part depicted on the motor projection area that controls its movement (Figure 2.25).

Inspection of the motor homunculus shows that equal areas of the body do not receive equal cortical space. Instead, parts of the body that are very mobile and capable of precisely tuned movement (the fingers, the tongue) are assigned greater cortical space than those employed for movements that are more gross and undifferentiated (the shoulder). Evidently, what matters is function, the extent and complexity of use (Penfield and Rasmussen, 1950).

SENSORY AREAS

Analogous methods have demonstrated the existence of cortical sensory areas. The ***somatosensory area*** is located in the parietal lobes (see Figure 2.26). Patients stimulated at a particular point of this area report a tingling sensation somewhere on the opposite side of their bodies. (Less frequently, they will report experiences of cold, warmth, or of movement.) Again, we find a neat topographic projection. Each part of the body's surface sends its sensory information to a particular part of the cortical somatosensory area, but again with an unequal assignment of cortical space. The parts of the body that are most sensitive to touch, such as the index finger and the tongue, enjoy a disproportionately large cortical space allocation. And again we find a crossover effect. Each part of the body is mapped onto the hemisphere on the side opposite to it: the right thumb onto the left hemisphere, the left shoulder onto the right hemisphere, and so on.

Similar projection areas exist for vision and for hearing and are located in the occipital and temporal lobes respectively (Figure 2.26). Patients who are stimulated in the visual projection area report optical experiences, vivid enough, but with little form or meaning—flickering lights, streaks of color. Stimulated in the auditory area, patients hear things, but again the sensation is rather meaningless and chaotic—clicks, buzzes, booms, hums.

ASSOCIATION AREAS

Less than one-quarter of the human cortex is devoted to the projection zones. The remaining regions are the **association areas,*** which are implicated in such higher mental functions as planning, perceiving, remembering, thinking, and speaking. Most of the evidence about these areas of the cortex comes from studies of patients who have incurred damage (technically, *lesions*) through tumor, hemorrhage, accident, or blockage of cerebral blood vessels (popularly known as *stroke*).

METHODS FOR STUDYING LOCALIZATION

The traditional interpretation of the effect of lesions in association areas is that they impair the organization of messages that come from the sensory projection areas or that go to the motor projection areas. But just how do we know exactly where the lesions are? To be sure, their exact location will eventually be known through an autopsy, but both the physician (and no doubt the patient) would surely prefer to get an answer while the patient is still alive. Standard X-rays are of some help, but they only reveal very gross pathologies. Fortunately, several modern techniques have been developed that provide us with a much more precise picture of the anatomical structure of a living patient's brain.

One such technique is the **CAT scan** (an abbreviation for *Computerized Axial Tomography*). It employs a narrow beam of X-rays that is aimed through the patient's head and hits a detector on the opposite side. This beam moves slowly in a circular arc, and the detector moves along with it. Since different brain tissues vary in density, they block the X-rays to different degrees. A computer eventually constructs a composite picture based on the X-ray views from all the different angles (see Figure 2.27).

* The term grew out of an earlier belief that neural messages from the different senses meet and become associated in these regions.

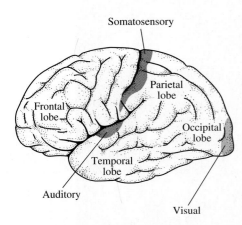

2.26 Sensory projection areas of the human cortex *The location of the somatosensory, auditory, and visual projection areas in the brain. (After Cobb, 1941)*

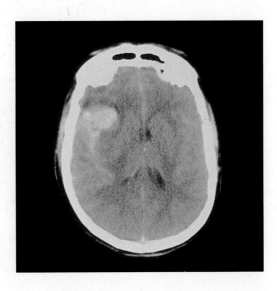

2.27 CAT scan *The CAT scan shows a subarachnoid hemorrhage, resulting from a ruptured blood vessel. The hemorrhage is the light area over the right side of the brain (left on image). It looks white because there was considerable bleeding; blood absorbs more radiation than ordinary brain tissue (Courtesy of the Radiography Dept., Royal Victoria Infirmary, Newcastle-upon-Tyre. Photo by Simon Fraser, Science Photo Library/Photo Researchers, Inc.)*

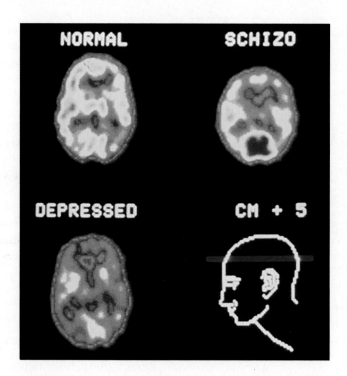

2.28   PET scans and disorders   *The scans show the difference in metabolic levels in normal, schizophrenic, and depressed individuals. Red indicates highest metabolic activity, with yellow next, followed by green, and then blue. During depression, for example, brain activity is considerably reduced, especially in the frontal areas. (NIH/SPL/Photo Researchers)*

Another development allows neurologists and psychologists to look into a living brain and observe some aspects of its functioning. This is the **PET scan** (or, to give its full name, *Positron Emission Tomography*), which utilizes the fact that brain tissue, like all other living tissue, uses more fuel the more active it is. The subject is injected with a radioactive sugar that resembles glucose (the only metabolic fuel the brain can use). Active cells of the brain take up this substance, which then signals its presence by emitting subatomic particles. (Needless to say, the dose is low enough so that there are no harmful effects). The more emission that occurs, the more metabolic activity is indicated. The resulting PET scan can thus tell the physician that a certain region of the brain is abnormally active or inactive and may suggest a tumor, a lesion, or a psychological disorder (see Figure 2.28). PET scans are also useful tools in studying localization of function in normal persons. For example, they show varying degrees of activity in the general region of the visual projection area depending on the complexity of the scene that is being viewed (see Figure 2.29).

By now the most widely used neurodiagnostic technique is **Magnetic Resonance Imaging (MRI)**, which relies on a physical principle of nuclear mag-

2.29   PET scan and visual stimulation   *These scans show the difference in metabolic brain activity depending on whether the patient's eyes were closed, or whether she was viewing a simple or complex scene. (Photograph by Dr. John Mazziotta et al./Photo Researchers)*

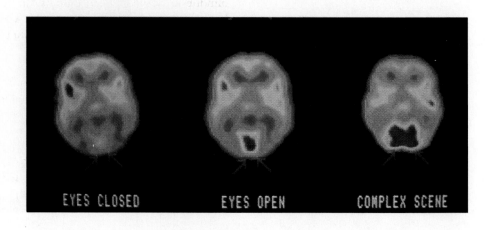

2.30 Magnetic Resonance Imaging (MRI) *A patient goes through the MRI procedure, while a medical specialist watches the image on a screen (Photograph © Paul Shambroom)*

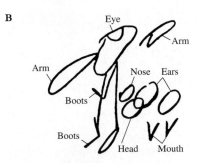

2.31 Drawings by a patient with agnosia *(A) Trying to copy an elephant. (B) Trying to draw a man. (From Luria, 1966)*

netic resonance. This refers to the fact that the nuclei at the center of atoms have their own resonant frequencies: If you perturb them, they sing like tuning forks as they bounce back to normal. The nuclei of the atoms that make up the neurons in the brain sing differently from those of other tissues. An MRI scan disturbs these atoms by passing a very high frequency alternating magnetic field through the brain by means of electromagnets surrounding the patient's head. As the magnetic field fluctuates, the chorus of atomic voices is detected by magnetic sensors within the scanner. A computer will then put the data together to form a picture of the brain that will show brain tumors and the blood clots and leaks that may signal strokes (see Figure 2.30).

As these and other medical procedures are refined in the next decade, they will offer a new window into the functioning of the normal human brain; at present, their greatest use is in locating cerebral lesions in clinical patients. By studying the disorders caused by such lesions, neuropsychologists have been able to make cautious inferences about the functions of the cortical association areas that have been damaged.

DISORDERS OF ACTION

Some lesions in the cortical association areas produce *apraxias* (from the Greek for "inability to act"), which are serious disturbances in the initiation or organization of voluntary action. In some apraxias, the patient is unable to perform certain well-known actions such as saluting or waving good-bye when asked to do so. In other cases, actions that normal persons regard as quite simple and unitary become fragmented and disorganized. When asked to light a cigarette, the patient may strike a match against a matchbox, and then strike it again and again after it is already burning; or he may light the match and then put it into his mouth. These deficits are in no sense the result of a motor paralysis, for the patient can readily perform each constituent of the action in isolation. His problem is in initiating the sequence or in selecting the right components and fitting them together (Luria, 1966; Kolb and Whishaw, 1990).

DISORDERS OF PERCEPTION

In several other disorders caused by lesions in certain cortical association areas, the patient suffers a disruption in the way she perceives the world or attends to it. One such disorder is *agnosia* (from the Greek for "without knowledge"). Whereas apraxia represents a disrupted organization of action, agnosia is characterized by a disorganization of various aspects of the sensory world. In visual agnosia, patients can see, but they are often unable to recognize what they see. They may have 20/20 vision, but they nevertheless suffer a kind of "psychic blindness." Some of these patients can perceive each separate detail of a picture, but they are unable to identify the picture as a whole. When shown a drawing of a telephone, one such patient painstakingly identified several parts and then ventured an appropriate guess: "A dial . . . numbers . . . of course, it's a watch or some sort of machine!" (Luria, 1966, p. 139). Agnosic patients have similar difficulties when asked to copy drawings. The individual parts are rendered reasonably well, but they cannot be integrated into a coherent whole (see Figure 2.31).

In some agnosias (technically known as *prosopagnosias,* from the Greek *proso,* "face"), the primary difficulty is in recognizing faces. Some of these patients are unable to distinguish familiar faces; others are even unable to recognize that a face *is* a face. When walking in the street, one such patient would pat the tops of fire hydrants, which he thought were the heads of little children. On one occasion he mistook his wife's head for a hat (Sacks, 1985; for further discussion, see Chapter 6).

3 5

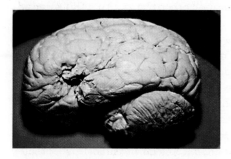

2.32 Tan's brain *The embalmed brain of Broca's famous aphasic patient "Tan," so-called because this was the only syllable he was able to utter. Note the area of damage on the lower side of the left frontal lobe, now known as Broca's area. (Photograph by M. Sakka, courtesy Musée de l' Homme et Musée Dupuytren, Paris)*

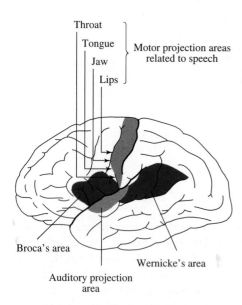

Throat
Tongue
Jaw
Lips

Motor projection areas related to speech

Broca's area

Wernicke's area

Auditory projection area

2.33 Broca's and Wernicke's areas *The diagram shows the two association areas most relevant to language. Destruction of Broca's area generally leads to expressive aphasia; destruction of Wernicke's area leads to receptive aphasia. Note the proximity to the relevant projection areas: Broca's area is closest to the regions that control the speech muscles, while Wernicke's area borders on the auditory projection zone.*

DISORDERS OF LANGUAGE

Certain lesions in the cortical association areas lead to serious disruptions of the most distinctively human of all human activities—the production and comprehension of speech. Disorders of this kind are called **aphasias** (from the Greek for "lack of speech"). In right-handers, they are almost always produced by lesions in certain cortical areas of the left hemisphere.

In one form of aphasia, the patient's primary difficulty is with the production of speech. This is **expressive aphasia,** which is essentially a language apraxia. In extreme cases, a patient with this disorder becomes virtually unable to utter or to write a word. Less extremely, a few words or phrases survive. These may be routine expressions such as "hello" or emotional outbursts such as "damn it!" In still less severe cases, only a part of the normal spoken vocabulary is lost, but the patient's speech becomes fragmented, as finding and articulating each word requires a special effort. The result is a staccato, spoken telegram: "Here . . . head . . . operation . . . here . . . speech . . . none . . . talking . . . what . . . illness" (Luria, 1966, p. 406).

The similarity to apraxias, which we discussed above, is very striking. There is no paralysis of speech muscles, for the patient is perfectly able to move lips and tongue. What is impaired is the ability to organize and plan these movements into a unified sequence, the ability to synthesize individual movements so as to form a word or to put one word after another so as to create a coherent sentence.

Expressive aphasias of the kind described here are generally produced by lesions in a region of the left frontal lobe called **Broca's area** (after a French physician, Paul Broca, who first noted its relation to speech in 1861; see Figures 2.32 and 2.33). This is an association area that borders on the part of the motor projection zone that controls the various speech muscles (jaw, tongue, lips, larynx, and so on) and presumably plays an important role in orchestrating their separate functions.

In expressive aphasia, patients generally understand what they hear but cannot answer. In another form of aphasia, the patients' problem is that they don't understand when they are spoken to, though they usually answer anyway. This condition is called **receptive aphasia,** which amounts to a kind of language agnosia. Unlike patients with expressive aphasia, those with receptive aphasia talk very freely and very fast, but while they utter many words, they say very little. The sentences they produce are reasonably grammatical, but they are largely composed of the little filler words that provide little information. A typical example is, "I was over the other one, and then after they had been in the department, I was in this one" (Geschwind, 1970, p. 904).

Receptive aphasia is usually associated with left-hemisphere lesions (in right-handers) in various association areas of the temporal and parietal lobes. Many authorities believe that the crucial locus is **Wernicke's area,** a region that borders on the auditory projection zone and is named after a nineteenth-century neurologist who first described various receptive aphasias (see Figure 2.33).

HOW NEAT IS THE HIERARCHY?

We have repeatedly noted that the nervous system is organized along the lines of a hierarchy, with higher centers controlling lower centers, which control yet lower ones. Where does the cortex fit in? Some nineteenth-century neurologists supposed that the cortex is at the very top of the hierarchy and hands down orders to all the rest. This view fits in with the view that those functions most severely disturbed by cortical lesions—language, thinking, memory, and perception—are the "higher" mental processes and that these presumably govern the "lower" ones. To that extent, our notion of the cortex as the neurological apex may be a good first approximation to the actual state of affairs. But it's worth noting that the final picture will probably turn out to be considerably more complicated than this.

For the nervous system is not organized according to a single hierarchy. It is not an absolute monarchy, with a cortical king who governs all below (e.g., Arbib, 1972). Instead, it is composed of a number of hierarchies whose controls and functions overlap, with some in the cortex and some in subcortical structures. These hierarchies interact continuously, with one in charge on one occasion but not on another. So it probably makes no sense to say that any one of them is the ruler. Instead, the operation of the nervous system may well be analogous not to an absolute monarchy but to the political system of a complex twentieth-century society such as ours. The United States in the 1990s is not governed by *one* hierarchy, but by a number of interlocking ones. There are the three branches of the federal government, as well as the armed forces and the bureaucracies of the government agencies, not to mention the hierarchies of the large corporations, the labor unions, the lobbyists, the media, and so on and so on. We are governed by a complex interaction of them all, and who will make the decisions depends on many factors, including what is to be decided.

So who's *really* in charge? That may be the wrong question. For just as rulers ultimately depend on those they rule, so the "higher" structures of the nervous system depend critically on the subordinate ones. The ultimate problem is to discover how all the various parts interact and work together.

ONE BRAIN OR TWO?

FOCUS QUESTIONS

- How do left-handers differ from right-handers in their general neurological organization?

- What is cerebral lateralization, and how is it studied?

- How do the two cerebral hemispheres appear to function differently?

Anatomically, the brain's two hemispheres appear to be quite similar, but there is abundant evidence that their functions are by no means identical. This asymmetry of function is called **lateralization,** and its manifestations include such diverse phenomena as language, spatial organization, and handedness—the superior dexterity of one hand over the other (Springer and Deutsch, 1981).

We have already seen that in right-handers aphasia is usually associated with lesions in the left hemisphere. Until fairly recently, neuroscientists interpreted this fact to mean that one hemisphere is *dominant* over the other. As a result, they called the (right-hander's) right hemisphere the "minor hemisphere," for they believed that it is essentially a lesser version of the left hemisphere.

More recent evidence has rescued the right hemisphere from this poor relation status, for it now appears that it has many important functions of its own. Right-handers with lesions in the right hemisphere often suffer from various difficulties in the comprehension of various aspects of space and form; they concentrate on details but cannot grasp the overall pattern. Some have trouble recognizing faces (Bogen, 1969).

The results are more ambiguous for the 12 percent or so of the population that is left-handed (and also generally left-footed and, to a lesser extent, left-

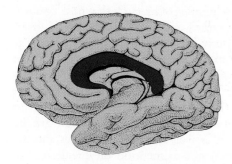

2.34   The split brain   *To control epilepsy, neurosurgeons sometimes sever the two hemispheres. This is accomplished by cutting the corpus callosum (in blue) and a few other connective tracts. The corpus callosum is shown here in a lateral cross section.*

eyed and left-eared as well; Porac and Coren, 1981). Somewhat more than half of the left-handers have speech predominantly lateralized in the left hemisphere; in the rest, language is usually represented in both hemispheres. But overall, there seems to be less lateralization in left-handers than in right-handers, so that the functional capabilities of the left-handers' two hemispheres are more on a par. Thus, in left-handers, aphasia may often be produced by lesions to either hemisphere. But by the same token, left-handed aphasics have a greater chance for recovery, for the intact hemisphere is better able to take over the responsibilities formerly assigned to the hemisphere that suffered damage (Brain, 1965; Springer and Deutsch, 1981).

EVIDENCE FROM SPLIT BRAINS

■ Some of the most persuasive evidence about the different functions of the two cerebral hemispheres comes from studies originated by Nobel laureate Roger Sperry on people with **split brains** (Sperry, 1974, 1982): those whose corpus callosum has been surgically severed (see Figure 2.34). The corpus callosum is a massive bundle of nerve fibers that connects the two hemispheres so that they can pool their information and function as a harmonious whole. This neurological bridge (and some other subsidiary ones) is sometimes cut in cases of severe epilepsy so that the seizure will not spread from one hemisphere to the other (Bogen, Fisher, and Vogel, 1965; Wilson et al.,1977). Once confined to a smaller cortical area, the seizures are less severe and less frequent. The surgery clearly relieves suffering, but it has a side effect—the two hemispheres of the split brain become functionally isolated from each other and in some ways act as two separate brains (Gazzaniga, 1967).

The effect of the split-brain operation is best demonstrated by setting a task that poses a question to one hemisphere and requires the answer from the other (see Figure 2.35). One method is to show a picture so that the neural message only reaches one hemisphere. This is done by flashing the picture for a fraction of a second to either the right or the left side of the patient's field of vision. The anatomical pathways of the visual system are such that if the picture is flashed to the right, it is projected to the left hemisphere; if presented to the left, it is projected to the right hemisphere (see Figure 2.36). The patient's job is merely to say what he sees. When the picture is on the right, he easily does so, for the information is transmitted to the same hemisphere that can formulate a spoken answer—the left hemisphere (which as we've seen is the primary site of lan-

2.35   A setup sometimes used in split-brain studies   *The subject fixates a center dot and then sees a picture or a word on the right or left side of the dot. He may be asked to respond verbally, by reading the word or naming the picture. He may also be asked to respond without words, for example, by picking out a named object from among a group spread out on a table and hidden from view, so that it can only be identified by touch. (After Gazzaniga, 1967)*

guage knowledge and of speech). The situation is different when the picture is flashed on the left. Now the visual image is sent to the right hemisphere, but this hemisphere can neither provide a spoken reply nor relay the information to the left hemisphere, which has the language capacity, because the bridge between the two has been cut (Gazzaniga, 1967).

This is not to say that the right hemisphere has no understanding of what it's been shown. One patient was unexpectedly shown a picture of a nude woman. When this picture was flashed to the left hemisphere, the patient laughed and correctly described what she had seen. When the same picture was presented to the right hemisphere, she said that she saw nothing, but immediately afterward she smiled slyly and began to chuckle. When asked what was so funny, she said, "I don't know . . . nothing . . . oh—that funny machine" (Gazzaniga, 1970, p. 106). The right hemisphere knew what it was laughing at. The left hemisphere heard the laughter but could only guess at the cause, for *it* didn't see what the right hemisphere had looked at.

LATERALIZATION IN NORMAL SUBJECTS

All the evidence for lateralization we've discussed thus far has come from patients with neurological deficits: some with lesions in one or another hemisphere, others with a severed corpus callosum. Can lateralization be demonstrated in normal populations? A considerable amount of recent research has shown that it can.

SELECTIVE STIMULATION OF THE TWO HEMISPHERES

One approach uses the same experimental procedure that was so successfully employed with the split-brain patients. Various stimuli are briefly presented to either the right or the left visual field of normal subjects. Some of the stimuli are items that are presumably better dealt with by the left hemisphere: words or letters. Others are items that call on the special capacities of the right hemisphere: faces or other complex forms. The subject's task is to recognize the items and indicate his response as quickly and as accurately as he can.

In studies of this sort, the experimenters' primary interest is in the subject's **reaction time,** that is, how long it takes him to respond. The logic of the experiment is simple. Suppose the stimulus is presented to the hemisphere that is most appropriate to it: words to the left, faces to the right. If so, this hemisphere can get to work immediately, decipher the stimulus, and come up with an answer. But suppose the stimulus is sent to the wrong cerebral address: words to the right and faces to the left. This calls for an extra step, for now the visual message must be forwarded to the other hemisphere by way of the corpus callosum. But this additional transmission step takes time. As a result, we would expect subjects to be faster in recognizing words presented to the left hemisphere than to the right hemisphere. By the same token, we would expect them to respond more quickly to faces shown to the right hemisphere than to the left. By now, a fair number of experiments have shown that this is essentially what happens (e.g., Geffen, Bradshaw, and Wallace, 1971; Moscovitch, 1972, 1979).

TWO MODES OF MENTAL FUNCTIONING

The preceding discussion indicates that language and spatial organization are usually handled in two different areas of the brain. Some psychologists believe that this difference in localization goes along with a distinction between

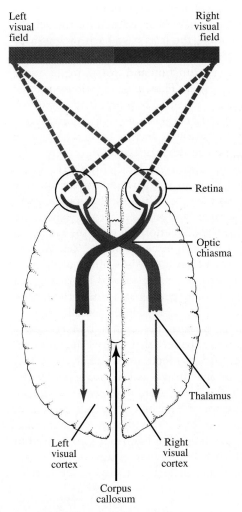

2.36 The visual pathway *The visual pathway is so arranged that all points in the right visual field send their information to the left hemisphere; all those in the left field send theirs to the right hemisphere. Information from one hemisphere is transmitted to the other by way of the corpus callosum.*

two fundamentally different modes of thought: one that involves words, the other spatial processes. This distinction is certainly in line with everyday observation. We often think in words—about scientific problems, about politics, about who likes whom; the list is endless. But we also mentally manipulate the world with little benefit of language—as when we visualize our living room with rearranged furniture or when we work a jigsaw puzzle. Many problems can be solved by either mode. We may find our way to a friend's home by referring to a mental map or by memorizing a verbal sequence, such as "first right turn after the third traffic light." But the two modes are not always intersubstitutable. How a corkscrew works is hard to describe in words; the pros and cons of a political two-party system are impossible to get across without them.

Many accounts of hemisphere lateralization have been written for the general lay audience. In the process of popularization, the facts have been progressively displaced by a rash of speculations that assert that the two hemispheres differ not just in their relative contributions to language function and spatial organization, but in many other underlying attributes as well. Thus it is sometimes claimed that the left hemisphere controls logical and sequential thought, that it analyzes, works with numbers, and deals in rationality. In contrast, the right hemisphere is said to be concerned with intuition, artistic creativity, and the comprehension of patterns that are grasped as a whole rather than being analyzed into their component parts. Some authors go so far as to relate right-left hemispheric differences to the (alleged) difference between Western science and logic on the one hand and Eastern culture and mysticism on the other. By now, the popular myth has it that our own society overly encourages "left-brained" at the expense of "right-brained" functions and that we need special efforts to train the neglected right hemisphere (e.g., Ornstein, 1977). One author recommends "Ten Ways to Develop Your Right Brain," which include occasionally drowning out the presentation of information with music and giving a thirty-second explanation of something and asking people to guess what you're getting at (Prince, 1978, cited in Springer and Deutsch, 1981). Whether such procedures actually help to strengthen intuitive thinking or complex pattern perception is exceedingly doubtful. But in any case, there is no reason to believe that the two hemispheres correspond to the distinctions (assuming such distinctions can really be made) between rational vs. intuitive thought, or analytic vs. artistic processes, or the difference between Western and Eastern philosophies of life (Levy, 1985; Efron, 1990). As Jerre Levy, a prominent investigator of hemispheric lateralization, puts it: ". . . The popular myths are misinterpretations and wishes, not the observations of scientists. . . . Normal people have not half a brain nor two brains but one gloriously differentiated brain with each hemisphere contributing its specialized abilities. We have a single brain that generates a single mental self" (Levy, 1985, p.44).

WHAT THE BRAIN CAN TELL US ABOUT THE MIND

■ The study of hemispheric lateralization illustrates an important trend in recent work on brain localization. Until recently, the main focus of twentieth-century investigators who studied the effects of brain lesions was on the light such effects might throw upon the functions that various parts of the brain perform. In effect they asked what the mind—or rather, damage to the mind—can tell us about the brain. But some modern workers, including many of those concerned with hemispheric lateralization, take the reverse approach. They ask what the brain can tell us about the mind.

To adherents of this approach—often called *cognitive neuropsychologists*—a crucial source of evidence comes from the *dissociation* of symptoms, a term that

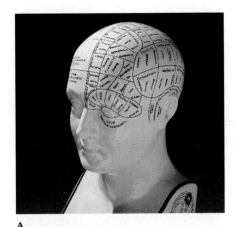

A

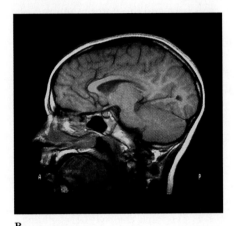

B

Cerebral localization then and now
(A) According to a now completely discredited theory developed during the nineteenth century, the degree to which people possessed such characteristics as foresight, courage, and the desire to have children could be assessed by looking at the shape of their skulls. The figure shows a model of a human head, indicating the supposed functions of the brain regions below. (Courtesy of The Science Museum / Science & Society Picture Library) (B) Modern neuropsychologists are more modest; they try to determine the function of different parts of the brain by correlating lesions in those regions with psychological losses. The figure shows a Magnetic Resonance Imaging (MRI) scan of a patient's head. (Photograph by Leonard Lessin / Peter Arnold, Inc.)

is used when a patient is impaired in one function but relatively unaffected in another. The neuropsychologists' reasoning is simple: If a patient with a lesion in one region of the brain suffers damage to one mental function but is unaffected in another function, while a person with a lesion in a different region shows the reverse pattern of impairments—which is just what happens with right- versus left-hemisphere lesions and spatial versus verbal ability—then we conclude that the two underlying psychological functions are essentially different.

Another example of such a dissociation of symptoms comes from certain patients with visual agnosias. Some of these patients are unable to identify or recognize inanimate objects. When confronted with pictures of vases and glasses and asked which go with each other, they fail completely. But when shown pictures of animate objects, such as dogs and cows, they do perfectly well. Other patients suffer from the reverse deficit: They have great difficulties in recognizing and identifying animate objects but little or none in dealing with inanimate ones. Findings of this sort suggest that our perception of animate and inanimate objects depends on different underlying psychological processes (McCarthy and Warrington, 1990; Shallice, 1988; but see Farah, 1990).

It's too early to say whether cognitive neuropsychology will succeed in determining which psychological processes belong together and which are independent of each other. Its adherents believe that it will, that the dissociation technique is a procedure that will carve cognition at its seams. To the extent that it will, psychology will be the richer.

SOME FINAL COMMENTS

Most of this chapter was about the neurological underpinnings of behavior. We have obviously come a long, long way since Descartes. Today we know a great deal about the biological foundation on which all human striving rests: the hundred billion neurons whose collective firings make up our human mind. Without these aggregates of neurons, there would be no *Hamlet,* no Sistine Chapel, no 9th Symphony, and of course no Auschwitz and no Cambodian massacres either.

The nervous system and its operation underlie whatever we do and think and feel. But does this mean that all psychological questions are at bottom neurological ones? Does it mean that all our ultimate answers will be in terms of action potential and neurotransmitters?

The proper reply is no. The answer to any question always depends on the level at which the question is phrased. Some questions are indeed most properly answered at the level of physiology (e.g., "What causes color blindness?"). But many others are properly stated at quite a different level. Suppose a historian asks why Napoleon didn't invade England. To answer with a paragraph—or book—about Napoleon's neurons and synaptic connections would be absurd. An appropriate answer might be that the weather was untoward, or that he didn't think he had enough ships, or that he didn't trust his admirals, or whatever. Any of these answers might be false, but they are at the right level. A statement about neuronal firing in Napoleon's frontal cortex would be completely off the mark and not only because we simply don't as yet know enough about the nervous system: Even if we could chart each firing, this answer is not going to satisfy the historian.

What holds for historians asking questions about a particular event holds for psychologists asking about the human (and even animal) mind. When they ask about how humans and animals act, perceive, think, remember, and feel, they typically want answers at the psychological level. Of course they're aware that all our actions take place within a framework set by our nervous system. But even so, they believe that psychological explanations are usually cast at a different (so to speak, higher) level than neurological explanations. Just how such psychological explanations are formulated will be the topic of many subsequent chapters.

One of the oldest of old and tired riddles is "Why did the chicken cross the road?" The answer—"Because it wanted to get to the other side"—is exceedingly silly, but it is surely much less silly than the answer "Because its cerebral neurons fired that way."

QUESTIONS FOR CRITICAL THINKING

1.   Given the all-or-none law, how can we explain the fact that our experience of the world is *not* all or none?

2.   Why might it be difficult—if not impossible—to isolate the exact region(s) of the brain responsible for any given thought or action?

3.   Given our greater understanding of brain function, does it still make sense to regard the mind as different from the brain?

4.   Human newborns can swim well (they can dog-paddle at birth) but soon lose this ability—in fact, most will need swimming lessons several years later. What might this tell us about the organization of the nervous system and possibly its evolution?

SUMMARY

1.   Since Descartes, many scientists have tried to explain human and animal movement by means of the *reflex* concept: A stimulus excites a sense organ, which transmits excitation upward to the spinal cord or brain, which in turn relays the excitation downward to a muscle or gland to produce action. Descartes' general classification of nervous function—*reception, integration,* and *reaction*—is still with us.

2.   Later investigators showed that the smallest unit of the nervous system is the *neuron,* whose primary anatomical subdivisions are the *dendrites, cell body,* and *axon.*

3.   A neuron's main function is to produce a *nerve impulse,* an electrochemical disturbance that is propagated along the membrane of the axon when the cell's normal *resting potential* is disrupted by a stimulus whose intensity exceeds the *threshold.* This stimulus produces a brief depolarization of the cell, which leads to an *action potential.* The action potential obeys the *all-or-none law:* Once threshold is reached, further increases of stimulus intensity do not effect its magnitude. But the nervous system can still distinguish between different intensities of stimuli all of which are above threshold. One means for doing this is *frequency:* The more intense the stimulus, the more often the neuron fires.

4.   To understand how neurons communicate, investigators have studied *reflex action,* which is necessarily based on the activity of several neurons. Results of studies with *spinal animals* led Sherrington to infer the processes that underlie conduction across the *synapse,* the gap between the axon of one neuron and the dendrites and cell body of the next. Conduction within neurons was shown to obey different laws than conduction between neurons (that is, across the synapse). Evidence included the phenomenon of *temporal summation.* Sherrington concluded that the excitation from several neurons funnels into a common reservoir over time to produce a *central excitatory state.*

5.   Further studies argued for a process of inhibition. Evidence came from *reciprocal inhibition* found in antagonistic muscles. Further work showed that a reflex can be activated either by increasing excitation or by decreasing inhibition.

6.   Sherrington's inferences of synaptic functions have been confirmed by modern electrical and chemical studies. We now know that transmission across the synapse is accomplished by *neurotransmitters,* chemical substances that are liberated at the axon terminals of one neuron and exert excitatory or inhibitory effects on the dendrites and cell body of another. They cross the *synaptic gap* and affect *receptor molecules* located on the *postsynaptic membrane.* This creates *graded potentials* that add up over time. When they reach threshold, they produce an action potential in the second neuron's axon.

7.   Important examples of neurotransmitters include *acetylcholine, norepinephrine,* and *dopamine.* The effect of transmitters is enhanced by *agonists* and reduced or blocked by *antagonists.*

8.   In addition to the nervous system, there is another group of organs whose function is to serve as an instrument of communication within the body. This is the *endocrine system,* whose glands secrete their *hormones* directly into the bloodstream, which will eventually carry them to various target organs.

9.   The brain tends to function hierarchically, with higher centers commanding lower centers. A demonstration of the hierarchical principal is the phenomenon of *disinhibition* produced by the destruction of higher centers that inhibit a reflex.

10.   A crude anatomical outline of the vertebrate nervous system starts out with the distinction between the *peripheral (somatic* and *autonomic)* and *central nervous systems.* The central nervous system consists of the *spinal cord* and the *brain.* Important parts of the brain are the *hindbrain* (including *medulla* and *cerebellum), midbrain,* and *forebrain* (including the *thalamus, hypothalamus, cerebral hemispheres,* and *cerebral cortex).* Of special interest is a group of subcortical structures of the forebrain called the *limbic system.*

11.   Hierarchical control in the central nervous system of mammals is shown by studies of animals whose brains have been cut at various points. An animal whose brain is cut so that only the hindbrain remains can still move but can't integrate its movements. An animal that has a hindbrain and a midbrain but not a forebrain shows integrated movements but can't pursue a goal. An animal that only lacks a cortex integrates its movements but pursues its goal ineptly.

12.   The *cerebral cortex* is generally believed to underlie the most complex aspects of behavior. The *projection areas* of the cortex act as receiving stations for sensory information or as dispatching centers for motor commands. The sensory projection areas for vision, hearing, and the bodily senses are respectively located in the *occipital, temporal,* and *parietal* lobes; the motor projection area is in the *frontal* lobe. The remaining regions of the cortex are called *association areas.* Their function concerns such higher mental processes as planning, remembering, thinking, and speaking.

13.   A number of modern neurological tools, including the *CAT scan,* the *PET scan,* and the *MRI* make it possible to diagnose and study lesions in the brains of living patients. Certain association area lesions lead to *apraxia,* a serious disturbance in the organization of voluntary action. Other lesions produce *agnosia,* a disorganization of perception and recognition. Still others cause *asphasia,* a profound disruption of language function, which may involve speech production, speech comprehension, or both. A lesion in *Broca's area* leads to *expressive aphasia;* one in *Wernicke's area* leads to *receptive aphasia.*

14.   In many ways, the two hemispheres are mirror images of each other. But to some extent, their function is not symmetrical. In most right-handers, the left hemisphere handles the bulk of the language functions, while the right hemisphere is more relevant to spatial comprehension. One source of evidence for this difference in hemispheric function, or *lateralization,* comes from the study of *split-brain* patients in whom the main connection between the two hemispheres, the *corpus callosum,* has been surgically cut. Further evidence is provided by the reaction times of normal persons when stimuli calling on verbal or spatial abilities are presented to either hemisphere.

15.   Until recently, most neuroscientists asked what damage to the mental functions can tell us about the brain. More recently, investigators concerned with *cognitive neuropsychology* have taken the opposite approach and asked what damage to the brain can tell us about the mental functions. A major tool in this endeavor is the study of the *dissociation* of symptoms.

CHAPTER 3

MOTIVATION

I n this chapter, we will examine some of the simple motives that human beings share with other animals. These motives steer our behavior in certain directions rather than others, toward food, say, rather than toward shelter.

Our main concern will be with motives that are essentially unlearned and that pertain primarily to the individual alone rather than to his interaction with others. Some of these motives can be understood as attempts at *self-regulation.* They include temperature maintenance, thirst, and hunger, which grow out of the organism's efforts to safeguard certain bodily necessities: a temperature that stays within certain limits, its water supply, its nutrient levels. Others are motives that are attempts at *self-preservation* in response to threat, such as the energetic exertions that accompany the emotions of fear and rage. Yet another motive is the need for sleep, which is sometimes thought to grow out of efforts at *self-restoration.*

These various motives are obviously very different, but they nevertheless have an underlying similarity, for they all direct behavior by making some acts more probable than others: When hungry, we generally seek food and eat it rather than engaging in other activities. The same holds for perception: When hungry, food and food-related stimuli in the environment are more likely to be looked for and noticed than are others. Similarly for feeling: When hungry, food is much more pleasant than when we are sated. This tendency to make some behaviors, perceptions, and feelings more probable than others is sometimes called *potentiation* (that is, increasing a potential). This chapter is an attempt to show how modern physiological psychologists try to account for these phenomena.

MOTIVATION AS DIRECTION

FOCUS QUESTIONS

- What is homeostasis?
- How does the concept of a feedback system help us to understand both homeostasis and motivation?

Most human and animal actions are directed. We don't simply walk, reach, shrink, or flee; we walk and reach *toward* some objects, shrink and flee *away* from others. The objects that are approached or withdrawn from may be in the organism's here and now, as when a kitten jumps toward a rolling ball. But often enough, the object exists in an as yet unrealized future. The hawk circles in the sky in search of prey, but there is none in sight as yet. In such a case, an inner motive (a purpose, a desire) apparently leads to actions that bring the hawk closer to its food.

Directed action seems difficult to reconcile with Descartes' notion of humans and animals as reflex machines, however complex their internal wiring. This problem is most pronounced for actions that are directed toward some future

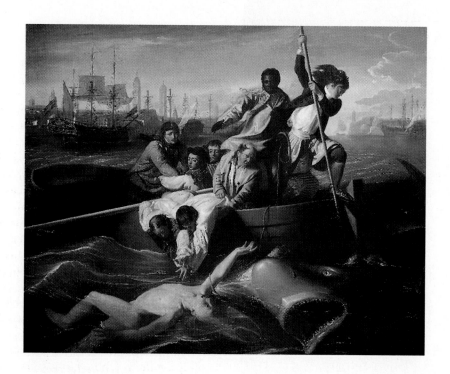

Motivation as directed action   This painting was commissioned by a man dramatically rescued from a shark attack in Havana harbor. As here depicted, each member of the small boat's crew directs his efforts towards the swimmer's rescue. (Watson and the Shark *by John Singleton Copley, 1778; gift of Mrs. George von Lengerke Meyer; courtesy of the Museum of Fine Arts, Boston)*

goal, for it is hard to see how an automaton can be imbued with purpose or desire. But difficulties arise even in the simplest case in which the direction is toward (or away from) an immediately present object. Consider the kitten reaching for the ball. What matters is not whether this flexor muscle is contracted or that extensor muscle relaxed, but rather whether the overall pattern of muscular activity gets the creature closer to the final end state—near the ball. The kitten may swipe at the ball with its right paw or its left, may crouch more on one side than on the other—all that matters is that, whatever the specific motor response, it will be directed toward the ball. Descartes' statues walked out and bowed when a visitor stepped on a hidden spring, but did they bow *to* the visitor? Suppose the visitor were to push the spring and then jump quickly to the left. The statue would surely lumber through its prescribed routine exactly as before, in stony disregard of the altered circumstance.

It is evident that a simple automaton is incapable of directed action. Can the machine be modified to overcome this lack? The answer is yes.

CONTROL SYSTEMS

■ Modern engineers have developed an immense technology based on machines that control their own activities and are in that sense directed. The basic principle upon which these devices are built is the notion of a *feedback system.* When such a machine is in operation, it performs some kind of action that may be mechanical, electrical, thermal, or whatever but that in all cases engenders some changes in the external environment. If these changes in turn influence the further operation of the machine, we have a control system based on *feedback.*

In *positive feedback systems,* the feedback strengthens the very response that produced it. The result is an ever-increasing level of activity. An example is what happens when a microphone is held too close to its amplifier. The microphone picks up whatever static is generated by the amplifier. It then feeds this static back to the amplifier, which makes the noise yet louder (that is, amplifies it), until it produces an unbearably loud wail that is the bane of poorly designed public-address systems.

Of greater relevance to our present concern is ***negative feedback*** in which the feedback stops, or even reverses, the original response of the machine that produced the environmental change. Negative feedback underlies a large number of industrial devices that can maintain themselves in a particular state (Figure 3.1). A simple example is the system that controls most home furnaces. A thermostat turns on a switch that controls the furnace for all temperatures below a given setting and turns it off for all that are above it. In the winter, the result is a steady house temperature, for the furnace will burn fuel only if the temperature is below the critical level; once this is reached, the furnace shuts off, deactivated by its own negative feedback. In a sense, the thermostatically controlled furnace has a goal: It "aims" at a particular temperature.

Negative feedback systems exist at all levels of the nervous system and are responsible, at least in part, for directed action. In this chapter we will see how such systems underlie motivated actions of many kinds. Some concern the organism's regulation of various vital functions—temperature maintenance, food and water intake, and the like. Others involve the organism's reaction to threats from outside, whether fearful escape or raging attack.

Can we apply the principles of negative feedback to the understanding of motivated action in which the direction is imposed from within? We will begin by considering those motives that grow directly out of the organism's regulation of its own internal state, such as its temperature, its water level, and its supply of nutrients.

HOMEOSTASIS

Descartes had emphasized the external environment—the stimuli that impinge on the organism from without and trigger its reactions. Some two hundred years after Descartes, another Frenchman, the physiologist Claude Bernard (1813–1878), emphasized the fact that the organism exists in an internal envi-

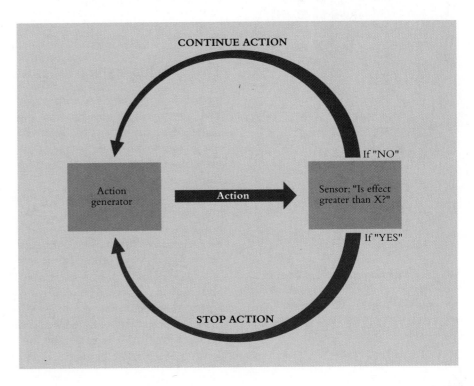

3.1 Negative feedback In negative feedback systems, the feedback stops or reverses the action that produces it. A sensing device indicates the level of a certain stimulus. If that level exceeds a certain setpoint, the action stops. The effect is self-regulation.

ronment as well as an external one—the organism's own bodily fluids, its blood and its lymph. Bernard pointed out that this internal environment is kept remarkably constant despite considerable fluctuations of the environment outside. This striking constancy is shown by the salt and water balance of the body, its oxygen concentration, its pH (a measure of acidity), its concentration of various nutrient substances such as glucose, and its temperature (in warm-blooded animals). In healthy organisms, all of these fluctuate within very narrow limits, and these limits define the organism's conditions for health and survival. Thus 60 to 90 milligrams per 100 cubic centimeters of blood is the acceptable range for the glucose concentration in the bloodstream of a healthy person. A drop below this level means coma and eventual death; a prolonged rise above it indicates disorders such as diabetes. The modern term for this stable internal equilibrium is **homeostasis** (literally, "equal state") and the mechanisms whereby it is achieved are sometimes said to reflect the "wisdom of the body" (Cannon, 1932).

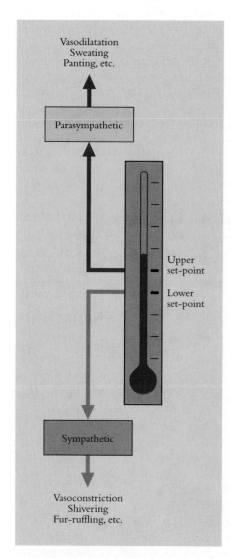

3.2 Reflexive temperature regulation in mammals *When the temperature deviates from an internal setpoint, various reflexive reactions will occur to restore the temperature to this setpoint.*

TEMPERATURE REGULATION

FOCUS QUESTION

■ What voluntary and involuntary methods are used to regulate internal body temperature?

A relatively simple example of homeostatic balance is temperature regulation in birds and mammals. These animals are called warm-blooded because they have a large repertoire of homeostatic adjustments that keep their internal body temperatures at a fairly constant level, despite wide temperature variations in the surrounding environment.

TEMPERATURE CONTROL FROM WITHIN

If the internal temperature of a warm-blooded animal is too high, various reflexive reactions produce heat loss. One is peripheral **vasodilatation,** a widening of the skin's capillaries. This sends warm blood to the body's surface and results in heat loss by radiation. Other reactions that lead to cooling are sweating (in humans) and panting (in dogs), both of which produce heat loss by evaporation.

An opposed pattern is called into play when the internal temperature is too low. Now there is no sweating or panting, and instead of peripheral vasodilatation there is **vasoconstriction.** The capillary diameters narrow, so that the blood is squeezed away from the cold periphery and heat is conserved. Other reflexive reactions include a ruffling of the fur to create a thick envelope of protective air. (The goose-flesh feeling is our feeble remnant of this reflex response, of little use to us now in our naked condition.) All of these reflexive reactions—as indeed all homeostatic adjustments—are essentially *compensatory.* They compensate for the swings of body temperature by pushing the system in the opposite direction (see Figure 3.2). In this regard, they are completely analogous to the thermostatic controls of a furnace or an air conditioner.

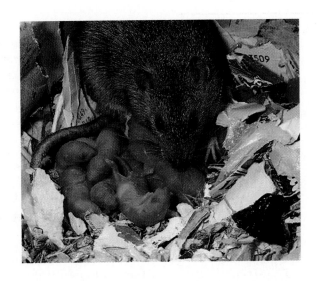

External temperature control and mother love in rats *After rat pups are born, they huddle under the mother's belly for warmth. Why does the mother allow this? It's not just maternal affection. The hormones circulating through the mother after she gives birth overheat her, so she is quite content to have the cool bodies of her offspring against her own. (Photograph by Jane Burton; © 1987, Bruce Coleman, Inc.)*

TEMPERATURE CONTROL BY BEHAVIOR

The homeostatic mechanisms we have just described are essentially involuntary. They may be actions, but we don't feel that they are *our* actions; in fact, some of them concern only a fraction of the body's subsystems. For example, vasodilatation and vasoconstriction do not involve the skeletal musculature at all. But there is no question that when the need arises, these reflexive compensatory mechanisms are supplemented by voluntary actions that involve the organism as a whole. If a rat is placed in a cold cage, it will search for suitable materials and build a nest. That humans perform similar voluntary acts in the service of temperature regulation goes without saying: They wear coats when they are cold and wear as little as custom permits (or turn on an air conditioner) when they are hot. The important point is that these voluntary actions are still in the service of that same internal environment whose constancy is so crucial to survival. But there is one important difference: Now the organism actively changes its external environment so that its internal environment can stay the same.

THE AUTONOMIC NERVOUS SYSTEM AND TEMPERATURE CONTROL

To understand how the nervous system marshals its forces to protect us against extreme heat and cold we'll begin by looking at the involuntary side of temperature regulation. What controls the various reactions of the internal organs that accomplish this? The most direct control is exerted by the *autonomic nervous system (ANS),* which sends commands to the *glands* and to the *smooth muscles*★ of the internal organs and blood vessels.

The ANS has two divisions: the *sympathetic* and the *parasympathetic.* These two divisions often act as antagonists. Thus, the excitation of the sympathetic division leads to an acceleration of heart rate and inhibition of peristalsis (rhythmic contractions) of the intestines. Parasympathetic activation has effects that are the very opposite; cardiac deceleration and stimulation of peristalsis. This same

---

★The individual fibers of these muscles look smooth when observed under a microscope, in contrast to the fibers of the skeletal muscles, which look striped.

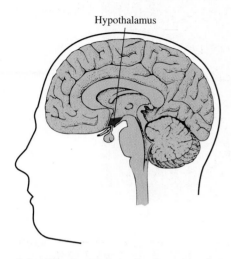

Hypothalamus

3.3   The hypothalamus   *Cross-section of the human brain with the hypothalamus indicated in blue. (After Keeton, 1980)*

3.4   Performing a learned response to keep warm   *A rat kept in a cold environment will learn to press a lever that turns on a heat lamp for a few seconds after each lever press. (Weiss and Laties, 1961)*

antagonism is seen in temperature regulation. The sympathetic division acts to counteract cold; it triggers vasoconstriction, shivering, and fur-ruffling. In contrast, the parasympathetic helps to cool the body when it is overheated; it stimulates panting, sweating, and vasodilatation (see Figure 3.10, p. 61). We'll have more to say about the tug-of-war between the two autonomic divisions when we discuss fear and rage. For now, we merely note that the autonomic nervous system is an important agent in directing the control of the internal environment.

SENSING THE INTERNAL ENVIRONMENT: THE HYPOTHALAMUS

■ The sympathetic and parasympathetic divisions control the various compensatory mechanisms that help to maintain the internal environment. But what governs *them?* A crucial center is the **hypothalamus** (see Figure 3.3), which represents a veritable triumph of anatomical miniaturization. In a full-grown person, it is only about the size of a pea, but it contains the controls for many of the biological motives.

Under normal conditions, temperature regulation is nearly perfect. This means that the hypothalamus can somehow sense the body's temperature, can sense deviations from the normal level, and can then determine in which direction it should throw the autonomic two-way switch (for example, choosing vasoconstriction over vasodilatation) to restore the thermal balance. But how does it do this?

The answer is that the hypothalamus contains its own thermometer: receptor cells that respond to the temperature of the bodily fluids in which the brain is bathed. When a cat's anterior hypothalamus is heated by a warm wire, there is panting and vasodilatation despite the fact that the cat's body temperature may be well below normal (Magoun et al., 1938). This suggests that the thermoreceptors are hooked up to the reflex controls so as to yield negative feedback—a hypothalamic thermostat. The heating wire fools the hypothalamus by changing its temperature independently of the temperature of the skin and body; the overheated hypothalamus then causes sweating, regardless of the body's actual temperature. The effect is analogous to what would happen if a blow dryer were directed at a home thermostat. The furnace would shut itself off, even though the house were actually freezing.

Vasoconstriction and vasodilatation are involuntary compensatory reactions, more in the domain of physiology than that of behavior. Does the hypothalamic feedback device have similar effects upon actions that reach out into the external world (for instance, wearing a fur coat)? Indeed it does. As one example, consider a study that utilized the fact that rats in a cold chamber will press a bar for a brief burst of heat (Weiss and Laties, 1961; see Figure 3.4). The question was whether rats that had learned this skill in a cold environment would bar-press for heat if one cooled their brains rather than their bodies. The test was to run cold liquid through a very thin U-shaped tube implanted in the neighborhood of the anterior hypothalamus (Satinoff, 1964). The rats turned on the heat lamp when their brains were cooled even though the outside temperature was reasonably neutral.

Tricking the hypothalamus (and certain regions just adjacent to it) can evidently affect integrated behavior patterns just as it does autonomic reactions like vasodilatation. The hypothalamus defines an internal need for the rest of the nervous system, and this need then becomes an important criterion that determines whether a given act is appropriate and, if so, potentiates it.

THIRST

FOCUS QUESTIONS

■ In what three ways does the body monitor its water supply?

■ How does the body attempt to maintain its water supply?

What holds for temperature holds for most other homeostatic regulations as well. Consider the body's water supply. We continually lose water—primarily through the kidneys but also through the respiratory system, the sweat glands, the digestive tract, and, occasionally, by hemorrhage.

How does the system act to offset these losses? One set of reactions is entirely internal. Thus, a loss of water volume leads to a secretion of the **antidiuretic hormone (ADH)** by the pituitary gland. ADH instructs the kidneys to reabsorb more of the water that passes through them. As a result, less water is passed out of the body in the urine. (Conversely, alcohol inhibits ADH, a fact that may explain why rest rooms are so heavily used at bars.)

But as with temperature regulation, internal compensatory readjustments can only restore the bodily balance up to a point. ADH can help protect the body against further water loss, but it cannot bring back what was lost already. Eventually, the corrective measures must involve some behavior by which the organism reaches out into the external world so as to readjust its internal environment. This behavior is drinking—in humans, an average of two to three quarts of water per day.

How does the body know that it needs water? There are a number of receptors that provide this information. Some are located in the brain and monitor the total volume of blood and other bodily fluids outside of the cells. Others are located inside the heart and its surrounding veins, and they are excited by drops in blood pressure that occur when there is a decrease in the total amount of body fluid. Still others keep track of the water *within* the body's cells. This depends on the concentration of certain minerals (especially sodium) that are dissolved in the fluid outside the cell.

It appears that there are at least three separate receptor systems that monitor the body's water levels; future research may find even more. Why so many? Here, as in the case of temperature regulation, we find that evolution has pro-

Thirst *Although surrounded by water, sailors in a lifeboat are nevertheless dying of thirst, for drinking the seawater would only lead to further dehydration. (Scene from* Mutiny on the Bounty, *1935; courtesy of Photofest)*

vided us with multiple defenses. There is a redundancy of mechanisms, so that if one fails another can take its place. We will find even greater redundancy when we turn to a more complex system of self-regulation: maintaining the body's nutrient levels by feeding.

HUNGER

FOCUS QUESTIONS

■ What signals indicate when to eat and when to stop eating?

■ What is the dual-center hypothalamic theory of feeding, and how is feeding affected by damage to specific areas of the hypothalamus?

■ How do both constitutional and behavioral factors contribute to obesity?

■ What are anorexia and bulimia, and what psychological factors may contribute to each?

All animals have to eat, and much of their lives revolve around food—searching for it, hunting it, ingesting it, and doing their best not to *be* it for others. There is no doubt that feeding is ultimately in the service of homeostasis, for no matter what food an animal eats or how he gets it, the ultimate biological consequence is always the same—to maintain appropriate nutrient supplies in the internal environment. But what are the actual mechanisms that determine whether humans and animals eat or stop eating? To put it another way, what makes us hungry and what satiated?

THE SIGNALS FOR FEEDING

There are numerous signals that control food intake. Among the most important of these are stimuli that arise from within the animal's own body and somehow inform the brain of the current state of the nutrient supplies. That some such messages are sent is certain. Without them, neither humans nor animals would be able to control their food intake, and they generally do. If food is freely available, they usually eat just about the right amount to keep a roughly constant weight as adults. What is regulated is caloric intake rather than the total volume of food that is eaten. This was demonstrated in a study in which the experimenter varied the caloric level of the diet fed to rats by adulterating their food with nonnutritive cellulose. The more diluted the food, the more of it was eaten, in a quantity roughly adequate to keep the total caloric content constant (Adolph, 1947).

SIGNALS FROM THE INSIDE

Receptors in the brain   How does the animal manage to adjust its food intake to its caloric needs? From the start, investigators focused on **glucose** (or blood sugar), which is the major source of energy for bodily tissues. The first hypothesis that comes to mind is that the critical signal is the glucose concentration in the bloodstream. But this cannot be what matters, for people with diabetes have abnormally high levels of blood glucose, yet they tend to be hungry much of the time. Perhaps what matters is not the amount of glucose as such, but the amount of glucose that is available for metabolic use (Mayer, 1955). Many authors believe that the receptors that detect changes in the way this metabolic fuel is utilized are in the brain itself, most likely in the hypothalamus. Evidence for such **glucose receptors** and their location comes from studies in which the hypothalamus was injected with a chemical that made its cells unable to respond to glucose. The result was ravenous eating. This treatment presumably silenced the glucoreceptors whose failure to fire was then interpreted as a fuel deficiency, which led to feeding (Miselis and Epstein, 1970).

Receptors in the stomach and intestines   Why does an animal stop eating? The receptors in the brain can't be the only reason. For they respond to fuel deficiency in the bloodstream, and this deficiency will not be corrected until after the meal has been at least partially digested. Yet humans and animals will terminate a meal much before that. What tells them that it's time to stop?

Common sense suggests that feeding stops when the stomach is full. This is true enough, but it is only part of the story, for animals will stop eating even when their stomach is only partially full. This will only happen, however, if they have ingested a nutritious substance. If the stomach is filled with an equal volume of nonnutritive bulk, the animal will continue to eat. This suggests that the stomach walls contain receptors that are sensitive to the nutrients dissolved in the digestive juices. They signal the brain that nutrient supplies to the internal environment are on their way as food is about to enter the intestines. The result is satiety (Deutsch, Puerto, and Wang, 1978).

Signals from the liver   Yet another source of information about the body's nutrient levels comes from the organ that acts as the manager of the body's food metabolism—the liver.

Immediately after a meal, glucose is plentiful. Since the body can't use it all, much of it is converted into other forms and put in storage. One such conversion goes on in the liver, where glucose is turned into **glycogen** (often called animal starch) and various fatty acids. Glycogen and fat cannot be used up as a metabolic fuel. This is fine right after a meal when glucose is still abundant, but the glucose will soon be used up so the stored energy has to be tapped eventually. When that happens, the chemical reaction goes the other way. Now the stored energy has to be turned into usable glucose.

Several studies suggest that the liver contains receptors that can sense in which direction the metabolic transaction goes, from glucose cash to stored energy deposits, or vice versa. If the balance tips toward storage, the receptors signal satiety and the animal stops eating. If the balance tips toward glucose production, the receptors signal hunger and the animal eats (Figure 3.5). The evidence

3.5   *The relation between the glucose-glycogen balance in the liver and eating*

GLUCOSE ➡ GLYCOGEN

↓

LIVER RECEPTORS

↓

DON'T EAT!

GLUCOSE ⬅ GLYCOGEN

↓

LIVER RECEPTORS

↓

EAT!

that this happens in the liver comes from hungry dogs that were injected with glucose. When the injection was into the vein that goes directly to the liver, the dogs stopped eating. When the injection was anywhere else, there was no comparable effect (Russek, 1971; Friedman and Stricker, 1976).

SIGNALS FROM THE OUTSIDE

The self-regulation of food intake is remarkable, but it is not perfect. Humans and animals eat to maintain nutritive homeostasis; put another way, they eat because their bodies need food. But they sometimes eat because they like the taste of a particular food. We eat dessert even though we may be full; our need for nutrients is gone, but not our appetite.

Such facts show that eating is not solely determined by stimuli that come from within the body. For these are supplemented by various external signals. We clearly do not eat for calories alone. Taste—and also smell and texture—is a powerful determinant of food intake for humans as well as animals. But palatability is not the only external signal for eating. Other signals are determined through learning. The expected mealtime is one example; the company of fellow eaters is another.

Sights, smells, tastes, and even company can restore one's appetite, but if the meal was large enough, even the tastiest dessert or the most encouraging cohorts will no longer tempt. The fact that the attractiveness of food depends on the degree of hunger reminds us of what hunger—and indeed all the biological motives—are all about. They potentiate and orchestrate all kinds of food-related behaviors whose ultimate biological function is to get us through life as healthy and as well-fed as possible. Animals don't know that their body needs various nutrients to convert into glucose and other vital metabolic necessities; after all, neither they nor most of us have ever read a text on digestive physiology. Nature has built that information into their and our nervous systems so that hunger is unpleasant and eating when hungry is pleasant. The fact that the most enjoyable dessert becomes unbearably cloying after two or three portions is another demonstration of the potentiating role of motives that determine what we feel no less than what we do.

Peasant Wedding Feast   (Peter Brueghel
the Elder, 1527; courtesy the Kunsthistorisches Museum)

HYPOTHALAMIC CONTROL CENTERS

■ We have seen that there are many different signals for food intake. It was natural to suppose that these various messages are all integrated at one point in the nervous system where a final decision is made to eat or not to eat. The natural candidate for such a feeding center was the hypothalamus, which was already known to house controls for temperature regulation and water balance and which gave evidence of containing glucoreceptors. Physiological psychologists soon devised a dual-center theory of hypothalamic control of feeding that was analogous to the temperature system. It postulates two antagonistic centers, one corresponding to hunger, the other to satiety.

DUAL-CENTERS FOR FEEDING

According to dual-center theory, the hypothalamus contains an "on" and an "off" command post for eating. Two anatomical regions are implicated. One is located in the *lateral region* of the hypothalamus; it was said to function as a hunger center whose activation leads to food search and eating. The other is the *ventromedial region,* which was thought to be a satiety center whose stimulation stops eating.

The evidence for these claims came from the effects of lesions. Rats whose lateral hypothalamus has been destroyed suffer from *aphagia* (from the Greek for "no eating"). They refuse to eat and drink and will starve to death unless forcibly tube-fed for weeks (Teitelbaum and Stellar, 1954). Interestingly enough, eventually there is some recovery of function. After a few weeks the animals begin to eat again, especially if tempted by such delectables as eggnog (Teitelbaum and Epstein, 1962).

Lesions to the ventromedial region produce effects that are in many ways the very opposite. Animals with such lesions suffer from *hyperphagia* (from the Greek for "excess eating"). They eat voraciously and keep on eating. If the lesion is large enough, they may become veritable mountains of rat obesity, finally reaching weights that are some three times as great as their preoperative levels (see Figure 3.6). Tumors in this hypothalamic region (although very rare) have the same effect on humans (Miller, Bailey, and Stevenson, 1950; Teitelbaum, 1955, 1961).

While ventromedial lesions lead to rapid weight gain, this levels off in a month or two after which the animal's weight remains stable at a new (and of course much greater) level. Once this new weight is reached, the animal eats enough to maintain it but no more (Hoebel and Teitelbaum, 1976). This suggests that the lesion produced an upward shift in a *setpoint* for weight regulation—a point that defines a kind of target value that determines food intake.

Details aside, dual-center theorists regard the two hypothalamic regions as mutually inhibitory centers of which one serves as an on-switch for eating, the other as an off-switch. There is a great deal of recent evidence that these switches are in turn activated by a number of internal and external signals. All of these signals act upon the feeding centers—some to trigger eating, others to inhibit it. Whether the organism eats will then depend on the summed value of them all: the level of various available nutrients in the blood stream, satiety signals from the stomach, food palatability, learned factors, and so on (Stellar, 1954).⋆

⋆The dual-center theory of feeding held center stage for several decades. But it has since come in for some reconsideration. The main grounds concern the effects of hypothalamic lesions. Critics believe that some of the effects of these lesions are not directly on behavior but rather on food metabolism (Stricker and Zigmond, 1976).

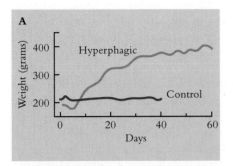

A

B

3.6 Hyperphagia (A) Curve showing the weight gain of hyperphagic rats after an operation creating a hypothalamic lesion. The weight eventually stabilizes at a new level. (After Teitelbaum, 1955) (B) Photograph of a rat several months after the operation. This rat weighed over 1,000 grams. (Courtesy of Neal E. Miller, Rockefeller University)

OBESITY

■ Both homeostatic and nonhomeostatic determinants of food intake are relevant to a problem partially created by the affluence of modern industrialized society—*obesity.* Obesity is sometimes defined as a body weight that exceeds the average for a given height by 20 percent. Judged by this criterion, about one-third of all Americans are obese. Most of them would rather be slim, and their wistful desires offer a ready market for a vast number of diet foods and fads. In part, the reason is health (at least it is sometimes said to be). But more important are social standards of physical attractiveness. There are no corpulent matinee idols, no fat sex goddesses (Stunkard, 1975).

Most authorities agree that there are several reasons why people become fat. In some cases, the cause is a bodily condition. In others, it is simply a matter of eating too much.

BODILY FACTORS IN OBESITY

Most of us take it for granted that body weight is a simple function of caloric intake and energy expenditure. To some extent this is undoubtedly true, but it is not the whole story. There is also good evidence that a number of other constitutional factors may predispose one person to get fat, even if he eats no more (and exercises no less) than his slender next-door neighbor. One reason may be a more proficient digestive apparatus; the person who manages to digest a larger proportion of the food he ingests will necessarily put on more weight than his digestively less efficient fellows. Another reason may be a lower metabolic level; the less nutrient fuel that is burned up, the more that is left for fatty storage. These constitutional differences may help to explain why some people gain weight much more readily than others (Sims, 1986).

In some individuals there may be a biochemical pattern in which too much of the nutrient intake is converted into fat, leaving too little to burn as metabolic fuel. As we already saw, this pattern necessarily leads to increased hunger and overeating, which in turn leads to further fat deposits and yet further overeating (Friedman, 1990 a, b).

Some recent studies suggest that such constitutional differences in metabolic efficiency depend partially on genetic makeup. One was a study on the effects of overeating on twelve pairs of identical male twins. Each of these men was fed about 1,000 calories per day above the amount required to maintain his initial weight. The activities of each subject were kept as constant as possible, and there was very little exercise. This regimen continued for a period of 100 days. Needless to say, all twenty-four men gained weight, but the amount they gained varied substantially: from about ten to thirty pounds. A further difference concerned the parts of the body where the newly gained weight was deposited. For some subjects, it was the abdomen; for others, it was the thighs and buttocks. The important finding was that the amount each person gained was very similar to the weight gain of his twin (see Figure 3.7). Similarly for the location on the body where the weight was deposited. If one twin gained in the abdomen, so did his twin; if another deposited the fat in his thighs and buttocks, his twin did too. These findings are a strong indication that people differ in how their bodily machinery handles excess calories and that this metabolic pattern is probably inherited (Bouchard et al., 1990).

BEHAVIORAL FACTORS

In some persons, obesity is evidently produced by a bodily condition. But for many others, the cause lies in behavior: They simply eat too much. The ques-

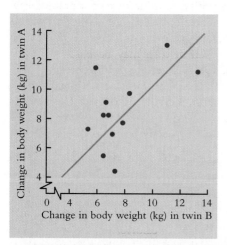

3.7 Similarity of weight gains in identical twins *Weight gains for twelve pairs of identical twins after 100 days of the same degree of overfeeding. Each point represents one twin pair, with the weight gain of twin A plotted on the vertical axis and the weight gain of twin B plotted on the horizontal axis. Weight gains are plotted in kilograms (1 kg = 2.2 lbs). The closer the points are to the diagonal line, the more similar the weight gains of the twins are to each other. (After Bouchard et al., 1990)*

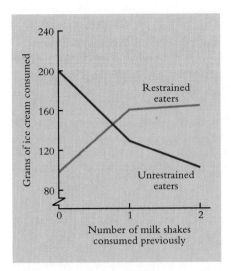

3.8 **The diet-busting effect in restrained eaters** *In the experiment, restrained and unrestrained eaters were asked to consume 0, 1, or 2 milk shakes in what they thought was an experiment on taste perception. They were later asked to judge the taste of ice cream and allowed to sample as much of it as they wished. The figure shows that restrained eaters ate considerably more ice cream if they had previously consumed one or more milk shakes. (After Herman and Mack, 1975)*

tion is why. It is virtually certain that there is no one answer, for chronic overeating has not one cause but many.

Restrained eating and obesity In our society many people who are overweight consciously try to restrain their eating. Since obesity is a social liability, they make resolutions, go on diets, buy low-calorie foods, and do what they can to clamp a lid on their intense desire to eat. But the clamp is hard to maintain, for any external stimulus for eating will threaten the dieter's resolve. In effect, there is a "disinhibition" of eating (Herman and Polivy, 1980).

An interesting demonstration of this disinhibition is provided by a study of "restrained" and "unrestrained" eaters. Persons judged as restrained said they were on a diet or expressed concerns about their weight. Restrained and unrestrained subjects participated in what was described as an experiment on the perception of tastes. Initially, some subjects had to taste (and consume) one or two 8 oz. milk shakes, while control subjects tasted none. After this, the subjects were asked to judge the taste of ice cream. While performing this task, they were left alone with an unlimited supply of ice cream. How much would they eat? Unrestrained eaters ate a sensible, homeostatically appropriate amount: The more milk shakes they had consumed, the less ice cream they ate in the subsequent test. But the exact opposite was true of the restrained eaters. The more milk shakes they had consumed, the more ice cream they ate now. The prior exposure disinhibited their restraint and led to a motivational collapse—a phenomenon all too familiar to would-be dieters—that some investigators have dubbed the "what-the-hell" diet-busting effect (Herman and Mack, 1975; see Figure 3.8).

The setpoint hypothesis The hypothesis regarding disinhibition of restrained eating tries to explain some of the effects of obesity. But it has little to say about its cause. One possibility is that people differ in their setpoints for weight. These may reflect differences in constitution, which in turn may be partially determined by heredity (Foch and McClearn, 1980). These setpoints determine the weight an individual's system aims at as it regulates its internal economy. But if so, then many a person who is fat by the standards of official what-your-weight-should-be tables may weigh exactly what their own setpoints say they should weigh. If they starve themselves, they'll drop to a weight below that level. But in the long run they probably won't stay there, for there'll always be a tendency to go back to the setpoint weight (Nisbett, 1972).

Some authors point out that the tendency to maintain a given body weight affects energy expenditure as well as caloric intake. Thus when obese people starve themselves, they don't lose anywhere near as much weight as they should on the assumption (known to all dieters) that 3,500 calories equals one pound. The reason is that the body compensates for the caloric loss by a drastic reduction in metabolism (Keesey and Powley, 1986). Repeated bouts of weight loss followed by weight gain lead to even greater efficiency in using food reserves. After several alternations between dieting and overeating, it takes considerably more days on the diet to get back to the original weight (Brownell, et al., 1986). This probably accounts for the "yo-yo" phenomenon sometimes observed in people who go on diets, break them, and then start dieting again (Carlson, 1991).

THE TREATMENT OF OBESITY

What can be done to help people who are overweight? Everyone knows that it's relatively easy to lose weight over the short run; the problem is to keep it off for good. Can it be done? Some authors are optimists and believe that obesity is a behavioral problem that can be remedied by training people to develop self-control and acquire appropriate habits of diet and exercise. Other authorities are

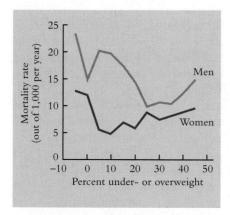

3.9 Relation of obesity to mortality
The figure presents the mortality rate in a sample of 5,209 people in Massachusetts for men and women from 45 to 74 years old between 1948 and 1964. The percent overweight is calculated by reference to mean weights for a given height. The figure shows that overweight does not increase the overall mortality risk, at least not for overweight percentages that are less than 50. (From Andres, 1980)

more pessimistic and believe that weight depends largely on a person's setpoint, which he can't escape in the long run. Attempts at treatment include psychoanalysis, various forms of behavior therapy (techniques for modifying the individual's behavior by the systematic use of certain principles of learning; see Chapters 4 and 19), and self-help groups (such as, Weight Watchers International). The extent to which any of these methods leads to long-term change is disputed, although there is some suggestion that the self-help groups do a fairly good job, especially for those who are only mildly overweight (Booth, 1980; Stuart and Mitchell, 1980; Stunkard, 1980; Wilson, 1980).

At this point it is difficult to decide whether the optimists or the pessimists have the better case (Logue, 1986). But suppose the pessimists turn out to be correct—suppose that there is a setpoint which decrees that weight is fate. If so, can we offer any hope to those who are overweight?

To begin with, one may question the widely held belief that being overweight is necessarily a disorder. It is often asserted that being overweight is a health hazard and that over one-third of the U.S. population are too heavy (U.S. Public Health Service, 1966). But apart from cases of gross obesity, the relation between overweight and life expectancy is still a matter of debate (Fitzgerald, 1981; see Figure 3.9). Some authors argue that for the great majority of individuals, obesity is a social and aesthetic problem, rather than a problem of physical health. (This is especially so for women, who are much more likely to regard themselves as overweight than are men; Gray, 1977; Fallon and Rozin,1985). Seen in this light, being slender is a social ideal, but we should not forget that it is an ideal of *our* society. Other cultures set different standards. The women painted by Rubens, Matisse, and Renoir were considered beautiful by their contemporaries; today they would be considered overweight. But does it really make sense to aspire to the body form of a fashion model if it is not one's own and perhaps can't be? Many people who regard themselves as overweight try to become lithe and slender but often fail anyway. Perhaps the best advice for them is to accept themselves as they are.

Changing conceptions of the relation between body weight and attractiveness *An underlying cause of many eating disorders in Western women is their belief that being slender is beautiful. But is it? It depends. (A) The Venus of Willendorf, a prehistoric statuette unearthed near Willendorf, Austria, that was sculpted some 30,000 years ago. Some archeologists believe that it depicts a fertility goddess; others, that it represents the female erotic ideal of the ice age. (Courtesy of Naturhistorisches Museum, Wien) (B) The Three Graces, painted by the Flemish master Peter Paul Rubens in 1639. (Courtesy of Museo del Prado) (C) Naomi Campbell, a fashion model of the 1990s. (Photograph by Mark Cardwell, Reuters/Bettmann)*

A

B

C

ANOREXIA AND BULIMIA

■ In some cases, the desire to be thin may be so extreme that it leads to eating disorders whose health hazards are much more serious than those produced by being somewhat overweight. One such condition is *anorexia nervosa,* which afflicts about 1 in 200 young women of the middle and upper classes in our society. Where the obese person is too fat and almost always eats too much, the anorexic is too thin (often dangerously so) and eats much too little. There are some cases of anorexia (literally "lack of appetite") that are caused by various organic conditions; for example in cancer patients, undergoing chemotherapy can produce nausea and various food aversions. In contrast, anorexia nervosa is not produced by any known organic pathology but is at least in part brought on by psychological factors. Its defining feature is "the relentless pursuit of thinness through self-starvation, even unto death" (Bruch, 1973, p. 4).

Anorexics are intensely and continually preoccupied by the fear of becoming fat. They eat only low-calorie food, if they eat at all. In addition, they often engage in strenuous exercise, often for many hours each day. Of course, this regimen leads to extreme weight loss, sometimes reaching levels that are less than 50 percent of the statistical ideal. Further symptoms include the cessation of menstruation, hyperactivity, sleep disorders, and avoidance of sex. In perhaps 10 percent of the cases, the end result of this self-starvation is death.

What leads to anorexia nervosa? Many authors believe that the primary causes are psychological and center on food and not eating because of our modern obsession with slimness (Logue, 1986). In some patients, the main cause is a fear of being sexually unattractive or of sex. In others, the primary focus involves a rebellion against the parents and a fierce desire to exercise some degree of autonomy and control. As one patient put it: "When you are so unhappy and you don't know how to accomplish anything, then to have control over your body becomes a supreme accomplishment. You make out of your body your very own kingdom where you are the tyrant, the absolute dictator" (Bruch, 1978, p. 61).

Other authorities believe that the primary problem is organic. One possibility is some kind of hypothalamic malfunctioning, together with a hormonal disturbance, as shown by the fact that anorexics have unusually low levels of reproductive and growth hormones. As yet, we don't know whether the hormonal imbalances are the effect or the cause of the psychological problems and the self-starvation diet (Garfinkel and Garner, 1982).

Another eating disorder is *bulimia,* which is characterized by repeated eating binges that are often followed by attempts to purge the calories just consumed by self-induced vomiting or by taking laxatives. Unlike anorexics, bulimics are of roughly normal weight, but their repeated binge-and-purge bouts can lead to a variety of problems. To begin with, many bulimics suffer considerable depression after a binge. In addition, the repeated binges may produce disruptions of the electrolyte balance that may ultimately lead to cardiac, kidney, and urinary infections. Bulimia is fairly common currently among college students (in one survey, it was found in 19 percent of the women and 5 percent of the men). The binge-and-purge cycle is a perfect expression of our contradictory attitudes toward food and eating. On the one hand, there are the easily available high-calorie foods that we are constantly urged to buy ("Treat yourself to a bar of _____ . You deserve it!"); on the other hand, we are constantly reminded that to be sexually attractive we must be thin (Logue, 1986).

We've seen that the regulation of food intake in all animals is a complexly regulated process characterized by multiple, overlapping mechanisms acting at a variety of levels of organization. But the eating disorders show us that in our own species in which a highly developed cerebrum modulates the hypothalam-

Thin is beautiful—or is it? Members of the Boston organization Boycott Anorexic Marketing believe that the glamorization of ultrathin models in advertising tends to encourage the development of eating disorders in young women. To call attention to this relationship, such groups sometimes annotate the ads of those they see as culprits. (Kate Moss in an advertisement for Calvin Klein; photograph courtesy of Jane Carter, 1994)

ic control centers, social and psychological factors can in some cases cause these mechanisms to bite the hand that tried to feed them, resulting in grave bodily harm and even death.

FEAR AND RAGE

FOCUS QUESTIONS

■ What broad functions are served by the two branches of the autonomic nervous system?

■ What is the emergency reaction, what physiological changes characterize it, and how are these changes used in lie detection?

■ What is the limbic system, and what kinds of behavior does it regulate?

■ What purpose does pain serve, and how does our knowledge of brain chemistry explain the various ways that pain is relieved and controlled?

Thus far, our emphasis has been on motives that are largely based on internal, homeostatic controls: A disruption of the internal environment impels the organism to perform some action that ultimately restores its internal balance. But there are a number of motives that have little to do with homeostatic equilibrium. Sex is one example. While internal hormone levels play an important role, the desire is essentially aroused (as it were, "turned on") by external stimuli of various kinds; homeostatic imbalances have nothing to do with it. We will discuss this in a later chapter that deals with motives that are primarily social (see Chapter 10). Here we will consider another motive that is almost entirely instigated from without rather than within: the reaction to intense threat, which results in attempts to escape or to fight back in self-defense and which is often accompanied by the violent emotions of rage and fear.

To the extent that this motive (much like sex) is nonhomeostatic and is primarily instigated by external stimuli, it is of course quite different from the motives of self-regulation, such as hunger, thirst, and temperature maintenance. But in one regard this motive is just the same as the homeostatic motives, for like them it has a potentiating function—it activates particular tendencies to react and decreases others. A man confronted by a hungry tiger has little on his mind except how to remove himself from the scene, or if he has a weapon and the skill to use it, how to remove the tiger. For the time being, food, drink, and sex will be very low on his list of priorities.

THREAT AND THE AUTONOMIC NERVOUS SYSTEM

■ What are some of the biological mechanisms that underlie our reactions to threat? We'll begin our discussion by looking at the functions of the autonomic nervous system. We previously saw how the interaction of sympathetic and parasympathetic excitations permits adjustments of the visceral machinery in the control of temperature. But the opposition between the two autonomic branches is more fundamental yet. According to the American physiologist Walter B. Cannon (1871–1945), they serve two broad and rather different functions. The parasympathetic system handles the *vegetative* functions of ordinary life: the conservation of bodily resources, reproduction, and the disposal of wastes. In effect, these reflect an organism's operations during times of peace—a

Walter B. Cannon *(Courtesy of the National Library of Medicine)*

3.10 **The sympathetic and parasympathetic branches of the autonomic nervous system** *The parasympathetic system (shown in red) facilitates the vegetative functions of the organism: It slows the heart and lungs, stimulates digestive functions, permits sexual activity, and so on. In contrast, the sympathetic system (shown in blue) readies the organism for an emergency: It accelerates heart and lung actions, liberates nutrient fuels for muscular effort, and inhibits digestive and sexual functions.*

Note that the fibers of the sympathetic system are interconnected through a chain of ganglionic fibers outside of the spinal cord. As a result, sympathetic activation has a somewhat diffuse character; any sympathetic excitation tends to affect all of the viscera rather than just some. This is in contrast to the parasympathetic system whose action is more specific. (After Cannon, 1929)

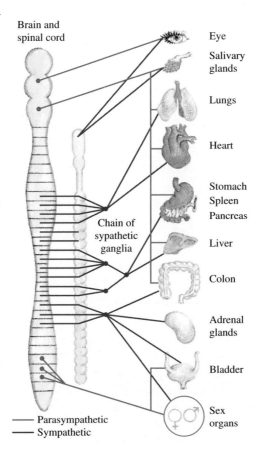

Brain and spinal cord

Chain of sypathetic ganglia

Eye
Salivary glands
Lungs
Heart
Stomach
Spleen
Pancreas
Liver
Colon
Adrenal glands
Bladder
Sex organs

— Parasympathetic
— Sympathetic

PARASYMPATHETIC SYSTEM

Constriction of pupil

Secretion of tear glands

Salivation

Inhibition of heart action

Constriction of respiratory passages

Stomach contraction: secretion of digestive fluids

Intestinal peristalsis

Contraction of bladder

Erection

SYMPATHETIC SYSTEM

Dilation of pupil

Inhibition of tear glands

Inhibition of salivation

Acceleration of heart action

Opens respiratory passages

Inhibits stomach contractions and digestive secretion

Inhibits intestinal peristalsis

Relaxes bladder

Inhibits erection

lowered heart rate, peristaltic movements of stomach and intestines, secretion of digestive glands. In contrast, the sympathetic system has an *activating* function. It summons the body's resources and gets the organism ready for vigorous action (Cannon, 1929).

As an example of this opposition, consider the role of the two autonomic divisions in governing the delivery of nutrient fuels and oxygen as well as the removal of waste products to and from the musculature. Parasympathetic excitation slows down the heart rate and reduces blood pressure. Sympathetic excitation has the opposite effect and also inhibits digestion and sexual activity. In addition, it stimulates the inner core of the adrenal gland, the **adrenal medulla,** to pour epinephrine (adrenaline) and norepinephrine into the bloodstream. These have essentially the same effects as sympathetic stimulation—they accelerate the heart rate, speed up metabolism, and so on. As a result, the sympathetic effects are amplified yet further (see Figure 3.10).

THE EMERGENCY REACTION

Cannon pointed out that intense sympathetic arousal has a special function. It serves as an **emergency reaction** that mobilizes the organism for a crisis—for flight or fight. Consider a grazing zebra, placidly maintaining homeostasis by nibbling at the grass and vasodilatating in the hot African sun. Suddenly it sees a lion approaching rapidly. The vegetative functions must now take second place, for if the zebra does not escape, it will have no internal environment left to regulate. The necessary violent exertions of the skeletal musculature will now require the total support of the entire bodily machinery, and this support is provided by intense sympathetic activation. There is more nutrient fuel for the muscles, and it is now delivered more rapidly. At the same time, waste products

3.11 Sympathetic emergency reaction
A cat's terrified response to a frightening encounter. (Photograph by Walter Chandoha)

3.12 Lie detection by use of autonomic measures *(A) Various devices measure autonomic arousal—a tube around the chest measures respiration rate, electrodes attached to the hand measure GSR, and an arm band measures blood pressure and pulse. (Photograph by Mary Shuford) (B) A recording of respiration, GSR, and a measure of blood pressure and pulse. The record was obtained from a store employee caught stealing merchandise. At issue was the amount of the theft. To determine this, all parties agreed to be guided by the results of a lie detector test. The subject was asked questions about the amount, such as "Did you steal more than $1,000?" and "Did you steal more than $2,000?" The record shows a high peak just after $3,000 and before $5,000. Later the subject confessed that the actual amount was $4,000. (After Inbau and Reid, 1953)*

are jettisoned more quickly, and all unessential organic activities are brought to a halt. If the zebra does not escape, it is not because its sympathetic system did not try.

Cannon produced considerable evidence suggesting that a similar autonomic reaction occurs when the pattern is one of attack rather than of flight. A cat about to do battle with a dog shows accelerated heartbeat, piloerection (its hair standing on end, normally a heat-conserving device), and pupillary dilation—all signs of sympathetic arousal, signs that the body is girding itself for violent muscular effort (Figure 3.11).

Cannon emphasized the biological utility of the autonomic reaction, but his principle cannot tell us which choice the animal will make, whether it will choose fight or flight. This depends in part upon built-in predispositions, in part upon the specific situation. For example, a rat first tries to escape but fights when finally cornered. Emergency situations may produce still different reactions from those we have already seen. Some animals become paralyzed by fright and stand immobile—an adaptive reaction since predators are more likely to detect and strike prey that is in motion. Other animals have even more exotic means of self-protection. Some species of fish pale when frightened, which makes them harder to spot against the sandy ocean bottom. This effect is produced by the direct action of adrenal epinephrine upon various pigmented substances in the animal's skin (Odiorne, 1957).

These reactions are of course also found in humans, as bodily concomitants of intense emotion. In fear, our hearts pound, our palms sweat, and we sometimes shiver—all sympathetic activities. It is hardly surprising that such autonomic responses (as pulse rate and respiration) are often used as indicators of emotional states. The **galvanic skin response (GSR)** is a particularly favored measure. It is a drop in the electrical resistance of the skin, particularly of the palm (related to, but not identical with, the activity of the sweat glands), that is a sensitive index of general arousal.

The GSR and other indices of autonomic activity are part of the technology of the polygraph test, sometimes called the "lie detector test." Such tests obviously cannot detect lies as such. What they do instead is uncover autonomic arousal to certain key questions or phrases. The responses to these critical items (e.g., "Did you stab anyone with a knife on . . . ?") are then compared with the responses to control items—questions that are likely to produce an emotional reaction but are irrelevant to the issue at hand (e.g., "Before age nineteen did you ever lie to anyone?").

The fundamental assumption on which the lie-detection enterprise rests is that innocent persons will be more concerned by the control items than by the critical questions and will therefore show more intense autonomic arousal to the former than to the latter (Figure 3.12). But this assumption is in serious dispute (Lykken, 1979, 1981). By and large, while polygraph operators do rather well in

A

B

Respiration

GSR
Blood pressure/pulse

$1,000 $2,000 $3,000 $5,000 $7,500 $10,000

"Did you steal more than _____?"

identifying guilty individuals, certain persons—especially those called sociopathic personalities—seem to have a special knack for beating lie detector tests (Waid and Orne, 1982; see Chapter 18). In addition, the polygraph does rather poorly in exonerating individuals who are innocent (Saxe, Dougherty, and Cross, 1985). Evidence of this kind, as well as ethical considerations, led Congress to pass legislation in 1988 that severely restricted the use of lie-detector tests in the courts, in government, and in industry.

CENTRAL CONTROLS

The autonomic nervous system, in both its sympathetic and parasympathetic branches, is by no means as autonomous as its name implies; rather, it is largely guided by other neural centers. Some of these centers are among the oldest and most primitive portions of the cerebral cortex. These primitive cortical structures comprise the *limbic system,* a group of structures in the brain intimately involved in the control of the emotional reactions to situations that call for flight, defense, or attack (Figures 3.13 and 3.14). Electrical stimulation of certain portions of the limbic system transforms a purring cat into a spitting, hissing Halloween figure. Stimulation of the same region in humans often produces feelings of great anxiety or of rage, as in a patient who said that she suddenly wanted to tear things to pieces and to slap the experimenter's face (Magnus and Lammers, 1956; King, 1961; Flynn et al., 1970).

Psychologically there seem to be different kinds of attack, and they are evidently initiated by different control centers. In cats, the stimulation of one hypothalamic region produces predatory attack: quiet stalking followed by a quick, deadly pounce. The stimulation of another region leads to the Halloween pattern: a counterattack in self-defense (probably related to what in humans is called rage). When this rage pattern is triggered, the cat ignores a nearby mouse and will spring viciously at the experimenter by whom it presumably feels threatened (Egger and Flynn, 1963; Clemente and Chase, 1973). Predatory

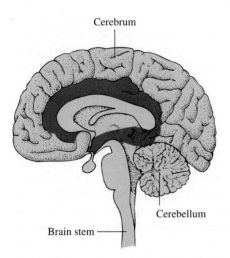

3.13 **Limbic system of the human brain** Schematic view of the limbic system (in blue) in cross section. (After Keeton and Gould, 1986)

3.14 **The limbic system and some related structures** *The brain is pictured here as if the hemispheres were essentially transparent. One of the structures particularly relevant to emotional reactions is the amygdala, a walnut-sized structure that has been implicated in the production of aggressive behavior and fear reactions. (After Bloom, Lazerson, and Hofstadter, 1988)*

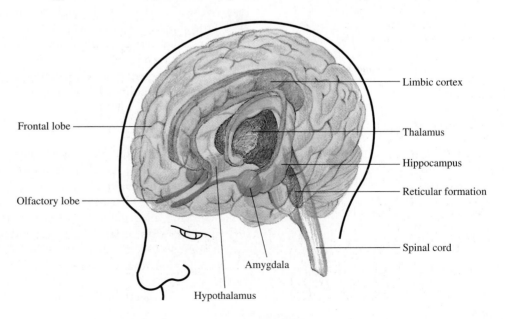

attack is another matter entirely: The lion who pounces on the zebra is probably not at all enraged but is merely engaged in the prosaic business of food gathering. (Whether the zebra is comforted by the fact that the lion is not angry at it is another question.)

DISRUPTIVE EFFECTS OF AUTONOMIC AROUSAL

■ Our preceding discussion emphasized the biological value of the emergency system. But strong autonomic arousal can also be disruptive and even harmful to the organism. This negative side of the matter is especially clear in humans. In our day-to-day lives we rarely encounter emergencies that call for violent physical effort. But our biological nature has not changed just because our modern world contains no sabertooth tigers. We still have the same emergency system that served our primitive ancestors, and its bodily consequences can take serious tolls.

The disruptive effect of fear and anger upon digestion or upon sexual behavior is a matter of common knowledge. During periods of marked anxiety there are often complaints of constipation or other digestive ills. The same holds for sexual dysfunction. This is hardly surprising, since digestive functions and many aspects of sexual activity (for example, erection) are largely controlled by the parasympathetic system and are thus inhibited by intense sympathetic arousal. Moreover, the aftereffects of emotional arousal can sometimes be more permanent, causing profound and long-lasting bodily harm. Various disorders such as peptic ulcer, colitis, asthma, and hypertension can often be traced back to emotional patterns in the patient's life and are then considered psychophysiological disorders in which a psychological cause produces a bodily effect. Such psychophysiological effects are sometimes even more grievous and irrevocable, as in cases of hypertension and coronary disease, which can lead to heart attacks and death (see Chapter 18).

PAIN AND THE ENDORPHIN SYSTEM

■ We've considered the biological basis of self-defense, but have thus far said little about the stimuli that set it off. Some of the stimuli that lead to fear or counterattack have surely acquired their significance through learning (to which we will turn in the next chapter). But some of them seem to produce the sympathetic emergency reaction without any prior experience. An important example of such a built-in trigger for fear and rage is pain.

PAIN AS AN AID TO SURVIVAL

It seems paradoxical, but pain—especially pain that is acute rather than chronic—has survival value, representing a biological boon rather than a bitter burden. This fact is highlighted by the rare cases of individuals born with a virtual insensitivity to pain. As a child, one such individual bit off the tip of her tongue while chewing, incurred serious burns when kneeling on a hot radiator, and suffered severe dislocations in her hips and spine because she failed to shift her weight appropriately or turn over in her sleep. Such traumas eventually led to massive infections that caused her death at the age of twenty-nine (Melzack, 1973).

PAIN RELIEF THROUGH ENDORPHINS

Pain's adaptive value is as a signal to react—to withdraw from the burning flame, to run away, to fight in self-defense, to nurse one's wounds (Bolles and Fanselow, 1982). But once the pain stimulus has set off the appropriate reaction, continued pain may get in the way of whatever it is that has to be done. Under the circumstances, it would be adaptive if the organism could now alleviate its own pain.

The existence of such a biological process of self-administered pain alleviation has long been suspected. There is good evidence that pain can be alleviated or even abolished by psychological means that serve as an *analgesic* (a pain reliever). There are many stories of athletes or soldiers who suffer injuries but don't feel the pain until the game or the battle is over. Related effects have been produced in the laboratory. Thus rats subjected to various forms of stress, such as being forced to swim in cold water, become less sensitive to pain (Bodnar et al., 1980). Similar results have been shown in humans: Paradoxically enough, mild electric shock to the back or limbs can serve as an analgesic. So can acupuncture, an ancient Chinese treatment in which needles are inserted in various parts of the body (see Figure 3.15; Mann et al., 1973). This procedure seems to suppress pain in animals as well as humans (Nathan, 1978). In all these cases, the question is why.

The answer seems to be a matter of brain chemistry. It's long been known that the experience of pain can be dulled or entirely eliminated by various drugs, such as morphine and other opiates. These drugs are typically applied from the outside. But on occasion, the brain is its own best pharmacist. For when assailed by various kinds of stress (one of which is extremely painful stimulation), the brain can sometimes produce its own brand of opiates, which it then administers to itself. These are the *endorphins,* (a contraction of the word *endogenous*—that is, internally produced—and the word *morphines*), a group of neurotransmitters that are secreted by certain neurons within the brain. Regular opiates such as morphine are chemically very similar to the endorphins and will therefore activate the same pain-inhibiting neurons (though, in fact, some of the brain's own endorphins are considerably more powerful than the artificially produced morphines dispensed by physicians; Snyder and Childers, 1979; Bloom, 1983).

A

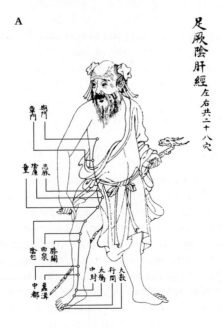

B

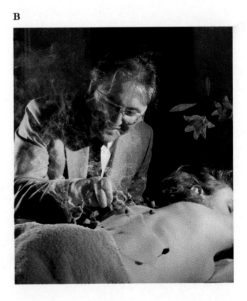

3.15 Acupuncture Acupuncture is a complex system of treatment that grew up in ancient China and was based on the idea that disease is a disturbance of vital energies that circulate in particular channels. Their balance was to be restored by manipulating metal needles at special points along these channels. (A) From a seventeenth-century Chinese treatise illustrating the liver tract with twenty-eight special points. (From Blakemore, 1977) (B) A contemporary patient receiving treatment. (Photograph © Pierre Boulat/Woodfin Camp & Associates)

To sum up, both pain and pain relief are biologically adaptive. Pain is a crucial warning signal that tells an animal that it had better do something quickly to avert bodily harm. But once the warning is given, further pain may be incapacitating. A wounded deer must be able to ignore its wounds if it wants to escape the hunters.

SLEEP AND WAKING

FOCUS QUESTIONS

- What brain systems seem to regulate when we sleep and when we are awake?

- How does active (or REM) sleep differ from quiet sleep?

- What purposes might sleep serve?

- When during sleep are we most likely to dream?

Thus far, our main concern has been with the *directive* function of motives. This direction can be primarily imposed from within, as in the case of the homeostatic motives, such as thirst and hunger. It can also be initiated by stimuli from the outside, as in fear and rage. Either way, the effects on behavior are readily described in terms of a negative feedback system. In the case of homeostatic motives, the organism acts so as to change the state of the internal environment; it eats or drinks until its water balance or nutrient level is restored. In the case of rage and fear, it acts to change the conditions of the external environment that prompted the disturbance: The cat runs away to remove itself from a barking dog, or it hisses and scratches in a frantic attempt to remove the dog.

Motives also have another function. They *arouse* the organism, which then becomes increasingly alert and vigorous. A given motive will thus act like both the tuner and the volume control of a radio. A thirsty animal seeks water rather than food or a sexual partner. And the thirstier it is, the more intensely it will pursue its goal. Psychologists have used various terms to describe this facet of motivation. Some call it **activation;** others prefer the term **drive.** They all agree that increased drive generally leads to increased behavioral vigor. Thus, rats will run faster to water the longer they have been water-deprived.

We will now look at some of the biological mechanisms of activation as we consider waking arousal and sleep.

WAKING

In a sense, the sympathetic branch of the autonomic nervous system can be considered an arousal system for various physiological processes of the body. Similar arousal systems operate to alert the brain, to activate the cortex so that it is fully responsive to incoming messages. In effect, they awaken the brain.

Just where these arousal systems are in the brain is still a matter of some debate. Until fairly recently, they were believed to have their origin in the midbrain but more recent work has focused on several structures in the mid- and hindbrain, which have branches that ascend to the rest of the brain. Activity in these regions not only leads to awakening but also produces increasing levels of arousal once awake (Aston-Jones, 1985).

Stimulation from the subcortical arousal systems is not the only source of cortical activation. Stimulation can also come from the cortex itself. Descending fibers from the cortex may excite the subcortical structures, which then activate the cortex more fully. This circuit—cortex to lower arousing systems to cortex—probably plays an important role in many phenomena of sleep and waking. We sometimes have trouble in falling asleep because we "can't shut off our thoughts." Here cortical activity triggers the subcortical arousal system, which activates the cortex, which again excites the lower level subcortical system, and so on. The role of the cortex in rousing itself is also shown by the fact that some stimuli—a baby's cry, the smell of fire, the sound of one's own name—are more likely to wake us than others, regardless of their intensity. The same circuit can also produce the lowering of arousal. When our cortex is unstimulated by events, the arousal level may drop so low that we find ourselves dropping off into the state that is the very opposite of high arousal—sleep.

SLEEP AND BRAIN ACTIVITY

■ The primary focus of this chapter is on motivation and thus on the direction and activation of behavior that motives bring about. In this context, sleep is of considerable interest because it seems to represent the very opposite of arousal. But it has a more direct relevance as well. The desire for sleep is one of the most powerful of motives; if kept awake long enough, the urge to sleep will eventually take precedence over most motives (which is one of the reasons why jailers sometimes use enforced sleeplessness to force confessions out of prisoners). What can we say about this state in which most of us spend a third of our lives? Sleep cannot be observed from within, since it is almost by definition a condition of which the sleeper is unaware. (The rare dreams in which we know that we are dreaming are an interesting exception.) Since we cannot study sleep from within, we must perforce study it from without. One way of doing this is by observing what the brain does while its owner is asleep.

Eavesdropping on the brain of waking or sleeping subjects is possible because the language of the nervous system is electrical. When electrodes are placed at various points on the skull, they pick up the electrical changes that are produced by the summed activity of the millions of nerve cells in the cerebral cortex that is just underneath. In absolute terms these changes are very small; they are therefore fed to a highly sensitive amplifier whose output in turn activates a series of pens. These pens trace their position on a long roll of paper that moves at a constant speed (Figure 3.16). The resulting record is an *electroencephalogram,* or EEG, a picture of voltage changes over time occurring in the brain.

Figure 3.17 shows an EEG record that begins with the subject in a relaxed state, with eyes closed, and "not thinking about anything in particular." The record shows *alpha waves,* a rather regular waxing and waning of electrical potential, at some eight to twelve cycles per second. This alpha rhythm is very characteristic of this state (awake but resting) and is found in most mammals. When the subject attends to some stimulus with open eyes or when he is involved in active thought (for instance, mental arithmetic) with his eyes closed, the picture changes. Now the alpha rhythm is *blocked;* the voltage is lower, the frequency is much higher, and the pattern of ups and downs is nearly random.

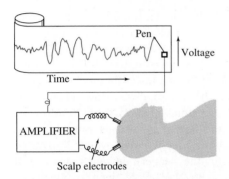

3.16 Schematic diagram of EEG recording *A number of scalp electrodes are placed on a subject's head. At any one time, there are small differences in the electrical potential (that is, the voltage) between any two of these electrodes. These differences are magnified by an amplifier and are then used to activate a recording pen. The greater the voltage difference, the larger the pen's deflection. Since the voltage fluctuates, the pen goes up and down, thus tracing a brain wave on the moving paper. The number of such waves per second is the EEG frequency.*

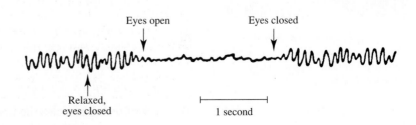

3.17 Alpha waves and alpha blocking *(After Guyton, 1981)*

AWAKE		QUIET SLEEP			ACTIVE SLEEP
	(Stage 1)	(Stage 2)	(Stage 3)	(Stage 4)	Dreaming

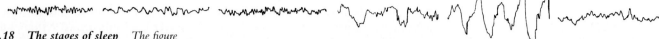

3.18 The stages of sleep *The figure shows EEG records taken from the frontal lobe of the brain, during waking, quiet sleep, and active sleep. (Courtesy of William C. Dement)*

THE STAGES OF SLEEP

■ Several decades of work involving continuous, all-night recordings of EEGs and other measures have shown that there are several stages of sleep and that these vary in depth. Just prior to sleep, there tends to be an accentuated alpha rhythm. As the subject becomes drowsy, the alpha comes and goes; there are increasingly long stretches during which the pattern is random. The subject is now in a light, dozing sleep from which she is easily awakened (Stage 1 in Figure 3.18). Over the course of the next hour she drifts into deeper and deeper stages, in which the EEGs are characterized by the complete absence of alpha and by waves of increasingly higher voltage and much lower frequency (Stages 2 through 4 in Figure 3.18). In the last stages, the waves are very slow. They occur about once every second and are some five times greater in amplitude than those of the alpha rhythm. At this point the sleeper is virtually immobile and will take a few seconds to awaken, mumbling incoherently, even if shaken or shouted at. During the course of the night, the sleeper's descent repeats itself several times. She drops from dozing to deep, slow-wave sleep, reascends to Stage 1, drops back to slow-wave sleep, and so on for some four or five cycles.

The oscillations between different sleep stages are not merely changes in depth. When the sleeper reascends into Stage 1, he seems to enter a qualitatively different state entirely. This state is sometimes called ***active sleep*** to distinguish it from the ***quiet sleep*** found during the other stages. Active sleep is a paradoxical condition with contradictory aspects. In some ways it is as deep as sleep ever gets. The sleeper's general body musculature is at its most flaccid, and he is at his least sensitive to external stimulation (Williams, Tepas, and Morlock, 1962). But judged by some other criteria, the level of arousal during active sleep is almost as high as during alert wakefulness. One sign is the EEG, which in humans is rather similar to that found in waking (Jouvet, 1967). Another is the appearance of dreams (of which more later), which are found in active rather than quiet sleep and during which we often feel as if we were active and thoroughly awake.

Of particular interest are the sleeper's eye movements during Stage 1 sleep; these can be recorded by means of electrodes attached next to each eye. During quiet sleep, the eyes drift slowly and no longer move in tandem. But during active sleep a different pattern suddenly appears. The eyes move rapidly and in unison behind closed lids, as if the sleeper were looking at some object outside. These jerky, rapid eye movements (REMs) are one of the most striking features of active sleep, which is often called ***REM sleep.*** Young human adults enter this stage about four times each night (Figure 3.19).

Observing sleep *All-night recordings of EEGs of patients in sleep labs have revealed the several stages of sleep. (Photograph by Grant Leduc/Monkmeyer)*

THE FUNCTIONS OF SLEEP

■ What functions are served by sleep, whether in its active or quiet form? Surprisingly enough, the answer is still unknown.

SLEEP DEPRIVATION

One way of trying to assess the benefits that sleep may bring is to observe what ills befall if it is prevented. This is the logic of sleep-deprivation experiments in

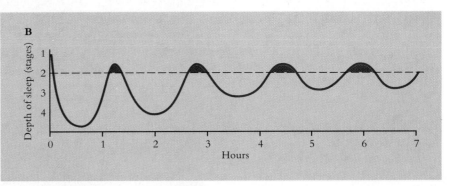

3.19 REM and non-REM sleep *(A) Eye movements during non-REM and REM sleep. The REM periods are associated with dreaming. (B) The alternation of non-REM and REM periods throughout the course of the night (REM periods are in color). Rapid eye movements and dreams begin as the person repeatedly emerges from deeper sleep to the level of Stage 1. (After Kleitman, 1960)*

which humans and animals are kept awake for days on end. The results suggest that there is indeed a need for sleep. If deprived of sleep, the organism seeks sleep just as it seeks food when it is starved. When sleep is finally allowed, the subjects sink down upon the nearest cot and try to make up for the sleep they have lost.

SLEEP AS A RESTORATIVE PROCESS

The sleep-deprivation experiments suggest that there is a need for sleep, but they do not tell us why. One possibility is that sleep is restorative, that it is a period during which some vital substance is resynthesized in the nervous system. In one form or another, this view was held at least as early as the Renaissance, as witness Shakespeare who regarded sleep as "a balm of hurt minds" that "knits up the ravel'd sleave of care." That sleep has some such function seems probable even though we have only a sketchy notion of what might be restored and how.

Some authors focus on the restorative functions of deep, slow-wave sleep (Stages 3 and 4). A number of studies suggest that slow-wave sleep is enhanced under conditions such as physical fatigue, where there is a greater need for bodily revival. There is some evidence that marathon runners sleep longer during the two nights after the race; their largest increase is in the time they spend during slow-wave sleep (Shapiro et al., 1981). This result fits in with the finding that a growth-promoting hormone that boosts protein synthesis (and thus helps to replace body tissue) is secreted primarily during slow-wave sleep (Takahashi, 1979). The matter is still under debate, for there is some evidence that the increase in slow-wave sleep may not be due to bodily fatigue at all. It appears that intense exercise leads to an increase in brain metabolism. If so, it is the brain rather than the body that requires rest and restoration (Horne, 1988).

SLEEP AS A CLOCK-DRIVEN PROCESS

Whether sleep really has a restorative function is by no means clear. But even if it does, that cannot be the whole story. For there is little doubt that the need for sleep partially depends on the time of day, regardless of the amount of prior sleep deprivation. People who go without sleep for several nights find that they feel more tired in the late evenings but more awake in the mornings, even though they didn't sleep the night (or nights) before. This shows that sleep is a **clock-driven** process (see Figure 3.20). In this regard, it resembles a number of other biological rhythms that seem to depend on built-in internal clocks. Some

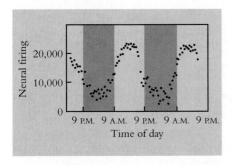

3.20 The ticking of the brain's biological clock *Activity of single cells in the superchiasmatic nucleus of a rat's hypothalamus. The regular day-night fluctuations in the firing rate of these cells demonstrate that the brain has a built-in biological clock. (From Carlson, 1991)*

Biological rhythms in the vegetable world
The figure shows a morning glory opening over a four-hour period. This timing is driven by the plant's circadian biological clock. (Photographs by Takahisa Hirano/Nature Production)

of these rhythms extend over a whole year, such as the seasonal patterns that determine migration, mating, and hibernation in many animals. Others are much shorter, such as the short rhythms of respiration and heart beat. In sleep, the rhythm spans about a twenty-four-hour day and is therefore called *circadian* (from the Latin, *circa,* "nearly," and *dies,* "day"). It originates from a clock circuit in the hypothalamus, which seems to be set by inputs from the optic nerve that inform the system of whether it is day or night. Disruptions of these clocks (e.g., through jet lag) can produce seriously debilitating motivational effects.*

SLEEP AS AN EVOLUTIONARY RELIC

The fact that sleep is related to the day-night cycle has led some investigators to suggest that it is a behavioral relic from earlier eons. They argue that while the desire for sleep is clearly an insistent motive, there is no reason to believe that it serves a vital bodily need. They agree that the sleepless person seeks sleep just as the starved one craves food. But they point out that while starvation eventually leads to death, there is no evidence that even prolonged sleep deprivation will have such dire effects; it will make people drowsy, a bit confused, and desperately anxious for sleep, but little more. They suggest that sleep may be an evolutionary relic, a built-in response system that once had an important adaptive function, although it no longer does. A daily period of enforced near-immobility spent in some hiding place may have been quite useful to our animal ancestors; it would have helped them to conserve their energies and have kept them out of the way of possible predators. It is of little use to us now that we have electric light bulbs and need fear no predators except those of our own kind, but it is no less powerful even so (Webb, 1974).

To sum up, while we know a great deal about the phenomena of sleep and some of the mechanisms that bring it about, we are as yet unsure about its functions. The desire for sleep is a powerful motive, and some twenty-five years of an aver-

*Some promising new treatments for certain emotional illnesses are based on the new realization that disturbances of biological clocks and sleep patterns can have radical effects upon moods (see Chapter 18).

age lifetime are devoted to it. But we're still not clear what it is really good for. (For discussion, see Webb, 1979, 1982; Horne, 1988).

DREAMS

■ REM sleep was discovered fairly recently, but its discoverers almost immediately related it to a phenomenon surely known to humans since prehistoric times: dreaming.

DREAMING AND REM SLEEP

When sleeping subjects are awakened during REM sleep, they generally report a dream: a series of episodes that seemed real at the time. Not so for quiet (that is, non-REM) sleep. When awakened from quiet sleep, subjects may say that they were thinking about something, but they rarely relate the kind of inner drama we call a dream (Cartwright, 1977). Further evidence links the duration of the dream to the length of the REM period. Subjects who are awakened five minutes after the onset of REM tend to describe shorter dreams than subjects awakened fifteen minutes after the REM period begins. This result argues against the popular notion that dreams are virtually instantaneous. In actual fact, the dream seems to take just about as long as the dream episode might have been in real life (Dement and Kleitman, 1957; Dement and Wolpert, 1958).

These findings suggest that the average adult dreams for about one-and-a-half hours every night, the time spent in REM sleep. How can we square this statement with the fact that in everyday life many people seem to experience dreams only occasionally and that some deny they ever dream? The answer is that dreams are generally forgotten within minutes after they have occurred. In one study, subjects were awakened either during REM sleep or five minutes after a REM period had ended. In the first condition, detailed dream narratives were obtained 85 percent of the time; in the second, no dreams were reported. (Wolpert and Trosman, 1958).

Dreams *Salvador Dali depicts a dreamlike world in which various bizarre and disjointed images are interpreted by the dreamer to have symbolic meaning. (*The Great Paranoic, *by Salvador Dali, 1936; courtesy Museum Boymans-van Beuningen, Rotterdam)*

Jacob's Dream *Dreams have often been regarded as a gateway between everyday reality and a more spiritual existence. An example is the biblical patriarch Jacob, who dreamed of angels descending and ascending a ladder between heaven and earth. (From the Lambeth Bible, England, twelfth century; courtesy of the Lambeth Palace Library)*

DO DREAMS HAVE A FUNCTION?

The ancients believed that dreams have a prophetic function. In our own time, several theorists have argued that their function is related to the sleeper's personal problems. The most influential account was that of Sigmund Freud, who maintained that during dreams a whole host of primitive and forbidden impulses—mostly concerning sex and aggression—start to break through the barriers we erect against them while awake. The result is a compromise. The prohibited materials emerge, but only in a heavily masked and censored form. Freud believed that this explains why our dreams are so often strange and apparently senseless. According to Freud, they are only odd on the outside. If we look beneath the surface, we can recognize the disguised meaning, the hidden, unacceptable, cleverly masked wishes (Freud, 1900).

During the last thirty years, more and more evidence has come up that has thrown considerable doubt on Freud's dream theory (for details, see Chapter 17). Today, many authors believe that dreams don't have the complex functions that Freud (let alone the ancients) maintained. An influential modern account is the ***activation-synthesis hypothesis,*** which holds that the dream is simply a reflection of the brain's aroused state during active sleep. During this period, the cerebral cortex is active, and its activity is manifested in conscious experience—the dream. But this dream experience necessarily has a special form. The cortex may be active, but it is largely shut off from sensory input. Under the circumstances, its activity is not constrained by the demands of external reality. Memory images become more prominent than they are in waking life, for they do not have to compete with the insistent here and now provided by the senses. The recent experiences of the day are evoked most readily, and they will then arouse a host of previous memories and intermingle with them. The cortex is sufficiently active to connect and interpret these raw materials so that we experience a running, inner narrative. But this is often accomplished in a primitive, disjointed way; perhaps the cortex is not active enough to provide more than a crude organization (Hobson and McCarley, 1977; Hobson, 1988).

What about the dreamer's own needs, conflicts, and preoccupations? These surely matter. For if the cerebral activity of active sleep is unconstrained by sensory reality, the content of dreams is likely to reflect the individuality of the dreamer. The raw materials of the dream are peculiarly *hers: her* thoughts, *her* memories, *her* emotions. Since objective sensory input is absent, these subjective sources are more prominent than they are in waking life. This is probably one of the reasons why dreams have so often been thought to have a deeper, more personal meaning (see Chapter 17).

WHAT DIFFERENT MOTIVES HAVE IN COMMON

FOCUS QUESTIONS

- Why is the concept of the optimal level of arousal so problematic in explaining the range of motivated behavior?

- What are drug addiction, tolerance, and withdrawal, and how does opponent-process theory explain them?

- Does the concept of the pleasure center mean that all motivated behavior has a common physiological basis?

The preceding sections have dealt with a number of motives that impel to action—hunger, thirst, fear, and so on. Some, such as hunger, are in the service of homeostasis and serve to maintain the internal environment. Others, such as fear and rage, are triggered by stimuli in the environment and are relevant to self-preservation. For a few others—the main example is sleep—the function is still unknown. These various motives are clearly very different, as are the goals toward which they steer the organism—food, water, escape from threat, a good night's sleep. Since all of them are motives, they all potentiate behavior (almost by definition), and so they affect what we do, what we see, and what we feel. But over and above this, is there something that all these motives and goals have in common?

THE PSYCHOLOGY OF REWARD AND THE AROUSAL LEVEL

A number of theorists have suggested that all—or at least most—motives can be described as a search for some *optimum level of arousal* or of general stimulation. One of the early controversies in this area was over the question of what the optimum level is.

Early theorists suggested that, in general, organisms seek minimum levels of stimulation, preferring peace and quiet to states of tension and arousal (Hull, 1943). But, in fact, this does not seem to be true. For there is little doubt that some experiences are actively sought after, like the taste of sweets and erotic stimulation. These are both felt to be positive pleasures rather than the mere removal of some irritant.

Similar conclusions emerge from work on curiosity and manipulation. Monkeys will go to considerable lengths to puzzle out how to open latches that are attached to a wooden board (see Figure 3.21). But when the latches are unlocked, nothing opens because the latches never closed anything in the first place. Since unlatching gets the animal nothing, the response was presumably its own reward. In this regard, monkeys act much like human beings, who in countless ways indicate that they often do things as ends in themselves, rather than as means to other ends.

To be sure, we do try to reduce arousal if our arousal level is unduly high, as in intense hunger or fear or pain. But in many other cases we apparently try to increase it, which suggests that there is an above-zero optimum level of arousal. If we are above this optimum (for example, in pain), we try to reduce arousal. But if we are below it, we seek stimulation to ascend beyond it. This optimum

3.21 Curiosity and manipulation
Young rhesus monkeys trying to open a latch. The monkeys received no special reward for their labors but learned to open the devices just "for the fun of it." (After Harlow, 1950; photograph courtesy of University of Wisconsin Primate Laboratory)

A

B

C

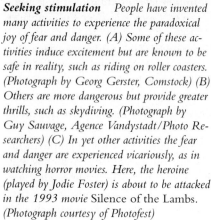

Seeking stimulation People have invented many activities to experience the paradoxical joy of fear and danger. (A) Some of these activities induce excitement but are known to be safe in reality, such as riding on roller coasters. (Photograph by Georg Gerster, Comstock) (B) Others are more dangerous but provide greater thrills, such as skydiving. (Photograph by Guy Sauvage, Agence Vandystadt/Photo Researchers) (C) In yet other activities the fear and danger are experienced vicariously, as in watching horror movies. Here, the heroine (played by Jodie Foster) is about to be attacked in the 1993 movie Silence of the Lambs. (Photograph courtesy of Photofest)

undoubtedly varies from time to time and from one motive to another as befits their different biological functions, as in hunger arousal versus sexual arousal. Optimum arousal levels may also differ from person to person. According to some authors, some people are sensation seekers who generally look for stimulation, while others prefer a quieter existence (Zuckerman, 1979; see Chapter 16).

DRUGS AND ADDICTION

The normal ways of coping with an arousal level that is too high or too low are by actively engaging with the world outside. If we are overaroused, we move toward quiescence: We still our hunger, escape from pain, or go to sleep. If we are under aroused, we seek stimulation. In some cases, this may reach rather high-pitched levels—by prolonged sex play, by watching an effective horror movie, by riding on a roller coaster. But there is another way to create a drastic change of arousal. We can use drugs that artificially give us a "high" or a "low."

Drugs that change arousal level Our present focus is on two major classes of drugs that have powerful effects: those that act as behavioral **depressants** and those that act as **stimulants.**

 Let's begin with the depressants. They include various sedatives (for example, barbiturates), alcohol, and the opiates (opium, heroin, and morphine).★ Their general effect is to depress the activity of all the neurons in the central nervous system. On the face of it that may seem surprising, since all of us have seen loud and aggressive drunks who seem anything but lethargic or depressed. The paradox is resolved if we recognize that their hyperexcitability is a case of disinhibition. At the first stage of inebriation (or at low doses of alcohol ingestion), the depression hits inhibitory synapses in the brain before it affects the excitatory ones. The usual constraints are relaxed, and the individual may engage in activities that he normally would not. Sexual inhibitions will be loosened, as will inhibitions against aggression. There may also be some initial euphoria. But with further alcohol ingestion, the depressive effects will hit all of the cerebral centers. Now the excitement produced by disinhibition will give way to a general slowdown of activity. Attention and memory will blur, and bodily

★Strictly speaking, the opiates belong to a separate class. For unlike alcohol and other sedatives, they serve as narcotics (that is, pain relievers) and act on separate opiate receptors. In addition, one of their number—heroin—seems to be able to produce an unusually intense euphoric "rush," sometimes likened to intense sexual excitement, when taken intravenously.

movement and speech will become increasingly uncoordinated, until finally the person will become completely incapacitated and lose consciousness.

The behavioral stimulants, which include amphetamine and cocaine, boost behavioral activity and can lead to an intense elevation of mood—a euphoric "rush" or "high" accompanied by feelings of enormous energy and increased self-esteem. This is especially so for cocaine, which some turn-of-the-century physicians (including Sigmund Freud) regarded as a miracle drug that produced boundless energy, exhilaration, and euphoria with no untoward side effects. This is unfortunately far from true, for the initial euphoria is bought at a considerable cost. Contrary to initial claims, amphetamines and cocaine often produce addictions that eventually become the user's primary focus in life. In addition, repeated use of cocaine (and amphetamines) can lead to extremely irrational states that resemble certain kinds of schizophrenia, in which there are delusions of persecution, irrational fears, and hallucinations (Siegel, 1984).

Tolerance and withdrawal   In many individuals, repeated drug use leads to **addiction.** One result is an increased *tolerance* for the drug, especially for the opiates, so that the addict requires ever-larger doses to obtain the same effect. A second consequence of addiction goes hand in hand with increased tolerance. When the drug is withheld, there are **withdrawal symptoms.** In general, these are the precise opposite of the effects produced by the drug itself. Thus heroin users deprived of their drug feel hyperexcitable; they are extremely irritable, are restless and anxious, and suffer insomnia. Similarly for the behavioral stimulants: The cocaine or amphetamine user's manic energy and elation give rise to severe emotional depression coupled with profound fatigue when the drug is withdrawn. The same antithesis holds for many physical symptoms. One characteristic of the opiates is that they lead to marked constipation. (They've been used for centuries to relieve diarrhea and dysentery.) But when the drug is withdrawn, the addict suffers violent diarrhea and related gastrointestinal symptoms (Julien, 1985; Volpicelli, 1989).

By its nature, addiction tends to be self-perpetuating. To begin with, the addict wants to regain the intense pleasure of his drug-induced euphoria (even though this euphoria will become harder and harder to obtain because of his increased tolerance). Even more important, perhaps, is the fact that the addict wants to escape the pangs of drug withdrawal. To dull those pains, he has to take another dose of the drug. But this may only strengthen the addiction and lead to even more intense withdrawal next time, and so on.

Further factors that underlie addiction are various local and psychological problems—in the family, at the workplace, or whatever (Alexander and Hadaway, 1982). Such problems often existed before the drug use began, and another dose or another drink is a way of escaping them for a while. But they can only be worsened by the addiction.

THE OPPONENT-PROCESS THEORY OF MOTIVATION

What accounts for the phenomena of drug use and drug addiction? Some suggestions come from the **opponent-process theory,** which offers a broad outline of how many motives are acquired.★ The opponent-process theory emphasizes the fundamental opposition of the various emotional feelings associated with pain and pleasure (such as fear and terror on the one hand, and joy and euphoria on the other). Its basic premise is that the nervous system has a general tendency to counteract any deviation from normal that is reminiscent of homeostasis. If

---

★The term *opponent process* was originally used in the field of color vision where it designates neural processes that pull in opposite directions (see Chapter 5).

there is too much of a swing to one pole of the pain-pleasure dimension, say toward joy and ecstasy, an opponent process is called into play that tilts the balance toward the negative side. Conversely, if the initial swing is toward terror or revulsion, there will be an opponent process toward the positive side. The net effect is that there will be an attenuation of the emotional state one happens to be in, so that ecstasy becomes mild pleasure and terror loses some of its force.

A further assumption of this theory is that repetitions of the initial emotional state will produce an increase in the power of the opponent process that is its antagonist (Solomon and Corbit, 1974; Solomon, 1980). This may explain the development of tolerance, the concomitant growth of the withdrawal state, and the resulting vulnerability to the vicious cycle of addiction. According to the theory, the emotional reaction produced by a behavioral stimulant such as amphetamine triggers an opponent process that pulls in the opposite direction. The more often the drug is taken, the stronger this opponent process becomes. The result is increased tolerance so that ever larger doses of the drug are required to produce an emotional high. The effect of the opponent process is revealed more starkly when the drug is withheld and there is no further pull toward the positive side of the emotional spectrum. Now all that remains is the opponent process whose strength has increased with every dose. This pulls the reaction in the opposite direction, resulting in the anguish of withdrawal (Solomon, 1980).

THE BIOLOGY OF REWARD

■ Thus far, we have discussed what the various motives that humans and animals strive to satisfy have in common psychologically. But one may also ask whether there are some underlying *physiological* commonalities. A number of investigators have asked whether there is a special region of the brain whose activation gives rise to what humans call "pleasure," a ***pleasure center*** that is triggered whenever a motive is satisfied, regardless of which motive it is. They have tried to answer this question by studying the rewarding effects of electrically stimulating various regions in the brain.

This general area of investigation was opened up in 1954 when James Olds and Peter Milner discovered that rats would learn to press a lever to give themselves a brief burst of electrical stimulation in certain regions of the limbic system (Olds and Milner, 1954; see Figure 3.22). Similar rewarding effects of self-stimulation have been demonstrated in a wide variety of animals, including cats, dogs, dolphins, monkeys, and human beings. To obtain it, rats will press a lever at rates up to 7,000 presses per hour for hours on end. When forced to opt between food and self-stimulation, hungry rats will typically opt for self-stimulation, even though it literally brings starvation (Spies, 1965).

3.22 Self-stimulation in rats The rat feels the stimulation of a pulse lasting less than a second. *(Courtesy of Dr. M. E. Olds)*

SPECIFIC AND GENERAL PLEASURE CENTERS

What explains the rewarding effect of self-stimulation? Two possibilities suggest themselves. One is that brain stimulation mimics certain *specific* natural rewards. Stimulation in one region might fool the brain into assuming there had been eating, stimulation in another that there had been copulation, and so on. Another possibility is that self-stimulation provides a more *general,* nonspecific kind of pleasure, something that all rewards share. Drinking, eating, and copulating are obviously different, but perhaps the different motivational messages they send to the brain ("have just drunk, eaten, copulated") ultimately feed into a common neurological system that responds to all of them in much the same way ("that sure felt good").

There is evidence that the stimulation of certain areas provides rather specific rewards. For example, animals will work to obtain electrical stimulation of the lateral zone of the hypothalamus (the "hunger center"), but how much they will work to get this reward depends on their hunger level. If they haven't eaten for a while, they will work much harder than they would otherwise. This suggests that the brain regards stimulation in this region as equivalent to food. Analogous effects are found for regions that are concerned with drinking or sexual behavior (Olds and Fobes, 1981).

As yet, we don't know how to put the various pieces of the brain-stimulation puzzle together to create a coherent picture of its physiological underpinnings. But there's reason to believe that when we do, we may understand much more than why rats (and dogs and dolphins) press levers that give certain portions of their brains small jolts of electric current. We may understand the neurological basis of natural rewards and motives, what it is in the brain that makes humans and animals record certain events as events they want to reexperience (such as eating when one is hungry, copulating when one is sexually aroused, and so on). And we may also understand something about the underlying biology of certain "unnatural" rewards like drugs to which some individuals may become addicted.

THE NATURE OF MOTIVES

To sum up, during the past fifty years, there has been enormous progress in our understanding of the psychology and physiology of the biological motives. But as yet, there is no agreement on what it is that the different biological motives have in common, in what ways a comfortable temperature, sufficient water and food, safety, a night's sleep, or sexual satisfaction are alike. Negative feedback can't be the answer, for while it underlies some motives, such as temperature regulation, thirst, and hunger, it can't easily account for others, such as sleep or sex. Nor can we find a common characteristic in arousal level. For some motives, such as sex, the optimum arousal level is high; for others, such as sleep, it is low. Perhaps all we can say is that these different satisfactions are things we seek and want, and for good biological reasons (though in the case of sleep that reason is still unknown).

It may be that there is no one characteristic that the various satisfactions of the biological motives have in common (although advocates of a general pleasure center would probably disagree). Like all scientists, psychologists are much happier when they get neat explanations, and one underlying explanation would be much neater than several different ones. But nature did not design organisms to make psychologists happy; organisms are designed to do what they need to do to survive and to propagate their genes.

A final point: This chapter was concerned with a number of built-in motives—the biological goals we must attain in order to survive. The specific nature of these goals depends not only on our biology but also on what we have learned and been taught. Just what we drink is not only a matter of our water balance: Except for Count Dracula, few members of our Western culture drink blood. By the same token, while we have to maintain certain nutrient levels, most of us would not be satisfied with a diet of grasshoppers. Similar concerns apply to what we fear and hate or how we behave in sexual matters and when, where, and with whom. In all these cases, experience builds upon biology and gives form to the built-in basics with which we start. We learn—from the experience of our own lifetime and, through culture, from the lifetime of hundreds of prior generations.

Evolution gave us a set of built-in, biological goals and a few built-in mechanisms for attaining them. Learning provides the way to modify these goals and to find ever more complex means to achieve them. We turn next to the mechanisms by which such learning occurs in humans and animals.

QUESTIONS FOR CRITICAL THINKING

1. Why is the concept of motivation as directed action hard to reconcile with Descartes' machine metaphor?

2. How is obesity treated, and how well do the treatments work? Should obesity even be considered a disorder?

3. Why does the notion of active sleep seem paradoxical?

4. Why does pleasure seeking appear to violate the principle of homeostasis?

SUMMARY

1. Most human and animal actions are motivated. *Motives* have a two-fold function: They *direct* behavior toward or away from some goal by *potentiating* certain perceptions, behaviors, and feelings rather than others. They also serve to *activate* the organism, which becomes more aroused the greater the strength of the motive.

2. The biological basis of directed action is *negative feedback* in which the system "feeds back" upon itself to stop its own action. Built-in negative feedback is responsible for many reactions that maintain the stability of the organism's internal environment, or *homeostasis.* Special cells in the hypothalamus sense various aspects of the body's internal state, such as temperature. If this is above or below certain *setpoints,* a number of self-regulatory reflexes controlled by the *sympathetic* and *parasympathetic* divisions of the *autonomic nervous system* are triggered (for example, shivering). In addition, directed, voluntary acts (such as putting on a sweater) are also brought into play.

3. Similar homeostatic mechanisms underlie a number of other biological motives, such as *thirst.* The organism is informed about its water balance by receptors that monitor the total volume of its bodily fluids and by receptors that respond to the concentration of certain minerals dissolved in these fluids. Water losses are partially offset by reflex mechanisms, including the secretion of the *antidiuretic hormone (ADH),* which instructs the kidneys to reabsorb more of the water that passes through them. In addition, the organism readjusts its own internal environment by directed action—drinking.

4. The biological motive that has been studied most extensively is *hunger.* Many of the signals for feeding and satiety come from the internal environment. Feeding signals include nutrient levels in the bloodstream (which probably affect *glucoreceptors* in the brain) and metabolic processes in the liver (especially the *glucose-glycogen* balance). Satiety signals include messages from receptors in the stomach and the intestines. Other feeding and satiety signals are external, including the taste, texture, and smell of the food.

5. Many authors believe that the control of feeding is lodged in two antagonistic centers in the hypothalamus whose excitation gives rise to hunger and satiety respectively. As evidence, they point to the effect of lesions. Destruction of the supposed hunger center leads to *aphagia,* a complete refusal to eat. Destruction of the supposed satiety center produces *hyperphagia,* a vast increase in food intake.

6. One feeding-related disorder is *obesity.* Some cases are produced by various constitutional factors, including genetically based metabolic efficiency. Others are the result of various behavioral factors. According to the *setpoint hypothesis,* overweight people have a higher internal setpoint for weight and therefore gravitate toward a weight that is at least in part determined by heredity.

7. Other eating disorders are *anorexia nervosa* in which there is a pattern of relentless self-starvation, sometimes to the point of death, and *bulimia,* which is characterized by repeated binge-and-purge bouts.

8. In contrast to thirst and hunger, which are largely based on homeostatic factors from within, a number of motives are instigated from without. An example is the intense reaction to external threat. Its biological mechanisms include the operations of the *autonomic nervous system.* This consists of two antagonistic branches. One is the *parasympathetic nervous system,* which serves the vegetative functions of everyday life, such as digestion and reproduction. It slows down the heart rate and reduces blood pressure. The other is the *sympathetic nervous system,* which activates the body and mobilizes its resources. It increases the available metabolic fuels and accelerates their utilization by increasing the heart rate and respiration. Intense sympathetic activity can be regarded as an *emergency reaction,* which underlies the overt reactions of *fight* or *flight* and their usual emotional concomitants, rage or fear.

9. The sympathetic emergency reaction is not always adaptive. It can produce temporary disruptions of digestive and sexual functions, and can also lead to more permanent psychophysiological disorders.

10. Among the stimuli that set off the sympathetic emergency reaction is *pain.* This has survival value for it is a signal to react to danger. But since continued pain may interfere with appropriate action, a counteracting process alleviates pain. The mechanism involves the *endorphins,* a group of neurotransmitters secreted within the brain that stimulate nerve tracts that inhibit the transmission of pain messages.

11. While the sympathetic system arouses the more primitive physiological processes of the body, several subcortical structures arouse and wake the brain. These waking systems are opposed by antagonistic processes that lead to sleep. During sleep, brain activity changes, as shown by the *electroencephalogram* or *EEG.* Each night, we oscillate between two kinds of sleep. One is *quiet sleep,* during which the cortex is relatively inactive. The other is *active sleep,* characterized by considerable cortical activity and *rapid eye movements* or *REMs,* a pattern of internal activity during which dreams are experienced.

12. *Sleep-deprivation* studies show that when one or the other kind of sleep is prevented, it is to some extent made up later on. This suggests that there is a need for each of the two sleep states, but the biological functions served by either are as yet unknown. One hypothesis is that one or both forms of sleep serve a *restorative function,* but this can't be the only reason, since sleep is a *clock-driven* process that partially depends on the time of day, regardless of the individual's state of exhaustion. Another hypothesis is that sleep represents an *evolutionary relic* of ancestral adaptive patterns.

13. Today most authors believe that organisms strive for an *optimum level of arousal.* If below this optimum, they try to increase arousal by various means. One way of coping with an arousal level that is too high or too low is by the use of drugs. Some drugs act as *depressants,* including alcohol and the opiates. Others, such as the *amphetamines* and *cocaine,* act as *stimulants.* In many individuals, repeated drug use leads to *addiction,* accompanied by increased *tolerance* and *withdrawal effects* if the drug is withheld.

14. The *opponent-process theory of motivation* tries to explain these and many other phenomena by arguing that all shifts of arousal level produce a counteracting process that acts to moderate the ups and downs. When the original instigator of the shift is removed, the opponent process is revealed more clearly, as in withdrawal effects.

15. Work on the rewarding effects of certain regions of the brain has led to speculations about possible *pleasure centers* in the brain. Stimulation may be either *specific* (and mimic certain natural rewards) or *general* (signalling something all rewards share).

CHAPTER **4**

LEARNING

T hus far, our discussion has centered on the built-in facets of human and animal behavior: the general neural equipment that provides the underpinning for everything we do and the specific, innate feedback systems that underlie directed action. But much of what we do and are goes beyond what nature gave us and is acquired through experience in our lifetime. People learn—to grasp a baby bottle, to eat with a knife and fork, to read and write, to love or hate their neighbors, and eventually, to face death. In animals, the role of learning may be less dramatic, but it is enormously important for them too.

What can psychology tell us about the processes whereby organisms learn? Consider Descartes' reflex-machine conception, which we discussed in the preceding chapters. Reflexes are built-in links between afferent neural messages coming from outside and efferent commands to the muscles or glands. In effect they represent connections that are **hardwired,** a term that derives from the computer industry and refers to a circuit that is built into the machine itself. Such hardwired connections underlie many of the behavior patterns of both animals and humans and are presumably established because they have proved to be adaptive in the species' evolutionary past. However, much of what we and animals do is not based on the evolutionary past but rather on what we and they experience in our own lifetimes. A squirrel has a built-in tendency to bury nuts in the fall and to look for them in the winter. But this alone will not get the squirrel through the winter; the animal must also remember where it buried the nuts in the first place. Hardwired connections are clearly not enough, for no squirrel is born knowing that it buried a walnut under Farmer MacDonald's tree.

A number of investigators have tried to reconcile the phenomena of learning with the reflex-machine conception. The adherents of this approach, whose modern exponents are sometimes called **behavior theorists,** argue that the organism's hardwired repertory of behaviors is supplemented by continual **rewirings** that are produced by experience. Some of these rewirings consist of new connections between stimuli. Thus, the sight of the mother's face may come to signify the taste of milk. Other rewirings involve new connections between acts and their consequences, as when a toddler learns that touching a hot radiator is followed by a painful burn. The behavior theorists set themselves the task of discovering how such rewirings come about.

The behavior theorists' interest in the learning process was admirably suited to the intellectual climate during the first part of this century, especially in the United States. For here was a society that was deeply committed to the individual's efforts to improve himself by pushing himself on to greater efforts and acquiring new skills—in numerous public schools and colleges, in night classes for recent immigrants, dance classes for the shy, courses for those who wanted to "win friends and influence people," and martial-arts classes for those less interested in winning friends than in defeating enemies. There was—and in many ways still is—an enormous faith in the near-limitless malleability of human beings, who were thought to be almost infinitely perfectible by proper changes in their environment, especially through education. Under the circumstances, it was hardly surprising that learning became (and remains) one of the paramount concerns of modern psychology, particularly in the United States.

How should the learning process be studied? At least initially, most behavior theorists felt that there were some basic laws that come into play, regardless of what is learned or who does the learning—be it a dog learning to sit on command or a college student learning integral calculus. This early conception was very influential. It led to the view that even the most involved learned activities are made up of simpler ones, much as complex chemical compounds are made up of simpler atoms. Given this belief, it was only natural that the early investigators concentrated their efforts on trying to understand learning in simple situations and in (relatively) simple creatures like dogs, rats, and pigeons. By so doing, they hoped to strip the learning process down to its bare essence so that its basic laws might be revealed.

As we will see, some of the beliefs of the early behavior theorists had to be modified in the light of later discoveries. They never succeeded in finding *one* set of laws that underlie *all* phenomena of learning in *all* organisms, including humans. But even so, their search led to the major discoveries that form the basis of much of what we know today. It is to these that we now turn.

HABITUATION

FOCUS QUESTIONS

- What is habituation?

- Why might habituation be adaptive?

- What are the two types of habituation?

Perhaps the simplest of all forms of learning is **habituation.** This is a decline in the tendency to respond to stimuli that have become familiar due to repeated exposure. A sudden noise usually startles us—an adaptive reaction, for sudden and unfamiliar stimuli often spell danger. But suppose the same noise is repeated over and over again. The second time, the startle will be diminished, the third time it will hardly be evoked, and after that, it will be ignored altogether. We have become habituated to the noise. Much the same holds for many other everyday events. We have become so accustomed to the ticking of a clock in the living room that we are utterly unaware of it until it finally stops. By the same token, city dwellers become completely habituated to the noise of traffic but are kept awake by the crickets when they take a vacation in the country.*

What is the adaptive significance of habituation? One of its major benefits is that it narrows down the range of stimuli that elicit escape reactions. After all, organisms have to eat and drink and mate to survive, and they can't do so if they spend all their time running away from imaginary enemies. Habituation allows them to ignore the familiar and focus their emergency reactions on things that are new and may signal danger (Wyers, Peeke, and Herz, 1973; Shalter, 1984).

Laboratory studies have shown that habituation comes in two varieties. One is a short-term effect that dissipates in a matter of minutes. A second is more long term; it may persist for days or weeks. That these two are different makes intuitive sense. We gradually habituate to a certain noise; but if a year elapses without the noise, that same sound might well frighten us again. These two

Habituation in Siamese fighting fish
Male Siamese fighting fish adopt a fighting posture when they see another male, but after awhile they habituate to his presence. (Photograph by Bette Splendens / Oxford Scientific Films)

---

*There is some debate about whether habituation is really a different kind of learning from certain others we'll describe later, such as classical and instrumental conditioning. According to some authors, it only refers to a certain experimental procedure used to establish the effect (Rescorla and Holland, 1976).

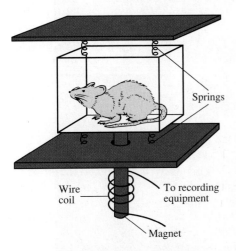

4.1 An apparatus that measures the startle response in rats *A small chamber is balanced on springs. The bottom of the chamber is attached to a magnet that is surrounded by a coil of wire. Sudden movements of the rat will lead to movements of the chamber that produce an electrical current in the wire. (After Hoffman and Fleshler, 1964)*

facets of habituation were demonstrated in a study of rats that were exposed to a high-pitched, loud tone presented for two seconds (Leaton, 1976). Initially, the stimulus produced a marked startle response. The rat literally jumped up in the air when it heard the tone (see Figure 4.1). To measure *short-term habituation,* the experimenters presented three hundred of these tones within the space of five minutes. Presented in this manner, the startle quickly wore off. After one hundred or so presentations, the animal ignored the now familiar tones. The experimenters next asked whether this nonchalance wore off after longer intervals. It evidently did, for when tested after a twenty-four-hour interval the rats jumped just as much as they did at the start of their last short-term training—a phenomenon called *spontaneous recovery.*

To demonstrate *long-term habituation,* the investigators presented the same tone just once a day over an eleven-day period. They found that the startle response gradually declined over days. This shows that there is a long-term memory effect as well as a short-term effect. In some fashion, the animal compares what it now hears and sees with what else it has previously heard and seen, either in its immediate or its more remote past. To the extent that the current stimulus matches what is in its memory, it is judged to be familiar and thus not "startling" (Wagner, 1979; Whitlow and Wagner, 1984). We will have occasion to revisit the distinction between short- and long-term memory storage in a later chapter (see Chapter 7).

CLASSICAL CONDITIONING

FOCUS QUESTIONS

- What steps are involved in demonstrating classical conditioning?

- Once a conditioned response is acquired, how can it be extinguished ("unconditioned") and how can it be reacquired?

- What is discrimination in classical conditioning?

In habituation, an organism learns to recognize an event as familiar, but it doesn't learn anything about the relation between that event and any other circumstances. Such learned relationships among events linked in space or time are often called *associations.*

There's little doubt that much of what we learn consists of various associations between events: between thunder and lightning, between the nipple and food, between the sound of a thumping motor and a large automobile repair bill. The importance of associations in human learning and thinking has been emphasized since the days of the Greek philosophers, but the experimental study of associations did not begin until the end of the nineteenth century. A major step in this direction was the work on conditioning performed by the great Russian scientist, Ivan Petrovich Pavlov (1849–1936).

PAVLOV AND THE CONDITIONED REFLEX

Ivan Petrovich Pavlov had already earned the Nobel Prize for his work on digestion before he embarked upon the study of conditioning that was to gain him even greater fame. His initial interest was in the built-in nervous control of the various digestive reflexes in dogs; most important to us, the secretion

Ivan Petrovich Pavlov in his laboratory, with some colleagues and best friend
(Courtesy of The Bettman Archive)

of saliva. He surgically diverted one of the ducts of the salivary gland, thus channeling part of the salivary flow through a special tube to the outside of the animal's body where it could be easily measured and analyzed. Pavlov demonstrated that salivation was produced by several innate reflexes that prepare for digestion. This is triggered by food (especially dry food) placed in the mouth.

In the course of Pavlov's work a new fact emerged. The salivary reflex could be set off by stimuli that at first were totally neutral. Dogs that had been in the laboratory for a while would soon salivate to a whole host of stimuli that had no such effect on their uninitiated fellows. Not only the taste and touch of the meat in the mouth, but its mere sight, the sight of the dish in which it was placed, the sight of the person who usually brought it, even that person's footsteps—eventually all of these might produce salivation. Pavlov soon decided to study such effects in their own right, for he recognized that they provided a means of extending the reflex concept to embrace learned as well as innate reactions. The approach was simple enough. Instead of waiting for accidental events in each animal's history, the experimenter would provide those events himself. Thus he would repeatedly sound a bell and always follow it with food. Later he observed what happened when the bell was sounded and no food was given (Pavlov, 1927; Figure 4.2).

4.2 Apparatus for salivary conditioning
The figure shows an early version of Pavlov's apparatus for classical conditioning of the salivary response. The dog was held in a harness; sounds or lights functioned as conditioned stimuli, while meat powder in a dish served as the unconditioned stimulus. The conditioned response was assessed with the aid of a tube connected to an opening in one of the animal's salivary glands. (After Yerkes and Morgulis, 1909)

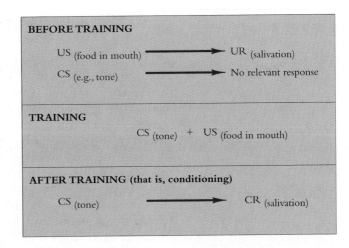

4.3   Relationships between CS, US, CR, and UR in classical conditioning

The fundamental finding was simple: Repeated bell-food pairings led to salivation when the bell was presented alone (that is, unaccompanied by food) on occasional test trials. To explain this, Pavlov proposed a distinction between unconditioned and conditioned reflexes. **Unconditioned reflexes** he held to be essentially inborn and innate; these are unconditionally elicited by the appropriate stimulus regardless of the animal's history. An example is food in the mouth, which unconditionally elicits salivation. In contrast, **conditioned reflexes** were acquired; thus they were conditional upon the animal's past experience and, according to Pavlov, based upon newly formed connections in the brain.

According to Pavlov, every unconditioned reflex is based upon a (presumably built-in) connection between an **unconditioned stimulus (US)** and an **unconditioned response (UR).** In Pavlov's laboratory, these were food in the mouth (the US) and salivation (UR). The corresponding terms for the conditioned reflex are **conditioned stimulus (CS)** and **conditioned response (CR).** The CS would be an initially neutral stimulus, that is, some stimulus (here, the bell) that does not elicit the CR without prior conditioning. The CR (here again, salivation) is the response elicited by the CS after some such pairings of CS and US. These various relationships are summarized in Figure 4.3 and constitute the basis of what is now known as **classical conditioning.**★

THE MAJOR PHENOMENA OF CLASSICAL CONDITIONING

■ Pavlov saw conditioning as a way of extending the reflex concept into the realm of learning. Later workers (especially in the United States) were not as convinced that the so-called conditioned reflex is in fact some kind of reflex, even one that is modified. As a result, they substituted the more neutral term "response" for "reflex," as in "unconditioned response." But until quite recently, most of them shared Pavlov's conviction that conditioning was essentially a change in what the animal does, and so they also focused on the acquisition of the conditioned response. As we will see, later workers came to see conditioning in rather different ways. But we will begin by describing Pavlov's empirical discoveries with a minimum of editorial comment, for these findings laid the foundation for all subsequent theories of classical conditioning and indeed of much of learning generally.

★The adjective "classical" is used, in part, as dutiful tribute to Pavlov's eminence and historical priority and, in part, to distinguish this form of conditioning from *instrumental conditioning* to which we will turn later.

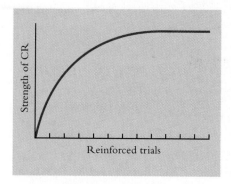

4.4 An idealized learning curve
Strength of the CR is plotted against the number of reinforced trials. The curve presents the results of many such studies, which by and large show that the curve is negatively accelerated: Strength of the CR rises with increasing number of trials, but each trial adds less strength than the trial just before it.

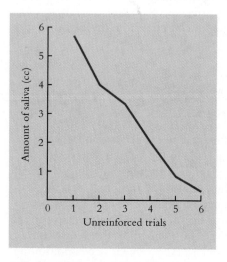

4.5 Extinction of a classically conditioned response *The figure shows the decrease in the amount of saliva secreted (the CR) with increasing number of extinction trials—that is, trials on which the CS is presented without the US. (After Pavlov, 1928)*

ACQUISITION OF CONDITIONED RESPONSES

Pavlov noted that the tendency of the CS to elicit the CR goes up the more often the CS and the US have been paired together. Clearly then, presenting the US together with (or more typically, subsequent to) the CS is a critical operation in classical conditioning. Such a pairing is said to *reinforce* the connection; trials on which the US occurs and trials on which it is omitted are called **reinforced** and **unreinforced trials** respectively.

Figure 4.4 is an idealized learning curve in which the strength of the CR is plotted against successive reinforced trials. In this and other conditioning trials, the general trend is very clear and unsurprising. The strength of the response increases with the number of reinforced trials: The more often a bell's ringing is followed by food for the dog, the greater the amount of saliva the dog produces when he hears the bell.

Once the CS–US relation is solidly established, the CS can serve to condition yet further stimuli. To give one example, Pavlov first conditioned a dog to salivate to the beat of a metronome, using meat powder as the US. After a number of such pairings, he presented the animal with a black square followed by the metronome beat, but without ever introducing the food. Eventually the sight of the black square alone was enough to produce salivation. This phenomenon is called **second-order conditioning.** The metronome, which served as the CS in first-order conditioning, now functioned as the US for a second-order conditioned response. In effect, the black square had become a signal for the metronome, which in turn had previously signaled the appearance of food.

EXTINCTION

The adaptive value of conditioning is self-evident. A zebra's chance of future survival is enhanced by conditioning. There's much to be gained by a conditioned fear reaction to a place from which a lion has pounced some time before (assuming, of course, that the zebra managed to survive the CS–US pairing in the first place). On the other hand, it would be rather inefficient if a connection once established could never be undone. The lion might change its lair, and its former prowling place might now be perfectly safe for grazing.

Pavlov showed that a conditioned reaction can be undone. He demonstrated that the conditioned response will gradually disappear if the CS is repeatedly presented without being reinforced by the US; in his terms, the CS–US link undergoes **experimental extinction.** Figure 4.5 presents an extinction curve from a salivary extinction experiment. As usual, response strength is measured along the *y*-axis, while the *x*-axis indicates the number of extinction trials (that is, trials without reinforcement). As extinction trials proceed, the salivary flow dries up. In effect, the dog has learned that the CS is no longer a signal for food.

A conditioned response that has been extinguished can be resurrected. One means is through **reconditioning,** that is, by presenting further reinforced trials. Typically, reconditioning requires fewer reinforced trials to bring the CR to its former strength than were necessary during the initial conditioning session, even if extinction trials had been continued until the animal stopped responding altogether. The conditioned response was evidently not really abolished by extinction but instead was somehow masked.

The fact that the conditioned response is only masked rather than abolished by extinction is also shown by the phenomenon of **spontaneous recovery.** An extinguished CR will usually reappear after a rest interval during which the animal is left to its own devices. This effect is reminiscent of a similar phenomenon in habituation. In both cases, the sheer passage of time leads to the spontaneous recovery of a response: In the one case, the resurrected response had previously been habituated; in the other, it had been extinguished.

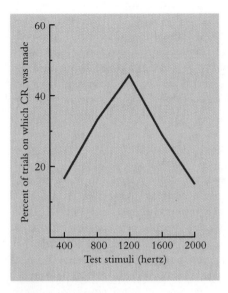

4.6 Generalization gradient of a classically conditioned response *The figure shows the generalization of a conditioned blinking response in rabbits. The CS was a tone of 1,200 hertz, and the US was electric shock. After the conditioned response to the original CS was well established, generalization was measured by presenting various test stimuli, ranging from 400 hertz to 2,000 hertz and noting the percent of the trials on which the animals gave the CR. The figure shows the results, averaged over several testing sessions. (After Moore, 1972)*

GENERALIZATION

So far our discussion has been confined to situations in which the animal is tested with the *identical* stimulus that had served as the CS during training. But of course in the real world the stimuli are never really identical. The master's voice may signal food, but the exact intonation will surely vary from one occasion to another. Can the dog still use whatever it has learned before? If it can't, its conditioned response will be of little benefit. In fact, animals do respond to stimuli other than the original CS, so long as these are sufficiently similar.

This phenomenon is called **stimulus generalization.** A dog may be conditioned to respond to a tone of 1,000 hertz (cycles per second); nevertheless, the CR will be obtained not just with that tone, but also with tones of different frequencies, like 900 or 1,100 hertz. But the CR evoked by such new stimuli will be weaker than the CR elicited by the original CS. The greater the difference between the new stimulus and the original CS, the larger this decrement will be. The resulting curve is called a **generalization gradient** (see Figure 4.6).

DISCRIMINATION

Stimulus generalization is not always beneficial. A tiger may be similar to a kitten; but someone who generalizes from one to the other is likely to be sorry. What he must do instead is discriminate—and not try to pet the tiger.

The phenomenon of **discrimination** is readily demonstrated in the laboratory. A dog is first conditioned to salivate to a CS, for example, a black square (CS$^+$). After the CR is well established, reinforced trials with the black square are randomly interspersed with nonreinforced trials with another stimulus, say, a gray square (CS$^-$). This continues until the animal discriminates perfectly, always salivating to CS$^+$, the reinforced stimulus, and never to CS$^-$, the nonreinforced stimulus. Of course the dog does not reach this final point immediately. During the early trials it will be confused, or more precisely, it will generalize rather than discriminate. It will tend to salivate to CS$^-$ (which, after all, is quite similar to CS$^+$); by the same token, it will often fail to salivate when presented with CS$^+$. Such errors gradually become fewer and fewer until perfect discrimination is finally achieved. Not surprisingly, the discrimination gets harder and harder the more similar the two stimuli are. As similarity increases, the tendency to respond to CS$^+$ will increasingly generalize to CS$^-$, while the tendency not to respond to CS$^-$ will increasingly generalize to CS$^+$. As a result, the dog will require many trials before it finally responds without error.

One might think that the difficulty in forming a discrimination is that the animal has trouble telling the two stimuli apart. But that is usually not the reason. The dog's problem is not that it can't form a sensory discrimination between CS$^+$ and CS$^-$. What is at fault is not its eyesight, for it can distinguish between the dark-gray and light-gray squares visually. Its difficulty is in discovering and remembering which stimulus is *right*—which goes with the US and which does not. Eventually the animal learns, but this doesn't mean that it has learned to see the stimuli differently. What it has learned is their significance; it now knows which stimulus is which.

EXTENSIONS OF CLASSICAL CONDITIONING

Thus far, we have mainly looked at laboratory phenomena such as dogs salivating to bells, lights, and metronomes. Needless to say, conditioning would be of little interest if it only applied to those phenomena. But in actual fact, its scope is very much larger than this.

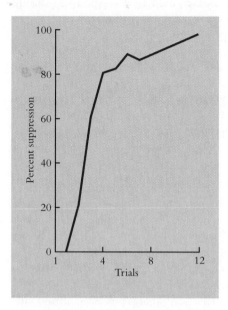

4.7 Response suppression *A rat is trained to press a lever at a steady rate to gain food. The figure plots the extent to which this response is suppressed after successive presentations of a three-minute light CS that is immediately followed by electric shock. After twelve such trials, suppression is at 100 percent, and the animal doesn't respond at all during the three minutes when the CS is presented. (Data from Kamin, 1969)*

To begin with, classical conditioning has been found in a large variety of animal species other than dogs, including ants and anteaters, cats and cockroaches, pigeons and people. Thus, crabs have been conditioned to twitch their tail spines, fish to thrash about, and octopuses to change color. Responses conditioned in laboratory studies with humans include the galvanic skin response (where the US is typically a loud noise or electric shock) and the blink-reaction of the eyelid (where the US consists of a puff of air on the open eye; Kimble, 1961).

Nor is classical conditioning restricted to the laboratory, for it plays a considerable role in our everyday lives. Many of our feelings and urges are probably the result of classical conditioning. We tend to feel hungry at mealtimes and less so during the times between; this is so even if we fast a whole day. Another example is sexual arousal. This is often produced by a partner's special word or gesture whose erotic meaning is very private and is surely learned.

CONDITIONED FEAR

Of special importance is the role of classical conditioning in the formation of various emotional reactions, especially those concerned with fear. A common consequence of a conditioned fear reaction is **response suppression.** The CS will evoke fear, which in turn will suppress whatever other activities the animal is currently engaged in. This is the basis of a widely used technique to study fear conditioning, the **conditioned emotional response (CER)** procedure. A hungry rat is first taught to press a lever for an occasional food reward. After a few training sessions, the rat will press at a steady rate. Now classical conditioning can start. While the animal is pressing, a CS is presented—a light or a tone that will stay on for, say, three minutes. At the end of that period, the CS terminates and the rat receives a mild, brief electric shock (the US). Some twenty minutes later, the same CS-US sequence is repeated. After this, there is another twenty-minute interval during which neither the CS nor the US are presented, followed by yet another CS-US sequence, and so on (Estes and Skinner, 1941; Kamin, 1965). After twelve such trials, the response is completely suppressed—the rat will no longer press the lever (see Figure 4.7).

It is a plausible guess that many adult fears are based upon classical conditioning, acquired in much the same way that fear is acquired in the laboratory. These fears may be relatively mild or very intense (if intense enough, they are called **phobias**). They may be acquired in early childhood or during particular traumatic episodes in later life. An extreme example is an Air Force pilot who bailed out of his plane but whose parachute failed to open until five seconds before he hit the ground. In such traumatic episodes, conditioning apparently occurs in a single trial. This seems reasonable enough, for it would certainly be unadaptive if the pilot had to bail out on ten separate occasions, each time barely escaping death, before he finally developed a conditioned fear reaction (Sarnoff, 1957; see Chapter 18).

INSTRUMENTAL CONDITIONING

FOCUS QUESTIONS

- What is instrumental conditioning, and how does it differ from classical conditioning?

- What was Thorndike's law of effect, and why did he consider it analogous to the doctrine of evolution?

- How did Skinner simplify the study of instrumental conditioning?
- What is the partial-reinforcement effect, and how does it explain some cases of persistent unwanted behavior?

Habituation and classical conditioning are two of the main forms of simple learning. Another is **instrumental conditioning** (which is also called **operant conditioning**). An example of instrumental conditioning comes from the zoo. When a seal learns to turn a somersault to get a fish from the zoo attendant, it has learned an *instrumental response.* The response is instrumental in that it leads to a sought-after effect—in this case, the fish.

There are some important differences between instrumental and classical conditioning. The most important is the fact that in instrumental learning, reinforcement (that is, reward) depends upon the proper response. For the seal the rules of the game are simple: no somersault, no fish. This is not true for classical conditioning. There the US is presented regardless of what the animal does. Another difference concerns response selection. In instrumental learning, the response must be selected from a sometimes very large set of alternatives. The seal's job is to select the somersault from among the numerous other things a seal could possibly do. Not so in classical conditioning. There the response is forced, for the US unconditionally evokes it.

We could loosely summarize the difference between the two procedures by a description of what is learned in each. In classical conditioning the animal must learn about the relation between two stimuli, the CS and the US: Given CS, US will follow. In instrumental learning, the animal has to learn the relation between a response and a reward: Given this response, there will be reinforcement. But such statements are only crude descriptions. To get beyond them, we must discuss instrumental learning in more detail.

THORNDIKE AND THE LAW OF EFFECT

■ The experimental study of instrumental learning began a decade or two before Pavlov. It was an indirect consequence of the debate over the doctrine of evolution. Darwin's theory was buttressed by impressive demonstrations of continuity in the bodily structures of many species, both living and extinct: Despite their apparent differences, a bird's wing, a seal's flipper, and a person's arm have the same bone structure. But his opponents could argue that such evidence was not enough. To them the essential distinction between humans and beasts was elsewhere: in the human ability to think and reason, an ability that animals did not share. To answer these critics, it was important to find proof of mental as well as bodily continuity across the animal kingdom.

For evidence, the Darwinians turned to animal behavior. At first, the method was largely anecdotal. Several British naturalists (including Darwin himself) collected stories about the intellectual achievements of various animals as related by presumably reliable informants. Taken at face value, the results painted a flattering picture of animal intellect, as in accounts of cunning cats scattering bread crumbs on the lawn to entice birds (Romanes, 1882). But even if such observations could be trusted (and they probably could not), they did not prove that the animals' performances were achieved in the way a human might achieve the same thing: by reason and understanding. To be sure of that, one would have to study the animals' learning processes from start to finish. To see a circus seal blow a melody on a set of toy trumpets is one thing; to conclude from this observation that it appreciates the tune is quite another.

There was clearly a need for controlled experimental procedures whereby the entire course of learning could be carefully scrutinized. That method was

Edward L. Thorndike *(Courtesy of The Granger Collection)*

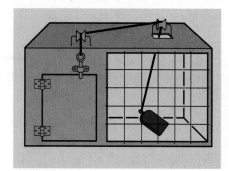

4.8 Puzzle box *This box is much like those used by Thorndike. The animal steps on a treadle attached to a rope, thereby releasing a latch that locks the door. (After Thorndike, 1911)*

provided in 1898 by Edward L. Thorndike (1874–1949) in a brilliant doctoral dissertation that became one of the classic documents of American psychology (Thorndike, 1898).

CATS IN A PUZZLE BOX

Thorndike's method was to set up a problem for the animal. To gain reward the creature had to perform some particular action determined by the experimenter. Much of this work was done with hungry cats. The animal was placed in a *puzzle box,* an enclosure from which it could escape only by performing some simple action that would unlatch the door, such as pulling a loop or wire, or pressing a lever (Figure 4.8). Once outside, the animal was rewarded with a small portion of food and then placed back into the box for another trial. This procedure was repeated until the task was mastered.

On the first trial, the typical cat struggled valiantly; it clawed at the bars, it bit, it struck out in all directions, it meowed, and it howled. This continued for several minutes until the animal finally hit upon the correct response by pure accident. Subsequent trials brought gradual improvement. The mad scramble became shorter and the animal took less and less time to perform the correct response. By the time the training sessions were completed the cat's behavior was almost unrecognizable from what it had been at the start. Placed in the box, it immediately approached the wire loop, yanked it with businesslike dispatch, and hurried through the open door to enjoy its well-deserved reward. The cat had certainly learned.

How had it learned? If one merely observed its final performance one might credit the cat with reason or understanding, but Thorndike argued that the problem was solved in a very different way. For proof he examined the learning curves. Plotting the time required on each trial (that is, the *response latency*) over the whole course of training, he usually found a curve that declined quite gradually (Figure 4.9). Had the animals "understood" the solution at some point during training, one might expect learning curves that showed a sudden drop as the cat finally got the point. ("Aha!" muttered the insightful cat, "It's the lever that lets me out," and henceforth howled and bit no more.) But what really happened was that the cat achieved the correct response pattern in small increments, with no evidence of a sudden insight followed by perfect performance.

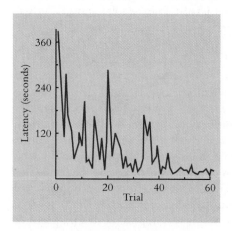

4.9 Learning curve of one of Thorndike's cats *To get out of the box, the cat had to move a wooden handle from a vertical to a horizontal position. The figure shows the gradual decline in the animal's response latency (the time it takes to get out of the box). Note that the learning curve is by no means smooth but has rather marked fluctuations. This is a common feature of the learning curves of individual subjects. Smooth learning curves are generally produced by averaging the results of many individual subjects. (After Thorndike, 1898)*

THE LAW OF EFFECT

Thorndike proposed that what the animal had learned was best described as an increase in the strength of the correct response. Initially, the cat had the tendency to perform a large set of responses, perhaps because of prior learning, perhaps because of built-in predispositions. As it happened, virtually all of these led to failure. As trials proceeded, the strength of these incorrect responses gradually weakened. In contrast, the correct response, which at first was weak, increasingly grew in strength. In Thorndike's terms, the correct response was gradually "stamped in," while futile ones were correspondingly "stamped out." The improvements in the learning curves "represent the wearing smooth of a path in the brain, not the decisions of a rational consciousness" (Thorndike, 1911).

According to Thorndike, some responses get strengthened and others weakened as learning proceeds. But what produces these different effects? Thorndike's answer was a bold formulation called the *law of effect.*

The relevant features of his analysis are schematized in Figure 4.10, which indicates the tendency to perform the various responses, whether correct (R_c) or incorrect (R_1, R_2, R_3, etc.). The critical question is how the correct response gets strengthened until it finally overwhelms the incorrect ones that are at first so dominant. Thorndike's proposal, the law of effect, held that the consequences

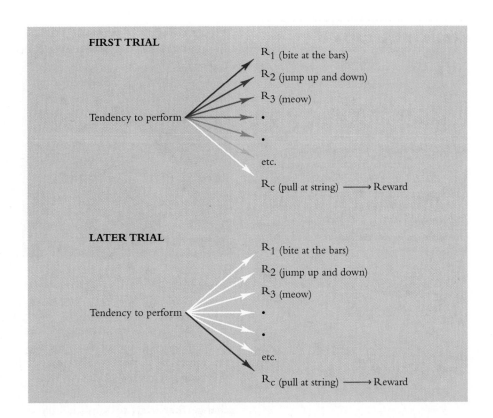

FIRST TRIAL

Tendency to perform

R$_1$ (bite at the bars)
R$_2$ (jump up and down)
R$_3$ (meow)
.
.
etc.
R$_c$ (pull at string) ——→ Reward

LATER TRIAL

Tendency to perform

R$_1$ (bite at the bars)
R$_2$ (jump up and down)
R$_3$ (meow)
.
.
etc.
R$_c$ (pull at string) ——→ Reward

4.10 The law of effect *The figure is a schematic presentation of Thorndike's theory of instrumental learning. On the first trial, the tendency to perform various incorrect responses (biting the bars, jumping up and down) is very strong, while the tendency to perform the correct response (pulling the string) is weak or nonexistent. As trials proceed, the strength of these responses changes. The incorrect responses become weaker and weaker, for none of these responses is immediately followed by reward. In contrast, there is a progressive strengthening of the correct response because this is followed more or less immediately by reward.*

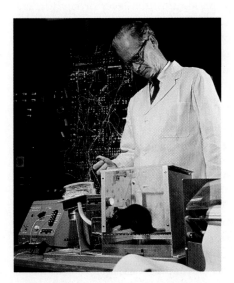

B. F. Skinner *(Photograph by Nina Leen, Life Magazine, © Time Warner, Inc.)*

(that is, the effect) of a response determine whether the tendency to perform it is strengthened or weakened. If the response is followed by reward, it will be strengthened; if it is followed by the absence of reward (or worse yet, by punishment) it will be weakened. There was no need to postulate any further intellectual processes in the animal, no need to assume that the animal noticed a connection between act and consequence, no need to believe that it was trying to attain some goal. If the animal made a response and reward followed shortly, that response was more likely to be performed at a subsequent time.

This proposal fits neatly into the context of evolutionary thinking so dominant at the time. Thorndike emphasized the adaptive nature of the animal's activity, which is gradually shaped to serve its biological ends. But the relationship to evolutionary theory is even closer, for, as Thorndike pointed out, the law of effect is an analogue of the law of the survival of the fittest. In the life of the species, the individual whose genetic makeup fits it best for its environment will survive to transmit its characteristics to its offspring. In the life of the individual, learning provides another adaptive mechanism through the law of effect, which decrees that only the fittest *responses* shall survive. As Thorndike put it, "It is a process of selection among reactions . . . by eliminating the unsuitable reaction directly by discomfort, and also by positively selecting the suitable one by pleasure. . . . It is of tremendous usefulness. . . . He who learns and runs away, *will live to learn another day* . . ." (Thorndike, 1899, p. 91). In short, the reward is to new and adaptive responses as survival is to new and adaptive mutations.

SKINNER AND OPERANT BEHAVIOR

Thorndike initiated the experimental study of instrumental behavior, but the psychologist who shaped the way in which many modern behavior theorists think about the subject is B. F. Skinner (1904–1990). Skinner was one of the first theorists to insist on a sharp distinction between classical and

A   B

4.11 Animals in operant chambers (A) *A rat trained to press a lever for water reinforcement. (Photograph by Mike Salisbury) (B) A pigeon pecking at a lighted key for food reinforcement. Reinforcement consists of a few seconds' access to a grain feeder that is located just below the key. (Photograph by Susan M. Hogue)*

instrumental conditioning. In classical conditioning, the animal's behavior is *elicited* by the CS; to that extent, the salivation is set off from the outside. But Skinner insisted that in instrumental conditioning the organism is much less at the mercy of the external situation. Its reactions are *emitted* from within, as if they were what we ordinarily call *voluntary.* Skinner called these instrumental responses **operants:** They operate on the environment to bring about some change that leads to reward. Like Thorndike, Skinner believed in the law of effect, insisting that the tendency to emit these operants is strengthened or weakened by its consequences (Skinner, 1938).

Behavior theorists have always searched for ever-simpler situations in the hope that the true laws of learning will show up there. Skinner's way of simplifying the study of operant behavior was to create a situation in which the same instrumental response could be performed repeatedly. The most common example is the experimental chamber (popularly called the Skinner box) in which a rat presses a lever or a pigeon pecks at a lighted key (Figure 4.11). In these situations, the animal remains in the presence of the lever or key for, say, an hour at a time, pressing and pecking at whatever rate it chooses. All of the animal's responses are automatically recorded; stimuli and reinforcements are presented automatically by programming devices. The measure of response strength is the **response rate,** that is, the number of responses per unit of time.

THE MAJOR PHENOMENA OF INSTRUMENTAL CONDITIONING

■ Many of the phenomena of instrumental learning parallel those of classical conditioning. Consider reinforcement. In classical conditioning, the term refers to an operation (establishing a CS–US contingency) that strengthens the CR. In instrumental learning, reinforcement refers to an analogous operation: having the response followed by a condition that the animal prefers. This may be the presentation of something good, such as grain to a hungry pigeon. The grain is an example of an **appetitive stimulus** (a stimulus for which the animal so to speak "has an appetite"). In Thorndike's terms, it is something that the animal does everything to attain and nothing to prevent. Reinforcement may also be the termination or prevention of something bad, such as the cessation of an electric shock. Such a shock is an example of an **aversive stimulus,** one that the animal does everything to avoid and nothing to attain.

4.12   Studying discriminative stimuli with the jumping stand   *The rat has to jump to one of two cards, say a triangle or a square, behind which is a ledge that contains food. If the choice is correct, the card gives way and the animal gets to the food. If the choice is incorrect, the card stays in place and the rat bumps its nose and falls into the net below. (After Lashley, 1930)*

We can also distinguish between ***positive reinforcement*** and ***negative reinforcement.*** Positive reinforcement refers to conditions in which the response produces an appetitive stimulus—a rat pressing a lever to get food. Negative reinforcement refers to conditions in which the instrumental response eliminates or prevents an aversive stimulus—a rat jumping over a barrier to escape an electric shock.

Just as in classical conditioning, the probability of an instrumental response increases with an increasing number of reinforcements. And, again as in classical conditioning, the response suffers extinction when reinforcement is withdrawn.

GENERALIZATION AND DISCRIMINATION

The instrumental response is not elicited by external stimuli but is, in Skinner's terms, emitted from within. But this doesn't mean that external stimuli have no effect. They do exert considerable control over behavior, for they serve as ***discriminative stimuli.*** Suppose a pigeon is trained to hop on a treadle to get some grain. When a green light is on, hopping on the treadle will pay off. But when a red light is on, the treadle-hopping response will be of no avail, for the pigeon gets no access to the food container. Under these circumstances, the green light becomes a positive discriminative stimulus and the red light a negative one (here indicated by CS$^+$ and CS$^-$ respectively). The pigeon will hop in the presence of the first and not in the presence of the second. But this discrimination is made in an instrumental and not a classical conditioning context. The green light doesn't signal food the way a CS$^+$ might in Pavlov's laboratory. Instead, it signals a particular relationship between the instrumental response and the reinforcer, telling the pigeon as it were "If you hop now, you'll get food." Conversely for the red light: The CS$^-$ tells the animal that there's no point in going through the treadle-hopping business right now.

A variety of techniques have been used to study the role of discriminative stimuli in affecting learned instrumental behaviors (see Figure 4.12). Many of the results mirror those of generalization and discrimination in classical conditioning. An example is the study of stimulus generalization using operant techniques. Figure 4.13 shows a typical stimulus generalization gradient for color in pigeons. The birds were trained to peck at a key illuminated with yellow light after which they were tested with lights of varying wavelengths. The resulting gradient is orderly. As the test light became less similar to the original CS$^+$, the pigeons were less inclined to peck at it (Guttmann and Kalish, 1956).

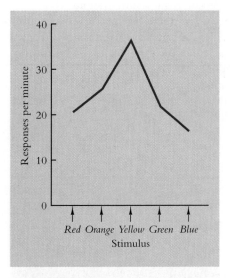

4.13   Stimulus generalization of an instrumental response   *Pigeons were originally reinforced to peck at a yellow light. When later tested with lights of various colors, they showed a standard generalization gradient, pecking more vigorously at colors more similar to yellow (such as green and orange) than at colors farther removed (such as red and blue). Prior to being reinforced on the yellow key, their tendency to peck was minimal and roughly equal for all colors. (After Reynolds, 1968)*

Shaping *The routines of circus animals are generally established through the method of successive approximation. (Photograph © Hank Morgan)*

SHAPING

How does an animal learn the instrumental response that will lead to reinforcement? The law of effect tells us that once that response has been made, then reinforcement will act to strengthen it. But what happens if that response isn't ever made in the first place? As it happens, pecking and lever pressing are fairly easy as such responses go; many animals hit upon them of their own accord. But we can make the response much more difficult. For example, we could set the rat's lever so high on the wall that it must stretch up on its hindlegs to depress it. Now the animal might never make the response on its own. But it could learn this response and even ones more outlandish if its behavior were suitably ***shaped.*** This is accomplished by the method of ***successive approximations.***

Take the problem of the elevated lever. First, we train the animal to approach the tray in which the food is delivered whenever the food-dispensing mechanism gives off its characteristic click. At random intervals, the click sounds and a food pellet drops into the tray; this continues until the rat shows that it is properly trained by running to pick up its pellet as soon as it hears the click. Shaping can now begin. We might first reinforce the animal for walking into the general area where the lever is located. As soon as it is there, it hears the click and devours the pellet. Very soon it will hover around the neighborhood of the lever. We next reinforce it for facing the lever, then for stretching its body upward, then for touching the lever with its paws, and so on until we finally complete its education by reinforcing it for pressing the lever down. The guiding principle throughout is immediacy of reinforcement. If we want to reinforce the rat for standing up on its hindlegs, we must do it the instant after the response; even a one-second wait may be too long, for by then the rat may have fallen back on all fours, and if we reinforce it then, we will reinforce the wrong response.

By means of this technique, animals have been trained to perform exceedingly complex response chains (see Figure 4.14). Pigeons have been trained to play Ping-Pong and dogs to plunk out four-note tunes on a toy piano. Such successes encouraged some enterprising psychologists to develop live advertising exhibits, featuring such stars as Priscilla, the Fastidious Pig to promote the sale of certain farm feeds (Breland and Breland, 1951). Priscilla turned on the radio, ate breakfast at a kitchen table, picked up dirty clothes and dropped them in a hamper,

A

B

4.14 Animals in show business (A) A pig trained by means of operant techniques to push a market cart. The animal was first reinforced for putting its front feet up on the handle, until it could raise up on the handle and push the cart while walking on its hind feet. (Photograph courtesy of Animal Behavior Enterprises) (B) Squirrels trained to stand on their hind legs, hold onto the bar, and, hence, to waterski for a fixed interval so as to get reinforced. (Photograph by Gerald Davis/Contact Press Images)

4.15   Conditioned reinforcement in chimpanzees   *Chimpanzee using a token to obtain food after working to obtain tokens. (Courtesy Yerkes Regional Primate Research Center of Emory University)*

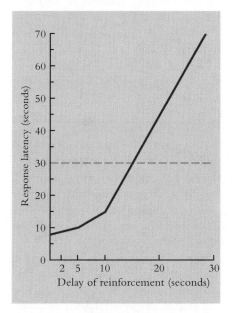

4.16   The effect of a delay in reinforcement   *The graph shows the response latency for rats pressing a lever after 50 trials on which they received a food reward following a delay of 0, 2, 5, 10, or 30 seconds. The dotted line indicates the animals' average latency at the very first trial. It is clear that animals trained with delays up to 10 seconds improved over trials, and the shorter the delay the greater was their improvement. But animals trained with a delay of 30 seconds did not improve; on the contrary, their performance was markedly worse after 50 trials than it was initially. (Data from Perin, 1943)*

vacuumed the floor, and finally selected the sponsor's feed in preference to Brand X—a convincing tribute to the sponsor and to the power of reinforcement.

CONDITIONED REINFORCEMENT

So far, our examples of reinforcement have included food or water or termination of electric shock, whose capacity to reinforce responses is presumably based upon built-in mechanisms of various kinds. But instrumental learning is not always reinforced by events of such immediate biological consequence. For example, piano teachers rarely reinforce their students with food or the cessation of electric shock; a nod or the comment "good" is all that is usually required. How does the Thorndikian approach explain why the word "good" is reinforcing?

Thorndike and Skinner would answer that a stimulus will acquire reinforcing properties if it is repeatedly paired with a primary reinforcer. It will then provide **conditioned reinforcement** if administered after a response has been made.

Numerous experiments give evidence that neutral stimuli can acquire reinforcing properties. For example, chimpanzees were first trained to insert poker chips into a vending machine to acquire grapes. Having learned this, they then learned to operate another device that delivered poker chips (Cowles, 1937; see Figure 4.15). Examples of this kind indicate that the critical factor in establishing a stimulus as a conditioned reinforcer is its association with primary reinforcement. It is then not surprising that the effect increases the more frequently the two have been paired. As we might also expect, a conditioned reinforcer will gradually lose its powers if it is repeatedly unaccompanied by some primary reinforcement. All of this argues that conditioned reinforcement is established by a process that is akin to, if not identical with, classical conditioning. The conditioned reinforcer serves as a CS that signals some motivationally significant US.

If conditioned reinforcers are so readily extinguished in the laboratory, why do they seem so much more permanent in human life? Nods do not lose their reinforcing value just because they haven't been paired with any primary reinforcer for a month or more. In part, the answer may be that the nod or the smile has enormous generality. It is associated not with one but with many different desirable outcomes. Even if extinguished in one context, it would still be maintained in countless others.

DELAY OF REINFORCEMENT

According to the law of effect, a response will be strengthened if it is followed by a reward. But the mere fact that a reward will follow is not enough. In general, the reward must follow the response rather quickly, for a reinforcer becomes less and less effective the longer its presentation is delayed after the response is made.

The relation between the delay and the effectiveness of a reward has been studied experimentally in various ways. One experimenter trained several groups of rats to press a lever that was withdrawn from the box immediately after the correct response. Food was delivered after different delays of reinforcement ranging from 0 to 30 seconds for the various groups. Learning was clearly faster the shorter the interval. These results are summarized in Figure 4.16, which shows the declining effectiveness of reinforcement with increasing delay. Note that there was no learning at all when the interval was 30 seconds; in instrumental learning, late is sometimes no better than never (Perin, 1943).

To what extent does the delay-of-reward principle apply to humans? It depends upon which aspects of human behavior we consider. At one level there is an enormous gap between what we see in the rat and what we know of ourselves. Rats and humans live according to different time scales entirely. Reinforcement may come many days after an action and still have an effect, as in the case of a monthly paycheck, because people can relate their present to their past by all sorts of symbolic devices. Unlike the rat, humans can transcend the here and now.

The fact that people sometimes overcome long delays of reinforcement should not blind us to the fact that they often do not. Many of our actions are dictated by immediate reward, regardless of the long-term outcome. To give only one example, consider cigarette smoking. By now, most smokers are undoubtedly convinced of the ultimate dangers they are courting. In fact, they may experience some discomfort: They may cough and have trouble breathing when they wake up. Yet despite all this, many of them continue to smoke. The problem is that the positive reinforcement of the act is immediate, while the discomfort or worse comes later. Transcending the gradient of reward is no easy task.

SCHEDULES OF REINFORCEMENT

So far, we've only dealt with cases in which reinforcement follows the response every time it is made. But outside of the laboratory, this arrangement is surely the exception and not the rule. The fisherman does not hook a fish with every cast, and even a star tennis player occasionally loses a match to one of her less accomplished rivals. All of these are cases of *partial reinforcement* in which a response is reinforced only some of the time.

One way of studying phenomena of this kind is in the operant situation. Here reinforcement can easily be scheduled in different ways—after every response, after some number of responses, after some interval, and so on. The *schedule of reinforcement* is simply the rule set up by the experimenter that determines the occasions on which a response is reinforced.

Ratio schedules One example of such a rule is the *fixed-ratio schedule* (abbreviated FR 2, FR 4, FR 50, as the case may be) in which the subject has to produce a specified number of responses for every reward, like a factory worker paid by piecework. Such schedules can generate very high rates of responding, but to get the organism to that level requires some finesse. The trick is to increase the ratio very gradually, beginning with continuous reinforcement and slowly stepping up the requirement. By such procedures, pigeons (and probably factory workers) have been led to perform at schedules as high as FR 500.

When the fixed ratio gets high enough, a new pattern develops. Following a reinforcement, the pigeon will pause for a while before it starts to peck again. The higher the ratio, the longer the pause (see Figure 4.17). In a way, the pigeon is like a student who has just finished one term paper and has to write another. It is very hard to start again, but once the first page is written, the next ones come more readily. The pause following reinforcement can be eliminated by changing the schedule to a *variable ratio (VR)*. In VR schedules, reinforcement still comes after a certain number of responses but that number varies irregularly, averaging out to a particular ratio (for example VR 50, that is, a reward on average after every fifty responses). Now there is no way whereby the pigeon can know which of its pecks will bring reward. It might be the first, the tenth, or the hundredth peck following the last reinforcement. Since the number of prior pecks is no longer a clue, the pause disappears. A glance at a gambling casino gives proof that VR schedules affect humans much as they do pigeons. The slot machines are set to pay off occasionally, just enough to maintain the high rate of behavior that keeps the casino lucrative to its owners and not to its clients.

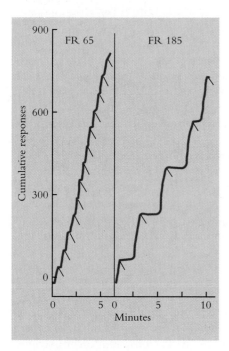

4.17 Performance on two fixed-ratio schedules *The figure records the pigeon's cumulative responses—how many key pecks it made after 5 minutes in the operant chamber, after 10 minutes, and so on. The steeper the record, the faster the response rate. The left-hand panel shows performance on FR 65, the right on FR 185. The small diagonal slashes indicate times when the animal received reinforcement. Note the characteristic pause after the fixed ratio has been run off and that the duration of this pause increases with increasing ratios. (Adapted from Ferster and Skinner, 1957)*

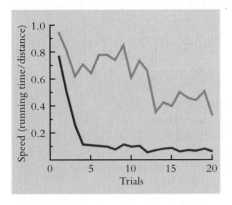

4.18   The partial-reinforcement effect
The figure shows runway speeds during extinction trials on two groups of rats. One group had previously been reinforced on every trial; the other had only been reinforced on 30 percent of the trials. The figure shows that the group trained under full reinforcement (in dark red) stops running considerably before the group that was trained under partial reinforcement (in blue). (After Weinstock, 1954)

Partial reinforcement and extinction   Some of the most dramatic effects of partial reinforcement are seen during subsequent extinction. The basic fact can be stated very simply: A response will be much harder to extinguish if it was acquired during partial rather than continuous reinforcement. This phenomenon is often called the **partial-reinforcement effect** (Humphreys, 1939).

A good illustration is provided by an experiment in which several rats were trained on a runway for food (Weinstock, 1954). All animals received the same number of trials but not the same number of reinforcements. One group was reinforced on every trial, another only on 30 percent of the trials. Figure 4.18 shows what happened to these two groups during extinction. The rats reinforced 100 percent of the time gave up very much sooner than their partially reinforced fellows. Numerous other experiments have given substantially the same result on all manner of subjects, including humans.

On the face of it, the partial-reinforcement effect is paradoxical. If the strength of an instrumental response increases with increasing reinforcements, we should expect that groups reinforced 100 percent of the time would continue to respond for longer than those reinforced only partially. In fact, the very opposite is true. Why? Speaking informally, we might suggest that the partially reinforced rat has come to expect that reward may occur even after several unrewarded trials; it has learned that "if at first you don't succeed, try, try again." In contrast, the rat reinforced 100 percent of the time has never encountered unreinforced trials before. If this interpretation of the partial-reinforcement effect is correct, we would expect an irregular sequence of reinforcements to be harder to extinguish than a regular one, even if the proportion of reinforcements is the same in both cases. This is precisely what happens. Thus ratio schedules engender greater resistance to extinction if they are variable rather than fixed.

To see the partial-reinforcement effect in action, consider a simple problem in child rearing. Many parents find that their six-month-old does not want to go to sleep. Put into his crib at night, he howls his vehement protests until he is lifted out again. Sooner or later his parents resolve that this has to stop. The baby is put back in the crib, and the wails begin. The parents stay firm for a while, but eventually they weaken (after all, the baby might be sick). Brought out of his crib, the baby gurgles happily, and the process of partial reinforcement has begun. Next time, the parents will have an even harder time. According to one study (and to common sense), the answer is consistent nonreinforcement. Two determined parents plotted an extinction curve for their twenty-one-month-old child's bedtime tantrums. One day they simply decided to put their little tyrant to bed and then leave the bedroom and not go back. On the first occasion, the child howled for forty-five minutes; the next few times the cries were much diminished, until finally after ten such "trials," the child went to sleep smiling and with no complaints at all (Williams, 1959).

AVERSIVE CONDITIONING

So far, our discussion of instrumental learning has largely centered on cases where the reinforcing stimulus is appetitive—the kind we normally call reward. But aversive stimuli are no less relevant to instrumental learning; they represent the opposite side of the coin—the stick rather than the carrot, punishment rather than reward. These aversive stimuli may be electric shock for laboratory rats or swats on the rear for infants. While the stimulus may differ, there is little doubt that organisms learn whatever they must to minimize such unpleasantries, to get as few shocks, swats, and insulting reproofs as they possibly can.

Punishment   Psychologists distinguish between several kinds of instrumental learning that depend on the use of aversive stimuli. The most familiar from

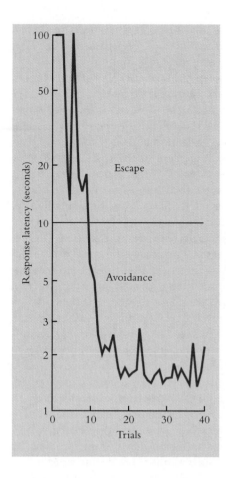

4.19 The course of avoidance learning in a dog *The figure shows response latencies of one animal (where latency is the time from the onset of CS to the animal's response). A warning stimulus indicated that shock would begin 10 seconds after the onset of the signal. For the first nine trials the dog escaped. It jumped over the hurdle after the shock began. From the tenth trial on, the dog avoided: It jumped before its 10 seconds of grace were up. The jumping speed increased until the animal jumped with an average latency of about 1½ seconds. (Latency is plotted on a logarithmic scale. This compresses the time scale so as to put greater emphasis on differences between the shorter response latencies.) (After Solomon and Wynne, 1953)*

everyday life is **punishment training.** Here, a response is followed by an aversive stimulus, which will then tend to suppress the response on subsequent occasions. Note that this is not identical to negative reinforcement. In negative reinforcement a response is *strengthened* by the cessation of an aversive stimulus, as in the case of a rat that jumps over a hurdle to escape an electric shock. In contrast, punishment training *weakens* (or suppresses) a response by the application of an aversive stimulus shortly after the unwanted response has been made. An example is a driver who gets a ticket for speeding. One factor that determines the resulting response suppression is the extent to which reinforcement is delayed, which we've already discussed in the context of reward. Consider a cat that has developed the unfortunate habit of using a large indoor plant as its private bathroom. The irate owner discovers the misdeed an hour or so later and smacks the cat when he sees it in the kitchen. It's hardly surprising that the punishment will not produce the hoped for hygienic result, for the animal has no way of connecting the crime with the punishment. For punishment to have its desired effect, it must be administered shortly after the unwanted response is performed.

Escape and avoidance Aversive stimuli can weaken response tendencies (as in punishment training), but they can also be used to strengthen them. This happens in **escape** and **avoidance learning.** In escape learning, the response stops some aversive event that has already begun. In avoidance learning, the subject can forestall the aversive event altogether. An example of escape learning is when a rat learns to press a lever to get rid of an electric shock. An example of avoidance learning is when a dog learns to jump over a hurdle when it hears a tone that signals impending shock; if it jumps within some grace period, it will manage to avoid the shock entirely (see Figure 4.19).

Avoidance learning in human life An enormous amount of ordinary human activity involves avoidance. We stop at red lights to avoid getting traffic tickets, pay bills to avoid interest charges, carry umbrellas to avoid getting wet, and devise excuses to avoid having lunch with a bore. We probably perform dozens of such learned avoidance responses each day, and most of them are perfectly useful and adaptive (Schwartz, 1989). But some avoidance learning is essentially maladaptive and is often based on more potent aversive stimuli than a boring lunch. An extreme example is phobias. As already mentioned, some people have intense fears—heights, open spaces, dogs, elevators, and so on. As a result, they will develop elaborate patterns to avoid these things. In some cases, the phobia may be caused by traumatic experiences in the past as in the case of a woman who was trapped for several hours in a swaying elevator stuck between the fortieth and forty-first floor of an office building and never used an elevator thereafter. Such an avoidance reaction is of little future use, for elevators ordinarily function perfectly well. But the trouble is that the avoidance response is self-perpetuating. It will not extinguish even if the aversive stimulus is no longer there. The reason is that the person (or animal) will not stay in the previously dangerous situation long enough to discover whether the danger is indeed still there. The woman

Avoidance learning *No doubt the infant will learn to avoid the flame. (Photograph by Erika Stone)*

who avoids elevators will never find out that they are now perfectly safe, for she won't ever use them again—a rather inconvenient behavior pattern if her own office happens to be above the forty-first floor.

Is there any way to extinguish avoidance responses? (The question is of considerable practical interest because it has implications for therapy of phobias and related conditions; see Chapter 19). In animals, the answer is yes. The technique is to force them to test reality so that they can discover that the aversive stimulus is no longer there. In a number of studies, animals were first trained to jump back and forth in a box to avoid a mild shock. After they had learned the avoidance response, they were exposed to the stimulus that previously had signaled impending shock. They immediately tried to jump to the other side of the box, but they couldn't; their avoidance response was blocked by a floor-to-ceiling barrier that forced them to remain in the compartment. They necessarily remained and were visibly frightened. But, in fact, there was no shock. After a few such trials without shock, the avoidance reaction was extinguished. The idea is much like getting back on the horse that threw you—a good prescription for aspiring jockeys, assuming the horse won't throw them again (Baum, 1970; Mineka, 1979).

COGNITIVE LEARNING

FOCUS QUESTIONS

- What is the cognitive theory of conditioning?

- What findings suggest that cognitive interpretations might apply to both classical and instrumental conditioning?

- What is learned helplessness, and how can it explain some aspects of human depression?

To the early theorists, the essential thing about classical and instrumental conditioning was that both procedures modify behavior. This held for classical conditioning, which Pavlov saw as an extension of reflex action whereby the elicitation of certain responses (the URs) is passed from one set of stimuli (the USs) to another (the CSs). It also held for instrumental conditioning, which Thorndike and Skinner regarded as the strengthening of certain responses by the mechanical effect of reinforcement.

From the earliest days of behavior theory, however, there was an alternative view which asserted that what really matters when animals (and humans) learn is not the *change* in behavior as such, but the acquisition of new *knowledge.* One of the most prominent exponents of this view was Edward C. Tolman (1886–1959), who argued that in both classical and instrumental conditioning an animal gains various bits of knowledge, or *cognitions.*

These bits of knowledge are organized so that they can be used when needed. This is very different from asserting that the animal acquires a tendency to perform a certain response. As Tolman saw it, the response an animal acquires in the course of a learning experiment is only an index that a given cognition has been gained. It is an indispensable measuring stick, but it is not what is being measured. Rather the essence of what is learned is something within the animal, a private event that will only become public when the animal acts upon its newly acquired knowledge. Today such cognitions are often called *representations,* which correspond to (represent) certain events, or relations between events, in the animal's world (Dickinson, 1987).

Edward C. Tolman *(Courtesy of the Psychology Department, University of California, Berkeley)*

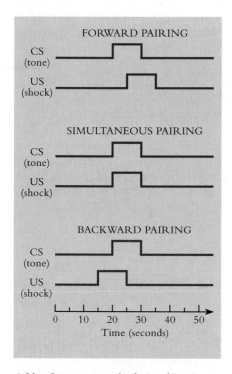

4.20   Some temporal relationships in classical conditioning

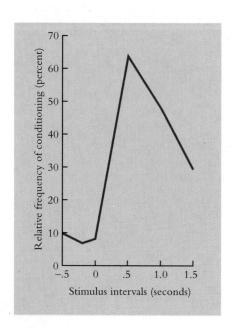

Evidence that animals acquire cognitions came from a number of experiments designed to determine whether instrumental learning can occur without the performance of the relevant response. Many early behavior theorists claimed that performance is an indispensable ingredient for instrumental learning, insisting that the animal learns by doing and in no other way. Several studies, however, suggest that this is not the case. For example, rats have been ferried from one end of a large room to another in transparent trolley cars. Later tests showed that they had learned something about the general features of the room even though they had not performed any relevant responses during their trolley-car ride (Gleitman, 1963). They had acquired what Tolman called a "cognitive map" that represents what is where and what leads to what (Tolman, 1948).

A COGNITIVE VIEW OF CLASSICAL CONDITIONING

■ The cognitive approach has had considerable impact on current conceptions of animal learning. One of its effects was a reinterpretation of classical conditioning. It appears that what is learned in classical conditioning is an association between two events: the CS and the US. But how is this association acquired? In line with many philosophers who had thought about association, Pavlov believed that a necessary condition is temporal *contiguity,* that is, togetherness in time. As we will see, the answer is not quite as simple as that.

One way of finding out whether the CS-US association is based on contiguity in time is to vary the interval between the two stimuli as well as the order in which they are presented. A number of procedures do just that. In some, the CS precedes the US *(forward pairing),* in others it follows the US *(backward pairing),* and in yet others the two stimuli are presented at the same time *(simultaneous pairing).* (See Figure 4.20.)

The general results of these procedures are as follows: Conditioning is best when the CS *precedes* the US by some optimum interval that is generally rather short (see Figure 4.21). Presenting the CS and the US simultaneously is generally much less effective, and the backward procedure is even worse. On the other hand, the effectiveness of forward pairing declines rapidly when the CS-US interval increases beyond the optimum interval (Rescorla, 1988).

How can we make sense of these facts? A reasonable suggestion is that the CS serves a signaling function: It prepares the organism for a US that is to come. Let us consider forward, simultaneous, and backward pairing in this light by likening the subject's situation to that of a driver setting out upon an unfamiliar road. Suppose our driver wants to go from Denver to Salt Lake City and that some 150 miles out of Denver there is a dangerous hairpin turn over a ravine. How should the driver be warned of the impending curve? Presumably there will be a sign, "Hairpin Turn," which should obviously appear just a bit before the turn (analogous to forward pairing with a short CS-US interval). If the interval is too long it will be almost impossible to connect the sign with that which it signifies. The driver will understandably lose some of her faith in the Highway Department if it sets up the sign, "Hairpin Turn," just outside the Denver city

4.21   The CS-US interval in classical conditioning   *The figure shows the results of a study on the effectiveness of various CS-US intervals in humans. The CR was a finger withdrawal response, the CS a tone, and the US an electric shock. The time between CS and US is plotted on the horizontal axis. Negative intervals mean that the US was presented before the CS (backward pairing), a zero interval means that the two stimuli were presented simultaneously, and a positive interval means that the CS began before the US (forward pairing). The vertical axis indicates the degree of conditioning. (After Spooner and Kellogg, 1947)*

limits while the turn itself is three hours away (forward pairing with a long CS-US interval). Her faith will be really shaken if she sees the sign prominently displayed just at the sharpest bend of the turn (simultaneous pairing). She will finally begin to suspect a degree of malevolence if she discovers the sign innocently placed on the road a hundred feet or so beyond the turn (backward pairing), though she should probably be grateful that she did not find it at the bottom of the ravine.

CONTINGENCY

It would seem that in classical conditioning an organism learns that one stimulus is a signal for another. The next task is to describe just what such a sign relationship between two events consists of.

Consider a dog in Pavlov's laboratory who is exposed to several presentations of a beating metronome followed by some food powder. The poor beast doesn't know that he is supposed to form a CS-US connection. All he knows is that every once in a while food appears. There are all sorts of stimuli in the laboratory. Of course he hears the metronome, but he also hears doors slamming and a babble of (Russian) voices in the background, and he feels the strap of the conditioning harness. How does he discover that it is the metronome that is the signal for food rather than the scores of other stimuli that he is also exposed to? After all, no one told him that metronome beats are Professor Pavlov's favorite conditioned stimuli.

A useful way of trying to understand what happens is to think of the animal as an amateur scientist. Like all scientists, the dog wants to predict important events. (When his human counterparts succeed, they publish; when the dog succeeds, he salivates.) How can he predict when food will appear? He might decide to rely on mere contiguity and salivate to any stimulus that occurs along with food presentation. But if so, he'd have to salivate whenever he was strapped in his harness or whenever he heard voices, for these stimuli were generally present when he was fed. But if the dog had any scientific talent at all, he would realize that the harness and the voices are very poor food predictors. To be sure, they occur when food is given, but they occur just as frequently when it is not. To continue in his scientific quest, the dog would look for an event that occurs when food appears and that does not occur when food is absent. The metronome beat is the one stimulus that fulfills *both* of these conditions, for it never beats in the intervals between trials when food is not presented. Science (or rather classical conditioning) has triumphed, and the dog is ready to announce his findings by salivating only when the CS is presented.

Contingency versus contiguity   The preceding account is a fanciful statement of an influential analysis of classical conditioning developed by Robert Rescorla (Rescorla, 1967). According to Rescorla, classical conditioning depends not only on CS-US pairings but also on pairings in which the *absence* of CS goes along with the *absence* of US. These two experiences—metronome/meat and no metronome/no meat—allow the dog to discover that the occurrence of the US is **contingent** (that is, dependent) upon the occurrence of the CS. According to Rescorla, conditioning does not occur because the US is *contiguous* with the CS but rather because it is *contingent* upon the CS. By determining this contingency, the animal can forecast what is going to happen next.

To determine if getting meat is contingent upon the metronome, the animal must somehow compute two probabilities: the probability of getting meat when the metronome is sounded and the probability of getting meat when it is not. If the first probability is greater than the second, then getting meat is contingent on the metronome (the metronome's ticking predicts that meat will arrive). If it is smaller than the second, getting meat is contingent upon the *absence* of the

TABLE 4.1 CONTINGENCY IN CLASSICAL CONDITIONING

Three tables illustrating three different CS/US contingency arrangements in a hypothetical experiment in which the CS is a tone and the US is meat powder. Each table presents a different tone/meat contingency based on twenty trials. The column labeled *p* shows the probabilities that meat will occur under a particular stimulus condition.

Meat contingent upon tone

	Meat	No Meat	p
Tone	8	2	.80
No Tone	2	8	.20

Meat contingent upon absence of tone

	Meat	No Meat	p
Tone	3	7	.30
No Tone	7	3	.70

Meat and tone independent

	Meat	No Meat	p
Tone	5	5	.50
No Tone	5	5	.50

metronome (the metronome's ticking predicts that meat will *not* arrive). Such a negative contingency is analogous to the relation between a sunny sky and rain—rain is more likely when the sun is *not* shining. An important final possibility is that the two probabilities are identical. If so, there is no contingency, and the two events are independent (see Table 4.1).

If this line of thinking is correct, then temporal contiguity as such will not produce conditioning. For according to this view, conditioning will only occur if the probability of a US when the CS is present is greater than the probability of a US when the CS is absent. To demonstrate this, Rescorla exposed rats to various combinations of a tone CS and a shock US in a conditioned suppression experiment. In one set of conditions, the probability of receiving a shock when the tone was sounded was always the same (about .40). What varied was the probability that a shock would occur when no tone was sounded. The results were clear-cut. If the likelihood of a shock when the tone was on was the same as the likelihood of a shock when the tone was off, there was no conditioning. But if the likelihood of a shock was smaller when the tone was off than when it was on, conditioning did take place. The greater the difference in these probabilities, the stronger the level of conditioning the animal achieved (see Figure 4.22). The critical factor is evidently not contiguity, because the sheer number of CS-US pairings was identical for all groups. What matters is whether the tone was an informative signal that told the animal that shock was more likely now than at other times (Rescorla, 1967, 1988).

The absence of contingency   What happens when there is no contingency whatsoever? On the face of it, there is nothing to learn. But in a situation in which there is fear and danger (for example, getting an electric shock) the animal does learn something after all: It learns it can never feel safe at any time.

The difference between signaled and unsignaled shock may be related to the distinction between *fear* and *anxiety* made by clinical psychologists concerned with human emotional disorders. As they use the terms, fear refers to an emotional state that is directed at a specific situation or object—flying in airplanes, snakes, or whatever. In contrast, anxiety is a chronic fear that has no particular object but is there at all times. A number of authors suggest that this unfocused anxiety state is in part produced by unpredictability. Patients whose dentists tell them "this may hurt" but at other times assure them "you won't feel anything now" will probably have fewer dental anxieties than those whose dentists never tell them anything (Seligman, 1975; Schwartz, 1989).

A COGNITIVE VIEW OF INSTRUMENTAL CONDITIONING

■ We have seen that what is learned in classical conditioning is a representation about the relation between two stimulus events, the CS and the US. There is reason to believe that a similar cognitive account applies to instrumental conditioning. As with classical conditioning, this interpretation goes back to Tolman. Thorndike and Skinner had argued that instrumental learning involves the strengthening of a particular response, such as pressing a bar in a Skinner box. In contrast, Tolman believed that the animal acquires an internal represen-

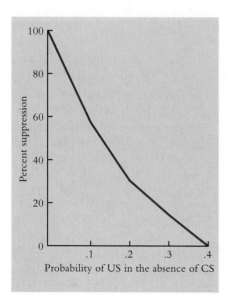

4.22 Contingency in classical conditioning   *The figure shows the results of fear conditioning as a function of contingency. The probability of the US in the presence of the CS was always .40, but the probability of the US in the absence of the CS varied from 0 to .40. Conditioning was measured by the degree of response suppression. (After Rescorla, 1966)*

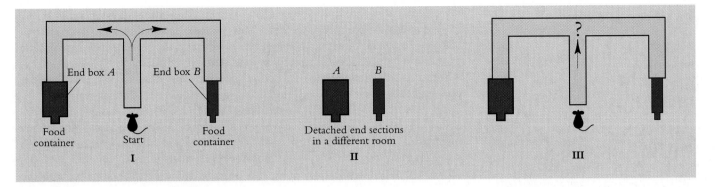

4.23 Proving that rats learn what leads to where (I) Floor plan of a maze in the first phase of an experiment during which rats could learn that a left turn leads to end box A, a right turn to end box B. (II) The second phase of the experiment in which the two end boxes were detached from the rest of the maze and the animals were shocked in one of them, say, A. (III) The third phase of the experiment in which the animals were returned to the original situation. If they could put the two experiences together, then, having learned that a left turn led to A and that A led to shock, they should turn right—that is, away from shock. The results showed that they did. (After Tolman and Gleitman, 1949)

tation of the relation between the response and the reinforcer that follows it: It doesn't just learn to press a bar; it learns that the bar leads to a food pellet. In effect, it acquires an association between an act and its outcome. This act-outcome representation may or may not be used on a later occasion, depending on the circumstances, such as the animal's needs and motives (Tolman, 1932).

EVIDENCE FOR ACT-OUTCOME ASSOCIATIONS

Early evidence that animals do acquire act-outcome cognitions of this sort comes from a study in which rats were run in an enclosed maze that had a black end box on one side and a white one on the other (see Figure 4.23). Both ends contained food, and the animals chose indifferently between them on several trials. Subsequently, the animals were placed into each box by hand without actually running the maze. In one end box they now found food as before; in the other they were shocked. After all this, the animals were again allowed to run down the original maze. Now virtually all of them chose the side away from the end box in which they had been shocked. Clearly, the rats had learned which turn led to which box, but this cognition led to selective action only after the two boxes had acquired their new significance. In effect, the animals had to combine two experiences. During the first phase of the experiment, they presumably learned to associate a particular turn with a particular end box. During the second phase, they further learned that a particular end box brought shock. The results of the final test indicate that they were able to put these two experiences together—an argument against the view that all instrumental learning depends on the strengthening or weakening of particular response tendencies (Tolman and Gleitman, 1949).

Similar *latent learning* effects have been obtained in a number of other studies. A classic example is an experiment in which rats were run through a maze without a reward for ten days. On the eleventh day food was finally placed in the goal box, and on the very next trial there was an abrupt decline in errors. Presumably the rats had learned something about the maze during the preceding days. But they did not show that they had learned until the reward was introduced. What they learned over the first ten days was only latent but not yet manifest (Tolman and Honzik, 1930).

A more recent experiment has provided some elegant further evidence for Tolman's general view (Colwill and Rescorla, 1985). Hungry rats were trained to make two different responses, each of which produced a different food reward. On some days, their experimental chamber contained a standard Skinner-box lever that projected from one wall. When this lever was pressed, it led to a pellet made of rat chow. On other days, instead of a lever there was a chain that dangled from the ceiling. When this chain was pulled, the rat was rewarded with a few drops of a sugar solution. After a few days of training, the rats were busily bar pressing and chain pulling, indicating that instrumental learning had been effective. But exactly what was it that had been learned? One possibility is that they acquired a tendency to perform the two responses. Another is that they acquired a cognition about the act-outcome relation: Bar pressing leads to rat-chow pellets, and chain pulling leads to sugar water.

To decide between these alternatives, the experimenters changed the desirability of one of the rewards after a week or so of instrumental training. They injected the rats with a mild toxin after they drank the sugar solution, creating a taste aversion for the sugar but not for the pellets (see Chapter 3 and pp. 108–109). The question was what the animals would do when again given the chance to press a bar or pull a lever. The results showed that the rats learned which response led to which reward. They no longer pulled the chain that led to the sugar water (now a no-longer-desirable reward) but continued to press the lever that produced the chow pellet (Colwill and Rescorla, 1985; see Figure 4.24).

CONTINGENCY IN INSTRUMENTAL CONDITIONING

We saw that classical conditioning depends on the contingency between the CS and the US rather than on their contiguity. A similar relation holds for instrumental conditioning. Here the relevant contingency is between an act and its outcome. If the act is lever pressing and the outcome is a food pellet, then the contingency is determined by comparing the probability of getting a pellet when the lever has been pressed with the probability of getting it when the lever has not been pressed. If the first probability is greater than the second, getting food is contingent upon lever pressing. If the two probabilities are equal, there is no contingency—lever pressing and getting pellets are independent.[*]

Response control in infants   One line of evidence for the role of contingency in instrumental conditioning comes from studies of human infants. A group of two-month-old infants was provided with an opportunity to make something happen. The infants were placed in cribs above which a colorful mobile was suspended. Whenever the infants moved their heads, they closed a switch in their pillows. This activated the overhead mobile, which promptly turned for a second or so and did so every time the pillow switch was closed. The infants soon learned to shake their heads about, thus making their mobiles turn. They evidently enjoyed doing so; they smiled and cooed happily at their mobiles, clearly delighted at seeing them move. A second group of infants was exposed to a similar situation, but there was one difference—they had no control over the mobile's movement. Their mobile turned just about as often as the mobile for the first group, but it was moved for them, not by them. After a few days, these infants no longer smiled and cooed at the mobile, nor did they seem particularly interested when it turned. This suggests that what the infants liked about the mobile was not that it moved but that they made it move. This shows that infants can distinguish between response-controlled and response-independent outcomes, which is a strong argument for the contingency approach. It also shows that infants, no less than we, prefer to exercise some control over their environment. The reason for this is by no means clear, but it appears that even a two-month-old infant wants to be master of her own fate (Watson, 1967; see Figure 4.25).

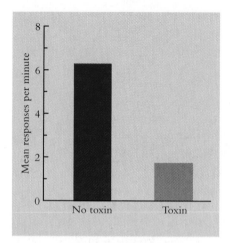

4.24   Act-outcome cognitions   *The figure shows the results on the final test of an experiment in which two different responses were reinforced by two different food rewards. Subsequently, one of the two rewards was paired with a toxin. There was a marked decline in the response leading to the reward that was devalued by the toxin (in blue) as compared with the response leading to the reward that was not devalued (dark red). (After Colwill and Rescorla, 1985)*

---

[*]If the second probability is greater than the first, then getting the pellet is contingent upon *not* pressing the lever. This kind of contingency is common whenever one wants the learner to refrain from doing something, for example: "I'll give you a cookie if you stop whining."

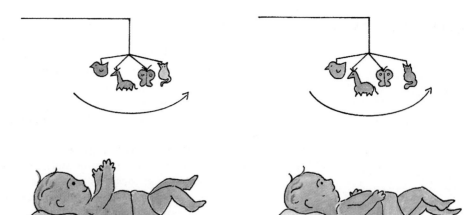

4.25 Response control *Infants who can make a mobile move, smile and coo at it, while those who have no control over its motion, stop smiling.*

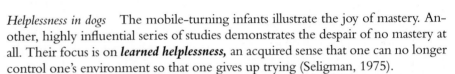

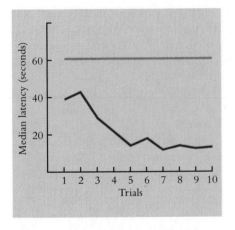

4.26 Learned helplessness *The figure shows the performance of two groups of dogs. On each trial, the animal could escape or avoid a shock. If it jumped within ten seconds after the CS, it avoided the shock altogether; if it did not jump within sixty seconds, the trial was terminated. The figure shows how quickly the animals jumped. The animals in Group A (dark red) had previously received electric shocks that they could escape by performing an instrumental response. The animals in Group B (blue) received the same shocks, but were unable to do anything about them. (After Maier, Seligman, and Solomon, 1969)*

Helplessness in dogs The mobile-turning infants illustrate the joy of mastery. Another, highly influential series of studies demonstrates the despair of no mastery at all. Their focus is on **learned helplessness,** an acquired sense that one can no longer control one's environment so that one gives up trying (Seligman, 1975).

The classic experiment on learned helplessness employed two groups of dogs, *A* and *B,* who received strong electric shocks while strapped in a hammock. The dogs in group *A* were able to exert some control over their situation. They could turn the shock off whenever it began by pushing a panel that was placed close to their noses. The dogs in group *B* had no such power. For them, the shocks were inescapable. But the number and duration of these shocks were exactly the same. For each dog in group *A* there was a corresponding animal in group *B* whose fate was "yoked" to that of the first dog. Whenever the group *A* dog was shocked, so was the group *B* dog. Whenever the group *A* dog turned off the shock, the shock was turned off for the group *B* dog. This arrangement guaranteed that the actual physical punishment meted out to both groups was precisely the same. What was different was what they could do about it. Group *A* was able to exercise some control; group *B* could only endure.

The question was how the group *B* dogs would fare when presented with a new situation that provided them with an opportunity to help themselves. To find out, both groups of dogs were presented with a standard avoidance learning task, a set up in which they could jump over a hurdle to avoid a shock (Figure 4.26). The dogs in group *A* learned just about as quickly as did naïve dogs who had no prior experimental experience of any kind. During the first trials, they waited until the shock began and then scrambled over the hurdle; later, they jumped before their grace period was up and thus avoided shock entirely. But the dogs in group *B,* who had previously suffered inescapable shock in the hammock, behaved very differently. Initially, they behaved much like other dogs; they ran about frantically, barking, and howling. But they soon became much more passive. They lay down, whined quietly, and simply took whatever shocks were delivered. They neither avoided nor escaped; they just gave up trying. In the hammock setup they had been objectively helpless; there really was nothing they could do. But in the setup with the hurdles, their helplessness was only subjective, for there was now a way in which they could make their lot bearable. But they never discovered it. They had learned to be helpless (Seligman and Maier, 1967).

Helplessness and depression Martin Seligman, one of the discoverers of the learned helplessness effect in animals, asserts that a similar mechanism underlies the development of certain kinds of depression in human patients. (For further discussion of depression, see Chapter 18.) He believes that such patients share certain features with animals who had been rendered helpless. Both fail to initiate actions and instead "just sit there"; both are slow to learn that something they did was successful; both lose weight and have little interest in others. To Seligman and his associates these parallels suggest that the underlying cause is the same in both cases. Like the helpless dog, the depressed patient has come to feel that his acts are of no avail. And Seligman argues that, like the dog, the depressed patient was brought to this morbid state of affairs by an initial exposure to a situation in which he was objectively helpless. While the dog received inescapable shocks in its hammock, the patient found himself powerless in the face of bereavement, business failure, or serious illness (Seligman, Klein, and Miller, 1976). In both cases, the problem is a lack of contingency between acts and unfortunate outcomes.

Some biological consequences of helplessness   The lack of contingency between acts and outcomes can have important medical consequences. Of particular interest are the biological effects of learned helplessness that are produced when humans and animals discover that they have no control over stressful events in their lives.

There's an old adage that patients who "give up hope" have a poorer chance of surviving than those who continue fighting. Several medical investigations suggest that there are some grounds for this belief. People who are hopeless and depressed are more likely to contract and succumb to major illness than those who try to cope. Thus, people who suffer the loss of a loved one are more likely to die in the year after their bereavement than control subjects of the same age. Finally, there is evidence that despair and helplessness in the face of important personal losses increase the risk of cancer in subsequent years (Horne and Picard, 1979; Shekelle et al., 1981; see Figure 4.27).

What might be responsible for these relationships? Some recent studies suggest that learned helplessness impairs the ***immune system*** of the body. The immune system produces a number of cells that fight various foreign invaders and tumors. Among these is a group called "killer cells," which deal with tumors. The killer cells recognize that the tumors are foreign and promptly dispatch them. Steven Maier and his associates have shown that the production of such killer cells is impaired when rats are put in a situation that induces learned helplessness. One group of animals was given a number of shocks from which they could escape by turning a tread wheel. A second group received the same shocks as the control rats but could do nothing about them. They suffered the same degree of physical stress, but unlike their counterparts in the control group, they learned that they had no control over their fate and so they became helpless. Later tests showed that animals who had been rendered helpless in this fashion produced fewer killer cells and were thus less able to stop tumor growth. This result fits in with other findings which show that learned helplessness in rats increases susceptibility to injected tumors (Visintainer, Volpicelli, and Seligman, 1982; Maier, Laudenslager, and Ryan, 1985).

Just why learned helplessness affects the immune system is still unknown. But whatever the mechanism, the fact that it does suggests that learning about the

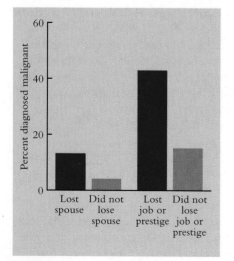

4.27 Psychological loss and lung cancer   *Diagnoses were performed on over 100 patients whose X-rays showed a lesion in the lungs. Some of these patients had suffered serious psychological losses in the previous five years, for example, loss of a spouse, parent, or sibling; retirement; loss of a job; or loss of prestige. Others had not experienced any such losses. The figure presents the percent of the cases whose lung lesions turned out to be malignant. As the figure shows, malignancy was more likely for the patients who had suffered one of the serious losses listed above (in dark red) than for those who had not suffered any of these losses (in blue). (After Horne and Picard, 1979)*

contingencies (and in the case of learned helplessness, the lack of contingencies) between one's own actions and subsequent events in the world has profound effects on bodily functioning.

VARIETIES OF LEARNING

FOCUS QUESTIONS

- What are biological constraints on learning, and what are some examples both from the laboratory and from everyday life?

- Why are some kinds of learning considered adaptive specializations, and what are some examples?

Until fairly recently, most investigators were primarily interested in discovering some general laws of learning—whether associative or cognitive or possibly both—regardless of the particular animal that did the learning. To be sure, many of them believed that humans and other primates are capable of more complex cognition than lower animals, but outside of that they had little concern with the diversity of the animal kingdom, for in their view general laws should hold across the zoological board. By the same token, they also felt that these laws should apply to whatever is learned, whether it is learning to hunt or to escape hunters, to recognize members of one's own species or to speak the language of one's own group.

During the past two decades, this position has come under serious attack from investigators who adopt what has been called the *adaptive evolutionary perspective* (e.g., Roper, 1983; Bolles and Beecher, 1988; Rozin and Schull, 1988). A major impetus to their view came from the discovery of the role of "belongingness" in the formation of associations by animals.

Arbitrary learning by operant techniques
Animals can be trained to prefer all manner of arbitrary responses by operant techniques as in the case of this cat that plays the piano. But there are important biological constraints that make some responses more difficult to learn than others. The cat has trouble learning to press the piano keys for food because its natural tendency is to importune people (or as a kitten, its mother) to feed it. (Photograph courtesy of Animal Behavior Enterprises)

BIOLOGICAL CONSTRAINTS ON ASSOCIATIVE LEARNING: BELONGINGNESS

In the early days of behavior theory, there was a widespread belief that animals are capable of connecting just about any CS to any US (in classical conditioning) or of associating virtually any response with any reinforcer (in instrumental conditioning). But during the last three decades, more and more evidence has accumulated that has undermined this position, which is sometimes called the *equipotentiality principle.* For as it turns out, not all associations are equally easy to learn. There are evidently certain built-in predispositions (often called *biological constraints*) that determine what a given animal can learn and what sorts of learning it will find difficult. These constraints are built into the system and help the animal adjust to the requirements of the environment in which it evolved (Rozin and Kalat, 1971, 1972; Seligman and Hager, 1972).

CS-US RELATIONS IN CLASSICAL CONDITIONING

According to the equipotentiality principle, the associations between the CS and the US are essentially arbitrary. But this turns out to be false. For there is now evidence that associations between two items are more readily formed if the items somehow belong together. An important example of the role of belongingness comes from classical conditioning, where a number of investigators have shown that certain CSs are more readily related to certain USs than to others. In their view, the animal has a built-in predisposition, sometimes called a **preparedness,** to form certain associations rather than others. The bulk of this evidence comes from learned taste aversions (Garçia and Koelling, 1966; Domjan, 1983).

Belongingness and learned taste aversions   It has long been known that rats are remarkably adept at avoiding foods they ate just before falling sick. This is the reason why it is very difficult to exterminate wild rats with poison: The rat takes a small bite of the poisoned food, becomes ill, generally recovers, and thereafter avoids that particular flavor: The animal has become bait shy. Similar effects are easily produced in the laboratory. The subjects (usually rats) are presented with a given flavor, such as water containing saccharin. After drinking some of this water, they are exposed to X-ray radiation—not enough to kill them, but enough to make them ill and nauseous. After they recover, they are given a choice between, say, plain water and a saccharine solution. They will now refuse to drink the saccharin even though they they much preferred this sweet-tasting drink prior to their illness.

Such learned taste aversions are usually believed to be based on classical conditioning in which the CS is a certain flavor (here, saccharin) and the US is being sick. The question is whether other stimuli such as lights or tones serve equally well as CSs for such taste aversions. A number of studies by John Garcia and his coworkers have shown that they do not, thus refuting the equipotentiality principle.

One of the earliest studies to make this point is an experiment by Garcia and Koelling in which thirsty rats were allowed to drink saccharine-flavored water. The water came from a drinking tube; whenever the rat licked the nozzle, a bright light flashed and a clicking noise sounded. Subsequently, some rats received a shock to their feet. Others were exposed to a dose of illness-producing X-rays. All of the animals developed a strong aversion to the saccharine water. When again presented with water that was sweet and was accompanied by bright flashes and clicks, they hardly touched the drinking nozzle. All rats had

Learned food aversions in birds   *In contrast to rats and humans, whose learned food aversions are usually based on taste and odor, most birds rely on visual cues. The figure shows the reaction of a bird who has just eaten a monarch butterfly, which contains distasteful and poisonous substances. The distinctive wing pattern of this butterfly provides the cue for an immediately acquired food aversion, for after one such mistake the bird will never again seize another monarch. (Courtesy of Lincoln P. Brower, University of Florida)*

TABLE 4.2 BELONGINGNESS IN CLASSICAL CONDITIONING

Training	In all groups: CS = saccharine taste + light + sound			
US:	Shock		X-ray illness	
Test Water with:	Saccharine taste	Light + sound	Saccharine taste	Light + sound
Results	No effect	Aversion	Aversion	No effect

presumably acquired a classically conditioned aversion. The US was either shock or illness. The CS was a stimulus compound comprised of the flavor, the light, and the noise. But did the rats learn to avoid all of these stimulus features or only some?

To find out, the experimenters tested the rats in a new situation. They gave some of the rats water that was saccharine-flavored but was unaccompanied by either light or noise. They gave others plain, unflavored water that was accompanied by the light and sound cues that were present during training. The results showed that what the rats had learned to avoid depended upon the US. If they had been shocked (and felt pain), they refused water that was accompanied by light and noise, but they had no objection to the sweet flavor. If they had been X-rayed (and became ill), the opposite was true—they avoided the saccharine flavor but were perfectly willing to drink when the water was preceded by light and noise (Table 4.2).

These results indicate that rats tend to link stimuli in certain fitting ways: In rats, taste goes with illness, sights and sounds with externally induced pain. This makes good biological sense. In the world of the rat, an omnivorous creature that selects its food mainly on the basis of its flavor, taste may well be the most reliable cue that warns of impending illness. If so, a built-in bias to associate sickness with preceding tastes is likely to have survival value. In effect, the rat cannot help but ask itself, "What did I eat?" whenever it has a stomachache (Garcia and Koelling, 1966).

If this is so, one might expect rather different results for animals who select their food on the basis of cues other than taste. An example comes from some species of birds that rely heavily on vision when choosing food. In one study, quail drank blue, sour water and were then poisoned. Some of the birds were later tested with blue, unflavored water; others were tested with water that was sour but colorless. The quail developed a drastic aversion to blue water. But they drank just about as much sour water as they had prior to being poisoned. Here, the learned food aversion was evidently based on color rather than on taste (Wilcoxin, Dragoin, and Kral, 1971). Thus, it appears that the built-in belongingness relation is species specific. Certain birds have a natively given bias to link sickness with visual cues, while rats and other mammals link it to taste. This bias prepares them to learn certain relations more readily than others (Seligman, 1970). In both cases, the preparedness fits in with the way the animal identifies food in its native habitat.

Learned taste aversions and the CS-US interval That the equipotentiality principle is clearly false constitutes yet another argument against the role of contiguity in conditioning. In Garcia and Koelling's experiment with rats, the noise and the flashing light were no less contiguous to the illness-producing X-rays than was the flavor of the water. But even so, only the flavor became an effective CS.

A further argument against the role of contiguity came from studies of the CS-US interval in learned taste aversions. In most studies of classical conditioning, the most effective CS interval tends to be relatively short, on the order of a few seconds or less. But Garcia and other investigators showed that in learned taste aversions the optimum interval is about an hour and that learning will occur with intervals as long as twenty-four hours (Garcia, Ervin, and Koelling, 1966; Rozin and Kalat, 1971; Logue, 1979). Just why it is possible to associate illness with tastes experienced an hour or more earlier is still a matter of debate (see Revusky, 1971, 1977, 1985; Rozin and Kalat, 1971; Domjan, 1980). But whatever the mechanism that underlies it, the biological utility of this phenomenon is clear enough: Both the beneficial and harmful effects of ingested food are delayed by the fairly slow processes of absorption and digestion. Under the circumstances, a mechanism that allows an animal to connect its internal malaise with tastes experienced some time ago makes excellent adaptive sense.

Taste aversions in humans   Taste aversions quite similar to those found in rats are also found in humans. When people get sick to their stomachs they often develop an aversion to the taste of food they ate before they became ill. They may know that their malaise was the result of an intestinal flu and that the raspberry ice cream or the clam chowder that they now find so repellent was in fact quite innocent. But this rational understanding does not alter their aversion, which may last for years (Logue, 1986).

The study of human taste aversions has implications for a number of real life concerns. One such area is the anorexia that is often found in cancer patients who undergo chemotherapy. The administration of the therapeutic drugs often produces nausea, which in turn may lead to an aversion to foods eaten prior to the treatment. This was demonstrated by a study in which cancer patients were given a novel-tasting ice cream before a chemotherapy session. Many of these patients developed a strong aversion to that novel flavor, even though they knew that their nausea was caused by the chemotherapy. This suggests some ways to alleviate the anorexia, such as minimizing meals—especially meals with novel foods—prior to treatments (Bernstein, 1978).

ACT-OUTCOME RELATIONS IN INSTRUMENTAL CONDITIONING

The preceding discussion showed that the CS-US relation in classical conditioning is not always arbitrary. A similar nonarbitrariness characterizes many instrumental learning situations (Shettleworth, 1972).

Consider a pigeon pecking away in a Skinner box. Here surely is the very prototype of arbitrary instrumental learning. But in fact, the relation between pecking and what is pecked at is far from arbitrary. One line of evidence comes from the fact that it is exceedingly hard to train pigeons to peck so as to escape or avoid electric shock (Hineline and Rachlin, 1969). This doesn't mean that shock escape or shock avoidance are inadequate reinforcers for pigeons—far from it. The birds readily learn to hop or flap their wings in order to get away from shock. What they have trouble learning is to peck to bring about the same outcome. According to Robert Bolles, this is because many animals have built-in defense reactions to danger. The pigeon is no exception. Its species-specific defense reaction is speedy locomotion, preferably airborne flight. The bird can learn new avoidance responses, but only to the extent that these fit in with its natively given danger reaction. Hopping, flying, and wing-flapping qualify, for they are merely modifications of the basic defense pattern. But pecking does not, and it is therefore very hard to learn as an escape or an avoidance response (Bolles, 1970).

ADAPTIVE SPECIALIZATIONS OF LEARNING

■ The preceding discussion demonstrates that the way in which animals associate events is not arbitrary. They come biologically prepared to acquire certain linkages rather than others. This clearly shows that the laws of associative learning must be modified to encompass the relationship between the CS and the US and between the reinforcer and the response. But some theorists go further: They assert that in addition to the general forms of learning—conditioning and cognitive learning—there are some forms of learning that are specific to the species that does the learning and to what it is that gets learned.

DIFFERENCES IN WHAT DIFFERENT SPECIES LEARN

Proponents of this position argue that diversity is the rule in the biological world as different species adapt to different ecological niches. Different animals have vastly different anatomies and built-in behavior repertories: lions stalk, antelopes run, and hyenas wait around and scavenge for left-overs. Proponents of the evolutionary perspective argue that a similar diversity may well apply to the processes of learning, that some animals can readily learn in ways that others cannot (Roper, 1983; Gallistel, 1990).

An oft-cited example is Clark's nutcracker, a food-storing bird of the American Southwest. In the summer this bird buries thousands of pine nuts in various hiding places over an area of several square miles. All through the winter and early spring, the nutcracker flies back again and again to dig up its thousand of hidden caches. To find them it relies primarily on memory—a prodigious feat that few of us could rival. There is no doubt that the nutcracker is anatomically specialized as a food hoarder: It has a special pouch under its tongue that it fills with pine nuts when flying to find a hiding place. Why couldn't there be a similar evolutionary adaptation of the learning and memory process? Some further evidence suggests that there is: Related birds such as jays and pigeons that don't store food show poorer spatial memory than the nutcracker (Shettleworth, 1983, 1984; Olson, 1991).

In birds the brain center essential for such functions is the hippocampus. Injury to this structure markedly impairs spatial memory: When lesioned in the hippocampus, food storing birds can't locate their caches. In line with the evolutionary perspective, it turns out that food-storing species possess a hippocampus that's twice the size of those found in species that don't store food.

A related fact concerns a sex difference in the size of this structure in the cowbird, a parasite that lays its eggs in the nest of another species. The female first finds a potential host nest, then returns to it a few days later to lay a single egg. During any one breeding season, she will repeat this process some forty times. This obviously requires some significant spatial ability; she first has to locate a potential host nest and must then find it again. No such ability is required in the male, who takes no part in the female's nest-finding activities. Appropriately enough, this behavioral difference between the sexes is mirrored in the size of their hippocampus. The female's is larger than the male's (Sherry, Jacobs, and Gaulin, 1992; Sherry et al., 1993).

A number of other phenomena of animal learning may well be understood as analogous biological adaptations. Seen in this light, the ability of many birds to learn the song of their own species and the remarkable navigation capacity of pigeons and geese are special forms of learning, their own particular biological adaptations to their environment (Marler, 1970; Gallistel, 1990).

Adaptive specialization of learning A *black-capped chickadee hiding a seed in one of many holes in a specially constructed laboratory tree. This bird has been shown to have a remarkable spatial memory: It hides over 100 seeds per day, each in a different location, and remembers where these seeds were deposited for up to 14 days. (From Dr. David Sherry; photograph courtesy of Susan Bradnam)*

SIMILARITIES IN WHAT DIFFERENT SPECIES LEARN

■ Some of the more extreme adherents of adaptive specialization are sufficiently impressed with the differences in what and how various species learn as to deny that there are any truly general learning processes. But in fact the similarities in how different creatures learn are no less striking than the differences. For example, there is evidence that the major phenomena of conditioning are found in honey bees just as they are in rats and pigeons (Couvillon and Bitterman, 1980). Such similarities suggest that while there are surely specialized adaptations, there are also some general mechanisms that govern learning throughout much of the animal kingdom. Such general learning processes would presumably underlie classical and instrumental conditioning, as well as the more complex cognitive processes found in higher mammals.

Given the fact that the nervous system of a bee is vastly different from that found in any animal with a backbone and has a totally different evolutionary history, it is quite unlikely that the same physiological mechanisms will underlie the way bees, rats, and pigeons learn. So how can we possibly explain the many similarities in the learning patterns of these and other animals? A possible answer is offered by the principle of *convergent evolution:* the idea that animals under similar environmental pressures often evolve similar adaptations.

Biologists appeal to this principle to explain why a very similar characteristic—such as the wing—evolves in organisms of very different ancestry—such as insects, birds, and bats. Although the wings of these creatures are anatomically very different (four specialized appendages of the outer skeleton in insects, two modified forelegs in birds, and two special skins between thumb and index finger in bats), they are wings all the same, for they all beat the air and serve as organs of flight. Their essential similarity is not produced by an underlying equivalence of anatomy or ancestry; it is instead created by equivalence of the world in which all three kinds of animals live. For all three must move through the air, and so they must obey the same laws of aerodynamics.

What holds for wings may also hold for some general laws of learning. Their physiological underpinnings may well be different in bees and rats. But whatever the underlying biology may turn out to be, one thing is the same and that is the world in which all these animals live. In that world, some significant events are contingent upon others and some important outcomes depend upon actions. Since this is so, one might well expect the evolution of mechanisms for extracting these relationships—that is, classical and instrumental conditioning. Many of the specific properties of conditioning that we have discussed already would be a natural consequence of the relationship between events in the real world. As one example, consider the superiority of forward to backward conditioning—a natural consequence of the fact that in our world time only flows in one direction, with the cause always preceding the effect.

Such considerations suggest that while there may be some species-specific differences in the what and how of learning, there are also some general process-

Convergent evolution *Animals that are exposed to similar environmental pressures may evolve similar adaptations. This holds for the convergent evolution of wings in animals of very different ancestry, such as insects, birds, and bats. It may also hold for some characteristics of learning, which may explain why many of the major phenomena of conditioning are found in such widely different animals as rats and honey bees. (A) A flying desert locust. (Photograph by Stephen Dalton/ NHPA) (B) A barn owl. (Photograph courtesy of Joe MacDonald/Bruce Coleman, Inc.) (C) A fishing bat. (Photograph by Stephen Dalton/Photo Researchers, Inc.)*

es such as classical and instrumental conditioning. Whether the physiological mechanisms that underlie such general processes are the same in different animals is still an open question.

COMPLEX COGNITION IN ANIMALS

FOCUS QUESTIONS

- What are cognitive maps, and what evidence suggests that some animals construct such maps?

- What evidence suggests that some animals can show insight and solve abstract problems?

The work on animal cognitions that we discussed earlier showed that animals may know something without manifesting this knowledge in their actions. But it did not focus directly on the intellectual capacities that this knowledge revealed. Evidence that bears on this point comes from a number of sources. One concerns spatial memory in animals; the other relates to insightful learning.

COGNITIVE MAPS

A number of contemporary investigators have extended Tolman's notion of a cognitive map that represents the spatial layout of the animal's world and indicates what is where and what leads to what (Tolman, 1948). By now we know that this spatial knowledge can be quite complex. One investigator studied rats in radial-arm mazes, consisting of a central platform from which 8 pathways extended like spokes in a wheel (Figure 4.28). Each arm of the maze contained a food pellet. A hungry rat was placed on the center platform and allowed to move about at will. It generally explored a bit, then chose one of the arms, ran to its end, found the food pellet, and ate it. The question was what it would do after it returned to the center? Its optimal strategy was *not* to revisit the arm on which it had just been, for this arm was now empty. Instead, it should visit each arm just once, thus getting the most food for the least effort. But to accomplish this, the rat must not only have learned the spatial layout; it must also have remembered where on that layout it had been and where it hadn't. The results show that the rats had these capacities. Given a radial maze of 8 arms, they chose an average of 7.9 different arms in 8 choices (Olton and Samuelson, 1976; Olton, 1978, 1979).

What rats can do, chimpanzees can do even better. Proof came from a chimpanzee version of an Easter-egg hunt. The experimenter took one animal at a time and carried it through a zig-zag course of a familiar, one-acre compound, while accompanied by an assistant who hid pieces of fruit in eighteen different locations. During this time, the chimpanzee merely watched through the bars of its carrying cage. A few minutes after the last piece of fruit had been hidden, the animal was released. It immediately dashed to one hiding place after another, unearthed the fruit hidden in each, and ate it. In general, the chimpanzee remembered most of the hiding places after only one trial of passive watching (Menzel, 1973, 1978).

Studies such as these suggest that the notion of a cognitive map may be more than a figure of speech. Perhaps something analogous to a map of the spatial environment is formed in the nervous system. Some authors have tried to find a physiological basis for such a mapping pattern in a certain region of the limbic

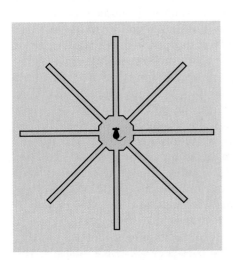

4.28 A radial-arm maze   *One pellet is placed at the end of each arm, so the rat is rewarded most for choosing each arm once. (From Olton and Samuelson, 1976)*

system in the brain containing neurons that seem to be sensitive to spatial information (O'Keefe and Nadel, 1978).

INSIGHTFUL BEHAVIOR

■ Thorndike had argued that problem solving in animals comes about by blind trial and error. But his conclusion was soon challenged by an early study of chimpanzees undertaken by the German psychologist Wolfgang Köhler (1887–1968). Köhler believed that animals can behave intelligently. To be sure, Thorndike's cats had shown little sign of understanding, but perhaps cats are not the best subjects if one wants to determine the upper reaches of animal intellect. A closer relative of human beings, such as chimpanzees, might prove a better choice. Even more important, Köhler believed that Thorndike had loaded the dice in favor of blind trial and error, for the problems he had posed his cats were often impossible to solve in any other way. Thus, even an intellectual supercat could never hit on the idea of yanking the wire that pulled the door latch except by pure chance; there was no other way, for all the strings and pulleys were hidden from the animal's view. To Köhler the real question was whether animals would behave intelligently when the conditions were optimum—when all of the ingredients of the solution were visibly present.

Köhler's procedure was simple. A chimpanzee was placed in an enclosed play area. Somewhere out of its reach was a desirable lure (usually some fruit, such as a banana). To obtain it, the ape had to employ some nearby object as a tool. In this the animals were remarkably successful. They learned to use sticks as rakes to haul in bananas placed on the ground just outside the cage, but beyond the reach of their arms. Sticks were equally useful to club down fruit hung too high overhead. Some chimpanzees used the sticks as a pole as well; they stood it upright under the banana, frantically climbed up its fifteen-foot length, and grasped their reward just as the stick toppled over (a considerable intellectual as well as gymnastic feat, demonstrating the virtues of a healthy mind in a healthy body). The chimpanzees also learned to use boxes as "climb-upon-ables," dragging them under the banana and then stepping atop them to claim their prizes. Eventually they even became builders, piling boxes on top of boxes and finally erecting structures that went up to four (rather shaky) stories, as Köhler spurred them on to ever-greater architectural accomplishments by progressively raising the height of the lure (Figure 4.29).

Wolfgang Köhler (Courtesy of The Warder Collection)

4.29 Tool using in chimpanzees (A) Using a stick as a pole to climb up to a banana. (B) Using a stick as a club to beat down a banana. (C and D) Erecting three- and four-story structures to reach a banana. (From Köhler, 1925)

A   B   C   D

4.30   Tool making in chimpanzees
Sultan making a double stick. (From Köhler, 1925)

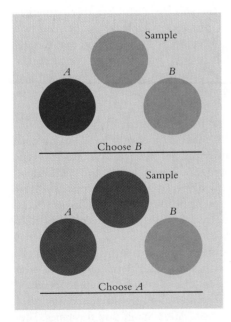

4.31   Matching to sample   *The figure shows the procedure of a typical matching-to-sample experiment. The top circle in each panel represents the sample. The subject's task is to choose the one circle from the two at the bottom that matches the sample in color. In the top panel of the figure, the correct choice is B; in the bottom panel, it is A.*

Occasionally the apes became tool-makers as well as tool-users. For example, when in need of a stick, they might break off a branch of a nearby tree. Even more impressive was the manufacture of a double stick. A particularly gifted chimpanzee called Sultan was faced with a banana far out of his reach. There were two bamboo sticks in his cage, but neither of them was long enough to rake in the lure. After many attempts to reach the banana with one stick or another, Sultan finally hit upon the solution. He pushed the thinner of the two sticks into the hollow inside of the thicker one and then drew the banana toward himself, his reach now enlarged by the length of two sticks (Figure 4.30).

Köhler denied that such achievements were the result of a mechanical strengthening and weakening of response tendencies. On the contrary, the animals behaved as if they had attained what he called **insight** into the relevant relationships—as if they *saw* what led to what. Köhler offered several lines of evidence. To begin with, when the problem was once solved, the animals usually performed smoothly and continuously thereafter as if they "knew what they were doing," in marked contrast to Thorndike's cats who went on fumbling for many trials. In further opposition to Thorndike's findings, the insightful solution often came quite suddenly, sometimes after a pause during which the chimpanzee only moved its head and eyes as if studying the situation. Once the correct response was made, further errors were rare.

ABSTRACT CONCEPTS IN ANIMALS

A number of studies have shown that various primates can respond to certain abstract, conceptual aspects of a situation that transcend perceptual characteristics. Some demonstrations have been obtained by David Premack who has tried to map the upper limits of the cognitive capacities in several chimpanzees, including his prize pupil, Sarah (Premack, 1976; Premack and Premack, 1983). An example of such an abstract concept is the notion "same-different." Consider a situation in which an animal is shown three items. One serves as the sample, the other two as alternatives. The animal's task is to choose the alternative that matches the sample. Suppose the alternatives are a triangle and a square. If so, the triangle is the correct choice if the sample is also a triangle; conversely, if the sample is a square. This procedure is called **matching to sample** (see Figure 4.31).

There is little doubt that animals other than primates can be taught to match if they are given enough trials to learn. Thus, pigeons can be taught to peck at a green rather than a yellow key if the sample is green and to peck at the yellow key if the sample is yellow. But does that mean that they understand what sameness means? The question is whether they somehow understand that the relation between two yellow keys is the same as the relation between two equal tones or two identical triangles, that in all cases the two items are the same. To test whether the animal has this abstract concept of sameness, we have to determine whether there is any transfer from one matching–to–sample situation to another one in which the particular stimulus items are quite different. Take the pigeon that has learned to match green-green. Does this training help the pigeon to match red-red or, better yet, triangle-triangle? By and large, the answer seems to be no (Premack, 1978; but see also Zentall and Hogan, 1974). It can recognize that two reds are the same. But it does not recognize that this sameness is the identical relation that exists between two other equal stimulus items.

The situation is quite different in chimpanzees. Having matched to sample on only three prior problems, Sarah and a few other animals readily handled new problems, performing perfectly on the very first trial. Even more impressive is the fact that Sarah learned to use two special tokens to indicate *same* and

115

4.32 The same-different problem
(After Premack and Premack, 1972)

different. She was first shown two identical objects, such as two cups, and was then given a token whose intended meaning was *same.* Her task was to place this *same* token between the two cups. She was then presented with two different objects, such as a cup and a spoon, was given yet another token intended to mean *different,* and was required to place this *different* token between the cup and the spoon. After several such trials, she was tested with several pairs of items, some identical and some different, had to decide whether to place the *same* or the *different* token between them, and did so correctly (see Figure 4.32).

Such accomplishments show that chimpanzees can develop a way of thinking about the world that goes beyond the specific perceptual relations of the concrete moment. Like pigeons, they can of course respond to these concrete relationships, for example, the relationship between, say, red and red, circle and circle, A-flat and A-flat. But unlike pigeons, chimpanzees can also deal with some **higher-order relationships,** the relations that hold between the various concrete relationships. They can therefore recognize that the relation between red and red is identical to that between circle and circle, and for that matter between hippopotamus and hippopotamus—that in all of these the relation is *sameness.*

GAINING ACCESS TO WHAT ONE KNOWS

The formation of abstract concepts is certainly one of the characteristics of what we normally call intelligence. But it is not the only one. Another criterion is whether the animal has some *access* to its own intellectual operations. This point is particularly relevant in the light of our previous discussion of adaptive specializations of learning.

Consider a pigeon who finds its way home over long distances. That bird is a brilliant navigator. It refers to the stars, to the sun, to a number of landmarks, and somehow calculates the correct path with remarkable accuracy. But we don't therefore regard the bird as especially intelligent. The reason is that we are convinced that it doesn't really know what it is doing. Its brain constitutes a marvelous navigational computer. But the bird can't use that computer for any purpose other than that for which it was installed by evolution. It has no access to its own intellectual machinery.

In this regard, a pigeon is quite different from a human being. At least to some extent, we do have access to our own mental functioning. We think and remember, and we also know that we think and remember. And we can use these and other intellectual capacities very broadly. This access to our own intellectual functions is by no means total; as we will see later on, it is especially limited in childhood (see Chapter 13). Our present point is only that this access is one of the defining features of intelligent behavior and is a characteristic of that intellectual generalist, the human being (Rozin, 1976a).

Some studies by Premack and his collaborators suggest that intellectual access is not confined to humans. They showed Sarah several videotaped scenes of a trainer struggling with different problems. In one scene, he tried to reach a banana suspended high above him. In another, he vainly stretched his arm toward a banana on the floor outside of a cage. After Sarah saw the tapes, she was shown different photographs of the trainer engaged in one of several actions. In one picture he was climbing on a box, in another he was shoving a stick under the wire mesh of the cage, and so on. Sarah's job was to pick the photograph that depicted the appropriate solution to the problem. Thus, if she was first shown a scene in which the trainer struggled to reach an overhead banana, she had to choose the picture of a man stepping on a box. Sarah did quite well, succeeding in twenty-one out of twenty-four trials (Figure 4.33).

Sarah's success in this task suggests that the chimpanzee's problem-solving ability goes further even than Köhler had thought. To be sure, Sarah can solve a

A

B

4.33 Knowing about problem solving
(A) End of brief videotaped segment showing Sarah's trainer reaching for bananas that are too high for him. (B) Two pictured alternatives. One shows the trainer reaching along the ground with a stick. The other shows him stepping on a box. Sarah tended to choose the picture that showed the correct solution—in the present case, the trainer stepping on the top of the box. (From Premack and Woodruff, 1978)

variety of spatial problems and can do so insightfully. But her ability may go beyond this. She not only solves problems, she also seems to know something *about* problem solving. She recognizes that the trainer has a problem, what this problem is, and how it should be dealt with successfully. To this extent, she has some access to her own intellectual processes (a point we'll return to later in discussing the extent to which monkeys, chimpanzees, and three-year-old humans have a "theory of mind"; see Chapters 10 and 13).

TAKING STOCK

What is the upshot of the scientific study of animal learning that began with the studies of Pavlov and Thorndike some ninety years ago? It is clear that they and their intellectual descendants have discovered many vital phenomena of learning. Whether the principles they uncovered in their study of habituation, classical conditioning, and instrumental conditioning underlie all forms of learning is still a matter of debate. For certain complex intellectual achievements in animals and humans, such as insightful understanding, abstract concepts, and—especially—human language, may well be acquired in some different ways. But there is no question that the study of how CS-US and response-reinforcer relations are acquired and represented in animals will give important clues about the fundamental nature of some basic learning processes found in both humans and animals.

When we began our discussion, our initial focus was on *action,* on how classical and instrumental conditioning change what animals *do:* how Pavlov's dogs came to salivate to ticking metronomes they had never heard before; how Thorndike's cats came to perform all sorts of novel tricks. But as we saw, these changes of overt behavior are only one aspect of what happened to these animals—they are the consequence of having learned rather than its essence. For unlike Pavlov and Thorndike, who focused on overt behavior, modern investigators of animal learning have shown that at bottom classical and instrumental conditioning (and many other forms of learning too) depend on *cognition.* Rats—and dogs and pigeons—learn which events predict which other events and which actions produce which outcomes. These and other phenomena make it clear that psychological functions involve not just what animals and humans *do,* but also what they *know.*

Psychology must necessarily deal with both action and knowledge. In our discussion of animal learning we have straddled them both, for the field represents a kind of bridge between these two major concerns. We will now cross the bridge completely and move on to the study of cognition as a topic in its own right.

QUESTIONS FOR CRITICAL THINKING

1. How is habituation different from boredom?

2. How is classical conditioning important in everyday life?

3. Why is avoidance learning self-perpetuating?

4. How can classical and instrumental conditioning account for chronic, self-destructive habits like nail biting and hair pulling?

SUMMARY

1.   The simplest of all forms of learning is *habituation,* a decline in the tendency to respond to stimuli that have become familiar through repeated exposure. In habituation the organism learns that it has encountered a stimulus before. In *classical conditioning,* first studied by I. P. Pavlov, it learns about the *association* between one stimulus and another. Prior to conditioning, an *unconditioned stimulus* or *US* (such as food) elicits an *unconditioned response* or *UR* (such as salivation). After repeated pairings of the US with a *conditioned stimulus* or *CS* (such as a buzzer), this CS alone will evoke a *conditioned response* or *CR* (here again, salivation) that is often similar to the UR.

2.   The strength of conditioning is assessed by the readiness with which the CS elicits the CR. This strength increases with the number of *reinforced trials,* that is, pairings of the CS and the US. When a CS-US relation is well established, the CS can be paired with a second neutral stimulus to produce *second-order conditioning.*

3.   Nonreinforced trials (when the CS is presented without the US) lead to *extinction,* a decreased tendency of the CS to evoke the CR. Some contend that *spontaneous recovery* shows that the CR is masked, not abolished, by extinction.

4.   To train the animal to respond to the CS but not to other stimuli, one stimulus (CS^+) is presented with the US, while another (CS^-) is presented without the US. The more similar the CS^+ is to the CS^-, the more difficult this *discrimination* will be.

5.   Classical conditioning can involve many responses other than salivation, such as, conditioning to feel fear as assessed by the *conditioned emotional response (CER)* procedure.

6.   In classical conditioning, the US is presented regardless of whether the animal performs the CR or not. In another form of simple learning, *instrumental conditioning* (or *operant conditioning*), something analogous to the US—a reward or *reinforcement*—is only delivered upon performance of the appropriate instrumental response.

7.   An early study of instrumental conditioning was conducted by E. L. Thorndike using cats that learned to perform an arbitrary response to escape from a *puzzle box.* As Thorndike saw it, what the animals learned involved no understanding but was rather based on a gradual strengthening of the correct response and a weakening of the incorrect one. To account for this, he proposed his *law of effect,* which states that the tendency to perform a response is strengthened if it is followed by a reward (reinforcement) and weakened if it is not.

8.   During the past sixty years or so, the major figure in the study of instrumental conditioning was B. F. Skinner, one of the first theorists to insist on a sharp distinction between classical conditioning in which the CR is *elicited* by the CS and instrumental (or *operant*) conditioning in which the instrumental response, or *operant,* is *emitted* from within. Operants are strengthened by *reinforcement,* but their acquisition may require some initial *shaping* by the method of *successive approximations.*

9.   While some reinforcers are stimuli whose reinforcing power is unlearned, others are *conditioned reinforcers* that acquire their reinforcing power from prior pairings with stimuli that already have that capacity. One of the factors that determines the strength of instrumental conditioning is the *delay of reinforcement:* The shorter the interval between the response and the reinforcement, the stronger the response will be.

10.   During *partial reinforcement,* the response is reinforced only some of the time. Responses that were originally learned under partial reinforcement are harder to extinguish than those learned when the response was always reinforced. The rule that determines the occasions under which reinforcement is given is a *schedule of reinforcement.*

11.   Reinforcement can be provided by the presentation of *appetitive stimuli* or by the termination or prevention of *aversive stimuli.* Aversive stimuli can weaken or strengthen instrumental responses, depending on the relation between the aversive stimulus and the

response. In *punishment training,* the response is followed by an aversive stimulus; as a result, the animal learns *not* to perform it. In *escape learning,* the response stops an aversive stimulus that has already begun; in *avoidance training,* it averts it altogether. In both cases, the animal will then learn to make the desired response.

12. Pavlov, Thorndike, and Skinner believed that the essential aspect of both classical and instrumental conditioning is that they modify *action. Cognitive theorists* such as Köhler and Tolman believe that when humans and animals learn they acquire new bits of knowledge or *cognitions.* According to many theorists, what is learned in classical conditioning is an association between two events, the CS and the US, such that the CS serves as a signal for the US. One line of evidence comes from studies of the effect of the CS-US interval. The general finding is that conditioning is more effective when the CS precedes the US by some optimum interval, which is typically rather short.

13. A number of investigators have asked how the animal learns that the CS is a signal for the US. The evidence shows that CS-US pairings alone will not suffice; there must also be trials on which the absence of CS goes along with the absence of US. This allows the animal to discover that the US is *contingent* (depends) upon the CS.

14. Unlike Thorndike and Skinner, who argued that instrumental learning involves the strengthening of an instrumental response, cognitive theorists believe that it is based on an association between an act and its outcome. Evidence for this view comes from studies in which animals are trained to perform two responses that lead to two different outcomes after which one of the outcomes is made less desirable. Subsequent tests indicate that the animals learned which response led to which result.

15. Contingency is crucial in instrumental conditioning just as it is in classical conditioning. In instrumental conditioning, the relevant contingency is between a response and an outcome. When there is no such contingency, the organism learns that it has no *response control.* Threatening conditions in which there is no response control may engender *learned helplessness,* which often generalizes to other situations.

16. According to Pavlov, Skinner, and other early behaviorists, the connections established by classical and instrumental conditioning are essentially *arbitrary.* This led them to believe that just about any CS can become associated with any US and that just about any response can be strengthened by any reinforcer, a position often called the *equipotentiality principle.* This position is challenged by the fact that certain CSs are more readily associated with some USs than with others, as shown by studies of *learned taste aversions.* These studies suggest that animals are biologically prepared to learn certain relations more readily than others. Similar preparedness effects occur in instrumental conditioning: Some responses are more readily strengthened by some reinforcers than by others.

17. According to some investigators there are some forms of learning that are species specific so that some animals can readily learn what others cannot. Adherents of this view point to specialized adaptations in various birds, including remarkable memory for hoarded food, song learning, and navigation abilities.

18. Cognitive theorists point out that animals are capable of rather complex cognitions. Evidence comes from work on spatial memory in rats and chimpanzees which shows that these animals can acquire rather elaborate *cognitive maps.* Further work concerns the ability to abstract *conceptual* relationships. Early evidence came from Köhler's studies of *insightful learning* in chimpanzees. Later work showed that chimpanzees can acquire certain *higher-order* concepts such as "same-different" and seem to have some access to their own cognitive operations.

PART TWO

COGNITION

CHAPTER **5**

S E N S O R Y
P R O C E S S E S

The approach to mental life we have considered thus far emphasizes action, whether natively given or modified by learning. It is an approach that asks what organisms do and how they do it. We now turn to another approach to mental functioning that asks what organisms know and how they come to know it.

Both humans and many animals are capable of knowledge, though in our own species, knowing (or cognition) is vastly more refined. We know about the world directly around us, perceiving objects and events that are in our here and now, like the rose that we can see and smell. We also know about events in our past at least some of which are stored in our memory and can be retrieved at some later time; the rose may fade, but we can recall what it looked like when it was still in bloom. Our knowledge can be transformed and manipulated by thinking; we can somehow sift and analyze our experiences to emerge with new and often abstract notions, so that we can think of the faded rose petals as but one stage in a reproductive cycle which in turn reflects the procession of the seasons. Finally, we can communicate our knowledge to others by the use of language, a uniquely human capacity that allows us to accumulate knowledge, each building upon the discoveries of the preceding generation.

T o survive, we must know the world around us. For most objects in the world are charged with meaning: Some are food, others are mates, still others are mortal enemies. The ability to distinguish between them—say, between a log and a crocodile—is literally a matter of life and death. To make these distinctions, we have to use our senses. We must do our best to see, hear, and smell the crocodile so that we can recognize it for what it is before it sees, hears, smells, and (most especially) touches and tastes us.

THE ORIGINS OF KNOWLEDGE

FOCUS QUESTIONS

- How do the empiricists think we acquire knowledge? the nativists?

- What are proximal and distal stimuli?

- What is psychophysics?

- What are absolute and difference thresholds? What does Weber's fraction reveal about difference thresholds?

- What is signal-detection theory? How can the beliefs and attitudes of subjects affect the way they respond during signal-detection experiments?

John Locke *(Courtesy of the National Portrait Gallery, London)*

The study of sensory experience grows out of an ancient question: Where does human knowledge come from? Most philosophers in the past subscribed to one of two opposed positions. The *empiricists* maintained that all knowledge is acquired through experience. In contrast, the *nativists* argued that many aspects of our knowledge are based on innately given characteristics of the human mind (or, as we would now say, of the brain).

THE EMPIRICIST VIEW

■   A major proponent of the empiricist position was the English philosopher John Locke (1632–1704). Locke maintained that all knowledge comes through the senses. There are no innate ideas; at birth, the human mind is a blank tablet, a *tabula rasa,* upon which experience leaves its marks.

> Let us suppose the mind to be, as we say, a white paper void of all characters, without any ideas:—How comes it to be furnished? Whence comes it by that vast store which the busy and boundless fancy of man has painted on it with an almost endless variety? Whence has it all the materials of reason and knowledge? To this I answer, in one word, from experience. In that all our knowledge is founded; and from that it ultimately derives itself (Locke, 1690).

Locke's view fit in well with the emerging liberalism that was the dominant sentiment of the rising middle classes during the eighteenth century. The merchants and manufacturers of Western Europe had little use for the hereditary privileges of a landed aristocracy or for the divine right of kings to govern (and worse, to tax) as they chose. Under the circumstances, they readily grasped at any doctrine that proclaimed the essential equality of all men. If all men enter life with a *tabula rasa,* then all distinctions among them must be due entirely to differences in their environments.

DISTAL AND PROXIMAL STIMULI

Given the assumption that all knowledge comes through the senses, it was natural enough to ask about the kind of knowledge that the senses can give us. What is the information that the senses receive? Consider vision. We look at a tree some distance away. Light reflected from the tree's outer surface enters through the pupil of the eye, is gathered by the lens, and is cast as an image upon the photosensitive region at the rear of the eye called the *retina.* The stimuli that are involved in this visual sequence can be described in either of two ways. We can talk about the *distal stimulus,* an object or event in the world outside, such as the tree. (This is typically at some *distance* from the perceiver, hence the term *distal.*) We can also talk about the *proximal stimulus,* the pattern of stimulus energies that takes its origins at the distal stimulus and finally impinges on a sensory surface of the organism (hence, the term *proximal,* that is, "nearby.") In our example, this proximal stimulus would be the optical image the tree casts on the retina.

As perceivers, our interest obviously centers upon the distal stimulus, the real object in the world outside. We want to know about the tree, not its retinal image. Our interest is in the tree's real size, its distance away from us, the kind of leaves it has, and so on. But we can only learn about the distal stimulus through the proximal stimuli to which it gives rise. There is no way of really seeing the tree out there without a retinal image of the tree. The same holds for the other senses. We can only smell a rotten egg (the distal stimulus) because of hydrogen sulfide molecules suspended in the air that flows over the sensory cells in our nasal cavities (the proximal stimulus).

5.1   Distal and proximal stimuli   *The
young girl and her father are distal stimuli,
real objects in the world outside. The proximal
stimuli they give rise to are the images they
cast on the retina. In the example, the little
girl is about one-third the size of her father.
But since the father is three times farther removed from the observer's eye than the child,
the size of the retinal image he casts is the
same as the one cast by the child.*

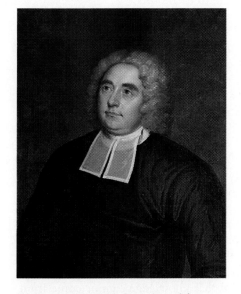

Bishop George Berkeley   *(Detail from*
The Bermuda Group *by John Smibert;
courtesy of Yale University Art Gallery, gift of
Isaac Lothrop of Plymouth, Mass.)*

The senses are the only portals we have to the world outside; the proximal
stimuli are the only messengers that are allowed to pass information through
them. Such heirs of Locke as Bishop George Berkeley (1685–1753) were quick
to show that this fact has enormous consequences. For one thing, the sensory
information provided by the proximal stimulus seems to lack many of the qualities that presumably characterize the external object (that is, the distal stimulus)
to which this information refers. For example, Berkeley pointed out that we
cannot tell the size of the physical object from the size of its retinal image. Our
tree might be a miniature plant nearby or a giant one in the distance. By the
same token, we cannot tell whether an object is in motion or at rest from its
retinal image alone, for motion of the image may be caused by motion of the
external object or by movements of the observer's eye. It appears that the
knowledge that comes by way of the retinal image is very meager (see Figure 5.1).

SENSATIONS

Considerations of this sort led later empiricists to assume that the raw materials
out of which knowledge is constructed are **sensations,** the primitive experiences
that the senses give us and upon which we must then build. Green and brown
are examples of visual sensations. An example of an auditory sensation would be
a loud A-flat. An example of a gustatory (that is, taste) sensation would be a bitter taste. According to the empiricists, all our perceptual experience is ultimately composed of such sensations—a mosaic of colored patches, tones of different
pitch and loudness, sweets and sours, and so on.

Can this description possibly do justice to the richness of our perceptual
world? The fact is that we do see trees (and innumerable other objects) and not
mere patches of green and brown. While Bishop Berkeley might argue that our
vision cannot inform us about depth or true size, in actual life we seem to have
little difficulty in telling how far an object is away from us. (Were it otherwise,
every automobile would become a wreck within minutes of leaving the show-
room.) And we can in fact perceive the true size of an object. After all, even
Berkeley would have had little trouble in distinguishing between a tiger in the
distance and a kitten close by.

How did the empiricists reconcile these facts with their assumptions about
the nature of sensation? Their answer was learning.

*5.2   The use of linear perspective in
Renaissance art*   The School of Athens
*by Raphael, 1509–1511. (Stanze della
Segnatura, Vatican; courtesy of Scala/Art
Resource)*

THE ROLE OF ASSOCIATION

The empiricists assumed that the organized character and the meaningfulness of
our perceptual world are achieved by prior experience. The key to this accomplishment was held to be **association,** the process whereby one sensation is
linked to another. The basic idea was very simple: If two sensations occur
together often enough, eventually one of them will evoke the idea of the other.
According to the empiricists, this associative linkage is the cement that binds the
separate components of the perceptual world to each other.★

An example is provided by the various **distance cues.** Some of these had been
noted by the painters of the Renaissance who discovered several techniques for
rendering a three-dimensional world on a two-dimensional canvas. Among
them was linear perspective—objects appear to be farther away as they decrease
in size (Figure 5.2). To an empiricist, the explanation is a matter of prior association. Visual cues of perspective generally precede reaching or walking; eventually, the visual cue alone will produce the memory of the appropriate movement
and thus the experience of depth.

THE NATIVIST REJOINDER

■   The major theoretical alternative to the empiricist conception is **nativism,**
which asserts that many aspects of perceptual experience are part of our
natural endowment and do not depend on learning. This general position has a
long ancestry with roots that go back as far as Plato. In more recent times, an
influential rejoinder to empiricism came from the German philosopher
Immanuel Kant (1724–1804). Kant argued that knowledge cannot come from

---

★ It is obvious that the notion of association was at the root of many of the theories of learning
we discussed in the last chapter. For example, Pavlov's conceptions of classical conditioning are in
many ways derived from the views of the early associationists.

sensory input alone; there must also be certain preexisting "categories" according to which this sensory material is ordered and organized. Examples are space, time, and causality—categories that, according to Kant, are built into the mind (or, as we would now say, into the nervous system). In Kant's view, there is no way in which we can see the world except in terms of these categories. It is as if we looked at the world through colored spectacles that we could never take off; if they were red, then redness would necessarily be part of everything we see. According to Kant, experience provides the sensory input that is then ordered according to these preexisting categories. But the categories themselves, and the way in which they order the sensory information, are natively given.

PSYCHOPHYSICS

The dispute between empiricists and nativists focused attention on the role of the senses and prodded later investigators into efforts to discover just how these senses function. The question they were concerned with can be stated very simply: What is the chain of events that begins with a stimulus and leads up to reports such as "a bitter taste," "a dull pressure," or "a brightish green"? The details of this sequence are obviously very different for the different senses. Vision differs from hearing, and both differ from taste—in the stimuli that normally excite them, in their receptors, in the qualities of their sensations. Even so, we can analyze the path from stimulus to sensory experience in quite similar ways, whatever the particular sense may be.

In all cases, one can crudely distinguish three steps in the sequence. First, there is the proximal stimulus. Second, there is the neural chain of events that this stimulus gives rise to. The stimulus is converted (technically, *transduced*) into an electrical signal, which is then translated into a nerve impulse. Once converted in this manner, the message is transmitted further and often is modified by other parts of the nervous system. Third, there is some sort of psychological response to the message, often in the form of a conscious, sensory experience (or sensation).

The sequence can be looked at from several points of view. One concerns the *psychophysical* relations between some property of the (physical) stimulus and the (psychological) sensory experience it ultimately gives rise to, quite apart from the intervening neural steps. Another approach concerns *psychophysiology*. Here the questions concern the neural consequences of a given stimulus input—how it affects the receptors and the neural structures higher up in the brain. For now, we will confine our discussion to psychophysical matters, leaving psychophysiological issues for later on.

The object of psychophysics is to relate the characteristics of physical stimuli to attributes of the sensory experience they produce. For example, there are a variety of stimuli to which the human organism is sensitive. They include chemicals suspended in air or dissolved in water, temperature changes on the skin, pressure on the skin or within various parts of the body, pressure in the form of sound waves, and electromagnetic radiations within the visible range (the spectrum). In each case, the sensory system will not respond unless the stimulus energy is above some critical level of intensity called the **absolute threshold.**

The range of stimuli to which a given sensory system reacts is actually quite limited. Human sight is restricted to the visible spectrum and human hearing to sound waves between 20 and 20,000 hertz (that is, cycles per second). But there are many organisms that respond to different ranges of stimulation and thus see and hear a world different from ours. Many insects see ultraviolet light, while dogs and cats hear sound waves of much higher frequency than we can. The bat has carried high-frequency hearing to a point of exquisite perfection. As it glides through the night it emits high-pitched screams of up to 100,000 hertz

Immanuel Kant   *(Courtesy of Culver Pictures, Inc., New York)*

that are used as a kind of sonar. They bounce off small objects in the air such as insects, echo back to the bat, and thus enable it to locate its prey.

Gustav Theodor Fechner *(Courtesy of the National Library of Medicine)*

MEASURING SENSORY INTENSITY

Measuring the magnitude of a stimulus is in principle easy enough. We measure the physical stimulus energy—in pounds, in degrees centigrade, in lumens, in decibels, or whatever. But such matters become more difficult when we try to assess psychological intensity, the magnitude of a sensation rather than that of a stimulus.

Gustav Theodor Fechner (1801–1887), the founder of psychophysics, believed that sensations cannot be measured directly. In his view, sensations and the stimuli that produce them belong to two totally different realms—to use the terms many philosophers employ, that of the body and that of the mind. If this is so, how can one possibly describe them by reference to the same yardstick? Fechner argued that while sensations can't be compared to physical stimuli, they can at least be compared to each other. A subject can compare two of his own sensations and judge whether the two are the same or are different.

Consider the sensation of visual brightness produced by a patch of light projected on a certain part of the eye. We can ask, what is the minimal amount by which the light intensity of this patch must be increased so that the subject experiences a sensation of brightness just greater than the one he had before? This amount is called the **difference threshold.** It produces a **just noticeable difference,** or **jnd.** The jnd is a psychological entity, for it describes a subject's ability to discriminate. But it is expressed in the units of the physical stimulus that produced it. (In our example, this would be lux, a unit of illumination.) Fechner had thus found an indirect means to relate sensory magnitude to the physical intensity of the stimulus.

Before proceeding we should note that the **absolute threshold** may be considered as a special case of a difference threshold. Here the question is how much stimulus energy must be added to a *zero* stimulus before the subject can tell the difference between the old stimulus ("I see nothing") and the new ("Now I see it").

E. H. Weber *(Courtesy of the National Library of Medicine)*

THE WEBER FRACTION

To Fechner, measuring jnd's was only the means to a larger goal—the formulation of a general law relating (physical) stimulus intensity to (psychological) sensory magnitude. He believed that such a law could be built upon an empirical generalization first proposed in 1834 by the German physiologist E. H. Weber (1795–1878). Weber proposed that the size of the difference threshold is a constant ratio of the standard stimulus. Suppose that we can just tell the difference between 100 and 102 candles burning in an otherwise unilluminated room. If Weber is right, we would also be able just to distinguish between 200 and 204 candles, 400 and 408, and so forth. Put in other words, the nervous system is sensitive to a percentage change rather than a change in absolute values—a 2 percent candle difference, rather than a difference of 2 or 4 or 8. Fechner was so impressed with this relationship that he referred to it as **Weber's law,** a label by which we still know it.

Fechner and his successors performed numerous studies to determine whether Weber's law holds for all of the sensory domains—or, more technically, **sensory modalities.** The answer seems to be yes, at least for much of the normal range of stimulus intensity within each sense. The nervous system is evidently geared to notice relative differences rather than absolute ones.

DETECTION AND DECISION

■ The goal of psychophysics is to chart the relationships between a subject's perceptual responses and various characteristics of the physical stimulus. But are these physical characteristics the only factors that determine what the subject does or says in a psychophysical experiment? What about her expectations or wishes? The early psychophysicists believed that such factors could be largely disregarded. But a more recent approach to psychophysical measurement insists that they cannot. This is *signal-detection theory,* a very influential way of thinking about the way people make decisions.

RESPONSE BIAS

To understand how beliefs and attitudes come into play in a psychophysical experiment, consider a study of absolute thresholds. On every trial, harried subjects are forced into a decision. Is a stimulus there or isn't it? The decision is often difficult, for at times the stimulus is so weak that the subjects may be quite uncertain of their judgment. Under the circumstances, their *response bias* will exert an effect. Such a response bias is a preference for one response over another (here "yes" or "no"), quite apart from the nature of the stimuli. Thus, some subjects will approach the task with a free-and-easy attitude, cheerfully offering "yes" judgments whenever they are in doubt. Others will take a more conservative line and will never respond with a "yes" unless they are quite certain. This will produce a difference in obtained thresholds that will necessarily be lower for the subjects who are more liberal with their "yes" responses. But this only reflects a difference in response bias, not in sensory sensitivity. Both groups of subjects can presumably hear or see or feel the stimuli equally well. They only differ in their willingness to report a stimulus when they are unsure.

SIGNAL DETECTION

Such considerations make it clear that thresholds obtained with traditional techniques reflect two factors. One is sensitivity—how well the subject can hear or see the stimulus. The other is response bias—how readily the subject is willing to say "yes, I heard" when not certain. How can these two factors be separated?

The early psychophysicists tried to cope with this problem by using only subjects who were highly trained observers. In absolute threshold studies, such subjects were models of conservatism; they would never say "yes" unless they were completely certain. To maintain this attitude, the experimenters threw in an occasional "catch trial" on which there was no stimulus at all (Woodworth, 1938).

Signal-detection theory has developed a more systematic way of dealing with response bias. To begin with, it has provided a somewhat different testing procedure, the *detection experiment,* in which catch trials are part of the regular procedure rather than just an occasional check to keep the subjects on their toes (Green and Swets, 1966).

One version of this procedure is related to the measurement of the absolute threshold. Here the question is whether the subject can detect the presence of a stimulus. We take a fairly weak stimulus and present it on half the trials. On the other half of the trials (interspersed in random order), we present no stimulus at all. We will now look at two kinds of errors. One is a *miss,* not reporting a stimulus when one is present. The other is a *false alarm,* reporting a stimulus when in fact none is present. By the same token, there are two different kinds of correct responses: reporting a stimulus when it is actually there (a *hit*) and not reporting one when none is present (a *correct negative*) (see Table 5.1).

TABLE 5.1 THE FOUR POSSIBLE OUTCOMES OF THE DETECTION EXPERIMENT

	Stimulus present	Stimulus absent
Responds "yes"	Hit	False alarm
Responds "no"	Miss	Correct negative

TABLE 5.2 PAYOFF MATRIX THAT WILL PRODUCE A "YES" BIAS

	Stimulus present	Stimulus absent
Subject says "yes"	+ 10¢	– 1¢
Subject says "no"	– 10¢	+ 5¢

THE PAYOFF MATRIX

The detection experiment can tell us what factors underlie response bias. One such factor is differential payoff. Suppose we (literally) pay a subject for every hit and correct negative but penalize him for every miss and false alarm according to a prescribed schedule of gains and losses called a **payoff matrix.** Thus the subject might gain 10 cents for every hit and 5 cents for every correct negative, while losing 10 cents for every miss and only 1 cent for every false alarm. Such a payoff matrix will lead to a bias toward "yes" judgments (Table 5.2). To make this clear, let's consider an extreme case. Suppose there are, say, fifty trials on which the subject has no sensory information on the basis of which he can decide whether the stimulus is present or not. If he consistently says "yes," he will on the average be correct on twenty-five trials (thus collecting $2.50) and wrong on the other twenty-five (thus losing $0.25) for a net gain of $2.25. In contrast, consistent "no" judgments will lead to a net loss (collecting $1.25 for the correct negatives and losing $2.50 for the false alarms).

EXTENSIONS TO OTHER FIELDS

Illustrations of the effect of payoff matrices abound in real life. There the differential payoff is usually reckoned in units larger than pennies. Consider a team of radiologists poring over an X-ray to look for a tiny spot that indicates the start of a malignant tumor. What are the penalties for error here? If the physicians decide there is no spot when there actually is one, their miss may cost the patient's life. If they decide that they see a spot when in fact there is none, their false alarm has other costs, such as the dangers of more elaborate clinical tests, let alone those of an operation. What the physicians ultimately decide will depend both on what their eyes tell them as they inspect the X-ray and also on the relative costs of the two possible errors they may commit.

Another example is the selection of college applicants. One error of admissions is a miss: An applicant is rejected who would have done well. Another error is a false alarm: An applicant is accepted who will be unable to graduate (see Chapter 15). The important point is that in virtually all decision making some errors are inevitable and that these errors can either be misses or false alarms. There is always a trade-off between these two kinds of errors. If one wants to minimize the misses (rejected applicants who would have done perfectly well had they been accepted), one has to change the response bias toward "yes," which then inevitably increases the number of false alarms (accepted applicants who will flunk out). Conversely, if one wants to minimize the number of false alarms, one necessarily must increase the number of misses. Just which trade-off is chosen depends on the payoff matrix.

A SURVEY OF THE SENSES

FOCUS QUESTIONS

■ What two sensory systems do we use to determine our orientation and movements?

■ Which kinds of sensations have receptors on the skin?

■ How does our sense of smell function as both an internal and a distance sense?

- What are pheromones, and what role(s) do they play in humans? nonhumans?

- What is the distal stimulus for hearing? What is the proximal stimulus, and how is it transduced into a nerve impulse?

The development of psychological methods, coupled with various physiological techniques, gave psychology a powerful set of tools with which to study the various senses. Our primary focus will be on just one sense, which we will consider in detail: vision. But we will first look briefly at several other sensory systems that provide us with information about various aspects of the world and about our own position within it.

KINESTHESIS AND THE VESTIBULAR SENSES

One group of senses informs the organism about its own movements and its orientation in space. Skeletal movement is sensed through *kinesthesis,* a collective term for information that comes from receptors in the muscles, tendons, and joints. Another group of receptors signals the rotation of the head. These are the receptors in the *semicircular canals,* which are located within the *vestibules* of the inner ear (Figure 5.3). The three canals contain a viscous liquid that moves when the head rotates. This motion bends hair cells that are located at one end of each canal. When bent, these hair cells give rise to nervous impulses. The sum total of the impulses from each of the canals provides information about the nature and extent of the head's rotation.

One vital function of the semicircular canal system is to provide a firm base for vision. As we walk through the world, our head moves continually. To compensate for this endless rocking, the eyes have to move accordingly. This adjustment is accomplished by a reflex system that automatically cancels each rotation of the head by an equal and opposite motion of the eyes. These eye movements are initiated by messages from the three semicircular canals, which are then relayed to the appropriate muscles of each eye. Thus, the visual system is effectively stable, operating as if it rested on a solid tripod.

THE SKIN SENSES

Stimulation of the skin informs the organism of what is directly adjacent to its own body. Not surprisingly, skin sensitivity is especially acute in those parts of the body that are most relevant to exploring the world that surrounds us directly: the hands and fingers, the lips and tongue. These sensitivities are reflected in the organization of the cortical projection area for bodily sensations. As we have seen, the allocation of cortical space is quite unequal, with a heavy emphasis on such sensitive regions as face, mouth, and fingers (see Chapter 2).

How many skin senses are there? Aristotle believed that all of the sensations from the skin could be subsumed under just one rubric, that of touch. But today most investigators believe that there are at least four different skin sensations: *pressure, warmth, cold,* and *pain.* How are these different sensory experiences coded by the nervous system? Here, as in the study of many other senses, the first line of inquiry was suggested by the German physiologist Johannes Müller (1801–1858), who developed the *doctrine of specific nerve energies:* If the sensory qualities are different, see whether there are different receptors that underlie them.

A

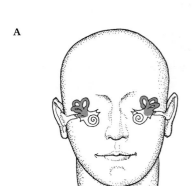

B

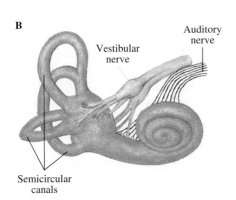

Vestibular nerve

Auditory nerve

Semicircular canals

5.3 The vestibular sense (A) The location of the inner ears, which are embedded in bone on both sides of the skull. The vestibules are indicated in orange. The rest of the inner ear is devoted to the sense of hearing. (After Krech and Crutchfield, 1958) (B) Close-up of the vestibular apparatus. (After Kalat, 1984)

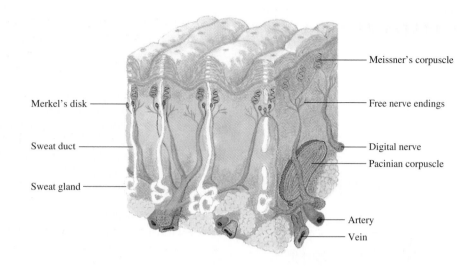

5.4   A cross section through the skin   *The figure shows a number of structures that serve as receptors in hairless skin; for example, on the fingertips and palms. (After Carlson, 1986)*

Are there different receptors that correspond to these different sensations? The answer is a qualified yes. There is good reason to believe that various sensations of pressure are produced by a number of different specialized receptors in the skin (see Figure 5.4). Some of these receptors are wrapped around hair follicles in the skin and sense movements of the hair. Others are capsules that are easily bent by slight deformations of the skin. Some of these capsules respond to continued vibration, others to sudden movement across the skin, still others to steady indentation. It's clear that there is not one touch receptor but several.

Less is known about the underlying receptor systems for warmth, cold, and pain. Some of these experiences are probably signaled by free nerve endings in the skin that have no specialized end organs. These free nerve endings have been thought to provide information about warmth, cold, and pain, but some of them may also be additional pressure receptors (Sherrick and Cholewiak, 1986).

THE SENSE OF TASTE

■ The sense of taste has a simple function. It acts as a gatekeeper for the organism's digestive system by providing information about the substances that may or may not be ingested. Its task is to keep poisons out and usher foodstuffs in. In most land-dwelling mammals, this function is performed by specialized receptor organs, the *taste buds,* which are sensitive to chemicals dissolved in water. The average person possesses about 10,000 such taste buds, located mostly in the tongue but also in other regions of the mouth. Fibers from these receptors convey the message to the brain, first to the medulla and then further up to the thalamus and cortex.

TASTE SENSATIONS

Most investigators believe that there are four basic taste qualities: *sour, sweet, salty,* and *bitter.* In their view, all other taste sensations are produced by a mixture of these primary qualities. Thus, grapefruit tastes sour and bitter, while lemonade tastes sweet and sour. What are the stimuli that produce these four basic qualities? As yet, we don't have a full answer. We do know that the salty taste is usually produced by inorganic molecules dissolved in water and the sour taste by acids. The story is more complicated for sweet and bitter sensations. Both are generally produced by complex organic molecules, but as yet there are no clear-cut rules that predict the resulting taste sensation. For example, "sweet"

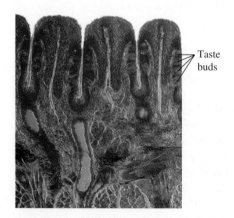

Section of a mammalian tongue   *The taste buds, which look like small hairy balls, are embedded in the walls of deep narrow pits in the tongue. (Courtesy of Ed Reschke)*

is produced by various sugars, but also by saccharin, a chemical compound that is structurally very different from sugar. Additional problems are posed by effects of concentration. Some substances, such as saccharin, that taste sweet in low concentrations taste bitter when their concentration is increased.

TASTE AND SENSORY INTERACTION

The sense of taste provides an illustration of a pervasive principle that holds for most (perhaps all) of the other senses and that we will here call *sensory interaction.* It describes the fact that a sensory system's response to any given stimulus rarely depends on that stimulus alone. It is also affected by other stimuli that impinge, or have recently impinged, upon that system.

One kind of sensory interaction occurs over time. Suppose one taste stimulus is presented continuously for fifteen seconds or more. The result will be *adaptation,* a phenomenon that is found in virtually all sensory systems. If the tongue is continually stimulated with the identical taste stimulus, sensitivity to that taste will quickly decline. For example, after continuous exposure to a quinine solution, the quinine will taste less and less bitter and may finally appear to be completely tasteless. This adaptation process is reversible, however. If the mouth is rinsed out and left unstimulated for, say, a minute, the original taste sensitivity will be restored in full.

In another form of interaction, the adaptation to one taste quality may lead to the enhancement of another, an effect that is sometimes regarded as a form of contrast. For example, adaptation to sugar makes an acid taste even sourer than before (Kuznicki and McCutcheon, 1979). A related effect is the change in the taste of ordinary tap water after prior adaptation to various substances. Adaptation to a salty solution will make water taste sour or bitter; adaptation to one that's sweet will make it taste biter (McBurney and Shick, 1971).

THE SENSE OF SMELL

Thus far, our discussion has centered on the sensory systems that tell us about objects and events close to home: the movements and position of our own bodies, what we feel with our skin, and what we put in our mouths. Our sense of smell also tells us about things close to home.

SMELL AS AN INTERNAL SENSE

We can smell the spaghetti on our plate, but we can also sense its flavor when we take a forkful in our mouths. That flavor—as indeed all flavors—depends largely on our sense of smell. For what we commonly call the "taste of food" is very rarely the sensation of taste alone; it is almost always a combination of taste, texture, temperature, and—most important of all—smell (Rozin, 1982). When our nose is completely stuffed up by a cold, food appears to be without any flavor. While we can still experience the basic taste sensations, the aroma is lost, and so the food seems "tasteless." If smell is gone, we can no longer distinguish between vinegar and a fine red wine, or between an apple and an onion. For a gourmet (or a chef or a wine taster), a sensitive nose is even more essential than a sensitive tongue.

SMELL AS A DISTANCE SENSE

But our sense of smell (along with our senses of hearing and vision) clearly collects information for us from much farther off as well, enlarging our world by responding to stimuli at a distance. Smell—or more technically, *olfaction*—provides information about chemicals suspended in air that excite receptors located in a small area at the top of our nasal cavity. As yet there is no agreement about the underlying principle that makes certain chemicals arouse one olfactory experience rather than another. At present, the best guess is that olfactory quality is not coded by particular receptors—with, say, one group of receptors responding to stimuli we call fragrant and another receptor group responding to stimuli we describe as putrid. Instead, the relevant sensory code for quality is probably a pattern of excitation across different receptor groups.

As a distance sense, smell plays a relatively minor part for humans. It is clearly less important to us than it is to many other species. In this regard we are similar to our primate cousins and to birds in that these animals all left the odor-impregnated ground to move up into trees, an environment in which other senses, especially vision, became more critical. In contrast, smell is of vital importance to many ground dwellers such as dogs. For them, it furnishes a guide to food and to receptive mates, and it may give warning against certain natural enemies. Modern psychophysical methods allow us to determine just how much more sensitive the dog's nose is compared to our own; it turns out that the dog-to-human ratio in sensitivity to smell is about a thousand to one (Marshall and Moulton, 1981; Cain, 1988).

Compared to dogs and most other land-dwelling animals, we are evidently olfactory incompetents. But that doesn't mean that smell is of no relevance to human life. It does warn us of impending danger, as when we sniff escaping gas; it greatly adds to our enjoyment of food; and it provides the basis of the perfume and deodorant industries. According to some reports, it even helps to sell luggage and used cars; plastic briefcases saturated with artificial leather scents and second-hand cars permeated with a "new car" odor are said to have greater market value (Winter, 1976). In addition, smell evidently plays a role in identifying other people. In one study, a psychologist asked men and women to wear T-shirts for twenty-four hours without taking a shower or using perfumes or deodorants. After the twenty-four hours were up, each (unwashed) T-shirt was sealed in a separate bag. Every subject was then asked to sniff the contents of three of these bags without looking inside. One contained his or her T-shirt, a second the T-shirt worn by another man, a third the T-shirt worn by another woman. About three-quarters of the subjects were able to identify their own T-shirt based only on its odor, and could also correctly identify which of the other T-shirts had been worn by a man or by a woman (Russell, 1976; McBurney, Levine, and Cavanaugh, 1977).

Pheromones   In many species, olfaction has a function beyond those we have discussed thus far. It represents a primitive form of communication. Certain animals secrete special chemical substances called **pheromones** that trigger particular reactions in other members of their own kind. Some pheromones affect reproductive behavior. In many mammals, the female secretes a chemical (often in the urine) that signals that she is sexually receptive. In some species, the male sends chemical return messages to the female. For example, boars apparently secrete a pheromone that renders the sow immobile so that she stands rigid during mating (Michael and Keverne, 1968).

Other pheromones signal alarm. It appears that some animals can smell danger. To be more exact, they can smell a substance secreted by members of their own species who have been frightened. Thus rats who suffer an electric shock in an experimental chamber seem to exude a chemical that induces fear in other rats that are exposed to a whiff of the air from that same chamber (Valenta and Rigby, 1968).

Are there pheromones in humans? There may be some vestigial remains. One line of evidence concerns the development of **menstrual synchrony.** Women who live together, for example, in college dormitories, tend to develop men-

(*Cartoon by Sidney Harris; © 1980, The New Yorker, Inc.*)

strual cycles that roughly coincide with each other, even though their periods were very different at the start of the school year (McClintock, 1971). Some recent studies suggest that this synchrony is primed by olfactory cues. Female subjects exposed to the body odor of a "donor" woman gradually shifted their menstrual cycles toward that of the donor, even though the subjects and the donor never saw each other (Russell, Switz, and Thompson, 1980).

Of potentially greater interest is the possibility of discovering an olfactory sex attractant that operates like a kind of pheromone. Thus far, there has been little to whet the financial appetites of perfume manufacturers or the erotic hopes of male or female Lonely Hearts. At best, there may be some faint remnants. One line of evidence comes from olfactory thresholds to certain musk-like substances similar to that secreted by boars. Sexually mature women are vastly more sensitive to the smell of these compounds than are men or sexually immature girls. This sensitivity fluctuates with the woman's menstrual cycle and seems to reach a peak during ovulation. An intriguing speculation is that the receptive female's greater sensitivity to this odor points to the existence of a human male pheromone in our evolutionary past. Perhaps it is still present in a greatly attenuated form, but if so its effects are almost certainly too weak to be of any practical significance. Drenching himself in boar's musk and wearing Tom Cruise's unwashed T-shirt (or Mel Gibson's or Denzel Washington's) will not transform the universally rejected suitor into a matinee idol pursued by all women (even those—or especially those—near enough to smell him).

A

B

5.5 The stimulus for hearing (A) The figure depicts a momentarily frozen field of vibration in air. An insect vibrating its wings rapidly leads to waves of compression in the surrounding air. These waves travel in all directions like ripples in a pond into which a stone has been thrown. (B) The corresponding wave pattern is shown in simplified form. The amplitude of the wave is the height of each crest; the wavelength is the distance between successive crests. (From Gibson, 1966)

HEARING

The sense of hearing, or **audition,** is a close relative of other receptive senses that react to mechanical pressure, such as the vestibular senses or touch. Like these, hearing is a response to pressure, but with a difference—it informs us of pressure changes in the world that may take place many meters away. In effect, then, hearing is feeling at a distance.

SOUND

What is the stimulus for hearing? Outside in the world there is some physical movement that disturbs the air in which it occurs. This may be an animal scurrying through the underbrush or a rock dropping from a cliff or a set of vibrating vocal cords. The air particles directly adjacent to the movement are agitated, push other particles that are ahead of them, and then return to their original position. Each individual air particle moves back and forth for just a tiny bit, but this is enough to set up a series of successive pressure variations in the air. These travel in a wave form analogous to the ripples set up by a stone thrown into a pond. When these **sound waves** hit our ears, they initiate a set of further mechanical pressure changes that ultimately trigger the auditory receptors. These initiate various further neural responses in the brain which ultimately lead to an experience of something that is heard rather than felt. (This is another example of the operation of Müller's doctrine of specific nerve energies.)

Sound waves can vary in both **amplitude** and **wavelength.** Amplitude refers to the height of a wave crest: the greater the intensity of the vibration, the higher this crest will be. Wavelength is simply the distance between successive crests. Sound waves are generally described by their **frequency,** which is the number of cycles per second. Since the speed of sound is constant within any given medium, frequency is inversely proportional to wavelength (Figure 5.5).

Both amplitude and frequency are physical dimensions. Our brain translates these into the psychological dimensions of **loudness** and **pitch.** Roughly speak-

TABLE 5.3   INTENSITY LEVELS OF VARIOUS COMMON SOUNDS

Sound	Intensity level (decibels)
Manned spacecraft launching (from 150 feet)	180
Loudest rock band on record	160
Pain threshold (approximate)	140
Loud thunder; average rock band	120
Shouting	100
Noisy automobile	80
Normal conversation	60
Quiet office	40
Whisper	20
Rustling of leaves	10
Threshold of hearing	0

ing, a sound will appear to be louder as its amplitude increases and will appear more high-pitched as its frequency goes up.

Amplitude and loudness   The range of amplitudes to which humans can respond is enormous. Investigators have found it convenient to use a scale that compresses this unwieldy range into a more convenient form. To this end, they developed a logarithmic scale that describes sound intensities in **decibels** (Table 5.3). Perceived loudness doubles every time the physical intensity (that is, the amplitude) goes up by 10 decibels. The physical stimulus intensity rises more steeply, increasing by a factor of 10 every 20 decibels (Stevens, 1955).

Frequency and pitch   The frequency of a sound wave is generally measured in **hertz** (Hz) (named after the nineteenth-century German physicist Heinrich Hertz), or waves per second. Young adults can hear tones as low as 20 hertz and as high as 20,000 hertz, with maximal sensitivity to a middle region in between. As people get older, their sensitivity to sound declines, especially at the higher frequencies.

GATHERING THE PROXIMAL STIMULUS

Most of the ear is made up of various anatomical structures whose function is to gather the proximal stimulus—they conduct and amplify sound waves so that they can affect the auditory receptors (Figure 5.6). Sound waves collected by the

5.6   The human ear   *Air enters through the outer ear and stimulates the eardrum, which sets the ossicles in the middle ear in motion. These in turn transmit their vibration to the membrane of the oval window, which causes movement of the fluid in the cochlea of the inner ear. Note that the semicircular canals are anatomically parts of the inner ear. (After Lindsay and Norman, 1977)*

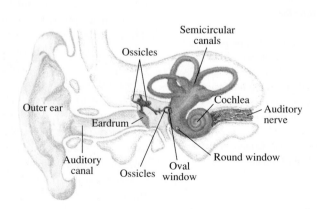

Rock and roll and hearing loss *As rock guitarist Pete Townshend learned too late, prolonged exposure to loud noise, like that produced by his band, The Who, can cause serious hearing loss, as well as tinnitus, or, ringing in the ears. Many rock musicians, as well as fans, now wear ear plugs to prevent damage. (Photograph © RDR productions, 1981; Rex USA)*

outer ear are funneled toward a taut membrane that they cause to vibrate. This is the ***eardrum,*** which transmits its vibrations across an air-filled cavity, the ***middle ear,*** to another membrane, the ***oval window,*** that separates the middle from the ***inner ear.*** This transmission is accomplished by way of a mechanical bridge built of three small bones that are collectively known as the ***ossicles.*** The vibrations of the eardrum move the first ossicle, which then moves the second, which in turn moves the third, which completes the chain by imparting the vibratory pattern to the oval window to which it is attached. The movements of the oval window set up waves in a fluid that fills the ***cochlea,*** a coiled tube in the inner ear that contains the auditory receptors.

Why did nature choose such a roundabout method of sound transmission? The major reason is that the cochlear medium is a fluid, which, like all liquids, is harder to set into motion than air. To overcome this difficulty, the physical stimulus must be amplified. This amplification is provided by various features of the middle-ear organization. One involves the relative sizes of the eardrum and of that portion of the oval window moved by the ossicles; the first is about twenty times larger than the second. The result is the transformation of a fairly weak force that acts on the entire eardrum into a much stronger pressure that is concentrated upon the (much smaller) oval window.

TRANSDUCTION IN THE COCHLEA

Throughout most of its length the cochlea is divided into an upper and lower section by several structures including the ***basilar membrane.*** The auditory receptors are called ***hair cells*** and are lodged between the basilar membrane and other membranes above. Motion of the oval window produces pressure changes in the cochlear fluid that in turn lead to vibrations of the basilar membrane. As the basilar membrane vibrates, its deformations bend the hair cells and provide the immediate stimulus for their activity (Figure 5.7).

How does the activity of the auditory receptors lead to the sensory properties of auditory experience? Much of the work in this area has focused upon the perception of pitch, the sensory quality that depends upon the frequency of the stimulating sound wave.

Basilar place and pitch According to the ***place theory*** of pitch, first proposed by Hermann von Helmholtz (1821–1894), different parts of the basilar membrane are responsive to different sound frequencies. In Helmholtz's view, the nervous system interprets the excitations from different basilar places as different pitches. The stimulation of receptors at one end of the membrane leads to the experience of a high tone, while the stimulation of receptors at the other end leads to the sensation of a low tone.

Today we know that Helmholtz was correct at least in part. The classic studies were performed by Georg von Békésy (1899–1972), whose work on audito-

5.7 Detailed structure of the middle ear and the cochlea (A) Movement of the fluid within the cochlea deforms the basilar membrane and stimulates the hair cells that serve as the auditory receptors. (After Lindsay and Norman, 1977) (B) Cross-section of the cochlea showing the basilar membrane and the hair cell receptors. (After Coren and Ward, 1989)

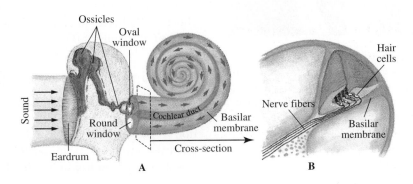

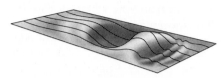

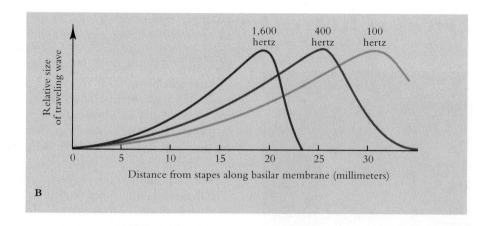

B

5.8 The deformation of the basilar membrane by sound *(A) In this diagram, the membrane is schematically presented as a simple, rectangular sheet. In actuality, of course, it is much thinner and coiled in a spiral shape. (B) The relation between sound frequency and the location of the peak of the basilar membrane's deformation. The peak of the deformation is located at varying distances from the stapes (the third ossicle, which sets the membrane in motion by pushing at the oval window). As the figure shows, the higher the frequency of the sound, the closer to the stapes this peak will be. (After Lindsay and Norman, 1977; Coren and Ward, 1989)*

Georg von Békésy (1899–1972)
(Courtesy of Nobel Stiftelsen)

ry function won him the Nobel Prize in 1961. Some of Békésy's experiments used cochleas taken from fresh human cadavers. Békésy removed part of the cochlear wall so that he could observe the basilar membrane through a microscope while the oval window was being vibrated by an electrically powered piston. He found that such stimulation led to a wavelike motion of the basilar membrane (Figure 5.8). When he varied the frequency of the vibrating stimulus, the peak of the deformation produced by this wave pattern occurred in different regions of the membrane: High frequencies corresponded to regions close to the oval window, low ones to regions close to the cochlear tip (Békésy, 1957).

Sound frequency and frequency of neural firing   The place theory of pitch faces a major difficulty. As the frequency of the stimulus gets lower and lower, the deformation pattern it produces gets broader and broader. At very low frequencies (say, below 50 hertz), the wave set up by the tone deforms the entire membrane just about equally so that all receptors will be equally excited. But since we can discriminate low frequencies down to about 20 hertz, the nervous system must have some means for sensing pitch in addition to basilar location.

It is generally believed that this second means for sensing pitch is related to the firing frequency of the auditory nerve. For lower frequencies, the basilar membrane vibrates at the frequency of the stimulus tone and this vibration rate is then directly translated into the appropriate number of neural impulses per second, as evidenced by gross electrical recordings taken from the auditory nerve. The impulse frequency of the auditory output is further relayed to higher centers that somehow interpret it as pitch.

It appears then that pitch perception is based upon two separate mechanisms: Higher frequencies are coded by the place of excitation on the basilar membrane, lower frequencies by the frequency of the neural impulses. It is not clear where one mechanism leaves off and the other takes over. Place of excitation is probably relatively unimportant at frequencies below 500–1,000 hertz and has no role below 50 hertz, while impulse frequency has little or no effect for tones above 5,000 hertz. In all probability, sound frequencies in between are handled by both mechanisms (Green, 1976; Goldstein, 1989).

EVOLUTION AND SENSORY EQUIPMENT

As we've repeatedly noted, the particular stimuli to which different animals are sensitive vary markedly. For the sensory equipment of any species is an adaptation to the environment in which it lives. This holds both for what an animal can sense and what it cannot. It's hardly surprising that vision is only rudimentary in moles who live in lightless burrows but is exquisitely acute in eagles who have to detect their prey while circling in the sky several thousands of feet above. Many animals have senses that we lack altogether. Thus sharks are sensitive to electric currents leaking through the skin of fish hiding within crevices, rattlesnakes have specialized organs that can detect infrared radiation given off by small mammals nearby, and carrier pigeons use the earth's magnetic field to find their way home on cloudy nights when they can't navigate by the stars (Gould and Gould, 1988; Dyer and Gould, 1983; Wiltschko, Nohr, and Wiltschko, 1981).

An instructive example of the way in which evolution fashions a species' sensory system comes from some recent studies that have some of the flavor of a detective story perhaps entitled "The Case of the Missing Ear." Students of insect behavior long believed that the praying mantis was deaf, for it didn't seem to possess any ears. But electrophysiological evidence showed that some of the insect's nerve tracts fired in response to sounds. Their primary sensitivity was in the ultrasonic region, to tones between 25,000 and 50,000 hertz, which humans of course can't hear. So the mantis was evidently not deaf after all. The next question was, Where are its ears? To find out, the investigators coated the entire animal with a heavy layer of Vaseline after which the nerve no longer responded to sound. They next scraped off different portions of the Vaseline until they finally found a critical groove in the animal's thorax. When this was opened, the nerve resumed its response to auditory stimulation.

An ear had been found, but this only deepened the puzzle. For there was only *one* ear, located in the animal's midline. In the animal kingdom, ears almost invariably come in pairs—a crucial prerequisite for sound localization. If the sound comes from the right, the right ear will be stimulated earlier and more intensely than the left; conversely, if the sound comes from the left. Information of this sort allows the the fortunate possessor of two ears to determine where a sound is coming from. Given its one-eared status, the mantis can't do that. But if this is true, what is its one ear good for? And why is its primary sensitivity in the ultrasonic range?

The answer is bats. As we saw in a previous section (see pp. 127–28), bats emit high-frequency sounds that operate like radar. These sounds echo back off the bodies of flying insects, thus enabling bats to locate their prey. The mantis's ear evidently serves as a bat detector. But if the mantis's single ear can't tell it where the bat is coming from, of what use is it? A clever study showed that sensing the likely direction of attack doesn't really matter. The investigators climbed on a ladder holding a mantis and then (gently) threw it into the air. When the mantis was aloft and flying, the investigators fired a batgun—a device that emits brief pulses of ultrasonic sound, much like the screams of a hunting bat. High-speed photographs showed that whenever the batgun fired, most of the insects adopted an evasive flight pattern reminiscent of those used by fighter pilots—a steep, spiraling power dive likely to get them out of harm's way regardless of where the bat was coming from. The ultimate proof came from a study that pitted the insects against live bats. Over thirty mantises were thrown into the air in a wooded area in which several bats were hunting. When attacked by the bats, all insects that went into the spiral escaped unharmed; those that did not were generally captured (Yager and Hoy, 1986; Yager and May, 1990; Yager, May, and Fenton, 1990).

Evasive flight pattern of a praying mantis *When the batgun fires (indicated by the arrow), the mantis takes evasive action, plummeting to the ground, away from what in nature would be a hungry bat. (From Yager and May, 1990)*

THE SENSES IN OVERVIEW

We've presented a brief sketch of all the senses except for vision, which we will take up in detail below. But before moving on, we should say a few words about the senses in general.

Hermann von Helmholtz (1821–1894)
(Courtesy of the National Library of Medicine)

In our discussion of the various senses, we have come across many ways in which they differ—from each other and, to some extent, across different species. But we have also encountered a number of important phenomena that are not specific to any particular sensory system but are found more generally.

First, in most sense modalities (and among many animals) the processing of external stimulus energies begins with various *accessory structures* that gather these physical energies and fashion a "better" proximal stimulus for the receptors to work on. An example is provided by the semicircular canals which contain a liquid that is set in motion by head rotation and then stimulates the hair cell receptors of the vestibular system.

Second, in all sense modalities, the next step involves the receptors that achieve the *transduction* of the physical stimulus energy into an electrical signal. In some sensory systems, particularly hearing and vision, the nature of this transduction process is reasonably well understood. In other systems, such as smell, it is still unknown.

Third, the processing of stimulus input does not stop at the receptor level. Coding typically occurs at further neural centers. The stimulus information is coded (or "translated") into the various dimensions of sensation that are actually experienced. Some of these dimensions involve intensity. In taste, we experience more or less bitter, in hearing—more or less loud. Other dimensions involve differences in quality. In taste, we can tell the difference between bitter, sweet, sour, and salty; in hearing, we can discriminate differences in pitch.

Fourth, any part of a sensory system is in continual *interaction* with the rest of that system. This process of interaction pertains both to the immediate past and to present activity in neighboring parts of the system. We considered some examples of sensory interaction in the taste system, including the phenomena of adaptation (with continued exposure, quinine tastes less bitter) and taste contrast (prior adaptation to a salty solution will make tap water taste sour or bitter).

VISION

FOCUS QUESTIONS

■ What are the distal and proximal stimuli for vision? In what ways can the eye alter the stimulus to enhance acuity?

■ What are the two kinds of receptor cells? How are they distributed on the retina, and how is their output transduced into a nerve impulse?

■ How does lateral inhibition explain the phenomenon of brightness contrast?

■ What are subtractive and additive color mixture?

■ What is the opponent-process theory?

■ What are feature detectors, what kinds of simple and complex features do they detect, and what findings appear to confirm their existence?

We now turn to a detailed discussion of vision, which in humans is the distance sense par excellence. The organization of this account will reflect characteristics that are common to most of the senses. Specifically, we will first describe the eye as a structure for gathering the visual stimulus, we well next examine the transduction of light energies by the visual receptors, then we will discuss some interaction processes found in vision, and finally we will consider the coding processes that are involved in experiencing a particular sensory quality—in the case of vision, color.

THE STIMULUS: LIGHT

Most visual sensations have their point of origin in some external (distal) object. Occasionally, this object will be a light source that emits light in its own right; examples (in rather drastically descending order of emission energy) are the sun, an electric light bulb, and a glow worm. All other objects can only give off light if some light source illuminates them. They will then reflect some portion of the light cast upon them while absorbing the rest.

The stimulus energy we call light comes from the relatively small band of radiations to which our visual system is sensitive. These radiations travel in a wave form that is somewhat analogous to the pressure waves that are the stimulus for hearing. This radiation can vary in its *intensity,* the amount of radiant energy per unit of time, which is a major determinant of perceived brightness (as in two bulbs of different wattage). It can also vary in *wavelength,* the distance between the crests of two successive waves, which is a major determinant of perceived color. The light we ordinarily encounter is made up of a mixture of different wavelengths. The range of wavelengths to which our visual system can respond is the *visible spectrum,* extending from roughly 400 ("violet") to about 750 ("red") nanometers (1 nanometer = 1 millionth of a millimeter) between successive crests.

GATHERING THE STIMULUS: THE EYE

The next stop in the journey from stimulus to visual sensation is the eye. Except for the *retina,* none of its major structures has anything to do with the transduction of the physical stimulus energy into neurological terms. Theirs is a prior function: to fashion a proper proximal stimulus for vision, a sharp *retinal image,* out of the light that enters from outside.

Let us briefly consider how this task is accomplished. The eye has often been compared to a camera, and in its essentials this analogy holds up well enough (Figure 5.9). Both eye and camera have a *lens,* which suitably bends (or *refracts*) light rays passing through it and thus projects an image upon a light-sensitve surface behind—the film in the camera, the retina in the eye. (In the eye, refraction is accomplished by both the lens and the *cornea,* the eye's transparent outer coating.) Both have a focusing mechanism: In the eye this is accomplished by a set of muscles that changes the shape of the lens; it is flattened for objects at a distance and thickened for objects closer by, a process technically known as *accommodation.* Finally, both camera and eye have a diaphragm that governs the amount of entering light: In the eye this function is performed by the *iris,* a smooth, circular muscle that sur-

5.9 Eye and camera As an accessory apparatus for fashioning a sharp image out of the light that enters from outside, the eye has many similarities to the camera. Both have a lens for bending light rays to project an inverted image upon a light-sensitive surface at the back. In the eye a transparent outer layer, the cornea, participates in this light-bending. The light-sensitive surface in the eye is the retina, whose most sensitive region is the fovea. Both eye and camera have a focusing device; in the eye, the lens can be thickened or flattened. Both have an adjustable iris diaphragm. And both finally are encased in black to minimize the effects of stray light; in the eye this is done by a layer of darkly pigmented tissue, the choroid coat. (Wald, 1950)

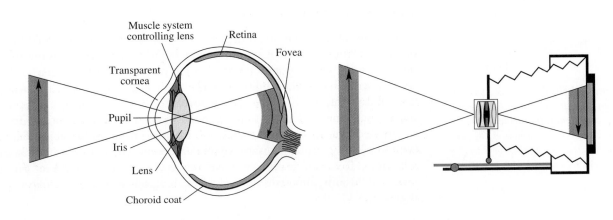

Muscle system controlling lens
Retina
Fovea
Transparent cornea
Pupil
Iris
Lens
Choroid coat

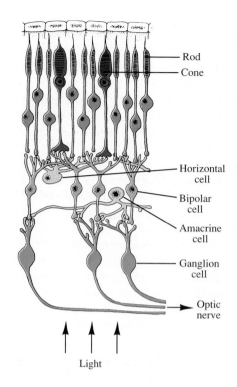

Rod

Cone

Horizontal cell

Bipolar cell

Amacrine cell

Ganglion cell

Optic nerve

Light

5.10   The retina   *There are three main retinal layers: the rods and cones, which are the photoreceptors; the bipolar cells; and the ganglion cells, whose axons make up the optic nerve. There are also two other kinds of cells, horizontal cells and amacrine cells, that allow for sideways (lateral) interaction. As shown in the diagram, the retina contains an anatomical oddity. As it is constructed, the photoreceptors are at the very back, the bipolar cells are in between, and the ganglion cells are at the top. As a result, light has to pass through the other layers (they are not opaque so this is possible) to reach the rods and cones, whose stimulation starts the visual process. (After Coren and Ward, 1989)*

rounds the pupillary opening and that contracts or dilates under reflex control when the amount of illumination increases or decreases substantially.

The image of an object that falls upon the retina is determined by simple optical geometry. Its size will be inversely proportional to the distance of the object, while its shape will depend on its orientation. Thus, a rectangle viewed at a slant will project as a trapezoid.

THE VISUAL RECEPTORS

We have arrived at the point where the path from distal object to visual sensation crosses the frontier between optics and psychophysiology—the transformation of the physical stimulus energy into a nervous impulse. The structures that accomplish this feat have their visual receptor organs in the retina.

The retina is made up of several layers of nerve cells, one of which is the receptor layer. Microscopic inspection shows two kinds of receptor cells whose names describe their different shapes—the *rods* and the *cones.* The cones are more plentiful in the *fovea,* a small roughly circular region at the center of the retina. While very densely packed in the fovea, they are less and less prevalent the farther out one goes toward the *periphery.* The opposite is true of the rods; they are completely absent from the fovea and are more frequent in the periphery. In all, there are some 120 million rods and about 6 million cones.

The receptors do not report to the brain directly, but relay their message upward by way of two intermediate neural links—the *bipolar cells* and the *ganglion cells* (Figure 5.10). The bipolar cells are stimulated by the receptors, and they, in their turn, excite the ganglion cells. The axons of these ganglion cells are collected from all over the retina, converging into a bundle of fibers that finally leaves the eyeball as the *optic nerve.* The region where these axons converge contains no receptors and thus cannot give rise to visual sensations; appropriately enough, it is called the *blind spot* (Figure 5.11).

VISUAL ACUITY

One of the most important functions of the visual sense is to enable us to tell one object from another. A minimum precondition for doing so is the ability to distinguish between separate points that are projected on the retina so that we do not see a blur. The ability to make such distinctions is called *acuity.* In normal daylight, this is greatest in the fovea, for it is there that the receptors are most closely bunched and thus provide the sharpest optical resolution. To "look at" an object means to move the eyes so that the image of that object falls upon both foveas. In peripheral vision we often see something without quite knowing what it is. To see it clearly, we swivel our eyes so that the image of the as yet unidentified something falls upon the foveal regions where our resolving power is greatest.

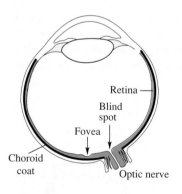

Retina

Blind spot

Fovea

Choroid coat

Optic nerve

5.11   Fovea and blind spot   *The fovea is the region on the retina in which the receptors are most densely packed. The blind spot is a region where there are no receptors at all, this being the point where the optic nerve leaves the eyeball. (After Cornsweet, 1970)*

THE DUPLEX THEORY OF VISION

The fact that rods and cones differ in structure suggests that they also differ in function. Almost a hundred years ago, this notion led to the development of the *duplex theory of vision,* a theory that by now has the status of established fact. The idea is that rods and cones handle different aspects of the visual task. The rods are the receptors for night vision; they operate at low light intensities and lead to *achromatic* (colorless) sensations. The cones serve day vision; they respond at much higher levels of illumination and are responsible for sensations of color. The biological utility of such an arrangement becomes apparent when we consider the enormous range of light intensities encountered by organisms like ourselves who transact their business during both day and night. In humans, the ratio between the stimulus energy at absolute threshold and that transmitted by a momentary glance at the midday sun is 1 to 100,000,000,000. Evolution has evidently provided a biological division of labor, assigning two separate receptor systems to the upper and lower portions of this incredible range.

VISUAL PIGMENTS

When light hits a visual receptor, its energy eventually triggers a nervous impulse. The first stage of this energy conversion involves a photochemical process. We are again reminded of the camera. In a photographic plate the sensitive elements are usually grains of silver salt such as silver bromide. When light strikes the film, some of it is absorbed by the silver bromide molecules with the result that the silver is separated from the compound (and eventually becomes visible after several darkroom manipulations). The visual receptors contain several *visual pigments* that perform an analogous function for the eye. One such substance is *rhodopsin,* which serves as the visual pigment for the rods.

Unlike a photographic emulsion, the visual pigments constantly renew themselves. Were it otherwise, a newborn infant would open his eyes, look at the bustling world around him, and never see again—his retina would be bleached forever. The bleached pigments are reconstituted to permit an unbroken succession of further retinal pictures.

INTERACTION IN TIME: ADAPTATION

We now turn to some phenomena which prove that the visual system (as indeed all sensory systems) is much more than the passive observer that Locke had assumed it to be. On the contrary, the visual system actively shapes and transforms the optic input; its components never function in isolation but constantly interact.

One kind of interaction concerns the relation between what happens now and what happened just before. The general finding is simple: There will be a gradual decline in the reaction to any stimulus that persists unchanged. For example, after continued inspection of a green patch, its greenness will eventually fade away. Similar adaptation phenomena are found in most other sensory systems. Thus, the cold ocean water feels warmer after we have been in it for a while.

What does the organism gain by sensory adaptation? Stimuli that have been around for a while have already been inspected; if they posed a danger, this would have been detected already. Since these stimuli are of lesser relevance to the organism's survival, it pays to give them less sensory weight. What is important is change, especially sudden change, for this may well signify food to a predator and death to its potential prey. Adaptation is the sensory system's way of pushing old news off the neurophysiological front page.

INTERACTION IN SPACE: CONTRAST

Adaptation effects show that sensory systems respond to change over time. If no such change occurs, the sensory response diminishes. What holds for time holds for space as well. For here, too, the key word is *change*. In vision (as in some other senses), the response to a stimulus applied to any one region partially depends on how the neighboring regions are stimulated. The greater the difference in stimulation, the greater the sensory effect.

BRIGHTNESS CONTRAST

It has long been known that the appearance of a gray patch depends upon its background. The identical gray will look much brighter on a black background than it will on a white background. This is **brightness contrast,** an effect that increases the greater the intensity difference between two contrasting regions. Thus, gray appears brighter on black than on dark gray and darker against white than against light gray (Figure 5.12). Contrast is also a function of the distance between the two contrasting regions—the smaller that difference, the greater the contrast (Figure 5.13).

LATERAL INHIBITION AND BRIGHTNESS CONTRAST

What is the physiological mechanism that underlies spatial interaction? Today we know it is **lateral inhibition,** the tendency of a region of the visual system to oppose the responses from an adjacent region, or inhibition exerted sideways. This is why neighboring regions in the retina tend to inhibit each other. A simplified version of how this mechanism works is as follows: When any visual receptor is stimulated, it transmits its excitation upward to other cells that eventually relay it to the brain. But this excitation has a further effect. It also stimulates some neurons that extend sideways along the retina. These lateral cells make contact with neighboring cells whose activation they inhibit.

5.12   Brightness contrast   Four (objectively) identical gray squares on different backgrounds. The lighter the background, the darker the gray squares appear.

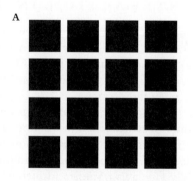

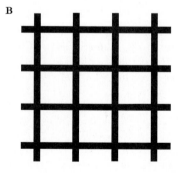

5.13   The effect of distance between contrasting regions   (A) The white lines in the grid are physically homogeneous, but they don't appear to be—each of the "intersections" seems to contain a gray spot. The uneven appearance of the white strips is caused by contrast. Each strip is surrounded by a black square, which contrasts with it and makes it look brighter. But this is not the case at the intersections, which only touch upon the black squares at their corners. As a result, there is little contrast in the middle of the intersections. This accounts for the gray spots seen there. (B) The same point is made by the second grid. Here there seem to be whitish spots at the intersections. The explanation is the same: The black lines are bounded by white and thus look darker by contrast. There is less contrast operating on the regions in the middle of the intersections. As a result, they don't appear as dark as the streets, creating the whitish spots. (After Hering, 1920)

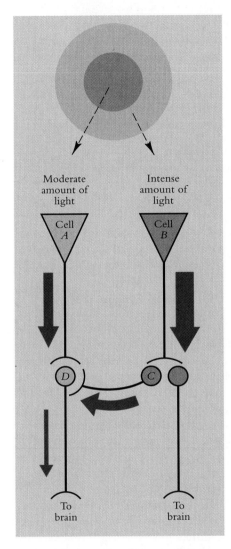

5.14 Lateral inhibition and contrast
Two receptor cells, A and B, are stimulated by neighboring regions of a stimulus. A receives moderate stimulation; B receives an intense amount of light. A's excitation serves to stimulate the next neuron in the visual chain, cell D, which transmits the message further toward the brain. But this transmission is impeded by cell B, whose own intense excitation exerts an inhibitory effect on its neighbors. B excites a lateral cell, C, which exerts an inhibitory effect on cell D. As a result, cell D fires at a reduced rate. (Excitatory effects are shown by dark green arrows, inhibitory ones by dark red arrows. In the human eye, the lateral inhibitors are the horizontal cells and the amacrine cells of the retina; see Figure 5.10.)

To see how lateral inhibition works, consider the retinal image produced by a gray patch surrounded by a lighter ring (Figure 5.14). For the sake of simplicity, we will only look at two neighboring receptor cells, A and B. A is stimulated by the gray patch and receives a moderate amount of light. B is stimulated by the lighter ring and receives much more light. Our primary interest is in the excitation that cell A, the one stimulated by the gray patch, relays upward to the brain. The more cell A is stimulated, the more excitation it will relay, and the brighter the patch will appear to be. The important point is that the excitation from cell A will not be passed on unimpeded. On the contrary, some of this excitation will be canceled by inhibition from neighboring cells. Consider the effect of cell B, whose stimulation comes from the lighter ring. That cell is intensely excited. One result of this excitation is that it excites a third cell, C, whose effect is inhibitory and exerted sideways (in short, a lateral inhibitor). The effect of this lateral cell C is to block the excitation that A sends upward.

Lateral inhibition is the basis of brightness contrast. Let's go back to the three cells in Figure 5.14. The more intensely cell B is stimulated, the more it will excite the lateral inhibitor, cell C. This explains why a gray patch on a black background looks brighter than the same gray patch surrounded by white. The black background does not stimulate cell B; as a result, the lateral inhibitor C is not active. But a white background does stimulate cell B, which excites cell C, which in its turn diminishes the excitation cell A sends upward to the brain to inform it of the apparent brightness of the gray patch. The upshot of all this is contrast: The brain gets a visual message that is an exaggeration; what is dark seems darker, what is light seems lighter.

COLOR

Despite their many differences, the sensory systems of hearing and of vision have some things in common. In both, the relevant stimulus energy is in wave form. And in both, wavelength is related to a qualitative psychological dimension—in one case pitch, in the other color. Much of the research in both domains has revolved around the question of how these two sensory qualities are coded. We will here consider only one of these domains, that of color.

CLASSIFYING THE COLOR SENSATIONS

A person with normal color vision can distinguish over seven million different color shades. What are the processes that allow him to make these distinctions? One step in answering this question is to find a classification system that will allow us to describe any one of these millions of colors by reference to a few simple dimensions. In this task we concentrate on what we see and experience, on psychology rather than physics. What we want to classify is our color sensations rather than the physical stimuli that produce them. In doing so, we cannot help but discover something about the way our mind—that is, our nervous system—functions. Whatever order we may find in the classification of our sensations is at least partially imposed by the way in which our nervous system organizes the physical stimuli that impinge upon it.

The dimensions of color Imagine seven million or so colored paper patches, one for each of the colors we can discriminate. We can classify them according to three perceived dimensions: hue, brightness, and saturation.

Hue is a term whose meaning is close to that of the word "color" as used in everyday life. It is a property of what are called the **chromatic colors** (for example, red and blue) but not of the **achromatic colors** (that is, black, white, and all of the totally neutral grays in between). Hue varies with wavelength (Figure

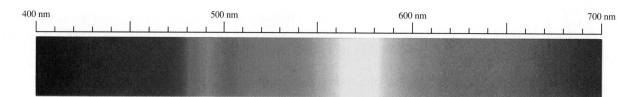

400 nm   500 nm   600 nm   700 nm

5.15 The visible spectrum and the four unique hues *The visible spectrum consists of light waves from about 360 to 700 nanometers (1 nm = one-millionth of a millimeter). White light contains all of these wavelengths. They are bent to different degrees when passed through a prism, yielding the spectrum with the hues shown in the figure. Three of the four unique hues correspond to part of the spectrum: unique blue at about 465 nm, unique green at about 500 nm, and unique yellow at about 570 nm. These values vary slightly from person to person. The fourth, unique red—that is, a red that has no apparent tinge of either yellow or blue—is called extraspectral because it is not represented by a single wavelength on the spectrum. It can only be produced by a mixture of wavelengths. (From Ohanian, 1993)*

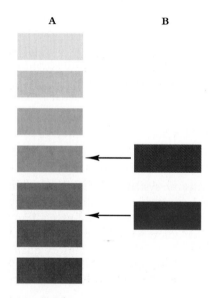

A   B

5.16 Brightness *Colors can be arranged according to their brightness. (A) This dimension is most readily recognized when we look at a series of grays, which are totally hueless and vary in brightness only. (B) But chromatic colors can also be classified according to their brightness. The arrows indicate the brightness of the blue and dark green shown here in relation to the series of grays.*

5.15). Thus, **unique blue** (a blue that is judged to have no trace of red or green in it) occurs on the spectrum at about 465 nanometers, **unique green** (which has no blue or yellow) at about 500 nanometers, and **unique yellow** (which has no green or red) at about 570 nanometers.

Brightness varies among both the chromatic and achromatic colors. Thus, ultramarine is darker than light blue and charcoal gray is darker than light gray (Figure 5.16). But the brightness dimension stands out most clearly if we consider achromatic colors alone. These differ in brightness only, while the chromatic colors may differ in hue (as we have seen) and in saturation (which we will discuss next). Note that white and black represent the top and bottom of the brightness dimension. Thus, white is hueless and maximally bright; black is hueless and minimally bright.

Saturation is the "purity" of a color, the extent to which it is chromatic rather than achromatic. The more gray (or black or white) that is mixed with a color, the less saturation it has. Consider the various blue patches in Figure 5.17. All have the same hue (blue). All share the brightness of a particular, achromatic gray (which is also the same gray with which the blue was mixed to produce the less saturated blue patches, *A, B, C,* and *D*). The patches only differ in one respect: the proportion of blue as opposed to that of gray. The more gray there is, the less the saturation. When the color is entirely gray, saturation is zero. This holds for all colors. Thus red and pink differ largely in saturation, so that pink appears like a "washed out" red.

The color circle and the color solid Some hues appear to be very similar to others. Suppose we only consider the color patches that look most chromatic—that is, those whose saturation is maximal. If we arrange these on the basis of perceptual

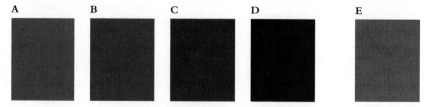

A   B   C   D   E

5.17 Saturation *The four patches A–D are identical in both hue and brightness. They only differ in saturation, which is greatest for A and decreases from A to D. The gray patch, E, on the far right matches all the other patches in brightness; it was mixed with the blue patch, A, in varying proportions to produce patches B, C, and D.*

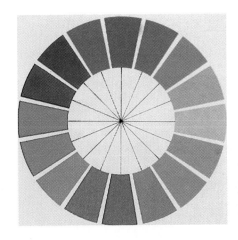

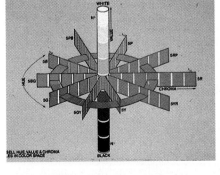

5.19 The three dimensions of color
Brightness is represented by the central axis, going from darkest (black) to brightest (white). Hue is represented by angular position relative to the color circle. Saturation is the distance from the central vertical axis: The farther the color is from this axis, the more saturated it is. The maximal saturation that is possible varies from hue to hue; hence, the different extensions from the central axis. (Munsell Color, courtesy of Macbeth, a division of Kollmorgen Corporation)

5.18 The color circle *The relationship between maximally saturated hues can be expressed by arranging them in a circle according to their perceptual similarity. Note that in this version of the color circle, the spacing of the hues depends upon their perceptual properties rather than the wavelengths that give rise to them. In particular, the four unique hues are equally spaced, each 90 degrees from the next. (Hurvich, 1981)*

similarity, the result is a circular series, the **color circle,** such that red is followed by orange, orange by yellow, yellow-green, green, blue-green, blue, and violet, until the circle finally returns to red (Figure 5.18).

The color circle embodies the perceptual similarities among the different hues. To complete our classificatory schema, we construct a **color solid,** which incorporates the color circle with the other two dimensions of perceived color, brightness and saturation (Figure 5.19). Each of our original seven million color patches can be fitted into a unique position in this solid (Figure 5.20). Our classificatory task is thus accomplished.

COLOR MIXTURE

With rare exceptions, the objects in the world around us do not reflect a single wavelength; rather, they reflect different ones, all of which strike the same region of the retina simultaneously. Let us consider the results of some of these mixtures.

Subtractive mixture   Before proceeding, we must recognize that the kind of mixture sensory psychologists are interested in is very different from the sort artists employ when they stir pigments together on a palette. Mixing pigments on a palette (or smearing crayons together on a piece of paper) is **subtractive mixture.** In subtractive mixture, one set of wavelengths is subtracted from another set. The easiest demonstration of this is with colored filters, such as those used in stage lighting, which allow some wavelengths to pass through them while holding others back. Take two such filters, *A* and *B*. Suppose filter *A* allows passage to all light waves between 420 and 520 nanometers but no others. The broad range of light that comes through this filter will be seen as blue. In contrast, fil-

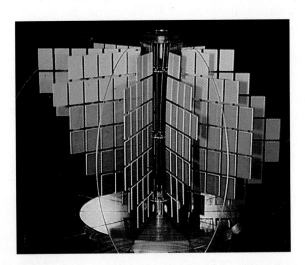

5.20 The color solid *Every color can be placed within a color solid that is based on the three dimensions of brightness, hue, and saturation. The inside of the solid is shown by taking slices that illustrate variations in hue, brightness, and saturation. (Munsell Color, courtesy of Macbeth, a division of Kollmorgen Corporation)*

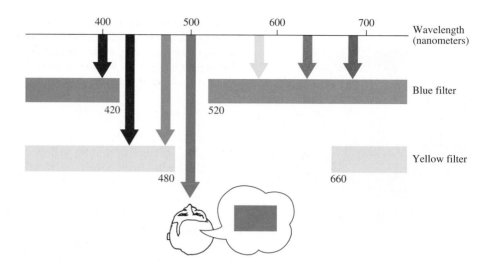

5.21 Subtractive mixture *In subtractive mixture, the light passed by two filters (or reflected by two mixed pigments) is the band of wavelengths passed by the first minus that region subtracted by the second. In the present example, the first filter passes light between 420 and 520 nanometers (a broad-band blue filter), while the second passes light between 480 and 660 nanometers (a broad-band yellow filter). The only light that can pass through both is in the region between 480 and 520 nanometers, which appears green.*

ter *B* passes light waves between 480 and 660 nanometers but excludes all others. The band of light waves that comes through this filter will be seen as yellow (Figure 5.21).

We now ask how we see light that has to pass through both filters. Filter *A* (the blue filter) blocks all light above 520 nanometers, while filter *B* (the yellow filter) blocks all light below 480 nanometers. As a result, the only light waves that can pass through this double barricade are those that can slip through the narrow gap between 480 and 520 nanometers, the only interval left unblocked by both filters. As it happens, light in this interval is seen as green. Thus, when the mixture is subtractive, mixing blue and yellow will yield green.

Thus far we have dealt with filters that let some wavelengths through while blocking others. The same account also applies to artists' pigments. Any pigment reflects only a certain band of wavelengths while absorbing the rest. Suppose we mix pigment *A* (say, blue) with pigment *B* (say, yellow). The result is a form of subtraction. What we will see is the wavelengths reflected by the blue pigment (420 to 520 nanometers) minus the wavelengths absorbed by the yellow pigment (everything below 480 nanometers). The effect is exactly the same as if we had superimposed a blue filter over a yellow one. All that is reflected is light between 480 and 520 nanometers, which is seen as green.

Additive mixture In subtractive mixture, one set of wavelengths is removed from another set. This occurs before the light ever hits the eye. In another kind of mixture, the procedure is the very opposite. This is **additive mixture,** which occurs when different bands of wavelengths stimulate the same retinal region simultaneously. Here the mixture occurs in the eye itself. Such additive mixtures can be produced in the laboratory by using filtered light from two or more dif-

Color mixture *The effect of (A) passing light through several filters (subtractive mixture) and (B) throwing different filtered lights upon the same spot (additive mixture). (Photographs by Fritz Goro/Life Magazine, © Time Warner, Inc.)*

A

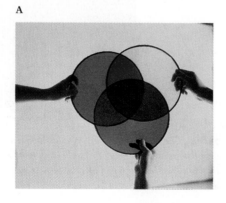

B

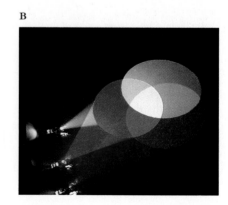

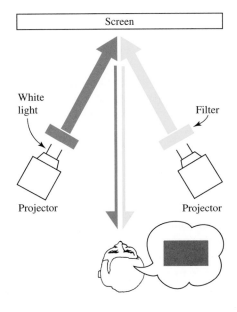

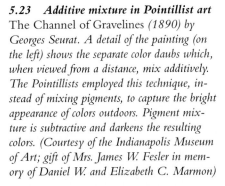

5.22 Additive mixture *In additive mixture, the light passed by two filters (or reflected by two pigments) impinges upon the same region of the retina at the same time. The figure shows two projectors throwing blue and yellow filtered light upon the same portion of the screen from which it is reflected upon the same region of the retina. In contrast to what happens in subtractive mixture, the result of adding these two colors is gray.*

ferent projectors that are all focused on the same spot. In this procedure, the light from each source remains unmixed until it reaches the retina; the mixture occurs after this point and is produced by processes within the nervous system (Figure 5.22).

In real life, additive mixture has many uses. One is color television, in which the additive mixture is accomplished by three different sets of photosensitive substances. Another example is provided by the Pointillist painter Georges Seurat. His works are composed of dots of different colors that are too close together to be seen separately, especially when the picture is viewed from a distance (Figure 5.23). The result is that, while the colors remain separate on the canvas, they blend together in the viewer's eye.

COMPLEMENTARY HUES

An important fact about additive color mixture is that every hue has a **complementary**, another hue that, if mixed with the first in appropriate proportions, will produce the color gray. An easy way to find complementaries is by reference to the color circle. Any hue on the circumference will yield gray if mixed (additively) with the hue on the opposite side of the color circle (see Figure 5.24). Of particular interest are the complementary pairs that involve the four unique colors, red, yellow, green, and blue. Blue and yellow are complementaries that produce gray upon additive mixture; the same holds for red and green. Hues that are not complementary produce mixtures that preserve the hue of their components. Thus, the mixture of red and yellow leads to orange

5.23 Additive mixture in Pointillist art The Channel of Gravelines *(1890) by Georges Seurat. A detail of the painting (on the left) shows the separate color daubs which, when viewed from a distance, mix additively. The Pointillists employed this technique, instead of mixing pigments, to capture the bright appearance of colors outdoors. Pigment mixture is subtractive and darkens the resulting colors. (Courtesy of the Indianapolis Museum of Art; gift of Mrs. James W. Fesler in memory of Daniel W. and Elizabeth C. Marmon)*

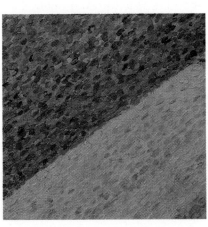

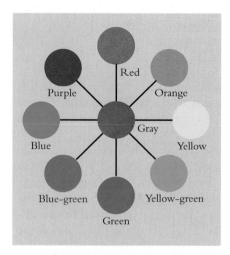

5.24 Complementary hues *Any hue will yield gray if additively mixed (in the correct proportion) with a hue on the opposite side of the color circle. Such hue pairs are complementaries. Some complementary hues are shown here linked by a line across the circle's center. Of particular importance are the two complementary pairs that contain the four unique hues: red-green and blue-yellow.*

(which still looks like a yellowish red), while that of blue and red yields a violet (which looks like a reddish blue; see Figure 5.24).

At the risk of repetition, note that all of this holds only for additive mixture. When blue and yellow are additively mixed in the right proportions, the observer sees gray. This is in contrast to what happens when the mixture is subtractive, as in drawing a blue crayon over a yellow patch. Now the result is green. The same holds for red and green. Additive mixture of the two yields gray; subtractive mixture produces a blackish brown.

COLOR ANTAGONISTS

The color-mixture effects we have just described suggest that color complementaries, such as blue and yellow on the one hand, and red and green on the other, are mutually opposed "antagonists" that cancel each other's hue. Some further phenomena lead to a similar conclusion.

One such phenomenon is the chromatic counterpart of brightness contrast. In general, any region in the visual field tends to induce its complementary color in adjoining areas. The result is *simultaneous color contrast.* For example, a gray patch will tend to look bluish if surrounded by yellow, yellowish if surrounded by blue, and so on (Figure 5.25).

In simultaneous contrast, the complementary relation involves two adjoining regions in space. In a related phenomenon, the contrast is with an immediately preceding stimulus; it is a contrast in time rather than in space. Suppose we stare at a green patch for a while and then look at a white wall. We will see a reddish spot. This is a *negative afterimage* (Figure 5.26). Negative afterimages have the complementary hue of the original stimulus (which is why they are called negative). Thus, fixation on a brightly lit red bulb will make us see a dark greenish shape when we subsequently look at a white screen.

Afterimages are caused by events that occur in the retina and associated visual mechanisms. This is why, when the eye moves, the afterimage moves along with it. One reason for the effect is retinal adaptation. When we fixate a white disk on a black background, the pigments in the retinal region that correspond to the disk will be stimulated more intensely than those in surrounding areas. During subsequent exposure to a homogeneous white surface, the more deeply stimulated regions will respond less vigorously and will thus report a lesser sensory intensity. The result is a dark gray negative afterimage. But peripheral adaptation is probably not the whole story. In addition, there may be a rebound phenomenon. While the stimulus was still present, the excited regions may well have inhibited an antagonistic process. White held back black, blue inhibited yellow, and so on. When the stimulus was withdrawn, the inhibited processes rebounded, like a coiled spring that is suddenly released.

5.25 Color contrast *The gray patches on the blue and yellow backgrounds are physically identical. But they don't look that way. To begin with, there is a difference in perceived brightness: The patch on the blue looks brighter than the one on the yellow, a result of brightness contrast. There is also a difference in perceived hue, for the patch on the blue looks somewhat yellowish, while that on the yellow looks bluish. This is color contrast, a demonstration that hues tend to induce their antagonists in neighboring areas.*

5.26 Negative afterimage *Stare at the center of the figure for a minute or two, and then look at a white piece of paper. Blink once or twice; the negative afterimage will appear within a few seconds, showing the rose in its correct colors.*

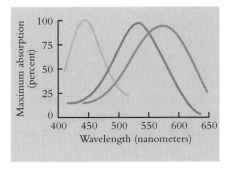

5.27 Sensitivity curves of three different cones in the primate retina *The retinas of humans and monkeys contain three different kinds of cones, each with its own photopigment that differs in its sensitivity to different regions of the spectrum. One absorbs more of the shorter wavelengths (and is thus more sensitive to light in this spectral region), a second more of the middle wavelengths, a third more of the longer ones. The resulting sensitivity curves are shown here. (After MacNichol, 1964)*

THE PHYSIOLOGICAL BASIS OF COLOR VISION

What is the physiological basis of color vision? We will consider this issue by subdividing it into two questions: First, how are wavelengths transduced into receptor activity? Second, how is the receptor output coded so that it yields the psychological attributes of color, such as the sensory experience of unique blue?

COLOR RECEPTORS

The raw material with which the visual system must begin is light of various intensities. Since we can discriminate among different wavelengths, there must be different receptors (that is, different types of cones) that are somehow differentially attuned to this physical dimension.

It turns out that normal human color vision depends on three different kinds of cone elements (which is why our color vision is often called trichromatic). While each of these cone types responds to a broad range of wavelengths in the visible spectrum, their sensitivity curves differ in that one cone type is most sensitive to wavelengths in the short-wave region of the spectrum, the second to wavelengths in the middle range, and the third to the longer wavelengths (Bowmaker and Dartnall, 1980; MacNichol, 1986; see Figure 5.27).

The critical fact about all three cone elements is that their sensitivities overlap extensively so that most of the wavelengths of the visible spectrum stimulate each of the three receptor elements. This being so, how can we manage to discriminate different wavelengths? We can, because each receptor element responds in differing degrees depending upon the wavelength of the stimulus light. If the light is from the blue end of the spectrum, there will be maximum output from the cone element whose sensitivity is greatest in the short-wave region. If the light is from the orange end, it will elicit maximum activity from the cone element whose sensitivity is greatest in the long-wave region. As a result, each wavelength will produce a different ratio of outputs from the three types of receptors. Assuming that the nervous system can tell which receptor type is sending which message, wavelength discrimination follows.

COLOR CODING: THE OPPONENT-PROCESS THEORY

The preceding analysis can explain how lights of different wavelengths are discriminated from each other, but can it account for the reason why these lights look the way they do? One attempt to explain the psychological properties of color is the **Young-Helmholtz theory** (named for Thomas Young and Hermann von Helmholtz who proposed it in the nineteenth century). According to this theory, each of the three receptor types gives rise to the experience of one basic color. Stimulation of the short-wave receptor produces blue, stimulation of the medium-wave receptor produces green, and stimulation of the long-wave receptor produces red. According to the trichromatic theory, all other colors are essentially mixtures of the three colors that are said to be primary—red, green, and blue.

This interpretation of the way colors appear runs into a number of problems. The Young-Helmholtz theory asserts that all colors are produced by the mixture of the three primaries—red, green, and blue. But in fact, many colors don't look like mixtures of different proportions of red, green and blue. Some do, such as purple, which looks like a mixture of red and blue. But many others do not.

The most troublesome example is yellow, which looks like a primary (that is, does not look like a mixture) but does not have primary status according to the trichromatic theory. An additional problem with this theory is that it cannot easily explain why the four unique hues form two complementary (and antagonistic) pairs: red-green and blue-yellow.

To account for phenomena of this kind we must assume some further neural mechanism that operates on outputs from the three cone types and ultimately codes them into the sensory qualities we know as color. Such a further mechanism is proposed by the **opponent-process theory** formulated by Leo Hurvich and Dorothea Jameson. This theory asserts that there are six psychologically primary color qualities—red, green, blue, yellow, black, and white—each of which has a different neural process that corresponds to it. These six processes are not independent, but instead are organized into three opponent-process pairs: red-green, blue-yellow, and black-white. The two members of each pair are antagonists. Excitation of one member automatically inhibits the other (Hurvich and Jameson, 1957).

The two hue systems   According to the opponent-process theory, the experience of hue depends upon two of the opponent-process pairs—red-green and blue-yellow. Each of these opponent-process pairs can be likened to a balance. If one arm (say, the blue process) goes down, the other arm (its opponent, yellow) necessarily goes up. The hue we actually see depends upon the position of the two balances (Figure 5.28). If the red-green balance is tipped toward red and the blue-yellow balance toward blue (excitation of red and blue with concomitant inhibition of green and yellow), the perceived hue will be violet. This follows, because the resulting hue will be a combination of red and blue, which is seen as violet. If either of the two scales is evenly balanced, it will make no contribution to the hue experience. This will occur when neither of the two antagonists is stimulated and also when both are stimulated equally and cancel each other out. If both hue systems are in balance, there will be no hue at all and the resulting color will be seen as achromatic (that is, without hue).

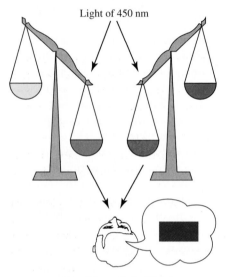

Light of 450 nm

Hue: Blue + Red = Violet

5.28   The opponent-process hue systems
The diagram shows how opponent-process theory interprets our response to light of a particular wavelength. In the example, the light is in the short-wave region of the visible spectrum, specifically, 450 nanometers. This will affect both the blue-yellow and red-green systems. It will tip the blue-yellow balance toward blue, and the red-green balance toward red. The resulting hue will be a mixture of red and blue (that is, violet).

THE PHYSIOLOGICAL BASIS OF OPPONENT PROCESSES

When the theory was first developed, the opponent processes were only an inference, based upon the perceptual phenomena of color vision. Today there is evidence that this inference comes close to the neurophysiological mark. The proof comes from single-cell recordings (in the retina or higher up), which show that some neurons behave very much as an opponent-process theory would lead one to expect.

As an example, take a study of single-cell activity in the visual pathway of the rhesus monkey, whose color vision is known to be very similar to ours. Some of its visual cells behave as though they were part of a blue-yellow system. If the retina is stimulated by blue light, these cells fire more rapidly. The opposite holds true if the same area is exposed to yellow light—the firing rate is inhibited (Figure 5.29). This is exactly what should happen if the underlying color mechanism mirrors the perceptual phenomena. Blue should have one effect and yellow the opposite. Other cells have been discovered that show a similar antagonistic pattern when stimulated by red or by green light (De Valois, 1965).

COLOR BLINDNESS

A small proportion of the total population consists of people who do not respond to color as most others do. Of these the vast majority are men, since many such conditions are inherited and sex-linked. Some form of color defect is found in 8 percent of all males as compared to only .03 percent of females.

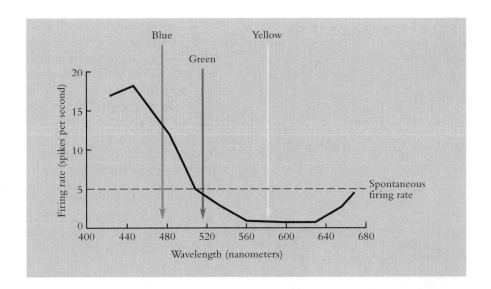

5.29 Opponent-process cells in the visual system of a monkey *The figure shows the average firing rate of blue-yellow cells to light of different wavelengths. These cells are excited by shorter wavelengths and inhibited by longer wavelengths, analogous to the cells in the human system that signal the sensation "blue." As the figure shows, shorter wavelengths lead to firing rates that are above the spontaneous rates obtained when there is no stimulus at all. Longer wavelengths have the opposite effect, depressing the cell's activity below the spontaneous firing rate. (Data from De Valois and De Valois, 1975)*

Deficiencies in color vision come in various forms: Some involve a missing visual pigment, others a defective opponent process, and many involve malfunction at both levels (Hurvich, 1981). Most common is a confusion of reds with greens; least common is total color blindness in which no hues can be distinguished at all. Color defects are rarely noticed in everyday life, for color-blind people ordinarily use color names quite appropriately. They call blood red and dollar bills green, presumably on the basis of other cues such as form and brightness. To determine whether a person has a color defect, he or she must be tested under special conditions in which such extraneous cues are eliminated (Figure 5.30).

How do people with color defects see colors? We may know that a particular person cannot distinguish between red and green, but that does not tell us how these colors look to him. He cannot tell us, for he cannot know what sensory quality is lacking. The question would have remained unanswerable had it not been for a subject who was red-green color blind in one eye and had normal color vision in the other. This subject (who happened to be one of the rare females with a color defect) was able to describe what she saw with the defective eye by using the color language of the normal one. With the color-blind eye she saw only grays, blues, and yellows. Red and green hues were altogether absent, as if one of the opponent-process pairs were missing (Graham and Hsia, 1954).

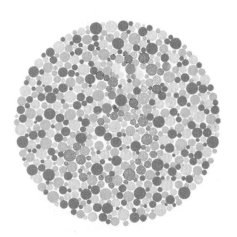

5.30 Testing for color blindness *A plate used to test for color blindness. To pick out the number in the plate, an observer has to be able to discriminate certain hues. People with normal color vision can do it and will see the number 3. People with red-green color blindness cannot do it.*

FEATURE DETECTORS

Thus far, our primary concern has been with the visual attributes of brightness and color. But there are other characteristics that are no less important for our perception of the visual world—the various attributes of ***contours*** that are crucial for the recognition of a particular form. Some contours are curved while others are straight, some are angled upwards while others are oriented downwards, and so on. These characteristics are sensed by specialized detector cells that respond to certain characteristics of the stimulus and no others. The discovery of these cells has been one of the most exciting achievements of visual physiology during the past four decades. Electrophysiologists often record from single nerve cells (see Chapter 2). By such techniques they have discovered how particular cells in a sensory system respond to simple stimuli, such as light of a given wavelength (see pp. 152–53). More recently, they have applied the same approach to the perception of contours, using stimuli that are much more complex and relational.

In some (relatively) lower animals, important aspects of form are detected at the level of the retina. In a classic study, recordings were taken from different ganglion cells of a frog's optic nerve while the animal was presented with various visual stimuli (Lettvin et al., 1959). The investigators found that certain ganglion cells respond only to particular and quite complex patterns of stimulation. For example, one kind of cell reacts most intensely to a small, dark object with convex edges that is moved into a particular retinal region and is then moved around within it. Moving stimuli that lack the appropriate shape have little or no effect, nor does a change in the general level of illumination. To a frog, the stimulus pattern that excites this particular cell (a "bug detector") represents its livelihood, for it is normally produced by a flying insect. This cell performs what amounts to a prewired sensory "abstraction," responding to buglike objects that move in a bug-like manner, with a concomitant disregard for all other features of the stimulus. Could a frog ask for anything more?

The frog's bug detector is an example of a *feature detector,* which selectively responds to certain characteristics of a stimulus pattern. Other detectors have been found that respond to such features as direction of movement, the orientation of lines and edges, and so on. In higher animals such as cats and monkeys (and undoubtedly humans as well) most of this analysis takes place at a level beyond the retina, primarily in the cortex.

Two physiologists, Nobel Prize winners David Hubel and Torsten Wiesel, studied the activity of single cortical cells of cats in response to various visual stimuli. They found some cells that react to lines or edges of a particular orientation. Such cells would be excited by a thin sliver of light slanted at, say, 45 degrees, but not otherwise, regardless of the line's specific retinal location (Figure 5.31). Still other cells detect even more complex features. An example is a cell that reacts to right angles (Hubel and Wiesel, 1959). Yet other cells respond to directional motion; they will fire if a stimulus moves from, say, right to left, but won't fire if it moves from left to right.

ADAPTATION OF FEATURE DETECTORS

Some evidence for the role of feature detectors in human perceptual experience comes from work on the phenomenon of adaptation. We previously encountered adaptation effects in the case of relatively simple sensory qualities such as hue. After prolonged fixation on a green patch, its apparent greenness will fade away and a neutral gray projected upon the same retinal region will look reddish (see pp. 150–51). Effects of this sort form the foundation of a theory of the opponent processes that underlie color. The same logic motivates the study of adaptation effects in more complex perceptual attributes (Anstis, 1975).

An example is the *aftereffect of visual movement.* If one looks at a waterfall for a while and then turns away to look at the riverbank, the bank and the trees upon it will seem to float upward, a dramatic effect that is readily produced in the perceptual laboratory (Figure 5.32). We might expect just this result on the assumption that the direction of perceived movement is signaled by the activity of two movement detectors that operate as opponent-process pairs. If these two detectors interact like the members of the color opponent-process pairs, then the stimulation of either one will automatically lead to the inhibition of the other. If one member of the pair has been stimulated for a long time (say, by exposure to a downward moving pattern), it will gradually adapt and will therefore fire less. As a result, the balance will swing toward the other member of the pair (that is, the upward movement detector). This changed balance will be revealed when the moving target is withdrawn and the subject looks at a stationary pattern. This (objectively stationary) pattern will now be perceived as moving upward. The effect is analogous to the red afterimage that follows prolonged fixation of a green patch. In both cases, there is adaptation of one member of an opponent-process pair.

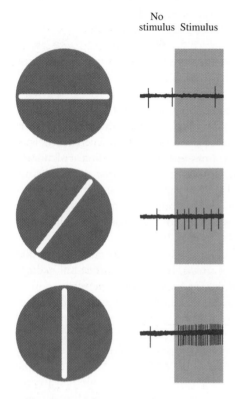

No
stimulus Stimulus

5.31 Feature detectors in the visual system of a cat *The response of a single cortical cell when stimulated by a slit of light in three different orientations. This cell, a simple unit, was evidently responsive to the vertical. A horizontal slit led to no response, a tilted slit led to a slight response, while a vertical slit led to a marked increase in firing. (After Hubel, 1963)*

FEATURE DETECTORS OF COMPLEX FORMS?

Organisms are evidently endowed with appropriate neural devices that allow them to respond to such stimulus features as directional motion, edges, and orientation. But how do they organize these features into the countless objects in the world? It may be that there are some prewired systems that can detect complex shapes of various kinds, particularly those that have a special significance in the life of a given species. Something of this sort is clearly true for many lower animals whose analyzers are apparently tuned to the detection of the relatively few objects that matter to them; the frog's bug detector is a case in point.

It is of course inconceivable that such built-in mechanisms can account for all the forms higher animals—and especially humans—perceive and recognize. For unlike frogs, humans must discriminate among a multitude of patterns, and it is hardly possible that we carry specialized detectors for all of them. Nevertheless, it may well be that even the primates—and indeed, we ourselves—possess some special cells geared to detect stimulus relationships that are more complex than color, edges, and directional movement. Thus certain cells in a monkey's cortex have been shown to respond to pictures of a monkey's face, but not at all to nonface stimuli (Desimone et al., 1984). While there is no evidence that humans have analogous face detectors, there is good reason to believe that the cortical systems that are responsible for recognizing faces are not the same as those that handle the perception of other visual forms. For as we saw in Chapter 2, certain cortical lesions may lead to a visual agnosia for faces (that is, to prosopagnosia) without affecting the perception of most other non-facelike objects (Farah, 1990). And as we'll see, there is evidence that infants prefer to look at shapes that resemble human faces rather than those that don't (see Chapter 13).

Perhaps we do possess some cells that do for us what the bug detector does for the frog. But there is little doubt that the vast majority of the forms we recognize are assemblages of lower-level features glued together by experience.

TAKING STOCK

We have looked at the way in which the different sensory systems respond to external stimuli, how they transduce the proximal stimulus and convert it into a neural impulse, how they code the incoming message into the various dimensions of our sensory experience, and how activity in any part of a sensory system interacts with the activity of other parts. All of this has led us to some understanding of how we come to see bright yellow-greens and hear high-pitched noises. But it has not yet addressed the question with which we started. How do we come to know about the objects and events outside—not just bright yellow-greens but grassy meadows, not just high-pitched noises but singing birds? That the sensory systems contribute the raw materials for such knowledge is clear enough. But how do we get from the sensory raw materials to a knowledge of the world outside? This question is traditionally dealt with under the heading of perception, the topic to which we turn next.

QUESTIONS FOR CRITICAL THINKING

1. Could any theory of knowledge be completely empiricist?

2. What might be the adaptive value of absolute thresholds?

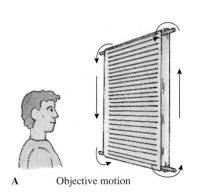

A   Objective motion

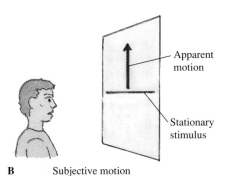

— Apparent motion

— Stationary stimulus

B   Subjective motion

5.32 Aftereffect of movement *(A) The subject first looks at a band of downward moving lines for a minute or two. (B) He then looks at a stationary horizontal line. This line will now appear to be moving upwards. This effect is probably produced by the adaptation of a movement detector that signals downward motion.*

3. How can an evolutionary view help make sense of the sensory capabilities of different species?

4. Why does snow under a tree often look bluish on a sunny day?

5. What visual phenomena suggest that vision is not a passive sense as the empiricists believed?

SUMMARY

1. The study of sensory processes grew out of questions about the origin of human knowledge. John Locke and other *empiricists* argued that all knowledge comes through stimuli that excite the senses. We can distinguish two kinds of stimuli: the *distal stimulus,* an object or event in the world outside, and the *proximal stimulus,* the pattern of physical stimulus energies that impinges on a given sensory surface. The only way to get information about distal stimuli outside is through the proximal stimuli these give rise to. This leads to theoretical problems, for we perceive many qualities—depth, constant size and shape—that are not given in the proximal stimulus. Empiricists try to overcome such difficulties by asserting that much of perception is built up through learning by *association.* This view has been challenged by *nativists,* such as Immanuel Kant, who believe that the sensory input is organized according to a number of built-in *categories.*

2. The path to sensory experience or *sensation* begins with a proximal stimulus. This is *transduced* into a nervous impulse by specialized receptors, is usually further modified by other parts of the nervous system, and finally leads to a sensation. One branch of sensory psychology is psychophysics, which tries to relate the characteristics of the physical stimulus to both the quality and intensity of the sensory experience.

3. The founder of psychophysics, Gustav Fechner, studied sensory intensity by determining the ability of subjects to discriminate between stimulus intensities. Important measures of this ability are the *absolute threshold* and the *difference threshold.* The difference threshold is the change in the intensity of a given stimulus that is just large enough to be detected, producing a *just noticeable difference,* or *jnd.* According to *Weber's law,* the jnd is a constant ratio of the standard stimulus.

4. A way of disentangling sensory sensitivity and *response bias* is provided by *signal-detection theory.* In a typical *detection experiment,* the stimulus is presented on half of the trials and absent on the other half. In this procedure, there can be two kinds of errors: *misses* (saying a stimulus is absent when it is present) and *false alarms* (saying it is present when it is absent). Their relative proportion is partially determined by a *payoff matrix.*

5. Different sense modalities have different functions and mechanisms. One group of senses provides information about the body's own movements and location. Skeletal motion is sensed through *kinesthesis,* bodily orientation by the *vestibular organs* located in the *inner ears.*

6. The various *skin senses* inform the organism of what is directly adjacent to its own body. There are at least four different skin sensations: *pressure, warmth, cold,* and *pain.*

7. The sense of *taste* acts as a gatekeeper to the digestive system. Its receptors are *taste buds,* whose stimulation generates the four basic taste qualities of *sour, sweet, salty,* and *bitter.*

8. Smell or *olfaction* is both an internal sense that provides information about substances in the mouth and (with the sense of taste) gives rise to the experience of flavor and a distance sense that gives information about objects outside of the body. In humans, olfaction is a relatively minor distance sense, but in many animals it is a vital guide to food, mates, and danger. In many species, it permits a primitive form of communication based on *pheromones.*

9. The sense of hearing or *audition* informs us of pressure changes that occur at a distance. Its stimulus is a disturbance of the air that is propagated in the form of *sound waves.* These can vary in *amplitude* and *frequency.*

10.   A number of accessory structures help to conduct and amplify sound waves so that they can affect the auditory receptors. Sound waves set up vibrations in the *eardrum* that are then transmitted by the *ossicles* to the *oval window,* whose movements create waves in the *cochlea* of the inner ear. Within the cochlea is the *basilar membrane,* which contains the auditory receptors that are stimulated by the membrane's deformation. According to the *place theory,* the sensory experience of pitch is based on the place of the membrane that is stimulated, each place being responsive to a particular wave frequency and generating a particular pitch sensation. But since very low frequency waves deform the whole membrane just about equally, modern theorists believe that both the place of deformation and firing frequency of the auditory nerve are important. Higher frequencies depend upon the place stimulated on the basilar membrane, while lower frequencies depend upon neural firing frequency.

11.   Vision is our primary distance sense. Its stimulus is light, which can vary in *intensity* and *wavelength.* Many of the structures of the eye, such as the *lens* and the *iris,* serve mainly as accessory devices to fashion a proper proximal stimulus, the *retinal image.* Once on the retina, the light stimulus is transduced into a neural impulse by the visual receptors, the *rods* and *cones. Acuity* is greatest in the *fovea* where the density of the receptors (here, cones) is greatest.

12.   According to the *duplex theory of vision,* rods and cones differ in function. The rods operate at low light intensities and lead to colorless sensations. The cones function at much higher illumination levels and are responsible for sensations of color.

13.   The first stage in the transformation of light into a neural impulse is a photochemical process that involves the breakdown of various *visual pigments* that are later resynthesized. One such pigment is *rhodopsin,* the photochemically sensitive substance contained by the rods.

14.   The various components of the visual system do not operate in isolation but interact constantly. One form of interaction occurs over time, as in various forms of *adaptation.*

15.   Interaction also occurs in space, between neighboring regions on the retina. An example is *brightness contrast.* This tends to enhance the distinction between an object and its background. The physiological mechanism that underlies these effects is *lateral inhibition.*

16.   Visual sensations have a qualitative character—they vary in color. Color sensations can be ordered by reference to three dimensions: *hue, brightness,* and *saturation.* Colors can be mixed *subtractively* (as in mixing pigments) or *additively* (as in simultaneously stimulating the same region of the retina with two or more stimuli). The results of additive-mixture studies show that every hue has a *complementary hue* that, when mixed with the first, yields gray. Two important examples are red and green, and blue and yellow. These two color pairs are color antagonists, a fact shown by the phenomena of the *negative afterimage* and *simultaneous color contrast.*

17.   The first question about the mechanisms that underlie color vision concerns the way in which the different light waves are transduced into a receptor discharge. There is general agreement that this is done by the joint action of three different cone types, each of which has a somewhat different sensitivity curve.

18.   A second question concerns the way the receptor output is coded to produce color quality. A leading approach is the *opponent-process theory* of Hurvich and Jameson. This assumes that there are neural systems that correspond to a pair of antagonistic sensory experiences—red-green and blue-yellow—which determine perceived hue. Further evidence for the opponent-process view comes from single-cell recordings of rhesus monkeys and some phenomena of *color blindness.*

19.   Attributes of visual *contour* are vital to the recognition of form. Many of these attributes are sensed by *feature detectors,* both in the retina and in the brain. These are cells that respond to certain relational aspects of the stimulus, such as edges and corners, as shown by single-cell recordings. The adaptation of such feature detectors may explain certain changes of perceptual experience after prolonged exposure to a certain kind of stimulus, as in the *aftereffect of visual movement.*

CHAPTER

6

PERCEPTION

In the previous chapter, we discussed some of the simpler attributes of sensory experience, such as red, A-flat, and cold. Locke and Berkeley thought that these experiences were produced by a passive registration of the proximal stimulus energies impinging upon the senses. But, as we have seen, the eye is more than a camera, the ear more than a microphone, for both sensory systems actively transform their stimulus inputs at the very start of their neurological journey, emphasizing differences and minimizing stimulation that remains unchanged. This active organization of the stimulus input is impressive enough when we consider the experience of simple sensory attributes, but it becomes even more dramatic when we turn to the fundamental problem traditionally associated with the term perception: how we come to apprehend the objects and events in the external reality around us, how we come to see, not just a bright red, but a bright red apple.

THE PROBLEM OF PERCEPTION

What must be explained in order to understand how we see the apple? Our initial reaction might be that the only problem is in grasping the perceptual meaning of the visual input, how we interpret it as an edible fruit—that grows on trees, that keeps the doctor away, that caused the expulsion from Eden, and so on. But how objects acquire perceptual meaning is by no means the only question, or even the most basic one, for the student of perception. The fundamental issue is not why a given stimulus is seen as a particular kind of object, but rather why it is seen as any object at all. Suppose we show the apple to someone who has never seen any fruit before. He will not know its function, but he will certainly see it as some round, red thing of whose tangible existence he has no doubt—in short, he will perceive it as an object.

How can he accomplish this feat? After all, the apple is a distal stimulus that (at least visually) is known to us only through the proximal stimulus it projects upon our retina, and this proximal stimulus is two-dimensional and constantly changing. It gets smaller or larger depending upon our distance from it; it stimulates different regions of the retina; it moves across the retina as we move our eyes. Before our observer can decide whether the object he's looking at is an apple (or a baseball or a human head, or whatever), he must somehow perceive the constant properties of this external object despite the continual variations in the proximal stimulus. To do this, he must organize the sensory world to which he is exposed into a coherent scene in which there are real objects (such as apples) and events (such as apples that fall from trees). To achieve this organization, he has to answer three important perceptual questions about what he sees (or hears and feels) in the world outside: Where is it? Where is it going? (And most important) What is it?

We will begin our discussion by turning to the first two questions, which concern the perception of depth and movement.

The problem of perception How do we come to perceive the world as it is—to see the flags as smaller than the boat, to see the wall extending continuously behind the people that block some portion of it from view, and so on? (Claude Monet, Terrace at Sainte-Adresse, 1867; courtesy of The Metropolitan Museum of Art, purchased with special contributions and purchase funds given or bequeathed by friends of the Museum, 1967)

THE PERCEPTION OF DEPTH: WHERE IS IT?

FOCUS QUESTIONS

■ What are the four major determinants of depth perception?

■ What evidence suggests that depth perception might be innate?

Quite apart from the question of what an object is (which we'll take up later), we have to know where it is located. The object may be a potential mate or a saber-toothed tiger, but we can hardly take appropriate action unless we can also locate the object in the external world.

Much of the work on the problem of visual localization has concentrated on the perception of depth, a topic that has occupied philosophers and scientists for over three hundred years. They have asked: How can we possibly see the world in three dimensions when only two of these dimensions are given in the image that falls upon the eye? This question has led to a search for *depth cues,* features of the stimulus situation that indicate how far the object is from the observer or from other objects in the world.

6.1 Retinal disparity Two points, A and B, at different distances from the observer, present somewhat different retinal images. The distance between the images on one eye, a_1b_1, is different (disparate) from the distance between them on the other, a_2b_2. This disparity is a powerful cue for depth. (After Hochberg, 1978a)

BINOCULAR CUES

A very important cue for depth comes from the fact that we have two eyes. These look out on the world from two different positions. As a result, they obtain a somewhat different view of any solid object they converge on. This *binocular disparity* inevitably follows from the geometry of the physical situation. The disparity becomes less and less pronounced the farther the object is from the observer. Beyond thirty feet the two eyes receive virtually the same image (Figure 6.1).

6.2   Linear perspective as a cue for depth
(Photograph by Roberta Intrater)

Binocular disparity alone can induce perceived depth. If we draw or photograph the two different views received by each eye while looking at a nearby object and then separately present each of these views to the appropriate eye, we can obtain a striking impression of depth.

MONOCULAR CUES

Binocular disparity is a very powerful (and probably innate) determinant of perceived depth. Yet we can perceive depth even with one eye closed. Even more important, many people who have been blind in one eye from birth see the world in three dimensions. Clearly then, there are other cues for depth perception that come from the image obtained with one eye alone—these are the ***monocular depth cues.***

Many monocular depth cues have been exploited for centuries by artists and are therefore called ***pictorial cues.*** Examples include ***linear perspective, interposition,*** and ***relative size*** (Figures 6.2, 6.3, and 6.4). In each case, the eye exploits an optical consequence of the projection of a three-dimensional world upon a flat surface. Objects that are farther away are also inevitably blocked from view

6.3   Interposition *When one figure interrupts the contour of another figure, it provides a monocular cue for depth. This is interposition. Because of interposition, the red rectangle in the figure is perceived to be in front of the blue one.*

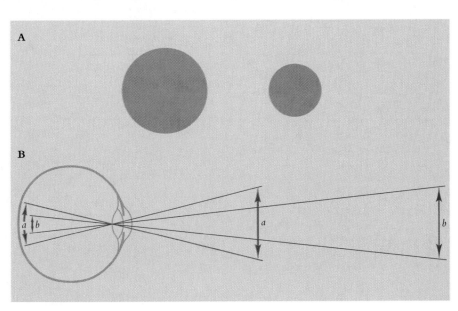

6.4   Relative size *(A) All other things being equal, the larger of two otherwise identical figures will seem to be closer than the smaller one. This is a consequence of the simple geometry of vision illustrated in (B). Two equally large objects, a and b, that are at different distances from the observer, will project retinal images of different size.*

6.5   Texture gradients as cues for depth
Uniformly textured surfaces produce texture gradients that provide information about depth: As the surface recedes, the texture density increases. Such gradients may be produced by sunflowers (A), or members of a gannet colony (B). (Photographs by Geoff Dore/© Tony Stone Worldwide and G. R. Roberts)

by any other opaque object that obstructs their optical path to the eye (interposition). Far-off objects necessarily produce a smaller retinal image than objects of the same size that are nearby (linear perspective and relative size).

An important set of pictorial cues is provided by ***texture gradients,*** whose role was emphasized by James J. Gibson (1904–1979), a very influential theorist in the psychology of perception. Such gradients are ultimately produced by perspective. Consider what meets the eye when we look at cobblestones on a road or clumps of grass in a meadow. Gibson pointed out that the retinal projection of such objects must necessarily show a continuous change, or texture gradient, that depends upon the spatial layout of the relevant surfaces (Figure 6.5). Such texture gradients are powerful determinants of perceived depth. Discontinuities in texture gradients provide information about further spatial relationships between the various textured surfaces. Thus, the change of texture density in Figure 6.6A produces the impression of an upward tilt, while that in Figure 6.6B yields perception of a sharp drop, a "visual cliff" (Gibson, 1950, 1966).

James J. Gibson   *(Courtesy of E. J. Gibson)*

6.6   The effect of changes in texture gradients   *Such changes provide important information about spatial arrangements in the world. Examples are (A) an upward tilt at a corner; and (B) a sudden drop. (After Gibson, 1950)*

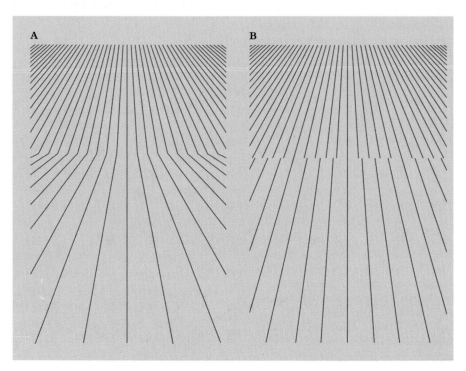

6.7 *Motion parallax* *When an observer moves relative to a stationary environment, the objects in that environment will be displaced (and will therefore seem to move) relative to that observer. (The rate of relative displacement is indicated by the thickness of the mauve arrows. The thicker these arrows, the more quickly the objects seem to move. The observer's movement is indicated by a blue arrow.) (After Coren and Ward, 1989)*

THE PERCEPTION OF DEPTH THROUGH MOTION

Thus far we have encountered situations in which both the observer and the scene observed are stationary. But in real life we are constantly moving through the world we perceive. This motion provides a vital source of visual information about the spatial arrangement of the objects around us, a pattern of cues that once again follows from the optical geometry of the situation.

As we move our heads or bodies from right to left, the images projected by the objects outside will necessarily move across the retina. This motion of the retinal images is an enormously effective depth cue, called **motion parallax.** As we move through space, nearby objects appear to move very quickly in a direction opposite to our own; as an example, consider the trees racing backward as one looks out of a speeding train. Objects farther away also seem to move in the opposite direction, but at a lesser velocity (Helmholtz, 1909; see Figure 6.7).

INNATE FACTORS IN DEPTH PERCEPTION

In many organisms, important features of the perception of space are apparently built into the nervous machinery. An example is the localization of sounds in space. One investigator studied this phenomenon in a ten-minute-old baby. The newborn consistently turned his eyes in the direction of a clicking sound, thus demonstrating that some spatial coordination between eye and ear exists prior to learning (Wertheimer, 1961).

There is evidence that some aspects of visual depth perception are also innately given (or come in at such an early age that if they are learned, they must be learned very quickly). The facets of depth that apparently come in first are those based on perceived movement, such as motion parallax. Another example is the response to **looming,** a rapid magnification of a form in the visual field that generally signals an impending impact. To study this looming effect experimentally, several investigators have simulated the visual consequence of rapid approach by various means, for example by a rapidly expanding shadow cast on a screen. When exposed to these expanding patterns, crabs flatten out, frogs jump away, and infant monkeys leap to the rear of their cages. Human infants as young as two or three weeks of age blink their eyes as if they sense a coming collision, stiffen, and cry (Schiff, 1965; Ball and Tronick, 1971; Yonas, 1981).

THE PERCEPTION OF MOVEMENT: WHAT IS IT DOING?

FOCUS QUESTION

- What two phenomena demonstrate that the perception of movement can occur without an object actually moving?

To see a large, unfriendly Doberman in front of you is one thing; to see him bare his teeth and rush directly at you is quite another. We want to know what an object is and where it is located, but we also want to know what it is doing. Put another way, we want to perceive events as well as objects. The basic ingredient of the perception of events is the perception of movement.

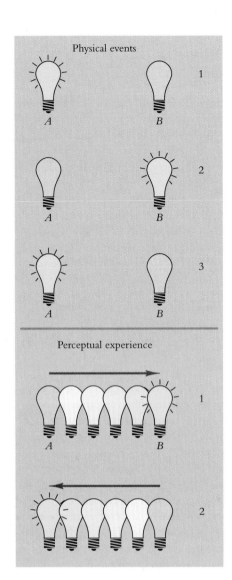

Physical events

Perceptual experience

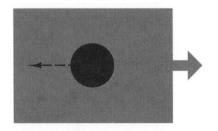

6.9 *Induced movement* *Subjects in an otherwise dark room see a luminous dot surrounded by a luminous frame. When the frame is moved to the right, subjects perceive the dot moving to the left, even though it is objectively stationary. (Duncker, 1929)*

6.8 *Stroboscopic movement* *The sequence of optical events that produces stroboscopic movement. Light A flashes at time 1, followed by light B at time 2, then back to light A at time 3. If the time intervals are appropriately chosen, the perceptual experience will be of a light moving from left to right and back.*

ILLUSIONS OF MOVEMENT

What leads to the perception of movement? One might guess that one sees things move because they produce an image that moves across the retina. But this answer is too simple. For in fact we sometimes perceive movement even when none occurs on the retina.

STROBOSCOPIC MOVEMENT

Suppose we briefly turn on a light in one location of the visual field, then turn it off, and after an appropriate interval (somewhere between 30 and 200 milliseconds) turn on a second light in a different location. The result is *apparent movement* (sometimes called *stroboscopic movement* or the *phi phenomenon*). The light is seen to travel from one point to another, even though there was no stimulation—let alone movement—in the intervening region (Figure 6.8). This phenomenon is perceptually overwhelming; given the right intervals, it is indistinguishable from real movement. It is an effect that has numerous technological applications, ranging from animated neon signs to motion pictures (Wertheimer, 1912). These results suggest that one stimulus for motion is relative displacement over time. Something is here at one moment and there at the next. If the time intervals are right, the nervous system interprets this as evidence that this something has moved.

INDUCED MOVEMENT

How does the perceptual system react when one of two objects is moving while the other is stationary? Consider a ball rolling on a billiard table. We see the ball as moving and the table at rest. But why not the other way around? To be sure, the ball is being displaced relative to the table edge, but so is the table edge displaced relative to the ball. One might guess that the reason is learning. Perhaps experience has taught us that balls generally move around while tables stay put. But the evidence indicates that what matters is a more general perceptual relationship between the two stimuli. The object that encloses the other tends to act as a frame, which is seen as stationary. Thus, the table serves as a frame against which the ball is seen to move.

In the billiard table example, perception and physical reality coincide, for the frame provided by the table is truly stationary. What happens when the objective situation is reversed? In one study subjects were shown a luminous rectangular frame in an otherwise dark room. Inside the frame was a luminous dot. In actual fact, the rectangle moved to the right while the dot stayed in place. But the subjects saw something else. They perceived the dot as moving to the left, in the opposite direction of the frame's motion. The physical movement of the frame induced the perceived movement of the enclosed figure (Figure 6.9).

The *induced movement* effect is familiar from everyday life as well. The moon seems to drift through the clouds, the base of a bridge to float against the river's current. In the second case, there may also be *induced motion of the self.* If the subject stands on the bridge that she perceives as moving, she perceives herself moving along with it. The same effect occurs when sitting in a train that's standing in a station. If a train on the adjacent track pulls out, we feel ourselves moving though in fact we—and the train we're in—are stationary.

FORM PERCEPTION: WHAT IS IT?

FOCUS QUESTIONS

- What is our main criterion for identifying an object?

- What is Gestalt psychology, and how do transposition of form and pattern support the Gestalt view of perception?

- What is a visual search task, and how does it help us determine what the primitive visual features are?

- What is perceptual segregation? How do figure-ground reversals and Gestalt laws of perceptual organization demonstrate visual segregation?

- Why is visual pattern recognition thought to rely on both top-down and bottom-up processing?

- What are perceptual hypotheses, and how do impossible figures demonstrate them?

We've asked how we see where an object is and know where it is going. But we have not dealt with the most important question of all: How do we perceive and recognize what an object is?

In vision, our primary means for recognizing an object is through the perception of its form. To be sure, we sometimes rely on color (a violet) and occasionally on size (a toy model of an automobile), but in the vast majority of cases, form is the major avenue for identifying what it is we see. This reliance on form begins at a very early age. In a recent study using three-year-olds, an experimenter held up an oddly shaped wooden object that was painted blue and said: "Do you see this? This is a dax" (see Figure 6.10A). The children were perfectly happy to accept this new bit of information. After all, they'd never seen a dax before, so why shouldn't they believe what they were told?

The children were then shown a series of other objects. Some of these new objects had the same shape, but were made of a different substance and varied in size, color, and texture; others had a different shape, but were made of the identical substance and were of the same size, color, and texture as the original. The children were then asked: "Can you show me a dax?" Their answers showed that even at the age of three objects are defined by their shape. Shown an object

6.10 A dax is a dax is a dax
Three-year-olds who are told that (A) is a dax, conclude that figures (B) and (C) are daxes too but that figure (D) is not. To humans, form is evidently the main criterion for identifying an object. Color, size, and texture are less relevant. (Adapted from Landau, 1994)

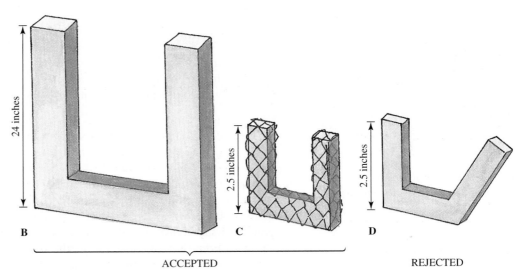

ACCEPTED   REJECTED

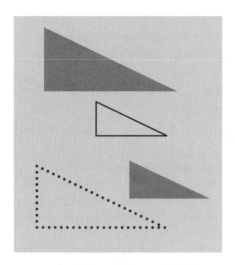

6.11 Form equivalence *The perceived forms remain the same regardless of the parts of which they are composed.*

of the same form, they unhesitatingly called it a dax, even if it was made of sponge rubber, was covered with chicken wire, or was ten times larger than the original (see Figure 6.10B and C). But an object of the same size, texture, and color as the original was rejected if its form was different (see Figure 6.10D). A dax is a dax is a dax—but only when it has the same shape (Landau, 1994).

The fact that the children recognized that a dax remains a dax, regardless of changes in color, texture, and size, illustrates one of the critical facts about form perception. Both humans and animals can often recognize a form even when many of its component parts are altered. Consider two similar triangles. It doesn't matter whether they are small, rendered as solids or as line drawings, made up of dots or dashes. The perceived form remains the same (Figure 6.11). A triangle is a triangle is a triangle, whatever the elements of which it is composed. This phenomenon is sometimes called the ***transposition of form*** or ***pattern.*** Similar effects occur in the temporal patterning of sounds: A melody remains the same even when all of its notes are changed by transposition to another key, and the same rhythm will be heard whether played on a kettledrum or a glockenspiel.

Phenomena such as these were among the chief arguments of **Gestalt psychology,** a school of psychology whose adherents believed that organization is basic to all mental activity and who bolstered their view by many appeals to form perception. In particular, they insisted that a form is not perceived by somehow summing up all its individual components. On the contrary, they argued that a form is perceptually experienced as a *Gestalt* (from the German for "form" or "entire figure"), a whole that is different from the sum of its parts. To recognize that a form is the same as one we have seen before, we must perceive certain relations among its component parts.

Most modern investigators of pattern recognition believe that the Gestalt psychologists had an important point. There is little doubt that a form is not just the sum of its parts: Three angles alone do not make a triangle, no more than a mouth, a nose, and two eyes suffice to make a face. The trouble is that it is hard to specify just what relations among the parts create the pattern. We can do it separately for each figure: For a triangle the three angles have to be properly aligned, for a face the nose has to be between the eyes, and so forth. But thus far no one has fully succeeded in formulating a general description of the relations between the parts that will do justice to all patterns. For these and similar reasons, most investigators of pattern recognition have focused less on the wholes than on the parts of which those wholes are composed. They hoped that by discovering the ways through which the proper parts are identified, the pattern can be identified as well.

We now turn to a discussion of the mechanisms by which particular patterns are recognized, whether it is in identifying a dax, the letter *W,* or a picture of an apple. We will consider some hypotheses about the processes by which the parts are transformed into patterns that we recognize as real objects and events in the world. While these hypotheses have not yet solved the transposition puzzle that Gestalt psychologists posed, they are important steps toward doing so.

THE INFORMATION-PROCESSING APPROACH

Form is evidently the major channel through which we identify objects. The question is how. Many modern psychologists who try to answer this question believe that form perception is based on several steps of ***information processing*** that transform (that is, process) the initial visual input into the cognitive end product: the perception of the objects in the world. This is generally thought to involve a series of successive stages of processing, in which each stage further transforms the outputs of the previous stage.

In part, the information-processing approach grew out of an analogy between the operations of the mind and the workings of a computer. Computers have some of the capabilities of human minds: They can acquire information, store it in memory, retrieve it, classify it, and transform it. By now the mind-as-computer has become a dominant scientific metaphor, largely replacing the metaphors of previous generations, starting with Descartes' water-powered statues as models of animal action through the more recent telephone switchboard analogies to explain the way the nervous system works. These earlier metaphors tried to explain transformations of energy: Certain energies (whether hydraulic or chemical or electrical) were converted into other energies until they were finally turned into a bodily movement. In contrast, the mind-as-computer metaphor tries to explain the transformation of symbols into other symbols.

Over the past four decades, the language of computers has also gradually crept into that of psychologists concerned with cognition; terms like *input, memory store, retrieval, subroutine,* and *coding* have become part of their everyday vocabulary. Attempts to understand such mental operations as recognizing a shape, recalling a name, or trying to solve a puzzle are often cast in the form of a flow chart. In the world of computer operators, such flow charts show the step-by-step operation of a computer program. Applied to the study of human cognitive processes, similar diagrams are meant to chart the flow of information as it is processed by the human mind (Neisser, 1967).

Much of our subsequent discussion of how forms are perceived will be organized along the lines of this information-processing approach.

THE ELEMENTS OF FORM

What's the first step in recognizing a form, whether it is a dax or an apple? Many investigators believe that the process begins with the response to certain primitive built-in features that serve as the elementary units of visual perception. In part, this belief is based on physiological findings we discussed in the previous chapter. Various cells in the brain act as feature detectors, which react to particular elements of visual form—lines or edges or a particular orientation. By now, there is good evidence that certain cortical cells signal other perceptual features. For example, some cells in the cortex are sensitive to binocular disparity (Hubel and Wiesel, 1970; Poggio and Fischer, 1978; Ferster, 1981). Other cells respond to directional movement; they fire if a line moves in one direction but won't fire if it moves in the direction that's opposite (e.g., Barlow and Hill, 1963; Vaultin and Berkeley, 1977).

Such evidence indicates that we're beginning to understand the built-in physiological mechanisms that underlie the primitive elements of visual perception. But how do we combine these building blocks so that we see not just colors, tilts, and edges, but the innumerable shapes and objects that we can perceive and recognize: circles and polygons, trees and houses, faces and hands? Many psychologists agree that this achievement comes in several stages, but their theoretical proposals vary in many specifics. What we will try to do here is to combine them in an (admittedly simplified) schematic overview.

FREE-FLOATING PRIMITIVES

How can we determine whether a given visual attribute is a primitive feature—a kind of sensory atom that serves as a building block for the perception of

Max Wertheimer *One of the most influential figures in the psychology of perception and the founder of Gestalt psychology. (Courtesy of Omikron)*

form? Single-cell recording studies may provide suggestions, but it would be much more convincing to have a psychological criterion, based on what human subjects actually perceive. Such a criterion has been provided in an influential series of studies by Anne Treisman (Treisman, 1986a, 1986b, 1988).

Treisman argues that a given attribute is a primitive visual feature if a difference in that attribute leads to an immediate discovery, so that the item that is different just "pops out." One way of demonstrating this effect is by means of a ***visual search task*** in which subjects have to indicate whether a certain target is or is not present in a briefly presented display. When the target is an *O* amidst a number of *V*s, subjects find it very quickly (see Figure 6.12) What's more, the number of *V*s in which the *O* is embedded hardly affects the search time. This indicates that the visual system doesn't have to inspect each of the figures in turn to determine whether it has or does not have the relevant properties that define an *O*; the difference between the *O*s and *V*s jumps out immediately. The same holds for differences in color, orientation, or direction of movement (Treisman and Gelade, 1980; Treisman and Souther, 1985).

Color, curvature, orientation, and some other attributes thus seem to be primitive features that are processed quite automatically. But the objects we perceive are obviously made up of more than one visual feature. A leaf on a tree will give rise to a number of different visual features: color, curvature, orientation, and—if it sways in the wind—movement. How are these different features put together? Treisman and her collaborators showed that this combination of features does not occur immediately but is accomplished in a later stage of processing. Subjects were presented with displays that contained items that combined several different features, for example a red *F* and a green *X*. The displays were flashed for about 200 milliseconds, and the subjects had to report what they saw. On a fair proportion of the trials, the subjects reported ***illusory conjunctions,*** such as having seen a green *F* or a red *X*. As Treisman sees it, these results indicate that at this early stage of processing, the various primitive features—color, shape, orientation, and so on—are free floating and exist in complete isolation from each other. It is as if each feature system had its own map with its own coordinate system, with no way of relating the different spatial maps to each other (Treisman and Schmidt, 1982).

According to Treisman, the integration of these separate feature systems is accomplished at a later stage of processing in which the several maps become coordinated and superimposed. Once this is done, there are no more illusory conjunctions, for now the system can determine what goes together with what—that there is a red *F* and a green *X* (rather than a green *F* and a red *X*), that the same leaf is at once green, curved with jagged edges, and fluttering in the breeze.

6.12 Pop-out in visual search An *O* embedded in an array of *V*s pops out immediately. Here, the visual system does not have to inspect each figure in turn to determine whether it is the target. Instead, it conducts a parallel search, inspecting all of the items simultaneously.

PERCEPTUAL SEGREGATION

The preceding discussion centered on the initial steps of form perception: deciding which primitive visual features go together. The next step is to decide what parts of the scene go together. Suppose the observer looks at the still life in Figure 6.13A. To make sense of the picture, her perceptual system must somehow group the many visual elements of the scene appropriately. For one thing, it has to determine what is focal (for example, the fruit and the bowl) and what can at least temporarily be relegated to the background (for example, the green shutters, the table, and perhaps the pitcher). But there is still more to be done. Some objects will necessarily be partially occluded by others that stand or lie in front of them. Consider the portions *A, B, C, D,* and *E* of Figure 6.13B. To determine what any given object can possibly be, we must first segregate the scene into its subcomponents, deciding whether portion *B* goes with *A*

6.13 Perceptual segregation *(A) A still life. (Photograph by Jeffrey Grosscup) (B) An overlay designating five different segments of the scene shown in (A). To determine what an object is, the perceptual system must first decide what goes with what: Does portion B go with A, with C, D, or E? Or with none of them?*

A

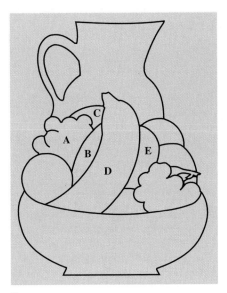

B

(half an apple combined with some grapes), with *C* (half an apple with a piece of orange), with *D* (half an apple with a banana), or finally with *E* (half an apple).

This **visual segregation** process is sometimes called **perceptual parsing,** since it performs the same function for vision that parsing performs for speech. When someone talks to us, our eardrums are exposed to a sound stream that is essentially unbroken. What hits the ears is a sequence of sounds such as:

Thestudentsaidtheteacherisafool.

The listener parses the sound pattern by grouping some sounds together with others, forming units called words:

The student said the teacher is a fool.

He may then parse further by grouping the words into larger units called phrases, as in:

The student, said the teacher, is a fool.

In some cases, he may even discover that there are alternate ways of parsing, as in:

The student said, the teacher is a fool.

The important point is that the parsing is not primarily in the stimulus. It is contributed by the listener, for the sound stream itself has no pauses between words and contains no commas. (When we don't understand a language, we don't "hear" the pauses, which is why foreigners speaking in their own language often sound as if they speak much faster than we do.) Until at least some basic parsing has been performed, the listener has no hope of comprehending what he has heard. To understand the meaning of the word *student*, he must first have segregated it from the surrounding sounds and heard it as a separate word.

What holds for words in speech, also holds for objects in the visual world: Visual segregation (or parsing) is the first step in organizing the world we see.

6.14 **Figure and ground** *The first step in seeing a form is to segregate it from its background. The part seen as figure appears to be more cohesive and sharply delineated. The part seen as ground seems more formless and to extend behind the figure.*

6.15 **Reversible figure-ground pattern** *The classic example of a reversible figure-ground pattern. It can be seen as either a pair of silhouetted faces or a white vase.*

6.16 **Figure-ground reversal in the visual arts** *The Trojan War as depicted by Salvador Dali. The scene of wild carnage conceals the image of the Trojan Horse, whose outline follows the gateway to the city. (Courtesy of Esquire)*

FIGURE AND GROUND

Visual segregation begins with the separation of the object from its setting, so that it is seen as a coherent whole that stands out against its background, as a tree stands out against the sky and the clouds. This segregation of *figure* and *ground* can easily be seen in two-dimensional pictures. In our still life, the apple is generally perceived as the figure, the tablecloth as the ground. But the same phenomenon also occurs with figures that have no particular meaning. Thus in Figure 6.14, the white splotch appears as the figure, which seems to be more cohesive and articulated than the blue region, which is normally perceived as the ground. This darker ground is seen as relatively formless and as extending behind the figure.

The differentiation between figure and ground is a perceptual achievement that is accomplished by the perceptual system. It is not in the stimulus as such. This point is made strikingly by *reversible figures* in which either of two figure-ground organizations is possible. A classic demonstration is shown in Figure 6.15, which can be seen either as a white vase on a blue background or as two blue faces in profile on a white background. This reversibility of figure-ground patterns has fascinated various artists, especially in recent times (see Figure 6.16).

According to one proposal, the figure-ground distinction corresponds to two different kinds of neural processing. One (in regions seen as figure) involves the analysis of fine detail, while the other (in regions seen as ground) involves a cruder analysis appropriate to the perception of larger areas (Julesz, 1978). To test this hypothesis, subjects were presented with brief exposures to vertical and slightly tilted lines that were flashed on either of three locations of a line drawing of the vase-profile figure (see Figure 6.17). The subjects' task was to judge the orientation of the lines. In accordance with the detail-processing hypothesis, the subjects were much more accurate when the line was projected onto the area the subjects happened to see as the figure than when it was projected onto the area they saw as the ground (Weisstein and Wong, 1986).

FORM PERCEPTION: WHAT IS IT?

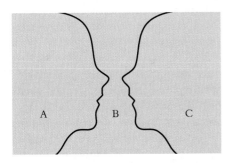

6.17 Fine detail is more readily seen in the figure than the ground *Subjects look at the vase-profiles figure as shown above and have to determine whether lines that are briefly flashed at points A, B, or C are tilted or vertical. If the vase is seen as the figure, they do much better when the stimuli are presented at B than at A or C. If the profiles are seen as the figure, they do much better when the lines are presented at A or C rather than at B. (After Weisstein and Wong, 1986)*

PERCEPTUAL GROUPING

Reversible figure-ground formations demonstrate that a single proximal pattern may give rise to different perceptual organizations. The same conclusion follows from the related phenomenon of perceptual *grouping.* Suppose we look at a collection of dots. We can perceive the pattern in various ways depending upon how we group the dots: as a set of rows, or columns, or diagonals, and so on. In each case, the figural organization is quite different even though the proximal stimulus pattern is always the same.

What determines how a pattern will be organized? Some factors that determine visual grouping were first described by Max Wertheimer (1880–1943), the founder of Gestalt psychology. Wertheimer regarded these grouping factors as the laws of *perceptual organization* (Wertheimer, 1923). A few of these are discussed below.

Proximity The closer two figures are to each other—the greater their *proximity*—the more they will tend to be grouped together perceptually. So these six lines generally will be perceived as three pairs of lines:

Proximity may operate in time just as it does in space. The obvious example is auditory rhythm: Four drum beats with a pause between the second and third will be heard as two pairs.

Similarity Other things being equal, we also tend to group figures according to their *similarity.* Thus, in the figure below, we group blue dots together with blue dots, and red dots together with red dots. As a result, we see rows rather than columns in the left panel, and columns rather than rows in the right panel.

What aspects of stimulus similarity lead to grouping? Color is clearly one. Another is orientation. When similarity of form (for example, *T*s versus *L*s) is pitted against orientation (upright *T*s versus *T*s tilted by 45 degrees), subjects generally group by orientation (Beck, 1966; see Figure 6.18). Certain simple

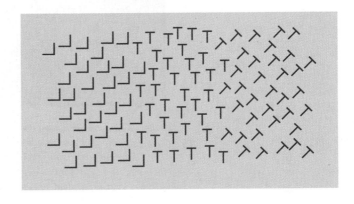

6.18 The effect of orientation and shape on perceptual grouping *The demarkation between the upright* Ts *and the tilted* Ts *is more easily seen than that between the upright* Ts *and the upright* Ls. *(From Beck, 1966)*

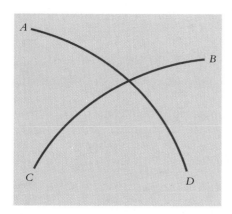

6.19   Good continuation   *The line segments in the figure will generally be grouped so that the contours continue smoothly. As a result, segment A will be grouped with D and segment C with B, rather than A with B and C with D.*

visual features such as color, brightness, and orientation are evidently more important for segmentation than more complex properties such as shape. This is because shape depends on more complex relations between the stimuli, such as the particular arrangement of the lines that defines the difference between a *T* and an *L* (Beck, 1982). This is just what we would expect if visual parsing is the first and thus most primitive step in visual organization.

Good continuation   Our visual system seems to "prefer" contours that continue smoothly along their original course. This principle of grouping is called ***good continuation*** (Figure 6.19). Good continuation is a powerful organizational factor that will often prevail even when pitted against prior experience (Figure 6.20). This principle is used by the military for camouflage (Figure 6.21A). It also helps to camouflage animals against their natural enemies. (Figure 6.21B).

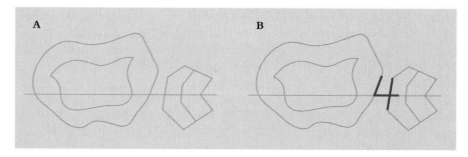

6.20   Good continuation pitted against prior experience   *In (A), virtually all subjects see two complex patterns intersected by a horizontal line. Hardly anyone sees the hidden 4 contained in that figure—and shown in (B)—despite the fact that we have encountered 4s much more often than the two complex patterns that are probably completely new. (After Köhler, 1947)*

6.21   Good continuation as the basis of camouflage   *In (A) camouflage is achieved by providing artificial contours that break up the outlines of the soldier's face and body. (Photograph by Larry Downing/Woodfin Camp & Associates) Good continuation helps to conceal the frog in (B) from predators, who tend to see the frog as continuous with its background. (Photograph © Michael Fogden, Oxford Scientific Films)*

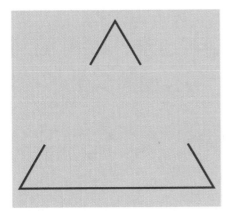

6.22 Closure *There is a tendency to complete—or close—figures that have a gap in them, as in the incomplete triangle shown here.*

Closure We tend to complete figures that have gaps in them. Figure 6.22 is seen as a triangle despite the fact that its sides are incomplete.

A closurelike phenomenon yields *subjective contours.* These are contours that are perceived, despite the fact that they don't physically exist (Figure 6.23). Some theorists interpret subjective contours as a special case of good continuation. In their view, the contour is seen to continue along its original path, and, if necessary, jumps a gap or two to achieve the continuation (Kellman and Shipley, 1991).

PATTERN RECOGNITION

We have considered the initial steps in perceiving the form of an object: First, we respond to the primitive features of the scene and parse it so that we see the object as a figure, whose parts seem to belong together and stand out against its background. The next step is to determine *what* the object is, whether it is the letter *A,* or a dax, or an apple. To accomplish this, the visual system has to take the figure that emerges from the parsing process and compare its features to those of objects in our visual memory until it finally finds a match. The end result of these various steps is called *pattern recognition.* One of the major problems of the psychology of perception is to determine how this is accomplished.

We'll begin our discussion by considering some possible ways in which the visual system might accomplish this task.

A MACHINE MODEL OF PATTERN RECOGNITION

Some thirty years ago, an important approach to pattern recognition grew out of the efforts of computer scientists to develop machines that could "read" letters and numerals. Devices of this kind would have numerous practical applications, for example, sorting mail for the postal service or organizing bank records.

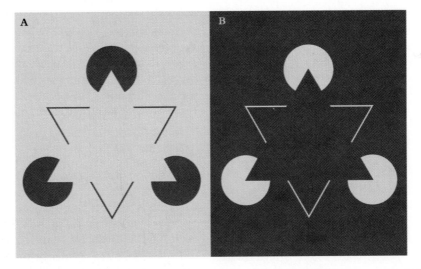

6.23 Subjective contours *Subjective contours are a special completion phenomenon in which contours are seen even where none exist. In (A) we see a tan triangle whose vertices lie on top of the three dark green circles. The three sides of this tan triangle (which looks brighter than the tan background) are clearly visible, even though they don't exist physically. In (B) we see the same effect with dark green and tan reversed. Here, there is a dark green triangle (which looks darker than the dark green background) with subjective green contours (Kanizsa, 1976)*

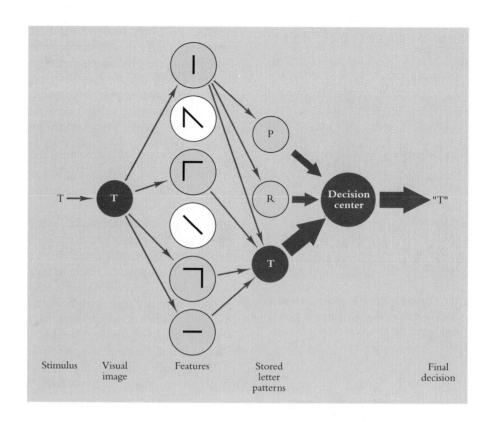

6.24 A pattern-recognition model *The physical stimulus "T" gives rise to a visual image. This is then analyzed for the presence or absence of various component features, such as vertical or horizontal lines, various corners, and so on. Each feature stimulates the stored letter patterns that contain it. In this example, one of the feature units stimulates the pattern "P," one the pattern "R," and four the pattern "T." As a result, the "T" is more actively excited than the "P" and "R," which leads to the decision that the letter is "T." (After Goldstein, 1984)*

Many attempts to design such artificial recognition systems involved a chain of processing steps that began with the analysis of visual features. This approach was partially influenced by the neurophysiological work on feature detectors in the nervous system (see Chapter 5). Under the circumstances, it seemed reasonable enough to endow systems of human (or machine) perception with a similar ability to extract elemental properties. A very influential system (or model) of this sort was one proposed by Oliver Selfridge (Selfridge, 1959). Suppose we have a machine that can scan the optical image of a letter. How can it decide that this letter is, say, a *T*? What the machine can do is start out by looking for the presence or absence of certain visual features (for example, horizontal, vertical, or diagonal bars, curves to the right or left, and so on). It can then consult a list stored in its memory in which each capital letter is entered, together with the visual features that define it. By comparing the features in the stimulus with those of the letters on the list, it can reach a decision (see Figure 6.24).

CONTEXT EFFECTS

Thus far we have discussed pattern recognition as a **bottom-up process,** which starts with primitive features and gradually builds up to larger units that are, so to speak, at the top. But there are reasons to believe that bottom-up processing is not enough. Pattern recognition often involves **top-down processes** in which the chain of events begins with the activation of higher units, which then affect units lower down. Evidence for this comes from the fact that recognition is often affected by higher-level knowledge and expectations.

One demonstration of top-down processing in perception is provided by what are called **context effects.** In some cases, the context is provided by experiences in the past (often the immediately preceding past). A good example is provided by ambiguous figures. Consider Figure 6.25A, which can be seen as either an old woman in profile or a young woman whose head is turned slightly

A

B

C

6.25 An ambiguous figure *(A) is ambiguous and is as likely to be seen as a young woman as it is an old woman. (B) and (C) are essentially unambiguous and depict the young woman and old woman respectively. If the subjects are first shown one of the unambiguous figures, they are almost sure to see the ambiguous picture in that fashion later on. (After Boring, 1930; Leeper, 1935)*

THE CAT

6.26 *The effect of context on letter recognition (After Selfridge, 1955)*

away. In one study, subjects were first shown one of two fairly unambiguous versions of the figure (Figures 6.25B and C). When later presented with the ambiguous figure (Figure 6.25A), they perceived it in line with the unambiguous version they had been shown before (Leeper, 1935).

In other cases, context effects depend on stimuli that are presented simultaneously with the stimulus in question. As an example, take the two words shown in Figure 6.26. The two middle "letters" of each word are physically identical, but they are usually seen as an *H* in *THE* and an *A* in *CAT.*

Similar context effects can make us hear speech sounds where in fact there are none. Something of this sort occurs in everyday life, for when people talk they sometimes cough or clear their throats so that the speech stream is interrupted. But even so, we usually hear and understand them and never notice that there were physical gaps in their actual utterance. In a laboratory demonstration of this phenomenon subjects listened to tape-recorded sentences in which the speech sounds were tampered with, as in the sentence:

The state governors met with their respective legi latures convening in the capital city.

In this sentence the experimenter replaced the middle *s* in the word *legislatures* with a cough-like noise. Yet virtually none of the subjects even noticed that any speech sound was missing. They somehow restored the deleted speech sound and "heard" the *s* that was provided by the total context (Warren, 1970).

Context effects demonstrate that there is some top-down processing. But this hardly means that bottom-up processing is unimportant—on the contrary. After all, if perceptual processing occurred only from the top down, we would always see what we expect and believe in—even if there were no stimulus whatever. To be sure, knowledge and expectations do help us interpret what we see and hear, but there has to be some sensory basis that informs these interpretations. Perceptual processing generally occurs in both directions—from the top down, but also from the bottom up—indicating that activation is usually *bidirectional.*

PERCEPTUAL PROBLEM SOLVING

Bidirectional models of the kind discussed above fit in with the belief that much of perception is essentially a form of problem solving in which the observer tries to discover (consciously or, more commonly, without awareness)

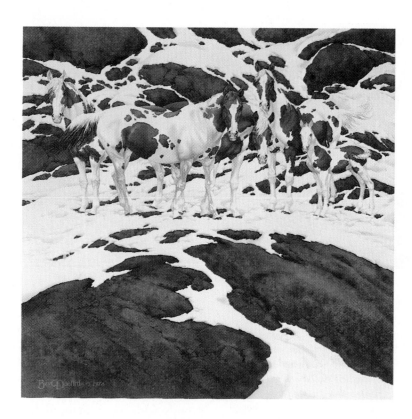

6.27 *Perceptual problem solving* *This is a picture of something. What? (By Bev Doolittle, 1979; courtesy of the Greenwich Workshop, Inc.)*

"By George, you're right! I thought there was something familiar about it." (Drawing by Chas. Addams; © 1957, 1985 The New Yorker Magazine, Inc.)

what it is that she sees. Seen in this light, the perceptual system starts out with both a stimulus and a hypothesis. The ***perceptual hypothesis*** is the perceiver's assumption about what the object out there really is. This hypothesis represents the top-down aspect of the process. It is tested as the system analyzes the stimulus (the bottom-up aspect) for some appropriate features. If these are found, the perceptual hypothesis gains plausibility and is either accepted or the stimulus is checked for further proof. If no such further confirming features are found, then a new hypothesis is considered, which is then tested by searching the stimulus for yet other features, and so on.

Occasionally, we become consciously aware that some such process operates. This sometimes happens when we are presented with a visual display that initially makes no sense. An example is Figure 6.27. At first glance most observers don't know what to make of it. But as they continue to look at the figure, they develop hypotheses about what it might be (e.g., maybe this part is the leg of some animal, maybe the animal has a spotted hide). If they are lucky, they eventually hit on the correct hypothesis (pintos on snow covered rocks). When they finally see the pintos, the top-down and bottom-up processes meet, and there is a perceptual insight, a visual "Aha!" Here the process of perceptual problem solving was quite conscious. But this is rare, for we usually see cars, trees, and people (and even pintos) without being aware that we are trying to solve any perceptual puzzles. But according to theorists who endorse the problem-solving approach to perception, much the same kind of thing occurs even then, though at much greater speed and outside of consciousness.

IMPOSSIBLE FIGURES

We've seen that the perceptual system is very clever. With a little top-down hint, it can reconstruct imperfect speech and discover hidden pintos. But even the cleverest system fails when it is confronted with a problem that is in principle insoluble. In perception such problems are posed by what are called ***impossi-***

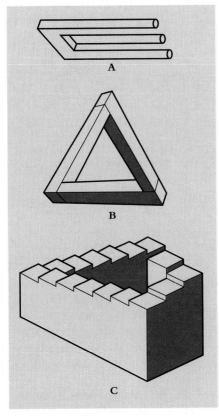

6.28 Impossible figures *(A) U-shape or three-pronged fork. (B) Impossible triangle. (C) Perpetual staircase. (Penrose and Penrose, 1958)*

ble figures in which there is no way of resolving a perceptual contradiction (Penrose and Penrose, 1958).

Take Figure 6.28A. At the left, it is a perspective drawing of two rectangular beams joined in a U-shaped form; at the right, it is a picture of three round rods. If we look at either the left or the right separately, the figure makes sense. But as our glance travels from left to right, there is a gross inconsistency, for the two halves of the figure don't add up to a whole. Consider the third horizontal line from the top. At the left, it is the bottom edge of the upper horizontal beam; at the right it becomes the top edge of the middle rod. Now the perceptual system is stumped, for there is no perceptual hypothesis that can make the figure into a coherent whole.

In other examples, the impossibility takes a bit longer to appreciate. Take Figure 6.28B, which at first glance looks like a triangular, three-dimensional object. The trouble is that the perspectives are drawn differently at the different corners. If we mentally trace a path from one corner of the object to the second, then to the third, and finally try to return to the first, we find that there is no way to do so because the corners don't mate properly. The perceptual problem posed by Figure 6.28C is even more subtle. Here the inconsistency is based on yet another trick of perspective. As the figure is drawn, we can start at any place and go around the entire stair arrangement, always climbing upwards, until we get back to the starting point.

Impossible figures underline the fact that perceptual problem solving consists of making a sensible whole out of separate parts, an integration that is often achieved over time. When we attend to any one region of an impossible figure, we are unaware that there's a problem. The difficulty comes when our attention (and our eyes) travels from one region to another, and we try to fit the two regions together. Under normal circumstances, this process of building up a mental picture of what we see out there occurs without any conscious awareness. But we become aware of it when it is somehow blocked or frustrated, as in the case of impossible figures (Hochberg, 1970).

PERCEPTUAL SELECTION: ATTENTION

FOCUS QUESTIONS

- What are parallel and serial visual processing, and how are they demonstrated in visual search experiments?

- What is the cocktail-party effect? What do the results from dichotic presentation of sound suggest about the role of attention in perception?

Our perceptual system shapes and organizes the patchwork of different sensations into a coherent whole that has depth, motion, and form as well as meaning and results from both bottom-up and top-down processing. But in this processing not all parts of the perceptual world are given equal weight. We focus on the figure, not on the ground; we are more likely to notice shapes that are moving than those that are stationary. Thus, in addition to its other characteristics, perception is selective. We don't look at all the stimuli that are there to be looked at or focus upon them all. Our ability to take in and interpret the myriad stimulations around us is finite, and so our perceptual system is forced to choose among them. The various ways in which we exercise such choices and perceive selectively are often grouped together under the general label *attention*.

A

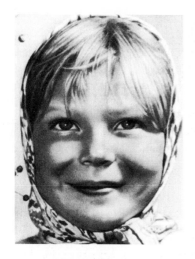

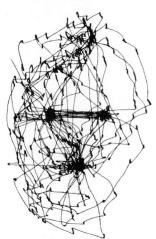

B

 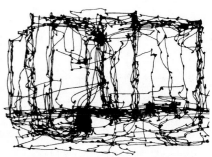

6.29 *Eye-movement records when looking at pictures* Both (A) and (B) are pictures that were looked at for 3 and 10 minutes respectively. With each picture is the record of the eye movements during this period. As the records show, most of the eye movements are directed toward the most visually informative regions. As a result, the eye-movement record is a crude mirror of the main contours of the picture. (From Yarbus, 1967)

SELECTION BY PHYSICAL ORIENTATION

The most direct means of selecting input is to orient the various sensory systems physically toward one set of stimuli and away from another. The organism does not passively touch, see, or hear; it actively feels, looks, and listens. It turns its head and eyes, explores the world with its hands (or paws or lips or prehensile trunk), and if it has the necessary motor endowment, pricks up its ears. These orienting adjustments of the sensory machinery are the external manifestations of attention.

In humans, the major means of physically selecting the stimulus input are movements of the eyes. Peripheral vision informs us that something is going on, say, in the upper left of our field of vision. But our peripheral acuity is not good enough to tell us what it is precisely. To find out, our eyes move so that this region falls into the fovea. A number of investigators have developed techniques for recording eye movements made when looking at pictures. The records show that the subjects glance most frequently at the regions that are visually most informative (Figure 6.29). This gaze pattern may be different for different observers, since what interests one person may not interest another. For example, a picture will be scanned quite differently if the observer is asked to estimate the ages of the people in it than when he's asked to estimate their economic status (see Figure 6.30A, B, and C).

These results show that the act of looking is purposeful. People don't scan the world in the wistful hope that their foveas will by chance hit on some interesting bit of visual news. They pick up some information from what they've vaguely seen in the periphery and from their general notions of what the scene is all about. They then move their eyes to check up on what they've seen and to refine their visual knowledge further (Yarbus, 1967; Rayner, 1978; Stark and Ellis, 1981).

CENTRAL SELECTION

Eye movements and other means for changing physical orientation determine the sensory input the perceptual system receives. But selective control of perception may also employ ***central selective processes,*** which determine whether a particular portion of the sensory input will be dealt with further and, if so, how it will be interpreted.

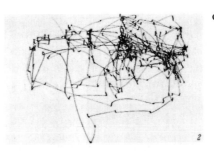

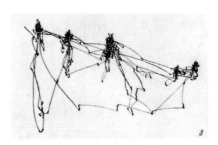

6.30 Eye movements as a function of what the observer is looking for *(A) A picture shown to subjects. Three-minute eye-movement records when the subjects were asked to estimate the wealth of the family (B) and when they were asked to estimate the ages of the people in the picture (C). (From Yarbus, 1967)*

6.31 Serial processing in visual search *When the task is to find a target that is defined by a conjunction of features (here a red O), the search is conducted serially. Each item is inspected in turn, and the search time increases as the number of false alternatives (red or green Vs, green Os) increases.*

SELECTIVE LOOKING

A widely used method for studying visual attention is the visual search procedure that we saw used in studying primitive features. As with those studies, a subject is briefly shown an array of letters, digits, or other visual forms (usually called distractors) and has to indicate as quickly and accurately as she can whether a particular target is or is not present among them.

Parallel and serial processing When the difference between the target and distractors involves just one feature, the search is very fast and seems almost effortless. An obvious example is searching for a green vertical among a number of green horizontals. Another is looking for an S in a group of other letters none of which contain any curves (e.g., A, E, F, H, and so on). Under these conditions, the search time is virtually independent of the number of distractors among which it appears. We saw earlier that some analysts take this as evidence that the single different feature is a primitive one. In information-processing terms the implication is that the search was conducted in **parallel:** All items in the display were processed simultaneously.

The situation is quite different when the target is defined by a **conjunction of features,** for example, a red *X* among distractors that include green *X*s, red *O*s, green *B*s, and so on. Now the system can't just look for the feature red or the feature diagonal; it has to find a red that goes with a diagonal, or a certain kind of diagonal (after all, the display might contain a red *R*). Under these conditions, search time is longer and increases with the number of distractors in the display. The implication is that the search is **serial:** The processing system examines each item, one by one, to determine whether it does or does not have the required conjunction of features. Anne Treisman believes that this process involves some kind of attentional focus. This focus is necessarily limited, it can't encompass the entire visual field at once. Rather, it serves as a mental searchlight that passes over the items in the display, one after another (Treisman, 1988; see Figure 6.31).

SELECTIVE LISTENING

A different method for studying selective attention focuses on listening to speech and is modeled on a phenomenon often observed in real life, the **cocktail-party effect.** During conversations at a noisy party, one tunes in on the voice of the person one is talking to. The many other voices are somehow filtered out and are consigned to a background babble. This effect has been studied experimentally by asking subjects to attend to one of two simultaneously presented verbal messages. The usual procedure is **dichotic presentation.** The subject wears two earphones and receives different messages through each of them. To guarantee selective attention, the subject is generally asked to *shadow* the to-be-attended message. This means that he has to repeat it aloud, word for word, as it comes over the appropriate earphone. Under these conditions, the irrelevant message tends to be shut out almost entirely. The subject can hear speechlike sounds, but notices little else. He is generally unable to recall the message that came by way of the unattended ear. In fact, he often does not even notice if the speaker on the unattended ear shifts into a foreign language or if the selection is read backwards (Cherry, 1953).

THE FILTER THEORY OF ATTENTION

Results of this sort suggest that selective attention acts as a kind of filter. This filter is presumably interposed between the initial sensory registration and later stages of perceptual analysis. If the information is allowed through the attentional filter, it can then be further analyzed—recognized, interpreted, and stored in memory. But if it does not pass through, much of it is lost.

Early versions of this theory suggested that the filtering effect is all-or-none. Subjects in a dichotic listening experiment were thought to understand no part of the message that entered by way of the unattended ear (Broadbent, 1958). This all-or-none theory turned out to be false, for there is good evidence that information that has some special significance is registered even if it is carried as part of the unattended message. The best example is the sight or sound of one's own name. No matter how intently we concentrate on the person next to us, we are quite likely to hear our own name in another conversation held on the other side of the room.

This everyday experience has been documented with the shadowing method. When subjects are forced to repeat a message that comes over one ear, word for word, they are almost completely oblivious to the irrelevant message that is fed into the other ear. But they do take notice when that irrelevant message contains the sound of their own name (Moray, 1959). This result suggests that the attentional filter does not block irrelevant messages completely. It only attenuates them, like a volume control that is turned down but not off. If the item is important enough (or perhaps familiar enough), then it may pass through the filter and be analyzed to some extent (Treisman, 1964).

Attentional selection *Without some attentional selection, performance of any complex task would deteriorate. (Photograph © Jeff M. Dunn)*

THE PERCEPTION OF REALITY

FOCUS QUESTION

■ What are perceptual constancies (such as those of size and shape), and how do empiricists, like Hermann von Helmholtz, and nativists, like James J. Gibson, explain them?

Of what use are all the mechanisms of perceptual organization we have considered throughout this chapter, whether innately given or based on learning? The answer is simple enough: They all help us to perceive reality. To be sure, the perceptual system may occasionally lead us astray, as in illusions of depth or movement, and sometimes it may actually leave us helpless, as in impossible figures. But these are fairly rare occasions. By and large, the processes that lead to the perception of depth, movement, and form serve the attainment of a larger goal—the perception of the real world outside.

To see the real world is to see the properties of distal objects: their color, form, size, and location, their movement through space, their permanence or transience. But as we have noted before, organisms cannot gain experience about the distal stimulus directly; all information about the external world comes to us from the proximal stimulus patterns that distal objects project upon the senses. The trouble is that the same distal stimulus object can produce many different proximal stimulus patterns. Its retinal image will get larger or smaller depending upon its distance; its retinal shape will change depending upon its slant; the amount of light it projects on the retina will increase or decrease depending on the illumination that falls upon it.

Under the circumstances, it may seem surprising that we ever manage to see the real properties of a distal object. But see them we do. The best proof is provided by *perceptual constancies:* An elephant looks large even at a distance; a postcard looks rectangular even though its retinal image is a trapezoid unless it is viewed directly head on. In these cases, we manage to transcend the vagaries of the proximal stimulus and react to certain constant attributes of the distal object such as its shape and its size.

EMPIRICISM AND NATIVISM REVISITED

How does the organism accomplish this feat? The attempts to answer this question are best understood as part of the continuing debate between the empiricist heirs of Locke on the one hand and the nativist descendants of Kant on the other.

THE EMPIRICISTS' ANSWER

Empiricists handle the problem of the constancies by asserting that the sensation produced by a particular stimulus is modified and reinterpreted in light of what we have learned through past experience. Consider perceived size. People five feet away look just about as tall as those at a fifty-foot distance. This is not merely because we know them to be average-sized rather than giants or midgets. The fact is that they really look equally tall provided there are cues that indicate their proper distance (Figure 6.32).

How can we explain this and similar phenomena? The most influential version of the empiricists' answer was formulated by Hermann von Helmholtz in the late nineteenth century. According to Helmholtz, the perceiver has two sources of information. To begin with, there is the sensation derived from the size of the object on the retina. In addition, there are a number of depth cues that indicate how far away the object is. Prior learning has taught the perceiver a general rule: The farther away things are, the smaller will be the sensation derived from the retinal image. The perceiver can now infer the true size of the object, given its retinal size, its distance, and the learned rule that relates the two. As a result she adjusts her perception of size, shifting it downward if the object is seen as close by and upward if it is seen as farther off. Helmholtz of course knew full well that we don't go through any conscious calculation of this sort when we look at objects and perceive their size. But he believed that some such

A

B

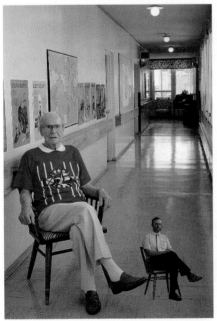

6.32   Perceived size and distance   (A) The actual image of the two men in the picture—which corresponds to the size of their retinal image—is in the ratio of 3 to 1. But this is not the way they are perceived. They look roughly equal in size, but at different distances, with one about three times farther off than the other. In (B) there are no cues that indicate that one man is farther away than the other—on the contrary. The figure was constructed by cutting the more distant man out of the picture and pasting him next to the other man, with the apparent distance from the viewer equal for the two. Now they look very different in size. (After Boring, 1964; Photograph by Jeffrey Grosscup)

process was going on anyway, and he therefore called it ***unconscious inference*** (Helmholtz, 1909).

It's worth noting that the unconscious inference theory is really an early version of the top-down processing hypothesis in perception. Both positions insist that perception is only partially determined by the sensory stimulation, that perception is in part a kind of mental construction, based on expectations and inferences of which the observer is often unaware. Thus contemporary theorists who argue that perception often involves a form of problem solving hold a view that is in many ways quite similar to that of Helmholtz (e.g., Hochberg, 1981, 1988; Rock, 1977, 1983, 1986).

THE NATIVISTS' ANSWER

The nativists' reply is that the perception of size is directly given. They argue that the stimulus for the perceived size of an object is not the size of the retinal image as such. It is rather some relationship between that size and certain other attributes that pertain to depth.

A very influential modern version of this approach is that of James J. Gibson (1950, 1966, 1979). Gibson believed that such vital characteristics of an object as its size, its shape, and its distance from the observer are signaled by various ***higher order patterns of stimulation*** to which the organism is innately sensitive.

As an example, let's return to size. To be sure, the size of the retinal image projected by an object must necessarily vary with its distance from the observer. But Gibson argued that this does not mean that there is no size information in the stimulus that hits the eye. One reason is that objects are usually seen against a background whose elements—leaves, pebbles, clumps of grass, or whatever—provide a texture. Since these elements are generally of about the same size, their size on the retina varies with distance and leads to texture gradients. As we've already seen, these texture gradients provide information about distance. But in addition, they also provide information about the relative size of objects in the world outside. For distance has the same effect on the retinal image of the object as it has on the retinal image of the adjacent textural elements of the object's background. In both cases, the retinal size decreases with increasing distance. As a result, there is a constant ratio between the retinal size cast by the object and the retinal size of its adjacent textural elements (see Figure 6.33).

The extent to which higher-order patterns of stimulation (such as the size ratio) provide information about various attributes of the world—of which size is only one—is still a matter of debate. Nor is it clear that perceivers are sensitive to all such higher order patterns or that the response to such patterns is part of our native endowment. These issues are by no means settled, as we will see when we turn to the empirical study of the various perceptual constancies.

SIZE AND SHAPE CONSTANCY

■ ***Size constancy*** is a term that describes the fact that the perceived size of an object is the same whether it is nearby or far away. A Cadillac Eldorado at a distance of 100 feet will look larger than a Volkswagen Beetle 20 feet away. An analogous phenomenon is ***shape constancy,*** which refers to the fact that we perceive the shape of an object more or less independently of the angle from which it is viewed. A rectangular door frame will appear rectangular even though most

A

B

6.33 *An invariant relationship that provides information about size* *(A) and (B) show a dog at different distances from the observer. The retinal size of the dog varies with distance, but the ratio between the retinal size of the dog and the retinal size of the textural elements made up of the bushes is constant. (Photographs by Jeffrey Grosscup)*

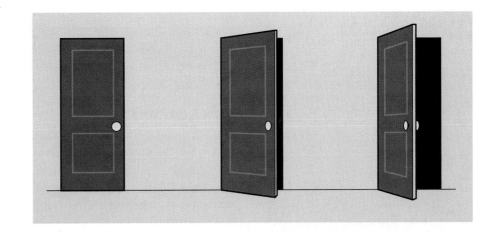

6.34 Shape constancy *When we see a door frame at various slants from us, it appears rectangular despite the fact that its retinal image is often a trapezoid. (After Gibson, 1950)*

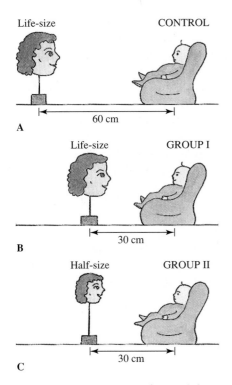

6.35 Size constancy in infants *(A) Six-month-old infants were exposed to a model of a human head at a distance of 60 cm until they habituated. (B) One group was then tested with the same head model at a distance of 30 cm—same distal size but altered retinal size. (C) A second group was tested with the same head model reduced to half its size but at the original distance of 30 cm— same retinal size but altered distal size. The infants in (C) spent more time looking at the model than those in (B), an indication of size constancy.*

of the angles from which it is regarded will produce a trapezoidal retinal image (see Figure 6.34).

How can we explain size and shape constancy? An essentially nativist approach such as Gibson's would try to account for the phenomena by looking for some stimulus pattern that remains the same despite changes in distance or angle of orientation. As we saw earlier in the chapter, in the case of distance such a proposed unchanging stimulus pattern is provided by the relation between the target stimulus and the texture of the background. Suppose we approach a door in a hallway. The door does not seem to change in size, even though its retinal image is expanding. In this case one thing remains unchanged: the ratio between the size of the images projected by the door and by the textural elements of the wallpaper in the hallway.

Such size ratios may well contribute to the constancy phenomenon, but they are probably not the only factor. For size constancy is found even when there are no apparent textural elements in either the target stimulus or the background that might provide the basis for a size ratio. As long as there are any cues to depth at all—such as perspective, interposition, binocular disparity, motion parallax, and so on—size constancy remains. As the number of these cues is progressively diminished, size constancy declines (Holway and Boring, 1947; Harvey and Leibowitz, 1967; Chevrier and Delorme, 1983).

An invariant size ratio is evidently unable to explain all cases of size constancy. But if so, what can? According to Helmholtz, we somehow take account of the object's distance and compensate for it (by unconscious inference). Helmholtz believed that the size-distance relationship is acquired through long experience. He argued that young children sometimes mistake objects at a considerable distance for miniatures. When they look from a tower, they see the people below as tiny dolls—a phenomenon that is also seen in adults (Helmholtz, 1909; Day, Stuart, and Dickinson, 1980). Gibson would reply that at those distances the crucial textural elements are too far away to be visible. This might explain why size constancy breaks down when the distance between observer and target gets large enough, but it cannot explain why that breakdown occurs at an earlier point in children than in adults (Zeigler and Leibowitz, 1957).

Perhaps Helmholtz was right in asserting that size constancy is learned. But if so, it must be learned fairly quickly, for size constancy seems to be present rather early in life (at least for moderate distances). Just how early is still a matter of some controversy, but it is certainly present by six months at the latest (Bower, 1966; McKenzie, Tootell, and Day, 1980; Day and McKenzie, 1981; see Figure 6.35). Much the same is true of shape constancy, which has been demonstrated in infants as young as three months of age (Caron, Caron, and Carlson, 1979; Cook and Birch, 1984).

6.36 Horemhab offering wine to Annu-bis, ca. 1339–1304 B.C. *The conventions of Egyptian art required the main parts of the human body to be represented in their most characteristic view. Thus, heads are shown in profile, arms and legs from the side, but eyes are depicted in full-face view, as are the shoulders and the chest. (Courtesy of the Metropolitan Museum of Art, New York, Rogers Fund, 1923)*

THE REPRESENTATION OF REALITY IN ART

FOCUS QUESTION

■ How did artists of different periods use perceptual phenomena to good advantage in their paintings?

The mechanisms of perceptual organization evolved to serve in the struggle for survival that all organisms must wage. They allow us to see reality as it actually is. But it is part of our humanity that we have managed to turn these perceptual mechanisms to a use that goes beyond the necessities of sheer survival: the representation of reality in art.

As we've seen, there are many perceptual phenomena (for example, the recognition of form) that are enormously affected by memories of the past and expectations of the future. Clearly, there is a wide region where it is not quite clear where seeing ends and knowing begins. The psychology of visual art is yet another illustration of the overlap between seeing and knowing.

SEEING AND KNOWING

Consider Figure 6.36, a wall painting from Egypt some three thousand years ago. Why did the artist depict the figures as he did, with eyes and shoulders in front view and the rest of the body in profile? His fellow Egyptians were surely built as we are. But if so, why didn't he draw them "correctly"?

The answer seems to be that Egyptian artists drew, not what they could see at any one moment or from any one position, but rather what they believed was the most enduring and characteristic attribute of their model. They portrayed the various parts of the human body from the vantage point that shows each form in its most characteristic manner: the front view for the eyes and shoulders, the profile for the nose and feet. The fact that these orientations are incompatible was evidently of no concern; what mattered was that all of the components were represented as the artist knew them to be (Gombrich, 1961).

THE RENAISSANCE: SCENES THROUGH A WINDOW FRAME

The illustrations of Egyptian art show the enormous role of the known in the visual representation of the seen. One may argue that this simply reflects the fact that these artists never set themselves the task of mirroring nature as it appears to the eye. Does the artist copy more precisely if one of his main purposes is to do just that?

The most striking examples come from the Renaissance masters who conceived the notion that a picture should look just like a real scene that is viewed through a window from one particular orientation (see Figure 6.37). The painting's frame is then the frame of this window into the artist's world. One major step toward achieving this end was the discovery of the geometrical laws of perspective that were discovered and codified by the Renaissance artist (Kubovy,

6.37 ***Perspective in Renaissance art*** The Annunciation by Crivelli *(ca. 1430–1495).*
Note the loving attention to perspective detail, such as roofs and arches extending far back. (Cour-
tesy of the National Gallery, London)

1986). This was supplemented by the systematic use of other pictorial cues for
depth such as interposition.

In effect, the Renaissance masters seemed to believe that to catch visual reality one's picture should correspond to the image the model casts on the eye. This
motivated their search for means to portray depth on a flat canvas. A similar
issue motivated such empiricists as Locke and Berkeley, whose concern was
with the nature of perception. The empiricists asked how the painters' means of
portraying depth—the pictorial cues—could lead to the experience of depth if
the image on the eye is two-dimensional.

THE IMPRESSIONISTS: HOW A SCENE IS
PERCEIVED

The Renaissance painters tried to represent a scene as it is projected on
the eye. Other schools of painting set themselves a different task. Consider
the French Impressionists of the late nineteenth century. They tried to recreate
certain perceptual experiences that the scene evokes in the observer, the impression it makes rather than the scene itself. One of their concerns was to render
color as we see it in broad daylight. Their method was to create a seeming

6.38   The Cathedral of Rouen by Claude Monet, 1893   *Monet, one of the leaders of the Impressionist movement, was engaged in a life-long attempt to catch fleeting sensations of light. If this painting of the cathedral at Rouen is viewed from a distance or out of foveal vision, the form becomes clearer and less impressionistic. What is lost is the brilliant shimmer of light and color. The oscillation between these two modes of appearance contributes to the total esthetic effect. (Courtesy of Musée d'Orsay)*

patchwork of different daubs of bright colors (see Figure 6.38). These are clearly separate when looked at directly. But when viewed from the proper distance, they change appearance, especially in the periphery where acuity is weak. The individual patches now blur together and their colors mix. But when the eyes move again and bring that area of the picture back into the fovea, the mixtures come apart and the individual patches reappear. Some authors believe that this continual alternation between mixed colors and separate dots gives these paintings their special vitality (Jameson and Hurvich, 1975).

This patchwork technique has a further effect. It enlists the beholder as an active participant in the artistic enterprise. Her active involvement starts as soon as she tries to see the picture as a whole rather than as a meaningless jumble of colored patches. This happens when the separate patches blur: when they are viewed from the periphery or from a few steps back. Now the picture suddenly snaps into focus and a whole emerges. This is both similar to and different from what happens in ordinary life. There we move our eyes to bring some part of the world to a region of greater acuity, the fovea. In the museum, we sometimes move our eyes (or our entire body) to bring a picture to a region of lesser acuity, away from the fovea. In either case, active movement leads to the perception of a figural whole (Hochberg, 1978b, 1980).

THE MODERNS: HOW A SCENE IS CONCEIVED

■ The Impressionists tried to engender some of the perceptual experiences a scene evokes in the observer. Later generations went further and tried to capture not just how the scene is perceived but how it is conceived, how it is known as well as seen. Modern art provides many examples, as in Pablo Picasso's

6.39 **Violin and Grapes** *by Pablo Picasso, 1912* *(Oil on canvas, 20" × 24"; collection of the Museum of Modern Art, New York; Mrs. David M. Levy bequest)*

still life showing superimposed fragments of a violin (Figure 6.39). Here perception and knowledge are cunningly merged in a sophisticated return to some of the ways of Egyptian artists (Gombrich, 1961).

Some Modern artists are not satisfied by adding conceptual elements to their visual representations. They want to create ambiguity by setting up visual puzzles that can't be solved. One way is to pit knowledge against visual perception, as in Picasso's faces that are seen in profile and front-face at the same time. Another is to build contradictions into the perceptual scene itself. An example is a painting by the turn-of-the-century Italian Giorgio de Chirico (Figure 6.40).

6.40 **The Enigma of a Day** *by Georgio de Chirico, 1914* *(Oil on canvas, 185.5 × 139.7 cm; collection of the Museum of Modern Art, New York; James Thrall Soby Bequest.)*

One reason for the disturbing quality of his work is the fact that de Chirico often used incompatible perspectives. In his *The Enigma of a Day,* the structure on the left converges to one horizon, the structure on the right to a different horizon, while the crate in the middle does not converge at all. The result is an insoluble visual problem, an eerie world that cannot be put in order.

De Chirico's streets do not look like real streets, and Picasso's violins are a far cry from those one sees in a concert hall. In this regard, these Modern painters appear quite different from many of their predecessors whose representations were closer to the world as it appears to the perceiver. But we have to realize that, with few exceptions, no artists, whether Renaissance masters, Impressionists, or Moderns, ever try to fool the observer into thinking that he is looking at a real scene. They neither can nor want to hide the fact that their painting is a painting. It may spring to life for a moment and look like a real person or a real sunset, or it may briefly conjure up a vivid memory of what a face or a violin looks like when viewed from several angles. But whether it emphasizes the seen or the known, it is also recognized as a flat piece of canvas daubed with paint.

According to some authors, this perceptual duality is an important part of the beholder's esthetic experience as he looks at a work of representational art. In a well-known poem by Robert Browning, a duke points to his "last duchess painted on the wall,/Looking as if she were alive." The key words are *as if.* One reason why visual art leads to an esthetic experience may be because it provides us with a halfway mark between seen reality and painted appearance, because it presents a visual *as if* (Hochberg, 1980).

In our discussion of visual art we have taken yet another step across the wide, shadowy region where perception and conception, seeing and knowing merge. In the next chapter we will cross the boundary altogether. There we will consider how we remember objects and events that no longer stimulate our senses.

QUESTIONS FOR CRITICAL THINKING

1. Why should our visual system be predisposed to operate according to Gestalt laws? In what circumstances might this predisposition backfire?

2. Why did early astronomers "see" constellations on starry nights?

SUMMARY

1. The fundamental problem of perception is how we come to apprehend the objects and events in the world around us. In the field of visual perception, the major issues concern the way in which we see *depth, movement,* and *form.*

2. The visual world is seen in three dimensions even though only two of these are given in the image that falls upon the eye. This fact has led to an interest in *depth cues.* Among these are *binocular disparity,* monocular cues such as *interposition* and *linear perspective, relative size,* and *texture gradients.* All of these cues are powerful determinants of perceived depth. More important still is *motion parallax,* which provides vital information about how far objects are from each other and how far they are from ourselves.

3.   Many aspects of depth perception are apparently built into the nervous machinery. Evidence comes from the behavior of very young humans or animals, as in reactions to *looming*.

4.   Retinal displacement alone cannot explain the perception of movement, as shown by the phenomena of *apparent movement* and *induced movement*.

5.   In vision, our primary means for recognizing an object is through its form, a fact already observed in young children. An important phenomenon in the psychology of form perception is *transposition of form*: A perceived form may remain the same even if all of its constituent parts are altered. This phenomenon is the keystone of *Gestalt psychology*, which emphasizes the importance of wholes created by the relationship between their parts.

6.   Many modern investigators believe that form perception is based on several steps of *information processing* that transform the initial visual input into its cognitive end product, the perception of objects in the world. This may begin with the automatic processing of *primitive features*, which can be identified by the fact that they "pop out" in a *visual search task*. At the first stage of processing, these features exist in free-floating isolation as shown by *illusory conjunctions*.

7.   Before the perceiver can recognize a form, he must first engage in a process of *visual segregation* and *parse* the visual scene. This involves the segregation of *figure* and *ground*, which are not inherent in the proximal stimulus but are imposed by the perceptual system, as shown by *reversible figures*. Further segregation produces perceptual *grouping*, which depends upon factors such as *proximity, similarity, good continuation,* and *closure*.

8.   An important approach to *pattern recognition* grew out of efforts of computer scientists to develop machines that could identify visual forms such as letters. Most such attempts start with the view that pattern recognition typically involves two kinds of processes. One is *bottom-up processing*, which starts with the stimulus and "works up" by subjecting it to a feature analysis that begins with lower-level units (such as slanted lines) that then activate higher-level units (such as letters). The other is *top-down processing*, which is based on expectations and hypotheses, as shown by perceptual *context effects*. It begins with the activation of higher-level units that then activate lower-level ones. Perceptual processing is usually *bidirectional*, however.

9.   Top-down processes provide *perceptual hypotheses* that are then tested by bottom-up processes. This kind of perceptual problem solving sometimes fails, as in the case of *impossible figures*.

10.   Perception is selective, for all aspects of a stimulus are not given equal weight. This selection is partially achieved by physical orientation, as in the case of eye movements. It is also achieved by a central process, *selective attention*. Methods for studying attention include *selective looking*, as demonstrated in *visual search procedures*, and *selective listening*, as in *dichotic presentation* in which one message is *shadowed*.

11.   Attempts to resolve the discrepancy between what the proximal stimulus gives us and what we actually see go back to two main approaches, the *empiricist* and the *nativist*. Empiricists explain this discrepancy by referring to *unconscious inference* based on a learned rule (in the case of size constancy, the rule that objects farther away cause smaller retinal sensations). Nativists emphasize *higher-order patterns of stimulation* that are directly given (in the case of size constancy, unchanging size ratios in the retinal image). Whether or not size and shape constancy are innate or based on learning is not clear cut, but if those constancies are based on learning, it must occur quite early in life.

12.   The psychology of visual art is a further illustration of the overlap between perception and thinking. The artist represents both what she sees and what she knows. *Renaissance* painters represented scenes as seen through a window frame; the *Impressionists* tried to recreate certain perceptual experiences the scene evokes in the beholder; while many *Modern artists* try to represent the scene as it is conceived and thought about.

CHAPTER

MEMORY

ur discussion of visual perception emphasized the way in which psychological events are organized in space. Locke and Berkeley to the contrary, our perceptual world is not a jumbled mosaic of isolated sensory fragments but an organized, coherent whole in which every piece relates to every other. We now turn to the subject of memory in which organization plays an equally prominent part. Where perception concerns the organization of space, memory—or at least many aspects of memory—concerns the organization of time.

Memory is the way in which we record the past for later use in the present. It is hard to think of humans (or any animal that is able to learn) without this capacity. Without memory, there would be no *then* but only a *now,* no ability to employ skills, no recall of names or recognition of faces, no reference to past days or hours or even seconds. We would be condemned to live in a narrowly circumscribed present, but this present would not even seem to be our own, for there can be no sense of self without memory. Each individual wakes up every morning and never doubts that he is he or she is she. This feeling of personal identity is necessarily based upon a continuity of memories that links our yesterdays to our todays.

STUDYING MEMORY

FOCUS QUESTIONS

- What are explicit and implicit memory?
- What are the three phases of the memory process?
- What are the two major methods used for studying memory retrieval?

How do psychologists study memory? The first step is to realize that there is no such thing as one memory system or one set of memory processes. The term *memory* is simply a blanket label for a large number of processes that form bridges between our past and our present. But these processes differ in important ways.

SOME PRELIMINARY DISTINCTIONS

An important first distinction concerns the length of time that is spanned in different tests of memory. Some of these intervals are measured in fractions of a second, others in seconds or minutes, and still others in months and years. Many psychologists believe that these different **retention intervals** are bridged by different memory systems. The major example concerns the distinction between **short-term** and **long-term memory.**

Card games and memory *Many card games make considerable demands on memory. Pictured here are children hard at work "playing" the game of "Memory." (Photograph by Kathy Hirsh-Pasek)*

Another distinction concerns our conscious awareness of remembering. We are sometimes aware that we are tapping our memory, but often we are not. Suppose someone asks us what we had for dinner last night. When we answer, we are perfectly aware that we are at least trying to remember (whether we succeed or not is another question). In such cases, we are dealing with ***explicit memory.*** But we often call upon our memory without being at all aware that we do. For example, when we speak or listen, we understand the words we speak or hear because we have learned their meaning in the past. This means that while speaking or listening we must tap a mental dictionary in our memory system. But we are not conscious of consulting some kind of memory, even though we surely did. In such cases we are dealing with ***implicit memory.***

Despite these significant distinctions, there are some general characteristics that pertain to all—or at least to most—kinds of memory. Before focusing on the different types of memory, let us start by examining what the various types of memory have in common.

ENCODING, STORAGE, RETRIEVAL

■ Any act of remembering implies success at three aspects of the memory process. Consider a person working on a crossword puzzle who is trying to think of an eight-letter word meaning "African anteater." If she comes up with the answer, *aardvark,* we can be sure that she succeeded in three aspects of remembering.

The first aspect of remembering has to do with acquiring the information in the first place. To remember, one must first have learned; the puzzle solver must first have encountered and noted this particular item of zoological exotica. During this acquisition phase, the item must be ***encoded.*** Taken from computer science, the term *encoding* refers to the form (that is, the code) in which an item of information is to be placed in memory. Our puzzle solver who once learned the word "aardvark" may have encoded it as a certain sound pattern or a particular letter sequence, in terms of its meaning or the context in which she first encountered the word, or all of these at once.

The next aspect of remembering is ***storage:*** To be remembered the encoded experience must leave some record in the nervous system (the ***memory trace***); it must be squirreled away and held in some more or less enduring form for later use (probably in doing the next crossword puzzle).

The final phase is ***retrieval,*** the point at which one "tries to remember," to dredge up a particular memory trace from among all the others we have stored. There are two major methods for studying retrieval. One is ***recall*** in which the subject is asked to produce an item or a set of items from memory, e.g., coming up with the answer to the question "What is the name of the boy who sat next to you in the third grade?" The experimental psychologist often tests for the recall of materials learned in the laboratory to assure that any failures aren't simply failures of original acquisition. The second method is ***recognition:*** A person is shown an item and has to indicate whether she has encountered it before, e.g., being able to answer the question "Is this one of the girls who played on your high-school field hockey team?" In the laboratory, the subject is usually asked to pick out the previously learned item from among several false alternatives. In multiple-choice or true-false tests a premium is obviously put on recognition, whereas essay or short-answer examinations emphasize recall.

Failures to remember can result from mishaps during any of the three phases of the memory process—encoding, storage, or retrieval. For example, if at the first encounter with *aardvark,* the learner encoded the term only as a sound pattern, there would be no memory trace of its meaning so that the puzzle item couldn't be solved. If both the sound and meaning were encoded and held for the length of the retention interval, the item might have been misfiled in memory—stored, say, with Asian carnivores rather than with African anteaters. If so, the item might be impossible to retrieve even though it is still stored in memory. That many of our failures to remember are failures of retrieval and not of storage often becomes clear at some later time. Our crossword expert might be unable to come up with the correct answer at the time, but when she later sees the solution, she realizes that she'd known it all along: "Of course. It's aardvark!"

Encoding, storage, and retrieval are the three aspects of the memory process. Encoding and retrieval represent the start and the end of this process; they are the two aspects that can be studied more or less directly and that we will focus upon in this chapter. (For some discussion of storage, see pp. 194, 208–10, 216–19).

ENCODING

FOCUS QUESTIONS

- What do stage theorists call the two memory systems they postulate, and what is the capacity of each?

- According to stage theory, how does information get transferred from short-term to long-term memory? Which memory system accounts for primacy effects and which for recency effects?

- Given the limited capacity of short-term memory, how do stage theorists explain how we manage to get so much information into long-term storage?

- How did the results of maintenance rehearsal tests call into question the traditional view of short-term memory as a storage depot?

- What are mnemonics, and how do they help us store information?

In our discussion of how memories are encoded, we'll start out by considering an important theory of memory, which we will here call the *stage theory*. As we'll see, this theory has been in some ways superseded, but its formulations still provide the framework for much of our current thinking about the topic.

THE STAGE THEORY OF MEMORY

Memory has often been compared to a storehouse. This conception goes back to the Greek philosophers and to St. Augustine, who described the "roomy chambers of memory, where are the treasures of countless images. . . ." This spatial metaphor, which likens memories to objects that are put into storage compartments, held for a while, and then searched for, is a recurrent theme in both ancient and modern thought. (Crowder, 1985; Roediger, 1980).

The *stage theory of memory,* developed some twenty years ago, represents a modern variation on this same spatial metaphor but casts it within the framework of an information-processing approach. Unlike Augustine, who believed that there is one memory warehouse, this theory asserts that there are several such storage systems, each with different properties (Broadbent, 1958; Waugh and Norman, 1965; Atkinson and Shiffrin, 1968).

The belief that there are several memory stores comes from the fact that memory may reach back for years but may also concern events that occurred just moments ago. We usually think of memory in terms of a past that is reckoned in hours, days, or years. But a moment's reflection tells us that memory

Overloading capacity *The limited cognitive capacity of the working memory system has its physical analogue in the demands sometimes made upon us in modern technological society as caricatured in this scene from Charlie Chaplin's 1936 film,* Modern Times. *(Courtesy of the Kobal Collection)*

comes into play as soon as the stimulus has disappeared from the scene. An example is a telephone number we look up and retain just long enough to complete the dialing; here the interval between acquisition and retrieval is a matter of mere seconds, but it is a memory all the same.

These simple facts provide the starting points for the stage theory of memory. One of its assertions is that there are several memory systems. Of these, the most important are *short-term memory,* which holds information for fairly short intervals, and *long-term memory* in which materials are stored for much longer periods, sometimes as long as a lifetime.

THE STORAGE CAPACITY OF SHORT- AND LONG-TERM MEMORY

There is reason to believe that memories for relatively recent events differ in important ways from memories for events that are more remote in time. One difference concerns the *storage capacity* of the two postulated memory systems. The storage capacity of short-term memory is markedly different from that of long-term memory. The capacity of long-term memory is enormous: The size of an average college student's reading vocabulary (about 80,000 words) is documentation enough. In contrast, the capacity of short-term memory is exceedingly limited.

One way to determine the capacity of short-term memory is by measuring the *memory span,* the number of items an individual can recall after just one presentation. For normal adults, this span is remarkably consistent. If the items are randomly chosen letters or digits, the subject can recall about seven items, give or take about two. This quantity, seven plus or minus two, has been called the *magic number,* a widely quoted term originated by George Miller (Miller, 1956). According to Miller, this number represents the holding capacity of the short-term memory system, the number of items that will fit into its store at any one time. There is some debate about whether this number, seven plus or minus two, is really an accurate description of short-term capacity, but all investigators are agreed that the capacity of short-term memory is very small indeed.

SHORT-TERM MEMORY AS A LOADING PLATFORM

What is the relation between short-term and long-term memory? The stage theory of memory asserts that the road into long-term memory necessarily passes through the short-term store. Seen in this light, short-term memory can be regarded as a loading platform into the huge long-term warehouse. A parcel that stays on the platform long enough may be picked up and placed in the warehouse, but the vast majority of the parcels never make it.

Forgetting recent memories Material in short-term memory is very short-lived. While reading the morning newspaper, we briefly note all kinds of extraneous matter: The coffee tastes bitter, a child is crying next door, there is a printer's error on the editorial page. But only a few moments thereafter these experiences are as if they had never been. One reason may be *decay:* The memory trace becomes eroded over time by some unknown physiological process, so its details become progressively less distinct (see p. 206). Another possibility is *displacement:* Items are somehow pushed out of memory by other items that enter later. The best evidence to date suggests that both factors play a role, that some packages on the platform rot away (decay), while others are shoved off by other packages (displacement). In either case, it is clear that they are generally not allowed to remain on the platform very long.

This rapid forgetting from short-term memory may be a blessing in disguise, for without it, our memory systems would be clogged with the clutter of useless

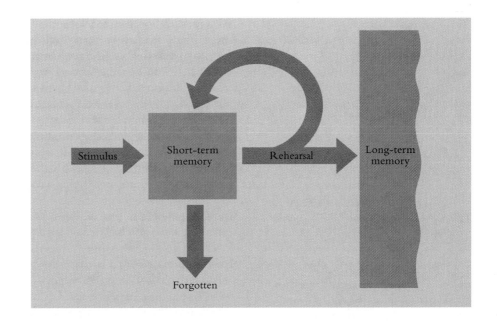

7.1 The relation between short-term and long-term memory systems as envisaged by stage theory *The figure is a schematic representation of the relation between the two memory systems as stage theorists conceive of them. Information is encoded and enters the short-term store. To enter the long-term store, it must remain in short-term memory for a while. The means for maintaining it there is rehearsal. (Adapted from Waugh and Norman, 1965)*

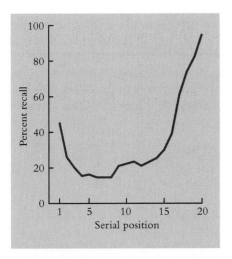

7.2 Primacy and recency effects in free recall *Subjects heard a list of twenty common words presented at a rate of one word per second. Immediately after hearing the list, the subjects were asked to write down as many of the words on the list as they could recall. The results show that the words at the beginning (primacy effect) and at the end (recency effect) were recalled more frequently than those in the middle. (After Murdock, 1962)*

information. Switchboard operators would be in poor shape if they were unable to forget a number immediately after they dialed it. Given its limited capacity, the loading platform has to be cleared very quickly to make room for new packages as they arrive (Bjork, 1970).

Transfer into long-term memory According to stage theory, some items on the platform are moved into the long-term store by an essentially mechanical transfer process. As we've seen, most packages disappear before this transfer can happen, but a few do remain on the platform for a while and thus become candidates for memorial tenure. Stage theorists believe that one reason why they remain long enough to be transferred is **rehearsal.** By repeating an item over and over again, a subject will hold it in short-term memory, which increases the probability that this item will be transferred into the long-term store (see Figure 7.1).

These hypotheses about the relations between short- and long-term memory systems fit rather well with some facts obtained by the method of **free recall.** The subject hears a list of unrelated items, such as common English words, presented one at a time and is asked to recall them in any order that she wants to. If the items are presented only once, and if their number exceeds the memory span, the subject cannot possibly produce them all. Under these circumstances, the likelihood that any one item will be recalled depends upon where in the list it was originally presented. Items that were presented at the beginning or the end of the list are much more likely to be recalled than those that were in the middle. The **primacy effect** denotes the enhanced recall of items at the beginning; the **recency effect** designates the greater recall for those at the end (see Figure 7.2).

Stage theorists believed that the recency effect is produced because items that were presented at the end of the list are retrieved from short-term memory. These items are generally reported easily. They are still clear in memory because they were presented just a few seconds ago and no further items arrived to displace them. This allows the subject to recite these items quickly, before they disappear from the short-term store. According to stage theory, the recency effect simply reflects the fact that three or four items are still in the short-term store when the subject begins to recall and that these items are the first he reports.

According to stage theory, the items at the beginning of the list are presumably retrieved from long-term memory. One reason for this interpretation of the primacy effect is that the early items have had more opportunity for rehear-

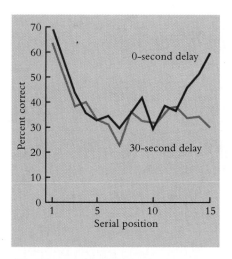

7.3 The recency effect and short-term storage *Subjects heard several fifteen-word lists. In one condition (dark red), free recall was tested immediately after they heard the list. In the other condition (blue), the recall test was given after a thirty-second delay during which rehearsal was prevented. The long delay left the primacy effect unaffected but abolished the recency effect, indicating that this effect is based on retrieval from short-term storage. (After Glanzer and Cunitz, 1966)*

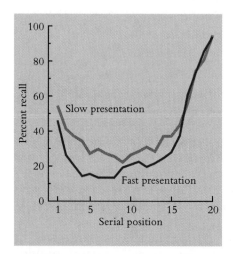

7.4 The primacy effect and long-term storage *The figure compares free-recall performance when item presentation is relatively slow (two seconds per item) and fast (one second per item). Slow presentation enhances the primacy effect but leaves the recency effect unaltered. The additional second per item presumably allows more time for rehearsal, which leads to long-term storage. (After Murdock, 1962)*

sal and thus for transfer into the long-term store. For example, if the first three items are *camera, boat,* and *zebra,* the subject could give his full attention to rehearsing *camera* after hearing it, silently repeating "camera, camera, camera. . . ." When the second word arrives, he'll rehearse that too, but his attention will now be divided in half ("camera, boat, camera, boat, . . ."). He'll have to divide his attention still further after hearing the third word ("camera, boat, zebra, camera, boat, zebra . . ."), and so through the list. The result is that the earlier words get more attention than the later ones. The more attention a word gets, the more likely that word will make it to the long-term warehouse. Since the attention is greater for the words at the beginning than for those that come later on, those first words have an advantage.

Supporting evidence for these interpretations comes from various manipulations that affect the primacy and recency effects. One important factor is the interval between the last item on the list and the signal to recall. If this interval is increased to thirty seconds (during which the subjects perform some mental tasks such as counting backwards so they can't rehearse), the primacy effect remains unchanged but the recency effect is completely abolished. This is just what one would expect if the last items are stored in short-term memory from which forgetting is very rapid (see Figure 7.3). Other procedures diminish the primacy effect. An example is the rate at which items are presented. If this rate is relatively fast, the subject has less time for rehearsal. As a result, there is less transfer to long-term storage. We would therefore expect a reduced primacy effect but no particular change in the recency effect, and this is again what happens (see Figure 7.4).

OVERCOMING THE SHORT-TERM BOTTLENECK

Stage theory asserts that in order to enter long-term storage, items must first pass through short-term memory. But as we have seen, the short-term loading platform has a limited capacity. It can handle only a small number of packages at any one time. In view of this bottleneck, how do we manage to deposit so much material in the long-term store? Stage theory's answer is *organization*. The capacity limit of the loading platform is on the number of packages, which is exceedingly small (perhaps 7 ± 2). But what these packages contain is up to us. If we can pack the input more efficiently, we may squeeze more information into the same number of memory units.

Recoding into larger chunks As an example, consider a subject who tries to recall a series of letters she heard only once:

CIAFBIIBMTWA.

This is quite difficult if interpreted as a series of twelve unrelated letters. But if it is reorganized by three-letter groupings, specifically

CIA FBI IBM TWA

the recall task is perfectly trivial.

In this example, the subject repackages the material to be remembered, **recoding** the input into larger units that are often called **chunks.** Each chunk imposes about the same load on memory as did each of the smaller units that are contained within it. But when eventually unpacked, each of these chunks yields much more information.

Much of the job of recoding items into larger chunks (or *chunking*) occurred in our early life. To an adult, a word is already a coherent whole, not merely a sequence of sounds. Still higher units of memorial organization are involved in

The role of chunking in remembering a visual display Could you possibly remember all the figures in this bewildering array? You might if you knew Netherlandish proverbs of the sixteenth century, for that is what the painting depicts. To mention only some, there is (going from left to right): a man who "butts his head against the wall," another who is "armed to the teeth" and "ties a bell to the cat," and two women of whom "one spins while the other winds" (malicious gossips). Going further left, we see a woman who "puts a blue cloak over her husband" (deceives him), a man who "fills the hole after his calf was drowned," and another who "throws roses [we say pearls] before swine." Recognizing these scenes as illustrations of familiar proverbs will organize the visual array and thus help you to remember its many parts. (Detail of Netherlandish Proverbs by Pieter Brueghel, 1559; courtesy of Gemäldegalerie, Staatliche Museen Preussischer Kulturbesitz, Berlin)

the memory for sentences. The memory span for unrelated words is about six or seven items, but we may well recall a fairly long sentence after only a single exposure. This fact even holds for sentences that make little sense, such as *The enemy submarine dove into the coffee pot, took fright, and silently flew away.* This dubious bit of naval intelligence consists of fourteen words, but it clearly contains fewer than fourteen memorial packages: *The enemy submarine* is essentially one unit, *took fright* is another, and so on.

A CHANGED EMPHASIS: ACTIVE MEMORY AND ORGANIZATION

The stage theory of memory largely dominated the field for several decades. But as time went on, there was a reevaluation. An important challenge to stage theory came from some findings on the effect of rehearsal. Stage theory asserts that when an item is rehearsed, it is more likely to enter long-term memory. According to the stage theory, this transfer from the short-term loading platform to the long-term warehouse depends largely on how long that item has been on the platform. The longer it sits there, the greater will be its probability of being transferred. According to this view, rehearsal helps because it keeps the item in the short-term store for a longer period and keeps it from rotting away or being displaced before that transfer can happen. But there is evidence that entering long-term memory is by no means as automatic as this.

SHORT-TERM MEMORY AS AN ACTIVE PROCESS

It turns out that one form of rehearsal does relatively little in the long run. This is called *maintenance rehearsal* through which the subject mentally holds on to the material for a little while but does nothing more. We use this form of rehearsal when we try to retain a telephone number just long enough to complete the call. We repeat the number to ourselves until we begin dialing but then we promptly forget it. Experimental evidence on the effect of maintenance rehearsal comes from an ingenious study that varied the time in which items remained in short-term memory. The subjects listened to a number of lists of words, and they were asked to monitor each list for words beginning with a certain letter. The lists varied in length. At the end of each list, the subjects had to report the last word on the list that began with a particular letter. Suppose the letter was *G* and that the list was as follows:

Daughter, Oil, Garden, Grain, Table,
Football, Anchor, Giraffe, Pillow, Thunder.

In this situation, the subject has to hold one *G*-word in short-term memory until the next one appears. Thus *Garden* will be replaced by *Grain*, which will make way for *Giraffe* and so on until the end of the list is reached at which time the subject has to come up with the last *G*-word—in the present case, *Giraffe*. This arrangement guarantees that some of the *G*-words are held longer in short-term memory than others are; thus *Grain* will stay longer than *Garden*. The question was whether this increased stay in the short-term store increased the chance that *Garden* would be transferred to long-term memory. To find out, the experimenters gave a final—and quite unexpected—test after the end of the session during which many such lists had been presented. They simply asked the subjects to report as many of the *G*-words they had heard as they could. The results showed that the time an item had been in short-term memory had no effect—*Garden* was recalled just as often as was *Grain* (Craik and Watkins, 1973). It appears that maintenance rehearsal confers little or no benefit in aiding recall.

WORKING MEMORY

The preceding discussion highlighted one of the problems of the stage theory of memory: Since maintenance rehearsal confers little or no benefit in aiding recall, the transfer from short- to long-term memory cannot be automatic. These and certain other phenomena we'll consider later led to a theoretical reorientation in the way psychologists think of memory processes. One change concerns the conception of short-term memory. Another is an emphasis on the role of processing and organization.

As we saw, stage theorists conceived of short- and long-term memory as depots in a traffic flow in which information was moved from a small short-term

Using working memory *Cardplayers have to call on working memory to decide which cards were played most recently and which should be played next. (*The Cardplayers, *by Paul Cezanne; courtesy of The Metropolitan Museum of Art, Bequest of Stephen C. Clark, 1960)*

loading platform to the more spacious long-term store. Today, however, most theorists believe that long-term memories are formed by a more active process in which the subject's own ways of encoding and organizing the material play a major role. As a result, they regard short-term memory not so much as a temporary storage platform but rather as a mental workbench on which various items of experience are encoded—sorted, manipulated, and organized. According to this view, whether the materials will be retained in memory long enough to become retrievable later does not depend upon a simple transfer from one storage container to another. Instead, it depends on how this material is processed (that is, encoded and recoded). The more elaborate the processing, the greater the likelihood of later recall and recognition.

Considerations of this sort led many psychologists to abandon the concept of short-term memory as a mere storage depot (Crowder, 1982). It also led many of them to prefer the term ***working memory*** to the older designation *short-term memory*. The newer term focuses on the way in which memories are processed rather than on the hypothetical structures in which these memories are held. Seen in this light, the key difference is between those portions of our memory system that are currently activated (and acted upon)—that is, working memory—and those that are currently dormant—that is, long-term memory. This new conception can easily account for the findings that first led to the belief in a short-term memory store with a limited storage capacity. As modern investigators think about it, what's limited is not the storage area but rather the amount of processing that can be accomplished. There is only so much cognitive processing (or mental effort) the system can engage in at any time. This may concern something we want to remember, if only for a moment, like a telephone number before it is dialed. Or it may be some mental task such as multiplying two-digit numbers in our heads, where we have to keep track of the numbers, the partial products, and the point we're at in the problem.

If this is correct, the appropriate metaphor for the limited capacity of a working memory system is not really a loading platform that can hold only so many parcels. It is rather an overworked operative at the memory workbench who can only pack so many parcels—can only do so much chunking and organizing and linking materials to prior memories—at any one time. It's as if he (or she or it) has only so many mental hands (Baddeley, 1976, 1986).

MNEMONICS

The development of techniques for improving one's memory, for helping one's workbench operative pack memory parcels most efficiently, is a very practical endeavor whose roots go back to ancient times. These techniques are often called ***mnemonics.***

Mnemonics through verbal organization   The ancients were well aware that it is much easier to remember verbal material if it is organized. They were particularly partial to the use of verse, or the organization of word sequences to maintain a fixed rhythm and rhyme. Without such aids, preliterate societies might never have transmitted their oral traditions intact from one generation to the next. Homeric bards could recite the entire *Iliad,* but could they have done so had it been in prose? Verse is still used as a mnemonic when it seems necessary to impose some sort of order upon an otherwise arbitrary set of items ("Thirty days hath September, / April, June, and November").

Mnemonics through visual imagery   Some of the most effective mnemonics ever devised involve the deliberate use of mental imagery. One such technique is the ***method of loci,*** which requires the learner to visualize each of the items she wants to remember in a different spatial location (locus). In recall, each location

7.5   Interactive and noninteractive depictions   *Subjects shown related elements, such as a doll sitting on a chair and waving a flag (A), are more likely to associate the words* doll, flag, *and* chair *than subjects who are shown the three objects next to each other but not interacting (B). (After Bower, 1970)*

is mentally inspected and the item that was placed there in imagination is thus retrieved. This method provides a scheme that allows orderly retrieval. It requires a deliberate effort to relate the items that must be memorized to distinctive features of the retrieval scheme and to do so through visual imagery. The efficacy of this mnemonic system has been tested by several experimental studies. Subjects who recalled by the method of loci recalled up to seven times more than their counterparts who learned in a rote manner. In one such study, college students had to learn lists of forty unrelated concrete nouns. Each list was presented once for about ten minutes during which the subjects tried to visualize each of the forty objects in one of forty different locations around the college campus. Tested immediately, they recalled an average of thirty-eight of the forty items; tested one day later, they still managed to recall thirty-four (Ross and Lawrence, 1968).

Why does imagery help?   Why are images such a powerful aid to memory? One of the reasons may be that they are yet another way of forming a new chunk in memory. By creating a mental image, the subject joins two unrelated items so that they form a new whole. When part of the chunk (the imagined locus) is presented, the entire chunk is retrieved, yielding the part required for recall.

Some evidence for this view comes from studies that show that mental images will only facilitate recall if they tend to unify the items to be associated into a coherent whole. Consider a subject who has to learn a list of noun-noun pairs such as eagle-locomotive and is instructed to use imagery as an aid to memory. She can construct mental pictures that bring the items into some kind of unitary relationship, for example, an eagle winging to his nest with a locomotive in his beak. But she may form an image whose constituents are merely adjacent and do not interact, such as an eagle at the side of a locomotive. Several recent experiments demonstrate that unifying mental images produce much better recall than nonunifying images (Wollen, Weber, and Lowry, 1972). A similar effect is found when the test items are real pictures. If shown a drawing of a doll standing on a chair waving a flag, subjects quickly reply "chair and flag" when asked to recall the objects that were pictured with the doll. Their recall score is substantially lower if they were shown a picture of the doll, chair, and flag, drawn as separate, unrelated objects (Figure 7.5).

The usefulness of mnemonics in everyday life   Mnemonic systems provide effective means for imposing organization upon otherwise disparate materials, such as a foreign vocabulary list or nonsense materials developed in the psychological laboratory. But we are not often confronted by such arbitrary pairings. A student reading a history text does not have to impose an organization. His job is to discover the organization that is already inherent in the material. When he does so, the various treaties and battles will fall into an appropriate mental scheme, linked to each other and to relevant historical matters that have been learned before. But imagery mnemonics will not help to provide this scheme. A visual image that links, say, General Custer and Chief Sitting Bull will be of little use in helping the student understand the conflict between the American Indians and the encroaching settlers.

In short, the best prescription for recall is to organize and understand the material at the time it is learned. If this material is devoid of inherent organization, some organization must be imposed upon it. In that case, mnemonic devices, especially imagery, are a useful tool. If the material is already organized, the best approach is to discover that organization and to chunk the various items in terms of it.

RETRIEVAL

FOCUS QUESTIONS

- What is the compatibility (or encoding-specificity) principle?

- What is memory search, and how does the tip-of-the-tongue phenomenon illustrate it?

- What is implicit retrieval, and how is it demonstrated? How can it explain the feeling of déjà vu?

That memory storage is not the same as memory retrieval is obvious to anyone who has ever blocked on a familiar name. We may know (that is, have stored) a name, a fact, an event, or whatever and still be unable to retrieve it on a particular occasion. In such cases, the memory trace is said to be inaccessible. Access to the trace may be restored by an appropriate **retrieval cue,** a stimulus that opens the path to the memory (Tulving and Pearlstone, 1966).

The recollection of temporarily inaccessible memories by appropriate retrieval cues is usually a rather humdrum event. We can't recall where we parked on a shopping trip, are reminded that our first stop was in a drugstore, and suddenly remember squeezing the car into a narrow space just across the street. But occasionally the effect is much more dramatic. Some people reported having been unable to recall some of the simplest geographical features of the hometown they left years before. They finally returned for a visit, barely reached the outskirts, and suddenly all of the memories flooded back, often with a sharp pang of emotions that had been felt years before. Physical places are only one source of retrieval cues that may bring back the past. A word, a mood, a smell, a visit from a school friend not met for decades—any of these may trigger memories we thought were utterly lost.

Retrieval cues in the movies *A scene from Charlie Chaplin's 1931 film,* City Lights, *which shows the little tramp with a millionaire (played by Harry Myers) who befriends him one night while drunk, doesn't recognize him the next morning when he is sober, but greets him as an old friend when he gets drunk again the following night. While nowhere as extreme as this, such state-dependent memory effects have been observed in the laboratory. (Eich, 1980; courtesy of Photofest)*

THE RELATION BETWEEN ORIGINAL ENCODING AND RETRIEVAL

What are the characteristics of an effective retrieval cue? It is obvious that not every reminder will in fact remind us, will in fact help us retrieve what is stored. The best guess is that success is most likely if the context at the time of retrieval approximates that during original encoding. This is sometimes

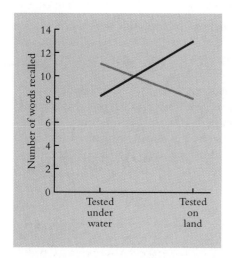

7.6 The effect of changing the retrieval situation *Scuba divers learned a list of 36 unrelated words above water (dark red) or 20 feet underwater (blue) and were then tested above or underwater. The figure shows that retention was better when the retrieval situation was the same as that in which encoding took place. (Godden and Baddeley, 1975)*

called the **compatibility principle** (or the **encoding-specificity principle;** Tulving and Osler, 1968; Tulving and Thomson, 1973; Hintzman, 1990).

A rather dramatic illustration of the compatibility principle is provided by a study of scuba divers who had to learn a list of unrelated words either on a boat or underwater and who were later tested for recall in either the same or the alternate environment in which they had learned. The results showed a clear-cut context effect: What was learned in the water was best recalled in the water, likewise for what was learned on deck (Godden and Baddeley, 1975; see Figure 7.6).

Similar effects can be obtained without going underwater. One experimenter presented subjects with a long list of words. A day later he brought them back for an unexpected recall test that took place in either the same room or in a different one, one that varied in size, furnishings, and so on. Recall was considerably better for subjects who were tested in the same physical environment. But the investigator found a simple way of overcoming this context effect. A different group of subjects was brought to the new room, but just prior to the recall test these subjects were asked to think about the room in which they had learned the lists—what is looked like, what it made them feel like. By doing so, they mentally recreated the old environment for themselves. On the subsequent recall test, these subjects performed no worse than those for whom there was no change of rooms. It appears that what matters is not so much that the retrieval cues physically match the conditions of acquisition; what counts is how the subject thinks about these conditions at the time he tries to recall (Smith, 1979).

MEMORY SEARCH

■ Many investigators believe that retrieval is generally preceded by an internal process call **memory search.** In most cases, this process occurs without our awareness and at great speed, as when answering the question: "Which president of the United States had the first name *Abraham?*" But there are times when we do become aware that some such process is going on, as we consciously sift and sort among our memories until we finally recall just who it was that did what to whom on which occasion many years ago.

SEARCH STRATEGIES

In a study of such conscious search processes, subjects were asked to try to recall the names of their high-school classmates after intervals of from four to nineteen years. Their recall accuracy was checked by consulting their high-school yearbooks. The subjects came up with a fair number of names in the first few minutes of this attempt. After this, they said that they couldn't remember any more. But the experimenters asked them to keep on trying anyway. And so they did, for ten sessions of one hour each. As they continued their efforts, they surprised themselves by dredging up more and more names, until they finally recalled about a third of the names of a class of three hundred (Williams and Hollan, 1982).

While going about this task, the subjects were asked to think aloud. Their comments fit the analogy of a physical search. They seemed to hunt for the sought-for names as one might search for a tangible object, inspecting one likely memory location after another. Their efforts were rarely haphazard, but seemed often based on well-formulated search strategies. For example, they mentally looked through their various classes, clubs, and teams, or scanned internal pictures to locate yet another person whom they would then try to name:

. . . It's like I want to think of, sort of prototypical situations and then sort of examine the people that were involved in those. And things like P.E. class, where there was . . . Ah . . . Gary Booth. Umm, and Karl Brist . . . Umm . . . I can think of things like dances. I guess then I usually think of . . . of girls . . . Like Cindy Shup, Judy Foss, and Sharon Ellis . . . I mean it's sort of like I have a picture of the high school dance. . . . (Williams and Hollan, 1982, p. 90)

THE TIP-OF-THE-TONGUE PHENOMENON

Needless to say, search isn't always successful. Some forgotten names are never retrieved, no matter how hard we try. But occasionally, we experience a kind of halfway point, when we seem about to recall something but don't quite. When this occurs, we feel as if the searched-for memory is on "the tip of the tongue," but we are unable to go beyond. There is no better description of this phenomenon than that by William James:

> Suppose we try to recall a forgotten name. The state of our consciousness is peculiar. There is a gap therein; but no mere gap. It is a gap that is intensely active. A sort of wraith of the name is in it, beckoning us in a given direction, making us at moments tingle with the sense of our closeness, and then letting us sink back without the longed-for term. If wrong names are proposed to us, this singularly definite gap acts immediately so as to negate them. They do not fit into its mold. And the gap of one word does not feel like the gap of another, all empty of content as both might seem necessarily to be when described as gaps. (James, 1890, vol. 1, p. 251)

There is evidence that the tip-of-the-tongue experience described by James is a good reflection of how close to the mark we had actually come in our memory search, that we were really "getting warm," though unable to reach the exact spot. In one study college students were presented with the dictionary definitions of uncommon English words such as *apse, sampan,* and *cloaca.* The subjects were asked to supply the words that fit these definitions. The experimenters were concerned with those occasions on which subjects were unable to recall the target word but felt that they were on the verge of finding it. Whenever this happened, they were asked to venture some guesses about what the target word sounded like. These guesses turned out to be closely related to the target. Given that the target word was said to be at the tip-of-the-tongue, its initial letter was guessed correctly over 50 percent of the time. Similar results were found when the subjects were asked to guess at the number of syllables. When asked to supply some other words that they thought sounded like the target, the subjects were usually in the correct phonological neighborhood. Presented with the definition "a small Chinese boat" for which the proper answer is *sampan,* subjects who said they almost remembered but not quite supplied the following as sound-alikes: *saipan, Siam, Cheyenne,* and *sarong* (Brown and McNeill, 1966; Koriat and Lieblich, 1974).

IMPLICIT RETRIEVAL

Up to now, we've considered only methods of retrieval that are *explicit,* specifically recall and recognition. In both procedures, the subject is asked a question that refers to her prior experience. She may be tested for recall: "Tell me the name of one of your former high-school teachers." Or she may be asked for recognition: "Was Mr. Halberdam one of your former high-school teachers?" In either case, the question explicitly refers to the subject's remembered past. But retrieval can be *implicit* rather than explicit. An example comes from the performance of well-practiced skills. In general, the pianist need not be consciously aware of when and where he learned to finger the keys as he strikes a

External aids to memory *People often rely on external memory aids. Some remind us of events in our past, such as family albums and high-school yearbooks. Others remind us of plans for future actions, such as calendars, memo pads, and shopping lists. (Brockton High-School yearbook, class of 1975, p. 108)*

chord, nor does the golfer need consciously to remember where and how she perfected her golf swing while swinging the club. We know of course that the achievements of these skilled performers are honed by constant practice and thus depend on memory. To play the chord or hit the ball, both pianist and golfer necessarily retrieve something from memory, but these retrievals are implicit rather than explicit, for there is typically no awareness of "remembering" at the time.

Implicit retrieval has been the subject of many laboratory investigations (see Schacter, 1987, 1992; Roediger, 1990). In one such study the subjects were shown a number of words after which they were given two tests of memory. The first was a test of explicit memory in which a standard recognition procedure was employed. The second was a test of implicit memory in which the subjects' task was to identify words that were flashed on a screen for 35 milliseconds. Some of these words were the same as those that had been on the original list. The results of this second test showed *repetition priming:* Words that had been on the original list were identified more readily than words that had not. The crucial finding was that this priming effect held even for words that the subjects failed to recognize during the previous test of explicit retrieval. In short, subjects may show signs of implicit memory for items that they cannot consciously—that is, explicitly—remember, if their retrieval is tested implicitly (Jacoby and Witherspoon, 1982).

Similar implicit retrieval effects have been shown using a number of other priming procedures. An example is *fragment completion* in which subjects are presented with a word in which letters are missing (such as C_O_O_I_E for CROCODILE) and have to complete it with the first appropriate word that comes to mind. Here priming is indicated by an increased tendency to use words that were shown on a previous list (Jacoby and Dallas, 1981; Tulving, Schacter, and Stark, 1982; Graf and Mandler, 1984).

IMPLICIT RETRIEVAL AND FEELINGS OF FAMILIARITY

Thus far most of our discussion of the difference between implicit and explicit retrieval has centered on laboratory studies. But this distinction may help to explain a phenomenon we have all experienced in everyday life: the feeling that something is familiar, though we can't for the life of us recall where or when we encountered it. According to one hypothesis, the explanation is implicit retrieval. Something is retrieved, so there is the sense of familiarity. But the retrieval remains implicit, so there is no *source memory* and no knowledge of where the memory came from.

An elegant laboratory demonstration of this effect was produced in a study on "How to Become Famous Overnight." The subjects first took what they thought was a pronunciation test by reading a long list of unfamiliar names aloud. A day later, they were presented with a second list of names. This time their task was to decide whether the names were of famous people or not. Half of the names on the list were of moderately famous people (e.g., Esther Williams). The other half were the names of people who were not famous at all but instead were picked from a telephone directory (e.g., Sebastian Weisdorf). The crucial point of the experiment was that some of these nonfamous names, such as Sebastian Weisdorf, had appeared on the original pronunciation list.

The results showed that familiarity sometimes breeds fame rather than contempt. At least it did for Sebastian Weisdorf, for he and others who had appeared on the first list were now erroneously judged to be famous. What happened was simple. The name Sebastian Weisdorf produced an implicit retrieval process with a consequent feeling of familiarity. But since the subject couldn't recall where or when she'd encountered that name before, she made the reasonable judgment: I probably read his name in a newspaper or heard it on TV—so he's famous.

In an important control experiment, the second list was presented immediately after the original pronunciation list. Now there was little confusion. To be sure, Sebastian's name triggered a sense of familiarity. But since the pronunciation list had been read just minutes before, the subject knew exactly why his name was familiar, and so she decided that Sebastian was not famous after all (Jacoby, et al., 1989).

Implicit retrieval may also help to explain the occasional experience of *déjà vu*—the feeling that we've met someone or visited some locale before, even though there is no question that we couldn't possibly have done so (e.g., we'd never been in the country where we encountered the familiar place). A possible interpretation is that the oddly familiar event aroused some memory trace—perhaps by association or through similarity or whatever—but that this arousal was entirely implicit. All that remained was an uncanny feeling of familiarity with no source memory whatsoever—the eerie sense of *déjà vu*.

WHEN MEMORY FAILS

FOCUS QUESTIONS

- What three major theories attempt to explain forgetting?
- What are proactive and retroactive inhibition?
- What are schemas and scripts, and how do they affect what we remember?
- What are the two major kinds of amnesia, and how do they differ?
- What are procedural and declarative knowledge, and which can those with anterograde amnesia acquire?

In popular usage, the word *forgetting* is employed as a blanket term whenever memory fails. But as we've seen, memorial failures have many causes. Some arise from faulty encoding, while others arise at the moment of recall. In this section, we will discuss three broad topics that deal with memory failure. One concerns the lapse of time. Why is it easier to remember the recent past than it is to remember events from long ago? A second is the role of reconstruction in remembering, since much of remembering turns out to be a form of problem solving in which we draw on what we expect and believe to supplement what we actually remember. The third topic is somewhat different and concerns what happens to memory in certain cases of brain damage.

Very Bad Memory

(Cartoon by Abner Dean)

FORGETTING

At least on the face of it, forgetting increases with **retention interval,** the time that intervenes between original learning and the time of the test. Yesterday's lesson is better remembered than last week's. This fact was well known to Hermann Ebbinghaus (1850–1909), who began the experimental study of human learning by constructing lists of nonsense syllables—two consonants with a vowel in between that do not form a word, such as *zup* and *rif*—and then serving as his own subject as he memorized their serial order. He was the first to plot a **forgetting curve** by testing himself at various intervals after

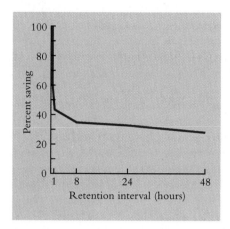

7.7 Forgetting curve *The figure shows retention after various intervals since learning. Retention is here measured in percentage saving, that is, the percent decrease in the number of trials required to relearn the list after an interval of no practice. If the saving is 100 percent, retention is perfect—no trials to relearn are necessary. If the saving is 0 percent, there is no retention at all, for it takes just as many trials to relearn the list as it took to learn it initially. (After Ebbinghaus, 1885)*

learning (using different lists for each interval) and then asking how much effort he had to expend to relearn the list to the level previously achieved. He found that there was a saving: Relearning the list took fewer trials than did the original learning. As one might expect, the saving declined as the retention interval increased. The decline was sharpest immediately after learning and became more gradual thereafter (Ebbinghaus, 1885; see Figure 7.7).

What accounts for the fact that the retention of the long-term memories seems to decline the longer the time since the memory was acquired? There are several theories designed to explain this and related phenomena.

DECAY

The most venerable theory of forgetting holds that memory traces gradually *decay* as time passes, like mountains that are eroded by wind and water. The erosion of memories is presumably caused by normal metabolic processes that wear down the memory trace until it fades and finally disintegrates.

Like most chemical reactions, many metabolic processes increase with increasing temperature. If these metabolic reactions are responsible for memorial decay, then forgetting should be a function of body temperature during the retention interval. One study tried to provide an indirect test of this theory by varying body temperature. This prediction was tested with cold-blooded animals, such as goldfish, whose bodies take on the temperature of their surroundings. By and large, the results were in line with the hypothesis: The higher the temperature of the tank in which the fish were kept during the retention interval, the more forgetting that took place (Gleitman and Rozin, as reported in Gleitman, 1971).

But other findings complicate this picture. There is good evidence that forgetting is determined not simply by normal metabolic processes during the retention interval, but by what actually happens to the subject during this time. Experiments on humans have shown that recall is substantially worse after an interval spent awake than after an equal period while asleep (Jenkins and Dallenback, 1924). Later studies suggest that the favorable effect of sleep on retention only holds for quiet, slow-wave sleep (Ekstrand, 1972; Ekstrand et al., 1977).

Such results pose difficulties for a theory that assigns all of the blame for forgetting to decay, for they show that the normal metabolic processes that occur over time do not cause all of the loss. To explain such findings within a theory of decay, one would have to assert that the processes that erode the memory trace are slowed down (or counteracted) during one or all of the sleep states.

INTERFERENCE

A rather different theory of forgetting is *interference*. According to this view, a forgotten memory is neither lost nor damaged, but is only misplaced among a number of other memories that interfere with the recovery of the one that was sought. Seen in this light, our inability to remember the name of a high-school friend is analogous to what happens when a clerk cannot find a letter he received a year ago. The letter is still somewhere in his files, but it has been hopelessly buried in a mass of other letters that he filed both before and since. The greater the length of time since original acquisition, the greater the opportunity for new acquisitions to interfere (or, in terms of the filing analogy, the greater the chance that the accumulation of other letters will get in the way).

Memorial interference is easily demonstrated in the laboratory. A major example is *retroactive inhibition* in which new learning hampers recall of the old. In a typical study, a control group learns some rote material, such as a list of nonsense syllables (List *A*), and is tested after a specified interval. The experimental group learns the same list as the control group and is tested after the

TABLE 7.1 RETROACTIVE INHIBITION EXPERIMENT

	Initial Period	Retention interval	Test period
Control Group	Learns list A	———————	Recalls list A
Experimental Group	Learns list A	Learns list B	Recalls list A

same retention interval. But in addition it must also learn a second list (List *B*) that is interpolated during the retention interval (Table 7.1). The usual result is a marked inferiority in the performance of the experimental group; the interpolated list interferes with (inhibits) the recall of List *A* (McGeoch and Irion, 1952; Crowder, 1976).

A similar effect is ***proactive inhibition*** in which interference works in a forward (proactive) direction. The usual procedure is to have an experimental group learn List *A* followed by List *B* and then to test for recall of List *B* after a suitable retention interval. The critical comparison is with a control group that learns only List B (Table 7.2). In general, the experimental group does worse on the recall test (e.g., Underwood, 1957). Such interference effects can have serious consequences. An example is the difficulty encountered by U.S. visitors in Britain when driving on the left side of the road. A more exotic example is recounted of a young woman who in moments of passion had the embarrassing tendency to cry out the name of a previous lover (Loftus, 1980, as cited in Baddeley, 1990).

CHANGE OF RETRIEVAL CUES

Decay theory holds that the memory trace gradually fades away with time, while interference asserts that the trace gets lost among other traces acquired both before and after the forgotten material was learned. There is a further alternative which argues that memorial success or failure is primarily determined by the retrieval cues presented at the time of recall.

We have already seen that a change in retrieval cues disrupts remembering. But can this effect explain why forgetting increases with an increasing retention interval? To maintain the hypothesis that the critical factor is cue alteration, one must assume that such an alteration becomes ever more likely with the passage of time. There are some cases for which this may well be true. Certain memories may have been acquired in a particular locale; over the years the neighborhood changes as some houses are torn down and new ones are built, thus altering the physical cues and thereby decreasing the chance of retrieval.

Some authors appeal to the retrieval-cue hypothesis to explain the phenomenon of ***childhood amnesia***—the fact that most of us can't recall events of our

The child's world is in many ways utterly different from the adult's According to some authors, childhood amnesia is partially produced by the enormous change in the retrieval cues available to the adult. (Photo courtesy of Suzanne Szasz)

TABLE 7.2 PROACTIVE INHIBITION EXPERIMENT

	Initial Period		Retention interval	Test period
Control Group	———————	Learns list B	———————	Recalls list B
Experimental Group	Learns list A	Learns list B	———————	Recalls list B

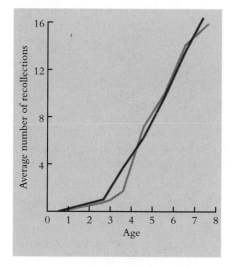

7.8 Number of childhood memories
College students were asked to recall childhood experiences. The figure plots the average number of events recalled as a function of the age at which they occurred for men (blue) and for women (dark red). Women recall a bit more at the earliest ages, which may reflect the fact that the maturation of girls is generally ahead of that of boys. (Data from Waldfogel, 1948)

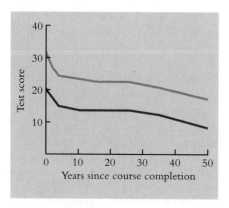

7.9 Forgetting a foreign language *The figure displays performance on a Spanish reading comprehension test administered from 0 to 50 years after taking Spanish in high school or college to subjects who had previously earned a grade of A (blue) or C (dark red). (After Bahrick, 1984)*

very early childhood. When college students are asked to report any events they can remember that occurred in early life, the average age of their earliest recollection is about three-and-a-half years (Waldfogel, 1948; Sheingold and Tenney, 1982; see Figure 7.8). One possible cause is a massive change of retrieval cues. The world of the young child is utterly different from the world she will occupy some ten or fifteen years later. It is a world in which tables are hopelessly out of reach, chairs can be climbed upon only with great effort, and adults are giants in size and gods in ability. Whatever memories the child may store at this time are necessarily formed and encoded within this context; thus the appropriate retrieval context is necessarily absent from the adult's environment (Schachtel, 1947; Neisser, 1967).

But encoding differences may also contribute to such memorial failures. According to some authors, infants and very young children store memories—especially explicit memories—less efficiently than older children and adults. This may be because some relevant neural structures are not yet sufficiently mature (Nadel and Zola-Morgan, 1984). It may also be because these very young children have not yet developed the necessary schemas within which experiences can be explicitly organized, encoded, and rehearsed (White and Pillemer, 1979). Thus, while cue change may account for some aspects of childhood amnesia, it almost surely does not account for it all (see also Howe and Courage, 1993).

WHEN FORGETTING SEEMS NOT TO OCCUR

The fact that there is forgetting doesn't mean that it always occurs. For memory doesn't always fail, even after very long intervals.

Long-lasting memories Some evidence was provided by Harry Bahrick, who studied the long-term retention of materials in semantic memory. Bahrick was interested in what people remember from what they learned in school. To this end, he gave a Spanish reading-comprehension test to nearly 800 people who had studied Spanish for three or four years either in high school or in college. They were tested at intervals that ranged from one week to fifty years since their last Spanish course. The results showed that quite a bit is forgotten in the first two or three years after learning. But after this, the test performance levels off until much later in life, where aging effects probably account for the bulk of the later memory loss (see Figure 7.9). Educators will probably be gratified by the fact that even after fifty years the test performance reflects how well the language was learned originally. On average, students who had earned an A performed better than those who had received a C, even after half a century had passed (Bahrick, 1984). Similar findings come from a more recent study on the retention of knowledge acquired in an advanced psychology course, which showed rather good retention of basic concepts—but not of proper names—after retention intervals up to twelve years (Conway, Cohen, and Stanhope, 1991).

The important finding is that some fraction of what had been learned originally remained intact without any further forgetting. In Bahrick's terms, these memories—vocabulary items, idioms, bits of grammar, psychological theories—moved into what he called a ***permastore.*** The semantic memory of an adult contains much information that is essentially permanent. We don't forget the meaning of ordinary words or the rules of arithmetic or many individual bits of information. In part, this may be because such materials are extremely well-learned in the first place. But in part, it may be because such items—and one hopes much of what we learn in school—have an inherent structure that protects them from being forgotten, a structure that Ebbinghaus's series of nonsense syllables certainly lacked (Neisser, 1989).

Childhood memories   *While there is child-hood amnesia for the events of the first two or three years, some early memories do remain, often in a jumbled and kaleidoscopic fashion. Thus the paintings of the Russian émigré artist Marc Chagall (1887–1985) show composite images of his early life in a Russian village, including a cow being milked, his mother, a child's naïve picture of a Russian village, and so on. (I and the Village, 1911, oil on canvas, 6'3⅝" × 59⅝". Collection of The Museum of Modern Art, New York, Mrs. Simon Guggenheim Fund)*

Flashbulb memories   Bahrick's findings concerned semantic memory. Are there episodic memories that are also essentially immune to being forgotten? According to Roger Brown and James Kulik, certain unexpected and emotionally important events produce *flashbulb memories,* which are extremely vivid and essentially permanent. They believe that such memories are like a photograph that preserves the scene when a flashbulb is fired. Some of the events that trigger the flash may be private and personal, such as an early morning telephone call that tells of a parent's death. Others may involve news of powerful national import such as the assassination of President Kennedy or the space shuttle disaster. Brown and Kulik found that most people recalled where they were at the time they learned of President Kennedy's assassination and also what they did, who told them, and so on. On the face of it, these detailed memories are surprising.

A

B

Events that have produced flashbulb memories   *(A) After the Kennedy assassination; (B) the space shuttle disaster. (Courtesy of the Bettmann Archive)*

That a president's assassination is an important and memorable event is obvious, but why should so many Americans recall the humdrum circumstances in which they personally found themselves at the time, such as "the weather was cloudy and gray," or "I was carrying a carton of Viceroy cigarettes, which I dropped"? According to Brown and Kulik, the reason is that such surprising and emotionally powerful events set off a mental flashbulb that preserves the entire scene along with perfectly mundane and unremarkable details (Brown and Kulik, 1977; see also Pillemer, 1984; McCloskey, Wible, and Cohen, 1988).

The flashbulb hypothesis has been the subject of considerable debate. The main issue is whether such memories are really created by a special mechanism that fixes the circumstances of the moment with a special "flashbulb" clarity. The best guess is that such a special mechanism does not exist. To begin with, there is some debate about the accuracy of these memories; they may be vivid, but that does not mean that they are fully correct (e.g., Neisser, 1982a, 1986; Thompson and Cowan, 1986; McCloskey, Wible, and Cohen, 1988). In addition, much of what was remembered may have been rehearsed in subsequent conversations with others, so that what was entered in memory did not in fact depend on a hypothetical flashbulb set off in the head. All in all, there is good reason to doubt the existence of a special flashbulb mechanism.

CONCEPTUAL FRAMEWORKS AND REMEMBERING

■ Thus far, our primary concern has been with memory failures that involve errors of omission in which we draw a blank, are unable to recall a name or recognize a face, and come up with nothing. We now turn to another kind of failure in which the memory error is one of *commission*. These are errors in which we give a distorted account by unwittingly reconstructing facts and events based on what we think and know rather than on what we really remember.

We've repeatedly stressed that remembering depends upon encoding and retrieval. These in turn are affected by still another factor: what the learner already knows. For all remembering takes place against a backdrop of prior knowledge that necessarily colors whatever enters memory. Without prior knowledge, we could not understand the words we hear, their connection with each other, or their relation to events in the world. Using prior knowledge in memory is analogous to top-down processing in perception. As in perception, such top-down effects can be enormously helpful. But again as in perception, our knowledge and expectations can lead us astray. For just as we can misperceive, so we can—and often do—misremember.

MEMORY DISTORTIONS

The most influential experiments on memory distortions were performed by the British psychologist Frederic Bartlett almost sixty years ago. Bartlett's subjects were asked to reproduce stories taken from the folklore of other cultures; thus, their content and structure were rather strange to Western ears. The reproductions showed many changes from the original. Some parts were subtracted; others were overelaborated; still others were additions that were completely new. In effect, the subjects had built a new story upon the memorial ruins of the original. This memorial reconstruction was generally more consonant with the cultural conceptions of the subjects than with the story they had actually heard. For example, certain supernatural plot elements were reinterpreted along more familiar lines.

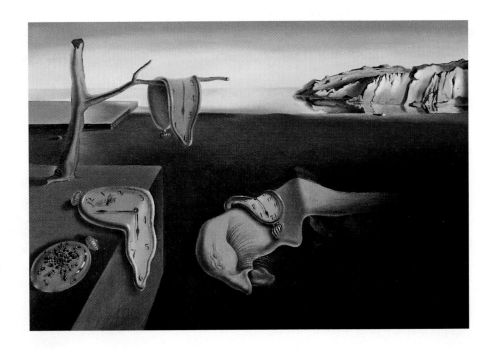

The Persistence of Memory *by Salvador Dali (1931). Memory persists, sometimes in distorted form. (Oil on canvas, 9½" × 13"; collection of the Museum of Modern Art; given anonymously)*

The effect of schemas and scripts Numerous experiments document Bartlett's claim that memories for events or narratives are strongly affected by the framework of prior knowledge in terms of which they are understood. In one study, subjects were asked to read a description of a home while taking either of two different viewpoints: that of a prospective home buyer or that of a burglar. Later recall showed that the different perspectives affected what was remembered: in the case of the "home buyers," a leaky roof; in the case of the "burglars," a valuable coin collection (Anderson and Pichert, 1978). In another study, there were errors of commission. Subjects were told about a person's visit to the dentist and then falsely recalled hearing some details that typically occur in a dentist's office (checking in with the receptionist, looking at a magazine in the waiting room, and so on), even though these were never explicitly mentioned (Bower, Black, and Turner, 1979).

In all these cases, the subjects' memory was affected by their knowledge of the world. They had some ideas of how home buyers, burglars, and dental patients are likely to behave, and they fit their particular recollections into the general outlines of this knowledge, filling in various gaps in memory without knowing that they did so. Following Bartlett, many contemporary psychologists describe such conceptual frameworks as *schemas.* As used in this context, the term refers to a general cognitive structure into which data or events can be entered, typically with more attention to broad brush strokes than to specific details. Many aspects of our experience are redundant: When prospective buyers look at a house, they inspect the roof and basement; when patients visit the dentist, they generally check in with a receptionist, and so on. A schema is an effective summary of this redundancy and can therefore help us interpret and supplement the details of our remembered experience (Schwartz and Reisberg, 1991). A special subcase of a schema is a *script,* which describes a characteristic scenario of behavior in a particular setting, such as a restaurant script (whose sequence includes being seated, looking at the menu, ordering the meal, eating the food, paying the bill, and leaving), or the visit-to-the-dentist script we just described (Schank and Abelson, 1977).

Eyewitness testimony The schema-induced distortions we've discussed thus far were not particularly damaging. To be sure, the subject's memory for the partic-

(Drawing by Chas. Addams; © 1979, The New Yorker Magazine, Inc.)

ular details was faulty, but that hardly mattered since she recalled the gist. Under the circumstances, there was no harm done, since our ultimate object is to remember what a statement is all about, not its detailed phrasing. One might even argue that schematized remembering is beneficial since its efficiency lets us package, store, and retrieve more material than we could otherwise manage in an information-cluttered world.

The trouble is that this enhanced efficiency has a down-side, for sometimes the details are of considerable importance. They certainly are to lawyers and judges, who are concerned with the accuracy of eyewitness testimony. Witnesses are sometimes quite confident of various circumstances they remember, even though their recollections don't fit the actual facts. An accident occurred months ago, and its details have dimmed over time. As the witness tries to retrieve this past event, he may fill in the gaps by an inference of which he is quite unaware. In these cases (and many others), schematic distortion can have very damaging effects.

A series of studies by Elizabeth Loftus and her associates has highlighted this problem of schematized memory processes in eyewitness testimony. An important factor is the way in which recall is elicited. In one study, subjects viewed a brief film segment of a car accident. Immediately afterward they were asked a number of questions that were in either of two forms:

"Did you see the broken headlight?"
or
"Did you see a broken headlight?"

The results showed that subjects who were questioned about *the* headlight were more likely to report having seen one than subjects who were asked about *a* headlight. This was so whether the film actually showed a broken headlight or not. Here the schema is provided by the nature of our language. In effect, the use of the definite article, *the,* makes the query a leading question, one which implies that there really was a broken headlight and that the only issue is whether the subject noticed it. No such presupposition is made when the indefinite article, *a,* is used (Loftus and Zanni, 1975).

Some authors believe that schemas can do more than just fill in gaps, as is shown by a study in which leading questions during a first interrogation changed how the witnessed event was reported later. Subjects were again shown film segments of a car accident. Shortly afterward some of them were asked leading questions such as, "Did you see the children getting on the school bus?" A week later, all subjects were asked the direct question, "Did you see a school bus in the film?" In actual fact, there was no school bus. But when compared to controls, subjects who were originally asked the leading question that presupposed the school bus were three to four times more likely to say that they had seen one. It would seem that a false memory of a bus had been implanted (Loftus, 1975).

Another study also suggests that schemas may actually alter memories: Subjects were shown slides of an automobile collision. Later on, the subjects were asked either of two questions: "How fast were the cars going when they hit each other?" or "How fast were the cars going when they smashed into each other?" A week later the subjects were asked whether they had seen any broken glass in any of the slides they had been shown. (In actual fact, there was none.) Subjects who had been asked about the cars that "smashed into each other" were much more likely to report having seen such glass than subjects who were asked about the cars that "hit each other" (Loftus and Palmer, 1974).

In this and the school-bus study, earlier memories seem to have changed to accord with later interpretation, as if the past were rewritten and updated to fit into the current view. Such retrospective alterations of memory, called *accommodative distortions,* are of considerable relevance not only to the psychology of memory but to the legal process as well. To students of memory, they highlight the importance of prior knowledge and expectations in memory. To legal scholars they reemphasize the crucial importance of how questions are worded, not only in the courtroom but also in prior interrogations. Whether such phenomena really prove that old memories are easily erased and updated is still a matter of debate. But whatever the ultimate verdict on this point, one thing is clear: Such retrospective alterations change how a memory is *reported* (Belli, 1989; Loftus and Hoffman, 1989; Tversky and Tuchin, 1989; Zaragoza and McCloskey, 1989).

THE LIMITS OF MEMORY

There is ample evidence that memory is often fallible and subject to distortion. But the phenomena of retrieval tell us that more is retained in memory than we typically dig out and recall on any one occasion. This fact has led to a search for special techniques for recovering memories that have some particular importance, such as trying to help witnesses remember what a suspect said or did.

Memory, hypnosis, and the courtroom　A case in point is hypnosis. A number of law enforcement agencies have used this as a device to prompt witness recall in criminal investigations. A witness is hypnotized, told that he is back at a certain time and place, and asked to tell what he sees. On the surface, the results—in both the real world and in laboratory studies—are quite impressive. A hypnotized witness identifies an assailant as he mentally returns to the scene of the crime; a hypnotized college student is brought back to the age of six and relives his sixth birthday party with appropriately childlike glee. There is little doubt that these hypnotized people are convinced that they are actually reexperiencing these events, that what they recall really happened. But upon investigation, it often turns out that the hypnotically prodded memories are false. In one courtroom case, a suspect turned out to have been abroad at the time the hypnotized witness recalled having seen him during an assault (Orne, 1979). Similar points apply to the description of childhood events elicited under hypnosis. Convinc-

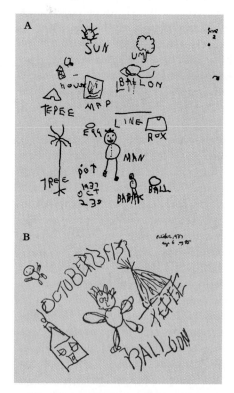

7.10 Remembering studied through drawings done while under hypnosis *(A) Drawings done at age six. (B) Drawings done while subject was hypnotized and told that he was six years old. Note some interesting differences between the pictures, for example, the tepee, which is much more detailed in (B); the spelling of* balloon; *and a sense of overall design present in (B) and altogether lacking in (A). (From Orne, 1951)*

ing details such as the name of a first-grade teacher generally turn out to be quite false when later checked against available records. Some subjects were asked to draw a picture while mentally back at the age of six. At first glance, their drawings looked remarkably childlike. But when compared to the subjects' own childhood drawings made at that very age, it is clear that they are much more sophisticated. They represent an adult's conception of what a childish drawing is, rather than being the real thing (Figure 7.10; Orne, 1951).

How can we explain these results? First of all, it is clear that hypnosis does not have the near-magical powers often attributed to it (Barber, 1969; Orne and Hammer, 1974; Hilgard, 1977). Hypnosis does not enable us to relive our past at will (nor, for that matter, does it permit feats of agility or strength of which we are otherwise incapable). What it does do is to make people unusually anxious to believe in and cooperate with another person, the hypnotist, and to do what he asks of them (within the bounds of certain mutually understood limitations). If he asks them to remember, they will do their very best to oblige. They will doggedly stick to the task and rummage through their minds to find any possible retrieval cue. And so of course would we all, whether hypnotized or not, providing that we wanted to remember badly enough. But what if we don't succeed? If we are not hypnotized, we will eventually concede failure. But hypnotized people will not. They try to please the hypnotist who has told them to recall and has assured them that they can. And so they do what the hypnotist asks. They produce memories—by creatively adding and reconstructing on the basis of what they already know. As we have seen, such reconstructions are a common feature in much so-called remembering. The difference is that under hypnosis subjects become unusually confident that their memories are real (probably because of the hypnotist's suggestion).

Some evidence for this interpretation comes from a study on the susceptibility of those under hypnosis to leading questions. The experimenter employed the familiar technique of showing subjects videotapes of an accident and later asking them to recall certain details, in some cases while hypnotized and in others while not. Some of the probes were leading questions, while others were more objective in phrasing. As we just saw, such leading questions lead to errors even without hypnosis. But they lead to even more errors in hypnotized subjects than in controls. When asked whether they had seen "the license plate . . ." (which in fact was not visible), some of the hypnotized subjects not only said yes but actually volunteered partial descriptions of the license plate number. Findings of this sort cast serious doubts on the use of hypnosis in real-life judicial settings (Putnam, 1979; Smith, 1983).

The tape-recorder theory of memory Over and above what these findings tell us about hypnosis, they also have implications for what is sometimes called the tape-recorder (or, to update it, the videotape-recorder) theory of memory. According to this view, the brain contains a virtually imperishable record of all we have ever heard or seen or felt. The only trick is to find a way to turn the recorder back to some desired portion of the tape. But the evidence indicates that this suggestion is exceedingly implausible. All techniques that claim to provide such memory "playbacks"—the major example is hypnosis—have been found wanting. Under the circumstances, our best guess is that the tape-recorder theory is false. To be sure, we retain much more than we can retrieve at any given moment. But this doesn't mean we retain every bit of sensory information we encounter. Some is never entered, some is lost if not rehearsed and organized, and some is altered to fit in with incoming material (Loftus and Loftus, 1980; Neisser, 1982b).

Are there false memories? A special problem that has lately received much public attention concerns the reality of so-called ***repressed memories.*** In recent years, a considerable number of people have reported memories of traumatic childhood events, usually involving sexual abuse. As these people tell it, these memories had been pushed out of consciousness—that is, repressed—for many years, sometimes for as long as two or three decades. The memories surface much later, often while the person is being treated by a therapist who in many cases employs hypnosis. Are these memories accurate—that is, a true recounting of the actual history of what happened? This question has serious social and legal significance, all the more since many of the accusers have brought civil suits against the alleged perpetrators—parents or other relatives—or charged them in criminal court.

The authenticity of such long-repressed memories has been questioned in a recent paper by Elizabeth Loftus (Loftus, 1993). As she points out, there is some debate about whether memories can be repressed to such a massive extent and for so long a time; some even doubt whether the phenomenon of repression exists at all (e.g., Holmes, 1990). A further question concerns the role of psychotherapy. Many people who report the resurrection of repressed memories of child abuse are under the care of therapists who are convinced that their patients' psychological problems stem from childhood abuse and that these problems can only be dealt with if the patient faces them squarely by uncovering the buried memories of that abuse (e.g., Bass and Davis, 1988). Under these circumstances, there is a strong possibility of accommodative distortion and memory reconstruction. This possibility is further enhanced by the fact that many of these therapists use hypnosis as a means of uncovering the repressed childhood past.

None of this is said to minimize the social and moral problems produced by childhood sexual abuse and incest, the prevalence of which is clearly greater than previously supposed. Nor can we deny that some—perhaps very many—of the memories of childhood sexual abuse are valid. But we cannot take the veracity of these memories for granted: We know that it is possible to remember events from very long ago, but we also know that the possibility for error is greater in remembering the distant past than in remembering recent events. Likewise, we saw in our discussion of retrieval failures that some memories will come to light only if appropriately triggered with well-chosen cues, but we also saw that close questioning of a subject can *create* "memories" about things that never occurred, especially if the questions are asked of a hypnotized subject. We therefore have to be very cautious in accepting the accuracy of memories of long-past events, especially if those memories emerged through therapists' suggestions and hypnosis (Loftus, 1993; Kihlstrom, 1993; for a sharply divergent position, see Bass and Davis, 1988).

THE LIMITS OF DISTORTION

In the last chapter we saw that perception is an active process. It depends on incoming stimuli, but it does not provide a mere copy of that stimulus, for the incoming sensory information is often reshaped and transformed. A similar point applies to memory. Memory depends on what is stored, but a given act of remembering provides us with more than a frozen slice of the past; it often reconstructs events to fill in gaps as we unwittingly try to fit our past into our present (Neisser, 1967).

But these acts of cognitive construction and reconstruction have some limits, in memory as well as in perception. For while there are numerous ways in which a memory can be distorted, such distortions don't always occur—far from it. After all, we do remember many details of experiences we've been exposed to, and many of those fit into no particular cognitive mold. And even in cases in which various schemas have led to distortions of recall, subsequent tests of recognition show that more is remembered than seems so at first (Alba and Hasher, 1983).

In sum, our memory is neither wholly distorted nor wholly accurate. The tape-recorder theory of memory is false. But so is the theory that everything we remember is changed and distorted by inference and reconstruction. In these regards, memory is again much like perception. Both are affected by processes that work from the top down as well as by those that start from the bottom up. Perception without any bottom-up processing (that is, without any reference to stimuli) would amount to continual hallucination. Memory without bottom-up processing (that is, without any reference to memory traces) would amount to perpetual delusion, a mere will-o'-the-wisp in which the remembered past is continually constructed and reconstructed to fit the schemas of the moment. Both top-down and bottom-up processes operate in both cognitive domains.

The use of schemas—that is, top-down processing—clearly has a cost, for it can lead to distortions of memory. But it also confers great benefits. Our cognitive machinery is limited: There's only so much that we can encode, store, and retrieve. As a result, we are forced to schematize and simplify so that we can impose order on the world we perceive and think about. But the very tools that help us to understand and remember occasionally backfire so that we misremember.

DISORDERED MEMORIES

■ Thus far, our discussion has largely centered on people with normal memories. But during the last thirty years, some of the most intriguing questions about human memory have been raised by studies of people with drastic defects in memory caused by various kinds of damage to the brain (Rozin, 1976b; Squire, 1987; Mayes, 1988).

ANTEROGRADE AMNESIA

Certain lesions in the temporal cortex (specifically, in the hippocampus and nearby regions of the limbic system) produce a memory disorder called **anterograde amnesia** (anterograde means "in a forward direction"). Patients with this disorder often have little trouble in remembering whatever they learned prior to the injury; their difficulty is in learning anything new thereafter. Such lesions can occur in various ways. They are found in certain chronic alcoholic patients who suffer from **Korsakoff's syndrome** (named after the Russian physician who first described it). They sometimes accompany senility. In the famous case of a patient generally known as H.M., they were a tragic side effect of neurosurgery undertaken to minimize severe epileptic seizures (see Figure 7.11).

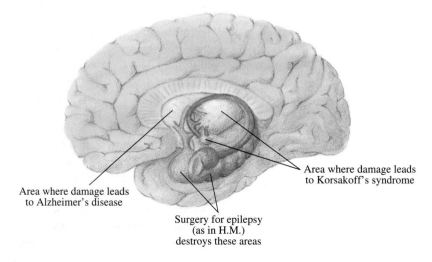

7.11   Regions of the brain where damage can cause memory loss   *A cutaway section of the human brain showing regions of the hippocampus and associated structures whose destruction caused H.M.'s massive memory deficits. Patients with Korsakoff's syndrome tend to have lesions in regions that lie higher up, including the thalamus, while patients with Alzheimer's disease show damage in the base of the forebrain. (Adapted from Mishkin and Appenzeller, 1987)*

Area where damage leads to Alzheimer's disease

Surgery for epilepsy (as in H.M.) destroys these areas

Area where damage leads to Korsakoff's syndrome

1950s   1960s   1970s   1980s

Remote and recent memory in amnesics
(A) Sample items adapted from the "famous faces" test in which patients are asked to identify faces of individuals who reached fame in a particular decade (Albert, Butters, and Levin, 1979; Butters and Albert, 1982). The names of those pictured are listed on page 219. (B) Results on the famous faces test for H.M. (blue) and normal controls (dark red) for the years from 1920 to 1960. Note that, as one would expect, the performance of H.M. was essentially equivalent to that of normals in identifying persons reaching prominence between 1920 and 1930. Like the normals, he did poorly for faces that predate 1930 when he was still a preschool child. But he performed much more poorly than the two controls on faces from the period after his operation (which was performed during the early 1950s). (Adapted from Marslen-Wilson and Teuber, 1975)

B

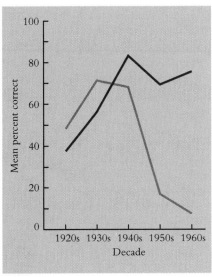

H.M.'s hippocampal lesion occurred when he was twenty-nine. Following the surgery he had a normal memory span and thus, apparently, a normal working memory. But he seemed to be incapable of adding any new information to his long-term store. He often could not recognize anyone he had not met before the surgery, no matter how often they met afterward. He was unable to find his way to the new house his family moved into after his operation. When told that his uncle had died, he was deeply moved but then forgot all about it and repeatedly asked when his uncle would come to visit. On each occasion he was told again of his uncle's death, and every time his grief was as intense as before; to him, each time he was told was the first (Milner, 1966; Milner, Corkin, and Teuber, 1968; Marslen-Wilson and Teuber, 1975; Corkin, 1984).

While H.M.'s long-term storage system was apparently almost completely closed to any new memories, his memories prior to the operation remained largely intact, especially for events that happened more than a year or so before the surgery. He could still read and write and engage in lively conversation. In many ways, his intellectual functioning was unimpaired. This is not uncommon in patients suffering damage to the hippocampus and related systems. Korsakoff's original patient could still play a competent game of chess though he could not remember how any given position on the chess board came about. But his memory loss was nevertheless profound and profoundly unsettling.

Some of H.M.'s comments give an idea of what such an amnesic state is like:

Right now, I'm wondering, Have I done or said anything amiss? You see, at this moment everything looks clear to me, but what happened just before? That's what worries me. It's like waking from a dream; I just don't remember. (Milner, 1966)

And on another occasion:

> . . . Every day is alone in itself, whatever enjoyment I've had, and whatever sorrow I've had. (Milner, Corkin, and Teuber, 1968)

RETROGRADE AMNESIA

Various brain injuries may lead to *retrograde amnesia* (retrograde means "in a backward direction") in which the patient suffers a loss of memories for some period prior to the accident or the stroke. That period may be relatively brief, perhaps a matter of days or weeks. But in some cases, the retrograde amnesia covers a much longer span and may be reckoned in years. Some retrograde effects often go along with anterograde amnesia. Thus H.M. had difficulty remembering events that happened one to three years before his operation, but his memory was perfectly normal for those that occurred before then (Mayes, 1988).

What accounts for the loss of memories for events preceding the cerebral injury? According to some authors, one of the causes is a problem with *trace consolidation.* This is a hypothetical process by which newly acquired memory traces gradually become firmly established (consolidated). This might explain why retrograde amnesia primarily affects memories that were formed shortly before the injury. Such memories would not have time to consolidate and would thus be more liable to destruction. The consolidation effect may be on storage—young traces need time to become resistant to being forgotten, for until then they are as vulnerable as a cement mixture before it has hardened. The effect may also be on retrieval—like a newly acquired library book that will be difficult to find until the librarian takes the time to fill out its card for the catalogue and to file it properly (Weingartner and Parker, 1984).

Whether retrograde amnesia can be explained in this manner is still a matter of debate. One trouble is the fact that retrograde amnesia often extends back for several years prior to the injury. If so, consolidation could not explain the deficit unless one assumes—and some authors do—that it is an exceedingly drawn-out process that may occur over very long time periods (Squire and Cohen, 1979, 1982; Squire, 1987).

EXPLICIT AND IMPLICIT RETRIEVAL REVISITED

■ For quite a while, it was thought that H.M. and other patients with the anterograde amnesic syndrome could not acquire any long-term memories at all. But further study demonstrated that this isn't true. They can be classically conditioned. They can also learn to trace the correct path through a maze and can acquire certain skills like mirror-tracing and reading mirror-imaged print. With practice, their performance gets better and better. But each time they are brought back into the experimental situation, they continue to insist that they have never seen the conditioning apparatus or the maze before and that they don't remember anything at all (Corkin, 1965; Weiskrantz and Warrington, 1979; Cohen and Squire, 1980).

How can we make sense of these findings? Anterograde amnesics are evidently quite competent at retaining skills such as mirror-tracing (they do just about as well as normals, despite their insistence that they don't remember anything about it; see Figure 7.12). On the other hand, they are utterly incompetent at many ordinary long-term memory tasks; for example, they don't recognize an experimenter they have met on twenty different occasions. The one kind of

7.12 *An example of what amnesics can learn* (A) In mirror drawing, the subject has to trace a line between two outlines of a figure while looking at her hand in a mirror (Kolb and Whishaw, 1990). Initially, this is very difficult, but after some practice the subject gets very proficient at it. The same is true for amnesics. The graphs in (B) show H.M.'s improvement on this task over a period of three days. (Milner, Corkin, and Teuber, 1968)

memory is spared; the other is not. What is the essential difference between such tasks?

Some authors believe that the essential distinction is between what computer scientists called *procedural* and *declarative knowledge*. Procedural knowledge is "knowing how"—how to ride a bicycle or how to read mirror writing—areas in which the amnesic's memory is relatively unaffected. According to this view, such skills are essentially programs (that is, procedures) for executing certain motor or mental operations. In contrast, declarative knowledge is "knowing that"—that there are three outs in an inning, that automobiles run on gasoline, that I had chicken for dinner last Thursday. To know something procedurally does not guarantee that one also knows it declaratively. Professional baseball players know how to swing a bat, but not all of them can explain just what it is that they know. Conversely, most physicists probably know (and can describe) the underlying mechanics of a baseball swing, but few will be able to perform competently when given a bat and asked to hit a ball. Neuroscientists who argue that this distinction explains what anterograde amnesics can remember and what they can't also believe that procedural and declarative memories depend on different neural systems (Cohen and Squire, 1980; Squire, 1986).

A somewhat different explanation centers on the distinction between explicit and implicit retrieval (see pp. 203–204). The memories may be there, but they can only be retrieved implicitly so that the patient doesn't know that he has them. As a result, he cannot answer questions like "Do you remember?" or "Do you recognize?" when they pertain to events that occurred after he sustained the cerebral damage. Some evidence that the amnesic's deficit concerns explicit but not implicit memory comes from priming procedures. When amnesic patients are shown a number of words and are later asked to recall or recognize them, they fail completely. But the results are quite different when they are presented, with fragments of the words and asked to complete them by forming the first words that come to mind. Now there is evidence that something was remembered. The patient who was previously shown ELEPHANT and BOOKCASE will properly complete the fragments _L_P_A_T and B_O_C_S_, even though he will not recognize either word if explicitly asked whether he's just seen it (Warrington and Weiskrantz, 1978; Diamond and Rozin, 1984). Interestingly enough, this effect will work only if the patient does not connect it with any intentional attempt to retrieve the word from memory. If he is explicitly asked to recall the previously presented words by using the fragments as cues, he will fail again (Graf, Mandler, and Squire, 1984).

TAKING STOCK

Answers to "famous faces" test
1950s: *Mamie Eisenhower, Jonas Salk, Adlai Stevenson.* 1960s: *Nikita Khrushchev, Mohammed Ali, Golda Meir.* 1970s: *Anwar Sadat, Betty Ford, Patty Hearst.* 1980s: *Robert Bork, Walter Mondale, Bjorn Borg.*

In looking back over this chapter, we are again struck by the intimate relationship between the fields of perception, memory, and thinking. It is often unclear where one topic ends and another begins. To give just one example, consider memory search. As we saw, trying to recall the names of one's high-school classmates apparently involves many of the same thought processes that are called upon when we try to figure out how to solve a geometry problem. To the extent that this is so, it is clear that much of memory involves thinking. And as we saw previously, the same is also true of perception. For there, too, the perceiver becomes a thinker as he tries to solve perceptual problems and make sense out of ambiguous or impossible figures. In the next chapter, we will consider the topic of thinking in its own right.

QUESTIONS FOR CRITICAL THINKING

1.   Some famous mnemonists (memory experts) can perform such astounding feats as memorizing instantly the names and birthdays of all the hundreds of people in their audience. Given what we know about memory, how do you think they do this?

2.   Actors often "walk through" their parts in order to remember their lines. What memory principle(s) might explain why this helps?

3.   What aspects of memory help explain the fondness of senior citizens for reminiscence?

4.   How much faith should we repose in "recovered" memories of early child abuse? What would be the repercussions should all such memories be believed?

SUMMARY

1.   Any act of remembering implies success in each of three phases: *encoding, storage,* and *retrieval.*

2.   According to the *stage theory of memory,* there are several memory systems. Of these, the most important are *short-term memory* in which information is held for fairly short intervals and *long-term memory* in which information is stored for much longer periods. According to stage theory, to get to the long-term memory system, material must first pass through the short-term store.

3.   An important difference between short-term and long-term memory is in their capacity. That of long-term memory is enormous; that of short-term memory is very limited as shown by studies of memory span. The recall of an item heard just before may be from the short-term or long-term store. Studies of free recall with lists of unrelated items have provided a way of determining from where such items are retrieved. According to stage theory, the *primacy effect* obtained by use of this procedure is associated with retrieval from long-term storage, while the *recency effect* reflects retrieval from short-term memory.

4.   Since the stage theory assumes that the only gateway to long-term memory is through short-term memory, there will obviously be a bottleneck. This is overcome by *recoding* the incoming material into larger *chunks.*

5.   An important challenge to stage theory came from the fact that *maintenance rehearsal,* in which material is simply held passively in short-term memory, confers little or no long-term benefits in aiding recall, which indicates that the transfer from short-term to long-term memory cannot be automatic. This realization led to a theoretical reevaluation in the way memory is conceived today. Short-term memory is now often called *working memory* and is regarded as a mental workbench on which items are held while they are encoded. *Mnemonics,* techniques for helping memory, include various forms of verbal organization and the use of *visual imagery.*

6.   Remembering depends in part upon the presence of appropriate *retrieval cues.* According to the principle of *compatibility* (also called *encoding specificity*), remembering is most likely if the context at the time of the retrieval is identical to that present at the time of original encoding.

7.   Retrieval from long-term memory is often preceded by a process of *memory search.* In some cases, the search reaches a halfway point, where we seem to recall something but not quite, and we experience the *tip-of-the-tongue phenomenon.*

8.   What we normally call remembering involves explicit retrieval, using such methods as recall or recognition in which subjects are explicitly asked questions that refer to

SUMMARY

memory. But retrieval can also be implicit, where subjects are not asked or even made consciously aware that they are referring to some prior experience. Laboratory methods to test for implicit retrieval include *repetition priming* and *fragment completion*.

9.   Other things being equal, forgetting increases the longer the time since learning. This point was first demonstrated by Ebbinghaus, who plotted the *forgetting curve* of associations between nonsense syllables. The causes of forgetting are still a matter of debate. One theory holds that traces gradually *decay* over time, though this view is complicated by the fact that forgetting is greater if the subject is awake rather than asleep during the retention interval. Another view argues that the fundamental cause of forgetting is *interference* produced by other, inappropriate memories. This approach leans heavily on two forms of interference produced in the laboratory, *retroactive* and *proactive inhibition*. Yet another theory asserts that forgetting is primarily caused by changes in *retrieval cues* at the time of recall. This position is sometimes used to explain the phenomenon of *childhood amnesia*.

10.   Under some circumstances, forgetting doesn't seem to occur. There is evidence that some memories last for a very long time, as in the case of a language learned in school some remnants of which seem to remain in a *permastore*. Other evidence for long-lasting memories are *flashbulb memories* (as in remembering where one was at the time one heard that President Kennedy was assassinated or that the space shuttle had exploded), though these often prove inaccurate.

11.   In many cases, remembering depends on prior knowledge, which affects encoding and later retrieval by relating the incoming material to various conceptual frameworks called *schemas* and *scripts*. Using such frameworks can sometimes lead to *memory distortions* as originally shown by Bartlett. Modern studies of eyewitness testimony have elaborated this point by demonstrating that what is remembered can be seriously affected by building various presuppositions into the request for recall. Related work has shown that hypnotized subjects will reconstruct memories to please a hypnotist. Although genuinely convinced that what they recall really happened, the hypnotized subject often turns out to be incorrect and to be easily affected by leading questions. *Accommodative distortions*, which don't just fill gaps but represent genuine alterations in one's memory, may underlie schema-based memory distortions.

12.   Certain injuries to the brain, particularly to the hippocampus and surrounding regions, can produce disorders of memory. In *anterograde amnesia*, the patient's ability to fix material in long-term memory is damaged. In *retrograde amnesia*, the loss is for memories just prior to the injury and is sometimes attributed to a disruption of *trace consolidation*. An important issue is why patients with severe anterograde amnesia can acquire certain long-term memories (learning a maze, benefiting from repetition priming) but not others (remembering that they have seen the maze or heard the word before). According to one hypothesis, the crucial distinction is between *procedural* and *declarative* knowledge; according to another, it is between *implicit* and *explicit retrieval*.

CHAPTER

8

THOUGHT AND KNOWLEDGE

In ordinary language, the word *think* has a wide range of meanings. It may be a synonym for *remembering* (as in "I can't think of her name") or for *attention* (as in the exhortation "Think") or for *belief* (as in "I think sea serpents exist"). It may also refer to a state of vague and undirected reverie as in "I'm thinking of nothing in particular." These many uses suggest that the word has become a blanket term to cover virtually any psychological process that goes on within the individual and that is essentially unobservable from without.

But thinking also has a narrower meaning, which is graphically rendered in Rodin's famous statue of *The Thinker*. Here, the meaning of *think* is best conveyed by such words as *to reason* or *ponder* or *reflect*. Psychologists who study thinking are mainly interested in this sense of the term. To distinguish it from the others, they refer to **directed thinking,** a set of mental activities that are used whenever we plan a course of action, try to solve a problem, evaluate the truth of an assertion, or weigh the costs and benefits as we decide between alternatives. As we do these things, we necessarily draw on the foundation upon which all thinking rests: what we already know.

ANALOGICAL REPRESENTATIONS

FOCUS QUESTIONS

- What are the two kinds of mental representation?

- What is eidetic imagery?

- How are visual images like—and unlike—pictures?

- What is spatial thinking, and how "spatial" is it?

Whenever we think, we draw on what we already know, and shuffle and rearrange it to come up with a solution, an answer. To fix a mower, we call on our knowledge of gasoline-powered motors; to avert a social disaster, we refer to what we know about a thin-skinned acquaintance. But how should that knowledge be characterized? Many (perhaps all) of the components of this knowledge can be regarded as **mental representations** of the world and the individual's experiences with it.

These mental representations are the main elements of thought. They are the internal equivalent of the many **external representations** we encounter in ordinary life, those signs or symbols that "stand for" something else, such as maps, blue-prints, menus, price lists, stories—the list is very large. In all these cases, the representation is not equivalent to that for which it stands; it just signifies it: We don't literally drive on the map, nor do we eat the menu.

Psychologists, philosophers, and computer scientists have found it convenient to distinguish between two broad classes of representations, the **analogical** and

Thinking *(Aristotle Contemplating the Bust of Homer, 1653, by Rembrandt; courtesy of The Metropolitan Museum of Art, purchased with special funds and gifts of friends of the Museum, 1961)*

the ***symbolic.***★ Analog representations capture some of the actual characteristics of (and are thus analogous to) that which they represent. In contrast, symbolic representations bear no such relationship to the item for which they stand. As we will see, human thought uses both kinds of representations.

Consider a picture of a mouse and compare it to an actual mouse. The picture is in some ways quite different from the real animal. It represents a mouse rather than actually being one. But even so, the picture has many similarities to the creature that it represents, for it looks quite a bit like a real mouse. It is an analogical representation. In contrast, take the word *mouse.* This word stands for the same long-tailed, big-eared, and bewhiskered creature that the picture represents. But unlike the picture, the word has no physical similarity to the mouse whatever. It is an abstract representation, for the relation between the sound "mouse" (or the written, five-letter word *mouse)* and the little, long-tailed animal that it represents is entirely arbitrary and symbolic.

The same distinction applies to many other external representations. Consider the road sign "winding road ahead" shown below:

This sign is an analogical representation, for it (crudely) depicts the winding road it warns about. No such pictorial analogy applies to the abstract—symbolic—representation "$."

The same distinction that holds for external representations also holds for mental, internal ones. Some of our internal representations are images that are in some ways picturelike; others are thoughts that are more abstract and symbolic. We will begin our discussion by considering thought based on analogical representations: mental images and the related topic of visual and spatial thinking.

★ Many psychologists and computer scientists use the term *digital* for what we here call "symbolic" because computers usually encode such symbolic, nonpictorial representations in a discrete, all-or-none fashion by various combinations of the digits 0 and 1.

MENTAL IMAGES

There is little doubt that much of our knowledge is based on analogical memories, often called *mental images,* that preserve some of the characteristic attributes of our senses. It's not just that we *know* that, say, people's waists are between their heads and their toes. Of course we do, but that isn't all. We are also able somehow to retrieve this "betweenness" from a mental image that has some of the characteristics of the original visual experience. As some authors (including Shakespeare) have put it, we see it in "our mind's eye." While similar claims have been made for other senses—hearing with the mind's ear (composers), feeling with the mind's fingers (blind persons)—our primary concern here will be with visual images.

RATING ONE'S OWN IMAGES

The first attempt to study visual imagery goes back a hundred years to Sir Francis Galton (1822–1911), the founder of the field of individual differences, who asked people to describe their own images and to rate them for vividness (Galton, 1883). The results showed that individuals differed widely. Some people said they could call up scenes at will and see them with the utmost clarity. Others (including some well-known painters) denied ever having images at all. One might expect that these differences in how people describe their own experiences would predict their performance on various tasks that seemed to call for visual memory. But in fact the results on this matter are ambiguous. Some studies do find the expected correlation, others find a reverse effect, while still others find no relationship at all (Marks, 1983; Reisberg and Leak, 1987; Di Vesta, Ingersoll, and Sunshine, 1971; Baddeley, 1976).

EIDETIC IMAGERY

Since self-judgments of imagery are of uncertain value, psychologists have turned to more objective procedures. In addition to asking what the image is like, they ask what it enables the subject to do. For example, is the image a mental picture from which he can read off information as if it were an actual visual scene outside? By and large, the answer is no. But there are some exceptions. The most striking is *eidetic imagery,* characterized by relatively long-lasting and detailed images of visual scenes that can sometimes be scanned and "looked at" as if they

Some representations are pictorial, others—abstract *(A) A photograph of Ambroise Vollard, a French art dealer at the turn of the century. (B) A cubist portrait of Monsieur Vollard by Pablo Picasso. Note that while Picasso's rendering is by no means literal, there is enough of a pictorial similarity to the model that the portrait is still recognizable. While this painting is a pictorial representation, the model's name—Ambroise Vollard—is not. It stands for him, but it is not like him, for both names and words are abstract representations rather than pictorial ones. (Picasso's* Portrait of Ambroise Vollard, *1909. Pushkin Museum, Moscow; courtesy of Scala/Art Resource)*

A

B

8.1   Test picture for study of eidetic imagery   *This picture from* Alice in Wonderland *was shown for half a minute to elementary schoolchildren, a few of whom seemed to have an eidetic image of it. (Illustration by Marjorie Torrey)*

had real existence outside. In one study, a group of school children was shown a picture for thirty seconds. After it was taken away, the subjects were asked whether they could still see anything and, if so, to describe what they saw (Leask, Haber, and Haber, 1969). Evidence for eidetic imagery is contained in the following protocol of a ten-year-old boy, who was looking at a blank easel from which a picture from *Alice in Wonderland* had just been removed (Figure 8.1).

Experimenter:	Do you see something there?
Subject:	I see the tree, gray tree with three limbs. I see the cat with stripes around its tail.
Experimenter:	Can you count those stripes?
Subject:	Yes (pause). There's about 16.
Experimenter:	You're counting what? Black, white or both?
Subject:	Both.
Experimenter:	Tell me what else you see.
Subject:	And I can see the flowers on the bottom. There's about three stems but you can see two pairs of flowers. One on the right has green leaves, red hair and a red hair band and there are some leaves in the upper left-hand corner where the tree is. (Haber, 1969, p. 38)

Eidetic imagery is relatively rare. Only 5 percent of schoolchildren tested seem to have it, and the proportion is almost surely smaller in adults. According to one author, this difference between children and adults may only indicate that children tend to rely more on imagery in their thinking, perhaps because their verbal and conceptual memory systems are not as yet sufficiently developed (Kosslyn, 1980, 1984). In any case, there is no reason to believe that this form of imagery is an especially useful form of mental activity. Contrary to popular belief, memory experts don't generally have eidetic imagery (or photographic memory as it is popularly named); their skill is in organizing material in memory, rather than in storing it in pictorial form.

PICTURE-LIKE ASPECTS OF VISUAL MEMORY

With the possible exception of eidetic imagery, our memory of visually presented objects and events is not a simple reembodiment of stored visual sensation. Our perceptions are not like photographs, and so our visual memories (which are presumably based on these perceptions) can't be either. But they may nevertheless contain certain pictorial attributes that are also found in visual perception. A number of studies suggest that this is indeed the case.

Image scanning   One line of evidence comes from studies on ***image scanning.*** In one such study, subjects were first shown the map of a fictitious island containing various objects: a hut, a well, a tree, a meadow, and so on (see Figure 8.2). After memorizing this map by copying it repeatedly, the subjects performed a reaction-time task. The experimenter named two objects on the map (say, the hut and the meadow). The subjects' task was to conjure up a mental image of the entire island and then to imagine a little black speck zipping from the first location to the second. The results showed that their reaction time was directly proportional to the distance between the two points. This result would be no surprise had the subjects scanned a physical map with their real eyes. That the same holds true when they scan an image with their mind's eye is rather remarkable (Kosslyn, Ball, and Reisser, 1978).

Images are not pictures   The preceding discussion makes it clear that visual images are analogical representations that share some of the properties of pictures. In particular, some of the major spatial characteristics of the depicted scene are maintained in the image. If two points in the scene are close to each other, they

8.2 **Image scanning** *Subjects were asked to look mentally at a map of a fictional island and then to imagine a speck zipping from one location to another. (After Kosslyn, Ball, and Reiser, 1978)*

are functionally close in the image; if they are far apart, they are also functionally far apart in the image. What holds for perceived distance, also holds for such spatial relations as "betweenness." If point *B* in the scene is between points *A* and *C,* this relation is preserved in the image. It is functionally "between" in the image, so that one cannot mentally scan from point *A* to point *C* without passing through point *B.* In sum: Images preserve the general spatial layout of the scene that is depicted in the image.

But while images are picture-*like,* they are *not* pictures. Some evidence for this view comes from a study by Chambers and Reisberg who presented their subjects with a figure (that they had never seen before) that is normally reversible: If it is seen as oriented toward the left, it looks like the head of a duck; if oriented toward the right, it looks like the head of a rabbit (Figure 8.3). The subjects' first task was to form a mental image of this figure. At a later time, when the picture was no longer physically present, they were asked to call up this image and describe what it looked like. All subjects "saw" either a duck or a rabbit with their mind's eye, and some said they saw it very vividly. They were then asked whether their image might look like something else. Not one of the subjects came up with a reversal, even after many hints and considerable coaxing. The results were very different when the subjects subsequently drew the figure and looked at their own drawing. Now everyone came up with the perceptual alternative. To Chambers and Reisberg these results indicated that a visual image is not a picture. It is instead a mental product that is based on a picture but that is already encoded to some extent—perhaps as a duck, perhaps as a rabbit. To the extent that it is so encoded, it has lost its pictorial innocence. It is no longer ambiguous because it has already been interpreted (see Chambers and Reisberg, 1985; for further discussion, see Finke, Pinker, and Farah, 1989; Reisberg and Chambers, 1990).

8.3 **Images are not pictures** *The rabbit-duck figure, first used in 1900 by Joseph Jastrow. (After Attneave, 1971)*

SPATIAL THINKING

Closely related to mental imagery is **spatial thinking,** the kind that we use when we want to determine a shortcut between two locations or when we mentally try to rearrange the furniture in the living room. How are such tasks accomplished? One means is by way of mental images. By consulting a mental picture, the traveler can read off shortcuts as she might from a mental map, and the decorator can save wear and tear on his back muscles by rearranging his images before moving the actual armchairs and sofas.

MENTAL MAPS

These kinds of spatial thinking may be based on picture-like images, but others involve processes that are much more symbolic and conceptual. In one study, subjects were asked to indicate the relative locations of two cities. One of the pairs was San Diego, California, and Reno, Nevada. The subjects judged San Diego to be west of Reno, although it actually is farther east. Another pair was Montreal, Canada, and Seattle, Washington. Here the subjects judged Montreal to be farther north, although its actual location is south of Seattle. These results suggest that the subjects didn't base their answers on picture-like mental maps resembling the real maps shown in Figure 8.4. If they had, they would have said that Reno is west of San Diego. But in fact, they (falsely) asserted the very opposite.

How can we explain the subjects' errors? The most plausible explanation is that their judgments were affected by what they knew about the relative locations of the states or countries that contain the cities about which they were asked (e.g., Nevada is east of California, and Canada is north of the United States). And this knowledge was based on abstract, symbolic representations rather than representations that are analogical and pictorial. What the subjects knew about San Diego and Reno can be summarized by the three propositions shown below:

California is west of Nevada.
San Diego is in California.
Reno is in Nevada.

This way of representing spatial knowledge could easily lead to error, for it might suggest that the east-west relation that holds for the states also holds for all the cities within them. This would be true if the larger geographical units (California and Nevada) were conceptual categories such as *bird*. (If we know that owls and robins are birds, it automatically follows that they both have wings, beaks, and feathers.) Of course, states and countries are not at all equivalent to categories such as *bird*: Reno is not *a* Nevada but is *in* Nevada. Even so,

8.4   Conceptual mental maps   Subjects tend to judge San Diego to be west of Reno and Montreal to be north of Seattle. But these judgments are in error. (A) A map of California and Nevada with colored lines of longitude (angular distance from an arbitrary reference point in Greenwich, England) which shows that in fact San Diego is east of Reno. (B) A map of the United States and southern Canada with colored lines of latitude (angular distance from the equator) which shows that Seattle is slightly north of Montreal. (Stevens and Coupe, 1978)

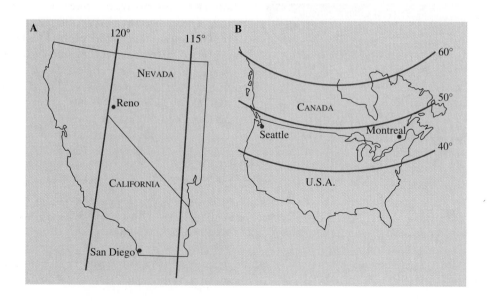

most of us often store spatial information in such a rough-and-ready conceptual way. (One hopes that airplane navigators are an exception.) To the extent that we do store some geographical information under category rubrics, our spatial knowledge cannot be exclusively—or even largely—picture-like (Stevens and Coupe, 1978).

SYMBOLIC REPRESENTATIONS

FOCUS QUESTIONS

- What are two constituents of symbolic representation?
- What kinds of memory make up the "data base" for symbolic thought?
- What is the network model of semantic memory, and what is one of its limitations?

Mental images are clearly not the only elements of thought, nor are they the most important ones. Around the turn of the century, several psychologists asked subjects to describe everything that "went through their minds" as they tried to solve various intellectual problems. The solution frequently came without a trace of imagery (and frequently also without words). The subjects reported that when their thought was both wordless and imageless, they often had a sense of certain underlying relationships, such as the experience of "this doesn't go with that" or a "feeling of *if* or *but*" (Humprey, 1951).

SYMBOLIC ELEMENTS

The attempt to describe the components of this more abstract level of thinking is relatively recent, at least for psychologists. But some of the key items of such a description are already in the vocabulary of related disciplines, such as logic and linguistics. Examples are the terms *concept* and *proposition*.

CONCEPTS

The term *concept* is generally used to describe a class or category that subsumes a number (sometimes an infinite number) of individual instances or subtypes. An example is *dog,* which includes *poodle, beagle, dachshund,* and *Alsatian.* Other concepts designate qualities or dimensions. Examples are *length* and *age.* Still others are relational, such as *taller than.* Relational concepts don't apply to any one item in isolation. One can't be *taller than* except in relation to something else to which one's height is being compared. For our present purposes, these and many other concepts are regarded as symbolic rather than analogic mental representations.★

PROPOSITIONS

Concepts describe classes of events or objects or relations between them. They are what we generally think about. In so doing, we tend to combine them in various ways. The British empiricists emphasized one such mental combination:

★ As we will see in the next chapter, some authors believe that many concepts are better described by a *prototype* that serves as a kind of mental average of the various members of the conceptual category (see Chapter 9).

the simple associative train of thought in which one idea leads to another. A more important way of relating concepts is by asserting something about them, for example, "Dogs generally bite postmen." Such statements are called *propositions*. They make some assertion that relates a **subject** (the item about which an assertion is made, e.g., *dogs*) and a **predicate** (what is asserted about the subject, e.g., *bite postmen*) in a way that can be true or false.

KNOWLEDGE AND MEMORY

■ Concepts and propositions are the elements of symbolic thought. Many of them are stored in memory, where they constitute our accumulated knowledge, the "data base" that sustains and informs our thoughts. How is this knowledge organized in memory, how is it retrieved, explicitly or implicitly, and when is it used?

GENERIC MEMORY

Psychologists often distinguish between episodic and generic memory. **Episodic memory** is the memory for particular events (episodes) of one's own life, what happened when and where, as when recalling that one ate fried chicken the other night. This contrasts with **generic memory**, which is memory for items of knowledge as such, independent of the particular occasion on which one acquired them. For example, we remember the capital of France, the square root of 9, and the fact that Aaron Burr shot Alexander Hamilton in a duel, but rarely do we remember how or when we first acquired these bits of knowledge. In effect, a person's generic memory is the sum total of his acquired knowledge—the meanings of words and symbols, facts about the world, what objects look like, and various general principles, schemas, and scripts.

One of the most important components of generic memory is **semantic memory**, which concerns the meanings of words and concepts. As some authors conceive it, our entire vocabulary is in this store: every word, together with its pronunciation, all of its meanings, its relations to objects in the real world, the way it is put together with other words to make phrases and sentences. How do we ever find any one bit of information in this bulky mental dictionary? One thing is certain: When we search for an item—say, a synonym for *quiet*—we don't go through *all* of the items in the semantic store, one after the other. If we did, the hunt might last for days or weeks. The fact that we can come up with *silent* in a second or less shows that we make use of a much more efficient retrieval system. To use a library analogy, the person who wants to take out a book doesn't have to rummage through all of the volumes on each shelf in order to find the one he wants. He can obtain his book much faster because there is an organized system according to which the books are arranged in the stacks.

A HIERARCHICAL NETWORK

Semantic memory is surely organized, but just what does its organization consist of? To answer this question many investigators propose a **network model** in which the words and concepts stored in semantic memory are linked through a complex system of relationships (somewhat analogous to the networks we encountered previously when discussing pattern recognition—see Chapter 6). In such networks, the words or concepts are indicated by *nodes,* while the associations between them are indicated by lines or arrows (see Figure 8.5).

One of the first such network models was hierarchical. It assumed a semantic hierarchy in which a particular word (say, *canary*) is stored under the higher-

8.5   Network structure in semantic memory models   *The figure shows a small section of a semantic memory model, with nodes ("elephant" "mammal" "trunk") connected through associative links. Some networks employ labeled associations that indicate the particular relations between the nodes (such as, is a, has a, and so on).*

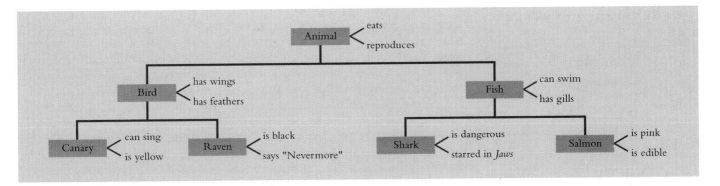

8.6 A hierarchical theory of semantic memory *To decide whether the sentence "Ravens have feathers" is true, given the organization of the entries here pictured, one has to "look up" the information at the second level, under* bird.

order category that subsumes it (here, *bird),* which in turn is stored under a yet higher category (here, *animal),* and so on. Certain properties, or *features,* that describe each of these terms are then stored under the node that is most appropriate. Under canary, one presumably stores such features as: "is yellow," "can sing." Under bird, one might store features such as: "has wings," "has feathers." Similarly for yet higher categories such as *animal* or *living thing* (see Figure 8.6; Collins and Quillian, 1969).

This hierarchical model was very neat but as so often, nature is much less neat than theorists would like it to be. To mention only one problem, membership in many semantic categories does not seem to be an all-or-none affair. Thus when subjects are asked to rate various birds according to the degree to which they are "typical birds," robins are rated to be most typical, chickens less so, and penguins birds by courtesy only (Rosch, 1973a, 1973b). These differences in typicality seem to affect the way in which semantic memory is accessed. For example, subjects are faster in agreeing that "X is a bird," if X is a typical bird like a canary rather than a marginal case like a penguin or an ostrich (Rips, Shoben, and Smith, 1973; Rips, Smith, and Shoben, 1978). Such effects suggest that the relation between items of information in the semantic memory is not as simple as the hierarchical position had supposed (e.g., Conrad, 1972; for further discussion, see Chapter 9).

THE PROCESS OF THINKING: SOLVING PROBLEMS

FOCUS QUESTIONS

■ What does it mean to say that problem solving is hierarchical?

■ How do experts and novices differ in problem solving?

■ What are mental sets, and what are their costs and benefits?

■ What are algorithms and heuristics? Under what circumstances might heuristics be more useful and why?

Thus far, our concern has been with the elements of which thought and knowledge are composed. We now turn from the question of *what* to the question of *how.* How does thinking operate as we try to solve the myriad of problems encountered in life, whether trying to fix a broken lawn mower, to smooth over an awkward social situation, or to solve an anagram?

NAGMARA

BOLMPER

SLEVO

STIGNIH

TOLUSONI

8.7 Anagrams *Rearrange the letters on each line to form a word. (For the solution, see p. 234).*

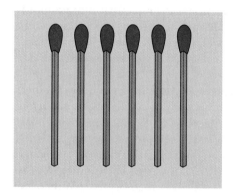

8.8 Matchstick problem *Assemble all six matches to form four equilateral triangles, each side of which is equal to the length of one match. (For the solution, see p. 243).*

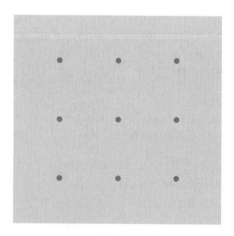

8.9 Nine-dot problem *Nine dots are arranged in a square. Connect them by drawing four continuous straight lines without lifting your pencil from the paper. (For the solution, see p. 242).*

ORGANIZATION IN PROBLEM SOLVING

■ Thinking is an activity, and like most activities of the organism it is organized. The would-be problem solver goes through a sequence of internal steps that are organized in a special way: They are directed toward a goal—the solution of the problem. Consider a taxi driver who is trying to decide on the best route from the city to the airport. The internal steps he goes through in making his decision are determined not merely by the step just before but by the original problem. This sets the overall direction that dominates all the later steps and determines how each of them is to be evaluated. The taxi driver considers the super highway and rejects it as he recalls some road construction along the way, thinks of a major avenue and dismisses it because of rush-hour traffic, and then decides on a cross-town highway. The original problem acts like a schematic frame, waiting to be filled in by a "fitting" solution.

Here, as in many other directed activities, the desired end determines the beginning. This same effect is seen in virtually all efforts at problem solving. Laboratory demonstrations include studies in which subjects have been asked to decipher anagrams (Figure 8.7), to manipulate various concrete objects so as to produce a desired result (Figure 8.8), or to find the solution to various geometrical problems (Figure 8.9). Considering this variety of problems, it is hardly surprising that there are differences in the way in which they are attacked and solved; a subject who tries to join nine dots with one continuous line will surely call upon a somewhat different set of mental skills than one who has to rearrange the letters *NAGMARA* into an English word. But in all cases, the problem solver's efforts are directed toward the goal.

The role of goal-determined organization in problem solving was highlighted in a classic study by the Gestalt psychologist Karl Duncker, who asked his subjects to "think out loud" while they tried to find the solution (Duncker, 1945). One of Duncker's problems was cast in medical terms:

> Suppose a patient has an inoperable stomach tumor. There are certain rays which can destroy this tumor if their intensity is large enough. At this intensity, however, the rays will also destroy the healthy tissue which surrounds the tumor (e.g., the stomach walls, the abdominal muscles, and so on). How can one destroy the tumor without damaging the healthy tissue through which the rays must travel on their way?

Duncker's subjects typically arrived at the solution in several steps. They first reformulated the problem so as to produce a general plan of attack. This in turn led to more specific would-be solutions. For example, they might look for a tissue-free path to the stomach and so propose to send the rays through the esophagus. (A good idea that unfortunately will not work—rays travel in straight lines and the esophagus is curved.) After exploring several other general approaches and their specific consequences, some subjects finally hit upon an appropriate general plan. They proposed to reduce the intensity of rays on their way through healthy tissue and then turn up this intensity when the rays reach the tumor. This broad restatement of what is needed eventually led to the correct specific means, which was to send several bundles of *weak* rays from various points outside so that they meet at the tumor where their effects will summate (see Figure 8.10).

HIERARCHICAL ORGANIZATION

We've seen that problem solving is organized in a goal-directed manner. This organization is also *hierarchical*. Various mental operations are performed as

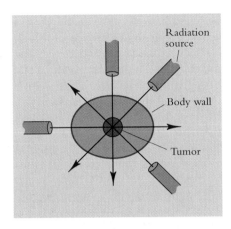

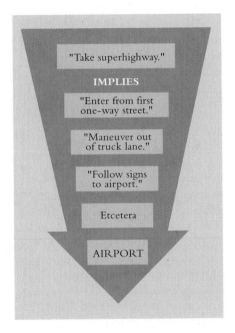

8.11 *Hierarchical organization of a plan* Plans have subcomponents that have subcomponents below them, as here illustrated by the taxi driver's task.

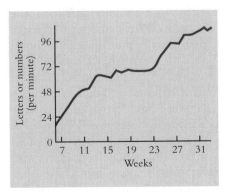

8.10 The solution to the ray-tumor problem Several weak rays are sent from various points outside so that they will meet at the tumor site. There the radiation of the rays will be intense, for all the effects will summate at this point. But since they are individually weak, the rays will not damage the healthy tissue that surrounds the tumor. (After Duncker, 1945)

lower-level operations (what computer scientists call **subroutines**) that are run under the control of higher-level ones. We have encountered the concept of hierarchical organization before, when discussing the neural organization of behavior (see Chapter 2) as well as the role of chunking in memory (see Chapter 7). A similar principle governs directed thinking. To the taxi driver, the idea "take the cross-town highway" is a sort of master plan that implies various subsidiary actions: entering from the appropriate one-way street, maneuvering out of the truck lane, following the signs to the airport exit, and so on. To the experienced driver, all of these substeps require no further thought, for they are by now highly familiar and routinized. The result is a hierarchical organization resembling that of a disciplined army. The colonel who orders his regiment to attack does not have to specify the detailed commands his second lieutenants issue to their platoons. Given the order from above, the subcommands follow (Figure 8.11).

The ability to subsume many details under a larger chunk is one of the crucial features of all directed activity, including the internal activity we call thought and in particular the activity of problem solving. Take the fact that many problems that seem insuperable to the novice are absurdly easy to the expert. One reason for this difference is that with long practice the necessary responses to many of the lower-level subtasks in a problem (like those faced by the taxi driver or by Duncker's subjects who tried to destroy the tumor) become automatic. Initially they may well have been quite difficult and quite distinct, but eventually they merged into lower-level chunks that are stored in memory as subroutines, so that when later called upon they can be run off with a minimum of attention. As we shall see, much of the difference between the expert problem solver in a given domain and the beginner is in the degree to which subcomponents of the activity have been turned into subroutines.

SKILLS AS THE DEVELOPMENT OF SUBROUTINES

How are subroutines formed? Their development in directed activity is particularly clear when we study how people become proficient at various skills. Some of these are mental skills, such as reading or doing arithmetic. Others involve the perceptual and motor systems, as in playing tennis.

The first experimental study in this area was done about a hundred years ago by William Bryan and Noble Harter. These psychologists were trying to discover how telegraph operators master their trade. Their subjects were Western Union apprentices whose progress at sending and receiving Morse code messages was charted over a period of about forty weeks. Figure 8.12 plots one student's improvement at receiving, measured in letters per minute. What is interesting about this learning curve is its shape. Following an initial rise, the curve flattens into a plateau, after which it may rise again until it reaches another plateau, and so on. According to Bryan and Harter, such plateaus are an indi-

8.12 An apprentice telegrapher's learning curve The curve plots the number of letters or digits the operator can receive per minute against weeks of practice. Note the plateau in the learning curve. The curve stays level from weeks 15 to 25 and then starts to rise again. According to Bryan and Harter, the new rise indicates the use of larger chunks. (After Bryan and Harter, 1899)

233

cation that the learner gradually transforms his task. At first he merely tracks individual letters, getting progressively faster in doing so as practice proceeds. But with time, the effective units he deals with become larger and larger: first syllables and words, then several words at a time, then simple phrases. The plateau represents the best the learner can do given that he is working with a unit of a lower level (say, letters); once this lower level is completely mastered, a higher level of organization—a larger chunk—is possible, and the learning curve shoots up once more (Bryan and Harter, 1897).

Similar effects are observed in the acquisition of many other skills, such as typing or driving a car. In such activities, becoming skillful involves a qualitative change in how the task is performed (Keele, 1982). To the novice, typing proceeds letter by letter; to the expert, the proper units are much larger, including familiar letter groupings, words, and occasionally phrases. Similarly, the beginning driver laboriously struggles to harmonize clutch, gas pedal, steering wheel, and brake to the considerable terror of innocent bystanders. After a while, those movements become quite routine and are subsumed under much higher (though perhaps equally dangerous) chunks of behavior, such as overtaking another car. An even simpler example is dressing. To the small child every article of clothing represents a major intellectual challenge; she beams with pride when she finally gets the knack of tying her shoelaces. To an adult the unit is "getting dressed," and its various components are almost completely submerged within the larger chunk. We decide to dress and before we know it we are almost fully clothed. Somehow our shoes get tied, but we never notice, unless a shoelace breaks.

MASTERS AND BEGINNERS

Clearly, some people solve certain problems better than others do. As we discussed above, one reason is experience; the trained mechanic is more likely to hit on the cause of automotive failure than is his young apprentice. But what exactly does experience contribute? One obvious factor is knowledge. But no less important is chunking. Experts approach a problem in different ways than beginners. They think in larger units whose components are already contained within them. As a result the subcomponents require no further thought.

An interesting demonstration of how chunking makes the master comes from studies of chess players (de Groot, 1965; Chase and Simon, 1973a, 1973b). The chess world ranks its members according to a ruthlessly objective hierarchy of merit based on a simple record of who beats whom. Grandmasters are at the top, followed by masters, then experts, down to Class *D* players at the lowest rungs of the chess ladder. Adrian de Groot, a Dutch psychologist who was also a chess master, posed various chess problems to members of each merit category (including two former world champions) and asked them to select the best move. All of the masters chose continuations that would have won the game, while few of the other players did. But why? De Groot and many later theorists believed that the reason was in the way the players organized the problem. The chess master structures the chess position in terms of broad strategic concepts (e.g., a king-side attack with pawns) from which many of the appropriate moves follow naturally. In effect, the master has a "chess vocabulary" of more and larger chunks. If so, one would expect him to grasp a chess position in a shorter time. This is indeed the case. Players of different ranks were shown chess positions for five seconds each and were then asked to reproduce them a few minutes later. Grandmasters and masters did so with hardly an error; lesser players (including mere experts) performed much more poorly (see Figure 8.13). This is not because the chess masters had better visual memory. When presented with bizarre positions that would hardly ever arise in the course of a well-played game, they recalled them no better than novices did. Their superiority was in

ANAGRAM

PROBLEM

SOLVE

INSIGHT

SOLUTION

Solution to Anagrams (see Figure 8.7, p. 232)

A	B	C
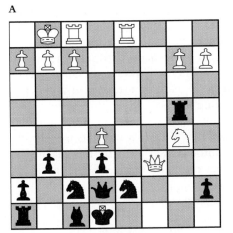	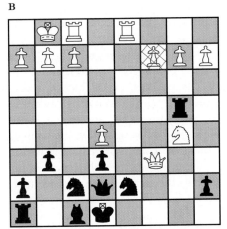	
Actual position	Typical master player's performance	Typical average player's performance

8.13 **Memory for chess positions in masters and average players** *(A) An actual chess position that was presented for five seconds after which the positions of the pieces had to be reconstructed. Typical performances by masters and average players are shown in (B) and (C) respectively, with errors indicated in red. (After Hearst, 1972)*

A	B
ZYP	RED
QLEKF	BLACK
SUWRG	YELLOW
XCIDB	BLUE
WOPR	RED
ZYP	GREEN
QLEKF	YELLOW
XCIDB	BLACK
SUWRG	BLUE
WOPR	BLACK
SUWRG	RED
ZYP	YELLOW
XCIDB	GREEN
QLEKF	BLUE
WOPR	GREEN
QLEKF	BLUE
WOPR	RED
ZYP	YELLOW
XCIDB	BLACK
SWRG	GREEN

8.14 **The Stroop effect** *The two lists, (A) and (B), are printed in four colors—red, green, blue, and yellow. To observe the Stroop effect, name the colors (aloud) in which each of the nonsense syllables in list (A) is printed as fast as you can, continuing downward. Then do the same for list (B), calling out the colors in which each of the words of the list is printed, again going from top to bottom. This will very probably be easier for list (A) than for list (B), a demonstration of the Stroop effect.*

the conceptual organization of chess, not in the memory for visual patterns as such.

Some later studies show that the superiority of the chess masters is not entirely produced by better chunking. They are also better at evaluating chess positions, and they look further ahead in their mental calculations (Charness, 1981; Holding and Reynolds, 1982; Holding, 1985). But chunking clearly plays a major role in this mental skill, just as it does in telegraphy, typing, and various athletic pursuits (e.g., Allard, Graham, and Paarsalu, 1980).

Processes similar to chunking may also underlie much of the cognitive growth that occurs in childhood. As infants grow into toddlers, and toddlers into children, they gradually acquire many concepts that adults take for granted, so that they eventually comprehend space, time, and causality in much the way their parents do. It may be that the way in which they achieve this has much in common with the route that beginners take in becoming masters in a particular skill. We will return to this issue in a later discussion of cognitive development (see Chapter 13).

AUTOMATIZATION

The routinization of subcomponents in skilled activities, however, has a cost as well as a benefit. Its benefit is simple: It allows us to **automatize** the performance of many motor and mental operations (such as reading) so we can devote our attention to other tasks. The cost shows up when the automatized operations are inappropriate for the task at hand, for once they are set in motion, they are difficult to turn off.

An example is reading. When we see a billboard on a highway, we can't help but read what it says, whether we want to or not. The forms on the sign proclaim that they are letters and words; this is enough to trigger our automatized reading routines (La Berge, 1975). A striking demonstration of this phenomenon is the **Stroop effect** (Stroop, 1935). Subjects are asked to name the colors in which groups of letters are printed and to do so as quickly as they can (Figure 8.14). In one case, the letter groups are unrelated consonants or vowels. In this condition, the subjects have little trouble. After a little practice, they become very proficient at rattling off the colors, "red, blue, yellow. . . ."

The subjects' task becomes vastly more difficult when the letters are grouped into words that are color names, such as *red, blue, yellow,* and so on. Diabolically enough, these are not the colors in which the color words are printed. Instead, *red* is printed, say, in green ink, *blue* in brown ink, *yellow* in red ink, and so on. Now the subjects respond much more slowly. Their task is to name the colors of the ink and say "green, brown, red," and so on, naming the *colors* in which the words are printed. But they can't help reading the *words* "red, blue, yellow, . . ." for reading is an automatized skill. As a result, there is violent response conflict. This conflict persists even after lengthy practice. One way subjects may finally manage to overcome it is by learning to unfocus their eyes. By this maneuver, they can still see the colors but can no longer recognize the words (Jensen, 1965; see also Reisberg, Baron, and Kemler, 1980).

OBSTACLES TO PROBLEM SOLVING

■ So far, we have primarily dealt with situations in which problem solvers succeed. How can we explain their all too many failures?

Problem solving is an organized, directed process that uses hierarchical chunking. But there are a number of risks built into this process. As we've just seen, the benefits of chunking can be offset by the cost of its accompanying automatization. But there are other risks as well. In order to use hierarchical chunks, one has to have a good sense of which chunks are appropriate and relevant; in order to work toward a goal, appropriate subgoals must be set. The trouble is that one's selections may be wrong. If so, the would-be problem solver may get stuck in a wrong approach and be unable to get unstuck. When finally told the answer, his reaction often shows that he was blind rather than ignorant: "How stupid of me. I should have seen it all along." He was victimized by a powerful **mental set** that was inappropriate for the problem at hand.

A well-known study shows how mental sets can make people rigid. They become **fixated** on one approach to a task, which makes it hard for them to think of it in any other way. The subjects were presented with a series of problems. They were told that they had three jars of known volume. Their job was to use these to obtain (mentally) an exact quantity of water from a well. In one problem, for example, the subjects had three containers—*A, B,* and *C*—which held 21, 127, and 3 quarts respectively. Their task was to use these three jars to obtain 100 quarts. After a while, they hit upon the correct method. This was to fill jar *B* (127 quarts) completely, and then pour out enough water to fill jar *A* (21 quarts). After this, they would pour out more water from jar *B* to fill jar *C* (3 quarts), empty jar *C,* and fill it again from jar *B.* The remaining water in jar *B* was the desired quantity, 100 quarts (Figure 8.15).

On the next few problems, the numerical values differed (see Table 8.1). But in all cases, the solution could be obtained by the same sequence of arithmetical

8.15 The standard method for solving the three-container problem (After Luchins, 1942)

TABLE 8.1 THE THREE-CONTAINER PROBLEM			
	Volume of empty jar (quarts)		
Desired quantity of water (quarts)	A	B	C
99	14	163	25
5	18	43	10
21	9	42	6
31	20	59	4

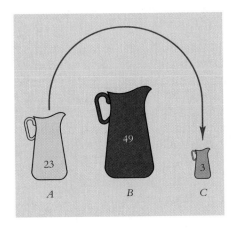

**8.16   A simpler method for solving cer-
tain three-container problems**   *(After
Luchins, 1942)*

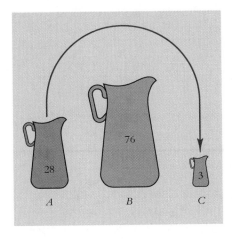

**8.17   A case where only the simple
method works**   *(After Luchins, 1942)*

8.18   Horse-and-rider problem   *The
task is to place (B) on (A) in such a way that
the riders are properly astride the horses. (After
Scheerer, Goldstein, and Boring, 1941; for
the solution, see p. 253).*

steps, that is, $B - A - 2C$. Thus, $163 - 14 - 2 \times 25 = 99$; $43 - 18 - 2 \times 10 = 5$,
and so on.

After five such problems, the subjects were given two critical tests. The first
was a problem that required them to obtain 20 quarts, given jars whose volumes
were 23, 49, and 3 quarts. Now most of the subjects showed a mechanization
effect produced by mental set. They dutifully performed the laborious arithmetical labors they had used before, computing $49 - 23 - 2 \times 3 = 20$. They did
so, even though there was a simpler method that takes only one step (Figure
8.16).

Subsequent to this was a second critical problem. The subjects were now
asked to obtain 25 quarts, given jars of 28, 76, and 3 quarts. Note that here the
only method that will work is the direct one, that is, $28 - 3 = 25$ (Figure 8.17).
But the mental set was so powerful that many subjects failed to solve the problem altogether. They tried the old procedure, which is inappropriate ($76 - 28 -
2 \times 3$ does not equal 25), and could not hit on an adequate alternative. The set
had made them so rigid that they became mentally blind (Luchins, 1942).

Similar effects have been demonstrated with other problems. In many of these
there is no need to induce the misleading set by instructions or prior practice,
for it is usually engendered by the perceptual arrangement of the problem itself.
Examples of such perceptually induced sets are the nine-dot problem (Figure
8.9, p. 232) and the horse-and-rider problem (Figure 8.18).

SET AND MOTIVATION

In fairy tales the hero is sometimes required to solve a riddle or suffer death, but,
being a fairy-tale hero, he invariably succeeds. In real life, he would have a harder time. For unfairly enough, problem solution becomes more difficult when
the need for it is especially great. This is because of the relation between set and
motivation. The greater the motivation toward solution, the stronger are the sets
with which the problem is approached. If these sets happen to be appropriate,
well and good. But if they are inappropriate, increased motivation will be a hindrance, for sets will then be that much harder to break. Since difficult problems—almost by definition—are problems that tend to engender the wrong set,
their solution will be impeded as motivation becomes intense.

Evidence for these assertions comes from several experiments which show
that flexibility goes down when motivation becomes intense enough. In one
such study, the subjects were posed a practical problem: to mount two candles
on a wall, given only two candles, a box of matches, and some thumbtacks

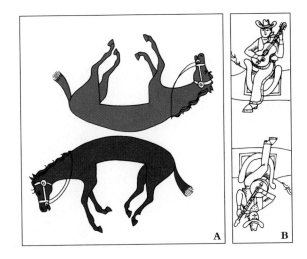

A

B

8.20 The water-lily problem *Water lilies double in area every twenty-four hours. On the first day of summer, there is one water lily as in (A). On the sixtieth day, the lake is all covered, as in (B). On what day is the lake half-covered?*

8.19 Functional fixedness *(A) The problem is to mount two candles on the wall, given the objects shown. (B) To solve the problem, one has to think of a new function for the box. (After Glucksberg, 1962; photographs by Jeffrey Grosscup)*

(Figure 8.19). The solution is to empty one of the boxes, tack it to the wall, and then place the candles upon it. The difficulty of this particular problem is caused by *functional fixedness.* This is a set to think of objects in terms of their normal function: A box is to put things in and not on top of. The tendency to maintain this set (that is, functional fixedness) was increased by motivation. Subjects who expected no particular reward solved the problem more quickly than subjects who were told that they might win twenty dollars (Glucksberg, 1962).

OVERCOMING OBSTACLES TO SOLUTION

The preceding discussion highlighted some of the conceptual and motivational obstacles that lie in the way of problem solution. Apart from acquiring some further knowledge and some relevant cognitive chunks (and keeping calm about the $20 reward that accompanies success), is there anything one can do to surmount these obstacles? Thus far, no one has found a problem solver's panacea. But some psychologists have offered a few suggestions.

WORKING BACKWARDS

One useful method for solving problems is to work backwards. As an example, consider the following problem:

> Water lilies double in area every twenty-four hours. On the first day of summer, there is one water lily on a lake. It takes sixty days for the lake to become covered with water lilies. On what day is the lake half covered?

Here the problem solver will run into trouble if she tries to work it out by brute force: On Day 1, there is one lily; on Day 2, there are two; on Day 3, there are four, and so on. The trick is to shift gears and look at the problem backwards. If the lake is fully covered on Day 60, it must be half-covered on the day before, since lilies double in area every day, which means that the answer is Day 59 (after Sternberg and Davidson, 1983; see Figure 8.20).

CHANGING THE REPRESENTATION

In many cases, a problem seems difficult because it is not correctly interpreted. To solve it, it has to be looked at in a new way. In effect, this is another case of changing set, but technically it is usually described as a change in the way the problem is **represented.**

Below is an example:

> Suppose Joe and Frank have the same amount of money. How much must Joe give Frank so that Frank has $10 more than Joe?

Here the crucial recognition is that Frank's gain is necessarily Joe's loss. Every dollar Joe gives to Frank must be represented as a net change of two dollars: one gained by Frank and one lost to Joe. Since we need a net change of $10, the answer is $5. (For another problem in which the solution depends on a change of representation, see Figure 8.21).

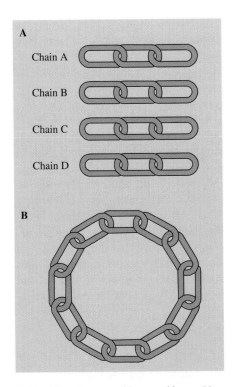

8.21 The cheap-necklace problem *You are given four separate pieces of chain that are each three links in length (A). It costs 2 cents to open a link and 3 cents to close a link. All links are closed at the beginning of the problem. Your goal is to connect all 12 links of chain into a single circle as shown in (B). The total cost must be no more than 15 cents. (From Wickelgren, 1974. The solution is described on p. 253).*

8.22 Archimedes in his bathtub *A sixteenth-century engraving celebrating a great example of creative restructuring. The Greek scientist Archimedes (287–212 B.C.) tried to determine whether the king's crown was made of solid gold or had been adulterated with silver. Archimedes knew the weight of gold and silver per unit volume but did not know how to measure the volume of a complicated object such as a crown. One day, in his bath, he noticed how the water level rose as he immersed his body. Here was the solution: The crown's volume is determined by the water it displaces. Carried away by his sudden insight, he jumped out of his bath and ran naked through the streets of Syracuse, shouting "Eureka! I have found it!" (Engraving by Walter H. Ryff, courtesy of The Granger Collection)*

RESTRUCTURING

We've already seen that the solution of a difficult problem often involves a shift in the way in which the problem is viewed. This shift may be very sudden and is then experienced as a flash of insight, a sense of "aha" that occurs when the misleading set is finally broken. **Restructuring** is especially clear in problems that impose a false set. To solve the nine-dot problem (Figure 8.9, p. 232) the subject has to move out of the square frame imposed by the dots. In a similar vein, the matchstick problem (Figure 8.8, p. 232) requires working in three dimensions rather than two.

Gestalt psychologists have proposed that this kind of perceptual restructuring lies at the heart of most problem solving in both animals and humans. So far, though little is known about the mechanisms that underlie the restructuring effect, there is reason to believe that it is a central phenomenon in the psychology of thinking. (For a contrary view, see Weisberg and Alba, 1981.)

CREATIVE THINKING

The creative thinker is one who generates a solution that is both new and appropriate. At the top of the pyramid are such giants as Archimedes, Descartes, and Newton, thinkers whose creations define whole chapters of intellectual history. On another level are the anonymous copywriters who develop new advertising slogans for spray deodorants. But whether great or humble, these real-life achievements are quite similar to those of the problem solver in the psychological laboratory. They represent a conceptual reorganization of what was there before.

According to the creators' own accounts, the critical insights typically occur at unexpected times and places. There is usually a period of intense preparation during which the thinker is totally immersed in the problem and approaches it from all possible angles. But illumination tends not to come then. Quite the contrary: After the initial onslaught fails, there is usually a period of retreat during which the problem is temporarily shelved. Rest or some other activity intervenes, and then suddenly the solution arrives, not at the writer's desk or the composer's piano, but elsewhere entirely—while riding in a carriage (Beethoven, Darwin), stepping onto a bus (the great mathematician Poincaré), or, in the most celebrated case of all, while sitting in a bathtub (Archimedes; see Figure 8.22).

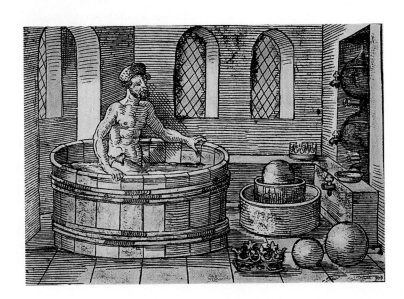

Such effects have sometimes been attributed to a process of *incubation* (Wallas, 1926). According to this view, a thinker does not ignore the unsolved problem altogether when she turns away from it in baffled frustration; she continues to work on it, but does so "unconsciously." This hypothesis adds little to our understanding, for it merely substitutes one mystery for another. Unless we know the why and wherefore of unconscious thought (whatever that may be), we know no more than we did before.

Many psychologists suspect that such incubation effects are produced in a less active way: Time away from a problem simply allows the problem solver to shake off false mental sets (Wickelgren, 1974; Anderson, 1990). Such false sets become increasingly restricting the longer she stays at the task, all the more so since her motivation is probably intense. Leaving the problem for a while may very well break these sets. As time elapses, the false set may be forgotten, and a drastic change of retrieval cues (the woods or the bathtub) will prevent its reinstatement. Once the false set is dropped, there is a chance that the true solution may emerge. Of course, that chance is much more likely to be realized if one is totally familiar with all the ins and outs of the problem and (especially) if one has the talents of a Beethoven or an Archimedes. Just taking a bath is unfortunately not enough.

ARTIFICIAL INTELLIGENCE: PROBLEM SOLVING BY COMPUTER

■ The preceding discussion emphasized the role played by hierarchical organization in thinking. But how does this organization come about? How does the problem solver hit upon the right plan of attack, and how does she recognize that it is right when she thinks of it? For that matter, how and when does restructuring occur? These questions are as yet unanswered, but there have been some promising leads.

One interesting avenue of research comes from attempts to program computers so as to simulate certain aspects of human thinking. The impetus for this work

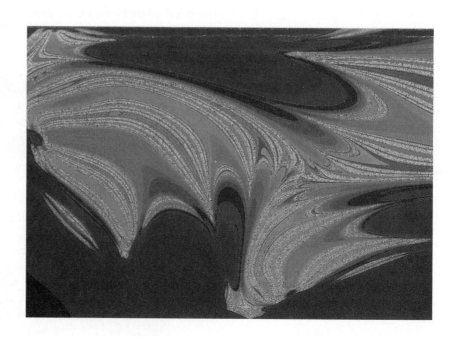

Computer-generated visual design By now, computers are used to assist in many human endeavors. The figure shows a computer design generated from a graphic program that incorporates various geometrical algorithms. *(Courtesy of Lifesmith Classic Fractals)*

"This one writes some fine lyrics, and the other one has done some beautiful music, but they just don't seem to hit it off as collaborators." (© 1978 by Sidney Harris—American Scientist Magazine)

stems from the belief, held by many psychologists, that humans and computers are similar in one important regard—they are both information-processing systems. We have already seen several examples of the information-processing approach in our discussions of perception and memory. When we talk of items that are temporarily activated in working memory, are recoded into fewer and more compact chunks, and are later retrieved by various hierarchical search procedures, we are describing a system in which information is systematically converted from one form into another. There is a formal similarity between this sequence of inferred events in human memory and the actual steps of a computer program that handles the storage, recoding, and retrieval of various materials (such as library titles, tax returns, and so on). In an analogous way, what we call "thinking" may be the systematic manipulation of the hierarchically arranged conceptual chunks stored in our brain.

To be sure, the underlying physical machinery is very different. Computers use hardware made of magnetic cores and transistors, while biological systems are built of neurons. But this difference does not prohibit a similarity in their operations. Two different computers may differ in that one is built with electronic tubes and the other with transistors, but they may be fed the same programs even so—and they will both compute the same functions. Similarly—for at least some purposes—it may not matter that digital computers are built of steel and ceramic chips, while an organism's mental machinery is built of neurons. To students of **artificial intelligence,** the important point is that both computers and human beings are information-processing systems (Turing, 1950). They therefore regard it as likely that the study of one will help in the understanding of the other.

ALGORITHMS AND HEURISTICS

Several investigators have deliberately forced their "thinking" programs to be as humanlike as possible. The most prominent among these are Allen Newell and Nobel laureate Herbert Simon, who have programmed computers to play chess, to discover and prove theorems in symbolic logic, and to decipher cryptograms. They began by studying how human subjects deal with these problems, uncovering their typical strategies by using the think-aloud technique we discussed earlier. Newell and Simon then incorporated these problem-solving plans into the instructions fed to their computer. Interestingly enough, the computer does fairly well if it attacks these problems as human subjects say they do (Newell and Simon, 1972).

Newell and Simon found it useful to distinguish between two major kinds of solution strategies. One is an **algorithm,** a procedure in which all of the operations required to achieve the solution are specified step by step. Examples are the various manipulations of arithmetic. An algorithm guarantees that a solution will be found in time, but this time may be very long in coming. Consider a person working on a crossword puzzle who is trying to find a synonym for "sharp-tongued" that will fit into _c_ _bi_. An algorithm exists: Insert every possible alphabetic combination into the four empty spaces and check each result against an unabridged dictionary. While this procedure is certain to produce "acerbic," it should appeal to few puzzle solvers, for it will require the inspection of nearly 460,000 possibilities.

In actual practice, crossword puzzles are solved by procedures that, though not as sure, are much less slow. These are **heuristics,** strategies that buy efficiency at the cost of possible error, in contrast to algorithms that are guaranteed to work but are totally blind to efficiency. Such heuristics are tricks and rules of thumb that have often worked in the past and may do so again, such as guessing at a suffix given the word's grammatical class (*ic* is a good bet for an adjective),

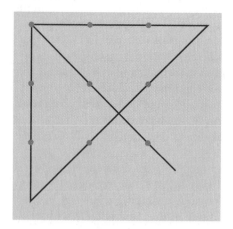

The solution of the nine-dot problem
The problem (see Figure 8.9, p. 232) is solved by going outside of the square frame into which the dots are perceptually grouped. The lines have to be extended beyond the dots as shown. Most subjects fail to hit on this solution because of a perceptual set imposed by the square arrangement.

forming hypotheses on the basis of likely letter sequences in the language (if *c* is the second letter, the first must be an *s* or a vowel), and so on. The various procedures for overcoming obstacles to problem solving that we have discussed before, such as working backwards, finding analogies, and changing the way the problem is represented, are heuristics of a similar sort—they are by no means guaranteed to work, but they often do. The great majority of problems people face are solved by such heuristic procedures rather than by algorithms, for human life is short and human processing capacity is limited. Physicians reach their diagnoses by first considering a few hypotheses that seem most plausible and then testing those. If instead they looked at every possibility, the patient would be dead before being diagnosed.

EXPERT SYSTEMS

A promising new trend in the field of artificial intelligence is the development of **expert systems.** These are problem-solving programs with a very narrow scope. They deal only with problems in a highly limited domain, such as some subfield of organic chemistry, law, or medicine. Because they are so specialized, their memories can be stocked with a considerable amount of know-how in their own area.

An example is MYCIN, a computer program designed to assist physicians in the treatment of infectious diseases. MYCIN is not just a stored table that lists drugs to combat this or the other microorganism. It can diagnose, suggest therapies, and estimate their effectiveness. The physician "informs" the computer of the patient's symptoms and of the results of various blood tests and bacterial cultures. The computer then consults its memory for lists of potentially useful drugs and chooses among them by following various decision rules (which consider the patient's age, other medications, side effects, and so on) and makes a recommendation, indicating the statistical probability of success. If "asked," it will indicate how it arrived at its decision. If appropriately "instructed," it will add to or modify its rules; for example, it may add a note that a particular antibiotic ought not to be administered to a patient with a certain allergy (Shortliffe et al., 1973; Duda and Shortliffe, 1983; Buchanan and Shortliffe, 1985).

SOME LIMITATIONS OF ARTIFICIAL INTELLIGENCE

Computer simulation has added a new and exciting dimension to the study of cognitive processes. But so far at least, it still has some serious limitations as an approach to human thinking.

Well-defined and ill-defined problems   The problems that existing computer programs can handle are *well-defined:* There is a clear-cut way to decide whether a proposed solution is indeed the right one. Examples are algebraic proofs (Are the terms identical on both sides of the equation?), chess problems (Is the opposing king checkmated?), and anagrams (Is the rearranged letter sequence a word that appears in the dictionary?).

In contrast, many of the problems people face in real life are *ill-defined.* Consider an architect who is asked to design a modern college dormitory. Exactly what is a correct solution? Some proposals can obviously be rejected out of hand—for example, a design with no provisions for bathrooms—but there is no definite criterion for what is acceptable. The situation is similar for many other problems, such as completing a sonnet or organizing a lecture or planning a vacation. In all of these cases, the critical first step is to define the problem so that it can be solved and so that the solution can be evaluated. The architect begins by asking questions about the number of students who are to be housed, the facilities that must be included, the surrounding terrain, the available budget—all in an attempt to transform an ill-defined problem into a well-defined one. The progress of human knowledge is often a matter not of problem solution but of problem definition and redefinition: The alchemist looked in vain for a way to change lead into gold; now the modern physicist tries to discover the atomic structure of matter. As of yet, computer programs do not define their own problems. It's by no means clear that computers will ever be able to do so in the way people do.

The lack of common sense Some computer scientists feel that the crucial difference between human and artificial intelligence concerns what is popularly called "common sense"—an understanding of what is relevant and what is not. People possess it, and computers do not. Consider a simple example: Let's assume that you build a computer program to perform some of the functions of a college registrar, such as keeping records of enrollments and grades. In principle it shouldn't be too hard to do so, and in many ways the program will do a much better job than a person might; it will never lose an entry or misfile it. Now let's suppose that you ask this computer a simple question: "How many psychology majors passed Computer Science 101 last semester?" The computer will search its memory and may come up with the answer "None." You become worried and restless and wonder whether psychology majors have some special disability. But if you understand the limitations of most computer programs, you will ask the computer a further question: "How many psychology majors enrolled in Computer Science 101 last semester?" When the computer comes up with the answer "None," you breathe a sigh of relief. But you will look at the computer wonderingly. A human registrar would never have answered the first question as the computer did. He would have understood the point of the question and would have responded relevantly and without extra prompting: "There were no psychology majors enrolled in the course." This is presumably because the human registrar—but not the computer—would immediately realize how misleading the original bare response "None" would be (Joshi, 1983; for a discussion of the problem of relevance, see Sperber and Wilson, 1986).

Computer scientists, well aware of the current limitations of artificial intelligence, sometimes tell a story about an interchange between an army general and the Pentagon's main computer in the war room:

Computer:	The Russians (or the Chinese, or the Iraquis, or whoever) are coming!
General:	By land or by sea?
Computer:	Yes.
General:	Yes what?
Computer:	Yes, SIR!!!

The computer can answer questions, but it cannot understand why the questions were asked. In this regard human intelligence is different from artificial intelligence. For human thinking involves a heady mixture of exactness and inexactness, of algorithmic and heuristic procedures that computers have not as yet achieved and perhaps never will. There may be a permanent difference in kind—not just a present difference in power—between human and computer thinking. For while computers are getting ever more powerful—with enormous memorial stores, incredible processing speeds, and huge interlocking networks of commands—it's by no means clear that they are coming closer to reproducing the kaleidoscopic reach, the flexibility and the creativity of human thought, though in the current infancy of artificial intelligence it is of course too early to be secure about any such pessimistic assessment.

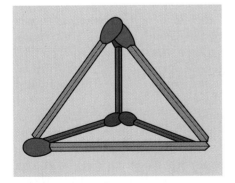

Solution of the matchstick problem *To arrange six matches (see Figure 8.8, p. 232) into four equilateral triangles, the matches have to be assembled into a three-dimensional pyramid. Most subjects implicitly assume the matches must lie flat. (After Scheerer, 1963)*

THE PROCESS OF THINKING: REASONING AND DECISION MAKING

FOCUS QUESTIONS

■ What are the two major kinds of reasoning, and what kinds of errors can occur with each?

■ What kinds of heuristics can lead to errors in decision making?

8.23 Syllogistic argument *Insisting upon the execution of the Cheshire Cat, the King of Hearts argued that anything that has a head can be beheaded, including the Cheshire Cat, which at this stage of the story consists of nothing but a head. (Lewis Carroll, Alice in Wonderland, p. 55)*

In problem solving, a goal is set that has to be reached by some as yet unknown means. As we've seen, the goals that constitute the problem can vary widely. Some are mechanical (e.g., fixing an electrical short circuit), others are numerical (e.g., the water jug problem), still others are social (e.g., looking for a graceful way to refuse an invitation) or spatial (e.g., the taxi driver's search for the fastest route), and so on. One form of problem solving is of special interest. This is reasoning, in which the goal is to determine what conclusions can logically be drawn from certain premises.

How do people reason? For many years, the assumption was that the processes they use are intimately related to the formal laws of logic. Thus, George Boole, a famous nineteenth-century mathematician, entitled his treatise on the laws of logic "An Investigation into the Laws of Thought," with little doubt that the laws that governed the one also govern the other (Henle, 1962). Today, this belief is no longer held as widely. For by now there is ample evidence that people are very prone to errors of reasoning. As a result, some psychologists argue that the laws of logic have more to say about how people *should* think than about how they really *do* think, for in their view humans are not quite as rational as one would like to believe.

DEDUCTIVE REASONING

■ In *deductive reasoning,* the reasoner tries to determine whether certain conclusions can be drawn—that is, *deduced*—from a set of initial assertions. Logically, the decision of whether the deduction is valid depends entirely on the initial assertions, coupled with some basic logical operations such as affirmation, negation, and so on. But do humans follow the appropriate laws of logic when they make their deductions?

A classical example of deductive reasoning is the analysis of *syllogisms,* an enterprise that goes back to Aristotle. Each syllogism contains two premises and a conclusion. The question is whether the conclusion logically follows from the premises (see Figure 8.23). Two examples of such syllogisms (one valid, one invalid) are:

All *A* are *B.*
All *B* are *C.*
Therefore: All *A* are *C.* (valid)

All *A* are *B.*
Some *B* are *C.*
Therefore: Some *A* are *C.* (invalid)

Or, stated in more concrete terms:

> All American Eagles are patriots.
> All patriots are red-blooded.
> Therefore: All American Eagles are red-blooded. (valid)

And:

> All heavenly angels are accomplished harp players.
> Some accomplished harp players are members of the American
> musicians' union.
> Therefore: Some heavenly angels are members of the American musicians'
> union. (invalid)★

Until the nineteenth century, most philosophers were convinced that the ability to evaluate syllogisms of this kind was an essential aspect of human rationality. Under the circumstances, it was a bit disheartening when experimental psychologists demonstrated that subjects make a considerable number of errors in evaluating syllogisms.

One cause of errors is produced by the subjects' tendency to perform inappropriate logical transformations. They hear the statement —"All *A* are *B*" and somehow interpret it as if it were symmetrical. As a result, they convert it to: "All *A* are *B,* and all *B* are *A.*" Such invalid conversions will then of course lead to invalid judgments (Revlin and Leirer, 1980). An example is "All owls are birds," which of course does not permit the conclusion "All birds are owls."

INDUCTIVE REASONING

In deductive reasoning, we typically go from the general to the particular. We apply some general rule ("All people are mortal") and ask how it applies to a particular case ("Pat Smith is mortal"). But much of the reasoning we engage in is ***inductive reasoning*** in which this process is reversed. Here we go from the particular to the general. We consider a number of different instances and try to determine—that is, *induce*—what general rule covers them all.

Induction is at the very heart of the scientific enterprise, for the object of science is to determine what different events have in common. To do so, scientists formulate various *hypotheses*—tentative assumptions about what constitutes the general rule from which the individual observations can be derived. Hypotheses are developed by laymen as well as scientists. All of us try to see some general pattern in the world around us, as in trying to explain the behavior of a moody daughter or a troublesome automobile. The hypotheses we come up with may not be particularly profound ("She's a teenager" or "It's a lemon"), but profound or not they are attempts to comprehend an individual case by subsuming it under a more general statement.

What do people do to determine whether their hypotheses are correct? A number of investigators have concluded that there is a powerful **confirmation bias.** By and large, people seek evidence that will confirm their hypotheses, but they only rarely set out to see whether their hypotheses are false.

An illustration is provided by a study in which subjects were presented with three numbers—2-4-6—and were told that these numbers are an example of a

"There it comes again."

(Illustration by Henry Gleitman)

★ Note that the validity of syllogisms only depends on whether the conclusion follows *logically* from the premises. The *empirical* plausibility of the conclusion (e.g., that the angels of heaven are unionized) has nothing to do with the matter.

The confirmation bias in science Galileo
vainly trying to persuade a group of university
professors to look through his telescope. (From
a National Theatre production of Galileo by
Bertolt Brecht; photograph by Zoe Dominic)

series that conforms to a general rule that the subjects were asked to discover. To
do this, they had to generate a three-number series of their own. Every time
they produced such a series, the experimenter would tell them whether it did or
didn't fit the rule. The subjects always indicated why they chose a particular
series, and after a number of trials they announced their hypothesis. This continued until the subject succeeded or finally gave up.

The rule the experimenter had in mind was exceedingly simple: "any three
numbers in increasing order of magnitude." It was so simple in fact that the subjects took quite a while before they discovered what it was. But the real issue
was how they went about their task. All of them soon developed one or another hypothesis. But whenever they did, they almost always generated a series that
fit this hypothesis—to confirm it. They very rarely generated a series that was
not consistent with their current hypothesis and would disconfirm it (Wason,
1960, 1968; Wason and Johnson-Laird, 1972).

The confirmation bias shown in the 2-4-6 experiment is a very pervasive
phenomenon. It is not restricted to the psychologist's laboratory, for it is also
found in the real-world behavior of scientists and engineers. They too tend to
seek confirmations of their hypotheses and are disinclined to seek evidence that
contradicts them. When Galileo provided visible proof that Jupiter has moons
that rotate around it, some of his critics were so incensed at this challenge to
their geocentric views of the universe that they refused even to *look* through his
telescope (Mitroff, 1974; Mahoney, 1976; Mahoney and DeMonbreun, 1981).

There is little doubt that the confirmation bias can be a genuine obstacle to
understanding, for in many ways, disconfirmations are more helpful in the
search for truth than are confirmations. *One* disconfirmation shows that a
hypothesis is false, but countless confirmations cannot really prove that it is true.

What accounts for the confirmation bias? A plausible guess is that humans
have a powerful tendency to seek order in the universe. We try to understand
what we see and hear, and to impose some organization upon it. The organization may not be valid, but it is often better than having none at all, for without
some such organization we would be overwhelmed by an overload of information. But this benefit also has a corresponding cost, for our confirmation bias

often condemns us to remain locked within our false beliefs and prejudices (Howard, 1983). We would be better off if we more readily considered their falsity and heeded Oliver Cromwell's advice to a group of clergymen: "I beseech you, in the bowels of Christ, think it possible you may be mistaken."

DECISION MAKING

Deductive reasoning is about certainties: If certain premises are true, then certain conclusions will follow. There are no exceptions. If it is true that Pat Smith is a person and that all people are mortal, then it inevitably follows that Pat Smith is mortal. The situation is very different in inductive reasoning in which we try to find a general rule when given a number of individual instances. Once we have arrived at this rule, we then try to apply it to new instances. But in contrast to deductions, inductions can never be certain; they can only be probable. This even holds for Smith's mortality. For in actual fact, the proposition "All people are mortal" is only an induction. To be sure, this induction is based on all of human history in which every single person who ever lived was ultimately observed to die. That Pat Smith will be an exception is therefore exceedingly unlikely—in fact, astronomically improbable. But death (or, for that matter, taxes) is not an *absolute* certainty in the sense in which deductively derived truths always are.

In ordinary life, we are usually concerned with probabilities that are much less clear-cut, and evaluating these probabilities is often crucial. Baseball batters have to estimate the likelihood that a pitcher will throw a fast ball; brokers must judge the probability that a certain stock will rise; patients who contemplate elective surgery must do their best to weigh the relevant medical risks. How do people estimate the relevant probabilities? And how do they use these estimates to decide whether to swing at the pitch, buy the stock, or undergo the surgery? These questions are the province of an area of psychology (and other social sciences) called **decision making.**

COGNITIVE SHORTCUTS FOR ESTIMATING PROBABILITIES

Technically, the probability that a particular event will happen is defined by a ratio: the frequency of that event (for example, the number of times a coin falls heads) divided by the total number of observations (the number of times the coin is tossed). But in actual practice we often don't know these frequencies. And even if we do, we often find it difficult to use them properly. According to Amos Tversky and Daniel Kahneman, we instead make use of various heuristics, which as we've seen are rules of thumb, cognitive shortcuts that often serve us well enough. But as Tversky and Kahneman point out, they sometimes lead to serious errors when they are used to estimate likelihoods (Tversky and Kahneman, 1973, 1974).

The representativeness heuristic One such rule of thumb is called the **representativeness heuristic.** When people have to make a judgment about the probability that a particular object or event belongs to a certain category, they often do this by comparing the similarity of the particular instance to a prototype of the category (that is, a representative case of that category). As a result, they may seriously misjudge the actual probabilities. A representativeness heuristic often comes into play when we have to make judgments about people. In one study, Kahneman and Tversky presented subjects with the following thumbnail sketch of an individual:

Jack is a forty-five-year-old man. He is married and has four children. He is generally conservative, careful, and ambitious. He shows no interest in political and social issues and spends most of his time on his many hobbies, which include carpentry, sailing, and mathematical puzzles.

One group of subjects was told that this description was drawn at random from a group of seventy engineers and thirty lawyers, and were asked to indicate their judgment of the probability that the person described by the sketch was an engineer. A second group of subjects was given the identical task with only one difference: They were told that the description was drawn at random from a group of seventy lawyers and thirty engineers.

The results showed that both groups estimated that the odds that Jack was an engineer were more than 90 percent. They evidently concluded that the thumbnail sketch described a person with hobbies and interests that were more stereotypical of an engineer than of a lawyer. To that extent Jack seemed more representative of an engineer than of a lawyer. That the subjects took this information into account in making their judgment is not too surprising. What is surprising is that the group that was told that engineers accounted for only 30 percent of all the cases did not take this fact into account at all. It appears that the subjects completely ignored the **base rate,** the proportion of the category—here, engineers—that were in the original sample. The concrete description and its similarity to the stereotype overwhelmed all other factors in the estimate. Such failures to take base rates into account illustrate the general tendency to give more weight to the vivid, prototypical, and concrete case than to the pale statistics (Kahneman and Tversky, 1972, 1973).

The availability heuristic   Another rule of thumb used in inductive reasoning is the **availability heuristic.** This is a cognitive shortcut for estimating the frequency of certain events by considering how many such events come readily to mind (are currently available to memory). One study involved guesses of how often certain letters appear in different positions in English words. As an example, take the letter *R*. Considering all the words in the language, does *R* occur more frequently in the first position or in the third position of all the words in the language? Over two-thirds of the subjects said that it is more common in the first than the third position. In actuality the reverse is true. The reason for the error is availability. The subjects made their judgments by trying to think of words in which *R* is the first letter (e.g., *r*ed, *r*ose, *r*ound) and of words in which it is the third (e.g., er*r*ing, bo*r*ing, ca*r*t, st*r*ong). They then compared the number they managed to generate in each category. But this method leads to a wrong estimate because our memorial dictionary (as well as Webster's) is organized according to the first rather than the third letter in each word. As a result, words that start with an *R* are much more easily retrieved (that is, more available) than those whose third letter is an *R*. As a result, their frequency is seriously overestimated (Tversky and Kahneman, 1973).

The availability heuristic can have serious practical consequences. What are the chances that the stock market will go up tomorrow or that a certain psychiatric patient will commit suicide? The stockbrokers and psychiatrists who have to decide on a particular course of action must base their choice on their estimate of these probabilities. But this estimate is likely to be affected by the availability heuristic. The stockbroker who remembers a few vivid days on which the market went up may overestimate the chances of an upswing; the psychiatrist who remembers one particular patient who unexpectedly slashed his wrists may underestimate the likelihood of eventual recovery of her other patients.

Vividness in memory is not the only factor that determines availability. Vividness in the way events are reported in the media have a similar effect. Consider estimates of various risks of death or bodily harm. In several studies,

"But we just don't have the technology to carry it out." (© 1976 by Sidney Harris— American Scientist Magazine)

people were asked which of two causes of death is the more frequent. They generally overestimated the frequency of dramatic and sensational events, such as motor accidents, fires, tornadoes, and homicides, and underestimated that of more unspectacular causes, such as diseases. For example, they thought that the number of lives claimed by homicide was about the same as those caused by stroke, whereas the actual ratio is 1 to 11. Here the extent of the perceived risk is determined by how frequently and dramatically such events are reported by the media through which we learn about them, which in turn determines their availability. Fires and murders make front page stories, while strokes rarely do (Slovic, Fischoff, and Lichtenstein, 1982).

ARE PEOPLE REALLY IRRATIONAL?

The preceding discussion has considered a body of evidence that throws a rather poor light on human rationality. People make many errors in deductive reasoning; they often misunderstand or misconvert the premises and so come up with an incorrect conclusion. They make errors in inductive reasoning; they are primarily concerned with demonstrating that their hypotheses are correct and don't try to discover whether they are wrong. They are also very prone to error when they have to make decisions in the face of uncertainty; they use a number of heuristics that may lead to mistakes in estimating the probability of events. Intellectually, we evidently have much to feel modest about. But if so, how could humanity possibly have achieved what it has in mathematics, philosophy, and science?

One reason is that most of our great intellectual achievements are at bottom collective. They depend on countless prior generations, each of which bequeathed some bits of new knowledge and some new ways of gaining yet further knowledge to the generation that followed it. Because of them, we possess an immense arsenal of intellectual tools, including various techniques of formal thinking. Our mental machinery has some limited capacity for deductive and inductive reasoning, but this capacity is not finely honed until experience—the individual's own and that of her ancestors before her—makes it so.

COGNITION AND CONSCIOUSNESS

FOCUS QUESTION

■ What phenomena suggest that people can think and act without being conscious of doing either?

The last few chapters have dealt with the ways in which we acquire, store, retrieve, and reorganize knowledge, as we perceive, remember, and think. But there is one topic that has come up in several contexts but has never been discussed in its own right—*consciousness.* This subject crops up in all areas of cognition. We see the brilliant colors of a sunset, have a clear auditory image of a soprano's aria, and experience frustration when we try to think our way through a difficult algebra problem. To be sure, these experiences are produced by something from the outside, but at bottom they are *our* experiences. We can describe them to others, but ultimately no one else can ever share them. They are private, by definition.

There is certainly much about consciousness that we don't understand: What exactly is consciousness? How is it possible for a biological mechanism, namely the human brain, to be conscious at all? Are other organisms conscious in the

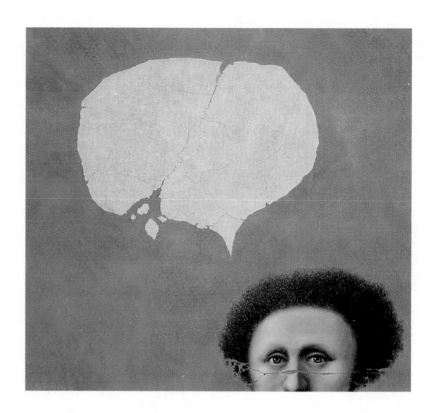

Nonconsciousness *Some hints of what consciousness is about come from studies of mental processes that go on in the absence of consciousness.* (Figure 14, *1982, by Alfredo Castañeda; courtesy of Mary-Anne Martin/ Fine Art, New York).*

same sense we are? Could machines (perhaps complex computers) be conscious? These questions remain the subject of debate, and, generally speaking, philosophers probably have more to say on such matters than psychologists do. (See, for example, Dennett, 1991; Rosenthal, 1993.)

Even so, psychologists have of late made some progress in this area. Ironically, though, this progress has come, not from examining consciousness itself, but rather by studying what happens when consciousness is *absent*. In a way, this is similar to some other areas of psychology in which advances were also made by investigating functions that are impaired or lacking. For example, much of what we know about memory comes through the study of forgetting. By describing what can be done *without* consciousness, psychologists have tried to understand what consciousness does when it comes into play and just what it contributes to our mental functioning.

MENTAL PROCESSES THAT GO ON BELOW THE SURFACE

■ As we've seen before on several occasions, people can perform many mental functions without being conscious that they do so. They can perceive, remember, reason, and understand with no awareness of what they are doing and with no conscious supervision of these complex activities.

Before proceeding, a word about the word *unconscious*. The popular conception of the term goes back to the ideas of Sigmund Freud, who applied it to ideas or memories that he believed are actively kept out of consciousness because they are threatening or because they provoke anxiety (see Chapter 17). But the mechanisms we will discuss here are in no sense pushed down into a mental cellar; we are not aware of them in just the sense in which we are usually unaware of the intricate machinery of digestion that operates after we eat a meal. They are simply *non*conscious rather than *un*conscious in Freud's sense.

PERCEPTION WITHOUT AWARENESS

An obvious starting point is perception. When we look at the world we see many familiar objects—a chair, a dog, a friend, and so on. We respond appropriately to them all: We don't sit on the dog, throw a bone to the friend, or ask the chair about its golf game. This means that the relevant visual stimuli triggered the relevant visual memories. But we ourselves were not conscious that this happened. Very occasionally we may become aware of this process, for example, when the light is poor and the object is at some distance. If so, we may ask (and ask ourselves), "Is that you, Joe?" and are quite conscious of the answer. But ordinarily most perceptual identifications take place outside of our awareness.

A similar point is made by a surprising neurological finding. This is the phenomenon of **blindsight,** which has been observed in some patients who suffer from damage to the occipital cortex, the region of the cerebral cortex to which the pathway from the eye and thalamus project (see Chapter 2). Lesions here will lead to a blindness in the area of the visual field that corresponds to the area of cortical destruction. If presented with visual stimuli in that region (which can be very large), the patient says he sees nothing and won't react even to flashes of very bright light. For all intents and purposes, this patient is blind in that area. But a series of studies by Larry Weiskrantz and his associates have shown that such patients are not truly without sight there. They presented various stimuli to the patients' affected field and asked them to point in the direction in which they were. The patients said the task was absurd: They were blind, so how could they guess? The investigators persisted, and the patients shrugged and guessed. It turned out that the guesses were surprisingly accurate. In further studies, the patients guessed whether stimuli placed in their blind field were, say, Xs or Os, or circles or squares. Here, too, their guesses were very much better than chance (Weiskrantz, 1986). Many investigators believe that the blindsight phenomenon depends on some connections between the visual system and other parts of the cortex (Weiskrantz, 1986; Rodman, Gross, and Albright, 1989; Cowey and Stoering, 1992). But whatever its underlying neurological cause, the important psychological point concerns the fact that a mental process may take place without our being aware that it does. In a sense, Weiskrantz's patients could *see* but they were not *aware* of seeing.

MEMORY AND UNDERSTANDING WITHOUT AWARENESS

What holds for perception, holds for other cognitive processes as well. Take memory: We've already seen that we often rely on inferences to fill in gaps in our recollection (see Chapter 7). Very often such reconstructions occur quite unwittingly, without our ever being aware that we are referring to what we know or expect. This same lack of awareness crops up whenever we listen and understand. For in all cases we necessarily consult our memories without knowing that we do so.

Consider the sentence:

Susan put the vase down too firmly on the table and it broke.

What does the word *it* refer to in this sentence? The sentence is ambiguous, for it could be the vase or (less probably) the table. But most of us see only one of the two meanings: To us, *it* has to be the vase. But how do we know? To draw this conclusion, we surely rely on our knowledge that vases are often fragile and tables usually are not. This holds for every word in the sentence and indeed for all sentences we hear or speak: To understand them, we must construct their meaning from the pieces we retrieve from memory. Examples like this demonstrate that our understanding of ordinary language (and of pictures, and scenes, and events) is dependent on what's in our memories.

To understand, we have to consult our memories, but these consultations go on underground. They are memory retrievals, but they are implicit (see Chapter 7). They had better be, for if we consciously searched our memories every time we heard a sentence, we would probably never get to the end of any paragraph. For most of us the potential ambiguity of the vase-and-table sentence never comes to mind.

While much of our everyday memory retrieval is implicit and without awareness, it's of course clear that we can also retrieve memories consciously. This is especially so for episodic memories: When did we meet Jane last and what did we do, and so on. Here, conscious memory search and recollection occur quite regularly. But as we've seen, this is much less common in certain cases of brain damage. Patients suffering from Korsakoff's syndrome often have no conscious awareness of events they have witnessed or of things they have done. Yet these patients do remember these events in some sense—they are influenced, in their present beliefs and behaviors, by the specific content of prior episodes as shown by various demonstrations of implicit retrieval (see Chapter 7). Apparently amnesics can remember and are influenced by their memories, with no awareness that they are recalling the past.

ACTION WITHOUT AWARENESS

People can evidently perceive objects, retrieve and use memories, and make judgments—all without conscious awareness. As we've seen in our discussion of automatization, they can also act without awareness and they often do. With increasing practice, many tasks become automatic so that we become less and less aware of their details. To return to a previous example, we all know how to tie our shoes, but most of us have forgotten the steps needed to accomplish this feat. If asked to list the steps for shoelace tying (as if instructing a child), many of us will not be able to provide an adequate account. We tie our shoes without consciously knowing how and usually without being aware that we're doing so. This and many other operations are tasks that are by now on "autopilot."

How does practice create automaticity? One proposal is that, with practice, fewer *decisions* are required as one steps through a complex task. The well-practiced shoelacer doesn't have to choose what to do next after the first loop is formed. Instead, she can simply, and quite implicitly, draw on the memory of what she has done many times before. A complete subroutine has been stored in memory, encapsulating all of the steps of the procedure. Once the routine is launched, no decisions are needed—she simply repeats the familiar steps. (For a theoretical proposal on how such subroutines are formed, see Logan, 1988).

These various lines of evidence suggest that much of our mental life goes on behind the scenes, backstage and out of sight. By and large, we seem to be unaware of the *processes* by means of which we perceive, remember, think, and understand. What we are aware of instead are the *products* that emerge from these processes (Nisbett and Wilson, 1977).

When automatization breaks down *We are normally unaware of such highly practiced operations as tying our laces. But we quickly become conscious of them when something disrupts the routine, as in the case of the figure skater Tonya Harding who had some problems with her laces during the 1994 Winter Olympics and had to ask the judges for additional time. (John Gaps III/AP Wide World)*

WHAT'S CONSCIOUSNESS GOOD FOR?

■ It appears that many mental processes operate quite well without our awareness. But if so, what is consciousness good for? So far, psychologists (and philosophers and neuroscientists) can only offer some speculations.

One suggestion comes from the study of automatization. Nonconscious processing is very fast and efficient—whether going through the step-by-step rou-

Solution of the horse-and-rider problem
Solving the horse-and-rider puzzle (see Figure 8.18, p. 237) requires a change of perceptual set. (A) must be rotated 90 degrees so that the two old nags are in the vertical position. One can now see that the head of each (vertical) can join (horizontally) with the hindquarters of the other. The final step is to slide (B) over the middle of (A) and the problem is solved. (After Scheerer, Goldstein, and Boring, 1941)

Solution to the cheap-necklace problem
The obvious (but incorrect) approach to the problem (Figure 8.21, p. 239) is to try to link the four chains together: A to B to C to D and then back to A. The trouble is that this procedure costs too much. To solve the problem, one has to shift the representation and see that one of the chains (say, A) can provide the connecting links to connect the other three chains. The first step is to destroy a chain by opening all three links in A (at a total cost of 6 cents). The first link is used to connect B and C (creating a 7-link chain), the second to join this new chain with D (making an 11-link chain), and finally the third to join the ends of this 11-link chain together. It costs 9 cents to close these 3 links, for a total cost of 15 cents. One of the reasons why this problem is quite difficult is that its solution requires a detour: In order to make a larger chain (that is, the final necklace) one has to destroy one of the smaller ones. (From Wickelgren, 1974)

tine of shoelace tying, or sending and receiving telegraphic messages, searching through memory, or drawing an obvious conclusion from the evidence. We achieve this efficiency in part simply by relying on familiar routines, rather than attending to each new decision. But as we saw earlier, by relying on routines we give up flexibility.

This leads to an obvious suggestion: Perhaps we need consciousness precisely for those tasks where we must preserve flexibility—that is, when we have to make choices. Nonconscious processing is fine when there are no choices and efficiency is the prime concern; much can be accomplished in a mind*less* fashion. Mind*ful*ness is required when we have to choose between one action and another. Mindfulness (that is, consciousness) becomes especially important when we must avoid becoming victims of habit, falling into the rut of continually relying on routine activities.

Seen in this light, consciousness is required for tasks that call for decisions, especially a succession of decisions—that is, tasks that don't allow a simple reliance on routine. It is also required to *choose* between actions, to fine tune our decisions, to make them exactly appropriate for the present situation. To take a lowly decision from everyday life: To avoid the embarrassment of telling and retelling the same joke to the same audience, we must *consciously* remember when we last told the joke and to whom (see Jacoby et al., 1989).

Another example is the principle of reciprocity, which guides behavior in many social systems (see Chapter 12): In general, favors and gifts have to be repaid. But to apply this principle requires episodic memory (What have you done for me lately?) and that is largely supplied by conscious recollection. Here is yet another case in which the choice among actions (specifically, social actions) depends on consciousness.

At best, these are but small and very tentative steps on the road to an answer. After all, the puzzle of consciousness has perplexed some of the greatest minds in human history, and it would be surprising if it were unraveled in the foreseeable future. But even so, modern psychologists and neuroscientists are increasingly turning their attention to this issue, which is surely one of the most important in their field. Whether they will ultimately progress beyond the speculations of the great philosophers of centuries past is as yet unclear. But it's interesting that the suggestion that consciousness is required for choice hearkens back to Descartes whose mechanism for action required a soul (consciousness?) whenever a choice between two acts was required.

TAKING STOCK

In looking back over the three domains of cognition—perception, memory, and thinking—we can only repeat a theme we have struck before. There are no clear boundaries that demarcate these three domains. In describing perception, we often cross over the border into memory. For the way we perceive familiar objects—let alone such ambiguous figures as the young woman-old woman picture—is based in part on how we perceived them in the past. But perception also shades into thinking. We look at an ambiguous picture and eventually solve the perceptual puzzle as we recognize in it the image of spotted horses dappled by sunlight. Nor is it clear where memory leaves off and thinking begins. Much of remembering seems like problem solving. We try to recall to whom we lent a certain book, conclude that it has to be Jane, for we know no one else who is interested in the book's topic, and then suddenly have a vivid recollection of the particular occasion on which she borrowed it (and the way she swore that she'd return it right away). But if remembering is sometimes much like thinking, thinking can hardly proceed without reference to the storehouse of memory. Whatever we think about—which route to take on a vacation trip, how to fill out a tax form—requires retrieval of items from various memory systems.

All of this shows that there are no exact boundaries between perception, memory, and thinking. These areas are not sharply separated intellectual domains, but are simply designations for somewhat different aspects of the general process of cognition. We will now turn to the one aspect of cognition that we have thus far discussed only in passing—language. It, too, is intertwined with the other domains of cognition, but unlike perception, memory, and thinking, which are found in many animals, language is unique to human beings.

QUESTIONS FOR CRITICAL THINKING

1. Given enough time and resources, can any problem be solved just using algorithms?

2. Is it really irrational to follow stereotypes and ignore base rates when considering the engineer-lawyer problem and its like?

3. Suppose that a particular kind of brain damage eliminated all *conscious* awareness but left unaffected all *nonconscious* thoughts and actions. How could you tell whether someone had suffered such brain damage? Would that person be able to tell you?

4. How could you tell whether a computer had consciousness?

5. What is consciousness good for?

SUMMARY

1. All thought draws on our knowledge. The components of knowledge can be regarded as *mental representations,* which are either *analogical* or *symbolic.* Analogical representations capture some of the actual characteristics of that which they represent (e.g., a mouse and a picture of a mouse), while symbolic representations bear no such relationship to that which they represent (e.g., a mouse and the word "mouse").

2. An important example of analogical representation in thinking is provided by mental images. With the possible exception of *eidetic imagery,* visual memories are not a simple reembodiment of stored visual perceptions. But they have some picture-like attributes as shown by studies of *image scanning. Spatial thinking* is both symbolic and analogical as shown by studies on *mental maps.*

3. The elements of symbolic thought are *concepts* and *propositions.* Many of these are stored in *generic* memory, where they constitute the "database" for our thoughts. Unlike *episodic memory,* which concerns memory for particular events in one's life, *generic memory* concerns items of knowledge as such. An important component of generic memory is *semantic memory,* whose organization has been described by various *network models.*

4. Problem solving is a directed activity in which all steps are considered in terms of how they fit into the overall structure set up by the task. This structure is typically hierarchical, with goals, subgoals, and so on. This hierarchical structure is not unique to problem solving but may be a general characteristic of any directed activity.

5. Increasing competence at any directed activity goes together with an increase in the degree to which the subtasks of this activity have become chunked and *automatized.* In learning to send and receive Morse code, as in the attainment of many skills, learning curves exhibit *plateaus* followed by a later rise, suggesting the acquisition of progressively

larger units. Similar chunking seems to occur in many forms of mental activity, including problem solving, and differentiates masters and beginners in many endeavors, such as playing chess.

6. Problem solving is not always successful. One reason may be a strong, interfering *mental set,* which makes the subject *fixated* and is especially hard to overcome under conditions of intense motivation.

7. Investigators of thinking have come up with a few suggestions to overcome obstacles to problem solving. One is working backwards from the goal; another is changing the mental representation of the problem. Sometimes the solution involves a radical *restructuring* by means of which a misleading set is overcome. Such restructurings may be an important feature of much creative thinking. Accounts by prominent writers, composers, and scientists suggest that restructuring often occurs after a period of *incubation.*

8. An influential approach to problem solving comes from work on *artificial intelligence* in which computer scientists try to simulate certain aspects of human thinking. A number of solution strategies, including the use of *algorithms* and *heuristics,* have been incorporated into several computer programs. Some further extensions feature the use of *expert systems.* Among the limitations of current artificial intelligence programs as an approach to human thinking are their difficulty in dealing with ill-defined problems and their lack of common sense, a knowledge about many aspects of the world together with an understanding of what is relevant to the problem at hand.

9. Studies of *deductive reasoning* show that people are prone to various errors in thinking. Errors of reasoning in dealing with *syllogisms* are caused by a number of factors, including the tendency to perform inappropriate logical transformations.

10. In deductive reasoning, the thinker tries to determine whether a particular consequence follows from a general rule or set of rules. In *inductive* reasoning, the direction is reversed, for here the thinker tries to determine whether a general rule can be inferred from particular instances. An initial, tentatively held induction is a hypothesis. A number of studies have pointed to a powerful *confirmation bias* that makes subjects seek evidence that will confirm their hypotheses rather than look for evidence that would show their hypotheses to be false.

11. *Decision making* involves the estimation of probabilities and the use of these estimates in deciding on a course of action. To make such estimates, people often use certain heuristics. These are cognitive rules of thumb that often serve us well enough but that may also lead to serious errors. One such rule of thumb is the *representativeness heuristic:* estimating the probability that an object belongs to a category by comparing the object to a prototype of the category, while ignoring other factors, such as *base rates.* Another rule of thumb is the *availability heuristic:* estimating the frequency of an event by how readily an example of such an event comes to mind.

12. In recent years, psychologists have paid increasing attention to the problem of *consciousness.* Most of the progress in this area has come from studying some psychological processes that operate when consciousness is absent. One example is *blindsight,* which occurs in persons who have lost some portion of their visual cortex but can nevertheless perform many visual discriminations without being conscious that they do. Similar *nonconscious processing* occurs on innumerable occasions in everyday life when people retrieve memories implicitly. Yet another everyday occurrence of nonconscious processing is the performance of automatized tasks. These phenomena suggest that consciousness functions as a monitor that helps us to make choices between alternatives.

CHAPTER **9**

LANGUAGE

**W**hen we consider the social forms and physical artifacts of human societies, we are struck by the diversity of cultures in different times and places. Some humans walk on foot, others travel on camels, and still others ride rockets to the moon. But in all communities and all times, humans are alike in having language. This essential connection, between having language and being human, is one reason why those interested in the nature of human minds have always been particularly intrigued with language.

To philosophers such as Descartes language was that function which most clearly distinguished between beasts and humans, and was "the sole sign and only certain mark of thought hidden and wrapped up in the body." Descartes held that humans were utterly distinct from the other animals because all humans have language, while no other animals have anything of the sort. But this claim comes up against an immediate objection: There are about 4,000 languages now in use on earth (Comrie, 1987). Obviously, these are different from one another, for the users of one cannot understand the users of another. In what sense, then, can we speak of "language in general" rather than of French or English or Hindi? The answer is that human languages are at bottom much more alike than they seem at first glance to be. For example, all languages convey thought by the same means: They all use words and sentences to organize ideas. In contrast, animal communications often have something like words (for instance, a cat can purr happily and hiss angrily), but they never have complicated sentences (such as *I'm going to stop purring and start hissing unless you give me that catnip immediately*).

Another similarity is in the ideas human languages can express. When the United Nations ambassador from France makes a speech, numerous translators immediately whisper its equivalent in English, Russian, Arabic, and so on to the listening ambassadors from other countries. The fact that the French speech can readily be translated suggests that, by and large, the same things that can be said in French can be said in English and Russian as well. This is true despite the fact that the Russian and English listeners may disagree with what the French diplomat is saying. But the translation will allow them to *know* that they disagree, so that they are in a position to stomp out of the room in a rage or make a counterspeech—which will also be translatable. In our discussion of language, we will use English as our main example. But it is important to keep in mind that what we say about English generally goes for the other human languages as well.

The biblical account of the origin of different languages *According to the Bible, all people once spoke a common language. But they built a tall structure, the Tower of Babel, and tried to reach the heavens. To punish them for their pride and folly, God made them unable to understand each other, each group speaking a different language.* (Tower of Babel *by Jan Brueghel, the Elder, 1568–1625; courtesy of Kunsthistorisches Museum, Vienna)*

MAJOR PROPERTIES OF HUMAN LANGUAGE

FOCUS QUESTION

■ What are the five major properties of all human languages?

There are five major properties of all human languages that psychology must describe: Language is *creative* (or *novel*), it is highly *structured* (or *patterned*), it is *meaningful,* it is *referential* (that is, it refers to and describes things and events in the real world), and it is *interpersonal* (or *communicative*—involving the thoughts of more than one person at a time).

LANGUAGE IS CREATIVE

At first glance, language might seem to be merely a complicated habit, a set of acts by ear and mouth that have been learned by memorization and practice. According to this view, the explanation of talking is simple: Each of the memorized speech acts is simply performed whenever the appropriate circumstances arise. Our mothers said *That's a rabbit* when they saw a rabbit. Having observed this, we now say *That's a rabbit* when we see a rabbit. But this position of language as habit is hard to maintain, for speakers can and will utter and understand a great many sentences that they have never uttered or heard before. To see this point, it is only necessary to realize that, in addition to *That's a rabbit,* each of us can also say and understand

> *That's a rabbit over there.*
> *A rabbit is what I see over there.*

Obviously, that's a rabbit.
How clearly I recall that the word for that animal is rabbit.
Well bless my soul, if that isn't a rabbit!

and so on, with hundreds of other examples. A little child who has memorized all these sentences must be industrious indeed. But the situation is really incredibly more complicated than this, for we can talk about objects and creatures other than rabbits, including aardvarks and Afghans, apples and armies, proceeding all the way to zebras and Zyzzogetons.

Furthermore, the sheer number of English sentences rules out habit as the explanation for language use. A good estimate of the number of reasonably short (20 words or fewer) English sentences is 10^{30}. Considering the fact that there are only 3×10^9 seconds in a century, a learner memorizing a new sentence every second would have learned only a minute fraction of them in the course of a lifetime. But the fact is that we can all say and understand most of them (Bloomfield, 1933; Chomsky, 1959).

In sum, we effortlessly create and interpret new sentences on the spot. Only a very few such as *How are you?*, *What's new?*, and *Have a nice day* are said and heard with any frequency. All the rest are at least partly new—new to the person who says them and new to his listeners as well. To express all the thoughts, we combine a limited—though large—number of words into sentences. Thus language is a system that allows us to reach a limitless end from limited means: Our stock of memorized, meaningful words is finite, but we nevertheless have the capacity to speak of an infinite number of new things and events. We can do so because our language system allows us to combine the old words in novel ways.

LANGUAGE IS STRUCTURED

■ While language use is creative in the sense that we can and do invent new sentences all the time, it is also restricted: There are unlimited numbers of strings of English words that—accidents aside—we would never utter. For example, we do not say *Is rabbit a that* or *A rabbit that's* even though these are fairly comprehensible ways to say *That's a rabbit*. Speakers construct their utterances in accord with certain abstract principles of language structure. These **structural principles** underlie the way in which we combine words to make up new sentences, and they are honored by every normal individual—without special thought and without any formal training in school. These principles are generally not known consciously, but are *implicit*. Even so, they govern our use of language and allow us to compose and understand boundless new sentences.

The power of an "H"   A scene from the stage version of My Fair Lady *in which the cockney flower girl, Eliza (Julie Andrews), is taught by Henry Higgins (Rex Harrison) to pronounce an "H" the way the British upper classes do. She thus becomes a lady. This shows that following prescriptive rules can sometimes confer important social advantages. (Labov, 1970b; photograph by Leonard Mc-Combe/LIFE Magazine, © Time Warner, Inc.)*

We should point out that the structural principles of language (sometimes called **descriptive rules**) have to be distinguished from certain **prescriptive rules** handed down from various authorities about how they think we *ought* to speak or write. Prescriptive rules are the so-called rules of grammar that many of us learned painfully at school in the fourth grade (and thankfully forgot in the fifth), such as "Never say *ain't*" or "A sentence cannot end with a preposition." These recipes for speech and writing often do not conform to the actual facts about natural talking and understanding. For example, most of us have no qualms about ending sentences with a preposition (as in the sentence, *Who did you give the packages to?*) or even two prepositions (as in *What in the world are you up to?*). In some cases it sounds rather odd not to do so, as Winston Churchill pointed out when spoofing this "rule" by insisting that "This is the kind of language up with which I will not put!"

The **structural principles** we will be concerned with in this chapter are those that every normal speaker honors without effort or formal instruction—for example, the principle by which we invariably say *the rabbit* rather than *rabbit the.* It is these regularities that are fundamental to understanding language as a universal human skill. In fact, most human cultures outside of America and Western Europe do not have prescriptions for "proper" speech at all.

LANGUAGE IS MEANINGFUL

■ Each word in a language expresses a meaningful idea (or concept) about some thing (e.g., *camera* or *rabbit*), action (*run* or *rotate*), abstraction (*justice* or *fun*), quality (*red* or *altruistic*), and so on. The purpose of language is to express all these meanings to others, so we have no choice but to learn a conventional word for each.

But people talk in whole sentences rather than just one word at a time. This is because the grammatical patterns that we discussed in the previous section also contribute to meaningfulness. For example, the words *dogs, cats, bite* express very different meaningful thoughts depending on how they are put together: *Dogs bite cats,* or *Cats bite dogs.*

LANGUAGE IS REFERENTIAL

■ Language users know more than how to put words together into meaningful and grammatical sentences. They also know which words refer to which things, scenes, and events in the world. If a child said *"That's a shoe"* (a sentence whose grammar is impeccable and whose meaning is transparent) but did so while pointing to a rhinoceros, we would not think she had learned English very effectively. This is the problem of **reference:** how to use language to describe the world of real things and events—saying *shoe* to make reference to a shoe, but saying *rhinoceros* to refer to a rhinoceros.

LANGUAGE IS INTERPERSONAL

■ Many aspects of human language are within the individual and are thus the property of each single human mind. But language is a process that goes beyond the individual, for it is a social activity in which the thoughts of one mind are conveyed to another. To accomplish these social ends, each speaker must know not only the sounds, words, and sentences of his language, but also certain **principles of conversation.** These principles govern the way in which language is used appropriately under varying circumstances.

Suppose, for example, that one sees a lion in the parlor and wants to tell a companion about this. It is not enough that both parties speak English. One has to estimate the listener's mental state, capacities, motivations, and relations to oneself in order to speak appropriately. If the companion is a sharpshooter with a revolver, one might say:

Quick, shoot! There is a lion in the parlor.

But if the companion is an artist, one might say:

Quick, draw! Lion of a gorgeous shade of ochre in the parlor.

To a biologist, one might say:

Quick, look! Member of the genus Panthera leo *in the parlor.*

And to an enemy,

Lovely morning, isn't it? See you later.

Adam gives names to the animals *The belief that knowledge of word meanings sets humans above animals goes back to antiquity. An example is the biblical tale illustrated in this painting by William Blake, which shows Adam assigning names to the animals. According to some ancient legends, this act established Adam's intellectual superiority over all creation, including even the angels. In one such tale, the angels were unable to call the animals by name, but Adam could: "'Oh Lord of the world! The proper name for this animal is ox, for this one horse, for this one lion, for this one camel!' And so he called all in turn, suiting the name to the peculiarity of the animal" (Ginzberg, 1909, vol. 1, p. 62). Notice that Adam thinks that words sound like what they mean. (William Blake's* Adam Naming the Beasts; *Stirling Maxwell Collection, Pollok House, Glasgow Museums & Art Galleries)*

The stimulus-free property of language use How many sentences can you think of to describe this painting? (Henri Rousseau's The Sleeping Gypsy, 1897, oil on canvas, 5' 1" × 6' 7." Collection, The Museum of Modern Art, New York. Gift of Mrs. Simon Guggenheim)

Clearly, what one says about a situation is not just a description of that situation, but depends upon one's knowledge, beliefs, and wishes about the listener. To communicate successfully, then, one must build a mental picture of "the other" to whom speech is addressed (Austin, 1962; Clark and Clark, 1977; Clark, 1978; Prince, 1981; Schiffrin, 1988).

The same problem arises for the listener, of course. To determine the sense of what one has heard, one must make an estimate of the speaker and the circumstances of her utterances. Suppose, for example, someone said "Can you pass me the salt?" To know how to respond appropriately, one must ask oneself (implicitly, of course) "Does this speaker think my arms are broken?" (in which case the answer should be "Yes, I can" or "No, I can't," depending on whether one's arms *are* in fact broken). But if one is hale and hearty, the ordinary supposition would be that this was just a polite way of requesting one to pass the salt. And now the answer should be, "Sure. Here you are," accompanied by the action of passing the salt (Searle, 1969; Clark, 1979; Sperber and Wilson, 1986).

THE STRUCTURE OF LANGUAGE

FOCUS QUESTIONS

- What are phonemes, and to what extent are they shared across cultures?

- What are morphemes? How do content morphemes differ from function morphemes?

- What is syntax?

All human languages are organized as a hierarchy of structures. At the bottom of the hierarchy, each language consists of little snippets of sound, and at the other end, of sentences and conversations. We begin by describing the basic building blocks: the 40 or so phonemes, the 80,000 or so morphemes, and the hundreds of thousands of words.

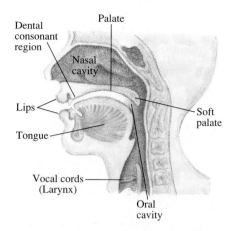

9.1 The human vocal tract *Speech is produced by the air flow from the lungs that passes through the larynx (popularly called the voice box) containing the vocal cords and from there through the oral and nasal cavities which together make up the vocal tract. Different vowels are created by movements of the lips and tongue, which change the size and shape of the vocal cavity. Consonants are produced by various articulatory movements that temporarily obstruct the air flow through the vocal tract. For some consonants the air flow is stopped completely. Examples are* p, *where the stoppage is produced by bringing both lips together, and* t *where it is produced by bringing the tip of the tongue to the back of the upper teeth. Some other consonants are created by blocking the air flow only partially, for example* th *(as in thick), which is produced by bringing the tip of the tongue close to the upper teeth but without actually touching them. (After Lieberman, 1975)*

PHONEMES

To speak, we move the various parts of the vocal apparatus from one position to another in a rapid sequence while expelling a column of air up from the lungs and out through the mouth (see Figure 9.1). Each of these movements shapes the column of air from the lungs differently and thus produces a distinctive speech sound (MacNeilage, 1972). Many of these differences among speech sounds are ignored by the listener. Consider the word *bus,* which can be pronounced with more or less of a hiss in the *s.* This difference is irrelevant to the listener, who interprets what was heard to mean 'a large vehicle' in either case. But some sound distinctions do matter, for they signal differences in meaning. Thus neither *butt* nor *fuss* will be taken to mean 'a large vehicle.' This suggests that the distinctions among *s, f,* and *t* sounds are relevant to speech perception, while the difference in hiss magnitude is not. The distinctions that are perceived to matter are called **phonemes.** They are the perceptual units of which speech is composed (Liberman, 1970; see Figure 9.2, which illustrates the hierarchy of linguistic structures).

Because of the construction of the human speech apparatus, children can learn to pronounce a couple of hundred different speech sounds clearly and reliably. But each language restricts itself to using only some of them. English uses about forty.★ Other languages select differently from among the possible phonemes. For instance, German uses certain gutteral sounds that are never heard in English, and French uses some vowels that are different from the English ones. Once children have learned the sounds used in their native tongue, they usually become quite rigid in their phonemic ways: It becomes difficult for them to utter or perceive any others. This is one reason why foreign speech often sounds like a vague and undifferentiated muddle, rather than like a sequence of separable sounds.

MORPHEMES AND WORDS

At the next level of the linguistic hierarchy (see Figure 9.2, p. 263), fixed sequences of phonemes are joined into morphemes. The **morphemes** are the smallest language units that carry bits of meaning. Like phonemes, the morphemes of a language can be combined only in certain ways. Some words consist of a single morpheme, such as *and, run,* or *strange.* But many morphemes cannot stand alone and must be joined with others to make up a complex word. Examples are *er* (meaning 'one who') and *s* (meaning 'more than one'). When these are joined with the morpheme *strange* (meaning 'alien' or 'odd') into the complex word *strangers* (*strange + er + s*), the meaning becomes correspondingly complex ('ones who are odd or alien'). Each of these morphemes has a fixed position within the word. Thus *er* has to follow *strange* and precede *s;* other orders (such as *erstranges* or *strangeser*) are not allowed (Aranoff, 1976).

The morphemes such as *strange* that carry the main burden of meaning are called **content morphemes.** The morphemes that add details to the meaning but also serve various grammatical purposes (such as the suffix *er* or the connecting word *and*) are called **function morphemes.**

The average speaker of English has acquired about 80,000 morphemes by adulthood (Miller and Gildea, 1987), knows the meaning of each, and how they

★The English alphabet provides only twenty-sex symbols (letters) to write these forty phonemes, so it often uses the same symbol for more than one. Thus, the letter O stands for two different sounds in hot and cold, an "ah" sound and an "oh" sound. This fact contributes to the difficulty of learning how to read English.

9.2 The hierarchy of linguistic structures *Every sentence is composed of phrases, which are composed of morphemes (simple units of meaning such as strange and the plural -s), which in turn are composed of phonemes (the units of speech sound, such as p and ə). The phonemes are described by symbols from the phonetic alphabet because English spelling is not always true to the sounds of words.*

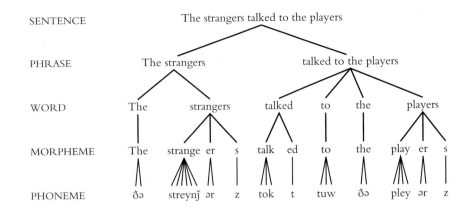

are positioned within words. If we counted vocabulary by morphemes rather than by words, normal people would be credited with several hundred thousand of these, for then *strange, stranger, strangers,* etc. would each count as a separate item.

PHRASES AND SENTENCES

The system of words in a language is very rich and allows us to express an enormous variety of meanings with great precision. Nevertheless, we cannot memorize a new word for each of the hundreds of millions of thoughts that we want to express. Therefore, we combine our limited—though large—stock of words into whole sentences. We may remark either *The lion kicked the gnu* or *The gnu kicked the lion.* Both these sequences of words are meaningful, but there is a difference in the meaning that is of some importance—at least to the lion and the gnu. The term **syntax** (from the Greek, *arranging together*) is the name for the system that arranges (or groups) words together into meaningful phrases and sentences. This topic has been extensively investigated by the American linguist, Noam Chomsky (Chomsky, 1975, 1980, 1986; for overviews of syntactic theory, see Newmeyer, 1983; Sells, 1985; Radford, 1988).

Just as a morpheme is an organized grouping of phonemes and a word is an organized grouping of morphemes, so a **phrase** is an organized grouping of words. The phrases are the building blocks of which sentences are composed. Consider the sentence

The French bottle smells.

This sentence is **ambiguous:** It can be understood in two ways depending on how the words are grouped into phrases; either

(The French bottle) (smells).

or   *(The French) (bottle) (smells).*

Thus by the choice of phrasing (that is, word grouping), the word *bottle* comes out a noun in the first interpretation, so that sentence is telling us something about French bottles. But *bottle* comes out a verb in the next interpretation, in which case the sentence is telling us about what the French put into bottles— namely, smells (that is, perfumes). For another example, see Figure 9.3.

The phrase is thus the unit that organizes words into meaningful groupings within the sentence. Just as for phoneme sequences and morpheme sequences, some phrase sequences (like those we just considered) are acceptable, while others are outlawed: for example, *(The French) (smells) (bottle).*

9.3 How phrase structure can affect meaning *On being asked what a Mock Turtle is, the Queen tells Alice "It's the thing Mock Turtle Soup is made from." Needless to say, this is a misanalysis of the phrase* mock turtle soup *as (mock turtle) (soup). It ought to be organized as (mock) (turtle soup)—a soup that is not really made out of turtles (and is in fact usually made out of veal). (Lewis Carroll,* Alice in Wonderland, *1969, p. 73)*

FOCUS QUESTIONS

- What are the reference, definitional, and prototype theories of meaning?
- What are propositions, and what are their elements?

We have seen that language consists of a small number of sound units (the forty or so phonemes) organized into fixed sequences (the 80,000 or so morphemes and hundreds of thousands of words), which in turn are organized into the boundless number of phrases and sentences. In sum, as we ascend the linguistic ladder there are more and more units at every level. How can the human mind deal with this ever expanding number of items? There is only one possible answer: We don't learn the billions of sentences in the first place. Instead, we acquire generalizations that allow us to construct any sentence. It is the fact that organization of units exists at each level of the hierarchy that makes language use possible in the first place. Without systematic knowledge of such patterns, we would not be able to learn, speak, or understand a language—there would just be too much to handle.

But why do humans go to the trouble of acquiring language? The answer, of course, is just that it allows us to convey boundless thoughts from one human mind to another human mind. Of primary interest, then, are the higher level units and patterns of language: the meaningful words, phrases, and sentences. In the following sections, therefore, we will take up the questions of word and sentence meaning in detail.

THE MEANING OF WORDS

The question, "What do words mean?" is one of the knottiest in the whole realm of language (see Putnam, 1975; Fodor, 1983, 1988). The subfield that deals with this question, *semantics,* has thus far been able to give only a few, rather tentative answers. As so often, the first step is to eliminate some of the answers that appear to be false.

MEANING AS REFERENCE

One of the oldest approaches to the topic equates word and phrase meaning with *reference.* According to this position, the meaning of a word or phrase is whatever it refers to in the world. Thus this view asserts that words and certain phrases are essentially names. Proper names such as *Steffi Graf, Australia,* and the *Eiffel Tower* are labels for a particular person, place, and object. The reference theory of meaning claims that expressions such as *tennis player, continent,* and *building* function in a similar manner. According to this view, the only difference between such expressions and true proper names is that the former are more general; *tennis player* refers to various male and female players and to champions as well as duffers: *Steffi Graf* refers to one player and no one else.

The reference theory of meaning runs into several difficulties. One difficulty is that some words or phrases are perfectly meaningful even though it is hard to know exactly what they refer to. Some of these are abstract expressions such as *justice, infinity,* and *historical inevitability.* One cannot point to a real "infinity" somewhere out there in the world. Others are imaginary, such as *unicorn* and *the crown prince of South Dakota*, which presumably have no real-world referents at all. Yet these expressions do not seem to be "meaningless" or "semantically empty."

A famous example of the distinction between meaning and reference was pointed out by the German philosopher, Gottlob Frege (1892): The expression *the morning star* has one meaning (namely, 'the last star visible in the eastern sky as dawn breaks'), and the expression *the evening star* has quite a different meaning (namely, 'the first star visible in the western sky as the sun sets'). Yet both of these expressions refer to one and the same object in the sky (namely, the planet Venus). Thus two expressions can have different meanings and yet refer to the same thing. It follows that there is a distinction between the meaning of a word or phrase and the things that this word or phrase refers to in the world. The meaning of a word is the idea or concept that it expresses. The referents of the word are all those things in the real (or imaginary) world that fall under that concept.

THE DEFINITIONAL THEORY OF MEANING

We have just concluded that the meaning of a word is a concept (or **category**). Some words describe concepts that refer to only one thing or creature in the real or imaginary world, such as *Madonna* or *Pinocchio*, while other words such as *dog* or *unicorn* are more general, describing categories that have many referents. But is the meaning of a word always just a simple concept, irreduceable to simpler elements? Most theories of word meaning assert that only a relative handful of the words in a language describe elementary, "simple" concepts. The rest are labels for bundles of concepts. Thus the words *feathers, flies, animal, wings* might describe simple concepts, but all of these ideas are bundled together in the (relatively) complex word *bird*. One approach of this kind is the **definitional theory of meaning.** It holds that meanings are analyzable into a set of subcomponents, organized in our minds much as they are in standard dictionaries. This approach starts out with the fact that there are various meaning relationships among different words and phrases. Some words are similar in meaning *(wicked-evil)*; others are opposites *(wicked-good)*; still others seem virtually unrelated *(wicked-ultramarine)*. According to the definitional proposal, these relationships can be explained by assuming that words are **bundles of semantic features** (Katz and Fodor, 1963; Katz, 1972). As an example, take the word *bachelor*. This word clearly has something in common with *uncle, brother, gander,* and *stallion*. As speakers of English, we know that all of these words carry the notion *male*. This point is forcefully made by considering various sentences that most English speakers will regard as odd (or, to use the technical term, *anomalous*). Thus, the sentence *My _____ is pregnant* sounds very peculiar if the missing word is any of the members of the bachelor-related group listed below:

My
      uncle
      brother
      gander   *is pregnant.*
      stallion
      bachelor

Demonstrations of this sort suggest that words like *stallion* and *bachelor* are not simple in meaning, but rather are composed of a number of meaning atoms—the semantic features. For *bachelor*, these might be 'never married,' 'human,' 'adult,' and 'male'; for *stallion*, they would include 'adult,' 'male,' and 'horse.' Words like *stallion* and *bachelor* will be perceived to be related because when an

Is this the entry for bird in your mental dictionary? "bird . . . n. . . . [ME, fr. OE bridd] . . . **2:** *Any of a class (Aves) of warm-blooded vertebrates distinguished by having the body more or less completely covered with feathers and the forelimbs modified as wings. . . .*

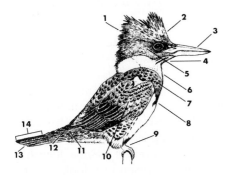

"bird 2 (kingfisher): 1 crest, 2 crown, 3 bill, 4 throat, 5 auricular region, 6 breast, 7 scapulars, 8 abdomen, 9 tarsus, 10 upper wing coverts, 11 primaries, 12 secondaries, 13 rectrix, 14 tail" (Merriam-Webster's Collegiate Dictionary, Tenth Edition)

Can a white rose be red? *The Queen had ordered the gardeners to plant a red rose bush, but they planted a white one by mistake. They're now trying to repair their error by painting the white roses red. On the definitional theory of meaning, this seems reasonable enough. For the expressions* red rose bush *and* white rose bush *differ by only a single feature—red* versus *white. But if so, why are they so terrified that the Queen will discover what they did? (From Lewis Carroll,* Alice in Wonderland, *1971, p. 62)*

individual looks up the features for each of these words in her mental dictionary (or **lexicon**), she will find that the meaning atom 'male' is listed for both of them. Taken together, the semantic features constitute a definition of a word. According to this theory, we carry such definitions in our heads as the meanings of words.

THE PROTOTYPE THEORY OF MEANING

The definitional theory faces a problem, for some members of a meaning category appear to exemplify that category better than others do. Thus a German shepherd seems to be a more doglike *dog* than a Pekinese, and an armchair seems to be a better example of the concept of *furniture* than a reading lamp. This seems to be at odds with the analysis we have described thus far, whose aim was to specify the necessary and sufficient attributes that *define* a concept. When a dictionary says that a bachelor is "an adult human male who has never been married," it claims to have said it all. Whatever fits under the umbrella of this definitional feature list is a bachelor. Whatever does not, is not. But if so, how can one bachelor be more bachelorlike (or one dog more doglike) than another?

The question is whether the semantic categories described by words are really as all-or-none as the definitional theory would have it. Several investigators have made a strong case for an alternative view, called the **theory of prototypes** (Rosch, 1973b; Rosch and Mervis, 1975; Smith and Medin, 1981).

The facts that the prototype theory tries to account for can easily be illustrated. Close your eyes and try to imagine a bird. It is pretty safe to guess that you just imagined something like a robin or a sparrow, not a buzzard, ostrich, or goose. There is something quintessentially *birdy* about a robin, while a goose does not seem such a good example of a bird. The definitional theory would have considerable trouble explaining why this is so. According to the definitional theory, some feature or features associated with the concept *bird* (such as 'has feathers,' 'lays eggs,' 'flies,' 'chirps') are both necessary and sufficient to pick out all birds and only birds. But if geese and robins are both said to be birds because they share these necessary and sufficient features, what makes the robin more birdy than the goose?

According to the prototype theory, the answer is that the meaning of many words is described as a whole set of features, no one of which is individually either necessary or sufficient. The concept is then held together by what some philosophers call a **family resemblance structure** (Wittgenstein, 1953). Consider the way in which members of a family resemble each other. Joe may look like his father to the extent that he has his eyes. His sister Sue may look like her father to the extent that she has his nose. But Joe and Sue may have no feature in common (he has his grandfather's nose and she has Aunt Fanny's eyes), and so the two of them do not look alike at all. But even so, the two are physically related through a family resemblance, for each has some resemblance to their father (see Figure 9.4).

In sum, a family resemblance structure is like a collection of attributes. Probably no single member of the family will have them all. Nor will any two members of a family have the same ones (except for identical twins). But all will have at least some. Some individuals will have many of the family features. They are often called the "real Johnsons" or "prototypical Smiths." They are the best exemplars of the family resemblance structure because they have, say, the most Johnson-attributes and the least Jones-attributes. Other family members are marginal. They have only the nose or the little freckle behind the left ear.

Many investigators believe that what holds for the Smiths and the Johnsons may hold for many word concepts, such as *bird,* as well. For in fact, there is little doubt that, except for professional biologists, most people don't really know the features that all birds have in common (and which could thus serve as a defini-

9.4 The Smith brothers and their family resemblance *The Smith brothers are related through family resemblance, though no two brothers share all features. The one who has the greatest number of the family attributes is the most prototypical. In the example, it is Brother 9, who has all the family features: brown hair, large ears, large nose, moustache, and eyeglasses. (Courtesy of Sharon Armstrong)*

Prototypes *Members of the bird category. (A) A prototypical bird—the robin. (B) An atypical bird—the ostrich. (C) An exceedingly atypical bird—the penguin. (Photographs by Kenneth W. Fink, Laura Riley, and Des and Jen Bartlett, all courtesy of Bruce Coleman)*

tion for *bird*). Thus, contrary to our first guess, not all birds fly (ostriches don't fly). And not everything that lays eggs is a bird (giant tortoises lay eggs). Not all birds chirp (crows do not chirp, they caw), and some chirpers (crickets) are not birds. What are we left with from our list of defining features? Nothing but a pile of feathers! But feathers alone do not make something a bird. Hats have feathers, too. And, after all, if one plucked all the feathers out of a robin, it would be a mutilated robin, but it would still be a bird for all that. (You think this unfair? What would *you* call it? A hippopotamus?)

According to prototype theorists, birdiness is largely a matter of the total number of bird features a given creature exhibits. No one of these features is necessary and none is sufficient, but animals that have few (such as penguins and ostriches) will be judged to be poor members of the bird family, while those that have many (such as robins) will seem to be exemplary members. According to the theory, these judgments are based on a comparison with an internal **prototype** of the concept. Such prototypes represent mental averages of all the various examples of the concept the person has encountered. In the case of birds, people in our culture have presumably seen far more robins than penguins. As a result, something that resembles a robin will be stored in their memory system and will then be associated with the word *bird*. When the person later sees a new object, he will judge it to be a bird to the extent that it resembles the prototype in some way. A sparrow resembles it in many ways and so is judged to be "a good bird"; a penguin resembles it just a little and hence is "a marginal bird"; a rowboat resembles it not at all and hence is judged to be no bird.

Evidence for the prototype view comes from the fact that when people are asked to come up with typical examples of some category, they generally produce instances that are close to the presumed prototype (e.g., *robin* rather than *ostrich*). A related result concerns the time required to verify category membership. Subjects respond more quickly to the sentence *A robin is a bird* than to *An ostrich is a bird* (Rosch, et al., 1976; Rosch, 1978; for a related discussion, see Chapter 8).

COMBINING DEFINITIONAL AND PROTOTYPE DESCRIPTIONS

It appears that both the definitional and the prototype approaches to word meaning have something to offer. The prototype view helps us to understand why robins are better birds than ostriches. But the definitional theory explains why an ostrich is nevertheless recognized as a bird. Perhaps we can combine both views of meaning rather than choosing between them.

A

B

C

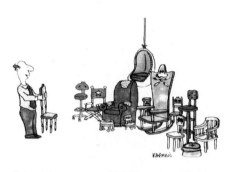

"Attention, everyone! I'd like to introduce the newest member of our family." (Drawing by Kaufman; © 1977, The New Yorker Magazine, Inc.)

Consider the word *grandmother.* This word designates people who are 'mothers of a parent.' Thus *grandmother* clearly has a set of necessary and sufficient features that neatly define it. The definitional theory seems just right for words like this. But now reconsider. Everyone knows that a grandmother is a person who bakes cookies, is old and gray, and has a kindly twinkle in her eye. When we say that someone is *grandmotherly,* we are referring to such prototypical attributes of grandmothers, not to genealogy. But some grandmothers lack these typical properties. Zsa Zsa Gabor is a mother of a parent, but she is hardly gray or twinkly. And we all know some kindly lady who is gray and twinkly but never had a child; she may be grandmotherly, but she is not a grandmother (Lakoff and Johnson, 1980; Landau, 1982).

The most plausible assumption is that people have two partly independent mental representations for the meaning of a word. They know about prototypical attributes that are good symptoms of being a grandmother, such as being old and gray. They probably store a list (or perhaps a picture) of such attributes (or prototypical features) as a handy way of picking out likely grandmother candidates. But they also store defining grandmother features (e.g., 'mother of a parent'). These definitional features determine grandmother limits and tell one how to use the prototype appropriately (Miller and Johnson-Laird, 1976; Smith and Medin, 1981; Armstrong, Gleitman, and Gleitman, 1983).

ORGANIZING WORDS INTO MEANINGFUL SENTENCES

■ While individual words describe things, events, and so forth, the word groups that constitute phrases describe the endless varieties of complex categories for which the 80,000 words would be insufficient. Thus, once in a lifetime, we might want to speak of *three of the spotted ostriches on Joe Smith's farm.* We could not possibly memorize enough word items for all such complex categories that we could construct and might want to talk about, so we combine the words together in patterned ways to express our more complex concepts.

Sentence meanings are even more complex. They have to do with the various relations *among* the concepts that we want to express. Basic sentences introduce some concept that they are about (this is called the **subject** of the sentence) and then *propose* or *predicate* something of that concept (called the **predicate** of the sentence). Thus when we say *The boy hit the ball,* we introduce *the boy* as the subject or topic, and then we propose or predicate of the boy that he *hit the ball.* This is why sentence meanings are often called **propositions:** *The boy hit the ball* proposes (of the boy) that he hit the ball.

A grammar lesson at the Mad Hatter's Tea Party *The meanings of words change in different linguistic constructions, so grammatical patterns are of great importance for communication.*

March Hare: *"You should say what you mean."*

Alice: *"I do—at least I mean what I say— that's the same thing, you know."*

Hatter: *"Not the same thing a bit! Why, you might just as well say that 'I see what I eat' is the same thing as 'I eat what I see'!"*

March Hare: *"You might just as well say that 'I like what I get' is the same thing as 'I get what I like.'"*

Lewis Carroll's poignant tale of how an animal's mind would be different if it had language Alice came to a forest where nothing had a name. She met a fawn that walked trustingly by her side: "So they walked together through the wood, Alice with her arms clasped lovingly around the soft neck of the Fawn, till they came out into another open field [where things had names]. And here the Fawn gave a sudden bound into the air, and shook itself free of Alice's arm. 'I'm a Fawn!' it cried out in a voice of delight. 'And dear me! You're a human child!' A sudden look of alarm came into his beautiful brown eyes, and in another moment it had darted away at full speed." *(Carroll,* Through the Looking Glass, *p. 227)*

More generally, a simple proposition is usefully thought about as a sort of miniature drama in which the verb is the action and the nouns are the performers, each playing a different role. In our proposition about *boy-hitting-ball, the boy* is the "doer," *the ball* is the "done-to," and *hit* is the action itself. The job of a listener is much like that of a playgoer. The playgoer must determine which actors are portraying the various roles in the drama and what the plot (the action) is. Similarly, for each of the millions of heard sentences, the listener must discover exactly who did what to whom (Healy and Miller, 1970).

LANGUAGE DEVELOPMENT

FOCUS QUESTIONS

- What is the reinforcement (or correction) theory of language learning, and why is it false?

- How do infants learn which phonemes are part of their own language?

- Why do function words appear so late in language development?

- What is telegraphic speech?

- Why do four- and five-year-old children sometimes make errors (like using "runned" for "ran") when they did not make such errors earlier?

Now that we have surveyed the boundless forms and contents of language, it seems impossible that any save the most brilliant person could possibly learn it. Yet we know that language is as natural and inevitable a part of human nature as chirping is to birds, roaring is to lions, and barking is to dogs. Whatever their talent, their motivation, or their station in life, normal children learn their native tongue to a high level of proficiency during the preschool years. This holds for children reared in poverty on the streets of New York and in the deserts of North Africa as much as it does for upper-class British children reared by nannies and sent to posh nursery schools.

IS LANGUAGE LEARNING THE ACQUISITION OF A SKILL?

■ Language learning is more than mere imitation. It is true that young children say "dog" and not "perro" or "chien" if they are exposed to English, so in this sense they are imitating the language community around them. But the real trick in word learning and use is creative: The word *dog* must apply to new dogs that the learners see. What served as a label for the pet bulldog must apply to the neighborhood poodle as well.

What goes for words goes for sentences too. Young children utter sentences they have never heard before. For instance, a mother may say to her child "I love you, Jane." But in response Jane may say "I hate you, Mommy" or "I'm going to crayon a face on this wall." These sentences are clear, though unwelcome, creative language acts of Jane's. They could not possibly have been learned by imitation.

Another popular hypothesis about language learning is that it is based on explicit **correction** or **reinforcement** by parents. According to this view, grammatical mistakes are immediately pointed out to the young learner, who subsequently avoids them. But in fact, this hypothesis is false (Morgan and Travis, 1989). In actual practice, mistakes in grammar and pronunciation generally go unremarked, as in the following exchange:

Two-year-old: Mamma isn't boy, he a girl.
Mother: That's right.

The situation is quite different if the child makes an error of fact. In that case, the mother often does provide a correction:

Two-year-old: And Walt Disney comes on Tuesday.
Mother: No, he does not.

(Brown and Hanlon, 1970)

These findings are perfectly reasonable. Parents are out to create socialized and rational beings, not little grammarians, and so they correct errors of conduct and fact, not errors of grammar.

THE SOCIAL ORIGINS OF SPEECH PRODUCTION

■ As we have just seen, imitation, correction, and reinforcement can't bear too much of the burden in explaining language learning. Children don't come to the task of acquiring their native tongue as little robots who can only notice and copy whatever they hear, whenever they hear it. How then are we to explain the growth of speech and comprehension? We will begin by tracing the child's progress during the first few years of life.

Infants begin to vocalize from the first moments of life. They cry, coo, and babble. They make sounds such as "ga" and "bagoo" that sound very much like words—except that these babbles have no conventional meaning. This is shown

Social origins of speech   (Photograph by Erika Stone)

Learning language requires a receptive human mind. *Ginger gets plenty of linguistic stimulation but is prepared by nature only to be man's best friend. (The FAR SIDE cartoon by Gary Larson is reprinted by permission of Chronicle Features, San Francisco, California.)*

by the fact that deaf infants, who cannot hear others' vocalizations, babble in the same way (Lenneberg, 1967). Moreover, deaf children in a home where sign language is used also babble manually; they produce gestures that look just like real signs, but as yet have no meaning (Petitto and Marentette, 1991). In the hearing infant, vocalization soon takes on a social quality, for three-month-olds will vocalize more when an adult vocalizes to them (Collis, 1975; L. Bloom, 1988).

Though true speech is absent in the first year of life, prelinguistic children have their own ways of making contact with the minds, emotions, and social behaviors of others. Quite early in life, babies begin to exchange looks, caresses, and sounds with caregivers. Several investigators have suggested that these are precursors and organizers of the language development to follow. The idea is that the gesture-and-babble interaction helps children to become linguistically socialized, to realize, for instance, that each participant in a conversation "takes a turn," and responds to the other (Bruner, 1974/1975; Tomasello and Ferrar, 1986; Baldwin, 1991).

Thus language knowledge is essentially social and interpersonal from the beginning (Fernald, 1992). Though the capacity to learn it is built into the brain of the individual child, usable knowledge of speaking and listening requires social interactions between more than one person at a time. To speak to another, one has to have an idea—no matter how primitive—that the other lives in the same, mutually perceived, world (Bates, 1976; Bates and MacWhinney, 1982).

DISCOVERING THE FORMS OF LANGUAGE

Infants' first attempts to speak are rather unimpressive. But careful analysis shows that they know more about language than they seem to at first glance. For at a very early age, they make some perceptual distinctions about the sounds they hear that are crucial to later language learning. Indeed, one remarkable study shows that infants are more attentive to hearing their caretaker's language than a foreign language by the fourth day of life (Mehler et al., 1988).

We have previously seen that all languages are built out of a few basic sound distinctions: the phonemes. But these linguistic sound atoms vary somewhat from language to language. Thus in English, there is a crucial difference between "l" and "r" (as in *lob* vs. *rob*). Though physically these sounds are quite similar, each of them falls within a different phoneme in English, whose speakers have no trouble producing and perceiving the distinction. In contrast, this distinction has no linguistic significance in Japanese, where "l" and "r" sounds fall within the same phoneme. In consequence, Japanese speakers can neither produce nor perceive a distinction between them. How does the infant learn which sound distinctions are the phonemes of his language?

The answer is that initially infants respond to just about all sound distinctions made in any language. They discover the phonemes of their native tongue by *learning to ignore* the distinctions that don't matter. Their first step in understanding, say, Japanese, is to learn not to become speakers of all the other 4,000 languages on earth (Jusczyk, 1985; Werker, 1991).

Evidence comes from studies which show that two-month-old babies can distinguish between such sounds as "ba" and "pa," "la" and "ra," and so forth. The experimenters used a version of the habituation method (see Chapter 13). The babies were given a pacifier, and whenever they sucked on it the syllable "ba" was broadcast over a loudspeaker. The infants quickly learned that their sucking led to the sound, and they began sucking faster and faster to hear it some more. After awhile, the babies habituated to the "ba" sound and their

A

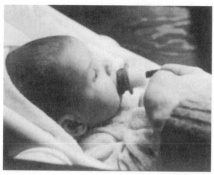

B

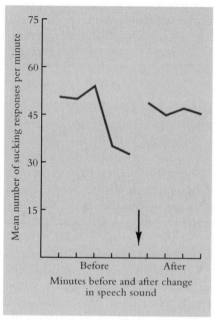

9.5 Sucking rate and speech perception in the infant *(A) An infant sucks to hear "ba" or "ga." (Photograph courtesy of Philip Morse, Boston University) (B) The graph shows the sucking rate of four-month-olds to "ba" or "ga." The infants soon become habituated, and the sucking rate drops. When a new stimulus is substituted ("ga" for "ba" and "ba" for "ga"), the infant dishabituates and sucks quickly once again. Similar results have been obtained for one-month-olds. The point of the shift is indicated by the arrow. (From Eimas et al., 1971)*

sucking rate diminished. At this point, the experimenters changed the broadcast sound from "ba" to "pa." The babies now started to suck again at a rapid rate. They had become dishabituated. This result indicates that they could discriminate between the two sounds (see Figure 9.5; Eimas et al., 1971).

Infants in the first year of life are sensitive to just about every contrast that occurs in *any* human language, but their sensitivity to foreign contrasts diminishes significantly by twelve months of age (Werker and Tees, 1984), and alteration in phonetic sensitivities is already observable at age six months (Kuhl et al., 1992). This is consistent with the idea that infants must be prepared by nature to learn any language on earth. After all, they arrive without a passport that tells them which language they are going to hear. But the diminished sensitivities of twelve-month-olds suggest that babies recalibrate their perceptions just as true speech and understanding begin, thus concentrating selectively on the distinctions that matter in their own linguistic community (Kemler-Nelson et al., 1989).

THE ONE-WORD SPEAKER

■ Children begin to understand a few words that their caregivers are saying as early as five to eight months of age. For example, some six-month-olds will regularly glance up at the ceiling light in response to hearing their mother say "light." Actual talking begins sometime between about ten and twenty months of age. Almost invariably, children's first utterances are one word long. Some first words refer to simple interactions with adults, such as *hi* and *peekaboo*. Others are names, such as *Mama* and *Fido*. Most of the rest are simple nouns, such as *duck* and *spoon*, adjectives such as *hot* and *big*, and action verbs such as *give* and *push*. And lest one think that child rearing is all pleasure, one of the first words is almost always a resounding *No*. The early vocabulary tends to concern things that can be moved around and manipulated or that move by themselves in the child's environment. For example, children are less likely to talk about ceilings than about rolling balls. And this early vocabulary refers more often to attributes and actions children can perceive in the outside world, such as shape or movement, than to internal states and feelings, such as pain or ideas (Nelson, 1973; Huttenlocher, Smiley, and Charney, 1983; Landau, 1994).

Missing altogether are the function words and suffixes, such as *the, and,* and *-ed*. These are among the most frequent items the child hears, but they are never uttered by beginners even so. There are several reasons for the lateness of these function items. One has to do with how hard they are to perceive. Infants are especially interested in such properties of the sound wave as high pitch. But the function words are usually not stressed and occur with low pitch in the caregiver's speech (Kelly and Martin, 1994; Cutler, 1994). A second reason is that the function morphemes are grammatical items. Since young children say only one word at a time, they presumably have little need to utter morphemes whose central role is to organize groups of words into sentence form (Gerken, Landau, and Remez, 1990).

WORD MEANING AT THE ONE-WORD STAGE

It is hard to find out precisely what young children mean by the words they say. To be sure, we hear the tots say "rabbit" and "ball" but what exactly do these words mean to their young users? One reason for our relative ignorance about these earliest word meanings is that the same scene or event can often be described in many ways, depending on the particular words chosen. The very

9.6 Symmetrical problems for child learners and investigators of child language *(A) The child's helpful mother points out a rabbit, saying "rabbit." The child sees a rabbit—but also sees an animal, an ear, and the ground beneath the rabbit. Which one does the mother mean by the word rabbit? (B) The mother's (and the investigator's) problem in understanding young children's speech is much the same. The child may say "rabbit" when she observes a rabbit, but for all the mother knows the child may have made an error in learning, and thus may mean something different by this word.*

same creature can be described as *Peter, the rabbit, the animal, the creature with a tail,* and so forth. Therefore, even if a young child says "rabbit" on seeing a rabbit, he may mean 'tail' or 'animal' or 'white' or even 'runs by' for all we know.

The same problem that makes it hard for investigators to find out exactly what children mean ought to make it hard for children themselves to discover these meanings. Even if the helpful mother points out a rabbit to her child, saying "rabbit," the child still has a big job to do. He has to make up his mind whether the word *rabbit* means a particular animal (in which case *rabbit* is a name, such as 'Peter Rabbit'), anything that falls within the animal kingdom (in which case *rabbit* means 'animal'), anything within a particular species (so *rabbit* means 'rabbit'), or even some property, part, or action of a rabbit (in which case *rabbit* means 'white' or 'tail' or 'hops'; see Figure 9.6).

Because such problems for the learner are real, beginners often **undergeneralize** the meaning of a word: They may know that the word *house* refers to small toy buildings but not that it also refers to large real buildings. And they may **overgeneralize** the meanings of other words. They may think that the word *Daddy* refers to any man, not just their own father. These overgeneralizations and undergeneralizations are common for the first seventy-five or so words the child utters, but very rare thereafter (Rescorla, 1980). At later stages of learning, the child is almost always exactly on the mark in using words to refer to the right things in the world. We shall return later to how the child manages to be right overwhelmingly often despite the real problem of rabbits, rabbit parts, and the like. But for now it is important to realize that even the young overgeneralizer is surprisingly correct in what he has learned. Though he just about always observes the ground whenever he observes a rabbit (and hears the word *rabbit*)—because rabbits can't fly and thus are always found near the ground—still, he virtually never mistakenly learns that *rabbit* means 'ground' (or that *ground* means 'rabbit'). He just makes the category a bit too broad or narrow at first. (For overviews of word-meaning acquisition, see Clark, 1993; L. Gleitman and Landau, 1994).

Child on mother's lap

Hidden speaker

Computer

Hidden tape deck

Hidden Observer

Hidden tape deck

9.7 Set-up for the selective looking experiment *The child sits on the mother's lap and listens to a taped sentence while two video screens show two cartoon characters performing different actions. A hidden observer notes which screen the child is looking at. The mother wears a visor that covers her eyes, to make sure she does not see which screen shows which action and thereby give inadvertent clues to the child. (Courtesy of Roberta Golinkoff)*

PROPOSITIONAL MEANING AT THE ONE-WORD STAGE

There is another question about children's first words: Are these little foreshortened sentence attempts? That is, do children have a proposition in mind when they say "Doggie!" as a dog runs by? Many investigators of child language believe young children have propositional ideas in mind even when they are speaking only one word at a time (Shipley, Smith, and L. Gleitman, 1969; Bretherton, 1988). The strongest evidence comes from recent experiments in which children as young as sixteen months of age (who themselves speak only one word at a time) look at brief movies that depict different happenings. The subjects sit on their mothers' laps and can see two video screens, one to their left and one to their right (see Figure 9.7). Each screen shows cartoon characters the babies know engaged in various actions (Figure 9.8). On the screen to the left, Big Bird is tickling Cookie Monster, and on the screen to the right, Cookie Monster is tickling Big Bird. Half the children hear a voice saying "Oh look! Big Bird is tickling Cookie Monster." The other children hear the reverse sentence ("Oh look! Cookie Monster is tickling Big Bird"). Hidden observers now record which screen the children turn their attention to. The finding is that the toddlers look primarily at the screen that matches the sentence they have heard. To understand what matches and what does not match, their only clue is the syntax of the sentence they have heard. Thus the experiment proves that even babies who can speak only in single words understand the logic of simple sentences in terms of the drama of who-did-what-to-whom (Hirsh-Pasek et al., 1985; Naigles, 1990; L. Gleitman, 1990).

THE TWO-WORD (TELEGRAPHIC) SPEAKER

Many drastic changes take place beginning at about the second birthday (Brown, 1973; Braine, 1976). The child's vocabulary begins to spurt, rising to many hundreds of words. Soon she begins to put words together into

9.8 Stimuli for the selective looking experiment *One screen shows Big Bird tickling Cookie Monster, the other shows Cookie Monster tickling Big Bird.*

A

B

C

9.9 The ambiguities of two-word speech
The two-word utterances of young children, while systematic and meaningful, are quite ambiguous. The three panels from the children's story Higgledy Piggledy Pop, *by Maurice Sendak, show why one young child might want to learn more about adult syntax. (A) An adventurous dog takes a job as nurse to Baby. He must get Baby to eat, or he will be fed to the lion down in the basement. Here Baby refuses the food, saying "No eat!" (I will not eat). (B) Here, the dog eats up the food Baby has refused. Baby finds this objectionable and so cries out "No eat!" (Don't eat my porridge!). (C) Baby has angrily pushed the button so the dog-nurse will fall down to the waiting lion, but Baby has accidentally fallen also. To avoid being eaten by the lion, Baby cries out "No eat!" (Don't eat me up!). (From Maurice Sendak, 1979)*

primitive sentences, and then we are aware most poignantly that another human mind is among us.

Though we can clearly recognize propositional ideas in these first "sentences," these hardly sound like adult speech. Generally, each rudimentary sentence is only two words long, and each of its components is a content word. The function morphemes are still largely missing, and so these sentences sound like the short ones we often use in telegrams and newspaper headlines: "Throw ball!" "Daddy shoe," "No eat!" (Brown and Bellugi, 1964).

These sentences show some organization, however, despite their simplicity. From the earliest moments of "telegraphic speech," the words seem to be serially ordered according to the propositional rules. The child who says "Throw ball" usually does not say "Ball throw" to mean the same thing (Braine, 1963; L. Bloom, 1970; deVilliers and deVilliers, 1973). Thus young English speakers will put the doer of the action first and will say "Mommy throw!" if they want the mother to throw the ball; and they will put the done-to last and say "Throw ball!" in approximately the same circumstances. So mothers of two-year-old learners of English would probably be right in feeling a bit miffed if their child said "Throw Mommy!"

Two-year-olds' correct use of word order to express different sentence meanings is consistent with the comprehension that they showed even earlier (in understanding who did what to whom in the Cookie Monster and Big Bird videos). In fact, these short sentences are ordinarily so clear in meaning that one may wonder why children bother to learn anything more. But see Figure 9.9 for a demonstration of how ambiguous two-word speech sometimes is.

LATER STAGES OF LANGUAGE LEARNING: SYNTAX

■ By two-and-a-half years or so, children progress beyond the two-word stage. Their utterances now become longer (Figure 9.10). They can say little sentences that contain all three terms of a basic proposition, and function

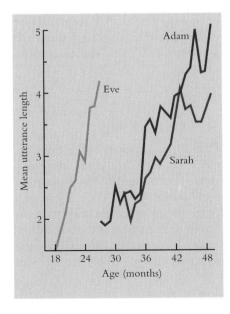

9.10 The average length of the utterances produced by three children *The mean utterance length in three children between one-and-a-half and four years of age. The utterance length is measured in morphemes, where* dolls *counts as two morphemes* (doll + s). *Note the variations among the children, who were all within a normal range. (After Brown, Cazden, and Bellugi-Klima, 1969)*

(Photograph by Roberta Intrater, 1980)

words have begun to appear. Their utterances are still short and simple, but—at least initially—they are quite correct as far as they go. Soon, however, a new phenomenon appears. Children start to make various kinds of errors in their word formation and in their syntax. An example concerns the *-ed* suffix, which represents pastness. At age two and three, children use correct regular forms of the past tense (as in *walked* or *talked*), as well as correct irregular ones (such as *ran, came,* and *ate*). But at age four and five, these same children sometimes say "runned," "comed," and "eated" (Ervin, 1964; Prasada and Pinker, 1993). And they resist change even even when they hear their parents use the correct form, as in the following exchange:

Child:	My teacher holded the baby rabbits and we patted them.
Mother:	Did you say your teacher held the baby rabbits?
Child:	Yes.
Mother:	What did you say she did?
Child:	She holded the baby rabbits and we patted them.
Mother:	Did you say she held them tightly?
Child:	No, she holded them loosely.

(Bellugi, 1971)

What has happened to this child who in earlier years said "held" but now doggedly keeps saying "holded"? The answer seems to be that the child is now seeking general patterns that hold over the whole vocabulary or set of sentence structures. If some words choose to be exceptions to these patterns, so much the worse for these words. Thus the child now overgeneralizes the use of certain structures, though she no longer overgeneralizes the meanings of words. (For an alternative view, see Rumelhart and McClelland, 1986; for discussion, see Pinker and Prince, 1988).

FURTHER STAGES OF LANGUAGE LEARNING: WORD MEANING

■ We have already discussed some of the difficulties children *should* confront when they try to discover which word stands for which meaning. But in reality, they experience very little difficulty. Five-year-olds have a vocabulary of 10,000 to 15,000 words, whereas at fifteen months they had a vocabulary of only about twenty-five words. This means they must be acquiring about ten words a day—every day, every week, every month. It is likely that none of us adults could do as well (Carey, 1978).

CAREGIVER AIDS TO WORD LEARNING

Part of the explanation for this remarkably rapid learning may come from the quite regular ways in which mothers talk to their children, for syntax often contains useful hints about what a word could mean. Let's return to the problem of learning which word means 'ear' and which means 'rabbit' (see Figure 9.6 above). It turns out that when mothers refer to the whole rabbit, they use simple sentences ("This is a rabbit") and often point to the rabbit at the same time. But when they want to refer to the ear, they first refer to the whole rabbit, and then use such words as *his* in referring to the part: "This is a rabbit; these are his ears" (Shipley, Kuhn, and Madden, 1983).

PERCEPTUAL AND CONCEPTUAL BIASES IN CHILD LEARNERS

We see that caregivers' speech style helps language learners to decide which words are about the whole objects and which words are about their parts. It turns out that children have some biases, or "best guesses," of their own that also contribute to their solution of the word learning problem.

Much of the child's word learning is explained by how she is disposed to carve up (*categorize*) the world that she observes. Some ways of conceptualizing experience are natural to humans while others are less natural (Rosch, 1973a; Keil, 1979; Fodor, 1983). Thus the child can learn more easily if she assumes that each word represents some "natural" organization of experience.

One indication of this is the fact that young children acquire the "basic-level" words (e.g., *dog*) before the superordinates *(animal)* or subordinates *(Chihuahua)* (Rosch, 1978). One might think this is just because the basic-level words are used most frequently to children. But this does not seem to be the explanation. In some homes, the words *Spot* or *Rex* (specific names) are used much more often than *dog* (a basic-level term) for obvious reasons. And it is true that in this case the young learner will soon utter "Spot" and not "dog." But she has first learned it as a basic-level term all the same. This is shown by the fact that she will then utter "Spot" to refer to the neighbor's dog as well as her own. She overgeneralizes *Spot* just enough to convert it from a specific name to the basic level of categorization—evidently, the most natural level for carving up experience (Mervis and Crisafi, 1978; Shipley and Kuhn, 1983).

WORD CLASSES AND WORD MEANINGS

Children are disposed to organize the world into overarching categories—things, events, properties, and so forth. But what is more, they appear to believe that language will classify words according to related categories—nouns, verbs, and adjectives—in a way that is consistent with the conceptual categories (Braine, 1976; Pinker, 1984).

This phenomenon was demonstrated in an experiment with three- and four-year-olds in which the experimenter showed children a picture in which a pair of hands seemed to be performing a kneading sort of motion with a mass of red confetti-like material that was overflowing a low, striped, container (Figure 9.11). The children were introduced to the picture in sentences that used nonsense words, but either as verbs ("In this picture can you see *sebbing*?"), common nouns *("Can you see a seb?"),* or mass nouns *("Can you see any seb?").*★ The children who had been asked to show *sebbing* made kneading motions with their hands, those asked to show a *seb* pointed to the container, and those asked about *any seb* pointed to the confetti (Brown, 1957; see also Katz, Baker, and MacNamara, 1974; Carey, 1982).

9.11 Word classes and word meanings
When asked "In this picture can you see any sebbing?" (verb), children pointed to the hands; when asked "Can you see a seb?*" (common noun), they pointed to the bowl; and when asked "Can you see any* seb?*" (mass noun), they pointed to the confetti. (Adapted from Brown, 1957)*

★ A **common** or **count noun** is one that (1) requires a specifier such as *the* or *two* (compare *The dog walks down the street* with the ungrammatical *Dog walks down the street*), and (2) generally refers to the kinds of entities that can be counted (e.g., *One dog, two dogs*). A **mass noun** (1) occurs without a specifier (compare *Water flows through the pipes* with the ungrammatical *A water flows through the pipes*), and (2) generally refers to stuff that can't be counted, e.g., *water, confetti,* or *sand.*

LANGUAGE LEARNING IN CHANGED ENVIRONMENTS

FOCUS QUESTIONS

■ Given what we know about isolated and deaf children, do we need to hear in order to learn language?

■ How important is sight for learning language?

Thus far, our focus has been on language development as it proceeds normally. Under these conditions, language seems to emerge in much the same way in virtually all children. They progress from babbling to one-word speech, advance to the two-word telegraphic stage, and eventually graduate to complex sentence forms and meanings. The fact that this progression is so uniform and universal has led many psycholinguists to the view that children are biologically pre-programmed to acquire language.

Further evidence for this view stems from studies of language development under certain unusual conditions, when children grow up in environments that are radically different from those in which language development usually proceeds. Which aspects of the early environment are essential for language learning? One line of evidence comes from reports of children who grew up in the wild or under conditions of virtual social isolation.

WILD CHILDREN

There are some remarkable examples of children who wandered (or were abandoned) in the forest and who survived, having been reared by bears or wolves. Some of these cases have been discussed by the psycholinguist Roger Brown (1958). In 1920, Indian villagers discovered a wolf mother in her den together with four cubs. Two were baby wolves, but the other two were human children, subsequently named Kamala and Amala. No one knows how they got there and why the wolf adopted them. Brown tells us what these children were like:

> Kamala was about eight years old and Amala was only one and one-half. They were thoroughly wolfish in appearance and behavior: Hard callus had developed on their knees and palms from going on all fours. Their teeth were sharp edged. They moved their nostrils sniffing food. Eating and drinking were accomplished by lowering their mouths to the plate. They ate raw meat. . . . At night they prowled and sometimes howled. They shunned other children but followed the dog and cat. They slept rolled up together on the floor. . . . Amala died within a year but Kamala lived to be eighteen. . . . In time, Kamala learned to walk erect, to wear clothing, and even to speak a few words. (Brown, 1958, p. 100)

The outcome was much the same for the thirty or so other wild children about whom we have reports. When they were found, they were all shockingly animal-like. None of them could be rehabilitated so as to use language at all normally, though some, including Kamala, learned to speak a few words (Figure 9.12).

9.12 A modern wild boy *Ramu, a young boy discovered in India in 1976, appears to have been reared by wolves. He was deformed, apparently from lying in cramped positions, as in a den. He could not walk, and drank by lapping with his tongue. His favorite food was raw meat, which he seemed to be able to smell at a distance. After he was found, he lived at the home for destitute children run by Mother Theresa in Lucknow, Uttar Pradesh. He learned to bathe and dress himself, but never learned to speak. He continued to prefer raw meat and would often sneak out to prey upon fowl in the neighbor's chicken coop. Ramu died at the age of about ten in February 1985. (*New York Times, Feb. 24, 1985; photographs courtesy Wide World Photos)*

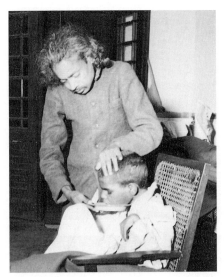

ISOLATED CHILDREN

Kamala and Amala were removed from all human society. Some other children have been raised by humans, but under conditions that were almost unimaginably inhumane, for their parents were either vicious or deranged. Sometimes, such parents will deprive a baby of all human contact. "Isabelle" (a codename used to protect the child's privacy) was hidden away, apparently from early infancy, and given only the minimal attention necessary to sustain her life. Apparently no one spoke to her (in fact, her mother was deaf and did not speak). Isabelle was six years old when discovered. Of course she had no language, and her cognitive development was below that of a normal two-year-old. But within a year, this girl learned to speak. Her tested intelligence was normal, and she took her place in an ordinary school (Davis, 1947; Brown, 1958). Thus Isabelle at seven years, with one year of language practice, spoke about as well as her peers in the second grade, all of whom had had seven years of practice.

Rehabilitation from isolation is not always so successful. A child, "Genie," discovered in California, was fourteen years old when found. Since about twenty months, apparently, she had lived tied to a chair, was frequently beaten, and never spoken to—but sometimes barked at, for her father said she was no more than a dog. Afterwards, she was taught by psychologists and linguists (Fromkin et al., 1974). But Genie did not become a normal language user. She says many words and puts them together into meaningful propositions as young children do, such as "No more take wax" and "Another house have dog." Thus she has learned certain basics of language. Indeed, her semantic sophistication—what she means by what she says—is far beyond young children. Yet even after years of instruction, Genie did not learn the function words that appear in mature English sentences, nor did she combine propositions together in elaborate sentences (Curtiss, 1977).

Why did Genie not progress to full language learning while Isabelle did? The best guess is that the crucial factor is the age at which language learning began. Genie was discovered after she had reached puberty, while Isabelle was only six. As we shall see later (pp. 285–87), there is some reason to believe there is a *critical period* for language learning. If the person has passed this period, language learning proceeds with greater difficulty.

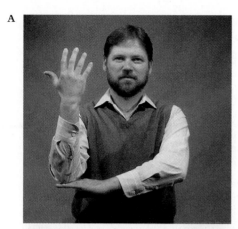

A

B

C

9.13   Some common signs in ASL   *(A) The sign for* tree. *One difference between ASL and spoken language is that many of the signed words physically resemble their meanings. This is so for* tree, *in which the upright forearm stands for the trunk and the outstretched fingers for the branches. But in many cases, such a resemblance is not present. Consider (B), which is the modern sign for* help, *whose relation to its meaning seems as arbitrary as that between most spoken words and their meanings. Even so, such a relation was once present, as shown in (C), a nineteenth-century sign for* help. *At that time, the sign was not arbitrary; it consisted of a gesture by the right hand to support the left elbow, as if helping an elderly person cross a street. (B) grew out of (C) by a progressive series of simplifications in which signs tend to move to the body's midline and use shorter, fewer, and more stylized movements. All that remains of (C) is an upward motion of the right palm. (Frishberg, 1975; photographs of and by Ted Supalla)*

LANGUAGE WITHOUT SOUND

The work on wild and isolated children argues that a necessary condition for learning language is some contact with other humans. If one's early life is spent entirely among animals, the effects are irreversible. If it is spent among people who do not talk to one, language may still be acquired later on if the crucial learning period has not been passed as yet. Our next question concerns the more specific factors of the learner's human environment. What aspects of this environment are essential for language to emerge?

It has sometimes been suggested that an important ingredient is exposure to language sounds. According to this view, language is intrinsically related to the way we organize what we hear. If so, language cannot develop in the absence of sound.

This hypothesis is false. For there is one group of humans that is cut off from auditory-vocal language—the deaf, who cannot hear it—yet this doesn't mean that they have no language. Most deaf people eventually learn to read and write the language of the surrounding community of hearing persons. But they also have a manual-visual, or *gestural, system.* One such system is *American Sign Language* (or *ASL*).

Are gestural systems genuine languages? One indication that they are is that these systems are not derived by translation from the spoken languages around them but are independently created within and by communities of deaf individuals (Klima et al., 1979). Further evidence comes from comparing ASL to the structure and development of spoken languages. ASL has hand shapes and positions of which each word is composed, much like the tongue and lip shapes that allow us to fashion the phonemes of spoken language (Stokoe, 1960). It has morphemes and grammatical principles for combining words into sentences that are similar to those of spoken language (Supalla, 1986; see Figure 9.13).

Finally, babies born to deaf users of ASL (whether or not the babies themselves are deaf) pick up the system from these caregivers through informal interaction rather than by explicit instruction, just as we learn our spoken language (Newport and Ashbrook, 1977).★ And they go through the same steps on the way to adult knowledge as do hearing children learning English. It is hard to avoid the conclusion that ASL and other gestural systems are true languages (Klima et al., 1979; Supalla and Newport, 1978; Newport, 1984, 1990).

Thus language does not depend on the auditory-vocal channel. When the usual modes of communication are denied to humans of normal mentality, they

★ In fact, the expert sign-language translators seen on television are usually hearing children of deaf parents. They grow up in a bilingual environment, with ASL learned from their parents and English learned by contact with hearing children and adults, so they achieve perfect knowledge of both and thus are the best translators.

come up with an alternative that reproduces the same contents and structures as other language systems. It appears that language is an irrepressible human trait: Deny it to the mouth and it will dart out through the fingers.

LANGUAGE WITHOUT A MODEL

The evidence we have reviewed shows that language emerges despite many environmental deprivations. Still, each case seemed to have one requirement—some adults who knew a language and could impart it to the young. But this must leave us puzzled about how language originated in the first place. Is it a cultural artifact (like the internal combustion engine or the game of chess) rather than a basic property of human minds, an invention that happened to take place in prehistoric times? Our bias has been the opposite, for we have argued that humans are biologically predisposed to communicate by language. But our case would have been much better if Kamala and Amala had invented a language of their own, down there in the wolf's den. Why didn't they? There are many ways to write off or ignore this case—maybe they were too busy learning to be good wolves, and maybe a human language is of no special use for learning to devour raw chickens. Is there a better test than those provided by the tragic cases of brutal mistreatment and neglect so far considered?

It certainly would be interesting if we could find a case of mentally normal children living in a socially loving environment but not exposed to language use by the adults around them. Feldman, Goldin-Meadow, and L. Gleitman (1978) found six children who were in such a situation. These children were deaf, and so they were unable to learn spoken language. Their parents were hearing; they did not know ASL and decided not to allow the children to learn a gestural language. This is because they shared the belief (held by some groups of educators) that deaf children can achieve adequate knowledge of spoken language by special training in lip reading and vocalization.* The investigators looked at these children before they had acquired any knowledge of English, for a number of prior studies had shown that under these circumstances deaf children will spontaneously gesture in meaningful ways to others (Tervoort, 1961; Fant, 1972). The question was which aspects of communication these youngsters would come up with as they developed.

The results showed that the children invented a sizeable number of pantomimic gestures that the investigators could comprehend. For example, they would flutter their fingers in a downward motion to express *snow,* twist their fingers to express a twist-top *bottle,* and flap their arms to represent *bird* (see Figure 9.14).

The development of this "language" showed many parallels to ordinary language learning: The children gestured one sign at a time in the period (about eighteen months of age) when hearing learners speak one word at a time. At two and three years of age they went on to two- and three-word sentences and so on. And in these basic sentences, the individual gestures were serially ordered by semantic role. This is strong evidence for a rudimentary syntactic organization, just like that of children who hear German or French—or see ASL—produced by adults.

On the other hand, we should not lose sight of the severe limitations of these homemade systems. First, they are limited to the basics of language as we know

A

B

9.14 Self-made signs in a deaf boy never exposed to sign language *A two-sign sequence. (A) The first sign means "eat" or "food." Immediately before, the boy had pointed to a grape. (B) The second sign means "give." The total sequence means "give me the food." (Goldin-Meadow, 1982; drawing courtesy of Noel Yovovich)*

* The degree of success with lip-reading and vocalization of English, as well as reading acquisition, by deaf children is variable, with the level attained closely related to the degree of deafness. Even the slightest hearing capability helps enormously. But there is growing evidence that the most natural alternative for profoundly deaf children is to learn and use ASL, for in this manual-visual medium they have no language handicap at all.

A

B

9.15 The meaning of "look" (A) A blindfolded, sighted three-year-old tilts her head upward in response to "Look up!" for to her the word look means 'perceive by eye.' (B) A congenitally blind three-year-old raises her arms upward in response to "Look up!" for to her the word look means 'perceive by hand.' (Drawings by Robert Thacker)

it, with function words and elaborately organized sentences absent (Goldin-Meadow, 1982). And there is a yet more serious limitation that goes back to the social and interpersonal nature of ordinary language use: The parents of these children used gestures to them very rarely, and the adults' sporadic gesturing was in terms of isolated "words" and pointing to things in view, with no syntactic organization (Goldin-Meadow and Mylander, 1983). The result was that social interaction in this medium was quite restricted, for it takes more than one individual—inventive as he or she may be—to make a living language. We can be thankful, then, that these children once they reached the age of four or five began to receive instruction in reading English and were eventually introduced to a full sign language (ASL) by meeting other deaf individuals.

In sum, these studies provide us with a fairly pure case of a group of children who were isolated from language stimulation but not from love and affection. The findings show that the capacity to organize thought using the word and syntax principles of language is a deep-seated property of the human mind, at least in its basics if not in its elaborations. In this sense, we have no need to ask further about the origins of human language. Our best guess is that as human nature originated in evolutionary history, language inevitably made its appearance too. Yet the same studies show us the necessarily interpersonal and interactive nature of human communication, which must become stymied and dysfunctional in the end if there is no "other" with whom it can be used.

CHILDREN DEPRIVED OF ACCESS TO SOME OF THE MEANINGS

■ Children usually learn the meanings of words in situations in which they can determine the referents of those words. Thus it is certainly easier to learn the meaning of the word *horse* if that word is said in the presence of a horse. Only the rarer, and late-acquired, words like *zebu* usually have to be looked up in the dictionary (and even for these, we are helped if the dictionary provides a picture). To the extent that referents of the words and sentences help the learner, we should expect that blind learners have significant difficulties in learning a language. For often the mother may be talking of things that are too large, gossamer, or distant for the blind child to feel with her hands (e.g., mountains, clouds, or birds).

In this sense, blind children seem to suffer an environmental deprivation symmetrical with the one previously considered: The isolated deaf children heard no language *forms* from their parents, but they were free to observe all the things and events in the world that language describes. In contrast, blind children hear the language forms from their parents, but they are cut off from some opportunities to observe their referents (and thus, presumably, to acquire word and sentence *meanings*).

All the same, recent evidence shows that blind children learn language as rapidly and as well as sighted children. One striking example is vision-related words like *look* and *see,* which blind children use as early (two-and-a-half to three years of age) and as systematically as sighted children. To be sure, there are some differences in how blind and sighted children understand these words. A young sighted listener, even if her vision is blocked by a blindfold, will tilt her covered eyes upward when asked to "Look up!" This suggests that to the sighted child, looking *must* refer to vision (Figure 9.15A). But a congenitally blind child, when also told to "Look up!" shows that she too has a sensible interpretation of *look,* though a somewhat different one. Keeping her head immobile, the blind youngster reaches upward and searches the space above her body with her hands (Figure 9.15B). Thus each of these children understands *look* differently.

But the meanings resemble each other even so. Both children realize that *look* has something to do with perceiving the world by use of the sense organs. The children arrive at meaningful interpretations of words even though their information about the world is often quite different.

This fits with the general picture of language learning as we have discussed it, for all learners—not just blind ones—must (and do!) build their language knowledge from relatively sparse information about referents. Thus one child may see a Great Dane and a poodle when he hears "dog." Another child may be introduced to this same word when seeing a collie and a terrier. Based on these quite different experiences, both children will acquire the same category, as we know from the fact that both will apply it to Chihuahuas and Huskies the first time they see them. In light of this marvelous ability of children to categorize the world in terms that are important to their own perceptual and conceptual lives, perhaps it is not so surprising that the blind child understands *looking* to mean 'exploring with the hands' (Landau and L. Gleitman, 1985; see also Urwin, 1983; Mulford, 1986; Bigelow, 1987).

Before leaving this topic, we should again strike a cautionary note (as we did with the self-invented gestural language of deaf children). Even though blind learners' language forms and word meanings are strikingly like those of sighted children, up until age three they manifest many problems in understanding the particulars of conversations going on around them. This creates significant frustration (sometimes leading to severe behavioral problems) in blind toddlers. This is not surprising. Imagine what it would be like if all your companions were involved in face-to-face conversation, but you were connected to them only by telephone. Like blind children, you would experience confusion about what was being talked about, have trouble identifying the referents of pronouns, and so forth (Landau and L. Gleitman, 1985).

In sum, we see that those with sensory deprivation are relatively unscathed in the acquisition of syntax and meaning. Language principles are part of our nature and emerge in relative indifference to the type of environmental support. But we see also that these deprivations (at least early in life) have a significant impact on the interpersonal use of language for successful communication.

THE CASE OF HELEN KELLER

■ The most dramatic and compelling picture of children cut off from contact with a language community comes to us from the case of Helen Keller (1880–1968). At eighteen months, she was a bright toddler, learning her first few words. But she then suffered a devastating illness (never adequately diagnosed) that left her both deaf and blind. Thus Helen, unlike the congenitally deaf and blind children we have discussed (who never experienced hearing or seeing), was aware of suffering a catastrophic loss. She later wrote (speaking of herself in the third person):

> With appalling suddenness she [Helen] moved from light to darkness and became a phantom. . . . Helplessly the family witnessed the baffled intelligence as Phantom's hand stretched out to feel the shapes which she could reach but which meant nothing to her. . . . Nothing was part of anything, and there blazed up in her frequent fierce anger. . . . I remember tears rolling down her cheeks but not the grief. There were no words for that emotion or any other, and consequently they did not register. (Keller, 1955)

Helen thus suffered the double affliction of sudden darkness and silence, and lived the next five years of her life in many ways isolated from the world of other people. But in the end, she entered Radcliffe, studied algebra, Greek, and literature, wrote classic and elegantly crafted books on her life and experiences,

Helen Keller conversing with Eleanor Roosevelt *Helen understood speech by noting the movements of the lips and the vibration of the vocal cords. (Photograph by Larry Morris/*New York Times*; courtesy of the Perkins School for the Blind)*

became an illustrious educator, and was personally close to many of the important people of her time, including Mark Twain, Eleanor Roosevelt, and Alexander Graham Bell (Lash, 1980).

Helen Keller gave the credit for this triumphant return to life to her great teacher, Anne Sullivan. Sullivan, herself half-blind and raised in appalling conditions in a "poor house," had acquired a partial manual system. It was through this medium that she began to unlock the stifled mind of Helen: She finger-spelled onto her eager pupil's palm. Helen reported her awakening in this famous passage (in which Anne Sullivan is holding one of Helen's hands under a waterspout):

> . . . as the cool stream gushed over one hand, she [Anne Sullivan] spelled into the other the word water. . . . I stood still, my whole attention fixed upon the motions of her fingers. . . . Suddenly I felt a misty consciousness as of something forgotten—a thrill of returning thought; and somehow the mystery of language was revealed to me. . . . Everything had a name, and each name gave birth to a new thought. As we returned to the house every object which I touched seemed to quiver with life. (Quoted in Lash, 1980)

As Anne Sullivan wrote, "She has learned that the manual alphabet is the key to everything she wants to know." Almost immediately, Helen was learning six new words a day. Eventually (though in the face of significant struggles because of the poor materials available for deaf children in these early days), Helen read raised letters and Braille, and went on to achieve a state of literacy and creativity with language that would put most of us to shame.

What can we learn from Helen Keller's case? It is not as though this child was completely unable to communicate or think before the arrival of Sullivan in her life. In Helen's biography, she underestimated her own status at that time, remembering herself as merely "a wild and destructive little animal." But Anne Sullivan saw something else. Like the deaf children we have described in the previous section, Helen had spontaneously invented many gestures to describe her wants and needs. For instance, "a desire for ice cream was shown by turning the freezer and a little shiver; . . . knotting hair on the back of her head symbolized her mother. . . . If she wanted bread and butter, she imitated the motions of cutting . . . and spreading." Sullivan recognized at least sixty such spontaneous "descriptive gestures" when she first met Helen (Lash, 1980).

So Helen's case is consistent with that of the deaf children we discussed earlier. Isolated from language forms, a human infant begins to invent her own. But Helen's case also reveals the crushing limitations of such a homemade language system for communicating with the surrounding community, which neither knows this idiosyncratic system nor understands its significance. Anne Sullivan, an incredibly sophisticated and talented teacher, differed from the loving but bewildered parents by capitalizing on the homemade signs in her first communicative contact with Helen. She wrote that "I use complete sentences . . . and fill out the meaning with gestures and her [Helen's] descriptive signs" (Lash, 1980). Anne Sullivan also knew that language learning has to be natural and communicative, and will not succeed by memorizing word lists out of context as had been common in the education of sensorily deprived children at that time. Thus she signed into Helen's palm "as we talk into the baby's ear." She wrote that the drill methods of her predecessors

> seem to be built up on the supposition that every child is a kind of idiot who must be taught to think. . . . Let him come and go freely, let him touch real things and combine his impressions for himself. . . . (Lash, 1980)

Thus we see that Sullivan's success depended not only on exploiting the child's natural disposition to organize language according to deep-seated principles of

Helen Keller and her teacher Anne Sullivan *(Photograph courtesy of the Perkins School for the Blind)*

form and meaning, but on introducing language in the context of its—just as deep-seated—functions for communicating about things, events, and feelings with others (see Bates and MacWhinney, 1982).

We should also note one other resemblance between Helen's case and that of the other children we have discussed. Unlike Genie who was first exposed to English during adolescence and who failed to learn anything but rudimentary basics, Helen received language stimulation quite early in life. As in the case of Isabelle, her rehabilitation began at about age six and was richly successful. The medium of transmission Sullivan used to teach Helen Keller—signing onto the palm or cheek—is still employed today with great success for children who are both deaf and blind (C. Chomsky, 1984).

LANGUAGE LEARNING WITH CHANGED ENDOWMENTS

FOCUS QUESTIONS

- What is the critical-period hypothesis of language learning?
- What characteristics of human language are shared by chimpanzees? Should they be considered to have language?

We have now shown that language learning can proceed quite successfully despite severe environmental differences and deprivations. This suggests that there is an innate "mental machinery" for language that runs its course unde-flected by any but the most radical environmental stresses (such as that suffered by Genie). But what happens if the nature of the learners themselves is changed? To the extent that language learning and use are determined by brain function, changing that brain should have strong effects (Lenneberg, 1967; Menyuk, 1977; L. Gleitman, 1986).

There are many indications that the nature and state of the brain have massive consequences for language functioning. An obvious instance is *aphasia* (see Chapter 2)—if there is damage to a certain part of the left hemisphere of the brain *(Broca's area),* the victim loses use of the function words; if the damage is to another part *(Wernicke's area),* the loss is to the content words (Figure 9.16).

We will now turn our attention to quite a different distinction in the mental machinery that learners bring to the task of learning a language, one we have already mentioned in passing. This is their chronological age when they are exposed to linguistic stimulation. As the brains of humans are still growing and developing almost to the time of puberty, there is room to believe that young vs. old learners of a language approach the task equipped with rather different mental apparatus. Does this matter?

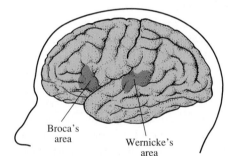

9.16   The language areas of the brain
Certain areas of the cerebral cortex (in most right-handers, in the left hemisphere) are de-voted to language functions. These include Broca's area, whose damage produces deficits in speech production, especially of function words (expressive aphasia), and Wernicke's area, whose damage leads to deficits in comprehension of word meanings (receptive aphasia). For more details, see Chapter 2. (After Geschwind, 1972)

THE CRITICAL PERIOD HYPOTHESIS

According to the *critical period hypothesis,* there is an especially sensitive period in early life when language acquisition is easy. But according to this hypothesis, some characteristics of the brain change as the critical period draws to its close, so that later learning (both of a first language and of others) becomes more difficult (Lenneberg, 1967).

Critical periods seem to govern the acquisition of a number of important behavior patterns in many animals. One example is the attachment of the young of various animals to their mothers, which generally can be formed only in early

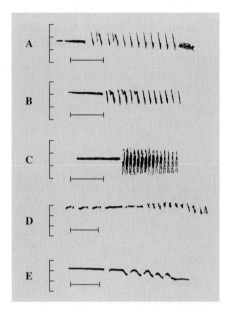

9.17 Critical period in the development of bird song *(A) A graphic presentation of the song of an adult, male white-crowned sparrow. The figure, a sound spectrograph, plots the frequency region of the bird's vocal output over time. Frequency is indicated by the vertical axis, in steps of 2,000 hertz. The horizontal time marker indicates half a second. The figure shows that the normal song begins with a whistle or two, continues with a series of trills, and ends with a vibrato. (B) The song of a bird raised in acoustic isolation but exposed to four minutes of normal song between the ages of 35 and 56 days. His adult song was almost normal. (C) The song of an isolated bird exposed to normal song between days 50 and 71. The adult song of this bird has some crude similarities to normal white-crowned sparrow song. There is a whistle followed by trills, but the details are very different. (D) and (E) show the songs of birds whose exposure to normal song occurred very early in life (days 3 to 7) or very late (after 300 days of age) respectively. Training at either of these times had no effect. (After Marler, 1970)*

childhood (see Chapter 14). Another example is bird song. Male birds of many species have a song that is characteristic of their own kind. They learn this song by listening to adult males of their own species. But this exposure will only be effective if it occurs at a certain period in the bird's life. This has been extensively documented for the white-crowned sparrow. To learn the white-crowned sparrow song in all its glory (complete with special trills and grace notes), the baby birds must hear an adult's song sometime between the seventh and sixtieth day of their life. The next forty days are a marginal period. If the fledgling is exposed to an adult male's song during that period but not before, he will acquire only some limited basics of the sparrow song, without the full elaborations heard in normal adults (see Figure 9.17). If the exposure comes still later, it has no effect at all. The bird will never sing normally (Marler, 1970).

Is there an analogy to this distinction in humans learning languages? Are adults less able to learn language than children because they have passed out of some critical period? Much of the evidence has traditionally come from studies of second-language acquisition.

SECOND-LANGUAGE LEARNING

In the first stages of learning a second language, adults appear to be much more efficient than children (Snow and Hoefnagel-Hohle, 1978). The adult will venture halting but comprehensible sentences soon after arrival in the new language community. In contrast, many young children seem to be filled with confusion, astonishment, and even horror when they suddenly hear speech that they cannot understand at all; often they stop talking altogether for some weeks or even months. But in the long run the outcome is just the reverse. After one to two years, very small children speak the new language fluently and soon sound just like natives. This is much less common in adults.

This point has been made by investigators who studied the long-run outcome of second-language learning, depending on the age of first exposure to the new language. The subjects were native Chinese and Korean speakers who came to the United States (and became immersed in the English-language community) at varying ages. These Far Eastern languages were chosen for study because they are quite dissimilar to English. The subjects were tested only after they had been in the United States for at least five years, so they had had ample exposure to English. Finally, all of them were students and faculty members at a large midwestern university, so they shared some social background (and presumably were all motivated to learn the new language so as to succeed in their university roles).

All of these subjects took a lengthy test. They listened to English sentences. Half of these were grossly ungrammatical (e.g. *The farmer bought two pig at the market; The little boy is speak to a policeman*). The other half were the grammatical counterparts of these same sentences. The task of the subjects was to indicate which sentences were grammatical in English and which were not. The results are shown in Figure 9.18. The learners who had been exposed to English before age seven performed just like native speakers of English. Thereafter there was an increasing decrement in performance as a function of age at first exposure. The older the subjects when they first came to the United States, the less well they seemed to have acquired English (Johnson and Newport, 1989).

IS THE CRITICAL PERIOD SPECIFIC TO LANGUAGE?

The notion of a critical period seems fairly plausible. What is less clear is that it is specific to language. One can take a broader view, which simply asserts that children are better at picking up any and all complex skills of which language is

LANGUAGE LEARNING WITH CHANGED ENDOWMENTS

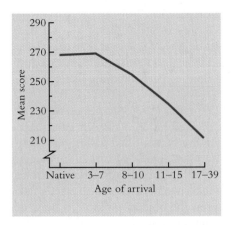

9.18 Critical period for second-language learning *Relation between age of arrival in the United States by 46 Korean and Chinese individuals, and their score (out of 276 test items) on a test of English grammar conducted five years later. (After Johnson and Newport, 1989)*

(The FAR SIDE cartoon by Gary Larson is reprinted by permission of Chronicle Features, San Francisco, California)

only one. As of now, we have insufficient evidence to choose between the narrow and the broad conceptions of the critical period. It may be specific to language alone. Or it may be nonspecific—so much so, perhaps, that to assert that such a period exists amounts to little more than the statement that you can't teach an old dog (or an old language learner) new tricks. Whatever the answer, some kind of internal clock is doubtless ticking away and affecting the ability to acquire a new language. Hence if you have a passionate desire to acquire, say, Tlingit or Malay or Finnish, you would be well advised to buy your airline tickets immediately, for every moment seems to count.

LANGUAGE IN NONHUMANS

We have considered the role of the human biological endowment in language learning and use. The outcomes should leave us quite pessimistic about whether we can teach other animals to converse with us in our language (or, for that matter, whether we can learn to communicate with them in their own species-specific manner). As we will now see, not even our nearest animal relative, the chimpanzee, comes close to attaining human language even with the best of good will and the most strenuous educational procedures. Just as language deprivation did not forever destroy in Helen Keller the capacity to become a fully human user of language, so we cannot expect that language enrichment, no matter how extensive and systematic, can create this capacity full-blown in a chimpanzee.

At the same time, there is considerable overlap between our biological endowments and those of other primates. For this reason, we should not be too surprised if some rudiments of language-like skills can be made to grow in them. If so, this may offer some insight into the origins of our own communicative organization.

THE MEDIUM OF TRANSMISSION FOR CHIMPANZEE COMMUNICATION

Chimpanzee vocal tracts differ from our own, so they cannot literally speak as we do (Hayes, 1952). Several investigators overcame this obstacle by employing visual systems of various kinds. Some use artificial systems based on colored plastic chips or symbols on a computer screen (Premack, 1976; Rumbaugh, 1977). Others have adopted items from ASL (Gardner and Gardner, 1969, 1975, 1978; Terrace et al., 1979).

VOCABULARY

Chimpanzees using any of the visual systems just mentioned can acquire a substantial number of "words." Consider Washoe, a chimpanzee introduced to words at about one year of age and treated just like a human child, with naps, diapers, and baths. She was taught ASL signs by having her hands physically molded into the desired position; other signs were learned by imitation (Fouts, 1972). After four years, she had learned about 130 signs for objects *(banana, hand)*, actions *(bite, tickle)*, and action modifiers *(enough, more)*. This rate cannot compare with the human child who learns about 10,000 words in this period, but it is impressive all the same (for discussion, see Savage-Rumbaugh et al., 1980).

Also of considerable interest is the finding that some of the chimpanzees use their new acquisitions in naturalistic interactions with their trainers, not just in laboratory tests. Moreover, Washoe appears to be teaching some of her human signs to an adopted chimpanzee baby (Fouts, Hirsch, and Fouts, 1982). If this result holds up, it is a very interesting case of "cultural transmission" by another species.

9.19 A test for propositional thought in chimpanzees *(A) A chimpanzee is shown a whole apple and two halves of an apple. Its task is to place one of three alternatives between them: a pencil, a bowl of water, or a knife. (B) The animal chooses the knife, the instrument which produced the change from the uncut to the cut state. In other trials, when the animals were shown a blank piece of paper and a scribbled-upon piece of paper, in general, they would put the pencil in the middle. When shown a dry sponge and a wet sponge, they chose the bowl of water. (From Premack, 1976; photographs courtesy of David Premack)*

PROPOSITIONAL THOUGHT

Are chimpanzees capable of propositional thought? We know that they have mental representations of various objects and events in the world, for as we just saw, they can be taught words for them. But do they have anything like a notion of this-does-something-to-that?

One line of evidence comes from David Premack's (1976) studies on the concept of causation in chimpanzees. Premack showed his animals pairs of objects. In each pair the second object was the same as the first but had undergone some change. One pair consisted of a whole apple and an apple that was cut in pieces; another pair was a dry towel and a wet towel; a third was an unmarked piece of paper and a piece of paper covered with pencil marks. The chimpanzee's task was to place one of several alternatives between the objects—a knife, a bowl of water, or a pencil. The question was whether the animals would choose the item that caused the change (Figure 9.19). Premack's star pupil, Sarah, performed correctly on 77 percent of the trials, far more than would be expected by chance. Perhaps these animals have some primitive notions of the relation between certain objects, acts, and outcomes—knives cut things up, water wets them, and pencils mark them. To the extent that the apes have these concepts, they have the germs of propositional thought.

SYNTAX

Human speech is characterized by abstract syntactic principles. Can chimpanzees do anything of this sort? Can they organize their signs for *Mama, tickle,* and *Washoe* so as to say either *Mama tickles Washoe* or *Washoe tickles Mama*? The Gardners believe that Washoe has some such ability. As evidence, they refer to apparently novel sequences of signs produced by Washoe on her own. For instance, she once signed *listen eat* on hearing an alarm clock that signals mealtime, and she signed *water bird* upon seeing a duck.

A number of critics feel that such observations prove little or nothing. They are anecdotes that can be interpreted in several ways. Take the sequence *water bird.* On the face of it, its use seems like a remarkable achievement—a chimpanzoid equivalent of a compound noun that presumably means something like *bird that lives on water.* But is this interpretation justified? Or did Washoe merely produce an accidental succession of two signs: *water* (perhaps water was seen just before) and *bird* (because of the duck)? It is hard to believe that she really understood the significance of the order (in English) in which the two words are uttered: a *water-bird* is a bird that lives on water, but *bird-water* is water for a bird. Since all we have is an anecdote, we cannot be sure.

Recent claims for another species, the pygmy chimpanzee, are even stronger. It is claimed that these animals quite often come up with novel combinations of words and that their language knowledge in general is broader than that of common chimpanzees taught by similar methods (Savage-Rumbaugh et al., 1986; Savage-Rumbaugh, 1987). Our final assessment of primate linguistic intelligence will depend to some degree on further documentation of such effects.

Current evidence allows us to conclude only that chimpanzees can learn words and show some propositional thought. There is little satisfactory evidence that they can create (or understand) syntactic structures that are the human vehicles for expressing propositional thought. Thus—at least so far, though the debate continues—they cannot be said to be "linguistic animals." (For discussion

A

B

Chimpanzees signing   *A young chimpanzee making the sign for (A) "hug" and (B) "apple." (Terrace, 1979; photographs courtesy of Herbert Terrace)*

of some of these issues, see Seidenberg and Pettito, 1979; Van Cantfort and Rimpau, 1982; Pinker, 1994).

IS IT LANGUAGE?

To sum up, recent years have seen a tremendous growth of scientific interest in the question of whether chimpanzees (and dolphins, gorillas, and other advanced animals) can acquire language. What current evidence supports is that there are some precursors and prerequisites (such as primitive propositional thought) to our language capacities that are observable in trained chimpanzees. However, these very findings have led to great controversy. Some scientists have concluded from them that there is little qualitative difference in this regard between us and these primates—only a difference in degree. Others conclude that the chimpanzees' accomplishments are too sporadic and limited to be of much interest for understanding the minds of either chimpanzees or humans. Many other scientists find no merit at all in calling these chimpanzee behaviors "language" in any useful sense. Their view is that these trained behaviors are no more convincing than the tricks of dancing circus poodles, whose accomplishments are never taken to prove that dogs, like humans, are two-legged animals.

Whether the chimpanzees' accomplishments should be called *language,* then, seems to depend on one's definition of that term. We can choose to say that trained chimpanzees use language. But in doing so, we have changed the technical meaning of the term so as to exclude from consideration the learning and speech of every nonpathological human. Worse, we have even changed the common-sense meaning of the term *language.* For one thing is certain: If any of our children learned or used language the way Washoe or Sarah does, we would be terror-stricken and rush them to the nearest neurologist.

LANGUAGE AND ITS LEARNING

In our survey of the nature of language, we emphasized that human communication systems are at rock bottom the same all over the world. To be sure, the words themselves sound different, so the speakers of different languages cannot understand each other. Still, every language turned out to consist of a hierarchy of structures that represent a complex interweaving of meaning and form. The effect is that, if we share a language, we can communicate about all the endless social, emotional, and intellectual matters that concern us as humans.

Language is marvelously ornate and intricate—so much so that we must be boggled by the idea that human babies can learn any such thing. And yet they do. In all the nurturant (and even most of the horribly abusive) circumstances in which human babies find themselves, language makes its appearance and flourishes. Our nearest primate cousins even given the utmost in social and linguistic support do not approach the competence and sophistication of the most ordinary three-year-old human child. What makes this learning possible?

We have argued throughout that language is the product of the young human brain, such that virtually any exposure will suffice to guide acquisition of any language in the world. In this sense, there appears to be a "bioprogram" for language learning (Chomsky, 1965; Lenneberg, 1967; L. Gleitman, 1981; Bickerton, 1984; Pinker, 1994). In retrospect, this is scarcely surprising. It would be just as foolish for evolution to have created human bodies without human "programs" to run these bodies as it would be to have created giraffe bodies without giraffe programs or white-crowned sparrow bodies without white-crowned sparrow programs.

Noam Chomsky

But we must close by reemphasizing that specific languages must be learned by human babies, even though the capacity to accomplish this is given in large part by nature. This is because the manifestations of the human language capacity are certainly variable, particularly in the sounds of the individual words. To reiterate a point with which we began: Greek children learn Greek, not Urdu or Swahili. For this reason, we have had to view the language acquisition task as a complex interaction between the child's innate capacities and the social, cognitive, and specifically linguistic supports provided in the environment. Perhaps, in light of the efficiency and sure-handedness with which (as we saw) human babies accomplish this feat, you might feel disposed to buttonhole the next baby you meet in the street to compliment her for being born a human being.

QUESTIONS FOR CRITICAL THINKING

1. Bats are biologically close to rats, but most people would probably consider them closer to birds. What does this suggest about our family-resemblance structures?

2. What do you think might be the minimum number of senses required to learn a language?

3. Many in the American deaf community believe that ASL is a separate language that makes the deaf a separate culture. What do you think?

4. Suppose that plastic surgeons could alter the vocal tracts of young chimps so that they could reproduce human speech sounds. Would their language ability develop any differently? Would it advance further than it would with unaltered vocal tracts?

SUMMARY

1. Language has five major properties. It is *creative* or novel: All normal humans can say and understand sentences they have never heard before. It is *structured:* Only certain arrangements of linguistic elements (phonemes, words, and so forth) are allowed. It is *meaningful:* Each word or combination of words expresses a meaningful idea (or concept). It is *referential:* It relates to things, scenes, and events in the extralinguistic world. It is *interpersonal:* It enables us to communicate with other people.

2. Languages are organized as a hierarchy of structures. The lowest-level units are *phonemes,* the sound elements of language. Different languages may use different phonemes, and each has specific arrangements of the phonemes it uses. Each language also has *morphemes,* which are the smallest language units that carry bits of meaning. There are *content morphemes,* which carry the bulk of meaning, and *function morphemes,* which carry the structure of the sentence. *Phrases* are groupings of morphemes that carry more complex meanings than single morphemes and words. Phrases are combined into *sentences* according to the principles of syntax. There are infinitely many phrases and sentences in a language.

3. Word and phrase meaning is not identical to word and phrase reference, for some expressions can refer to the same thing and yet have different meanings. The *definitional theory of meaning* holds that each word describes a bundle of more elementary semantic features. Each word is "defined" as some small set of features that are individually necessary and jointly sufficient to pick out that word from all other words in the language. The *prototype theory of meaning* responds to the fact that it is hard to find necessary and sufficient definitions for all words. The most widely held theory of word meaning today combines the definitional and prototype theories. The definitional part picks out properties that a concept must have. The prototype part concerns the most "typical" properties, the ones that most members of the concept share.

SUMMARY

4.   Human thought is in terms of whole *propositions,* consisting of a *subject* or topic, and a *predicate* (that which is said about the subject or topic).

5.   Language learning is more than skill acquisition, for the learning cannot be fully described as a habit acquired through imitation and reinforcement. The proof is that children come to know more sentences than they ever could have heard.

6.   Infants are responsive to linguistic stimulation almost from birth. For instance, they have been shown to be responsive to differences among just about all the phonemes used in the various languages of the world. Learning a specific language's phoneme structure involves learning not to notice those distinctions not made in one's native language.

7.   Most infants begin talking in *one-word sentences* at about one year of age and rapidly acquire a large vocabulary. They seem to have propositional ideas in mind, and some appreciation of syntactic structure, even at this early stage.

8.   At about two years of age, children begin using rudimentary *two-word* or *telegraphic sentences* that contain content words but typically omit function morphemes and words. Still, these short sentences have a good deal of structure.

9.   Language learning takes place successfully in many radically different environments. It fails only if children are removed from all human company or violently isolated and abused. Even if one is deaf, one learns a language. In this case, it will be a signed (visual-manual) language rather than a spoken (auditory-vocal) one.

10.   Children isolated from opportunities to learn the language around them invent some of it for themselves. An example is deaf children not exposed to signed languages who invent pantomimic gestures for words and combine these into propositions.

11.   In contrast to the cases of changed environmental conditions, which children of normal mentality generally overcome, are cases of changed conditions of mentality. When the brain is unusual or deficient, radical changes in language learning are seen.

12.   An important case of a "changed brain" that learns a language is the second-language learner who is chronologically older than the usual first-language learner. The less mature brain and the mature brain appear to have different capacities. The finding is that the younger the second-language learner, the more likely he or she is to acquire the new language adequately.

13.   Because experimental evidence makes it clear that language learning is based on special properties of the young human brain, we should not expect to find that human language can be fully or even adequately learned by other higher animals such as chimpanzees. Nevertheless, chimpanzees have been shown to have rather good word-learning capacities, though nowhere as good as those of a two-and-a-half-year-old human. They also seem to be able to think propositionally to some degree. There is little or no credible evidence, however, that chimpanzees can acquire even the rudiments of syntactic principles.

14.   Summarizing all the evidence, language learning results from the interaction between a young human brain and various social, cognitive, and specifically linguistic supports provided in the environment. Language is perhaps the central cognitive property whose possession makes us "truly human." If aliens came from another planet but spoke like us, we would probably try to get to know them and understand them—rather than trying to herd them or milk them—even if they looked like cows.

PART THREE

SOCIAL BEHAVIOR

CHAPTER **10**

THE BIOLOGICAL BASIS OF SOCIAL BEHAVIOR

In the preceding chapters, we asked what organisms do, what they want, and what they know. But thus far we have raised these questions in a limited context, for we have largely considered the organism as an isolated individual, abstracted from the social world in which it lives. But many aspects of behavior are impossible to describe by considering a single organism. Courtship, sex, parental care, competition, and cooperation do not take place in isolation. They are not merely actions; they are interactions in which each participant's behavior is affected by the behavior of others.

In humans, the role of social factors is even more powerful than in other animals. Most of our motives—the desire to be loved, to be esteemed, and in some cases, unhappily, to inflict pain—are social. Even motives that seem to involve only the isolated individual, such as hunger, thirst, and temperature maintenance, are social. For the ways we satisfy these motives are enormously affected by the social context—created by our forebears—in which we live. Thus, we eat food that is raised by a complex agricultural technology based on millenia of human discovery, and we eat it delicately, with knife and fork, according to the etiquette of a long-dead king.

The study of social behavior is the study of lives inextricably intertwined with those of others both living and dead. It is the study which proves that, to quote John Donne's famous sermon, "no man is an island complete unto himself."

 classic question posed by philosophers is, "What is the basic social nature of humankind?" Are greed, competition, and hate (or for that matter, charity, cooperation, and love) unalterable components of the human makeup, or can they be instilled or nullified by proper training? To answer these questions, we will have to consider not just humankind but some of its animal cousins as well.

THE SOCIAL NATURE OF HUMANS AND ANIMALS

FOCUS QUESTIONS

- How did Malthus's formula for population growth provide Darwin with the principle underlying natural selection?

- What does it mean to say that a behavior has adaptive value?

- What is ethology, and how did early ethologists explain species-specific behavior?

- What are displays, and what purpose do they serve?

- How would sociobiologists explain animal and human behavior?

Are human beings so built that social interaction is an intrinsic part of their makeup? Or are they essentially solitary creatures who turn to others only because they need them for their own selfish purposes? The English social philosopher Thomas Hobbes (1588–1679) argued for the second of these alternatives. In his view, man is a self-centered brute who, left to his own devices, will seek his own gain regardless of the cost to others. Except for the civilizing constraints imposed by society, men would inevitably be in an eternal "war of all against all." According to Hobbes, this frightening "state of nature" is approximated during times of anarchy and civil war. These were conditions Hobbes knew all too well, for he lived during a time of violent upheavals in England when Stuart royalists battled Cromwell's Puritans, when commoners beheaded their king in a public square, and when pillaging, burning, and looting were commonplace. Hobbes argued that in such a state of nature, human life is a sorry lot. There are "no Arts; no Letters; no Society; and which is worst of all, continuall fear, and danger of violent death; And the life of man solitary, poore, nasty, brutish, and short" (Hobbes, 1651, p. 186). Hobbes argued that under the circumstances, people had no choice but to protect themselves against their own ugly natures. They did so by entering into a "social contract" to form a collective commonwealth, the State.

Hobbes's psychological starting points are simple enough: People are by nature asocial and destructively rapacious. Society is a means to chain the brute within. Only when curbed by social fetters does humanity go beyond animal nature to become truly human. Given this position, the various social motives that bind us to others (such as love and loyalty) presumably are imposed through culture and convention. They are learned, for they could not possibly be part of our intrinsic makeup.

Thomas Hobbes *(Painting by John Michael Wright; courtesy of The Granger Collection)*

NATURAL SELECTION AND SURVIVAL

During the nineteenth century, Hobbes's doctrine of inherent human aggression and depravity was garbed in the mantle of science. The Industrial Revolution seemed to give ample proof that life is indeed a Hobbesian battle of each against all, whether in the marketplace, in the sweatshops, or in the far-off colonies. Ruthless competition among people was regarded as just one facet of the more general struggle for existence waged among all living things. This harsh view of nature had gained great impetus at the start of the nineteenth century when Thomas Malthus announced his famous law of population growth. According to Malthus, human and animal populations grow by geometrical progression (for example, 1, 2, 4, 8, 16, . . .), while the food supply grows arithmetically (for example, 1, 2, 3, 4, 5, . . .). As a result, there is inevitable scarcity and a continual battle for survival.

When Charles Darwin (1809–1882) read Malthus's essay, he finally found the explanatory principle he had been seeking to account for the evolution of living things. He, as others before him, believed that all present-day plants, animals, and even humans, were descended from prior forms. The evidence came from various sources, such as fossil records that showed the gradual transformation from long-extinct species to those now living. But what had produced these changes? Within each species there are individual variations; some horses are faster, others are slower. Many of these variations are part of the animal's hereditary makeup and thus are bequeathed to its descendants. But will an individual animal have descendants? That depends on how it fares in the struggle for existence. As a matter of fact, most organisms don't live long enough to reproduce. Only a few seedlings grow up to be trees; only a few tadpoles achieve froghood. But certain characteristics may make survival a bit more likely. The faster horse is more likely to escape predatory cats than its slower fellow, and it is thus more

Charles Darwin *(Painting by J. Collier; courtesy of The National Portrait Gallery, London)*

Genetic survival   *The peacock's long tail feathers are a cumbersome burden that may decrease his chances of escaping predators and thus his own personal survival. But this is more than offset by his increased chances of attracting a sexual partner, thereby assuring survival of his genes. (Photograph © Ed Reschke, 1988; all rights reserved.)*

A woven nest   *Many animals have genetically determined behavior patterns characteristic of their species. An example is nest weaving in the thick-billed African weaverbird. (Photo courtesy of Brian M. Rogers/Biofotos)*

likely to leave offspring who inherit its swiftness. This process of **natural selection** does not guarantee survival and reproduction; it only increases their likelihood. In consequence, evolutionary change is very gradual and proceeds over eons (Darwin, 1872a).

PERSONAL AND GENETIC SURVIVAL

Natural selection leads to the "survival of the fittest." But just what does it mean to be fit? Thus far, our examples of better "fitness" involved attributes that make personal survival more likely: the faster horse, the more ferocious cat, and so on. But personal survival as such is not what the evolutionary game is about. The trick is to have reproductive success—to have offspring who will pass your genes along. A horse that manages to live two or three times longer than any of its fellows but that for some reason or another is infertile or stays celibate has not survived in an evolutionary sense. Personal survival (at least until sexual maturity) is a prerequisite for genetic survival, but it alone is not enough.

Seen in this light, it's clear that "fitness" is determined by all characteristics that enhance reproductive success, whether or not such characteristics contribute to the individual's own personal survival. Consider the magnificent tail feathers of the peacock. His long, cumbersome tail may somewhat decrease his chance to escape predators, but it hugely contributes to his evolutionary fitness. The peacock has to compete with his fellow males for access to the peahen; the larger and more magnificent his tail, the more likely she will respond to his sexual overtures. From an evolutionary point of view, the potential gain was evidently greater than the possible loss; as a result, long tail feathers were selected for. Much the same holds for many other characteristics that are of advantage in sexual competition. This is especially so among males (for reasons we'll discuss later on). Some of these characteristics are rather general, such as strength and aggressiveness. Others, such as the brightly colored plumage of many male birds and the large antlers of the stag, are more specialized. But whatever the particulars of a given attribute, its contribution to the animal's fitness is the extent to which it leads to reproductive success.

INHERITED PREDISPOSITIONS TO BEHAVIOR

The inherited characteristics that increase the chance for biological survival (that is, reproduction) may concern bodily structures such as the horse's hooves or the stag's antlers. But Darwin and his successors pointed out that natural selection may also involve behavior. Squirrels bury nuts and beavers construct dams; these behavior patterns are characteristic of the species and depend on the animals' genes, the basic units of heredity. Whether these genes are selected for or not depends upon the **adaptive value** (that is, the biological survival value) of the behavior they give rise to. A squirrel who has a genetic predisposition to bury nuts in autumn is presumably more likely to survive the winter than one who doesn't. As a result, it is more likely to have offspring who will inherit the nut-burying gene (or genes). The end product is an increase in the number of nut-burying squirrels.

Granted that behavior can be shaped by evolution, what kind of behavior is most likely to evolve? And, most important to us, what kind of built-in predispositions are most likely to characterize humankind? Many nineteenth-century thinkers answered in Hobbesian terms. They reasoned that people are animals and that in the bitter struggle for existence all animals are shameless egoists by sheer necessity. At bottom, they are all solitary and selfish, and human beings are no exception. To the extent that humans act sociably and on occasion even unselfishly—mating, rearing children, living and working with others—they learn to do so in order to satisfy some self-centered motive such as lust or hunger.

On the face of it, this Hobbesian view seems to fit evolutionary doctrine. But on closer examination, Darwinian theory does not imply anything of the sort. It holds that there is "survival of the fittest," but "fittest" only means most likely to survive and to have offspring; it says nothing about being solitary or selfish. Darwin himself supposed that certain predispositions toward cooperation might well be adaptive and would thus be selected for. We now know that something of this sort is true, for animals as well as human beings. As we shall see, there is considerable evidence that, Hobbes to the contrary, humans and animals are by nature social rather than asocial and that much of their social behavior grows out of natively given predispositions rather than running counter to them.

Konrad Lorenz *(Photograph by Nina Leen)*

BUILT-IN SOCIAL BEHAVIORS

■ Most systematic studies of built-in social behavior have been conducted within the domain of *ethology,* a branch of biology that studies animal behavior under natural conditions. Led by the Europeans Konrad Lorenz (1903–1989) and Niko Tinbergen (1907–1988), both Nobel Prize winners, ethologists have analyzed many behavior patterns that are built-in and *species-specific,* that is, characteristic of a particular species. Many of these built-in and species-specific behavior patterns are social; they dictate the way in which creatures interact with others of their own kind. Some involve a positive bond between certain members of the same species—courtship, copulation, care of the young. Others concern reactions of antagonism and strife—the struggle for social dominance, competition for a mate, and dispute over territory.

FIXED-ACTION PATTERNS

The early ethologists believed that many species-specific social reactions are based on genetically pre-programmed *fixed-action patterns,* which in turn are elicited by genetically pre-programmed *releasing stimuli.* An example of such a fixed-action pattern is the begging response of newly hatched herring gulls. They beg for food by pecking at the tips of their parents' beaks. The parent will then regurgitate some food from its crop and feed it to the young. But what is the critical stimulus that "releases" the chick's begging pecks? To find out, Tinbergen offered newly hatched gull chicks various cardboard models of gull heads and observed which ones they pecked at the most. The most successful model was one that was long and thin and had a red patch at its tip (see Figure 10.1). These are the very characteristics of an adult herring gull's beak, but the newly hatched chick has never encountered a parent's beak previously. Tinbergen concluded that evolution had done a good job in programming the chick to respond to certain stimulus features so as to recognize the parent's beak at first sight (Tinbergen, 1951).

Niko Tinbergen *(Photograph by Nina Leen)*

In many species, the releasing stimuli for any one animal's behavior are produced by another animal's behavior. What matters then is not just what some other animal looks like (e.g., the red spot on the gull parent's beak) but also what that other animal does. An important example of such behaviorally produced stimulus releasers are *displays.* Displays produce an appropriate reaction in another animal of the same species and are thus the basis of a primitive, innate communication system. The gull chick's begging peck is an elementary signal whose meaning is genetically given to both chick and parent: "Feed me! Feed me now!" (Tinbergen, 1951).

10.1 Stimulus releasers for pecking
(A) The figure indicates the pecking rate of a herring gull chick when presented with various models. As the figure shows, a flat cardboard model is more effective than a real head, and a disembodied bill works almost as well. (Adapted from Keeton and Gould, 1993) (B) Best of all was a stick with spots on it moving back and forth horizontally, which the gull chick pecks at while ignoring a full representation of the parent's head. (Photograph courtesy of John Sparks, BBC [Natural History]).

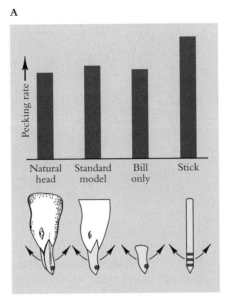

A

B

THE SOCIOBIOLOGICAL APPROACH

The analysis of chick pecking we have just discussed concentrated on the causes of behavior that are in the organism's own past (often the immediately preceding past): the particular stimuli that elicit the behavior, the physiological mechanisms that underlie it, and the developmental factors (such as learning) that help to shape it further. But there is another level of causation that precedes the particular organism's own past by countless generations: the animal's evolutionary history, which created the built-in bias toward that behavior through natural selection. In the last twenty years, a new branch of biology called ***sociobiology*** has arisen that focuses on these long-past causes, with primary emphasis on the evolutionary basis of various social behaviors (Wilson, 1975). Most behavioral scientists agree that sociobiology has provided valuable insights about social behavior in animals. What is much more controversial is the sociobiologists' contention that similar analyses can be applied to human social patterns, a topic to which we turn later (see pp. 317–19, 328–29).

BIOLOGICAL SOURCES OF AGGRESSION

FOCUS QUESTIONS

- How do nonhuman animals manifest aggression, and what do they become aggressive about?

- How do the sexes differ in aggressiveness, and what hormonal factor may explain this difference?

- How does territoriality limit aggression? What other features of animal societies act similarly?

- How do dominance hierarchies affect the behavior of individuals, and how does rank within the hierarchy affect evolutionary fitness?

*10.2 **Defending the nest*** *A royal tern attacks an egret that has come too close to its nest. (Photograph © M. P. Kahl)*

We will begin our discussion of built-in social patterns by considering the biological basis of aggression. In humans, some of the causes of aggression are events in the immediate present, such as threats and frustrations that provoke anger and hostility. Our present concern is with sources that lie in our inherent makeup, the biological roots of aggression that derive from our evolutionary past. To uncover these, we have to study animals as well as humans, for the biological sources of human aggression are likely to be obscured by cultural factors and tradition.

CONFLICT BETWEEN SPECIES: PREDATION AND DEFENSE

■ Most psychobiologists restrict the use of the term **aggression** to conflict between members of the same species. When an owl kills a mouse, it has slaughtered for food rather than murdered in hatred. As Lorenz points out, the predator about to pounce upon its prey does not look angry; the dog who is on the verge of catching a rabbit never growls, nor does it have its ears laid back (Lorenz, 1966).

Somewhat closer to true aggression is the counterattack lodged by a prey animal against a predatory enemy (see Figure 10.2). Flocks of birds sometimes **mob** an intruding cat or hawk. A colony of lovebird parrots will fly in a body upon a would-be attacker, flapping their wings furiously and uttering loud, shrill squeaks. In the face of this commotion, the predator often withdraws to look for a less troublesome meal (Dilger, 1962). Defense reactions may also occur when a hunted animal is finally cut off from retreat. Even normally reticent creatures may then become desperate fighters, as in the case of the proverbial cornered rat.

CONFLICT BETWEEN LIKE AND LIKE

■ There is probably no group among the animal kingdom that has forsworn aggression altogether; fighting has been observed in virtually all species. Fish chase and nip each other; lizards lunge and push; birds attack with wing, beak, and claw; sheep and cows butt heads; deer lock antlers; rats adopt a boxing stance and eye each other warily until one finally pounces upon the other and begins a furious wrestling match with much kicking and leaping and occasionally serious bites (see Figure 10.3).

Among vertebrates, the male is generally the more aggressive sex. In some mammals, this difference in combativeness is apparent even in childhood play.

*10.3 **Aggressive fighting*** *Male rats generally fight in fairly stereotypical ways, including (A) a "boxing position" that often escalates into (B) a leaping, biting attack. (From Barnett, 1963)*

A

B

Young male rhesus monkeys, for instance, engage in more vigorous rough-and-tumble tusslings than do their sisters (Harlow, 1962). A related result concerns the effect of **testosterone,** a male sex hormone. High testosterone levels in the bloodstream accompany increased aggressiveness in males; the reverse holds for decreased levels. This generalization seems to hold over a wide range of species, including fish, lizards, turtles, birds, rats and mice, monkeys, and human males (Davis, 1964).

SECURING RESOURCES

What do animals fight about? Their struggles are generally about scarce resources—something valuable in their world that is in short supply. Such a resource may be a food source or a water hole; very often it is a mate. To secure a modicum of such resources many animals stake out a claim to a particular region, which they will then defend as their exclusive preserve, their private **territory.**

Take male songbirds, for example. In the spring, they endlessly patrol their little empires and furiously repel all male intruders who violate their borders. Contrary to the poet's fancy, the male bird who bursts into full-throated song is not giving vent to inexpressible joy, pouring out his "full heart in profuse strains of unpremeditated art." His message is more prosaic. It is a warning to male trespassers and an invitation to unattached females: "Have territory, will share."

A biological benefit of territoriality is that it secures an adequate supply of resources for the next generation. The songbird who chases his rivals away will probably leave more offspring than the one who doesn't, for his progeny will have a better start in life. Once his claim is staked out he can entice the female, offering his territory as a kind of dowry.

A side effect of territoriality is that it often serves to keep aggression within bounds. Good fences make good neighbors, at least in the sense that they keep the antagonists out of each others' hair (or fins or feathers). One mechanism that accomplishes this is rather simple. Once a territory is established, its owner has a kind of home-court advantage in further disputes (Krebs, 1982). On his home ground he is courageous; if he ventures beyond it, he becomes timid and is readily repulsed. As a result, there may be occasional border skirmishes but few actual conflicts. This behavior pattern is utilized by circus trainers who make sure that they are the first to enter the training ring and that the animals come in later. As a result, the ring becomes the trainer's territory and even the great cats are more readily cowed (Hediger, 1968).

Aggressive encounter between male bighorn rams (Courtesy of Stouffer Productions, Animals Animals)

Red deer stag roaring *(Photograph ©
Manfred Danegger)*

LIMITING AGGRESSION

A certain amount of aggression may be biologically adaptive. This is especially so for males who compete for access to females. For example, a more aggressive songbird will conquer a larger and more desirable territory, which will help him attract a mate. In addition, his territory confers further advantages such as more seeds or more worms, which further help his progeny who will get more and better food in their early days as nestlings. As a result, we would expect some selection for aggressiveness. But this holds only up to a point, for while aggression may confer some benefits, it also has its costs. Combat is dangerous and can lead to death or serious injury. And the male who is continually fighting with his sexual rivals will have little time (let alone energy) left to mate with the female after his competitors have fled. Under the circumstances, natural selection strikes a compromise; there is aggression, but a number of factors keep it firmly in hand.

One way of avoiding catastrophic damage to life and limb is to assess the strength of the enemy. If he seems much stronger (or more agile, or better armed) than oneself, the best bet is to proclaim a cease-fire and concede defeat, or better yet, never to start the battle at all. Red deer stags compete for females by roaring at each other, sometimes for days on end. The stag that can roar longest and loudest will generally prevail—a reasonable decision, since a stronger roar is most likely produced by a stronger stag (Krebs and Davies, 1987). Similar strategies for avoiding the costs of a bloody defeat are found in many species of sheep and deer whose males engage in a ritualized form of combat as if under an internal compulsion not to inflict serious wounds (see Figure 10.4).

The limitation on violence appears in other ways as well. Many conflicts are settled by blustering diplomacy before they erupt into actual war. For example, male chimpanzees try to intimidate each other by staring, raising an arm, or uttering fearsome shouts. This approach is found throughout the animal kingdom: Whenever possible, try to get your way by threat or bluff rather than by actual fighting. This holds even for creatures as large as elephants and as fierce as tigers. Both these and other creatures make use of ***threat displays,*** a much less costly method for achieving one's aim than actual combat (see Figure 10.5).

10.4   *Ritualized fighting*   *Two South
African wildebeest males in a harmless ritualized dual along an invisible but clearly defined
mutual border between their territories. (Photograph by Hans Reinhard, © Bruce
Coleman, Inc., 1988)*

A   B

10.5 Threat displays *(A) Some species threaten by making themselves appear larger and more impressive. (Photograph by Rod Williams, © Bruce Coleman, Inc., 1991) (B) Other species threaten by shouting at the top of their lungs, like howler monkeys, who scream at each other for hours on end. (Photograph © Ferrero)*

In some cases, serious fighting will occur even so, for animals no less than human generals may miscalculate their chances of victory. But some ways of limiting the cost of defeat still remain. In wolves, the loser may "admit defeat" by adopting a special submissive gesture, such as begging like a puppy or rolling on his back. This is an ***appeasement display*** that is functionally equivalent to our white flag of surrender. Unlike some human warriors, the victorious wolf is without rancor. He generally accepts the loser's submission, and all fighting stops (Lorenz, 1966). The adaptive value of such submissive signals is clear enough. They allow today's loser to withdraw from the field of battle so that he can come back in a year or two when he is older and wiser, and when he may very well win a rematch. The evolutionary rule is simple enough: Don't fight unless the probable gains (in reproductive success) outweigh the costs. If you lose and run away (or make an appeasement display), you may live to fight (and mate) another day.

DOMINANCE AND SUBMISSION

Animals that live in groups often develop a social order based on ***dominance hierarchies.*** Such hierarchies can be quite complex among troops of primates. For example, in baboons, the dominant male has usually achieved his status through victory in several aggressive encounters. After this, his status is settled for a while, and lower-ranking baboons generally step aside to let the "alpha male" pass, and nervously scatter if he merely stares at them.

Why should animals spend so much time to achieve and maintain dominance? The answer is that rank has considerable privileges. The alpha male has first choice of sleeping site, enjoys easier access to food, and has priority in mating (see Figure 10.6). Such perquisites undoubtedly make life more pleasant for the alpha male than for his less fortunate fellows. But even more important may be the long-run evolutionary value of rank, for in terms of genetic survival, the higher-ranking animal is more "fit." Since he has easier access to females, he will presumably leave more offspring (Smith, 1981; Silk, 1986).

Thus far, our primary focus has been on dominance relations among primate males. This followed the initial emphasis of investigators in this area who

10.6 Dominance hierarchies *A dominant male baboon with a harem of females and young. (Courtesy of Bruce Coleman)*

303

Appeasement displays in humans *A Yanamamö Indian youngster smiles appeasingly at another boy who threatens him. (Photograph © I. Eibl-Eibesfeldt, Forschungsstelle f. Humanethologie)*

focused on male-male aggression. To be sure, the males' aggressive encounters are quite obvious, as they fight and strut and bellow. Many authors took this as evidence that the social order among most primates (and by implication, our own) was ultimately based on political struggles among males. But recent research shows that this conclusion is off the mark. For in many primate societies, females compete no less than males and develop hierarchies that are often more stable than those of males. Moreover, female rank has important long-term consequences, for mothers tend to bequeath their social rank to their offspring, especially to their daughters (Hrdy and Williams, 1983; Walters and Seyfarth, 1986).

TERRITORIALITY IN HUMANS AND HUMAN CULTURE

Is any of the preceding discussion of animals relevant to human behavior? At least on the surface there are parallels that have led some writers to suppose that concepts such as territoriality, dominance hierarchy, and the like apply to humans as well as to animals. There are certainly some aspects of human behavior that resemble territoriality. Even within the home, different members of a family have their private preserves—their own rooms or corners, their places at the dinner table, and so on. Other territorial claims are more temporary, such as a seat in a railroad car, whose possession we mark with a coat, a book, or a briefcase if we have to leave for a while.

A related phenomenon is **personal space,** the physical region all around us whose intrusion we guard against (Figure 10.7). On many New York subways, passengers will carefully choose their seats so as to leave the greatest possible distance between themselves and their nearest neighbor.

A desire to maintain some minimum personal space is probably nearly universal, but the dimensions seem to depend upon various social factors. By and large, appropriate personal distance increases with age and socioeconomic status (Collier, 1985). It is also affected by the standards of a particular culture. In North America, acquaintances stand about two or three feet apart during a conversation; if one moves closer, the other feels crowded or pushed into an unwanted

10.7 Personal space *(A) Relatively even spacing in ring-billed gulls (Photograph by Allan D. Cruikshank © 1978/Photo Researchers) (B) Some ethologists believe that the maintenance of personal space in humans is a related phenomenon. Vacationers at a beach on the Baltic Sea in Germany keep a precise distance between each couple or family unit. (Photograph by J. Messerschmidt/Bruce Coleman)*

A

B

intimacy. For Latin Americans, the acceptable distance is said to be much less. Under the circumstances, misunderstanding is almost inevitable. The North American regards the Latin American as overly intrusive; the Latin American in turn feels that the North American is unfriendly and cold (Hall, 1966).

One may ask whether these observations truly parallel the evidence from other species. There is no doubt that many people—though not all—care deeply about private ownership, whether of things, real estate, or more subtle private preserves. The question is whether this concern stems from the same evolutionary roots as does the territoriality of the songbird. Most current theorists believe that, while the overt behaviors may sometimes be similar, the underlying mechanisms are not. Territoriality in robins is universal and innately based, but in humans it is enormously affected by learning, which certainly suggests that cultural factors play a vital role.

THE BIOLOGICAL BASIS OF LOVE: THE MALE-FEMALE BOND

FOCUS QUESTIONS

- Why is sexual reproduction biologically advantageous?
- What are courtship rituals, and what function(s) do they serve?
- Which sex tends to make the final decision about mating and why?
- What hormones modulate sexual behavior? To what degree do they affect behavior in humans?
- What are the common mating systems, how do they differ, and how would sociobiologists account for them?

The preceding discussion has made it clear that there is some biological foundation for strife and conflict. The tendencies toward destruction are kept in bounds by a set of counteracting tendencies such as territoriality and ritualized fighting. As we shall see, they are also controlled and modified by learning, especially during childhood in humans, and their expression is greatly affected by situational factors (see Chapters 11 and 14).

But over and above these various checks on aggression, there is a positive force that is just as basic and deeply rooted in the biological makeup of animals and humans. The poets call it love. Scientists use the more prosaic term *bonding,* the tendency to affiliate with others of one's own kind.

The forces of social attraction are most obvious between mate and mate, and between child and parent. But positive bonds occur even outside of mating and child care. Examples are the social relationships cemented by *grooming* in monkeys and apes, who sit in pairs while the groomer meticulously picks lice and other vermin out of the groomee's fur (Figure 10.8). The animals evidently like to groom and be groomed over and above considerations of personal hygiene; it is their way of forming a social bond, and it works. Grooming occurs most commonly among kin (brothers and sisters, cousins, and so on), although it may also occur among unrelated animals. But whether they be kin or unrelated, animals who groom most often are also the most closely bonded by other measures of primate togetherness: They sit together, forage for food together, and stick together in alliances against common antagonists (Walters and Seyfarth, 1986).

It has sometimes been suggested that a comparable human practice is small talk in which we exchange no real information but simply talk for the sake of

10.8   Grooming in baboons   *(Photograph by P. Craig-Cooper, Nature Photographers Ltd.)*

"relating" to the other person. Other people are part of our universe, and we need them and want their company. Much the same is probably true for our primate cousins. They groom each other, whether or not they have vermin. We talk to each other, whether or not we really have something to say.

SEXUAL BEHAVIOR

■ In some very primitive organisms, reproduction is asexual; thus amoebas multiply by a process of simple cell division. This form of procreation seems to work well enough, for amoebas are still among us. It appears that contrary to one's first impression, sex is not necessary (at least, not for reproduction). But if so, why do the vast majority of animal species reproduce sexually? Perhaps sexual reproduction is more enjoyable than the asexual varieties, but its biological advantage lies elsewhere. It comes from the fact that it assures a greater degree of genetic variability.

An amoeba that splits into two has created two replicas of its former self. Here natural selection has no differences to choose between, for the second amoeba can be neither better nor worse in its adaptation to the environment than the first, since the two are genetically identical.

Things are quite different in sexual reproduction. Here specialized cells, *sperm* and *ovum,* must join to form a fertilized egg, or *zygote,* which will then become a new individual. This procedure amounts to a kind of genetic roulette. To begin with, each parent donates only half of the genetic material: Within some limits, mere chance determines which genes are contained in any one sperm or ovum. Chance enters again to determine which sperm will join with which ovum. As a result, there will be inevitable differences among the offspring. Now natural selection can come into play, perhaps favoring the offspring with the sharper teeth or the one with the more sexually attractive display, which will then enhance the survival of the gene that produced these attributes.

SEXUAL CHOICE

■ For sexual reproduction to occur, sperm and ovum have to meet in the appointed manner, at the proper time and place. Many structures and behavior patterns have evolved to accomplish these ends. Our first concern is with those that underlie sexual choice and determine who mates with whom.

ADVERTISING ONE'S SEX

The first job of a would-be sexual partner is to proclaim his or her sex. Many animals have anatomical structures whose function is precisely that, for example, the magnificent tail feathers of the male peacock or the comb and wattle of the rooster (see Figure 10.9).

In humans, structural displays of sex differences are less pronounced, but they are present nonetheless. A possible example is the female breast, whose adipose tissue does not really increase the infant's milk supply. According to some ethologists, it evolved as we became erect and lost our reliance upon smell, a sense that provides the primary information about sex and sexual readiness in many mammals. Under the circumstances, there had to be other ways of displaying one's sex. The prominent breasts of the female may be one such announcement among hairless, "naked apes" (Morris, 1967).

10.9 Advertising one's sex *The comb and wattle of this barred rock rooster proclaim that he is a male. (Photograph by Garry D. McMichael, 1987/Photo Researchers)*

A

B

C

10.10 Courtship rituals *(A) The male bower bird tries to entice the female into an elaborate bower decorated with berries, shells, or whatever else may be available, such as colored clothespins. (B) Grebes engage in a complex aquatic ballet. (C) The male tern courts by feeding the female. (Photographs from left to right by Philip Green; Bob and Clara Calhoun/Bruce Coleman; Jeff Foott/Bruce Coleman)*

COURTSHIP RITUALS

Advertising one's intentions   In many animals, sexual display involves various species-specific behavior patterns, called **courtship rituals.** These are essentially ways of advertising one's amorous intentions. Some of these rituals are mainly a means to exhibit the structural sex differences, as in the male peacock spreading his tail feathers. Others are much more elaborate. Thus penguins bow deeply to each other while rocking from side to side, and certain grebes complete an elaborate aquatic ballet by exchanging gifts of seaweed (Figure 10.10).

In some species, courtship rituals may also involve alternating bouts of approach and withdrawal, of coy retreat and seductive flirtation. What accounts for these apparent oscillations between yes and no? There is an underlying conflict between attraction and fear; neither animal can really be sure that the other is not hostile. Each must therefore inform the other that its intentions are not aggressive. This is especially true of the male, who in many species performs various appeasement rituals that allay the female's fears.

Indicating one's species   Courtship rituals have a further function. They not only increase the likelihood that boy meets girl, but they virtually guarantee that the two will be of the same species. This is because these rituals are highly species-specific, as in the case of the gift-exchanging grebes. In effect they are a code whereby both members of the pair inform the other that they belong, say, to the duck species *anas platyrhynochos,* rather than to *bucephala clangula* or *tachyeres patachonicus,* or some other duck species that no self-respecting *anas platyrhynochos* would ever want to mate with. The effect of such species-specific courtship codes is that they make it more likely that the mating will produce fertile offspring. For, contrary to popular view, different species can interbreed if they are related closely enough. But the offspring of such "unnatural" unions is often infertile; an example is the mule, a result of crossing a horse with a donkey. Species-specific courtship rituals probably evolved to avoid such reproductive failures.

The evolutionary origin of courtship rituals   We've discussed the general function of courtship rituals, but what can we say about the evolutionary history of a particular ritual or display? Displays leave no fossils, so there is no direct method for reconstructing their biological past. One possible approach is to compare displays in related species. By noting their similarities and differences, the ethologist tries to reconstruct the evolutionary steps in their history, much as a comparative anatomist charts the family tree of fins, wings, and forelegs.

An example of how this comparative method works is an analysis of an odd courtship ritual in a predatory insect, the dancing fly (Kessel, 1955). At mating time, the male dancing fly secretes a little ball of silk which he brings to the female. She plays with this silk ball while the male mounts her and copulates. How did this ritual arise? The courtship patterns in a number of related species give a clue. Most flies of related species manage with a minimum of precopulatory fuss; the trouble is that the female may decide to eat the male rather than mate with him. However, if she is already eating a small prey animal, the male is safe. Some species have evolved a behavior pattern that capitalizes on this fact. The male catches a small insect and brings it to the female for her to eat while he mates with her. In still other species, the male first wraps the prey in a large silk balloon. This increases his margin of safety, for the female is kept busy unwrapping her present. The dancing fly's ritual is probably the last step in this evolutionary sequence. The male dancing fly wastes no time or energy in catching a prey animal, but simply brings an empty ball of silk, all wrapping and no present. Copulation can now proceed unimpeded since the female is safely occupied—perhaps the first creature in evolutionary history to realize that it is the thought and not the gift that matters (Figure 10.11).

WHO MAKES THE CHOICE

The preceding discussions have centered on the various factors that bring male and female together. But, interestingly enough, the two don't have an equal voice in the ultimate decision. In most species, it is the female who makes the final choice in deciding whether or not to mate. The biological reason is simple—the female shoulders the major cost of reproduction. If she is a bird, she supplies not only the ovum but also the food supply for the developing embryo. If she is a mammal, she carries the embryo within her body and later provides it with milk. In either case, her biological burden is vastly greater than the male's. If a doe's offspring fails to survive, she has lost a whole breeding season. In comparison, the stag's loss is minimal—a few minutes of his time and some easily replaced sperm cells. Under the circumstances, natural selection would favor the female who is particularly choosy about picking the best possible male, that is, the male whose genetic contribution will best ensure their offsprings' survival. From the male's point of view, the female seems coy or "plays hard to get." But in fact this is not just playacting, for, to the female, reproduction is a serious business with heavy biological costs (Trivers, 1972).

There are a few interesting exceptions. One example is the sea horse, whose young are carried in a brood pouch by the male (see Figure 10.12). In this animal, the male exhibits greater sexual caution and discrimination than the female. A similar effect is found in the phalarope, an arctic seabird whose eggs are hatched and whose chicks are fed by the male. Here a greater part of the biological burden falls on the male, and we should expect a corresponding increase in his sexual choosiness. This is just what happens. Among the phalaropes, the female does the wooing. She is brightly plumaged, and aggressively pursues the dull-colored, coyly careful male (Williams, 1966).

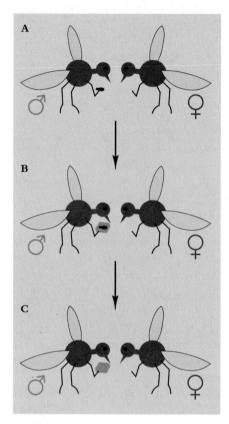

10.11   The evolution of courtship in dancing flies *(A) In some species, the male catches a prey animal and gives it to the female to eat during copulation; this keeps her busy so she is less likely to eat him. (B) In other species, the male first wraps the prey in a balloon of secreted silk. This keeps the female even busier, since she has to unwrap the prey. (C) Finally, in the dancing fly, the male gives the female a ball of silk without anything in it. (After Klopfer, 1974)*

REPRODUCTION AND TIMING

■ Once male and female have met, the next step is to arrange for the union of their respective sperm and ovum. Terrestrial animals have evolved a variety of sexual mechanics to accomplish this end. In general, the male introduces his sperm cells into the genital tract of the female, where the ovum is fertilized. The problem is synchronization. The sperm has to encounter a ready ovum, and the fertilized egg can develop only if it is provided with the appro-

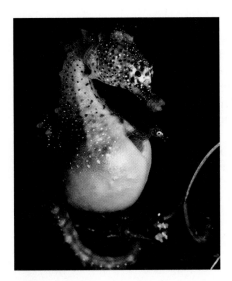

10.12 Male seahorse "giving birth" *(Photograph © Rudie H. Kuiter, Oxford Scientific Films)*

priate conditions. Under these circumstances, timing is of the essence. In birds and mammals, the timing mechanism depends on a complex feedback system between brain centers and hormones.

ANIMAL SEXUALITY AND HORMONES

Hormonal cycles Except for the primates, mammals mate only when the female is in heat, or *estrus.* For example, the female rat goes through a fifteen-hour estrus period every four days. At all other times, she will resolutely reject any male's advances. If he nuzzles her or tries to mount, she will kick and bite. But during estrus, the female responds quite differently to the male's approach. She first retreats in small hops, then stops to look back, and wiggles her ears provocatively (McClintock and Adler, 1978). Eventually, she stands still, her back arched, her tail held to the side, in all respects a willing sexual partner.

What accounts for the difference between the female's behavior during estrus and at other times? The crucial fact is a simple matter of reproductive biology. The time of estrus is precisely the time when the female's ova are ripe for fertilization. Evolution has obviously provided a behavioral arrangement that is exactly tuned to reproductive success.

Hormonal changes and behavior Hormonal changes can affect behavior dramatically. When male rats are castrated, they soon lose all sexual interest and capacity, as do female rats without ovaries. But sexual behavior is quickly restored by appropriate injections of male or female hormones, specifically testosterone and estrogen.

Many investigators believe that behavioral effects of hormones are caused by neurons in the hypothalamus that contain receptors with which certain hormone molecules from the bloodstream combine. When this occurs, it leads to neural changes in the hypothalamus that trigger sexual appetite and behavior. This hypothesis was tested by injecting minute quantities of various hormones into several regions of the hypothalamus. The total amounts were negligible and could hardly affect the overall hormone concentration in the blood. Was the hypothalamic sexual control system fooled by the local administration of the hormone, as is its thermostatic counterpart when it is locally cooled or heated (see Chapter 3)? It evidently was. A spayed female cat went into estrus when estrogen was implanted in her hypothalamus (Harris and Michael, 1964). Analogous effects have been obtained with **androgens** (that is, male hormones) administered to castrated male rats (Davidson, 1969; McEwen et al., 1982; Feder, 1984).

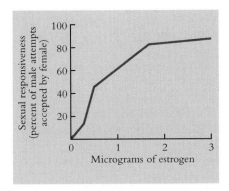

10.13 Estrogen and sexual behavior
The effect of estrogen injections on the sexual responsiveness of female rats was measured by the number of male attempts at mounting that were accepted by the female. The females' ovaries had been removed, so they could not produce estrogen themselves. The hormone was injected daily in the doses shown above. Sexual behavior was measured eight days after hormone treatment began. (After Bermant and Davidson, 1974)

HUMAN SEXUALITY AND HORMONES

The major difference between animal and human sexuality concerns the flexibility of sexual behavior. When does it occur, how, and with whom? Compared to animals, we are much less automatic in our sexual activities, much more varied, much more affected by prior experience. Human sexuality is remarkably plastic and can be variously shaped by experience and by cultural patterns (see Chapter 14).

The difference between animal and human sexual behavior is especially marked when we consider the effects of hormones. In rats and cats, sexual behavior is highly dependent upon hormone levels; castrated males and spayed females stop copulating a few months after the removal of their gonads (Figure 10.13). In humans, on the other hand, sexual activity may persist for years, even decades, after castration or ovariectomy, provided that the operation was performed after puberty (Bermant and Davidson, 1974).

The liberation from hormonal control is especially clear in human females. To be sure, women are subject to a physiological cycle, but this has relatively little impact on sexual behavior, at least when compared to the profound effects seen in animals. The female rat or cat is chained to an estrus cycle that commands her to be receptive during one period and prevents her from being so at all other times. There are no such fetters on the human female, who is capable of sexual behavior at any time during her cycle and also more capable of refusing.

Although we are evidently not the vassals of our hormones that most animals are, this is not to say that hormonal factors have no effect. Androgen injections into men with abnormally low hormone levels will generally increase their sex drive (Davidson, 1986).

EVOLUTION AND MATING SYSTEMS

■ In many species, the male and female part company after copulation and may very well never meet again. But in others, the partners remain together for a breeding season or even longer. In many cases, their arrangement involves *polygyny,* and the resulting family consists of one male, several females, and their various offspring. In a very few others, the mating system is *polyandry,* which works the other way around, with one female and several males. And in still others, the mating pattern is *monogamy,* with a reproductive partnership based on a special, more or less permanent tie between one male and one female.

MATING SYSTEMS IN ANIMALS

What accounts for the different mating systems found in different parts of the animal kingdom? A clue comes from the different patterns found in mammals and birds. Some 90 percent of all birds are monogamous: They mate and stay together throughout a breeding season. In contrast, more than 90 percent of all mammals are polygynous, with one male monopolizing a number of females. Why should this be so?

Evolutionary biologists seek the answer through some kind of evolutionary economics: The patterns that evolved are such as to maximize each individual's reproductive success. Consider the reproductive problem faced by birds. In many species, successful incubation requires both parents: one who sits upon the eggs, another who forages for food to nourish the bird that's sitting. After hatching, finding food for a nestful of hungry chicks may still require the full-time efforts of both birds. Under the circumstances, monogamy makes reproductive sense for both sexes: The father has to help the mother after she lays her eggs or else no chicks will survive into adulthood.

The situation is quite different for most mammals. Here there is no incubation problem; since the fetus grows within the mother's womb, she is still able to forage for her own food during the offspring's gestation. In addition, the mother has the exclusive job of feeding the offspring after birth, for only females can secrete the milk on which the infants live. Now the reproductive calculus leads to a different conclusion. The male does not have to invest time and effort in taking care of his offspring; instead, his best bet for maximizing his own reproductive success lies in mating with as many females as he possibly can. To accomplish this, he has to become attractive to females (by developing the most impressive antlers or whatever), and he has to win in the competition with many other males, all of whom have the identical goal. The end result is polygyny, with one successful male monopolizing a number of females.

Birds as monogamous *Birds tend to mate and stay together during a mating season as both parents are needed for successful incubation of their young. Here a black-bowed albatross male courts a female on the nest that will serve as home for their offspring. (Photograph by Robert W. Hernández/The National Audubon Society Collection/Photo Researchers)*

A   B

10.14 Sexual dimorphism *Polygynous
species tend to be dimorphic. (A) A Hooker's
sea lion bull with his harem. Note the bull's
markedly larger size. (Photograph by Francisco
J. Erize/Bruce Coleman Ltd.) (B) In Titi
monkeys, which are monogamous, males and
females are very similar in size and form.
(Photograph © Jim Clare, Partridge Films/
Oxford Scientific Films)*

There's an interesting anatomical correlate of mating arrangements in the animal kingdom. Almost invariably, polygyny is accompanied by **sexual dimorphism,** a pronounced anatomical difference in the size or bodily structures of the two sexes. The more polygynous the species, the more dimorphic it tends to be, with the males larger and often more ornamented than the females, as shown by the peacock's tail, the stag's antlers, and the male elephant seal's disproportionate size (Figure 10.14A). In contrast, monogamous species such as the gibbon show no such dimorphism (Figure 10.14B).

MATING PATTERNS IN HUMANS

A number of authors have tried to extend this general line of reasoning to account for the evolution of human sexual and mating behavior. One area of application concerns mate selection.

Mate selection   What determines who is a more desirable sexual or marital partner? Everyday observation suggests that in our society men and women choose on the basis of somewhat different criteria. One difference is the physical attractiveness of the partner, which seems to be more important to men than to women. Another is age: By and large, men seem to prefer younger women, women to prefer men who are older than they. Yet another difference concerns the social and financial status of the partner, which seems to matter much more to women than it does to men. A number of studies by David Buss have shown that these male-female differences are not unique to our own society, but are found throughout the world, in countries as diverse as China, India, France, Nigeria, and Iran. In all cases, the results were the same: In evaluating the desirability of a potential mate, physical attractiveness and youth were more important to men, signs of good financial and social prospects were more important to women (Buss, 1989, 1992; Buss and Barnes, 1986).

Buss and his co-workers argue that these findings are consistent with an evolutionary point of view. As they see it, the mating preferences of both men and women were shaped by natural selection. The male's preference for a young female grows out of the fact that younger women tend to be more fertile than older ones (physical attractiveness is here seen as an outward sign of health and youth), while the female's preference for males of higher social and economic status is based on the potential benefits these resources may bring to her offspring. While Darwinian concerns may not be particularly relevant in deter-

Polygynous tendencies in humans *The archetype of the philandering male is Don Juan, played here by John Barrymore. (From the 1926 film* Don Juan, *with Mary Astor; courtesy of the Motion Picture and Television Photo Archive)*

mining the behavior of modern men and women, they did produce the mating preferences in our long dead prehistoric ancestors. They have therefore become a built-in preference pattern, even though their original biological point may no longer be relevant today.

Is this the only possible interpretation of Buss's findings? Some authors suggest that the greater value women seem to place on the status of their prospective mates may be a matter of economics rather than biology. Throughout much of the world men exercise greater economic influence and control than women do. (Just why is another issue.) To the extent that this is so, the male's economic position becomes critical to women because it determines both her and her children's economic future. This line of reasoning suggests that the gender difference in mate selection should be smaller in societies in which women have achieved a greater degree of economic parity. Whether this is actually so is still a matter of debate (Wallen, 1989).

Mating systems Another issue concerns human mating patterns. Sociobiologically oriented theorists start out with the observation that humans are somewhat dimorphic: On average, the human male is about 10 percent larger than the female. Since such dimorphism is correlated with polygyny in animals, one might expect some similar tendency in humans.

To bolster their case, sociobiologists refer to a number of findings that in their view point in this direction. One is the anthropological evidence. A review of 185 cultures showed that the majority formally allowed polygyny. Only 16 percent of the cultures had monogamous marriage arrangements that permitted only one spouse to each partner (Ford and Beach, 1951).★ Related findings come from a number of studies of our own culture. These strongly suggest that, on average, men have a greater desire for a variety of sexual partners than do women (Symons, 1979).

Sociobiologists argue that these differences are ultimately rooted in our biological nature. In their view, men want greater sexual variety because for them it is reproductively adaptive: The more women they mate with, the more children they father. In contrast, women are much more cautious in evaluating potential sexual partners and more interested in a stable, familial relationship—a good reproductive strategy, since, as we've seen, the biological parental investment of a human female is greater than a male's. Such built-in patterns are presumably no longer relevant in a modern world in which birth control techniques have managed to uncouple sex from reproduction. But according to the sociobiologists, these remnants of our biological past are still with us just the same. They were once reproductively adaptive, and they continue to influence our behavior even though their adaptive role is diminished or altogether gone.

This sociobiological account has been severely challenged. One line of attack concerns the role of culture. Many critics argue that differences in sexual attitudes are a product of society rather than of biological predispositions and reflect a cultural rather than a built-in double standard. In their opinion, polygyny is a natural outgrowth of cultural conditions in which men are dominant and women are perceived as property. As to the differences in men's and women's desire for sexual variety, they regard it as a product of early social training: Boys are taught that many sexual conquests are a proof of "manliness," while girls are taught to value home and family and to seek a single partner.

Critics of the sociobiological approach have no quarrel with the sociobiologists' efforts to understand animal behavior from an evolutionary perspective.

★ Note that this 16 percent figure applies to 185 different *cultures,* indicating that 30 of these cultures were monogamous. Of course, the percentage would be much higher if it were based on *individuals* rather than cultures, since the monogamous modern cultures (including our own) are much more populous than most of the ones described in the anthropological literature.

Their critique is aimed at the attempt to extend these concepts to the human level. After all, terms such as *monogamy* have quite a different meaning when applied to, say, geese and humans. In geese, the term describes the fact that two parents stay together for one breeding season to hatch and raise their young; in humans, the term describes an arrangement that only makes sense in the context of a network of social and legal patterns. Evolution may have shaped many of our impulses and desires, but we simply don't know how these in turn have shaped the culture in which humans live and mate and bring up their children. Since this is so, it is rank speculation to assert that the reproductive economics that underlie an elephant seal's attempts to set up a harem are at bottom the same as those that account for the philandering found in some human males (Kitcher, 1985).

THE BIOLOGICAL BASIS OF LOVE: THE PARENT-CHILD BOND

FOCUS QUESTIONS

- Why do offspring tend to bond so strongly to their parent(s)? Why is the bond especially strong in birds and mammals?

There is another bond of love whose biological foundations are no less basic than those of the male-female tie—the relation between mother and child (and in many animals, the relation between father and child as well). In birds and mammals some kind of parental attachment is almost ubiquitous. In contrast to most fish and reptiles that lay eggs by the hundreds and then abandon them, birds and mammals invest in quality rather than quantity. They have fewer offspring, but they then see to it that most of their brood survives into maturity. They feed them, clean them, shelter them, and protect them during some initial period of dependency. While under this parental umbrella, the young animal can grow and become prepared for the world into which it must soon enter and can acquire some of the skills that will help it survive in that world. This period of initial dependency is longest in animals that live by their wits, such as monkeys and apes, and it is longest of all in humans.

THE INFANT'S ATTACHMENT TO THE MOTHER

In most birds and mammals, the young become strongly attached to their mother. Ducklings follow the mother duck, lambs the mother ewe, and infant monkeys cling tightly to the mother monkey's belly. In each case, separation leads to considerable stress: The young animals give piteous distress calls, and quack, bleat, and cry continuously until the mother returns. The biological function of this attachment is a simple matter of personal survival. This holds for humans as well as animals. For there is little doubt that in our early evolutionary history a motherless infant would probably have died an early death—of exposure, starvation, or predation. There are very few orphanages in nature.

The mechanisms that lead to this attachment will be discussed later (see Chapter 14). For now, we will only say that while some theorists believe that the main factor is the child's discovery that the mother's presence leads to the alleviation of hunger, thirst, and pain, there is strong evidence that the attach-

Orangutan mother and child (Photograph © Zefa Germany/The Stock Market, 1994)

ment is more basic than that. For the distress shown by the young—whether birds, monkeys, or humans—when they are separated from their mother occurs even when they are perfectly well-fed and housed. It appears that the infant's attachment to its mother is based on more than the satisfaction of the major bodily needs. The infant evidently comes predisposed to seek social stimulation, which is rewarding in and of itself.

THE MOTHER'S ATTACHMENT TO THE INFANT

For the infant, the function of the mother-child bond is simple personal survival. For the mother, the biological function is again a matter of survival, but for her, the survival is genetic rather than personal, for unless her young survive into adulthood, her genes will perish. But what are the mechanisms that produce the mother's attachment? (And in many species, the father's attachment too). Robins and gibbons behave like proper parents: They care for their young and protect them. But they surely don't do this because they realize that their failure to act in this way would lead to genetic extinction. The real reason must lie elsewhere. One possibility is that there are some built-in predispositions toward parental behavior. If such predispositions do exist, they would then be favored by natural selection.

There is good evidence that the young of many animal species have a set of built-in responses that elicit caretaking from the parents. To give only one example, many baby birds open their mouths as wide as they can as soon as the parent arrives at the nest. This "gaping" response is their means of begging for food (see Figure 10.15). Some species of birds have special anatomical signs that help to elicit a proper parental reaction. An example is the Cedar Waxwing, whose bright red mouth lining evidently provides a further signal to the parent: I'm young, hungry, and a Cedar Waxwing!

Child care in humans is obviously more complex and flexible than it is in Cedar Waxwings, but it too has biological foundations. The mother-child relation grows out of a number of built-in reaction patterns, of child to mother and mother to child. The human infant begins life with a few relevant reflex patterns, including some that help him find the mother's nipple and suck at it once it is found. He also has an essentially innate signal system through which he tells

10.15 Gaping in young birds (A) The gaping response of the young yellow warbler serves as a built-in signal that elicits the parents' feeding behavior. (Photograph by John Shaw/Bruce Coleman) (B) Cuckoos are parasites who lay their eggs in other birds' nests. The figure shows a young cuckoo being fed by its foster parent, a reed warbler. The young cuckoo, at about twenty-four hours old, instinctively ejects any eggs or young of its host from the nest, so that it alone is the sole occupant. Its large orange-red gaping mouth provides a powerful stimulus in eliciting feeding. The unwitting warbler will continue to feed the cuckoo even when it has grown to several times the "parent's" size. (Courtesy of Ian Wyllie, Monks Wood Experiment Station)

A   B

B

10.16   The stimulus features of "babyness"   *"Cute" characteristics of the "baby schema" are common to humans and a number of animals. (A) These include a rounded head shape, protruding forehead, and large eyes below the middle of the head (after Lorenz, 1943). (B) The Disney character Mickey Mouse became "cuter" over the years by subscribing more and more to the baby "schema," with his eyes and head becoming larger. (© Walt Disney Productions)*

A

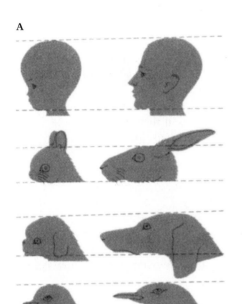

the mother that he is in distress: He cries. Analogous ***distress calls*** are found in many animals, for when the young chirp, bleat, mew, or cry, the mother immediately runs to their aid and comforts them.

According to ethologists, evolution has further equipped the infant with a set of stimulus features that function as innate releasers of parental, and especially maternal, feelings. The cues that define "babyness" include a large, protruding forehead, large eyes, an upturned nose, chubby cheeks, and so on. Endowed with these distinctive properties, the baby looks "cute" and "cuddly," something to be picked up, fussed over, and taken care of. The case is similar for the young of various animals who share aspects of the same "baby schema." Various commercial enterprises exploit these facts by devoting themselves to the deliberate manufacture of cuteness. Dolls and Walt Disney creatures are designed to be babied by children, while certain lap dogs are especially bred to be babied by adults (Figure 10.16).

Nature has provided the infant with yet another trick to disarm even the stoniest of parental hearts: the smile. In some fashion, smiling may begin within the first month; it is often considered a built-in signal by which humans tell each other "I wish you well. Be good to me."

The evolutionary origin of the human smile   *According to some authors, the human smile grew out of the "fear grin." This is an appeasement display found in monkeys and other primates, which usually signifies submission but may also indicate reassurance when directed by a dominant animal to a subordinate (van Hooff, 1972). (A) The fear grin in a young chimpanzee. (Photograph © Tom McHugh/Photo Researchers, Inc., 1978) (B) A smile in an infant. (Photograph © Luis Castaneda/The Image Bank)*

A

B

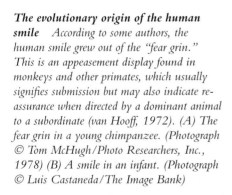

COMMUNICATING MOTIVES

FOCUS QUESTIONS

■ How do ethologists determine the meaning of a display?

■ What human displays appear to be universal? What evidence supports the view that such displays are innate?

The preceding discussion has given ample testimony that many animal species exist within a social framework in much the same way that humans do. What one creature does often has a crucial effect on the behavior of another of its own kind. As we have seen, the major means of exerting such social influences is the signaling display.

EXPRESSIVE MOVEMENTS: ANIMAL DISPLAY

■ Displays represent a simple mode of communication whereby animals inform each other of what they are most likely to do in the immediate future. The crab waves its claws, and the wolf bares its fangs; these threat messages may save both sender and receiver from bodily harm if the message is heeded.

How do ethologists determine what message is conveyed by a given display? Since the sender is an animal, they cannot ask it directly. They can try, however, to infer the message by noting the correlation between a given display and the animal's behavior just before and after its occurrence. For example, if a certain posture is generally followed by attack, then it is usually called a threat display; if it is usually followed by mating, it is probably a courtship signal, and so on.

Some ethologists interpret such correlations between displays and subsequent behavior by assuming that in effect displays communicate the animal's present motive state—its readiness to fight or to mate, its need for food or parental attention, and so forth. For this reason, displays are sometimes said to "express" the animal's inner state and are therefore described as *expressive movements.*

THE EXPRESSION OF EMOTIONS IN HUMANS

■ In humans, built-in social displays are relegated to a lesser place. After all, we have the much richer communication system provided by human language. But even so, we do possess a set of displays that tells others something about our feelings and needs—our various emotional expressions.

THE UNIVERSALITY OF EMOTIONAL EXPRESSIONS

Humans have a sizable repertory of emotional expressions, most of them conveyed by the face. We smile, laugh, weep, frown, snarl, and grit our teeth. Are any of these expressive patterns our human equivalent of displays? If so, they should be universal to all humans and innately determined (Ekman, 1973; Ekman and Oster, 1979; Fridlund, Ekman, and Oster, 1983).

In one study, American actors posed in photographs to convey such emotions as fear, anger, and happiness. These pictures were then shown to members of

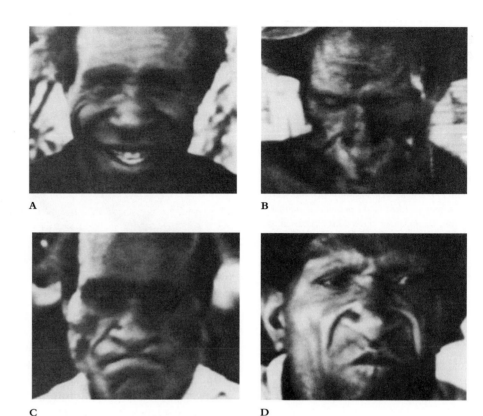

10.17 Attempts to portray emotion by New Guinea tribesmen *Acting out emotions appropriate to various situations: (A) "Your friend has come and you are happy"; (B) "Your child has died"; (C) "You are angry and about to fight"; (D) "You see a dead pig that has been lying there for a long time." (© Paul Ekman, 1971)*

A

B

C

D

different cultures, both literate (Swedes, Japanese, Kenyans) and preliterate (members of an isolated New Guinea tribe barely advanced beyond Stone Age culture). When asked to identify the portrayed emotion, all groups came up with quite similar judgments. The results were much the same when the procedure was reversed. The New Guinea tribesmen were asked to portray the emotions appropriate to various simple situations such as happiness at the return of a friend, grief at the death of a child, and anger at the start of a fight. Photographs of their performances were then shown to American college students who readily picked out the emotions the tribesmen had tried to convey (Figure 10.17).

These results indicate that some emotional expressions may be common to all humans. This conclusion fits observations of children born blind. These children cry, smile, and laugh under essentially the same conditions that elicit these reactions in sighted children. In fact, much the same is true even of children born both blind and deaf. It would be hard to argue that these children had learned the emotional expressions considering that their sensory avenues of both sight and sound had been blocked off from birth (see Figure 10.18).

At least in part, such built-in expressions may serve a function similar to animal displays. They act as social signals by which we communicate our inner states to others, a way of saying what we are likely to do next.

THE ROLE OF CULTURE

These findings do not imply that smiling and other emotional expressions are unaffected by cultural conventions. According to some accounts, Melanese

A

B

10.18 The smile in blind children *(A) Smile in a child born blind. (Courtesy of The Lighthouse, N.Y.C.) (B) Smiling in a child born both blind and deaf. (Photograph © Tommy Thompson, 1992, Courtesy of Florida School for the Deaf and Blind, St. Augustine, Florida)*

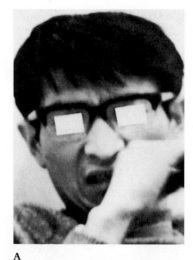 

A   **B**

10.19 Spontaneous facial expressions (A) A Japanese and (B) an American student watched a film that depicted a rather gruesome scene. The figure shows their expressions when they were alone. Under these conditions, their facial expressions were virtually identical. But when they watched in the presence of another person, the Japanese masked his expression of unpleasant emotions more than the American did. (From Ekman and Friesen, 1975)

chieftains frown fiercely when greeting each other at a festive occasion, and Samurai mothers are said to have smiled upon hearing that their sons had fallen in battle (Klineberg, 1940). But such facts do not disprove the claim that facial expressions are built-in social signals; they only show that such signals can be artificially masked and modified. How and when such artifice comes into play, however, depends on the culture.

Some evidence for this view comes from studies in which American and Japanese subjects were presented with a harrowing documentary film of a primitive puberty rite. As they watched the film, their facial expressions were recorded with a hidden camera. The results showed that when alone, the facial reactions of the Japanese and American subjects were virtually identical (see Figure 10.19). But the results were quite different when the subject watched the film in the company of a white-coated experimenter. Now the Japanese looked more polite and smiled more than the Americans (Ekman, 1977; for further discussion, see Fridlund, 1990).

SOCIAL COGNITION IN PRIMATES

FOCUS QUESTIONS

- What evidence suggests that knowledge of kinship and social relations is not restricted to humans?

- Might other primates have a "theory of mind"?

Human social life obviously involves both motives and cognition (as we will discuss in the next chapter). Our lives revolve around what we desire from and of other people, be they friends or enemies, strangers or lovers, parents or children, but also around what we know and think about them. Some recent studies of monkeys and apes indicate that there are many forerunners of such social cognitions in the animal world.

Consider the vervet, a small monkey that lives in groups of some fifteen animals or so and that makes its home primarily in the savanna woodlands of Africa. To a vervet, the most important thing in the world—right after not being eaten by an eagle or a leopard—is other vervets. Vervet monkeys can recognize other vervets in their troop by sight and sound. A demonstration comes

10.20 *Understanding kinship relationships in primates* *This group of female vervet monkeys is looking at the mother of an infant who just gave an alarm call. Apparently, they know who in their group is related to whom. (Photograph courtesy of Dorothy Cheney)*

from some elegant field studies performed by Dorothy Cheney and Robert Seyfarth. Cheney and Seyfarth set up camp near several vervet groups in Southern Kenya, tape recorded the screams of many of the vervets, and then played them back to their fellows at strategic times. On one occasion, they broadcast the distress cry of a juvenile to its mother and two other nearby females who also had offspring in the group. At the time all of the offspring were out of sight. The first result concerned the mother who looked in the direction of the (hidden) loud speaker and approached it, indicating that she recognized her screaming youngster's voice. More interesting yet was the behavior of the other two females. They did not look at the loudspeaker, nor did they look at each other, but instead looked *at the mother.* This suggests that they not only recognized the child's voice, but also recognized whose child it was, as if to say "It's *your* kid. So what are *you* going to do about it?" (see Figure 10.20; Cheney and Seyfarth, 1982).

Evidence of this sort indicates that monkeys have a considerable degree of knowledge of the kinship relationships in their group (e.g., Dasser, 1988). Further studies suggest that they also know a great deal about the dominance relationships in their group—who's up, who's down, and who's in-between. As a result, they can pretty well predict who's likely to chase or cuff them and who is not, and they can then behave according to these beliefs. But do monkeys think that other monkeys also have thoughts and beliefs? To ask this question is to ask whether these animals have what has often been called a "theory of mind," that is, whether they attribute states of mind such as beliefs and desires to others (Premack, 1978, 1988; Fodor, 1992; see also Chapter 4).★ One way of determining whether they do is to see whether they can use deliberate deception to induce a false belief in another individual. There is a suggestion that some monkeys and apes are intelligent enough (and immoral enough) to do so.

Some suggestive evidence comes from several anecdotes about vervet monkeys. On one occasion, two vervet troops clashed at the boundary of their two territories. One of the two battling groups was about to lose when one of the combatants suddenly ran up a nearby tree and gave a leopard alarm call. In actual fact, there was no leopard around, but every one of the vervets acted as if there was and frantically raced for the nearest tree. The result was a return to the status quo, with defeat averted and the old borders restored. The alarm caller's deception may have saved the day (Cheney and Seyfarth, 1990).

More compelling evidence comes from a laboratory study in which a chimpanzee saw a desirable piece of fruit being placed in one of two containers while the other was left empty. Unfortunately, the containers were too far removed to be reached through the bars of the cage. As a result, the apes had to rely on the good offices of an attendant who stood outside the cage in easy reach of the containers. The trouble was that this attendant had not been there when the food was placed, so that he didn't know which of the two containers held the food. As a result, there was only one way in which the chimpanzees could get the food: They somehow had to tell the attendant—by looking at the correct container or by pointing with hand or foot—which of the two containers was the correct one.

After a while, the animals learned to do this rather well, but then the experimenter introduced an unkind complication. He now used two attendants, one "good," the other "bad." The good one was all a chimpanzee could possibly ask for: Whenever he found food in a container, he gave it to the ape. The bad attendant was a self-seeking egotist: Whenever he found food in a container, he ate it himself. This eventually led the chimpanzees to develop a different strate-

★ We will later encounter that same question raised about children below four or four-and-a-half years of age (see Chapter 13).

gy. They now gave proper signals to the good but not to the bad attendant. One of four chimpanzees went further and actively misled the bad attendant by pointing to the *incorrect* container with her foot (Woodruff and Premack, 1981; for some complicating evidence, see Premack, 1988). To the extent that these animals could deliberately deceive another individual, they demonstrated that they believed others have beliefs and that these beliefs may be (and in the case of the bad attendant, should be) different from their own. It is perhaps ironic that a certain level of immorality requires a fairly high degree of intellectual comprehension: Adam and Eve could not lie until *after* they had eaten from the tree of knowledge.

Such findings suggest that chimpanzees (and perhaps monkeys too) have something like a theory of mind. But there is little doubt that this chimpanzoid theory is rather primitive and doesn't begin to approach the complexities of our own adult conceptions of how other people think, feel, and believe. Our own human social interactions depend not just on what any of us think and believe about other people, but also on what we think or believe they think and believe about us. Such mutual cognitions are a commonplace of everyday life (e.g., "I think most of my acquaintances like me, and they probably think I like them too, but Joe and Jane seem to feel otherwise, and I don't really know why . . ." and so on). To us, the fact that others have thoughts and wishes and beliefs is an axiom. As we will see in the next chapter, it is an axiom from which most of our social behavior flows directly.

SELF-SACRIFICE AND ALTRUISM

FOCUS QUESTIONS

■ How do sociobiologists explain altruism?

■ What might explain altruism toward non-kin?

The preceding pages have provided ample evidence that animals are certainly social: They fight and compete with each other, mate, reproduce, and communicate. Some even make judgments about what their fellows think and use that information to their own advantage. Still further work by ethologists suggests that under certain conditions they may even behave as if they were "unselfish altruists."

It's of course well known that many animals go to considerable lengths to defend their offspring. Various birds have evolved characteristic ways of feigning injury such as dropping one wing and paddling around in circles to draw a predator away from their nests (see Figure 10.21). On the face of it, such acts appear heroically unselfish, for the parents court the danger that the predator will seize them. But here again we come up with the difference between personal and genetic survival. For what seems unselfish from the vantage of the individual looks different from a biological point of view (Wilson, 1975). The mother bird who does not divert a potential attacker may very well live longer because she has played it safe. But from an evolutionary perspective what counts is not her own survival but the survival of her genes. And these are more likely to perish if she flies off to safety; while she hides in the bushes, the marauding cat will eat her chicks. As a result, she will have fewer offspring to whom she can pass on her genes, including the very gene or genes that underlie her maternal indifference. Those of her offspring that do survive will in turn have fewer offspring, and so on, until her genetic attributes disappear.

10.21 A misleading display *In feigning injury, the killdeer, a small American bird, runs and flies erratically from predators that approach its nest, often flopping about as if it has a broken wing. (Photograph by Wayne Lankinen/Bruce Coleman)*

10.22 Alarm call *Ground squirrels give
alarm calls when they sense a nearby predator.
Such alarm calls are more likely to be given
by females than males. The females usually
have close relatives living nearby. As a result,
their alarm call is more likely to benefit genetically related rather than unrelated individuals,
which suggests that it is based on kin selection. (Photograph by Georg D. Lepp/Bio-
Tec Images)*

ALTRUISM IN ANIMALS

■ Seen in this light, parental self-sacrifice can be understood in evolutionary
terms. Can a similar analysis be applied to unselfish acts that benefit individuals other than one's own children? Such apparently altruistic acts are found
in various animal species.★ A case in point is the warning signal given off by
many species at the approach of a predator (see Figure 10.22). When a robin
sees a hawk overhead, it gives an ***alarm call,*** a special cry that alerts all members
of the flock and impels them to seek cover. This alarm call is based on a built-in,
inherited tendency and is essentially unlearned. All robins emit this cry when in
danger, and they do so even if raised in complete isolation from their fellows.
There is no doubt that this alarm benefits all robins who hear it. They crouch
low and hide, so their chances of escape are enhanced. But what does it gain the
bird who sounds the alarm? Doesn't it place him in greater danger by increasing
the likelihood that the hawk will detect *him?* Why does the robin play the hero
instead of quietly stealing away and leaving his fellows to their fate? There are
several possible factors, each of which may play a role.

ENLIGHTENED SELF-INTEREST

One possibility is that this act of avian heroism is not as unselfish as it seems, for
it may well increase the warner's own chance of personal survival in the long
run. If a particular robin spies a hawk and remains quiet, there is a greater
chance that some bird in the flock will be captured, most likely another bird.
But what about tomorrow? A hawk who has seized a prey in a particular location will probably return to the very same place in search of another meal. And
this meal may be the very same robin who originally minded his own business
and stayed uninvolved (Trivers, 1971).

KIN SELECTION

There is another alternative. Let us assume that our heroic robin is unlucky, is
seized by the hawk, and dies a martyr's death. While this act may have caused
the robin to perish as an individual, it may well have served to preserve some of
that bird's genes. This may be true even if none of the birds in the flock are the
hero's own offspring. They may be relatives who carry some of his genes, brothers and sisters who share half of the same genes, or nieces and nephews who
share one-fourth. If so, the alarm call may have saved several relatives who carry
the alarm-calling gene and who will pass it on to future generations of robins.
From an evolutionary point of view, the alarm call had survival value—if not for
the alarm caller or its offspring, then for the alarm-calling gene (Hamilton,
1964; Maynard-Smith, 1965).

According to this view, altruistic behavior will evolve if it promotes the survival of the individual's kin. This ***kin-selection*** hypothesis predicts that unselfish
behavior should be more common among relatives than unrelated individuals.
There is some evidence that this is indeed the case. Certain deer snort loudly
when alarmed, which alerts other deer that are nearby. Groups of does tend to
be related; bucks, who disperse when they get old enough, are less likely to be
related. The kin-selection hypothesis would then predict that does should be
more likely to give the alarm snort than bucks. This is indeed what happens.
Similar results have been obtained for various other species (Hirth and
McCullough, 1977; Sherman, 1977).

★ In modern biological usage, the term *altruism* is reserved for cases in which the good deed
benefits neither the doers nor their own offspring.

RECIPROCAL ALTRUISM

There is yet another possible mechanism that leads to biologically unselfish acts—*reciprocal altruism.* Some animals—and we may well be among them—may have a built-in Golden Rule: Do unto others, as you would have them do unto you (or unto your genes). If one individual helps another, and that other later reciprocates, the ultimate upshot is a benefit to both. For example, male baboons sometimes help each other in aggressive encounters, and the one who received help on one occasion is more likely to come to the other's assistance later on (Packer, 1977).

A built-in predisposition toward reciprocity may well be one of the biological foundations of altruism in some animals (and perhaps ourselves as well). If the original unselfish act doesn't exact too great a cost—in energy expended or in danger incurred—then its eventual reciprocation will yield a net benefit to both parties. A tendency toward reciprocal altruism of this kind, however, presupposes relatively stable groups in which individuals recognize one another. It also presupposes some safeguards against "cheating," accepting help without reciprocating. One such safeguard might be a link between a disposition toward altruism and a disposition to punish cheaters (Trivers, 1971).

ALTRUISM IN HUMANS

■ There is little doubt that humans are capable of considerable self-sacrifice. Soldiers volunteer for suicide missions, and religious martyrs burn at the stake. In addition to these awesome deeds of heroism are the more common acts of altruism—sharing food and money, offering help, and the like. Can such human acts of altruism be understood in the biological terms that apply to the alarm calls of birds and monkeys?

THE SOCIOBIOLOGISTS' VIEW

According to Edward Wilson, the founder of sociobiology, the answer is yes, at least to some extent. While Wilson emphasizes the enormous variations among human social systems, he notes that there are certain common themes which he regards as grounded in our genetic heritage. Of these, the most important is based on kinship. Wilson and other sociobiologists suggest that, by and large, we will be most altruistic to our closest relatives. According to Wilson, the person who risks death in battle or through martyrdom probably helps to ensure the survival of the group of which he is a member—and thus of his own genes, since this group probably includes his own kin. As with the robin, the individual hero may die, but his genes will survive (Wilson, 1975, 1978).

Sociobiologists believe that this position is supported by the fact that kinship is of considerable importance in just about all human societies, as attested to by the elaborate terms used to describe the precise nature of kinship relations: brother, sister, uncle, aunt, cousin, second-cousin-once-removed, and so on. At least in our culture, the likelihood that one person will make a sacrifice for another increases the closer the two are genetically related to each other (Essock-Vitale and McGuire, 1985.

SOME PROBLEMS OF FACT AND THEORY: BIOLOGY OR CULTURE?

This sociobiological analysis of human altruism is highly controversial. To begin with, studies of different cultures show that the degree to which relatives help

Braving death for an ideal *During the Civil War, a vastly outnumbered group of black Union soldiers attacked an impregnable fortress held by the Confederate forces, suffering enormous casualties. They were willing to die for the abolition of slavery and to show that blacks are just as capable of sacrificing themselves for an ideal as whites are. From the 1989 film* Glory, *directed by Edward Zwick. (Photograph courtesy of Photofest)*

Human martyrdom *In France's darkest hour, Joan of Arc arose to lead the French against the British during the Hundred Years' War. After several brilliant successes, she was finally captured and burned at the stake by the British. Can we really attribute the actions of a Joan of Arc to kin selection or reciprocal altruism? (From the 1957 film* Saint Joan, *directed by Otto Preminger and starring Jean Seberg; photo courtesy of Photofest)*

each other is not a simple function of their genetic closeness. It often depends much more on whether individuals *regard* themselves as close and related than on whether they actually are so genetically. Some evidence comes from the study of several cultures in which newly married couples live in the groom's father's household and eventually create an extended family with many brothers, sisters, uncles, aunts, and so on. A young boy in this family will get to know his paternal uncles—they will live in the same hut or one nearby. But he won't have much to do with his maternal uncles; they stayed behind in his maternal grandfather's household. Genetically, he is of course equally close to both, but when questioned about whom he is more likely to help or be helped by, he immediately says that it is the paternal uncle, whom he has known and lived with all his life (Sahlins, 1976).

Critics of sociobiology feel that these and similar findings show that human social behavior depends crucially on culture rather than genetics. To understand human altruism, we have to understand it in its own social terms. The Polynesian boy who feels close to his paternal but not his maternal uncle is responding to kinship as his culture describes it, rather than as something defined by his genes. The same holds for self-sacrifice. The ancient Romans fell on their swords when defeated, not to save their brothers' genes, but to save their honor. The early Christians defied death because of a religious belief rather than to maintain a particular gene pool. We cannot comprehend the ancient Romans without considering their concept of honor, nor can we explain the martyrdom of the early Christians without reference to their belief in the hereafter.

To sum up, Wilson and other sociobiologists have argued that human social behaviors such as altruism and self-sacrifice are at bottom biological adaptations that guarantee the survival of the reproductively fittest—in principle no different from the social patterns found in primates and in lower animals. The critics of this view do not deny the powerful influence of biology on human behavior. But they insist that human social behavior is so thoroughly infused by culture— by moral and religious beliefs, by customs, by art—that the analogy to animal behavior is more misleading than informative. This issue is still being hotly debated in the fields of psychology, biology, and anthropology, and we cannot solve it here. But we will return to it when we discuss altruistic behavior as it is studied by modern social psychologists (see Chapter 12).

SOME PROBLEMS OF ETHICS

There is a final issue that concerns some of the ethical implications of the sociobiological position. Suppose the sociobiologists' assertions about humans are true—that men are biologically predisposed toward philandering and women toward coyness, and that all of us are genetically biased in favor of our own kin. All of these suppositions are vehemently disputed (see, for example, Lewontin, Rose, and Kamin, 1984; Kitcher, 1985, 1987). But for the sake of argument, let's assume that they are true. What then? Does this mean that these (supposed) biological facts justify sexism or vindicate the double standard or support a blind hostility toward everyone who is different from ourselves? The answer is an emphatic no. If the facts are as the sociobiologists claim they are (and we have repeatedly said that this is highly debatable), then philandering may be a biological predisposition in males and may be in that sense *natural*. But what is natural isn't necessarily good. A preference for sweets is biologically built in and has a perfectly understandable evolutionary function, for what's sweet is generally also nutritious. But in these days of caloric plenty, most of us learn to curb our natural appetite for sweets or suffer various unpleasant consequences. The same surely holds for whatever callous and self-seeking built-in tendencies we may have but that as civilized men and women we must morally deplore.

This point is recognized by a number of sociobiologists. Sarah Hrdy, an authority on primate behavior, stated it succinctly by quoting the character played by Katharine Hepburn in the film *The African Queen:* "Nature, Mr. Allnutt, is what we were put on this earth to rise above!" (Hrdy, 1988, p. 126).

ETHOLOGY AND HUMAN NATURE

Over three hundred years have passed since Hobbes described the "war of all against all," which he regarded as the natural state of all humankind. We are still far from having a definite description of our basic social nature. But at least we know that Hobbes's solutions are wrong or oversimplified. Humans are not built to be solitary. Other people are a necessary aspect of our lives, and a tendency to interact with others is built into us from the very outset. What holds for humans holds for most animals as well. The robin is pre-programmed to deal with other robins, the baboon with other baboons. Some of these interactions are peaceful, while others are quarrelsome. What matters is that there is always some intercourse between like and like. This social intercourse is an essential aspect of each creature's existence, as shown by an elaborate repertory of built-in social reactions that govern reproduction, care of offspring, and intraspecies competition at virtually all levels of the animal kingdom. No man is an island; neither is any other animal.

QUESTIONS FOR CRITICAL THINKING

1. How is Darwin's view of fitness similar to—and different from—Hobbes's view?

2. A few small animals reproduce asexually (they clone themselves) in the spring and summer, then reproduce sexually in the fall when the weather gets colder. How is their behavior consistent with the presumed advantage of sexual reproduction?

3. What nonevoluntary factors can explain human mate preferences?

4. If sociobiologists are correct about biological influences on human behavior, then to what degree can we modify culturally our sex roles, mate preferences, aggressiveness, and relations to our young?

SUMMARY

1. Are humans inherently asocial and self-centered? Thomas Hobbes believed that they are. An alternative position, championed by Charles Darwin among others, is that both humans and animals have built-in social dispositions. The study of such innate bases of social reactions has largely focused on animal behavior and has been undertaken within the domain of *ethology*. An influential theoretical approach is *sociobiology*, which tries to explain the emergence of social behaviors in both animals and humans within the framework of evolutionary principles.

2. Most animals exhibit various *species-specific* behaviors, which were once thought to be based on *fixed-action patterns* that are triggered by *releasing stimuli*. An example is the begging response of newly hatched herring gulls. Many of these species-specific reactions are *displays,* which serve as communicative signals.

3. One realm of social behavior that has important biological roots is *aggression,* a term generally reserved for conflict between members of the same species. To secure a supply of resources for themselves and their descendants, many animals (usually the males) stake out a *territory* that they then defend. Various methods have evolved to keep aggression within bounds, including territoriality, which separates potential combatants in space, and *dominance hierarchies,* which separate them in social status. Further limitations on aggression include *threat* and *appeasement displays.*

4. While there are certain parallels between aggression among animals and among humans—for example, territoriality and *personal space*—there is reason to suppose that most of the underlying mechanisms are different in that human aggression depends in great part upon learning and culture.

5. Built-in predispositions figure heavily in various aspects of sexual reproduction. Various displays advertise the animal's sex, its readiness to mate, and its species. Examples are *courtship rituals,* which are highly species-specific and tend to prevent animals from interbreeding with members of other species.

6. Sexual behavior is partially controlled by several sex hormones. Female animals (other than humans) only mate when they are in *estrus,* the time during which the ovum is ready for fertilization. In humans, sexual behavior is more flexible and less dependent upon hormonal conditions than it is in other animals. Thus, human females are capable of sexual behavior at any time in their cycle.

7. Animals have evolved a number of different mating systems. In some, the pattern is *polygyny,* with one male and several females. In others, it is *monogamy,* with a more or less permanent tie between one male and one female. In a very few others, it is *polyandry,* with one female and several males. According to sociobiologists, the mating systems that evolved are such as to maximize each participant's reproductive success. Thus birds tend to be monogamous, while mammals are likely to be polygynous. Polygyny is generally accompanied by *sexual dimorphism,* a pronounced anatomical difference in the size or bodily structures of the two sexes.

8. The majority of human cultures practice (or practiced) polygyny, and evidence from our own culture suggests that men have a greater desire for sexual variety than do women and that men prefer younger women while women prefer older, successful men. Viewed from a sociobiological perspective, these differences are rooted in our biological nature. Seen from a cultural perspective, they are the product of early social training, which in turn is an outgrowth of cultural and economic conditions.

9. In birds and mammals innate factors are an important determinant of another bond, that between parents—primarily mothers—and offspring. Parental reactions are elicited, at least in part, by various stimulus releasers produced by the young, such as *distress calls* and the human infant's smile.

10. The key to most animal social behavior is communication by display. Since displays communicate an animal's present motive state, they are often described as *expressive movements.* Displays are found in humans as well as animals. The major example is emotional expression. Many facial expressions seem to be partially based on built-in predispositions; one demonstration is smiling in children born blind. But such facial expressions are also affected by cultural conventions and can be voluntarily inhibited or "faked."

11. There has been some recent interest in *social cognition* in animals, especially monkeys and apes. These animals have a considerable knowledge of the kinship and dominance relations in their group and may have some primitive version of a "theory of mind" that allows them to attribute beliefs and desires to others.

12. Some inherited behavior patterns, such as the *alarm calls* of certain birds, seem to be biologically unselfish, since they don't directly contribute to the survival of the individuals or their offspring. The survival value of these behaviors often depends on *kin selection,* for such acts may save a number of relatives who carry the "altruist's" genes. Another mechanism that may lead to biologically unselfish acts is *reciprocal altruism.* Some authors have tried to explain human altruism in similar sociobiological terms. This attempt, like other attempts by sociobiologists to interpret human social patterns based on analogies to animal behavior, is highly controversial.

CHAPTER

11

SOCIAL COGNITION AND EMOTION

I n the preceding chapter, we considered the built-in bases of social behavior. Toward that end, we turned to the animal kingdom and looked at social interactions among robins and grebes, rats and baboons. None of these animals lives in isolation from its fellows, and their interactions tell us something about the biological foundations upon which all social life rests, whether in animals or ourselves. Both animals and humans compete in aggressive encounters, court and mate, provide for their young, and have a repertoire of built-in displays. But these similarities aside, there are of course enormous differences. While the social behavior of animals is relatively rigid and inflexible, that of humans is greatly affected by learning—through personal experience as well as the experience of previous generations. And our social interactions are vastly more complex than those of any other animal.

In part, this is simply because human social behavior occurs within an elaborate web of cultural patterns. Unlike rats or baboons, we attend school, vote, buy stock, go to church, and join protest demonstrations. These and countless other actions only make sense because of a whole set of institutions around which most of our social life is organized.

But in addition there are cognitive factors. For most of our social interactions depend on how we understand the situation in which they occur. As we've seen, something of that sort also goes on at the animal level, especially among the primates, who show a considerable degree of social understanding and may even possess some forerunners of a theory of (see Chapter 10). But their level of social cognition—surprising as it may be—can't begin to compare to the richness and complexity of our own. A monkey's theory of mind is at best a mere rudiment of a human's. The world we live in is built upon an intricate network of interlocking social cognitions. We take for granted that others have desires and beliefs, and know that they in their turn know that we too have desires and beliefs. This cognitive mutuality can reach dizzying heights, as in the calculations of a poker player musing about an opponent: "I think that he thinks that I think that he's bluffing."

The contrast between human and animal social behavior becomes even clearer when we turn away from primates to other animals, such as birds. Take the herring gull, which pecks at its neighbor when it comes too close. This is sometimes regarded as analogous to our desire to maintain our personal space, and in some ways it may be. But the differences between their actions and ours are no less striking than the similarities. Consider personal space in a railroad car. Suppose you are all alone in the car and a stranger approaches and sits next to you. Your reaction will depend upon your interpretation of his action. Is it an attempt to start a conversation, an unwelcome intrusion, a sexual invitation? Or is it simply a response to the fact that all other seats in the car happen to be covered with soot? The point is that humans don't respond to other people's actions automatically; they respond to those actions as they interpret them. The herring gull has no such subtle problems; any other gull that invades its personal space has to be repelled and that is that.

We react to any situation as we understand it to be The misunderstandings that may occur can form the plot of tragedy as well as comedy. In Shakespeare's Othello, *the hero strangles his wife because he wrongly believes she committed adultery. In the movie* Tootsie, *the hero disguises himself as a woman with resulting complications in his social relations. (Left: from a production of* Othello *at the 1987 Stratford Festival in Ontario, Canada, with Howard Rollins and Wenna Shaw; photograph by Michael Cooper. Right: from the 1982 film* Tootsie, *with Dustin Hoffman and Jessica Lange; courtesy of Photofest)*

The purpose of this chapter is to give some sense of the complexity of social cognition in humans. We will organize our account around one of the central questions of modern social psychology: How does an individual interpret social events and how does this interpretation affect his or her actions?

SOCIAL COGNITION AND SOCIAL REALITY

FOCUS QUESTIONS

- What did Asch's experiment reveal about the confidence we have in our own beliefs? Given the findings from social comparison research, would subjects have reacted differently had Asch's stimuli been ambiguous?
- What is cognitive dissonance?

An individual's response to a social situation depends upon what he understands that situation to be. Romeo killed himself in front of Juliet's tomb because he thought that Juliet was dead; had he known that she was only drugged, the play would have had a happy ending. This simple point forms the basis for much of modern social psychology. But many modern social psychologists make an important further assertion: The way in which we interpret and try to comprehend such social events—that is, the nature of *social cognition*—is in principle no different from the way in which we interpret and try to comprehend any event whatsoever, whether social or not.

THE INTERPERSONAL NATURE OF BELIEF

Seen in this light, many facets of social psychology are simply an aspect of the psychology of thinking and cognition in general. But over and above this, social cognition has certain features that make it uniquely social. For there is no doubt that much of what we know, we know because of others. The primary medium of this cognitive interdependence is of course human language, which allows us to share our discoveries and pass them on to the next generation. As a result, we look at the world not just through our own eyes but also through the eyes of others, and we form our beliefs on the basis of what we've

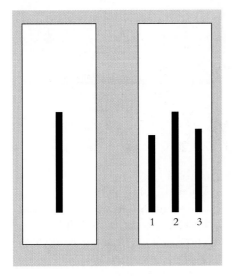

11.1   The stimulus cards in Asch's social pressure experiment   *The cards are drawn to scale. In the actual experiment, they were generally placed on the ledge of a blackboard, separated by forty inches. (Asch, 1956)*

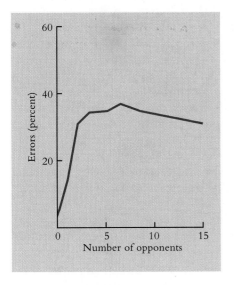

11.2   The effect of social pressure   *The extent to which the subject yielded in relation to the size of the group pitted against him is demonstrated by this figure. In this situation, the effect of group size seems to reach a maximum at three, though other studies (such as Gerard, Wilhelmy, and Conolley, 1968) have found that conformity continues to rise beyond this point as the number of opponents increases. (After Asch, 1955)*

heard them say or what they have written. In fact, our very notion of physical reality is at least in part a matter of mutual agreement. This point was made very dramatically in a classic study performed by Solomon Asch (Asch, 1956).

In Asch's experiment, nine or ten subjects were brought together in a laboratory room and shown pairs of cards placed a few feet in front of them. On one card was a black line, say, 8 inches long. On the other card were three lines of varying lengths, say 6 1/4, 8, and 6 3/4 inches (Figure 11.1). The subjects were asked to make a simple perceptual judgment. They had to indicate which of the three lines on the one card was equal in length to the one line on the other card. Then the experimenter told the subjects that this procedure was only a minor prelude to another study and casually asked them, in the interest of saving time, to indicate their judgments aloud by calling them out in turn (the three comparison lines were designated by the numbers 1, 2, and 3 printed underneath them). This procedure continued for a dozen or so pairs of cards.

Considering the sizable differences among the stimuli, the task was absurdly simple except for one thing: There was only one "real" subject. All of the others were the experimenter's secret confederates. They had arranged their seating order so that most of them would call out their judgments before the real subject's turn came around. After the first few trials, they unanimously rendered false judgments on most of the trials thereafter. For example, the confederates might declare that a 6 1/4-inch line equaled an 8-inch line, and so on, for a dozen more trials. What did the real subject do?

Asch found that the chances were less than one in three that the real subject would be fully independent and would stick to his guns on all trials on which the group disagreed with him (Figure 11.2). Most subjects yielded to the group on at least some occasions, in fine disregard of the evidence of their senses—with rather uncomfortable implications for the democratic process. When interviewed after the experiment, most of the yielding subjects made it clear that the group didn't really affect how they *saw* the lines. No matter what everyone else said, the 8-inch line still looked longer than the 6 1/4-inch line. But the subjects wondered whether they were right, became worried about their vision and sanity, and were exceedingly embarrassed at expressing their deviance in public (Asch, 1952, 1956; Asch and Gleitman, 1953).

For our present purposes, our concern is not so much with what the subjects did, but rather with how they felt. In this regard, most of them were alike. Some yielded and some were independent (see Chapter 12), but assuming they did not suspect a trick (and a few of them did), they were generally very much disturbed. Why all the furor? The answer is that Asch's procedure had violated a basic premise of the subjects' existence: However people may differ, they all share the same physical reality. Under the circumstances, it is small wonder that Asch's subjects were deeply alarmed by a discrepancy they had never previously encountered. (Needless to say, the whole experiment was carefully explained to them immediately afterwards.)

The belief that others see, feel, and hear pretty much as we do is a cognitive axiom of our everyday experience. When this axiom is violated, as it is in Asch's experiment, a vital prop is knocked out from under us, a prop so basic that we never even realized it was there.

A

B

C

The subject in a social pressure experiment (A) The true subject (center) listens to the instructions. (B) On hearing the unanimous verdict of the others, he leans forward to look at the cards more carefully. (C) After twelve such trials, he explains that "he has to call them as he sees them." (Photographs by William Vandivert)

Solomon E. Asch (Courtesy of Swarthmore College)

SOCIAL COMPARISON

The Asch study shows what happens when the clear evidence of one's senses is contradicted by the verdict of a unanimous group. But suppose that our own perception does not provide a clear-cut answer. This will happen, for example, if the lines differ by only a small amount. If left to our own devices, we will try to obtain some further sensory evidence. We may look at the lines once more but from a different angle or try to measure them with a ruler. But if we can't do that, then it's only reasonable to listen to what others have to say. Their judgments can then be used in lieu of further information provided by our own eyes or hands. If the others now disagree with us, we may well change our own answer on their say-so. Several studies have shown that this is precisely what occurs in an Asch-type experiment in which the discrimination is fairly difficult. There is more yielding and very little emotional disturbance (Crutchfield, 1955; for further discussion of conformity effects, see Chapter 12).

This general line of reasoning may explain why people seek the opinion of others whenever they are confronted by a situation that they do not fully understand. To evaluate the situation, they need more information. If they cannot get it first hand, they will try to compare their own reactions to those of others (Festinger, 1954; Suls and Miller, 1977). The need for such *social comparison* is especially pronounced when the evaluations pertain to social issues, such as the qualifications of a political candidate or the pros and cons of sex education in public schools.

COGNITIVE PROCESSES AND BELIEF

The preceding discussion showed that people try to make sense of the world they encounter. But how? In effect, they do this by looking for some consistency among their own experiences and memories, and then by turning to other people for comparison and confirmation. If all checks out, then well and good. But what if there is some incongruity? The Asch study showed what happens when there is a serious incongruity between one's own experiences (and the beliefs based upon them) and those reported by others. But suppose the incongruity is among one's own experiences, beliefs, or actions? Many social psychologists believe that this will trigger some tendency to restore *cognitive consistency*—to reinterpret the situation so as to minimize whatever inconsistency may be there.

What kinds of mechanisms might explain this general tendency to reinterpret aspects of our experience so that they fit together sensibly? A very influential approach was developed by Leon Festinger, who proposed that any perceived inconsistency among various aspects of knowledge, feelings, and behavior sets

(Drawing by Rea; © 1955, 1983, The New Yorker Magazine, Inc.)

up an unpleasant internal state that he called ***cognitive dissonance,*** which people try to reduce whenever possible (Festinger, 1957).

One of the earliest examples is provided by a study of a sect that was awaiting the end of the world. The founder of the sect announced that she had received a message from the "Guardians" from outer space. On a certain day, there would be an enormous flood. Only the true believers were to be saved and would be picked up at midnight of the appointed day in flying saucers. (Technology has advanced considerably since the days of Noah's Ark.) On doomsday, the members of the sect huddled together, awaiting the predicted cataclysm. The arrival time of the flying saucers came and went; tension mounted. Finally, the leader of the sect received another message: To reward the faithful, the world was saved. Joy broke out, and the believers became more faithful than ever (Festinger, Riecken, and Schachter, 1956).

Given the failure of a clear-cut prophecy, one might have expected the very opposite. A disconfirmation of a predicted event should presumably lead one to abandon the beliefs that produced the prediction. But cognitive dissonance theory says otherwise. By abandoning the belief that there are Guardians, the person who had once held this belief would have to accept a painful dissonance between his present skepticism and his past beliefs and actions. His prior faith would now appear extremely foolish. Some members of the sect went to such lengths as giving up their jobs or spending their savings; such acts would lose all meaning in retrospect without the belief in the Guardians. Under the circumstances, the dissonance was intolerable. It was reduced by a belief in the new message, which bolstered the original belief. Since other members of the sect stood fast along with them, their conviction was strengthened all the more. They could now think of themselves not as fools, but as loyal, steadfast members of a courageous little band whose faith had saved the earth.

ATTITUDES

FOCUS QUESTIONS

■ What are attitudes, and how are they measured? To what extent do they correspond to actual behavior?

■ What factors determine whether people can be persuaded to adopt a particular position?

■ In what circumstances can our behavior change our attitudes? What do these circumstances show about our need for consistency and, in turn, the nature of cognitive dissonance?

Attitudes Attitudes are a combination of beliefs, feelings, and evaluations, coupled with some predisposition to act accordingly. (Left: photograph by Sylvia Johnson/Woodfin Camp, 1989. Right: photograph by Susan McElhinney, 1980/Woodfin Camp)

Many social beliefs are accompanied by strong feelings. Take the conviction that abortion is murder—a far cry from the many beliefs we hold that are completely unencumbered by emotion, such as our nonchalant assurance that the sum of the angles of a triangle is 180 degrees. Emotionally tinged social views of the former kind are generally called **attitudes.** Since various people often have different attitudes, they tend to interpret many social situations differently; the same crowd may look like a group of peaceful demonstrators to one observer and like a rioting mob to another.

As modern social psychologists use the term, an attitude is a rather stable mental position held toward some idea or object or person. Examples are attitudes toward nuclear power, the legalization of marijuana, school integration, or packaged breakfast foods. Every attitude is a combination of beliefs, feelings, and evaluations and some predisposition to act accordingly. Thus, people who differ in their attitudes toward nuclear power will probably have different beliefs on the subject (e.g., "nuclear power plants are—or are not—unsafe") and will evaluate the topic differently (from extreme pro to extreme con); these differences will also make them more likely to take some actions rather than others (e.g., to support or to protest the construction of a new nuclear plant).

ATTITUDES AND BEHAVIOR

■ Attitudes can be measured in a number of ways. The most widely used methods involve some form of self-report. For example, the subject might be given an **attitude questionnaire** with items that relate to the matter at hand. Thus, in a questionnaire on nuclear power and related issues, subjects might be given a statement such as: "Accidental explosions in nuclear plants pose some danger, but this risk is relatively small compared to the economic and social benefits of cheap and abundant energy." They would then be asked to select a number between, say, +10 and −10 to indicate the extent of their agreement or disagreement. The sum of a person's responses to a number of statements that all tap the same concerns will then provide a quantitative expression of that person's attitude.

Do attitudes as measured by self-report predict what people actually do? This question has led to controversy, for some early reports suggested that the relationship is much weaker than one might think. During the 1930s when there was considerable prejudice against Asians, Richard LaPiere traveled through the

Attempts at persuasive communication
Two advertising messages that try to change consumer attitudes toward various products. (A) links love with an expensive gift; (B) asserts that a certain bread will appeal to any ethnic group whatever. (Courtesy of De Beers, Best Foods Baking Group)

country with a Chinese couple and stopped at over fifty hotels and motels and at nearly two hundred restaurants. All but one hotel gave them accommodations, and no restaurant refused them service. Later on the very same establishments received a letter that asked whether they would house or serve Chinese people. Ninety-two percent of the replies were "No" (LaPiere, 1934). It appears that there was a major inconsistency between people's attitudes as verbally expressed and their actual behavior.

The results of this and related studies led some social psychologists to doubt whether the attitude concept is particularly useful. If attitudes don't predict behavior, what is the point of studying them in the first place? (Wicker, 1969). But upon further analysis, this pessimism proved to be unwarranted. For later studies showed that under many circumstances attitudes do indeed predict what people do. Thus voter preferences during the four presidential campaigns of 1952 to 1964 as expressed in preelection interviews were a pretty good predictor of later behavior in the voting booth: 85 percent of the people interviewed voted in line with their previously expressed preference. For the most part, those who shifted had initial preferences that were rather weak (Kelley and Mirer, 1974).

It appears that attitudes often do predict behavior. But if so, how can we explain the fact that they don't always do so? An important factor is how specifically the attitude is defined. The less specific one's definition, the less likely it is to predict a particular bit of behavior. A demonstration comes from a study on women's attitudes toward birth control. Positive attitudes toward birth control in general showed only a negligible correlation with the use of oral contraceptives during a two-year period. But attitudes toward using birth control pills in particular correlated quite well with their actual use during this period (Davidson and Jaccard, 1979).

ATTITUDE CHANGE

■ While attitudes have a certain resilience, their stability is threatened at every turn, especially in modern mass society where our attitudes and beliefs are under continual assault. Hundreds of commercials urge us to buy one product rather than another, political candidates clamor for our vote, and any number of organizations exhort us to fight for (or against) arms control, or legalized abortion, or environmental protection, and so on. When we add these mass-produced appeals to the numerous private attempts at persuasion undertaken by our friends and relatives (let alone our would-be lovers), it is hardly surprising that attitudes sometimes do change. Social psychologists have spent a great deal of effort in trying to understand how such attitudinal changes come about.

PERSUASIVE COMMUNICATIONS

A number of investigators have studied the effectiveness of **persuasive communications.** These are messages that openly try to convince us to stop smoking, to outlaw abortion, to favor capital punishment, or—on a more humble level—to choose one brand of toothpaste rather than another. Among the factors that determine whether a given message has its desired effect are—not surprisingly—the person who sends the message and the message itself (Cialdini, Petty, and Cacioppo, 1981; McGuire, 1985).

The message source One factor that determines whether someone will change your mind on a given issue is who that someone is. To begin with, there is the element of credibility. Not surprisingly, communications have more of an effect if they are attributed to someone who is an acknowledged expert than to someone who is not. Thus a recommendation that antihistamines should be sold over the counter was more effective when ascribed to the *New England Journal of Medicine* than to a popular mass circulation magazine; a positive review of an obscure modern poem was more likely to lead to upward reevaluations of that poem if the review was attributed to T. S. Eliot rather than to another student (Hovland and Weiss, 1952; Aronson, Turner, and Carlsmith, 1963).

Expertise is important, but so is *trustworthiness.* For the would-be persuader will have a much harder time if we believe that he has something to gain from persuading us. When a used-car salesman tells you *not* to buy a car from his lot, you are likely to believe him. (Unless you believe that the other lot to which he refers you belongs to his brother-in-law.)

The message   However important the messenger, the message she delivers is surely more important yet. What are the factors that determine whether that message will change attitudes? According to Petty and Cacioppo there are two routes to persuasion. One is what they call the **central route to persuasion** in which we follow the message with some care and mentally elaborate its arguments with yet further arguments and counterarguments of our own. We take this route if the issue is one that matters to us and if we're not diverted by other concerns. Here content and information are what matter, and strong arguments will indeed be more effective in changing our minds than will weak arguments. But the situation is quite different if the message comes by way of the **peripheral route to persuasion.** We'll be induced to take this route if we don't care much about the issue or if the message isn't clearly heard because of background noise or if we are otherwise distracted. In such circumstances, content and arguments matter little. What counts instead is how or by whom or in what surroundings the message is presented (Petty and Cacioppo, 1985).

The central route to persuasion involves reasoned thought. But just what is the peripheral route? According to some authors, it often represents a kind of mental shortcut. After all, there are only so many things we can pay attention to, and so we use some rules of thumb, or **heuristics,** to help us decide whether to accept or reject the message (Eagly and Chaiken, 1984; Chaiken, 1987). Such heuristics may include the speaker's apparent expertise, or likability ("nice people can be trusted"), or the sheer number or length of the arguments that are presented, regardless of how good they are. Such heuristics in reacting to persuasive communications are reminiscent of heuristics in decision making; both are mental shortcuts we resort to because our cognitive capacity is limited (see Chapter 8 for a further discussion of heuristics).

COGNITIVE DISSONANCE AND ATTITUDE CHANGE

We've already seen that attitudes can affect behavior. But the relation can also go the other way. For in some situations, what an individual does will lead to a change in her attitudes. According to some social psychologists, this effect is produced by a tendency to reduce cognitive dissonance analogous to that which we've considered in the context of a change in beliefs. Suppose there is some inconsistency between a person's attitudes and her behavior. How can she reconcile the inconsistency? She can't change her behavior, for that's past and done with. All she can do is readjust her present attitude.

Justification of effort   An illustration of this kind of readjustment comes from retrospective explanations of prior efforts. People often make considerable sacrifices to attain a goal—backbreaking exertion to scale a mountain, years and

Another attempt to persuade   *An American advertisement from around 1900. (Frontispiece from* The Wonderful World of American Advertising, 1865–1900 *by Leonard de Vries and Ilonka van Amstel, Chicago: Follett, 1972)*

Justification of effort Newly accepted members of a group tend to value their group membership all the more if their initiation was especially harsh, as in the case of soldiers who have gone through boot camp. (Courtesy of the U.S. Army)

years of study to become a cardiologist. Was it worth it? According to dissonance theory, the goal will be esteemed more highly the harder it was to reach. If it were not, there would be cognitive dissonance. Support comes from common observation of the effects of harsh initiation rites, such as fraternity hazing. After the ordeal is passed, the initiates seem to value their newly found membership all the more. Similar effects have been obtained in the laboratory. Subjects admitted to a discussion group after going through a fairly harsh screening test put a higher value on their new membership than subjects who did not undergo such a screening (Aronson and Mills, 1959; Gerard and Mathewson, 1966).

Forced compliance A related result is the effect of **_forced compliance._** The basic idea is simple. Suppose someone agrees to give a speech in support of a view that is contrary to his own position, as in the case of a bartender arguing for prohibition. Will his public act change his private views? The answer seems to depend upon why he agreed to make the speech in the first place. If he was bribed by a large sum, there will be little effect. As he looks back upon his public denunciation of alcohol, he knows why he did what he did—$1,000 in cold cash is justification enough. But suppose he gave the speech with lesser urging and received only a trifling sum. If we later ask what he thinks about prohibition, we will find that he has begun to believe in his own speech. According to Festinger, the reason is the need to reduce cognitive dissonance. If the bartender asks himself why he took a public stand so contrary to his own attitudes, he can find no adequate justification; the few dollars he received are not enough. To reduce the dissonance, the compliant bartender does the only thing he can: He decides that what he said wasn't really all that different from what he believes.

A number of studies have demonstrated such forced compliance effects in the laboratory. In a classic experiment, subjects were asked to perform several extremely boring tasks, such as packing spools into a tray and then unpacking them, and turning one screw after another for a quarter turn. When they were finished, they were induced to tell another subject (who was about to engage in the same activities) that the tasks were really very interesting. They were paid either $1 or $20 for lying in this way. When later asked how enjoyable they had found the tasks, the well-paid subjects said that they were boring, while the poorly paid subjects said that they were fairly interesting. This result is rather remarkable. One might have guessed that the well-paid liar would have been more persuaded by his own arguments than the poorly paid one. But contrary to this initial intuition—and in line with dissonance theory—the exact opposite was the case (Festinger and Carlsmith, 1959). A number of other studies have performed variants on the original experiment with essentially the same results (e.g., Rosenfeld, Giacalone, and Tedeschi, 1984).

DISSONANCE RECONSIDERED

The reevaluation of prior decisions and the effect of forced compliance seem to be ways of reducing dissonance. But just what is the dissonance that is here reduced? One might regard dissonance as essentially equivalent to a logical inconsistency, like the inconsistency between the belief that the earth moves around the sun and the belief that the earth is at the center of the solar system. There is little doubt that cognitions are often adjusted to become consistent in just this sense. A person who hears the mumbled sentence "The woman shaved himself" is likely to hear it as "The man shaved himself" or "The woman shaved herself," so that noun and pronoun agree. The question is whether all cases of dissonance reduction boil down to an analogous tendency to keep cognitions logically consistent. The answer seems to be no, for recent evidence suggests that dissonance reduction is not always a cognitive matter. A number of studies indicate that we often try to reduce the dissonance between our acts and beliefs for more emotional reasons. One such factor is an effort to maintain a ***favorable self-picture*** (Aronson, 1969; Steele and Liu, 1983; Cooper and Fazio, 1984).

Consider the retrospective reevaluation of whether some achievement was worth its cost. People who have made a great sacrifice to attain some goal will value it more than those who achieved the goal with little effort. One hypothesis is that this dissonance reduction is produced by a tendency toward logical consistency—the worth of the goal has to match its cost, just as the noun must fit the pronoun. But there is a noncognitive reason that is just as plausible. An individual who goes through a difficult initiation rite to join a club and later discovers that the club is rather dull might well feel like a fool. To maintain a favorable self-picture, she adjusts her attitude to fit her own acts and overvalues her group membership.

PERCEIVING OTHERS

FOCUS QUESTIONS

- What are traits, and how are they like the attributes of physical objects?

- What are implicit personality theories? How do they affect the traits we are likely to ascribe to others?

- What is illusory correlation, and how might it explain the perpetuation of stereotypes?

Thus far our discussion of how people interpret the social world has focused upon the way in which they try to harmonize various events with their beliefs and attitudes. A similar approach has been applied to find out how we form impressions of other people and how we try to understand why they do what they do.

FORMING IMPRESSIONS

In the course of ordinary life we encounter many other people. The vast majority of them play the role of anonymous extras in each of our private dramas, especially in the big cities where we briefly cross the paths of countless strangers of whom we will never know anything. But a sizable number of other people do impinge upon our lives, as bit players (a traffic cop of whom we ask directions), supporting cast (a casual acquaintance), and starring leads (friends, lovers, bosses, enemies). These we cannot help but evaluate and try to understand, as they, in their turn, evaluate and try to understand us. Much of the plot of our own dramas (and of theirs) depends upon the outcome of these mutual social attempts at understanding. How are they achieved?

Perceiving the characteristics of another person is in some ways analogous to perceiving certain stable attributes of a physical object, such as its shape or size. In our previous discussion of visual perception, we saw that to do this the observer must abstract the crucial relationships within the stimulus input so that he can see the form of the object, say, a catlike shape (see Chapter 6). He must also disregard various transient aspects of the situation, such as distance and angle of regard, in order to perceive the stable characteristics of the object—its size and shape. By doing all this, the observer attains perceptual constancy and can answer such life-and-death questions as whether he is dealing with a kitten nearby or a tiger far away.

"I have the impression that they're not very substantial people." (Drawing by Chas. Addams; © 1939, 1967, The New Yorker Magazine, Inc.)

Something analogous occurs when we perceive—or rather, infer—such attributes of a person as his violent temper or warmth and so on. In effect, we are making a judgment as to what the person is "really" like, a judgment independent of the particular moment and occasion. His personal attributes (often called *traits*) are inferred invariant properties that seem to characterize his behavior in different situations. When we say that a person is irascible, we don't mean that he will utter an impolite expletive when someone deliberately steps on his toe. We mean that he will generally be short-tempered over a wide range of circumstances. To put it another way, the attempt to understand what another person is like boils down to an effort to note the *consistencies* in what he does over time and under different circumstances (see Chapter 16). The question is how this consistency is abstracted from the few bits of behavior of the other person we can actually observe.

IMPRESSIONS OF OTHERS AS PATTERNS

Several theorists assume that the processes whereby we try to understand another person are in many ways analogous to the way in which we perceive various attributes of physical objects. Consider visual form. This is a perceptual whole that depends upon the *relation* among the elements of which the form is composed; thus, a triangle can be composed of dots or crosses and still be perceived as the same triangle (see Chapter 6). According to Solomon Asch, a similar principle describes our conceptions of other people. In his view, these conceptions of others are not a simple aggregate of the attributes we perceive them to have. Instead, they form an organized whole whose elements are interpreted in relation to the overall pattern (Asch, 1952).

To test his hypothesis, Asch performed several studies of how people form impressions of others. His technique was to give subjects a list of attributes that they were told described a single person. Their task was to write a short sketch of the person so characterized and to rate this person on a checklist of antonyms (generous/ungenerous, good-natured/irritable). In one study, some subjects were given a list of seven traits: *intelligent, skillful, industrious, warm, determined, practical, cautious.* Other subjects received the same list except that *cold* was substituted for *warm.* The resulting sketches were quite different. The "warm person" was seen as "driven by the desire to accomplish something that would be of benefit," while the "cold person" was described as "snobbish, . . . calculating and unsympathetic." The checklist results were in the same direction. The person described as warm was seen as generous, happy, and good-natured. The "cold person" was characterized by the appropriate antonyms (Asch, 1946).

According to Asch, the warm/cold trait acted as a focus around which the total impression of the person was organized. Other traits seemed to be of lesser importance. For example, it made little difference whether the list of traits included *polite* or *blunt.*

IMPRESSIONS OF OTHERS AS COGNITIVE CONSTRUCTIONS

Asch tried to understand impression formation by an analogy to theories of perceptual patterning. A number of more recent authors have championed a view that is in many ways a modern version of Asch's approach, but they appeal to concepts derived from modern theories of memory and thinking rather than to principles of visual perception. In their view, our impressions of others are cognitive constructions based on various *schemas*—sets of organized expectations about the way in which different behaviors of people hang togeth-

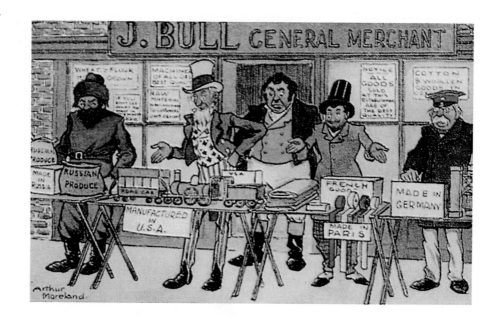

Stereotypes   *A British poster circa 1900, protesting competition from foreign goods on the home market in a cartoon featuring national stereotypes.*

er. If we believe that someone is outgoing and gregarious, we will also expect him to be relatively talkative. He may or may not be, but the pattern we perceive is partially imposed by our schema of what an outgoing and gregarious person is like. Such schemas about persons are sometimes called ***implicit theories of personality*** (Bruner and Tagiuri, 1954; Schneider, 1973).

A demonstration of how such cognitive constructions operate used subjects who read several lists of attributes. One described a person said to be an extrovert, another a person who was an introvert. On a later recognition test, subjects falsely recognized adjectives that had not been on the original list if they fit in with the appropriate label. Thus terms such as *spirited* and *boisterous* that had not been presented previously were misremembered as being part of the original list that described the extrovert; terms such *shy* and *reserved* were falsely remembered as part of the list that described the introvert (Cantor and Mischel, 1979).

Phenomena of this kind suggest that the processes of social cognition, that is, the ways in which we gain knowledge of social events, are much like those of cognition in general. Suppose we briefly looked into a tool chest and were then shown a set of objects and asked which of them we had seen. We'd surely be more likely to misremember having seen a hammer than a baby bottle (assuming neither was actually in the chest). Our cognitive schema of a tool chest includes a hammer, just as our schema of an extrovert includes the attribute "boisterous."

Stereotypes and illusory correlations   Given our limited cognitive capacity, schematic thinking provides us with a valuable mental tool that ordinarily works reasonably well. But the uncritical use of this tool can lead to errors that have serious social consequences. This is particularly clear in the case of social ***stereotypes,*** when schemas are simplified and applied to whole groups. Such stereotypes are categories by means of which we try to simplify the complex world in which we live, so that we talk about Greeks or Jews or African Americans (or student radicals, upwardly mobile yuppies, or little old ladies in tennis shoes) as if they were all alike. Such group stereotypes are often negative, especially if they are applied to minority groups.

The schema approach cannot explain how particular stereotypes come about, but it has some suggestions for how they are perpetuated. One possible factor is ***illusory correlation.*** Many characteristics of the world are correlated; they go together more often than would occur by chance alone—clouds and rainfall, accidents and sirens, and so on. But some of the correlations we perceive are illusory, a creation of our minds rather than a real relationship in the world outside. Such illusory correlations come about because certain co-occurrences are more readily noted and remembered than are others. One reason may be because they are the ones that are expected.

Some evidence for this idea comes from a study in which subjects were presented with a number of statements that described members of different occupational groups, for example, "Doug, an accountant, is timid and thoughtful" or "Nancy, a waitress, is busy and talkative." Some of the characteristics were judged to fit the stereotype (e.g., accountant—perfectionist; stewardess—attractive; salesman—enthusiastic), while others did not. But the sentences were so constructed that each occupation was systematically paired with each kind of adjective, so that in fact no correlation was encountered. The subjects were later asked to estimate how often each adjective described each occupational group in the sentences they had just read. Their estimates indicated that they believed that accountants were more often described as timid than were waitresses, stewardesses more often as attractive than librarians, and so on—a good example of an illusory correlation, suggesting how stereotypes can be maintained even in the face of contradictory evidence (Hamilton and Rose, 1980).

ATTRIBUTION

FOCUS QUESTIONS

- What is the fundamental attribution error?
- How does our appraisal of the importance of situational versus dispositional factors change based on whether we are actors or observers, or whether we succeed or fail?

As previously pointed out, the attempt to understand what another person is like is really an attempt to find the pattern, the consistency, in what he does. An important step toward that end is to infer what caused his behavior on any particular occasion—for the meaning of any given act depends upon the cause. But

Situation versus disposition? In ice hockey, it's not always clear whether a player who skates into another at full speed is deliberately trying to hurt him. The usual attribution is that he is, resulting in one of the many fights that characterize hockey. (Courtesy AP/Wide World Photos)

what cause do we see in what the other person does? Consider a football player who violently bumps an opponent in the course of the game. If the bumping occurred while the play was in progress, not much is revealed about the bumper's personality; he was behaving according to the rules of the game. But if the bump occurred some seconds after the official blew his whistle and the play was over, the situation is different. Now the act is more revealing and may be attributed to a grudge or a nasty disposition. The bumpee will conclude that the bumper's action was internally caused and will then self-righteously become a bumper when his own turn comes.

ATTRIBUTION AS A RATIONAL PROCESS

■ The study of how such attributions are reached is one of modern social psychology's important concerns (e.g., Heider, 1958; Kelley, 1967; Jones and Nisbett, 1972; Kelley and Michela, 1980). According to Harold Kelley, one of the first investigators in this area, the process through which such decisions are reached is analogous to the way in which a scientist tracks down the cause of a physical event (Kelley, 1967). An effect (such as an increase in gas pressure) is attributed to a particular condition (such as a rise in temperature) if the effect occurs when the condition is present but does not occur when that condition is absent. Kelley believed that when people try to explain the behavior of others, they implicitly refer to a similar principle of the covariation of cause and effect. To answer the question "Why did he bump me?" the aggrieved player has to consider the circumstances under which bumping is known to occur. Does it generally occur in circumstances just like now? Would most other football players do the same under much the same circumstances? If the answer to these and similar questions is yes, the act will probably be attributed to *situational factors:* essentially external causes, such as the social pressures of team play. But if the answer is no, the act will be attributed to some ***dispositional quality,*** something internal to the actor that is characteristic of him: He is a dirty player who took a cheap shot (Heider, 1958; Kelley, 1967).

As used in this context, *dispositional quality* refers to any underlying attribute that characterizes a given individual and makes him more disposed than others to engage in the particular bit of behavior we just observed. One kind of dispositional quality is the presence or absence of some ability (for example, falling because one is clumsy) or of some general personality trait (for example, leaving a very small tip for a waiter because one is stingy).

ERRORS IN THE ATTRIBUTION PROCESS

■ Kelley's analysis indicates that the rational way of trying to explain another person's behavior is to consider that behavior in the context of the total situation. But this is not always done. For there are a number of biases that lead to errors in the attribution process.

THE FUNDAMENTAL ATTRIBUTION ERROR

One error concerns the relative weights we give to situational and dispositional factors. While we do consider situational factors in judging the behavior of others, the evidence shows that we do so rather less than we should. There seems to be a strong bias to attribute behavior to dispositional qualities in the person while underrating the role of the external situation. This bias is so pervasive that it has been called the ***fundamental attribution error*** (Ross, 1977). The person on welfare is often judged to be lazy (a dispositional attribute) when he is really

"I've heard that outside working hours he's really a rather decent sort." (Chas. Addams; © 1975, The New Yorker Magazine, Inc.)

Attribution People sometimes confuse the actor with his role, as in the case of Boris Karloff, who often portrayed monsters such as Frankenstein's but who in real life was a gentle and cultured person. (Photographs courtesy of the Kobal Collection)

unable to find work (a situational attribute). Much the same holds for our interpretation of public affairs. We look for heroes and scapegoats and tend to praise or blame political leaders for acts over which in fact they had little control.

This general underemphasis of situational factors in interpreting why another person does what she does is illustrated in an experimental study in which college students were asked to participate in a simulated TV quiz show. Students were run in pairs and drew cards to decide who would be the "quiz master" and who the contestant. The quiz master had to make up questions, drawn from any area in which she had some expertise; the contestant had to try to answer them. Some of the questions were quite difficult (e.g., "What do the initials W. H. in W. H. Auden's name stand for?"). Under the circumstances, it's hardly surprising that the contestants' average score was only four correct answers out of ten.

The entire procedure was witnessed by other students who served as observers. When later asked to rate the two participants, the observers judged the quiz masters to be considerably more knowledgeable than the contestants. But why should this be so? To be sure, the contestants had been unable to answer many of the questions their partners asked. But the situation was obviously rigged, for the contestants were at the mercy of whatever questions their quiz masters posed. What happened clearly depended on the situation, on the role each participant was assigned. The observers knew that this role was determined by lot, for they witnessed the entire procedure. But even so, they couldn't help regarding the quiz masters as more knowledgeable than the contestants—a tribute to the power of the fundamental attribution error (Ross, Amabile, and Steinmetz, 1977).

THE ACTOR-OBSERVER BIAS

The tendency to underrate the importance of situational factors only occurs when we try to understand the behavior of others. The results are quite different when we ourselves are the actors rather than the observers. When we now try to explain our own acts, the causes seem less in us and more in the external situation. Someone trips, and we think he's careless or clumsy. But when we ourselves trip, we say the floor is slippery. This is the *actor-observer difference* in attribution—situational when we ourselves are the actors, dispositional when we are the observers (Jones and Nisbett, 1972).

One interpretation of the actor-observer difference is simply that we know ourselves better than we know anyone else. Let's say that on one evening we undertip a waiter in a restaurant. Should we make the dispositional attribution that we're stingy? Others who have never seen us in a similar situation might well conclude that we are. But we ourselves will disagree. We have observed ourselves in many restaurants and know that we normally tip properly. But if this is so, our recent act says nothing about our personal characteristics; rather, it must be caused by the situation—perhaps the waiter was rude, or we suddenly discovered that we didn't bring enough cash. Our attribution is different when we see someone else do the very same thing. We'll interpret *his* action dispositionally and conclude that he is stingy. After all, we haven't seen him in remotely as many restaurants as we've seen ourselves (Nisbett et al., 1973).

There is another factor that contributes to the difference between actors and observers—the two have different physical perspectives (see Figure 11.3, p. 342). To the observer, what stands out perceptually is the actor and his actions. The situation that calls out these actions is seen much less clearly, in part because the stimuli to which the actor responds are not as readily visible from the observer's vantage point. The reverse holds for the actor. He is not focused on his own behavior. One reason is that he cannot see his own actions very clearly (some, such as his own facial expressions, are literally invisible to him). What he attends

3 4 1

11.3 The actor-observer difference *A schematic figure of a study on the effect of visual perspective on the actor-observer difference. Two actors (actually confederates) were engaged in a conversation and observed from three vantage points: from behind Actor A, from behind Actor B, and from midway between them. The results showed that the observer who watched from behind Actor A felt that B controlled the conversation, while the observer behind Actor B felt the reverse. The observer who watched from midway between the two felt that both were equally influential. (After Taylor and Fiske, 1975)*

Actor A   Actor B

to is the situation around him—the place, the people, and how he interprets them all. If we assume that whatever serves as the main center of attention (the figure rather than the ground) is more likely to be seen as the cause for whatever happens, then the differences in attribution follow: dispositional for the observer (who thus commits the fundamental attribution error), situational for the actor (Heider, 1958).

Some evidence for this position comes from a study in which two strangers met and engaged in a conversation that was videotaped. When later played back, only one of the two participants was shown (on the pretense that one of the cameras had malfunctioned while the sound was unaffected). As a result, one of the participants saw just what he had seen before: his fellow conversationalist. But the other saw something different: himself. When asked to describe his own behavior, the participant who saw the videotape of his partner gave the usual pattern of attribution—he said that his own actions were caused by the situation. The results were different for the participant who saw himself. The reversed perspective led to a reversal of the usual actor-observer difference. Having watched himself, the subject described his own behavior in dispositional terms (Storms, 1973).

THE SELF-SERVING BIAS

The two accounts of the actor-observer bias we've just discussed—different information and perspectives—are essentially cognitive; they argue that the bias results from limitations on what the individual can see, remember, and understand. But there is another interpretation that argues that in addition there are motivational factors. For our thoughts are all too often colored by our desires.

The best evidence comes from work on the ***self-serving attributional bias,*** which shows that people often deny responsibility for failures and take credit for successes, attributing the first to situational and the second to dispositional factors. The tennis player explains a loss by complaining that her serve was off and that the light was in her eyes, but she takes a win as proof of her ability and stamina. The student who fails says that the exam was unfair and happened to cover just those parts of the course that he hadn't studied for, but he believes that a good grade is a tribute to his talent and hard work.

The self-serving bias is especially pronounced in the world of competitive sports. One study found evidence in the sports pages. The investigators analyzed

Self-serving bias *John McEnroe, a tennis star of the 1980s, was notorious for protesting calls that went against him. (Courtesy of Reuters/Bettman Newsphotos)*

the post-game comments of college and professional football and baseball players and coaches following important games. Eighty percent of the statements made by the winners were internal attributions: "Our team was great," "Our star player did it all," and so on. In contrast, the losers were less likely to give internal attributions (only 53 percent), but often explained the outcomes by referring to external, situational factors: "I think we hit the ball all right. But I think we're unlucky" (Lau and Russell, 1980, p. 32).

PERCEIVING ONESELF

FOCUS QUESTIONS

- What is the "looking-glass self"? What evidence suggests that our knowledge of ourselves is attained through social interaction?

We have discussed some of the ways in which we see various qualities in others, as well as some of the ways in which we come to see such qualities in ourselves. We all have a conception of our own selves, what we are really like and why we do what we do—"I am a certain kind of person with such and such capacities, beliefs, and attitudes"—even if we sometimes glorify those capacities with a self-serving bias. But how do such self-concepts arise in the first place?

(Photograph by Suzanne Szasz)

THE SELF-CONCEPT

One crucial element is some reference to other people. For there is little doubt that there can be no full-fledged "I" without a "you" or a "they," for a crucial component of the self-concept is social. According to many authors, the child begins to see herself through the eyes of the important figures in her world and thus acquires the idea that she is a person—albeit at first a very little person—just as they are (Mead, 1934). As the social interactions become more complex, more and more details are added to the self-picture. In effect, the child sees herself through the mirror of the opinions and expectations of those others—mother, father, siblings, friends—who matter to her. Her later behavior cannot help but be shaped by this early "looking-glass self" (Cooley, 1902). Examples of such effects include the roles in which society casts children from the moment of birth: race, gender, ethnicity, and so on. (For different theoretical approaches to the development of the self-concept, see Chapters 13 and 14.)

SELF-PERCEPTION AND ATTRIBUTION

According to the looking-glass theory, we learn who we are by finding out through others. But isn't there a more direct method? Can't we discover who we are and what we feel simply by observing ourselves?

According to some authors, the answer is no. In their view, our conceptions of self are attained through an attribution process no different from that which allows us to form conceptions of other people. The advocates of this *self-perception theory* maintain that, contrary to common-sense belief, we do not know our own selves directly (Bem, 1972). In their view, self-knowledge can only be achieved indirectly, through the same attempts to find consistencies, discount irrelevancies, and interpret observations that help us to understand other people.

The foot-in-the-door effect and the environment The photo shows young children induced to do their bit for conservation. Whether the cans they collect now make much of a difference matters less than that these acts are likely to lead to greater efforts in the future as the children come to think of themselves as environmentalists. (Photograph by S. C. Delaney/EPA)

One line of evidence concerns the relation between attitude and behavior. Common sense argues that attitudes cause behavior, that our own actions stem from our feelings and our beliefs. To some extent, this is undoubtedly true. Those in favor of segregation are unlikely to join civil rights demonstrations. But under some circumstances, the cause-and-effect relation is reversed. For as already noted in our discussion of cognitive dissonance, sometimes our feelings or beliefs are the result of our actions.

A demonstration comes from the "foot-in-the-door" technique, originally perfected by traveling salesmen. In one study, suburban homeowners were asked to comply with an innocuous request, to put a three-inch square sign advocating auto safety in a window of their homes. Two weeks later, another experimenter came to visit those homeowners who had agreed to display the small sign. This time they were asked to grant a much greater request, to permit the installation of an enormous billboard on their front lawns, proclaiming "Drive Carefully" in huge letters while obstructing most of the house. The results showed that agreement depended upon prior agreement. Once having complied with the first, small request, the subjects were much more likely to give in to the greater one (Freedman and Fraser, 1966).

One interpretation of this and similar findings is a change in self-perception (Snyder and Cunningham, 1975). Having agreed to put up the small sign, the subjects now thought of themselves as active citizens involved in a public issue. Since no one forced them to put up the sign, they attributed their action to their own convictions. Given that they now thought of themselves as active, convinced, and involved, they were ready to play the part on a larger scale. Fortunately for their less-involved neighbors, the billboard was in fact never installed—after all, the request was only part of an experiment. But in real life we may not be let off so easily. The foot-in-the-door approach is a common device for persuading the initially uncommitted; it can be used to sell encyclopedias or political convictions. Extremist political movements generally do not demand violent actions from newcomers. They begin with small requests like signing a petition or giving a distinctive salute. But these may lead to a changed self-perception that ultimately may ready the person for more drastic acts.

In short, our attitudes are affected by what we do and are expected to do. To some extent at least, the role makes the man or the woman. If one is appointed a judge, one begins to feel judicious.

EMOTION: PERCEIVING ONE'S OWN INNER STATES

FOCUS QUESTIONS

■ What is the James-Lange theory of emotions, and in what way does it reverse the usual view? How is this theory problematic?

■ What is the attribution-of-arousal theory? What evidence supports it, and what makes this theory problematic?

■ What are fundamental emotions? How many are postulated, and what evidence supports their innateness? Can they be modified by culture?

It appears that we come to know some of our own attitudes by a process of self-attribution. Some social psychologists have proposed that a similar process may affect the subjective experience of emotion. We say that we feel love, joy, grief, or anger. But are we always sure exactly what emotion we experience? In one of Gilbert and Sullivan's operettas, a character notes that the uninitiated may mis-

The misattribution of one's own inner state According to one of the characters in Gilbert and Sullivan's operetta Patience, *"There is a transcendentality of delirium—an acute accentuation of the supremest ecstasy—which the earthy might easily mistake for indigestion." (From a production by the New York Gilbert and Sullivan Players; photograph by Lee Snider, 1987)*

take love for indigestion. While this is probably an overstatement, something of the sort may be valid for all of us. We often have to interpret our internal states, have to decide whether the knot in our stomach is fear (say, of an impending examination), or is impatient anticipation (say, of a lovers' meeting). According to some psychologists, such interpretive processes are involved whenever we experience an emotion (Schachter and Singer, 1962; Mandler, 1975, 1984). To put their views in perspective, we will begin with a discussion of some earlier theories of emotion.

THE JAMES-LANGE THEORY

■ The topic of emotion has perplexed generations of investigators. Psychologists and biologists have had reasonable success in uncovering some of the objective, bodily manifestations of emotional states; examples are the emotional concomitants of fear and rage (see Chapter 3) and emotional expressions such as the smile (see Chapter 10). But what can we say about the way our emotions are experienced subjectively, how they feel "inside"?

One approach to the problem was proposed by William James. To James, the crucial facet of emotion was that it is an aspect of what a person does. In fear, we run; in grief, we weep. The common-sense interpretation is that the behavior is caused by the emotion. James stood common sense on its head and maintained that the causal relation is reversed; we are afraid *because* we run.

> Common-sense says, we lose our fortune, are sorry and weep; we meet a bear, are frightened and run; we are insulted by a rival, are angry and strike. The hypothesis here . . . is that we feel sorry because we cry, angry because we strike, afraid because we tremble. . . . Without the bodily states following on the perception, the latter would be purely cognitive in form, pale, colorless, destitute of emotional warmth. We might then see the bear, and judge it best to run, receive the insult and deem it right to strike, but we should not actually feel afraid or angry. (James, 1890, v. 2, p. 449)

This is the core of what is now known as the *James-Lange theory of emotions.* (Carl Lange was a contemporary of James who offered a similar account.) In effect, the theory asserts that the subjective experience of emotion is neither more nor less than the awareness of our own bodily changes in the presence of certain arousing stimuli. These bodily changes might be produced by skeletal movements (running) or visceral reactions (pounding heartbeat), though later adherents of James's theory emphasized the visceral responses and the activity of the autonomic nervous system that underlies them (Figure 11.4).

11.4   The sequence of events as conceived by the James-Lange theory of emotions *According to the James-Lange theory, the subjectively experienced emotion is simply our awareness of our own response to the anger- or fear-arousing situation. We see a dangerous object (an attacking dinosaur will do as well as any other); this triggers a bodily response (running, pounding heart), and the awareness of this response is the emotion (here, fear).*

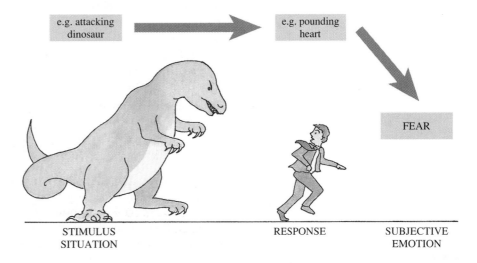

e.g. attacking dinosaur

e.g. pounding heart

FEAR

STIMULUS SITUATION

RESPONSE

SUBJECTIVE EMOTION

3 4 5

The James-Lange theory has been the focus of considerable controversy. One major criticism was raised by Walter Cannon, the pioneer in the study of autonomic functioning (see Chapter 3). Cannon pointed out that sympathetic reactions to arousing stimuli are pretty much the same, while our emotional experiences vary widely. Take the relation between rage and fear. Cannon pointed out that these two emotions are accompanied by just about the same autonomic discharge. So the James-Lange theory must have a flaw, since we are certainly able to distinguish between these two emotional experiences (Cannon, 1927).

A different objection concerns the effect of autonomic arousal. In several early studies, this was accomplished by injecting subjects with adrenaline. This triggered sympathetic activation with all its consequences—palpitations, tremor, and sweaty palms. According to the James-Lange theory, these are among the internally produced stimuli that give rise to the intense emotions of fear and rage. But in fact the subjects did not experience these emotions. Some simply reported the physical symptoms. Others said they felt "as if" they were angry or afraid, a kind of "cold emotion" that they knew was not the real thing (Landis and Hunt, 1932). These findings seemed to constitute a further argument against the James-Lange theory. The visceral reactions are evidently not a sufficient condition for the emotional experience.

THE ATTRIBUTION-OF-AROUSAL THEORY

In contrast to the James-Lange theory, which emphasizes the role of internal bodily feedback, an alternative account focuses on cognitive factors. After all, emotional experiences are usually initiated by certain external events—a letter with tragic news, a loved one's return. Events such as these bring grief or joy, but before they can possibly affect us emotionally they must be appraised and understood. Suppose we see a man who throws a spherical object toward us. Our emotional reaction will surely be different if we think the object is a ball than if we believe that it is a hand grenade. The emotion depends on some cognitive interpretation of the situation that in turn depends on what we see, what we know, and what we expect (Arnold, 1970).

Can a cognitive approach to emotion be combined with the James-Lange emphasis on bodily feedback? Proponents of a theory set forth by Stanley Schachter and Jerome Singer believe that it can. According to this *attribution-of-arousal theory* (sometimes called cognitive arousal theory) various stimuli may trigger a general state of autonomic arousal, but this arousal will provide only the raw materials for an emotional experience—a state of undifferentiated excitement and nothing more. This excitement is shaped into a specific emotional experience by cognitive appraisal and interpretation. In effect, this amounts to an attribution process. A person's heart beats rapidly and her hands tremble—is it fear, rage, joyful anticipation, or a touch of the flu? If the individual has just been insulted, she will interpret her internal reactions as anger and will feel and act accordingly. If she is confronted by William James's bear, she will attribute her visceral excitement to the bear and experience fear. If she is at home in bed, she will probably assume that she is sick. In short, according to Schachter and Singer's theory, emotional experience is produced, not by autonomic arousal as such, but rather by the interpretation of this arousal in the light of the total situation as the subject sees it (Schachter and Singer, 1962; Schachter, 1964; Mandler, 1984; see Figure 11.5).

THE MISATTRIBUTION OF AROUSAL

To test this general conception, Schachter and Singer performed a now classic experiment in which subjects were autonomically aroused but did not know

11.5 The sequence of events as conceived by Schachter and Singer's cognitive evaluation theory of emotions *According to Schachter and Singer, subjectively experienced emotion is the result of an evaluation process in which the subject interprets his own bodily reactions in the light of the total situation. Any number of external stimuli (ranging from attacking dinosaurs to competition in a race) may lead to the same general bodily reaction pattern—running and increased heart rate. The subjective emotion depends upon what the subject attributes these bodily responses to. If he attributes them to a danger signal (the dinosaur), he will feel fear. If he attributes them to the race, he will feel excitement.*

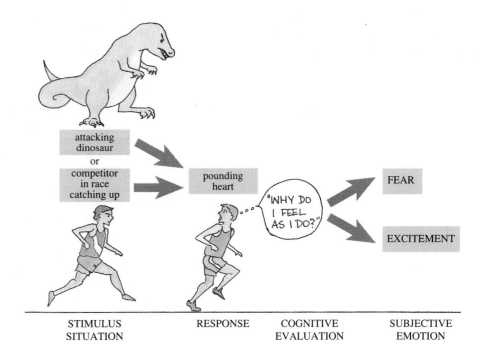

STIMULUS SITUATION · RESPONSE · COGNITIVE EVALUATION · SUBJECTIVE EMOTION

what caused the arousal. The subjects were injected with a drug that they believed to be a vitamin supplement but that was really adrenaline (epinephrine). Some subjects were informed of the drug's real effects, such as increase in heart rate, flushing, tremor, and so on. Other subjects were misinformed. They were told only that the drug might have some side effects, such as numbness or itching. After the drug had been administered, the subjects sat in the waiting room while waiting for what they thought was a test of vision. In actual fact, the main experiment was conducted in this waiting room with a confederate posing as another subject while the experimenter watched through a one-way screen. One condition was set up to produce anger: The confederate was sullen and irritable and eventually stalked out of the room. Another condition provided a context for euphoria: The confederate was ebullient and frivolous; he threw paper planes out of the window, played with a hula hoop, and tried to engage the subject in an improvised basketball game with paper balls. Following their stay in the waiting room, the subjects were asked to rate their emotional feelings (Schachter and Singer, 1962).

The critical question was whether the prior information about the drug's effects would influence the subjects' reactions. Schachter and Singer reasoned that those subjects who had been correctly informed about the physiological consequences of the injection would show less of an emotional response than those who had been misinformed. The informed subjects would attribute their tremors and palpitations to the drug rather than to the external situation. In contrast, the misinformed subjects had to assume that their internal reactions were caused by something outside—the elation of the euphoric confederate or the sullenness of the angry one. Given this external attribution, their emotional state would be in line with the environmental context—euphoric or angry as the case might be. The results were more or less as predicted. The misinformed subjects in the euphoria situation described themselves as more joyful than their correctly informed counterparts and were somewhat more likely than those counterparts to join in the confederate's mad antics. Analogous results were obtained in the anger situation.

BEYOND ATTRIBUTION-OF-AROUSAL THEORY

■ The attribution-of-arousal theory has come in for some criticism. A number of authors have pointed to various problems with the original study, such as that the effects they obtained were rather small or inconclusive and that several later investigators did not succeed in replicating the full range of results predicted by attribution-of-arousal theory (Reisenzein, 1983). But the main point at issue goes beyond the details raised by that experiment. It concerns the theory's contention that visceral arousal can lead to any and all emotional experiences, depending upon the person's interpretation of the situation. Some later studies suggest that emotional experience is not quite as flexible as this. Thus injections of epinephrine may be more likely to lead to negative emotional experiences (such as fear and anger) than to positive ones (such as euphoria) regardless of the context in which they occur (Marshall and Zimbardo, 1979; Maslach, 1979; for a rebuttal, see Schachter and Singer, 1979).

The issue is by no means settled, but a plausible position is one that stands midway between the James-Lange and attribution-of-arousal theories. As we saw, the Schachter-Singer attribution-of-arousal approach starts out with the assumption that all human emotions have the same bodily underpinning. Some investigators, however, claim that there are differences in the autonomic patterns that accompany such emotions as anger, sadness, and fear (e.g., Ax, 1953; Funkenstein, 1956; Schwartz, Weinberger, and Singer, 1981). Other investigators make similar claims but base them mainly on differences in facial expressions. According to these authors, different bodily and facial patterns characterize a number of different *fundamental emotions* (Ekman, 1971, 1984; Izard, 1977). If so, the autonomic raw materials may not allow themselves to be shaped into virtually any emotional experience as Schachter and Singer had supposed.

FUNDAMENTAL EMOTIONS AND FACIAL EXPRESSION

The hypothesis that there are a few distinctive facial expressions that reveal a corresponding set of fundamental emotions goes back to Charles Darwin (Darwin, 1872b), who considered these expressions to be vestiges of basic adaptive patterns shown by our evolutionary forerunners. In effect, he argued that these expressions are a kind of read-out of an underlying emotional state that is a remnant of an ancestral reaction pattern. On this read-out view of facial expressions, our "anger" face, often expressed by lowered brows, widened eyes, and open mouth with exposed teeth, reflects the facial movements our ancestors would have made when biting an opponent. Similarly, our "disgust" face, often manifested as a wrinkled nose and protruded lower lip and tongue, reflects how our ancestors rejected odors or spit out foods (for elaborations, see Ekman, 1980, 1984; Izard, 1977; Tomkins, 1963.)

Just how many fundamental emotions are there? On the facial read-out approach this question can be answered by determining how many distinct facial expressions there are (see Figure 11.6). In Chapter 10, we saw that many of the same facial expressions are used and recognized in many cultures, that they emerge at a very early age, and that they are displayed in blind and deaf children who could not have learned them by observation (see Chapter 10). They must therefore be regarded as part of our built-in human heritage. From these expressions lists of fundamental emotions have been constructed. The numbers vary; one account lists seven: happiness, surprise, anger, sadness, disgust, fear, and contempt (Ekman, 1984). Others list from eight to ten and may include emotions like shame and guilt (e.g., Izard, 1971, 1991; Plutchik, 1980).

The face and emotion A grieving Cypriot woman. (Photo by Constantine Manos/ Magnum)

Further complications are added by the fact that human facial expressions are at least partially under voluntary control. As a result, they can be faked even if we're not emotional or if we experience a different emotion from that which we express. Hamlet was surely not the first to note that one may smile and smile and be a villain. In addition, read-out theorists hold that facial expressions can be at least partially suppressed, using various learned *display rules,* which typically represent a culture's view about what facial signals may or may not be shown overtly and in what contexts (Ekman, Friesen, and O'Sullivan, 1988; Ekman, 1985; Ekman and Friesen, 1986).

FUNDAMENTAL EMOTIONS AND COGNITION

There are a number of further problems about the way in which emotional experiences arise. One concerns the fact that the number of fundamental emotions is rather small. The largest number that has been suggested is ten. But we surely can distinguish between many more emotional experiences than this—for example, between sadness, resignation, regret, grief, and despair, and between happiness, jubilation, rapture, and serene delight. But how can we do this if we possess at most ten different fundamental emotions?

Advocates of the read-out approach argue that the fundamental emotions are often mixed and blended in various proportions, generating an additional number of complex emotions. Thus "jealousy" can be regarded as a mix of fear and anger, while anxiety is composed of the emotions of fear, guilt, sadness, and shame (Izard, 1991).

Further distinctions may be made by just the kind of interpretive process that Schachter and Singer described. A situation arouses the bodily states (and expressive reactions) corresponding to one of the fundamental emotions. This in turn produces an emotional experience—say of fear, or anger, or joy, or sadness. But its exact nature is then further shaped by the situation as the individual interprets it to be. And since the number of situations that the individual can face is countless, the number of emotional experiences that he can feel is countless as well—each with its own complexity and subtle shadings.

TAKING STOCK

On looking back, we should note that many of the phenomena we've considered in this chapter may involve the operation of either (or both) cognition and motivation, or to use two old-fashioned terms, reason and passion. Consider the effect of forced compliance: Is it caused by a force toward cognitive consistency

11.6 Six fundamental emotions The photos depict the facial expressions that some investigators regard as characteristic of six fundamental human emotions: (A) happiness, (B) surprise, (C) sadness, (D) anger, (E) disgust, and (F) fear. (From Matsumoto and Ekman, 1989; photographs courtesy of David Matsumoto)

A

B

C

D

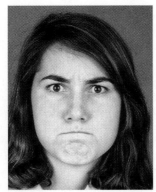

E

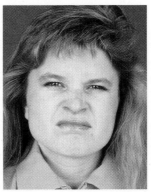

F

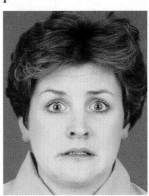

(that is, dissonance reduction) or by an attempt to minimize guilt? Or take the actor-observer bias in attribution: Is it produced by such cognitive factors as differential information and distinct perspectives or by the self-serving bias? Finally consider emotion: Here, if anywhere, motivational factors should be paramount, but we saw that even here—the very stronghold of passion—cognitive processes operate jointly with motivational ones to determine what we experience.

Both reason and passion determine what we think and feel and do. As we try to make sense of our social world, we try to be rational thinkers, but our cognitive limitations often force us to rely on schemas that may lead to various errors and biases. We are also people with motives and passions and a need to maintain self-esteem, so that we are sometimes wishful thinkers rather than rational ones.

QUESTIONS FOR CRITICAL THINKING

1. How would someone studying cognitive dissonance explain why we don't like it if our two best friends dislike each other?

2. Could we ever shed our biases so that we could determine the relative importance of situation versus disposition in understanding behavior?

3. People often go off somewhere alone in order to "find themselves." If indeed we are "looking-glass selves," then who are we looking for in solitude?

4. How might the James-Lange theory explain how we can feel one way but act another?

5. How would attribution-of-arousal theorists explain emotions like contentment and relief in which arousal is minimal?

SUMMARY

1. Social behavior depends in part on how people interpret the situations they encounter. The processes that lead to such interpretations are in many ways similar to those that underlie cognitive processes in general.

2. Our conception of what is real is heavily affected by confirmation from others, as shown by Asch's study on the effects of group pressure and by the need for *social comparison,* especially in ambiguous situations.

3. To make sense of the world, people look for *cognitive consistency.* According to *cognitive dissonance theory,* they will do what they can to reduce any inconsistency (dissonance) they perceive by reinterpreting information to fit in with their beliefs, attitudes, and actions.

4. The interpretation of the situations people encounter is affected by their *attitudes,* which vary from one person to another. Attitudes are rather stable mental positions held toward some idea, object, or person, which combine beliefs, feelings, and predispositions with action.

5. Social psychologists have studied a number of approaches to changing attitudes. One concerns the effectiveness of *persuasive communications.* This depends in part on various characteristics of the message's source, including that source's trustworthiness and credibility. It also depends on characteristics of the message itself. Some contend that strong arguments will be more likely to change attitudes if the message comes in through the *central route* than if it enters through the *peripheral route,* where there is more reliance on rough-and-ready *heuristics.*

SUMMARY

6.   Another approach asserts that attitude change is often produced by an attempt to reduce cognitive dissonance. There is some evidence, however, that the dissonance reduction effects observed in *justification of effort* and *forced compliance* studies are a way of protecting the individual's *favorable self-picture* rather than a means to remove logical inconsistency.

7.   The way we perceive others is in some ways similar to the way we perceive and think of inanimate objects or events. Some theorists believe that impressions of others can be regarded as patterns whose elements are interpreted in terms of the whole. More recent theorists emphasize the role of social cognition, which leads to the formation of *schemas* and *implicit theories of personality*.

8.   Attribution theory tries to explain how we infer the causes of another person's behavior, attributing them either to *situational factors* or to *dispositional qualities*. In part, this process is quite rational and depends on the conditions in which the behavior in question is seen to occur. But it can also lead to various errors. In judging others, we tend to make the *fundamental attribution error*, overestimating the role of dispositional qualities and underestimating that of situational factors. This attribution bias is reversed when we ourselves are the actors rather than the observers. Reasons for the *actor-observer difference* include the fact that we know ourselves better than anyone else and that actors and observers have different perspectives. An additional reason is the *self-serving bias,* which tends to make people deny responsibility for their failures while taking credit for their successes.

9.   According to self-perception theory, similar attribution processes determine how we perceive ourselves. In line with this theory is evidence that people realign their self-perceptions to fit their behavior, as shown in studies using the *foot-in-the-door technique*.

10.   An influential application of self-perception theory is Schachter and Singer's *attribution-of-arousal theory*, which is a revision of the *James-Lange theory of emotions*. According to the James-Lange theory, our subjective experience of emotion is simply an awareness of our own bodily changes (both autonomic and skeletal) in the presence of certain arousing stimuli. In contrast, proponents of the attribution-of-arousal theory argue that the emotion we feel is an interpretation of bodily responses and especially of our own autonomic arousal in light of the situation to which we attribute it.

11.   Many investigators doubt that one arousal process underlies all emotions. They suggest that there are some six to ten *fundamental emotions* that correspond to different facial expressions. According to the *read-out theory*, these facial expressions are a direct read-out of an underlying emotional state. This theory is complicated by the fact that facial expressions can be at least partially suppressed in keeping with culturally acquired *display rules*.

CHAPTER **12**

SOCIAL INTERACTION

I n the previous chapter, we discussed the ways in which we try to understand the social world around us. Our primary emphasis was on social cognition: our attitudes and how they are changed, our impressions of people, our interpretation of why they do what they do, and finally, the way that we ourselves interpret our own actions and experiences. In this chapter, our focus will be on action, or more precisely, *interaction*, as we ask how people deal with each other, influence each other, and act in groups.

We will consider four major kinds of interaction: Some are *one on one,* as when two friends have dinner or a customer tries to bargain with a used-car salesman; others are *many on one,* where many persons act upon one individual, as when a group of teenagers pressures one in their midst to wear the same clothes as all the others; still others are *one on many,* where one person acts on many others, as in various forms of leadership; we will finally consider interactions that can be described as *many on many,* as in riots or panics when many people affect many others and are affected by them in turn.

RELATING TO OTHERS: ONE-ON-ONE INTERACTIONS

FOCUS QUESTIONS

- What is the social exchange view of social interaction?

- How does the reciprocity principle exemplify the social exchange view? How does reciprocity serve as a means of persuasion?

- What is the bystander effect, and what factors contribute to it?

- What factors determine whether we find another person attractive?

How do people interact one on one? To a large extent, the answer depends on the relationship the actors have with each other. We deal one way with comparative strangers, another with people we know and like, and yet another with those we know but don't like. Still, according to many social scientists, there are some common threads that run through most of our relationships, no matter how tenuous or strong they may be. We'll begin by looking at the ways in which we interact with comparative strangers.

SOCIAL EXCHANGE AND RECIPROCITY

A number of theorists believe that one common principle that underlies the way people deal with others is ***social exchange.*** According to this view, each partner in a relationship gives something to the other and expects to receive something in return. Just what is exchanged depends on the relationship. If it is economic, as between buyers and sellers or employees and employers, the exchange will involve goods or labor for money. If it is between friends, lovers, or family members, the exchange will involve valued intangibles such as esteem, loyalty, and affection. According to social exchange theory, all (or at least, most) human relationships have this underlying give-and-take quality. If one partner gives but receives nothing in return, the relationship will disintegrate sooner or later (Kelley and Thibaut, 1978).

The social exchange perspective is essentially economic and thus quite appropriate to the realm of material transactions. In the marketplace, money provides a common standard by which the value of commodities can be assessed. As a result, the value of what is given and received can be compared. This is much harder (and perhaps impossible) to accomplish when the exchange involves such "commodities" as praise or loyalty, let alone love. Whether the social exchange approach applies to all social interactions is therefore a matter of debate but that it applies to some is indubitable. One important example is the operation of the *reciprocity principle*. This is a basic rule that affects many aspects of social behavior. We feel that we somehow must repay whatever we have been given: a favor for a favor, a gift for a gift, a smile for a smile. As one author points out, this sense of social indebtedness is so deeply ingrained that it has been built into the vocabulary of several languages: thus, "much obliged" is a virtual synonym for "thank you" (Cialdini, 1984).

RECIPROCITY AND PERSUASION

According to Robert Cialdini, the reciprocity principle can become a powerful tool of persuasion (Cialdini, 1984). Cialdini points out that incurring a favor necessarily leads to a sense of indebtedness. We feel that we must repay a donor, even if we never wanted his gift in the first place. As a result, we are sometimes manipulated into compliance—saying "yes," or buying some merchandise or making donations—all despite the fact that we never really wanted to. As an example, Cialdini describes the techniques the Hare Krishna Society used to employ in soliciting donations. Members of this sect would approach airport travelers and press a flower into their hands. Travelers would typically want to return the unwanted gift, but the Krishna member would not take the flower back, insisting sweetly that "It is our gift to you." The member's next step would be to request a donation to the society. Many travelers felt that under the circumstances they had no choice. Since they took the gift (no matter how unwillingly), they felt that they had to reciprocate. Their only defense—and many travelers resorted to it—was to beware of Krishnas bearing gifts!

The reciprocal-concession effect   Still another kind of behavior often affected by the reciprocity rule is bargaining. The seller states his price. The potential buyer says "No." Now the seller makes a concession by offering the item (the house, the car, or whatever) at a lower price. This very concession exerts a pressure on the buyer to increase her offer; since he offered a concession, she feels that she ought to give a little on her side too.

The reciprocal-concession effect has been the subject of several laboratory investigations. In one study, an experimenter approached people walking on a university campus and first made a very large request. He asked them to work as unpaid volunteer counselors in a juvenile detention center for two hours a week over a two-year period. Not a single subject agreed. The experimenter then made a much smaller request: that they accompany a group of boys or girls from the juvenile detention center on a single two-hour trip to the zoo. When this smaller request came on the heels of the large request that had been refused, 50 percent of the subjects consented. In contrast, only 17 percent of the subjects acceded to the smaller request when this was not preceded by the prior, larger demand. In the first case, there was an apparent concession; in the second, there

Social exchange   *The process of social exchange is most obvious when it is economic.*

The gifts of the Magi *The social exchange position can be stretched too far, for sometimes we give without expectation of return. (* The Star of Bethlehem, *1888–91, by Edward Burne-Jones; courtesy of The Birmingham Museums and Art Gallery)*

was not. The sheer fact that the experimenter seemed to make a concession was enough to make the subjects feel that they should now make a concession of their own (Cialdini et al., 1975). This method for achieving compliance has been dubbed the ***door-in-the-face technique*** by way of contrast to the foot-in-the-door technique in which compliance with a small request makes the subject more likely to comply with the larger one (see Chapter 11). Both techniques take their names from the tricks of door-to-door salespeople (Cialdini, 1984).

Reciprocity and self-disclosure Clearly, the reciprocity principle can be used to persuade people to give of their time or money. But it can also be used to persuade people to give of themselves. Take ***self-disclosure,*** revealing something personal about oneself. In some ways, telling another person something about your own life is a bit like giving a present: A number of studies confirm that the other person generally feels obliged to disclose a bit about himself in return. A number of studies confirm what common sense surely predicts: As relationships deepen, self-disclosure becomes more frequent and intimate (Jourard, 1964; Altman, 1973; Rubin et al., 1980; Hansen and Schuldt, 1984).

There is a gender difference in patterns of self-disclosure. By and large, women are more willing to reveal themselves to other women than men are to men, at least in Western culture (Morton, 1978). According to some authors, friendships between women are in some ways more intimate and qualitatively different than those between men. What matters to women is sharing emotions; what matters to men is sharing some common activity (Sherrod, 1989). But these differences are clearly affected—and very probably produced—by cultural factors. Thus Chinese students in Hong Kong were more self-disclosing than a comparable group of Americans and showed none of the gender difference so familiar in our own culture (Wheeler, Reis, and Bond, 1989).

ALTRUISM

Social exchange theory suggests (and the reciprocity principle derived from it insists) that no one ever gets anything for nothing. There is no such thing as a free lunch. But this harsh judgment on human nature seems to be contradicted by the fact that people sometimes act unselfishly. Or do they?

The Kitty Genovese tragedy   *Many people watched Kitty Genovese being murdered on a street corner in Queens, but no one intervened. (The Streetlight by Roger Brown, 1983; private collection, New York; courtesy of Phyllis Kind Gallery, New York/Chicago)*

There is ample evidence that people often fail to help others who are in distress. The widespread indifference of pedestrians to the beggars and the homeless all around them is by now a daily fact of American city life. The classic example of public apathy to a stranger's plight is the case of Kitty Genovese who was attacked and murdered on an early morning in 1964 on a street corner in Queens, New York. The assault lasted over half an hour during which time she screamed and struggled while her assailant stabbed her repeatedly until she finally died. It later came out that thirty-eight of her neighbors had watched the episode from their windows, but none of them had come to her aid. No one even called the police (Rosenthal, 1964). Why was there this appalling inactivity?

THE BYSTANDER EFFECT

One factor may be a lack of altruistic motivation. Perhaps people in a big city simply don't care about the fate of strangers, no matter how terrible it may be. But according to Bibb Latané and John Darley, the failure to help is often produced by the way people understand the situation. It's not that they don't care but that they don't understand what should be done. Here, as in many other contexts, social action (and interaction) is heavily affected by social cognition.

Ambiguity   Consider the passerby who sees a man lying unconscious on a city street. How can he tell whether the man is ill or drunk? The situation is ambiguous. A similar confusion troubled some of the witnesses to the Genovese slaying. They later reported that they weren't quite sure what was going on. Perhaps it was a joke, a drunken bout, a lover's quarrel. If it were any of these, intervention might have proved very embarrassing.

Pluralistic ignorance   The situation is further complicated by the fact that the various witnesses to the Genovese tragedy realized that many others were seeing just what they did. For as they watched the drama on the street unfold, they saw the lights go on in many of the windows of adjacent buildings. As a result there was *pluralistic ignorance.* Each of the witnesses looked to the others to decide whether there really was an emergency. Each was ignorant of the fact that the others were just as unsure as they. The sheer fact that the various witnesses could see each other through the windows reassured them that nothing urgent was going on.

Diffusion of responsibility The fact that each observer knew that others observed the same event made it difficult to realize that the event was an emergency. But this fact had yet another consequence. It made intervention less probable even for those witnesses who did recognize (or at least suspect) that the situation was an emergency. For these persons were now faced with a ***diffusion of responsibility.*** No one thought that it was her responsibility to act. After all, while many of the observers might have felt some impulse to help, they also had self-centered motives that held them back: Some didn't want to get involved; others were afraid of the assailant; still others were apprehensive about dealing with the police. The conflict between the desire to help and to mind one's own business was finally resolved in favor of inaction through the knowledge that others witnessed the same event. Everyone assumed that since so many others saw just what they did, surely one of them would do something about it or had already done it (such as calling the police). As a result, no one did anything (see Figure 12.1).

This general line of reasoning has been tested in a number of experiments. In one, subjects were asked to participate in what they thought was a group discussion about college life with either one, three, or five other people. The subjects were placed in individual cubicles and took turns talking to each other over an intercom system. In actuality, there was only one subject; all the other discussants were tape recordings. The discussion began as one of the (tape-recorded)

12.1 The bystander effect

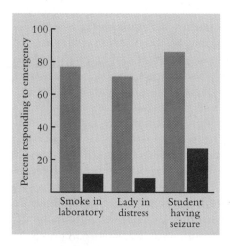

12.2 Group inhibition of bystander intervention in emergencies *When people are alone (in blue) they are more likely to respond in an emergency than when they are—or think they are—with others (in dark red), in part because of diffusion of felt responsibility. (Data from Darley, 1968; Latané and Rodin, 1969)*

confederates described some of his own personal problems, which included a tendency toward epileptic seizures in times of stress. When he began to speak again during the second round of talking, he feigned a seizure and gasped for help. The question was whether the subject would leave his own cubicle to assist the stricken victim (usually, by asking the experimenter's help). The results demonstrated the ***bystander effect:*** The larger the size of the group that the subject is in (or thinks he is in), the less likely he is to come to the victim's assistance (Darley and Latané, 1968; see Figure 12.2).

The bystander effect has been obtained in numerous other situations. In some, a fellow subject seems to have an asthma attack; in others, the experimenter appears to faint in an adjacent room; in still others, the laboratory fills with smoke. But whatever the emergency, the result is always the same: The larger the group the subject is in (or thinks he is in), the smaller the chance that he will take any action—in dramatic accord with the diffusion of responsibility hypothesis (Latané and Nida, 1981; Latané, Nida, and Wilson, 1981).

THE COSTS OF HELPING

The work on the bystander effect indicates that people often don't recognize that a need for help exists and that even when they do, they may not act because they think that others will. But suppose the situation is not ambiguous and that responsibility for helping is not diffused? Will they then help a stranger in distress?

One factor that determines whether they will or won't is the physical or psychological cost to the prospective helper. The greater that cost, the smaller the chance that he will in fact help. In some cases, the cost is physical danger. In others, it is simply time and effort. In one study, students had to go from one campus building to another to give a talk. They were told to hurry, since they were already late. As they rushed to their appointments, these students passed by a shabbily dressed man who lay in a doorway groaning. Only 10 percent

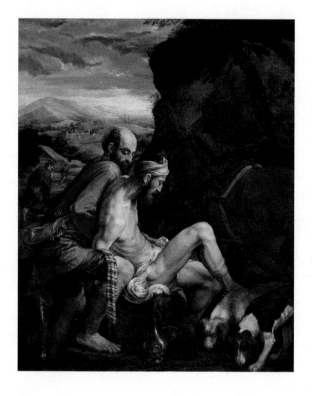

The Good Samaritan *(Painting by Jacopo Bassano, 1517/18–1592. Photograph © The National Gallery, London)*

Altruism *Helping victims of a highway collapse during the San Francisco earthquake of 1989. (Courtesy of the New York Public Library Picture Collection)*

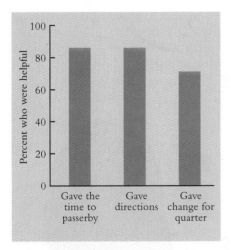

12.3 **Small acts of helping in a large city** *Various minor and prosaic acts of helping strangers are by no means uncommon even in a big city. (Data from Gerard, Wilhelmy, and Conolley, 1968)*

stopped to help the victim. Ironically enough, the students were members of a theological seminary, and the topic of their talk was the parable of the Good Samaritan who came to the aid of a man lying injured on a roadside. It appears that if the cost—here in time—is high enough, even theological students may not behave altruistically (Darley and Batson, 1973).

What is costly to one potential helper may not be equally so to another. Take physical danger. It is probably not surprising that bystanders who intervene in cases of assault are generally much taller, stronger, and better trained than bystanders who do not intervene and are almost invariably men (Huston et al., 1981).

THE SELFISH BENEFITS OF UNSELFISHNESS

Providing help can yield benefits as well as costs. Some of the benefits are various signs of social approval, as in the case of a wealthy donor who is sure to make a lavish contribution as long as everyone watches. Other benefits have to do with avoiding embarrassment. Many city dwellers give two or three quarters to a beggar not because they want to help him but because it's easier to give than to say no. Occasionally the benefits of giving involve romance. In one study, the investigators posed as motorists in distress, trying to flag passing cars to provide help with a flat tire. The passing cars were much more likely to stop for a female than for a male, and the cars that stopped were generally driven by young men alone. The best guess is that the young men's altruism was not entirely unalloyed by sexual interest (West, Whitney, and Schnedler, 1975).

IS THERE ANY GENUINE ALTRUISM?

The preceding discussion paints a somewhat unflattering portrait of human nature. It seems that we often fail to help strangers in need of assistance and that when we do, our help is often rather grudging and calculated, and based on some expectation of later reciprocation. But that picture is too one-sided. For while people can be callous and indifferent, they are also capable of true generosity and altruism (see Figure 12.3). Sometimes people share food, give blood, contribute to charities, and administer artificial respiration to accident victims. Yet more impressive are the unselfish deeds of living, genetically unrelated donors who give one of their kidneys to a stranger who will otherwise die (Sadler et al., 1971). And still others are commemorated by Jerusalem's Avenue of the Righteous, dedicated to the European Christians who sheltered Jews during the Nazi Holocaust, risking (and often giving) their own lives to save those to whom they gave refuge (London, 1970).

Such acts of altruism suggest that human behavior is not always selfish. This probably undermines the claim that all social interactions can be understood as a form of exchange. To be sure, acts of altruism in which the giver gets *no* benefits at all—no gratitude, no public acclaim—are fairly rare. The true miracle is that they exist at all. One aspect of our humanity is that we can go beyond the calls of social exchange and reciprocity.

ATTRACTION

■ Thus far, we've primarily looked at social interactions with virtual strangers. What happens when the interactions are with people to whom we are closer and about whom we have stronger feelings? We'll begin by asking about the factors that attract us to others.

"Do you really love me, Anthony, or is it just because I live on the thirty-eighth floor?" (Drawing by Claude; © 1959, 1987, The New Yorker Magazine, Inc.)

PROXIMITY

One of the most important determinants of attraction and liking is sheer **proximity.** By now, dozens of studies have documented the fact that if you want to predict who makes friends with whom, the first thing to ask is who is nearby. Students who live next to each other in a dormitory or sit next to each other in classes develop stronger relations than those who live or sit only a bit farther away. Similarly, members of a bomber crew become much more friendly to fellow crewmen who work right next to them than to others only a few feet away (Berscheid and Walster, 1978; Berscheid, 1985).

What holds for friendship also holds for mate selection. For example, there is evidence that more than half of the couples who took out marriage licenses in Columbus, Ohio, during the summer of 1949 were people who lived within sixteen blocks of each other when they went out on their first date (Clarke, 1952). Much the same holds for the probability that an engagement will ultimately lead to marriage; the farther apart the two live, the greater the chance that the engagement will be broken off (Berscheid and Walster, 1978).

Why should proximity be so important? One answer is that you can't like someone you've never met, and the chances of meeting that someone are much greater if he is nearby. But why should getting to know him make you like him?

One reason may be *familiarity.* There is a good deal of evidence that people tend to like what's familiar. This seems to hold for just about any stimulus, whether it's a word in a foreign language or a melody or the name of a commercial product—the more often it is seen or heard, the better it will be liked (Zajonc, 1968; Brickman and D'Amato, 1975; Moreland and Zajonc, 1982). Familiarity probably plays an important role in determining what we feel about other people as well. The hero of a well-known musical comedy explains his affection for the heroine by singing "I've grown accustomed to her face." In a more prosaic vein, the laboratory provides evidence that photographs of strangers' faces are judged to be more likable the more often they have been seen (Jorgensen and Cervone, 1978). Another study applied this general idea to the comparison of faces and their mirror images. Which will be better liked? If familiarity is the critical variable, then our friends should prefer a photograph of our face to one of its mirror image, since they've seen the first much more often than the second. But we ourselves should prefer the mirror image, which for us is by far the more familiar. The results were as predicted by the familiarity hypothesis (Mita, Dermer, and Knight, 1977; see Figure 12.4).

12.4 Familiarity and liking *The figure shows two versions of a rather well-known lady. Which do you like better—the one on the right or the one on the left? (Courtesy Réunion des Musées Nationaux) (Please turn to p. 370.)*

SIMILARITY

Do people like others who are similar to themselves, or do they prefer those who are very different? To put it differently, which bit of folk wisdom is more nearly correct: "Birds of a feather flock together" or—perhaps in analogy with magnets—"Opposites attract." It appears that birds have more to teach us in this matter than magnets do, for the evidence suggests that, in general, people tend to like others who are *similar* to themselves. For example, elementary school students prefer other children who perform about as well as they do in academics, sports, and music (Tesser, Campbell, and Smith, 1984), and "best friends" in high school resemble each other in age, race, year in school, and high-school grades (Kandel, 1978).

Whether similarity of personality characteristics such as sociability and extraversion play a similar role in determining attraction is still unclear. But there is no doubt that such relatively more objective attributes as race, ethnic origin, social and educational level, family background, income, and religion do affect marital choice and stability. This also holds for such behavioral patterns as the degree of gregariousness and drinking and smoking habits. One widely cited study showed that engaged couples in the United States are generally similar along all of these dimensions (Burgess and Wallin, 1943). The authors interpreted these findings as evidence for **homogamy**—a powerful tendency for like to marry like. Another study showed that homogamy plays a role in determining a couple's stability; couples who remained together after two-and-a-half years were more similar than those who had broken up (Hill, Rubin, and Peplau, 1976).

Is homogamy really produced by the effect of similarity on mutual liking? Or is it just a byproduct of proximity, of the fact that "few of us have an opportunity to meet, interact with, become attracted to, and marry a person markedly dissimilar from ourselves"? (Berscheid and Walster, 1978, p. 87). The answer is as yet unknown. But whether similarity is a cause of the attraction or is a side effect of some other factors that led to it initially, the end product is the same: Like pairs with like, and no heiress ever marries the butler except in the movies. We're not really surprised to discover that when a princess kisses a frog he turns into a prince. What would really be surprising is to see the frog turn into a peasant whom the princess then marries all the same.

Homogamy American Gothic *by Grant Wood, 1930 (Photograph © 1992 The Art Institute of Chicago, all rights reserved)*

PHYSICAL ATTRACTIVENESS

There is little doubt that for a given time and culture there is considerable agreement as to how *physically attractive* a particular man or woman is. Nor is there any doubt that this factor is overwhelmingly important in determining a person's appeal—or at least his or her initial appeal—to members of the opposite sex. The vast sums of money spent on cosmetics, fashion, diets, and various forms of plastic surgery are one kind of testimony; our everyday experience is another. Under the circumstances, one may wonder whether there is any need to document the point experimentally, but in any case, such documentation does exist. In one study, freshmen were randomly paired at a dance and later asked how much they liked their partner and whether they wanted to go out with him or her at some future time. The main factor that determined each person's desirability as a future date was his or her physical attractiveness (Walster et al., 1966). Similar results were found in a study of the clients of a commercial video-dating service who selected partners after consulting files that included a photograph, background information, and detailed information about interests, hobbies, and personal ideals. When it came to the actual choice, the primary determinant was the photograph: Both male and female clients selected on the basis of physical attractiveness (Green, Buchanan, and Heuer, 1984).

Matching for attractiveness   Physical attractiveness is clearly a very desirable quality. But if we all set our sights on only those who occupy the very top of this dimension, the world would soon be depopulated—there are simply not enough movie queens and matinee idols to go around. One would therefore assume that people behave in a more sensible fashion. They may well covet the most attractive of all possible mates, but they also have a fairly reasonable perception of their own social desirability (which is determined in part by their own physical attractiveness). In consequence, they will seek partners of roughly comparable social assets; while trying to get a partner who is most desirable, they also try to avoid rejection. This **matching hypothesis** predicts a strong correlation between the physical attractiveness of the two partners (Berscheid et al., 1971). This hypothesis is well supported by everyday observations ("They make such a fine couple!") and has been repeatedly documented in various empirical observations (Berscheid and Walster, 1974; White, 1980; Feingold, 1988).

What underlies physical attractiveness?   Our discussion has assumed that physical attractiveness is a given and that people pretty much agree on who is and who is not attractive. But why should this be? Why should one set of particular features, one set of bodily proportions, represent the apex of attractiveness for so many people in our time and culture? As yet we don't know.

So far we are only beginning to discover just what it is that constitutes physical attractiveness in our own culture. According to one study, American college men judge photographs of women (whether white, black, or Asian) as more attractive if their faces have certain features that are perceived as "cute" and tend to be found in children, such as relatively large and widely separated eyes, a small nose, and a small chin. If this result holds up in other cultures, a sociobiologist might suggest that this is because perceived youthfulness is a sign of fertility. The trouble is that there are a number of other features judged to be attractive that are associated with maturity rather than immaturity, for example, wide cheekbones and narrow cheeks (Cunningham, 1986).

In any case, there is little reason to suppose that the standards of attractiveness—of face or body—are the same across different times and places. To be sure, some similarities do exist. Signs of ill health and deformity (which might suggest a poor genetic bet) are considered unattractive in all cultures. The same holds for signs of advancing age (which generally signal lower fertility, especially in females). In addition, all cultures want males to look male and females to look

Attractiveness in American society   *Cher accepting the Oscar for Best Actress in 1988. (Photograph © 1988, Smeal/Ron Galella Ltd.)*

Attractiveness   *People ornament themselves in virtually every culture but choose different ways of doing so. (A) Balinese dancer (Photograph by George K. Fuller), (B) Ahka girl from a village in Thailand (Photograph by George K. Fuller), (C) Masai girl in Kenya (John Moss/Photo Researchers)*

A

B

C

female, although the specific cues that weigh in this judgment (and that are considered attractive) vary widely. Beyond this, however, the differences probably outweigh the similarities.

LOVE

Attraction tends to bring people closer together. If they are close enough, their relation may be that of *love*. According to some authorities, psychologists might have been "wise to have abdicated responsibility for analysis of this term and left it to poets" (Reber, 1985, p. 409). But wise or not, in recent years psychologists have tried to say some things about this strange state of mind that has puzzled both sages and poets throughout the ages.

Psychologists have tried to distinguish between different kinds of love. Some of the resulting classification systems are rather complex. But most agree that there are at least two crude categories. One is romantic—or passionate—love, the kind of love that one "falls into," that one is "in." The other is companionate love, a less violent state that emphasizes companionship and mutual trust and care.

ROMANTIC LOVE

Romantic love has been described as essentially passionate: "a wildly emotional state [in which] tender and sexual feelings, elation and pain, anxiety and relief, altruism and jealousy coexist in a confusion of feelings" (Berscheid and Walster, 1978). The extent to which the lovers feel that they are in the grip of an emotion they can't control is indicated by the very language in which they describe their love: They "fall in love," "are swept off their feet," and "can't stop themselves."

These tumultuous emotions are sharply focused on the beloved, who is almost always seen through a rosy glow. The lover constantly thinks about the beloved and continually wants to be in his or her company, sometimes to the point of near obsession. Given this giddy mixture of erotic, irrational, obsessed passions and idealized fantasy, it's understandable why Shakespeare felt that lovers have much in common with both madmen and poets. They are a bit mad because their emotions are so turbulent and their thoughts and actions so obsessive; they are a bit poetic because they don't see their beloved as he or she really is but as an idealized fabrication of their own desires and imaginings.

The rocky course of romantic love It has often been observed that romantic love seems to thrive on obstacles. Shakespeare tells us that the "course of true love never did run smooth" but if it had, the resulting love might have been lacking in ardor. The fervor of a wartime romance or of an extramarital affair is probably fed in part by danger and frustration, and many a lover's passion becomes all the more intense for being unrequited. In all these cases, there is increased arousal, whether through fear, frustration, or anxiety. This arousal continues to be interpreted as love, a cognitive appraisal that fits in perfectly with our ideas about romantic love, for these include suffering as well as rapture. An interesting demonstration of this phenomenon is the so-called Romeo-and-Juliet effect (named after Shakespeare's doomed couple whose parents violently opposed their love). This describes the fact that parental opposition tends to intensify the couple's romantic passion rather than to diminish it. In one study, couples were asked whether their parents interfered with their relationship. The greater this interference, the more deeply the couples fell in love (Driscoll, Davis, and Lipitz, 1972). The moral is that if parents want to break up a romance, their best

Romantic love *The blindness of romantic love is epitomized by Titania, Queen of the Fairies, in Shakespeare's* Midsummer Night's Dream. *Titania is made to fall in love with Bottom whose head has been turned into that of an ass. (*Titania Awakes, Surrounded by Attendant Fairies, Clinging Rapturously to Bottom, Still Wearing the Ass's Head, 1793/94, *by Henry Fuseli; Kunsthaus, Zurich (Switzerland), Society of Zurich Friends of Art; © 1994 Kunsthaus Zurich. All rights reserved.)*

Companionate love *When passion and obsession ebb, the companionship and affection of companionate love may follow. (Photograph © FPG International)*

bet is to ignore it. If the feuding Montagues and Capulets had simply looked the other way, Romeo and Juliet might well have become bored with each other by the end of the second act.

COMPANIONATE LOVE

It's widely agreed that romantic love tends to be a short-lived bloom. That wild and tumultuous state, with its intense emotional ups and downs, with its obsessions, fantasies, and idealizations, rarely if ever lasts forever. Eventually there are no further surprises and no further obstacles except those posed by the inevitable problems of ordinary life. The adventure is over, and romantic love ebbs. Sometimes it turns into indifference (if not active dislike). But sometimes—and hopefully more often—it is transformed into a related but gentler emotion—*companionate love.* This is sometimes defined as the "affection we feel for those with whom our lives are deeply intertwined" (Hatfield and Walster, 1981, p. 124). In companionate love, the similarity of outlook, mutual caring, and trust that develop through day to day living become more important than the fantasies and idealization of romantic love, as the two partners try to live as happily ever after as it is possible to do in the actual world. This is not to say that the earlier passion doesn't occasionally flare up again. But this passion no longer has the obsessive quality that it once had, where the lover is unable to think of anything but the beloved (Neimeyer, 1984; Hatfield, 1988; Caspi and Herbener, 1990).

SOCIAL INFLUENCE: MANY-ON-ONE INTERACTIONS

FOCUS QUESTIONS

- What is social facilitation? In what circumstances does the presence of others help or hinder our performance?

- Why do people conform? Why might some degree of conformity or obedience be beneficial?

- What was the Milgram experiment? To what degree did the subjects obey the experimenter? What factors appeared to promote or deter their obedience?

Up to now, our discussion has focused upon one-on-one interactions: some between comparative strangers, others between friends and lovers. In such interactions, other people often affect what we do, as in the case of a salesman trying to sell a car to a potential customer or a would-be lover trying to persuade his beloved to reciprocate his affections. But there are instances in which the interaction is more complex and in which the social effects come from many people simultaneously.

Such situations are usually discussed under the general heading of *social influence.* In these cases, the interaction is of the form of many on one: The influence of many others converges upon one individual. In some cases, the influence of others may make us tailor our behavior to conform to theirs. In others, it will make us obey them and comply with their orders. And in still other instances, the others exert their influence upon us in an even simpler way—by their mere presence as an audience.

SOCIAL FACILITATION: SOCIAL INFLUENCE BY THE PRESENCE OF OTHERS

It has long been known that the presence of other people has an effect on us. An example is laughter: Every comedian knows that laughter is contagious; each guffaw triggers another and yet another, a fact that led to the use of canned TV laughter on the theory that if the home audience hears the (dubbed) laughs of others, they will laugh along (Wilson, 1985). Similar effects have been demonstrated by many investigators who compared people on various tasks that they performed either alone or in the presence of others. The initial results suggested that the social effect is always beneficial. When with others who are engaged in the same task, people race bicycles faster, learn simple mazes more quickly, and perform more multiplication problems in the same period of time. Such effects have been grouped under the general title *social facilitation* (Allport, 1920).

Other studies, however, have indicated that the presence of others can sometimes be a hindrance instead of a help. While college students are faster at solving simple mazes when working with others, they are considerably slower when the mazes are more complex (Hunt and Hillery, 1973; Zajonc, 1965, 1980). An audience can evidently *inhibit* as well as facilitate. How can such divergent results be reconciled?

According to Robert Zajonc, the explanation is that the presence of others leads to a state of increased drive or arousal. Such an increase would resolve the apparent contradiction if we assume that it strengthens the tendency to perform highly dominant responses—the ones that seem to come "automatically." If so, then we should expect that the presence of others would improve performance when the dominant response is also the correct one—as in performing simple motor skills or learning simple mazes. But when the task gets harder—as in the case of complex mazes—then the dominant response is often incorrect. As a result, we should expect performance to get worse when others watch us, for in that case the dominant response (enhanced by increased arousal) will inhibit the less dominant but correct reaction. And this is just what happens.

As an example from ordinary life consider an accomplished professional actor. Such a person generally thrives in front of an audience—the bigger the audience, the happier he is. For him, the dominant responses are precisely those demanded by his role; he knows his part and how to make the most of it, and so the audience brings his performance to even higher peaks. But the situation is very different for an unpracticed young amateur who is still stumbling over his lines and unsure of his part. His dominant responses are inappropriate to what he ought to be doing, and so he coughs, gives an embarrassed smile, and takes a few undecided half steps. He becomes aroused by the audience, but this arousal makes his performance even worse than it would be otherwise (Zajonc, 1965, 1980).

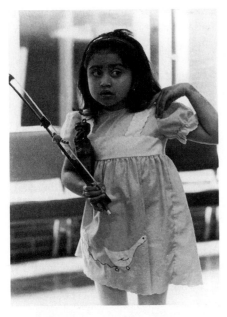

Social facilitation *Audiences generally enhance the performance of an accomplished professional. But the effect on novices is not always beneficial. (Photograph by Gale Zucker/Stock, Boston)*

CONFORMITY

Social facilitation (and inhibition) may well be the simplest form of social influence. It shows that our behavior is affected by the mere presence of others just about regardless of what they do. But in other forms of social influence what others do matters very much indeed. An important example is *conformity* in which we go along with other people. We may regard ourselves as independent nonconformists, but in some situations we all conform whether in speech or dress or manner. In the last chapter, we saw that people may go along with a group even when the group is patently wrong, as in Asch's experiment when the subjects yielded to a majority that judged an 8-inch line to be equal to one whose length was 6 1/4 inches (Asch, 1952, 1955, 1956; see Chapter 11).

THE CAUSES OF CONFORMITY

Why do people conform? The evidence suggests that there are two main reasons: One is that they want to be right; another is that they want to be liked (or at least that they don't want to appear foolish).

One basis for following others is when we ourselves aren't sure what is right. In such cases, the group exerts influence because it provides information that we feel that we ourselves don't have. This holds for information about any difficult judgment, whether it is sensory, social, or moral. If we are nearsighted and aren't wearing glasses, we'll ask others to read distant street signs; if we are not sure of what to wear (or what to say or who to vote for), we watch what others do to get some clues for how we ourselves should act. If people are made to believe that they are more competent and knowledgeable in some area than others are (for example, in seeing hidden figures), they are less likely to conform (e.g., Wiesenthal et al., 1976; Campbell, Tesser, and Fairey, 1986).

Another reason for going along with the crowd is not so much cognitive as motivational. For we sometimes conform even if we believe that we are right and the others are wrong. Consider the original Asch study in which a unanimous majority made a grossly incorrect judgment. The subject sees the world as it is, but she has every reason to believe that the others see it differently. If she now says what she believes, she can't help but be embarrassed; after all, the others will probably think that she's a fool and may then laugh at her. Under the circumstances, many subjects prefer to disguise what they really believe and go along.

THE EFFECT OF AN ALLY

A unanimous majority evidently exerts a powerful effect on a solitary individual that makes him want to conform. What happens when the individual is no longer alone?

The ally effect   Not being alone sustains one against a majority but also in other struggles, such as against evil witches and all-powerful wizards. (From the 1939 movie, The Wizard of Oz, with Judy Garland, Ray Bolger, Jack Haley, and Bert Lahr; courtesy of Photofest)

NURIT KARLIN

"Twenty-two is out of step. Pass it on."

To answer this question, Asch varied his experiment by having one of the confederates act as the subject's ally; all of the other confederates gave wrong answers while the ally's judgments were correct. Under these conditions, the real subject yielded very rarely and was not particularly upset.

The moral seems simple enough: One person who believes as we do can sustain us against all others. But on closer examination, things are not quite as simple as that. For in another variation, the confederate again deviated from the majority, but she didn't do so by giving the correct answer. On the contrary, she gave an answer that was even further from the truth than was the group's. Thus, on a trial in which the correct answer was 6 1/4 inches and the group answer was 6 3/4 inches, the confederate's answer might be 8 inches. This response was obviously not arrayed on the side of the subject (or of truth), but it helped to liberate the subject even so. He now yielded very much less than when confronted by a unanimous majority. What evidently mattered was the group's unanimity; once this was broken, the subject felt that he could speak up without fear of embarrassment (Asch, 1952). Similar studies have been performed in other laboratories with essentially similar results (Allen and Levine, 1971; Allen, 1975; Nemeth and Chiles, 1988).

One person who shares our view can sustain us against all others. But if we can't find a supporter, the next best thing is to find another person who also opposes the majority, even if her opposition comes from the other side than our own. Thus, totalitarian systems have good reason to stifle dissent of any kind, whether of the right or the left. The moment one voice is raised in dissent, the unanimity is broken and then others may (and often do) find the courage to express their own dissent, whatever its form.

BLIND OBEDIENCE

There is another way of influencing the behavior of others that is much more direct than any we've considered thus far. It is by getting people to obey what we command them to do. Of particular interest is the case of *blind obedience* to orders that violate one's own conscience, actions in which the individual subordinates his own understanding of the situation to that of some authority.

A certain degree of obedience is a necessary ingredient of living in a society. In any society, no matter how primitive, some individuals have authority over others, at least within a limited sphere. Obedience is particularly relevant as

Obedience *The commandant of a concentration camp in Germany stands amid some of his prisoners who were burned or shot as the American army approached the camp during the last days of World War II. Most Nazis who held such positions insisted that they were "just following orders." (Courtesy of United Press International)*

societies get more complex, where the spheres within which authority can be exerted become much more differentiated. Teachers assign homework, doctors order intravenous feedings, and policemen stop automobiles. The pupils, nurses, and motorists generally obey. Their obedience is based on an implicit recognition that the persons who issued the orders were operating within their legitimate domain of authority. If this domain is overstepped, obedience is unlikely. Policemen can't order motorists to recite lists of irregular French verbs or to take two aspirins and go to bed.

Some tendency to obey authority is thus a vital cement that holds society together; without it, there would be chaos. But the atrocities of this century—the Nazi death camps, the Cambodian massacres, the so-called ethnic cleansing in Bosnia—give terrible proof that this disposition to obedience can also become a corrosive poison that destroys our sense of humanity. Some of these atrocities could not have been committed without the obedience of tens or hundreds of thousands and the acquiescence of many more.

OBEDIENCE: PERSONALITY STRUCTURE OR SITUATION?

What makes people obey and thus participate in any of the unspeakable acts of which history tells us? One interpretation is that some personalities are more prone to obey than others, that the crucial determinant is within the person rather than in the situation.

An influential version of the person-centered hypothesis was proposed shortly after World War II by a group of investigators who believed they had discovered a personality type that is predisposed toward totalitarian dogma and is thus more ready to obey unquestioningly. Such ***authoritarian personalities*** are prejudiced against various minority groups and also hold certain sentiments about authority, including submission to those above, harshness to those below, and a general belief in the importance of power and dominance (Adorno et al., 1950).

While these studies have been criticized on various theoretical and methodological grounds (e.g., Snyder and Ickes, 1985), some of their major claims seem to have a basis in fact. Minority prejudice probably does tend to go together with authoritarian sentiments, and people with such sentiments do show a number of political characteristics that might be expected: They tend to be more obedient to authority, vote for conservative and law-and-order candidates, and accept the attitudes of those in power (Elms and Milgram, 1966; Izzett, 1971; Poley, 1974).

Can the person-centered hypothesis explain the atrocities of recent times? Are those who obey the order to massacre countless innocents sick individuals completely different from the rest of us? Some of them probably are (Dicks, 1972). But the frightening fact is that many seem to be cast in a much more ordinary mold; what is horrifying about them is what they do and not who they are. In a well-known account of the trial of Adolf Eichmann, the man who supervised the deportation of six million Jews to the Nazi gas chambers, the author comments on the grotesque "banality of evil": "The trouble with Eichmann was precisely that so many were like him, and that the many were neither perverted nor sadistic, that they were, and still are, terribly and terrifyingly normal" (Arendt, 1965, p. 276).

THE MILGRAM STUDIES

The importance of situational factors in producing obedience is highlighted by the results of what may be the best known study in modern social psychology, conducted by Stanley Milgram (1963). Milgram's subjects were drawn from a

A

B

C

D

broad spectrum of socioeconomic and educational levels; they were recruited by a local newspaper ad offering $4.50 per hour to persons willing to participate in a study of memory. Milgram's subjects arrived at the laboratory where a white-coated experimenter told them that the study in which they were to take part concerned the effect of punishment on human learning.

The subjects were run in pairs and drew lots to determine who would be the "teacher" and who the "learner." The task of the learner was to master a list of associations. The task of the teacher was to present the stimuli, to record the learner's answers, and—most important—to administer punishment whenever the learner responded incorrectly. The learner was conducted to a cubicle where the experimenter strapped him in a chair, to "prevent excess movement," and attached the shock electrodes to his wrist—all in full view of the teacher. After the learner was securely strapped in place, the teacher was brought back to the main experimental room and seated in front of an imposing-looking shock generator. The generator had thirty lever switches with labeled shock intensities, ranging from 15 volts to 450 volts in 15-volt increments. Below each of the levers there were also verbal descriptions ranging from "Slight Shock" to "Danger: Severe Shock." The labels below the last two levers were even more ominous; they were devoid of any verbal designation and were simply marked "XXX" (Figure 12.5).

The teacher presented the items that had to be memorized. He was instructed to move on to the next item on the list whenever the learner responded correctly but to administer a shock whenever an error was made. He was told to increase the level of punishment with each succeeding error, beginning with 15 volts and going up by one step for each error thereafter until 450 volts was reached. To get an idea what the learner experienced, the teacher first submitted to a sample shock of 45 volts, the third of the thirty-step punishment series, which gave an unpleasant jolt. During the experiment, all communications between teacher and learner were conducted over an intercom, since the learner was out of sight, strapped to a chair in the experimental cubicle.

Needless to say, the shock generator never delivered any shocks (except for the initial sample) and the lot drawing was rigged so that the learner was always a confederate, played by a mild-mannered, middle-aged actor. The point of the experiment was simply to determine how far the subjects would go in obeying the experimenter's instructions. Since the learner made a fair number of errors, the shock level of the prescribed punishment kept on rising. By the time 120 volts was reached, the victim shouted that the shocks were becoming too painful. At 150 volts he demanded that he be let out of the experiment. At 180 volts, he cried out that he could no longer stand the pain. At 300 volts, he screamed that he would give no further answers and insisted that he be freed. On the next few shocks there were agonized screams. After 330 volts, there was silence.

The learner's responses were of course predetermined. But the real subjects—the teachers—did not know that, so they had to decide what to do. When the victim cried out in pain or refused to go on, the subjects usually turned to the experimenter for instructions. In response, the experimenter told the subjects that the experiment had to go on, indicated that he took full responsibility, and pointed out that "the shocks may be painful but there is no permanent tissue damage."

12.5 The obedience experiment (A) The "shock generator" used in the experiment. (B) The learner is strapped into his chair and electrodes are attached to his wrist. (C) The teacher receives a sample shock. (D) The teacher breaks off the experiment. (Copyright 1965 by Stanley Milgram. From the film Obedience, distributed by Penn State Audio-Visual Services.)

Revisiting Figure 12.4   The familiarity-leads-to-liking hypothesis would predict a preference for the left panel—a retouched photograph of the Mona Lisa (see p. 360). The panel on the right is a mirror image of that photograph, which is presumably the less familiar of the two.

How far do subjects go in obeying the experimenter? The results were astounding: About 65 percent of Milgram's subjects continued to obey the experimenter to the bitter end. This proportion was unaffected even when the learner mentioned that he suffered from a mild heart condition. This isn't to say that the obedient subjects had no moral qualms—quite the contrary. Many of them were seriously upset. They bit their lips, twisted their hands, sweated profusely—but obeyed even so. Similar results were obtained when the study was repeated with subjects from other countries—Australia, Germany, and Jordan (Kilham and Mann, 1974; Mantell and Panzarella, 1976; Shanab and Yahya, 1977).

Is there a parallel between obedience in these artificial laboratory situations and obedience in the all-too-real nightmares of Nazi Germany, Cambodia, or Bosnia? In some ways, there is no comparison, given the enormous disparities in scope and degree. But Milgram believed that some of the underlying psychological processes may be the same in both cases.

Being another person's agent   In Milgram's view, one of the crucial factors is the fact that all of us are brought up in a world in which there is a continual stress on obedience to legitimate authority, first within the family, then in school, and still later within the institutional settings of the adult world. As a result, we all become well practiced in adopting the attitude of an agent who performs an action that is initiated by someone else. The responsibility belongs to that someone else and not to us. The good child does what she is told; the good employee may raise a question but will accept the boss's final decision; the good soldier is not even allowed to question why. All of them come to feel that they are just an agent who executes another's will: the hammer that struck a nail, not the carpenter who wielded it.

The feeling that one is a mere instrument with little or no sense of personal responsibility can be increased yet further. One means is by increasing the ***psychological distance*** between one's own actions and their end result. This phenomenon was studied in Milgram's laboratory. In one variation, two teachers were used. One was a confederate who was responsible for administering the shocks; the other was the real subject who was asked to perform such subsidiary tasks as reading the stimuli over a microphone and recording the learner's responses. In this new role, the subject was still essential to the smooth functioning of the experimental procedure. If he stopped, the victim would receive no further shocks. But even so, the subject might be expected to feel further removed from the ultimate consequence of the procedure, like a minor cog in a bureaucratic machine. After all, he didn't do the actual shocking! Under these conditions, over 90 percent of the subjects went all the way (Milgram, 1963, 1965; see also Kilham and Mann, 1974).

If obedience is increased by decreasing the subject's sense of personal responsibility, does the opposite hold as well? To answer this question, Milgram decreased the psychological distance between what the subject did and its effect upon the victim. Rather than being out of sight in an experimental cubicle, the victim was now seated directly adjacent to the subject who was told to administer the shock in a brutally direct manner. He had to press the victim's hand upon a shock electrode, holding it down by force if necessary. (His own hand was encased in an insulating glove to protect it from the shock; see Figure 12.6). Now compliance dropped considerably, in analogy to the fact that it is easier to drop bombs on an unseen enemy than to plunge a knife into his body when he looks you in the eye. But even so, 30 percent of the subjects still reacted with perfect obedience. (For further discussion of this and related issues, see Miller, 1986).

12.6   Obedient subject pressing the learner's hand upon the shock electrode *(Copyright 1965 by Stanley Milgram. From the film* Obedience, *distributed by Penn State Audio-Visual Services)*

Cognitive reinterpretations In addition to emphasizing his role as a mere instrument, the obedient person develops an elaborate set of further cognitive devices to reinterpret the situation and his own part in it. One of the most common approaches is to put on psychic blinders and try to shut out the awareness that the victim is a living, suffering fellow being. According to one of Milgram's subjects, "You really begin to forget that there's a guy out there, even though you can hear him. For a long time I just concentrated on pressing the switches and reading the words" (Milgram, 1974, p. 38). This dehumanization of the victim is a counterpart to the obedient person's self-picture as an agent of another's will, someone "who has a job to do" and who does it whether he likes it or not. The obedient person sees himself as an instrument; by the same token, he sees the victim as an object. In his eyes, both have become dehumanized (Bernard, Ottenberg, and Redl, 1965).

The slippery slope The cognitive reorientation by which a person no longer feels responsible for her own acts is not achieved in an instant. Usually, inculcation is by gradual steps. The initial act of obedience is relatively mild and does not seriously clash with the person's own moral outlook. Escalation is gradual so that each step seems only slightly different from the one before. This of course was the pattern in Milgram's study, which created a *slippery slope* that subjects slid down unawares. A similar program of progressive escalation was evidently used in the indoctrination of death-camp guards. The same is true for the military training of soldiers everywhere. Draftees go through "basic training," in part to learn various military skills, but much more importantly, to acquire the habit of instant obedience. Raw recruits are rarely asked to point their guns at another person and shoot. It's not only that they don't know how; it's that most of them probably wouldn't do it.

Milgram's study, the person, and the situation Modern social psychologists generally interpret Milgram's results as a pointed reminder that the situation in which people find themselves is a powerful determinant of what they do and may be more important than the sort of people that they are. Everyone knows that this is true for many ordinary situations of everyday life; virtually everybody stops at a red light, regardless of any quirks in their personalities. But that a situation such as Milgram's would lead two-thirds of his subjects to impose serious pain and harm on another person was a sobering surprise. Before Milgram published his results, he described his study to several groups of judges, including a group of forty psychiatrists. All of them predicted that he would encounter a great deal of defiance. In their view, only a pathological fringe of at most 2 percent of the subjects would go to the maximum shock intensity. As we now know, their predictions were far off the mark. In effect, they are yet another example of the fundamental attribution error—the belief that what people do is largely caused by who they are and to a much lesser extent by the situation in which they find themselves (see Chapter 11).

LEADERSHIP: ONE-ON-MANY INTERACTIONS

FOCUS QUESTIONS

- What is the "great person" view of leadership, and what is its alternative?

- What do laboratory studies suggest makes for a successful leader?

The preceding section dealt with interactions that are many-on-one, such as those in which groups exert influence on an individual and produce conformity and compliance. We will now turn the tables and look at the reverse condition, the effect of one on many, where one individual exerts his or her influence on a number—sometimes a very large number—of others. The most important example of such one-on-many interactions is *leadership.*

Leadership occurs in a multitude of social contexts, including politics, the military, business and commerce, academia, sports teams, social clubs, and even the family. The ways this leadership may be exercised vary even more widely (Hollander, 1985; Bass, 1990). One difference concerns the size of the group being led, which may be as large as the People's Republic of China or as small as a boys' gang. Another concerns the leader's authority: Is that leader the ultimate authority (as was Stalin), or does that person report to another higher up in a chain of command (as a colonel reports to a general)? A further difference is whether the leader tries to influence his followers directly or whether he exerts his influence through a special group of loyal subordinates. Considering these many differences, is there anything one can say about leadership in general?

GREAT PERSON OR SOCIAL FORCES?

From one perspective, history is essentially created by exceptional individuals, who, for better or worse, determine the course of human events. In the nineteenth century, the proponents of this great-person theory often cited the case of Napoleon Bonaparte. According to some contemporary writers such as Thomas Carlyle, Napoleon was a political and military genius whose brilliant mind and unyielding will overcame all opposition for over two decades (Carlyle, 1841). But from another perspective, the success or failure of individuals is determined by the situations in which they find themselves. Thus, to the great Russian novelist Leo Tolstoy, Napoleon's initial successes were caused by circumstance: the ineptitude of the opposing generals, the zeal of the French soldiers, the huge armies under his command. And when he finally failed, it was not because his genius deserted him, but because of the ferocious Russian winter, the long supply lines, and so on (Tolstoy, 1868). The same controversy has

Leadership—person or situation? (A) *Some historians focus on the personality of the individual leader. To them, Napoleon was a military and political genius who shaped history. (B) Others see the leader in the context of the total situation in which he finds himself. To them, instead of history being made by Napoleon, Napoleon was massed by history.* (Napoleon on the Battlefield of Eylau, February 9, 1807, *1808, by Jean-Antoine Gros, Louvre, Paris)*

B

A

"There are no great men, my boy—only great committees." (Drawing by Chas. Addams; © 1975, The New Yorker Magazine, Inc.)

emerged in the discussion of many other historical events. Would there have been a Bolshevik Revolution if Vladimir Lenin had remained in exile from Russia? Would the British have sued for peace with Hitler if Churchill had died before 1940? The two poles of the argument have surfaced again and again: On the one hand the genius of the leader seems to prevail, on the other the historical situation—sometimes described as "the spirit and needs of the times," sometimes as "economic necessity"—seems to control destiny (Hook, 1955; Jennings, 1960; Burns, 1978).

At a more mundane level, this debate among historians has its counterpart in an issue we considered in a previous discussion of attribution (see Chapter 11): Do we (and should we) attribute a person's actions to her dispositional qualities or to the situation? To be sure, the behaviors studied in the social psychologist's laboratory don't have the momentous quality of those performed by history's leaders; answering a quiz master's questions is hardly on a par with fighting the Battle of Waterloo. But the underlying questions are quite similar. Do we attribute the subject's poorer performance to something in her (she is not as smart and knows less) or to something in the situation (she's not the one who picked the questions)? Similarly for issues in history: Do we attribute Napoleon's defeat to something in him (e.g., his genius finally flagged) or to something in the situation (e.g., the combined armies of England, Russia, and his other enemies were too powerful)?

Put another way, the question is whether all—or most—successful leaders share any personal characteristics. The great-person theory would predict that they do, that a Napoleon would in all likelihood have achieved leadership even if he'd never entered the military. What evidence can social psychology offer?

LEADERSHIP IN THE LABORATORY

To determine whether there are, in fact, such leadership qualities, social psychologists have tried to relate various personal characteristics of group members to whether they are perceived as leaders and whether they are effective in this role. Leadership perception and performance have been assessed in many ways, including ratings by subordinates, peers, and supervisors. They have also been assessed by a number of laboratory studies in which small groups of four to six are given some joint task that has to be solved by discussion. Thus subjects may be told that they are explorers stranded 200 miles away from their base. To get back, they have to jettison some of their equipment (pup tent, tools, etc.). Each member first tells the others which item he would jettison first, which second, and so on. Then the group comes up with a consensus list. To assess leadership *perception,* each member is rated by all others on the degree to which he influenced the group. To assess leadership *performance,* each member's initial list is compared with the group's consensus list: To the extent that one member's list is closer to the final list than another's, his leadership is judged as more effective (Cammalleri et al., 1973; Bottger, 1984).

The next step is to see whether leadership perception and performance are related to any other personal characteristics. The verdict to date seems to be that there are indeed such relationships, although they are not as all-powerful as the great-person theory might lead one to suspect. Thus people who are seen as leaders tend to be more intelligent, more outgoing, and more dominant than those who are not regarded as leaders (e.g., Lord, deVader, and Alliger, 1986; Kenny and Zaccaro, 1983). But overall, the role of the situation seems to be at least as important as the leader's personal characteristics (Bass, 1981; Hollander, 1985). What are the characteristics of the situation that make a leader effective? Relatively favorable situations are those in which the leader has considerable authority, the task to be performed is clear-cut, and the group members get along with each other and with the leader.

But there is a complication: The person who becomes an effective leader of one group will not necessarily become the leader of another. This is especially true if the two groups have different missions. On reflection, this is pretty much what one might expect. The qualities that make for leadership in a corporate board meeting are surely different from those that make for leadership in a research laboratory. And both are different from those that make for leadership in a boys' gang. (For a more detailed proposal on the proper match-up between leaders and situations, see Fiedler, 1978).

How does any of this relate to the questions raised by speculative historians? Would the Nazi movement have risen to power in Germany without Adolf Hitler? Would Britain have continued to fight without Churchill's oratory? Social psychology obviously cannot answer momentous questions of this sort. Even to try would be exceedingly presumptuous. For surely issues of this sort require the combined efforts of all the social sciences—anthropology, economics, history, political science, social psychology, sociology—and even then, there may very well be no answers. For history—like life itself—has no control groups. It is a science that can only predict the past.

CROWD BEHAVIOR: MANY-ON-MANY INTERACTIONS

FOCUS QUESTIONS

■ How can deindividuation explain why people behave differently in crowds than they do alone?

■ What is the prisoner's dilemma? How can it explain the behavior of a panicked crowd without assuming that the participants are all irrational?

A

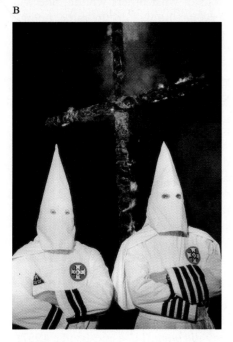

B

Deindividuation (A) Some deindividuation effects are harmless. (Photograph © 1983
by Michael Sheil/Black Star) (B) Others represent a menace to a humane, democratic society. (Photograph © Detroit Free Press,
1988, Pauline Lubens/Black Star)

In this chapter we've considered three broad classes of social interaction. The first class involved one-on-one interactions between two persons who might be relative strangers or friends and lovers. In the second group, the interactions were of many on one, cases of social influence in which the impact of a number of others converged on an individual to produce social facilitation or inhibition, conformity or obedience. In the third, we looked at the effects of one on many in which one person influenced or led a group of others. We now turn to a fourth class of social interactions in which the relation is many on many. These are group interactions in which a number of people interact with a number of others simultaneously. An important example is *crowd behavior.*★ There is little doubt that under some circumstances people in crowds behave differently from the way they do when alone. In riots or lynch mobs, they express aggression at a level of bestial violence that would be inconceivable if they acted in isolation. In other situations, crowds may become frantically fearful, as in panics that may sweep a tightly packed auditorium when someone shouts "Fire." Yet another example is provided by occasional reports of crowds that gather to watch some disturbed person on a high ledge of a tall building and then taunt the would-be suicide and urge him to jump.

What does the crowd do to the individual to make him act so differently from his everyday self? In analogy to the attempt to explain blind obedience, we can distinguish between two contrasting views. One focuses on emotional factors and holds that the crowd transforms the individual completely so that he loses his individuality and becomes essentially irrational. Another position stresses cognitive aspects. It holds that crowd behavior is not quite as irrational as it appears at first, but that it can be explained—at least in part—as a function of the individual's cognitive appraisal of the total situation.

THE EMPHASIS ON THE IRRATIONAL: DEINDIVIDUATION

An early exponent of the role of irrational factors was Gustav Le Bon (1841–1931), a French writer of conservative leanings whose disdain for the masses was reflected in his theory of crowd behavior. According to Le Bon, people in a crowd become wild, stupid, and irrational, giving vent to primitive impulses that are normally suppressed. Their emotion spreads by a sort of contagion and rises to an ever-higher pitch as more and more crowd members become affected. Thus, fear becomes terror, hostility turns into murderous rage, and the crowd member becomes a savage barbarian—"a grain of sand among other grains of sand, which the wind stirs up at will" (Le Bon, 1895).

A number of social psychologists have tried to translate some of these ideas into modern terms. To them, the key to crowd behavior is *deindividuation,* a state in which an individual in a group loses awareness of himself as a separate individual. This state is more likely to occur when there is a high level of arousal and anonymity. Deindividuation tends to disinhibit impulsive actions that are normally under restraint. Just what the impulses are that are disinhibited by deindividuation depends on the group and the situation. In a carnival, the (masked) revelers may join in wild orgies; in a lynch mob, the group members will kill and torture (Festinger, Pepitone, and Newcomb, 1952; Zimbardo, 1969; Diener, 1979).

★ The many-on-one and many-on-many distinction is not hard and fast. At bottom, most many-on-many interactions are probably composed of a large number of many-on-one interactions, as each member in a panicky crowd or a rioting mob is influenced by the collective force of the mass of others.

To study deindividuation experimentally, one investigation focused on the effect of anonymity in children who were trick-or-treating on Halloween. Some came alone; others came in groups. Some were asked for their names by the adults in the homes they visited; others were not. All children were then given an opportunity to steal pennies or candy when the adult left the room on some pretext. The children were much more likely to steal if they came in groups and were anonymous. Thus an increase in wrongdoing may have occurred because anonymity made the child less aware of himself as a separate individual—that is, made him deindividuated—with a resulting disinhibition of petty thievery. But there may have been a simpler and perfectly rational reason: Being anonymous, the child was less afraid of being caught (Diener et al., 1976).

COGNITIVE FACTORS AND THE PANICKY CROWD

■ Is crowd behavior really as irrational as the deindividuation approach suggests? Our primary focus will be on panics. Panics prove that people in groups sometimes act in ways that have disastrous consequences that none of them foresaw or desired. This shows that crowd behavior can be profoundly maladaptive, but does it prove that the individual members of the crowd acted irrationally? Several social psychologists have argued that it does not (Brown, 1965). They point out that in certain situations, such as fires in crowded auditoriums, the optimum solution for all participants (that is, escape for all) can only come about if they all trust one another to behave cooperatively (that is, not to run for the exits). If this trust is lacking, each individual will do the next best thing given her motives and her expectations of what others will do. She will run to the exit because she is sure that everyone else will do the same, hoping that if she runs quickly enough she will get there before them. The trouble is that all others make the same assumption that she does, and so they will arrive more or less together, jam the exit, and perish.

According to this cognitive interpretation, intense fear as such will not produce crowd panic, contrary to Le Bon's assertion. What matters are people's beliefs about escape routes. If they think that the routes for escape (the theater exits) are open and readily accessible, they will not stampede. Nor will panic develop if all escape routes are thought to be completely blocked, as in a mine collapse or a submarine explosion. Such disasters may lead to terror or apathetic collapse, but there will be none of the chaos that characterizes a panicky crowd. For panic to occur, the exits from danger must be seen to be limited or closing. In that case, each individual may well think that she can escape only if she rushes ahead of the others. If everyone thinks this way, panic may ensue (Smelser, 1963).

Panic *In June of 1985, a riot broke out at a soccer match in Brussels resulting in the collapse of a stadium wall that killed 38 spectators and injured more than 200 others. The photo gives a glimpse of the resulting panic. (Photograph by Eamonn McCabe, The Observer)*

THE PRISONER'S DILEMMA

Roger Brown believes that some facets of escape panic can be understood in terms of a problem taken from the mathematical theory of games (Brown, 1965). It is generally known as the ***prisoner's dilemma*** (Luce and Raiffa, 1957). Consider the hypothetical problem of two men arrested on suspicion of bank robbery. The district attorney needs a confession to guarantee conviction. She hits on a diabolical plan. She talks to each prisoner separately and offers each a simple choice—confess or stay silent. But she tells each man that the consequences will depend, not just on what he does, but also on his partner's choice. If both confess, she will recommend an intermediate sentence of, say, eight years in prison for each. If neither confesses, she will be unable to prosecute them for robbery, but she will charge them with a lesser crime, such as illegal possession

TABLE 12.1 PAYOFF MATRIX FOR THE PRISONER'S DILEMMA

		Prisoner B:	
		Stays silent	Confesses
Prisoner A:	Stays silent	1 year for A 1 year for B	20 years for A No jail for B
	Confesses	No jail for A 20 years for B	8 years for A 8 years for B

of a gun, and both will get one year in jail. But suppose one confesses and the other does not. In this case the two men will be dealt with very differently. The one who confesses will be treated with extra leniency for turning state's evidence; he will receive a suspended sentence and won't go to jail at all. But the one who remains silent will feel the full force of the law. The D.A. will recommend the maximum penalty of twenty years.

As the situation is set up, there are four possible combinations of what the prisoners may do. Both may remain silent; Prisoner A may confess while B does not; B may confess while A does not; or both may confess. Each of the four sets of decisions has a different consequence, or payoff, for each of the two prisoners. The four sets of decisions and the payoffs associated with each yield a payoff matrix as shown in Table 12.1.

Given this payoff matrix, what can the prisoners do? If both remain silent, the consequence is reasonably good for each of them. But how can either be sure that his partner won't double-cross him? If A remains silent while B tells all, B is even better off than he would be if both kept quiet; he stays out of jail entirely, while poor, silent A gets twenty years. Can A take the chance that B will not confess? Conversely, can B take this chance on A? The best bet is that each of them will decide that it's too risky to trust the other, for they both know that the other will be mightily tempted to defect. As a result, neither takes the chance, and so they both defect from the common good and confess. The D.A. gets her conviction, and both men get eight years.

In a sense, the prisoners' behavior is maladaptive, for the outcome is far from optimal for each. But this doesn't mean that either of the two men behaved irrationally—on the contrary. Paradoxically enough, each picked the most rational course of action considering that he couldn't be sure how his partner would decide. Each individual acted as rationally as possible; the ironic upshot was an unsatisfactory outcome for both. In the best of all possible worlds they would have been able to trust each other, would have remained silent, and been in jail for a much shorter period. (But in the best of all possible worlds they wouldn't have robbed the bank in the first place.)

THE PRISONER'S DILEMMA AND PANIC

The underlying logic of the prisoner's dilemma applies to various social interactions whose payoff matrix is formally analogous. Brown has shown how it pertains to panic. In such cases there are more than two participants, but the essential ingredients are much the same. Each individual in the burning auditorium has two choices—she can wait her turn to get to the exit, or she can rush ahead. What are the probable outcomes? As in the case of the prisoners, they partially depend upon what others in the auditorium (especially those nearby) will do. If the individual rushes to the exit and everyone else does too, they will all probably suffer severe injuries and run some risk of death. If she

TABLE 12.2 PAYOFF MATRIX FOR AN INDIVIDUAL AND OTHERS IN A BURNING AUDITORIUM

		Others (O):	
		Take(s) turns	Rush(es) ahead
Individual (I):	Take(s) turn	Minor injuries for *I* Minor injuries for *O*	Increased chance of death for *I* No injuries for *O*
	Rush(es) ahead	No injuries for *I* Increased chance of death for *O*	Severe injuries for *I* Severe injuries for *O*

takes her turn and others decorously do the same, the outcome is better; they will probably all escape, though they may suffer some minor injuries. The best outcome for the individual is produced if she ruthlessly pushes herself ahead while the others continue to file out slowly. In this case she will surely escape without a blister, but the chances for the others to escape are lessened. Suppose the situation is reversed so that the individual waits her turn while everyone near her runs ahead? Now the others may very well get out without injury while she herself may die. These sets of decisions and their associated outcomes represent just another version of the prisoner's dilemma, and they are shown in the payoff matrix of Table 12.2. Given this payoff matrix, most people will probably opt to rush ahead rather than wait their turn. As in the case of the two prisoners, this solution is grossly maladaptive, but from the point of view of each separate individual it is, sadly enough, quite rational.

SOCIAL DILEMMAS

In the classic prisoner's dilemma only two criminals are involved in the choice. But as the panic scenario illustrates, the dilemma can be expanded to include any number of individuals, each of whom has to decide whether to cooperate or to defect. Thus the prisoner's dilemma and its payoff structure can be applied to many serious social and economic issues (Dawes, 1980).

Consider the **social dilemma** posed by industrial pollution. Suppose ten companies make various plastic toys and in the process create sulfurous gases. Antipollution devices can be installed to remove the sulfur, but they are expensive. What will the companies do? If all ten toy manufacturers make the same environmentally sound choice, none will have a price advantage, and air and water quality will remain the same. If they all attempt to look out for themselves alone and omit antipollution devices, none still will have a price advantage but the environment will be terribly degraded. If the other nine toy manufacturers can be counted on to make the environmentally sound choice, one toy producer could omit the antipollution devices, undercut the competition on price, and only degrade air and water quality slightly. But if all the other manufacturers choose to ignore environmental degradation, then that one high-minded toy producer will probably be driven out of business.

In the modern world we face social dilemmas in many areas, including industrial pollution, deforestation, and the depletion of energy reserves. Is there anything we can do to encourage individuals to make the socially beneficial decision? As we saw in Chapter 5, we can skew the payoff matrix to create a bias. (This is largely what our district attorney did to encourage the prisoners to throw loyalty to the wind.) In the case of social dilemmas we can skew the payoff matrix by imposing penalties such as taxes or fines on individuals or compa-

Social dilemmas *A roadside dump in Edgerton Kansas. (Photograph © Dave Gleiter/FPG International)*

nies that pollute, or we can enhance the appeal of altruistic behavior through education. Many of the social scientists who have studied social dilemmas suggest that teaching the ultimate benefits of cooperation and increasing our trust that others won't exploit us may be the most effective ways of changing the outcomes (e.g., Orbell, van de Kragt, and Dawes, 1988; Rapoport, 1988). Whether such methods will be sufficient to save "spaceship earth" from the follies of its inhabitants is another question (Dawes, 1980).

THE GENERALITY OF SOCIAL PSYCHOLOGY

FOCUS QUESTION

■ How universal—across both time and place—are the findings from social psychology?

In this and the preceding chapter we asked how the individual interprets the social world in which he lives and how he interacts with the other people in it. This led to a survey of many topics, including the way we perceive the motives and acts of others as well as those of our own selves, how we interact with others, how we conform and obey, and how we behave in crowds.

Social psychology has clearly contributed to our understanding of social behavior. But how broadly applicable is this understanding? Does it bring us closer to an understanding of basic human nature, or is it necessarily limited to our own time and place?

Some authors argue that the discoveries of modern social psychology are limited to our social and cultural circumstances and cannot be generalized beyond them. Perhaps consistency, attribution of motives, self-perception, obedience, diffusion of responsibility, and so on are patterns of behavior that are specific to twentieth-century industrialized society, in particular, to that of modern North America. If so, they may not describe how people act and think in other places and at other times (Gergen, 1973; Jahoda, 1979).

This kind of culture-specific critique may be a valuable corrective to the notion that a genuine science of the psychology of social behavior can be developed in isolation from other social disciplines, such as anthropology, sociology, economics, political science, and history. To understand the social situation the individual confronts, one has to refer to many cultural (or sociological or historical or political or economic) factors that transcend the individual (Pepitone, 1976; Price-Williams, 1985). We will return to this issue when we discuss the topic of personality, where we will consider different concepts of the self as they affect various aspects of cognition, emotion, and behavior (see Chapter 17).

Nevertheless, there are good reasons to believe that human social nature is much more stable than the culture-specific critique assumes it to be. Such diverse political theorists as Aristotle, Hobbes, and Machiavelli are still read despite the fact that they lived many centuries ago and under very different political systems than our own; they wrote about characteristics of human social behavior that we can recognize even today. History provides many other examples of enduring social reactions. There are records of panics in Roman amphitheaters when the stands collapsed, of riots during sporting events in Byzantium, and of murderous mobs in medieval Europe. The cast and costumes differ, but the basic plots remain much the same. Some of the ancients even used certain of our modern propaganda devices. When the city of Pompeii was destroyed by a volcano in 79 A.D., it was evidently in the midst of a municipal

Electioneering in Pompeii Electoral inscriptions on the outer walls of houses in Pompeii. (From The Buried Cities of Pompeii and Herculaneum; photograph by Carlo Bevilacqua, © 1978 Instituto Geografico De Agostini; courtesy of the New York Public Library)

election. Modern archeologists have found some of the election slogans on the excavated walls: "Vote for Vatius, all the whoremasters vote for him" and "Vote for Vatius, all the wife-beaters vote for him." While the techniques of the anti-Vatius faction may be a bit crude for our modern taste, they certainly prove that the psychology of the smear campaign has a venerable history (Raven and Rubin, 1976).

Phenomena of this sort suggest that there are some invariant properties of human social behavior that have genuine generality.

QUESTIONS FOR CRITICAL THINKING

1. Is all human altruism actually just well-disguised self-interest?

2. Why would couples tend to conform to the matching hypothesis, when each of us presumably seeks the most attractive partner?

3. What do Milgram's findings suggest about whether authoritarianism is largely a personality trait?

4. How could parents rear children so that they would not become blindly obedient adults?

5. What explains our propensity to deindividuate in the first place? Might this propensity offer some advantage?

SUMMARY

1. Social interactions can be classified as those that are *one on one* (our relations with both strangers and persons to whom we are closer), those that are *many on one* (including various manifestations of social influence), those that are *one on many* (including leadership), and those that are *many on many* (including crowd behavior).

2. According to some theorists, all one-on-one interactions depend on *social exchange.* Evidence comes from the operation of the *reciprocity rule,* which applies not only to material things such as food and gifts but also to intangibles such as *self-disclosure.*

3. In investigating *altruism,* social psychologists have found that people often fail to help others in an emergency. One reason is the *bystander effect:* The greater the number of people who are present, the less likely that any one of them will provide help, in part because of *pluralistic ignorance,* in part because of *diffusion of responsibility.*

4. Social psychologists have studied some of the factors that attract people to each other. They include *proximity, familiarity, similarity,* and *physical attractiveness.* There is evidence in favor of the *matching hypothesis,* which predicts a strong correlation between the physical attractiveness of the two partners. Love is an especially close relation between two partners. Some authors distinguish between *romantic love,* in which the emotions are intensely focused, and *companionate love,* which is less turbulent and more long-lasting.

5. A number of many-on-one situations involve *social influence.* In some cases, all that matters is the mere presence of others, which produces *social facilitation* and inhibition.

6. Another case of social influence is *conformity.* One reason for conformity is informational: We may believe that the group has knowledge we don't possess. Another reason is motivational: We go along because we want to be liked. A dissenting minority often leads to a massive reduction in the force toward conformity and may produce genuine changes in what people think and feel.

SUMMARY

7.   Still another form of social influence is obedience. Blind obedience has sometimes been ascribed to factors within the person, as in studies on the *authoritarian personality*. But situational factors may be even more important, as shown by Milgram's obedience studies. His findings suggest that obedience depends on the *psychological distance* between one's own actions and their end result. When this distance is increased—by decreasing one's sense of responsibility, by *dehumanization,* and by means of various *cognitive reinterpretations*—obedience increases too.

8.   An important example of *one-on-many* interactions is *leadership.* A major question in politics, warfare, and contemporary social psychology is what used to be called the *great-person* versus *social-forces* controversy: Does successful leadership depend on the special qualities of the leader or on the situation? The answer is that it is generally an interaction between the two.

9.   In many-on-many interactions, a number of people interact with a number of others simultaneously. An example is crowd behavior, as in panics or riots. According to one account, the behavior of such crowds is essentially irrational and is based on *deindividuation*. According to another interpretation, it is not as irrational as it appears at first. The *prisoner's dilemma* shows that under certain conditions there can be collective irrationality even though all of the participants behave rationally as individuals. This has been applied to behavior in panics and to *social dilemmas.*

PART FOUR

DEVELOPMENT

CHAPTER **13**

PHYSICAL AND COGNITIVE DEVELOPMENT

How do psychologists try to explain the phenomena they describe? Thus far, we've primarily dealt with two main approaches. The first is concerned with mechanism—it tries to understand how something works. The second approach focuses on function—it tries to explain what something is good for. But there is yet another approach to explanation in psychology that focuses on development. This approach deals with questions of history—it asks how a given state of affairs came into being.

In the next two chapters, our concern will be with this developmental perspective on psychological phenomena. We will ask how various psychological processes arise in the organism's history—how we come to see and remember, reason and think, feel and act as we now do; how it is that we are no longer children, but for better or worse have become adults in mind as well as in body.

t the beginning of the nineteenth century, many thinkers became increasingly interested in all forms of progressive change. They lived at a time of dramatic upheavals—the French Revolution, which ushered in a period of continued political unrest, and the Industrial Revolution, which transformed the social and economic structure of Europe and North America. These massive changes suggested an underlying pattern of social development—"progress" (Bury, 1932). Given this background, many scientists became interested in development wherever they saw it: in the history of the planet as it changed from molten rock to continents and oceans; in the history of life as it evolved from early forms to myriad species of fossils and plants. One aspect of this intellectual movement was an increasing concern with the life history of individual organisms, starting from their embryonic beginnings and continuing as they developed toward maturity.

All animals develop, and so do we. The duckling becomes a duck, the kitten a cat, the human baby an adult. In this regard all humans are alike. It doesn't matter whether they are Gandhi or Hitler, Joan of Arc or Isaac Newton—they all started life as infants. Is there any common pattern in the developmental history of each human life? If so, what is it? The attempt to answer these questions is the province of developmental psychology.

WHAT IS DEVELOPMENT?

FOCUS QUESTIONS

- When does the human embryo become a fetus? What are the major stages in fetal development?

- What are the basic sensory and motor capabilities of the newborn?

- What are the major stages of motor and intellectual development in the infant?

Many aspects of human development share certain characteristics, at least in a very general way, whether they involve _physical development_, the maturation of various bodily structures; _motor development_, the progressive attainment of various motor skills; _cognitive development_, the growth of the child's intellectual functioning; or _social development_, changes in the ways the child deals with others. We will consider three very general features that many aspects of development have in common: differentiation, growth, and orderly progression. We'll begin our discussion by looking at differentiation as this is revealed in the physical development of the embryo and in childhood behavior.

DEVELOPMENT AS DIFFERENTIATION

The concept of differentiation grows out of some early discoveries in embryology, the study of an organism as it develops from a single egg and assumes the complex shape and function of its adult form. The German biologist Karl Ernest von Baer (1792–1876) pointed out that embryological development involves a progressive change from the more general to the more particular, from the simpler to the more complex—in short, **differentiation.**

In embryonic development, anatomical differentiation is directly apparent. Initially there is one cell, then several cell layers, then the crude beginnings of the major organ systems, until the different organs and their component parts gradually take shape. Von Baer argued that this is the reason why embryos of very different species are so similar at early stages of development and utterly dissimilar at later stages (see Figure 13.1). Initially, the embryo only manifests the very general body plan characteristic of a broad class of animals. Thus a very young chick embryo looks much like the embryo of any other vertebrate animal at a similar stage of its development. The embryonic structures that will eventually become wings are quite similar to those structures that in a young human embryo will eventually become arms. As embryonic development proceeds, special features begin to emerge, and the chick embryo begins to look like a bird, then like some kind of fowl, and still later like a chicken (Gould, 1977).

Von Baer's differentiation principle was initially regarded as a description of anatomical development and nothing else. But a number of psychologists suggested that a similar principle also applies to the development of behavior. Consider the development of grasping movements in human infants. When reaching for a small block, they initially curl their entire hand around the block; still later, they oppose the thumb to all four fingers. By the time they are one year old, they can victoriously coordinate hand, thumb, and one or two fingers to pick up the block with an elegant pincer movement (although such ultimate triumphs of manual differentiation as picking up a tea cup while holding the little finger extended will probably have to wait until they are old enough to read a book on etiquette) (Halverson, 1931; see Figure 13.2).

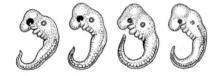
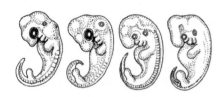
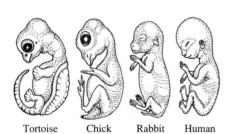

Tortoise　Chick　Rabbit　Human

13.1 Differentiation during embryonic development _The figure shows three stages in the embryonic development of four different vertebrates—tortoise, chick, rabbit, and human. At the first stage, all of the embryos are very similar to each other. As development proceeds, they diverge more and more. By the third stage, each embryo has taken on some of the distinctive characteristics of its own species. (From Keeton and Gould, 1993. Redrawn from Romanes, 1882)_

DEVELOPMENT AS GROWTH

One of the most obvious characteristics of development is growth. Organisms grow as they change from a fertilized egg to a fetus, and after birth, they continue to grow in many different dimensions, ranging from sheer physical size to mental complexity.

GROWTH BEFORE BIRTH

Each human existence begins at conception when a sperm and egg cell unite to form the fertilized egg. This egg divides and redivides repeatedly, producing a

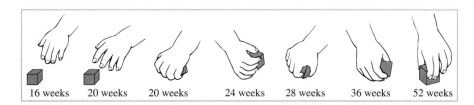

16 weeks 20 weeks 20 weeks 24 weeks 28 weeks 36 weeks 52 weeks

23 weeks *28 weeks* *58 weeks*

13.2 The development of manual skills *The diagram shows the progressive differentiation in the infant's use of the hand when holding an object. At sixteen weeks of age, he reaches for the object but can't hold on to it. At twenty weeks, he grasps it using the hand as a whole, with no differentiated use of the fingers. Between twenty-four and thirty-six weeks, the fingers and thumb become differentiated in use, but the four fingers operate more or less as a whole. By fifty-two weeks of age, hand, thumb, and fingers are successfully differentiated to produce precise and effective pincer movements. (Adapted from Liebert, Polous, and Strauss, 1974) Photos illustrate the same point at twenty-three, twenty-eight, and fifty-eight weeks. (Photographs by Kathy Hirsh-Pasek)*

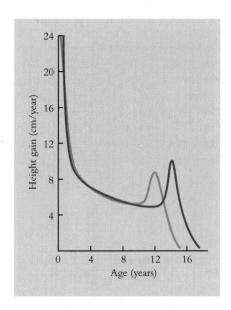

13.3 Physical growth *Heights of British boys (dark red) and girls (blue) from birth until nineteen years of age. Physical growth continues for almost twenty years after birth, with a special spurt at adolescence. (From Tanner, 1970)*

cellular mass that attaches itself to the wall of the uterus. Two weeks after conception the mass of cells (now called an ***embryo***) begins to differentiate into separate cell layers. From now until birth, growth and development proceed at a rapid pace. At one month after conception, the embryo is a fifth of an inch long and looks like a little worm. At two months after conception the mass of cells is about one inch in length and is now called a ***fetus.*** Just one month later, the fetus has grown to about three inches in length and has begun to look like a miniature baby with some functioning organ systems and a number of early reflexes, including sucking movements when the lips are touched. In another four months (that is, seven months after conception), the fetus has grown to sixteen inches, has a fully developed reflex pattern, can cry, breathe, swallow, and has a good chance of survival if it should be delivered at this time.

These stages of our prenatal life attest to the massive changes in sheer size and structural complexity that take place over this period. In addition to these gross gains, however, there are also many subtler ones that have far-reaching effects. Some of the most important of these concern the developing nervous system. In the later stages of prenatal growth, the neurons begin to mature, and their axons and dendrites form increasingly complex branches and interconnections with other nerve cells (Schacher, 1981).

GROWTH AFTER BIRTH

Physical growth continues for almost two decades after birth, with a special spurt at adolescence (see Figure 13.3). The growth of the child's body is accom-

A   B   C

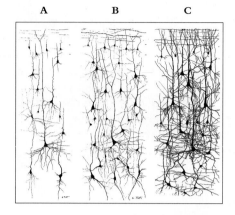

13.4 Growth of neural interconnections
Sections of the human cortex in (A) a newborn, (B) a three-month-old, and (C) a fifteen-month-old. (Conel, 1939, 1947, 1955)

panied by the no less striking growth of her mind—in the way she perceives, thinks, speaks, understands, and reacts to others. The details of these accomplishments will be discussed in later sections. For now we only note that many of these feats are based on the continuation of events that began before birth. Of particular importance is the growth of neural interconnections beginning in fetal life and continuing long into infancy, as illustrated in Figure 13.4, which shows sections of the human cortex in a newborn, a three-month-old, and a fifteen-month-old child (Conel, 1939, 1947, 1955). According to a recent analysis, there is a tenfold increase in the average number of synapses per cortical neuron in the first year of life (Huttenlocher, 1979). This increasing neural complexity may well be one of the reasons for the increase in mental capacities as development proceeds.

THE SLOW RATE OF HUMAN GROWTH AND ITS EFFECTS

Nine months after conception the fetus enters the outer world. But is it really ready to do so? Left to its own devices, it obviously is not. It is singularly helpless and inept, more so by far than the young of most other mammals. To be sure, a newborn calf has to suckle and follow its mother, but it can walk at birth, and it can pretty well manage on its own after a fairly short period. But in humans (and to a lesser extent, in monkeys and apes), a considerable degree of development continues far beyond birth. For example, in most mammals the newborn's brain is just about fully formed—not so in primates and most especially not so in humans. Human newborns have achieved only 23 percent of their adult cranial capacity at birth and are still only at 75 percent of this final value when they are about two-and-a-half years old (Catel, 1953, cited in Gould, 1977). What holds for brain growth also holds for other aspects of physical development. At birth the bones of the skull are not yet joined together and certain wrist bones are still made of cartilage. In many ways, we are all born premature.

A number of authors believe that this retarded rate of development is what most distinctively makes us human, for the inevitable result is a protracted period of dependency. In some ways, this is quite inconvenient—for child and parent alike. But in many others, there are great benefits. For such a long period of dependency is tailor-made for a creature whose major specialization is its capacity for learning and whose basic invention is culture—the ways of coping with the world that each generation hands on to the next. As there is so much to learn, the young have much to gain by being forced to stay a while with those who teach them.

Capacity for learning *Learning from culture is not accomplished overnight. A ten-month-old baby is trying to master the intricacies of eating with a spoon. (Photograph courtesy of Kathy Hirsh-Pasek)*

THE NEWBORN'S EQUIPMENT

What do newborns bring into the world to serve as a foundation for further psychological development? Here, we will only ask about motor and sensory capacities.

The infant's response capacities   Initially infants have little control of their motor apparatus. Newborns can do very little—they thrash around in an uncoordinated manner and can't even hold up their heads. By four months of age they'll be able to sit up with support and reach for objects (which they often miss). But how do they manage in the meantime?

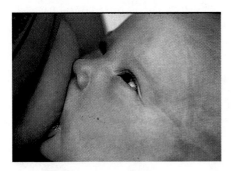

A vital reflex in the newborn *The sucking reflex is initiated when an appropriate object is inserted three or four centimeters into the mouth. (Photograph by Kenneth Garrett 1984/Woodfin Camp*

Part of the answer is that newborns have a neurological survival kit that will see them through their first period of helplessness: a set of early reflexes. Some reflexes of the very young infant have to do with clinging to the person who supports him. An example is the *grasp reflex*—when an object touches the infant's palm, he closes his fist tightly around it. If the object is lifted up, the infant hangs on and is lifted up along with it, supporting his whole weight for a minute or more. This and some related reflexes are sometimes regarded as a primitive heritage from our primate ancestors whose infants cling to their mothers' furry bodies.

Other infantile responses pertain to feeding. An example is the *rooting reflex.* When the cheek is lightly touched, the baby's head turns toward the source of stimulation, her mouth opens, and her head continues to turn until the stimulus (usually a finger or nipple) is in her mouth. When this point is reached, sucking begins.

The infant's sensory capacities While newborns' motor capacities are initially very limited, their sensory channels function nicely from the very start. Evidence comes from changes in their rates of breathing, of sucking, and of similar indices in response to stimulation. Newborns can hear; they can discriminate between tones of different pitch and loudness. They also prefer their mother's voice to that of a strange female (DeCasper and Fifer, 1980; Aslin, 1987). Newborns can see: While quite short-sighted and unable to focus on objects farther off than about four feet, they can readily discriminate brightness and color, and they can follow a moving stimulus with their eyes (Bornstein, 1985; Aslin, 1987). In addition, they are sensitive to touch, smell, and taste (Crook, 1987).

All in all, infants seem to come rather well equipped to sense the world they enter. But do they come equipped to interpret what it is they see, hear, or touch? This is a disputed issue to which we will return in a later section. For now we merely note that young infants are quite competent to receive sensory inputs. Whether they have some built-in knowledge of what these inputs might signify (as nativists would argue) or have to acquire this knowledge by relating various sensory inputs to each other (as empiricists would have it) is another matter.

DEVELOPMENT AS ORDERLY PROGRESSION

In prenatal growth some events necessarily come before others. The embryo consists of primitive tissue layers before it develops organs; the skeleton is made of cartilage before it becomes bone. Developmental psychologists argue that similar patterns of orderly progression characterize psychological development after birth.

In *motor development* there is a regular sequence of achievements that begins with the ability to hold the head erect, followed by the ability to roll over, then to creep, crawl, sit up, stand up, take a step or two, and finally to walk, first shakily and then with increasing confidence. There is a good deal of variability in the age at which a given baby masters each skill. But a few months more or less make little difference for later development. What matters is that each step in the sequence comes before the next. No baby can walk before he can sit. (The

A

FETAL POSITION
0 month

CHIN UP
1 month

CHEST UP
2 months

REACH AND MISS
3 months

SIT WITH SUPPORT
4 months

SIT ON LAP
GRASP OBJECT
5 months

SIT ON HIGH CHAIR
GRASP DANGLING OBJECT
6 months

SIT ALONE
7 months

STAND WITH HELP
8 months

CREEP
10 months

WALK WHEN LED
11 months

PULL TO STAND
BY FURNITURE
12 months

CLIMB STAIR STEPS
13 months

STAND ALONE
14 months

WALK ALONE
15 months

B

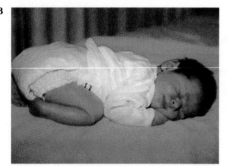

2 days

2 months

6 months

8 months

13.5   The development of locomotion   *(A) The average age at which babies master locomotor skills, from holding their chins up to walking alone. These ages vary considerably. (From Shirley, 1961) (B) A pictorial record of these milestones in the life of one child. (Photographs courtesy of Kathy Hirsh-Pasek)*

average age at which children reach each of these milestones of motor development is shown in Figure 13.5.)

Similar progressions are found in aspects of intellectual development. In the acquisition of language there is also an orderly sequence (see Chapter 9). Initially the baby coos, then he babbles, then he utters his first word or two, then he develops a small vocabulary but is limited to one-word utterances, after which both vocabulary and sentence complexity increase until they finally reach adult levels. As with motor development, there is a good deal of variability among different infants. Some may begin to talk by ten months, others as late as twenty, but age of initial language onset is no predictor of later linguistic competence. The important point is that linguistic development follows the same general progression for all children. Here, as in so many other areas, development proceeds by an orderly sequence of steps, and this holds for the growth of our minds as well as our bodies.

10 months

10 months

14 months

PIAGET'S THEORY OF COGNITIVE DEVELOPMENT

FOCUS QUESTIONS

- What are Piaget's four stages of intellectual growth, and at what ages do they generally occur?

- What are schemas for Piaget, and how do they emerge from the processes of assimilation and accommodation?

- How and when does the infant start to manifest mental representation?

- What is the egocentrism of the preoperational period, and how can it be demonstrated?

- What cognitive activities distinguish the periods of concrete and formal operations?

Children as miniature adults *Children dressed as did the adults of their time and class as shown in this 1786 Dutch painting. (Helena van der Schalke,* by G. ter Borch, *Courtesy of the Rijksmuseum, Amsterdam)*

Thus far, our discussion of development has focused on physical growth and changes in motor behavior. But the child grows in mind as well as body—in what he knows, how he comes to know it, how he thinks about it, and in the fact that he can tell it to others (sometimes interminably so). This intellectual growth from infancy to adulthood is generally called ***cognitive development.***

We will organize our discussion of the child's mental growth around the work of the Swiss psychologist Jean Piaget (1896–1980). He was the first to develop methods for studying the ways in which infants and children see and understand the world, the first to suggest that these ways are profoundly different from those of adults, and the first to offer a systematic theoretical account of the process of mental growth from infancy to adulthood. As we will see, Piaget's formulations have aroused considerable controversy: Many of his empirical claims have been disputed, and most of his theoretical proposals have come under serious attack. But even so, we cannot begin the study of cognitive development without first considering Piaget's views, since these shaped the way in which all subsequent investigators thought about the subject.

Piaget believed that mental growth involves major qualitative changes. This hypothesis is relatively recent. According to the eighteenth-century empiricists, the child's mental machinery is fundamentally the same as the adult's, the only difference being that the child has fewer associations. Nativists also minimized the distinction between the child's mind and the adult's, for they viewed the basic categories of time, space, number, and causality as given *a priori*, being part of the native mental equipment that all humans have at birth. Thus both empiricists and nativists regarded the child as much like an adult; the first saw him as an adult-in-training, the second as an adult-in-miniature. In contrast, Piaget looked for qualitative differences and tried to chart the orderly progression of human intellect as the child grows into an adult.

Piaget's original training was as a biologist, which may be one of the reasons why his conception of intellectual development bears many resemblances to the way an embryologist thinks of the development of anatomical structures. The human fetus doesn't just get larger between, say, two and seven months—its whole structure changes drastically. Piaget argued that mental development is characterized by similar qualitative changes. He proposed that there are four main stages of intellectual growth, whose overall thrust is toward an increasing emancipation from the here and now of the immediate, concrete present to a conception of the world in increasingly symbolic and abstract terms. These stages are the period of ***sensory-motor intelligence*** (from birth to about two

3 9 1

years), the ***preoperational period*** (two to seven years), the period of ***concrete operations*** (seven to eleven years), and the period of ***formal operations*** (eleven years and on). The age ranges are very approximate, however, and successive stages are often thought to overlap and blend into each other.★

SENSORY-MOTOR INTELLIGENCE

 According to Piaget, at first there is nothing but a succession of transient, unconnected sensory impressions and motor reactions. As he saw it, mental life during the first few months contains neither past nor future, no distinction between stable objects and fleeting events, and no differentiation between the "me" and the "not me." The critical achievement of the first two years is the development of these distinctions.

OBJECT PERMANENCE

Consider an infant holding a rattle. To an adult, the rattle is an object, a thing, of whose existence he has no doubt, whether he looks at it or briefly looks away. The adult is sure of its existence, for he is certain that he will see it once more when he looks at it again. But does the rattle exist as a thing in the same sense to the infant? Does the infant have the notion of ***object permanence***?

According to Piaget, there is little object permanence in the first few months of life. The infant may look at a new toy with evident delight, but if it disappears from view, he shows little concern (see Figure 13.6). It seems as if what's out of sight is also out of mind and does not really exist for the infant. Needless to say, infants eventually come to live in a world whose objects do not capriciously appear and disappear with each movement of their eyes. At about eight months of age, they start to search for toys that have been hidden or that have fallen out of their cribs.

According to Piaget, the notion that objects exist on their own, and continue to exist even if they are not seen, heard, felt, or reached for, is a major accomplishment of the sensory-motor period. This notion emerges as the infant gradually interrelates his various sensory experiences and motor reactions. Eventually he coordinates the sensory spaces provided by the different modalities—of vision, hearing, touch, and bodily movement—into one real space in which all of the world's objects—himself included—exist.

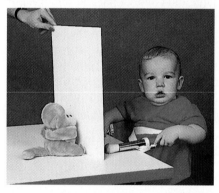

13.6 Object permanence *(A) A six-month-old looks intently at a toy. (B) But when the toy is hidden from view, the infant does not search for it. According to Piaget, this is because the infant does not as yet have the concept of object permanence. (Photographs by Doug Goodman, 1986/Monkmeyer)*

SENSORY-MOTOR SCHEMAS

The newborn starts life with a rather limited repertoire of built-in reactions, such as gross bodily movements in response to distress, sucking and swallowing reflexes, and, after a few days, certain orienting responses such as head and eye movements. In Piaget's view, these recurrent action patterns are the first mental elements—or ***schemas***—through which the infant organizes the world that impinges upon her. At first, these various schemas operate in isolation. A one-month-old infant can grasp a rattle and can also suck it or look at it. But she will perform these actions only if the stimulus object is directly applied to the relevant sensory surface. She will suck the rattle if it touches her mouth and will grasp it if it's pressed into her palm. But she is as yet unable to grasp whatever she's sucking or to look at whatever she's grasping. The coordination of all these

---

★ These stages roughly correspond to the categories employed by modern developmental psychologists, regardless of their stand on Piaget's theory: infancy (from birth to about two-and-a-half years), early childhood (two-and-a-half to six years), middle childhood (six to eleven years), and adolescence and beyond (twelve years and up).

PIAGET'S THEORY OF COGNITIVE DEVELOPMENT

Assimilation and accommodation *The three-month-old has assimilated the rattle into her sucking schema and has accommodated the schema so that it now includes the rattle as a suckable object. (Photograph by Steve Skloot/Photo Researchers)*

Jean Piaget *(Photograph by Yves De-Braine, Black Star)*

patterns is not complete until she's about five months of age. How is this integration achieved?

According to Piaget, the answer lies in the two processes that in his view are responsible for all of cognitive development: ***assimilation*** and ***accommodation.*** At any given point, the child has to be able to interpret the environment in terms of the mental schemas she has at the time; the environment is assimilated to the schema. But the schemas necessarily change as the child continues to interact with the world around her; they accommodate to the environment. In the case of the sucking response, the initial schema only applies to the nipple. But with time, the infant starts to suck other objects, such as her rattle. Piaget would say that by doing this she has assimilated the rattle into her sucking schema. The rattle is now understood and dealt with as a "suckable." But the process does not stop there. After all, rattles are not the same as nipples; while both are suckable, they are not suckable in quite the same way. This necessarily leads to new discriminations. As a result, the sucking schema adjusts to (that is, accommodates) the new object to which it is applied. This process continues, with further assimilations followed by yet further accommodations, until finally looking, reaching, grasping, and sucking have all merged into one unified exploratory schema (Piaget, 1952).

BEGINNINGS OF REPRESENTATIONAL THOUGHT

According to Piaget, the last phase of the sensory-motor period (about eighteen to twenty-four months) marks a momentous change in intellectual development. Children begin to conceive of objects and events that are not immediately present by representing (that is "re-presenting") some prior experience with these to themselves. Such ***mental representations*** may be internalized actions, images, or words. But in all cases, they function as symbols that stand for whatever they may signify yet are not equivalent to it.

One demonstration of this change is the achievement of full object permanence. At eighteen months or so, children actively search for absent toys and are surprised (and sometimes outraged) if they don't find them under the sofa cover where they saw the experimenter hide them; it is reasonable to infer that they have some internal representation of the sought-for object. Even more persuasive are examples of ***deferred imitation*** in which children imitate actions that occurred some time past, such as a playmate's temper tantrum observed a day ago. A related phenomenon is make-believe play, which is often based on deferred imitation.

THE PREOPERATIONAL PERIOD

■ Given the tools of representational thought, the two-year-old has taken a gigantic step forward. A year ago, he could interact with the environment only through direct sensory or motor contact; now he can carry the whole world in his head. But while his mental world now contains stable objects and events that can be represented internally, it is still a far cry from the world of adults. The two-year-old has overcome the initial chaos of separate sensations and motor impressions. But according to Piaget, this was only to exchange it for a chaos of ideas (that is, representations) that he is as yet unable to relate in any coherent way. The achievement of the next five years is the emergence of a reasonably well-ordered world of ideas. In Piaget's view, this requires higher-order schemas, which he calls ***operations,*** that allow the internal manipulation of ideas according to a stable set of rules. In his view, genuine operations do not appear until about seven or so, hence the term ***preoperational*** for the period from two to about seven years.

393

A

B

13.7 Conservation of liquid quantity
(A) Patrick, aged four years, three months, is asked by the experimenter, "Do we both have the same amount of juice to drink?" Patrick says yes. (B) The experimenter pours the juice from one of the beakers into a new, wider beaker. When now asked, "Which glass has more juice?" he points to the thinner one. (Photographs by Chris Massey)

FAILURE OF CONSERVATION

Conservation of quantity and number A revealing example of preoperational thought is the young child's failure to **conserve quantity.** One of Piaget's experimental procedures uses two identical glasses, *A* and *B*, which stand side by side and are filled with the same amount of some colored liquid. A child is asked whether there is more orangeade in one glass or the other, and the experimenter obligingly adds a drop here, a drop there until his subject is completely satisfied that there is "the same to drink in this glass as in that." Four-year-olds can easily make this judgment.

The next step involves a new glass, *C*, which is much taller but also narrower than *A* and *B* (see Figure 13.7). While the child is watching, the experimenter pours the entire contents of glass *A* into glass *C*. He now points to *B* and *C*, and asks, "Is there more orangeade in this glass or in that?" For an adult, the question is almost too simple to merit an answer. The amounts are obviously identical, since *A* was completely emptied into *C*, and *A* and *B* were set to equality at the outset. But four- or five-year-olds don't see this. They insist that there is more orangeade in *C*. When asked for their reason, they explain that the liquid comes to a much higher level in *C*. They seem to think that the orangeade has somehow increased in quantity as it was transferred from one glass to another. They are too impressed by the visible changes in appearance that accompany each transfer (the changing liquid levels) and do not yet realize that there is an underlying reality (the quantity of liquid) that remains constant throughout.

By the time children are about seven years old, they respond much like adults. They hardly look at the two glasses, for their judgment needs little empirical support. "It's the same. It seems as if there's less because it's wider, but it's the same." The experimenter may continue with further glasses of different sizes and shapes, but the judgment remains what it was: "It's still the same because it always comes from the same glass." To justify their answer, the children point to the fact that one can always pour the liquid back into the original glass (that is, *A*), and thus obtain the same levels. They have obviously understood that the various transformations in the liquid's appearance are reversible. For every transformation that changes the way the liquid looks, there is another that restores its original appearance. Given this insight, children at this age recognize that there is an underlying attribute of reality, the quantity of liquid that remains constant (is *conserved*), despite the various perceptual changes. (For comparable results with malleable solids like clay, see Figure 13.8).

A related phenomenon is **conservation of number.** The child is first shown a row of six evenly spaced bottles, each of which has a glass standing next to it. The child agrees that there are as many bottles as there are glasses. The experimenter now rearranges the six glasses by setting them out into a much longer row while leaving the six bottles as they were. Here the turning point comes a

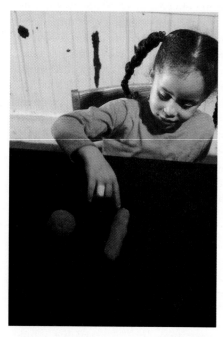

13.8 Conservation of mass quantity *In parallel to the failure to conserve liquid quantity is the preschooler's failure to conserve mass. Jennifer, aged four years and four months, is shown two clay balls which she adjusts until she is satisfied that there is the same amount of clay in both. The experimenter takes one of the balls and rolls it into a "hot dog." When now asked which is more, Jennifer points to the hot dog. (Photograph by Ed Boswell)*

bit earlier, at about five or six. Up to that age, children generally assert that there are more glasses because "they're more spread out" (see Figure 13.9). From about six on, there is conservation; the child has no doubt that there are just as many bottles in the tightly spaced row as there are glasses in the spread-out line. In all these conservation tasks, the older child's explanation emphasizes reversibility—liquid can be poured back in the taller glass, and the long line of glasses can be reassembled into a compact row.

Attending to several factors simultaneously   Why are preschool children unable to appreciate that the amount of a substance remains unaffected by changes of shape or that the number of objects in a given set does not vary with changes in the spatial arrangement? According to Piaget, part of the problem is the child's inability to attend to all of the relevant dimensions simultaneously. Consider conservation of liquid quantity. To conserve, the children must first comprehend that there are two relevant factors: the height of the liquid column and the width. They must then appreciate that an increase in the column's height is accompanied by a decrease in its width. Initially, they center their attention only on the height and do not realize that the change in height is compensated for by a corresponding change in width. Later on, say at five, they may well attend to width on one occasion and to height on another (with corresponding changes in judgment). But to attend to both dimensions concurrently and to relate them properly requires a higher-order schema that reorganizes initially discrete perceptual experiences into one conceptual unit.

In Piaget's view, this reorganization occurs when the child focuses on the transformations from one experience into another, rather than on the individual experiences by themselves. The child sees that these transformations are effected by various reversible overt actions, such as pouring the contents of one glass into another. The overt action eventually becomes internalized as a reversible operation so that the child can mentally pour the liquid back and forth. The result is conservation of quantity (Piaget, 1952).

In summary, the preoperational child is the prisoner of his own immediate perceptual experience and tends to take appearance for reality. When a seven-year-old watches a magician, she can easily distinguish between her perception and her knowledge. She perceives that the rabbits come out of the hat, but she knows that they couldn't possibly do so. Her four-year-old brother has no such sophistication. He is delighted to see rabbits anytime and anywhere, and if they want to come out of a hat, why shouldn't they?

EGOCENTRISM

In Piaget's theory, the inability of preoperational children to consider two physical dimensions simultaneously has a counterpart in their approach to the social

13.9   Conservation of number   (A) The experimenter points to two rows of checkers, one hers, the other Tyler's. She asks, "Do I have as many checkers as you?" and Tyler (aged four years, five months) nods. (B) One row of checkers is spread out and the experimenter says, "Now, do we still have the same?" Tyler says no and points to the spread-out row, which she says has more. (Photographs by Chris Massey)

A

B

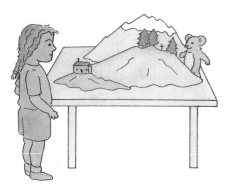

13.10   The three-mountain test of egocentrism   *The child is asked to indicate what the teddy bear sees. The results suggest that the child thinks the teddy bear sees the scene just as she does, including the little house, which is of course obstructed from the teddy bear's vantage point. (After Piaget and Inhelder, 1967)*

world. They cannot understand another person's point of view, for they are as yet unable to recognize that different points of view exist. This characteristic of preoperational thought is called *egocentrism.* As Piaget used the term, it does not imply selfishness. It is not that children seek to benefit at the expense of others; it is rather that they haven't fully grasped that there are other selves.

An interesting demonstration of egocentrism involves a literal interpretation of "point of view." If two adults stand at opposite corners of a building, each knows that the other sees a different wall. But according to Piaget, preoperational children don't understand this. In one study, children were shown a three-dimensional model of a mountain scene. While the children viewed the scene from one position, a small doll was placed at various other locations around the model. The child's job was to decide what the doll saw from its vantage point (see Figure 13.10). To answer, the child had to choose one of several drawings that depicted different views of the mountain scene. Up to four years of age, the children didn't even understand the question. From four to seven years old, their response was fairly consistent—they chose the drawing that showed what they saw, regardless of where the doll was placed (Piaget and Inhelder, 1956).

CONCRETE AND FORMAL OPERATIONS

■   Seven-year-olds have acquired mental operations that allow them to abstract some of the essential attributes of reality such as number and substance. But according to Piaget, these operations are primarily applicable to the relations between concrete events (hence the term *concrete operations*). They do not really suffice when these relations must be considered entirely in the abstract. Eight- and nine-year-olds can perform various manipulations on specific numbers, but they generally fail to understand that certain results will hold for any number whatsoever. They may realize that 4 is an even number and 4 + 1 is odd, and similarly for 6 and 6 + 1, 8 and 8 + 1, but they are by no means sure that the addition of 1 to *any* even number must always produce a number that is odd. According to Piaget, the comprehension of such highly abstract and formal relationships requires *formal operations,* operations of a higher order, which emerge at about eleven or twelve years of age. Given formal operations, the child's thought can embrace the possible as well as the real. He can now entertain hypothetical possibilities, can deal with what might be no less than what is.

An illustration of the role of formal operations comes from a study in which children had to discover what makes a pendulum go fast or go slow. They were shown how to construct a pendulum by hanging some object from a string. They were also shown how to vary the length of the string, the weight of the suspended object, and the initial force that set the pendulum in motion. Children between seven and eleven typically varied several factors at a time. They might compare a heavy weight suspended from a long string with a light weight suspended from a short string and would then conclude that a pendulum swings faster the shorter its length and the lighter its weight. Needless to say, their reasoning was faulty, for the way to determine whether a given factor (e.g., weight) has an effect is to hold all others (e.g., length) constant. Children younger than about eleven cannot do this, for they can operate only on the concretely given. They are unable to consider potential cause-and-effect relationships, which must first be deliberately excluded and then tested for later on. In contrast, older children can plan and execute an appropriate series of tests. Their mental operations proceed on a more formal plane, so they can grasp the notion of "other things being equal" (Inhelder and Piaget, 1958).

The entry into the period of formal operations is the last important milestone in the child's intellectual progression that Piaget and his co-workers charted in some detail. Their account of the developmental steps that led up to this point has been enormously influential. But this doesn't mean that it has gone unchallenged. We will now consider some of the efforts to look at Piaget's description of human cognitive development with a more critical eye.

WHAT IS THE COGNITIVE STARTING POINT?

FOCUS QUESTIONS

■ What do studies of occlusion (using the habituation procedure) suggest about whether young infants have some concept of space or time? Do these findings support Piaget's view?

■ What findings suggest that infants even younger than a year may recognize the existence of other minds?

One critical challenge to Piaget's work concerns his views of what is given at the very start of life. A number of modern developmental psychologists contend that Piaget—who in this regard was much like the early British empiricists—had seriously underestimated the infant's native endowment. These critics deny that the infant's mind is the mere jumble of unrelated sensory impressions and motor reactions that Piaget declared it to be, for they believe that some of the major categories by which adults organize the world—such as the concepts of space, objects, number, and the existence of other minds—have primitive precursors in early life. They have buttressed their position by systematic studies of perception and action in very young infants.

SPACE AND OBJECTS IN INFANCY

Do humans come equipped with some built-in notion of space and objects? Some experiments with very young infants suggest that they do.

THE EFFECT OF OCCLUSION

One series of studies focused on the perceptual effect of *occlusion.* Consider Figure 13.11A, which shows an object that partially obscures (occludes) the view of an object behind it. When adults encounter this sight, they will surely perceive it as a child behind a gate. They are completely certain that when the gate is opened so that the partial occlusion is removed, they will see a whole child (Figure 13.11B) and would be utterly astounded if the opened gate revealed a child with gaps in her (Figure 13.11C). This ability to perceive partly hidden objects as they really are is continually called upon in our everyday life. Most of the things we see are partly concealed by others in front of them, but we perceive a world of complete objects rather than disjointed fragments (see Chapter 6).

What accounts for the adult's ability to perceive partly hidden objects? To some extent, it is surely a matter of learning. We know that people have no gaps in them and that even if they do, they can't stand unsupported in mid-air. But does this mean that Piaget is correct and that the infant starts life with no idea at all that there are external objects outside? Some authors believe it does not. In their view, the infant comes equipped with some primitive concept of a physical world that contains unitary objects whose parts are connected and stay connected regardless of whether the object is partially hidden. Their evidence comes

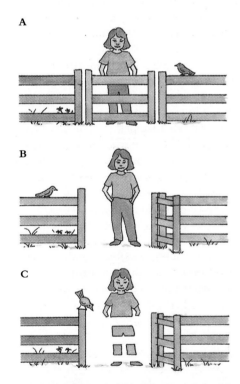

A

B

C

13.11   The perceptual effect of occlusion
(A) A child occluded by a gate is perceived as a whole person behind a gate, so that she will look like (B) when the gate is opened, rather than being perceived as (C), a child with gaps in her body.

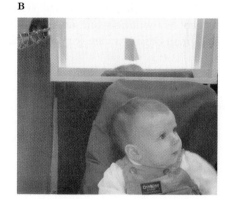
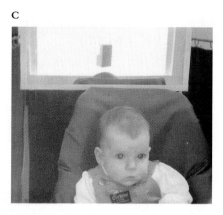

13.12   The habituation procedure
(A) A four-month-old's face, looking at a small slowly rotating pyramid in front of her (the pyramid can be seen in the mirror that is behind the infant and above her head).
(B) Habituation: The infant becomes increasingly bored and looks away. (C) Dishabituation: The infant sees a new object (the rotating cube shown in the mirror) and looks again. This dishabituation effect provides evidence that the infant perceives a difference between the first and the second stimulus (that is, the pyramid and the cube). (Photographs courtesy of Phillip Kellman)

from experiments which show that under some conditions four-month-old infants seem to perceive occluded objects in much the same manner that adults do. Most of these experiments employed the ***habituation procedure*** (Figure 13.12).

In one such study, the infants were shown a rod that moved back and forth behind a solid block that occluded the rod's central portion (Figure 13.13A). This display was kept in view until the infants became bored (that is, *habituated*), and stopped looking at it. The question was whether the infant perceived a complete, unitary rod, despite the fact that this rod was partially hidden. To find out, the experimenters presented the infants with two new and unoccluded displays. One was an unbroken rod that moved back and forth (Figure 13.13B). The other consisted of two aligned rod pieces that moved back and forth in unison (Figure 13.13C). If the infants saw the original display as a complete rod that moved behind the block, they would presumably regard the broken rod as a novel stimulus. If so, they would look at it for a longer time than they looked at the (now unobstructed) complete rod. This is just what happened. The fact that the top and bottom of the rod in the original display were seen to move together behind the block apparently led to the perception that they were connected. This suggests that some notion of a real physical object exists even at four months of age (Kellman and Spelke, 1983; Kellman, Spelke, and Short, 1986).

KNOWING ABOUT OBJECTS

The preceding discussion suggests that very young infants see objects rather than disjointed fragments. Do they also understand certain rock-bottom principles of the physical world, such as the fact that two objects can't occupy the same space at the same time?

13.13   The perceptual effect of occlusion in early infancy   *Four-month-olds were shown a rod that moved back and forth behind an occluding block as shown in (A). After they became habituated to this display and stopped looking at it, they were shown two new displays, neither of which was occluded. (B) was an unbroken rod that moved back and forth. (C) was made of two aligned rod pieces that moved back and forth together. The infants spent much more time looking at (C) than at (B). (After Kellman and Spelke, 1983)*

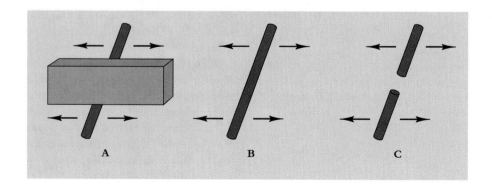

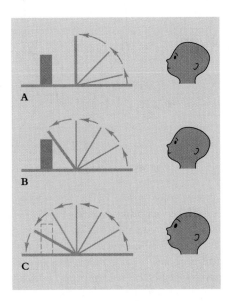

13.14   Knowing about objects   *A four-and-a-half-month-old infant is looking at a stage on which he sees an upright, brightly colored box. In front of the box is a screen that initially lies flat and then starts to rotate upward (A). In the first condition (B), the screen stops rotating as soon as it hits the box. In the second condition (C), when the screen is at a point high enough to hide the box, the box is surreptitiously removed and the screen continues to rotate backwards. The infant seems to find this quite surprising as shown by the fact that he continues to look at the stage much longer than he did in the first condition. Infants seem able to distinguish possible from impossible events. (After Baillargeon, 1987a)*

To answer that question, four-and-a-half-month-olds were shown a miniature stage in the middle of which was a medium-sized yellow box. In front of the box was a screen that was hinged on a rod attached to the stage floor. Initially, that screen was laid flat so that the box behind it was clearly visible, but the screen was then rotated upwards like a drawbridge, hiding the box from view (Figure 13.14A). There were two conditions. In one condition, the screen rotated backwards until it reached the no longer visible box, stopped, and then rotated forwards and returned to its initial position at which point the box became visible again (Figure 13.14B). In the other condition, the screen rotated backwards until it reached the occluded box and then kept on going as though the box were no longer there. Once it finished the full 180 degree arc, it reversed direction and swiveled all the way backwards, at which point the box was revealed again (the box being surreptitiously removed and replaced as required; see Figure 13.14C; Baillargeon, Spelke, and Wasserman, 1985; Baillargeon, 1987a).

To an adult, these two conditions present the observer with two radically different events. The first of these makes perfect physical sense: Since two objects can't occupy the same space at the same time, the screen necessarily stops when it encounters the solid box. But the second event is physically impossible: If one assumes the box is still where it was originally seen to be, the screen couldn't possibly pass through it.

This is all very well for adults, but do infants see the world the same way? The answer seems to be yes. They spent much less time looking at the stage in the first condition than they did in the second. In the first condition, the screen did what it was supposed to: It came to a halt when it came up against the—presumably still present—solid box. But in the second condition, the screen behaved rather oddly, for it apparently passed through a solid object. The four-month-olds evidently found the second condition more surprising—or puzzling—than the first. This suggests that these young infants had some notion of object permanence, for they evidently believed that the yellow box they had seen before continued to exist even though it was now occluded. It also suggests that young infants have some notions of the principles that govern objects in space; they evidently know that two objects (here, the screen and the yellow box) can't occupy the same place at the same time.

SOCIAL COGNITION IN INFANCY: THE EXISTENCE OF OTHER MINDS

To an adult, the existence of other minds is a basic axiom (e.g., Austin, 1970). We know that we have beliefs and desires, and take for granted that others also do. According to Piaget and the British Empiricists, this knowledge is entirely a product of learning. But while it's true that an enormous amount of what we know about others is acquired through learning, there is reason to believe that this learning builds upon a substantial substructure that is natively given.

To begin with, there is evidence that infants come into the world with some built-in predisposition to look at human faces. One group of investigators studied babies immediately (that is, nine *minutes*) after they were born. The experimenter held each baby in his lap and moved several patterns in front of their eyes. The infants turned their heads and looked longer at the pattern if it was of a schematic rather than of a scrambled face. Further studies suggest that this very early face recognition process is based on a subcortical mechanism that drops out within a month or two and is then replaced by more sophisticated recognition machinery that comes into its own as the visual cortex matures (Goren,

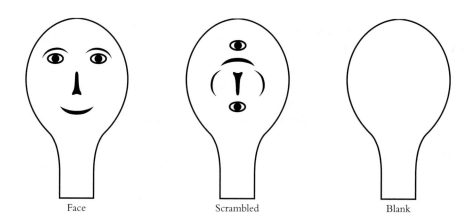

13.15 Rudimentary face recognition in newborns *Newborn babies look longer at a pattern showing a schematic face than at a scrambled or a blank pattern. (From Johnson and Morton, 1991)*

Face　　　Scrambled　　　Blank

Sarty, and Wu, 1975; Johnson and Morton, 1991; see Figure 13.15). The ability to recognize that certain sensory patterns characterize other human beings—that some visual patterns specify faces, that some auditory patterns define voices—is a necessary foundation on which all further social cognition rests. Before long the baby will know not just that such and such a sensory pattern characterizes another person but that it belongs to a particular person—its mother, father, or some other important caretaker.

The ability to recognize others is only the barest first step in understanding that there are other minds. An important next step is the infant's recognition that others live in the same physical world and can more or less see what she sees, hear what she hears, and so on. Evidence comes from work on shared attention. Thus nine-month-olds will tend to look in the direction of their mothers' gaze (Scaife and Bruner, 1975). When they are between twelve and eighteen months their ability to recognize where the mother is looking and what she is looking at becomes a conceptual achievement that goes beyond the perceptual here and now. In one study, each infant was held in his mother's lap while she looked at one of a number of toys arranged in front of her in a semicircle. But the child was held with his head toward the mother's body so that he could not see the target; all he could see was his mother's eyes. Evidently, that was enough—as soon as the mother's hold was released the infant squirmed around and looked at just the toy the mother had looked at a moment before (Butterworth and Cochran, 1980; Butterworth and Jarrett, 1991).

COGNITIVE DEVELOPMENT IN PRESCHOOLERS

FOCUS QUESTIONS

■ Why do some investigators question Piaget's view of cognitive development as proceeding by distinct stages?

■ What do studies of counting, numerical reasoning, theories of mind, perception, and belief imply about how cognitive development proceeds?

The preceding discussion showed why many critics feel that Piaget underestimated the infant's native cognitive endowments. If these critics are right, the starting point of mental growth is higher than Piaget assumed it to be. But what about the process of development from then on? As Piaget described it, cognitive development goes through several distinct stages that are in some ways analogous to the stages found in embryological development. This stage notion of development has been the subject of considerable debate. No one doubts that there is mental growth, that the child changes in the way she thinks as she gets older. But is this growth best described as a progression through successive stages?

THE MEANING OF MENTAL STAGE

Piaget used the term *stage* in analogy to how it is understood in embryology. Embryological stages tend to be discrete rather than continuous. There is a qualitative difference between a tadpole and a frog; to be sure, the change from one to the other takes a while, but by the time the creature is a frog, its tadpole days are emphatically over. Piaget's basic claim was that the same discreteness characterizes cognitive development. A number of critics have questioned whether it really does.

As Piaget's account is usually understood, many cognitive capacities that mark one period of development are totally absent at prior periods. But this is questionable. Consider conservation of quantity or number. According to a simple discrete-stage hypothesis, these should be totally absent at an early age, say, five years old and younger. They should then emerge virtually full blown when the curtain finally opens on the next act of the developmental drama, the period of concrete operations. But a number of modern investigators deny that cognitive development is essentially all or none. As these critics see it, various cognitive achievements such as conservation have primitive precursors that appear several years earlier than the Piagetian calendar would predict (Gelman, 1978; Gelman and Baillargeon, 1983).

We will now consider two areas of cognitive growth during the preschool period—number and social cognition—from the perspective of these modern investigators.

NUMERICAL SKILLS IN PRESCHOOLERS

Some initial rudiments of counting appear as early as two and a half. At this age, children may not yet know the conventional number terms. But nevertheless they may have grasped some aspect of what the counting process is all about. For example, some children employ an idiosyncratic number series. Thus one two-year-old consistently used "one, two, six," and another used "one, thirteen, nineteen." But what is important is that they used these series consistently. They realized that each of these number tags has to be applied to each object in the set on a one-to-one basis, that the tags must always be used in the same order, and that the last number applied is the number of items in the set. And this realization is the foundation on which counting rests (Gelman and Gallistel, 1978; Gelman, 1982).

NUMERICAL REASONING

A child who can count (even if rather idiosyncratically) has taken a big step. But there is more to numerical understanding than counting. The child must also grasp some principles of numerical reasoning. She must understand that adding an item increases the total number of items in the set that is being counted, that subtracting one decreases it, and that adding one and then subtracting one leaves everything unchanged. The comprehension of these basic numerical truths will not suffice to make the child an arithmetician, but they are basic to all further advances in the numerical domain. The evidence suggests that preschoolers

A

B

C

*13.16 Gelman's mouse-plate test (A)
The experimenter points to the plate that has
two mice and says it is the "winner," while
three-year-old Carly watches. (B) After the
experimenter covers the plates and rearranges
the plates by a sleight-of-hand trick, (C)
Carly points to the correct "winner" and then
looks at the experimenter with surprise and
says, "Hey—they're spreaded out!" (Photographs courtesy of Hilary Schmidt)*

gradually acquire these concepts. When comparing two sets of items, three- and
four-year-olds can correctly point to the one that is smaller or larger if the number of items are small enough (Gelman, 1982; Gelman and Gallistel, 1978).

How can such results be reconciled with Piaget's claim that preschoolers fail
in tasks that call for conservation of number? We have previously described the
standard Piagetian finding: When preschoolers are asked to compare two rows
that contain the same number of, say, toy soldiers, they often say that the longer
row contains more soldiers, in an apparent confusion of length and number. But
more recent studies show that children as young as three have surprising precursors of number conservation if the test conditions are suitably arranged
(Gelman, 1972).

In one procedure, the children were shown two toy plates, each with a row of
toy mice attached with velcro. One plate had two mice, while the other had
three. One plate was designated the "winner," the other the "loser." Each plate
was then covered by a can and shuffled around while the children were instructed to keep track of the winner—a small-fry version of the venerable shell game.
After each trial, the plates were uncovered, and the children received a prize if
they could correctly identify the winner and the loser. After several such trials,
the real test was conducted. The experimenter surreptitiously substituted a new
plate for the original winner. In one case, the new plate contained the same
number of mice as the original, but the row was made longer or shorter. In the
other case, the row length stayed unchanged, but a mouse was added or subtracted. The results showed that spatial arrangement made little difference. But
changes in number had dramatic consequences even at three and four years of
age. The children were surprised, asked where the missing mouse was, and
searched for it (Gelman, 1972; see Figure 13.16).

Other studies suggest that the children's apparent lack of conservation in
Piaget's original studies may have been produced by the way in which the
experimenter questioned them. In a typical number conservation experiment, a
six-year-old is shown two rows, say, of buttons arranged in a neat one-to-one
manner. When asked, "which row has more buttons, or do they both have the
same?" she quickly answers "The same!" Now the experimenter spreads out the
buttons in one row, pushes the buttons in the other row more closely together,
and asks again: "Which row has more buttons, or do they both have the same?"
But this is the same question he asked her before. The child may now interpret
the fact that he repeated his question as an indication that her first answer,
"they're the same" was wrong, and so she changes it. To be sure, this misinterpretation is only possible because the child is not really sure of her answer. If the
number of buttons is small enough, the confusion will not arise (Siegal, 1991).

Here as in other cognitive realms, the achievements of later periods are built
upon foundations established much earlier. If we look carefully enough, we see
that the accomplishments of the concrete-operational period do not come out
of the blue but have preludes in much earlier childhood years. It may well be
true that there are milestones of intellectual growth which, as Piaget argued,
must be passed in an orderly sequence. But there are no neat demarcations
between stages and no sharp transitions. The stages of cognitive development
are not as all or none as the changes from tadpole to frog (let alone from frog to
prince).

SOCIAL COGNITION IN PRESCHOOLERS:
DEVELOPING A THEORY OF MIND

■ We've considered cognitive development during the preschool years as it
pertains to the understanding of the world of things. But cognitive development also takes place in another realm—the understanding of the social

world. During the same preschool period the child acquires the beginnings of what some theorists call a ***theory of mind,*** a term originally coined by Premack and Woodruff to interpret some phenomena observed in chimpanzees and then adopted more widely in the discussion of social cognition in children and adults (Premack and Woodruff, 1978; Wellman, 1990; Leslie, 1992; Fodor, 1992).★

In adults a theory of mind is a set of interrelated concepts we use as we try to make sense of our own mental processes and those of others, including the fact that both we and others have beliefs and desires, that beliefs can be true or false, that the beliefs and desires of others are not necessarily the same as our own, and that others know all this and also know that we know it too. These are rock-bottom axioms whose understanding is an absolute prerequisite for all social interactions, whether practiced at the poker table, in foreign embassies, or in a used-car lot. The used-car salesman knows that his prospective customers know that his financial interests are not identical to theirs, and he also knows that they worry that he'll misrepresent his own beliefs about the road worthiness of his cars.

EGOCENTRISM REVISITED

Needless to say, three-year-olds are not yet capable of the advanced social machinations of international diplomacy and used-car sales. But have they got the first rudiments of a theory of mind?

Piaget would have answered with an emphatic "no." In his view, preschoolers couldn't possibly have anything resembling a theory of mind, since they are still dominated by egocentrism and haven't fully grasped that there are other selves. As a result, they are unable to appreciate the difference between another's point of view and their own. But recent studies show that a modicum of this ability is found in children between two and four.

One study used a picture-showing task. Children from one to three years of age were asked to show a photograph to their mother who was seated opposite them. At two-and-a-half and three years of age, all children turned the picture so that it faced the mother, which implies that they had some conception of the difference between one person's angle of regard and another's. If they had been totally egocentric, they should have shown their mothers the back of the picture, while continuing to look at it from the front (Lempers, Flavell, and Flavell, 1977).

PERCEPTIONS AND DESIRES

Evidence of this sort shows that the child has at least a rudimentary understanding that there are other minds. But how deep does this knowledge go? There is little doubt that even at three years of age the child has begun to be a little psychologist.

To begin with, she has some primitive understanding of how perception works. Two- and three-year-olds can hide things (to be sure, quite ineptly) so that another person can't find them, or they can help someone see a small picture by bringing it closer to his eyes (Flavell, Shipstead, and Croft, 1978; Lempers, Flavell, and Flavell, 1977). They evidently know that perception depends on the presence of an external stimulus.

★ As they use the term, "an individual has a theory of mind if he imputes mental states to himself and others" (Premack and Woodruff, 1978). Premack and Woodruff make a good case that chimpanzees have such a theory of mind (though, to be sure, a rather primitive one), and there is some suggestion that monkeys also have some limited capacity to attribute beliefs and desires to other monkeys (Premack and Woodruff, 1978; Cheney and Seyfarth, 1990; see Chapters 4 and 10). It is called a "theory" because it is an informal attempt at an explanation.

A

B

C

13.17 The false-belief test *(A) The child watches as the experimenter makes the puppet "hide" the ball in the oatmeal container. (B) While the puppet is gone, the experimenter and the child move the ball to the box. (C) When the child is now asked, "Where does the puppet think the ball is?" she points to the box. (Photographs by Kimberly Canidy)*

BELIEFS

The child's task becomes much harder when we turn to *belief.* Adults take it for granted that another person's actions will depend not just on what he sees and desires, but also on what he believes. At first glance, the same seems to be true for the three-year-old. Suppose you tell Annie that Johnny wants to play with his puppy and thinks that it is under the piano. If you then ask her where Johnny will look, she'll say he'll look under the piano (Wellman and Bartsch, 1988). She seems to understand the concept of belief. But does she really?

A number of authors point out that there are two crucial components to the notion of belief. One is that beliefs can be true or false; the other is that different people can have different beliefs. According to several authors, the three-year-old doesn't understand this and won't until she is about four or four-and-a-half. To the extent that she doesn't, there is something seriously lacking in her theory of mind. Evidence for this comes from studies utilizing **false-belief tests** (Dennett, 1978; Wimmer and Permer, 1983).

In a typical study of this kind, the child and a teddy bear sit in front of two boxes, one red and the other green. The experimenter opens the red box and puts some candy in it. She then opens the green box and shows the child—and the teddy—that this box is empty. The teddy bear is now taken out of the room (to play for a while) and the experimenter and the child move the candy from the red box into the green one. The teddy bear is brought back into the room, and the child is asked: "Where will the teddy look for the candy?" Virtually all three-year-olds and some four-year-olds will answer "In the green box." If you ask them why they say so, they'll say, "Because that's where it is." They evidently don't yet understand that beliefs can be false and that others may not share our own. At about four-and-a-half, they get the idea: "He'll look in the red box because that's where he thinks the candy is" (Wellman, 1990; Wimmer and Perner, 1983; Cassidy, 1993; see Figure 13.17).

Many authors have interpreted such results as an indication that the young child doesn't yet have a genuine theory of mind. But more recent evidence suggests that here, as in some other areas of cognitive development, the young preschooler knows more than it first appears. Some authors suggest that three- and four-year-olds do have a theory of mind, but they perform badly because they are confused by the experimental situation. One trouble is that they are pulled by their desire. To figure out what the teddy would do or think requires some mental cogitation; it's much easier to go in the direction of what it is that they want, the candy rather than the empty box (Fodor, 1992). To test this notion children were given a false-belief test, but this time the object that was moved was something the children did not want—some broccoli. (They were also told that the teddy would have to eat whatever he found in the box). When now asked where the teddy would look, even the three-year-olds gave proof that they did understand something about beliefs. They correctly answered "In the red box." They were no longer seduced by desire and could therefore show that they did understand something about beliefs (Cassidy, 1993).

SEQUENCE OR STAGES?

■ What can we conclude about Piaget's stages of mental development? The evidence as a whole suggests that the child's mental growth does not proceed as neatly as a simple stage theory might lead one to expect (Flavell, 1985).

Does this mean that Piaget's cognitive milestones have no psychological reality? Not really: The sequence may not be as neat as one might wish, but there is little doubt that some such sequence exists. Consider the difference between

seven-year-olds and preschoolers. Despite all the precursors of concrete operations at four or even earlier, there is no question that seven- and eight-year-olds
have something preschoolers lack—the ability to apply their insights to a much
wider range of problems (Fodor, 1972). Three-year-olds can tell the difference
between two and three mice regardless of how they are spaced on the table. But
they haven't fully grasped the underlying idea—that number and spatial arrangements are in principle independent and that this is so for *all* numbers and *all* spatial arrangements. As a result, they fail—and will continue to fail until they are
six or seven years old—the standard Piagetian test for conservation of number in
which they have to recognize that two rows of, say, nine buttons contain the
same number of buttons, regardless of how the rows are expanded or com-
pressed. This task baffles the preschool child, who finds the number in each row
too large to count and gets confused. Seven-year-olds have no such problems.
They can count higher, but that's not the issue. They know that there is no need
to count, that the number of buttons in each row has to be identical, regardless
of the way they are arranged. As a result, they can conserve number in general.

What holds for conservation of number holds for many other intellectual
achievements. Most of them have precursors, often at much earlier ages than
Piaget led us to suppose. But these preschool abilities usually represent isolated
pockets of knowledge that can't be applied very widely. The seven- or eight-
year-old's understanding of physical, numerical, and social reality is considerably
more general, so much so that it seems qualitatively different from what went on
before. By simplifying the task in various ways, experimenters can induce
preschoolers to perform more creditably. But the fact remains that by the time
the child is seven or eight years old, no such simplification is necessary. A seven-
or eight-year-old conserves with barely a glance at the containers in which the
liquid is sloshed around. He *knows* that the liquid quantity is unaffected no matter how the containers are shaped.

THE CAUSES OF COGNITIVE GROWTH

FOCUS QUESTIONS

- Can coaching or experience speed cognitive development?

- Why do many developmental psychologists think that Piaget's processes of assimilation and accommodation are inadequate to explain cognitive development?

- For the information-processing theorist, how do the issues of expertise, memory
  strategies, and metacognition all help us understand why young children's memories are poor?

We described cognitive development as it proceeds from early infancy into the
school years. But what explains these changes? As so often in the field of cognition, the attempts to come up with an adequate explanation have fluctuated
between the two poles of the nature-nurture controversy.

THE NATIVIST APPROACH: MATURATION

As in the study of physical development, some investigators are inclined
toward a nativist interpretation. There is, of course, no doubt that native
endowment plays some role in cognitive development as well. The human
infant begins life with a potential that is quite different from that of his near and

13.18 Development as maturation?
(A) Emerging from its crysalis for a butterfly and (B) walking for a child are largely matters of maturation. (C) Is the cognitive growth that underlies a seven-and-a-half-year-old's success in a Piagetian conservation task to be understood in similar terms? (Photographs by Pat Lynch/Photo Researchers; Ray Ellis/Photo Researchers; Chris Massey)

distant cousins in the rest of the animal kingdom, and no amount of training and nurturing can ever erase these differences in the equipment with which the varying species begin. Worms won't fly, platypuses won't form higher-order chunkings, and polar bears won't conserve liquid quantity, no matter what environments they are reared in. Our native equipment is thus a necessary pre-condition for all development. But can this endowment explain the orderly progression of cognitive development?

Some theorists believe that it can. They believe that development is largely driven by some form of physical **maturation,** a preprogrammed growth process based on changes in underlying neural structures that are relatively independent of environmental conditions. Could cognitive development be a matter of maturation (in part or whole) in the sense in which walking is (Figure 13.18)? As we saw earlier, there is a tenfold increase in the number of synaptic connections in the cortex between birth and twelve months of age, with further changes that last into the school years (see p. 388). If the brain gets more complex, wouldn't cognition follow suit (Siegler, 1989)?

A number of authors have argued that maturational changes of this kind underlie many aspects of human cognitive development. This view is buttressed by the fact that, at least in broad outline, mental growth seems rather similar in children of different cultures and nationalities. While children of different cultures master intellectual tasks such as conservation at somewhat different ages, they usually pass these landmarks in the same order. Thus Arab, Indian, Somali, and British children show the same progression from nonconservation of quantity to conservation (Hyde, 1959). This is reminiscent of physical maturation. Different butterflies may emerge from their chrysalis at slightly different times, but none is a butterfly first and a chrysalis second. The timing of the transitions may well be affected by environmental conditions: in humans, by culture; in butterflies, by temperature. But according to the maturational hypothesis, the order of the stages is determined by the genetic code.

THE EMPIRICIST APPROACH: SPECIFIC LEARNING

The simplest alternative to a maturation-centered approach is one that emphasizes learning by exposure to the environment. The most extreme version of this view is that of the empiricists who followed in the footsteps of John Locke (see Chapter 5). To them, the human mind starts out as a blank tablet, a *tabula rasa,* upon which experience gradually leaves its mark. But can such a radical empiricist position explain the systematic sequence of cognitive development that Piaget and other investigators have chronicled?

Piaget argued that simple learning theories of the kind espoused by the early empiricists—and by their modern heirs such as Pavlov and Skinner—will not do. According to such theories, learning is the acquisition of relatively specific skills that in principle could be mastered at any age. But this is precisely what Piaget denied. According to Piaget, four-year-olds cannot possibly be taught how to use a measuring cup correctly, no matter how attractive the reinforcements or how many the number of trials. He argued that four-year-olds lack the prerequisite concepts of number and quantity (which they cannot attain before the concrete-operational level), so that any attempt to teach them is as fruitless as trying to build the third story of a house without a second story underneath it. This view has obvious relevance to educational policy. If Piaget is right, then there is little point in efforts to teach children this or that aspect of the curriculum before they are "ready" for it.

In an attempt to test this claim, several investigators have tried to determine whether children can be trained to reach certain cognitive landmarks such as conservation ahead of schedule. The results are a bit ambiguous. Formerly, most investigators concluded that specific training has little impact. In some cases, conservation was speeded up by special coaching, but later checks revealed that the children had not really understood the underlying principles and quickly reverted to their previous, nonconserving ways (e.g., Smedslund, 1961). But some later studies showed more substantial effects. In some cases, these were brought about by mere observation; for example, six-year-old nonconservers who watched conservers perform showed subsequent conservation of mass or number (Botvin and Murray, 1975; Murrary, 1978). But the most likely interpretation is that the children already had most of the necessary conceptual ingredients at the time they were "trained." If so, then watching another child did not really teach conservation; it only helped to uncover what was already there (Gold, 1978; Gelman and Baillargeon, 1983).

Related findings come from a study conducted in a Mexican village whose inhabitants made pottery and whose children helped and participated in this activity from early on. When tested for conservation of mass, these children turned out to be more advanced than their North American counterparts (or those studied by Piaget in Switzerland). Having spent much of their lives working at a potter's wheel, they were more likely to know that the amount of clay is the same whether it is rolled into a ball or stretched into a long, thin sausage (Price-Williams, Gordon, and Ramirez, 1969). But these effects of pottery making were relatively specific. They led to an advance on tests of conservation of mass but to little else. (For further discussion, see Greenfield, 1976; Price-Williams, 1981; Rogoff, Gauvain, and Ellis, 1984.)

All in all, there is little doubt that environment plays some role in cognitive development. To acquire liquid conservation, one presumably has to live in a world in which liquids exist. If a frozen planet like Jupiter had inhabitants whose cognitive potential was like our own, their young would never know that when water is poured from a wide jar into a tall, thin beaker the amount of water stays unchanged. But this is not to say that the environment shapes human (or Jovian) children in the simple, passive way proposed by an extreme empiricist.

PIAGET'S APPROACH: ASSIMILATION AND ACCOMMODATION

Piaget's own view was that neither maturation nor specific learning could by themselves account for cognitive development. As he saw it, the child's mental progress is propelled by the twin engines of developmental change that we mentioned earlier, assimilation and accommodation. At any one stage, the environment the child faces is interpreted in terms of the mental schemas she has at that time—the environment is assimilated to the schemas. But these schemas cannot help but change as the child continues to interact with the world around her—the schemas accommodate to the environment. Without active involvement, there will be no such accommodation and hence no mental growth.

Piaget's conception of these two opposite processes, assimilation and accommodation, may be a useful way of emphasizing the fact that organism and environment interact in producing mental growth. But is it an explanation? Many psychologists argue that it is not, for Piaget offered no mechanism whereby schemas are changed through accommodation. Lacking such a mechanism, Piaget's proposal still leaves us with the unanswered question of why children go from one stage of thought to another.

THE INFORMATION-PROCESSING APPROACH: CHUNKING AND STRATEGIES

▪ A recent suggestion for explaining cognitive development is in terms of information processing. According to this approach, all cognitive activities are ways of handling—that is, *processing*—information. Whenever a person perceives, remembers, or thinks, she has to acquire, retrieve, or transform information (see Chapters 6, 7, and 8). If adults think differently (and with greater success) than children, this is presumably because they process information differently.

In recent years, concepts derived from this information-processing approach have been applied to many aspects of cognitive development, including perception, language, thinking, and memory (Siegler, 1983). Here, we will focus on just the development of memory and the awareness that other people have minds like our own.

THE CHILD AS A LIMITED MENTAL PROCESSOR

On many conventional tests of recall, younger children do worse than older ones. Take memory span—the number of items a subject can reproduce after just one presentation. This number is roughly equal to the child's age until she is about five: one item at eighteen months, three at three-and-a-half years, and four at four-and-a-half years, compared to a span of seven or eight in adulthood (see Figure 13.19).

What has happened during development that makes us so much better at remembering than young children are? Several theorists (sometimes called neo-Piagetians) believe that the reason is largely a matter of maturation. Initially, the child's mind is like a small computer with limited storage and processing capacity. But as her brain grows, so does her memory capacity. This in turn allows her to develop a whole set of cognitive skills that she could never have acquired previously (Pascale-Leone, 1978; Case, 1978, 1985). But there is reason to believe that maturational processes are only part of the story.

THE CHILD AS NOVICE

There is evidence that the young child's poor performance at memory tasks is caused, at least in part, by the fact that she knows so little and has rather limited strategies for remembering the little that she does know (Flavell and Wellman, 1977; Brown et al., 1983; Chi, 1978, 1985).

In a previous section, we saw that in the course of acquiring skills, the performance of the learner changes qualitatively. For example, skilled typists have formed various higher-order chunks, so that they no longer respond to individual letters but to letter groupings and words (see Chapter 8). It may be that much of cognitive development can be understood as a similar process that all human beings go through as they go from infancy to adulthood.

This view assumes that the difference between child and adult is in large part a matter of expertise—the adult has had the time to develop many conceptual chunkings that the child still lacks. But suppose we found some task on which the child is the expert and the adult the novice? One investigator studied memory for chess positions in adults and ten-year-olds. Experts generally do much better in this task than novices because they can draw on more and larger chunks (see Chapter 8). But the study had a novel twist because here the children were the experts (they were recruited from local chess clubs), while the

13.19 Memory span in young children
(After Case, 1978)

The child as expert *Ten-year-old chess champion Etienne Bacrot plays an adult opponent. To make the competition a bit more even, she wears a blindfold. (Photograph by Benainous, © Gamma)*

adults were the novices. Now that the tables were turned, what mattered was specific mastery rather than overall level of cognitive development. The children recalled many more chess positions than did the adults (Chi, 1978).

According to some authors, such findings suggest that intellectual growth is largely produced by the acquisition of more and more knowledge. But some of this knowledge is in the form of cognitive capital goods—tools for acquiring new knowledge. These are strategies for learning and thinking that become increasingly efficient and more widely applicable as the child gets older. As a result, he can become an expert in many areas.

THE CHILD AS A POOR STRATEGIST

When an adult is presented with a series of items and told to repeat them a moment later, she does her best to "keep them in mind." She rehearses, perhaps by repeating the items mentally, perhaps by organizing them in various ways. But the very young child doesn't do this, for he hasn't yet learned how. Some first precursors of rehearsal are found at age three. In one study, three-year-olds watched while an experimenter placed a toy dog under one of two containers. The experimenter told the children that he'd leave the room for a little while, but that they should tell him where the dog was hidden as soon as he came back. During the interval, some children kept looking at the hiding place and nodding "yes"; others kept their eyes on the wrong container while shaking their heads "no"; yet others kept their hands on the correct container. They all had found a way of building a bridge between past and present by performing an overt action—keeping the toy dog in their minds by marking its location with their bodies. Piaget, who believed that all mental activity is ultimately an outgrowth of overt action, might well have been pleased at this outcome (Wellman, Ritter, and Flavell, 1975).

Keeping one's hand on the to-be-remembered object may be a forerunner of rehearsal, but it's still a far cry from the real thing. Genuine rehearsal does not occur spontaneously until around age five or six. One experiment used subjects of five, seven, and ten years of age. The stimuli were pictures of seven common objects (e.g., a pipe, a flag, an owl, etc.), and the experimenter slowly pointed at

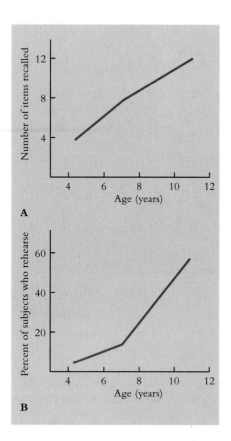

A

B

13.20 Strategies for memorizing in children *(A) Nursery-school children, first-graders, and fifth-graders were shown a number of pictures and were asked to try to remember them. The figure shows recall as a function of age. (B) While the subjects watched the stimuli, the experimenters observed them for signs of rehearsal—naming the pictures, moving their lips while watching, and so on. The figure shows the proportion of all children who rehearsed. In the older children, there was quite a bit of rehearsal, but there was very little for the first-graders and virtually none for the nursery-school children. Absence of rehearsal has also been found for retarded subjects. (Data from Appel et al., 1972)*

three of them in turn. The children's job was to point at the three pictures in the same order after a fifteen-second interval. During this interval their eyes were covered (by a specially designed space helmet), so they couldn't bridge the interval by looking at the pictures or by surreptitiously pointing at them. Not surprisingly, the older children did better on the recall test than the younger ones (Figure 13.20). Was this because they had greater memory capacity? The main cause lay elsewhere. One of the experimenters was a trained lip reader who observed that almost all of the ten-year-olds were silently mouthing the words—that is, rehearsing—compared to only 10 percent of the five-year-olds. The older children remembered more than the younger ones, not because they had more "memory space," but because they used it better (Flavell, Beach, and Chinsky, 1966).

METACOGNITION

When young nonrehearsers are taught to rehearse, they will recall as well as children of the same age who rehearse on their own. But there is one problem. When later presented with another memory task, many of these subjects will abandon the rehearsal method they have just been taught. This is especially likely if the new task is somewhat different from the old. A child might be taught to remember a set of names by reciting it aloud, but he won't apply the same principle to a shopping list. What is evidently lacking is a "master plan" for dealing with memory tasks in general, a strategy for using strategies (Flavell, 1970, 1977).

Normal adults adopt this higher-order strategy as a matter of course whenever they try to learn. They know that remembering telephone numbers or traffic directions or the names of the twelve cranial nerves are at bottom similar memory tasks. They also know that trying to commit them to memory requires certain mental activities—perhaps rehearsal or rhythmic and semantic grouping, all of which are lower-order strategies that are subsumed under the general memory master plan. But young children lack this general insight. They don't recognize what all memory tasks have in common. As a result, they don't realize that what helps in mastering one will also help in mastering the other. The adult's strategy of using strategies is an example of the higher-order cognitive processes that go under the general label of *metacognition.*

Human adults can reflect on the cognitive operations whereby they gain knowledge. They know, they know that they know, and they also know a good deal about how they come to know it. But in children, metacognition is less well developed. Take memory, for example. An adult has a fairly realistic idea of what he may or may not recall. When briefly shown pictures of four common objects, he will predict that he can recall them correctly after one presentation; when shown ten such pictures, he will predict that he cannot. First- and second-graders are much less realistic about what they can and cannot do (Yussen and Levy, 1975).

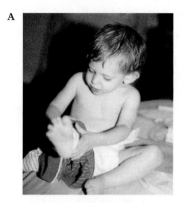

From apprentice to master (A) At two, getting the right body part through the right hole of a shirt is still a major problem. (B) Only six months later, dressing is well on the way to becoming automatic, (C) though complete mastery is not quite there yet. (Photographs courtesy of Kathy Hirsh-Pasek)

Metacognition is not limited to memory. Older children and adults manifest it in perception, so that they can do more than perceive—they can recognize the role of perspective, know the difference between reality and illusion, and become artists and art connoisseurs (Flavell, Flavell, and Green, 1983). They also manifest it in language, so that they can do more than talk and understand—they can play with language, as in puns or poems, recognize that some sentences are ill-formed, and become poets or linguists (Gleitman, Gleitman, and Shipley, 1972). They also manifest metacognition in thinking and problem solving. Of course, they think and solve problems, but they can do more—they can use general strategies for reaching solutions, know when they need more information, recognize a paradox, and become scientists or logicians. It may well be that metacognitive processes of this kind are one of the distinguishing hallmarks of adult human intelligence (Gleitman, 1985).

COGNITIVE DEVELOPMENT FROM A CROSS-CULTURAL PERSPECTIVE

FOCUS QUESTIONS

- What do cross-cultural studies suggest about whether cognitive development proceeds similarly across cultures?

- What might explain why members of some nonliterate cultures perform poorly on tests of abstract reasoning?

Thus far our primary emphasis has been on cognitive development among children in the Western world. Studies of cognitive development in non-Western cultures, especially those in which there is no formal schooling, have provided another perspective on theories of cognitive development.

We previously discussed evidence indicating that children from different cultures show a similar progression on the standard Piagetian tests (e.g., from nonconservation to conservation). But other studies suggest that there are also important cross-cultural differences in development. In some cultures (for example, that of Australian aborigines and of New Guinea tribesmen), a substantial number of adults fail tests of concrete operations, and evidence of formal operations is rare in cultures in which there is no formal schooling (Cole, 1975; Price-Williams, 1981). A related finding is the inability of most members of such cultures to deal with certain abstract problems such as syllogistic reasoning. Thus unschooled Kpelle farmers in Liberia were informed that "Spider and Black Deer always eat together. Spider is eating." When asked, "Is Black Deer eating?" they would typically fail to give the simple syllogistic "Yes." Instead, they would be noncommittal: "But I was not there. How can I answer such a question." If pushed, they would reply "Yes" but on irrelevant grounds: "The reason is that Black Deer always walks about all day eating green leaves in the bush. When it rests for a while, it gets up again and goes to eat" (Cole, et al., 1971, p. 187).

Such results are sometimes taken as signs that members of certain preliterate cultures are somehow deficient in abstract thinking because they lack some important experiences (especially formal schooling) that are a necessary prerequisite for the development of the relevant cognitive skills (Greenfield, 1966). But a number of investigators disagree. They point out that some of the peoples that do so poorly on standard cognitive tasks (such as Piaget's) are capable of

411

some remarkable intellectual feats in the context of their own everyday lives. An example comes from the !Kung San hunter-gatherers of the Kalahari desert, who perform remarkable feats of inference while hunting game: weighing the chances of tracking down a wounded giraffe against the cost of a drawn-out search, searching for clues in the pattern of crushed grasses, judging whether the blood on a twig fell before or after the twig was bent, and then evaluating the various interpretations to decide on a course of action (Blurton-Jones and Konner, 1976). It is clear that people who can perform such tasks are capable of abstract thought. But if so, how can we explain their poor performance on standard cognitive tests?

One possibility is that the test does not adequately assess non-Western peoples, in part, because the subjects often don't know just what kind of an answer the experimenter wants. Examples come from tests of classification. In one classic study the subjects were Central Asian Russian peasants some of whom had a few years of schooling while others had none. All of the subjects were shown sets of four pictures. In each set, three were of members of a well-defined category, such as tools (e.g., a saw, an ax, and a shovel) and a fourth (e.g., a piece of wood) did not belong to that category but was functionally related to two of the other items. The subjects were asked to pick out the three pictures that belonged together. The farmers who had some schooling behaved much as Western subjects do. They chose according to the abstract semantic category and grouped all the tools together. The unschooled farmers behaved quite differently. They chose on the basis of the concrete situation in which the objects would be used together, picking out the ax, the piece of wood, and the saw; those three go together (the tree must be felled, then sawed into pieces), but the shovel is irrelevant (Luria, 1971). Similar results have been found in studies of Kpelle subjects in Liberia. When unschooled Kpelle subjects were asked to sort objects (including tools and foods) into groups, they arranged them by function—a knife with an orange, a hoe with a potato, and so on. Asked why they sorted the objects as they did, they replied: "That is the way a wise man would do it." When the experimenter asked "How would a fool do it?" he received the response that he had originally looked for—food in one pile and tools in another (Glick, 1975).

Results of this kind suggest that cross-cultural differences in cognitive performance are partially artifacts of our procedures and the way we interpret them, produced by looking at non-Western behavior through Western eyes. But that is probably not all. For in part, they may also reflect a genuine difference in the way schooled and unschooled peoples think. Thus, schooled West African children are more likely to conserve than unschooled ones (Greenfield, 1966), and schooled children in such diverse regions as Morocco, Yucatan, and Liberia do better on various tests of free recall than their unschooled counterparts (Cole, et al., 1971; Wagner, 1974, 1978).

Schooling evidently makes a difference, but why? First, schooled people are more likely to understand just what the experimenter has in mind. (For exam-

A

B

Polynesian navigators *The seafarers of the Caroline Islands in the Pacific Ocean guide their sailing canoes over hundreds of miles of open ocean without benefit of compass or Western navigational mathematics. Instead, they rely on an elaborate navigational method that is based on a knowledge of star positions, ocean swells and currents, and the behavior of birds, and is carefully handed on from generation to generation. The figure shows a master navigator (A) guiding a boat, (B) teaching the star positions to students of all ages. (Reproduced from S. D. Thomas,* The Last Navigator, *New York: Holt, 1987. By permission of the publisher)*

ple, they are used to being asked a question by someone who already knows the answer but wants to find out whether they know the answer or not). But another reason is more far-reaching. Western schools teach their students concepts and techniques that apply to many different contexts. If the Western student studies trigonometry, he doesn't expect to apply what he learns about sines and cosines to his everyday life outside of school. But he does assume—or at least his teachers hope that he assumes—that what he learns applies to all trigonometric relationships. The same applies to other parts of mathematics and to science, logic, and many other topics. They teach very general rules and operations that can be applied to a large number of problems. To the extent that he can do this, he operates at a more abstract level than an unschooled Kpelle or !Kung tribesman. As a result, he can use and create general strategies for reasoning and problem solving that apply across the board, thus acquiring the skills that are demanded by his complex technological society. But that kind of schooling will not serve him well if he wants to survive in the !Kung culture; courses in calculus and logic will be of little use in learning how to hunt giraffes (Scribner and Cole, 1973).

TAKING STOCK

As we review the various lines of evidence, we conclude that cognitive development is the joint outcome of both maturational and environmental factors. Certain earlier aspects of cognitive growth seem to be driven largely by maturation: Examples are the sensory-motor achievements of the first two years, the acquisition of language, and (perhaps) the development of certain simple concrete operations. These earlier achievements will unfold in a broad range of environments (though, if the environment is hostile enough, they may be impaired). The situation is different for various aspects of cognitive development that typically come in later on and that involve broadly generalizable, abstract skills, especially those that are often identified with Piaget's formal operations. For these, environmental and cultural conditions are of paramount importance. The conditions of our own culture and its formal schooling help the child to develop higher-order concepts that can serve as a foundation for yet higher ones and to acquire increasingly effective strategies for learning and thinking that become ever more widely applicable (and thus more abstract) as the child gets older.

QUESTIONS FOR CRITICAL THINKING

1. Why do the early embryonic stages of animals look so much alike?

2. How would you describe the mental life of a fetus at, say, six months?

3. Would a child blind from birth have the concept of an object?

4. Why can't we remember our own births?

5. Could you—and if so, how would you—develop a culture-free test of cognitive development?

SUMMARY

1.   Embryological development involves progressive anatomical *differentiation*. According to many theorists, the differentiation principle also applies to the development of behavior. An example is the development of grasping during the infant's first year.

2.   Development can be considered a process of growth. After conception, the fertilized egg divides, redivides, and differentiates. In the process, it becomes an *embryo*, and then, two months later, a *fetus*. At birth, the infant comes equipped with a set of early reflexes and good sensory capacities. However, human newborns are further removed from adulthood than are the newborns of most other animal species. This leads to a long period of postnatal growth and dependency, which may be one of the factors that led to the development of human culture.

3.   A general characteristic of development is that it is progressive. An example is *motor development* in which such steps as creeping, crawling, and walking occur in much the same sequence for all babies.

4.   All humans go through a process of *cognitive development*. According to Jean Piaget, they do so by passing through the same sequence of developmental stages.

5.   In Piaget's account, the first stage is the period of *sensory-motor intelligence,* which lasts until about two years of age. During this period, the infant develops the concept of *object permanence,* builds up coordinated *sensory-motor schemas,* becomes capable of genuine *imitation,* and acquires increasingly complex *mental representations.*

6.   The next period lasts till about six or seven. It is the *preoperational period* during which children are capable of representational thought but lack mental *operations* that order and organize these thoughts. Characteristic deficits include an inability to *conserve* quantity and number, and *egocentrism,* an inability to take another person's perspective.

7.   At about seven, children begin to acquire a system of mental *operations* that allows them to manipulate mental representations with consequent success in conservation tasks and similar tests. But until they are about eleven, they are still in the period of *concrete operations,* which lacks an element of abstractness. After eleven, they enter the period of *formal operations.* As a result, they can consider hypothetical possibilities and become capable of scientific thought.

8.   One critical challenge to Piaget's views concerns his beliefs of what is given at the very start of life. A number of critics deny that the infant's mind is the mere jumble of unrelated sensory impressions and motor reactions that Piaget declared it to be, for they believe that some of the major categories by which adults organize the world—such as the concepts of space, objects, and the existence of other minds—have primitive precursors in early life.

9.   Studies of visual perception in infancy using the habituation procedure suggest that humans come equipped with some built-in notions of space and objects. Infants show appropriate reactions to perceptual *occlusion* and have some notions of the principles that govern objects in space.

10.   Other criticisms suggest that Piaget also underestimated the preschoolers' general cognitive abilities, as well as their *social cognition.* Three- and four-year-olds show less egocentrism than Piaget would have predicted. They also have the rudiments of a *theory of mind.* While they have difficulties on *false-belief tests* until they're about four-and-a-half years of age, these may be side effects of the experimental situation.

11.   Trying to explain cognitive growth has turned out to be even more difficult and controversial than trying to describe it. The nativist approach assumes that development is largely driven by *maturation.* Empiricists assume that the answer is *specific learning.* Piaget himself rejected both empiricist and nativist extremes, arguing that development involves a constant interchange between organism and environment, as the environment

is *assimilated* to the child's current schema and the schema in turn *accommodates* to aspects of the environment. A current approach sees cognitive development as a change in *information processing* and argues that increased mental growth is based in part on the acquisition of better and larger chunks and of various strategies for thinking and remembering that depend on the development of *metacognition*.

12.   Studies of cognitive development in non-Western cultures, especially those in which there is no formal schooling, have provided another perspective on theories of cognitive development. While some preliterate people do poorly on standard cognitive tasks, this may be because these subjects don't adequately assess these tasks, in part, because they don't know what kind of answer the experimenter is looking for. This is especially likely given the remarkable intellectual feats of these people in the context of their own everyday lives, as shown by the abilities of !Kung hunters to track game.

CHAPTER **14**

SOCIAL DEVELOPMENT

I n the preceding chapter we discussed physical and cognitive development: the ways in which we progress from embryos to full-grown adults, from crawling infants to energetic tricyclists, from babbling babes to sophisticated eight-year-olds who understand all about liquid conservation. But children don't just grow in size and thought; they also develop in their relations to other people. To find out how they do this is the task of psychologists who study social development.

Physical, cognitive, and social development are different aspects of the human journey from birth to maturity. But even so, they are alike in one respect: In all three, we see an ever-increasing enlargement of the developing individual's universe. In biological development, the infant enlarges her physical horizons. As she grows in sheer size and strength, she develops the ability to move freely within her environment and becomes emancipated from her initial limitations in physical space. Cognitive development leads to an analogous expansion of horizons, but now of the mental rather than the physical world, as the growing child comes to transcend the immediate here and now to live in a world of ever more abstract ideas.

In social development, there is a similar pattern of continued expansion. In the first weeks of life, the baby's social world is limited to just one person, usually the mother. In time, her social horizons become enlarged to include both parents, then the rest of the family, then young peers in the nursery and in school. As adolescence sets in, friends of the opposite sex assume more and more importance, sexuality begins in earnest, and the individual soon becomes a parent in her own right and starts the reproductive cycle all over again. But the expansion of the child's social world goes yet further. As she grows older, she comes to understand the system of social rules through which she is linked, not just to her own family circle, but to a larger social universe. A major concern of this chapter is to chart the course of this social expansion through which babes in arms grow into citizens of the world.

Are there any general statements that describe this developmental progression? Much of the early work in the field was inspired by the theoretical scheme proposed by Sigmund Freud, the founder of psychoanalysis, whose work we'll consider in some detail in a later chapter (see Chapter 17). For now, we'll merely list two of his major claims that are particularly relevant to our present concerns. One is that the child's first social relationships are ultimately based on the gratification of basic creature needs, including certain infantile precursors to sexual satisfactions. Another is the belief that the relationship of young children to their parents determines all of their future social relationships. As we will see, both claims have turned out to be very questionable at best.

Attachment (Mother and Child, c. 1890, by Mary Cassatt; Courtesy of Wichita Art Museum, Wichita, Kansas; the Roland P. Murdock Collection)

ATTACHMENT

FOCUS QUESTIONS

■ What is the "cupboard theory" of infant attachment?

■ According to Bowlby, what are the two facets of infant attachment? How did he explain the paradoxical tendency of punished or abused children to cling even more tightly to their parents?

■ Why is imprinting generally confined to a sensitive (or critical) period?

■ How attached are children to their fathers? In what way does this attachment differ from that of the child to the mother?

■ How do understimulation and social neglect affect children? Do the effects extend into adulthood? Can they be reversed?

Social development begins with the first human bond that is sometimes said to lay the foundations for all later relationships with others: the infant's **attachment** to the person who takes care of him.★ The infant wants to be near his mother, and if unhappy, he is comforted by her sight, her sound, and her touch. In this regard, human children have much in common with the young of many other species. Rhesus infants cling to their mother's body, chicks follow the hen, and lambs run after the ewe. As the young grow older, they venture farther away from the mother, gaining courage for ever more distant explorations. But for quite a while, the mother continues to provide a secure home base, a place to run back to should unmanageable threats be encountered.

THE ROOTS OF ATTACHMENT

■ What accounts for the infant's attachment to the mother? Until some thirty years ago, it was widely believed that the love for the mother is a secondary consequence of her association with basic creature satisfactions such as the alleviation of hunger, thirst, and pain. The most influential version of this approach was probably that of Sigmund Freud, who believed that the infant's upset at the mother's absence is based on the crass fear that his bodily needs would now go unsatisfied (see Chapter 17). The British psychiatrist John Bowlby called this the **cupboard theory** of mother love; it boils down to the view that the first love object is the breast or the bottle (Bowlby, 1969, 1973).

IS THE NEED FOR THE MOTHER PRIMARY?

The cupboard theory of the infant's tie to her mother has been criticized on several grounds. One problem is the fact that babies often show great interest in other people, even those who have never fed them or satisfied their other bodily needs. They seem to enjoy seeing others smiling or playing peek-a-boo. Does anyone seriously propose that infants want someone to play peek-a-boo with them because this game has previously been associated with food? It seems much more reasonable to assume that the infant comes predisposed to seek social satisfaction, which is rewarding in and of itself.

★ Since the caregiver is typically the child's mother (she almost always was in earlier eras), we will from here on refer to the child's caregiver by that traditional term, *mother,* despite the fact that the actual caregiver may well be another person, such as the father or a babysitter.

14.1 *The need for contact comfort* *A frightened rhesus monkey baby clings to its terry-cloth mother for comfort. (Photograph by Martin Rogers/Stock, Boston)*

14.2 *Contact comfort in humans* *(Photograph by Suzanne Szasz)*

Another demonstration that love of mother goes beyond bodily needs comes from the work of Harry Harlow (1905–1981). Harlow raised newborn rhesus monkeys without their mothers. Each young monkey lived alone in a cage that contained two stationary figures. One of these models was built of wire; the other was made of soft terry cloth. The wire figure was equipped with a nipple that yielded milk, but no similar provision was made for the terry-cloth model. Even so, the monkey infants spent much more time on the terry-cloth "mother" than on the wire figure. The terry-cloth figure could be clung to and could provide what Harlow called "contact comfort" (Figure 14.1). This was especially clear when the infants were frightened. When placed in an unfamiliar room or faced with a mechanical toy that approached with clanking noises, they invariably rushed to the terry-cloth mother and clung to her tightly. The infants never sought similar solace from the wire mothers, who were their source of food and nothing more (Harlow, 1958).

These results are in complete opposition to the cupboard theory. The monkey infant evidently loves its mother (whether real or terry cloth), not because she feeds it, but because she feels so "comforting." Some of the characteristics of the figure toward whom the monkey can direct its attachment are evidently preprogrammed. In monkeys, these presumably include the way the figure feels to the touch. Whether touch is equally important to human infants is as yet unclear, but very likely it plays some role. Frightened young humans run to their mothers and hug them closely just as rhesus infants do (Figure 14.2). Children also like stuffed, cuddly toys such as teddy bears, whom they hold tightly when they feel apprehensive. Perhaps Linus's security blanket is a kind of terry-cloth mother. It may or may not be; but contrary to the cupboard theory, it is not a substitute tablecloth.

BOWLBY'S THEORY OF ATTACHMENT

An important alternative to the cupboard theory was developed by John Bowlby, who proposed that attachment results because infants are born with a number of interrelated built-in tendencies that make them seek direct contact with an adult (usually the mother).

One facet of attachment seeking is positive. The infant evidently enjoys being with his mother and interacting with her. From birth on, he is well-equipped for social interaction. He quickly comes to recognize and prefer his mother's voice and even her smell (MacFarlane, 1975; DeCasper and Fifer, 1980). If he is contented, he is generally calm, he gurgles, and (starting at about six weeks) he will produce a full-blown social smile. The mother—and other important adults—will happily reciprocate; when the baby smiles, they smile back. As the infant gets older and acquires some locomotor control, he will do whatever he can to be in the adult's company—reaching toward the mother and father to be picked up, crawling toward them, and so on (Campos et al., 1983).

According to Bowlby, attachment seeking has a second, more negative cause. This is a built-in fear of the unknown and unfamiliar, which is yet another reason why the young of most mammals and birds become attached and stay close to some object that has become familiar to them. In the real world, the most likely object of attachment will be the mother. She has been around throughout the infant's short life and has therefore become familiar. And she has certain appropriate preprogrammed stimulus properties for the young of her species: If she is a duck, she quacks; if she is a rhesus monkey, she is furry.

Bowlby suggests that such a built-in fear of the unfamiliar has a simple survival value. Infants who lack it will stray away from their mothers and will be more likely to get lost and perish. In particular, they may well fall victim to predators, for beasts of prey tend to attack weak animals that are separated from their fellows.

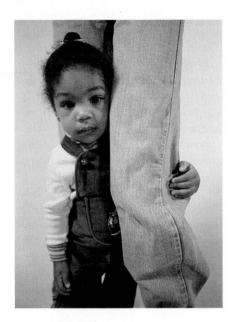

(Photograph by J. Blyenberg/Leo de Wys)

Needless to say, infants don't know enough about the world to fear specific predators. But Bowlby argues that the built-in fear is initially quite unspecific. He conjectures that the fear aroused by the mother's absence is analogous to what psychiatrists call **free-floating anxiety.** This is a state in which the patient is desperately afraid but doesn't know what he is afraid of; he therefore becomes all the more afraid. Given this anxiety, even mild external threats become enormous to the child; the increased need for reassurance may lead to wild clinging and "childish" dependency, as in the dark or during a thunderstorm. This may occur even when the threat comes from the parents themselves. A child who is severely punished by his parents may become even more clinging and dependent than before. The parents caused the fear, but they are the ones who are approached for reassurance. This is analogous to the dog who licks the hand that whipped him. The whipping led to fear and pain, but whom can the dog approach for solace but his master?

IMPRINTING

According to Bowlby, the fear of the unfamiliar produces an attachment to a familiar object. In the real world of animals, this object is generally the mother. But it needn't be. Harlow's studies have already shown us that the focus of filial devotion is not rigidly determined by the genes, as witness the love borne for the terry-cloth mother.

A similar point is made by **imprinting** in birds, which has been studied extensively by the European ethologist Konrad Lorenz. Imprinting is a kind of learning that occurs very early in life and provides the basis for the chick's attachment to its mother. When a newly hatched duckling is first exposed to a moving stimulus, it will approach and follow this stimulus as soon as it is able to walk (at about twelve hours after hatching). If the duckling follows the object for about ten minutes, an attachment is formed; the bird is imprinted. In nature, the moving stimulus is the duckling's mother and all is well. But in the laboratory, the duckling may be exposed to a moving duck on wheels or to a rectangle sliding back and forth behind a glass window or even to Konrad Lorenz's booted legs. In each case, the result is the same. The duckling becomes imprinted on the rectangle or on Lorenz; it follows one of these objects as if it were its mother, uttering piteous distress calls whenever it is not nearby. The real mother may quack enticingly so as to woo her lost offspring back, but to no avail; the

Imprinting in ducklings *Imprinted ducklings following Konrad Lorenz. (Courtesy of Nina Leen)*

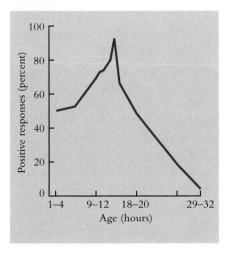

14.3 Imprinting and the critical period
The curve shows the relation between imprinting and the age at which a duckling was exposed to a male moving model. The imprinting score represents the percentage of trials on which the duckling followed the model on a later test. (After Hess, 1958)

14.4 A diagrammatic sketch of the "Strange Situation" M *indicates the mother, and* S *the stranger. (Adapted from Ainsworth et al., 1978)*

imprinted duckling continues to follow the wooden duck or the moving rectangle or Lorenz (Hess, 1959, 1973).

Imprinting occurs most readily during a sensitive period that in ducklings lasts for about two days, with a maximum sensitivity at some fifteen hours after hatching (Hess, 1959). Subsequent to this period, imprinting is difficult to achieve (see Figure 14.3). According to Lorenz, this phenomenon reflects a decline in the plasticity of some part of the young bird's brain—a decline that is somehow tied to a physiological clock (Gottlieb, 1961). Another possible explanation is that ducklings are difficult to imprint after the sensitive period because by then they have become thoroughly afraid of all new objects. When exposed to the wooden duck, the bird flees instead of following. Having lived for several days, it has learned something about what is familiar, and it can therefore appreciate—and fear—what is strange. Some evidence for this position comes from the fact that older ducklings can be imprinted on new objects if they are forced to remain in their presence for a while. One group of investigators exposed five-day-old ducklings to a moving rectangle. The ducklings tried to flee and huddled in a corner. After a while, their fear diminished. At this point, they began to follow the rectangle and gave distress calls when it was withdrawn. They had become imprinted even though they were long past the sensitive period (Hoffman, 1978; for still another interpretation, see Bateson, 1984).

PATTERNS OF ATTACHMENT

The attachment to the mother has a corollary: A separation from her evokes distress. During the first few months of life, the infant will accept a substitute, perhaps because there is as yet no clear-cut conception of the mother that differentiates her from all other people. But from somewhere between six and eight months of age, the infant comes to know who his mother is; he now cries and fusses when he sees her leave. The age at which children begin to register this protest against separation is pretty much the same across such diverse cultures as African Bushmen in Botswana, U.S. city dwellers, Indians in a Guatemalan village, and members of an Israeli kibbutz (Kagan, 1976).

ASSESSING ATTACHMENT

The reaction to separation provides a means for assessing the kind of attachment a particular infant has to her mother. A widely used procedure is the "Strange Situation" devised by Mary Ainsworth and her colleagues for children of about one year of age (Figure 14.4). The child is first brought into an unfamiliar room that contains many toys, and she is given an opportunity to explore and play while the mother is present. After a while, a stranger enters, talks to the mother, and then approaches the child. The next step is a brief separation—the mother goes out of the room and leaves the child alone with the stranger. A reunion follows—the mother comes back and the stranger leaves (Ainsworth and Bell, 1970; Ainsworth et al., 1978).

The behavior of one-year-olds in the Strange Situation falls into three major categories. The first group (over two-thirds of the children in one of Ainsworth's studies) is described as "securely attached." As long as the mother is present, these children explore, play with the toys, and even make wary overtures to the stranger. They show some distress when the mother leaves, but greet her return with great enthusiasm. The children in the second group show various behavior patterns that Ainsworth and her colleagues regard as signs of "insecure attachment." Some of these children are described as "resistant." They don't explore even in the mother's presence, they become intensely upset and

A

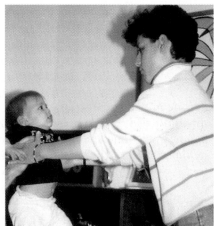

B

C

14.5 Stranger anxiety *An eleven-month-old taken from his father's lap by a stranger (Photographs by Stephanie Arch, courtesy of Kathy Hirsh-Pasek)*

(Photograph courtesy of Photo Researchers, Inc.)

very panicky when she leaves, and they act emotionally ambivalent during the reunion, running to her to be picked up and then angrily struggling to get down. A third group of children was described as "avoidant." They are distant and aloof from the very outset, show little distress when the mother leaves, and ignore her when she returns.

Ainsworth and other adherents of attachment theory believe that behavior in the Strange Situation reflects fairly stable characteristics, at least for the first few years of life. Thus children who were rated as securely attached in the Strange Situation at fifteen months of age were judged to be more outgoing, popular, and well-adjusted in nursery school at age three and a half (Waters, Wippman, and Sroufe, 1979).

ASSESSING THE ROLE OF THE FATHER

Thus far, we've concentrated entirely on the child's attachment to the mother. Is the father left out in the cold? To find out, one investigator used Ainsworth's Strange Situation with fathers as well as mothers and found signs of distress when the father left and some clinging and touching when he returned (see Figure 14.5). It appears that the emotional life of the child is not exclusively wrapped up in the mother. But the mother seems to be more important, at least at an early age. There was more distress at the mother's departure than at the father's and more enthusiasm at her return (Kotelchuk, 1976).

It appears that young children become attached to fathers as well as to mothers, but further evidence indicates that the attachments to the two parents have some different characteristics. A number of studies have shown that fathers are more likely to play with their infants (and young children) than mothers are. In addition, their play is more physical and vigorous; they may lift or bounce their babies or toss them in the air. In contrast, mothers generally play more quietly with their infants and stress verbal rather than physical interactions. As a result, while the mother may be the parent the child is more likely to run to for care and comfort, the father is often the preferred playmate. This difference in the response to the two parents begins in early infancy, when there are more smiles for the mother and more giggles for the father. By the time the children are toddlers, two out of three pick the father as the one they want to play with. Mother is security and comfort; father is fun (Lamb, 1977; Clarke-Stewart, 1978; Parke, 1981).

THE EFFECT OF EARLY MATERNAL SEPARATION

■ A number of authors believe that early separations from the mother may lead to lasting psychological damage. Thus John Bowlby (in common with many other attachment theorists) asserts that any disturbance of the initial attachment of the child to the mother will render the person more emotionally insecure in later life. In his view, separation is psychologically dangerous, for the continuity of the child's relationship to the first attachment figure is a necessary element of the child's ultimate mental health (Bowlby, 1973). This position has various social consequences. It has made many women uneasy about becoming working mothers and leaving their children with another person or in a day-care center. It has also affected legal policies in cases of child placement, with a bias in favor of keeping children in homes (in which they had presumably formed attachments) despite evidence of neglect or abuse (Maccoby, 1980).

Given current social and economic conditions in the United States, it is hardly surprising that John Bowlby's views have led to considerable controversy. What with the majority of mothers now employed outside the home and a growing number of single-parent households, family life in the United States today is not that pictured in *Little House on the Prairie,* let alone in "Father Knows Best." According to one estimate, by the year 2000 one out of every five mothers of infants under one year of age will be in the labor force (Cole and Cole, 1993). Some form of out-of-home child care is clearly indispensable. But what are the consequences of this economic and sociological necessity for the psychological welfare of our children?

In line with Bowlby's views, some authors argue that children who have had extensive nonmaternal care (more than twenty hours per week) during their first year of life are more likely to show insecure patterns of attachment in the Strange Situation and were less compliant to adults (Barglow, Vaughn, and Molitor, 1987; Belsky, 1988; Belsky and Braungart, 1991). Does this mean that day care interfered with their optimum social and emotional development? Some authors don't think so. For one thing, they dispute the interpretation of these children's behavior in the test situation. Consider noncompliance to adult demands. Perhaps the day-care children were less compliant and obedient because they had become more independent and self-reliant. This interpretation is in line with other evidence that indicates that day-care children match or in

Attachment and day care While some contend that any early separation from the primary caregiver may adversely affect the child, others contend that its not the fact of day care that's important so much as it is the quality of day care (Photograph © Stephen Shames/ Matrix; The Caring Center, West Philadelphia)

some cases outstrip their non–day-care peers on measures of sociability, persistence, and achievement (Clarke-Stewart, 1989, 1993).

All of this makes good sense. The social world includes peers as well as primary caregivers, and some early experience with children of one's own age may well provide special benefits. But this conclusion probably has to be modified, for several studies suggest that what matters is the quality of the day care rather than the fact of day care as such. Children who, when four years old, attended centers that were well-equipped and spacious, with good adult-child ratios, well-trained teachers, and small classes showed better social and emotional development at eight years of age than children who had attended day-care centers that were poorer in these regards, even when such factors as social class and income were equated. But this result doesn't really prove that what happens at an earlier age still exerts an effect some years later. It may be that parents who select high-quality day care for their children also differ in some other regards from parents who don't make that selection. They may interact differently with their children or feel differently about them, and these differences may well persist over the four-year span (Vandell, Henderson, and Wilson, 1988).

WHEN THERE IS NO ATTACHMENT AT ALL

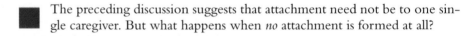 The preceding discussion suggests that attachment need not be to one single caregiver. But what happens when *no* attachment is formed at all?

HUMANS REARED IN INADEQUATE INSTITUTIONS

It appears that human infants reared under conditions of comparative social isolation suffer from severe social inadequacy. The evidence comes from studies of infants who were reared in orphanages that supplied adequate nutrition and bodily care but provided rather little in the way of sensory and social stimulation. In one such institution the infants were kept in separate cubicles for the first eight months or so as a precaution against infectious disease. Their brief contacts with adults were restricted to the times when they were fed or diapered. Feeding took place in the crib with a propped-up bottle. There was little social give and take, little talk, little play, and little chance that the busy attendant would respond to any one baby's cry (Goldfarb, 1955; Provence and Lipton, 1962; Dennis, 1973).

When these infants were compared to others who were raised normally, there were no differences for the first three or four months. Thereafter, the two groups diverged markedly. The unstimulated infants showed serious impairments in their social development. Some were insatiable in their demands for individual love and attention. But the majority went in the opposite direction and became extremely apathetic in their reactions to people. They rarely tried to approach adults, either to hug and caress them or to get reassurance when in distress. A few others sat in a corner of their cribs, withdrawn and expressionless, and rocked their bodies.

It appears that many of these early deficits persist into later life. A number of studies have shown that in a fair number of cases—although by no means all—there are a number of intellectual deficits, for example in language and in abstract thinking, which persist into adolescence and beyond. There are also various long-term effects in the social and emotional sphere: heightened aggression, delinquency, and indifference to others (Yarrow, 1961).

ARE THE EFFECTS OF EARLY SOCIAL DEPRIVATION REVERSIBLE?

■ It's clear that serious social deprivation in early life has unfortunate effects. But is that because the experience occurred early in life? And is the effect of that early experience irreversible? According to Freud—and many others—the answer to both questions is yes. To Freud there was no question that "the events of [the child's] first years are of paramount importance for his whole subsequent life." In effect, this position is in some ways analogous to the Calvinist doctrine of predestination. According to John Calvin, each person is predestined to be blessed or damned before he is ever born. To Freud, the die is cast by the age of five or six.

UNDOING THE PAST

Some further evidence suggests that the dead hand of the past is not quite as rigid as Freud had supposed. The evidence is by no means clear-cut, but the results of one study give grounds for optimism. The subjects were children at an overcrowded orphanage. There were few staff members and little individual attention. After about one-and-a-half years, some of the children were transferred out of the orphanage to an institution for mentally retarded women. Ironically, this institution provided the necessary means for emotional and intellectual rehabilitation. There was a richer and more stimulating environment, but most important, there were many more caregivers. Each of the transferred children was "adopted" by one adult—either an institutionalized woman or an attendant—who became especially attached to the child. This new emotional relationship led to improvements in many spheres of behavior. While the intelligence-test scores of the children who remained in the orphanage dropped during the succeeding years, those of the transferred children rose considerably. Similarly for their social adjustment: When they reached their thirties, the transferred subjects had reached an educational and occupational level that was about average for the country at the time. In contrast, half of the subjects who remained behind never finished the third grade (Skeels, 1966).

REASSESSING THE ROLE OF EARLY EXPERIENCE

In light of all this, we must evidently reassess our views on the all-importance of early social experience. That experience certainly provides a vital foundation upon which further social relationships are built. But experiences in infancy or childhood do not affect adult behavior directly. What happens instead is that each step in a sequence of social developments paves the way for the next. The early years are crucial in the sense that certain social patterns are much more likely to be acquired then, such as the capacity to form attachments to other people. These early attachments are a likely prerequisite for the formation of later ones. The child who has never been loved by his parents will be frightened by his peers and probably hampered in his further social development. But while the earlier attachments (to mother and father) lay the foundation for later ones (to friends, lovers, and one's own children), the two are nevertheless quite different. As a result, there may be ways of acquiring the social tools for dealing with one's later life that circumvent the handicaps of one's early childhood. For, while the past affects the present, it does not predetermine it.

To sum up, the easiest way of getting to the second floor of a house is by way of the first floor. But in a pinch one can always bring a ladder and climb in through a second-floor window.

Socialization *Most authors agree that parents exert some effect on the personality development of their children. What is at issue is what effects they have and how they achieve them. (Photographs courtesy of George Gleitman)*

FOCUS QUESTIONS

- What are the three main mechanisms postulated for socialization?

- What are three parenting styles? Do they have a lasting impact? Which seems preferable and why?

- In what way do children participate in their own upbringing?

The infant's attachment to her caregiver marks her entrance into the social world. This is the starting point of *socialization,* the process by which the child acquires the patterns of thought and behavior that are characteristic of the society in which she is born.

MECHANISMS OF SOCIALIZATION

How is socialization achieved? Different theorists emphasize different mechanisms. Some stress the role of reward and the fear of punishment. Others point to the importance of imitation. Still others argue for the importance of the child's growing understanding of what she's supposed to do and why. The best guess is that all three of these kinds of mechanisms contribute to the child's socialization.

REINFORCEMENT THEORY

According to both operant behavior and psychoanalytic theory (see Chapters 4 and 17), the child is socialized by a calculus of pain and pleasure. She will continue to do (or wish or think or remember) whatever previously brought her gratification and will refrain from whatever led to punishment and anxiety.

SOCIAL LEARNING THEORY

But many psychologists believe that a theory exclusively based on such learning by reinforcement cannot possibly do justice to the socialization process. For we are animals with a culture, which makes us altogether unlike any of the animals studied in the learning laboratory. Thorndike's cats had to discover how to get out of the puzzle box by themselves (see Chapter 4): No other cat told them how to do it; no other cat could. But in the course of a lifetime, human beings learn a multitude of solutions that were discovered by those who came before them. They do not have to invent spoken language or the alphabet; they do not have to discover fire or the wheel or even how to eat baby food with a spoon. Other people show them.

A group of psychologists who are sometimes called social learning theorists regard *observational learning* as one of the most powerful mechanisms of socialization. The child observes another person who serves as a model and then proceeds to imitate what the model does, thus learning how to do something he didn't know before (Figure 14.6). The child sees an adult hammer a nail into a board and tries to duplicate the same feat (with any luck, not on the new dining room table). Many cultures explicitly use such imitative patterns as a way of inducting the child into adult ways. In one Central American society, young girls are presented with miniature replicas of a water jar, a broom, and a grind-

14.6   Learning by imitation   *Performing a traditional tea ceremony is learned by imitating an accomplished model. (Photograph by Michael Heron/Woodfin Camp)*

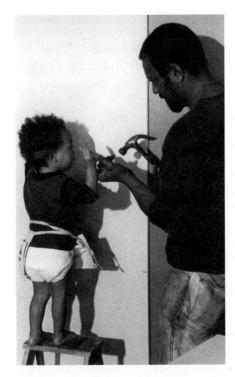

Modeling in real life   *(Photograph by Frostie/Woodfin Camp)*

ing stone. They observe how their mothers use the real objects and through constant imitation acquire the relevant skills themselves (Bandura and Walters, 1963).

How does a person learn a new response by imitation? There is little doubt that imitative learning is not a species of classical or instrumental conditioning. As social learning theorists point out, imitation may occur even though the observer does not copy the model's actions at the time that he sees them (learning without performance) and even though he neither receives a reward himself nor sees the model receive one (learning without reinforcement).

COGNITIVE DEVELOPMENTAL THEORY

Still another perspective on socialization is offered by the cognitive approach, which emphasizes the role of understanding in interpersonal conduct and thought. Cognitive theorists believe that there are many situations in which the child behaves neither as a creature impelled by irrational forces, as a puppet controlled by schedules of reward and punishment, nor as a sheep that follows an adult leader.

The child has some understanding of her own actions; she not only knows that some things are "bad" and others "good" but has some sense of why they are bad or good. Initially her understanding is quite dim, but as her mental development unfolds, so does her rational comprehension of how one does (or should) relate to others. As a result, much of social development is a consequence of cognitive development.

To illustrate the cognitive theory of socialization, consider imitation. Cognitive theorists argue that understanding plays a crucial role, both in learning by imitation and in performing a response one has learned by watching others. There's little doubt that imitative learning involves considerable cognitive complexity. One of the requirements seems to be a realization of the correspondence between one's own body and that of the model's. Suppose a boy imitates his father hitching up his trousers. In order to do so, he has to relate his own clothes and body to those of his father: My trouser belt is to my hands as his trouser belt is to his hands, and so on. In effect, the imitator takes the model's role. But he can do so only if the model's behavior fits into what Piaget would have called a well-developed cognitive "schema" (Piaget, 1951; Aronfreed,

Agents of socialization *Early lessons in social behavior are taught not only by parents, but also by older siblings.*

1969). Under the circumstances, it is hardly surprising that children imitate more accurately as they get older, for their ability to utilize what they see the model do presumably increases with their cognitive development (Yando, Seitz, and Zigler, 1978).

The child's imitation of an adult model is not blind and irrational. The novice climber who follows a guide is not like a sheep that runs after a leader; he follows because he knows that the guide will bring him safely up and down the mountain slope. The child who imitates is no less rational, for she proceeds from the perfectly reasonable premise that, by and large, adults know more than she does (Kohlberg, 1969).

THE FIRST AGENTS OF SOCIALIZATION: THE PARENTS

■ Thus far, we have looked at socialization from the standpoint of the child who is being socialized, and we have considered how he learns the lessons that society tries to teach him—whether by reinforcement, by modeling, by understanding, or by all three. We now shift our focus to those that serve as society's first teachers: the child's parents. Do different ways in which they rear their children produce differences in the children's behavior? If so, how lasting are the effects?

FEEDING AND TOILET TRAINING

To answer questions of this sort, one must first decide which particular aspects of the parents' behavior one wants to focus on. Until forty or so years ago, developmental psychologists interested in these general issues concerned themselves with certain specific aspects of child rearing that Sigmund Freud and his followers had made much of, such as breast feeding and toilet training. They asked about the effects of different practices associated with feeding, weaning, and toilet training. Does breast feeding produce happier (or unhappier) infants? What about early weaning or early toilet training? As it turned out, the answer is that these child-rearing particulars have little or no effect (Orlansky, 1949; Zigler and Child, 1969; Zigler, Lamb, and Child, 1982).

DIFFERENT PARENTAL STYLES

In recent years, developmental psychologists have taken a different approach. Instead of concentrating on specific child-rearing practices, they have turned their attention to the general home atmosphere in which the child is raised (Baumrind, 1967, 1971; Maccoby and Martin, 1983).

In a number of studies, parents were asked to describe the way they dealt with their children and were also observed with them in various situations. Several patterns of child rearing emerged. One is the **autocratic pattern** in which the parents control the child strictly and often quite sternly. The rules they set down are essentially edicts whose infraction leads to severe (and frequently physical) punishment. Nor do they attempt to explain these rules to the child, who has to accept them as a simple manifestation of parental power: "It's because I say so, that's why."

At the opposite extreme is the **permissive pattern** in which children encounter few don'ts and even fewer do's. The parents try not to assert their authority, impose few restrictions and controls, tend not to have set schedules (for, say, bedtime or watching TV), and rarely use punishment. They also make few demands on the children—such as putting toys away, doing schoolwork, or helping with chores.

Autocratic parents brandish parental power; permissive parents abdicate it. But there is a third approach that is in some ways in between. It is called the *authoritative-reciprocal pattern* because the parents exercise their power but also accept the reciprocal obligation to respond to the child's point of view and his reasonable demands. Unlike the permissive parents, they govern; but unlike the autocratic ones, they try to govern with the consent of the governed.

Parents whose pattern is authoritative-reciprocal set rules of conduct for their children and enforce them when they have to. They are fairly demanding, assign duties, expect their children to behave maturely and "act their age," and spend a good deal of time in teaching their children how to perform appropriately. But they also encourage the child's independence and allow a good deal of verbal give and take.

Are there any differences between children that are raised in these three different styles? One investigator observed preschoolers in various settings. She found that children raised autocratically were more withdrawn, lacked independence, and were more angry and defiant (especially the boys). Interestingly enough, children at the opposite end of the spectrum had similar characteristics. Thus children whose parents were permissive were not particularly independent, and (if boys) they were more prone to anger. In addition, they seemed very immature and lacked social responsibility. In contrast, the children raised in the authoritative-reciprocal mode were more independent, competent, and socially responsible. Here, as so often, the happy medium seems the best approach.

There is evidence that the parental pattern experienced when the child was three or four is related to the way the child behaves in later years. When observed at the age of eight or nine, children whose parents had been judged to be either autocratic or permissive five years earlier seemed to be relatively low in intellectual self-reliance and originality. Once again, the children raised in the authoritative-reciprocal style fared best. They were more self-reliant when faced by intellectual challenges, strove for achievement, and were socially more self-confident and at ease (Baumrind, 1977). More recent studies have shown that the benefits of the authoritative-reciprocal style extend into the high-school years, where this parental pattern is associated with better grades as well as better social adjustment (Dornbusch et al., 1987; Steinberg, Elman, and Mounts, 1989).

"They never pushed me. If I wanted to retrieve, shake hands, or roll over, it was entirely up to me." (Drawing by Frascino; © 1971, The New Yorker Magazine, Inc.)

THE CHILD'S EFFECT ON THE PARENTS

Thus far, we have discussed socialization as something that is done *to* the child. But in recent years, developmental psychologists have become increasingly insistent that socialization is a two-way street. For the child is more than a lump of psychological clay that is shaped by various social agencies. In fact, he actively participates in his own rearing. His own behavior affects that of the parent, whose behavior then in turn affects him. To the extent that this is true, the parents don't just socialize the child. They are also socialized by him (Bell, 1968; Bell and Harper, 1977).

One of the main reasons why socialization works in both directions is that infants differ from the very day they are born. For example, there are differences in *temperament* that probably have a built-in, genetic basis (see Chapter 16). One infant may be relatively placid and passive; another may be more active and assertive. These differences persist over at least the first two years of life and may last much beyond. The mother will respond quite differently to these two infants. If we later study the correlation between what the mother did and how the child behaves, we will find a correlation. But in this case, the order of cause and effect is the reverse of the one that is actually expected. A difference in the child led to a difference in the way his parents dealt with him (Thomas, Chess, and Birch, 1970; Osofsky and Danzger, 1974; Olweus, 1980). This is another way of saying that children help to make their own environments. To the extent that they are genetically different in either temperament or ability, their parents, siblings, and eventually their peers cannot help but treat them differently (Scarr and McCartney, 1983).

THE DEVELOPMENT OF MORALITY

FOCUS QUESTIONS

■ What may be the origins of empathy in young children?

■ What are Kohlberg's stages of moral reasoning? How well does his theory describe the moral reasoning of both men and women? members of non-Western cultures?

Initially, the child's social world is largely confined to the family. His first lessons in social behavior are taught in the limited family context: Pick up your toys, don't push your baby brother, and so on—circumscribed commands and prohibitions that apply to a very narrow social setting. But his social sphere soon grows to include young peers: at home, in day-care centers, in preschool settings, still later in the schools. These peers become increasingly important, and their approval is then sought as eagerly (if not more eagerly) than that of his parents. Eventually the child's social universe expands still further as he acquires rules of social thought and action that are vastly broader than the simple commands and prohibitions of his toddler years. For these rules pertain not just to the people he meets face to face but to countless others he has never met and probably will never meet. Among the most important of these rules are those of moral conduct.

Internalization *A four-year-old reproaches her doll: "Bad girl! Didn't I tell you to keep out of the dirt?" In imitating how her mother scolds her, the child is taking the first steps toward internalizing the mother's prohibitions. (Photograph by Suzanne Szasz)*

NOT DOING WRONG

■ All societies have prohibitions that its members must learn to obey despite various temptations to the contrary. It's easy enough to set up external sanctions that enforce the prohibitions from the outside. Children rarely steal from the cookie jar when their parents are present. The trick is to make them resist temptation when they are not being watched. The person who does not steal or cheat because he thinks that he will be caught is not moral; he's merely prudent. One aim of socialization is to instill moral values that are *internalized*, so that the individual will shun transgressions because he feels that they are wrong and not because he is afraid of being punished.

What leads to the internalization of right and wrong? Sigmund Freud believed that internalization is produced by self-punishment in the form of guilt and anxiety.★ The child kicks his little brother, and the parents punish him. As a result, the forbidden act (or, for that matter, the mere thought of that act) becomes associated with anxiety. Thus, the child will feel a pang of anxiety the next time he starts to attack his younger brother. To stop this painful feeling, he must stop that which triggered it: the thought, let alone the execution, of the forbidden behavior. In Freud's view, these internalized inhibitions are a remnant of our childhood that remains with us for the rest of our lives and makes sure

★ Freud called the primary agent of these internalization processes the **superego,** an unconscious remnant of the internal conflicts the child experienced during the Oedipus conflict (see Chapter 17).

that we commit no wrong. The external authorities that once punished our transgressions have long stopped watching the cookie jar. But they no longer have to because they now inhabit our minds, where we can no longer hide from them.

Given this general view of the inhibition of the forbidden, one would predict that the internalization of prohibition is most pronounced in children whose parents relied on sheer power in raising them—whether this power was exercised by the use of physical punishment or deprivation of privileges or threats of withdrawal of love and of abandonment. But this prediction turns out to be false. For a number of studies suggest that prohibitions are *less* internalized in children whose parents primarily relied on power in its various forms than in children whose parents took pains to explain just why a misdeed was wrong and why the child ought to behave differently. The children of power-asserting (autocratic) parents were more likely to cheat for a prize when they thought no one was looking, and they were less likely to feel guilt about their misdeeds or to confess them when confronted (Hoffman, 1970).

DOING GOOD

■ Our discussion of moral action has dealt with the inhibition of forbidden acts. But moral action pertains to do's no less than to don'ts, to doing good as well as not committing evil. In a previous chapter we considered the fact that humans are capable of positive moral actions that call for some personal sacrifice and altruism (see Chapter 10). We now ask how this capacity develops in the child.

Thus far, we are still far from an answer. A number of studies show that even very young children try to help and comfort others, and occasionally share with them (Rheingold, Hay, and West, 1976; Radke-Yarrow, Zahn-Waxler, and Chapman, 1983). The question is why.

EMPATHY

Why do children sometimes act unselfishly? Some evidence comes from studies of *empathy.* Empathy is a direct emotional response to another person's emotions; we see a patient writhe in pain in a hospital bed, and we ourselves experience vicarious distress (Aronfreed, 1968). Some precursors to such empathic reactions are found even in the first two days of life. On hearing a newborn's cry, one-day-old infants cry too and their hearts beat faster (Simner, 1971; Sagi and Hoffman, 1976).

What accounts for such empathic reactions at this tender age? According to one hypothesis, the reason is classical conditioning. In this view, the response of crying becomes conditioned to the sound of crying. Initially, crying was evoked by some pain or discomfort. But soon the sound of the infant's own crying became a conditioned stimulus for further crying. Since another baby's cry resembles the infant's own, it will elicit her own cry as a conditioned response (in addition to various other distress reactions, such as increased heart rate). An alternative hypothesis is that some empathic reactions are innately given, a position that is by no means implausible given the facts of built-in alarm and distress reactions in many animals (see Chapter 10). As yet it is too early to choose between these two views. But whichever turns out to be correct, it is clear that some forerunner of what may later become a feeling for others is found at the very start of life.

The mere fact that one feels empathy doesn't mean that one will do anything about it. For to help one's fellows, one has to do more than just feel for them. One also has to act on this feeling. And one has to know how.

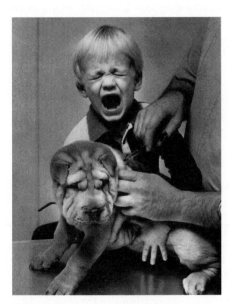

Feeling distress at the distress of another
The young boy cries as the veterinarian gives an injection to his puppy. (Photograph by Janet Kelly/Reading Eagle-Times, © Reading Eagle Company)

Consider a two-year-old girl who sees an adult in pain—say, an uncle who has cut his finger with a knife. In all likelihood, she will feel empathy and become distressed herself. But what will her **empathic distress** make her do? A number of anecdotes suggest that she will give her uncle whatever *she* finds most comforting herself—for example, her favorite doll. While appreciating her kindly sentiments, the uncle would probably have preferred a Band-Aid or a stiff drink. But the child is as yet too young to take his perspective and doesn't realize that her uncle's needs are not the same as her own (Hoffman, 1977a, 1979, 1984).

As we develop, we become increasingly able to tell what other people are likely to feel in a given situation and how to help if help is needed. But even that is not enough to ensure that we will act unselfishly. For helping is only one means of getting rid of the empathic distress that is caused by the sight of another person's pain. There is an easier but more callous method: One can simply look away. This often occurs in the big city, with its many homeless and victims of violence, where empathy may seem a luxury one can no longer afford. It may also occur in war or other situations where people "harden their hearts" to become immune to the sufferings of others (see Chapter 12). Such arguments indicate that while empathy is a likely precursor of altruism, it does not guarantee it.

MORAL REASONING

■ Thus far, our focus has been on the development of moral behavior. What about the development of moral thought? What happens to the child's conception of right and wrong as he grows up?

KOHLBERG'S STAGES OF MORAL REASONING

An influential account of moral development was devised by Lawrence Kohlberg. His basic method is to confront subjects with a number of stories that pose a moral dilemma. An example is a story about a man whose wife will die unless treated with a very expensive drug, a drug that costs $2,000. The husband scraped together all the money he could, but it was not enough. He promised to pay the balance later, but the pharmacist still refused to give him the drug. In desperation, the husband broke into the pharmacy and stole the drug. The subjects were asked whether the husband's act was right or wrong and why (Kohlberg, 1969).

Kohlberg analyzed the subjects' answers and concluded that moral reasoning proceeds through a series of successive stages. Roughly speaking, there is a progression from a primitive morality guided by personal fear of punishment or desire for gain ("If you let your wife die, you'll get in trouble"), through stages in which right or wrong are defined by convention, by what people will say ("Your family will think you're an inhuman husband if you don't"), to the highest stage in which there are internalized moral principles that have become one's own ("If you didn't steal the drug, you wouldn't be blamed and you would have lived up to the outside rule of the law, but you wouldn't have lived up to your own standards of conscience"). As one might expect, there is a rough correlation between Kohlberg's levels and age. But even in adulthood only a small proportion of subjects give answers that correspond to Kohlberg's highest level. In a recent study that made use of a revised set of Kohlberg's criteria, no subject below the age of twenty was judged to have reached Stage 5, and Stage 6 was not found at all (Colby et al., 1983; Colby and Kohlberg, 1986). Considering that Kohlberg considers this final stage to be the level that characterized such moral giants as Mahatma Gandhi and Dr. Martin Luther King, the failure of his

TABLE 14.1 KOHLBERG'S STAGES OF MORAL REASONING	
Stage of moral reasoning	*Moral behavior is that which:*
Preconventional morality	
Level 1	Avoids punishment.
Level 2	Gains reward.
Conventional morality	
Level 3	Gains approval and avoids disapproval of others.
Level 4	Is defined by rigid codes of "law and order."
Postconventional morality	
Level 5	Is defined by a "social contract" generally agreed upon for the public good.
Level 6	Is based on abstract ethical principles that determine one's own moral code.

SOURCE: Adapted from Kohlberg, 1969.

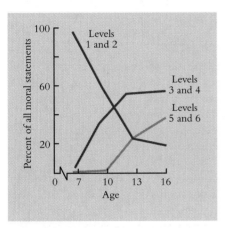

14.7 Level of moral reasoning as a function of age *With increasing age, the level of moral reasoning changes. In this figure, the percent of all moral judgments made by children at various ages falls into one of three general categories defined by Kohlberg. At seven, virtually all moral judgments are in terms of avoiding punishment or gaining reward (Kohlberg's levels 1 and 2). At ten, about half the judgments are based on criteria of social approval and disapproval or of a rigid code of laws (Kohlberg's levels 3 and 4). From thirteen on, some of the children refer to more abstract rules—a generally agreed-upon social contract or a set of abstract ethical principles (Kohlberg's levels 5 and 6). (After Kohlberg, 1963)*

subjects (and no doubt, most of us) to attain it is probably not too surprising (Figure 14.7; Table 14.1).

MORAL REASONING IN MEN AND WOMEN

Are there sex differences in moral orientation? An influential discussion by Carol Gilligan suggests that there may be. In her view, men tend to see morality as a matter of justice, ultimately based on abstract, rational principles by which all individuals can be treated fairly. As one eleven-year-old boy put it in describing the moral dilemmas posed by Kohlberg: "It's sort of like a math problem with humans." Women in contrast see morality in more concrete, social terms. To them, the focus is on compassion, on human relationships, on special responsibilities to those with whom one is intimately connected. Given these different emphases, one might expect women to score lower than men when moral reasoning is assessed by Kohlberg's yardstick. For as Gilligan sees it, Kohlberg's system has a built-in sex bias in which the moral outlook usually adopted by men is judged to be more advanced than that which is more characteristic of women. Kohlberg calls the highest steps on his moral staircase "postconventional morality," which is defined by just those abstract, rational principles that tend to fit in with the way in which men see the moral order. The moral outlook of women, on the other hand, with their emphasis on helping others, would be judged to be on one of Kohlberg's lower steps. Under the circumstances, it would not be surprising to find that women obtain lower scores on Kohlberg's tests than men (Gilligan, 1982).

Psychologists interested in moral reasoning were quick to ask whether men really achieve "higher" levels of moral reasoning as defined by Kohlberg. It turns out that they don't. According to several authors, a systematic check of the work performed on the topic reveals no reliable sex differences in moral reasoning on Kohlberg's test; of 108 studies, only 8 showed a superiority of males over females, while 4 or 5 went in the opposite direction (Brabeck, 1983; Walker, 1984; but see Baumrind, 1986, Walker, 1989). But if so, what remains of Gilligan's critique?

Gilligan states that she herself never said that women can't reason at Kohlberg's "highest" level; the point is that they usually choose not to do so. As she sees it, the female perspective emphasizes human relationships, attachments, and personal responsibilities rather than the abstract conceptions of rights and justice emphasized by the male perspective (Gilligan, 1986). That such a differ-ence in emphases exists is suggested by various empirical findings, including the fact that girls seem to place a greater value on going out of one's way to help other people and show more emotional empathy than do boys (Hoffman, 1977b). Just why women emphasize the perspective of care rather than of abstract justice is still unsettled. The best guess is that it is a result of different patterns of socialization that stress different values for boys and girls (Hoffman, 1984).

Is either perspective preferable to the other? Virtually everyone agrees that the answer is no and that an appropriate conception of morality must include both justice and compassion. As Kohlberg points out, both of these orientations are built into the New Testament's Golden Rule. That rule is formulated in two ways. One insists on justice: "Do unto others as you would have them do unto you." The other urges care and compassion: "Love thy neighbor as thyself" (Kohlberg and Candee, 1984).

MORAL REASONING AND CULTURAL FACTORS

Gilligan's description of the difference between the moral perspectives of men and women is paralleled by the differences found among cultural groups. A number of studies have shown that when members of technologically less advanced societies are asked to reason about moral dilemmas, they generally come up with comparatively low scores on Kohlberg's scale; they justify acts on the basis of concrete issues such as what neighbors will say or concern over one's wife, rather than more abstract conceptions of justice and morality (Kohlberg, 1969; Tietjen and Walker, 1985). How should we interpret such results? Does it mean that the inhabitants, say, of a small Turkish village are less moral than the residents of Paris or New York? A more plausible interpretation is that the Turkish villager spends his life in a small community in continual face-to-face encounters with all its members. Under the circumstances, the most likely out-come is a more concrete morality that gives the greatest weight to care, respon-sibility, and loyalty, which is just what we might expect (Simpson, 1974; Kaminsky, 1984).

Moral reasoning in men and women
The belief that men and women focus on different aspects of morality has ancient roots. A classical example is Sophocles's tragedy Antigone, *which revolves around the irreconcilable conflict between Antigone, who insists on burying a slain brother, and her uncle Creon, the king, who issues a decree forbidding anyone from doing so on pain of death. To Antigone, the ultimate moral obligation is to the family; to Creon, it is to the state and its laws. (From a 1982 produc-tion at the New York Shakespeare Festival, with F. Murray Abraham and Lisa Banes; photograph by Martha Swope)*

THE DEVELOPMENT OF SEX AND GENDER

FOCUS QUESTIONS

■ How do gender-role stereotypes affect early child rearing?

■ On what two psychological traits are sex differences most often held to be biologi-cal? What nonbiological factors might help explain these differences?

■ How do the three main theories of socialization explain the acquisition of gender identity and gender roles?

■ What biological factors may predispose someone to a homosexual orientation?

■ From an evolutionary viewpoint, how might a homosexual orientation be adap-tive?

Thus far, our emphasis has been on social development considered as growth and expansion. But social development is more than that. Like physical and cog-nitive development, it involves growth, but this growth is not just a matter of increasing size. It is also accompanied by increasing differentiation. For as the child gets older, she becomes increasingly aware of the fact that people differ from each other and from herself. In so doing, she also gains a clearer conception of her own self and of her own personality—what she is really like, in her own eyes and in those of others.

Seen in this light, social development goes hand in hand with the development of a sense of personal identity. One of the most important elements of this is sexual identity—of being male or female and all that goes with it.

Biologically, sexual identity seems simple enough. It may refer to genetic sex: having XX or XY chromosome pairs. It may also refer to morphological (that is, structural) sex: having clitoris, vagina, and ovaries or penis, scrotum, and testes. But what does sexual identity mean psychologically? It refers to three issues. One is *gender identity*—our inner sense that we are male or female. A second is *gender role*—a whole host of external behavior patterns that a given culture deems appropriate for each sex. A third is *sexual orientation*—the inclination toward a sexual partner, which in most of us—though of course not all of us—is directed toward the opposite sex. Gender identity, gender role, and sexual orientation are among the most important determinants of a person's social existence.* How do they come about?

GENDER ROLES

Gender roles pervade all facets of social life. The induction into one or the other of these roles begins with the very first question that is asked when a human being enters the world: "Is it a boy or a girl?" As soon as the answer is supplied—which now, due to fetal ultrasound, may be months before birth—the process of gender typing begins, and the infant is ushered onto one of two quite different social trajectories. Some of the patterns of gender typing have probably changed in the wake of modern feminism, but many differences in child rearing persist.

Social learning of gender roles
(Photograph by Suzanne Arms/Jeroboam)

The stereotypes in our own culture are obvious. The infant is dressed in either pink or blue; the child plays with either dolls or trucks; at least until recently the adult woman's place was in the home, while the man's was in the marketplace—or the buffalo hunting grounds or whatever. Society not only has different expectations about what the two sexes should *do;* it also has different conceptions of what they should *be.* In our own culture, men are expected to be more aggressive and tough, more restrained emotionally, and more interested in things than in people. In contrast, women are expected to be submissive, more emotionally expressive, and more interested in people than in things.

There is no doubt that these gender-role stereotypes have a considerable effect on how we perceive people, even newborns and very young infants. In one study, mothers of young infants were asked to participate as subjects in an experiment on "how children play." The mothers were introduced to a six-month-old baby, little "Joey" or "Janie," and they were asked to play with him or her for a few minutes. In fact, the six-month-old was a baby actor who was dressed up as a boy or girl regardless of its actual sex. The results showed that the

---

* It has become customary to distinguish between sex and gender. *Sex* generally refers to aspects of male-female differences that pertain to reproductive functions (for example, having ovaries versus testes, vagina versus penis) or genetically related factors (for example, differences in height or muscular strength). It is also used to designate erotic feelings, inclinations, or practices (for example, heterosexuality and homosexuality). *Gender,* on the other hand, refers to social or psychological aspects of being seen as a man or woman or regarding oneself to be so. Thus it is one thing to be male and another to be a man; one thing to be female, another—a woman (Stoller, 1968). A special note about the term *sex difference:* This term is used here strictly to designate male-female differences, with no presuppositions about whether they have biological or cultural origins.

subjects' behavior depended on whether they thought they were playing with "Joey" or "Janie." To "Joey" they offered toys such as a hammer or a rattle, while "Janie" was invariably given a doll. In addition, the subjects physically touched and handled "Joey" and "Janie" differently. In dealing with "Joey," they often bounced "him" about, thus stimulating the whole body. In contrast, their response to "Janie" was gentler and less vigorous (Smith and Lloyd, 1978).

Children soon behave as adults expect them to. Starting at about age one and a half, they begin to show gender-typed differences. By three years of age, they prefer different toys and play mainly with peers of their own sex (Huston, 1983). As they grow older, they become increasingly aware of male and female stereotypes. In one study, both male and female children had to decide whether certain characteristics were more likely in a man or a woman. Over 90 percent of a group of U.S. eleven-year-olds thought that the adjectives *weak, emotional, appreciative, gentle, soft-hearted, affected, talkative, fickle,* and *mild* probably described a woman and that the adjectives *strong, aggressive, disorderly, cruel, coarse, adventurous, independent, ambitious,* and *dominant* probably described a man. Boys and girls endorsed just about the same gender-role stereotypes (Best et al., 1977).

Many of these gender-role stereotypes are reinforced by parents and peers. When young children play with toys that are deemed to be inappropriate—as when a boy plays with a dollhouse—their parents are likely to express disapproval. This is especially so for fathers, who sternly object to any such behaviors in their sons. By and large, girls are allowed more latitude in such matters. A girl can be a tomboy and get away with it; a boy who is a sissy is laughed at or taunted (Langlois and Downs, 1980).

Gender-role stereotypes *Once parents and others recognize an infant's sex, they will treat him or her differently. Notice the difference in the cards sent to parents congratulating them on the birth of a son or daughter. (© Hallmark Cards, Inc.)*

CONSTITUTIONAL FACTORS AND SEX DIFFERENCES

■ What accounts for the difference in current gender roles? We will consider both constitutional and social factors in an attempt to understand how biology and society conspire to make boys into men and girls into women.

It's self-evident that gender roles are influenced by anatomical and physiological differences that pertain to reproduction, and there are of course differences in average size, strength, and physical endurance. But what about *psychological* differences? There is no doubt that such differences do exist and that some of them fit cultural stereotypes. The question is whether any of these differences—in aggression, independence, emotional expressiveness, social sensitivity, and so on—are biologically given, whether they accompany the sexual anatomy the way menstruation goes along with a female XX chromosome pair.

Before proceeding, two cautions: The first is that any psychological difference between the sexes is one of *averages.* The average three-year-old girl seems to be more dependent than her male counterpart; she is more likely to ask for help, to cling, and to seek affection (Emmerich, 1966). But this doesn't mean that this generalization applies to *every* boy and girl, because there are certainly many three-year-old girls who are less dependent than many three-year-old boys. After all, the same applies even to many physical differences like height and weight. Thus, while it's clear that men are on the average taller than women, it's equally clear that a considerable number of women are taller than many men.

A second caution is about interpretation. Suppose we obtain a sex difference. What accounts for it? It may indeed reflect a biological predisposition, but it may also reflect the society in which the children are raised. In our society and many others, boys are encouraged to be independent, to be "little men," and any differences in a trait like dependency may simply reflect this cultural fact. Here, as in so many other areas, nature and nurture are difficult to disentangle.

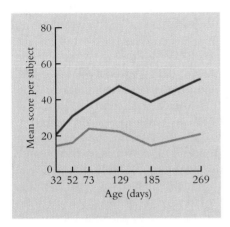

14.8 The development of rough-and-tumble play in male and female rhesus monkeys *Roughhouse play in two male and two female rhesus monkeys during the first year of life. The scores are based on both frequency and vigor of this activity, in which monkeys wrestle, roll, or sham bite—all presumably in play, since no one ever gets hurt. Roughhouse play is considerably more pronounced in males (dark red) than in females (blue), a difference that increases during the first year of life. (After Harlow, 1962)*

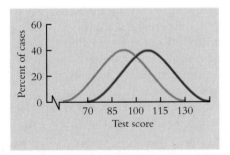

14.9 Sex differences in spatial ability *Results on a spatial-mathematical test, which included questions such as "How many times between three and four o'clock do the hands of a clock make a straight line?" The curve plots the percentage of subjects who receive a particular score (with men in dark red and women in blue). As the curve shows, the men perform better than the women, though the two curves overlap considerably. (Data from Very, 1967, with test scores adjusted by a method called "normalization")*

AGGRESSION

If there is one sex difference that is constitutional in origin, at least in part, it is aggression. Males are on average more active and assertive than females. This difference is apparent from the very start; male infants are more irritable and physically active than female infants, and mothers often report that their boys were more active than their girls in utero. At two or three, boys are much more likely to engage in rough-and-tumble play and mock fighting than are girls (a difference also seen in apes and monkeys; see Figure 14.8). By four or five, they are more ready to exchange insults and to greet aggression with retaliation.

The difference continues into adulthood. While acts of physical violence are relatively rare among both sexes, they are very much more common among men than women; thus among adolescents, arrests for violent crimes occur five times more often among males than females (Johnson, 1979). A similar pattern of results holds in different social classes and in such widely different cultural settings as Ethiopia, India, Kenya, Mexico, Okinawa, and Switzerland (Whiting and Whiting, 1975; Maccoby and Jacklin, 1974, 1980; Parke and Slaby, 1983).

It is probably not surprising that this sex difference is more pronounced for physical aggression than for other forms of aggression. When aggression is measured by rating the degree of verbal hostility or by asking how intense a shock a subject is willing to administer to another person, the difference is not as striking (Hyde, 1981). But even so, it is still quite marked.

That this sex difference in aggression—especially physical aggression—is found so early in life, is observed in so many different cultures, and is also seen in our primate relatives suggests a constitutional origin—all the more so given that aggressiveness is enhanced by the administration of male sex hormones (see Chapter 10). But a constitutional origin of a sex difference does not mean that social and cultural factors play no part—on the contrary. As we will describe below, the various agents of socialization—parents, teachers, peers, and the cultural media—all combine to magnify whatever sex differences were there to begin with.

PATTERNS OF INTELLECTUAL APTITUDES

There is another psychological difference that is often said to be based on biological givens—a different pattern of intellectual abilities. On the average, men do better on tests of spatial and mathematical ability (Figure 14.9; Maccoby and Jacklin, 1974, 1980; Halpern, 1992). Until fairly recently, it was generally believed that the reverse held for verbal abilities. According to some recent studies, the superiority of women over men on verbal tasks may be much smaller than had previously been assumed, though this is a matter of some dispute (Hyde and Linn, 1988; Halpern, 1992).

What accounts for the sex difference in cognitive aptitudes, especially in spatial-mathematical abilities? In part, it may simply reflect a difference in the way boys and girls are brought up. But various lines of evidence suggest that social factors are only part of the story. An example is a study of SAT scores in 40,000 male and female adolescents. The investigators found the usual sex difference on spatial and mathematical tasks even when they limited their comparison to boys and girls who had taken the same high-school math courses and had expressed the same degree of interest in mathematics (Benbow and Stanley, 1983; Benbow, 1988).

A number of authors feel that such sex differences in mathematical aptitude are ultimately produced by a difference in certain spatial abilities. An example is the ability to visualize objects in space, which is often assessed by asking subjects to rotate a three-dimensional object in their imagination to decide whether it is a rotated version of another figure or whether it is its mirror image. Since a number of branches of mathematics rely on such abilities—for example, geometry, topology, trigonometry, and much of calculus—it does not seem too far-fetched to assume that the sex difference in this ability underlies those in quantitative aptitude and achievement (Burnett, Lane, and Dratt, 1979; Hunt, 1985a; Halpern, 1992).

A number of investigators have searched for a constitutional basis for the male-female difference in spatial abilities. One of several suggestions is that the key to the puzzle is in different maturation rates. There is some evidence that children who mature later tend to do better on spatial tests than children who mature earlier. An intriguing hypothesis is that this effect is related to the different functions of the two cerebral hemispheres. As we've previously seen, the right hemisphere is specialized for spatial tasks, the left for language (see Chapter 2). By making the assumption that the right hemisphere matures more slowly than the left and that neurological maturation comes to an effective end at the time of puberty, we can account for most of the evidence. The usual male-female difference in cognitive orientation would then follow from the fact that girls generally reach puberty before boys. If so, their right (spatial) hemisphere is stopped at an earlier point of neurological organization (Waber, 1977, 1979).

Social factors and sex differences *Social effects augment constitutional differences. (Photograph © Yvonne Hemsey, The Gamma Liaison Network)*

SOCIAL FACTORS AND SEX DIFFERENCES

■ While some psychological sex differences may have biological roots, even more important are the ways in which boys and girls are socialized. We will begin our discussion by taking a second look at the two characteristics for which there is some evidence of a biologically based sex difference: aggression and spatial aptitudes. We'll see that even here there is some reasonable evidence that social effects augment and interact with whatever constitutional differences may have been there to start with.

ARE CONSTITUTIONAL DIFFERENCES REALLY CONSTITUTIONAL?

A ready example of the interaction of culture with constitution lies in aggression. Boys may very well be more disposed toward aggression than girls, but it appears almost certain that cultural pressures magnify any preexisting sex differences. Boys are encouraged to be tough and are given toy guns, while girls are expected to be well-behaved and receive dolls and doll houses. Parents will generally allow (and even foster) a degree of aggressiveness in a boy that they would never countenance in a girl. Thus fathers often encourage their sons to fight back when another boy attacks them (Sears, Maccoby, and Levin, 1957).

This process continues in adolescence, where aggressive behavior in boys is tolerated or indulgently smiled at, while the same behavior in girls is discouraged in favor of a more dependent, approval-seeking pattern. The scales are tipped still further by the way in which the two sexes are usually portrayed by the media, with strong, silent heroes and charming, help-mate heroines. While males and females may start life with different biological dispositions toward aggression, by the time they are adults society has exaggerated this initial difference manifold (Parke and Slaby, 1983).

Similar considerations may apply to the sex difference in spatial aptitude. In our society, girls are expected to do better in English than in math. This belief is shared by teachers, parents, and the pupils themselves, who all conspire to make it come true, so that even the girl who does have the appropriate genetic potential may do worse on spatial and mathematical tests than her ability warrants. In addition, many male and female students share a widespread feeling that math-related courses and careers are a male province and that the women who succeed in them are somehow unfeminine. A recent review quotes a female mathematics professor's description of this stereotype:

> Many people on hearing the words "female mathematician" conjure up an image of a six-foot, gray-haired, tweed-suited, oxford-clad woman. This image, of course, doesn't attract the young woman who is continually bombarded with messages, both direct and indirect, to be beautiful, "feminine" and catch a man. (Quoted in Halpern, 1992, p. 216).

The upshot is similar to the gender difference in aggression. While the male-female difference in intellectual aptitudes may originally be based on built-in constitutional factors, it is certain to be greatly magnified by social expectations and stereotypes.

THEORIES OF GENDER TYPING

Social factors are evidently of great importance in fashioning our sense of being men or women, and they shape our behavior accordingly. But exactly how do these social factors exert their effects? Each of the three main theories of socialization—psychoanalysis, social learning theory, and the cognitive developmental approach—has attempted an answer (see Figure 14.10).

PSYCHOANALYTIC THEORY

According to Freud's psychoanalytic theory, the basic mechanism for determining gender identity is *identification.* The child models himself or herself on the

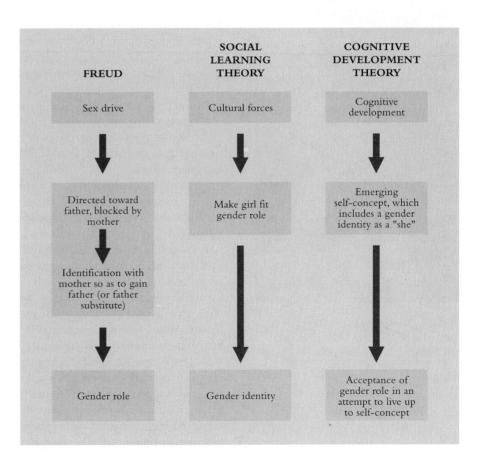

14.10 Three theories of sex typing
The figure summarizes the three major theories of sex typing (for females).

same-sex parent in an effort to become like him or her. In Freud's view, identification is the end product of a mother-father-child triangle that he called the Oedipal conflict, which culminates at about age five or six. This identification also has implications for sexual orientation, as we discuss below. (We will discuss the Oedipal conflict when we discuss psychoanalytic theory; see Chapter 17).

SOCIAL LEARNING THEORY

A very different position is held by social learning theorists, who argue that children behave in gender-appropriate ways for the simplest of possible reasons: They are rewarded if they do so and are punished if they don't. For the most part, they learn what each sex is supposed to do by *imitation.*

But whom shall they imitate? They quickly discover that they must choose a model of their own sex (usually a parent or caretaker). For example, a girl imitates her mother and is rewarded for rocking the baby (at that point a doll may have to do), for prettying herself up, and for being Mommy's little helper. The boy who imitates these maternal acts will be ridiculed and called a sissy. He will do better by imitating his father, who rewards him for doing boylike things (Mischel, 1970).

Why do parents push their sons and daughters into different social molds? A social learning theorist would probably reply that the parents' behavior (as well as that of peers, teachers, and so on) is also shaped by various reinforcers, all of which act to maintain a particular gender-typed social structure. In effect, the socialization of children is simply an apprenticeship for the roles they will adopt as adults.

COGNITIVE DEVELOPMENTAL THEORY

Yet another proposal was offered by Lawrence Kohlberg, who regarded gender typing in the context of cognitive development. Kohlberg's emphasis was on the child's emerging awareness of his or her gender identity—the sense of being male or female. While social learning theory emphasizes what boys and girls must learn to *do* to fit the role of man or woman, Kohlberg focuses on what boys and girls must *understand* to recognize that they belong to the category man or woman (Kohlberg, 1966).

According to Kohlberg, the concept of gender is quite vague until the child is five or six years old. The four-year-old has only a shadowy notion of what the categories "male" and "female" mean. He has no real comprehension of how these categories pertain to genital anatomy. When presented with dolls that have either male or female genitals and varying hair length and asked to tell which are the boys and which the girls, preschoolers generally decide on the basis of hair length (McConaghy, 1979; but see Bem, 1989).

A related phenomenon is the fact that four-year-olds don't really understand that gender is one of the permanent and (for all intents and purposes) unchangeable attributes of the self. Children develop a sense of gender identity by about age three. But it takes them another two years or so to achieve the concept of *gender constancy*—the recognition that being male or female is irrevocable. When shown a picture of a girl, four-year-olds say that she could be a boy if she wanted to or if she wore a boy's haircut or wore a boy's clothes. But in Kohlberg's view, the problem is not with gender as such. For many four-year-olds also say that a cat could be a dog if it wanted to or if its whiskers were cut off. This suggests that the lack of gender constancy is just another reflection of the preschooler's failure to comprehend the underlying constancies of the universe. After all, children at this stage of cognitive development don't consistently conserve liquid quantity, mass, or number (see Chapter 13).

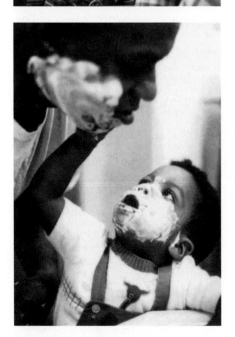

Male and female models (*Top: photograph by Suzanne Szasz. Bottom: photograph by Burk Uzzle/Woodfin Camp*)

A four-year-old and her doll Is she trying to live up to her gender identity or simply acting like a parent? (Photograph by Erika Stone)

According to Kohlberg, the child's identification with the parent of the same sex *follows* the acquisition of gender identity. Once they recognize that they are boys or girls, they will try to live up to their sense of gender identity, to act in a manner that befits their own self-concept. They will now look for appropriate models—and the most readily available ones are usually their mothers and fathers—that can show them how to get better and better at being a male or a female.

SEXUAL ORIENTATION

The majority of men and women are *heterosexual;* they exclusively seek a partner of the opposite sex. But for a significant minority, the sexual orientation is otherwise. Some of them experience erotic and romantic feelings exclusively toward members of their own sex; such people are *homosexual.* Others experience such feelings for both their own and the opposite sex; such people are *bisexual.* ⋆

Regardless of this variation in sexual orientation, however, virtually all gay and bisexual men think of themselves as men and are so regarded by others; the analogous point holds for lesbians (Marmor, 1975). This clearly illustrates the fact that sexual orientation, gender identity, and gender role are in principle independent.

THE PREVALENCE OF HOMOSEXUALITY

Perhaps the most comprehensive study of sexual patterns among Americans was an anonymous survey conducted in the 1940s by a research team led by biologist Alfred Kinsey. Kinsey and his associates found that 4 percent of American men are exclusively homosexual during their lifetime (Kinsey, Pomeroy, and Martin, 1948). The comparable prevalence of exclusive homosexuality among women seems to be lower—about 2 percent (Kinsey et al., 1953). But when Kinsey counted in those men and women whose orientation was predominantly homosexual but who had had some heterosexual experience, the percentages increased to about 13 percent for men and 7 percent for women. Some feel that these estimates are too high, arguing that Kinsey's survey sample was not adequately representative (Reisman and Eichel, 1990). One study, using quite stringent criteria that focused entirely on actual behavior, reported only a 2 percent rate of exclusive male homosexual orientation (Hamer et al., 1993a, b). But recent surveys of both men and women in other Western cultures accord basically with Kinsey's estimates of exclusive homosexuality (e.g., ACSF Investigators, 1992; Johnson et al., 1992). In general, it's probably not surprising that studies that focus on activity (engaging in sexual behavior with members of one's own sex) and on perceived identity (regarding oneself as gay or lesbian) tend to report lower percentages than studies that ask about feeling and desire.

It's evident that a substantial number of men and women are erotically and romantically oriented toward a partner of their own sex despite the fact that our society sharply stigmatizes such behavior. This cultural taboo against homosexual behavior is by no means universal, however. According to one cross-cultural survey, two-thirds of the societies studied regarded homosexuality as normal and

---

⋆ Since relatively little systematic study has been directed toward bisexuality, our primary focus here will be homosexuality. (For some discussions, see Paul, 1984, 1985).

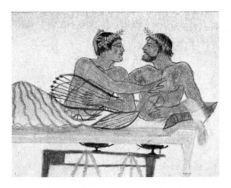

Homosexual behavior in antiquity
Among the ancient Greeks homosexual rela-
tions between men were widely practiced and
accepted, as the mural from the Tomb of the
Diver (c. 480 B.C.–470 B.C.), found in
what was a Greek settlement in southern
Italy, suggests. (Courtesy of National Archae-
ological Museum, Paestum, Italy)

acceptable, at least for some people or for some age groups (Ford and Beach, 1951). In certain historical periods the practice was glorified and extolled, as in classical Greece where Pericles, the great Athenian statesman, was regarded as rather odd because he was *not* attracted to beautiful boys.

In this context it's important to realize that much of the sexual behavior of gays and lesbians revolves around feelings of romance and love just as does that of heterosexual people. There is a widely held belief that the homosexual orientation only leads to brief and furtive liaisons, especially among gay men. While this may be true for some subgroups, it does not seem to describe a majority of the gay and lesbian population. On the contrary, many gays and lesbians form lasting bonds and become couples, despite the fact that our culture does not offer any recognized route for such relationships (Mattison and McWhirter, 1987; Green and Clunis, 1988).

WHAT CAUSES HOMOSEXUALITY: ENVIRONMENTAL FACTORS?

Experience in early life   Some of the attempts at an explanation of what causes homosexuality focus on the role of childhood experience. But there is very little evidence to support this view. In one study, about 1,000 gays and lesbians provided various items of information about their life histories. There was some difference in how gay people and heterosexuals viewed their parents. Compared to heterosexual controls, gay people had a less satisfactory relationship with their parents, especially with those of their own sex. But on closer analysis, it turned out that these familial relationships did not have much of an effect on the development of sexual orientation. If gay men don't get along too well with their fathers (although in fact many of them do), this is probably because the fathers can't accept various aspects of their sons' sexual orientation. If so, the unsatisfactory father-son relationship is a result of the son's sexual orientation, not its cause. Something of the same sort applies to the mother-daughter relationship in lesbians. Such findings give little support to the psychoanalytic framework, with its emphasis on the crucial role of the early family constellation (Bell, Weinberg, and Hammersmith, 1981).

Experience in later childhood or adolescence   Further evidence undermines the widely held stereotype that homosexuality is produced when a boy is "seduced" by an older man or a girl by an older woman. In the same interview study, the main predictor of eventual homosexuality was the way people *felt* about sexuality in childhood and early adolescence rather than what they *did*. Homosexual feelings and erotic fantasies usually preceded any actual homosexual encounters people might have had (Bell, Weinberg, and Hammersmith, 1981). Many individuals report that "I've been that way all my life" (Saghir and Robins, 1973), and just as future heterosexuals imagine starstruck romances with members of the opposite sex, so do those who will become homosexual imagine same-sex love and romance. Same-sex desires and the corresponding fantasies usually emerge before biological puberty, sometimes as early as age three or four (Green 1979; Hamer et al., 1993; Zuger, 1984).

But perhaps the most decisive evidence against the idea that early sexual experience determines sexual orientation comes from other cultures. In a number of cultures there are socially prescribed periods of homosexual behavior, usually between boys and older men, which begin in childhood and last through adolescence. Despite this intensive homosexual experience, which occurs amid the boys' puberty and sexual awakening, at adulthood most of the young men show the expected heterosexual orientation and pursue marriage and fatherhood (Herdt, 1990; Stoller and Herdt, 1985).

WHAT CAUSES HOMOSEXUALITY: BIOLOGICAL FACTORS?

Childhood experience does not seem to provide the answer to what causes homosexuality. As an alternative, a number of investigators have looked to biology.

Genetics and inheritance patterns   One approach has considered genetic dispositions. One line of evidence comes from twin studies: A man's chance of having a homosexual orientation is fully 52 percent if his identical twin has one, but decreases to 22 percent if his gay twin brother is fraternal (Bailey and Pillard, 1991). Likewise, a woman's chance of having a homosexual orientation is 48 percent if her identical twin sister has one, but only 16 percent if her lesbian twin sister is fraternal (Bailey et al., 1993).

A potential breakthrough in understanding how sexual orientation—or at least male homosexual orientation—may be inherited comes from a team of researchers led by geneticist Dean Hamer (Hamer et al., 1993). Hamer's team obtained results which suggest that the homosexual orientation in males might largely be attributed to a gene or genes in a specific area of the X-chromosome. These results are preliminary, but even if they hold up, the question remains of just what the X-linked genes do to produce the homosexual orientation.

One thing the X-linked genes may do is code for differences in brain structure. For among the most dramatic recent developments in understanding sexual orientation is the finding of differences in brain structure between individuals with heterosexual and homosexual orientations. Most investigators have concentrated upon the hypothalamus and compared heterosexual to homosexual men. One study by Simon Le Vay examined an area in the anterior hypothalamus that affects sexual behavior in animals and which was previously found to be twice as large in the brains of men than in those of women (Le Vay, 1991; Allen et al., 1989). When Le Vay looked at the brains of gay men, he found that this area of the hypothalamus was about the size of the same area in heterosexual women—only about half as large as this area in the brains of the heterosexual men.★

At present, the reasons for the brain differences are unknown; they might be genetic, hormonal, or both. Nor is it known whether the structures that differ in individuals with heterosexual versus homosexual orientations are indeed themselves the crucial areas that originally determined sexual orientation; they may have developed secondarily as a function of other differences. The jury is still out—but hard at work.

EVOLUTION AND HOMOSEXUALITY

The preceding discussion suggests that both homosexual and heterosexual orientations are at least partially based on biological predisposition. On the face of it, this seems to pose a puzzle. For one might suppose that individuals with a homosexual orientation reproduce less than those with a heterosexual one.

A lesbian couple   (© 1991 Joan E. Biren)

★ One might ask why these studies have focused only on gay men and say nothing about lesbians. The answer is both grim and straightforward. To perform these studies requires comparisons between the brains of persons whose sexual orientation can be verified. But the only time sexual orientation is normally a part of the medical record is in diagnosed cases of HIV infection. Thus in all of these studies, the brains of the homosexual males were obtained from men who died of AIDS. A number of considerations indicate that these brain differences cannot be attributed to any overall degenerative changes resulting from the disease, since they were limited to the hypothalamic area and not found in other cerebral regions (Le Vay, 1991).

From the standpoint of natural selection, then, wouldn't a homosexual orientation be expected to disappear?

This point is sometimes raised as a way to claim that a homosexual orientation must be biologically disadvantageous, in the sense of reducing the number of genes its bearer will leave to posterity. This argument presupposes that people with a homosexual orientation have far fewer children than heterosexuals. But this may not be true. It is very likely that through much of human history people who would now be regarded as gay or lesbian mated with people of the opposite sex and did have children. And it is likely that much the same is true today, for many people whose basic orientation is homosexual marry even so, in part because of the great pressure exerted by the social stigma attached to homosexuality. In addition, there are many people whose orientation is bisexual and who are thus just as likely to have children as are heterosexuals. If it's true that bisexuality is genetically related to homosexuality (which seems plausible, though there is no evidence as yet), there is yet another argument against the reproductive disadvantage of homosexuality.

Some sociobiologists have proposed that a homosexual orientation may enhance biological fitness in a more subtle way. We've previously seen that reproductive success can be assessed in terms of *inclusive fitness,* which considers not just one's own offspring but also that of one's kin (see Chapter 10). For example, individuals who don't have children themselves might be more free to tend to their sisters and brothers, and nieces and nephews, and thus ensure that they thrive. The result might well be a greater (though indirect) proliferation of one's genes than would be possible through one's own children.

This caretaking role is institutionalized in the role of the *berdache* found in Native American and Eskimo villages (Williams, 1986). The berdache is a man who often dresses like a woman, has sexual relations with both single and married men in the village, and is often regarded as a shaman. He also acts as a matchmaker and marital therapist, generously distributes resources to those in need, even acting as a "spare parent" if a mother or father should die. Having a berdache in the family is considered quite beneficial to the other family members. The berdache may, as the theory suggests, also benefit his own reproductive success indirectly through the relatives whose welfare he aids (Weinrich, 1987).

TWO SIDES OF THE COIN

So what leads to homosexuality? A biological, genetically based predisposition is very likely a major factor that determines the direction of the child's emerging sexual desire. But cultural conditions undoubtedly contribute a heavy share in shaping how children see themselves as they grow up. So as yet there is no clear answer to this question. It may well be that the question simply represents the other side of the question, "What leads to heterosexuality?" This second question is rarely asked because most people take the heterosexual preference for granted. Yet if we did know how to explain the origin of heterosexuality, we would be much closer to an understanding of how homosexuality comes about as well.

Stating the two questions in this parallel form may help us see another point. People sometimes ask whether gay men and lesbians can somehow be transformed into heterosexual men and women. The answer is that such a transformation is extremely difficult if not impossible. Nor do most gay men and lesbians wish for such a change. Like heterosexuality, homosexuality is much more than a sexual preference that can be done or undone more or less at will. It represents a fundamental part of an individual's makeup, a makeup that essentially defines him or her.

Whatever the causes of a homosexual or bisexual orientation, one thing is clear: Such an orientation is not a psychological disorder or defect. It is only abnormal in the sense of being the orientation of a minority, say, of some 10 percent or so of the population—but so is left-handedness. Gays and lesbians are neither better nor worse than heterosexuals. While their number includes great artists (e.g., Leonardo da Vinci), writers (e.g., Gertrude Stein), and warriors (e.g., Alexander the Great), the great majority of them are rather ordinary people whose names will not be recorded in history books. The same no doubt holds for left-handers—and for heterosexuals.

DEVELOPMENT AFTER CHILDHOOD

FOCUS QUESTIONS

- What are the "eight ages of man" that Erik Erikson proposed?
- How universal is the Western view of adolescence as a period of emotional upheaval?
- How has the social role accorded the elderly changed over the last one hundred years?

Thus far, our primary focus in describing human development has been on infancy and childhood. This emphasis reflects the orientation of the major figures over the history of the field. Thus Piaget tried to describe the growth of the mind until the achievement of formal operations at about the age of eleven. Freud was even more narrowly focused on childhood; to him, the most important events of social development took place before the age of five or six. Both Freud and Piaget, in common with most developmental psychologists, understood the term *development* in much the sense in which it is generally used by biology: the processes by which the newly formed organism changes until it reaches maturity.

In recent years, a number of authors have argued that this interpretation of the term *development* is too narrow. In their view, there is no reason to assume that human personality stops developing after childhood, for humans continue to change as they pass through the life cycle. The problems faced by an adolescent boy are not the same as those of a young man about to get married or become a father, let alone those of a middle-aged man at the peak of his career or of a seventy-year-old at the close of his. This being so, it seems reasonable to chart the course of psychological development after puberty is reached in the hope that one can find some psychological milestones in adult development analogous to those that students of child development have tried to describe for earlier ages (Baltes, Reese, and Lipsitt, 1980).

What are the stages of development after childhood? Most later investigators have been strongly affected by proposals of the psychoanalyst Erik Erikson. According to Erikson, all human beings pass through a series of major crises as they go through the life cycle. At each stage, there is a critical confrontation between the self the individual has achieved thus far and the various demands posed by his or her social and personal setting. In all, Erikson sets out "eight ages of man," of which the first few occur in early childhood and roughly correspond to Freud's oral, anal, and phallic stages (see Chapter 17). These are fol-

Erik Erikson   A pioneer in the study of development after childhood. (© 1990 Olive Pierce/Black Star)

TABLE 14.2 ERIKSON'S EIGHT AGES OF MAN

Approximate age	Developmental task of that stage	Psychosocial crisis of that stage
0–1 ½ years	Attachment to mother, which lays foundation for later trust in others	Trust versus mistrust
1 ½–3 years	Gaining some basic control of self and environment (e.g., toilet training, exploration)	Autonomy versus shame and doubt
3–6 years	Becoming purposeful and directive	Initiative versus guilt
6 years–puberty	Developing social, physical, and school skills	Competence versus inferiority
Adolescence	Making transition from childhood to adulthood; developing a sense of identity	Identity versus role confusion
Early adulthood	Establishing intimate bonds of love and friendship	Intimacy versus isolation
Middle age	Fulfilling life goals that involve family, career, and society; developing concerns that embrace future generations	Productivity versus stagnation
Later years	Looking back over one's life and accepting its meaning	Integrity versus despair

SOURCE: Based on Erikson, 1963.

lowed by adolescence, early adulthood, middle age, and the final years (Erikson, 1963; see Table 14.2).

Erikson's developmental scheme has influenced many investigators of adult development. We will continue to refer to his organization as we briefly discuss some issues in the study of adolescence and adulthood.

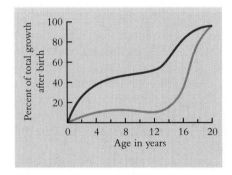

14.11   The growth spurt at adolescence
The figure shows the percentage of total growth after birth attained between the ages 0 and 20 years for overall height (dark red) and size of genital and reproductive organs (blue), averaged for males and females. (After Tanner, 1970)

ADOLESCENCE

The term *adolescence* is derived from the Latin for "growing up." It is a period of transition in which the individual changes from a child to an adult. There are biological changes: a physical growth spurt, a change in bodily proportions, and the attainment of sexual maturity (see Figure 14.11). Biological maturing ultimately leads to social and economic changes: from dependence on one's family to ever-increasing independence. And of course there are the numerous psychological changes that accompany the process of growing up. These include the progressive maturing of sexual attitudes and behavior that will ultimately allow the adolescent to start his or her own family, and the acquisition of various skills that will eventually enable him or her to become a fully functioning member of adult society. In effect, adolescence is simply a protracted version of what in birds is a rather abrupt procedure—the point at which fledglings are forced to fly out of the nest and to make their own way.

THE NATURE OF THE TRANSITION

Compared to other animals, humans attain sexual maturity rather late in their development. This is just another facet of an important difference between ourselves and our animal cousins—a lengthened period of immaturity and dependence that provides time for each generation to learn from the one before. When is this period over?

Biology has set a lower limit at roughly age fifteen for girls and seventeen for boys when physical growth is more or less complete. But the point that marks the beginning of adulthood is decreed by social conditions as well as biology. As an example, a study of colonial New England families shows that the age at which sons become autonomous from their parents changed over the course of four generations. The sons of the first settlers stayed on their parents' farm until their late twenties before they married and became economically independent. As farmland became scarcer and other opportunities opened in the surrounding villages and towns, the sons left home, learned a trade, married, and became autonomous at a younger age (Greven, 1970). But with the onset of mass education in the mid-nineteenth century, this pattern was reversed again. Instead of leaving to become an apprentice or take a job, more and more youths continued to live with their families and remained in school through their late teens. This allowed them to acquire the skills required for membership in a complex, technological society, but it postponed their social and economic independence and their full entry into the adult world (Elder, 1980).

Culture evidently has an important say in the when and how of the transition period. It also sets up special occasions that mark the end of that period or highlight certain points along the way. A number of human societies have *initiation rites* that signify induction into adulthood (Figure 14.12). In some preliterate cultures, these are violent, prolonged, and painful, especially in certain puberty rites for boys that involve ceremonial beatings and circumcision. According to some anthropologists, such initiation rites are especially severe in cultures that try to emphasize the dramatic distinction between the roles of children and adults, as well as between those of men and women. In our own society, the transition to full adulthood is much more gradual, with milestones that refer not just to biological changes but also to various educational and vocational attainments. It is therefore not too surprising that we have not one initiation rite but many (none of which would ever be regarded as especially severe): confirmations and bar (or bas) mitzvahs, "sweet sixteen" parties, high-school and college graduations, and so on. Each of them represents just one more step on a protracted road to adulthood (Burton and Whiting, 1961; Muuss, 1970).

A **B**

14.12 Initiation rites *These rites signify induction into adulthood, as in (A) a bar mitzvah, or (B) a South African ceremony in which young men of about 19 are initiated into full manhood by having to live in isolation for 2 months after a ritual circumcision. During this period, they are smeared with white clay to indicate that they are in a state of transition and in contact with ancestral spirits. (A): photograph by Blair Seitz, 1986/Photo Researchers. (B): photograph by A. Bernhaut/Photo Researchers)*

Cultural factors also determine the time at which other benchmarks of development are reached. An example is the age at which virginity is lost, which has steadily decreased in our own society during the past few decades, reflecting a change in sexual mores for both men and women. This change is undoubtedly caused by many factors, not the least of which is the existence of increasingly effective methods of birth control that allow the separation of the emotional and recreational functions of sexuality from its reproductive ones.

IS ADOLESCENCE ALWAYS TURBULENT?

There is a traditional view of adolescence which holds that it is inevitably a period of great emotional stress. This notion goes back to the Romantic movement of the early nineteenth century, when major writers such as Goethe wrote influential works that featured youths in desperate conflict with a cynical, adult world that drove them to despair, suicide, or violent rebellion. This position was later endorsed by a number of psychological theorists, including Sigmund Freud and many of his followers. To Freud, adolescence was necessarily a period of conflict, since this is the time when the sexual urges repressed during the closing phase of the Oedipal conflict can no longer be denied and clash violently with the unconscious prohibitions previously set up. Further conflicts center on struggles with the older generation, especially the same-sex parent, that were repressed in childhood but now come to the fore (see Chapter 17).

This traditional view of adolescence has been seriously challenged by several modern writers who argue that the turbulence of the period is by no means inevitable. Whether there is marked emotional disturbance depends on the way the culture handles the transition. Some evidence for this view comes from studies of preliterate cultures in which the shift from childhood to adulthood is very gradual. Among the Arapesh of New Guinea, the young increasingly participate in adult activities as they get older. The child begins by tilling her parents' garden and eventually tills her own. Given the relatively simple social and economic structure of Arapesh life, the change is not very drastic. Correspondingly, there seems to be no psychological crisis among the Arapesh during adolescence (Mead, 1939).

However enviable, the gentle adolescent transition of the Arapesh is difficult to achieve in our modern industrial society. It's hard to see how a five-year-old can help his father at his job if that job happens to be computer programming. Accordingly, one might expect a fair level of disturbance during adolescence in our own society. And, indeed, such emotional disturbance is a theme often sounded by the mass media and much twentieth-century literature (for example, J. D. Salinger's *Catcher in the Rye*). But in fact, a number of studies suggest that such turbulence is by no means universal among modern adolescents. Several investigators find that for many adolescents "development . . . is slow, gradual, and unremarkable" (Josselson, 1980, p. 189). What probably matters is the particular social and psychological setting, which surely differs from individual to individual in a complex society such as ours.

Puberty *by Edward Munch, 1895 (Copyright © The Munch Museum/The Munch-Ellingsen Group/ARS, 1994)*

TRYING TO FIND A PERSONAL IDENTITY

It appears that adolescence is not necessarily a time of troubles. But even so, it does pose a number of serious problems as the adolescent has to prepare to become an autonomous individual in his or her own right. A number of writers have tried to understand some characteristic adolescent behavior patterns in light of this ultimate goal.

  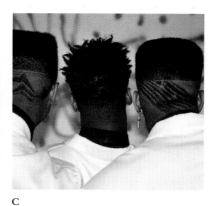

A   B   C

14.13 Adolescent fads *New adolescent fads spring up to maintain the differentiation between the adolescents' own world and that of the adults around them. They then disappear rather quickly to be replaced by yet newer fads. The photos show some such fads prominent at various times. (A) seventies— streaking, (B) eighties—punk fashions, (C) nineties—black rap singers' hairstyles. (Photographs by T. Lowell/Black Star, © Spencer Grant/The Picture Cube, © Jeff Greenberg/The Picture Cube)*

Establishing a separate world Unlike fledglings, adolescents in our society remain in the nest for quite a while after they can fly (or perhaps more precisely, get their driver's licenses). This probably makes it all the more essential for them to establish some elements of a separation between themselves and the world of their parents. As one means to this end, many adolescents adopt all kinds of external trappings of what's "now" and what's "in," such as distinctive tastes in dance steps, clothing, and idiom (Figure 14.13). These often change with bewildering rapidity as yesterday's adolescent fads diffuse into the broader social world and become today's adult fashions (as witness men's hairstyles). When this happens, new adolescent fads spring up to maintain the differentiation (Douvan and Adelson, 1958).

The identity crisis of adolescence According to Erikson, the separation from the adult's sphere is only one manifestation of what adolescents are really trying to achieve. Their major goal throughout this period is to discover who and what they really are as they go through what he calls an *identity crisis.* In our complex culture, there are many social roles, and adolescence is a time to try them on to see which one fits best—which vocation, which ideology, which group membership. The adolescent's primary question is, "Who am I?" and to answer it, he strikes a succession of postures, in part for the benefit of others, who then serve as a mirror in which he can see himself. Each role, each human relationship, each worldview is first temporarily adopted on an all-or-none basis with no room for compromise. Each is at first a costume. When the adolescent finds that some costume fits, it becomes the clothes of his adult identity (Erikson, 1963).

ADULTHOOD

Erikson describes a number of further stages of personality development. In young adulthood, the healthy individual has to achieve the capacity for closeness and intimacy through love or else suffer a sense of isolation that will permit only shallow human relationships. In early middle age, he has to develop a sense of personal creativity that extends beyond his own self. This includes a concern for others, for his work, for the community of which he is a part. And toward the end of life, there is a final crisis during which each person has to come to terms with his own life and accept it for what it was, with a sense of integrity rather than of despair. Erikson eloquently sums up this final reckoning: "It is the acceptance of one's own and only life cycle as something that had to be and that, by necessity, permitted of no substitutes. . . . healthy children will not fear life if their elders have integrity enough not to fear death" (Erikson, 1963, pp. 268–69).

449

The ages of man Jacob Blessing the
Sons of Joseph *by Rembrandt, 1656
(Copyright by Staatliche Museem, Kassel.
Photograph by M. Busing)*

*(Top: Photograph by Roberta Intrater.
Bottom: Photograph © Benn Mitchell/Image
Bank)*

HOW UNIVERSAL ARE THE STAGES OF ADULT DEVELOPMENT?

There is enough consistency in the results obtained by various investigators of adult development to suggest that the stages and transitions they describe apply fairly widely to people in our time and place. But are they universal? When we considered various stage theories of child development, we asked whether these stages occur in all cultures. The same question can be asked about adult development. Is there a midlife transition among the Arapesh? Does an Eskimo villager of fifty go through an agonizing reappraisal of what he's done with his life to date? If the answer is no, then we have to ask ourselves what the various stages described by Erikson and other students of the adult life span really are.

Thus far there is little concrete evidence one way or the other, so we can only guess. Certain adult milestones are clearly biological. In all cultures, humans reach puberty, mate, have children, begin to age, go through female menopause or male climacteric, age still further, and finally die. But the kind of crises that confront persons at different points of the life cycle surely depend on the society in which they live.

An example of the effect of social conditions on adult crises is the transition into old age. Over a century ago in the United States, different generations often lived close together as part of an extended family. There was much less segregation by age than there is now; children, parents, and grandparents frequently lived under the same roof or close to each other in the same neighborhood. In times of economic hardship, older people contributed to the family's resources even when they were too old to work—by caring for the children of working mothers, helping with the housekeeping, and so on. Older people—especially women—had yet another function: They were often sought out for advice on matters of child rearing and homekeeping. But today, the elderly have no such recognized family role. They usually live apart, are effectively segregated from the rest of society, are excluded from the workforce, and have lost their role as esteemed advisers. Given these changes, it follows that the transition into old age today is quite different from what it was 150 years ago. People still age as they did then—although the proportion of people who live into their seventies and eighties has increased radically—but they view aging differently (Hareven, 1978).

Facts of this sort suggest that various aspects of the stages proposed by students of adult development may be quite specific to our society and can therefore not be said to be universal. But if so, can we say anything about the life cycle that goes beyond the narrow specifics of our own time and social condition? Perhaps the best suggestion comes from a lecture by Erikson in which he tried to define adulthood:

> . . . In youth you find out what you *care to do* and who you *care to be*. . . . In young adulthood you learn whom you *care to be with*. . . . In adulthood, however, you learn what and whom you can *take care of*. . . . (Erikson, 1974, p. 124)

Seen in this light, the later phases of the life cycle can perhaps be regarded as the culmination of the progressive expansion of the social world that characterizes the entire course of social development from early infancy on. In a way, it is a final expansion in which our concern turns from ourselves to others and from our own present to their future (and in some cases, the future of all humanity).

This may or may not be a good description of what genuine adulthood *is*. But it seems like an admirable prescription for what it *ought* to be.

(Photograph by Eve Arnold, Magnum)

QUESTIONS FOR CRITICAL THINKING

1. How would Bowlby's attachment theory explain the Stockholm Syndrome in which hostages or prisoners of war grow attached to their captors?

2. What factor associated with children who do not form close attachments in early life might account for the deficits found in understimulated and socially neglected orphans? (Hint: Parents whose children are placed in orphanages may not be representative of the population.)

3. Would certain parenting styles suit some cultures better than others?

4. Recent critics have argued that morality in American society is in decline. How could we discover whether this contention is valid?

5. How could we determine whether a sex difference is truly constitutional?

SUMMARY

1. The infant's *social development* begins with the first human bond he forms—his *attachment* to his mother (or other caregiver). Studies of infant humans and monkeys indicate that this attachment is not caused by the fact that the mother feeds them, but rather because she feels so "comforting."

2. Developmental psychologists have tried to assess the quality of the child's attachment to the mother by observing the behavior of infants and young children in the "Strange Situation." There is some evidence that the quality of attachment at about fifteen months of age predicts behavior two years later.

3. Some theorists have proposed that the attachment to the mother can only be formed during a sensitive period in early life. In part, this position derives from work on *imprinting* in birds. According to this view, if such an early attachment is not formed, later social development may be seriously impaired, as indicated by studies of children reared in deprived orphanages. But later work on adopted children suggests that this impairment is not necessarily irrevocable and that there are good reasons to reassess the belief in the all-importance of early experience.

4. *Socialization* is the process by which children acquire the patterns of thought and behavior that characterize their society. Modern attempts to explain the mechanisms that underlie socialization include social learning theory, which emphasizes modeling, and cognitive developmental theory, which emphasizes the role of understanding as opposed to imitation.

5. The process of socialization begins with child rearing by parents. What seems to matter is the general home atmosphere, as shown by the effects of *autocratic, permissive,* and *authoritative-reciprocal* patterns of child rearing. On the other hand, how the parents treat the child is partially determined by the child's own characteristics, as suggested by studies on infant *temperament.*

6. One aspect of moral conduct concerns the *internalization* of prohibitions. Another aspect of moral conduct involves altruistic acts. Studies of *empathy* and *empathic distress* suggest that some precursors of altruism may be present in early infancy.

7. The study of *moral reasoning* has been strongly affected by Kohlberg's analysis of progressive stages in moral reasoning. According to a later critique by Carol Gilligan, there are some important sex differences in moral orientation, with men emphasizing

SUMMARY

justice and women stressing human relationships and compassion. Related differences have been found between different cultural groups.

8. Socialization plays a role in determining various senses of being male or female, including *gender identity, gender role,* and *sexual orientation.*

9. Certain psychological differences between the sexes may be based on biological differences. One is physical *aggression,* which tends to be more pronounced in men. Another is a tendency for men to perform better on spatial tests of mental ability than women do. Such biologically based differences—if any—are undoubtedly magnified by socially imposed gender roles.

10. Each of the three main theories of socialization—psychoanalysis, social learning theory, and cognitive developmental theory—tries to explain how social factors shape our sense of being male or female. Psychoanalysis asserts that the basic mechanism is *identification.* Social learning theory proposes that it is *imitation* of the parent of the same sex. Cognitive developmental theorists believe that identification comes after the child acquires gender identity, which presupposes an understanding of *gender constancy.*

11. The causes of *sexual orientation* are not yet clear. There is little evidence to support the view that *homosexuality* is produced either by a particular pattern of relations with parents in early childhood or by childhood sexual experiences. Current evidence points to *differences in brain structure* and a *genetic link.* But whatever its causes, this sexual orientation (no less than heterosexuality) is a fairly stable condition that can be changed only with great difficulty, if at all.

12. Development continues after childhood is past. Some theorists, notably Erik Erikson, have tried to map later stages of development. One such stage is *adolescence,* which marks the transition into another stage—*adulthood.*

PART FIVE

INDIVIDUAL DIFFERENCES

CHAPTER 5

INTELLIGENCE: ITS NATURE AND MEASUREMENT

People are different. They vary in bodily characteristics such as height, weight, strength, and hair color. They also vary along many psychological dimensions. They may be proud or humble, adventurous or timid, gregarious or withdrawn, intelligent or dull—the list of psychological distinctions is very large. Thus far such individual differences have not been our main concern. Our emphasis has been on attempts to find general psychological laws—whether in physiological function, perception, memory, learning, or social behavior—that apply to all people. To be sure, we have occasionally dealt with individual differences, as in the discussions of handedness, color blindness, and variations in child rearing. But our focus was not on these differences as such; rather, it was on what they could tell us about people in general—on how color blindness could help to explain the underlying mechanisms of color vision or how variations in child rearing might help us understand some aspects of socialization. In effect, our concern was with the nature of humankind, not with particular men and women.

We now change our emphasis and consider individual differences as a topic in its own right. We will first deal with the measurement of psychological attributes, specifically intelligence and personality traits. We will then turn to the discussion of psychopathology and attempts to treat it, a field in which the fact that people are in some ways different— sometimes all too different—is starkly clear.

I n twentieth-century industrialized society, particularly in the United States, the description of individual differences is a flourishing enterprise that has produced a multitude of psychological tests to assess various personal characteristics, especially those that pertain to intellectual aptitude. As we will see, the interest in individual differences grew in part from an effort to apply evolutionary ideas to humanity itself. But even more important was the social climate of the late nineteenth century, which provided a fertile soil for such concerns. The study of individual differences makes little sense in a society in which each person's adult role is fully determined by the social circumstances of his or her birth. In a caste society there is no need for vocational counselors or personnel managers. In such a society farmers beget farmers, soldiers beget soldiers, and princes beget princes; there is no point in administering mental tests to assist in educational selection or job placement. The interest in human differences arises only if such differences matter, if there is a social system that will accommodate them.

In a complex, industrialized society like our own, with its many different socioeconomic niches and some mobility across them, there is a real use for the systematic assessment of human characteristics. Such a society will try to find a means, however imperfect, for selecting the proper person to occupy the proper niche.

Mental tests were meant to supply this means. They were devised as instruments to help in educational and occupational selection or for use in various forms of personal guidance and diagnosis. As such, they are often regarded as one of the major contributions of psychology to the world of practical affairs. However, for this very reason, the discussion of test results and applications necessarily touches upon social and political issues that go beyond the usual confines of scientific discourse. Under the circumstances, it is hardly surprising that some of the questions raised by testing, especially intelligence testing, are often debated in an emotionally charged atmosphere. Should a student be denied admission to a college because of his or her Scholastic Aptitude Test score? Are such tests fair to disadvantaged ethnic or racial groups? Are scores on such tests determined by heredity, by environment, by both? This chapter will not be able to provide definite answers to all of these questions. Some involve judgments about social and political matters; others hinge on unresolved issues of fact. Our primary purpose is to provide the background against which such questions have to be evaluated.

MENTAL TESTS

FOCUS QUESTIONS

- Why did the concept of variability figure so large in Darwin's theory of natural selection?

- What is Galton's correlation coefficient?

- What are test validity and reliability? How is each determined?

- If a test is valid and reliable, will it necessarily be useful? Why or why not?

Mental tests come in different varieties. Some are tests of *achievement;* they measure what an individual can do now, his present knowledge and competence in a given area—how well he understands computer language or how well he can draw. Other tests are of *aptitude;* they predict what an individual will be able to do later, given the proper training and the right motivation. An example is a test of mechanical aptitude, which tries to determine the likelihood that an individual will do well as an engineer after an appropriate training period. *Intelligence tests* are sometimes considered tests of a very general cognitive aptitude, including the ability to benefit from schooling. Still another is a test of *personality,* which tries to assess an individual's characteristic behavior dispositions—whether she is generally outgoing or withdrawn, confident or insecure, placid or moody, and so on.

We will consider the nature of mental tests in general, regardless of what in particular they try to measure. But to understand the reasoning that underlies the construction and use of mental tests, we must first take a detour and look at the general problem of variability and of its measurement.

THE STUDY OF VARIATION

The study of how individuals differ from each other grew up in close association with the development of statistical methods. Until the nineteenth century, the term **statistics** meant little more than the systematic collection of various state records (*state*-istics) such as birth and death rates or the physical measurements of army recruits. In poring over such figures, the Belgian scientist Adolphe Quetelet (1796–1874) saw that many of them fell into a pattern (see Table 15.1). From this, he determined the **frequency distribution** of various sets

TABLE 15.1 QUETELET'S DISTRIBUTIONS OF CHEST MEASURES OF SCOTTISH SOLDIERS	
Measures of the chest in inches	Number of men per 10,000
33	4
34	31
35	141
36	322
37	732
38	1,305
39	1,867
40	1,882
41	1,628
42	1,148
43	645
44	160
45	87
46	38
47	7
48	2

of observations, that is, the frequency with which individual cases are distributed over different intervals along some measure. For example, he plotted the frequency distribution of the chest expansion of Scottish soldiers, noting the number of cases that fell into various intervals, from 33 to 33.9 inches, 34 to 34.9 inches, and so on.

VARIABILITY

Quetelet noticed two facts about his results. One was that his scores tended to cluster around a central value. One of the most common measures of this *central tendency* is the *mean*, or simple average, which is obtained by summing all of the values and dividing by the total number of cases. But the clustering tendency is by no means perfect, for there is *variability* around the average. All Scottish soldiers are not alike, whether in their chest sizes or anything else. An important measure of variability in a distribution is the *variance (V)*. This is computed by taking the difference between each score and the mean, squaring this difference, and then taking the average of these squared differences. For many purposes, a more useful measure of variability is the *standard deviation (SD)*, which is simply the square root of the variance.★

Quetelet's main contribution was the realization that, when put on a graph, the frequency distributions of various human physical attributes have a characteristic bell-shaped form. This symmetrical curve approximates the *normal curve*, which had already been studied by mathematicians in connection with games of chance. The normal curve describes the probability of obtaining certain combinations of chance events. Suppose, for example, that someone has the patience to throw six coins for over a hundred trials. How often will the coins fall to yield six heads, or five, four, three, two, one, or none? The expected distribution is shown in Figure 15.1, which also indicates what happened when a dedicated statistician actually performed the experiment. As more and more coins are thrown on any one trial, the expected distribution will approach the normal curve (Figure 15.2).

According to Quetelet, the variability found in many human characteristics can be explained in similar terms. He believed that nature aims at an ideal value—whether of height, weight, or chest size—but that it generally misses the mark, sometimes falling short and sometimes overshooting. For example, one's height depends upon a host of factors, some of which lead to an increase, others

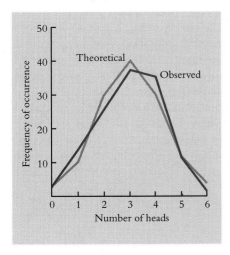

15.1 Theoretical and observed distribution of number of heads in 128 throws of six coins *(After Anastasi, 1958)*

★ For a fuller description of these and other statistical matters that will be referred to in this chapter, see the Appendix, "Statistics: The Collection, Organization, and Interpretation of Data."

15.2 The normal curve *(A) The probability of the number of heads that will occur in a given number of coin tosses. (B) When the number of coins tossed approaches infinity, the resulting distribution is the normal curve. The fact that this curve describes the distribution of many physical and mental attributes suggests that these attributes are affected by a multitude of independent factors, some pulling one way and some another.*

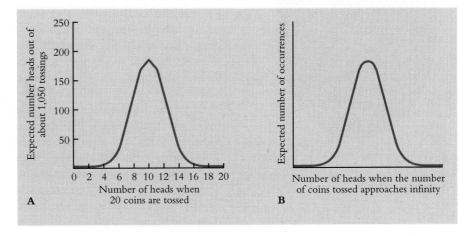

to a decrease. But each of these factors is independent of the others, and the operation of each is determined by chance. Thus nature is in effect throwing a multitude of coins to determine any one person's height. Each time the coin comes up "heads," it adds, say, a millimeter, and each time it comes up "tails," it subtracts one. The result is a frequency distribution of heights that approximates a normal curve.

VARIABILITY AND DARWIN

After Darwin published the *Origin of Species,* variability within a species was suddenly considered in a new perspective. Darwin showed that variability provides the raw material on which natural selection can work. Suppose that the average finch on a paricular island has a fairly long and narrow beak. There is some variability; a few finches have beaks that are shorter and wider. These few will be able to crack certain hard seeds that the other finches cannot open. If these hard seeds suddenly become the primary foodstuffs in the habitat (perhaps because of a change in its climate), the short-beaked finches may find themselves at a reproductive advantage. They will outlive and thus outbreed their long-beaked comrades and eventually a new species may be born (or more precisely, hatched). Seen in this light, variability is far from being an error of nature that missed the ideal mark as Quetelet had thought. On the contrary, it is the very stuff of which evolution is made. It gives natural selection something to select *from* (Figure 15.3).

CORRELATION

Could this line of reasoning be applied to variations in human characteristics? It might, if these characteristics could be shown to be hereditary, at least in part. This assumption seemed reasonable enough for the physical attributes, such as chest size that Quetelet tabulated, but is it appropriate for mental characteristics such as intellectual ability? A half-cousin of Darwin's, Francis Galton (1822–1911), spent much of his life trying to prove that it is. Most of the subsequent work in the area rests on the statistical methods he and his followers developed to test his assertions.

An important part of Galton's program called for the assesment of similarity among relatives. It was obvious from the start that children tend to be like their parents to some extent. The problem was to find some measure of this relationship.

As an example take a person's weight. How is this related to his height? The first step is to construct a **scatter diagram** in which one axis represents weight and the other height. Each person is represented by one point corresponding to his position along the weight and height axes (see Figure 15.4A). Inspection of the scatter diagram reveals that the two variables are related: as height goes up, so does weight. But this covariation, or **correlation,** is far from perfect. We can draw a **line of best fit** through the points in the scatter diagram, which allows us to make the best prediction of a person's weight given his height. But this prediction is relatively crude, for there is considerable variability around the line of best fit.

Galton and his stiudents developed a mathematical expression that summarizes both the direction and the strength of the relationship between the two measures. This is the **correlation coefficient,** which varies between +1.00 and –1.00 and is symbolized by the letter **r.** The plus or minus sign of the correlation coefficient indicates the direction of the relationship. In the case of height and weight this direction is positive: As height increases so does weight (Figure 15.4A). With other measures, the direction is negative: As the score on one measure increases, the score on the other declines (Figure 15.4B).

15.3   Evolution of the honeycreeper
These related species of Hawaiian honeycreepers display dramatic differences in beak size and shape. Like the finches that provided an important impetus to Darwin's theory of natural selection, these honeycreepers are thought to have evolved from a common ancestor. (Courtesy of H. Douglas Pratt)

Francis Galton   *A pioneer in the study of individual differences. (Courtesy of the National Library of Medicine)*

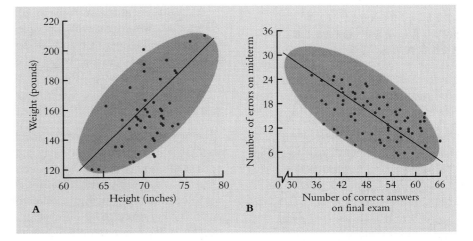

15.4 Correlation *(A) A scatter diagram of the heights and weights of fifty male undergraduates. Note that the points fall within an ellipse, which indicates variation around the line of best fit. The correlation for these data was +.70. (Technically, there are two lines of best fit. One predicts weight from height; the other predicts height from weight. The line shown on the diagram is an average of these two.) (B) A scatter diagram of the test performances of seventy students in an introductory psychology course. The diagram plots number of errors in a midterm against number of correct answers on the final. The correlation was −.53. If errors (or correct answers) had been plotted on both exams, the correlation would, of course, have been positive.*

The strength of the correlation is expressed by its absolute value (that is, its value regardless of sign). A correlation of $r = .00$ indicates no relation whatsoever. An example might be the relation between a student's height and his scholastic aptitude score. If we plot the scatter diagram, the points will form no pattern. There is thus no way of predicting a student's scholastic aptitude from his height, so there is no single line of best fit (Figure 15.5).

As the absolute value of r increases, the dots on the scatter diagram form an ellipse around the line of best fit. As the correlation goes up, the ellipse gets thinner and thinner. Note that as the ellipse gets thinner, there is less departure from the line of best fit. Thus, the thinner the ellipse, the less error there is as we try to predict the value of one variable (say, weight) when given the value of the other (say, height). When the absolute value of r reaches 1.00 (+1.00 or −1.00), the ellipse becomes a straight line. There is no more variation at all around the line of best fit; the correlation is perfect, and prediction is error-free. However, such perfect correlations are virtually never encountered in actual practice; even in the physical sciences there is bound to be some error of measurement.

While correlations are a useful index of the degree to which two variables are related, they have a limitation. The fact that two variables are correlated says nothing about the underlying causal relationship between them. Sometimes, there is none at all. Examples are correlations that are produced by some third factor. The number of umbrellas one sees on a given day is surely correlated with the number of people who wear raincoats. A Martian observing the human scene might conclude that umbrella-carrying causes raincoat-wearing or vice versa; our own earthly wisdom tells us that both are caused by rain.

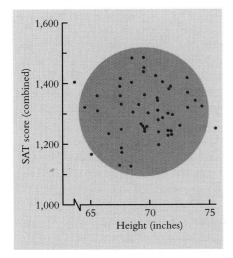

15.5 A correlation of zero *A scatter diagram of Scholastic Aptitude Test scores and the heights of fifty undergraduate males. Not surprisingly, there was no relation, as shown by the fact that the points fall within a circle. The correlation was +.05, which for all essential purposes is equivalent to zero.*

EVALUATING MENTAL TESTS

An important application of the correlation techniques developed by Galton and his students was to mental testing for which they provided the underlying statistical methodology.

A mental test is meant to be an objective yardstick to assess some psychological trait or capacity on which people differ (for example, artistic and mechanical aptitude; see Figures 15.6 and 15.7). But how can one tell that a given test actually accomplishes this objective?

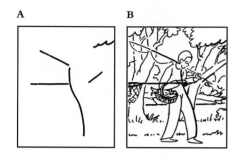

15.6 A test of art aptitude *The person tested is presented with (A). Using the lines in this card as a start, he has to make a completed drawing. (B) A completed sample. The test score is based on ratings by an experienced art teacher. These scores correlated quite well (+.66) with grades in a special art course for high-school seniors. (Cronbach, 1970b. Test item from the Horn Art Aptitude Inventory, 1953; courtesy of Stoelting Co., Chicago)*

RELIABILITY

One important criterion of the adequacy of a test is its **reliability,** the consistency with which it measures what it measures. Consider a bathroom scale. If the scale is in good condition, it will give virtually identical readings when the same object is repeatedly weighed. But if the scale is gradually losing its elasticity, repeated weighings will give different values. If it does this, we throw away the scale. It has proved to be unreliable.

The same logic underlies test reliability. One way of assessing this is by administering the same test twice to the same group of subjects, with, say, a few weeks in between. The correlation between test and retest scores will then be an index of the test's reliability.

One trouble with the **test-retest method** is that the performance on the retest may be affected by what the subject learned the first time around. For example, some people may look up the answers to questions they missed or avoid slip-ups they made the first time. To avoid these problems testers sometimes develop **alternative forms** of a test; reliability is then assessed by using one form on one occasion and another on a second.

Most standard psychological tests now in use have **reliability coefficients** (that is, test-retest correlations or correlations between alternative forms) in the .90s or in the high .80s. Tests with lower reliability are of little practical use in making decisions about enduring characteristics of individuals.

VALIDITY

High reliability alone does not guarantee that a test is a good measuring rod. Even more critical is a test's **validity,** which is most simply defined as the extent to which the test measures what it is supposed to measure. Again consider the spring scale. If the spring is made of good steel, the scale may be highly reliable. But suppose someone decides to use this scale to measure length. This bizarre step will produce an instrument of high reliability but virtually no validity. It measures some attribute very precisely and consistently but that attribute is not length. The weight scale is an accurate tool that happens to be irrelevant to the job at hand. As a test of length, the scale is invalid.

In the case of the spring scale, we can readily define the physical attribute that it is meant to measure and this lets us assess validity. But how can we define the psychological attribute that a mental test tries to assess?

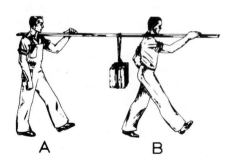

15.7 A test of mechanical comprehension *One of the items asks, "Which man carries more weight?" (Sample item from the Bennett Test of Mechanical Comprehension; courtesy of The Psychological Corporation)*

Predictive validity One approach is to consider the test's **predictive validity,** its ability to predict future performance. If a test claims to measure scholastic aptitude, a score on that test should predict later school or college performance. The same holds for tests of vocational aptitude, which ought to predict how people later succeed on the job. One index of a test's validity is the success with which it makes such predictions. This is usually measured by the correlation between the test score and some appropriate criterion. For scholastic aptitude, a common criterion is the grade-point average the student later attains. For vocational aptitude, it is some measure of later job proficiency. For example, aptitude tests for salespeople might be validated against their sales records.

Validity coefficients (that is, the correlations between test scores and criteria) for scholastic aptitude are generally in the neighborhood of .50 or .60, which means that the prediction is far from perfect. This is hardly surprising. For one thing, the tests probably don't provide a perfect index of one's "capacity" (ignoring for the time being just what this capacity might be). But even if they did, we would not expect validity coefficients of 1.00, for we all know that school grades depend on many factors in addition to ability (for example, motivation).

Construct validity Predictive validity is not the only way of assessing whether a test measures what it claims to measure. Another approach is to establish that the test has **construct validity** (Cronbach and Meehl, 1955). This is the extent to which the performance on the test fits into a theoretical scheme—or construct—about the attribute the test tries to measure. For example, suppose someone tries to develop a test to assess behavioral tendencies toward depression (see Chapter 18). The validity of such a test would not be established by correlating it with any one factor, such as feelings of helplessness. Instead, the investigator would try to relate the test to a whole network of hypotheses about depression. To the extent that the results do indeed fit into this larger pattern, they confer construct validity on the test. Thus present-day chemical tests of pregnancy have both construct and predictive validity. They have construct validity because modern medical science knows enough about the hormonal changes during pregnancy to understand why the chemical reacts as it does. They also have predictive validity, for they correlate almost perfectly with the highly visible manifestations of pregnancy that appear a short time later.

STANDARDIZATION

To evaluate a test, we need another item of information in addition to its reliability and validity. We have to know something about the group on which the test was **standardized.** Suppose we learn that Rita's verbal aptitude score is 130. This number by itself provides very little information. It can, however, be interpreted by comparing it with the scores obtained by other people. These other scores provide the **norms** against which an individual's test scores are evaluated. To obtain these norms, the test is first administered to a large sample of the population on which the test is to be used. This initial group is the **standardization sample.** A crucial requirement in using tests is the comparability between the subjects who are tested and the standardization sample that yields the norms. If these two are drawn from different populations (an extreme example would be children versus adults), the test scores may not be interpretable.

UTILITY

There is one final measure of the worth of a mental test, even when the test has already been judged to be adequately valid, reliable, and standardized. This concerns the test's *utility:* Is the test worth the time, energy, and cost required to admininster it? Suppose we have two tests of shyness, A and B. Both are well-standardized, but while test A has validity and reliability coefficients over .90, test B has coefficients of only .80. Test A appears to be better than test B, but there is a catch: Test A takes three days and costs $1,000 to administer, while test B is a quick ten-minute questionnaire that only costs $30. The benefits of discovering just exactly how shy you are may not be worth the additional $970; you may be perfectly happy with a ballpark result that is obtained faster and costs very much less.

USING TESTS FOR SELECTION

■ Suppose we have a test of good reliability, reasonable validity, and satisfactory utility. How will it be used? One important application in our society is as a selection device. A well-known example is an aptitude test for pilot training developed by the Army Air Force during World War II. A large number of separate subtests were constructed for this purpose, including tests of motor coordination, reaction time, perceptual skills, and general intellectual ability. These subtests were administered to over 185,000 men who went through pilot training. The initial question was how each of these subtests correlated with the criterion—success or failure in training. The scores of each subtest were then combined to produce a composite score that gave the best estimate of the criterion. The use of this composite pilot aptitude test score led to an appreciable improvement in trainee selection. Without the test, the failure rate was 24 percent. By using the test to identify promising candidates, the failure rate was cut to 10 percent. This was accomplished by setting a *cutoff score* on the test below which no applicant was accepted (Flanagan, 1947).

Given a reasonable validity coefficient, the use of tests evidently helps to reduce the number of selection errors. The overall number of such errors declines as the validity coefficient of the test increases. But some errors will always be present, for validity coefficients are never at 1.00; in fact, most vocational aptitude testers count themselves lucky if they manage to obtain validity correlations of .40 or .50.

INTELLIGENCE TESTING

FOCUS QUESTIONS

■ How did Binet and Simon view intelligence, and how did this perspective influence their design of the first formal test of intelligence?

■ What levels of functioning are typical of mild, moderate, severe, and profound degrees of mental retardation? What degree of mental retardation is most common?

■ How do intelligence-test scores change over the life span? Why were the early studies faulty in claiming precipitous declines after age twenty?

■ Which intellectual abilities are most likely to decline with age, which most likely to be retained?

What is *intelligence?* In a crude sense, of course, we all have some notion of what the term refers to. The dictionary is full of adjectives that distinguish levels of intellectual functioning such as bright and dull, quick-witted and slow. Intelligence tests try to get at some attribute (or attributes) that roughly corresponds to such distinctions. One might think that the design of these tests began with a precise conception of what it was they were meant to test. But this was not the case. There was no consensus as to a definition of intelligence, and those definitions that were offered were usually so broad and all-inclusive as to be of little use. Intelligence was said to be a capacity, but what is it a capacity for? Is it a capacity for learning, for transfer, for abstract thinking, for judgment, comprehension, reason, or perhaps all of these? There was no agreement. Edward Thorndike suggested that intelligence might be defined "as the quality of mind . . . in respect to which Aristotle, Plato, Thucydides, and the like differed most from Athenian idiots of their day" (Thorndike, 1924). While this seemed sensi-

Alfred Binet *(Courtesy of the National Library of Medicine)*

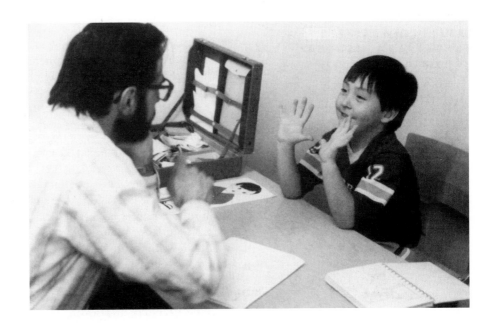

A boy taking the Stanford-Binet (Form L-M)   *(Photograph by Mimi Forsyth/ Monkmeyer)*

ble enough, it hardly went beyond the intuitive notions people had long before psychologists appeared on the scene.

MEASURING INTELLIGENCE

Given the difficulty in defining intelligence, devising tests for this hard-to-define attribute was an undertaking of a rather different sort from constructing a specialized aptitude test for prospective pilots. The pilot aptitude test has a rather clear-cut validity criterion. But what is the best validity criterion for intelligence tests? Since the nature of intelligence is unclear, we can't be sure of what the appropriate validity criterion might be.

But our theoretical ignorance notwithstanding, we do have intelligence tests and many of them. They were developed to fulfill certain practical needs. We may not understand exactly what it is that they assess, but the test consumers—schools, armies, industries—want them even so. The fact is that for many practical purposes these tests work quite well.

TESTING INTELLIGENCE IN CHILDREN

The pioneering step in intelligence testing was taken by a French psychologist, Alfred Binet (1857–1911). As so often in the field of individual differences, the impetus came from the world of practical affairs. By the turn of the century, compulsory elementary education was the rule among the industrialized nations. Large numbers of schoolchildren had to be dealt with, and some of them seemed untalented or even mentally retarded. If they were indeed retarded, it appeared best to send them to special schools. But mere backwardness was not deemed sufficient to justify this action; perhaps a child's prior education had been poor, or perhaps the child suffered from some illness. In 1904, the French minister of public instruction appointed a special committee, including Binet, and asked it to look into this matter. The committee concluded that there was a need for an objective diagnostic instrument to assess each child's intellectual state and to determine which pupils needed special programs. Much of what we now know about the measurement of intelligence comes from Binet's efforts to satisfy this need.

Intelligence as a general cognitive capacity   Binet and his collaborator, Théophile Simon, started with the premise that intelligence is a rather general attribute that manifests itself in many spheres of cognitive functioning. This view led them to construct a test that included many tasks that varied in both content and difficulty—copying a drawing, repeating a string of digits, recognizing coins and making change, explaining absurdities. The child's performance on all these subtests yielded a composite score. Later studies showed that this composite measure correlated with the child's school grades and with the teacher's evaluations of the child's intelligence. The test evidently had some predictive validity.

The intelligence quotient, IQ   Binet made another assumption about intelligence. He believed that it develops with age until maturity is reached. This fits in with our intuitive notions. We know that an average six-year-old is no intellectual match for an average nine-year-old. It's not just that she knows less; she's not as smart. This conception provided the basis for the test's scoring system. Binet and Simon first gave their test to a standardization sample composed of children of varying ages whose test performance provided the norms. Binet and Simon noted which items were passed by the average six-year-old, which by the average nine-year-old, and so on. (Items that were passed by younger but not by older children were excluded.)

This classification of the test items generated a ladder of tasks in which each rung corresponded to subtests that were passed by the average child of a given age. Testing a child's intelligence was thus tantamount to a determination of how high the child could ascend this ladder before the tasks finally became too difficult. The rung she attained indicated her **mental age** (usually abbreviated MA). If she successfully coped with all items passed by the average eight-year-old and failed all those passed by the average nine-year-old, her MA was said to be eight years.

The MA assesses an absolute level of cognitive capacity. To determine whether a child is "bright" or "dull" one has to compare her MA with her chronological age (CA). To the extent that her MA exceeds her CA, we regard the child as "bright" or advanced; the opposite is true if the MA is below the CA. But a particular lag or advance clearly has different import depending upon the child's age. To cope with this difficulty, a German psychologist, William Stern (1871–1938), proposed the use of a ratio measure, the **intelligence quotient** or **IQ.** This is computed by dividing the MA by the CA. The resulting quotient is multiplied by 100 to get rid of decimal points. Thus,

$$IQ = MA/CA \times 100.$$

By definition, an IQ of 100 indicates average intelligence; it means that the child's MA is equivalent to his CA and thus to the average score attained by his age-mates. By the same token, an IQ greater than 100 indicates that the child is above average, an IQ of less than 100 that he is below average.

Stern's quotient measure has various drawbacks. The major problem is that the top rung of Binet's mental age ladder was sixteen (in some later revisions of the test the ceiling was higher). In some ways this makes good sense, for intelligence does not grow forever, any more than height does. But since CAs keep on rising beyond the MA ceiling, the IQ (defined as a quotient) cannot help but decline. Consider the IQ of an adult. If her CA is 48 and her MA is 16, the use of the standard computation results in an IQ of 33 (16/48 × 100 = 33), a score that indicates severe mental retardation—an obvious absurdity.

Eventually a new approach was adopted. In the last analysis, an intelligence score indicates how an individual stands in relation to an appropriate comparison sample—his own age-mates. The intelligence quotient expresses this comparison as a ratio, but there are more direct measures of getting at the same thing. One example is an individual's ***percentile rank,*** that is, the proportion of persons in the comparison group whose score is below his. A more commonly used measure that provides the same information is the ***deviation IQ.*** We will not go into the details of how this measure is arrived at; suffice it to say that an IQ of 100 indicates a score equal to the average of the comparison sample (and thus a percentile rank of 50); that for most standard tests, IQs of 85 and 115 indicate percentile ranks of about 16 and 84, and IQs of 70 and 130 percentile ranks of 2 and 98.

TESTING INTELLIGENCE IN ADULTS

The Binet scales were originally meant for children, but demands soon arose for the assessment of adults' intelligence. This eventually led to the development of a test standardized on an adult population—the Wechsler Adult Intelligence Scale (Wechsler, 1958). This scale was divided into a verbal and a performance subtest. The verbal test includes items that assess general information, vocabulary, comprehension, and arithmetic. The performance test includes tasks that require the subject to assemble the cut-up parts of a familiar object so as to form the appropriate whole, to complete an incomplete drawing, or to rearrange a series of pictures so that they are in the proper sequence and tell a story (Figure 15.8).

COMPREHENSION
1. Why should we obey traffic laws and speed limits?
2. Why are antitrust laws necessary?
3. Why should we lock the doors and take the keys to our car when leaving the car parked?
4. What does this saying mean: "Kill two birds with one stone."

INFORMATION
1. Who wrote *Huckleberry Finn?*
2. Where is Finland?
3. At what temperature does paper burn?
4. What is entomology?

ARITHMETIC
1. How many 15¢ stamps can you buy for a dollar?
2. How many hours will it take a cyclist to travel 60 miles if he is going 12 miles an hour?

A. Verbal tests
3. A man bought a used stereo system for ³/₄ of what it cost new. He paid $225 for it. How much did it cost new?
4. Six men can finish a job in ten days. How many men will be needed to finish the job in two-and-a-half days?

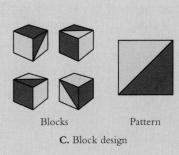

Blocks   Pattern

C. Block design

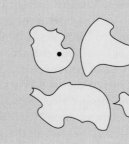

B. Picture completion

15.8   Test items similar to some in the Wechsler Adult Intelligence Scale. *(A) Verbal tests. These include tests of information, comprehension, and arithmetic. (B) Picture completion. The task is to note the missing part. (C) Block design. The materials consist of four blocks, which are all dark green on some sides, all light green on other sides, and half dark green and half light green on the rest of the sides. The subject is shown a pattern and has to arrange the four blocks to produce this design. (D) Object assembly. The task is to arrange the cut-up pieces to form a familiar object. (Courtesy of The Psychological Corporation)*

D. Object assembly

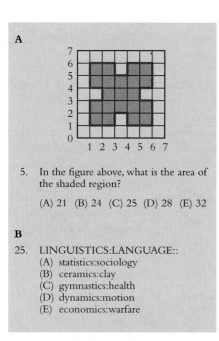

A

5. In the figure above, what is the area of
    the shaded region?

    (A) 21 (B) 24 (C) 25 (D) 28 (E) 32

B

25. LINGUISTICS:LANGUAGE::
     (A) statistics:sociology
     (B) ceramics:clay
     (C) gymnastics:health
     (D) dynamics:motion
     (E) economics:warfare

**15.9 Two items from the Scholastic
Aptitude Test (SAT)** *(Courtesy of the
College Entrance Examination Board and
the Educational Testing Service)*

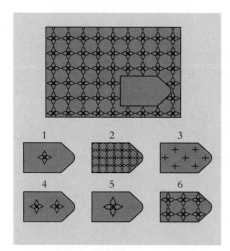

**15.10 An example item from the Raven
Progressive Matrices Test** *The task is to
select the alternative that fits into the empty
slot above. (Courtesy of H. K. Lewis)*

GROUP TESTS

Both the Binet and the Wechsler scales are administered individually—a lengthy
and expensive business. This economic fact of life led to the development of
group tests of various cognitive and scholastic aptitudes, usually of the paper-
and-pencil multiple-choice format. Some examples are the Scholastic Aptitude
Test (SAT), taken by most college applicants, and the Graduate Record
Examination (GRE), a more difficult version of the SAT designed for applicants
to graduate schools (Figure 15.9). A test that emphasizes abstract, nonverbal
intellectual ability is the Progressive Matrices Test (Figure 15.10).

SOME NEW DEVELOPMENTS IN INTELLIGENCE TESTING

A new test for children In recent years, a new test for children has come to
prominence, the *Kaufman Assessment Battery for Children (K-ABC)*. Like virtually
all intelligence tests, this is an outgrowth of those devised by Binet and Wechsler. But it has two novel aspects. To begin with, its construction is based on
some modern formulations that try to understand intelligence within the conceptual framework of information processing (see Chapters 7, 8, and 13). Some
of its subtests assess the child's capacity for sequential cognitive processing, for
example, his ability to recall a number of digits in the same sequence as he heard
them or to copy the exact sequence in which the examiner tapped the table
with his hand. Others assess his ability to process simultaneously presented information; for example, his ability to select the picture that best completes a
visual analogy or to recall the location of items arranged randomly on a page.
Another novelty is that the test gives particular attention to the assessment of
handicapped children and is appropriate for cultural and linguistic minorities.
Toward that end, it includes a nonverbal scale with questions that are presented
in pantomime and have to be answered with various motor gestures. This scale
is particularly useful for testing children who cannot speak English (or can't
speak it well) or who are hearing-impaired, and its scores seem to be less
affected by sociocultural conditions than those of the Stanford-Binet or of
Wechsler's scales for children (Anastasi, 1984, 1985; Coffman, 1985; Kaufman,
Kamphaus, and Kaufman, 1985; Page, 1985).

AN AREA OF APPLICATION: MENTAL RETARDATION

■ How valid are intelligence tests? One way of answering this question is by
looking at their effectiveness in predicting school success, which as we've
seen is fairly good, with correlations of around +.50. But another criterion
grows out of Binet's original purpose, which was to design an instrument for the
diagnosis of mental retardation. How well did he and his followers succeed? On
the whole, the tests seem to perform this function rather well, at least as a first
step toward diagnosis. The usual demarcation for retardation is an IQ of about
70 or below. Thus defined, about 2.5 percent of the population of the United
States would be regarded as retarded (Grossman, 1983). But test performance is
by no means the only criterion of retardation. Equally important are social and
cultural competence, the ability to learn and cope with the demands of society,
to take care of oneself, to earn a living. This competence obviously depends in
part upon the nature of the society in which a person lives. A complex technological culture like ours puts a higher premium on various intellectual skills than
does an agrarian society. Someone classified as mildly retarded in twentieth-

century North America probably would have managed perfectly well in, say, feudal Europe.

A widely used classification system distinguishes several degrees of retardation: mild (IQ of approximately 50–55 to 70), moderate (35–40 to 50–55), severe (20–25 to 35–40), and profound (20–25 and below). The more severe the retardation, the less frequently it occurs: In 100 retarded persons, one would expect the degree of retardation to be mild in 90, moderate in 6, severe in 3, and profound in 1 of the cases (Robinson and Robinson, 1970).

Table 15.2 presents a description of the general level of intellectual functioning in each of these categories at various ages. Among other things, the table shows that mentally retarded people do not have to be excluded from useful participation in society. This is especially true for those whose degree of retardation is mild, and they account for almost 90 percent of all the cases. If provided with appropriate education and training, such people can ultimately achieve an acceptable level of adjustment in adult life (Tyler, 1965).

TABLE 15.2 CHARACTERISTICS OF THE MENTALLY RETARDED*

Degree of retardation	IQ range	Level of functioning at school age (6–20 years)	Level of functioning in adulthood (21 years and over)
Mild	50–55 to approx. 70	Can learn academic skills up to approximately sixth-grade level by late teens; can be guided toward social conformity.	Can usually achieve social and vocational skills adequate to maintain self-support, but may need guidance and assistance when under unusual social or economic stress.
Moderate	35–40 to 50–55	Can profit from training in social and occupational skills; unlikely to progress beyond second-grade level in academic subjects; may learn to travel alone in familiar places.	May achieve self-maintenance in unskilled or semiskilled work under sheltered conditions; needs supervision and guidance when under mild social or economic stress.
Severe	20–25 to 35–40	Can talk or learn to communicate; can be trained in elemental health habits; profits from systematic habit training.	May contribute partially to self-maintenance under complete supervision; can develop self-protection skills at a minimum useful level in controlled environment.
Profound	below 20–25	Some motor development present; may respond to minimal or limited training in self-help.	Some motor and speech development; may achieve very limited self-care; needs nursing care.

*Descriptive terms and score intervals are from a classificatory system recommended by the American Association for Mental Deficiency.
SOURCE: Grossman, 1983, p. 13.

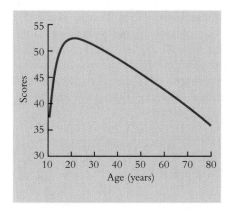

15.11 Mental test scores as related to age *The scores are based on comparisons of different age groups. They are expressed in units that allow comparisons of different tests and are based on averaged results of three different studies. (After Jones and Kaplan, 1945)*

INTELLIGENCE AND AGE

What is the relation between intelligence-test performance and age? To be sure, age was the basis on which Binet standardized his original test, but he only used the age range of three to sixteen years. Many investigators have tried to plot the growth of intelligence from middle childhood to old age. To do so, they administered the same test to people in different age groups matched by sex and socioeconomic level. Figure 15.11 presents a composite curve based on several such studies. The figure should hearten the young and bring gloom to all who are past age twenty. There is a sharp increase in mental ability between ages ten and twenty, and an accelerating decline thereafter.

Later investigators (perhaps prompted by the fact that they were over thirty) concluded that the situation could not be as bleak as that. They argued that the steep decline in intelligence across the adult years could be the by-product of an irrelevant factor: On the average, the older age groups in these studies had a lower level of education. Such a difference might have been present even though the groups were matched by years of schooling, for curricula have probably improved over time. One way of getting around this difficulty is by shifting from the ***cross-sectional*** method that compares people in different age groups to the ***longitudinal*** method in which the same people are tested at different ages. The results of such longitudinal studies suggest that age (or at least middle age) is not as deleterious to mental functioning as it seemed (Schaie and Strother, 1968; Schaie, 1979). There is a continued rise on tests for verbal meaning, for reasoning, and for educational aptitude until about age fifty. After this, there is a moderate decline.

It appears that the precipitous decline of intelligence with age shown in Figure 15.11 was an artifact; this was avoided by the longitudinal comparisons. But does this mean that there is no decline in intelligence until age sixty or even later? Further work has shown that it depends on just what abilities are being tested. Many facets of verbal abilities do show little decline until age seventy. The results of tests of vocabulary are even more encouraging to those of later years; there is no drop in vocabulary even at age eighty-five (Blum, Jarvik, and Clark, 1970). In contrast, nonverbal abilities tapped by such tests as the Progressive Matrices decline earlier, usually around age forty (Green, 1969). The most pronounced drops are found for tests that depend on quick recall, especially when there is no memory organization available to help retrieval. An example from everyday life is memory for names, whose gradual worsening is bemoaned by many persons as they get older. An example from the laboratory is the word fluency test, in which the subject has two minutes to write down as many words as he can think of that start with a particular letter. Such mental calisthenics are best left to the young; declines in word fluency are very steep and are seen as early as thirty (Schaie and Strother, 1968).

Some authors believe that the age curves obtained for different subtests of intelligence reflect an important distinction between two underlying intellectual abilities (Cattell, 1963). One is ***fluid intelligence,*** which is the ability to deal with essentially new problems. The other is ***crystallized intelligence,*** which is the repertoire of information, cognitive skills, and strategies acquired by the application of fluid intelligence to various fields. Examples of tasks that emphasize fluid intelligence are scrambled sentences and number series. Consider the set of words shown below:

Tree pick an climbed man our apple the to

When a person is asked to rearrange these words to make a meaningful sentence, she has to reason it out. Here fluency, speed, and flexibilty will help out greatly. The same holds for number series, such as the one below in which the task is to find the number that is next in the series:

$$3 \quad 8 \quad 12 \quad 15 \quad 17$$

In contrast, tasks that primarily rely on crystallized intelligence are exemplified by tests of vocabulary (e.g., what does "amanuensis" mean?) or of calculation (e.g., $6 \times 7 - 4 \times 5 = ?$). Such tasks depend less on processing speed and more on stored knowledge.

According to the theory, fluid intelligence declines with age, beginning in middle adulthood or earlier. But crystallized intelligence does not drop off. On the contrary, it continues to grow until old age as long as the person is in an intellectually stimulating environment. From the point of view of actual functioning in middle age and beyond, the drop in the one ability may be more than compensated for by the increase in the other. The older person has "appropriated the collective intelligence of the culture for his own use" (Horn and Cattell, 1967). By so doing, he has not only amassed a large store of knowledge, but he has also developed better ways of organizing this knowledge, of approaching problems, and of filing new information away for later use.

These cognitive achievements are similar to those we discussed in Chapter 8 in which we considered the distinction between masters and apprentices. The masters have chunked and organized the material at a different level than the apprentices. On balance, then, the slight loss in fluid intelligence can be tolerated if made up for by an increase in crystallized intelligence.

WHAT IS INTELLIGENCE? THE PSYCHOMETRIC APPROACH

FOCUS QUESTIONS

- What is the psychometric approach to understanding intelligence?

- What is Spearman's g factor, and what does it imply about the nature of intelligence? What is an alternative view of intelligence?

We have seen that intelligence tests were developed even though there was no consensus on a definition of intelligence and thus no clear-cut validity criterion for any test that claims to measure it. But even so, many psychologists would agree that such instruments as the Stanford-Binet and the Wechsler tests do distinguish people in ways that correspond with our intuitive conceptions of the term *intelligence*. There is no doubt that either scale would easily differentiate between Aristotle and the Athenian village idiot. Can we get any further than this?

According to one group of investigators, further inquiries into the nature of intelligence can build on the fact that intelligence tests do make some distinctions between people and that these distinctions do fit our initial sense of what intelligence is about. These investigators believe that we can refine our knowledge of the nature of intelligence by a careful further study of these distinctions. This line of reasoning underlies the **psychometric approach** to the study of intelligence. It amounts to a bootstrap operation in which one scrutinizes the results provided by the measuring instrument in order to find out what the instrument really measures.

THE STRUCTURE OF MENTAL ABILITIES

■ To understand the psychometric approach, consider how it addresses a central question about intelligence: Is intelligence a unitary ability? In principle one could imagine several kinds of mental ability that are quite unrelated. Perhaps different cognitive tasks draw on distinctly different cognitive gifts. It may also be that the truth is in between, that human intellectual abilities are composed of both general and more particular capacities. How can we decide among these alternatives?

The psychometric approach tries to answer these questions by starting with people's scores on various tests. These scores presumably reflect some underlying abilities—perhaps one, perhaps several. But these underlying capacities are not observable directly; they can only be inferred from the scores. Students of psychometrics have tried to perform this inference by looking at the intercorrelations among different tests.

To get an intuitive idea of this general approach, consider a man who looks at a lake and sees what appear to be serpentlike parts:

A

He can entertain various hypotheses. One is that all visible parts belong to one huge sea monster (a hypothesis that is analogous to the assumption that there is a unitary intellectual ability):

B

He might also assume that there are several such beasts (analogous to separate mental abilities):

C

Or finally, he might believe that there are as many sea animals as there are visible parts (analogous to the hypothesis that every test measures a totally different ability):

D

How can he choose among these alternatives, given that he has no way of peering below the waters? His best bet is to wait and watch how the serpentine parts change over time and space. If he does this, he can find out which parts go together. If all parts move jointly (B), the most reasonable interpretation is that they all belong to one huge sea monster. (For the purposes of our example, we will assume that sea serpents are severely arthritic and are unable to move their body portions separately.) If the first part goes with the second, while the third goes with the fourth (C), there are presumably two smaller creatures. If all parts move separately (D), the best bet is that there are as many sea serpents as there are visible parts. In effect, our sea-serpent watcher has studied a correlation pattern; this pattern allows him to infer the invisible structure (or structures) under the surface.

SPEARMAN AND THE CONCEPT OF GENERAL INTELLIGENCE

The psychometric equivalent of the joint movements of sea-serpent portions is the correlation pattern among different tests of mental abilities. As an example, consider the correlations among four subtests of the Wechsler Adult Scale: information *(I)*, comprehension *(C)*, arithmetic *(A)*, and vocabulary *(V)*. These intercorrelations are all quite high, which suggests that there may be a common factor that runs through all four of these subtests. In essence, those people with a greater fund of information turn out to be exactly those people who are likely to get higher scores in comprehension. They are also probably better at arithmetic, and they generally have a larger vocabulary as well. Conversely, those people who do poorly on any one of these tests, are also likely to do poorly on the others. This makes it plausible to assume that these subtests share something in common, that they all measure the same underlying attribute. This was exactly the conclusion reached by the English psychologist Charles Spearman (1863–1945), who developed the first version of **factor analysis,** a statistical technique by which one can "extract" this common factor that all of the various tests share. In Spearman's view, this factor was best described as **general intelligence,** or **g,** a mental attribute that is called upon in any intellectual task a person has to perform. According to Spearman, if one has a lot of *g,* this will help in any intellectual endeavor. If *g,* however, is in short supply, intellectual performance will suffer across the board.

GROUP-FACTOR THEORIES

Spearman's theory of intelligence is sometimes described as "monarchic." As he saw it, there is one factor, *g,* that reigns supreme over all intellectual functions. But this view was soon challenged by other investigators. They argued that the intercorrelations among test scores are better explained by a *set* of underlying mental abilities rather than by one overarching *g*-factor. Spearman called this **group-factor theory** an "oligarchic" conception of intelligence, since it views intelligence as the composite of separate abilities without a sovereign capacity that enters into each. L. L. Thurstone (1887–1955), who originated most of the concepts and techniques that underlie this approach, regarded these group factors as the "primary mental abilities." Some of the more important of these are spatial, numerical, verbal, and reasoning abilities.

WHAT IS INTELLIGENCE? BEYOND IQ

FOCUS QUESTIONS

- What is tacit knowledge, and how might it explain nonacademic intelligence?

- How might membership in a non-Western culture distort the outcome of intelligence tests?

Bodily-kinesthetic intelligence *The incredible precision of a ballet dancer's movements is captured in this time-lapse photograph. According to Howard Gardner, the ability to learn such complex motor patterns is one of several "multiple intelligences" that are largely independent of each other. (Photograph © Globus Studios/The Stock Market)*

The tests devised by Binet and his successors surely tap some aspects of what is ordinarily meant by intelligence. But no less surely some other aspects of its meaning are left out, and many of these aspects concern people's competence in dealing with the real world in which they live. People with high IQs are likely to get good grades in school, but some of them may lack "common sense" or "street smarts," or "know how," as exemplified in the stock figure of the impractical, absent-minded professor. A related ability is social competence: the ability to persuade others and to judge their moods and desires. Shrewd salespeople have this ability and so do successful politicians, even if they don't have the most spectacular IQ.

A demonstration of the separation of academic and nonacademic intelligence comes from a study of experienced racetrack handicappers who were asked to predict the favorites and their probable pay-offs in forthcoming races. This is a tricky mental task that involves complex reasoning in which such facts as track records, jockeys, track conditions, sires and dams of the horses, and so on have to be juggled and put together. On the face of it, one might suppose that the ability to perform such mental calculations is just what intelligence tests do measure. But the results proved otherwise, for the handicappers' success turned out to be completely unrelated to their IQs (Ceci and Liker, 1986).

PRACTICAL INTELLIGENCE

Some attempts have been made to develop tests for nonacademic, practical intelligence. Robert Sternberg and Richard Wagner asked business executives to rate the relative importance of various skills in heading up a company department (e.g., delegating authority, promoting communication). They found that success at the skills the executives rated most highly correlated rather well with various criteria of business success, such as percentage salary increase, and that their responses correlated only weakly with IQ if at all (Wagner, 1987; Wagner and Sternberg, 1987; Sternberg and Wagner, 1993). Sternberg and Wagner believe that this demonstrates a kind of practical intelligence that differs from the abilities measured by a standard intelligence test. In their view, this practical intelligence is based on what they call *tacit knowledge*—knowledge that is never explicitly taught but picked up along the way and that some people acquire to a greater degree than others. But it's important to realize that this practical intelligence is specific to a particular domain. The business executive acquires tacit knowledge that is relevant to running a company, but not to navigating a ship or handicapping horses.

This is probably the same phenomenon we encountered when discussing chunking in masters and beginners (see Chapter 8). Chess grandmasters can readily beat "mere" experts because they've acquired larger and better chess chunks—tacit knowledge in this very specific and specialized domain.

THE NOTION OF MULTIPLE INTELLIGENCES

15.12 Drawing ability in a retarded savant *A drawing by Nadia, a severely retarded child with remarkable drawing ability. This horse was drawn when she was four years old. (From Selfe, 1977)*

A different attempt to expand the notion of intelligence to embrace abilities outside of the traditional academic domain is Howard Gardner's concept of ***multiple intelligences*** (Gardner, 1983). Like those who argue in favor of group-factor theories, Gardner believes that there are several essential, independent mental capacities. He lists six such abilities (which he calls "intelligences"): linguistic, logical-mathematical, spatial, musical, bodily-kinesthetic, and personal intelligence. The first three are familiar enough, for they are assessed by most standard intelligence scales (and emerged as primary factors in Thurstone's group-factor analyses), and everyone knows pretty much what's meant by musical ability. By bodily-kinesthetic intelligence, Gardner refers to the ability to learn and create complex motor patterns, as in dancers and skilled athletes. By personal intelligence, he refers to the ability to understand others and oneself.

One line of evidence for Gardner's claim that these "intelligences" are largely independent of each other comes from studies of different brain lesions, which may affect some abilities (e.g., language) while leaving others unimpaired (e.g., mathematical ability). Thus certain lesions will make a person unable to recognize drawings (spatial intelligence), while others will make him unable to perform a sequence of movements (bodily-kinesthetic intelligence), and still others will produce major changes in personality (personal intelligence).

Further arguments for Gardner's theory of multiple intelligences comes from the study of ***retarded savants*** (formerly called *idiot savants*). These are mentally retarded people who have some remarkable talent that seems out of keeping with their low level of general intelligence. Some display unusual artistic talent (see Figure 15.12). Others are calendar calculators; they are promptly able to come up with the right answer if asked questions like, "What was the date of the third Monday in 1682?" (see Figure 15.13). Still others have unusual mechanical talents, such as the ability to build a functional full-sized merry-go-round or scale models of ships. And yet others have unusual musical skills as in the case of a woman who could play "Happy Birthday" in the style of different composers (Hill, 1978).

Some of the evidence Gardner cites in support of his general contention of independent intelligences can be questioned. For example, the incidence of

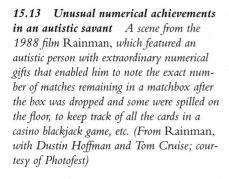

15.13 Unusual numerical achievements in an autistic savant *A scene from the 1988 film* Rainman, *which featured an autistic person with extraordinary numerical gifts that enabled him to note the exact number of matches remaining in a matchbox after the box was dropped and some were spilled on the floor, to keep track of all the cards in a casino blackjack game, etc. (From* Rainman, *with Dustin Hoffman and Tom Cruise; courtesy of Photofest)*

"Son, your mother is a remarkable woman."

retarded savants is quite low, perhaps one or two in every thousand institutional-ized retarded persons (Hill, 1978). Why are such cases so rare if the various "intelligences" are really as independent as Gardner claims? Nor is it clear that the abilities of many savants are quite as extraordinary as they seem at first. Thus many calendar calculators do not possess special numerical or mathematical skills. They may do wonders with dates, but they are unable to add or subtract single digit numbers. And the savant who could play "Happy Birthday" in the style of Mozart, Verdi, or Schubert may not have been quite as musically cre-ative as she appeared. According to one author, she may have played some appropriate bass lines she knew from memory and adjusted them to fit the har-mony (Viscott, 1979). In short, while the accomplishments of these savants are unusual enough (given that they are mentally retarded), they don't come close to the musical, or artistic, or mathematical achievements of even lesser com-posers, artists, and mathematicians, who are generally quite intelligent in the ordinary sense of the term. That Beethoven and Michelangelo represent the absolute top of musical and artistic ability is self-evident, but a glance at the let-ters and diaries of these giants indicates that their verbal and logical intelligence was also far from negligible, which tends to undermine the claim that these var-ious capacities are truly independent.

Whatever the ulitmate verdict on Gardner's theory, there is no doubt that he has performed a very valuable service by drawing attention to a whole set of abilities that are all too often ignored by our society, which values (and perhaps overvalues) the kind of intelligence that helps people succeed in our education-al system. Still, while it is quite clear that these various abilities should be highly esteemed, it is not clear that the same term—intelligence—should be applied to all of them.

THE CULTURAL CONTEXT OF INTELLIGENCE

■ Sternberg's work on practical intelligence and Gardner's on multiple intel-ligences point up certain limitations of standard intelligence tests. These limitations become more glaring when trying to assess intelligence in members of other cultures. To begin with, many standard intelligence tests emphasize quick and decisive responses. But not all cultures share our Western preoccupa-tion with speed (or our taste for fast food). To give just two examples, Indians and Native Americans place a higher value on being deliberate; in effect they'd rather be right than quick. In addition, they prefer to qualify, or to say "I don't know" or "I'm not sure," unless they're absolutely certain of their answer. But such deliberations and hedging won't help their test scores; on standard intelligence tests you get more points if you guess (Sinha, 1983; Triandis, 1989).

Further factors have to do with formal Western schooling, which teaches the students the kinds of questions teachers (and tests) tend to ask. We saw previously that unschooled Kpelle subjects in Liberia group objects, not according to an abstract semantic category (e.g., tools vs. foods) but rather on the basis of the concrete situation in which the objects would be used together (e.g., a knife with an orange; see Chapter 13). A similar concreteness is seen in the response of an unschooled Russian peasant who was asked: "From Shakhimardan to Vuadil it takes three hours on foot, while to Fergana it is six hours. How much time does it take to go on foot from Vuadil to Fergana?" The reply was: "No, it's six hours from Vuadil to Shakhimardan. You're wrong. . . . It's far and you wouldn't get there in three hours." (Luria, 1976, quoted in Sternberg, 1990, p. 229). If this had been a question on a standard intelligence test, the poor peasant would have scored poorly. But why? He had not gone to school, so he didn't know that questions of this sort are trying to get at arithmetical reasoning and nothing else, that it doesn't matter what the actual distances between the towns really are. It turned out that he was quite able to perform the relevant calculation, but couldn't accept the form in which the question was presented.

All of this makes it clear that we have to be very careful in applying the IQ measure. It is a useful instrument for predicting school success in Western cultures and probably reflects some important aspect of human cognitive functioning. But it does not reflect all such aspects. IQ can indicate an ability (or, if group factor theory is right, a set of abilities) that intelligence tests measure, and it does a pretty good job of predicting success in a Western school system. It can also indicate the speed and efficiency of various cognitive operations that are relevant to the tasks set in school. But ultimately IQ indicates mental competencies that can only be judged in their appropriate environmental and cultural context. (For further discussion, see Sternberg, 1985, 1990).

NATURE, NURTURE, AND IQ

FOCUS QUESTIONS

- Does the fact that twins have similar IQs imply that intelligence is hereditary? Why or why not?

- What evidence supports an environmental role in determining IQ?

- Does the fact that IQ appears to be genetically determined within a group imply that IQ differences between groups are due to heredity?

- Why should a hereditarian conclusion about racial or ethnic differences in IQ make little difference in social policy?

As we've seen, while intelligence tests do a pretty good job in predicting school success in Western cultures, there is no general agreement on just what it is that they really measure. But this state of affairs has not deterred psychologists—nor indeed, the general public—from making intelligence-test performance one of the major foci of the nature-nurture controversy, debated with a stormy passion rarely found in any other area of the discipline (see Block and Dworkin, 1976; Eysenck vs. Kamin, 1981; Fancher, 1987).

"Immigration Restriction. Prop Wanted"

Anti-immigration sentiment in the United States   *A cartoon that appeared in the January 23, 1903, issue of the* Philadelphia Inquirer *calling for more restrictive immigration laws. (Courtesy of the New York Public Library)*

SOME POLITICAL ISSUES

The vehemence of the debate over intelligence-test performance is understandable considering that mental testing is a field in which the concerns of the scientist impinge drastically upon those of the practical world. In our society, those who are well off tend to do better on intelligence tests than those who are disadvantaged. The same holds for their children. What accounts for this difference? There is some tendency for social groups to be biased in favor of different answers to this question. This bias was especially marked some eighty years ago when the prevailing social climate was much more conservative. Then—and to a lesser extent even now—advantaged groups were more likely to believe that intelligence is largely inherited. This assertion was certainly comforting to those who benefited from the status quo, since it suggested that they got what they "deserved."

In contrast, advocates for the disadvantaged took a different view. To begin with, they often disparaged the tests themselves, arguing that the tests are not fair to their own subculture. In addition, they argued that intellectual aptitudes are much more determined by nurture than nature. In their view, differences in intelligence, especially those between different ethnic and racial groups, are determined predominantly by environmental factors such as early home background and schooling. Seen in this light, the children of the poor obtain lower test scores, not because they inherit deficient genes, but rather because they inherit poverty.

These contrasting views led to different prescriptions for social policy. An example of the impact of a hereditarian bias is the rationale behind the United States' immigration policy between the two World Wars. The Immigration Act of 1924 set definite quotas to minimize the influx of what were thought to be biologically "weaker stocks," specifically those from southern and eastern Europe. To "prove" the genetic intellectual inferiority of these immigrants, a congressional committee pointed to the scores of these groups on the army intelligence test, which were indeed substantially below those attained by Americans of northern European ancestry.

In actual fact, these differences were primarily related to the length of time that the immigrants had been in the United States prior to the test; their average test scores rose with every year and became indistinguishable from native-born Americans after twenty years of residence in the United States. This result undermines the hypothesis of a hereditary difference in intelligence between, say, northern and eastern Europeans. But the congressional proponents of differential immigration quotas did not analyze the results so closely. They had their own reasons for restricting immigration, such as fears of competition from cheap labor. The theory that the excluded groups were innately inferior provided a convenient justification for their policies (Kamin, 1974).

A more contemporary example of the relation between psychological theory and social policy is the argument over the value of compensatory educational programs for preschool children from disadvantaged backgrounds. Such programs have been said to be failures because they often don't lead to improvement in later scholastic performance. Assuming this is true (and this is debatable), the question is why. A highly controversial paper by Arthur Jensen suggested that the difference in intellectual performance between the advantaged and disadvantaged groups is partially caused by a genetic difference between the groups. Given this hereditarian position, Jensen argued that environmental alterations can at best mitigate the group difference; they cannot abolish it (Jensen, 1969).

Jensen's thesis has been vehemently debated on many counts, some of which we will discuss below. For now, we will only note that the failure of any given program (assuming it was really a failure) does not prove the hereditarians' claim. Perhaps the preschool experience that was provided was not of the right sort; perhaps it was inadequate to counteract the overwhelming effects of ghetto life (Hunt, 1961). In any case, there is by now a growing consensus that Jensen and others have underestimated the effectiveness of preschool education on school performance in later years (Zigler and Berman, 1983). Such preschool experiences may or may not raise the children's intelligence-test scores. But regardless of their effect on IQ scores, these programs do have positive effects. Thus low-income children who have participated in such programs seem to perform more acceptably in later grades (from fourth to twelfth grades) than children who had no such experience; they are less likely to be held back in grade, less likely to drop out of school, and so on (Lazar and Darlington, 1982).

GENETIC FACTORS

■ Thus far, our emphasis has been on the social and political aspects of the nature-nurture issue in intelligence, the considerations that bias people to take one or another side of the issue. But what exactly are the facts? What is the evidence about the contributions of heredity and environment in producing differences within groups (for instance, among American whites) and between groups (for instance, between American whites and blacks)?

GENETIC TRANSMISSION

Before turning to the relationship between intelligence-test performance and genetic endowment, we must say a few words about the mechanisms that underlie the transmission of genetic characteristics from one generation to the next.

The mechanism of genetic transmission   Each organism starts life with a genetic blueprint, a set of instructions that steers its development from fertilized cell to mature animal or plant. The genetic commands are contained in the **chromosomes** in the cell's nucleus. In organisms that reproduce sexually, the chromosomes come in corresponding pairs, with one member of each pair contributed by each parent. In humans, there are twenty-three such chromosome pairs.

Every chromosome stores thousands of genetic commands each of which is biologically engraved in a **gene,** the unit of hereditary transmission. Any given gene is located at a particular place on a given chromosome. Since chromosomes come in pairs, both members of each pair have corresponding loci at which there are genes that carry instructions about the same bodily characteristic (for example, eye color). These two related genes—one contributed by each parent—may or may not be identical. Consider eye color. If both the genes for eye color are identical (blue-blue or brown-brown), there is no problem; the eye color will follow suit. But suppose they are different. Now the overt expression of the genetic blueprint depends upon still other relationships between the two members of the gene pair. In humans, the gene for brown eyes is **dominant;** it will exert its effect regardless of whether the other member of the gene pair calls for brown or blue eyes. In contrast, the gene for blue eyes is **recessive.** This recessive gene will lead to blue eyes only if there is an identical gene (that is, another gene for blue eyes) on the corresponding locus of the paired chromosome (see Figure 15.14).

Phenotype and genotype   A key distinction in any discussion of hereditary transmission is that between **phenotype** and **genotype.** The phenotype corresponds to the overt appearance of the organism—its actual structure and behavior. But this

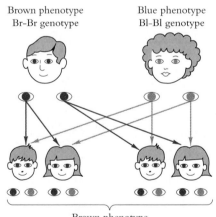

Brown phenotype
Br-Br genotype   Blue phenotype
Bl-Bl genotype

Brown phenotype
Br-Bl genotype

15.14   Phenotype and genotype in the transmission of eye color   *Eye color of the children of a brown-eyed and a blue-eyed parent if the brown-eyed parent's genotype is brown-brown. All of the children's eyes (phenotypes) will be brown, although their genotypes will be brown-blue. In the figure, genotypes are indicated by a pair of schematic eye-color genes under each face.*

479

phenotype is by no means equivalent to the organism's genotype, which describes the set of the relevant genes. There are several ways in which a genotype may be kept from overt (that is, phenotypic) expression. One depends on gene dominance, as we saw. Another is by the interaction between genotype and environment. This interaction is especially important during the early stages in the organism's development, since a particular genetic command can only be executed if certain physical characteristics (oxygen concentration, hormone levels, temperature) both inside and outside of the developing body are within a certain range.

As an example, consider the dark markings on the paws, tail, and eartips of a Siamese cat. These markings are not present at birth, but they appear gradually as the kitten matures. The genealogical records kept by cat breeders leave no doubt that these markings in the mature animal are almost entirely determined by heredity. But this does not mean that they emerge independently of the environment. These dark markings will only appear if the kitten's extremities are kept at their normal temperature, which happens to be lower than that of the rest of the animal's body. If the extremities are deliberately warmed during early kittenhood by such devices as leggings and tail and earmuffs, they will not turn darker—in apparent defiance of the creature's genotype (Ilyin and Ilyin, 1930). Similar findings have been obtained with some other animals (see Figure 15.15).

This example underlines the fact that genes do not operate in a vacuum. They are instructions to a developing organism, instructions that will be followed only within a given range of environmental conditions. It therefore makes no sense to talk of heredity alone or environment alone, for there is no trait that does not depend upon both. There can be no organism without a genotype, and this genotype cannot ever express itself independently of the environment.

The inheritance of psychological characteristics   It is obvious that many physical characteristics (e.g., height, eye color) are determined by heredity, but the same is true for many psychological characteristics as well. An important example is a severe form of mental retardation, ***phenylketonuria*** or ***PKU,*** that is determined by a single gene. In the United States, about one baby in every fifteen thousand is born with this defect. PKU is caused by a deficiency in an enzyme that allows the body to transform ***phenylalanine,*** an amino acid (a building block of proteins), into another amino acid. When this enzyme is missing, phenylalanine is instead converted into a toxic agent that accumulates in the infant's bloodstream and damages his developing nervous system. Analyses of the incidence of PKU among the siblings of afflicted children and among others in their family trees indicate that this disorder is produced by a single recessive gene.

Although PKU is of genetic origin, it can be treated by appropriate environmental intervention. The trick is a special diet that contains very little phenylalanine. If this diet is introduced at an early enough age, retardation can be minimized or avoided altogether.

This result demonstrates the fallacy of the popular belief that what is inherited is necessarily unchangeable. Genes lay down certain biochemical instructions

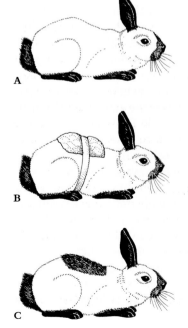

15.15   The effect of temperature on coat color   *Normally only the feet, tail, ears, and nose of the Himalayan rabbit are black (A). But when an ice pack is applied to a region of the back (B), the new fur grown at an artificially low temperature also comes in black (C). (After Winchester, 1977)*

that determine the development of a particular organ system. If we understand the genetic command clearly enough, we may eventually find ways to circumvent it. In the case of PKU, we are already on the way to doing so (McClearn and DeFries, 1973).

Polygenic inheritance   Hereditary traits produced by the action of one gene pair are usually all-or-none, such as being brown-eyed or being afflicted with PKU. But how can we explain the inheritance of attributes that vary continuously, such as height and intelligence? The answer is ***polygenic inheritance*** in which the trait is controlled not by one but by many gene pairs. Take height. Some gene pairs pull toward increased stature, others toward lesser stature; the individual's ultimate genetic potential for height (for now, ignoring environmental effects) is then determined by the combined action of all the height-controlling gene pairs. To the extent that intelligence (or any other psychological attribute that varies continuously) is partially determined by hereditary factors the same logic applies to it.

GENETICS AND IQ

How can we find out whether differences in human intelligence (at least as measured by intelligence tests) have a genetic basis? To do so, we have to infer the underlying genotypes from the observable phenotypic performance. One strategy is to examine the similarities between relatives, an approach that dates back to Francis Galton. Galton found that personal distinction (which he called "eminence" and measured by reputation) runs in families; eminent individuals were more likely to have eminent relatives than the average person (Galton, 1869). Similar results have been repeatedly obtained with intelligence-test scores. For example, the correlation between the IQs of children and parents, or between the IQs of siblings, runs in the neighborhood of +.45 (Bouchard and McGue, 1981). From Galton's perspective, such findings document the inheritance of mental ability. But the environmentalist has a ready reply. Consider eminence. The relatives of an eminent person obviously share his or her social, educational, and financial advantages. As a result, there is a similarity of environmental background, as well as an overlapping set of genes. The same argument applies to the interpretation of the correlations between the IQs of close relatives.

A similar problem arises in another connection. IQs tend to be fairly stable; the ten-year-old with an IQ of 130 will probably get a roughly similar score at age fifteen. Supporters of the genetic theory of intelligence have often argued that this constancy of the IQ shows that intelligence tests measure an inborn capacity, "native intelligence," which is an essentially unalterable characteristic of an individual and is genetically based. This argument has been used as a justification of such educational practices as early assignment to one or another school track. But IQ constancy is no proof that intelligence is fixed or inborn. To the extent that this constancy occurs, it only demonstrates that a child tends to maintain her relative standing among her age-mates over time. This may be because of a genetically given attribute that remains unchanged with age. But it may also be because the child's environmental advantages (or disadvantages) stay pretty much the same as time goes on. If a child is born in a slum, the odds are pretty good that she will still be there at twelve; the same holds if she is born in a palace. Once again, the evidence is inconclusive.

During the last fifty years, however, psychologists have developed a variety of research designs to disentangle hereditary and environmental factors. We will consider two main attempts to accomplish this end: the study of twins and the study of adopted children.

*15.16 Identical twins Identical twins
tend to be very much alike in both physical
and mental characteristics. The photo shows
two such twins, Faye and Kaye Young, who
both played professional basketball for the
New York Stars. As Faye put it: "We've always participated the same amount of time
and done the same things and have progressed
the same." (Photograph © Kathryn
McLaughlin Abbe and Frances McLaughlin
Gill, 1980)*

Twin studies   **Identical twins** originate from a single fertilized egg that splits into
two exact replicas that then develop into two genetically identical individuals
(see Figure 15.16). In contrast, **fraternal twins** arise from two different fertilized
eggs, when each of two eggs in the female reproductive tract is fertilized by a
different sperm cell. Under the circumstances, the genetic similarity between
fraternal twins is no greater than that between ordinary siblings. Since this is so,
a comparison between identical twins and fraternal twins of the same sex is of
considerable interest, if one is willing to assume that the twins' environments are
no more similar if they are identical than if they are fraternal. Given this
premise, it follows that if identical twins turn out to be more similar on some
trait than fraternals, one can conclude that this trait is in part genetically determined.

The overall results show that the correlation between the IQs of identical
twins is substantially larger than that between the IQs of fraternal twins. Based
on roughly 10,000 twin pairs in all, the average correlations are +.86 for identi-
cals and +.60 for fraternals (Bouchard and McGue, 1981). Some further findings
on familial similarity in IQ scores are presented in Table 15.3.

TABLE 15.3 CORRELATIONS BETWEEN THE IQS OF FAMILY MEMBERS	
Identical twins reared together	+.86
Fraternal twins reared together	+.60
Siblings reared together	+.47
Child and biological parent by whom child is reared	+.42
Child and biological mother separated from the child by adoption	+.31
Child and unrelated adoptive mother	+.17

SOURCE: Data on twins, siblings, and children reared with biological parents from Bouchard
and McGue, 1981; data on adopted children from Horn, Loehlin, and Willerman, 1979.

On the face of it, this pattern of results seems like clear-cut evidence for a genetic component in the determination of IQ. But a number of criticisms have been leveled at these and related studies. One argument bears on the assumption that the similarity in the environments of identical and fraternal twins is essentially equal. But is it really? Since identical twins look alike, there may be a tendency to treat them the same way. Ultimately, parents and teachers may develop the same expectations for them. In contrast, fraternal twins are no more or less similar in appearance than ordinary siblings and may thus evoke a more differentiated reaction from others. If this is so, the comparison of the IQ correlations between identical and fraternal twins is not as neat a test of the nature-nurture issue as it seemed at first (Anastasi, 1971; Kamin, 1974).

In a study designed to meet this criticism, over three hundred twins were classified as identical or fraternal according to two criteria. One was by a comparison of twelve blood-type characteristics. This is a reliable and objective method for assessing genotypic similarity. To be judged identical, both members of a twin pair must correspond on all of the twelve indices. Another criterion involved the subjects' own belief in whether they are identical or fraternal. This belief is presumably based on how similar the twins think they are and how similarly they feel that they are treated. In a sizable number of twins this subjective judgment did not correspond to the biological facts as revealed by the blood tests. Which of the two ways of classifying a twin is a better predictor of the similarity in intelligence-test scores? The results suggest that the primary determinant is the true genotype. When the classification was by blood tests, there was the usual effect; identical twins scored more similarly than did fraternals. But when the classification was based on the twins' own judgments, this effect was markedly reduced. This result suggests that the greater intellectual similarity of identical as compared to fraternal twins is not an artifact of different environments. The best guess is that the effect occurs because intelligence-test performance is in part genetically determined (Scarr and Carter-Saltzman, 1979).

Even more persuasive are the results obtained when considering identical twins that were reared apart. A research center in Minnesota has studied over fifty such twins who were separated in early life, reared apart during their formative years, and reunited as adults. The twins were subjected to over fifty hours of intense medical and psychological assessment, including several tests of mental ability. The results showed a correlation of about +.75, which is not sub-

"Separated at birth, the Mallifert twins meet accidentally." (Drawing by Chas. Addams; © 1981, The New Yorker Magazine, Inc.)

483

stantially less than the correlations between identical twins reared together (Bouchard et al., 1990).

Adopted children   Another line of evidence comes from studies of adopted children. One study was based on three hundred children who were adopted immediately after birth (Horn, 1983; Horn, Loehlin, and Willerman, 1979, 1982). When these children were later tested, the correlation between their IQs and those of their biological mothers (whom they had never seen) was greater than the corresponding correlation between their IQs and those of their adoptive mothers (+.28 versus +.15). Other investigators have shown that this pattern persists into adolescence. When the adopted child is tested at age fourteen, the correlation between his IQ and that of his biological mother's education is greater than that between the child's IQ and the educational level of the adoptive mother (+.31 versus +.04; Skodak and Skeels, 1949).

ENVIRONMENTAL FACTORS

■ There is evidently a genetic component that helps determine differences in intelligence-test performance. But heredity alone does not account for all of the variance. Environmental factors also play a role.

Some of the evidence comes from an inspection of the same kind of data that demonstrate the importance of heredity: the similarities between members of the same family. The IQs of adopted children correlate +.17 with those of their (genetically unrelated) adoptive mothers. To be sure, this correlation is fairly low and smaller than that between these same children and their biological mothers (+.31), but even so, it demonstrates that the similarity in environments exerts some effect. Another argument for the role of environment comes from the fact that the correlation between the IQ scores of fraternal twins seems to be a bit higher than the correlation of scores between ordinary siblings (+.60 versus +.47). While the similarity in the hereditary makeup of fraternal twins is no greater than that of ordinary siblings, that of their environments obviously is; if there were any changes in the family circumstances (changed economic circumstances, death of a parent, divorce), they hit both twins at the same age.

IMPOVERISHED ENVIRONMENTS

Further evidence for environmental factors comes from studies of the effects of impoverished environments. Examples of what impoverished environments can do come from children who worked on canal boats in England during the 1920s and hardly attended school at all or who lived in remote regions of the Kentucky mountains. An environmentalist would argue that these are poor conditions for the development of the intellectual skills tapped by intelligence tests. If so, exposure to such an environment should have a cumulatively adverse effect; the longer the child remains in the environment, the more depressed his IQ should be. This is precisely what was found. There was a sizable negative correlation between IQ and age. The older the child, the longer he had been in the impoverished environment, and thus the lower his IQ (Gordon, 1923; Asher, 1935).

ENRICHED ENVIRONMENTS

Impoverishing the environment is evidently harmful. Enriching it has the opposite effect. An example is a community in East Tennessee that was quite isolated from the U.S. mainstream in 1930 but became less and less so during the follow-

Environmental deprivation *A migratory family from Texas in 1940 living in a trailer in an open field without water or sanitiation. The evidence suggests that the longer a child lives under such conditions the more depressed her IQ will be. (Photograph by Dorothea Lange; courtesy of the National Archives)*

ing decade, with the introduction of schools, roads, and radios. Between 1930 and 1940, the average IQ of individuals in this community rose by 10 points, from 82 to 92 (Wheeler, 1942).

Further evidence comes from adoption studies. We saw previously that they show the importance of genetic factors. But they also document the contribution of environment. One group of investigators studied the mean IQs of adopted children, most of whom were placed in foster homes before they were three months old. At age four, their mean IQ was 112, at age thirteen it was 117. The authors argue that these values are considerably higher than the mean IQ that would have been predicted for this group of children, given the fact that the occupational and educational levels of the biological parents were known to be below average. Since the adopting parents were above average on these indices as well as on IQ, it seems only natural to assume that the home background they provided led to an increase in the IQs of their adopted children (Skodak and Skeels, 1945, 1947, 1949). Similar results have been obtained in several other studies, both in France and in the United States (Schiff et al., 1982; Scarr and Weinberg, 1983).

GROUP DIFFERENCES IN IQ

Thus far, we have focused on IQ differences within groups and have considered the nature-nurture debate as it pertained to these. But the real fury of the controversy rages over another issue—the differences in average IQ that are found between groups, such as different socioeconomic classes or racial-ethnic groups.

Numerous studies have shown that the average score of American blacks is about 10 to 15 IQ points below the average of the white population (Loehlin, Lindzey, and Spuhler, 1975). The fact that there is such a difference is not in dispute. What is at issue is what this difference means and how it comes about.

Before proceeding, we should emphasize that the differences are between averages. There is considerable overlap between the two distributions. From 15 to 25 percent of blacks score higher than 50 percent of whites (Shuey, 1966). The numerical variations *within* either group are clearly much greater than those *between* groups.

ARE THE TESTS CULTURE-FAIR?

Some psychologists have tried to deal with the between-group difference by explaining it away. They have suggested that it is primarily an artifact of a cultural bias built into the tests themselves (Sarason, 1973). According to this view, the intelligence tests now in use were designed to assess the cognitive skills of the white middle class. When these tests are administered to another group with different customs, values, and even dialects—such as inner-city African-American children—there cannot help but be a cultural bias that makes the yardstick no longer applicable. This point is obvious when the test item calls for verbal information, as in vocabulary or analogy tests. If different subgroups have different degrees of exposure to the relevant information, any difference in test scores becomes uninterpretable. Further problems stem from different motivations in the test-taking situation and to different attitudes toward the tester. Yet another complication is posed by different degrees of language comprehension. According to some linguists, many American blacks speak a dialect of English—so-called black English—the syntax, phonology, and lexicon of which differ in some important ways from "standard" English (e.g., Labov, 1970). Since intelligence tests are usually administered in standard English, the African-American children who take them are under a linguistic handicap.

Such considerations suggest that some component of the black-white test score difference is attributable to cultural bias, either in the tests themselves, in their administration, or both. The question is whether this accounts for all of the difference. There are reasons to believe that it does not. The evidence comes from studies in which one or another possible source of cultural bias has been eliminated or at least minimized. An example is an attempt to test African-Americans in black English. To this end, the Stanford-Binet was translated into black English and was then administered orally to black children by black examiners (Quay, 1971). The performance of these children was virtually identical to that of a group tested with the regular version. The dialect difference is evidently not the crucial variable.

BETWEEN-GROUP DIFFERENCES: HEREDITY OR ENVIRONMENT?

The **between-group** difference in average IQ is evidently not just an artifact. But what accounts for it? In the thirty years before 1965, the consensus among social scientists in the United States was that the effect resulted from the massively inferior environmental conditions that were (and in many ways still are) the lot of most African-Americans—systematic discrimination, poorer living conditions, lower life expectancies, inadequate diets and housing, and inferior schooling. But the issue was reopened in the sixties and early seventies by, among others, Arthur Jensen, who felt that the hypothesis of a genetic contribution to the between-group difference had been dismissed prematurely (Jensen, 1969, 1973, 1985).

As currently conceived, human racial groups (some authors prefer the term racial-ethnic groups) are populations whose members are more likely to interbreed than they are to mate with outsiders. This restriction on the gene flow between different subgroups may be imposed by geographical barriers, such as oceans or mountains, or by social taboos, such as prohibitions on intermarriage. The restrictions are not complete, but if they last long enough, they may result in a population that differs from other groups in the statistical frequency of various genes. This is undeniable for genes that determine such characteristics as skin color, pattern of hair growth, or various blood groups. But does the same hold for behavioral traits like intelligence-test performance? More specifically, is

NATURE, NURTURE, AND IQ

the difference in average IQs of blacks and whites partially attributable to different frequencies of IQ-determining genes in the two populations?

Within-group genetic determination One of Jensen's arguments was based on the finding that IQ has a substantial **within-group** genetic determination. Jensen suggested that, given this fact, it was plausible to suppose that the between-group difference (that is, the difference between the black and white averages) could be interpreted in similar terms. A number of critics disagreed. They countered by saying that the fact that within-group genetic determination is high does not imply that between-group differences are genetically determined (Layzer, 1972).

One writer gave an example of two samples of seed, randomly drawn from a bag that contains several genetically different varieties. One sample is placed in barren soil and the other in soil that is extremely fertile. When the plants are fully grown they will differ in height. There will be *within-group* differences as measured by the variance within each of the two samples. There will also be a *between-group* difference as indicated by a difference in the average height of the plants in the two samples. The within-group difference can be attributed to genetic variation; the samples were drawn from a genetically mixed bag so that there is high within-group genetic determination. But the between-group variation must be primarily of environmental origin since the two sets of seeds were planted in soils of different fertility (Lewontin, 1976; see Figure 15.17).

The moral is simple: Differences within and between groups may be produced by very different causal factors. This holds for plants and the heights they attain at maturity. And it may also apply to human racial-ethnic groups and IQ.

Matching for environment If the black-white difference in IQs is really a result of environmental factors, that difference should disappear if one compares black and white groups who are equated in these regards. It is reasonable to suppose that the relevant factors include socioeconomic variables like education, parents' education, income, occupational level, and so on. A number of studies have tried to match black and white children on indices of this kind and then have compared the IQ averages of the two matched groups. The general result was that the black-white difference was markedly reduced (Loehlin, Lindzey, and Spuhler, 1975).

On the face of it, such results seem like vindications of the environmentalists' view: Equate the soil and the two sets of seeds will grow up much alike. But

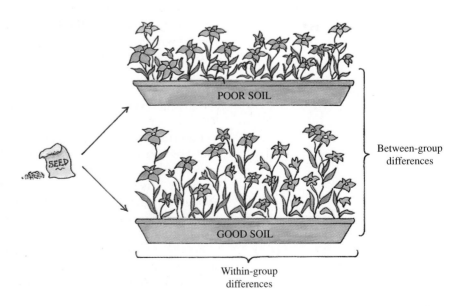

15.17 Between-group and within-group differences *Between-group differences may be caused by very different factors than within-group differences. Here, the between-group difference reflects an environmental factor (soil) while the within-group difference reflects genetic variation (seed).*

POOR SOIL

GOOD SOIL

SEED

Between-group differences

Within-group differences

487

hereditarians will emphasize another finding. While equalizing socioeconomic variables diminishes the black-white difference, it does not abolish it. In their view, this residual difference makes the genetic hypothesis all the more plausible. But environmentalists reply that the environments of the black and white children were not truly matched, despite the social scientists' very best efforts. For matching parental education, income, and occupational level is not enough. The very fact that one child is black and the other white means that they grow up in different environments, since our society is riddled with racial discrimination that will hit the one child but not the other.

A somewhat better approximation to an equalized environment is found in a study of the illegitimate offspring of U.S. servicemen stationed in Germany after World War II. The investigators compared two groups of such children whose white, German mothers were roughly similar in socioeconomic background. One group of children was fathered by black soldiers and the other by white ones. When the children were tested with a German version of the Wechsler scale, the main finding was that both groups had about the same average IQ (Eyferth, 1961). This result seems to contradict the genetic interpretation of the black-white difference, for the children received half of their genes from a black father. To maintain the genetic hypothesis, one would have to postulate a special kind of mating selection—whatever the reasons, the choice of mates might have been such that black fathers and white fathers had about the same average IQ. This possibility cannot be completely ruled out, but it does not seem very plausible (Flynn, 1980).

The effect of environmental change Some investigators have taken another tack. Instead of trying to match environments, they have asked what happens when the environment is changed. A widely cited example is Scarr and Weinberg's study of ninety-nine black children who were adopted at an early age by white middle-class parents, most of whom were college educated (Scarr and Weinberg, 1976). The mean IQ of these children was 110. This value exceeds the national average for black children by about 25 IQ points. (For further discussion, see Scarr and Carter-Saltzman, 1982; Scarr and Weinberg, 1983.)

Some tentative conclusions about between-group differences in IQ Perhaps the fairest thing to say in summarizing this debate is that there is not a single study whose results or interpretations cannot be challenged, nor is there a single argument (whether genetic or environmental) for which there is no counterargument. Under the circumstances, no conclusion can be anything but tentative. Even so, the weight of the evidence seems to tilt toward the environmentalist side, especially when one's intuitions about the effects of three hundred years of slavery and racist oppression are thrown into the balance.

But suppose that the genetic interpretation is correct after all. Suppose that some significant fraction of the black-white IQ difference is in fact determined by the genes. What then? What effects should this have on our thinking about social issues and socioeconomic policy? In this author's view, relatively little. There are several reasons for this.

First, the genetic interpretation does not imply that environmental intervention—in home or school—will have no effect. There is no one who denies that environmental factors are responsible for some proportion of the between-group variance. There are thus no grounds for abandoning appropriate educational efforts for improving cognitive skills (and presumably raising IQs). The trouble is that thus far we have only the skimpiest ideas about the kinds of environmental changes that would do the trick.

Second, what about the portion of the variance that, according to the hereditarians, is determined by the genotype? Is that unchangeable? Some participants on both sides of the controversy seem to feel that, almost by definition, environmentally determined traits are alterable while genetically determined ones are fixed. But this is far from true. Some environmentally produced effects are almost impossible to change, including some that are acquired through certain forms of learning. Examples are the long-lasting effects of imprinting (see Chapter 14) and the difficulty most adults have in shedding the phonological system of their mother tongue when trying to speak another language without an accent (see Chapter 9). Nor is it true that genetically determined traits are necessarily unchangeable. The widely cited counterexample is PKU, an inherited form of mental retardation which, as we have seen, can be treated by an appropriate diet. Conceivably, other approaches may be found to alter the effects of some of the genes that underlie the distribution of IQs.

Third, there are reasons to believe that the black-white IQ difference, regardless of what causes it, is not a major factor in producing the economic inequality between whites and blacks. To be sure, IQ is correlated with adult income, but according to at least some writers, this correlation accounts for only 12 percent of the total variance in individual incomes in the United States (Jencks et al., 1972). Given this relatively low value, the emphasis on IQ in discussions of social inequality may well be misplaced.

We should make a final point (which has been stressed by Jensen no less than by his environmentalist critics). In a democratic society the emphasis is on individuals and their own abilities and attributes. A given individual's subgroup may have a greater or smaller average gene frequency for this or the other trait, but this has no bearing on how a particular person should be judged. When people are assessed according to the average characteristics of the group to which they belong, rather than according to the characteristics that they themselves possess, one of the most essential premises of a democratic society is violated.

TAKING STOCK

What has been the upshot of the work on human individual differences in cognitive aptitudes that Francis Galton began over a hundred years ago? One consequence was the developement of a whole host of sophisticated techniques for the creation and evaluation of mental tests. Modern intelligence tests document the variabililty of certain intellectual skills, and they have found wide (though not always salutary) applications for selection and clinical guidance. People differ in their test performance, and these differences correlate substantially with success in our Western school system.

We have tests, and there is no denying their practical significance. But many questions remain about the nature of the differences they reveal. Investigators who take a psychometric perspective ask whether intelligence-test performance is best ascribed to one underlying ability or to several (Spearman's g versus group factors). Those influenced by the information-processing approach try to discover the cognitive operations that underlie this ability (or these abilities), such as speed of processing, cognitive components, or strategies. Yet other questions are raised by the fact that the term *intelligence* can also refer to mental abilities that only make sense within a given environmental and cultural context.

A rather different question goes back to the nature-nurture controversy we've encountered so often before: Are the differences revealed by intelligence tests produced by heredity or environment? As usual, the answer is both, for humans are shaped both by their genes, their environment, and the interaction between them. But while there is clear-cut evidence that genetic factors are of considerable importance in determining variation *within* groups (as shown by the comparison of identical and fraternal twins and adopted children), there is but little evidence for a genetic account of the difference *between* groups.

So far, our discussion has been concerned with differences between individuals that have to do with abilities, especially cognitive abilities. But people don't just differ in what they can do, but also in what they want to do, how they do it, and how they feel about it. Those and many other differences between people—whether they are usually sociable or solitary, pleasant or surly, anxious or self-confident—belong to the topic of human personality and are the subject matter of the field of personality, the topic to which we turn next.

QUESTIONS FOR CRITICAL THINKING

1. How would our overall view of intelligence and its importance change if it were renamed "academic potential"?

2. How might the general-intelligence and group-factor approaches be reconciled?

3. Would a finding that intelligence is polygenically inherited favor the group-factor or multiple-intelligence views of intelligence over the general-intelligence view?

4. Technically, the only way to make a perfectly culture-fair IQ test is to ensure that equally intelligent members of Culture A and Culture B get exactly the same scores on the test. Why is this strategy problematic?

5. Several studies have found that on average Asian-Americans score five points higher on IQ tests than do European-Americans. Would the same conclusions regarding European-American versus African-American IQ differences apply to Asian-Americans versus European-Americans?

SUMMARY

1. Many physical and psychological characteristics vary from one individual to another. This pattern of variation is often displayed by *frequency distributions.* The scores in a frequency distribution tend to cluster around a *central tendency,* often measured by the *mean.* The *variability* around this central tendency is indicated by the *variance,* or its square root, the *standard deviation.* The graphed frequency distributions of many physical and psychological characteristics have a shape approximating that of the *normal curve,* which describes the probability of obtaining certain combinations of chance events.

2. The extent to which two characteristics vary together is measured by the *correlation coefficient,* or *r.* Perfect correlation is indicated by an *r* of +1.00 or −1.00, no correlation by an *r* of .00.

3. An important application of the correlation technique was the development of mental testing. A mental test is meant to be an objective yardstick to assess some psychological trait or capacity on which people differ. One criterion of such a test's adequacy is its *reliability,* the consistency with which it measures what it measures, as given by *test-retest correlations* and similar indices. An even more important criterion is a test's *validity,* the extent to which it measures what it is supposed to measure. *Predictive validity* is assessed by determining the correlation between the test and an appropriate criterion. *Construct validity* is the extent to which performance on a test fits into some relevant theoretical scheme. A test's *utility* is its usefulness when weighed against the time, energy, and expense required to administer it.

4. Tests with good reliability, reasonable predictive validity, and acceptable utility may be useful as a selection device. But since validity coefficients are less than 1.00, there are inevitable selection errors.

5. Alfred Binet, the originator of intelligence tests, was primarily interested in assessing children. His tests measured *mental age*, or *MA*. The standing of a child relative to her age-mates was determined by comparing her MA with her chronological age, or CA. A useful measure of this relative position is the *intelligence quotient*, or *IQ*, which equals MA / CA × 100. Modern testers prefer another measure, the *deviation IQ*. This is based on a comparison between an individual's score and that of her age-mates and can be used with both children and adults.

6. Different intelligence-test scales have been developed for various uses. Some are meant to test children, others to test adults; some can be administered individually, others in groups.

7. Intelligence tests can be used to diagnose several levels of *mental retardation*, varying from mild to profound.

8. Investigators have also studied the relation between intelligence-test performance and age. The evidence suggests a distinction between *fluid intelligence*, which declines with age, and *crystallized intelligence*, which tends to drop off more slowly if at all.

9. Investigators using the *psychometric approach* try to discover something about the underlying nature of intelligence by studying the pattern of results provided by intelligence tests themselves. One issue is the structure of mental abilities. To determine whether intelligence is one unitary ability or is composed of several unrelated abilities investigators have looked at the correlations between different subtests. *Factor analysis* of these correlations led to a number of competing theories of mental structure, including Spearman's theory of *general intelligence*, or *g*, and *group-factor theory*.

10. Some investigators have concerned themselves with aspects of the term *intelligence* that go beyond IQ, such as practical and social intelligence, and with the cultural spheres in which intelligence is used and assessed. Another related approach has led to the notion of *multiple intelligences*, buttressed by evidence from studies of brain lesions and of *retarded savants*.

11. Intelligence-test performance has become one of the major foci of the nature-nurture controversy, fueled in great part by various social and political forces. The factual questions concern the relative contributions of heredity and environment in producing differences within and between groups in contemporary America.

12. Intelligence-test performance seems to be determined by both environmental and genetic factors, though the issue is not regarded as fully settled by all psychologists. Evidence for the role of genetic factors comes from the fact that the correlation between IQs of *identical twins* are higher than those for *fraternal twins* and that this correlation is remarkably high even when identical twins are reared apart. Further evidence for a hereditary contribution comes from adopted children whose IQs correlate more highly with those of their biological than their adoptive parents. Evidence for environmental effects is provided by increases and decreases in the mean IQ of populations whose cultural or educational level has risen or fallen. A similar point is made by adoption studies that show IQ increases in adopted children after being placed in enriching foster homes.

13. In recent years, much interest (and polemic) has focused on IQ differences between different racial-ethnic groups. The mean IQ of American blacks is about 10 to 15 points lower than that of American whites. Some authors have argued that this is in part a consequence of a genetic difference between the two groups. Environmentalists reply that the difference is markedly reduced by various environmental changes such as interracial adoption. A similar point is made by the fact that the mean IQs of illegitimate children of white German mothers fathered by U.S. soldiers after World War II are just about the same whether the fathers were black or white.

CHAPTER **16**

CH16-19

PERSONALITY I: ASSESSMENT, TRAIT THEORY, AND THE BEHAVIORAL-COGNITIVE APPROACH

I n the preceding chapter, our focus was on differences in cognitive ability. But people also differ in their nonintellectual attributes. They differ in their predominant desires, in their characteristic feelings, in their typical modes of expressing these needs and feelings, and in the way these affect their outlook on the world they live in. All of these distinctions fall under the general heading of personality differences.

The fact that personality differences exist is hardly a recent discovery; it was probably known since prehistoric times. Cro-Magnons surely knew that all Cro-Magnons were not the same; they probably liked some, disliked others, and spent some of their time gossiping about the Cro-Magnons in the cave next door. But it's unlikely that they did so self-consciously, unlikely that they had any explicit ideas about the ways in which one person is different from another. Such explicit formulations came later. In the main, they were the work of various writers who concerned themselves with the representation of character.

An example is a series of sketches entitled "The Characters" that was written in the fourth century B.C. by the Greek philosopher Theophrastus (ca. 370–287 B.C.). "The Characters" featured such diverse types as the Coward, the Flatterer, the Boor, and so on. At least some of his types are as recognizable today as they were in ancient Greece:

> The Garrulous man is one who will sit down close beside somebody he does not know, and begin with a eulogy of his own life, and then relate a dream he had the night before, and after that tell dish by dish what he had for supper. As he warms to his work he will remark that we are by no means the men we were, and the price of wheat has gone down, and there's a ship of strangers in town. . . . Next he will surmise that the crops would be all the better for some more rain, and tell him what he's going to grow on his farm next year, adding that it's difficult to make both ends meet . . . and "I vomited yesterday" and "What day is it today?" . . . And if you let him go on, he will never stop. . . . (Edmonds, *The Characters of Theophrastus,* 1929, pp. 48–49)

Even more influential than such literary efforts were those of the playwrights. The very origin of the word *personality* suggests a possible relationship between the dramatic rendering of character and the psychologists' attempts to describe and understand it. The word comes from *persona,* the mask that Greek and Roman actors wore to indicate the characters that they played.

In their comic drama, the Greeks and the Romans tended to think of people as types, a tradition that has continued in various forms to the present day. Their comedy created a large cast of stock characters: the handsome hero, the pretty young maiden, the restless wife, her jealous husband, the angry old man, the sly servant, the panderer, the kind-hearted prostitute, the boastful soldier, the pedant, and so on. Many of these types were resurrected in later times and other countries. An example is the comic theater of Renaissance Italy, the *commedia dell' arte,* which boasted a large stable of such stock characters, each invariably played by the same actor and always with a mask that indicated who he was. While modern movie and television actors usually don't wear masks (Batman is

Masks used by actors in Roman comic drama (Capitolone Museums, Rome; courtesy of Scala/Art Resource)

A

B

Characters in sixteenth and seventeenth century Italy's Commedia dell' arte
(A) Pantalone, the rich, stingy, old merchant, who is invariably deceived by his servants, his children, and his young wife. (B) Pulcinella, a sly and boisterous comic. (Courtesy of Casa Goldoni, Venezia; photographs by Paul Smit, Imago)

one exception), they often represent stock characters even so. The hero and villain of the Western and the busybody and conniving schemer of the television soap opera are only a few of such instantly recognizable types.

Over the ages, there have been many discussions of the appropriate conception of dramatic and literary character. One concerned the use of type characters in drama and literature. Some critics argued that such characterizations are necessarily flat and two-dimensional and could not possibly do justice to an individual; in reality, even the most passionate lover is not just passionate, for he surely has other attributes as well. They therefore felt that drama and literature should avoid all such stock characters and instead only present fully rounded, complex characters, such as Hamlet, who are essentially like no one else. Such rounded characters are as difficult to describe perfectly as a person in real life, and are therefore capable of surprising us (Forster, 1927). But other critics disagreed and felt that, while simplified types could not possibly do full justice to any individual, they accomplished another and equally important aim: They showed what all people of a certain kind have in common rather than that which distinguishes them as individuals (Johnson, 1765).

Another argument concerns the relative importance of internal versus external forces in determining what a character does. Some critics insisted that all dramatic action ultimately springs from within and grows out of the character's own essential nature, while others disagreed and pointed to the role of the external situation, as in the case of realistic modern dramas, such as *Death of a Salesman,* whose heroes do what they do because their social or economic situation forces them to. Yet another issue concerns the character's self-knowledge. Do her actions spring from goals of which she is aware, or is she reacting to unconscious forces that she herself does not recognize? (Bentley, 1983).

These arguments about drama and literature are mirrored in current debates between psychologists who embrace different theories of personality. As we will see, the drama of types is a distant cousin of modern *trait theory,* which holds that personality is best understood by the description and analysis of underlying personality traits. The insistence that a character's actions are prompted by external circumstances is related to some formulations of the *behavioral-cognitive approach,* which defines personality differences by the way in which different people act and think about their actions, and insists that these acts and thoughts are largely produced by the situation that the individuals face now or have faced on previous occasions. And the belief that people may act because of unconscious impulses is of course a dominant view of *psychodynamic theory,* which argues that the crucial aspects of personality stem from deeply buried, unconscious conflicts and desires (see Chapter 17). The insistence that characters be rounded and to some extent unpredictable would be congenial to a *humanistic approach* to personality, which maintains that what is most important about people is how they achieve their own selfhood and actualize their human potentialities (see Chapter 17). Finally, that the concept of character and selfhood may differ from one culture to another is a tenet of the *sociocultural approach* to personality (see Chapter 17).

Before turning to these theories of personality, however, we must first consider some of the methods by which differences in personality have been assessed.

METHODS OF ASSESSMENT

FOCUS QUESTIONS

■ What are structured personality tests? What are two of the best-known such tests, and how well do they predict behavior?

■ How were the items for the MMPI selected? How do some of the items provide a check on examinees who might wittingly or unwittingly misrepresent themselves?

■ What are unstructured personality tests? What are two of the most widely used, how is each administered and interpreted, and how valid—and useful—are they?

There is an implicit assumption that underlies Theophrastus's sketches or, for that matter, any drama that uses character types, and that assumption is shared by most authors who concern themselves with personality: The personality patterns they ascribe to their characters are assumed to be essentially consistent from one time to the next and from one situation to another. The hero is generally heroic, the villain villainous, and the garrulous talkative regardless of who is listening (or rather, trying not to listen). The traits by which modern students of personality describe people are more subtle than those that define the stock characters of the classical or Renaissance stage, but for many investigators the key postulate of this trait theory still exists. They assume that certain traits characterize a person's behavior in a variety of situations. This is just another way of saying that a knowledge of an individual's personality traits will permit us to pre-

Character types in the Nō drama of Japan *In the traditional Nō drama of Japan, character is indicated by a mask. The mask shown in the figure is that of a mystical old man with godlike powers. Before donning the mask, the actor who performs this part must go through various rituals of purification, because after he puts it on, the actor "becomes" the god. (Photograph by George Dineen/Photo Researchers)*

dict what he is likely to do, even in situations in which we have never observed him (Allport, 1937).

Personality tests were devised in an attempt to supply the information that would make such prediction possible. In a way, they are analogous to an actor's audition; the director asks him to try out for a part by reading a page or two from a scene. Such an audition is a test that tries to determine (by no means perfectly) whether the actor can play a certain part. In contrast, a personality test is a test that tries to determine (again, far from perfectly) whether a person *is* that part.

STRUCTURED PERSONALITY TESTS

As in the case of intelligence measurement, the impetus for the development of personality tests came from the world of practical affairs. The first personality test was meant to identify emotionally disturbed U.S. Army recruits during World War I. This test was an "adjustment inventory" consisting of a list of questions that dealt with various symptoms or problem areas (for instance, "Do you daydream frequently?" and "Do you wet your bed?"). If the subject reported many such symptoms, he was singled out for further psychiatric examination (Cronbach, 1970a).

The parallel between tests of intelligence and those of personality ends when we turn to the question of how these tests are validated. Binet and his successors had various criteria of validity: teachers' evaluations, academic performance, and, perhaps most important, chronological age. It turns out that validity criteria are much harder to come by in the field of personality measurement.

THE MMPI: CRITERION GROUPS FROM THE CLINIC

To provide an objective validity criterion, some later investigators turned to the diagnostic categories developed in clinical practice. Their object was to construct a test that could assess a person's similarity to this or the other psychiatric criterion group—paranoid patients, depressives, schizophrenics, and so on. The best-known test of this sort is the ***Minnesota Multiphasic Personality Inventory, or MMPI,*** which first appeared in 1940 (see Table 16.1; Hathaway and McKinley, 1940). The original MMPI together with its new revision, the MMPI-2, are widely used in both clinical practice and research (Butcher et al., 1989; Lanyon and Goldstein, 1982; Greene, 1991) and constitute the psychological tests most frequently administered in professional settings (Lubin et al., 1985).

Constructing the MMPI The authors of the MMPI began by compiling a large set of test items taken from previously published inventories, from psychiatric examination forms, and from their own clinical hunches. The intent from the outset was to make the test "multiphasic," that is, diagnostic of a number of different kinds of psychopathology. These items were then administered to several patient groups who had already been diagnosed, as well as to a group of nonpatient subjects. The next step was to eliminate all items that did not discriminate between the patients and the non-patient controls and to retain those items that did. The end result was the MMPI—an inventory of 566 items the responses to which are collated and tallied to form ten major scales. The score on each of these scales indicates how the subject's answers compare with those of the relevant criterion group (Table 16.1).

Using the MMPI Interpreting an MMPI record is a complicated business. Clinicians don't merely look at the absolute scores obtained on any one scale.

TABLE 16.1 SOME MMPI SCALES WITH REPRESENTATIVE EXAMPLE ITEMS *

Scale	Criterion group	Example items
Depression	Patients with intense unhappiness and feelings of hopelessness	"I often feel that life is not worth the trouble."
Paranoia	Patients with unusual degree of suspiciousness, together with feelings of persecution and delusions of grandeur	"Several people are following me everywhere."
Schizophrenia	Patients with a diagnosis of schizophrenia, characterized by bizarre or highly unusual thoughts or behavior, by withdrawal, and in many cases by delusions and hallucinations	"I seem to hear things that other people cannot hear."
Psychopathic deviance	Patients with marked difficulties in social adjustment, with histories of delinquency and other asocial behaviors	"I often was in trouble in school, although I do not understand for what reasons."

* In the example items here shown, the response appropriate to the scale is "True." For many other items, the reverse is true. Thus, answering "False" to the item "I liked school" would contribute to the person's score on the psychopathic deviance scale.

Instead, they consider the various scale values in relation to each other. This is most easily done by inspecting **score profiles,** which present the scores on every scale in graphic form (Figure 16.1). In interpreting a patient's score on the depression scale, for example, a clinician compares the patient's answers against the items that differentiated a group of patients diagnosed to be in a depressive state from normal persons.

Validity scales One trouble with self-administered personality inventories is that subjects can easily misrepresent themselves. To cope with this and related problems, the originators of the MMPI added a set of further items that make up

16.1 MMPI profile The profile is of an adult male seeking help in a community health center. The scales are those described in Table 16.1. The scores are based on the performance of the standardization group. Scores above 70 will occur in about 2.5 percent of the cases; scores above 80 in about .1 percent. The profile strongly suggests considerable depression and neurotic anxiety. (After Lanyon and Goldstein, 1971)

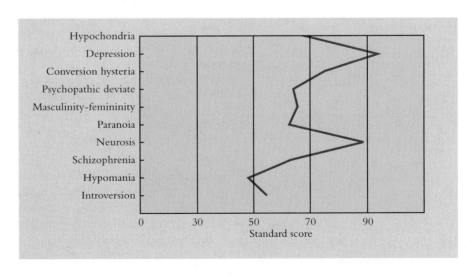

several *validity scales.* One is a simple lying scale. It contains items like "I gossip a little at times" and "Once in a while I laugh at a dirty joke." The assumption is that a person who denies a large number of such statements is either a saint (and few of those take personality tests) or is lying. Another validity scale consists of a number of bizarre statements like "There are persons who are trying to steal my thoughts and ideas" and "My soul sometimes leaves my body." To be sure, some of these statements will be endorsed by severely disturbed psychiatric patients, but even they will only agree with a small proportion of them. As a result, we can be reasonably sure that a person who checks an unusually large number of such items is either careless, has misunderstood the instructions, or is trying to fake psychiatric illness. If the score on these and similar validity scales is too high, the test record is discarded as invalid.

THE CPI: CRITERION GROUPS FROM NORMAL LIFE

While the MMPI can be employed to test normal subjects, it has some limitations when used in this way. The main problem is that the criterion groups that defined the scales were composed of psychiatric patients. This prompted the development of several new inventories constructed according to the same logic that led to the MMPI but with normal rather than with pathological criterion groups. One of the best known of these is the *California Psychological Inventory,* or *CPI.* The CPI is especially aimed at high-school and college students. It tests for various personality traits such as dominance, sociability, responsibility, a sense of well-being, and so on.

As an example of how scales for these and other traits were derived, consider dominance. High-school and college students were asked to name the most and the least dominant people within their social circles. The people who comprised these two extremes were then used as the criterion groups that defined the dominance-submission dimension. Other traits were defined in a similar manner, and several validity scales were added to assess the subjects' test-taking attitudes (Gough, 1975).

THE VALIDITY OF PERSONALITY INVENTORIES

The originators of the MMPI, the CPI, and other personality inventories based on criterion groups, took considerable pains to provide their instruments with a solid, empirical foundation. To evaluate the success of their efforts, we must look at the validity of these tests.

Predictive validity   The usual way to assess validity is to determine the degree to which a test can predict some real-world events. There is evidence that personality tests do indeed have some *predictive validity.* For instance, among college women during the fifties and sixties, the sociability scale of the CPI correlated with how often the subject went out on dates and whether she joined a sorority. Other scales correlate with how subjects are rated by their peers (Hase and Goldberg, 1967).

The trouble is that while personality inventories can predict behavior, their efficiency in doing so is not terribly high. The correlations between test scores and validity criteria are generally in the neighborhood of +.30. This doesn't compare very well with the validation coefficients of intelligence tests (usually assessed by correlating IQ and academic performance), which are about +.50. The contrast is even sharper if we compare the usefulness of these personality tests with the predictive efficiency of common-sense measures such as relevant past behavior in related situations. The result is simple: The best predictor of future performance (for example, of psychiatric breakdown or delinquency) is

preting the TAT stories in the light of all available information, of which the case history is probably the most important.

Some illustrations of this impressionistic and global approach to TAT interpretation are provided by the stories elicited by one of the cards, which shows a boy looking at a violin that lies on a table in front of him. A forty-five-year-old business man, who was an important executive in his firm and believed to have an even brighter future, gave this story:

> This is a child prodigy dreaming over his violin, thinking more of the music than anything else. But of wonderment that so much music can be in the instrument and in the fingers of his own hand. . . . I would say that possibly he is in reverie about what he can be or what he can do with his music in the times that lie ahead. He is dreaming of concert halls, tours, and . . . the beauty he will be able to express and even now can express with his own talents.

A clerk in the same firm was about the same age, but had been in the same position for many years and was regarded as unlikely to advance further. He produced this story:

> . . . This is the son of a very well-known, a very good musician. . . . The father has probably died. The only thing the son has left is this violin which is undoubtedly a very good one. . . . To the son, the violin is the father and the son sits there daydreaming of the time that he will understand the music and interpret it on the violin that his father had played.

According to the interpreter, the difference in the two stories reflects the difference between the achievements and aspirations of the two men. Both presumably identify with the boy in the picture but in different ways. The successful executive concentrates upon the work to be accomplished (the music), visualizes eventual success (the concert halls), and sees himself as part of it (the fingers of his own hand). In contrast, the clerk focuses on the difference between the boy and his dead successful father whom he may not be able to emulate (very well-known, very good musician) so that he only daydreams of future success and understanding (Henry, 1973).

Interpretations of this sort are very beguiling. But are the facets of personality suggested by the test interpretation really there? Are these interpretations equally astute when the tester does not have the benefit of hindsight, when she does not know the salient facts of the subject's life history?

VALIDITY OF PROJECTIVE TECHNIQUES

By now, there must be nearly ten thousand published articles that are explicitly devoted to the Rorschach and the TAT. Considering all this effort, the upshot has been disappointing. According to some experts, these techniques have some limited validity; according to others, they have little or none (Holt, 1978; Kleinmuntz, 1982; Rorer, 1990).

Validity and the Rorschach   Individual Rorschach indices—especially those that don't refer to content—show little or no relation to external validity criteria. In one study of psychiatric patients, over thirty different measures from the Rorschach records (for instance, the number of responses using the whole inkblot) were studied to see whether there was any relation to later diagnosis. There was none. Similar results apply to nonpsychiatric populations. For example, a preponderance of responses that involve human movement is said to indicate creativity, but a group of eminent artists were no different from ordinary persons in this regard (Zubin, Eron, and Shumer, 1965).

16.3   A picture of the type used in the TAT

Studies of this kind have sometimes been criticized as too "atomistic," for they focus on single aspects of a subject's Rorschach record. Wouldn't it be better to use the test as a whole and to allow the judge to read the entire record verbatim (or even to administer the test) and then predict the criterion on the basis of this overall, global knowledge? One study that meets these conditions used twelve eminent Rorschach experts who tried to assess the personalities of various patients on the basis of their complete Rorschach records. These Rorschach-based assessments were then compared to the pooled judgment of a number of psychiatrists who had read each patient's case history, obtained in six or so interviews of several hours each. The mean correlation between the Rorschach experts' predictions and the psychiatrists' judgments was +.21. Apparently then, global assessment on the basis of the verbatim record does have some modest validity (Little and Shneidman, 1959).

Some efforts by John Exner suggest that the clinical usefulness of the Rorschach may be increased by using a more rigorous system of administration, scoring, and interpretation (Exner, 1974, 1978; Exner and Clark, 1978). The system he developed to accomplish this has led to a considerable improvement in the test's reliability, as shown by a large increase in its test-retest stability. Whether it will also increase the test's diagnostic power (that is, its validity) is as yet unclear.

Validity and the TAT The TAT has fared no better than the Rorschach in validity studies that assess its ability to predict psychiatric diagnosis. In one case study, the TAT was administered to over a hundred male veterans, some in mental hospitals and others in college. The TAT results showed no difference between normals and patients, let alone between different psychiatric groups (Eron, 1950).

While the TAT may have little value as a diagnostic tool for psychiatric classification, the test does seem to have some validity for more limited purposes. A number of studies have shown that the TAT may be a fair indicator of the presence of certain motives, though probably not of all. One group of investigators worked with subjects who had not eaten for various periods of time. When presented with TAT-like pictures, some of which suggested food or eating, hungry subjects came up with more stories whose plots concerned hunger or food-seeking than a control group of sated subjects (Atkinson and McClelland, 1948). Related findings have been obtained with various other motives, including aggression, sexual arousal, the need for achievement, and so on. The success of these efforts represents a kind of construct validation of the TAT as an assessment device for at least some motives.

Projective techniques and utility We have seen that when the Rorschach or TAT is used in conjunction with knowledge of the subject's background and life history, they do have some modest predictive validity for diagnosis. But is predictive validity enough? The real issue is **incremental validity,** how much additional (that is, *incremental*) information these techniques provide over and above that which is contained in case histories and similar data that have to be gathered anyway (Meehl, 1959). To give and score a Rorschach or a TAT is time-consuming; so if the effort is to be worthwhile, these tests ought to provide a reasonable increment in information. But the available evidence suggests they don't. Several studies have shown that when clinical psychologists were asked to make inferences about a subject's personal characteristics, they were just as accurate with only the case history to go on as they were when provided with additional data in the form of the Rorschach or TAT records (Kostlan, 1954; Winch and More, 1956).

A   B

Stock characters in the Hollywood Western (A) *The hero (played by William S. Hart) and a woman in distress in* Wild Bill Hickok, *and (B) the hero (played by Roy Rogers) and the villain (played by George Hayes) in* Young Buffalo Bill. *(Courtesy of Movie Stills Archives)*

THE TRAIT APPROACH

FOCUS QUESTIONS

■ What is the trait approach to personality?

■ What are Norman's "Big Five" dimensions of personality? What was Eysenck's alternative, two-dimensional personality framework?

■ What is situationism? Why might it be limiting to explain behavior in terms of either traits or situations exclusively?

■ What is self-monitoring, and how do high self-monitors differ from low self-monitors?

■ How is "person constancy" like the object constancy of perception, and what does it imply about the validity of trait theory?

■ What evidence supports the role of heredity in personality? What does such evidence imply about Eysenck's personality traits?

Transcending type in the modern Western *Some modern filmmakers deliberately play on the stock conceptions of earlier days, as in the recent Western* Unforgiven *in which Gene Hackman plays a sadistic sheriff and Clint Eastwood a sympathetic gunman. (Photograph © Warner Bros., Inc.; courtesy of Photofest)*

Personality tests have a very practical purpose: They are meant as an aid in diagnosis and counseling. But psychologists who study the topic of personality have aims that go beyond such applications, no matter how socially useful those might be. They want to understand the kinds of differences that personality tests uncover, to find a useful framework within which to describe such differences, and to discover how they come about. In their efforts to answer these questions, they appeal to several so-called personality theories.

Most of the theories of personality that have been developed thus far aren't really theories in the conventional sense. They are not specific enough to make the clear-cut predictions that would help us choose between them. What they are instead are different orientations from which the subject of personality is approached. We will begin with the *trait approach,* which tries to describe individuals by a set of characterizing attributes.

Trait theory is first of all an attempt to be descriptive. It tries to find some way to characterize people by reference to some underlying basic traits. But just which traits are basic? The comic theaters of classical and Renaissance days—and modern trait theory—imply not merely that a particular person has a characteristic personality, but that this personality can be categorized along with those of others who are in some ways equivalent. But what are the categories along which people should be grouped together? The early playwrights (and many film makers) picked a few attributes that were easy to characterize and caricature—the tight-lipped silence of the Western hero who speaks only with his guns, the virtuous chastity of the eternal heroine, the cowardice of the braggart soldier (who in Shakespeare's hands transcends his type and becomes Falstaff). But are these the personality traits that are really primary for the description of human personality?

The trait theorists' search for an answer is a bit like an attempt to find a few general principles that underlie the multitude of masks on, say, an Italian Renaissance stage. At first glance, these masks are very different, as different as the many people we encounter in real life. Is there a way to classify these masks according to a few basic dimensions? Put another way, can we classify human personality by reference to a few fundamental traits?

The seven dwarfs as character types
Doc, Sleepy, Grumpy, Dopey, Sneezy, Happy, and Bashful. (From Walt Disney's Snow White; *courtesy of the Kobal Collection)*

THE SEARCH FOR THE RIGHT TAXONOMY

■ In a way, much the same question is faced during the early stages of any science. At this point, a major task is the development of a useful *taxonomy,* or classification system. Consider the early biologists. They recognized that various creatures differ in a multitude of ways—in their size and color, in the absence or the presence of a skeleton, in the number and kind of appendages, and so on. The biologists had to decide which of these distinctions provided the most useful classification categories. The psychologist who studies personality differences faces exactly the same issues. The dictionary lists 18,000 trait names (Allport and Odbert, 1936). But without some kind of taxonomy, how can we decide which of these are basic traits, important for classifying all people?

CLASSIFICATION THROUGH LANGUAGE

One step towards a taxonomy of personality traits grew out of an examination of the language used to describe personality attributes (Allport and Odbert, 1936). Advocates of this procedure argue that the adjectives we use to describe people (e.g., shy, friendly, stingy, generous, arrogant, humble, and so on) embody the accumulated observations of many previous generations. A systematic sifting of such trait adjectives might therefore give clues about individual differences whose description has been important enough to withstand the test of time (Goldberg, 1982).

This line of reasoning led to the development of a widely used personality inventory by Raymond Cattell (1957), who identified some sixteen primary dimensions of personality. Each of these dimensions was defined by a pair of adjectives that describe the opposite poles of the dimension, such as outgoing versus reserved, suspicious versus trusting, tense versus relaxed, happy-go-lucky versus sober, and so on (Cattell, 1966).

Later work by other investigators managed to reduce the number of primary dimensions to a smaller set. A widely quoted study by Warren Norman featured five major dimensions of personality, often dubbed the "Big Five": extroversion (sometimes called extraversion), emotional stability, agreeableness, conscientiousness, and cultural sensitivity (see Table 16.2).

NEUROTICISM/EMOTIONAL STABILITY AND EXTROVERSION/INTROVERSION

Many later studies have come up with other five-factor descriptions of personality that are quite similar to Norman's (see Brody, 1988; Goldberg, 1990, 1993;

TABLE 16.2 THE NORMAN FIVE-FACTOR TAXONOMY OF PERSONALITY TRAITS

Factor names	Scale dimensions
Extroversion	Talkative/Silent Frank, open/Secretive Adventurous/Cautious Sociable/Reclusive
Agreeableness	Good-natured/Irritable Not jealous/Jealous Mild, gentle/Headstrong Cooperative/Negativistic
Conscientiousness	Fussy, tidy/Careless Responsible/Undependable Scrupulous/Unscrupulous Persevering/Quitting, fickle
Emotional stability	Poised/Nervous, tense Calm/Anxious Composed/Excitable Not hypochondriacal/Hypochondriacal
Culture	Artistically sensitive/Artistically insensitive Intellectual/Unreflective, narrow Polished, refined/Crude, boorish Imaginative/Simple, direct

SOURCE: Adapted from Norman, 1963.

John, 1990). But others have suggested that the underlying dimensions of personality may be even fewer. The most influential alternative is that proposed by Hans Eysenck, who tried to encompass the whole spectrum of personality differences in a space defined by just two dimensions: neuroticism/emotional stability and extroversion/introversion (which correspond to two of Norman's dimensions).

Neuroticism is equivalent to emotional instability and maladjustment. It is assessed by affirmative answers to questions like "Do you ever feel 'just miserable' for no good reason at all?" and "Do you often feel disgruntled?" *Extroversion* and *introversion* are terms that refer to the main direction of a person's energies, toward the outer world of material objects and other people or toward the inner world of one's own thoughts and feelings. The extrovert is sociable, impulsive, and enjoys new experiences, while the introvert tends to be more solitary, cautious, and slow to change. Extroversion is indicated by affirmative answers to questions such as "Do you like to have many social engagements?" and "Would you rate yourself as a happy-go-lucky individual?"

As Eysenck sees it, neuroticism/emotional stability and extroversion/introversion are independent dimensions. To be sure, introverts and many neurotics have something in common: They are both unsociable and withdrawn. But, in Eysenck's view, their lack of sociability has different roots. Healthy introverts are not afraid of social activities: They simply do not like them. In contrast, neurotically shy people keep to themselves because of fear: They want to be with others but are afraid of joining them.

16.4 Eysenck's two-dimensional classification of personality *Two dimensions of personality—neuroticism/emotional stability and extroversion/introversion—define a space into which various trait terms may be fitted. Eysenck points out that the four quadrants of this space seem to fit the venerable four-fold classification of temperaments proposed by the ancient Greek physician Hippocrates (ca. 400 B.C.): introverted and stable—phlegmatic; introverted and unstable—melancholic; extroverted and stable—sanguine; extroverted and unstable—choleric. (After Eysenck and Rachman, 1965)*

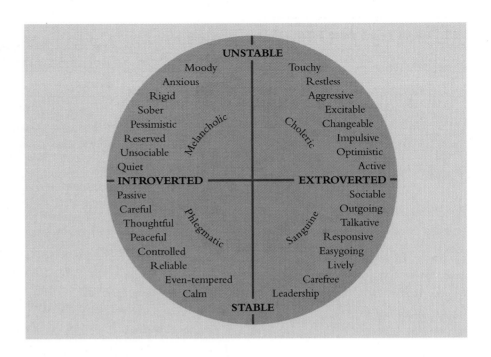

Eysenck's two-dimensional classification defines a conceptual space into which many trait terms can be fitted (see Figure 16.4). To the extent that it or similar systems succeed, they are analogous to the classification schemes that have proved so successful in the field of sensory psychology, such as, the color solid, which accommodates all possible colors on the basis of just three dimensions—brightness, hue, and saturation (see Chapter 5).

THE TRAIT-SITUATION CONTROVERSY

Different trait theorists may argue about the kind and number of trait dimensions with which to describe personality. Yet on one thing they all agree: There are personality traits that are stable and enduring properties of the individual. This basic credo has come under serious attack. One reason was the predictive validity of personality tests. For while tests such as the MMPI and the CPI predict behavior, they don't predict it all that accurately. Critics of the trait approach suggest that the tests don't do as well as one might wish because that which they are trying to measure—a set of stable personality traits—isn't really there. To put it another way, they contend that there is no real consistency in the way people behave at different times and in different situations.

THE ATTACK ON TRAIT THEORY

The challenge to the trait concept was launched over twenty-five years ago by Walter Mischel, whose survey of the research literature led him to conclude that people behave much less consistently than a trait theory would predict (Mischel, 1968). A classic study concerns honesty in children (Hartshorne and May, 1928). Grade-school children were placed in a variety of settings in which they had the opportunity to lie, cheat, or steal: in athletic events, in the classroom, at home, alone, or with peers. The important finding was that the child who was dishonest in one situation (cheating on a test) was not necessarily dishonest in another setting (cheating in an athletic contest). There was some consistency, but it was rather unimpressive; a later reanalysis of the results came up with an average intercorrelation of +.30 between honest behavior in one setting and honesty in another (Burton, 1963). The more similar the two settings, the greater were the correlations. Thus honesty in one classroom situation was more consistent with honesty in another classroom situation than with honesty assessed at home.

Mischel argued that a similar lack of cross-situational consistency is found for many other behavior patterns, such as aggression, dependency, rigidity, and reactions to authority. The intercorrelations among different measures of what seems to be the same trait are often low and sometimes nonexistent. In Mischel's view, the fact that personality tests have relatively low validities is just another demonstration of the same phenomenon. A personality test taps behavior in one situation, while the validity criterion of that test assesses behavior in another context. Since cross-situational consistency tends to be low, so are validity coefficients.

Situationism The failure to find behavioral consistency has been taken as an argument against the importance of personality characteristics in determining what a person will do. But if these are not relevant, what is? One answer is offered by **situationism,** the notion that human behavior is largely determined by the characteristics of the situation itself rather than by the characteristics of the person. That this is so for some situations is indubitable. Given a red light, most drivers stop; given a green light, most go—regardless of whether they are friendly or unfriendly, stingy or generous, dominant or submissive, and so on. Situations of this sort produce predictable reactions in virtually all of us. According to situationism, the same principle applies to much or nearly all of human behavior. Consider the enormous effect of social roles, which often define what an actor must do with little regard to who the actor is (see Chapter 11). To predict how someone will act in a courtroom, there is little point in asking whether she is sociable or extravagant with money, or whether she gets along with her mother. What we really want to know is the role that she will play—judge, prosecutor, defense attorney, or defendant. Seen in this light, what we do depends not on who we are, but on the situation in which we find ourselves.

This is not to say that situationists deny the existence of individual differences. They certainly agree that various demographic and socioeconomic factors—such as age and sex, marital status, ethnic background, occupation, and income—are powerful determinants of human behavior. Nor do they dispute the important effect of differences in ability, especially cognitive ability. As they see it, all of these factors determine the kinds of situations a person is likely to

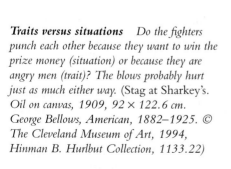

Traits versus situations *Do the fighters punch each other because they want to win the prize money (situation) or because they are angry men (trait)? The blows probably hurt just as much either way. (Stag at Sharkey's. Oil on canvas, 1909, 92 × 122.6 cm. George Bellows, American, 1882–1925. © The Cleveland Museum of Art, 1994, Hinman B. Hurlbut Collection, 1133.22)*

encounter (or to have encountered) and thus to learn from. But in their view, it is these situations, rather than personality traits, that determine what people actually do.

Consistency as an illusion If situationism is correct, the underlying consistency of the personalities of our friends and acquaintances (and perhaps our own) is more or less illusory. But if so, how can one explain the fact that most people have been subject to this particular illusion since the days of Greek drama and no doubt much before?

According to critics of trait theory, one explanation is that people's personalities seem to be stable because we repeatedly see them in the same social setting. But the critics make an even more important point. In their view, personality traits are mental constructions devised by the observer who watches another person's actions and tries to make sense out of them. They believe that people are often faced with an overload of information, which they then try to reduce and simplify (e.g., Shweder, 1975; Nisbett and Ross, 1980; Ross and Nisbett, 1991). As a result, they are prone to various kinds of errors of inference that produce the belief that there are consistent personality traits.★ Critics of trait theory argue that such errors show that personality descriptions are more in the eyes of the beholders than in the people they behold (Cantor and Mischel, 1977, 1979).

IN DEFENSE OF TRAITS

The emphasis on situations provided a useful corrective to those who sought to explain everything people do as a manifestation of their own inner nature. But if pushed to the extreme, this position becomes just as questionable as the one it tried to correct. For in this form situationism can be interpreted as asserting that personality does not exist at all. Whether any psychologist has actually gone to this extreme is doubtful; certainly Mischel never did (Mischel, 1973, 1979). But the very possibility that someone might climb all the way out on this particular theoretical limb was enough to produce a spirited counterreaction against Mischel's attack on the trait concept.

Consistency over time The reaction to the situationist position took several forms. Many authors felt that even if there is little personal consistency across *situations,* there is considerable consistency over *time* (Block, 1971, 1977). Proof comes from a number of longitudinal studies that show a fair degree of behavioral consistency over sizable stretches of the life span. Thus in one study, dependability in males as judged in high school correlated quite well with ratings of the same attribute made by different judges some ten or more years later (r = +.55; Block, 1971). In another study, male adults between seventeen and eighty-five years of age were given the same personality inventory at six- and twelve-year intervals. The correlations between their scores on the first and second administration of the inventory (on traits such as dominance, sociability, and emotional stability) ranged from +.59 to +.87 (Costa, McCrae, and Arenberg, 1980).

Consistency across situations Others have argued that there is behavioral consistency across situations, despite Mischel's critique. According to Seymour Epstein, cross-situational consistency is much higher than Mischel had supposed. In Epstein's view, studies that seem to show low cross-situational consistency

Consistency as an illusion *At a class reunion people may think that their old classmates haven't changed at all. They really have changed, but they act as they once did because they have returned to the old situation. Here we see Kathleen Turner in the 1986 film* Peggy Sue Got Married, *as she once again puts on the crown and holds the flowers as "homecoming queen" at her twenty-fifth class reunion. (Courtesy of the Kobal Collection)*

★ We previously considered some of these errors in our discussion of attribution processes and person perception, for example, the fundamental attribution error, illusory correlations, and oversimplified schemas and stereotypes (see Chapter 11).

Consistency across situations? *In some situations, most people behave the same way. In others, people behave differently. A major task of personality psychology is to discover whether they behave consistently across situations. (Left: Photograph by Bob Krist/Black Star. Right: Photograph by Jan Halaska/ Photo Researchers)*

usually employ only a small sample of behaviors. As a result, the assessment of the relevant trait is necessarily unreliable. And the correlation between two (unreliable) measures of this trait cannot help but be low or nonexistent. To determine whether people behave consistently from one situation to another, the behavior in each situation (e.g., cheating in class and cheating on the athletic field) must be measured not just once, but on a number of different occasions.

To buttress his position, Epstein observed subjects' moods and behavior on about thirty days. He found that correlations from one day to any other day were very low. He then compared correlations based on the average score on any two days, then on any three days, and so on. As the number of observations increased, the correlations rose from about +.30 to +.80 (Epstein, 1979, 1980).

The definition of consistency Another issue concerns the definition of cross-situational consistency. Whether such consistency is found may well depend on what behaviors the experimenter defined as different or equivalent for the purposes of assessing a given trait. A number of authors argue that behavioral inconsistency is often more apparent than real, for two reactions that are at first glance quite dissimilar may turn out to be a manifestation of the same underlying trait when examined more closely (e.g., Moskowitz, 1982; Buss and Craik, 1983; Rorer and Widiger, 1983).

Some examples come from the study of development. Consider aggression. In males, aggression is fairly consistent between childhood and adolescence, but it takes different overt forms at different ages. Young boys pummel each other with their fists; young men rarely do more than shout in anger (Kagan and Moss, 1962).

Aggression in boys and men *The same trait is often (though not always) expressed differently at different ages. (Left: Photograph by Wayne Miller/Magnum. Right: Photograph by Paul Kennedy/Leo de Wys)*

THE INTERACTION BETWEEN PERSON AND SITUATION

A number of psychologists feel that the debate between situationists and trait theorists has focused on the wrong distinction. As originally formulated, the question was whether an individual's actions are better predicted by the situation or by personal characteristics. But there is a third alternative: The critical factor may be the *interaction* between person and situation (e.g., Magnusson and Endler, 1977).

A study in which subjects were asked to describe their usual reaction to various threats offers an example of such an interaction (Endler and Hunt, 1969). Some of these perils involved loss of self-esteem (failing an examination), others physical danger (being on a high ledge on a mountain top), still others a threat whose nature was still unclear (getting a police summons). The results showed that both individual differences and situations affected behavior to some extent. Some people seemed more generally fearful than others, and some situations ("being approached by cars racing abreast") evoked more fear than others ("sitting in a restaurant").

What is more interesting, though, is that the bulk of these effects were produced by the person-by-situation interaction. In other words, people tend to be frightened (or angered or reassured) by different things. This finding undercuts the usefulness of general traits such as "anxiety." To predict behavior better such traits should be qualified, as in "anxiousness in an interpersonal setting," "anxiousness when facing physical danger," "anxiousness in the face of the unknown." By this use of the person-by-situation interaction, the notion of stable personality differences can be maintained. But there is a price, for the process of qualification may be endless. Consider "anxiousness when facing physical dangers." Should this be further qualified so that we separately consider "anxiousness when facing inanimate nature," "anxiousness when facing threatening strangers," and "anxiousness in the presence of animals," with the last of these subdivided into "anxiousness with cats," "anxiousness with dogs," "anxiousness with horses"? The end result of such subdivisions can only be an enormous subdivision of ever more finely drawn traits (Cronbach, 1975; Nisbett, 1977).

CONSISTENCY AS A TRAIT

By now there is general agreement that, when properly defined, traits do exist. We've seen that a major criterion for determining whether such traits are present is cross-situational consistency in behavior. But recently psychologists have come to realize that consistency itself—the degree to which people do much the same thing in different situations—also varies from person to person. To the extent that this is true, cross-situational consistency may be regarded as a trait in its own right.

Some people are more consistent than others In most of us, what we do is affected by both our personal characteristics and by the demands of the situation. But the extent to which one or the other of these predominates varies from person to person. It goes without saying that there are some social situations that affect most people equally and allow little play for personal variations. At a funeral, everyone is quiet and restrained (Price and Bouffard, 1974; Monson, Hesley, and Chernick, 1982). What about situations that are more ambiguous? Here some people will tend to behave much more consistently than others.

Self-monitoring Some people adjust their behavior to fit the social situation more than do others. One of the factors that determines the extent to which

Person-by-situation interaction Like some other fantasy heroes, Superman is utterly fearless when faced by physical danger, but is shy and timid—at least as his alter ego, Clark Kent—when around women. (Photographs courtesy of Photofest)

TABLE 16.3 SOME REPRESENTATIVE ITEMS FROM THE SELF-MONITORING SCALE
1. I can look anyone in the eye and tell a lie with a straight face (if for a right end). (True)★
2. In different situations and with different people, I often act like very different persons. (True)
3. I have trouble changing my behavior to suit different people and different situations. (False)
4. I can only argue for ideas which I already believe. (False)

★ In the items shown, the key after each question is in the direction of self-monitoring. Thus high self-monitors would presumably answer "True" to questions 1 and 2, and "False" to questions 3 and 4.

SOURCE: Snyder, 1987.

they do this, is the degree to which they try to control the impression they make on others, so that they can be "the right person in the right place at the right time." The tendency to do this is assessed by the ***self-monitoring scale,*** developed by Mark Snyder. (For some representative items, see Table 16.3). High self-monitors care a great deal about the appearance of the self they project in a social situation. By constantly adjusting to the situation, they are necessarily inconsistent; they'll act like cultured highbrows when with art lovers and boisterous sports fans when with a group of college athletes. In effect, they always seem to ask themselves: "How can I be the person this situation calls for?" In contrast, low self-monitors are much less interested in how they appear to others. They want to be themselves whatever the social climate in which they find themselves. As a result, their behavior is much more consistent from situation to situation (Snyder, 1987).

On the face of it, the high self-monitor seems to cut a rather less admirable figure than his low self-monitoring counterpart. But as Snyder points out, whether such value judgments apply depends on the way in which the self-monitoring pattern fits into the rest of the individual's life. The high self-monitor is probably rather pleasant to be with, and his diplomatic skill and adaptability may well be an asset in dealing with the many roles created by a complex society such as ours. The virtues of the low self-monitor are even more apparent; there's much to be said for the man of integrity who is the same today as he'll be tomorrow and to himself is ever true.

The extremes of the self-monitoring scale *(A) Woody Allen as the high self-monitor, Zelig, the man who can fit in with anybody, anywhere, anytime. (B) Woody Allen as the hero of most of his other movies, the ultimate low self-monitor who stays true to himself regardless of the situation. (Pictured with Calvin Coolidge and Herbert Hoover in* Zelig, *1983, with Diane Keaton in* Annie Hall, *1977; both courtesy of the Kobal Collection)*

A

B

But at the extremes, neither approach is particularly appealing. An extremely high self-monitor may very well be a shallow, unprincipled poseur. And an extremely low self-monitor may manage to turn the virtues of his pattern into vices as consistent adherence to principle becomes blind and stubborn rigidity. To march to the music of a different drummer is not necessarily admirable. It depends on what the music is (Snyder, 1987).

PERSON CONSTANCY

In looking back it's worth noting that the trait-situation controversy has its counterpart in a similar debate we encountered when discussing social psychology (see Chapters 11 and 12). The critics of trait theory have argued that traits alone do not predict what people will do. Similar claims have been made in the social realm, where the tendency to attribute an individual's actions to his dispositional qualities and underestimate the role of the situation (the fundamental attribution error) has been noted. The difficulty in predicting behavior from attitudes and the belief that unusual acts (such as blind obedience in the Milgram experiment) reflect unusual personality characteristics also indicate that emphasizing traits can be mistaken. The person-situation debate comes up again and again, and the social psychologists—and their like-minded colleagues in the field of personality—have highlighted one pole of this polarity by emphasizing the crucial and often underrated role of the situation.

In the light of all this, what can we say about the other end of the polarity—the assumption that there is an underlying unity in how any one individual acts and thinks and feels, a basic consistency that we call "personality" and that plays a role in determining behavior? The evidence indicates that this assumption—which goes back to the ancient dramatists and before—still stands.

We all have an intuitive belief in something like "person constancy," a phenomenon analogous to "object constancy" in perception (see Chapter 6). A chair is perceived as a stable object whose size remains the same whether we are near to it or far away and whose shape remains unchanged regardless of our visual orientation. These constancies are not illusions; they reflect a genuine stability in the external world. The stability of persons is in some ways analogous. For we somehow manage to peer through a welter of ever-changing situations to perceive an individual's behavioral consistency. The constancy of personality is not as sturdy as that of chairs, but it has some reality even so.

To be sure, we sometimes err and may see more uniformity and coherence than is actually there so that we exaggerate person constancy in others and in ourselves (Shweder, 1975; Nisbett and Wilson, 1977; Nisbett, 1980; Kihlstrom and Cantor, 1984). But the fact that there are errors in our perception of persons, doesn't mean that their personality is entirely in our own eyes. After all, there are visual illusions, but their existence does not disprove the fact that by and large we see the world as it really is. What holds for the world of vision probably holds for person perception as well, and this is probably why trait theory has continued to have so much appeal (Kenrick and Funder, 1988). Person constancy is a fact. Jane remains Jane whether she is at home or at the office, whether it is today or yesterday or the day after tomorrow. And at some level she is different from Carol and Margaret and six billion other humans alive today, for her personality—just like theirs—is unique.

TRAITS AND BIOLOGY

■ To the extent that person constancy exists, we are probably justified in holding on to some version of the trait approach. People vary in their characteristic modes of behavior, and their variations can be described and

Person constancy and caricature *Most artists have always believed that there is a constancy of behavioral as well as of bodily features, as illustrated in this 1743 print by William Hogarth. (Detail from "Characters and Caricaturas,"* subscription ticket for Marriage à la Mode; *reproduced by courtesy of the Trustees of the British Museum)*

16.5 Temperamental differences in different breeds of dogs (A) Basset hounds are calm (Photograph by Wilfong Photographic/Leo de Wys), (B) terriers are excitable, and (C) spaniels are very sociable and affectionate. (Photographs by H. Reinhard/Bruce Coleman)

assessed, however imperfectly, by the trait vocabulary. But how do such variations arise?

Thus far, we've talked about traits as if they were merely descriptive labels for broad groups of behavior patterns. But some trait theorists go further. In their view, traits are general predispositions to behave in one way or another that are ultimately rooted in the individual's biological makeup.

PERSONALITY AND TEMPERAMENT

A number of modern investigators believe that personality traits grow out of the individual's **temperament,** a characteristic reaction pattern that is present from a rather early age. Like Hippocrates who coined the term some 2,500 years ago, they believe that such temperamental patterns are largely genetic and constitutional in origin (though they obviously don't share his archaic ideas of their underlying humoral basis). Such characteristic behavior patterns may begin in the first few months of life. An example comes from a study of 141 children, observed for about a decade following birth:

> Donald exhibited an extremely high activity level almost from birth. At three months . . . he wriggled and moved about a great deal while asleep in his crib. At six months he "swam like a fish" while being bathed. At twelve months he still squirmed constantly while he was being dressed or washed. . . . At two years he was "constantly in motion, jumping and climbing." At three, he would "climb like a monkey and run like an unleashed puppy." . . . By the time he was seven, Donald was encountering difficulty in school because he was unable to sit still long enough to learn anything. . . . (Thomas, Chess, and Birch, 1970, p. 104)

More recent investigators have tried to describe temperament within the framework of traditional trait classifications. An example is a temperament scale developed by Buss and Plomin that includes two major dimensions called sociability and emotionality (Buss and Plomin, 1984). According to Buss and Plomin, these two traits are the core components of the main axes of Eysenck's system—extroversion/introversion and neuroticism/emotional stability. They feel that in young children, extroversion is best represented by sociability (which presumably affects the attachment bond between mother and child, reactions to strangers, and the like), while neuroticism (emotional instability) is mainly represented by a greater tendency to be fearful (anxiety and guilt are reactions that come in later years). In line with these views, both sociability and emotionality show a fair degree of stability over the first twenty years of life, as demonstrated by correlations of +.48 between fearfulness assessed at age five and again assessed in adulthood, and of +.53 between sociability at age six and at age fifteen (Bronson, 1966, 1967).

PERSONALITY AND THE GENES

Consistencies of this sort suggest the operation of genetic factors. Such hereditary effects are no news to animal breeders. Different strains of dogs show marked differences in temperament produced by centuries of breeding: Basset hounds are calm, terriers are excitable and aggressive, while spaniels become easily attached to people and are very peaceable (Scott and Fuller, 1965; see Figure 16.5). We wouldn't expect to find such enormous differences in human temperaments, since there are fortunately no people breeders working to create pure-bred human strains. But some fairly sizable genetic effects on human personality exist even so.

The evidence comes from the same methods that have been used to study hereditary effects in the determination of intelligence—the study of twins. In

Some people seek sensations (Top: Photograph © Helga Lade/Peter Arnold, Inc.; Bottom: Photograph © Philippe Blondel, Agence Vandystadt/Photo Researchers, Inc.)

Others prefer a more quiet existence (Photograph by Alan Carey/The Image Works)

just about all cases, identical twins turn out to be more alike than fraternal twins on various personality attributes (e.g., Buss and Plomin, 1984; Zuckerman, 1987). In one study, a personality questionnaire was administered to over 12,000 pairs of twins in Sweden. The results showed average correlations of +.50 between identical twins on scores both of extroversion and of neuroticism. The corresponding correlations for fraternal twins were +.21 and +.23 (Floderus-Myrhed, Pedersen, and Rasmuson, 1980). Given these findings, there is little doubt that hereditary factors make a sizable contribution to differences in personality makeup.

PERSONALITY AND PHYSIOLOGICAL AROUSAL

To say that personality traits are in part inherited is to say that they have some physical basis. But just what is this physical basis? Here the search for an answer has just begun.

Extroversion-introversion An interesting approach comes from attempts to link certain personality traits to aspects of neurophysiological arousal. The pioneer in this area is Hans Eysenck, who has tried to relate the extroversion-introversion dimension to many phenomena outside of the personality domain.

As Eysenck sees it, introversion corresponds to a higher level of central nervous system arousal than does extroversion; in effect, introverts are thought to be more awake than extroverts. As a result, they are less distractible and better able to attend to the task at hand (Harkins and Green, 1975). A related finding is that introverts are more reactive to external stimuli than extroverts are; according to Eysenck, this is one of the reasons why they shy away from the world while extroverts embrace it enthusiastically. Thus introverts have lower pain tolerance (Bartol and Costello, 1976) and when studying prefer a lower noise level and fewer opportunities for socializing (Campbell and Hawley, 1982). On the other hand, extroverts prefer to be stimulated; they seek diversion from job routine, enjoy going on trips without planned routes, and are more active sexually, both in terms of frequency and of number of different partners (Wilson, 1978). They need external stimulation more than do the naturally aroused introverts.

In a recent study, these findings were linked directly to cerebral functioning. The investigators measured the electrical reaction to auditory clicks in several areas of the brain stem that are thought to help activate the cortex. In line with Eysenck's theory, introverts showed a faster response—indicating greater arousal—than extroverts (Bullock and Gilliland, 1993).

Sensation-seeking A related topic concerns **sensation seeking.** This is the tendency to seek varied and novel experiences, to look for thrills and adventure, and to be highly susceptible to boredom, as shown by affirmative answers to items such as: "I would like to try parachute jumping," "I sometimes like to do 'crazy' things just to see the effect on others," and "I wish I didn't have to waste so much of a day sleeping" (Zuckerman, 1979). Marvin Zuckerman, who developed the scales that contained these items, has provided convincing evidence of their validity. People who score at the high end of these scales are more likely to participate in risky sports such as scuba diving, get more restless in a monotonous, confined situation, are less likely to be afraid of snakes, and drive at faster speeds than people at the lower end (Zuckerman, 1983).

According to Zuckerman, the biological basis of sensation seeking is similar to that which Eysenck suggests for extroversion. In Zuckerman's view, sensation seekers are people who are underaroused in certain systems of the brain, specifically those in the systems that control the neurotransmitter norepinephrine (usually abbreviated NE). One of his lines of evidence comes from a study in which the level of NE in the spinal fluid was correlated with various measures on personality scales. The results showed a negative correlation: the greater the sensation-seeking tendency, the lower the NE level (Zuckerman et al., 1983). This fits in with the general hypothesis. Persons whose NE level is low are presumably underactive in their NE systems. In effect, they are underaroused; as a result they seek thrills and take risks to jog their depleted and sluggish NE systems into greater activity.

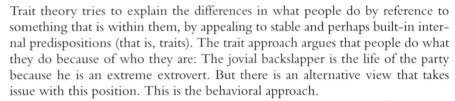

THE BEHAVIORAL-COGNITIVE APPROACH

FOCUS QUESTIONS

- What is the behavioral-cognitive approach to personality?

- How do social learning theorists view personality, and how do they explain the ways in which personalities can differ?

- How does the need to exert control over events affect our sense of well-being?

- What is attributional style, and how does it affect the likelihood of suffering from depression?

- What is delay of gratification, and why might the ability to cope with it be important in the development of adolescent and adult competence?

Is personality coherent? Some early versions of the behavioral-cognitive approach argued that the consistency of personality is an illusion. (Pablo Picasso's Girl before a Mirror. Boisegeloup, March 1932. Oil on canvas, 64 × 51¼". The Museum of Modern Art, New York. Mrs. Simon Guggenheim Fund. Photograph © 1994 The Museum of Modern Art, New York.)*

Trait theory tries to explain the differences in what people do by reference to something that is within them, by appealing to stable and perhaps built-in internal predispositions (that is, traits). The trait approach argues that people do what they do because of who they are: The jovial backslapper is the life of the party because he is an extreme extrovert. But there is an alternative view that takes issue with this position. This is the behavioral approach.

In contrast to trait theory, the behavioral approach asserts that human actions are determined from without: They are reactions to the external forces that impinge upon the person. In recent times, this has often been called the behavioral-cognitive approach, since many recent adherents of the behavioral position assign increasing importance to cognitive factors such as expectations and beliefs.

In part, this position grows out of the situationist critique of trait theory we considered previously, for its adherents hold that people do what they do because of the situation in which they find themselves or in which they have found themselves on previous occasions. The life of the party acts his part precisely because he is at a party, a situation in which he will be reinforced for being outgoing and boisterous, as he has no doubt been reinforced on many previous occasions. This general view is traditionally associated with **behaviorism,** a very influential theoretical outlook that dominated American psychology for the first half of this century, emphasizing the role of environment and of learning, and insisting that people, no less than animals, must be studied objectively—from the outside (see Chapter 4).

If the trait approach can be likened to dramatic productions with character types who wear one mask that defines them throughout, the behavioral view corresponds to the dramatic approach of a repertory company in which every member takes many parts. Today an actor plays one role, tomorrow he learns to play another, depending upon the play. Nor is the way he plays them determined by anything from inside. Actors of the behavioral school don't worry about inner motivations or subtle subtexts. If required to enact an emotion, they pay a great deal of attention to its visible bodily manifestations; they tremble or

A

B

C

Repertory roles *Lawrence Olivier is often regarded as the prototype of the repertory actor who could play any part. He once said that "in finding a character . . . I do it from the outside in," an approach quite different from that of the Actor's Studio. (A) As Hamlet (from the 1948 film he directed), (B) as Archie Rice, a cheap music hall entertainer (from the 1960 film,* The Entertainer*), (C) as the Mahdi, the fanatical leader of a nineteenth-century Sudanese sect (from the 1966 film* Khartoum*). (Courtesy of Photofest)*

sway or clench their fists or breathe more rapidly, depending upon the particular emotion they want to enact. For in their view, all that matters is their outer behavior, because that's all the audience ever hears or sees. Here again, they are much like behavior theorists, who believe that the only way to understand people is by studying them objectively—from the outside.

SOCIAL LEARNING THEORY

■ Another more modern version of behaviorism takes a cognitive approach to personality and accepts terms like *expectation* and *belief* as a matter of course. Those who subscribe to this modified approach are often called **social learning theorists** and include such figures as Albert Bandura and Walter Mischel.

At first glance, one might well think that social learning theorists would downplay the role of personality differences in predicting human behavior. For it was they (most prominently, Walter Mischel) who attacked trait theory by arguing that differences between situations are more important than differences between individuals in determining what people do. But by now, virtually everyone—whether trait or social learning theorist—has abandoned the extremes of the trait-situation controversy and agrees that both persons and situations matter, as well as the interaction between the two. Thus social learning theorists do accept the notion of personality differences after all. But how do they express that notion?

In essence, they contend that many of the personal qualities that characterize individuals are essentially cognitive: different ways of seeing the world, thinking about it, and interacting with it acquired in the course of an individual's history. Mischel lists some of the cognitive qualities on which people may differ. One concerns the individual's **competencies**—the kinds of things a person can do and understand. Another concerns her **encoding strategies**—the way she tends to interpret situations. A third refers to her **expectancies**—her beliefs about what follows what: what acts will produce what outcomes, what events will lead to what consequences, and so on. A fourth difference concerns her **subjective values**—which outcomes she values. A final difference involves what Mischel calls **self-regulatory systems**—the way in which a person regulates her own behavior by various self-imposed goals and plans (Mischel, 1973, 1984).

CONTROL

We will consider only a few of the cognitive categories along which personalities may differ. Here we'll talk about a certain kind of expectancy: people's beliefs about the control they can exert on the world around them. But before discussing what different individuals believe about control, a few words are in order about the fact that just about all of us generally seem to desire control.

In a previous discussion, we saw that animals and babies behave as if they want to have a sense of control over their lives. Babies smile if an overhead mobile turns around because they made it turn; if it turns around regardless of what they do, they stop smiling. Dogs can cope with electric shocks if they can escape them; other dogs who get the same number of shocks no matter what they do will suffer from learned helplessness (see Chapter 4). What holds for animals and babies also holds for human adults. They too prefer control.

A widely cited illustration of this common desire for control is a series of studies of elderly people in a nursing home. Patients on one floor of a nursing home were given small houseplants to take care of, and they were also asked to choose the time at which they wanted to participate in some of the nursing home activities (for example, visiting friends, watching television, planning social events). Patients on another floor were also given plants but with the understanding that they would be tended by the staff. They also participated in the same activities as the first group of patients, but at times chosen by the staff rather than by them. The results were clear-cut. According to both nurses and the patients' own report, the patients that were allowed to exert control were more active and felt better than the patients who lacked this control; this difference was still apparent a year later (Langer and Rodin, 1976; Rodin and Langer, 1977).

ATTRIBUTIONAL STYLE

The actual control an individual exercises over vital events in his life is important. But no less important is the extent to which he *believes* that these events are under his control. These beliefs are intimately related to his ***attributional style,*** a characteristic pattern in designating the causes of whatever good or bad fortunes may befall him. This style can be measured by a specially constructed ***Attributional Style Questionnaire (ASQ)*** in which a subject is asked to imagine himself in a number of situations (for example, failing a test) and to indicate what would have caused those events if they had happened to him (Peterson et al., 1982).

Much of the interest in attributional style comes from its use in predicting whether a person is likely to suffer from depression, a psychological disorder that can range from a mild case of "feeling blue" to an intense, chronic, and ultimately hospitalizable condition characterized by utter dejection, apathy, hopelessness, and such physical symptoms as loss of appetite and sleeplessness (for details, see Chapter 18). Being prone to depression is correlated with a tendency to attribute unfortunate events to internal, global, and stable causes—that is, to causes that refer to something within the person, that will generalize to other situations, and that will continue over time (for example, being unattractive or unintelligent) (Peterson and Seligman, 1984).★

According to proponents of this approach, the internal-global-stable attributional style for unfortunate events creates a predisposition that makes the person vulnerable to depression. This vulnerability will then be transformed into the actual disorder by a stressful event. (For a further discussion of this approach

Loss of control *Patients in a Florida nursing home. (Photograph by Michael Heron, 1983/Woodfin Camp)*

★ This attributional account of depression is a reformulation of an earlier model of depression based on helplessness (e.g., Seligman, 1975).

Delay of gratification   (Photograph by George Gleitman)

to mental disorders, see Chapter 18.) To test this hypothesis, the investigators administered the ASQ to students enrolled in a large college class and also assessed the students' mood both before a mid-term exam and at several points thereafter (Metalsky et al., 1982; Metalsky, Halberstadt, and Abramson, 1987). The question was how a poor grade would affect the students' mood. The results were in line with the vulnerability-stress conception. A lasting depressive mood was primarily found in students who had the appropriate internal-global-stable attributional style (the vulnerability) and also received a poor grade (the stress).

SELF-CONTROL

Expectancies about control represent one category of personality differences that social learning theorists have considered. Another concerns differences in patterns of self-regulation, especially *self-control.* Control refers to an individual's ability to do what he wants to do. Self-control refers to his ability to refrain from doing some of the things he wants to do (or doing some things he would rather not do) in order to get what he really wants at some time in the future.★

An important example of self-control is *delay of gratification.* Much of our ordinary life requires us to postpone immediate rewards for the sake of some more important reward in the future. Some of the postponements involve delays of years or even decades, as in the case of a student who plans a career as a neurosurgeon or a fledgling politician who wants to become president. Others are reckoned in shorter intervals, such as waiting for a paycheck at the end of the week or waiting one's turn in a cafeteria line. Many authors have pointed out that it's hard to imagine any culture that does not require some such system of self-imposed delays, whether they involve food or sex and reproduction. Farmers have to sow before they reap, and most cultures have elaborate rules that prescribe the when and where of sexuality and procreation (e.g., Freud, 1930; Mischel, 1986).

What is often called "will power" is presumably just this ability to forgo some immediate gratification in order to pursue some ultimate goal. According to popular wisdom, some people have this ability to a greater degree than others. But do they really? That is, is this ability consistent over time and across different situations?

Delay of gratification in young children   Walter Mischel and his associates studied this ability in young children and showed that it is related to a number of personality attributes in later life (Mischel, 1974, 1984). Their subjects were children between four and five years of age who were shown two treats, one of which they had previously said they preferred to the other (for example, two marshmallows or two pretzels versus one). To obtain the more desirable treat, they had to wait for an interval of about fifteen minutes. If they didn't want to wait or grew tired of waiting during the delay interval, they were given the less desirable treat immediately but then had to forgo the more desirable one. The results showed that the length of time the children were able to wait depended on just what happened during that period. If the marshmallows were hidden from view, the subjects waited ten times longer than if they were visibly exposed (Mischel, Ebbesen, and Zeiss, 1972).

★ Some manifestations of self-control involve forgoing a particular gratification altogether for the sake of some other reward or to avoid some aversive state of affairs. An example is giving up smoking.

Further study showed that the mere physical presence or absence of the rewards was not the primary factor. What really mattered was what the children did and thought during the interval. If they looked at the marshmallow, or—worse—thought about eating it, they usually succumbed and stopped waiting. But they could delay if they found (or were shown) some way of distracting their attention from the desired treat—for example, by thinking of some "fun things," such as Mommy pushing them on a swing. They could also delay if they thought about the desired objects in some way other than consuming them—for example, by focusing on the pretzels' shape and color rather than on their crunchy taste. By mentally transforming the goals in this fashion, the children managed to have their cake (or pretzel) and ultimately eat it too. By the time they were seven or eight, some of the children seemed to understand their own cognitive strategies for achieving self-control. One child explained why one mustn't look at the marshmallows: "If she's looking at them all the time, it will make her hungry . . . and she'd want to [stop waiting] . . ." (Mischel and Baker, 1975; Mischel and Moore, 1980; Mischel and Mischel, 1983; Mischel, 1984).

As Mischel points out, such results suggest that "will power" is not really the grimly heroic quality it is often said to be. At least in children, the trick is not in buckling up and bearing what's difficult and aversive, but in transforming what's unpleasant into what is pleasant while yet sticking to the task at hand (Mischel, 1986).

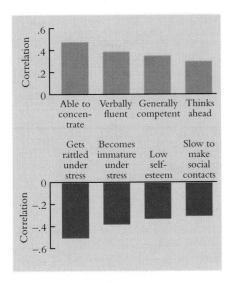

16.6 Childhood delay and adolescent competence *The figure indicates the relation between the ability to delay gratification at age four or five and personality traits at about age sixteen by showing correlations between various personality traits of adolescents as rated by their parents and the length of time they delayed gratification as preschoolers. Bars in blue show positive correlations; bars in dark red show negative correlations. (Data from Mischel, 1984)*

Childhood delay and adolescent competence   These various findings show that whether a child delays gratification depends on how he construes the situation. But it apparently also depends on some qualities in the child himself. The best evidence comes from follow-up studies that have demonstrated some remarkable correlations between the children's ability to delay at four years of age and some of their characteristics ten years later as rated by their parents. The results showed that the ability to tolerate lengthy delay of gratification in early childhood augurs well for later development. It correlates significantly with academic and social competence and with general coping ability in adolescence. Thus subjects who delayed longer in early childhood were judged to be more verbally fluent, attentive, self-reliant, able to plan, and capable of thinking ahead, and less likely to go to pieces under stress than were subjects whose delay times were shorter (Mischel, Shoda, and Peake, 1988; see Figure 16.6).

Why should a four-year-old's willingness to wait fifteen minutes to get two pretzels rather than one be an indicator of such important personal characteristics as academic and social competence a full decade later? So far, we can only guess. One possibility is that some of the same cognitive characteristics that underlie this deceptively simple waiting task in childhood are similar to those demanded by successful performance in the more serious undertakings of adolescence and adulthood. To succeed in school, the student must be able to subordinate short-term goals to long-term purposes. Much the same is true of her social relations. The person who is at the whim of every momentary impulse will probably be unable to keep friendships, sustain commitments, or participate in any kind of team play, for reaching any long-term goal inevitably means some renunciation of lesser goals that beckon in the interval, whether in childhood or later life. One possibility is that there is some built-in disposition that underlies the child's behavior and also the adult's. But it may also be that the common personal quality is produced by learning. Some children may acquire certain general cognitive skills (say, at keeping their attention on distant goals without getting too frustrated in the bargain) that they can continue to apply to more complex goal-directed efforts as they get older.

PERSONALITY I ■ CH. 16

TAKING STOCK

Looking back over our discussion, it's clear that social learning theorists have taken a considerable interest in relatively stable and generalized personal characteristics, as revealed by studies of attributional style and delay of gratification. But if so, how do they differ from trait theorists?

There are two answers. One has to do with the situation. By now, everyone agrees that both traits and situations matter, but even so, social learning theorists, true to their behaviorist lineage, are more likely to stress the role of situational factors (or of a person-situation interaction) than trait theorists are.

The second answer is even more important. For unlike trait theorists, who are generally inclined to believe that the major personality traits have a built-in, genetic basis, social learning theorists are more likely to assume that most such attributes are a result of learning. In this regard, social learning theory still shares the environmentalist bias that is a hallmark of American behaviorism. For both behaviorists and their social learning theory descendants hold to an empiricist worldview, which in its extreme form asserts that virtually anyone can become anything by proper (or in some cases, improper) training. This view was well-expressed in a widely quoted pronouncement by the founder of American behaviorism, John B. Watson:

> Give me a dozen healthy infants, well-formed, and my own specified world to bring them up in and I'll guarantee to take any one at random and train him to become any type of specialist I might select—doctor, lawyer, artist, merchant-chief, and, yes even beggarman thief, regardless of his talents, penchants, tendencies, abilities, vocations, and race of his ancestors. (Watson, 1925)

This is just another way of climbing out to the most extreme pole of the nature-nurture controversy as it pertains to individual differences. Put in terms of our theatrical metaphor, it's a way of saying that any actor can take any part at all, put on any mask whatever, as long as he's properly coached.

Needless to say, such an extreme position is no longer held by anyone. As in most other areas of psychology, there is virtually no one who believes that behavior is determined by nature alone or by nurture alone. In this sense, the nature-nurture controversy is resolved. Similarly for the trait-situation controversy. What's left are different biases. For different psychologists will still make different bets about which factors—traits or situations, a built-in, genetic disposition or the individual's learning history—will be most illuminating in understanding this or another facet of a person. Trait theorists generally make one bet, and social learning theorists make the other. But biases only play a role when we don't yet know the actual facts. For when these are in—and they are coming in ever more quickly—there will be no more room for betting.

In this chapter, we've considered the trait approach, which tries to describe differences in personality in terms of a few underlying attributes that may well be based on built-in predispositions, and the behavioral-cognitive approach, which focuses on the individual's outwardly observable acts and emphasizes the role of the situation and of learning. Both approaches have made important contributions to our understanding, but they are not the only approaches to the subject matter. In the next chapter, we will consider three further perspectives from which personality can be viewed: the psychodynamic, the humanistic, and the sociocultural. As we will see, each perspective on the field has its own validity. For like a statue, the subject matter of personality can be viewed from several different angles, all of which contribute to our overall appreciation.

QUESTIONS FOR CRITICAL THINKING

1. Why might unstructured tests have lower reliability and validity than structured tests?

2. What might explain why the Rorschach and TAT are used so much when there is so little evidence for their utility?

3. Are we predisposed to "see" traits even when behavior is inconsistent? If so, why?

4. To what extent might our own perception of constancy in others be a trait in itself? How could its existence be verified?

5. How would a behavioral-cognitive theorist explain the stability of traits like temperament and the neurophysiological findings of Eysenck's trait dimensions?

SUMMARY

1. People differ in their predominant desires, in their characteristic feelings, and in their typical modes of expressing these desires and feelings. All of these distinctions fall under the general heading of personality differences. The five main attempts to understand these differences are the *trait approach,* the *behavioral-cognitive approach,* the *psychodynamic approach,* the *humanistic approach,* and the *sociocultural approach* to personality.

2. One approach to personality assessment is by objective personality tests, such as the *Minnesota Multiphasic Personality Inventory,* or *MMPI.* The MMPI assesses traits by means of a number of different scales, each of which measures the extent to which a person's answers approximate those of a particular psychiatric criterion group. In actual practice, MMPI records are interpreted by inspecting the person's score profile, including his response to various validity scales. A number of other personality inventories, such as the *California Psychological Inventory* or *CPI,* were constructed in an analogous manner but using normal rather than pathological criterion groups.

3. The validity of personality inventories has been evaluated by using indices of *predictive validity.* The results show that while these tests predict, they don't predict very well, for their validity coefficients are relatively low.

4. A very different way of assessing personality is by means of *projective techniques.* Two prominent examples are the *Rorschach inkblot test* and the *Thematic Apperception Test,* or *TAT.* While these tests are often used in clinical practice, they have been criticized because of their relatively low predictive validity and even lower utility, as shown by their low *incremental validity* coefficients.

5. Personality *traits* are attributes that define distinctions in the predominating desires and feelings, and the typical modes of expressing these, that are characteristic of different persons. The underlying assumption of trait theory is that such traits are fundamentally consistent over time and across situations.

6. One of the first tasks of the trait approach is to find an appropriate taxonomy for personality attributes. Many investigators have tried to develop such a taxonomy, and

five major dimensions, often called the "Big Five," have been identified: extroversion, emotional stability, agreeableness, conscientiousness, and cultural sensitivity. An alternative scheme proposed by Eysenck features two main dimensions—*neuroticism/emotional stability* and *extroversion/introversion.*

7. The concept of stable personality traits has been seriously challenged by critics who argue that people behave much less consistently than a trait theory would lead one to predict. One alternative is *situationism,* which claims that human behavior is largely determined by the situation in which the individual finds herself. Proponents of this view believe that the underlying consistency of human personalities is more or less illusory and that personality traits are mental figments devised by an observer who watches other people's actions and tries to make sense out of them.

8. While most observers have concluded that there is strong support for behavioral consistency over time, there is still disagreement over the degree to which there is *behavioral consistency across situations.* Some authors argue that the failure to find cross-situational consistency is caused by assessments that are based on too few observations. Others argue that many inconsistencies in behavior are apparent rather than real.

9. Many commentators argue that behavioral consistencies will show up best if one looks at the *interaction* between person and situation.

10. Consistency of behavior can be regarded as a trait in its own right. Some people tend to be more consistent than others. To the extent that people monitor their behavior to fit the social situation, they will behave inconsistently; the tendency to do so is assessed by the *self-monitoring scale.*

11. While some trait theorists view traits as merely descriptive categories, others see them as predispositions to behave in certain ways that are ultimately rooted in the individual's biological makeup. Some evidence for this view grows out of studies of *temperament,* a characteristic reaction pattern of an individual that is present from early childhood on.

12. There is evidence that some personality traits have a genetic basis. Twin studies, for example, show that the correlations on tests of extroversion and neuroticism are considerably higher in identical than in fraternal twins.

13. Some investigators have tried to link certain personality traits to aspects of neurophysiological arousal. According to Hans Eysenck, introversion corresponds to a higher level of central nervous system arousal than does extroversion. As a result, introverts prefer lower levels of physical and social stimulation, while extroverts prefer to enhance their level of stimulation. Much the same may hold for the trait of *sensation seeking,* which is thought to relate to underarousal of certain regions of the brain.

14. In contrast to trait theory, adherents of the *behavioral approach* assert that people do what they do because of the situation that they are in or have been in on previous occasions.

15. *Social learning theory* is a more liberalized behavioral approach to personality. Social learning theorists, such as Albert Bandura and Walter Mischel, are interested in what people think no less than in what they do, which is why their orientation is sometimes called the *behavioral-cognitive approach.* They emphasize the role of situational factors in determining behavior. Unlike trait theorists, who tend to believe that major personality traits have a built-in basis, social learning theorists believe that most such attributes are the result of learning.

16. Social learning theorists are interested in various cognitive characteristics along which personalities may differ. One of these concerns the beliefs people have about the control they can exert on the world around them. One difference concerns their characteristic *attributional style*—the causes to which they tend to attribute events that happen to them. Some of the interest in attributional style comes from its use in predicting depression. Being prone to depression is correlated with a tendency to attribute unfortunate events to internal, global, and stable causes.

17. While control refers to a person's ability to do what he wants to do, *self-control* refers to his ability to refrain from doing what he wants to do in order to get something he wants even more. There is evidence that four-year-olds who are able to tolerate *delay of gratification* for the sake of a more desirable reward show more social and academic competence in adolescence.

CHAPTER **17**

PERSONALITY II: PSYCHODYNAMIC, HUMANISTIC, AND SOCIOCULTURAL APPROACHES

T he preceding chapter described many of the ways in which people differ in their characteristic modes of thought, desires, and behavior—that is, in their distinctive patterns of personality. Trait theorists try to understand these differences by reference to underlying trait dimensions, while adherents of the behavioral-cognitive approach stress the importance of the situation and of learning. We will now consider several alternatives to these approaches that take another tack entirely: the *psychodynamic,* the *humanistic,* and the *sociocultural.*

THE PSYCHODYNAMIC APPROACH: FREUD AND PSYCHOANALYSIS

FOCUS QUESTIONS

- What is the psychodynamic approach to personality?

- What is Freud's three-fold conception of personality? How does each part originate, and what function does it serve?

- What evidence does Freud offer for the validity of psychoanalysis? Why is such evidence problematic?

- How do neo-Freudians differ from Freud in their beliefs about biologically programmed psychosexual stages, the mechanisms of oral and anal character formation, and the universality of the Oedipus complex?

- How do contemporary researchers regard Freud's theories of dreaming and repression?

Adherents of the **psychodynamic approach** do not deny that some people are more sociable than others, that some are more impulsive or emotionally labile or whatever. But they feel that explaining such tendencies as the expression of a personality trait or as the result of simple learned patterns is rather superficial. In their view, what people do and say—and even what they consciously think—is only the tip of the iceberg. As they see it, human acts and thoughts are just the outer expression of a whole set of motives and desires that are often derived from early childhood experiences, that lie buried beneath the surface, that are generally pitted against each other, and that are for the most part unknown to the person himself. They believe that to understand a person is to understand these hidden psychological forces (often called *psychodynamic* forces) that make him an individual divided against himself.

We saw previously that the trait approach bears a certain similarity to dramatic forms that employ stock characters, such as the comedies of the classical age. In such plays, everything was exactly what it appeared to be. Once the character entered, the audience knew pretty much what to expect. If the actor wore the mask of the cowardly soldier, he would brag and run away; if he wore the mask of the miserly old man, he would jealously guard his money. In contrast, the

Acting with the subtext *Certain modern approaches to acting such as those developed by New York's Actor's Studio emphasize the importance of subtexts. The photo shows a scene from the film,* The Godfather, Part II, *featuring Lee Strasberg, the late head of the Actor's Studio, and Al Pacino, one of its illustrious graduates. In the scene, a gangster overlord plans a deadly double-cross of another, while telling him: "You're a wise and considerate young man." (From* The Godfather, Part II, *1974; courtesy of the Kobal Collection)*

The dramatic presentation of inner conflicts *In some cases, actors play a character who is not fully aware of her own subtext, so she, like one of Freud's patients, is really lying to herself. An example is Blanche, in this scene from Tennessee Williams's play* A Streetcar Named Desire. *She is both sexually attracted to and repelled by her brutal brother-in-law Stanley. (From the stage version of* A Streetcar Named Desire, *1947, with Marlon Brando and Jessica Tandy; photograph courtesy of the Museum of the City of New York)*

psychodynamic perspective is related to a more modern approach to drama in which nothing is quite what it seems. In playing a character, actors who follow this approach pay attention to the *subtext,* the unspoken thoughts that go through the character's head while he speaks his lines. And many actors are interested in a still deeper subtext, which consists of thoughts and wishes of which the character is unaware. According to the psychodynamic approach, this deepest level of subtext is the essence of all human personality.

THE ORIGINS OF PSYCHOANALYTIC THOUGHT

■ We will begin our discussion with the views of Sigmund Freud (1856–1939), the founder of **psychoanalysis,** for all current versions of the psychodynamic approach are ultimately derived from his. Initially, our primary emphasis will be on exposition, postponing critical analysis until later.

In some ways, Freud can be regarded as a modern Hobbesian. Hobbes had insisted that at bottom humans are savage brutes whose natural impulses would inevitably lead to murder, rape, and pillage if left unchecked (see Chapter 10). To curb this beast within, they entered into a social contract in some distant past and subordinated themselves to a larger social unit, the state. Like Hobbes, Freud regarded the basic human instincts as a "seething cauldron" of pleasure seeking that blindly strives for gratification regardless of the consequences. This savage, selfish human nature has to be tamed by civilization.

Unlike Hobbes, however, Freud did not believe that the subjugation of the brute in humankind was a onetime event in political history. Rather, he argued that it occurs in every lifetime, for the social contract is renewed in the childhood of every generation. Another difference concerns the nature of the taming process. According to Hobbes, people's baser instincts are curbed by external social sanctions; they want to rob their neighbors but don't do so because they are afraid of the king's men. According to Freud, the restraints of society are incorporated internally during the first few years of childhood. The first curbs on behavior are based on a simple (and quite Hobbesian) fear of direct social consequences—of a scolding or spanking. But eventually the child inhibits her misdeeds because she feels that they are bad, and not just because she fears that

The Dream of Reason Produces Monsters
*An engraving by Francisco Goya (1799),
which suggests that the same mind that is capable of reason also produces unknown terrors.
(Courtesy of the National Library of Medicine)*

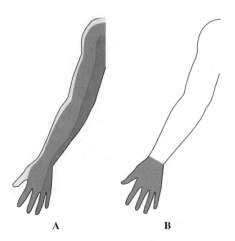

A   B

*17.1 Glove anesthesia (A) Areas of the
skin of arms that send sensory information to
the brain by way of different nerves. (B) A
typical region of anesthesia in a patient with
hysteria. If there were a nerve injury (in the
spinal cord), the anesthesia would extend the
length of the arm, following the nerve distribution shown in (A).*

she will be caught and punished. At this point, the taming force of society has
become internalized. The king's men are now within, internalized embodi-
ments of society's dictates whose weapons—the pangs of conscience—are no
less powerful for being mental.

According to Freud, the taming process is never fully complete. The forbidden impulses cannot be ruled out of existence. They can be denied for a while,
but eventually they will reassert themselves, often through new and devious
channels, leading to yet further repressive measures that will probably fail in
their turn as well. As a result, there is constant conflict between the demands of
instinct and of society, but this war goes on underground, within the individual
and usually without his knowledge. As a result, the individual is divided against
himself, and his unconscious conflicts express themselves in thoughts and deeds
that appear irrational but that make sense if understood in terms of the underground drama.

HYSTERIA AND HYPNOSIS

When Freud began his medical practice, many of his patients suffered from a
disorder then called **hysteria.** The symptoms of hysteria presented an apparently
helter-skelter catalogue of physical and mental complaints—total or partial
blindness or deafness, paralysis or anesthesia of various parts of the body, uncontrollable trembling or convulsive attacks, distortions, and gaps in memory.
Except for these symptoms, the patients were in no sense "insane"; they were
generally lucid and did not have to be institutionalized. Was there any underlying pattern that could make sense of this confusing array of complaints?

The first clue came with the suspicion that hysterical symptoms are **psychogenic,** the results of some unknown psychological cause rather than the product of organic damage to the nervous system. This hypothesis grew out of the
work of Jean Charcot (1825–1893), a French neurologist, who noticed that
many of the bodily symptoms of hysteria make no anatomical sense. For example, some patients suffered from anesthesia of the hand but lost no feeling above
the wrist. This **glove anesthesia** (so called because of the shape of the affected
region) could not possibly be caused by any nerve injury, since an injury to any
of the relevant nerve trunks would also affect a portion of the arm above the
wrist (Figure 17.1). This ruled out a simple organic interpretation and suggested
that glove anesthesia has some psychological basis. While such findings showed
that the hysterical symptoms are somehow psychological, they did not mean
that the symptoms are therefore unreal. The patients weren't faking; their symptoms were real enough to them and often caused considerable suffering.

In collaboration with another physician, Josef Breuer (1842–1925), Freud
came to believe that hysterical symptoms are a disguised means of keeping certain emotionally charged memories under mental lock and key. When such
memories are finally recovered, there is **catharsis,** an explosive release of previously dammed up emotions (Freud and Breuer, 1895). Originally, Freud and
Breuer tried to uncover these memories while the patients were in a hypnotic
trance, but Freud eventually abandoned this method, in part because not all
patients were readily hypnotized. He decided that crucial memories could be
recovered even in the normal, waking state through the method of **free association.** The patients are told to say anything that enters their mind, no matter how
trivial and unrelated it may seem, or how embarrassing, disagreeable, or indis-
creet. Since Freud presumed that all ideas are related by an associative network,
he concluded that the emotionally charged "forgotten" memories would be
evoked sooner or later. But a difficulty arose, for it seemed that the patients did
not really comply with Freud's request: There was a **resistance** of which the
patient was often unaware.

Sigmund Freud *(Courtesy of the National Library of Medicine)*

The patient attempts to escape . . . by every possible means. First he says nothing comes into his head, then that so much comes into his head that he can't grasp any of it. Then we observe that . . . he is giving in to his critical objections, first to this, then to that; he betrays it by the long pauses which occur in his talk. At last he admits that he really cannot say something, he is ashamed to. . . . Or else, he has thought of some thing but it concerns someone else and not himself. . . . Or else, what he has just thought of is really too unimportant, too stupid, and too absurd. . . . So it goes on, with untold variations, to which one continually replies that telling everything really means telling everything. (Freud, 1917, p. 289)

Freud believed that the intensity of resistance was often an important clue to what was really important: When a patient seemed to struggle especially hard to change a topic, to break off a train of thought, she was probably close to the recovery of an emotionally charged memory. Eventually it would come, often to the patient's great surprise. But if this was so, and if the recovery of these memories helped the patient to get better (as both Freud and his patients believed), why then did the patients resist the retrieval of these memories and thus obstruct their own cure? Freud concluded that the resistance was the overt manifestation of some powerful force that opposed the recovery of the critical memories into consciousness. Certain experiences in the patient's life—certain acts, impulses, thoughts, or memories—that were especially painful or anxiety provoking had been pushed out of consciousness, in Freud's terms *repressed,* and the same repressive forces that led to their original expulsion were mobilized to oppose their reentry into consciousness during the psychiatric session.

Freud believed that the repressed material is not really eradicated but remains in the *unconscious.*★ This is a metaphorical expression which only means that the repressed ideas still exert a powerful effect. Again and again, they push up from below, like a jack-in-the-box, fueled by the biological urges that gave rise to them in the first place or triggered by associations in the here and now. As these repressed ideas well up again, they also bring back anxiety and are therefore pushed down once more. The result is a never-ending unconscious conflict.

The task Freud set for himself was the analysis (as he called it, the *psychoanalysis*) of these conflicts, the discovery of their origins, of their effects in the present, of their removal or alleviation. But he soon came to believe that the same mechanisms that produce the symptoms of psychopathology also operate in normal persons, that his discoveries were not just a contribution to psychiatry, but laid the foundation for a general theory of human personality.

UNCONSCIOUS CONFLICT

■ Our sketch of Freud's theory of the nature and development of human personality will concentrate on those aspects that represent the highlights of a complex (though scientifically marred) theoretical formulation that was continually revised and modified during the course of his long career. In this description, we will separate two aspects of Freudian theory: We will begin with his conception of the mechanisms of unconscious conflict; we will then deal

---

★ The term *unconscious* as Freud used it is not equivalent to *nonconscious.* Freud employed it to apply to ideas or memories that in his view are actively kept out of consciousness because they are threatening or because they provoke anxiety. In contrast, the term *nonconscious* is applied to the many mental processes that go on outside of consciousness, for example, tying one's shoelaces. We are simply not aware of these mental processes in just the sense in which we are usually unaware of our heartbeat (see Chapter 8).

with Freud's theory of the origins of these conflicts in the individual's life history and of their relation to the development of sexual identity and morality.

THE ANTAGONISTS OF INNER CONFLICT

Freud's theories concern hypothesized forces whose antagonism produces unconscious conflict and the effects produced when these forces clash. But who fights whom in unconscious conflict?

When conflict is external, the antagonists are easily identified: David and Goliath, St. George and the Dragon, and so on. But what, according to Freud, are the warring forces when the conflict is inside of the individual? In essence, they are different behavioral tendencies, such as a patient's sexually tinged desire to be at a dance and her conflicting reactions of guilt at leaving a dying father. One of the tasks Freud set himself was to classify the tendencies that participate in such conflicts, to see which of them are usually arrayed together and fight on the same side. Freud eventually devised a threefold classification of conflicting tendencies within the individual, which he regarded as three more or less distinct subsystems of the human personality: the *id,* the *ego,* and the *superego.* In some of his writings, Freud treated these three systems as if they were three separate persons inhabiting the mind. But this is only a metaphor that must not be taken literally; id, ego, and superego are just the names he gave to three sets of very different reaction patterns. They are not persons in their own right (Freud, 1923).

The id   The **id** is the most primitive portion of the personality, from which the other two are derived. It contains all of the basic biological urges: to eat, drink, eliminate, be comfortably warm, and, most of all, to gain sexual pleasure.★ The id's sole law is the ***pleasure principle***—satisfaction now and not later, regardless of circumstances and whatever the cost.

The id's blind strivings for pleasure know no distinction between self and world, between fantasy and reality, between wishing and having. Its insistent urges spill out into reflex motor action, like emptying the bladder when it is full. If that doesn't work, the clamoring for pleasure leads to primitive thoughts of gratification, fantasies of wish fulfillment that cannot be distinguished from reality.

The ego   At birth, the infant is all id. But the id's shrill clamors are soon met by the harsh facts of external reality. Some gratifications come only after a delay. The breast or the bottle are not always present; the infant has to cry to get them.

The confrontations between hot desire and cold reality lead to a whole set of new reactions that are meant to reconcile the two. Sometimes the reconciliation is by appropriate action (saying "please"), sometimes by suppression of a forbidden impulse (not touching one's genitals). These various reactions become organized into a new subsystem of the personality—the ***ego.*** The ego is derived from the id and is essentially still in its service. But unlike the id, the ego obeys the ***reality principle.*** It tries to satisfy the id (that is, to gain pleasure), but it does so pragmatically, in accordance with the real world and its real demands. As time proceeds, the opposition between need and reality leads to the emergence of more and more skills, all directed to the same end, as well as a whole system of thoughts and memories that grows up concurrently. Eventually, this entire system becomes capable of looking at itself and now deserves the name Freud gave it, *ego* or "self." Until this point, there was no "I" but only a mass of undifferentiated strivings (named after the Latin impersonal pronoun *id,* literally "it").

Inner conflicts as envisaged by Plato   *The Greek philosopher Plato anticipated Freud's tripartite division of the mind by over two thousand years. In one of his dialogues, he likened the soul to a chariot with two horses that often pull in opposed directions. The chariot's driver is Reason, the two horses are Spirit (our nobler emotions) and Appetite. This Renaissance medallion depicts Plato's image of the internal conflict.*

★ These urges are sometimes called "instincts," but that is a misnomer caused by an unfortunate translation of Freud's original term.

A

B

Ego and superego in popular culture *(A)*
*If Freud were asked to describe Walt Disney's
creations in psychoanalytic terms, he would
probably describe* Fantasia's *sorcerer's apprentice (a.k.a. Mickey Mouse) as the ego and the
sorcerer as the superego. (From* Fantasia,
*1940; photograph © The Walt Disney
Company) (B) In his film* Pinocchio, *the
character of Jimminy Cricket serves as a
"kinder, gentler" superego. (From* Pinocchio,
1940; photograph courtesy of Photofest)

The superego   The id is not the ego's only master. As the child grows older, a
new reaction pattern develops from within the ego that acts as a kind of judge
that decides whether the ego has been "good" or "bad." This new mental
agency is the ***superego,*** which represents the internalized rules and admonitions
of the parents and, through them, of society. Initially, the ego only has to worry
about external reality. It may inhibit some id-inspired action but only to avert
some future trouble: You don't steal cookies because you might be caught. But a
little later, the forbidden act is suppressed even when there can never be any real
punishment. This change occurs because the child starts to act and think as if he
himself were the parent who administers praise and reproof. A three-year-old
is sometimes seen to slap his own hand as he is about to play with mud or commit some other heinous deed; he sometimes mutters some self-righteous pronouncement like "Dirty. Bad." This is the beginning of the superego, the ego's
second master, which praises and punishes just as the parents did. If the ego lives up
to the superego's dictates, the reward is pride. But if one of the superego's rules
is broken, the superego metes out punishment just as the parents scolded or
spanked or withdrew their love. There is then self-reproach and a feeling of guilt.

In summary, Freud's threefold division of the personality is just a way of saying that our thoughts and actions are determined by the interplay of three major
factors: our biological drives, the various ways we have learned to satisfy these
drives and master the external world, and the commands and prohibitions of
society. Freud's contribution is his insistence that the conflicts among these
three forces are inside the individual, that they are derived from childhood
experiences, and that they are waged without the individual's conscious awareness.

REPRESSION AND ANXIETY

We now turn to Freud's formulation (here drastically simplified) of the rules by
which these inner wars are waged. In rough outline, the conflict begins when
id-derived urges and various associated memories are pushed underground, are
repressed. But the forbidden urges refuse to stay down. They find substitute
outlets whose further consequence is a host of additional defenses that are erected to reinforce the original repression, hold off the id-derived flood, and allow
the ego to maintain its self-regard (Freud, 1917, 1926; Freud, 1946).

What underlies repression? Freud came to believe that the crucial factor is
intense ***anxiety,*** an emotional state akin to fear (see Chapter 3). According to
Freud, various forbidden acts become associated with anxiety as the child is
scolded or disciplined for performing them. The parents may resort to physical
punishment, or they may merely register their disapproval with a frown or rep-
rimand; in either case, the child is threatened with the loss of their love and
becomes anxious. The next time he is about to, say, finger his penis or pinch his
baby brother, he will feel a twinge of anxiety, an internal signal that his parents
may leave him and that he will be abandoned and alone.

Since anxiety is intensely unpleasant, the child will do everything he can in
order to remove it or to ward it off. If the cause is an external stimulus, the
child's reaction is clear. He runs away and thus removes himself from the fear-
inducing object. But how can he cope with a danger that comes from within?
As before, he will flee from whatever evokes fear or anxiety. But now the flight
is from something inside himself. To get rid of anxiety, the child must suppress
that which triggers it—the forbidden act.

Freud's concept of repression applies to the thought no less than the deed. We
can understand that a four-year-old boy who is punished for kicking his baby
brother will refrain from such warlike acts in the future. But why does the boy
stop thinking about them, and why does he fail to remember the crucial incident, as Freud maintains? One answer is that thinking about an act is rather

similar to performing it. This is especially so given the young child's limited cognitive abilities. He has not as yet fully mastered the distinction between thought and action. Nor does he know that his father can't really "read his mind," that his thoughts are private and thus immune from parental prosecution. The inhibition therefore applies not just to overt action, but to related thoughts, memories, and wishes.

SUPPLEMENTARY MECHANISMS OF DEFENSE

Repression can be regarded as the primary, initial **mechanism of defense** that protects the individual against anxiety. But repression is often incomplete. Often enough the thoughts and urges that were pushed underground refuse to stay buried and surge up again. But as they do, so does the anxiety with which they are associated. As a result, various further mechanisms of defense are brought into play to reinforce the original dam against the forbidden impulses.

One such supplementary defense mechanism is **displacement.** When a geyser is dammed up, its waters usually penetrate other cracks and fissures and eventually gush up elsewhere. According to Freud, the same holds for repressed urges, which tend to find new and often disguised outlets. An example is **displaced aggression,** which develops when fear of retaliation blocks the normal direction of discharge. The child who is reprimanded by her parent turns on her playmate or vents her anger on the innocent household cat. According to many social psychologists, the same mechanism underlies the persecution of minority groups. They become convenient scapegoats for aggressive impulses fueled by social and economic unrest.

In displacement, the forbidden impulse is rechanneled into a safer course. Certain other mechanisms of defense are attempts to supplement the original repression by blocking off the impulse altogether. An example is **reaction formation** in which the repressed wish is warded off by its diametrical opposite. The young girl who jealously hated her sister and was punished for hostile acts may turn her feelings into the very opposite; she now showers her sister with an exaggerated love and tenderness, a desperate bulwark against aggressive wishes that she cannot accept. But the repressed hostility can still be detected underneath the loving exterior; her love is overly solicitous and stifling, and the sister probably feels smothered by it.

In reaction formation, there is an attempt (albeit not terribly successful) to keep the forbidden wishes at bay. Some other mechanisms represent a different line of defense; the repressed thoughts break through but they are reinterpreted and are not recognized for what they are. One example of this is **rationalization** in which the person interprets some of his own feelings or actions in more acceptable terms. The cruel father beats his child mercilessly but is sure that he does so "for the child's own good." Countless atrocities have been committed under the same guise of altruism: Heretics have been tortured to save their immortal souls, and cities have been razed to protect the world against barbarism. Rationalization is also employed at a more everyday level, as a defense not only against repressed wishes but against any thought that would make the individual feel unworthy and anxious. An example is the sour-grapes phenomenon. The jilted lover tells his friends that he never really cared for his lost love; eventually he comes to believe this himself.

Another example of a defense mechanism in which cognitive reorganization plays a major role is **projection.** Here the forbidden urges well up and are recognized as such. But the person does not realize that these wishes are his own; instead, he attributes them to others. "I desire you" becomes "You desire me," and "I hate you" becomes "You hate me"—desperate defenses against repressed sexual or hostile wishes that can no longer be banished from consciousness (Freud, 1911).

Rationalization *The expression "sour grapes" comes from a fable by Aesop, which tells of a fox who desperately desired some grapes that hung overhead. When the fox discovered that the grapes were so high that he could not reach them, he said that he never really wanted them, for they were much too sour. (From* Baby's Own Aesop *by Walter Crane, engraved and colored by Edmund Evans; reproduced from the print collection of the New York Library, Astor, Lenox, and Tilden Foundations)*

In yet another defense mechanism, *isolation,* the dangerous memories are allowed back into consciousness; what's held back is their relation to the patient's motives and emotions. The memories themselves are retained, but they are isolated (so to speak, compartmentalized) from the feelings that go along with them. This mechanism is sometimes seen in people who have suffered severe distress, such as concentration camp survivors or rape victims. Some of these people are able to relate their experiences in precise detail but are unable to recall the emotions that accompanied them.

THE ORIGINS OF UNCONSCIOUS CONFLICT

Freud believed that the unconscious conflicts he uncovered always derived from certain critical events in the individual's early life. His observations of his patients convinced him that these crucial events are remarkably similar from person to person. He concluded that all human beings go through a largely similar sequence of significant emotional events in their early lives, that some of the most important of these involve sexual urges, and that it is this childhood past that shapes their present (Freud, 1905).

STAGES OF PSYCHOSEXUAL DEVELOPMENT

Freud's theory of *psychosexual development* emphasizes different stages, each of which is built upon the achievements of those before. (In this regard it resembles Jean Piaget's theory of cognitive growth, which we took up in Chapter 13). In Freud's view, the child starts life as a bundle of pleasure-seeking tendencies. Pleasure is obtained by the stimulation of certain zones of the body that are particularly sensitive to touch: the mouth, the anus, and the genitals. Freud called these regions *erogenous zones,* for he believed that the various pleasures associated with each of them have a common element that is sexual. As the child develops, the relative importance of the zones shifts. Initially, most of the pleasure seeking is through the mouth (the *oral stage*). With the advent of toilet concerns, the emphasis shifts to the anus (the *anal stage*). Still later, there is an increased interest in the pleasure that can be obtained from stimulating the genitals (the *phallic stage*). The culmination of *psychosexual development* is attained

Hidden meanings   *This painting,* Hide and Seek, *by the Russian emigré artist Pavel Tchelitchew shows the different aspects of childhood development as hiding in the branches of a gnarled tree. (*Hide and Seek, *1941–42, oil on canvas, 6′6½″ × 7′3¾″, collection of the Museum of Modern Art; reproduced by permission)*

in adult sexuality when pleasure involves not just one's own gratification but also the social and bodily satisfaction brought to another person (the *genital stage*).

How does the child move from one stage to the next? In part, it is a matter of physical maturation. For example, bowel control is simply impossible at birth, for the infant lacks the necessary neuromuscular readiness. But there is another element. As the child's bodily maturation proceeds, there is an inevitable change in what the parents allow, prohibit, or demand. Initially, the child nurses, then he is weaned. Initially, he is diapered, then he is toilet trained. Each change automatically produces some frustration and conflict as former ways of gaining pleasure are denied.

ORAL AND ANAL CHARACTERS

According to Freud, many patterns of adult personality can be understood as remnants of reactions at one or another stage of childhood psychosexual development. An example is what Freud called the *oral character*, which is said to go back to oral fixation (a lingering attachment to oral pleasure seeking after a new stage has been attained). During the oral stage, the infant feels warm, well-fed, and protected, leading an idyllic existence in which all is given and nothing is asked for in return. According to Freud and his student Karl Abraham, certain adults are oral characters, whose relations to others recapitulate the passive dependency they enjoyed while suckling at the mother's breast (Abraham, 1927).

Freud and Abraham believed that there is also an *anal character*, whose personality derives from severe conflicts during toilet training. These conflicts may lead to various forms of reaction formation in which the child inhibits rather than relaxes his bowels (Freud, 1908; Abraham, 1927). This pattern then broadens and becomes manifest in more symbolic terms. The child becomes compulsively clean and orderly ("I must not soil myself"). Another effect is obstinacy. The child asserts himself by holding back on his potty ("You can't make me if I don't want to"), a stubbornness that may soon become a more generalized "no." Another characteristic is stinginess. According to Freud, this is a general form of withholding, a refusal to part with what is one's own (that is, one's feces). This refusal also generalizes, and the child becomes obsessed with property rights and jealously hoards his possessions. Freud believed that excessive conflicts during the anal stage may lead to an adult personality that displays the three symptomatic attributes of the anal character—compulsive orderliness, stubbornness, and stinginess.

THE OEDIPUS COMPLEX

We now turn to that aspect of the theory of psychosexual development that Freud himself regarded as the most important—the family triangle of love, jealousy, and fear that is at the root of internalized morality and out of which grows the child's identification with the parent of the same sex. This is the *Oedipus complex*, named after the mythical king of Thebes who unknowingly committed two awful crimes—killing his father and marrying his mother. According to Freud, an analogous family drama is reenacted in the childhood of all men and women. Since he came to believe that the sequence of steps is somewhat different in the two sexes, we will take them up separately. We will start with his theory of how genital sexuality emerges in males (Freud, 1905).

At about three or four years of age the phallic stage begins. The young boy becomes increasingly interested in his penis, which becomes a source of both pride and pleasure. He masturbates and this brings satisfaction, but it is not enough. His erotic urges seek an external object. The inevitable choice is his mother (or some mother substitute). But there is an obstacle—the boy's father. The little boy wants to have his mother all to himself, as a comforter as well as an erotic partner, but this sexual utopia is out of the question. His father is a rival, and he is bigger. The little boy wants his father to go away and not come back—in short, to die.

At this point, a new element enters into the family drama. The little boy begins to fear the father he is jealous of. According to Freud, this is because the boy is sure that the father knows of his son's hostility and that the father will surely answer hate with hate. With childish logic the little boy suspects that his punishment will fit his crime: The same organ by which he sinned will be the one that is made to suffer. The result is *castration anxiety.* As a result, the boy tries to push the hostile feelings underground, but they refuse to stay buried. They return, and the only defense that is left is projection: "I hate father" becomes "Father hates me." This naturally increases the boy's fear, which increases his hate, which is again pushed down, comes back up, and leads to yet further projection. This process spirals upward, until the father is finally seen as an overwhelming ogre who threatens to castrate his son.

As the vicious cycle continues, the little boy's anxiety eventually becomes unbearable. At this point, he throws in the towel, renounces his mother as an erotic object, and renounces genital pleasure, at least for a while. Instead, he *identifies* with his father. He concludes that by becoming like him, he will eventually enjoy an erotic partnership of the kind his father enjoys now, if not with his mother, then at least with someone much like her.

Freud believed that once the tumult of the Oedipal conflict dies down, there is a period of comparative sexual quiet which lasts from about five to twelve years of age. This is the *latency period* during which boys play only with boys, devote themselves to athletics, and want to have nothing to do with the opposite sex. All of this changes at puberty. The hormone levels rise, the sex organs mature rapidly, and the repressed sexual impulses can no longer be denied. But as these urges come out of their closet, parts of the Oedipal family skeleton come out as well, dragging along many of the fears and conflicts that had been comfortably hidden away for all these years.

According to Freud, this is one of the reasons why adolescence is so often a period of deep emotional turbulence. The boy is now physically mature, and he is strongly attracted to the opposite sex, but this very attraction frightens him, and he doesn't know why. Sexual contact with women arouses the unconscious wishes and fears that pertain to mother and father. In healthy individ-

Oedipus Rex *From a 1955 production directed by Tyrone Guthrie with Douglas Campbell in the title role, at Stratford, Ontario. (Courtesy Billy Rose Theatre Collection, The New York Public Library at Lincoln Center, Astor, Lenox, and Tilden Collections)*

"Why can't you be more like Oedipus?"
(Drawing by Chas. Addams; © 1972, The
New Yorker Magazine, Inc.)

uals, the Oedipus complex has been resolved well enough so that these fears can be overcome. The boy can eventually accept himself as a man and achieve *genital sexuality* in which he loves a woman as herself rather than as some shadowy substitute for his mother and in which his love involves giving as well as taking.

THE ELECTRA COMPLEX

We have traced Freud's account of the male psychosexual odyssey to adult sexuality. What about the female? In Freud's view, she goes through essentially identical oral and anal phases as does the male. And in many ways, the development of her phallic interests (Freud used the same term for both sexes) is symmetrical to the male's. As he focuses his erotic interests on the mother, so she focuses hers upon the father. As he resents and eventually comes to fear the father, so she the mother. In short, there is a female version of the Oedipus complex (sometimes called the **Electra complex** after the Greek tragic heroine who goaded her brother into slaying their mother).

WINDOWS INTO THE UNCONSCIOUS

Freud arrived at his theory of unconscious conflict by studying the behavior of disturbed individuals, usually hysterics. But he soon concluded that the same clash of unconscious forces that results in neurotic symptoms is also found in the life of normal persons. Their inner conflicts are under control, with less resulting anxiety and no crippling effects, but the conflicts are present nonetheless. We will consider two areas to which Freud appealed for evidence: lapses of memory and slips of the tongue in everyday life, and the content of dreams.

ERRORS OF SPEECH AND MEMORY

Freud drew attention to what he called the "psychopathology of everyday life" in which we momentarily forget a name that might call up embarrassing memories or in which we suffer a slip of the tongue that unwittingly reveals an underlying motive (Freud, 1901). Suppressed intentions sometimes emerge to make us become "absent minded" about things we don't really want to do. Freud cites the example of a friend who wrote a letter that he forgot to send off for several days. He finally mailed it, but it was returned by the post office, for there was no address. He addressed it and sent it off again only to have it returned once more because there was no stamp.

This is not to say (though psychoanalytic writers often seem to say it) that all such slips of the tongue, mislayings of objects, and lapses of memory are motivated in Freud's sense. The host who cannot call up a guest's name when he has to introduce him to another guest is unlikely to have some hidden reason for keeping that name out of his consciousness. The name is probably blocked because of simple, and quite unmotivated, memory interference (see Chapter 7).

DREAMS

One of Freud's most influential works was his theory of dreams (Freud, 1900). He argued that dreams have a meaning that can be deciphered if one looks deeply enough. In his view, dreams concern the dreamer's past and present, and they arise from unknown regions within. He saw dreams as somewhat analo-

An artist's dream   *A painting that depicts a dream in which an artist is at a friend's house when the door suddenly opens and a man to whom he was once apprenticed enters, joined by a nude woman who was one of his most beautiful models. Freud would probably have noted the Oedipal theme, considering that the dream featured a former mentor and his nude model. (The frontispiece of* Les rêves et les moyens de les diriger, *by Marquis d'Hervey de Saint Denis, 1867)*

gous to hysterical symptoms. On the surface, they both appear meaningless and bizarre, but they become comprehensible when understood as veiled expressions of an unconscious clash between competing motives.

Freud began with the assumption that at bottom every dream is an attempt at **wish fulfillment.** While awake, a wish is usually not acted upon right away, for there are considerations of both reality (the ego) and morality (the superego) that must be taken into account: "Is it possible?" and "Is it allowed?" But during sleep these restraining forces are drastically weakened and the wish then leads to immediate thoughts and images of gratification. In some cases the wish fulfillment is simple and direct. Starving explorers dream of sumptuous meals; men stranded in the desert dream of cool mountain streams. According to a Hungarian proverb quoted by Freud, "Pigs dream of acorns, and geese dream of maize."

Simple wish-fulfillment dreams are comparatively rare. What about the others, the strange and illogical nightly narratives that are far more usual? Freud argued that the same principle of attempted wish fulfillment could explain these as well. But here a new process comes into play. The underlying wish touches upon some forbidden matters that are associated with anxiety. As a result, various mechanisms of defense are invoked. The wish cannot be expressed directly; it is censored and is only allowed to surface in symbolic disguise. The dreamer never experiences the underlying **latent dream** that represents his own hidden wishes and concerns. What he does experience is the carefully laundered version that emerges after the defense mechanisms have done their work—the **manifest dream.** The end product is reminiscent of hysterical symptoms and various pathologies of everyday life. It represents a compromise between forbidden urges and the repressive forces that hold them down. The underlying impulse is censored, but it surreptitiously emerges in a veiled disguise.

In some dreams, the underlying wish finds expression in various displaced forms. There is **symbolism** in which one thing stands for another. Some symbols are widely shared because certain physical, functional, or linguistic similarities are recognized by most people (for example, screwdriver for penis and box for vagina). But there is no simple cipher that can be generally applied. After all, many physical objects are either long and pointed or round and hollow; a pat equation with male and female genitals will be of little use. Instead, most symbolic relationships depend upon the dreamer's own life experience and can only be interpreted by noting her free associations to the dream.

A CRITICAL LOOK AT FREUDIAN THEORY

■ Thus far, we have presented Freud's views with a minimum of critical comment. We now shift our perspective to consider some of his assertions in the light of present-day thought and evidence.

METHODOLOGICAL AND CONCEPTUAL ISSUES

By what criteria can one determine whether Freud's assertions are in fact correct? Freud's own criterion was the evidence from the couch. He considered the patient's free associations, his resistances, his slips of the tongue, his dreams, and then tried to weave them into a coherent pattern that somehow made sense of all the parts. But can one really draw conclusions from this kind of clinical evidence alone? Clinical practitioners cannot be totally objective no matter how hard they try. As they listen to a patient, they are more likely to hear and remember those themes that fit in with their own views than those that do not? (This point is especially pertinent to Freud who never took notes during psychoanalytic sessions.) Would a clinician with different biases have remembered the same themes?

Yet another problem is conceptual. Scientific theories lead to certain predictions; if these fail, the theory is refuted. But are Freud's assertions theories in this sense? What specific predictions do they lead to? Consider the hypothetical case of a boy raised by a harsh, rejecting mother and a weak, alcoholic father. What will the boy be like as an adult? Will he seek dominating women who will degrade him as his mother did? Will he try to find a warm, comforting wife upon whom he can become dependent and thus make up for the mothering he

Dreams and symbolism   *The 1927 German silent film* The Secrets of a Soul *by Georg Pabst tried to depict a case history in psychoanalytic terms. Its subject was a middle-aged man suffering from impotence. The film portrays several of the patient's dreams. In this one, he tries to plant a tree, a symbol for impregnating his wife. (Courtesy of the Museum of Modern Art/Film Stills Archive)*

A picture of Freud's consultation room
In classical psychoanalysis, the patient reclines on the couch while the analyst sits behind him, out of sight. Freud adopted this method to avoid influencing the patient's flow of associations by his own facial expressions. He also had a personal motive: "I cannot bear to be gazed at for eight hours a day." (Freud, 1913; photograph by Edmund Engelman)

never had as a child? There is no way of predicting on psychoanalytic grounds. Each outcome makes perfectly good sense—after it has occurred.

Another problem with many psychoanalytic arguments is that the analyst's theory often determines whether a patient's statement should or should not be accepted at face value. Suppose a woman insists that she hates her mother. The analyst will probably believe her. But if she swears that she loves her mother, the analyst may conclude that she, like Shakespeare's lady, "doth protest too much." He may then interpret her protestations of love as meaning the exact opposite, as reflecting a reaction formation against her "real" feelings of hate. The trouble with this kind of two-way reasoning is that it becomes difficult to find any sort of disproof. (For a discussion of this and related issues, see Grünbaum, 1984.)

Such considerations suggest that if we want to test Freud's assertions, we must look for further evidence and must be more rigorous in the way in which we interpret it. We will begin by considering some criticisms from theorists who agreed with Freud's thesis that there is unconscious conflict, but who were skeptical of his particular assertions of what these conflicts are.

BIOLOGY OR CULTURE?

A number of psychoanalytically oriented theorists took strong exception to Freud's insistence that the pattern of unconscious conflicts is biologically based and will therefore be found in essentially the same form in all men and all women.

The emphasis on social factors Since Freud believed that the key to emotional development is in biology, he assumed that its progression followed a universal course. In his view, all humans pass through oral, anal, and phallic stages and suffer the conflicts appropriate to each stage. This conception has been challenged by various clinical practitioners, many of whom used Freud's own psychoanalytic methods. These critics felt that Freud had overemphasized biological factors at the expense of social ones. This point was first raised by one of Freud's own students, Alfred Adler (1870–1937). It was later taken up by several like-minded authors who are often grouped together under the loose label **neo-Freudians,** including Erich Fromm (1900–1980), Karen Horney (1885–1952), and H. S. Sullivan (1892–1949).

According to the neo-Freudians, human development cannot be properly understood by focusing on the particular anatomical regions—mouth, anus, genitals—through which the child tries to gratify her instinctual desires. In their view, the important question is how humans relate, or try to relate, to others—whether by dominating, or submitting, or becoming dependent, or whatever. Their description of our inner conflicts is therefore in social terms. For example, if they see a mother who toilet trains her child very severely, they are likely to interpret her behavior as part of an overall pattern whereby she tries to push the child to early achievement; the specific frustrations of the anal stage as such are of lesser concern to them. Similarly for the sexual sphere: According to Freud, the neurotic conflict centers on the repression of erotic impulses; according to the neo-Freudian critics, the real difficulty is in the area of interpersonal relationships. Neurosis often leads to sexual symptoms, not because sex is a powerful biological motive that is pushed underground, but rather because it is one of the most sensitive barometers of interpersonal attitudes. The man who can only relate to other people by competing with them may well be unable to find sexual pleasure in his marriage bed, but the sexual malfunction is an effect of his neurotic social pattern rather than its cause.

The same emphasis on social factors highlights the neo-Freudian explanation for how these conflicts arise in the first place. In contrast to Freud, the neo-Freudians deny that these conflicts are biologically ordained; they contend, rather, that these conflicts depend upon the specific cultural conditions in which the child is reared. According to the neo-Freudians, the conflicts that Freud observed may have characterized his patients, but this does not mean that these same patterns will be found in people who live at other times and in other places.

The rejection of cultural absolutism   One set of relevant findings came from another discipline, **cultural anthropology,** which concerns itself with the practices and beliefs of different peoples throughout the world. There are evidently considerable variations in these patterns, with accompanying variations in the kind of person who is typical in each setting. Personality characteristics that are typical in our culture are by no means universal, a result that was beautifully attuned to the antibiological bias of the neo-Freudians (a point to which we will return later).

CRITIQUE OF FREUD'S THEORIES OF DEVELOPMENT

Some related criticisms concern Freud's theories of psychosexual development. It's rather ironic that Freud, whose views of childhood development had such a powerful influence on Western thought, never himself studied children. His theories of early development were mostly based on his adult patients' recollections, dreams, and free associations. But by now of course, the study of childhood development is a flourishing enterprise (see Chapters 13 and 14). What light has it shed on the role of early childhood events in producing adult personality?

Oral and anal characters   The verdict on the oral character is simple. There is little or no evidence that differences in the way the infant was fed have much of an effect on later personality (assuming adequate nutrition). Later adjustment and development appear to be much the same whether the infant was fed by breast or by bottle, was weaned early or weaned late. (For an overview, see Zigler and Child, 1972.)

Some who study childhood development contend that the concept of the anal character may have more validity. They cite evidence that the critical anal

Freud at age sixteen with his mother, Amalie Nathanson Freud Freud was his mother's first-born and her favorite, a fact that may have affected his theory of the human family drama. As he put it, "A man who has been the indisputable favorite of his mother keeps for life the feeling of a conqueror, that confidence of success that often induces real success." (E. Jones, 1954, p. 5; photograph courtesy of Mary Evans/Freud copyrights)

traits—neatness, obstinacy, and stinginess—do in fact correlate to a significant extent (Fisher and Greenberg, 1977). But no correlation whatever has been found between age of toilet training and the personality traits that define the anal character (Beloff, 1957). In fact, there is little evidence that shows any long-term effects growing out of toilet-training practices, either in our own or other cultures (Orlansky, 1949). For example, there seems to be no relation between the severity of toilet training in different cultures and the degree of hoarding or economic competition (Cohen, 1953). There is thus little evidence for Freud's claim that the toilet is a prep school for becoming a banker or a captain of industry.

But if so, what can we make of the fact that the three so-called anal traits form a cluster and seem to be transmitted from parent to child? Our best guess is that they are transmitted as part of a general pattern of middle-class values and attitudes, communicated by the general social atmosphere in which the child is raised, and instilled as one facet of what the parents want the child to become. Seen in this light, obstinacy, orderliness, and stinginess may well be a result of the parents pushing their child toward independence and achievement. They are not by-products of getting the child out of diapers.

The universal Oedipus complex Freud's theories of the Oedipus complex in childhood have not fared much better. Our major source of information in this area comes from studies of other cultures. On the whole, the evidence was welcome grist to the neo-Freudian mill: The Oedipus conflict is not universal but depends upon cultural variations in the family constellation.

This point was first raised some seventy years ago by the English anthropologist Bronislaw Malinowski on the basis of his observations of the Trobriand Islanders of the western Pacific (Malinowski, 1927). The family pattern of the Trobriand Islanders is quite different from our own. Among the Trobrianders, the biological father is not the head of the household. He spends time with his children and plays with them, but he exerts no authority. This role is reserved for the mother's brother, who acts as disciplinarian. The Trobriand Islanders thus separate the roles that in Freud's Vienna were played by one and the same person.

According to Freud, this different family pattern should make no difference. There should still be an Oedipus complex in which the father is the hated villain, for, after all, it is he who is the little boy's sexual rival. But this did not turn out to be the case. Malinowski saw no signs of friction between sons and fathers, though he did observe a fair amount of hostility directed at the maternal uncle. The same held for dreams and folk tales. The Trobriand Islanders believe that there are prophetic dreams of death; these generally involve the death of the maternal uncle. If we accept Freud's notion that dreams involve unconscious wishes and preoccupations, we are forced to conclude that the Trobriand boy hates his uncle, not his father. In sum, the child has fears and fantasies about the authoritarian figure in his life, the man who bosses him around. This is the father in Freud's Austria but the uncle on the Trobriand Islands. His fears are not about his mother's lover as such, for the Trobriand boy does not hate the father, who plays this role.

FREUD'S THEORIES OF DREAMS, REPRESSION, AND DEFENSE

Thus far, we have looked at critiques that came from within the psychodynamic fold. They disagreed with Freud's theories about what internal conflicts were about and where they came from. But they accepted his notion of unconscious conflict and its effect on mental processes—acts, wishes, thoughts, perceptions—that are kept out of consciousness by an elaborate system of internal censorship. We'll now consider two lines of research that bear on this conception. One concerns Freud's theory of dreams, the other his theory of repression and defense.

Freud's theory of dreams   Stated in the most general terms, Freud's theory asserts that dreams tend to reflect the current emotional preoccupations of the dreamer, including those of which he is unaware, often portrayed in a condensed and symbolic form. This is probably quite true. Thus, patients who await major surgery reveal their fears in what they dream about during the two or three nights before the operation. Their fears are rarely expressed directly; few, if any, of their dreams are about scalpels or operating rooms. The reference is indirect, in condensed and symbolized form, as in dreams about falling from tall ladders or standing on a high, swaying bridge, or about a decrepit machine that needs repair (Breger, Hunter, and Lane, 1971).

Such evidence indicates that dreams often express whatever motives are currently most important. But Freud's theory went much further than this, for it insisted that the manifest dream represents a wish fulfillment and is a censored and disguised version of the latent dream that lies underneath. This conception of dreams has been much criticized. To begin with, there is considerable doubt that all (or even many) dreams are attempts at wish fulfillments, whether disguised or open. In one study, subjects were made extremely thirsty before they went to sleep. Since thirst is hardly a forbidden urge, there is no reason to suppose an internal censorship. However, none of the subjects reported dreams of drinking. Since they were so thirsty, why didn't they gratify themselves in their dreams (Dement and Wolpert, 1958)?

Another problem is the fact that the same urge is sometimes freely expressed in dreams, but heavily disguised on other occasions. Tonight, the sleeper dreams of unabashed sexual intercourse; tomorrow night, she dreams of riding a team of wild horses. For sake of argument, let us agree that riding is a symbol for

The Nightmare   *This painting by Henry Fuseli (painted in 1783 and said to have decorated Freud's office) highlights what seems to be one of the difficulties of Freud's dream theory. If all dreams are wish fulfillments, what accounts for nightmares? According to Freud, they are often dreams in which the latent dream is not sufficiently disguised. The forbidden wish is partially recognized, anxiety breaks through, and the sleeper suffers a nightmare. (Courtesy of The Detroit Institute of Arts)*

intercourse. Why should the censor disguise tomorrow what is so freely allowed tonight?

One investigator, C. S. Hall, has come up with a plausible suggestion (Hall, 1953). According to Hall, the dream symbol does not *disguise* an underlying idea; on the contrary, it *expresses* it. In Hall's view, the dream is a rather concrete mental shorthand that embodies a feeling or emotion. Riding a horse, plowing a field, planting a seed—all of these may be concrete renditions of the idea of sexual intercourse. But they are not meant to hide this idea. Their function is much the same as the cartoonist's picture of Uncle Sam or John Bull. These are representations of the United States and of England, but they are certainly not meant as disguises for them. During sleep, more specifically during REM sleep (see Chapter 3), we are incapable of the extreme complexity and abstractness of waking mental life. We are thus reduced to a more concrete and archaic form of thinking. The wishes and fears of our waking life are still present at night, and we dream about them. But the way in which these are now expressed tends to be more primitive, a concrete pictorialization that combines fragments of various waking concerns and serves as a kind of symbolic cartoon.

Such findings do not dispute Freud's belief that dreams involve complex cognitive processes many of which are hidden from view. But they argue against the central tenet of his theory: that they are disguised representations of forbidden urges that are held underground in their threatening, unmasked form.

Laboratory studies of anxiety and recall   The concept of repression is the cornerstone of psychoanalytic thought. What evidence bears on this hypothesis? There have been many efforts to produce repression and related effects in the laboratory (see Eriksen and Pierce, 1968). But this task is far from easy. According to psychoanalytic theory, motivated forgetting is a defense against anxiety. One would therefore expect that materials that are associated with anxiety would be recalled less readily than neutral items. But how can the experimenter be sure that the critical material is really anxiety-provoking for the subject?

To cope with this problem, several investigators selected material to fit each subject's own pattern of anxieties. One way of doing this is by an initial word-association test. The subject is given a list of words; she has to reply to each with the first word that comes to mind. If her reaction to any one stimulus word is unusually slow or if it is accompanied by increased heart rate or a marked galvanic skin response, that word is presumably emotion-arousing for her. Using this method, one experimenter selected a set of neutral and emotional words for each subject (Jacobs, 1955). When these were later used as the responses in a paired-associate task, the subject had more trouble in producing the emotional than the neutral items. One way of explaining the result is to assume that as the emotionally loaded word was about to be retrieved from memory, it triggered anxiety, which blocked further efforts at retrieval. (For a review and methodological critique, see Holmes, 1990).

Seen in this light, repression may turn out to be a special case of retrieval failure. We have previously seen that recall is enormously dependent upon the presence of an appropriate retrieval cue. We forget the street names of the city we grew up in, but most of them come back when we revisit the city after many years. The same may hold for memories that Freud said are repressed. Perhaps they are not really held back by some imperious censor; perhaps they are rather misfiled under a hard-to-reach rubric and cannot be retrieved for this reason. One might want to add some further assumptions about the role of anxiety in maintaining this state of affairs. Perhaps anxiety blocks refiling; perhaps it impedes the use of appropriate retrieval cues (Erdelyi and Goldberg, 1979).

The retrieval-blocking interpretation of repression is part of a more general approach taken by some contemporary psychologists who have tried to fit the concept of the unconscious into the framework of modern cognitive psychology. They agree with the psychoanalysts' assertion that much of mental life is affected by processes of which we are not conscious, pointing to such phenomena as blind sight, implicit retrieval, and automatization as illustrations (see Chapter 8). They do not, however, share Freud's belief that these unconscious processes are necessarily defenses against anxiety or have the sexual and aggressive quality that Freud attributed to them. To quote one author, our modern view of nonconscious mental life suggests that, while quite extensive, it is often "kinder, gentler, and more rational than the seething unconscious of Freud" (Kihlstrom, 1990).

FREUD'S CONTRIBUTIONS IN RETROSPECT

We have seen that many of Freud's beliefs have not been confirmed. There are good grounds to doubt Freud's essentially Hobbesian view of human nature. There is little evidence for his general theory of psychosexual development, and there is good reason to believe that he overemphasized biological givens at the expense of cultural factors. We have also seen that Freud can be criticized not just for what he asserted but for the way in which he tried to prove his claims. By now, there is general agreement that the psychoanalytic couch is not a source of objective fact and that many of Freud's theoretical proposals are rather vague and metaphorical, so that it is not clear how one can decide whether they are right or wrong. All in all, this is a formidable set of criticisms. But even so, many psychologists would maintain that, wrong as he probably was in any number of particulars, Sigmund Freud must nevertheless be regarded as one of the giants of psychology, one of the few our field has known thus far.

There are at least two reasons. The first concerns one major conception of Freud's that still stands, however much it may have to be modified and reinterpreted—the notion that there is some kind of internal conflict of which we are often unaware. Freud was not the first to recognize that we are often torn in opposite directions and that we frequently deceive ourselves about what we want (Ellenberger, 1970). But he was the first for whom this insight was the cornerstone of an entire point of view. Whether his own therapeutic procedure, psychoanalysis, is an appropriate tool to make the unknown known and thus to restore a measure of free choice to the emotionally crippled victims of inner

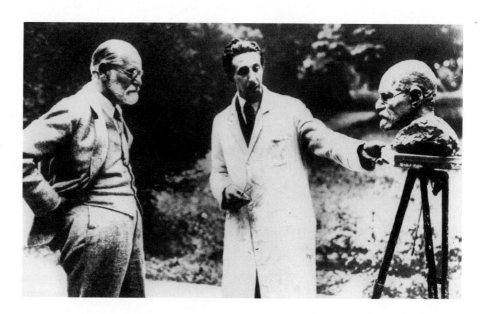

Freud looking at a bust of himself sculpted for his seventy-fifth birthday by O. Nemon (Courtesy of Wide World Photos)

conflict is still debatable (see Chapter 19). But whether his therapy works or not, Freud's contribution remains. He saw that we do not know ourselves, that we are not masters of our own souls. By pointing out how ignorant we are, he set a task for later investigators who may ultimately succeed, so that we may then be able to follow Socrates's deceptively simple prescription for a good life, "Know thyself."

The other major reason why Freud has a lasting place among the greats of intellectual history is the sheer scope of his theoretical conception. His was a view of human nature that was virtually all-embracing. It tried to encompass both rational thought and emotional urges. It conceived of neurotic ailments as a consequence of the same psychological forces that operate in everyday life. It saw humans as biological organisms as well as social beings, as creatures whose present is rooted in their past and who are simultaneously children and adults. The range of psychological phenomena that Freud tried to comprehend within his theory is staggering—neurotic symptoms, personality patterns, social groupings, family relations, humor, slips of the tongue, dreams, artistic productions, aspects of religious thought. Freud's theory has many faults, but this long list highlights some of its virtues. It dealt with matters of genuine human significance; it concerned both human beings and their works; it was an account that was about humanity as a whole.

We now know that many of Freud's views have not been confirmed, but there is no doubt that these views have influenced virtually all thinkers in these areas who have come after him. For Freud was one of those rare intellectual figures who cast his shadow over a whole century. And right or wrong, he provided a guide for posterity by showing us the kinds of questions we must answer before we can claim to have a full theory of human personality.

THE PSYCHODYNAMIC APPROACH: PERSONALITY DIFFERENCES

FOCUS QUESTIONS

- How does Karen Horney explain people's neurotic, self-sabotaging behavior?
- What is ego psychology? What does George Vaillant's longitudinal study suggest about the coping strategies people use over their life spans?

While the primary focus of psychodynamic theory (and of Freud's theory in particular) is about human personality in general, it does offer many proposals about the way in which people (especially "normal" people) differ from each other and also how those differences come about. Freud's theory of oral and anal personalities is one example. More recent attempts at theorizing by various neo-Freudians classify and analyze personality differences in terms of the person's dominant patterns of defense. The neo-Freudians, like Freud himself, believe that anxiety is an inevitable part of human existence and that some defenses against anxiety will therefore be found in everyone. What makes people different is the pattern of defenses they have erected.

PATTERNS OF NEUROTIC CONFLICT

A major figure in the analysis of these patterns of defenses was Karen Horney (1885–1952), who argued that many people in modern Western society suffer from *basic anxiety*—an "all-pervading feeling of being alone and

Self-destructive behavior (From B. Kliban, Luminous animals. *Copyright 1983, B. Kliban, Penguin Books*)

helpless in a hostile world" (Horney, 1937, p. 89). Horney believed that this anxious feeling should not be traced to childhood struggles with infantile sexual conflicts. She felt that instead its roots are in our culture, which often makes incompatible demands on the individual.

According to Karen Horney, the neurotics' basic anxiety leads them to the frantic pursuit of various goals, sought less for themselves than as a way to deaden this anxiety. Some neurotics try to assuage their anxiety by seeking love, others by seeking prestige or possessions, still others by withdrawing from any genuine emotional involvements, and yet others by deadening the anxiety with alcohol or drugs (Horney, 1937, 1945, 1950). Such efforts often fail, but they generally persist and harden into enduring patterns of personality. The question is why. Horney's answer is that the neurotic conflict creates a self-perpetuating vicious circle.

An example of such a vicious circle is the neurotic search for love. If a man needs a woman's love to deaden his sense of basic anxiety, his demands for affection will be unconditional and excessive. But if so, they can't possibly be fulfilled. The slightest failure to accede to his wishes will be interpreted as a rebuff and a rejection. This will increase his feelings of anxiety, which will make him even more desperate for affectionate reassurance, which will further increase the chances of rebuff, and so on and so forth. Add to this the fact that such rebuffs—whether real or imagined—lead to hostility, which he can't possibly acknowledge lest he lose her altogether. Add to this the further fact that since his basic anxiety makes him devalue himself, he may well begin to devalue her. How could she be as wonderful as he thought at first, if she loves him? As Groucho Marx once said, "I wouldn't want to belong to any club that would accept me as a member." All of these further factors combine to enhance the love-seeking neurotic's sense of anxiety, which then refuels his desperate need for love and affection.

COPING PATTERNS AND MENTAL HEALTH

■ The patterns we have just described characterize people with emotional conflicts that in some cases are quite serious. But can they help us understand normal people? Contemporary psychodynamically oriented theorists would say that they can. For in their view, unconscious conflict and defense mechanisms are found in normals as well as in people with profound emotional disorders; what distinguishes the two is the extent to which those conflicts are appropriately resolved.

Several investigators have studied characteristic patterns of defense using normal people. Much of this work was influenced by an emerging new movement in psychoanalysis, called *ego psychology,* whose initial impetus probably came from Freud's daughter Anna Freud (1895–1982). Its leaders include Heinz Hartmann (1894–1970), as well as Erik Erikson (1902–1994), whose work we encountered in a previous chapter (see Chapter 14). Adherents of this position share the neo-Freudian concern with cultural and interpersonal factors. But they add a further element by stressing the healthy aspects of the self as it tries to cope with the world—to deal with reality as it is rather than to distort it or hide from it (Freud, 1946; Hartmann, 1964).

Anna Freud (Photograph courtesy of the Bettmann Archive)

LONGITUDINAL STUDIES OF COPING PATTERNS

To find out how coping patterns are employed over the course of the life span, a number of investigators have performed *longitudinal studies,* that is, studies in which the same person is examined at different ages. Longitudinal studies that cover a span of twenty to thirty years represent an arduous undertaking; subjects

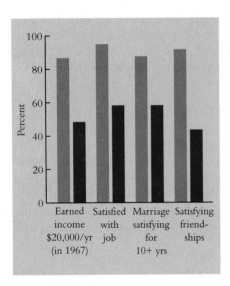

17.2 Maturity of defense mechanisms and life adjustment *Adult success at work and love, as shown by men with predominantly mature (blue) and immature (dark red) adaptive styles. (After Vaillant, 1971)*

drop out of the study for any number of reasons, and the investigators who begin the study are rarely the ones who finally complete it. In longitudinal studies of personality, the raw material is usually in the form of interview records conducted at different times. These records are later rated for various characteristics, such as certain personality traits or the use of this or another mechanism of defense.

An example of such a longitudinal study is George Vaillant's analysis of the case reports of ninety-four male college graduates studied at different points in their life span. They were extensively interviewed at age nineteen, and then again at thirty-one, and yet again at forty-seven. Vaillant studied the predominant patterns of defense—that is, ways of coping—each man used at these three ages. He classified these coping patterns according to their level of psychological maturity. At the bottom of the hierarchy were mechanisms that are often found in early childhood and during serious psychiatric breakdown—such as denial or gross distortions of external reality. Further up the ladder were patterns often seen in adolescence and in disturbed adults—such as projection, hypochondria, and irrational, emotional outbursts—"acting out." Still higher were the mechanisms studied by Freud and seen in many adults—repression, isolation, reaction formation, and the like. At the top of the hierarchy were coping patterns that Vaillant saw in "healthy" adolescents and adults—such as humor, suppression (a conscious effort to push anxiety-evoking thoughts out of mind, at least for the time being, as opposed to repression, which is an unconscious process), and altruism (in which one tries to give to others what one might wish to receive oneself).

Vaillant's findings are simple enough. It's not particularly surprising (though it is certainly reassuring) that as his subjects grew older, their coping mechanisms generally became more mature. There was growth and change, but there was also some continuity; men whose coping patterns were better integrated at nineteen, were somewhat more likely to have mature patterns in their forties, which then predicted various objective indices—satisfaction in marriage, rewarding friendships, more gratifying jobs, and better physical health (see Figure 17.2). As so often, it is by no means clear just what in those men's lives was cause and what was effect, but regardless of whether the mature coping defenses produced success in marriage and career or vice versa, it is worth knowing that the two—mature coping and personal success—tend to be correlated (Vaillant, 1974, 1976, 1977).

COPING AND THE UNCONSCIOUS

On the face of it, the preceding discussion of adaptive patterns may appear rather distant from the orientation of psychodynamic theorists, especially as represented by Freud. After all, Freud emphasized unconscious processes that operate in a murky underground of which we are unaware. In contrast, the coping responses of normal people seem much more ordinary, and they are at least sometimes in plain view. Is there any relation between these two?

Ego-oriented psychoanalysts—and most modern psychologists—would answer yes. For whatever their many differences, the defense mechanisms of the neurotic and the shoulder-shrugging reaction of the mature adult who refuses to worry about things he can't help anyway have one thing in common—they are both ways of trying to cope with and adapt to the strains and stresses of existence.

The fact that some of these adaptive reactions are fully conscious while others are not doesn't necessarily mean that there is a sharp break between them. For a number of psychologists have pointed out that what Freud called "unconscious

Improvisation *Some actors are famed for their ability to improvise on the spur of the moment. An example is Robin Williams, who improvised many of his lines in the film* Good Morning Vietnam, *1987. (Courtesy of the Kobal Collection)*

mechanisms" may be regarded as ways of not attending, in line with the "kinder, gentler, and more rational" unconscious we discussed previously (Bowers, 1984; Erdelyi, 1985; Kihlstrom, 1987). The person who is in favor of a particular political candidate is much more likely to attend to arguments on his behalf than to arguments that favor his opponent. The first he will tend to remember; the second he is likely to forget. Similarly, the woman who has just suffered a painful divorce may prefer not to think about her ex-husband. When some topic comes up that starts to remind her about him, she will deliberately try to think about something else and may forget what it was that started the new train of thought. This method of turning away from one's own pain may not be as exotic as the complicated repressive maneuvers that Freud attributed to his patients, but it belongs to the same family.

Most of us physically avoid some situations we would rather not face; by the same token, some of us mentally avoid (that is, don't attend to) sights or thoughts or memories we find unpleasant or frightening. Seen in this light, the so-called unconscious mechanisms lose some of their mystery. They are just one more way of dealing with the world.

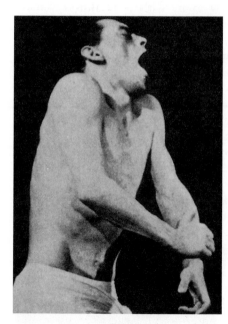

Spontaneity in the theater *Several modern movements emphasize spontaneity and creativity in the theater. An influential example is the theatrical school founded by the Polish director Jerzy Grotowski, who requires his actors to perform in a kind of trance, to give themselves totally in a confrontation with the play and the audience. The figure is taken from one of his productions,* The Constant Prince, *by Pedro Calderón de la Barca. (Reproduced by permission of Jerzy Grotowski)*

THE HUMANISTIC APPROACH

FOCUS QUESTIONS

- What is the humanistic approach to personality?

- How does the concept of motivation espoused by Maslow and other humanists differ from that of behaviorists and psychoanalysts?

- What did Maslow mean by "self-actualization"? Is there any scientific evidence for self-actualization?

Some forty years ago, a new perspective on human motivation and personality—the ***humanistic approach***—gained some prominence. According to its adherents, neither trait theorists, behaviorists, nor psychodynamic theorists have much to say about healthy, striving human beings. In their view, psychoanalysts look at people as if they are all emotional cripples, behaviorists regard them as if they are blind, unthinking robots, and trait theorists see them as material to file in sterile pigeon holes. Humanistic psychologists believe that all of these views have lost sight of what is truly human about human beings. Healthy humans want to feel free to choose and determine their own lives rather than to exist as mere pawns pushed around by stimuli from without and unconscious impulses from within. They seek more than food and sex and safety, strive for more than mere adjustment—they want to grow, to develop their potential, to become ***self-actualized.***

Returning to our theatrical analogy, the humanistic approach can be likened to certain modern movements in theater that emphasize spontaneity and improvisation. Actors who belong to this school insist that what is most important is genuine, authentic feeling. At least in principle (though rarely in actual practice), such actors might depart from the playwright's words and the director's stagings to provide the audience and themselves with a sense of freedom and spontaneity. To the extent that this occurs, there is no mask left at all; the actor and the part have become one.

547

THE MAJOR FEATURES OF THE HUMANISTIC MOVEMENT

■ According to Abraham Maslow (1908–1970), the humanistic movement represents a kind of "third force" in American psychology—the other two being behaviorism and psychoanalysis. For expositional purposes, we will begin by presenting some of the major features of this movement before discussing them more critically.

A POSITIVE VIEW OF HUMAN MOTIVATION

A major contrast between humanistic psychologists and the behaviorists and psychoanalysts that they oppose is in their contrasting conception of human motivation. According to Maslow, behaviorists and psychoanalysts see human beings as engaged in a never-ending struggle to remove some internal tension or make up for some deficit. The result is an essentially pessimistic and negative conception of human nature. Seen in this light, people always want to get away from something (pain, hunger, sexual tension) rather than to gain something positive. This perspective necessarily leads to an emphasis on the physiological needs—hunger, thirst, escape from pain, sex. Maslow called these *deficiency needs*; in all such cases, we experience a lack and want to fill it. According to Maslow, an analogous deficiency sometimes underlies social needs such as the desire for prestige or security; an example is the woman who hungers for the admiration of all men around her and feels empty without it. But as Maslow pointed out, release from pain and tension does not account for everything we strive for. We sometimes seek things for their own sake, as a positive goal in themselves. There is the joy of solving a puzzle, the exhilaration of galloping on a horse, the ecstasy of fulfilled love, the quiet rapture in the contemplation of great art and music or a beautiful sunrise. All of these are experiences that human beings seek, and it is these positive, enriching experiences—rather than the filled stomach or the sexual release at orgasm—that make us most distinctively human. A hungry rat and a sexually aroused monkey seek food and orgasmic release pretty much as we do, but the joy of Beethoven's Ninth Symphony is ours alone. Maslow insisted that to understand what is truly human, psychologists must consider motives that go beyond the deficiency needs (Maslow, 1968).

Thus, Maslow proposed a *hierarchy of needs* in which the lower-order physiological needs are at the bottom, safety needs are further up, the need for attach-

Self-actualization shown through self-portraits To actualize one's self may take a whole lifetime. Some great artists have given us a graphic record of the process at different points in their lives, as in these self-portraits by Rembrandt. One was created at the age of thirty-four, when he was very successful and saw himself as a Renaissance gentleman artist and virtuoso. The other was painted at about age sixty, when he tried to reaffirm his identity through his art and portrayed himself as a painter holding the tools of his craft (Wright, 1982). (*Left:* Self-Portrait at the Age of thirty-four; *courtesy of the National Gallery. Right:* Portrait of the Artist; *courtesy of English Heritage, The Iveagh Bequest*)

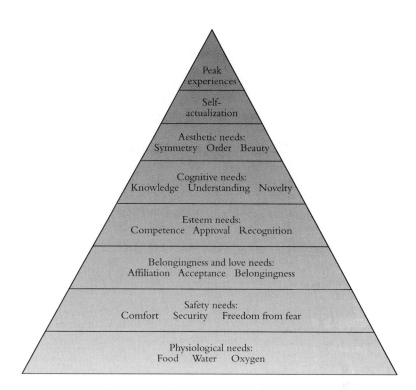

17.3 Maslow's hierarchy of needs
People will strive for higher-order needs (esteem or artistic achievement) generally after lower-order needs (hunger, safety) have been satisfied. (After Maslow, 1954)

ment and love is still higher, and the desire for esteem is yet higher. At the very top of the hierarchy is the striving for self-actualization—the desire to realize oneself to the fullest (of which more later) (see Figure 17.3).

Maslow believed that people will only strive for higher-order needs (say, self-esteem or artistic achievement) when lower-order needs (such as hunger) are satisfied. By and large this is plausible enough; the urge to write poetry generally takes a back seat if one hasn't eaten for days. But as Maslow pointed out, there are exceptions. Some artists starve rather than give up their poetry or their painting, and some martyrs proclaim their faith regardless of pain or suffering. But to the extent that Maslow's assumption holds, the motive at the very top of his hierarchy—that is, the drive toward self-actualization—will become a primary concern only when all other needs beneath are satisfied.

SELF-ACTUALIZATION

Given the satisfaction of the lower-level needs, the stage is set for the motive at the very top of Maslow's hierarchy, the desire for ***self-actualization.*** Maslow and other humanistic psychologists describe this as the desire to realize one's potential, to fulfill oneself, to become what one can become (Maslow, 1968, 1970). But exactly what does this mean?

Maslow gave some examples by presenting case histories of a number of people that he and his collaborators regarded as "self-actualized." Some of them were individuals that he had personally interviewed; others were historical figures (for example, Thomas Jefferson and Ludwig van Beethoven) or more recent luminaries (such as Eleanor Roosevelt and Albert Einstein), whose lives were studied by means of historical or other documents. Unlike most other investigators in the field, Maslow was not interested in these subjects' specific attributes or behavior patterns; all he looked for were some overall patterns that he felt were shared by them all. As Maslow saw it, these self-actualizers had many admirable characteristics. Among other things, they were realistically oriented, accepted themselves and others, were spontaneous, cared more about the problems they were working on than about themselves, had intimate relationships with a few people rather than superficial relationships with many, and had democratic values—all in all, an admirable list of human qualities (Maslow, 1968, 1970).

According to Maslow, another characteristic of self-actualized persons is that they are more likely than other people to have what he called ***peak experiences.*** Peak experiences are profound and deeply felt moments in a person's life in which there is a "feeling of great ecstasy and awe . . . with the conviction that something extremely important and valuable had happened . . ." (Maslow, 1970, p. 164). Such moments might come while with a lover, or while watching the sea or a sunset, or while listening to music or watching a play—but regardless of when and where they occur, they seem to have some important and lasting effects on the individual who thereafter is likely to see himself and others in a more spontaneous and healthier way.

EVALUATING THE HUMANISTIC APPROACH

■ In trying to evaluate the humanistic approach to personality, we must begin by asking about its empirical and conceptual foundations.

EMPIRICAL AND CONCEPTUAL DIFFICULTIES

Consider some of the assertions made by the proponents of the humanistic approach. How do we know that self-actualizers are in fact as Maslow described them to be—for example, realistically oriented, accepting of themselves and others, spontaneous, problem-centered, democratic, and so on; or that peak experiences have lasting and often beneficial effects on later life; or that self-actualizers have more peak experiences than other people? As yet, there is no real evidence that would allow us to draw such conclusions.

An even more serious criticism is the fact that many of the core conceptions of the humanistic approach are exceedingly unclear. Just what is meant by *self-actualization,* or by "letting yourself go and being yourself," or by a peak experience? Since these terms are only vaguely defined, it is difficult to know how to evaluate any assertions about them.

Consider Maslow's study of self-actualizers. Maslow chose a number of persons as exemplars, including a number of prominent and historical figures. But by what criteria did he select them? Among the historical figures he chose were Thomas Jefferson, Abraham Lincoln (in his later years), Eleanor Roosevelt, and Albert Einstein. Most of us would agree that these were admirable and creative people, and we can understand what is meant when someone says that they fulfilled their potential and "actualized themselves." But why can't the same term be applied to many other individuals, some of whom are far from admirable and may be veritable monsters? What about Napoleon, or Al Capone, or even Adolf Hitler? It's very likely that these persons felt that they had become what they were meant to become (at least until St. Helena, or Alcatraz, or the final days in the Berlin bunker.) But if so, why shouldn't we regard *them* as self-actualized? Given their belief that human growth has an inherent tendency toward good rather than evil, Maslow and Rogers would presumably rule out—by definition—moral monsters such as Capone or Hitler. But this line of reasoning can certainly be questioned. The development of personality may be a growth process, but this alone is not enough grounds for optimism. Given soil, sun, and water, a rose seedling will indeed become a rose. But if the seedling is a certain weed, it may self-actualize and become a full-grown stand of poison ivy.

"I'm quite fulfilled. I always wanted to be a chicken." (Drawing by Joseph Farris; © 1989, The New Yorker Magazine, Inc.)

THE HUMANISTIC APPROACH

The theater of protest   *The humanistic approach to personality is reminiscent of protest movements in the literary and political spheres. Examples are various modern dramatic productions that attack contemporary attitudes, as in Peter Weiss's play* Marat/Sade *in which contemporary society is likened to an insane asylum. (From the 1966 film* Marat/Sade, *directed by Peter Brook; courtesy of the Kobal Collection)*

HUMANISTIC PSYCHOLOGY AS A PROTEST MOVEMENT

It appears that many of the major tenets of the humanistic approach to personality rest on rather shaky foundations. But if so, why should we take it seriously? One answer is that the humanistic approach is best considered as a protest movement. It reacts against both behaviorism and psychoanalysis because it regards them as representatives of sterile mechanisms that treat people as marionettes pushed and pulled by forces from without and within. It reacts against trait psychology because it regards this approach as devoted to an endless cataloguing that reduces humans to mere ciphers. And it reacts against the general focus of much contemporary psychology, which it regards as narrow and pessimistic, oriented toward human sickness and deficiency rather than toward health and upward striving.

In some ways, the humanistic approach to personality is reminiscent of some prior movements in the political and literary spheres. Some two hundred years ago, the Romantic poets in England and Germany elevated feeling over reason, celebrated individualism and natural man, and deplored the effects of eighteenth-century science and technology. Some, such as William Blake and Samuel Coleridge, sought peak experiences in mystical visions or in opium dreams. Others railed against the cold, mechanical science that had left the universe dry and bare. An example is John Keats's lament that "Newton has destroyed all the poetry of the rainbow by reducing it to the prismatic colors" (in Abrams, 1953, p. 303). And many of them agreed with the social philosopher Jean Jacques Rousseau (1712–1778), whose writings helped to shape the French and American Revolutions, that "man is by nature good, and . . . only our institutions have made him bad!" (in Durant and Durant, 1967, p. 19).

The similarity between these sentiments and many of the themes of the humanistic psychologists is clear enough. The Romantics protested against what they regarded as a cold, mechanical approach to nature and politics; the humanistic psychologists lodge similar complaints against contemporary approaches to psychology.

Romanticism in the arts *The Romantic artists of the early nineteenth century stressed the full expression of the emotions. An example is this painting by Caspar David Friedrich. (*Frau in der Morgensonne; *courtesy of Museum Folkwang, Essen)*

To be sure, the Romantic poets did much more than protest; they also made lasting contributions to literature. And Rousseau influenced the political landscape of Europe for a century after his death. Is there a corresponding positive contribution of humanistic psychology? Some critics feel that apart from Rogers's work on the practice and evaluation of psychotherapy, the humanists' concepts are as yet too vague and their assertions as yet too unproven to count as serious positive scientific accomplishments (e.g., Smith, 1950). Others argue that the humanists often serve as moral advocates rather than dispassionate scientists. They tell us what personality *should* be rather than what it is.

But there is one accomplishment of which we can be sure. The humanistic psychologists remind us of many phenomena that other approaches to the study of personality have largely ignored. People do strive for more than food and sex or prestige; they read poetry, listen to music, fall in love, have occasional peak experiences, try to actualize themselves. Whether the humanistic psychologists have really helped us to understand these elusive phenomena better than we did before is debatable. But there is no doubt that what they have done is to insist that these phenomena are there, that they constitute a vital aspect of what makes us human, and that they must not be ignored.

THE SOCIOCULTURAL PERSPECTIVE

FOCUS QUESTIONS

■ What is the sociocultural perspective on personality?

■ What findings from cultural anthropology suggest that crucial aspects of personality are culture-dependent? Conversely, what findings suggest that some important aspects of personality may be universal?

■ How might a culture's collectivist or individualist orientation affect the personality traits—such as loyalty, conformity, and degree of self-expression—of its members?

■ What evidence suggests that there is cultural variation in the conception of the self?

Whatever their many differences, all of the approaches to personality we've discussed thus far have one thing in common: a focus on the individual. But surely all individuals exist in a social and cultural context that is critical in shaping and defining who they are. Yet by and large personality theorists have ignored that context and focused their efforts almost entirely on the individual, whether by categorizing him (trait theory), by studying how different situations shape him (social learning theory), by trying to uncover his hidden motives (psychodynamic theory), or by celebrating his uniqueness (humanistic psychology). None of these approaches concerns itself particularly with the culture of which the person necessarily is a part. Some modern critics feel that this is a serious lack. They point out that virtually all of the data on which modern personality theory is based come from the study of middle-class western Europeans or North Americans. Can we really be sure that what holds true for these people can be generalized to people in different times, different places, and different cultures?

As we might expect, the answer is both yes and no. For it turns out that in some regards people throughout the world are very different from each other, while in other respects they are much the same.

HUMAN DIVERSITY

■ Much of the evidence that bears on these matters comes from *cultural anthropology,* a discipline that studies ways of living that characterize different societies throughout the world. An early pioneer in this enterprise was Franz Boas (1858–1942), who convinced many anthropologists to study the preliterate cultures of the world before they disappeared altogether. Among his students were Ruth Benedict (1887–1948) and Margaret Mead (1901–1978), two of the most influential figures in this area; their work documents the enormous variety of human character and personality, shaped as they are by drastically different cultural traditions.

DIFFERENT PERSONALITY PATTERNS

Ruth Benedict's *Patterns of Culture* (1934) describes the characteristic personality patterns found in three very different preliterate societies. Among the Kwakiutl Indians of the Canadian Northwest, the dominant theme was rivalry and boastful self-glorification. Among the Pueblo Indians of the American Southwest, the primary theme was self-control, cooperation, and very little aggression within the community. And among the Dobu Islanders, there was a great deal of mutual enmity and distrust, and a near-universal conviction that everyone practices sorcery against everyone else.

Other findings pointed to a variety of gender roles in different cultures. Thus Margaret Mead compared the personality traits of men and women in three preliterate New Guinea tribes that lived within a hundred-mile radius of one another. Among the Arapesh, both men and women were mild, cooperative, and, so to speak, "maternal" in their attitudes toward each other and especially toward children. Among the neighboring Mundugomor, both sexes were ferociously aggressive and quarrelsome. In yet another tribe, the Tchambuli, the usual sex roles were reversed: The women were the hale and hearty breadwinners who fished and went to market unadorned. While the women managed the worldly affairs, the men gossiped, adjusted elaborate hairdos, carved and painted, and practiced intricate dance steps (Mead, 1935, 1937). Here was further evidence that the ways of modern Western society are not necessarily universal characteristics of human nature.

Of course neither Benedict nor Mead suggested that every member of a given culture exhibits the pattern they described. Not every Kwakiutl was vehe-

Margaret Mead in Samoa, 1925 *(Courtesy of the Institute for Intercultural Studies)*

PERSONALITY II ■ CH. 17

mently boastful; not every Arapesh was gentle and cooperative. What they tried to describe is a typical and common personality pattern that characterizes a given cultural group.

HUMAN SAMENESS

■ The anthropological evidence suggests that the typical personality patterns of the Kwakiutl, Arapesh, Ifaluk, and ourselves are in many ways very different. But a number of authors point out that there are also many respects in which the dominant personalitiese of these various societies must be alike, for whatever their cultural differences, they all share a common humanity.

The broad pattern of evidence thus suggests that the differences between the members of various cultures are not as unbridgeable as one might have supposed. Ironically enough, these differences may actually be a tool for discovering some universal principles of human nature. That at least is the underlying rationale of the *cross-cultural method.*

UNIVERSAL PATTERNS OF PERSONALITY

Several anthropologists have criticized Benedict's and Mead's accounts as oversimplifications. For example, they take issue with some of Mead's work by pointing out that there are probably some universal sex roles after all; for example, warfare is generally conducted by the men, even among the Tchambuli. They argue that this may very well be due to biological factors, for aggression is in part under hormonal control; as androgen levels rise, both human and animal males become more aggressive (see Chapter 10). To these critics, some aspects of aggression are part of our biological nature regardless of the culture we belong to. What culture does is to determine how this aggression is to be channeled and against whom, whether it is to be valued, and how much of it will be allowed. (For recent discussions of Mead's work, see Freeman, 1983, 1986; Brady, 1983; Patience and Smith, 1986.)

Some other considerations concern personality traits. Let's assume that we could administer personality tests to some of the people studied by Mead and Benedict. Even granting that some of their descriptions may be overdrawn, one would still guess that the average Kwakiutl male would score much more highly on such traits as dominance and irritability than his Arapesh counterpart. To that extent, the typical personality patterns of the cultures surely differ. But one thing may still be the same: the *dimensions* along which these personalities vary. Some relevant evidence comes from translated personality tests administered in such diverse societies as those in Bangladesh, Brazil, Hong Kong, and Japan. When the results were analyzed, the pattern that emerged was much the same as that found in the United States and in Britain. This was especially true for Eysenck's two main dimensions of extroversion and neuroticism. This is not to say that people in these different cultures do not differ on these personality traits, for they certainly do. For example, extroversion scores are very much higher in the United States than in Japan. What is the same is the way the responses to the items hang together; as a result, the same dimensions of personality emerge. To use an analogy, people come in different shapes and sizes, but their diversity can nevertheless be described by just a handful of tailor's measurements. To be sure, people in Sweden tend to be taller than people in Japan, but the same measuring tape can be used for them all. (Eysenck and Eysenck, 1983; for some qualifications see Bond, 1979; Yang and Bond, 1990).

In some ways, these results should not be surprising. Traits such as extroversion and emotional stability may well be based on built-in characteristics related

554

A

B

Cultural differences in socialization
(A) In pastoral, horticultural, and agricultural societies, children are expected to perform chores from a very early age. Here, a South American Indian woman weaves a mat, while her young son—as best he can—does likewise. (Photograph by Boris Malkin, Anthro-Photo) (B) In contrast, hunting-gathering societies allow their children a much freer rein. Here, San boys from the Kalahari desert in Botswana play at digging for spring hares, as they've seen their elders do during real spring hare hunts. When these children grow older, they will do in earnest what they do now in play. (Photograph by Irwin DeVore, Anthro-Photo)

to temperament, which we know is in part genetically based (see Chapter 16). If so, these trait dimensions correspond to a broad framework that should in principle fit all humankind. What varies is just where within this framework a particular person falls. And this in part depends on the culture of which an individual is a member.

THE CROSS-CULTURAL METHOD: STUDIES OF THE EFFECTS OF CHILDHOOD

We've repeatedly run across the notion that what happens in early childhood determines later personality. This view is most prominently associated with Freud, but it is found in the writings of many other authors as well and permeates much of modern Western thinking. Those who embrace the cross-cultural method examine this view by studying the relation between a culture's beliefs and practices—family structures, child-rearing patterns, rituals and religious thought—and the typical personality characteristics of its members. In effect, they take advantage of cultural differences to ask how—and whether—certain cultural variations, especially in the area of child rearing, shape personality.

In an interesting application of the cross-cultural method, psychologists have considered the effect of socioeconomic factors on child rearing. One study demonstrated a relationship between the economy on which a society is based and its methods of child rearing: Cultures that make their living through agriculture tend to stress compliance, conformity, and responsibility in raising their children, whereas hunting and fishing societies tend to stress self-reliance and initiative (Barry, Child, and Bacon, 1959). Other studies demonstrated that some differences in child rearing in our own society may be associated with social class. The evidence suggests that parents encourage their children to behave at home as they themselves do at work. Since members of the working class tend to be more closely supervised than are members of the middle class, working-class parents tend to emphasize control from outside and are more likely to use physical punishment, an extreme version of physical control. Because the work of the middle class tends to be self-directed, they are inclined to encourage self-control in their children as well (Kohn, 1969; Hess, 1970).

COLLECTIVISM AND INDIVIDUALISM

The relations between child-rearing patterns and socioeconomic factors just described seems clear enough. But does either of the two cause the other? Most likely there is no direct cause-and-effect link. Instead, they are both strands in a complex web of patterns of thought and action handed down from one generation to the next. It is this web that constitutes the culture, and according to many anthropologists, its strands cannot be studied in isolation. As they see it, a culture is a kind of social Gestalt, whose parts only make sense by reference to the whole, much as a note takes its character from the melody in which it appears. If so, the best way to compare cultures would be along some dimension that considers the culture as a whole.

Many authors believe that current cultures and ethnic subgroups can be distinguished according to their position on the dimension of ***collectivism-individualism*** (Triandis, 1989). Collectivist societies include many of the societies of Latin America, and most of the cultures of Asia and Africa. Individualist societies include the dominant cultures of the United States, western Europe, Canada, and Australia.

In collectivist societies, the emphasis is on the needs, demands, and values of the family and immediate community. It is these primary groups that determine

A

B

Japanese collectivism versus U. S. individualism *(A) Tokyo school children. (Photograph © Yves Gellie/Odyssey Matrix, 1990) (B) Kindergartners from P.S. 75, New York City. (Photograph courtesy of Marian Johnson, 1994)*

what is expected and what is frowned upon and that provide the major motives and rewards. In individualist societies, the emphasis is on a person's own private goals and aspirations. In such societies, one's important life choices—of occupation, friends, and spouse—are much less affected by the wishes of family and neighbors, for the ultimate goal is to be true to oneself. Thus students from individualist California are more likely to agree with statements that emphasize self-reliance, such as "Only those who depend on themselves get ahead in life," than are students from collectivist Hong Kong or Costa Rica. In contrast, students from Hong Kong and Costa Rica will be more likely to agree with statements that affirm a concern for one's family and close friends, such as "I would help within my means if a relative told me he (she) is in financial difficulty" and "I like to live close to my friends" (Triandis et al., 1988).

Once again, it is important to realize that terms that describe a culture don't necessarily apply to all of its members. They designate what is typical or average. There are surely some students from Hong Kong who would marry against their parents' wishes and some from California who would not. But the *average* student from Hong Kong will be more likely to behave along collectivist lines than the *average* student from California.

IN-GROUPS AND OUT-GROUPS

Collectivists and individualists (that is, members of collectivist and individualist societies) tend to differ in some further ways. Consider group pressure. On the face of it one might expect collectivists to be more subject to group pressure than individualists. But it turns out that this depends on the nature of the group. Collectivists are more affected than individualists by pressure from members of their **in-group,** a group to which they are tied by traditional bonds—their family (including second cousins and great-aunts and so on),★ classmates, close friends, and fellow workers. But in contrast, they are less affected than individualists by members of the **out-group,** a group that is best defined by exclusion, being constituted by those who do *not* belong to the in-group.

A related phenomenon is the permanence of an individual's social bonds. Collectivists belong to relatively few in-groups, but their bonds to those are strong and long-lasting. It's no accident that in Japan (a collectivist society) workers tend to remain in whatever organization they started out with, wearing their company's colors and singing company songs, such as "A bright heart overflowing with life links together Matsushita Electric" (Weisz, Rothbaum, and Blackburn, 1984). In contrast, members of individualist cultures belong to a whole set of overlapping in-groups, but their relation to these groups is more fragile and less enduring. In part, this is a consequence of their different values. To the individualist, what matters most is the freedom to pursue her own goals and preferences. As these change, so do her social relationships. As a result, individualists generally make friends more easily than collectivists do, but their friendships tend to be impermanent and to lack intimacy. Freedom is very precious, but for some individualists its price is loneliness.

All of this has to be qualified somewhat. It's true that members of collectivist societies are more likely to subordinate their own aspirations to the demands of their in-group than members of individualist cultures like our own are. But that doesn't mean that Westerners are unable to submerge their individuality

★ Of course, individualists and collectivists both have families to which they have strong ties. In a collective society the family is greatly extended. Typical individualists, on the other hand, take family to mean the *nuclear* family: two parents and their children. Individualists often feel affection for their own parents, but they don't feel obliged to live with them or close to them after they've started their own families.

for the sake of some common good. They can and do—sometimes. This is especially true in major emergencies, such as floods, earthquakes, and similar disasters, which often bring out rare qualities of heroism and group spirit. And millions of Americans have shown in one generation after another that they, the citizens of what may well be the most individualist society on earth, are capable of the most extreme acts of self-sacrifice and collectivism in times of war. Americans are less concerned about what their neighbors think and don't sing songs in praise of General Motors, but they too are capable of collective acts and feelings.

INDIVIDUALISM AND SELF-EXPRESSION

Historians point to a number of sources for our modern concept of individualism. Some point to special environmental factors, such as the presence of the frontier in eighteenth- and nineteenth-century America (Tocqueville, 1835). Others trace it to the Protestant Reformation, which insisted that each individual bears a direct relation to God (Weber, 1920). Still others go further back and see its origin in the Italian Renaissance. In that period artists began the practice of signing their own works as if to say "Look here! It's mine!" Until then, painters were craftsmen whose job was simply to paint a pious picture of the Madonna or a good likeness of their patron. But since the Renaissance, the artist's task has changed, for his job now is to make his work different from that of others, to be creative and original, to express himself (Burckhardt, 1860).

John Sabini has argued that our Western individualism has much in common with the value we place on artistic creativity. We celebrate personal uniqueness,

Individualism versus collectivism in art (A) After the middle ages, artists expressed their own individuality in their works, as in this self-portrait by Albrecht Dürer painted in 1499. (From Alte Pinakothek, Munich. Courtesy of Giraudon/Art Resource, New York) (B) In contrast, medieval painters, print makers, and architects saw themselves primarily as craftsmen who often dedicated themselves to some collective effort and were content to remain anonymous. Their lack of interest in individuality is illustrated in this French woodcut circa 1250, depicting the building of the biblical Tower of Babel, in which all workers look virtually alike. (From The Pierpont Morgan Library, New York; courtesy of The Pierpont Morgan Library/Art Resource, New York.) (C) Great medieval cathedrals, like Notre Dame in Paris (shown here), are the result of just such collective efforts. (Photograph courtesy of Robert McLean)

A

B

C

appreciate sincerity, approve of spontaneity, and applaud individual accomplishment. The unique self is regarded as a thing of value in itself, for we value self-expression, regardless of what it is that is expressed (Sabini, 1995). In this regard, we are quite different from collectivists. Americans try to excel and are asked to "be the best you can be." In contrast, collectivists like the Japanese try to become "so identified with their in-group that [their] individuality is not noticed." Where American children are urged to stand out, Japanese children are taught to "stand in" (Weisz, Rothbaum, and Blackburn, 1984; Barlund, 1975).

CULTURAL DIFFERENCES IN THE CONCEPT OF THE SELF

Some authors believe that differences among cultures indicate that our Western conception of the self and human personality has only limited application to cultures other than our own. In their view, many other cultures don't see the individual as we do—as ultimately separate and independent from the social framework in which she lives. They neither see nor value this socially abstracted personal independence, but define the self through its interdependence with others (e.g., Markus and Kitayama, 1991). Richard Shweder and his collaborators have tried to demonstrate this difference by comparing the responses of Western and non-Western subjects when asked to describe a close acquaintance. Americans were likely to use abstract trait terms, such as, "She is friendly." In contrast, subjects in India were inclined to describe what a person does in a particular social context, as in "She brings cakes to my family on festival days," or "He has trouble giving to his family" (Shweder and Bourne, 1986).

Whether Shweder's findings really prove that different cultures have a different conception of the self is debatable; the real difference may be in how the subjects talk about people rather than in how they think about them (e.g., Sabini, 1995). A more persuasive argument comes from some detailed accounts of life on the Indonesian island of Bali, provided by the anthropologist Clifford Geertz. As Geertz describes it, Bali's culture (at least until about 1950 or so) is at one extreme of the collectivism-individualism dimension and may well possess a different conception of selfhood (Geertz, 1983).

Consider people's names. In Bali, individuals have personal names (our equivalent of Henry or Lila), but they are rarely used. Instead, they have an elaborate system of other labels. One is a birth-order name (first-child, second-child, and so on) that parents and siblings use to address children and adolescents. Another is a complex naming system that refers to one's descendants, based on the name of one's first child (e.g., "Father of Henry"). When one's first grandchild is born, one's own name changes (e.g., "Grandfather of Ellen"). And if one lives until the first great-grandchild is born, one's name changes again (e.g., "Great-grandfather of Philip"). In addition, there is a complex system of status titles (e.g., high caste, middle caste, and so on) and social role indicators (e.g., elder of such and such a village). There is quite a difference between this and the American "Hello, I'm Joe."

This complex system of names and titles is part and parcel of a pattern of social life ruled by an elaborate system of ritual and etiquette that enters into every sphere of human existence, whether familial, economic, political, or religious. Individuality is suppressed; all that matters is the proper outward form. To quote Geertz:

> . . . Anything idiosyncratic, anything characteristic of the individual merely because he is who he is physically, psychologically, or biographically is muted in favor of his

Westernization of non-Western cultures
Solar-powered television in Nigeria. (Photograph © John Chiasson, Liaison International)

assigned place in the continuing pageant that is Balinese life. . . . Physically men come and go, mere incidents in a happenstance history, of no genuine importance even to themselves. But the masks they wear, the stage they occupy, the parts they play . . . remain, and they comprise not the facade but the substance of things, not least the self . . ." (Geertz, 1983, p. 62).

This description of Balinese life is one of the best expositions of what some authors mean when they argue that modern psychology's notions of personality and the self are a Western invention that may not apply to cultures (or at least, to all cultures) other than our own.

How does any of this bear on the various approaches to personality we discussed in this and the preceding chapter? It certainly reminds us that some aspects of these personality theories are bound up with our own individualist Western notions of what a person is. But that is to be expected. All of these theoretical approaches try to understand what makes people different: Trait theory concentrates on differences in largely built-in characteristics, social learning theory focuses on differences in what people have learned, and psychodynamic theory looks at differences in unconscious motivations. The humanistic approach is even more Western in its emphasis, for its focus is on human uniqueness, which it both studies and exalts. It is clear that all of these approaches could only arise in a culture in which people are differentiated over and above their differences in age, gender, race, and religion. In Bali such differences are suppressed; in many other non-Western, collectivized societies they are muted. Under the circumstances, we may have to be cautious about supposing that what makes sense in the West makes sense everywhere.

In closing, let us suppose that the sociocultural critique is valid in all regards (and this is by no means undisputed, e.g., Sabini, 1995). If this were so, then our various personality theories would only make sense for people in Western societies. While this would obviously limit their range of application, we shouldn't forget that this range is still very large indeed—encompassing perhaps a billion people. And for better or worse—probably for both—that number may well get larger as much of the world becomes progressively westernized, watching U.S. television, listening to rock music, and wearing jeans.

Even so, the sociocultural critique has provided a valuable corrective. It reminds us that we are not the only society in an ever-shrinking world and that others have different perspectives, a reminder that is all the more valuable as the United States becomes increasingly aware of its own multicultural nature.

TAKING STOCK

In this and the previous chapter, we considered a number of approaches to personality. One is the trait approach, which tries to describe personality by reference to a few basic characteristics, many of which have a built-in basis. Another is the behavioral approach, which focuses on the individual's outwardly observable acts and argues that these acts are produced by the situation that the individual faces now or has faced on previous occasions. Yet another is the psychodynamic approach, which centers on submerged feelings, unconscious conflicts, and desires. Still another is the humanistic approach, which asks how people achieve selfhood and realize their potential. And we concluded with a discussion of the sociocultural perspective, which suggests that certain conceptions of human individuality and the self may be a product of our Western culture that may not apply to cultures other than our own.

Today there are relatively few theorists who would espouse any of these approaches in their most extreme form. By now most adherents of the behavioral approach have shifted to a more cognitive conception of the subject matter, most psychodynamic theorists see unconscious defenses and conscious coping mechanisms as parts of a continuum, virtually everyone grants that what people do depends on both traits and situations, and many theorists recognize that there are both cultural differences and universals.

But even so, some important differences in approach clearly remain. This is probably fortunate. For these different theoretical orientations reflect different perspectives on the same subject matter, and each of these orientations has some validity. Some aspects of personality are clearly built in (trait theory); others are learned (social learning theory); some reflect buried conflicts (psychodynamic theory); others reveal the need for self-actualization (humanistic approach); and yet others may be limited to a particular cultural worldview (the sociocultural perspective). We cannot envisage what a complete theory of personality will look like in the year 2096, but it will surely have to describe all of these aspects of human functioning, for they are all there.

In this regard, the different perspectives on personality are again similar to different approaches to the presentation of character in literature or on the stage. Is the human drama best described by the use of a number of stock types, perhaps designated by a few well-chosen masks, or by well-rounded characters that are like themselves alone and no others? There is no simple yes or no, for people are both similar to and different from each other. Is character best described by the Classicists, who stress human reason, or by the Romantics, who emphasize feeling? Again there is no answer, for both emotion and rationality are part of our very nature. Should actors portray the inner life and concentrate on what lies behind the mask, or should they focus on the outward mask, since that is what the audience sees? Here too there is no answer, for we all have both an inner and an outer life.

We are similar to others, but we are also different. We are pulled by outer and inner forces, but we are also free to make our own choices. We are rational, but we are also impelled by feeling. We are both the masks we wear and something else beneath. We are members of a particular culture, but we are also members of the human race. Each of the approaches to personality—and to dramatic character—focuses on one or another of these aspects of our nature. Each of these aspects exists. And to that extent each of these approaches is valid.

QUESTIONS FOR CRITICAL THINKING

1.   Given what we know about the factors that promote persuasion and conformity, why might a patient in psychoanalysis be predisposed to accept an analyst's interpretations?

2.   Practitioners of "psychohistory" attempt to explain and predict the behavior of famous individuals—mostly politicians—by a psychoanalytic reconstruction and examination of their childhoods. Do such efforts seem likely to prove valid?

3.   Starving prisoners in Nazi concentration camps often took mock showers with dirty ditch water in an attempt to preserve some measure of dignity. How would this accord with Maslow's hierarchy of needs?

4.   Can cultures be meaningfully interpreted as having personalities?

SUMMARY

1.   The *psychodynamic approach* to personality is derived from Sigmund Freud's *psychoanalytic theory*. Freud asserted that all people experience *unconscious conflicts* originating in childhood. His theories grew out of studies of a *psychogenic* mental disorder then called *hysteria*. Freud proposed that hysterical symptoms are a means of keeping *repressed* thoughts or wishes unconscious. He believed that the symptoms would be eliminated once the repressed materials were recovered and devised a procedure, *psychoanalysis,* directed toward this end.

2.   Freud distinguished three subsystems of the human personality. One is the *id,* a blind striving toward biological satisfaction that follows the *pleasure principle.* The second is the *ego,* a system of reactions that tries to reconcile id-derived needs with the actualities of the world, in accordance with the *reality principle.* The third is the *superego,* which represents the internalized rules of the parents and punishes deviations by feelings of guilt.

3.   According to Freud, internal conflict is initially prompted by *anxiety,* which becomes associated with forbidden thoughts and wishes, usually in childhood. To ward off this anxiety, the child resorts to repression and pushes the forbidden materials out of consciousness. Repression is the initial, primary *mechanism of defense* against anxiety. But the repressed materials generally surface again, together with their associated anxiety. To push these thoughts and wishes down again, further, supplementary defense mechanisms come into play, including *displacement, reaction formation, rationalization, projection,* and *isolation.*

4.   Freud believed that most adult unconscious conflicts are ultimately sexual in nature and refer to events during childhood *psychosexual development.* According to Freud, the child passes through three main stages that are characterized by the erogenous zones through which gratification is obtained: *oral, anal,* and *phallic.* In Freud's view, differences in adult personality can be understood as residues of early reactions that occurred during psychosexual development. An example is the *oral character,* whose nature he believed

goes back to a powerful oral fixation. Another example is the *anal character,* whose attributes include compulsive neatness, obstinacy, and stinginess.

5. During the phallic stage, the male child develops the *Oedipus complex.* He directs his sexual urges toward his mother, hates his father as a rival, and comes to dread him as he suffers increasing *castration anxiety.* He finally renounces his sexual urges, *identifies* with his father, and represses all relevant memories. At adolescence, repressed sexual urges surface, are redirected toward adult partners, and the person generally achieves *genital sexuality.* In female children, the *Electra complex* develops, with love toward the father and rivalry toward the mother.

6. Freud tried to apply his theory of unconscious conflict to many areas of everyday life, including slips of the tongue, memory lapses, and dreams. He believed that all dreams are at bottom *wish fulfillments.* Since many of these wishes prompt anxiety, their full expression is censored. As a result, the underlying *latent dream* is transformed into the *manifest dream* in which the forbidden urges emerge in a disguised, sometimes symbolic form.

7. Some early critiques of Freudian theory came from within the psychoanalytic movement. Among the most influential of these were the *neo-Freudians,* who disputed many of Freud's theories about the nature and origins of unconscious conflict. In particular, they denied the notion of a universal Oedipus complex independent of culture.

8. Attempts to find evidence for repression and unconscious conflict have not met with unqualified success. While dreams are often relevant to personal preoccupations and may feature symbolism, there is little evidence that they are disguised representations of hidden urges. Laboratory studies of repression suggest that when motivated forgetting occurs, it may be a special case of retrieval failure. There are clearly nonconscious mental activities, but they are not necessarily a defense against anxiety, nor do they have the sexual and aggressive quality that Freud attributed to them, prompting some critics to hypothesize a "kinder, gentler unconscious."

9. Later psychodynamic theorists take a neo-Freudian orientation. In contrast to Freud, they generally focus on interpersonal rather than biological forces in the individual and are generally more interested in the individual's present situation than his childhood past. An example is Karen Horney, who studied self-perpetuating vicious circles in adult neurotic conflicts. Some modern psychodynamic theorists have studied characteristic patterns of defense and coping in normal persons, which show considerable consistency over an individual's lifetime.

10. Another major orientation to personality is the *humanistic approach,* which maintains that what is most important about people is how they achieve their own selfhood and actualize their human potential. The humanistic approach emphasizes what it considers positive human motives, such as *self-actualization,* and positive personal events, such as *peak experiences,* rather than what it calls *deficiency needs.* According to Abraham Maslow, people only strive for higher-order needs when lower-order needs are satisfied.

11. A number of authors have argued that much of modern personality theory is based on the study of middle-class western Europeans and North Americans and may not be applicable to cultures other than our own. The *sociocultural approach* is an attempt to provide a corrective. Testimony to the remarkable diversity of human beings has come from the work of *cultural anthropologists,* most prominently Ruth Benedict and Margaret Mead. Considerable diversity has been shown in characteristic personality patterns and in gender roles. But, as *cross-cultural methods* demonstrate, there is also evidence for some sameness across cultures, sameness that includes similar psychological dimensions.

12. A number of investigators have tried to use the *cross-cultural* method as a tool to discover the effects of child rearing on adult personality. Some have looked at socioeconomic factors and contrasted child-rearing styles in hunting and agricultural societies, and in different socioeconomic classes in our own culture.

13. According to many psychologists and anthropologists, an important psychological dimension along which different cultures can be classified is *collectivism-individualism.* In collectivist societies the emphasis is on the needs, demands, and values of the family

SUMMARY

and the community. In individualist societies, the focus is on the person's private aims and aspirations, and special value is placed on self-expression. While collectivists are more affected by social pressure than individualists, this only holds if the social force is applied by the *in-group*. For individualists the in-group/out-group distinction is not so sharply drawn. Some authors interpret these and other differences as demonstrations that different cultures have different conceptions of the self.

CHAPTER **18**

PSYCHOPATHOLOGY

I n the two preceding chapters, we considered normal variations in human personality. We now turn to conditions that depart from normal functioning and are considered *malfunctions*. The study of disorders in psychological functioning is the province of ***psychopathology*** or, as it sometimes is called, ***abnormal psychology.*** There is considerable debate about how psychopathology is to be defined. Some consider it simply a problem of statistical deviance, when normal kinds of behavior reach such an extreme that we label them pathological. Others take the term *psychopathology* more literally and regard its manifestations as something akin to illness. But if these manifestations are illnesses, then what kinds of illnesses are they? Are they simply the psychological aspects of some hidden bodily disorder, such as a defect in brain function or a biochemical imbalance? Or should they be considered distinctly *mental* illnesses, whose origins are psychological, such as learned defenses against anxiety?

As we shall see, there is no one answer to these questions. The biggest reason is that the conditions that comprise psychopathology are a very mixed lot. For some, the term *illness* seems quite appropriate; for others, this is not so clear. In any case, there is little doubt that many of the conditions that come to the attention of the psychopathologist—the psychiatrist, clinical psychologist, social worker, or other mental-health specialist—often cause considerable anguish and disability.

Our conceptions of psychopathology go back to antiquity, and so we will begin by discussing some of their historical roots.

DIFFERENT CONCEPTIONS OF MADNESS

FOCUS QUESTIONS

- What was the early demonological view of psychopathology?

- What is the somatogenic view of mental disorder?

- What is the DSM-IV, and how does it define a mental disorder? Why doesn't the DSM-IV use statistical normality to assess what is abnormal?

- What were the three classic supercategories of mental disorder? How has modern diagnosis changed the way that mental disorders are characterized, and how has this affected the use of these supercategories?

- What is the diathesis-stress model of disorder, and how does it explain the causes of mental disorder?

Mental disorders existed long before the mental-health profession appeared on the scene. Early mythological and religious writings are proof enough. The Greek hero, Ajax, slew a flock of sheep that he mistook for his enemies; King Saul of Judea alternated between bouts of murderous frenzy and suicidal depressions; and the Babylonian King Nebuchadnezzar walked on all fours in the

An early example of mental disorder
King Nebuchadnezzar as depicted by
William Blake (1795). (Courtesy of the Tate
Gallery, London)

belief that he was a wolf. Such phenomena were evidently not isolated instances. According to the Bible, young David feigned madness while seeking refuge from his enemies at the court of a Philistine king. This king had obviously encountered psychopathology before and upbraided his servants, "Do I lack madmen, that you have brought this fellow to play the madman in my presence?"★

PSYCHOPATHOLOGY AS DEMONIC POSSESSION

■ What leads to mental disorder? One of the earliest theories held that the afflicted person was possessed by evil spirits. It followed that the cure for the malady was to drive the devils out, and one of the earliest approaches was to provide a physical escape hatch for them. According to some anthropologists, this may explain why Stone Age people sometimes cut large holes into their fellows' skulls; many such ***trephined*** skulls have been found, often with signs that the patient managed to survive the operation (Figure 18.1).

Later treatment regimens attempted to calm the unruly demons or devils by music or chase them away with prayers or exorcisms. If the patient was lucky, the exorcism procedures were fairly mild; more often the techniques were less benign. One idea was to make things as uncomfortable for the evil spirit as possible so as to induce it to escape. Accordingly, the patient was chained, immersed in boiling water or ice baths, starved, or flogged. It is hardly surprising that such procedures usually drove the patient into worse and worse derangement.

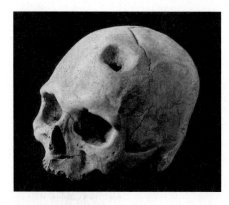

*18.1 **Trephining** A trephined prehistoric skull found in Peru. The patient apparently survived the operation for a while, for there is some evidence of bone healing. (Courtesy of The American Museum of Natural History)*

★ The terms *madness* and *insanity* are sometimes used colloquially to refer to severe cases of psychopathology. *Madness* is simply archaic and doesn't refer to any particular mental illness. The term *insanity,* however, is current—but it isn't a psychological term. It is a legal term, used to refer to a judgment by a court that one cannot be held responsible for one's actions. Of course, opinions of mental-health specialists may contribute to the court's decision, and the defense of not guilty by reason of insanity (NGRI) is occasionally used when a criminal defendant was so disabled by mental illness at the time of a crime that the focus in any sentencing is on treatment rather than incarceration (Simon and Aaronson, 1988).

PSYCHOPATHOLOGY AS A DISEASE

■ The demonological theory of mental illness is a thing of the past. Even in its heyday, there was an alternative view which held that such conditions resulted from natural causes and were a kind of disease. This theory of mental disorder goes back to antiquity and was held by many even during the Middle Ages, when the demonological theory was at its height (Allderidge, 1979; Neugebauer, 1979). But this belief did not necessarily lead to more humane treatment of the afflicted. It might have done so if a ready cure had been available, but until recently, there was little hope of that. As a result, the "madmen" were treated with little sympathy, for they seemed to have no common bond with the rest of humanity, and there was little likelihood that they ever would have. They were seen as a nuisance at best and a menace at worst. In either case, the interests of society seemed best served by "putting them away."

To this end, a number of special hospitals were established throughout Europe. But until the beginning of the nineteenth century (and in some cases, even later), most of these were hospitals in name only. Their real function was to serve as a place of confinement in which all kinds of social undesirables were segregated from the rest of humankind—criminals, beggars, the elderly, epileptics, incurables of all sorts, and the mentally disturbed (Rosen, 1966). After they had been in the "hospital" for a few years, it became hard to distinguish among them. Their treatment was barbaric. One author describes conditions in the major mental hospital for Parisian women at the end of the eighteenth century: "Madwomen seized by fits of violence are chained like dogs at their cell doors, and separated from keepers and visitors alike by a long corridor protected by an iron grille; through this grille is passed their food and the straw on which they sleep; by means of rakes, part of the filth that surrounds them is cleaned out" (Foucault, 1965, p. 72).

To most of their contemporaries, this treatment seemed only natural; after all, "madmen" were like dangerous animals and had to be caged. But since such animals are interesting to watch, some of the hospitals took on another function—they became zoos. At London's Bethlehem hospital (which became known as "Bedlam," for that's how it sounded when pronounced with a Cockney accent), the patients were exhibited to anyone curious enough to pay the required penny per visit. In 1814, there were 96,000 such visits (Figure 18.2).

18.2   The mentally disturbed on exhibit
*An eighteenth-century depiction of a tour of Bedlam. (**The Madhouse,** 1735/1763, William Hogarth; courtesy of the Bettmann Archive)*

A number of reformers gradually succeeded in eliminating the worst of these practices. Historians have given much of the credit to the French physician, Philippe Pinel (1745–1826), who was put in charge of the Parisian hospital system in 1793 when the revolution was at its height. Pinel wanted to remove the inmates' chains and fetters (albeit treating inmates from upper-class families preferentially), but the government gave its permission only grudgingly (Figure 18.3). A high functionary argued with Pinel, "Citizen, are you mad yourself that you want to unchain these animals?" (Zilboorg and Henry, 1941, p. 322). The functionary's concern about the prospect of the inmates running free is echoed even today; many people attach a severe stigma to mental illness and believe that mental hospitals are a good idea, just so long as neither the hospitals nor the patients come into *their* neighborhoods.

MENTAL DISORDER AS AN ORGANIC ILLNESS

Pinel and other reformers sounded one main theme: Madness is a disease. Following from this assertion, inmates became patients who needed treatment rather than imprisonment. And developing such treatments first required discovering the causes of the disease (or rather, diseases, since it was already known that there were several varieties of mental disorder). Today, almost two hundred years after Pinel, we are still searching for the causes of most of them.

At first, the notion of mental disorder as an illness implied a bodily cause, most likely some disease of the brain. Proponents of this **somatogenic** hypothesis (from the Greek *soma,* meaning "body") could point to such relevant discoveries as the effects of cerebral strokes in impairing speech (see Chapter 2). But the somatogenic position gained its greatest impetus at the end of the nineteenth century in the discovery of the organic cause of a once widely prevalent, severe, and debilitating disorder, **general paresis.** It is characterized by a general decline in physical and psychological functions, culminating in a grossly disturbed gait and marked personality aberrations that may include childish delusions ("I am the Prince of Wales") or profound hypochondriacal depressions ("My heart has stopped beating"). Without treatment, the cognitive deterioration progresses, paralysis ensues, and death occurs within a few years (Dale, 1975).

18.3   Pinel ordering the removal of the inmates' fetters *(Copyright Stock Montage, Inc.)*

Insanity as seen by an artist   *This painting undoubtedly shows aspects of what Francisco Goya saw when he visited an insane asylum in Spain, but it may also have been affected by the then current views of the classification of mental disorder. Most early descriptions included the raving maniac (here the nude men wrestling in the center), the hopeless melancholic (the despairing figures on the left), and those with grotesque delusions (the men with crowns demanding allegiance from their subjects). (The Insane Asylum, c. 1810, Francisco Goya, Accademia S. Fernando, Madrid; courtesy of Art Resource)*

By the end of the nineteenth century, the conviction had grown that general paresis has its roots in a syphilis infection that was contracted many years prior to the appearance of overt symptoms. In some untreated syphilitics (according to recent estimates, perhaps 5 percent), the outward signs of the infection may disappear, but the spirochete that caused it remains, invading and damaging the nervous system. Experimental proof came in 1897 when the Viennese physician Richard von Krafft-Ebbing inoculated several paretic patients with matter taken from syphilitic sores. None of them developed any of the early symptoms of syphilis, a clear sign that they had contracted the disease previously.★ Once the cause of the disease was known, the discovery of its cure and prevention was just a matter of time. The preferred modern treatment is penicillin. Its effectiveness is unquestioned. While general paresis at one time accounted for more than 10 percent of all admissions to mental hospitals, as of 1970, it accounted for less than 1 percent (Dale, 1975).

The discovery of the cause of general paresis was a triumph for the somatogenic view and aided many of its proponents in their claim that all mental disorders would ultimately be shown to have an organic basis, most likely in the brain. They could point to senility (a group of disorders now known as the *dementias*) in which there is atrophy of cortical cells. And they could point to a cognitive syndrome specific to chronic alcoholism, which results from the effects on the brain of a vitamin deficit produced by the alcoholism. The question became not whether there was value to the somatogenic view, but whether it could account for *all* mental disorders.

MENTAL DISORDER AS A PSYCHOLOGICAL ILLNESS

The achievements of the somatogenic approach were impressive, but by the end of the nineteenth century it became clear that it could not explain the full spectrum of mental disorders. One of the main stumbling blocks was a condition

---

★ Modern medical and scientific practitioners are considerably more sensitive than our forebears to the ethical issues raised by this and similar studies. Today such a procedure would require the patients' informed consent.

then known as hysteria, which we already encountered in our discussion of psychoanalysis (see Chapter 17).

The story of hysteria (now called *conversion disorder*) is part of the background that led to Freud's theories. For now, we will only reiterate the key discoveries. Patients with hysteria had odd complaints that seemed organic but did not conform consistently to the clinical picture of organic disorders. For example, hysterics would appear with limbs that were routinely "paralyzed" but that moved perfectly well during hypnosis. This suggested that hysteria was a *psychogenic* disorder, that is, a disorder whose origin is psychological rather than organic. A number of cases studied by French hypnotists of the nineteenth century appeared to originate in traumatic incidents. For example, one patient trapped underneath a derailed railroad car developed hysterical paralysis of his legs. His legs were actually in perfect physical condition, but his *belief* that they had been crushed ultimately produced his symptoms. Freud's theories were cast in a similar psychogenic mold, but they were much more elaborate, centering on repressed sexual fantasies in early childhood that threatened to break into consciousness and could only be restrained by drastic defensive maneuvers of which the somatic symptom was one (see Chapter 17).

We will turn to the modern conception of conversion disorder later (see p. 598). For now, the important point is that by 1900, most theorists had become convinced that the disorder was psychogenic. In other words, there were illnesses that did not conform to a strictly somatogenic account—they seemed to have mental causes as well as mental manifestations.

THE MODERN CONCEPTION OF MENTAL DISORDER

Whatever their views on the somatogenic or psychogenic distinction, most contemporary mental-health specialists agree on one thing—these conditions are *disorders*. They are called *mental* disorders because their primary symptoms are psychological, and they all represent a departure from normal psychological functioning (Wakefield, 1992). The commonly accepted definition was provided by the American Psychiatric Association in its now standard manual for categorizing such conditions, the *Diagnostic and Statistical Manual for Mental Disorders* (known in its most recent edition as the *DSM-IV*). As the DSM-IV defines it:

> "... Each of the mental disorders is conceptualized as a clinically significant behavioral or psychological syndrome or pattern that occurs in a person and that is associated with present distress (a painful symptom) or disability (impairment in one or more important areas of functioning) or with a significantly increased risk of suffering death, pain, disability, or an important loss of freedom." (American Psychiatric Association, 1994).

Some special questions arise from the fact that the terms *psychopathology* and *abnormal psychology* are often used interchangeably. Does this mean that psychopathology necessarily involves behavior that deviates from some statistical norm? Mental-health practioners would answer no. They would concede that in actual practice mental disorder often involves aberrations from what people usually do in a given situation; the disordered person may hear voices, suffer from severe mood swings, or behave in ways that are clearly bizarre. It was surely for reasons of this sort that the term *abnormal* became a near-synonym for *psychopathological*. But most modern practitioners would argue that deviation from a statistical norm is not what defines psychopathology. Consider the Black Death, which wiped out half of the population in the fourteenth century. At that time,

Psychopathology is not defined by statistical abnormality According to the psychopathology model, deviation from some statistical norm does not define psychopathology. The Black Death killed half to three-quarters of the population of many European countries during the fourteenth century, but that did not make it any less pathological. (Triumph of Death *by Pieter Bruegel the elder, Prado, Madrid; photograph courtesy of Scala/Art Resource)*

having the plague may well have been statistically normal. But this did not change the plague's status as a disease. The same applies to behavior. Certain patterns of behavior may qualify as a mental disorder no matter how common they are.

THE UNDERLYING PATHOLOGY MODEL

How can the various mental disorders be understood? Many mental-health professionals believe that one might try to understand them according to the same broad set of rules by means of which we try to understand most physical disorders, whether tuberculosis, diabetes, or whatever.

Just what are these rules? We will class them together under a very general category that we'll here call the ***underlying pathology model.*** (Different practitioners subscribe to different subcategories of this model of which more below.) According to this pathology model, various overt signs and symptoms are produced by an underlying cause—the pathology. The main object of the would-be healer is to discover (and ultimately to remove) the underlying pathology. After this is done, the symptoms will presumably disappear. As here used, the term *underlying pathology model* makes no particular assumption about the kind of pathology that underlies a particular mental disorder. It might be somatogenic or psychogenic or perhaps a little of both.

SUBCATEGORIES OF THE PATHOLOGY MODEL

There are a number of different approaches to psychopathology, which can be regarded as subcategories of the pathology model. We will briefly present a few of these. As we will see, some of these models are probably more appropriate to some forms of mental disorder than to others.

571

THE MEDICAL MODEL

Some authors endorse the *medical model,* a particular version of the pathology model, which assumes, for one thing, that the underlying pathology is organic. Its practitioners therefore employ various forms of somatic therapy such as drugs. In addition, it takes for granted that would-be healers should be members of the medical profession (Siegler and Osmond, 1974).

THE PSYCHOANALYTIC MODEL

Adherents of the *psychoanalytic model* follow the general conception of psychopathology developed by Sigmund Freud and other psychoanalysts. In their view, the manifestations of mental disorders are produced by psychological causes. The underlying pathology is a constellation of unconscious conflicts and various defenses against anxiety, often rooted in early childhood experience. Treatment is by some form of psychotherapy based on psychoanalytic principles, which allows the patient to gain insight into his own inner conflicts and thus removes the root of the pathology.

THE LEARNING MODEL

The *learning model* tends to view mental disorders as the result of some form of maladaptive learning. According to some practitioners (usually called behavior therapists), these faulty learning patterns are best described and treated by the laws of classical and instrumental conditioning.

A popular current variant on the learning model is the *cognitive-behavioral model,* which regards certain disorders as caused by faulty thinking habits, such as pessimistic or catastrophic thinking. Practitioners of this model, often called cognitive therapists, deal with disorders by changing the way in which the patient thinks about himself, his situation, and his future.

CLASSIFYING MENTAL DISORDERS

■ Mental disorders differ: in their manifestations, their severity, their duration, and their outlook for recovery. Into how many pieces do we need to slice the mental disorders pie? To answer this question, practitioners have tried to set up classificatory schemes for mental disorders analogous to the diagnostic systems in other branches of medicine. Here, as elsewhere in science, the purpose of a taxonomy is to bring some order into what at first seems a host of diverse phenomena. If the taxonomy is valid, then conditions that have been grouped together will turn out to have the same cause, and better yet, the same treatment.

The great German psychiatrist Emil Kraepelin (1855–1925) began the practice of diagnosing mental disorders just like physical disorders. In psychopathology, as in physical medicine, the diagnostic process begins with a *clinical interview* in which the practitioner asks the patient to describe her problems and concerns, and observes the patient throughout. The first consideration is the patient's set of complaints or *symptoms.* Patients who say, "I hear voices," "I feel nervous all the time," and "I feel hopeless" are providing symptoms. The practitioner then looks for any *signs* that might accompany these symptoms. If the same patients, respectively, turn toward a stapler as though it were speaking, shake visibly, and look teary-eyed, these would be signs that parallel the patients' symptoms. Sometimes symptoms do not correspond to signs, and such discrepancies are also important. In some cases of conversion disorder, for example, a patient might state, "My head hurts so bad it's like a buzzsaw running through my brain" but the patient seems to be quite calm and unconcerned while saying it.

Emil Kraepelin *The major figure in psychiatric classification, Kraepelin distinguished between two groups of severe mental disorders, schizophrenia and manic-depressive psychosis (now called bipolar disorder). (Courtesy of Historical Pictures Service)*

In physical medicine, a single symptom like "I always feel tired," or a single sign like a low red blood cell count, is rarely sufficient to reach a conclusion about what ails the patient. This is because feeling tired is a symptom of many disorders, and the low red blood cell count is a sign of many others. However, the combination may narrow the choices considerably (to disorders like anemia, among others). The same holds for psychopathology, and so the mental-health practitioner looks for a pattern of signs and symptoms that tend to go together. These patterns are called **syndromes.** An example of such a syndrome in psychopathology is a pattern of signs like disorganized speech, altered gait, and subdued facial expressions, together with symptoms like agitation, persecutory beliefs, and hallucinations. This syndrome is characteristic of schizophrenia.

The practitioner also attempts to obtain other information during the interview with the patient and, if possible or necessary, from family and friends. When did the problems start (the illness *onset*)? Has the patient's everyday functioning stayed the same, improved, worsened, or been irregular with good spells and bad spells (the *course* of the illness)? The patient's signs and symptoms, taken together with their onset and course, will begin to point to a disorder or disorders. Finally, the practitioner renders an opinion as to the specific disorder(s), and this opinion is called the patient's **diagnosis.** The diagnosis is not set in stone, but serves as the practitioner's best judgment about the patient's current state. A proper diagnosis can imply the outlook for the patient, it can suggest the most effective treatments, and it can also sometimes point to the disorder's cause.

How many disorders are there? Until about twenty-five years ago, the majority of mental-health specialists believed that most mental disorders could be subsumed under three broad supercategories. First were **organic brain syndromes,** such as the dementias or brain damage from chronic alcoholism. Second was **neurosis,** which referred to any disorder that was thought to be characterized by underlying anxiety-related conflicts. Examples of neuroses were the disorders now called phobias, panic disorder, obsessive-compulsive disorder, and the dissociative disorders. Neurotic patients might be severely distressed or handicapped by their symptoms, but they had not lost contact with reality. In contrast, **psychosis** referred to conditions such as schizophrenia and bipolar disorder (formerly called manic-depressive illness), which in their severe forms could render the patients' thoughts, moods, and deeds grossly disturbed and no longer in touch with reality (American Psychiatric Association, 1968).

Today, the term *neurosis* is no longer widely used in psychiatric classification. A major reason was the change to diagnoses based on specific, observable criteria, such as those cited above, rather than on theoretical inferences about underlying processes. The term *psychosis* is still used, but only descriptively; it refers not to an underlying set of disorders the causes of which are inferred, but to any disorder so severe that the victim loses contact with reality. The same holds for a number of other terms that are no longer used in official diagnosis, such as *sociopathy, hysteria,* and *senility.*

This new emphasis on observable criteria was embodied in the DSM-IV. Both it and its immediate predecessors—DSM-III and DSM-IIIR (American Psychiatric Association, 1980, 1987)—departed from earlier diagnostic manuals by placing greater stress on the description of disorders rather than on theories about their origin. As a result, a number of disorders that were once grouped together because of a belief—usually based on psychoanalytic theory—that they were at bottom alike are now classified under different diagnostic categories. An example is provided by various conditions that were once regarded as subcategories of neurosis, such as phobias or obsessive-compulsive disorders (see pp. 591–92). A major consequence of these changes is the substantially increased diagnostic reliability of the new manual (Matarazzo, 1983; American Psychiatric Association, 1994).

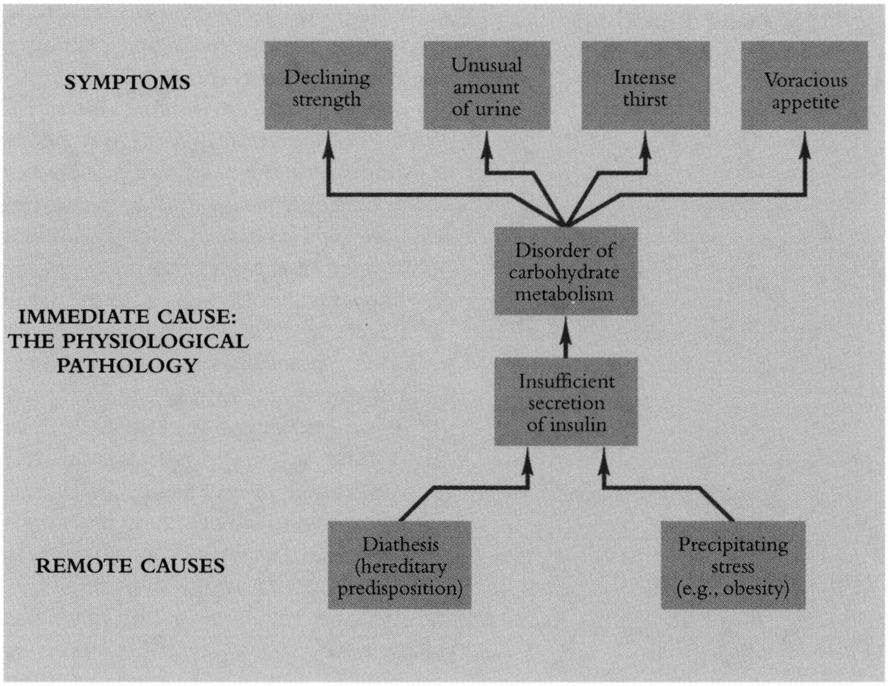

SYMPTOMS

| Declining strength | Unusual amount of urine | Intense thirst | Voracious appetite |

IMMEDIATE CAUSE: THE PHYSIOLOGICAL PATHOLOGY

Disorder of carbohydrate metabolism

Insufficient secretion of insulin

REMOTE CAUSES

Diathesis (hereditary predisposition)

Precipitating stress (e.g., obesity)

18.4   The underlying pathology model as applied to diabetes

EXPLAINING DISORDER: DIATHESIS, STRESS, AND PATHOLOGY

■ To explain how the underlying pathology approach may be applied to mental disorders, we'll first turn to the analysis of a disease that is already well understood. Our example will be an organic illness—diabetes (see Figure 18.4).

Again, our first step is to examine the overt signs and symptoms. In diabetes, the symptoms include declining strength, a marked increase in the frequency of urination, enormous thirst, and, in many cases, a voracious appetite. A frequent sign is a high sugar level in the urine. The next step is to look for the pathology underlying this syndrome. Diabetes was discovered to be a disorder of carbohydrate metabolism, produced by an insufficient secretion of insulin. These pathological conditions represent the immediate cause of the syndrome. But a full understanding of diabetes requires a further step, an inquiry into the more remote causes that led to the present pathology.

When the causal chain is traced backward, two general factors emerge. One is a predisposition (technically called a *diathesis*) toward the illness. The other is a set of environmental conditions that *stress* the system and precipitate the defective insulin mechanism. Obesity is one such stressor. In diabetes, the diathesis is based in part on genetic factors that create a marked susceptibility to the disease, which is then triggered or worsened by a stressor. The treatment follows from the analysis of the cause-and-effect relations. Since the diabetic's pancreas does not secrete enough insulin, this substance can be supplied from the outside (orally or by injection). Further regulation of the faulty metabolic controls is then imposed by an appropriate diet (Dolger and Seeman, 1985).

This discussion illustrates the *diathesis-stress* model, a conception that extends to mental as well as physical disorders. Many kinds of psychopathology are thought to result from the presence of a diathesis that leaves one vulnerable to a particular disorder or set of disorders and some kind of stressor that turns potentiality into actuality. The nature of the diathesis depends on the particular disorder. For some disorders, as we'll see, a diathesis may be genetic, as in schizophrenia (see pp. 580–81). For others, it may be environmental, as in phobia, which is sometimes thought to go back to an anxiety-producing incident in the patient's past (see p. 591).

Figure 18.4 provides a schematic summary of our discussion of diabetes, a physical ailment with few direct psychological manifestations. The figure gives us an idea of how a disease is analyzed when it is reasonably well understood. This is the framework we will use when we ask whether a particular mental disorder is an illness and if so, in what sense. How such disorders are treated will be taken up in the next chapter. We now turn to some of the most important mental disorders.

SCHIZOPHRENIA

FOCUS QUESTIONS

- What are the signs and symptoms of schizophrenia? How do the subtypes of schizophrenia differ?

- What two kinds of brain abnormality are implicated in schizophrenia?

- What evidence suggests a genetic basis for schizophrenia?

- Why do many researchers consider the prenatal period crucial to the development of schizophrenia?

One of the most serious disorders in all of psychopathology is *schizophrenia* (from the Greek *schizo,* "split," and *phrene,* "mind"). The term was coined by the Swiss psychiatrist, Eugen Bleuler (1857–1939), to designate what he regarded as the main attribute of this disorder—an abnormal disintegration of mental functions (Bleuler, 1911).★

Schizophrenia is quite prevalent, being found worldwide in about 1 percent of humanity (Torrey, 1987). According to one estimate, between 1 and 2 percent of Americans will need treatment for this disorder at some period during their lifetimes. At any one time, about 400,000 people are hospitalized with this condition, accounting for about half of all of the beds in the country's mental hospitals. The diagnosis is usually made not at the first subtle signs of the disorder but much later, when the condition has become so severe that evaluation and diagnosis in a clinic or hospital is required (Andreasen and Black, 1991; Babigian, 1975; Goldstein and Tsuang, 1990).

Many investigators believe that schizophrenia is a disease, in the straightforward, somatogenic sense of the term. To evaluate this position, we will discuss the disorder within the same framework we used when we considered a frankly organic disease, diabetes. We will discuss the pattern of signs and symptoms, the underlying pathology, the less immediate causes such as genetic predisposition, and the precipitating factors.

Eugen Bleuler *(Courtesy of the National Library of Medicine)*

SIGNS AND SYMPTOMS

The fragmentation of mental life characteristic of schizophrenia can be seen in disruptions in cognition, of motivation and emotion, and of social relationships. Few patients who are diagnosed as schizophrenics exhibit all of

★ This etymological derivation is responsible for a widespread confusion between schizophrenia and multiple personality ("split personality"), now called *dissociative identity disorder.* While both are varieties of psychopathology, the two conditions are wholly distinct.

these manifestations. Until fairly recently, this led to considerable disagreement in diagnosis, since different clinicians used different yardsticks to determine how many features had to be present and to what degree before someone was said to suffer from schizophrenia. With the new taxonomy introduced with DSM-III and continued in DSM-IV came more specific criteria for diagnosis, such as gross distortion in the perception of reality, symptoms present for at least six months, and so on.

DISORDERS OF COGNITION

A key sign of schizophrenia is a pervasive thought disturbance. The schizophrenic doesn't "think straight"; she can't maintain one unified guiding thought, but rather skips from one idea to the next. An example is a fragment of a letter written by one of Bleuler's patients:

> I am writing on paper. The pen I am using is from a factory called "Perry & Co." This factory is in England. I assume this. Behind the name of Perry Co., the city of London is inscribed; but not the city. The city of London is in England. I know this from my school-days. Then, I always liked geography. My last teacher in that subject was Professor August A. He was a man with black eyes. I also like black eyes. There are also blue and gray eyes and other sorts too. I have heard it said that snakes have green eyes. All people have eyes. There are some, too, who are blind. These blind people are led about by a boy. (Bleuler, 1911, p. 17)

This example shows that the schizophrenic may have difficulty in suppressing irrelevant ideas that come from within. Similar problems arise with irrelevant stimuli that assail her from without. We have seen that in ordinary perception one focuses on some aspects of the world while deemphasizing others. We somehow filter out the irrelevant stimuli so that we can follow a conversation without being continually distracted by other people's voices or radiator clankings or whatever (see Chapter 6). But schizophrenics seem to be less efficient in attending selectively. They hear (and see and feel) too much, perhaps because they can't exclude what is extraneous (McGhie and Chapman, 1961).

LOSS OF PERSONAL CONTACT

A common feature of schizophrenia is a withdrawal from contact with other people. In some patients this withdrawal begins quite early; they have had few friends and little or no adolescent sexual experience. What brings on this withdrawal is still unknown. One possibility is that it is a defense against the overstimulation to which they are exposed because of their inability to filter out the irrelevant. Another possibility is that it grows out of pathological family relations during childhood and adolescence.

Whatever led up to it, the schizophrenic's withdrawal from social contacts has drastic consequences. The individual starts to inhabit an inner world that becomes more and more private. The withdrawal from others provides fewer and fewer opportunities for *social reality testing* in which one's ideas are validated against those of others. As a result, the schizophrenic's thoughts become ever more idiosyncratic, until the patient may have trouble communicating with others even if he wants to; they may very well rebuff him because they can't understand him and think he's "weird." The result is further withdrawal, which leads to further idiosyncrasy, still further withdrawal, and so on. The final consequence of this vicious cycle is a condition in which the patient can no longer distinguish between his own thoughts and fantasies and the external reality experienced by all those around him. He has lost touch with the world.

A

B

Paintings by schizophrenics *Paintings by schizophrenics often have an odd, eerie quality. In many cases, the usual artistic conventions are disregarded, and the picture includes written comments, digits, and other idiosyncratic material. (A) Saint-Adolf-Grand-Grand-God-Father (1915), a painting by Adolf W., who was institutionalized in early adulthood and elaborated a fantastic autobiography that featured himself as Saint Adolf II, a young god who travels through space and has many adventures. (B) Guardian Angels by Else B., an institutionalized schizophrenic. In all her works, the legs of angels are painted as though they had fused at the top, to make sure that "nothing happens there."*
(Prinzhorn, 1972; courtesy of Galerie Rothe Heidelberg)

ELABORATING THE PRIVATE WORLD

In our previous discussions, we considered just how much we seek consistency in others and in the world (see Chapters 6, 11, 16, 17). This is no less true for the schizophrenic, who tries to make sense of a world that is increasingly sealed off from the outside. This can result in what Bleuler called *restitutional symptoms,* which include developing elaborate, organized systems of eccentric beliefs *(delusions)* and hearing voices of people who are not there *(hallucinations).*

Delusions   Once having initiated the break with the social world, many schizophrenics develop *ideas of reference.* They begin to believe that external events are specially related to them personally. The patient observes some strangers talking and concludes that they are talking about him; he sees people walk by and decides that they are following him; he hears a radio commercial and is sure that it contains a secret message aimed at him. Eventually, he may weave these false ideas, or delusions, into an entire *delusional system* in which he may believe, for example, that agents of the government are talking about him, following him everywhere, and have taken over the media to spread secrets about him. Such delusions are especially common in a subcategory called *paranoid schizophrenia.*

Hallucinations   Delusions are beliefs that result from the misinterpretation of real events. In contrast, *hallucinations* are perceptions that occur in the absence of actual sensory stimulation. The most common type are *auditory hallucinations* in which the patient "hears" voices—of God, the devil, relatives, or neighbors. If the patient can make out what they say, he will report that they are talking about him, shouting obscenities at him, threatening him, or making accusations about him.

Some authors believe that such hallucinations reflect an inability to distinguish between one's own memories and perceptions, between experiences that originate from within and those that originate from without. The patients may be talking to themselves, but they will then interpret their own inner speech as originating from outside. They "heard themselves talk" and thought they heard voices (McGuigan, 1966; Green and Preston, 1981).

Schizophrenia   The delusional world of some schizophrenics may resemble the bizarre images created by some surrealist artists. (Frederico Castellión, The Dark Figure, 1938; courtesy of the Whitney Museum of American Art, New York; photograph by Geoffrey Clements, NY)

DISORDERS OF MOTIVATION AND EMOTION

Thus far we have emphasized the schizophrenic's thoughts. When we look at her motives and feelings, we find similar evidence of disruption and fragmentation. In the early phase of the disorder, there is often a marked emotional oversensitivity in which the slightest rejection may trigger an extreme response. As time goes on, this sensitivity declines. In many patients it dips below normal until there is virtual indifference to their own fate or that of others. This apathy is especially pronounced in long-term schizophrenics, who stare vacantly, their faces expressionless, and answer questions in a flat and toneless voice.

In some cases, emotional reaction is preserved but the emotion is strikingly inappropriate to the situation. A patient may break into giddy laughter at the news of a brother's death "because she was so pleased at receiving letters with black borders"; another becomes enraged when someone says hello (Bleuler, 1911).

DISORDERS OF BEHAVIOR

Given the disruptions in the schizophrenics' thoughts, motives, and feelings, it is hardly surprising that there is often disruption in normal movements and actions. Some patients—in a subtype of schizophrenia called *catatonic schizophrenia*—exhibit very unusual motor reactions. They can become stuporous, remaining virtually motionless for long periods of time. They may be standing or sitting or "frozen" in some unusual posture and will often maintain this position for hours on end (Figure 18.5). With no notice, they can become frenzied, running haphazardly, shouting nonsensically, and acting violently.

In another subtype, *disorganized schizophrenia* (formerly, *hebephrenia*), thought, emotion, and behavior become virtually chaotic. The predominant symptoms are incoherence of speech and marked inappropriateness of behavior and emotion. In many ways, the disorganized schizophrenic is the closest match to the popular stereotype of madness. His speech is often bizarre and babbling, and while he is talking he giggles, makes silly smiles or odd grimaces, assumes odd postures, and may have sudden fits of laughing and crying. Such patients often deteriorate profoundly, lose all concern over personal appearance, and ignore the most elementary rules of social conduct; for example, they may urinate and defecate in public.

18.5   Patient with a diagnosis of catatonic schizophrenia who spent virtually all waking hours in this crouched position.   (Photograph by Bill Bridges/Globe Photos)

THE SEARCH FOR THE UNDERLYING PATHOLOGY

■ We have described the various manifestations that define schizophrenia. As in diabetes or any other organic disease, the next step is to look for the underlying *psychological malfunction* from which these signs and symptoms spring. Once found, then—if there is reason to suspect that the disorder is somatogenic—one searches for the organic pathology of which this psychological malfunction is an expression.

WHAT IS THE PSYCHOLOGICAL MALFUNCTION?

A widely held view is that the schizophrenic's major psychological malfunction is cognitive. The details of the proposed explanations vary, but most of them agree that the patient's major deficit is an inability to keep things in their proper context. Normal people perceive other persons, objects, and events without los-

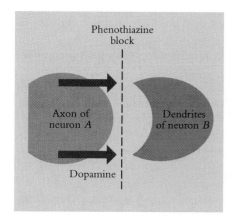

18.6 *The dopamine-blockade hypothesis of phenothiazine action*

PET scans of schizophrenics *PET scans comparing the normal and the schizophrenic brain reveal certain abnormalities of brain structure and increased metabolic activity in different areas of the schizophrenic's brain. (NIH/Science Source/Photo Researchers)*

ing track of the context and without being distracted by extraneous stimuli; they execute plans without interference by irrelevant responses. Not so the schizophrenic, who has considerable difficulty in holding onto one line of thought or action and is forever being lured off the main path (Chapman and Chapman, 1973; Patterson et al., 1986).

WHAT IS THE ORGANIC PATHOLOGY?

By now, most investigators believe that the core psychological malfunctions in schizophrenia are themselves expressions of an organic pathology. The search for the immediate causes centers on two possible kinds of malfunctions. One is physiological, emphasizing a disorder in certain neurotransmitter systems in the brain. The other is anatomical and focuses on some possible abnormalities in the brain structure of those who suffer from schizophrenia (Meltzer, 1987).

Malfunctioning neurotransmitters Some investigators believe that the immediate organic pathology involves some malfunction in one or more neurotransmitter system in the brain. A likely neurotransmitter candidate is **dopamine.** According to the **dopamine hypothesis,** the immediate organic cause of schizophrenia is abnormally increased dopamine activity in the brain. The increased activity may result from any of several mechanisms, including an overabundance of dopamine, an oversensitivity of dopamine receptors, or the facilitation of dopamine transmission by other transmitters such as norepinephrine (Van Kammen and Kelley, 1991) or serotonin (Kahn et al., 1993).

One strong line of evidence for the dopamine hypothesis comes from the effects of a number of medications known as **antipsychotics.** Among the most commonly used today are Thorazine and Haldol. These drugs are known to block dopamine at the synapse (Figure 18.6). This dopamine blockade is more pronounced in some kinds of antipsychotics than in others. As predicted by the dopamine hypothesis, the stronger the blockade, the more therapeutic the drug (Snyder, 1976). Conversely, if a decrease in dopamine activity makes schizophrenics better, an increase should presumably make them worse. This is indeed the case (Davis, 1974).

Structural defects The highly resolved images now permitted by magnetic resonance imaging scans (MRI; see Chapter 2) confirm that a certain proportion of schizophrenics suffer from some structural abnormalities in their brains. One such abnormality is an enlargement of the ventricles, the fluid-filled cavities within the brain. The ventricles enlarge when the brain does not fill the cranial space, which suggests a large-scale deficiency or even a progressive loss of brain tissue (Andreasen et al., 1986; Meltzer, 1987). Although abnormalities have been reported in numerous areas, the most persuasive findings involve the frontal and temporal lobes. Studies of these areas during autopsy show various abnormalities at the cellular level, for example, cell derangement and missing or abnormally sized neurons. These neuronal defects obviously affect brain function, and indeed, PET scans of brain metabolism and cerebral blood-flow studies suggest abnormally low levels of functioning in just these areas (Bloom, 1993).

Crow's two-syndrome hypothesis Both the dopamine and the anatomical-defect hypotheses face a problem: Each fits some cases of schizophrenia, but not all. For example, many schizophrenic patients respond to dopamine-blocking medications, but a number do not. In contrast, a significant number of schizophrenics show signs of cerebral atrophy, but many do not. One proposal by British psychiatrist Timothy Crow tries to handle these facts by proposing a **two-syndrome hypothesis** of schizophrenia (Crow, 1982, 1985). This hypothesis begins by making a distinction between positive and negative symptoms. ***Positive symptoms*** are those that involve what the patients do (and see and think) that normals don't; they include hallucinations, delusions, and bizarre behaviors. In contrast, ***negative symptoms*** are those that involve a lack of normal functioning, such as apathy, poverty of speech, emotional blunting, and the inability to experience pleasure or be sociable.

According to the two-syndrome hypothesis, schizophrenia is really a composite of two underlying pathologies, which Crow named Type I and Type II. Crow proposed that Type I schizophrenia is caused by a malfunction of neurotransmitters (especially dopamine) and produces the positive symptoms: delusions, hallucinations, and thought disorders. Type II, he suggested, is produced by cerebral damage and atrophy and leads to the negative symptoms: flat affect, social withdrawal, and apathy. Support for this view comes from the fact that, by and large, patients with mostly positive symptoms tend to respond well to standard antipsychotic medications and show no cerebral damage. The reverse holds for patients with negative symptoms, who are generally not improved by treatment with standard antipsychotics and are more likely to show signs of cerebral damage (Crow, 1980, 1985).

ULTIMATE CAUSES OF SCHIZOPHRENIA

■ We have considered several analyses of the basic pathology in schizophrenia, including hypotheses about the underlying psychological malfunction and some guesses about organic deficits or defects. These hypotheses about pathological processes are about the immediate causes of the disorder. But what explains these psychological, physiological, or anatomical deficits? This is the question of more ***ultimate*** causes, causes that are further back in time. As we saw in our discussion of diabetes, we must consider both the immediate causes (a metabolic malfunction brought on by insulin insufficiency) and more ultimate ones (genetic factors, environmental effects) if we are to understand a disorder fully and make a diathesis-stress interpretation possible. We will follow the same approach in our discussion of schizophrenia.

HEREDITARY PREDISPOSITION

Does schizophrenia have a hereditary basis? This question has been studied by the same means used to assess the role of heredity in other human traits such as intelligence (see Chapter 15). The basic approach is to consider family resemblance. In schizophrenia, as in intelligence, this resemblance is considerable. For example, the likelihood that a person who has a schizophrenic sibling is schizophrenic himself or will eventually become so is about 8 percent; this compares to 1 to 2 percent lifetime risk of schizophrenia in the general population (Andreason and Black, 1991; Rosenthal, 1970).

But again, as with intelligence, studies of family resemblances aren't decisive on the nature-nurture issue, for they can be interpreted either way. More conclusive evidence requires techniques that disentangle the contributions of heredity and environment using the familiar strategies of studying twins and adopted children. It turns out that if one of a set of twins is schizophrenic, then the other twin is much more likely to be schizophrenic as well. The probability of this event, technically called ***concordance***, is 55 percent if the twins are identical, compared to 9 percent if they are fraternal (Gottesman and Shields, 1972, 1982; Gottesman, McGuffin, and Farmer, 1987; Tsuang, Gilbertson, and Faraone, 1991; see Figure 18.7). Further evidence comes from adoption studies. Children born to schizophrenic mothers and placed in foster homes within a week or so

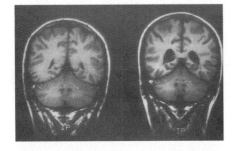

MRI scans of the brains of twins *Magnetic resonance imaging (MRI) scans of the brains of two twenty-eight-year-old identical twins. One (right) is hospitalized for schizophrenia; the other (left) is well. The schizophrenic twin has enlarged cerebral ventricles; the other does not. The fact that just one twin has schizophrenia shows that heredity is not the only factor in producing this disorder. (Courtesy of Drs. E. Fuller Torey and Daniel R. Weinberger, NIMH Neuroscience Center, Washington, D.C.)*

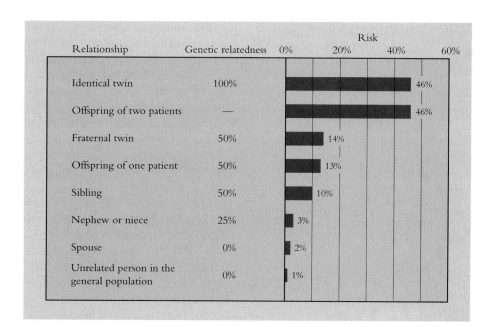

Relationship	Genetic relatedness	Risk
Identical twin	100%	46%
Offspring of two patients	—	46%
Fraternal twin	50%	14%
Offspring of one patient	50%	13%
Sibling	50%	10%
Nephew or niece	25%	3%
Spouse	0%	2%
Unrelated person in the general population	0%	1%

18.7 Genetic factors in schizophrenia
Risk estimates for schizophrenia as a function of relationship to a schizophrenic patient. (From Nicol and Gottesman, 1983)

after birth are much more likely to become schizophrenic. In fact, the odds are about 8 percent that the child of a schizophrenic mother who is adopted by nonschizophrenic parents will become schizophrenic, the same percentage as for children who remain with the schizophrenic biological parent (Kety, 1983; Kendler and Gruenberg, 1984; Tsuang et al., 1991).

Some contemporary investigators believe that these genetic findings coupled with some further evidence suggest that schizophrenia is a *neurodevelopmental disorder* (Waddington et al., 1991). According to this theory, pathological genes produce abnormalities in the brain during fetal development. These abnormalities, in turn, lead to behavioral and cognitive eccentricities from the outset that may eventuate in schizophrenia. One line of evidence comes from the fact that many cases of schizophrenia show preludes in childhood. Children at special hereditary risk for schizophrenia tend to have low activity levels, motor immaturity, and poor cuddliness; by adolescence, they have a host of subtle cognitive and perceptual deficits (Marcus et al., 1993). Those children who will later develop the negative symptoms of schizophrenia tend to manifest behavior problems such as isolation, passivity, and social unresponsiveness; those who will later develop the positive symptoms show irritability, distractibility, and aggression (Cannon, Mednick, and Parnas, 1990; Parnas and Jorgensen, 1989).

ENVIRONMENTAL INFLUENCES

The preceding discussion indicates that schizophrenia has a genetic basis. But there is no doubt that other factors also play a role. One line of evidence comes from identical twins. Their concordance for schizophrenia is considerable, but is much less than 100 percent. Since identical twins have the same genotype, there must be some nongenetic factors that also have a say in the determination of who becomes schizophrenic and who does not.

Family environment Some psychoanalytically oriented investigators concentrated upon the personality of the schizophrenic's parents, describing schizophrenics' mothers as rejecting, cold, dominating, and prudish, and their fathers as detached, humorless, weak, and passive (Arieti, 1959). But even if schizophrenics have less benign family backgrounds than do normal children, this does not prove that the family environment caused the patient's disorder. It may also be an effect, and for two reasons. First, having a schizophrenic in the family can be tragic for the family. Parents often blame themselves and each other for their disturbed child and become frustrated in their attempts to "reach" their child (Torrey, 1983). Second, schizophrenic children are more likely to come from more disturbed families because at least one of the parents may possess the same pathological genes that eventuated in schizophrenia in their child, whether or not the parent is schizophrenic. In fact, there is some evidence that even the nonschizophrenic parents and siblings of schizophrenics manifest biological markers for the propensity (Holtzman et al., 1988; Tsuang et al., 1991).

Prenatal environment   In recent years, considerable attention has been focused on environmental stresses in the uterus and during delivery. An important line of evidence comes from obstetric reports on the effects of various complications during pregnancy and birth, which evidently increase the likelihood that a genetic predisposition will eventually be expressed as schizophrenia (Cannon, 1991; Zorilla and Cannon, 1995). Further studies implicate a viral infection of the mother: patients with schizophrenia are more likely to have been born shortly after an influenza epidemic, suggesting that the mother's infection (probably in the second trimester) may be a contributing stress (Sham et al., 1992). It may well be that these and other prenatal factors are the most important environmental factors that precipitate the diathesis into the full-blown disease.

THE PATHOLOGY MODEL AND SCHIZOPHRENIA

■ We have considered schizophrenia under the same headings that are used to analyze physical illnesses—the pattern of signs and symptoms, the underlying pathology, the role of ultimate causes such as genetic predisposition, and precipitating factors. What can we conclude? To guide our evaluation, we will refer to a schematic diagram of the main factors in the schizophrenic disorder that is analogous to the one we used to analyze diabetes (Figure 18.8).

18.8   The pathology model as applied to schizophrenia   The diagram shows that the causal analysis by which nonbehavioral disorders such as diabetes are described can be applied to mental disorders such as schizophrenia. The basic logic applies regardless of whether the disorder ultimately turns out to be in part somatogenic or not.

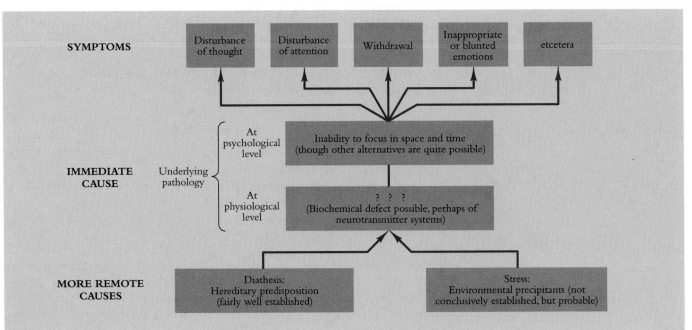

The schizophrenic syndrome can be considered the manifestation of a psychological deficit, perhaps a defect in the ability to retain the context of one's current thoughts and actions. The best guess is that this psychological malfunction reflects an organic pathology whose exact nature is still unknown. Most investigators believe that this organic pathology has two sources: One is a biochemical defect, most likely involving some neurotransmitter system. The other is anomalous or deficient brain tissue, perhaps through progressive atrophy. The pathology that represents the immediate cause of the disorder is in turn produced by more ultimate causes. One is a hereditary diathesis. Another may be a set of environmental stresses, including familial pressures and problems during pregnancy and delivery, that trigger the pathological process in persons with the initial diathesis.

What is the outlook for schizophrenic patients? To date, the prospects are not very encouraging. One study tracked down two hundred people who were suffering from schizophrenia in the 1930s and 1940s some thirty years later. Of these patients, 20 percent were doing well, while 45 percent were incapacitated; 67 percent had never married, and 58 percent had never worked (Andreasen and Black, 1991; Cutting, 1986).

Clearly schizophrenia is devastating in its overall impact, but we hasten to note that about one in five schizophrenics does well and continues to do well. We can hope that the odds will improve as researchers converge on the causes of the disease and perfect new treatments. Indeed, some new treatments give grounds for optimism, as we will discuss in the next chapter.

MOOD DISORDERS

FOCUS QUESTIONS

- What are the two major types of mood disorder, and what are the signs and symptoms of each?

- What is seasonal affective disorder, what biological factor may produce it, and when is it most frequently observed?

- Why do researchers believe that both genetic and biochemical defects are involved in the mood disorders? How do the actions of antidepressant medications suggest the probable biochemical defect?

- What two major theoretical accounts suggest a psychogenic contribution to depression?

While schizophrenia can be regarded as essentially a disorder of thought, in another group of disorders the dominant disturbance is one of mood. These are the *mood disorders* (sometimes called the *affective disorders*), which are characterized by two emotional extremes—the vehement energy of mania, the despair and lethargy of depression, or both.

BIPOLAR AND UNIPOLAR SYNDROMES

An initial distinction is that between *bipolar disorder* (essentially equivalent to what was formerly called *manic-depressive psychosis*) and *major depression.* In bipolar disorder, the patient swings from one energetic and emotional extreme to the other, sometimes with intermittent periods of normality, and experiences both manic and depressive episodes that may be as short as a few

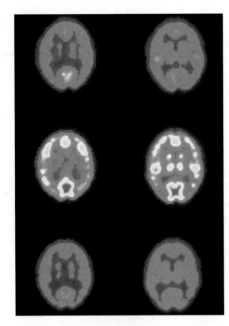

PET scan of a rapid-cycling bipolar patient *The top and bottom row are scans obtained on days in which the patient was depressed; the middle row on a day in which he was mildly manic. Reds and yellows indicate a high rate of metabolic activity; blues and greens indicate low rates. (Courtesy Dr. John Mazziotta)*

hours or as long as several months or more. Bipolar disorder occurs in about 0.5 to 1 percent of the population and is diagnosed more often in women by a ratio of 3 to 2 (Andreasen and Black, 1991). Much more frequent are cases of ***major depression*** (sometimes called ***unipolar disorder,*** since the mood extreme is of one kind only). According to several estimates, about 10 percent of all men and 20 percent of all women in America will suffer from a major depressive episode (defined as one that lasts for at least two weeks) at some time during their lives (Hirschfeld and Cross, 1981; Weissman and Boyd, 1985).

MANIA

In their milder form, manic states are often hard to distinguish from buoyant spirits. The person seems to have shifted into high gear: She is more lively and infectiously merry, is extremely talkative and always on the go, is charming, utterly self-confident, and indefatigable. It is hard to see that something is wrong unless one notices that she jumps from one plan to another, seems unable to sit still for a moment, and quickly shifts from unbounded elation to brittle irritation if she meets even the smallest frustration. These pathological signs become greatly intensified as the manic episode becomes more severe (***acute*** or ***psychotic mania***). Now the motor is racing and all brakes are off. The person may begin to stay up all night, engage in an endless stream of talk that runs from one topic to another and knows no inhibitions of social or personal (or for that matter, sexual) propriety. Patients in the manic state are incessantly busy. They may burst into shouts of song, smash furniture out of sheer overabundance of energy, do exercises, sleep only rarely, engage in reckless sexual escapades, go on drinking or drug-abuse bouts, spend all their money on gambling, conceive grandiose plans for rebuilding the hospital or redirecting the nation's foreign policy or making millions in the stock market—a ceaseless torrent of activity that continues unabated over many days and sleepless nights and which will eventually sap the patients' health (and that of those around them) if they are not sedated.

DEPRESSION

In many ways, major depression is the polar opposite of mania. The patient's mood may be utterly dejected, his outlook hopeless; he has lost interest in other people and believes he is utterly sinful or worthless. In describing the depths of his own depression, the novelist William Styron wrote:

> All sense of hope vanished, along with the idea of a futurity; my brain, in thrall to its outlaw hormones, had become less an organ of thought than an instrument registering, minute by minute, varying degrees of its own suffering. The mornings themselves were becoming bad now as I wandered about lethargic . . . but afternoons were still the worst, when I'd feel the horror, like some poisonous fogbank, roll in upon my mind, forcing me into bed. There I would lie for as long as six hours, stuporous and virtually paralyzed, gazing at the ceiling and waiting for that moment of evening when, mysteriously, the crucifixion would ease up just enough to allow me to force down some food and then, like an automaton, seek an hour or two of sleep again. (Styron, 1990, pp. 58–59)

Depressed patients often exhibit various physical symptoms. These can include a loss of appetite and weight loss, weakness, fatigue, poor bowel functioning, sleep disorders (most often early-morning awakenings), and loss of interest in sex. It is as if both bodily and psychic batteries have run down completely.

These physical symptoms seem to predominate in the depressions that occur in non-Western cultures, while mood symptoms like feelings of worthlessness and sinfulness are largely confined to Western depressions. The reasons for this difference are unknown, but several hypotheses have been proposed. These include the implicit blame that individualist Western cultures affix on people who are not faring well and the various ways that the cultures handle death and mourning (Kleinman and Good, 1985).

DEPRESSION AND SUICIDE

Depression, like schizophrenia, can be lethal. Given the depressive's bottomless despair it is not surprising that suicide is a very real risk. Some attempt the act, and more than a few succeed.

Women are three times as likely to attempt suicide as men, but when men make the attempt, they are much more likely to succeed; in fact, four times as many men as women kill themselves. One reason for the difference is in the choice of methods. The methods that women tend to use don't have the absolute finality of those generally used by men. While women are more likely to cut their wrists or swallow a bottle of sleeping pills, men tend to use methods that are irreversible, such as shooting themselves or jumping off a roof top (Fremouw, Perczel, and Ellis, 1990).

Contrary to what one might expect, the risk of suicide is relatively low while the patient is still in the depths of his depression. At that point his gloom is deepest, but so is his inertia. The risk increases as the patient begins to recover. Suicide rates are greatest during weekend leaves from the hospital and shortly after discharge (Beck, 1967). At this point the patient's mood may still be bleak, but he has regained some of his energy and ability to act. He has recovered just enough to do the one thing that will prevent all further recovery.

SEASONAL AFFECTIVE DISORDER

Many people who live in cold climates have experienced the phenomenon of "cabin fever," a lethargy that ensues as the days grow short with precious few hours of sunlight. Clinical investigators observed that this phenomenon often reached serious proportions. The typical picture is one of depressions that start in late fall when the days become shorter and remit—or even switch to mania— when the days lengthen in March or April. Such ***seasonal affective disorders*** are evidently linked to the amount of sunlight the patients receive (see Figure 18.9).

18.9 Seasonal affective disorder and day length (A) Percentage of patients with seasonal affective disorder who report being depressed in any given month. (B) Mean minutes of daylight per month. (From Rosenthal et al., 1984)

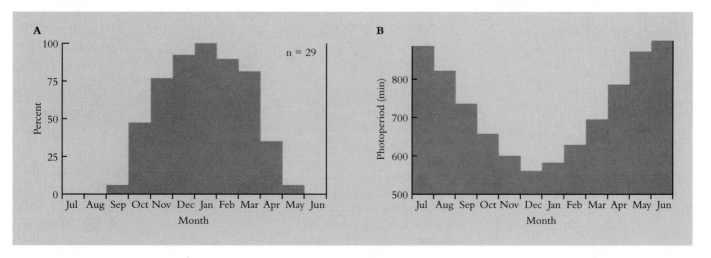

When they travel south in the winter, their depression lifts within a few days; when they travel north in the fall or winter, their depression gets worse. And needless to say, seasonal affective disorder is nonexistent in equatorial countries where there are no seasons and all days are equally long. Given these findings, it was only natural to attempt a treatment using bright artificial lights to replace the sun on one's "dark days." According to several studies, this treatment relieves even severe seasonal depressions within a few days or weeks, but the patient will relapse just as fast if the light therapy is discontinued. It's probably not surprising that one of the first regions in which this therapy was employed was Alaska (Rosen et al., 1990; Rosenthal et al., 1984; Hellekson, Kline, and Rosenthal, 1986; Lewy et al., 1987).

What might account for this striking effect of light on mood in people with seasonal affective disorder? As yet, we don't know. But one possibility is that the effect is somehow connected with the sleeping-waking cycle and with the secretion by the pineal gland of a chemical called *melatonin* (both of which are modulated by light). Indeed, there is some evidence that all depression may involve a disturbance in sleep rhythms, including the overly quick onset of REM sleep (Kupfer, Foster, and Reich, 1976; Wehr and Goodwin, 1981).

ORGANIC FACTORS

■ What produces the mood extremes of bipolar disorder and depression? According to one view, some of these conditions—especially the bipolar variety—are produced by some internal, organic pathology.

GENETIC COMPONENTS

The belief that such an organic pathology exists is based on several pieces of evidence. First, as in schizophrenia, certain drugs have rather specific therapeutic effects. And again, as in schizophrenia, there is good reason to suppose that at least some of the mood disorders have an important hereditary component. This is undoubtedly true for the bipolar condition. Concordances for identical twins with this affliction have been found to be some four times higher than those for fraternal twins (Andreasen and Black, 1991; Siever, Davis, and Gorman, 1991). Another line of evidence comes from detailed "genetic linkage" studies of extended families with numerous cases of bipolar disorder. In these families, the pattern of occurrence of bipolar disorder was linked to a particular enzyme deficiency as well as a type of color blindness. Both of these anomalies are due to defective genes on the X-chromosome, and the hunch is that the gene(s) causing bipolar disorder may be close by (Hodgkinson, Mullan, and Gurling, 1990).

While there is evidence that genetic factors play a role in unipolar cases as well, their contribution is probably not as powerful as it is in the bipolar condition. Further genetic evidence indicates that despite their surface similarity, the two conditions are at bottom quite different. Both tend to "breed true": People with one disorder (that is bipolar or unipolar) tend to have relatives with that condition but not the other. This suggests that there are separate inheritance pathways for each and makes it likely that they are largely separate disorders (Gershon et al., 1985; Torgersen, 1986; Wender et al., 1986).

BIOCHEMICAL HYPOTHESES

The genetic evidence is a strong argument for the view that there is some biological factor that underlies mood disorders, especially the bipolar ones. This

Depression and despair *Edward Adamson, a professional artist, founded a studio in a British mental hospital for the use of the institutionalized patients. Many of their works forcefully express these patients' depression and despair, as in the case of this painting entitled* Cri de Coeur *or* Cry from the heart. *(Cri de Coeur, by Martha Smith; reproduced from Adamson, 1984)*

Depression *(Photograph by Rhoda Sydney, Leo de Wys)*

view is further bolstered by the fact that in people suffering from bipolar disorder the switch from one mood to another is often quite divorced from external circumstances. The most plausible interpretation is that there is some internal, biological switch. But thus far, we know rather little about the biochemistry of bipolar disorder. Some investigators speculate that the disorder is due to instabilities of neuronal membranes (Hirschfeld and Goodwin, 1988; Meltzer, 1986). Such instabilities may also explain the actions of those medications that are successful in controlling the bipolar's mood swings.

Another hypothesis proposes a biochemical defect that involves the supply of some important neurotransmitters at certain critical sites of the brain. When there is a shortage, there is depression. Some investigators believe that this transmitter is **norepinephrine;** others believe that it is **serotonin;** still others suspect that both of these substances are involved (Schildkraut, 1965; Schildkraut, Green, and Mooney, 1985).

One line of evidence for the role of these neurotransmitters came from an analysis of the metabolic breakdown of these substances in the spinal fluid or the urine. If the level of these by-products is low, there should be a correspondingly low supply of the neurotransmitters from which they are derived. Just as predicted, the relevant metabolic by-products were in fact lower in at least some depressed patients than in controls. In addition, the norepinephrine levels in bipolar patients were below average when the patients were depressed and increased when the patients became manic (Muscettola et al., 1984; Schildkraut, Green, and Mooney, 1985). Further confirmation comes from the effect of various **antidepressant medications** all of which increase the amounts of norepinephrine and serotonin available for synaptic transmission.

PSYCHOGENIC FACTORS

The organic pathology—whatever it may turn out to be—might account for the extremes of some patients' moods, the fact that they are speeded up or slowed down in virtually all respects. But can it explain the depressive's hopeless despair and self-loathing? How does an inadequate supply of norepinephrine or serotonin lead to the belief that one is the "most inferior person in the world"?

MOOD OR COGNITION?

What comes first, mood or cognition? The question is again one of cause and effect. Theorists who regard the disorder as primarily somatogenic believe that what the patient thinks follows from her mood. If a transmitter insufficiency (or some other biochemical state) makes her feel sluggish and gloomy, she looks for reasons to explain her own mood. Eventually she finds them: The world is no good and neither is she. The end result is that her cognitions match her feelings. (For an analogous approach to the nature of emotional feelings in normal people, see Chapter 11).

Does this approach really do justice to the phenomenon? Theorists who believe in a psychogenic explanation think not. They grant that mood disorders such as bipolar disorder are probably mostly constitutional, but they insist that psychological factors play a vital role in at least some cases of major depression. In their view, the patient's view that she and the world are no good comes first and her depression comes second, as an effect of these cognitions rather than as their cause.

BECK'S COGNITIVE THEORY OF DEPRESSION

This cognitive view underlies a very influential approach to the understanding and treatment of depression developed by Aaron Beck (Beck, 1967, 1976). Beck believes that the patient's condition can be traced to a trio of intensely negative and irrational beliefs about himself, about his future, and about the world around him: that he is worthless, that his future is bleak, and that whatever happens around him is sure to turn out to be for the worst. According to Beck, these beliefs form the core of a negative cognitive schema in terms of which the patient interprets whatever happens to him. Facing minor setbacks, the depressive makes mountains out of molehills (insisting that he has ruined his car when he's only scratched a fender); facing major accomplishments he makes molehills out of mountains (insisting that he's inept even though he's just won an important professional prize). These negative schemas are ultimately derived from a succession of unfortunate experiences in earlier life; a harshly critical attitude in the home or in school, the loss of a parent, rejection by peers, and so on. But whatever their origins, such negative schemas become self-fulfilling; expecting defeat, the depressive eventually will be defeated. To counteract this system of essentially irrational beliefs, Beck has developed a psychological treatment called *cognitive therapy* by means of which the patients are made to confront and overcome the essential irrationality of their beliefs (we will discuss this in a later section—see Chapter 19; Beck, 1967; Beck et al., 1979).

LEARNED HELPLESSNESS AND DEPRESSIVE ATTRIBUTIONS

Whereas Beck's cognitive theory grew out of clinical observations of depressed patients, a related cognitive account, proposed by Martin Seligman, had its source in studies of animal learning. The initial findings that led to Seligman's approach concerned *learned helplessness,* first observed in the animal laboratory (Seligman, 1975; see Chapter 4).

Learned helplessness and depression   When normal dogs are placed in a box in which they have to jump from one compartment to another in order to escape an electric shock, they learn to do so with little difficulty. This contrasts with a second group of dogs who are first exposed to a series of painful shocks about which they can do absolutely nothing. When this second group is later placed in the box, their performance is drastically different from that of normal dogs. They do not look for some means of escape. Nor do they ever find the correct response—jumping over the hurdle. Instead, they simply give up; they lie down, whimper, and passively accept their fate. They have learned to become helpless (see Chapter 4; Seligman, Maier, and Solomon, 1971).

Seligman argued that learned helplessness in animals is in many ways similar to at least some forms of depression. Like the helpless dogs, depressed patients have given up. They just sit there passively, unable to take any initiative that might help them cope. Some further similarities concern the effects of antidepressant drugs. As we've seen, these drugs alleviate the symptoms of many depressed patients. It turns out that they have a similar effect on animals rendered helpless; the helplessness disappears, and the animals behave much like normals (Porsolt, LePichon, and Jalfre, 1977).

Seligman supposed that the essential similarity between the helpless dogs and the depressed people is the expectation that one's own acts are of no avail. In dogs, the cause is a series of inescapable shocks that the animals can do nothing about. In humans, the precipitating factor may be some personal catastrophe—rejection, bankruptcy, physical disease, the death of a loved one. In some people,

Hamlet on depression   *Probably no patient in real life has described his preoccupation with death, suicide, and dissolution as eloquently as that greatest depressive in all of English literature, Prince Hamlet:*
"O that this too too sullied flesh would melt,
Thaw, and resolve itself into a dew,
Or that the Everlasting had not fixed
His canon 'gainst self-slaughter. O God,
  O God,
How weary, stale, flat, and unprofitable
Seem to me all the uses of this world!
Fie on 't, ah fie, fie! 'Tis an unweeded
  garden
That grows to seed. . . ."
(Hamlet, Act I, scene ii, photograph from the 1948 film version of the play starring Sir Laurence Olivier).

this may lead to a generalized sense of impotence, a belief that there is nothing one can do to shape one's own destiny, that one is a passive victim with no control over events—that one is helpless.

Attributional style and depression   The helplessness interpretation of depression runs into a number of problems. To begin with, it can't explain why being helpless doesn't necessarily lead to depression. People who are about to undergo an operation are helpless in the sense of being utterly dependent on their surgeons, but if they believe they will recover they will generally not become depressed. A further problem is the depressive's self-hatred. If he thinks that he is helpless, then why does he blame himself? (Abramson and Sackheim, 1977). Considerations of this sort led to a revised version of the helplessness theory, which proposed that what really matters is the individual's **attributional style,** the way in which he habitually tries to explain events—especially bad events—that happen to him (see Chapter 16). Does he attribute unfortunate events to internal, global, and stable causes—that is, to causes that refer to something within himself, that will generalize to other situations, and that will continue over time (for example, being unattractive or unintelligent)? If so, he has an attributional style that will predispose him to depression (Abramson, Seligman, and Teasdale, 1978). There is good evidence that this despondent explanatory style is indeed characteristic of depressed persons (as shown by results with the Attributional Style Questionnaire described in Chapter 16; Peterson and Seligman, 1984).

A recent extension of this general approach stresses hopelessness. Its main point is that in some cases of depression, hopelessness is a major cause rather than a symptom. If the patient believes that he has absolutely nothing to look forward to and that the future is utterly bleak, he will probably start a downward spiral that will eventually have bodily manifestations and end in full-fledged depression. The precise differences between this and related psychogenic views (such as Beck's and other offshoots of the learned helplessness approach) are still being spelled out (Alloy, Hartlage, and Abramson, 1988; Abramson, Metalsky, and Alloy, 1989).

SEX DIFFERENCES IN THE INCIDENCE OF DEPRESSION

One very evident fact about depression deserves special mention. Major depression is diagnosed about twice as often in women as in men, even after accounting for differences in income and socioeconomic level. What accounts for this difference? We cannot know for certain, but there are several possibilities. Some are biological. Women may suffer more from depression because of hormonal factors, such as drops in estrogen and progesterone levels during the premenstrual period, the postpartum period, and menopause. Men's hormonal makeup, in contrast, may lead them to "act out" distress rather than to manifest it in depression.

Some other factors are behavioral. According to a recent study, when men are depressed, they try to distract themselves: "I avoid thinking of reasons why I'm depressed," or "I do something physical." In contrast, women who are depressed seem to dwell on their despondency: "I try to determine why I'm depressed," "I talk to other people about my feelings," and "I cry to relieve the tension." The result of these different ways of dealing with one's own feelings is that the initial depression is more likely to escalate and last longer in women than in men (Nolen-Hoeksema, 1987). These differences in the ways in which men and women try to cope with difficult life situations are probably based on cultural factors. The culture expects men to be self-reliant and active, while women are supposed to be more passive and dependent. To the extent that women follow

Sorrow   *(Vincent Van Gogh, 1882; courtesy of the Vincent Van Gogh Foundation/ National Museum Vincent Van Gogh, Amsterdam)*

this cultural expectation, they may gradually come to believe that they can't control their own fate and shouldn't even try—the very condition that renders them liable to learned helplessness and depression.

MOOD DISORDERS AND THE DIATHESIS-STRESS CONCEPTION

■ Major depressions are often preceded by some stressful event, whether it involves marital or professional difficulties, serious physical illness, or a death in the family (Leff, Roatsch, and Bunney, 1970; Paykel, 1982). But it's clear that environmental stress cannot be the whole story. After all, there are many people who suffer major setbacks and serious losses but who don't fall into a depressive collapse. There is evidently a diathesis—some people are more prone to mood disorders than others—that may be based on biological factors, such as an insufficiency of available norepinephrine or serotonin. But the predisposition may well be psychological in nature—such as a negative view of oneself or the world or a depressive attributional style. In either case, the diathesis makes the individual more vulnerable to later stress.

Seen in this light, psychological and biological factors are intermingled, so that the distinction between somatogenic and psychogenic origins becomes somewhat blurred. Negative cognitions and learned helplessness can produce a depletion of norepinephrine and serotonin, but the causal chain can also run the other way around. Either way, there will be a predisposition for later depression, which will be manifested in both behavior and biochemistry.

ANXIETY DISORDERS

FOCUS QUESTIONS

- What are the specific phobias, and how do conditioning theorists explain their development?

- What are the signs and symptoms of obsessive-compulsive disorder? What findings provide evidence for a biological predisposition?

- What is generalized anxiety disorder, and what theories are offered to explain it?

- What is panic disorder, and why does it so often lead to agoraphobia? How does the cognitive account explain the escalating signs and symptoms of a panic attack?

- What disorder is associated with especially traumatic events? How do the signs and symptoms change over the course of the disorder? How successful is treatment for severe cases?

In major depressions, the primary symptom is a profoundly dejected mood: The patient believes that her condition is awful and that there is no hope that it will ever get better. In another group of conditions, the *anxiety disorders,* the primary symptoms are anxiety or defenses against anxiety: The patient is chronically apprehensive, fears the worst, and must guard vigilantly against it. While such symptoms often cause serious distress and impair the person's functioning, they generally do not become so extreme as to render the person psychotic.

A

B

Phobias (A) The fear of dirt (Painting by Vassos); and (B) the fear of heights (Painting by Leon Spilliaert).

PHOBIAS

A relatively common anxiety disorder is a *phobia,* which is characterized by an intense and irrational fear of some object or situation. During the nineteenth century, some of these irrational fears were catalogued and assigned exotic-sounding Greek or Latin names. Some phobias are of particular objects or events; these are the *specific phobias.* Examples are fear of high places (acrophobia), enclosed places (claustrophobia), crowds (ocholophobia), germs (mysophobia), cats (ailurophobia), and even the number 13 (triskaidekophobia)—the list is potentially endless. The crucial point in the definition is that the fear must be irrational—there really is no danger at all or the danger is exaggerated out of all proportion. An African villager who lives in the jungle and is worried about leopards has an understandable fear; a San Francisco apartment dweller with a similar fear has a phobia. In most cases, this irrationality is quite apparent to the sufferer, who knows that the fear is groundless but continues to be afraid all the same.

In phobia, the irrational fear exerts an enormous effect on every aspect of the sufferer's life, for he is always preoccupied with his phobia. On the face of it, it is not entirely clear why this should be so. Why can't the phobic simply avoid the situations that frighten him? If he is afraid of leopards and snakes, he should stay away from the zoo; if he is terrified of heights, he should refrain from visits to the top of the World Trade Center. Some phobias may be minor enough to be handled this easily, but most cannot. In some cases this is because the phobia tends to expand: The fear of leopards becomes a fear of the part of the city where the zoo is located, of all cats and catlike things, or of all spotted objects, and so on. Still others do not allow avoidance, such as the fear of flying in an executive who has to travel.

THE CONDITIONING ACCOUNT OF SPECIFIC PHOBIAS

What is the mechanism that underlies the specific phobias? One notion goes back to John Locke, who believed that such fears were produced by the chance association of ideas, as when a child is told stories about goblins that come by night and is forever after terrified of the dark (Locke, 1690). Several modern authors express much the same idea in the language of conditioning theory. In their view, phobias result from classical conditioning; the conditioned stimulus is the feared object (e.g., cats) and the response is the autonomic upheaval (increased heart rate, cold sweat, and so on) characteristic of fear (Wolpe, 1958).

A number of phobias may indeed develop in just this fashion. Examples include fear of dogs after dog bites, fear of heights after falling off a ladder, and fear of cars or driving after a serious automobile accident (Marks, 1969). Conditioning theorists can readily explain why phobias acquired in this manner expand and spread to new stimuli. The fear response is initially conditioned to a particular stimulus. If this stimulus subsequently occurs in a new context, the fear will be evoked and thus conditioned to a whole set of new stimuli. An example is a woman who developed a fear of anesthetic masks after experiencing a terrifying sensation of suffocation while being anesthetized. This same sense of suffocation reoccurred later when she was in a stuffy, crowded elevator. This is turn led to a dread of elevators, whether empty or crowded. The phobia later generalized to any and all situations in which she could not leave at will, even when playing cards (Wolpe, 1958, p. 98).

591

Compulsive hand washing in literature
A scene from the Old Vic's 1956 production of Macbeth *with Coral Browne. It shows Lady Macbeth walking in her sleep and scrubbing imaginary blood off her hands, as she relives the night in which she and her husband murdered the king. (Courtesy of the Performing Arts Research Center, The New York Public Library)*

OBSESSIVE-COMPULSIVE DISORDER

In phobias, anxiety is aroused by external objects or situations. In contrast, anxiety in *obsessive-compulsive disorder* is produced by internal events—persistent thoughts or wishes that intrude into consciousness and cannot be stopped. An example of such an *obsession* is a mother who has recurrent thoughts of strangling her children. Several studies have found that the most common obsessive themes are of dirt and contamination, aggression and violence, religion, sex, bodily functions like elimination, and the need for balance and symmetry.

A number of *compulsions* may be understood psychodynamically, as attempts to *counteract* the anxiety-producing impulse that underlies an obsession: in Freud's terms, a way of *undoing* what should not have been done. This may explain some cases of compulsions like ritualistic cleaning, handwashing, and counting. The mother with uncontrollable thoughts of committing infanticide might feel compelled to count her children over and over again, as if to check that they are all there, that she hasn't herself done away with any. The patient is quite aware that her behavior is irrational but she can't help herself even so. Lady Macbeth knew that "what's done cannot be undone," but she nevertheless continued to wash the invisible blood off her hands.

Minor and momentary obsessional thoughts or compulsions are commonplace. After all, most people have on occasion checked the stove repeatedly. But in obsessive-compulsive disorder, such thoughts and acts are the patient's major preoccupation and are crippling. The disorder is fairly common, afflicting as many as 2 to 3 percent of the population sometime in their lives. It is also quite serious: Most cases worsen over time and are accompanied by bouts of major depression (Barlow, 1988).

There is some suggestion that there is a biological predisposition to develop obsessive-compulsive disorder. To begin with, there seems to be some genetic basis as shown by the fact that the concordance is higher for identical than for fraternal twins (Black and Noyes, 1990). The neurological mechanism apparently involves the neurotransmitter serotonin: Medications that increase serotonin activity reduce obsessive-compulsive manifestations, but just why they do this is unclear (Insel, 1990; Winslow and Insel, 1990; Zohar et al., 1988).

GENERALIZED ANXIETY DISORDER

In the anxiety disorders we have discussed thus far, anxiety is relatively focused, for it occurs in response to a fairly specific condition. In phobia, anxiety is aroused by the feared object; in obsessive-compulsive disorder, it is aroused by a thought or the belief that one hasn't performed some important act. In contrast, there are several conditions in which anxiety is not related to anything in particular, but isn't any less upsetting for all that.

In *generalized anxiety disorder*, anxiety is all-pervasive, or free-floating. The patient is constantly tense and worried, feels inadequate, is oversensitive, can't concentrate or make decisions, and suffers from insomnia. This state of affairs is generally accompanied by uncomfortable physical states—rapid heart rate, irregular breathing, excessive sweating, and chronic diarrhea.

Generalized anxiety disorder is probably the most common of the anxiety disorders, occurring in as many as 6 percent of the population in any one year (Weissman, 1985). However, little information is available on any genetic predisposition, and there is uncertainty about its cause. Some theorists believe it is psychogenic. A psychoanalytic interpretation holds that the disorder occurs when there are no defenses against anxiety or when those defenses are weak and collapse, so that unacceptable impulses are able to break into consciousness and to precipitate anxiety reactions. Conditioning theorists contend that generalized anxiety disorder is much like a phobia. The difference is that anxiety is conditioned to a very broad range of stimuli so that avoidance is virtually impossible (Wolpe, 1958). The trouble is that these stimuli are not easily specified, and thus the conditioning interpretation of this disorder is hard to evaluate.

Some investigators offer evidence in favor of a somatogenic interpretation. They believe that the condition is linked to certain abnormalities in the secretion of the neurotransmitter GABA (for gamma aminobutyric acid). Support comes from findings that the medications that lower anxiety work by locking onto specific receptor sites in the brain where GABA is plentiful (Costa, 1985).

PANIC DISORDER

Panic disorder is like generalized anxiety disorder in being characterized by anxiety that is not directed at anything in particular. The difference is in the frequency and intensity of the anxiety. Patients with panic disorder don't suffer from the nagging, chronic tensions and worries that beset people with generalized anxiety disorder. But when anxiety strikes them, it strikes with a vengeance.

The patient suffers sudden attacks that come out of the blue and bring terrifying bodily symptoms that she doesn't understand: labored breathing, choking, dizziness, tingling in the hands and feet, sweating, trembling, heart palpitations, and chest pain. These bodily sensations are accompanied by feelings of intense apprehension, terror, and a sense of impending doom. The patient often has an intense experience of unreality and fears that she is losing control, is going insane, or is about to die. Panic disorder is diagnosed if such attacks occur once

The Scream (Edward Munch, 1893; courtesy Nasjonalgalleriet, Oslo)

a week or more often; based on that criterion, it is found in about 2 to 3 percent of women and 1 percent of men (Robins et al., 1984).

Panic disorders can be frightening enough, but in addition, sufferers often develop a profound fear of *having* panic attacks, especially in places such as shopping malls where they might be embarrassing or in circumstances that might prove dangerous such as driving. As a result, people with the condition can rarely venture outside their designated "safe" places—their houses or even just their bedrooms. A common result is **agoraphobia** (from the Greek word *agora* meaning "marketplace"), a fear of being alone and outside of the home, especially in a public place.

What accounts for panic disorder? Some authors hold to a cognitive theory of the condition. They believe that it is produced by a vicious cycle that begins with a misinterpretation of certain bodily reactions to fear. In fear reactions, the sympathetic nervous system produces a number of circulatory and respiratory responses such as quicker heartbeats and faster and shallower breathing. This is normal enough, but the person with the panic disorder overreacts to her own internal sensations. She believes that the shortness of breath and quickened heart beat are a sign of an impending heart attack. This makes her more fearful, which intensifies the bodily reactions, which makes her even more fearful, and so on, spiraling upward toward the full-blown attack. This pattern becomes even worse after the patient has her first panic attack, for now every normal anxiety reaction becomes a potential signal of a further panic (Clark, 1986).

POST-TRAUMATIC STRESS DISORDER

■ Human beings sometimes undergo especially stressful traumatic events. One consequence can be a ***post-traumatic stress disorder.*** This has long been known as a disorder found in soldiers after intense combat and reached wide public attention because of its prevalence among Vietnam war veterans (Figley, 1978). But the disorder can occur at any age and can be produced by a wide range of extreme stressors including fires, automobile accidents, rape, con-

The Dead Mother, 1899–1900, by Edward Munch *(Courtesy of Eigentum der Kunsthalle, Bremen)*

centration camp incarceration, or handling bodies after airplane crashes (Wolf and Mosnaim, 1990).

Regardless of what the trauma was, the signs and symptoms of post-traumatic stress disorder are similar. Immediately after the trauma, there is usually a period of numbness during which the sufferer feels wholly estranged, socially unresponsive, and oddly unaffected by the event, a reaction technically known as *dissociation*. This initial period is often followed by recurrent nightmares and waking flashbacks of the traumatic event. These are often so intense and intrusive that the sufferer may momentarily believe that he is back *in* the situation. Below is a description of the flashbacks of soldiers who served as body handlers:

> . . . A dental X-ray technician reported seeing skulls when he saw the teeth of smiling people. A young lieutenant could not enter a local fast food establishment because the smell of burning food elicited a vomiting response. Some intrusions did not require an external stimulus. Soldiers reported seeing bodies when they closed their eyes. Their dream content consisted of nightmarish horror shows where zombie-like bodies were coming to kill the dreamer. One soldier reported seeing himself in a dream where he searched through human body parts and found his own ID tag. (Garrigan, 1987, p. 8)

Other consequences may include sleep disturbances and some changes in sympathetic nervous system and endocrine functioning. Still another may be "survival guilt" if friends or relatives were harmed or killed by the same traumatic event (Friedman, 1990). If the trauma is severe enough, the manifestations of post-traumatic disorder may remain for years and even decades, even with the best available treatments.

DISSOCIATIVE DISORDERS

FOCUS QUESTIONS

- What are the signs and symptoms of the various dissociative disorders?

- How does post-traumatic stress disorder resemble a dissociative disorder?

- Might the dissociative disorders fit a diathesis-stress model? What is the likely stressor in dissociative identity disorder, and why can't we be certain about its role?

Post-traumatic stress disorder shows that people can distance themselves psychologically, or *dissociate,* from ongoing events. This phenomenon is the defining feature of a number of syndromes now called *dissociative disorders.**** An example is *dissociative amnesia* in which the individual is unable to remember some period of her life, or sometimes all events prior to the onset of the amnesia, including her own identity. Such episodes usually last less than one week (Andreasen and Black, 1991). In other cases, the dissociation produces *dissociative fugue* in which the person wanders away from home, and then, days or even months thereafter, suddenly realizes that he is in a strange place, doesn't know how he got there, and has total amnesia for the entire period.

Still more drastic are cases of *dissociative identity disorder* (formerly known as "multiple personality disorder"). Here the dissociation is so massive that it

---

* Some authors suggest that the dissociative disorders are really severe cases of post-traumatic stress disorder or, alternatively, that the dissociations seen in post-traumatic stress disorder should be reclassified under the rubric of the dissociative disorders.

results in two or more distinct personalities. The "auxiliary" personalities, which can number from just a few to several dozen, seem to be built upon a nucleus of memories that already had some prior separate status. An example is a shy and inhibited person who has had fantasies of being carefree and outgoing from childhood on. These memories eventually take on the characteristics of a separate self. Once formed, the new self may appear quite suddenly, as in the famous case of Eve White, loosely depicted in the movie *The Three Faces of Eve:*

> After a tense moment of silence, her hands dropped. There was a quick, reckless smile and, in a bright voice that sparkled, she said, "Hi there, Doc." . . . There was in the newcomer a childishly daredevil air, an erotically mischievous glance, a face marvelously free from the habitual signs of care, seriousness, and underlying distress, so long familiar in her predecessor. This new and apparently carefree girl spoke casually of Eve White and her problems, always using she or her in every reference, always respecting the strict bounds of a separate identity. When asked her own name she immediately replied, "Oh, I'm Eve Black." (Thigpen and Cleckley, 1957, as described in Coleman, 1972, p. 246).

Some twenty years later, Eve White wrote an autobiography in which she described herself more fully. It turned out that at one time in her life she had as many as twenty-two subpersonalities rather than just three (Sizemore and Huber, 1988). The various personalities seen in such cases are not confined to differences in mood and attitudes. Sometimes the individual segregates different skills to different personalities, such that one plays the piano, while another cooks, and yet a third speaks French. The personalities can know of each other, have amnesia for each other, or exhibit any combinations of acquaintanceship.

Until twenty years ago, dissociative identity disorder was considered very rare, with fewer than two hundred cases reported before 1975. Now cases number in the thousands of whom the large majority are females (Kluft, 1987). A rash of reported cases followed *Sybil,* a popular book about one case of dissociative identity disorder, subsequently made into a television movie (Schreiber, 1973). Some critics argued that the flood of such diagnoses reflected a fad among therapists who inadvertently led their patients—many of whom had read the book themselves—to develop the signs and symptoms of dissociative identity disorder. This may well have been true in some cases, but dissociative identity disorder is now considered an entirely valid diagnosis for many patients.

FACTORS UNDERLYING DISSOCIATIVE DISORDERS

■ The mechanism that underlies the dissociative disorders is still obscure. Some authors suggest that phenomena like the development of auxiliary personalities may represent an unusual form of self-dramatization, without the awareness that any role playing is going on (Ziegler, Imboden, and Rodgers, 1963; Sarbin and Allen, 1968). Others try to understand dissociation in the context of human information processing and stress its similarity to phenomena like implicit memory and procedural knowledge (Kihlstrom, 1992; see Chapter 7).

There is less debate about the psychological function played by dissociation. Most authors hold to one or another variant of Freud's view. He believed that dissociation is a defense against something the individual is unable to face. The post-traumatic stress reaction is a case in point. Rape victims sometimes report that they are outside of their own bodies watching themselves being raped. Similarly for people who watch their houses burn; they sometimes experience a strange calm and report the feeling that "it's like it's not really happening to me."

A movie recreation of a case of dissociative identity disorder Joanne Woodward in The Three Faces of Eve *portraying Eve White (above) and Eve Black (below). (Courtesy of the Museum of Modern Art/Film Stills Archive)*

DISSOCIATIVE DISORDERS AND THE DIATHESIS-STRESS CONCEPTION

There is some evidence that dissociative disorders may fit a diathesis-stress conception. People seem to differ in their propensity to dissociate and in the intensity of the circumstances that make them do so. The evidence comes from work on hypnosis, which some investigators regard as a form of guided dissociation (Hilgard, 1986). If this is so, one might suspect that people with dissociative disorders should be more hypnotizable than others, and this indeed turns out to be the case (Ganaway, 1989). This seems to be especially so for patients with dissociative identity disorder. According to one investigator, such patients were unusually adept at self-hypnosis during childhood and created a new personality (often many more than just one) during their hypnotic trance as a form of escape from threatening traumatic events (Bliss, 1980).

The readiness toward dissociation—which may be constitutional or based on learned defense patterns—represents the predisposition or diathesis toward the disorder. To activate it into the full-fledged disorder, there has to be some unusual stress. This does indeed seem to be the case. Thus, most cases of dissociative amnesia occur after the same kinds of cataclysmic events that may lead to post-traumatic stress disorder. The same holds for dissociative fugues, which can also develop suddenly after personal misfortunes or financial pressures (Andreasen and Black, 1991).

There is reason to believe that the most serious and disabling of the dissociative conditions, dissociative identity disorder, results from the most harrowing stresses in early life. In a large percentage of the case histories, there are terrifying stories of repeated brutal physical and sexual abuse in childhood, often including incest (Putnam et al., 1986). These findings have led the majority of practioners to believe that child abuse, and especially sexual abuse, is a likely antecedent of dissociative identity disorder. But some others urge caution in accepting this interpretation, for virtually all of the reports of early childhood abuse are based on the patients' uncorroborated memories of early childhood (see Chapter 7; Frankel, 1993). As yet, the evidence is not all in.

SOMATOFORM AND PSYCHOPHYSIOLOGICAL DISORDERS

FOCUS QUESTIONS

- What are the somatoform disorders? How does hypochondriasis differ from both somatization disorder and somatoform pain disorder?

- What are psychophysiological disorders?

- What is the Type A behavior pattern, and what kinds of behavior account for the health risks associated with it?

In a number of psychological disorders the predominant symptoms are bodily complaints. We will take up examples drawn from two categories of such disorders: the *somatoform* and the *psychophysiological*.

SOMATOFORM DISORDERS

■ It appears that while some people experience anxiety directly and others dissociate from it, still others turn it into bodily complaints. At least this is the most common interpretation of the **somatoform disorders** (those disorders that take bodily form). There are several kinds of such disorders, but in each the patient exhibits or describes concerns about his bodily functions in the absence of any known physical illness. Probably the best known of the somatoform disorders is **hypochondriasis** in which the sufferer believes he has a specific disease and goes to doctor after doctor to be evaluated for it. Somewhat similar is the person with **somatization disorder.** She brings to the doctor a host of miscellaneous aches and pains in various bodily systems that do not add up to any known syndrome in physical medicine. And then there is **somatoform pain disorder** in which the sufferer describes chronic pain for which no physical basis can be found.

The most dramatic of the somatoform disorders is **conversion disorder.** Conversion disorder (formerly known as *conversion hysteria* or *hysterical neurosis*) represented the first and most dramatic argument for the psychogenic approach to psychopathology and was the foundation on which psychoanalytic theory was built. According to Freud, people with these disorders resolve some intolerable conflict by developing an hysterical ailment, such as being unable to see or hear or move an arm, even though there is nothing organically wrong (see Chapter 17).★ The soldier who is terrified of going into battle but cannot face the idea of being a coward may become hysterically paralyzed. This allows him to give in to his impulse of refusing to march. But it also lets him do so without guilt or shame—he is not marching because he cannot march.

A century ago, such cases were fairly common, but today they account for a much smaller fraction of mental disorders. How can we explain this changing fashion in psychopathological conditions? Some suggest that the reason is education: Because of a general increase in medical sophistication among lay persons, there are fewer people who believe that one can suddenly be struck blind or become paralyzed without some other accompanying bodily signs, say, of a stroke (Watson and Buranen, 1979). One historian has suggested that disorders such as chronic fatigue and somatoform pain disorder have become the conversion hysterias of the late twentieth century (Shorter, 1992). Diagnoses of conversion disorder might also be expected to decline because of medical advances that allow better detection of the physical disorders that might otherwise have been interpreted as cases of conversion disorders. Support for this notion comes from follow-up studies of patients whose symptoms were diagnosed as conversions. A fair proportion of these patients were later found to have had organic disorders after all, many of which involved neurological damage (Slater and Glithero, 1965; Watson and Buranen, 1979). And in today's medical malpractice climate, a physician diagnosis "conversion disorder" at her own risk.

PSYCHOPHYSIOLOGICAL DISORDERS

■ Thus far, our concern has been with psychopathological disorders whose primary symptoms are psychological. But certain other conditions can lead to genuine organic damage. For example, ulcer, high blood pressure, and

★ The term *conversion* was coined by Freud, who believed that the repressed energies that fueled the patient's unconscious conflict were converted into a somatic symptom much as a steam engine converts thermal energy into mechanical energy. Until recently, this condition was called *conversion hysteria.* The authors of DSM-III dropped the term *hysteria* because of its erroneous implication that conversion disorders were found only in women. ("Hysteria" is derived from the Greek *hystera,* for womb.)

asthma may be produced by organic causes, as in the case of an asthmatic allergic reaction. Yet they may also be produced (or aggravated) by emotional factors. If so, they are called *psychophysiological conditions* (or, to use an older term, *psychosomatic disorders*).

But whether their origin is organic or mental or a bit of both, their results are equally damaging. In this regard, the symptoms of a psychophysiological condition are quite different from the somatic complaints of a patient with a conversion disorder. That patient's paralysis of the legs may disappear after his underlying conflict is resolved; after all, his locomotor machinery is still intact. But the patient with a psychophysiological ulcer (or asthma or high blood pressure) has a disorder that plays for keeps. His ulcer will bleed and hurt just as much as an ulcer caused by gastric disease; if it perforates his stomach wall, he will suffer the same case of peritonitis; and if he dies, his death will be no less final.

CORONARY HEART DISEASE

Perhaps the best-documented example of a disorder brought on or aggravated by psychological factors is **coronary heart disease,** a progressively increasing blockage of the arteries that supply blood to the heart muscles. This may result in severe chest pains (angina), indicating that the muscles in a certain region of the heart don't get enough oxygen to maintain their current work load. It may also result in the death of some portion of the heart muscle tissue (a "heart attack") that received no oxygen at all. There are a number of biological factors that increase the risk of coronary heart disease, such as cholesterol level, obesity, smoking, and gender (men are more prone to the disease than women). But in addition, psychopathologists have identified certain characteristic behavior patterns that provide a major additional risk factor.

The Type A personality   One example is the **Type A behavior pattern.** People with this pattern are highly competitive and hard-driving, always in a hurry, and are irritable, impatient, and hostile. In the words of Friedman and Rosenman, the two cardiologists who first described this pattern, such individuals are "aggressively involved in a chronic, incessant struggle to achieve more and more in less and less time, and if required to do so, against the opposing efforts of other things or other persons" (Friedman and Rosenman, 1974, p. 67). In contrast, those with the **Type B behavior pattern** are less hurried and competitive, and more easygoing and friendly than their Type A counterparts. The Type A person runs up escalators whereas the Type B lets the escalator do the work. In traffic jams, the Type A fumes and curses, while the Type B in the next lane sits back and listens to a radio broadcast of a baseball game. Needless to say, many people are not extreme A or B types, but fall somewhere in between.

Several large-scale studies have shown that people with a Type A pattern are more likely to contract coronary heart disease than Type B individuals. In one such study, over 3,000 men with no sign of coronary heart disease were evaluated to determine their behavior type. The single best predictor of whether these men developed coronary heart disease during the subsequent eight years was their original assessment: Type A's were twice as likely to become victims than Type B's. Could this be because Type A's smoked more or had higher blood pressure or had higher cholesterol levels? The answer is no, for the relation between behavior pattern and heart disease held up even when these other risk factors were statistically held constant (Rosenman et al., 1975). Further work showed that the same relation held for women. Compared to men, women—whether Type A or Type B—are much less likely to suffer coronary heart disease, for reasons that are still a matter of debate. But compared to Type B women, Type A women are more at risk; they are two to three times more like-

"I don't care if they are moving better over there. This is the fast lane. This is where I live." (Drawing by Handelsman; © 1983, The New Yorker Magazine, Inc.)

ly to suffer a heart attack and this regardless of whether they are working women or not (Haynes, Feinleib, and Kannel, 1980).

Impatience or hostility? It appears that some aspects of the Type A behavior pattern predict coronary heart disease. But just what is the crucial part of the pattern? Is it the Type A's impatience, his relentless need for achievement, or his irritability? Some investigations suggest that these different components of the behavior pattern are not as tightly linked—to each other or to the disease—as they were initially thought to be (Mathews, 1982; Shekelle et al., 1983). Many investigators feel that the major pathological ingredient is hostility, manifested as a combination of continual anger, cynicism, and distrust of other people, that is found in some—but by no means all—Type A's (Dembroski et al., 1989). Those who say yes to questions like "Most people are honest chiefly through fear of being caught" or "When someone does me wrong I feel I should pay him back if I can, just for the principle of the thing" are more likely to fall victim to cardiac disease than those who do not. Other facets of the Type A pattern, such as the sense of hurry and competitiveness seem to be of lesser importance (Williams, 1987; Krantz et al., 1988; Barefoot et al., 1989).

THE DIATHESIS-STRESS CONCEPT AND PSYCHOPHYSIOLOGICAL DISORDERS

Emotional stress can lead to hypertension or coronary heart disease, but it can also lead to various other psychophysiological disorders such as stomach ulcers. Is there any way to predict which disorder will be produced in any one person by stress? What determines whether "she will eat her heart out" or whether "she'll tie her stomach into knots?" The answer is diathesis and stress.

There is reason to believe that the susceptibility to a given psychophysiological disorder depends on a preexisting somatic diathesis that may be of genetic origin. Given enough emotional stress, the body will cave in at its most vulnerable point. Some evidence for this view comes from studies which show that elevated blood pressure tends to run in families, in mice as well as men. In humans, a blood-pressure correlation between children and parents is seen as early as infancy. The best guess is that there is a genetic factor that is partially responsible for the initial blood-pressure elevation. This may bias the individual to respond to stress with his arterial muscles rather than with his lungs or stomach. If the stress is prolonged enough, the individual will develop chronic high blood pressure rather than suffer from asthma or an ulcer (Henry and Cassel, 1969).

A CATEGORIZING REVIEW

We have looked at a number of different mental disorders. The pathology model provides a convenient framework to review the way in which these disorders are generally considered today. This review is summarized in Table 18.1, which classifies disorders by the nature of their main symptoms and of their presumed underlying pathology (which in many cases is still controversial). Either the main symptoms or the pathology or both can be organic. But they can also be mental, that is, defined by behavioral rather than by organic attributes.

TABLE 18.1 A CLASSIFICATION OF SOME MENTAL DISORDERS

		Symptoms	
		Primarily organic	Primarily mental
Presumed underlying disorder	Primarily organic	Diabetes Measles Rickets	General paresis Schizophrenia★ Bipolar disorders★
	Primarily mental	Psycho-physiological disorders	Phobias Dissociative disorders

★ Whether the underlying pathology of these disorders is primarily organic or psychogenic is still a matter of debate. In some cases, organic and behavioral causes are so intertwined that it's impossible to say which is primary.

SOCIAL DEVIANCE

FOCUS QUESTIONS

- What is sociopathy, and what factors may cause it?

- Why are individuals with antisocial personality disorder not clearly classifiable as having a mental disorder?

The conditions we've considered thus far are clearly mental disorders. There is much about them that we still don't understand, but they seem to fit reasonably well within the general underlying pathology framework nevertheless. There are a number of other diagnostic categories, however, that don't fit so readily. The psychiatric classification system includes several conditions that are certainly deviant and usually undesirable, such as antisocial personality and alcohol and drug dependence. But it is by no means clear that these are really mental disorders. Nor is it clear that the underlying pathology model is the most appropriate framework for them.

Society calls some forms of deviance criminal while calling others disorders, and it has set up institutions to deal with each—the judicial system for the first and the mental-health system for the second. In actual fact, the two classifications overlap and both shade off into normality. Figure 18.10 (on p. 602) provides a graphic description of how the terms "normal," "bad," and "ill" are usually applied. Some kinds of people can be classified unambiguously: you and I (definitely "normal," or at least, so we hope), a professional criminal ("bad"), and a severe case of schizophrenia ("ill"). But there are also areas of overlap. Some people occupy a gray area between normality and criminality. An example might be a person who is a habitual reckless driver. Others lie between mental disorder and normality. An example would be someone with a serious drinking problem. Still others are in the zone between criminality and mental disorder. They are somehow both "ill" and "bad" at the same time. Our present concern is with one such group of individuals, the **sociopaths,** or as they are described in DSM-IV, persons with **antisocial personality disorder.**★

★ An earlier designation was *psychopath*. Some versions of this term are still in current use. One example is the MMPI scale, which attempts to measure psychopathic deviance.

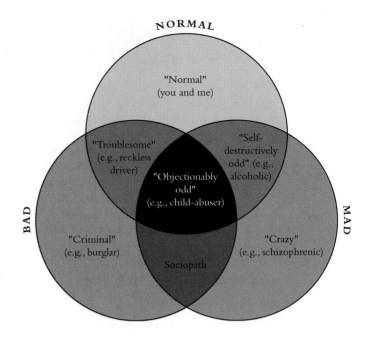

18.10 BAD, MAD, and NORMAL, and their areas of overlap *(After Stone, 1975)*

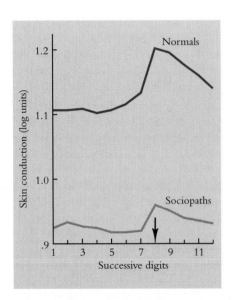

18.11 Anticipation of electric shock in normals and sociopaths *Normals and sociopaths were repeatedly presented with a series of twelve consecutive digits from 1 to 12. Whenever the digit 8 appeared, the subjects suffered an electric shock. To determine whether there were any differences in anticipatory anxiety prior to the advent of shock, the galvanic skin response (GSR) was measured. The results are shown in units of log conductance (a measure of GSR activity) for each of the 12 digits in the series. The sociopaths showed a much lower base-response level. In addition, they showed less anticipatory reaction to the digits just prior to the critical digit. (After Hare, 1965)*

THE SOCIOPATH

■ *The clinical picture* The sociopath is an individual who gets into continual trouble with others and with society. He—or somewhat less frequently, she—is grossly selfish, callous, impulsive, and irresponsible. Sociopaths are not truly socialized. They are loners, lacking any genuine feelings of love or loyalty for any person or group. But they are often quite adept at the machinations and strategies of personal interaction, manifesting a superficial charm and sometimes a greater than average intelligence.

Some possible causes of sociopathy What accounts for antisocial personality disorder? Many investigators have noted the sociopath's lack of concern for the consequences of his actions. Sociopaths are comparatively fearless. This is especially true when the danger is far off. One investigator told sociopaths and normals that they would receive a shock at the end of a ten-minute period. The subjects' apprehensiveness was assessed by their galvanic skin response (GSR). As the time grew closer, the control subjects grew increasingly nervous. In contrast, the sociopaths showed little anticipatory fear (Lippert and Senter, 1966; see Figure 18.11). If future pain had just as little import when the sociopath was young, his inadequate socialization becomes partially comprehensible. Whoever tried to teach him the don'ts of childhood had no effective deterrents.

The strange fearlessness of sociopaths has been observed by several writers who have noted their "extraordinary poise," their "smooth sense of physical being," and their "relative serenity" under conditions that would produce agitation in most of us (Cleckley, 1976). How does this difference between sociopaths and normals come about? Several investigators believe that there is a difference in some underlying physiological functions. One line of evidence concerns the EEG (electrical recordings from the brain; see Chapter 3). It appears that a fairly high proportion of sociopaths have abnormal EEGs that resemble those of children. One possible interpretation is that this cortical immaturity of sociopaths is the physiological counterpart of their essential childishness—their desire for instant gratification and their belligerent tantrums when thwarted.

Another hypothesis is that the sociopath is cortically underaroused, as if he were not fully awake under normal conditions. Proponents of this hypothesis argue that because of this underarousal, sociopaths actively seek stimulation—they are easily bored and court thrills and danger to rouse themselves to some optimal level of stimulation, much as the rest of us might pinch our arms to keep ourselves from dozing off (Quay, 1965; Hare, 1978).★

Such physiological differences suggest that there may be a constitutional predisposition toward sociopathy. This predisposition may well be genetic, as shown by the fact that identical twins have higher concordance rates on sociopathy than fraternal twins. Early environment may also play a role. There is considerable evidence that sociopaths are more likely to have a sociopathic or alcoholic father than are normals. An additional factor is discipline; inconsistent discipline in childhood or no discipline at all correlates with sociopathy in adulthood (Robins, 1966).

SOCIOPATHY AND THE DISORDER CONCEPT

By now, we are starting to get some understanding of how sociopathy might come about. But does that justify our calling it a mental disorder? There is some doubt whether it really does. Certainly the sociopath often comes to grief, but so do ordinary criminals and for the same reason: They get caught. Why should we call the one ill and the other bad? Why should one be the province of the mental-health system while the other is the business of the courts? The question is especially pertinent given the fact that most mental-health practitioners are pessimistic about the possibility of therapy for sociopaths. An additional difficulty lies in differential diagnosis, for in actual practice it can be difficult to distinguish sociopaths from ordinary criminals. Under the circumstances, it is not obvious what is gained by classifying sociopathy as a mental disorder.

THE SCOPE OF PSYCHOPATHOLOGY

Sociopathy is only one of the questionable categories in the psychiatric catalogue. Similar questions can be raised about drug addiction or alcoholism or a number of other deviant patterns. Are these really mental disorders in the sense in which schizophrenia and obsessive-compulsive disorder are? When the term is applied so widely that it includes virtually all forms of human behavior that cause personal unhappiness, it has become so vague that it is in danger of losing its meaning.

The imperialism of modern psychopathology that makes it try to subsume ever more conditions is not solely the fault of an ambitious mental-health establishment, however. Instead, it is in part the product of a society that insists on quick and simple solutions. We think that by designating a given human or social problem a mental disorder we have somehow taken a stride toward its solution. But we've really done nothing of the sort. For calling a problem—alcoholism, sexual exhibitionism, drug addiction, or even premenstrual syndrome—a mental disorder does not necessarily make it so. Nor does it mean that we therefore know what to do about it.

★ This suggests a relation to sensation seeking, which shows a similar pattern (see Chapter 16).

QUESTIONS FOR CRITICAL THINKING

1. Should couples with schizophrenia in one or both of their families be discouraged from having children?

2. Might depression (at least, mild depression) be biologically adaptive in any way?

3. Many of us have phobias about snakes, roaches, heights, and the dark. Why don't we have phobias about much riskier things—such as electric sockets and automobiles—instead?

4. Why do people dissociate? When might this be a very useful ability?

5. Might patients be stigmatized if their illnesses (like heart disease and hypertension) were labeled "psychophysiological"? Would there be a compensating advantage?

6. Should sociopaths who commit violent crimes be sent to prison or to psychiatric hospitals, and why?

SUMMARY

1. The field of *psychopathology*, which is sometimes called *abnormal psychology*, deals with a wide assortment of disorders that generally cause considerable anguish and seriously impair the person's functioning.

2. In certain periods of history, mental disorder was seen as a form of demonic possession. In others, as in our own, it was regarded as a form of illness. Some of these disorders are *somatogenic*, being the result of a bodily malfunction, as in *general paresis*, which was discovered to result from a syphilitic infection contracted years before. Other mental disorders are thought to be *psychogenic*, resulting from psychological rather than organic causes, a view that seemed to apply to many cases of *conversion disorder*.

3. A very general conception of psychopathology is provided by the *underlying pathology model*, which makes psychopathology analogous to physical disorders. A given disorder has various signs and symptoms that form a pattern or *syndrome*; these, plus the course of the illness, are the bases for diagnosis and classification. The classification system now in use is set out in *DSM-IV*, the current diagnostic manual of psychiatry.

4. According to the underlying pathology model, the signs and symptoms of a disorder are thought to result from some underlying and relatively immediate cause, the pathology. Many disorders seem well described by the *diathesis-stress* conception, which proposes the interaction of various predispositions (diatheses) with various stressors. As formulated here, the underlying pathology model is largely descriptive and makes no assertion about the nature of the signs and symptoms, their psychogenic or somatogenic causes, or the appropriate modes of treatment. Three subcategories of the underlying pathology model are the *medical model*, the *psychoanalytic model*, and the *learning model*.

5. Probably the most serious condition in psychopathology is *schizophrenia*. Its main symptoms are disorders of cognition, social withdrawal, disruption of emotional responding, and, in many cases, the construction of a private world accompanied by *delusions* and *hallucinations*. Subcategories of schizophrenia used in current classification include the *paranoid, catatonic,* and *disorganized* subtypes.

6. One question about the pathology of schizophrenia is how best to characterize the schizophrenic's underlying *psychological malfunction.* Many authors believe that it is fundamentally a disorder of thought, based on an inability to retain the context of one's thoughts and actions.

7. The search for the biological basis of schizophrenia has focused on two possible kinds of pathology. One involves a malfunctioning of neurotransmitters, specifically an

oversensitivity to *dopamine.* Evidence comes from the therapeutic effect of *antipsychotic medications,* which are known to block dopamine at neuron synapses. Another organic pathology involves an atrophy of brain tissue found in some schizophrenics. According to the *two-syndrome hypothesis,* schizophrenia is really a composite of two underlying pathologies: one type (Type I schizophrenia) is caused by a neurotransmitter malfunction and produces *positive symptoms,* such as delusions and hallucinations; the second type (called Type II schizophrenia) is caused by cerebral atrophy and leads to *negative symptoms,* such as withdrawal and apathy. Support for this view comes from the fact that patients with mostly positive symptoms respond well to standard antipsychotics and show little cerebral damage, while patients with mostly negative symptoms are not improved by standard antipsychotics and are more likely to show brain damage.

8.   More ultimate causes of schizophrenia include a genetic factor. The evidence is provided by *concordance* studies of identical and fraternal twins and by studies of children of schizophrenic mothers adopted shortly after birth. But this genetic factor is only a predisposition; its conversion into the actual schizophrenic disorder depends on some precipitating environmental stress. Some investigators believe that the critical environmental factors include pathological interactions within the family and a *neurodevelopmental disorder* in which a genetic predisposition produces abnormal fetal brain development that leaves the individual vulnerable to later stress.

9.   In another group of conditions, the dominant disturbance is one of *mood,* as in the frenzied energy of *mania* or the despair and lethargy of *depression.* One form of mood disorder is *bipolar disorder,* with recurrent swings from one emotional extreme to the other. Another is *unipolar disorder,* or *major depression,* for the mood extreme is generally depression. Still another is *seasonal affective disorder,* which seems to be related to the amount of light patients are exposed to, with depressions that start in the fall and end in the spring.

10.   According to one view, mood disorders, especially bipolar disorder, are produced by an organic pathology, a belief bolstered by evidence that such conditions have a genetic component. Bipolar disorder may arise from instabilities of neuronal membranes. For major depression, one hypothesis proposes a defect in the supply of certain neurotransmitters, in particular, *norepinephrine* and *serotonin.* Other investigators stress the role of psychogenic factors, such as cognitive outlook. An influential example of such a psychogenic view is the *learned helplessness theory* of depression. Some of its more recent extensions stress the role of *attributional style* and of *hopelessness.*

11.   Another group of conditions are the *anxiety disorders.* One such disorder is *specific phobia,* in which there is an intense and irrational fear of some object or situation. In *obsessive-compulsive disorder,* the anxiety is produced by internal wishes or events, such as obsessions that cannot be stopped. In *generalized anxiety disorder* it is all pervasive and free floating. In *panic disorder,* which is often accompanied by *agoraphobia,* there are sudden, vehement attacks that strike out of the blue. In *post-traumatic stress disorder,* there is a reaction to especially stressful events such as fires, war, and rape, which usually starts with an initial period of *dissociation,* followed by severe aftereffects, including recurrent nightmares, waking flashbacks, and "survival guilt."

12.   Another way of handling anxiety is through *dissociation.* Chief among the dissociative disorders is *dissociative identity disorder,* which has been somewhat controversially linked to early childhood sexual abuse.

13.   Another group are the *somatoform disorders,* characterized by the presence of bodily signs and symptoms that have no apparent organic basis. The somatoform disorders include the classic but now rare disorder that inspired psychoanalysis, *conversion disorder.* In *psychophysiological conditions,* psychogenic causes have genuine organic consequences. An example is *coronary heart disease,* which is more likely in people with elements of the *Type A behavior pattern.*

14.   The problem of defining psychopathology is acute for conditions such as *antisocial personality disorder* (or *sociopathy*) in which deviance overlaps mental disorder and criminality. The causes of sociopathy are still unknown; hypotheses include cortical immaturity, a chronic state of underarousal that leads to attempts to seek continued stimulation, and a genetic predisposition.

CHAPTER **19**

TREATMENT OF PSYCHOPATHOLOGY

hat can be done to help those who suffer from mental disorders? There is no scarcity of therapeutic methods, each with its own adherents. Some rely on biological interventions such as medications. Others approach the condition at the psychological level through various kinds of psychotherapy. Until recently, the proven benefits of these interventions were relatively modest. Of late, the outlook is more optimistic. There are no miracle cures, but at least some disorders seem to respond reasonably well to certain biological and/or psychological treatments.

BIOLOGICAL THERAPIES

FOCUS QUESTIONS

- What medications control the major manifestations of schizophrenia?

- What three classes of medication are the mainstays of treating depression? How do they seem to work?

- How is bipolar disorder treated? the anxiety disorders?

- Why can't the effectiveness of a medication be tested simply by giving it to patients and observing whether they improve? How does the double-blind technique solve the problems involved?

One approach to treatment is to make direct changes in various bodily systems. Such **biological therapies** characterize medicine's classical attack on any disease. Thus, once mental disorder was conceived as an illness, it was only natural to try to heal it with the traditional tools of the physician's trade. Until fairly recently, such attempts were largely unsuccessful, with the would-be cures often far worse than the disease. We already mentioned a very early example: *trephining, the removal of pieces of skull bone,* a prehistoric practice that persisted into the Middle Ages. Other early procedures involved a relentless succession of bloodlettings and purgatives, all intended somehow to restore harmony among the bodily humors. Later developments were hardly milder. For example, Benjamin Rush (1745–1813), one of the signers of the Declaration of Independence and the acknowledged father of American psychiatry, submersed patients in hot or cold water until they were just short of drowning, or twirled them on special devices at speeds that rendered them unconscious (see Figure 19.1 on the next page). Such methods were said to reestablish balance between bodily and mental functions. They almost certainly had no such salutary effects, although they were probably welcomed by hospital attendants, since such methods undoubtedly terrified the inmates and thus helped to "keep order" (Mora, 1975).

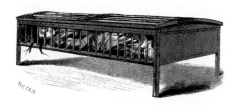

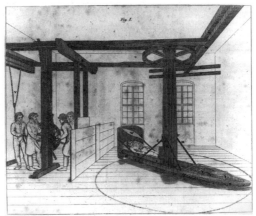

A

B

C

19.1   Early methods for treating mental disorder   *(A) A crib for violent patients. (Courtesy of Historical Pictures Service) (B) A centrifugal-force bed. (Courtesy of National Library of Medicine) (C) A swinging device. (Courtesy of Culver Pictures)*

DRUG THERAPIES

■ The bleak outlook for biological therapies did not brighten until the turn of the century. The first step was the conquest of the global, progressively disabling syndrome of general paresis, accomplished by attacking the syphilitic infection that caused it (see Chapter 18). But the major advances have come only during the last forty years or so with the discovery and development of a number of medications that seem to control, or at least moderate, the manifestations of schizophrenia and the mood and anxiety disorders.

These medications have had an enormous impact upon mental-health care. They have allowed many patients to be treated without hospitalization, and for many disorders, they are now routinely prescribed not only by psychiatrists, but by primary-care physicians, such as general and family practitioners (Olfson and Klerman, 1993).

DRUG TREATMENT OF SCHIZOPHRENIA: ANTIPSYCHOTICS

In the last chapter, we saw that one of the major arguments for a biochemical theory of schizophrenia was the effectiveness of certain drugs called **antipsychotics.** The most common of these drugs include Thorazine and Haldol. (Here, and in further text discussions, we only give the drug's trade name. Its technical name, the biochemical family it belongs to, and some related drugs that have similar effects are shown in Table 19.1.) These medications tend to reduce many of the major manifestations of schizophrenia, such as thought disorder and hallucinations. They are believed to act mainly by blocking synaptic receptors in pathways of the brain that are sensitive to dopamine. It is this blockade and the resultant decrease in dopamine activity that are generally thought to produce the therapeutic effects.

The social reality of treating schizophrenics   Because they allowed many schizophrenic patients to be managed outside of mental hospitals, the classic antipsychotics lent impetus to a movement called **deinstitutionalization,** which was intended to obtain better and less expensive care for patients in their own communities—at local community mental-health centers rather than at large, centralized hospitals. In part, this movement worked. Whereas in the 1950s mental hospitals in the United States housed about 600,000 patients, by the

| | | | TABLE 19.1 SOME COMMONLY USED PSY- CHOTROPIC MEDICATIONS |

Primary Function	Drug Class	Chemical Name	Trade (Commercial) Name
Antidepressants	MAO inhibitors	Phenelzine Tranylcypromine	Nardil Parnate
	Tricyclics	Clomipramine Imipramine	Anafranil Tofranil
	Selective serotonin reuptake inhibitors	Fluoxetine Sertaline	Prozac Zoloft
Antipsychotics	Butyrophenones	Haloperidol	Haldol
	Phenothiazines	Chlorpromazine	Thorazine
Antimanic medications		Lithium carbonate	Eskalith
Anxiety-reducing medications (anxiolytics)	Benzodiazepines	Chlordiazepoxide Diazepam	Librium Valium

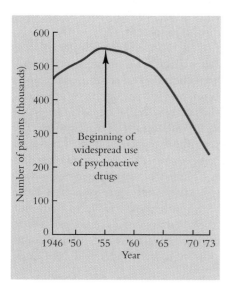

19.2 *Number of residents in state and local government mental hospitals, 1946–1973 in the United States* (Based on data from U.S. Public Health Service)

1980s this number had dropped to 125,000. The new drugs made it possible to discharge schizophrenic patients more quickly than ever before. According to one estimate, prior to the introduction of these drugs, two out of three schizophrenic patients spent most of their lives in the state asylum. In the 1980s, their average stay was about two months (Lamb, 1984; Davis, 1985a; see Figure 19.2).

But it soon became apparent that the situation was not as hopeful as it first appeared. For while the antipsychotic medications help to alleviate the symptoms of the disorder, they still leave much to be desired as a treatment. They only hold the manifestations of schizophrenia in check so long as they are taken; they neither cure the disease nor alter its progress. They tend to work more on positive symptoms like delusions and hallucinations and do little for negative symptoms like apathy, emotional blunting, and poor sociability. In addition, they have potent side effects that can include sedation, constipation, dry mouth, blurred vision, difficulty in urination, cardiac irregularities, tremors and muscle spasms, restlessness, a shuffling gait, and a curiously inexpressive, masklike face. Some patients who take them over the long term will eventually develop permanent motor disorders (Hollister and Csernansky, 1990).

One result of all these side effects is that many schizophrenic patients refuse to take their medicines reliably, and the flare-up of their signs and symptoms can eventuate in repeated hospitalizations, producing a "revolving-door patient." Even when patients do take their antipsychotics regularly, 30 to 50 percent of them have recurrent outbreaks of the illness and need further hospitalization or a change of dosage or type of medication (Andreasen and Black, 1991). As a consequence, although fewer schizophrenics remain in mental hospitals and do not stay in the hospital as long (Lamb, 1984; Davis, 1985a), the number of times they are readmitted for short stays has increased by 80 percent since the 1960s (Rosenstein, Milazzo-Sayre, and Manderscheid, 1989).

What do schizophrenic patients do when they are discharged from the hospital? Some stay at home with their aging parents. Others live in less than ideal

***Some adverse effects of deinstitutionaliza-
tion*** *Some of the homeless in American
cities may be persons discharged from mental
hospitals who are unable to make an adjustment to the world outside. (Courtesy of
AP/Wide World Photos)*

board-and-care homes, while still others become drifters and join the swelling
ranks of the homeless. According to a recent report, some 40 percent of New
York City's homeless people suffer persistent mental disorder or have a history of
mental illness (Golden, 1990). Such findings make it clear that, while the
antipsychotic drugs help to alleviate the symptoms of schizophrenia, they do not
provide a cure. Given the current inadequacy—and in many cases, the complete
lack—of appropriate community services, this represents, at least for now, a failure to achieve the intentions of deinstitutionalization (Jones, 1983; Lamb, 1984;
Westermeyer, 1987).

DRUG TREATMENT OF DEPRESSION: ANTIDEPRESSANTS

Shortly after the introduction of antipsychotics, two major groups of drugs were
found that seemed to act specifically on depression. These antidepressants were
of two major classes, the **monoamine oxidase (MAO) inhibitors** such as Nardil
and the **tricyclic antidepressants** such as Tofranil (see Table 19.1). Of these, the
tricyclics became the most widely used, mostly because the chemistry of MAO
inhibitors requires that patients conform to difficult dietary restrictions.

Most investigators believe that both the MAO inhibitors and tricyclic antidepressants work by increasing the amount of norepinephrine and serotonin available for synaptic transmission. (The mechanisms whereby they accomplish this
mission are different; for details, see Figure 19.3). These medications are very
effective in counteracting depression in up to 65 percent of the patients who
take them (Hollister and Csernansky, 1990). Not all of them work for all
patients, however. Some patients may have somewhat different biochemical
deficits and thus may do better with an MAO inhibitor than a tricyclic antidepressant, or vice versa. Furthermore, even within each class of antidepressant,
some patients may respond better to one medication than another. There is
some evidence that by using blood tests and the like a patient can be matched to
the proper antidepressant drug (Maugh, 1981; Davis, 1985b), but the selection
of medication is in most cases a matter of clinical judgment.

The use of medication for treating depression changed dramatically in 1988
with the introduction of the first "designer drug" for depression, Prozac
(Kramer, 1993). Prozac was engineered in the laboratory to act minimally upon
norepinephrine and maximally upon serotonin, and it became the most prominent of the new class of antidepressants known as **selective serotonin reuptake
inhibitors** (see Table 19.1). They reduce the manifestations of depression as fast
and as completely as the MAO inhibitors or the tricyclics, but they have far
fewer side effects and are thus safer to prescribe—so safe that most are now prescribed (and perhaps overprescribed) not by psychiatrists but by personal physicians (Olfson and Klerman, 1993). But while these antidepressants have been
regarded by many as panaceas, like all medications they, too, have their side
effects. The most substantial side effect from Prozac can be a loss of sexual
desire, which can occur in up to 30 percent of patients, but which can be countered in some patients with additional medication (Hollander and McCarley,
1992; Jacobsen, 1992).

DRUG TREATMENT OF BIPOLAR DISORDER: LITHIUM

Another pharmacological development is the use of lithium salts such as **lithium
carbonate** in the treatment of bipolar disorder (see Table 19.1). Most manic
episodes subside within five or ten days after patients start lithium therapy. There
is some further evidence that the drug can also forestall the depressive episodes

in bipolar disorder. Just what accounts for these effects is largely unknown. According to one hypothesis, lithium carbonate may reregulate neurotransmission by stabilizing the influence of calcium on neuronal membranes (Meltzer, 1986; Wood and Goodwin, 1987).

DRUG TREATMENT OF ANXIETY: ANXIOLYTICS

When patients suffer from disabling anxiety, they are often treated with medications that are popularly called tranquilizers and technically known as *anxiolytics* (see Table 19.1). The most common kinds of anxiolytics work by increasing neurotransmission at synapses containing the neurotransmitter GABA. Some of these medications, such as Valium and Xanax, are prescribed so often that their names have almost become household words. They are useful as short-term treatments for generalized anxiety disorder, post-traumatic stress disorder, alcohol withdrawal, insomnia, muscle spasms and tension headaches, and various other stress-related disorders. They are rarely used for long-term treatment because, unlike the medications we have reviewed thus far, they are highly addictive and interact dangerously with alcohol. Some newer anxiolytics such as Buspar are not addicting and have become popular substitutes for the older group of anxiolytics for patients who are prone to drug abuse or will have to take the medications over a long period of time.

EVALUATING A MEDICATION

How can we assess the effectiveness of a medication? We will discuss this issue in detail, because some of the issues raised by drug evaluation methods extend beyond tests of drug therapy. In large part, they apply to the evaluation of any therapeutic procedure whatever, including psychotherapy.

Suppose we want to find out whether a given drug, say Thorazine, is effective in treating the manifestations of schizophrenia. The most obvious approach is to administer the drug to a group of schizophrenic patients for some period and then make a before-and-after assessment. In fact, many of the clinical studies are of just this kind. But a little reflection shows that relying only on this procedure would be mistaken.

CONTROLLING FOR SPONTANEOUS IMPROVEMENT

One problem with a simple before-and-after assessment is that it ignores the possibility that the patient's condition would have cleared up without treatment, whether permanently or just for a while. Such spontaneous improvements occur in many disorders (though not often in schizophrenia). To control for this factor, one has to compare two groups of patients drawn from the same population. One group would receive the drug for, say, six weeks; a control group would not. Both groups would be assessed at the start and the end of the study (and perhaps at intervals in between). Initially, they ought to be equivalent. The question is whether they will be different when the six weeks are up.

CONTROLLING FOR PLACEBO EFFECTS

Suppose that after six weeks the patients who were given Thorazine seem to be less bothered by hallucinations and delusions than the untreated controls. That the treated group fared better than the untreated one minimizes the odds that the change was due to spontaneous improvement. Indeed, one might guess at

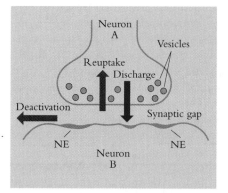

19.3   A schematic presentation of two ways in which a drug may increase the available supply of a neurotransmitter   *A neurotransmitter, norephinephrine (NE), is discharged by Neuron A into the synaptic gap and diffuses across the gap to stimulate Neuron B. The more NE accumulates at the membrane of Neuron B, the more that neuron will fire. The amount of NE at the synapse is diminished in several ways. One is* reuptake, *a process in which NE is pumped back into Neuron A. Another is* deactivation, *a process whereby certain enzymes (such as monoamine oxidase or MAO) break down the neurotransmitter and render it ineffective. Tricyclics and MAO inhibitors are antidepressants that increase the amount of available NE (and serotonin) at the synaptic junction but that accomplish this in different ways. Tricyclics do so by interfering with neurotransmitter uptake; MAO inhibitors do so by preventing MAO from breaking the transmitters down. Second-generation antidepressants like Prozac work similarly, except that they act selectively upon serotonin neurons.*

this point that the benefits of treatment were caused by the drug directly. Unfortunately, we still cannot make this claim, because we have not controlled for the possibility that the result was due to the **placebo effect.**

In medicine, the term *placebo* refers to some inert (that is, medically neutral) substance that is administered to a patient who believes it to have certain therapeutic powers, although it actually has none. Numerous studies have shown that, given this belief, many patients will make some kind of improvement after taking disguised sugar pills or receiving injections of harmless salt solutions. Such placebo effects probably account for many of the cures of ancient physicians whose medications included such items as crocodile dung, swine teeth, and moss scraped from the skull of a man who died a violent death (Shapiro, 1971).

Given the power of the placebo effect, how can we be sure that the improvement in the drug-treated group of our example is caused by the properties of the drug itself? Perhaps a sugar pill—or a bit of crocodile dung—would have done as well. To exclude this possibility, we must administer a placebo to the control patients. They will thus no longer be "untreated." On the contrary, they will receive the same attention, will be told the same thing, and will be given the same number of pills at the same time as the patients in the true drug group. There will be only one difference between the two groups: The control patients will swallow pills that, unbeknownst to them, contain only inert materials. As a result of this stratagem, we achieve simultaneous control for two factors—spontaneous improvement and placebo effects. Now that these two factors are controlled, a difference in the way the two groups appear after treatment can finally be attributed to the effect of the drug itself. Figure 19.4 shows the results of such a study, comparing the effects of Thorazine and a placebo after one, three, and six weeks of treatment. As the figure shows, Thorazine was clearly superior. But as the figure also shows, some slight improvement is found in the placebo group as well, thus highlighting the need for such a control in the evaluation of drug effectiveness.

What explains placebo effects? Some of them may be the result of **endorphins,** chemicals produced by the brain itself that act like opiates and reduce pain (see

Placebos in medieval medicine   *Medieval apothecaries prescribed many "medicinal" substances that were of no proven benefit to their patients. They must have had a placebo effect, though, because the patients (that survived) kept coming back. (Courtesy of Osterreichische Nationalbibliotek, Vienna)*

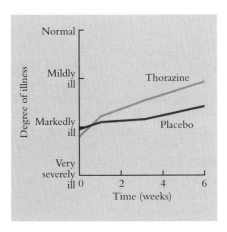

19.4 Controlling for placebo effects
Severity of illness over a six-week period during which patients were treated with either Thorazine or a placebo.

Chapter 3). Evidence for this view comes from a study in which pain was reduced by a placebo medication that the patients believed was a pain reliever. But this relief stopped as soon as the patients received a dose of a drug that is known to counteract the effects of any opiate (Levine, Gordon, and Fields, 1979).

CONTROLLING FOR EXPECTATIONS

By definition, a placebo control implies that all of the patients in the group think that they are being treated with the real medicine. But to guarantee this desired state of ignorance, the physicians—and the psychologists and social workers and nurses and attendants—must also be kept in the dark about who is getting a placebo and who the real medication, for the true information may affect their ratings of the patients' progress. If they believe in the medicine's effectiveness, they may exaggerate signs of improvement in members of the medicated group.

The staff members' knowledge may also have a more indirect effect. They may unwittingly communicate it to the patients, perhaps by observing the medicated ones more closely or by being less concerned if a placebo-treated patient fails to take her morning pill. By such signals, the patients may find out whether the physicians expect them to get better or not. If so, there is no genuine placebo control. To guard against such confounding effects of expectation, modern medication evaluators use the **double-blind technique** in which neither the staff members nor the patients know who is assigned to which group. The only ones who know are the investigators who run the study.

LIMITATIONS OF DRUG THERAPY

In our discussion of common kinds of psychotropic medications, we have taken pains to indicate their effectiveness. But we have also noted their two chief limitations, that they do not help everyone and that many of them have unpleasant side effects. These side effects can be regarded simply as a cost exacted by the drugs. But how great are the drugs' benefits? Critics contend that currently the beneficial results of drug therapy are quite limited. This is especially so for patients taking the classic antipsychotics and antimanic medications, who must remain on a maintenance dose to minimize their disability but who often quit taking their medicine because they find the side effects so unpleasant.

This criticism is less compelling in the case of antidepressants and anxiolytics, which sometimes do for patients with mood and anxiety disorders what insulin does for patients with diabetes: They don't cure the disease, but they sometimes do a fine job of controlling it.

Despite their limitations, the modern drug therapies are a major step forward. They have restored some patients to normal functioning and have allowed those who would otherwise have spent much of their lives in hospital wards to manage, however imperfectly, in a family or community setting. No less important is the fact that these drugs—especially the antipsychotics—have completely changed the atmosphere of mental hospitals, especially the large state-run facilities. Until a few decades ago, straitjackets were common, as were feces-smeared and shriek-filled wards; today, such scenes are comparatively rare because the medications can so effectively control the more florid manifestations of mental disorder. As a result, the modern mental hospital can function more as a therapeutic center than a warehouse. It can provide important social and psychological services, including vocational counseling and psychotherapy, all of which would have been unthinkable in the "snake-pit" settings of former times.

PSYCHOSURGERY

■ Until the advent of the major psychotropic drugs, psychiatrists relied on several other biological therapies, all of which involved drastic assaults on the nervous system. Some of these consisted of *psychosurgery,* or surgery on the brain. In prefrontal lobotomy, for example, the neurological connections between the thalamus and the frontal lobes are severed, in whole or in part. This operation was meant to liberate the patient's thoughts from the pathological influence of his emotions on the dubious neurological assumption that thought and emotion were localized in the frontal lobes and the thalamus, respectively. Evaluations of these early surgical procedures revealed ambiguous and even deleterious results on cognitive functions and led to extreme caution in their application (Maher, 1966; Robbin, 1958; Valenstein, 1986).

Psychosurgery has reemerged, but the psychosurgery of today has been refined considerably, both in the surgical procedures used and the patients judged suitable for them (Rappaport, 1992). The surgeries themselves now precisely locate and create lesions in very specific brain areas instead of disconnecting or destroying whole lobes or regions. In the vast majority of cases, psychosurgery is reserved for those patients who are severely disabled and show no improvement after all other medical or psychotherapeutic alternatives have been exhausted. In patients with intractable depression, severe obsessive-compulsive disorder, and chronic pain, psychosurgery is often beneficial, and the risks are usually tolerable compared to the severe level of the patients' ongoing disability (Davies and Weeks, 1993; Hay et al., 1993).

CONVULSIVE TREATMENTS

■ Another form of biological therapy involves the deliberate production of convulsive seizures. Today, the most widely used form of the convulsive method is *electroconvulsive therapy (ECT),* sometimes colloquially called "shock treatment." For about half a second a current of moderate intensity is passed between two electrodes attached to each side of the patient's forehead. The result is a thirty- to sixty-second convulsive seizure similar to that seen in epilepsy (Figure 19.5). When this treatment first came into use, patients were conscious and sometimes suffered serious bruises or bone fractures while thrashing about during their convulsions. Modern ECT actually looks very mild. Patients are given a short-acting anesthetic to render them temporarily unconscious, and muscle relaxants to reduce the manifestations of the seizure to a few slight muscle twitches. The usual course of ECT treatments is six to ten sessions over a period of a week or two. After each treatment, the patient may experience a brief period of nausea and confusion but is usually fine within a few hours (Andreasen and Black, 1991).

ECT was originally meant as a treatment of schizophrenia, but evaluation studies soon showed that it is most effective in depression. Here, its efficacy is considerable. It works for as many as 70 to 80 percent of patients who have not responded to any antidepressant medication (Janicak et al., 1985; Andreasen and Black, 1991) or who cannot take such medications because of overdose potential or other medical problems. In addition, ECT seems to act more quickly than antidepressant medications usually do (Weiner, 1984b, 1985).

Despite these advantages, the use of ECT is highly controversial. The main reason is the potential for memory impairment that in some cases lasts for months or even longer (Squire, 1977; Breggin, 1979; for discussion, see Weiner, 1984a, 1984b). Under the circumstances, ECT is generally used only after drug

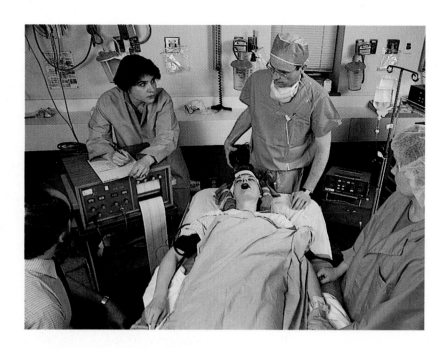

19.5 Patient about to undergo electro-convulsive shock treatment *(Photograph by James D. Wilson/Woodfin Camp)*

therapy has failed or when there seems to be a serious chance of suicide. In the latter case, the fast-acting quality of ECT treatment may be an overriding advantage (Andreasen and Black, 1991). Because of the speed with which ECT brings relief, several ways of minimizing psychological or physical damage have been attempted. One is to apply the current in very brief pulses to just one cerebral hemisphere (typically, the nondominant one), which apparently lessens memory impairment and other side effects but does not diminish the therapeutic effect (Inglis, 1969; Welch et al., 1982; Squire and Zouzounis, 1986).

What accounts for the therapeutic effects of ECT? As yet, we have little more than speculation. According to one hypothesis, ECT leads to heightened activation of certain neural pathways, which increases the availability of norepinephrine and serotonin in the brain (Weiner, 1984b, 1985).

PSYCHOTHERAPY

FOCUS QUESTIONS

- According to Freud, what makes classical psychoanalysis therapeutic? How do neo-Freudian, psychodynamic therapists depart from Freud's formula?

- What would a behavior therapist think causes a psychological disorder? a cognitive therapist? a humanistic therapist? How does each construe the goals of therapy, and what techniques does each use to attain those goals?

- What ingredients seem common to all psychotherapies? How does technical eclecticism capitalize on the varieties of psychotherapy?

- How does a therapist show cultural competence, and how can its lack impede the course of therapy?

Biological manipulations represent one approach to the treatment of psychopathology. But as we have already seen, there is another approach to the

An early attempt at psychotherapy *The biblical King Saul was subject to severe bouts of rage and depression but was apparently calmed by listening to young David playing the harp. (Rembrandt's* David Playing the Harp Before Saul; *photograph © Foundation Johan Maurits van Nassau. Courtesy of Mauritshuis, The Hague, inv. nr 621)*

treatment of such disorders that forgoes all direct ministrations to the patient's body and instead relies on psychological means alone. Such attempts to treat mental disturbance by psychological rather than biological methods are here grouped together under the general label ***psychotherapy.***

There are many different approaches to psychotherapy. A major difference among them is in their conceptions of psychopathology. Some approaches are based upon psychoanalysis and emphasize unconscious conflicts. Others rely on behavioral findings from animal and human experimentation. Still others take a cognitive approach and argue that many mental disorders arise from faulty thinking. A final, humanistic outlook espouses the importance of the concept of free will and views "disorder" as a failure to build a life that is expanding, fulfilling, and meaningful.

Given how much these perspectives differ in their basic view of psychopathology, it is hardly surprising that they differ greatly in how they say disorders should be treated. Here we will discuss five forms of psychotherapy that are conducted with individual patients: classical psychoanalysis, modern offshoots of psychoanalysis, behavior therapy, cognitive therapy, and humanistic therapy.

CLASSICAL PSYCHOANALYSIS

■ ***Classical psychoanalysis*** is the method Sigmund Freud developed at the turn of this century. According to some writers, this technique is the ancestor of virtually all forms of modern psychotherapy, whether they acknowledge this heritage or not (London, 1964). Freud's basic assumption was that his patients' ills (in his terms, their neuroses) stemmed from unconscious defenses against unacceptable urges that date back to early childhood. By adulthood, many of these defenses are useless relics, a mental blanket the neurotic has drawn over his head that prevents him from seeing both the outer world and his own inner world as they really are. These defenses become manifest as psychological symptoms, bodily malfunctions, or tendencies to repeat outdated and by now utterly unadaptive patterns of behavior (see Chapter 17).

Freud believed that to overcome his neurosis, the patient must drop his mental blanket, must achieve access to his buried thoughts and wishes, and gain insight into why he buried them. By so doing, he will master the internal conflicts that crippled him for so long. Once these are resolved, his symptoms will presumably wither away by themselves. In effect, Freud's prescription for the neuroses is the victory of reason over passion: "Where id was, there shall ego be."

THE RECOVERY OF UNCONSCIOUS MEMORIES

The origin of psychoanalytic technique dates back to Freud's attempts to treat hysteria by helping the patient recover some emotionally charged memories (see Chapter 17). Initially, Freud and his then collaborator, Josef Breuer, probed for these memories while their patients were hypnotized. Later on it became clear that such memories could be dug up even in the normal waking state by the method of *free association.* The patient was asked to say whatever came into his mind, and sooner or later the relevant memory was likely to emerge. Various forms of *resistance,* usually unconscious, by which the patient tried to derail a given train of thought—by changing the topic, forgetting what he was about to say, and so on—often gave important clues that the patient was about to remember something he had previously tried to forget. In addition to free association, Freud later asked his patients to tell him their dreams, and he began to interpret nearly any action—whether a slip of the tongue, or the wiggling of a foot on the couch, or a particular choice of words, or whether the patient was late or early for the sessions—as clues to the identity of their neurotic conflicts.

In popularized movie or TV versions, this dredging up of forgotten memories is often presented as the essence of psychoanalysis. The distraught heroine finally remembers a childhood scene in which she was spanked for a little sister's misdeed, suddenly a weight lifts from her shoulders, she rises from the couch reborn, is ready to face life and love serenely, and will live happily—or at least unneurotically—ever after. But as Freud described it, what actually happens is much less dramatic. The discovery of the patient's unconscious conflicts comes bit by bit, as a memory surfaces here, a dream or a slip of the tongue suggests a meaning there, and as the analyst offers an occasional interpretation of the resistances that crop up in a given session. To help the patient see how all of these strands of her mental life are woven together is one of the analyst's main tasks.

PSYCHODYNAMIC THERAPY

■ Many present-day psychotherapists still use techniques that bear Freud's imprint. Although a few still practice psychoanalysis just as Freud did, most practitioners have modified Freud's theories and procedures in various ways. Most of them—known variously as psychoanalytic, ego-analytic, or dynamic psychotherapists—subscribe to neo-Freudian views or to related approaches such as ego psychology (see Chapter 17). Like Freud, they believe that the ultimate key to what they call "neurosis" is unconscious conflict. But unlike Freud's classical form of psychoanalysis, these therapies emphasize the resolution of current problems by focusing on interpersonal and cultural factors. If early development is discussed in therapy, it centers on the patterns of interaction in one's family and the difficulties in establishing autonomy from one's parents as setting the stage for one's current problems (Eagle and Wolitsky, 1992; Liff, 1992).

A psychoanalytic session (Photograph by Will and Demi McIntyre/Science Source/Photo Researchers)

(Cartoon by Sidney Harris)

BEHAVIOR THERAPY

■ Not all psychotherapists derive their techniques from psychoanalysis. In fact, two major therapeutic approaches are reactions against psychoanalysis but for reasons that are diametrically opposed. The first is **behavior therapy,** which maintains that the theoretical notions underlying psychoanalysis are vague and untestable, while its therapeutic effectiveness is a matter of doubt. The other group consists of various humanistic therapies, which regard psychoanalysis as too mechanistic in its approach. Freud, who had a fine sense of irony, would have been wryly amused to find himself in the middle of this two-front war in which one side accuses him of being too scientific and the other of not being scientific enough.

Behavior therapists hold that the various conditions Freud called "neurosis" are caused by maladaptive learning whose remedy must be a form of reeducation. Taken by itself, this view is hardly original. What makes it different is that the behavior therapists take the emphasis on learning and relearning much more seriously than anyone had before them. They see themselves as applied scientists whose techniques for reeducating troubled people are adapted from principles of classical and instrumental conditioning discovered in the laboratories of Pavlov, Thorndike, and Skinner (see Chapter 4).

Like the learning theorists from whom they trace their descent, behavior therapists are basically tough-minded and pragmatic. They emphasize overt, observable behavior rather than hypothetical underlying causes such as unconscious thoughts and wishes, which they regard as hard to define and impossible to observe. Their concern is with what a person does, especially if it causes him distress. If so, the behavior therapists want to modify such behaviors—to get the person with agoraphobia over his fear of open places, to help the person with obsessive-compulsive disorder overcome the hand-washing rituals that are rubbing away his skin. To accomplish these ends, behavior therapists resort to various techniques for learning and unlearning—deliberate exposure to anxiety-producing stimuli, conditioning of incompatible reactions, or whatever. But their treatment does not include any attempt to have the patient gain insight into the origin of these symptoms. As these therapists see it, such insights, however valid, have no therapeutic value. What is wrong, and must be fixed, is the patient's behavior in the here and now.

Behavior therapy in the real world *A person with acrophobia who visits a rooftop in the presence of the therapist. (Photograph © Steve Mellon, 1994)*

EXPOSURE TECHNIQUES

One set of behavior therapy techniques is based on concepts drawn from classical conditioning. The major target of these techniques is unrealistic fear found in cases of specific phobia, such as disabling fears of heights, enclosed spaces, or cockroaches. Behavior therapists regard such fears as classically conditioned responses that are evoked by various eliciting stimuli, such as looking down a flight of stairs, being in an elevator, or finding roaches in one's cupboard (see Chapters 4 and 18). Exactly how the original conditioning took place—whether in a single episode or through a series of cumulative experiences—is immaterial. What matters is how this connection between stimulus and fear can be broken, regardless of how it was forged originally.

The most obvious way of removing the classically conditioned connection is through ***extinction.*** Imagine a rat that has been shocked on seeing a flashing light. To extinguish the fear, all we have to do is to present the conditioned stimulus (the light) without the unconditioned stimulus (the shock). But this is easier said than done, for the animal has learned to avoid the fear-arousing stimulus and runs away as soon as the light starts flashing. As a result, it can't "test reality" and discover that the formerly dangerous stimulus no longer signals shock. Therefore, its fear won't be extinguished. What holds for the rat, also holds for the person with a phobia. He is afraid of heights or of enclosed spaces or of roaches. His fear makes him avoid these stimuli, which is why he can't ever find out that his terrors are unjustified. And if he tries to face the phobic stimuli, he is often so traumatized that he becomes reconditioned.

One way of getting the rat (or the person suffering from a phobia) to test reality is to make the rat expose itself to the flashing light (or the snakes or open spaces). If the rat is forced to remain in the compartment in which it was formerly shocked and is repeatedly presented with the flashing light that is now no longer followed by shock, then its fear of the light will eventually disappear (Baum, 1970). Just this principle underlies what behavior therapists call "exposure techniques." The most widely used exposure technique is ***systematic desensitization,*** developed by the psychiatrist Joseph Wolpe. Its basic idea is to connect the stimuli that now evoke fear to a new response that is incompatible with fear and that will therefore displace it (Wolpe, 1958). The competing re-

Desensitization *(Courtesy of Henry Gleitman and Mary Bullock)*

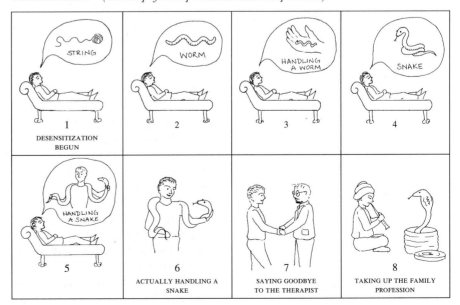

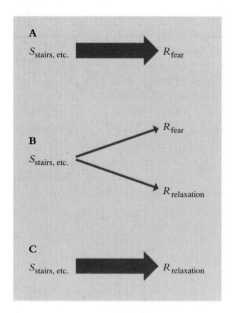

19.6 Systematic desensitization *(A)
The state of affairs in phobia. Various stimuli
such as flights of stairs arouse the response of
fear. (B) These stimuli are conditioned to the
response of relaxation. As this connection becomes stronger, the connection between the
stimulus and the fear response is weakened.
(C) The state of affairs when counterconditioning is complete. The relaxation response
has completely displaced the old fear response.*

sponse is usually muscular relaxation, a pervasive untensing of the body's musculature that is presumably incompatible with the autonomic and skeletal reactions
that accompany fear. This requires that the patient learn to relax his musculature
on cue through meditation-like tensing and untensing exercises performed in
the clinic and often assisted by using audiotapes at home. Once the patient can
relax thoroughly on cue, the goal is to condition the relaxation to the fear-
evoking stimuli, whether the stimuli is snakes, open spaces, or high roof tops
(see Figure 19.6).

AVERSION THERAPY

Another behavior therapy technique, **aversion therapy,** tries to attach negative
feelings to stimulus situations that are initially appealing so that the patient will
no longer want to engage in them. The object of this endeavor is to eliminate
behavior patterns that both patient and therapist regard as undesirable. Examples
are overeating, excessive drinking, or engaging in certain sexual deviations such
as exhibitionism.

The basic procedure of aversion therapy is very simple. One pairs the stimulus
that one wants to render unpleasant with some obnoxious unconditioned stimulus. In aversion therapy for excessive drinking the patient takes a sip of alcohol
while under the effect of a nausea-producing drug, so that he tastes the liquor
while he desperately wants to vomit.

Whether aversion therapy works over the long term is debatable. No one
doubts that it works in the therapist's office; the question is whether it is effective outside, when the shocking device is no longer attached or the nausea-
producing drugs are no longer administered (Rachman and Teasdale, 1969;
Emmelkamp, 1986). There is some suggestion that the nausea-producing procedure has lasting effects in some cases of alcoholism. According to one review,
two-thirds of alcoholics treated in this manner remained abstinent for a year,
one-third for three years (Wiens and Menustik, 1983). In effect, the patients
acquired a learned taste aversion so that the actual taste and smell of alcohol
became repellent (see Chapter 4).

COGNITIVE THERAPY

Exposure and aversion therapies focus on behaviors that are more or less
overt and try to modify them by techniques based on the principles of
simple learning. In exposure techniques like desensitization, the emphasis is on
some external stimulus (such as heights) that is connected with anxiety, a connection the therapy tries to sever. In aversion therapy, the emphasis is on some
overt response (such as excessive drinking), a response the therapy tries to eliminate. But what treatment is appropriate when the patient's problems cannot be
so readily described by referring to fear-evoking stimuli or to overt, undesirable
responses? Many patients' difficulties stem from anxiety that is triggered by
their own thoughts and feelings. An example is the person with an obsessive-
compulsive disorder whose own obsessional thoughts lead to intense anxiety
that can only be relieved by ever more frantic compulsive rituals. Here the
critical features of the disorder derive from covert rather than overt sources—
thoughts and feelings that go on "in the patient's head." How does a behavior-
oriented approach to therapy handle cases such as these?

A number of therapists deal with such problems by a frontal attack on the way
the patient thinks. They try to replace the patient's irrational beliefs and attitudes that caused his emotional stress by a more appropriate mode of thinking

that is in better accord with reality. This general form of therapy goes under various labels. A relatively recent version is cognitive therapy, originally developed as a treatment for depression by the psychiatrist Aaron Beck (Beck, 1967).

On the face of it, the goal of all cognitive approaches seems similar to the psychoanalytic quest for emotional insight. But cognitive therapists see themselves as more closely allied to behavior therapy. While they make little use of conditioning principles and concentrate on what the patients think rather than on what they do overtly, their techniques share many of the characteristics of behavior therapy. Cognitive therapists are extremely directive. They are primarily concerned with the patient in the present rather than with his history, and they focus on the beliefs that affect what the patient does and feels.

THE MAJOR TECHNIQUES OF COGNITIVE THERAPY

The basic technique of cognitive therapists is to confront patients with the contradictions inherent in their maladaptive beliefs. To accomplish this end, the therapist is active and even dominant throughout the proceedings, and—like many modern behavior therapists—gives the patient "homework assignments." One such task might be to discover irrational thoughts that come in the form of certain illogical phrases and sentences the patients say to themselves, such as "it's all my fault," and "if no one loves me, I'm no good," and so on. Such automatic and ultimately self-defeating thoughts may explain why patients sometimes feel unaccountably upset. For example, an event like seeing an old acquaintance across the street might lead to a wave of anxiety, with the patient in the dark about why he is anxious. But the therapist can put light on the situation—seeing the old friend triggered an automatic and irrational thought that led to the anxiety:

> The anxiety seemed incomprehensible until [the patient] "played back" his thoughts: "If I greet Bob, he many not remember me. He may snub me, it has been so long, he may not know who I am. . . ." (Ellis, 1962, quoted in Beck, 1985, p. 1436)

The job of the therapist is to help the patient identify the automatic thought and to recognize its irrationality. After all, Bob may very well remember him. And if he doesn't, it may be because Bob's memory is faulty. But suppose the patient is right, and Bob never liked him in the first place and might well have snubbed him. Is that the end of the world? Is it really necessary to be liked by everybody? Once these irrational beliefs are ferreted out, the patient has to tell himself repeatedly that they are false. If he can stop himself from such self-defeating automatisms, he will feel better, which will allow him to function at a higher level, which will make him feel better still, leading to a beneficent cycle of emotional improvement.

HUMANISTIC THERAPY

A number of practitioners charge that behavior therapy (and to a lesser extent, psychoanalysis) describes human beings too mechanistically and treats them too manipulatively. These *humanistic therapists* try to deal with the individual at a more global level, not as a bundle of conditioned reflexes to be extinguished, nor as a collection of warring, unconscious impulses to be reconciled, but rather as a whole person who must be understood as one person among many and in the context of his entire life.

CLIENT-CENTERED THERAPY

One example of a humanistically oriented approach is *client-centered therapy* (Rogers, 1951, 1970), which was developed during the early 1940s by psychologist Carl Rogers (1902–1987). One of its main premises is that the process of personality development is akin to growth. In this view, Rogers followed theorists like Abraham Maslow (1908–1970) and other adherents of a humanistic approach to personality in believing that all people have a native impulse toward the full realization of their human potential (Maslow, 1968; see Chapter 17). In this sense, he held that human nature is inherently good. But, alas, such self-actualization is fairly rare, for personality growth is often stunted. There are many people who dislike themselves, are out of touch with their own feelings, and are unable to reach out to others as genuine fellow beings. Rogers' remedy was to provide the appropriate psychological soil in which personal growth could resume; this soil was the therapeutic relationship.

Rogers initially tried to achieve this client-centered quality by a variety of *nondirective techniques* (Rogers, 1942). He would never advise or interpret directly, but would only try to clarify what the client really felt, by echoing or restating what the client himself seemed to say or feel. Rogers subsequently decided that there was no way of being truly nondirective, that one couldn't help but convey some evaluation with even the blandest nod. But more important, Rogers came to believe that the therapist's main contribution does not lie in any particular approach or technique; it is rather to supply the one crucial condition of successful therapy, himself or herself as a genuinely involved, participating fellow person. The Rogerian therapist's main job is to let the client know that she understands how the world looks through his eyes; that she can empathize with his wishes and feelings; and, most important of all, that she accepts and values him. In Rogers' view, this awareness that another person unconditionally accepts and esteems him ultimately helps the client to accept and esteem himself (Rogers, 1961). Perhaps this is just a modern restatement of the old idea that love can redeem us all.*

SOME COMMON THEMES

■ The various forms of psychotherapy differ in some important regards in what they try to do. Psychoanalytically oriented therapists emphasize understanding; they aim to help the patient realize the pattern of his thoughts and actions so that he can confront his unconscious conflicts and overcome them. Behavior therapists emphasize doing. They try to help their patients eliminate undesirable responses and build desirable ones. Cognitive-behavioral therapists are most concerned with thinking. They want to enable their patients to overcome patterns of irrational and self-defeating thoughts. Humanistic therapists stress feeling. Their hope is to help their clients accept themselves, express what they want and feel in the here-and-now, and set about doing things that give their lives transcendent meaning.

These differences among the various therapeutic schools are real enough. But of late there have been trends toward a rapprochement between the different schools of therapy. Some psychoanalytically oriented practitioners have come to use techniques that were formerly the exclusive preserve of behavior therapists, such as modeling and homework assignments (Wachtel, 1977, 1982). And from

Self-knowledge through psychotherapy (Hand with Reflecting Sphere, *1935, by M.C. Escher; © M.C. Escher Heirs, courtesy of Cordon Art, Baarn, Holland)*

* Rogers's humanistic approach has often been attacked by behavior therapists who regard him as "antiscientific." Under the circumstances, it is somewhat ironic that Rogers was one of the pioneers of psychotherapy evaluation, the first major figure in the field of psychotherapy who looked for evidence that his techniques were actually having some effect.

Psychotherapy—the purchase of friendship? (© 1950, 1952, United Feature Syndicate, Inc.)

the opposite side, many behavior therapists have come to realize that the client-therapist relation is an important part of treatment, that something like Freud's "transference" comes into play even in mechanistic conditioning therapies such as desensitization (Lazarus, 1971, 1981). The endpoint of this integration is seen in a survey of influential psychotherapists who strongly advocated what they call *technical eclecticism*—basically, doing whatever works—as the trend in therapy (Norcross and Freedheim, 1992). This eclectic orientation dovetails with recent changes in the practice of psychotherapy that were prompted by economic considerations, as we will see below (see pp. 628–30).

But quite apart from such trends toward an eclectic approach to psychotherapy, there are some common underlying themes that run through the beliefs and practices of all the various therapies:

Emotional defusing All psychotherapies aim at some kind of emotional reeducation. They try to help the patient rid himself of various intense and unrealistic emotional reactions, such as the fear in specific phobia. To this end, these reactions are evoked during the therapeutic session. Since this happens in the presence of an accepting, nonjudgmental therapist, the reactions are weakened.

Interpersonal learning All major schools stress the importance of interpersonal learning and believe that the therapeutic relationship is an important tool for bringing this about. This relationship shows the patient how she generally reacts to others, and it provides a test for trying new and better ways of reacting.

Self-knowledge Most psychotherapists try to help their patients achieve greater self-knowledge, though different therapeutic schools differ in what kind of self-knowledge they try to bring about. For psychoanalysts, the crucial emotional insights the patient must acquire refer to his own past; for Rogerians, they concern one's feelings in the present; for behavior therapists, the relevant self-understanding is the correct identification of the stimuli to which fear has been conditioned.

Therapy as a step-by-step process There is general agreement that psychotherapy is a gradual affair and that this is so regardless of whether the therapy emphasizes insight, emotion, or overt action. There are few sudden flashes of insight or emotional understanding that change a patient overnight. Instead, each new skill or newfound insight must be laboriously applied in one life situation after another before the patient can call it her own.

Therapy as socially accepted healing By and large, psychotherapists operate within a social context that gives them the status of officially designated healers for many mental disorders. As a result, the stage is set for a number of nonspecific gains of psychotherapy. One is an intimate, confiding relationship with another person. This alone may be a boon to some people who have no close bonds to anyone and for whom psychotherapy may amount to "the purchase of friendship" (Schofield, 1964). Another nonspecific gain is the hope that one will get better. This may lead to self-perpetuating improvements, because as the patient thinks better of himself, he may have small successes in the outside world, which may lead him to greater hope, with even better odds of continued success.

EXTENSIONS OF PSYCHOTHERAPY

In Freud's time, psychotherapy was still considered a somewhat arcane art, practiced by a few initiates (mostly physicians) and limited to a selected group of well-educated adult patients. Since then, psychotherapy has been

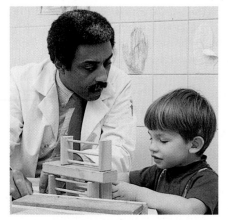

A

B

Play therapy, an extension of psychotherapy adapted for children *(A) In play therapy, the therapist tries to help the child understand and express his feelings about his parents and other family members through play with various toys. (B) Puppets are sometimes used to act out problems, as in this example of a therapy session with victims of child abuse. (Top: photograph by Michal Heron, 1979/Monkmeyer Press. Bottom: photograph by Bart Bartholomew, 1984/Black Star)*

broadened and extended to cover increasingly more terrain. One set of extensions widened the patient population to include children, retarded persons, various kinds of sociopaths, and psychotics. Another extension was a shift from the original one-therapist/one-patient formula to various modes of group therapy that feature all conceivable permutations: one therapist and several patients, several therapists and several patients, several patients and no therapist, and so on.

One early reason for treating patients in groups was that there simply weren't enough trained therapists for all the people who wanted their services; seeing clients in groups was one way of making the supply fit the demand. But group therapy was appealing for deeper reasons as well. For instance, therapy groups seemed to fill a void, at least temporarily, left by the weakening of family and religious ties of modern urbanized society.

EXPANSION OF THERAPEUTIC METHOD

Shared-problem groups One approach is to organize a group of people all of whom have the same problem. They may all be alcoholics or drug addicts or ex-convicts. The members meet, share relevant advice and information, help newcomers along, exhort and support each other in their resolve to overcome their handicaps. The classic example is ***Alcoholics Anonymous (AA),*** which provides the alcoholic with a sense that he is not alone and helps him weather crises without suffering a relapse. In such we-are-all-in-the-same-boat groups, the primary aim is to manage the problem that all members share. No specific attention is paid to emotional problems that are unique to any one individual.

Therapy groups The rules of the game are very different in groups explicitly organized for the purpose of ***group therapy.*** Here, a group of selected patients, usually around ten, are treated together under the guidance of a trained thera-

"When Jud accuses Zack, here, of hostility toward his daughter, like he seems to every session, why, it's plain to me he's only rationalizing his own lack of gumption in standing up to a stepson who's usurping the loyalty of his second wife. The way he lit into him just now shows he's got this here guilt identification with Zack's present family constellation. Calling Zack egotistical ain't nothing but a disguise mechanism for concealing his secret envy of Zack's grit and all-around starch, and shows mighty poor ego boundaries of his own, it appears to me." (Drawing by Whitney Darrow, Jr.; © 1976, The New Yorker Magazine, Inc.)

pist. This form of therapy may have some advantages that individual treatment lacks. According to its proponents, in group therapy the therapist does not really treat the members of the group; instead, he helps them to treat each other. The specific techniques of the therapist may vary from psychoanalytically oriented insight therapy to various forms of behavior therapy to Rogerian client-centered approaches. But whatever techniques the therapist favors, the treatment of each group member really begins as she realizes that she is not all that different from the others. She learns that there are other people who are painfully shy, who have hostile fantasies about their parents, or whatever. Further benefits come from a sense of group belongingness, of support, and of encouragement. But most important of all is the fact that the group provides a ready-made laboratory in interpersonal relations. The patient can discover just what she does that rubs others the wrong way, how she can relate to certain kinds of people more effectively, and so on (Sadock, 1975).

Marital and family therapy   In the therapy groups we've considered thus far, the members are almost always strangers before the sessions begin. This is in marked contrast to what happens in **marital and family therapy.** Here the people seeking help know each other very well (sometimes all too well) before they enter therapy.

In recent years, family therapy has become a major therapeutic movement (Satir, 1967; Minuchin, 1974; Kerr and Bowen, 1988). It is probably no coincidence that this growth has occurred during a time of turmoil in American families, evidenced by spiraling divorce rates and reports of child and spousal abuse, and by the increasing numbers of single-parent households.

Family and marital therapists regard the family as an emotional unit that can influence the onset and continuing manifestation of many mental disorders and social problems. Seen from this perspective, the key to marital and family distress is not necessarily in the pathology of any individual spouse or family member. Rather, it lies in the relationships within the family system: between the husband and wife or the various members of the family. In a dislocated shoulder, both the upper arm and shoulder socket may be perfectly sound, but until their mutual relationship is appropriately readjusted, there will necessarily be pain and the shoulder won't be able to function. Many marital (or couple) and family therapists feel that their task is like that of the orthopedist who resets the dislocated shoulder: They try to help the couple or the family readjust their interrelations.

THE EXPANSION OF THERAPEUTIC GOALS

Group methods and other extensions made psychotherapy available to a much larger number of people. But did all of them really need it? The answer depends on what one believes the goals of therapy are.

For Freud, the matter was simple. Most of his patients were incapable of any kind of full life. They were disabled by terrorizing phobias or all-consuming compulsions and were rendered unable to work and love. Freud wanted to heal these patients so that they could once again live normally. But he never regarded his treatment as automatically producing happiness or fulfillment or the discovery of meaning in their lives. These the patients had to find for themselves and they might very well fail to do so even when no longer saddled with their inner conflicts.

Later therapists broadened treatment goals. Consider humanistic therapists such as Rogers. To be sure, Rogerian therapists try to remove or alleviate their clients' distress. But their ambitions go further. They aim at more than a cure (the goal of psychoanalysts, at least in their early days) and at more than the modification of unwanted behavior patterns (the goal of behavior therapists).

"We're not living happily ever after." (Drawing by Chas. Addams; © 1959, 1987, The New Yorker Magazine, Inc.)

Their ultimate object is to help their clients to "grow" and to "realize their human potential." But if so, then therapy can be appropriate for just about anyone, regardless of whether he suffers some form of psychopathology or not (Orne, 1975). After all, who among us can claim to have achieved his full potential?

CULTURAL COMPETENCE IN PSYCHOTHERAPY

Because the originators of the common theories and techniques we have discussed were all Europeans and North Americans, many observers have suggested that psychotherapy may ill-serve patients whose backgrounds are from other cultures. The increasing awareness of multiculturalism has led many authors to stress the importance of *cultural competence* in psychotherapy. They argue that the therapist must understand the patient's culture well enough to modify the goals of therapy to conform to the values that the patient brings to therapy.

For example, Asian-American patients put more emphasis on formality in all their affairs. Their social roles tend to be structured largely by age and sex, with a father's authority rarely challenged within the family (Sue and Kirk, 1973). The therapist whose own values place a premium on individual autonomy over family loyalties might inadvertently run afoul of the patient's cultural traditions and endanger the therapy. Another example comes from Native Americans who tend to value happiness and sharing over competition and private ownership (Bryde, 1972). Here a therapy that stresses assertiveness over conciliation and diplomacy may well backfire. Part of cultural competence in psychotherapy requires that the therapist question the patient sensitively about her cultural values and religious beliefs and the extent to which she is assimilated to the dominant culture (Atkinson, Morten, and Sue, 1983; Sue, 1980).

EVALUATING THERAPEUTIC OUTCOME

FOCUS QUESTIONS

■ Does psychotherapy work better than no therapy at all?

■ What is meta-analysis, and what does it suggest about the effectiveness of psychotherapy?

■ Do some kinds of therapy work better than others? Why (or why not)?

■ How have recent economic and legal considerations altered the practice of psychotherapy?

We have just surveyed what different kinds of therapists do. We now ask whether what they do does any good. This question often arouses indignant protests from therapists and patients alike. For many of them feel utterly certain that they help or have been helped. They therefore see no point in questioning what to them is obvious. But their testimonials alone are not convincing. For one thing, both patients and therapists have a serious stake in believing that psychotherapy works. If it doesn't, the patient has wasted his money and the therapist has wasted her time. Under the circumstances, neither may be the most objective judge in assessing whether there was a significant change.

But even granting that change occurred, what caused this change? At this point, our previous explanation of how medications are evaluated should raise some obvious questions. Was the change produced by the psychotherapy itself, or would it have occurred anyway? Assuming that people naturally have ups and downs in their lives, patients often seek out therapy when they are at their worst, so it is natural that they would more likely return to an "up" phase while in therapy. And, assuming that the psychotherapy did play a direct role, was the improvement caused by the therapeutic techniques themselves or indirectly by placebo-like factors such as hope, expectations of cure, and the decision to "turn over a new leaf"?

DOES PSYCHOTHERAPY WORK?

The early impetus for discussions of psychotherapeutic outcomes came from a sharp attack launched by the British psychologist Hans Eysenck (Eysenck, 1961) on the efficacy of psychoanalysis and similar "insight" therapies. Eysenck surveyed some two dozen articles that reported the number of "neurotic" patients (mostly, patients with depression or anxiety disorders, in today's nomenclature) who improved or failed to improve after psychotherapy. Overall, about 60 percent improved, a result that might be considered fairly encouraging. But Eysenck argued that there was really nothing to cheer about. According to Eysenck's analysis, the spontaneous recovery rate in neurotics who received no treatment was, if anything, even higher—about 70 percent. If so, psychotherapy apparently has no curative effects.

In retrospect, it appears that Eysenck's appraisal was unduly harsh. In particular, he evidently overestimated the rate of spontaneous improvement. According to one review, the median rate of patients who get better without therapy is, depending upon the diagnostic composition of the group of patients, around 30 percent compared to an average improvement rate of 60 percent for neurotic patients who received psychotherapy, a difference that constitutes what the author called "some modest evidence that psychotherapy 'works'" (Bergin, 1971, p. 229; see also Luborsky, Singer, and Luborsky, 1975).

META-ANALYSES OF THERAPY OUTCOME

Several recent analyses of the effectiveness of psychotherapy provide an even more optimistic picture. For the most part, they are based on a statistical technique called *meta-analysis* by means of which the results of many different studies can be combined. In the most comprehensive analysis of this kind, 475 different studies, comprising 25,000 patients in all, were reviewed (Smith, Glass, and Miller, 1980). The conclusion drawn by averaging across these studies was that the "average person who receives therapy is better off at the end of it than 80 percent of the persons who do not" (Smith, Glass, and Miller, 1980, p. 87). Later analyses used somewhat more stringent criteria in eliminating studies that were methodologically suspect, and these yielded similar results (e.g., Andrews and Harvey, 1981; Shapiro and Shapiro, 1982). Further studies showed that these improvements are still found when patients are surveyed months or years after treatment (Nicholson and Berman, 1983).

COMPARING DIFFERENT THERAPIES

The preceding discussion indicates that patients who receive psychotherapy will, on average, be better off than patients who do not. To the extent that this is so, psychotherapy works. But as we've seen, there are any number of different psychotherapies: psychodynamic, humanistic, behavioral, cognitive, and so on. Do any of them get better results than the others? This question has been asked by several investigators. Their answer is unlikely to provide comfort for the adherents of any one school of psychotherapy. Most studies of psychotherapeutic outcomes suggest that the differences in the effectiveness of the various psychotherapies are slight or nonexistent. This view is sometimes called the ***dodo bird verdict*** after the dodo bird in *Alice in Wonderland* who organized a race between various Wonderland creatures and concluded that "Everyone has won and all must have prizes" (see Figure 19.7; Luborsky, Singer, and Luborsky, 1975). While a few reviewers feel that the behavioral and cognitive therapies have a slight advantage (e.g., Shapiro and Shapiro, 1982), many others judge that the outcome similarities far outweigh the differences (e.g., Smith, Glass, and Miller, 1980; Sloane et al., 1975; Elkin et al., 1989).

COMMON FACTORS

One explanation for the equality of treatment outcome among psychotherapies centers on the shared themes that underlie many of the beliefs and practices of the various schools, such as attempts at ***emotional defusing,*** and efforts to provide ***interpersonal learning*** and an ***empathic relationship*** with another human being, conducted within an accepted social framework (see pp. 622–23). To the extent that these features are indeed therapeutic and are common to the various schools, we would expect them to exert similar beneficial effects.

SPECIFIC FACTORS

There may also be some effects that are not so readily picked up by the outcome studies (for the most part, meta-analytic) that we've discussed thus far. These suggested that all psychotherapies are equally effective, regardless of the banner under which they are practiced. But the real issue may not be which therapy is most effective, but rather which treatment is most effective for which patient under which set of circumstances (Paul, 1967). Meta-analysis may not be the best way to answer this question, for it tends to lump different disorders together. Some critics feel that this is like combining apples and oranges and coming up with only moderate evidence for fruit.

According to some practitioners, some treatments do have a specific effect, being more effective for some patients and some conditions than for others. They believe that psychotherapy works best and goes beyond the effect of the common factors, if specific therapies are matched to the disorder and the patient (Beutler and Clarkin, 1990; Norcross, 1991; Norcross and Freedheim, 1992). This position is sometimes called ***prescriptionism,*** for it argues that specific therapies be prescribed for patients suffering from particular mental disorders just as specific medications are prescribed for particular physical illnesses.

ACCOUNTABILITY FOR PSYCHOTHERAPY

While attacks such as Eysenck's provoked the initial studies of therapeutic effectiveness, a more recent impetus has been the demand for economic accountability. Beginning in the 1970s, private insurance companies that had for years reimbursed patients for both inpatient care and outpatient psychotherapy began to question the costs and benefits of each (Garfield, 1992).

Did patients do any better with one kind of care than another, or with twelve years of therapy rather than twelve weeks? These questions struck at the pocketbook of both patient and practitioner, and they forced drastic changes in the practice of psychotherapy. Instead of justifying psychotherapy based on theories about psychopathology or commentaries about meaning and existence, practitioners suddenly had to show that what they practiced improved patients using the most concrete of dependent variables: How fast could the patient be dis-

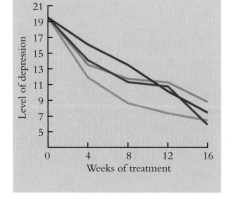

19.7 The dodo bird verdict *The figure shows the results of a study of 279 depressed patients receiving either cognitive therapy, interpersonal therapy (Klerman et al., 1984), antidepressant medication (Tofranil), or a placebo. The results after four months show that, while all treated patients were better off than the placebo controls, the particular treatment they received made little difference. (Gibbons et al., 1993)*

"Everyone has won and all must have prizes." (From Lewis Carroll, Alice in Wonderland, *1865/1963)*

charged? How rapidly could she return to work? How long was the patient able to function without further use of professional services? If the costs of therapy were to be reimbursed, the therapy had to be the most cost-effective. And if a patient was making no progress in therapy, the solution was not to conduct more therapy but to discontinue it entirely.

The ramifications also became legal. Could a therapist be guilty of malpractice for not offering a patient the best treatment or at least a proven treatment? Indeed, this was the outcome of a widely cited court case that pitted biological against psychoanalytic approaches to the treatment of depression. The case concerned a patient who was severely depressed and was admitted to a psychoanalytically oriented private hospital where he received no antidepressant medication, only intensive psychoanalytically based psychotherapy. During his hospital stay his condition worsened: He lost forty pounds, and his overall physical condition deteriorated. Even so, the therapy was continued, and the patient's deterioration was interpreted as reflecting the difficulties of working through the patient's defenses. After seven months, the patient's family became alarmed, removed him from this hospital, and placed him in another in which he was immediately treated with antidepressant medication. He recovered within three months and began initiating a lawsuit against the first hospital (*Osheroff v. Chestnut Lodge;* see Klerman, 1990).

The lawsuit was settled out of court, but the result stirred the medical community to form a set of standards of effective treatment. One of the first concerned the acceptable care for depression. It provides that depressives are best treated by a combination of antidepressant medication and psychotherapy. If psychotherapy is attempted alone, it should be only for mild to moderate depressions and only if improvement is seen quickly; otherwise antidepressant medication must be instituted (American Psychiatric Association, 1993). These standards will probably come to govern all mental-health practitioners, and similar standards of care are expected for other disorders.

Given these legal and economic factors, most psychotherapists today rarely engage patients in long-term psychoanalysis or humanistic therapy. Instead, they try to provide therapies that have a reasonable chance of working and working quickly. Most psychotherapy today reflects this pragmatic concern with expense and expediency; it consists of brief problem-solving sessions, various psychoeducational interventions such as stress-management classes, and time-limited behavioral therapy (Vandenbos, Cummings, and DeLeon, 1992).

A CENTURY OF THERAPY

Where does all of this leave us? It has been more than a hundred years since Krafft-Ebbing's discovery that general paresis is caused by syphilis and since Freud and Breuer's classic studies of hysteria. What can we say today about the treatment of mental disorder?

All in all, there has been considerable progress.

Let's begin with psychotherapy. There is little doubt that psychotherapy produces some nonspecific benefits. It helps people by providing someone in whom they can confide, who lends advice about troubling matters, who listens to them, and who instills hope that they will get better. The critic may reply that such gains merely reflect placebo effects and similar matters. According to this view, the benefits are not produced by any specific psychotherapeutic technique but might just as easily have been provided by a wise uncle, the understanding family doctor, or the local clergy.

Even if this were true—and it is certainly not the whole story—it may not be relevant. For wise uncles are in short supply today. The extended family in which uncles, nieces, and grandparents lived nearby is largely a thing of the past. The same is true of the family doctor, who has vanished from the scene, together with his bedside manner. Nor do many people today have a member of the clergy as a confidant. All of this suggests that psychotherapy has come to fill a social vacuum. Some of its effect may well be placebo-like, but a placebo may be better than nothing. And for the present, the psychotherapeutic professions seem to be the officially designated dispensers of such placebos.

But this is by no means all. For over and above placebo effects there seem to be some genuine, specific psychotherapeutic benefits that produce improvement, though rarely a complete cure. The specific ingredients that bring these effects about have not been identified with certainty but they probably include emotional defusing, interpersonal learning, and some insight—all acquired within the therapeutic situation and somehow transferred to the patient's life beyond.

How about biological therapies? Here the progress has been dramatic. Antipsychotic drugs control some of the worst manifestations of schizophrenia, the antidepressants and antimanic drugs (and where appropriate, electroconvulsive therapy) do the same for the mood swings of depression and mania, as do the anxiolytics for excessive anxiety. These advances are far from what one might wish. The drugs don't begin to effect a cure, and all have side effects. But we're much further along than we were a century ago.

How far is far? As so often, it depends on where we look. If we look back and compare our current practices with those at the time of the American Revolution when Benjamin Rush dunked his patients into ice cold water or whirled them around until they were unconscious, we've come a long way. But

SUMMARY

if we look ahead to some diagnostic manual of the future in which schizophrenia, mood and anxiety disorders, and all the rest of the current DSM-IV entries have neatly catalogued therapies that are sure to work, we must recognize that we have a much longer way to go. But considering our progress over the last hundred years, there is much to celebrate.

QUESTIONS FOR CRITICAL THINKING

1. Drug companies are developing versions of medications that are implantable under the skin and are effective for months at a time. What benefits and complications—medical, political, and legal—might these drugs bring?

2. Why might patients with mental disorders do so poorly overall at taking their medications regularly?

3. What does psychotherapy assume about the nature of the self? Could psychotherapy ever have arisen in a collectivist culture?

4. How could you decide whether a psychodynamic, behavioral, or cognitive account of a disorder was more accurate? Does the fact that one therapy works better than another imply that the underlying view of the disorder's origin is correct?

5. More and more difficulties in living (for example, being depressed at not finding a job) are being classified as mental disorders. Moreover, even some actions previously considered purely criminal (child abuse, rape) are often interpreted as reflecting mental disorder. What are the social implications of this change? Should a line be drawn limiting what is considered a mental disorder, and if so, where should that line be drawn?

6. On average, antidepressant medications and psychotherapy work about equally well for most depressions. What factors might determine which treatment a patient should receive?

7. Classical psychoanalysts tend to reject concrete criteria, such as length of hospitalization or length of time out of work, in assessing therapeutic outcome. Instead, they maintain that classical psychoanalysis produces a kind of outcome—insight about oneself—that is difficult to measure but much more profound. How could their claim be evaluated?

SUMMARY

1. *Biological therapies* constitute one major form of treatment of mental disorder. The classic *antipsychotics* like Thorazine and Haldol are helpful in holding in check the major positive symptoms of schizophrenia.

2. Classic *antidepressants* such as *MAO inhibitors* and *tricyclics* counteract depression. These antidepressants all have many undesirable side effects. *Selective serotonin reuptake inhibitors* like Prozac were designed to maximize their effects on serotonin neurotransmission. They have become popular because they have fewer side effects than the classic antidepressants and are equally effective for depression.

3. *Lithium carbonate* is useful in cases of bipolar disorder, especially in forestalling or reducing the intensity of manic episodes.

4. The effectiveness of drug treatment—as indeed of all therapies—requires careful evaluation that controls for spontaneous improvement and *placebo effects,* and that also guards against both the physicians' and the patients' expectations by use of *double-blind techniques.* Such studies have demonstrated genuine effects of certain drug therapies, some of which are quite specific to a particular mental disorder.

5. Other biological therapies include *psychosurgery,* a procedure that was once performed rather promiscuously and to the detriment of the recipients but is now conducted much more selectively and precisely. *Electroconvulsive therapy (ECT)* is markedly effective in cases of severe and potentially suicidal depression and for cases of depression that have not responded to antidepressant medications.

6. Another approach to the treatment of mental disorder, *psychotherapy,* relies on psychological means alone. Much of it is derived from *classical psychoanalysis* but has been expanded and diversified in both its guiding principles and techniques.

7. Psychoanalysts try to help their patients to recover repressed memories and wishes so that they can overcome crippling internal conflicts. Their tools include *free association* and the interpretation of the patient's *resistance* to it.

8. In *psychodynamic therapy,* therapists follow Freud's basic principles but generally place greater emphasis on current interpersonal and social problems rather than on psychosexual matters in the patient's childhood.

9. A different approach is taken by *behavior therapists* whose concern is with unwanted, overt behaviors rather than with hypothetical underlying causes. Many of the behavior therapists' techniques are derived from the principles of classical and instrumental conditioning. Therapies based on classical conditioning include *systematic desensitization,* which tries to countercondition the patient's fear by a policy of gradual exposure. Another is *aversion therapy* in which undesirable behaviors, thoughts, and desires are coupled with unpleasant stimuli.

10. Some recent offshoots of behavior therapy share its concrete and directive orientation but not its emphasis on conditioning. One example is *cognitive therapy,* which tries to change the way the patient thinks about his situation.

11. Another group of practitioners, the *humanistic therapists,* charge that both behavior therapy and psychoanalysis are too mechanistic and manipulative and that they fail to deal with their patients as whole persons. An example of a humanistic approach is Rogers' *client-centered therapy,* which is based on the idea that therapy is a process of personal growth.

12. The last few decades have seen an enormous extension of psychotherapy. One extension is of method. An example is *group therapy* in which patients are treated in groups rather than individually. Another example is *marital and family therapy,* whose practitioners believe that family distress is not in the pathology of any one individual but in the relationships within the family system and who therefore try to rectify these faulty relationships. Another extension concerns therapeutic goals. While the original purpose of psychotherapy was to cure pathology, some practitioners gradually broadened this goal to include personal growth. Therapists are now encouraged to develop *cultural competence,* so that they can adapt their therapies to the specific cultural values and customs that patients bring with them.

13. In recent years, investigators have begun to assess the effectiveness of psychotherapies through a statistical technique called *meta-analysis* by means of which the results of many different studies can be combined. The results of such analyses indicate that the various psychotherapies are more effective than placebo treatments, which in turn are better than no treatment at all. Comparing the effect of different psychotherapies is enormously difficult, but the main finding is that therapies tend to be fairly effective and that they are effective to about the same extent (the *dodo bird verdict*).

14. The dodo-bird verdict, however, comes from studies that combine many types of patients and disorders. Work is underway to determine the extent to which therapy can be matched to the patient and the disorder. Practitioners who adopt the *prescriptionist*

SUMMARY

position believe that in addition to placebo effects and various common factors such as *emotional defusing, interpersonal learning,* and an *empathic relationship* with another person, particular therapies have some specific effects on particular conditions.

15. Economic factors and legal issues have forced psychotherapists to reexamine their own efforts and provide only those services that have demonstrated effectiveness. This is leading to the development of generally accepted professional standards of care for specific mental disorders.

EPILOGUE

We have come to the end of our journey. We have traveled through the sprawling fields of psychology, a loosely federated intellectual empire that stretches from the domains of the biological sciences on one border to those of the social sciences on the other. We have gone from one end of psychology to another. What have we learned?

In looking back over our journey, there is little doubt that we have encountered many more questions than answers. To be sure, very much more is known today about mind and behavior than was known in the days of, say, Thorndike and Köhler, let alone those of Descartes, Locke, and Kant. For by now psychology has assuredly become a science, and in fact, a science of quite respectable accomplishments. But this does not change the fact that what we know today is just a small clearing in a vast jungle of ignorance. As we come to know more, the clearing expands, but so does the circumference that borders on the uncharted wildness.

What can we say? We can point at what we know and congratulate ourselves. Or we can consider what we do not know and bemoan our ignorance. Perhaps a wiser course is one recommended by Sigmund Freud on thinking about some aspects of human intellectual history (Freud, 1917).

Freud suggested a parallel between the psychological growth of each human child and the intellectual progress of humanity as a whole. As he saw it, the infant is initially possessed by an all-prevading sense of his own power and importance. He cries and his parents come to change or feed or rock him and so he feels that he is the cause of whatever happens around him, the sole center of a world that revolves around him alone. But this happy delusion of his own omnipotence cannot last forever. Eventually the growing infant discovers that he is not the hub of the universe. This recognition may come as a cruel blow, but he will ultimately be the better for it. For the child cannot become strong and capable without some awareness that he is not so as yet, without first accepting the fact that he can't have his way just by wishing. His first achievements will be slight—as he lifts his own cup or a bit later says his first word—but they are real enough and will lay the foundation for his later mastery of his environment.

Freud thought that a similar theme underlies the growth of humankind's awareness of the world in which we live. On two crucial occasions in our history, we had to give up some cherished beliefs in our own power and importance. With Copernicus, we had to cede our place in the center of the physical universe: The sun doesn't circle us, but we the sun. With Darwin, we had to perform a similar abdication in the biological sphere: We are not specially created but are descended from other animals. Each of these intellectual revolutions ran into vehement opposition, in large part because each represented a gigantic blow to humanity's self-love and pride. They made us face our own ignorance and insignificance. But however painful it may have been initially, each recognition of our weakness ultimately helped us gain more strength, each confession of ignorance eventually led to deeper understanding. The Copernican revolution forced us to admit our minute place in the celestial scheme of things, but this admission was the first step in a journey of ever-increasing physical horizons, a journey that in our own time brought human beings to the moon. The Darwinian revolution made us aware that we are just one biological species among millions, the product of the same evolutionary process that brought forth sea urchins and penguins as well as us. But this awareness opened the way for continually expanding explorations of the biological universe, explorations that have already given us much greater control of our own bodily condition and of the fragile environment in which humans and other species exist.

In this century we have had to suffer yet another blow to our self-pride. We learned that we are not sure of what goes on in our own minds. Modern psychology, for all its accomplishments, has made it utterly clear that thus far we know even less about our own mental processes and behavior than we know about the physical and biological world around us. Here, too, we have to confess that we are weak and ignorant. We can only hope that this confession will have some of the effects of our previous ones, that here again strength will grow out of weakness and knowledge out of folly and ignorance. If so, we may finally understand why we think and do what we think and do, so that we may ultimately master our inner selves as we have learned to master the world around us.

There are few goals in science that are worthier than this.

APPENDIX

STATISTICS: THE COLLECTION, ORGANIZATION, AND INTERPRETATION OF DATA

large body of psychological knowledge has been summarized in this book, and a good part of the discussion was devoted to the ways in which this knowledge was obtained. But there are certain methodological issues that were dealt with only in passing. These concern *statistical methods,* the ways in which investigators gather, organize, and interpret collections of numerical data.

Suppose some investigators want to find out whether three-year-old boys are more aggressive than three-year-old girls. To answer this question is a very big job. To start with, the investigators will have to come up with some appropriate measure of aggression. They will then have to select the subjects. The investigators presumably want to say something about three-year-olds in general, not just the particular three-year-olds in their study. To make sure that this can be done, they have to select their subjects appropriately. Even more important, their groups of boys and girls must be as comparable as possible, so that one can be reasonably sure that any differences between the two groups is attributable to the difference in sex rather than to other factors (such as intellectual development, social class, and so on).

The investigators are now ready to collect their data. But having collected them, they will have to find some way of organizing these data in a meaningful way. Suppose the study used two groups of, say, 50 boys and 50 girls, each observed on 10 separate occasions. This means that the investigators will end up with at least 1,000 separate numerical entries (say, number of aggressive acts for each child on each occasion), 500 for the boys and 500 for the girls. Something has to be done to reduce this mass of numbers into some manageable, summarized form. This is usually accomplished by some process of averaging scores.

The next step involves statistical interpretation. Suppose the investigators find that the average aggression score is greater for the boys than for the girls (it probably will be). Can they be sure that the difference between the groups is large enough not to be dismissed as a fluke, a chance event? For it is just about certain that the data contain *variability.* The children in each group will not perform equally; furthermore, the same child may very well behave differently on one occasion than another. As a result, the scores in the two groups will almost surely overlap; that is, some girls will get a higher aggression score than some boys. Could it be that the difference *between* the groups (that is, the difference between the two averages) is an accidental chance product of the variability that is seen to hold *within* the two groups? One of the key functions of statistical methods is to deal with questions of this sort, to help us draw useful general conclusions about organisms despite the unavoidable variability in their behavior.

The preceding example indicates the main tasks to which statistical methods have been applied. In this appendix, we will sketch the logic that underlies these methods as psychologists use them.

DESCRIBING THE DATA

The data with which statistics deals are numerical, so a preliminary step in statistical analysis is the reduction of the actual results of a study to numbers. Much of the power of statistics results from the fact that numbers (unlike responses to a questionnaire, videotapes of social interactions, or lists of words recalled by a subject in a memory experiment) can be manipulated with the rules of arithmetic. As a result, scientists prefer to use response measures that are in numerical form. Consider our hypothetical study of aggression and sex. The investigators who watched the subjects might rate their aggression in various situations (from, say, "extremely aggressive" to "extremely docile") or they might count the number of aggressive acts (say, hitting or insulting another child), and so on. This operation of assigning numbers to observed events (usually, a subject's responses) is called *scaling.*

There are several types of scales that will concern us. They differ by the arithmetical operations that can be performed upon them.

CATEGORICAL AND ORDINAL SCALES

■ Sometimes the scores assigned to individuals are merely *categorical* (also called *nominal.*) For example, when respondents to a poll are asked to name the television channel they watch most frequently, they might respond "4," "2," or "13." These numbers serve only to group the responses into categories. They can obviously not be subjected to any arithmetic operations.

Ordinal numbers convey more information, in that their relative magnitude is meaningful—not arbitrary, as in the case of categorical scales. If individuals are asked to list the ten people they most admire, the number 1 can be assigned to the most admired person, 2 to the runner-up, and so on. The smaller the number assigned, the more the person is admired. Notice that no such statement can be made of television channels: Channel 4 is not more anything than channel 2, just different from it.

Scores which are ordinally scaled cannot, however, be added or subtracted. The first two persons on the most-admired list differ in admirability by 1; so do the last two. Yet the individual who has done the ranking may admire the first person far more than the other nine, all of whom might be very similar in admirability; in other words, given an ordinal scale, differences of 1 are not necessarily equal psychologically. Imagine a child who, given this task, lists his mother first, followed by the starting lineup of the Chicago Cubs baseball team. In this example, the difference of 8 between person 2 and person 10 probably represents a smaller difference in judged admirability than the difference of 1 obtained between persons 1 and 2 (at least so the mother hopes).

INTERVAL SCALES

■ Scales in which equal differences between scores, or intervals, *can* be treated as equal units are called *interval scales.* Reaction time is a common psychological variable that is usually treated as an interval scale. In some memory experiments, a subject must respond as quickly as possible to each of several words, some of which he has seen earlier in the experiment; the task is to indicate whether each word has appeared before by pressing one of two buttons. An unknown, but possibly constant, part of the reaction time is simply the time required to press the response button; the rest is the time required for the decision-making process:

$$\text{reaction time} = \text{decision time} + \text{button-press time} \qquad (1)$$

Suppose a subject requires an average of 2 seconds to respond to nouns, 3 seconds to verbs, and 4 seconds to adjectives. The difference in decision time between verbs and nouns (3 − 2 = 1 second) is the same as the difference in decision time between adjectives and verbs (4 − 3 = 1 second). We can make this statement—which in turn suggests various hypotheses about the factors that underlie such differences—precisely because reaction time can be regarded as an interval scale.

RATIO SCALES

■ Scores based on an interval scale allow subtraction and addition. But they do not necessarily allow multiplication and division. Consider the centigrade scale of temperature. There is no doubt that the difference between 10 and 20 degrees centigrade is equal to that between 30 and 40 degrees centigrade. But can one say that 20 degrees centigrade is *twice* as high a temperature as 10 degrees centigrade? The answer is no, for the centigrade scale of temperature is only an interval scale. It is not a **ratio scale,** which allows statements such as 10 feet is 1/5 as long as 50 feet, or 15 pounds is 3 times as heavy as 5 pounds. To make such statements one needs a true zero point. Such a ratio scale with a zero point does exist for temperature—the Kelvin absolute temperature scale, whose zero point is about −273 degrees centigrade.

Some psychological variables can be described by a ratio scale. This is true of various forms of sensory intensity—brightness, loudness, and so on. For example, it makes sense to say that the rock music emanating from your neighbor's apartment is four times as loud as your roommate singing in the shower. But there are many psychological variables that cannot be so readily described in ratio terms. Let's go back to reaction time. This cannot be considered a ratio scale for the decision process. In our previous example we saw that the reaction time for adjectives was 4 seconds, while that for nouns was 2 seconds. But we cannot say that the 4-second response represents twice as much *decision* time as the 2-second response, because of the unknown time required to press the response button. Since this time is unknown, we have no zero point.

The fact that very few variables are ratio scaled does not, of course, prevent people from describing ordinal- or interval-scaled variables in ratio terms. A claim by an advertiser that drug *A* is "twice as effective" as drug *B* may mean that *A* works twice as fast, or for twice the time, or is successful on twice as many people, or requires only half the dose. A potential consumer needs to know the advertiser's meaning of "effective" to evaluate the claim. Similarly, a 4-second reaction time in the word-recognition experiment is certainly twice as long as a 2-second reaction time; there is no harm in saying so, as long as it is understood that we are not talking about the decision time but rather about the total reaction time.

COLLECTING THE DATA

The kinds of scales we have just discussed concern the ways in which psychological variables are described in numerical terms. The point of most psychological investigations is to see how such variables are related to various factors that may produce them. Psychologists—and most other scientists—employ three major methodological tools to achieve this end: the experiment, the observational study, and the case study.

THE EXPERIMENT

An *experiment* is a study in which the experimenter deliberately manipulates one or more variables to determine the effect of this manipulation on another variable. As an example, consider an experiment conducted to determine whether visual imagery aids memory. Participants in the experiment listen to a list of words, which they are instructed to memorize; later they are asked to recall as many words as possible. Two groups of subjects are chosen. One is the *experimental group;* this is the group to which the experimenter's manipulation is applied. It consists of subjects who are instructed to form visual images that connect each word to the preceding word. Other subjects form the *control group,* a group to which the experimenter's manipulation is not applied. These control subjects are not given imagery instructions. Many experiments have more than one experimental group (in this example, different groups might be told to do their visual imagining in different ways) or more than one control group (here, a second control group might be instructed to rehearse by repeating each word over and over).

Like many other experiments, this one can be thought of as a situation in which the experimenter varies something (here the instructions given to the subjects) and observes the effect of this variation on certain responses of the subjects (the number of words they correctly recall). The variable that is manipulated by the experimenter (imagery instructions) is called the *independent variable.* The subject's response (number of words recalled) is called the *dependent variable,* since the investigator wants to know whether it is dependent upon his manipulation of the independent variable. Speaking loosely, independent variables are sometimes regarded as causes, dependent variables as effects.

The results of our experiment are graphically presented in Figure A.1. The values of the independent variable are indicated on the horizontal, or *x*-axis, and the values of the dependent variable on the vertical, or *y*-axis. The figure displays the average number of items recalled for subjects who used visual imagery in memorizing and for those who did not. We will have more to say about this experiment presently.

A.1 The results of an experiment on memorizing *Subjects in the imagery group, who formed visual images of the words they were to memorize, recalled an average of 11 words. Subjects in the control group, who received no special instructions, recalled an average of 8 words.*

THE OBSERVATIONAL STUDY

Much psychological research departs from the experimental method in that investigators do not produce the effects directly, but only observe them. They do not so much design the experiment as discover it. Such an investigation is called an *observational study.* Consider the question "What is the effect of prenatal malnutrition on IQ?" This question can only be answered by locating children whose mothers were malnourished during pregnancy and measuring their IQs; to provide pregnant women with inadequate diets deliberately is obviously worse than unethical. But even though the investigators do not manipulate the mother's diet (or indeed, anything else), some of the methodological terms used before can still be applied. We can consider the mother's diet as the independent variable, and the child's IQ as the dependent variable. A group analogous to the experimental group would consist of children whose mothers were malnourished during pregnancy. An analogue to the control group is a group of children whose mothers' diet was adequate.

Observational studies like this one are sometimes called "experiments of nature." Because nature does not always provide exactly those control groups that the investigator might wish for, observational studies can be difficult to interpret. For example, children whose mothers were malnourished during pregnancy are often born into environments that might also be expected to have negative effects on IQ. Women whose diet is inadequate during pregnancy are likely to be poor; they are therefore less likely to provide some of the physical advantages (like good food and health care) and educational advantages (like books and nursery schools) that may well be helpful in developing intelligence.

THE CASE STUDY

In many areas of psychology, conclusions are based on only one person who is studied intensively. Such an investigation is called a *case study.* Individuals who display unusual psychological or physiological characteristics, such as rare forms of color blindness, exceptionally good or poor memory, or brain injuries, can sometimes provide information about normal vision, memory, or brain function that would be difficult or impossible to obtain from normal individuals. Take the patient known as H.M., who suffered severe amnesia after brain surgery (see Chapter 7). Before the operation his memory was normal; afterward he could remember virtually nothing about events that occurred after the operation. This patient has been extensively studied because of his unusual memory disorder. Since his amnesia is apparently the result of the destruction of a particular structure in the brain, the hippocampus, a comparison of H.M.'s performance with that of normal individuals allows us to make inferences about the role of the hippocampus in normal memory.

Some of the most famous case studies in psychology are those described by Sigmund Freud, whose extensive psychoanalytic interviews of his patients led him to develop his theories of dreams, defense mechanisms, and other psychological processes (see Chapter 17).

SELECTING THE SUBJECTS

How does one select the subjects for a psychological study? To answer the question, we have to consider the difference between a population and a sample.

SAMPLE AND POPULATION

Psychologists—again like other scientists—usually want to make statements about a larger group of persons (or animals) than the particular subjects they happen to use in their study. They want their conclusions to apply to a particular *population:* all members of a given group—say, all three-year-old boys, all schizophrenic patients, all U.S. voters, and in some cases, all humans. But they normally can't study all members of the given population. As a result, they have to select a *sample,* that is, a subset of the population they are interested in. Their hope is that the results found in the sample can be generalized to the population from which the sample is drawn.

It is important to realize that generalizations from a given sample to a particular population can only be made if the sample is representative (that is, typical) of the population to which one wants to generalize. Suppose one does a study on memory by using college students. Can one generalize the results to adults in general? Strictly speaking one cannot, for college students are on the average younger than the population at large and are more accustomed to memorizing things. Under the circumstances, the safest course may be to restrict one's generalizations to the population of college students.

Most experimenters would probably argue that college students don't differ too greatly from the general population (at least in memory skills) so that results obtained with them do apply in general, at least approximately. But there are many cases in which inadequate sampling leads to gross blunders. The classic example is a 1936 poll which predicted that Franklin D. Roosevelt would lose the presidential election. In fact, he won by a landslide. This massive error was produced by a *biased sample*—all persons polled were selected from telephone directories. But in 1936 having a telephone was much more likely among persons of higher than of lower socioeconomic status. As a result, the sample was not representative of the voting population as a whole. Since socioeconomic level affected voting preference, the poll predicted falsely.

RANDOM AND STRATIFIED SAMPLES

To ensure that one can generalize from sample to population, investigators use a *random sample.* This is a sample in which every member of the population has an equal chance of being picked—as in a jury drawn by lot from all the voters of a given district (if none are disqualified or excuse themselves). The random sampling procedure applies with special force to the assignment of subjects in an experiment. Here every effort has to be made to assign subjects randomly to the various experimental or control groups.

For some purposes, even a random sample may not be good enough. While every member of the population has an equal chance of being selected, the sample may still turn out to be atypical by chance alone. This danger of chance error becomes less and less the greater the size of the sample. But if one is forced to use a small sample (and one often is because of lack of time or money), other sampling procedures may be necessary. Suppose we want to take a poll to determine the attitudes of American voters toward legalized abortion. We can expect people's attitudes to differ depending (at least) on their age, sex, and religion. If the sample is fairly small, it is important that each subgroup of the population be (randomly) sampled in proportion to its size. This procedure is called *stratified sampling* and is common in studying psychological traits or attitudes that vary greatly among different subgroups of the population.

SAMPLING RESPONSES

The distinction between sample and population does not only apply to subjects. It also applies to the subjects' responses. Consider the investigators who studied aggressive behavior in 50 three-year-old boys. Each of these boys was observed on 10 occasions. Those 10 occasions can be regarded as a sample of all such occasions, just as the 50 boys can be regarded as a sample of all three-year-old boys (or at least of all middle-class U.S. boys). The investigators will surely want to generalize from this sample of occasions to the population of all such occasions. To make sure that such a generalization is warranted, one has to see to it that the occasions are not atypical—that the child isn't especially tired, or sick, and so on.

ORGANIZING THE DATA: DESCRIPTIVE STATISTICS

We have considered the ways in which psychologists describe the data provided by their subjects by assigning numbers to them (scaling) and the ways in which they collect these data in the first place (experiments, observational studies, case studies). Our next task is to see how these data are organized.

THE FREQUENCY DISTRIBUTION

Suppose we have designed and performed an experiment such as the imagery study described previously. The data will not automatically arrange themselves in the form shown in Figure A.1. Instead, investigators will first be faced with a list of numbers, the scores (number of words recalled correctly) for each subject in a given group. For example, if there were 10 subjects in the control group, their scores (in words correct) might have been

$$8, 11, 6, 7, 5, 9, 5, 9, 9, 11.$$

A first step in organizing the data is to list all the possible scores and the frequency with which they occurred, as shown in Table A.1. Such an arrangement is called a *frequency distribution.*

The frequency distribution can be expressed graphically. A common means for doing this is a *histogram,* which depicts the frequency distribution by a series of contiguous rectangles (Figure A.2). The values of the dependent variable (here, the number of words recalled) are shown by the location of each rectangle on the horizontal or *x*-axis. The frequency of each score is shown on the verti-

TABLE A.1 FREQUENCY DISTRIBUTION

Score	Frequency
11	2
10	0
9	3
8	1
7	1
6	1
5	2

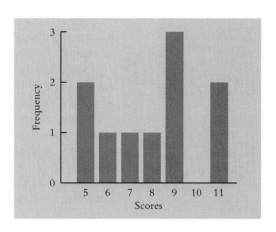

A.2 Histogram *In a histogram, a frequency distribution is graphically represented by a series of rectangles. The location of each rectangle on the x-axis indicates a score value, while its height shows how often that score value occurred.*

cal or y-axis, that is, by the height of each rectangle. This is simple enough for our example, but in practice graphic presentation often requires a further step. The number of possible values the dependent variable can assume is often very large. As a result, exactly equal values rarely occur, as when reaction times are measured to the nearest millisecond (thousandth of a second). To get around this, the scores are generally grouped by intervals for purposes of graphic display. The histogram might then plot the frequency of all reaction times between, say, 200 and 225 milliseconds, between 226 and 250 milliseconds, and so on.

MEASURES OF CENTRAL TENDENCY

■ A frequency distribution is a more concise description of the result of the experiment than the raw list of scores from which it was derived, but for many purposes we may want a description that is even more concise. We often wish to summarize an entire distribution by a single, central score; such a score is called a *measure of central tendency.* Three measures of central tendency are commonly used to express this central point of a distribution: the mode, the median, and the mean.

The *mode* is simply the score that occurs most frequently. In our example, the mode is 9. More subjects (to be exact, 3) recalled 9 words than recalled any other number of words.

The *median* is the point that divides the distribution into two equal halves, when the scores are arranged in increasing order. To find the median in our example, we first list the scores:

$$5, 5, 6, 7, 8, 9, 9, 9, 11, 11$$
$$\uparrow$$

Since there are ten scores, the median lies between the fifth and sixth scores, that is, between 8 and 9, as indicated by the arrow. Any score between 8 and 9 would divide the distribution into two equal halves, but it is conventional to choose the number in the center of the interval between them, that is, 8.5. When there is an odd number of scores this problem does not arise.

The third measure of central tendency, the *mean (M),* is the familiar arithmetic average. If N stands for the number of scores, then

$$M = \frac{\text{sum of scores}}{N}$$
$$= \frac{5 + 5 + 6 + 7 + 8 + 9 + 9 + 9 + 11 + 11}{10} = \frac{80}{10} = 8.0$$

Of these three measures, the mode is the least helpful, because the modes of two samples from the same population can differ greatly even if the samples have very similar distributions. If one of the 3 subjects who recalled 9 words recalled only 5 instead, the mode would have been 5 rather than 9. But the mode does have its uses. For example, in certain elections, the candidate with the most votes—the modal candidate—wins

The median and the mean differ most in the degree to which they are affected by extreme scores. If the highest score in our sample were changed from 11 to 111, the median would be unaffected, whereas the mean would jump from 8.0 to 18.0. Most people would find the median (which remains 8.5) a more compelling "average" than the mean in such a situation, since most of the scores in the distribution are close to the median, but are not close to the mean (18.0).

Distributions with extreme values at one end are said to be *skewed.* A classic example is income, since there are only a few high incomes but many low ones. Suppose we sample ten individuals from a neighborhood and find their yearly incomes (in thousands of dollars) to be:

$$5, 5, 5, 5, 10, 10, 10, 20, 20, 1,000$$

The median income for this sample is 10 ($10,000), since both the fifth and sixth scores are 10, and this value reflects the income of the typical individual. The mean income for this sample, however, is (5 + 5 + 5 + 5 + 10 + 10 + 10 + 20 + 20 + 1,000)/10 = 109, or $109,000. A politician who wants to demonstrate that his neighborhood has prospered might—quite honestly—use these data to claim that the average (mean) income is $109,000. If, on the other hand, he wished to plead for financial aid, he might say—with equal honesty—that the average (median) income is only $10,000. There is no single "correct" way to find an "average" in this situation, but it is obviously important to know which average (that is, which measure of central tendency) is being used.

When deviations in either direction from the mean are equally frequent, the distribution is said to be *symmetric.* In such distributions, the mean and the median are equal. Many psychological variables have symmetric distributions, but for variables with skewed distributions, like income, measures of central tendency must be chosen with care.

MEASURES OF VARIABILITY

In reducing an entire frequency distribution to an average score, we have discarded a lot of very useful information. Suppose we (or the National Weather Service) measure the temperature every day for a year in various cities and construct a frequency distribution for each city. The mean of this distribution tells us something about the city's climate. That it does not tell us everything is shown by the fact that the mean temperature in both San Francisco and Albuquerque is 56 degrees Fahrenheit. But the climates of the two cities nonetheless differ considerably, as indicated in Table A.2.

The weather displays much more variability in the course of a year in Albuquerque than in San Francisco. A simple measure of variability is the *range,* the highest score minus the lowest. The range of temperatures in San Francisco is 15, while in Albuquerque it is 42.

A shortcoming of the range as a measure of variability is that it reflects the values of only two scores in the entire sample. As an example, consider the following distributions of ages in two college classes:

Distribution *A:* 19, 19, 19, 19, 19, 20, 25
Distribution *B:* 17, 17, 17, 20, 23, 23, 23

TABLE A.2 TEMPERATURE DATA FOR TWO CITIES (DEGREES FAHRENHEIT)				
City	Lowest month	Mean	Highest month	Range
Albuquerque, New Mexico	35	56	77	42
San Francisco, California	48	56	63	15

TABLE A.3 CALCULATING VARIANCE		
Score	*Score − mean*	*(Score − mean)^2*
8	$8 - 8 = 0$	$0^2 = 0$
11	$11 - 8 = 3$	$3^2 = 9$
6	$6 - 8 = -2$	$(-2)^2 = 4$
7	$7 - 8 = -1$	$(-1)^2 = 1$
5	$5 - 8 = -3$	$(-3)^2 = 9$
9	$9 - 8 = 1$	$1^2 = 1$
5	$5 - 8 = -3$	$(-3)^2 = 9$
9	$9 - 8 = 1$	$1^2 = 1$
9	$9 - 8 = 1$	$1^2 = 1$
11	$11 - 8 = 3$	$3^2 = 9$

Each distribution has a mean of 20. Intuitively, distribution *A* has less variability, since all scores but one are very close to the mean. Yet the range of scores is the same (6) in both distributions. The problem arises because the range is determined by only two of the seven scores in each distribution.

A better measure of variability would incorporate every score in the distribution rather than just two scores. One might think that the variability could be measured by the average difference between the various scores and the mean, that is, by:

$$\frac{\text{sum of (score} - M)}{N}$$

This hypothetical measure is unworkable, however, because some of the scores are greater than the mean and some are smaller, so that the numerator is a sum of both positive and negative terms. (In fact, it turns out that the sum of the positive terms equals the sum of the negative terms, so that the expression shown above always equals zero.) The solution to this problem is simply to square all the terms in the numerator, thus making them all positive.★ The resulting measure of variability is called the **variance (V):**

$$V = \frac{\text{sum of (score} - M)^2}{N} \tag{2}$$

The calculation of the variance for the control group in the memorization experiment is shown in Table A.3. As the table shows, the variance is obtained by subtracting the mean (*M,* which equals 8) from each score, squaring each result, adding all the squared terms, and dividing the resulting sum by the total number of scores (*N,* which equals 10), yielding a value of 4.4.

Because deviations from the mean are squared, the variance is expressed in units different from the scores themselves. If our dependent variable were a distance, measured in centimeters, the variance would be expressed in square centimeters. As we will see in the next section, it is convenient to have a measure of

---

★ An alternative solution would be to sum the absolute value of (score − *M*), that is, consider only the magnitude of this difference for each score, not the sign. The resulting statistic, called the **average deviation,** is little used, however, primarily because absolute values are not too easily dealt with in certain mathematical terms that underlie statistical theory. As a result, statisticians prefer to transform negative into positive numbers by squaring them.

variability that can be added to or subtracted from the mean; such a measure ought to be expressed in the same units as the original scores. To accomplish this end, we employ another measure of variability, the **standard deviation,** or **SD.** The standard deviation is derived from the variance (V); it is obtained by taking the square root of the variance. Thus

$$SD = \sqrt{V}$$

In our example, SD is about 2.1, the square root of the variance which is 4.4.

CONVERTING SCORES TO COMPARE THEM

Suppose a person takes two tests. One measures her memory span—how many digits she can remember after one presentation. The other test measures her running ability—how fast she can run 100 yards. It turns out that she can remember 8 digits and runs 100 yards in 17 seconds. Is there any way to decide whether she can remember digits better (or worse or equally well) than she can run 100 yards? On the face of it, the question seems absurd; it seems to be like comparing apples and oranges. But in fact, there is a way, for we can ask where each of these two scores is located on the two frequency distributions of other persons (presumably women of the same age) who are given the same two tasks.

PERCENTILE RANKS

One way of doing this is by transforming each of the two scores into a **percentile rank.** The percentile rank of a score indicates the percentage of all scores that lie below that given score. Let's assume that 8 digits is the 78th percentile, which means that 78 percent of the relevant comparison group remembers fewer digits. Let's further assume that a score of 17 seconds in the 100-yard dash is the 53d percentile of the same comparison group. We can now answer the question with which we started. Our subject can remember digits better than she can run 100 yards. By converting into percentile ranks we have rendered incompatible scores compatible, allowing us to compare the two.

STANDARD SCORES

For many statistical purposes there is an even better method of comparing scores or of interpreting the meaning of individual scores. This is to express them by reference to the mean and standard deviation of the frequency distribution of which they are part by converting them into **standard scores** (often called **z-scores**).

Suppose you take a test that measures aptitude for accounting and are told your score is 36. In itself, this number cannot help you decide whether to pursue or avoid a career in accounting. To interpret your score you need to know both the average score and how variable the scores are. If the mean is 30, you know you are above average, but how far above average is 6 points? This might be an extreme score or one attained by many, depending on the variability of the distribution.

Let us suppose that the standard deviation of the distribution is 3. Your score of 36 is therefore 2 standard deviations (6 points) above the mean (30). A score that is expressed this way, as so many standard deviations from the mean, is called a standard score, or z-score. The formula for calculating a z-score is:

$$z = \frac{(\text{score} - M)}{SD} \tag{3}$$

Your aptitude of 36 has a z-score of $(36 - 30)/3 = 2$; that is, your score is 2 standard deviations above the mean.

The use of z-scores allows one to compare scores from different distributions. Still unsure whether to become an accountant, you take a screen test to help you decide whether to be an actor. Here your score is 60. This is a larger number than the 36 you scored on the earlier test, but it may not reveal much acting aptitude. Suppose the mean score on the screen test is 80, the standard deviation 20; then your z-score is $(60 - 80)/20 = -1$. In acting aptitude, you are 1 standard deviation below the mean (that is, $z = -1$); in accounting aptitude, 2 standard deviations above (that is, $z = +2$). The use of z-scores makes your relative abilities clear.

Notice that scores below the mean have negative z-scores, as in the last example. A z-score of 0 corresponds to a score that equals the mean.

Percentile rank and a z-score give similar information, but one cannot be converted into the other unless we know more about the distribution than just its mean and standard deviation. In many cases this information is available, as we shall now see.

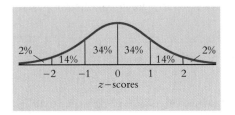

A.3   Normal distribution *Values taken from any normally distributed variable (such as those presented in Table A.4) can be converted to z-scores by the formula z = (score − mean)/(standard deviation). The figure shows graphically the proportions that fall between various values of z.*

THE NORMAL DISTRIBUTION

Frequency histograms can have a wide variety of shapes, but many variables of psychological interest have a **normal distribution** (often called a **normal curve**), which is a symmetric distribution of the shape shown in Figure A.3. The graph is smooth, unlike the histogram in Figure A.2, because it approximates the distribution of scores from a very large sample. The normal curve is bell-shaped, with most of its scores near the mean; the farther a score is from the mean, the less likely it is to occur. Among the many variables whose distributions are approximately normal are IQ, scholastic aptitude test scores (SAT), and women's heights (see Table A.4).★

These three variables, IQ, SAT score, and height, obviously cannot literally have the "same" distribution, since their means and standard deviations are different (Table A.4 gives plausible values for them). In what sense, then, can they

TABLE A.4 NORMALLY DISTRIBUTED VARIABLES							
				z-scores			
Variable	*Mean*	*Standard deviation*	*−2*	*−1*	*0*	*1*	*2*
IQ	100	15	70	85	100	115	130
SAT	500	100	300	400	500	600	700
Height (women)	160cm	5cm	150	155	160	165	170

★ Men's heights are also normally distributed, but the distribution of the heights of all adults is not. Such a distribution would have two peaks, one for the modal height of each sex, and would thus be shaped quite differently from the normal curve. Distributions with two modes are called **bimodal.**

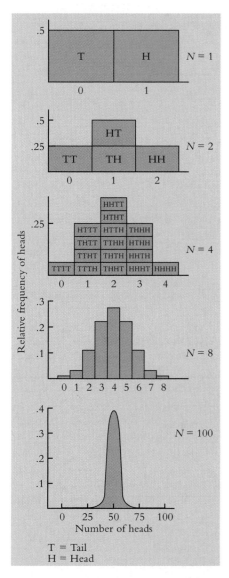

A.4 Histograms showing expected number of heads in tossing a fair coin N times
In successive panels, N = 1, 2, 4, and 8. The bottom panel illustrates the case when N = 100 and shows a smoothed curve.

all be said to be normal? The answer is that the distribution of *z*-scores for all these variables is the same. For example, an IQ of 115 is 15 points, or 1 standard deviation, above the IQ mean of 100; a height of 165 centimeters is 5 centimeters, or 1 standard deviation, above the height mean of 160 centimeters. Both scores, therefore, have *z*-scores of 1. Furthermore, the percentage of heights between 160 and 165 centimeters is the same as the percentage of IQ scores between 100 and 115, that is, it is 34 percent. This is the percentage of scores that lie between the mean and one standard deviation above the mean for any normally distributed variable.

THE PERCENTILE RANK OF A *Z*-SCORE

When a variable is known to have a normal distribution, a *z*-score can be converted directly into a percentile rank. A *z*-score of 1 has a percentile rank of 84, that is, 34 percent of scores lie between the mean and *z* = 1, and (because the distribution is symmetric) 50 percent of the scores lie below the mean. A *z*-score of −1 corresponds, in a normal distribution, to a percentile rank of 16: only 16 percent of the scores are lower. These relationships are illustrated in Figure A.3 and Table A.4.

HOW THE NORMAL CURVE ARISES

Why should variables such as height or IQ scores—and many others—form distributions that have this particular shape? Mathematicians have shown that whenever a given variable is the sum of many smaller variables, its distribution will be close to that of the normal curve. An example is height. Height can be thought of as the sum of the contributions of the many genes (and some environmental factors) that influence this trait; it therefore satisfies the general condition.

The basic idea is that the many different factors that influence a given measure (such as the genes for height) operate independently. A given gene will pull height up or push it down; the direction in which it exerts its effort is a matter of chance. If the chances are equal either way, then a good analogy to this situation is a person who tosses a coin repeatedly and counts the number of times the coin comes up heads. In this analogy, a head corresponds to a gene that tends to increase height, a tail to a gene that tends to diminish it. The more often the genetic coin falls heads, the taller the person will be.

What will the distribution of the variable "number of heads" be? Clearly, it depends on the number of tosses. If the coin is tossed only once, then there will be either 0 heads or 1 head, and these are equally likely. The resulting distribution is shown in the top panel of Figure A.4.

If the number of tosses (which we will call *N*) is 2, then 0, 1, or 2 heads can arise. However, not all these outcomes are equally likely: 0 heads come up only if the sequence tail-tail (*TT*) occurs; 2 heads only if head-head (*HH*) occurs; but 1 head results from either *HT* or *TH*. The distribution of heads for *N* = 2 is shown in the second panel of Figure A.4. The area above 1 head has been subdivided into two equal parts, one for each possible sequence containing a single head.★

As *N* increases, the distribution of the number of heads looks more and more like the normal distribution, as the subsequent panels of Figure A.4 show. When *N* becomes as large as the number of factors that determine height, the distribu-

---

★ The distribution of the number of heads is called the **binomial distribution,** because of its relation to the binomial theorem: the number of head-tail sequences that can lead to *k* heads is the $(k + 1)$st coefficient of $(a + b)^N$.

tion of the number of heads is virtually identical to the normal distribution. Similar arguments justify the assumption of normality for many psychological variables.

DESCRIBING THE RELATION BETWEEN TWO VARIABLES: CORRELATION

The basic problem facing psychological investigators is to account for observed differences in some variable they are interested in. Why, for example, do some people display better memory than others? The experimental approach to the problem, described earlier, is to ask whether changes in an independent variable produce systematic changes in the dependent variable. In the memory experiment, we asked whether subjects using visual imagery as an aid to memorizing would recall more words on the average than those who did not. In an observational study, however, our approach must be different, for in such a study we do not manipulate the variables. What is often done here is to observe the relationship between two—sometimes more—variables as they occur naturally, in the hope that differences in one variable can be attributed to differences in a second.

POSITIVE AND NEGATIVE CORRELATION

■ Imagine that a taxicab company wants to identify drivers who will earn relatively large amounts of money (for themselves and, of course, for the company). The company's officers make the plausible guess that one relevant factor is the driver's knowledge of the local geography, so they devise an appropriate test of street names, routes from place to place, and so on, and administer the test to each driver. The question is whether this test score is related to the driver's job performance as measured by his weekly earnings. To decide one has to find out whether the test score and the earnings are *correlated*—that is, whether they tend to vary together.

In the taxicab example, the two variables will probably be *positively correlated*—as one variable (test score) increases, the other (earnings) will generally increase too. But other variables may be *negatively correlated*—when one increases, the other will tend to decrease. An example is a phenomenon called Zipf's law, which states that words that occur frequently in a language tend to be relatively short. The two variables—word length and word frequency—are negatively correlated, since one variable tends to increase as the other decreases.

Correlational data are often displayed in a *scatter plot* (or scatter diagram) in which values of one variable are shown on the horizontal axis and variables of the other on the vertical axis. Figure A.5A is a scatter plot of word frequency versus word length for the words in this sentence.* Each word is represented by a single point. An example is provided by the word *plot,* which is 4 letters long

---

* There is no point for the "word" A.5A in this sentence. The frequencies of the other words are taken from H. Kucera and W. N. Francis, *Computational Analysis of Present-Day American English* (Providence, R. I.: Brown University Press, 1967).

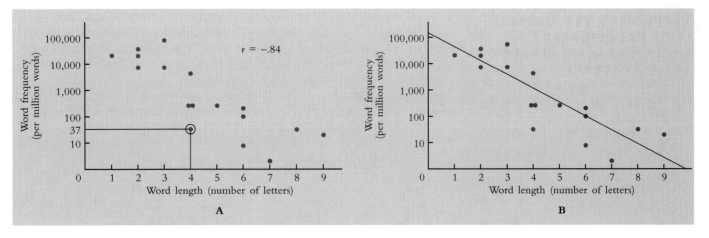

A.5 *Scatter plot of a negative correlation between word length and word frequency*

and occurs with a frequency of 37 times per million words of English text (and is represented by the circled dot). The points on the graph display a tendency to decrease on one variable as they increase on the other, although the relation is by no means perfect. It is helpful to draw a straight line through the various points in a scatter plot that comes as close as possible to all of them (Figure A.5B). The line is called a ***line of best fit,*** and it indicates the general trend of the data. Here, the line slopes downward because the correlation between the variables is negative.

The three panels of Figure A.6 are scatter plots showing the relation between other pairs of variables. In Figure A.6A hypothetical data from the taxicab example show that there is a positive correlation between test score and earnings (since the line of best fit slopes upward), but that test score is not a perfect predictor of on-the-job performance (since the points are fairly widely scattered around the line). Points above the line represent individuals who earn more than their test score would lead one to predict, points below the line individuals who earn less.

The examples in Figures A.5 and A.6A each illustrate moderate correlations; panels B and C of Figure A.6 are extreme cases. Figure A.6B shows data from a hypothetical experiment conducted in a fourth-grade class to illustrate the relation between metric and English units of length. The heights of five children are measured twice, once in inches and once in centimeters; each point on the scatter plot gives the two height measurements for one child. All the points in the

A.6 *Scatter plots of various correlations*
(A) The scatter plot and line of best fit show a positive correlation between a taxi-driving test and earnings. (B) A perfect positive correlation. The line of best fit passes through all the points. (C) A correlation of zero. The line of best fit is horizontal.

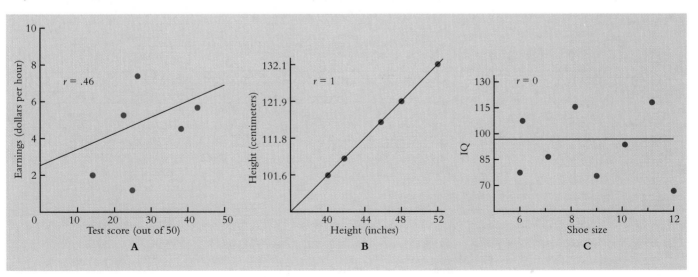

figure fall on the line of best fit, because height in centimeters always equals 2.54 times height in inches. The two variables, height in centimeters and height in inches, are perfectly correlated—one can be perfectly predicted from the other. Once you know your height in inches, there is no information to be gained by measuring yourself with a meterstick.

Figure A.6C presents a relation between IQ and shoe size. These variables are unrelated to each other; people with large shoes have neither a higher nor a lower IQ than people with small ones. The line of best fit is therefore horizontal, because the best guess of an individual's IQ is the same no matter what his or her shoe size—it is the mean IQ of the population.

THE CORRELATION COEFFICIENT

■ Correlations are often described by a *correlation coefficient,* denoted *r,* a number that can vary from +1.00 to −1.00 and that expresses the strength and the direction of the correlation. For positive correlations, *r* is positive; for negative correlations, it is negative; for variables that are completely uncorrelated, *r* = 0. The largest positive value *r* can have is +1.00, which represents a perfect correlation (as in Figure A.6B); the largest possible negative value is −1.00,

---

TABLE A.5 CALCULATION OF THE CORRELATION COEFFICIENT

1. Data (from Figure A.6A).

Test score (X)	Earnings (Y)
45	6
25	2
15	3
40	5
25	6
30	8

2. Find the mean and standard deviation for X and Y.

For X, mean = 30, standard deviation = 10
For Y, mean = 5, standard deviation = 2

3. Convert each X and each Y to a z-score, using $z = \dfrac{(\text{score} - M)}{SD}$

X	Y	z-score for X (z_x)	z-score for Y (z_x)	$z_x z_y$
45	6	1.5	0.5	0.75
25	2	−0.5	−1.5	0.75
15	3	−1.5	−1.0	1.50
40	5	1.0	0.0	0.00
25	6	−0.5	0.5	−0.25
30	8	0.0	1.5	0.00
				2.75

4. Find the product $z_x z_y$ for each pair of scores.

5. $r = \dfrac{\text{sum } (z_x z_y)}{N} = \dfrac{2.75}{6} = .46$

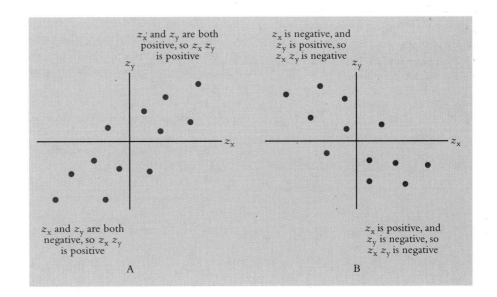

A.7 Correlation coefficients (A) Two positively correlated variables. Most of the points lie in the upper-right and lower-left quadrants, where $z_x z_y$ is positive, so r is positive. (B) Two negatively correlated variables. Most of the points lie in the upper left and lower right quadrants, where $z_x z_y$ is negative, so r is negative.

which is also a perfect correlation. The closer the points in a scatter plot come to falling on the line of best fit, the nearer *r* will be to +1.00 or −1.00 and the more confident we can be in predicting scores on one variable from scores on the other. The values of *r* for the scatter plots in Figures A.5 and A.6A are given on the figures.

The method for calculating *r* between two variables, *X* and *Y,* is shown in Table A.5 (on the previous page). The formula is:

$$r = \frac{\text{sum } (z_x z_y)}{N} \qquad (4)$$

The variable z_x is the *z*-score corresponding to *X*; z_y is the *z*-score corresponding to *Y*. To find *r,* each *X* and *Y* score must first be converted to a *z*-score by subtracting the mean and then dividing by the standard deviation. Then the product of z_x and z_y is found for each pair of scores. The average of these products (the sum of the products divided by *N,* the number of pairs of scores) is the correlation coefficient *r.*

Figure A.7 illustrates why this procedure yields positive values of *r* for positively related variables and negative values of *r* for negatively related variables. For positively correlated variables, most points are either above or below the mean on both variables. If they are above the mean, both z_x and z_y will be positive; if they are below, both z_x and z_y will be negative. (This follows from the definition of a *z*-score.) In either case the product $z_x z_y$ will be positive, so *r* will be positive. For negatively correlated variables, most points that are above the mean on one variable are below the mean on the other—either z_x is positive and z_y is negative or vice versa. The product $z_x z_y$ is therefore negative, and so is *r.*

INTERPRETING AND MISINTERPRETING CORRELATIONS

It is tempting, but false, to assume that if two variables are correlated, one is the cause of the other. There is a positive correlation between years of education and annual income in the population of North American adults;

many people, including some educators, argue from these data that students should stay in school as long as possible in order to increase their eventual earning power. The difficulty with this reasoning is not the existence of counterexamples (such as Andrew Carnegie, the American industrialist and millionaire who never finished high school), which merely show that the correlation is less than 1.00. It is rather that it is difficult to infer causality from this correlation because both variables are correlated with yet a third variable. Years of schooling and income as an adult are not only correlated with each other, they are also correlated with a third variable–the parents income. Given this fact, can we make any assertions about what causes adult income? Perhaps income is determined by one's education (it probably is, in part). But perhaps the relationship between income and education is a spurious byproduct of the parents' income. Perhaps this third factor partially determines both one's education and one's income, and there is no real causal connection between the two.

Another demonstration of the fact that correlation is not equivalent to causation occurs while waiting for a bus or a subway whose schedule is unknown. There is a negative correlation between the number of minutes a rider will have to wait for the next subway and the number of people waiting when the rider enters the station: The more people who are waiting, the sooner the subway will arrive. This negative correlation is fairly substantial, but even so, one would hardly try to cut down one's waiting time by arriving at the station with fifty friends. Here, the third, causal variable (time since the last train or bus left) is fairly obvious.* But even when it is harder to imagine just what the third variable might be, it is still possible that such a third variable exists and is responsible for the correlation. As a result, correlations can never provide solid evidence of a causal link.

INTERPRETING DATA: INFERENTIAL STATISTICS

We have seen that a psychologist collecting data encounters variability. In memory experiments, for example, different individuals recall different numbers of items, and the same person is likely to perform differently when tested twice. An investigator wishes to draw general conclusions from data in spite of this variability, or to discover the factors that are responsible for it.

ACCOUNTING FOR VARIABILITY

As an example of how variability may be explained, consider a person shooting a pistol at a target. Although he always aims at the bull's eye, the shots scatter around it (Figure A.8A). Assuming that the mean is the bull's eye, the variance of these shots is the average squared deviation of the shots from the center; suppose this variance is 100.

Now we set about explaining the variance. If the shooting was done outdoors, the wind may have increased the spread; moving the shooter to an indoor shooting range produces the tighter grouping shown in Figure A.8B. The new

* I thank Barry Schwartz for this example.

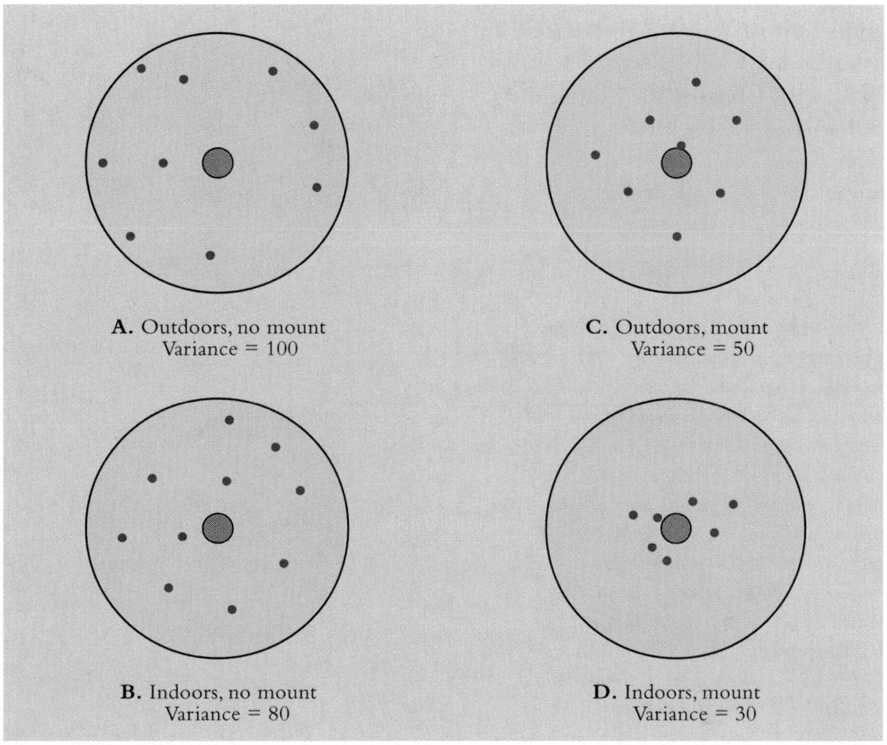

A. Outdoors, no mount
Variance = 100

C. Outdoors, mount
Variance = 50

B. Indoors, no mount
Variance = 80

D. Indoors, mount
Variance = 30

A.8 Results of target shooting under several conditions   *In each case, the bull's eye is the mean, and the variance is the average squared deviation of the shots from the bull's eye.*

variance is 80, a reduction of 20 percent—this means that the wind accounts for 20 percent of the original variance. Some of the variance may result from the unsteady hand of the shooter, so we now mount the gun. This yields a variance of 50 (Figure A.8C), a reduction of 50 percent, so 50 percent of the variance can be attributed to the shaky hand of the shooter. To find out how much of the variance can be accounted for by both the wind and the shaking, we mount the gun *and* move it indoors; now we may find a variance of only 30 (Figure A.8D). This means we have explained 70 percent of the variance, leaving 30 percent unaccounted for.★ Not all changes in the situation will reduce the variance. For example, if we find that providing the shooter with earmuffs leaves the variance unchanged, we know that none of the original variance was due to the noise of the pistol.

VARIANCE AND EXPERIMENTS

Figure A.9 (on the next page) shows how this approach can be applied to the experiment on visual imagery described earlier (see page A4). Figure A.9A shows the distribution of scores for all twenty subjects in the experiment lumped together; the total variance of this overall distribution is 6.25. But as we saw, ten of these subjects had been instructed to use visual imagery in memorizing, whereas another ten control subjects were given no special instructions. How much of the overall variance can be accounted for by the difference in these instructions? In Figure A.9B, the distributions are no longer lumped together. They are instead presented as two separate histograms; the subjects who received imagery instructions are shown in blue, while those who did not are indicated in rust. As the figure shows, there is less variability with either the imagery group or the control group than in the overall distribution that lumped both kinds of subjects together. While the variance in the overall distribution is

★ I am grateful to Paul Rozin for suggesting this example.

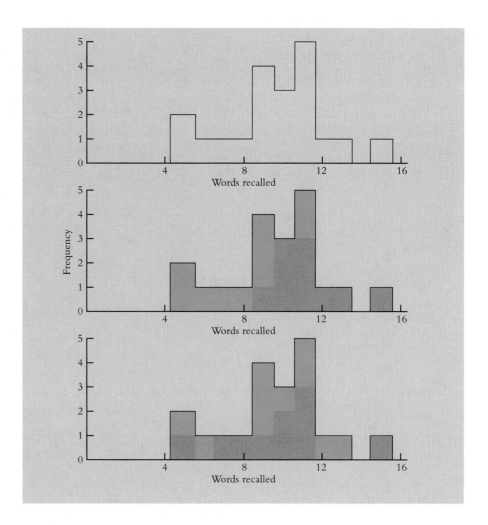

A.9 Accounting for variance in an experiment on memorizing *(A) The distribution of number of words recalled is shown for all twenty subjects lumped together; the variance of this distribution is 6.25. (B) The distributions of the experimental and control groups are displayed separately. The number of words recalled by the group that received imagery instructions is shown in blue; the number recalled by the control group that received no special instructions is shown in rust. Within each of these groups, the variance is about 4.00. (C) The distribution of words recalled is plotted separately for men and women regardless of how they were instructed. Blue indicates the number of words recalled by women, rust the number recalled by men. The variance is 6.25.*

6.25, the variance within the two subgroups averages to only 4.0. We conclude that the difference between the instructions the subjects were given accounted for 36 percent of the variance and that 64 percent (4 ÷ 6.25) still remains unexplained.

Figure A.9C shows a situation in which an independent variable (in this case, sex) accounts for little or none of the variance. In this figure, the subjects' scores are again presented as two separate histograms—one for the scores of the men (regardless of whether they were instructed to use imagery or not) and the other for the scores of the women (again, regardless of the instructions they received). The men's scores are shown in rust, the women's, in blue. Now the variance of the two subgroups (that is, men vs. women) averages to 6.25, a value identical to that found for the overall distribution. We conclude that the subject's sex accounts for none of the overall variance in memorizing performance.

VARIANCE AND CORRELATION

The technique of explaining the variance in one variable by attributing it to the effect of another variable can also be applied to correlational studies. Here, the values of one variable are explained (that is, accounted for) when the values of the other variable are known. Recall the taxicab example. In it a correlation of .46 was found between taxi drivers' earnings and their scores on a screening test. Since the correlation is neither perfect nor zero, some but not all of the variance in job performance can be explained by the aptitude test scores. The greater the magnitude of the correlation coefficient, r, the more variance is accounted for. The rule is that the proportion of variance that is explained equals r^2. If $r = .46$, one variable accounts for $(.46)^2 = .21$ of the variance of the other. (Just why this proportion is r^2 is beyond the scope of this discussion.) To put this another way, suppose all the cab drivers were identical on the one variable, their performance on the geographical text. This means that the variance on that variable would be zero. As a result, the variability on the second variable, earnings, would be reduced. The formula tells us by how much. The original variance on earnings can be determined from the data in Figure A.6A. It is 4. Its correlation with the geography test is .46. Since the effect of this variable, the geography test, is completely controlled, the variability on earnings will be $4 - (.46)^2 \times 4 = 3.16$. The drop in the variance from 4 to 3.16 is a reduction of 21 percent. The aptitude test does help us to predict taxicab earnings, for it accounts for 21 percent of the variance. But a good deal of the variance, 79 percent, is still unexplained.

HYPOTHESIS TESTING

Much behavioral research attempts to answer two-alternative questions. Does the amount of food a person eats depend on the effort required to eat it? Can people learn while they are sleeping? Is drug X more effective than aspirin? Each of these questions suggests an experiment, and the procedures described in the previous section could be used to discover how much of the variance in the dependent variable could be accounted for by the independent variable. But how can the results of such experiments lead to simple yes-or-no answers to the questions that inspired them?

TESTING HYPOTHESES ABOUT SINGLE SCORES

We will begin by testing a hypothesis about single scores. Consider the problem in interpreting a lie-detector test. In such a test, a person is asked a series of questions and various measures of physiological arousal are taken as he answers. An answer that is accompanied by an unusually high degree of arousal is taken as possible evidence that the person is lying. The question is how high is "unusually high?"

To answer this question we will first rephrase it. Can we reject the hypothesis that the given score came from the distribution of responses the same individual gave to neutral questions? (An example is "Is your name Fred?") Suppose the average arousal score to such control questions is 50, that the standard deviation of these neutral responses is 10, and that the arousal scores are normally distributed. We now look at the arousal score to the critical item. Let us say that this is 60. How likely is it that this score is from a sample drawn by chance from the population of responses to neutral questions? To find out, we convert it to a z-score by computing its distance from the mean and dividing it by the standard deviation. The resulting z-score is $(60 - 50)/10$ or 1. Since the distribution is normal, Figure A.3 tells us that 16 percent of this person's arousal scores would be as high or higher than this. Under the circumstances we don't feel justified in rejecting the hypothesis that the score in question comes from the distribution of neutral responses. Put another way, we don't feel justified in accusing the person of lying. Our feelings might be different if the score were 70 or above. For now the z-score is $(70 - 50)/10$ or 2 standard deviations above the mean of the neutral distribution. The chances that a score this high or higher is from a sample drawn from the population of neutral responses is only 2 in 100. We might now feel more comfortable in rejecting the hypothesis that this score is simply a chance event. We are more likely to assume that it is drawn from another distri-bution—in short, that the person is lying.

In this example we had to decide between two hypotheses. We looked at a given score (or a set of scores) obtained under a particular experimental condi-tion (in this case, a loaded question). One hypothesis is that the experimental condition has no effect, that the score is merely a reflection of the ordinary vari-ability around the mean of a control condition (in this case, neutral questions). This is the **null hypothesis,** the hypothesis that there really is no effect. The **alternative hypothesis** is that the null hypothesis is false, that the score is far enough away from the control mean so that we can assume that the same exper-imental condition has some effect. To decide between these two hypotheses, the data are expressed as a *z*-score, which in the context of hypothesis testing is called a **critical ratio.** Behavioral scientists generally accept a critical ratio of 2 as the cutoff point. If this ratio is 2 or greater, they generally reject the null hypothesis and assume there is an effect of the experimental condition. (Such critical ratios of 2 or more are said to be **statistically significant,** which is just another way of saying that the null hypothesis can be rejected.) Critical ratios of less than 2 are considered too small to allow the rejection of the null hypothesis.

This general procedure is not foolproof. It is certainly possible for a subject in the lie-detection example to have an arousal score of 70 (a critical ratio of 2) or higher even though he is telling the truth. According to Figure A.3, this will happen about 2 percent of the time, and the person administering the test will erroneously "detect" a lie. Raising the cutoff value to the critical ratio of 3 or 4 would make such errors less common, but would not eliminate them entirely; furthermore, such a high critical value might mean failure to discover any lies the subject does utter. One of the important consequences of the variability in psychological data can be seen here: The investigator who has to decide between two interpretations of the data (the null hypothesis and the alternative hypothesis) cannot be correct all the time.

TESTING HYPOTHESES ABOUT MEANS

In the preceding discussion, our concern was with hypotheses about single scores. We now turn to the more commonly encountered problems in which the hypotheses involve means.

In many experiments, the investigator compares two or more groups—sub-jects tested with or without a drug, with or without imagery instructions, and so on. Suppose we get a difference between the two groups. How do we decide whether the difference is genuine rather than a mere chance fluctuation?

Let us return to the experiment in which memory for words was tested with and without instructions to imagine the items visually. To simplify the exposi-tion, we will here consider a modified version of the experiment in which the same subjects serve in both the imagery and the nonimagery conditions. Each subject memorizes a list of 20 words without instructions, then memorizes a second list of 20 words under instructions to visualize. What we want to know is whether the subjects show any improvement with imagery instructions. There is no separate control group in this experiment, but, because a subject's score in the imagery condition can be compared with her score in the uninstructed con-dition, each subject provides her own control.

Table A.6 gives data for the ten subjects in the experiment. For each subject, the table lists the number of words recalled without imagery instructions, the number recalled with such instructions, and the improvement (the difference between the two scores). The mean improvement overall is 3 words, from a mean of 8 words recalled without imagery to a mean of 11 words with imagery. But note that this does not hold for all subjects. For example, for Fred and

TABLE A.6 NUMBER OF ITEMS RECALLED WITH AND WITHOUT IMAGERY INSTRUCTION, FOR 10 SUBJECTS

Subject	Score with imagery	Score without imagery	Improvement
Alphonse	11	5	6
Betsy	15	9	6
Cheryl	11	5	6
Davis	9	9	0
Earl	13	6	7
Fred	10	11	−1
Germaine	11	8	3
Hortense	10	11	−1
Imogene	8	7	1
Jerry	12	9	3
Mean	11	8	3

Variance of improvement scores $= \dfrac{\text{sum of } (\text{score} - 3)^2}{10} = 8.8$

Standard deviation of improvement scores $= \sqrt{8.8} = 2.97$

Hortense, the "improvement" is negative—they both do better without imagery instructions. The question is whether we can conclude that there is an imagery facilitation effect overall. Put in other words, is the difference between the two conditions statistically significant?

To show how this question is answered, we will follow much the same logic as that used in the analysis of the lie-detection problem. We have a mean—the average difference score of ten subjects. What we must realize is that this mean—3—is really a sample based on the one experiment with the ten subjects we have just run. Suppose we had run the experiment again, with another set of ten subjects—not just once, but many times. Each such repetition of the experiment would yield its own mean. And each of these means would constitute another sample. But what is the population to which these samples refer? It is the set of all of these means—the average differences between imagery and non-imagery instructions obtained in each of the many repetitions of the experiment we might possibly perform. And the mean of these means—a kind of grand mean—is the mean of the population. Any conclusions we want to draw from our experiment are really assertions about this population mean. If we say that the difference we found is statistically significant, we are asserting that the population mean is a difference score that is greater than zero (and in the same direction as in the sample). Put another way, we are asserting that the difference we found is not just a fluke but is real and would be obtained again and again if we repeated the experiment, thus rejecting the null hypothesis.

The null hypothesis amounts to the claim that the mean we actually obtained could have been drawn by chance from a distribution of sample means (that is, the many means of the possible repetitions of our experiment) around a population mean of zero. To test this claim, we have to compute a critical ratio that can tell us how far from zero our own mean actually is. Like all critical ratios, this is a z-score that expresses the distance of a score from a mean in units of the standard deviation (the SD). Thus, $z = (\text{score} - M)/SD$. In our present case, the score is our obtained mean (that is, 3); the mean is the hypothetical population mean of zero (assumed by the null hypothesis). But what is the denominator? It is the standard deviation of the distribution of sample means, the means of the many experiments we might have done.

The standard deviation of such a distribution of sample means is called the *standard error* of the mean *(SE)*. Its value is determined by two factors: the standard deviation of the sample and the size of that sample. Specifically,

$$SE = \frac{SD}{\sqrt{N-1}} \qquad (5)$$

It is clear that the variability of a mean (and this is what the standard error measures) goes down with increasing sample size. (Why this factor turns out to be $\sqrt{N-1}$ is beyond the scope of this discussion.) A clue as to why comes from the consideration of the effects of an atypical score. Purely by chance, a sample may include an extreme case. But the larger the size of that sample, the less the effect of an extreme case on the average. If a sample of three people includes a midget, the average height will be unusually far from the population mean. But in a sample of 3,000, one midget will not affect the average very markedly.

We can now conclude our analysis of the results of the memorization experiment. The critical ratio to be evaluated is:

$$\text{Critical Ratio} = \frac{\text{obtained sample mean} - \text{population mean}}{SE}$$

Since the population mean is assumed to be zero (by the null hypothesis), this expression becomes:

$$\text{Critical Ratio} = \frac{\text{obtained sample mean}}{SE} \qquad (6)$$

This critical ratio expresses the mean difference between the two experimental conditions in units of the variability of the sample mean, that is, the standard error.★ To compute the standard error, we first find the standard deviation of the improvement scores; this turns out to be 2.97, as shown in Table A.6. Then equation (5) tells us

$$SE = \frac{SD}{\sqrt{N-1}} = \frac{2.97}{\sqrt{10-1}} = .99$$

The critical ratio is now the obtained mean difference divided by the standard error, or $3/.99 = 3.03$. This is clearly larger than 2.0, so we conclude that the observed difference in memory between the imagery and control conditions is much too great to be attributed to chance factors. Thus, using visual imagery evidently does improve recall.

CONFIDENCE INTERVALS

In statistical hypothesis testing we ask whether a certain sample mean could be drawn by chance from a distribution of sample means around some assumed

---

★ There are several simplifications in this account. One is that the critical ratio described here does not have an exactly normal distribution. When the sample size is large, this effect is unimportant, but for small samples (like the one in the example) they can be material. To deal with these and related problems, statisticians often utilize measures that refer to distributions other than the normal one. An example is the *t*-test, a kind of critical ratio based on what is called the *t*-distribution.

A.10 A candidate's poll results and her confidence intervals *The results of a mythical poll conducted for a no-less-mythical presidential candidate Smith by randomly sampling 200 people in each of five regions of the United States. The figure shows the pro-Smith proportions in each region, together with the confidence intervals around them, and indicates that she is ahead in all five samples. But there are two regions where she cannot be confident that she is ahead in the population—the South and the Southwest, where the confidence intervals of the pro-Smith proportion dip below 50 percent.*

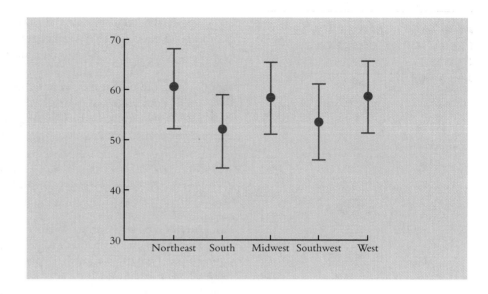

population mean. (When testing the null hypothesis, this assumed population mean is zero.) But there is another way of phrasing this question. Can we be reasonably confident that the mean of the population falls within a certain specified interval? If we know the standard error of the mean, the answer is yes. We have already seen that about 2 percent of the scores in a normal distribution are more than two standard deviations above and about 2 percent are lower than two standard deviations below the mean of that distribution. Since this is so, we can conclude that the chances are roughly 4 in 100 that the population mean is within an interval whose largest value is two standard errors above the sample mean and whose lowest value is two standard errors below. Because we can be fairly (96 percent) confident that the actual population mean will fall within this specified range, it is often called the **confidence interval.**

As an example, consider the prediction of political elections. During election campaigns, polling organizations report the current standing of various candidates by statements such as the following: "In a poll of 1,000 registered voters, 57 percent favored candidate Smith; the margin of error was 3 percent." This margin of error is the confidence interval around the proportion (that is, ± 3 percent).

To determine this confidence interval, the pollsters compute the standard error of the proportion they found. (In this case, .57). This standard error is analogous to the standard error of a mean we discussed in the previous section. Given an N of 1,000, this standard error happens to be .015.★ Since 2 × .015 is .03 or 3 percent, the appropriate confidence interval for our example is the interval from 54 to 60 percent. Under the circumstances, candidate Smith can be fairly confident that she has the support of at least 50 percent of the electorate since 50 percent is well *below* the poll's confidence interval (see Figure A.10).

★ The standard error of a proportion (e.g., the proportion of polled voters who express pro-X sentiments) is analogous to the standard error of the mean, and measures the precision with which our sample proportion estimates the population proportion. The formula for the standard error of a proportion p is:

$$SE_p = \sqrt{\frac{p \times (1 - p)}{N}}$$

In our example, $p = .57$ and $N = 1,000$, so $SE_p = .015$.

SOME IMPLICATIONS OF STATISTICAL INFERENCE

■ The methods of testing hypotheses and estimating confidence intervals that we just described are routinely employed in evaluating the results of psychological research. But they have several characteristics that necessarily affect the interpretation of all such results.

THE PROBABILISTIC NATURE OF HYPOTHESIS TESTING AND CONFIDENCE INTERVALS

Since there is always some unexplained variance in any psychological study, there is always some probability that the conclusions are wrong as applied to the population. If we use a confidence interval of ± 2 SE, the chances that the population mean (or proportion, or whatever) falls outside of that interval are less than 4 or 5 in 100. Do we want to be more confident than this? If so, we might use a confidence interval of ± 3 SE, where the equivalent chance is only 1 in 1,000. The same holds for critical ratios. We can say that a critical ratio of 2 means that a difference is statistically significant, but that only means that the chances are less than 2 in 100 that the difference as large or larger than this arose by chance. If we want to be more certain than this, we must insist that the critical ratio be larger—perhaps 3 (a chance factor of 1 in 2,000) or 4 (5 in 100,000), and so on. As long as there is some unexplained variance, there is some chance of error.

The probabilistic nature of statistical reasoning has another consequence. Even if we can come to a correct conclusion about the mean of a population (or a proportion, as in polls), we cannot generalize to individuals. Thus, a study which shows that men have higher scores than women on spatial relations tests is not inconsistent with the existence of brilliant female artists or architects. Sample means for the two groups can differ significantly, even though there is considerable overlap in the two distributions of scores.

THE CONSERVATIVE NATURE OF HYPOTHESIS TESTING

Another characteristic of statistical hypothesis testing is that it is essentially conservative. This is because of the great stress placed on the null hypothesis in reaching a decision: One has to be quite sure that the null hypothesis is false before one entertains the alternative hypothesis. There are other imaginable strategies for reaching statistical decisions, but the conservative one has a perfectly rational basis. Let's suppose that some independent variable *does* produce a difference between two groups that is quite genuine and not the result of chance, but that the critical ratio is too low to reject the null hypothesis. If so, we will have falsely concluded that no difference exists in the population. As a result, we will have failed to discover a small effect. But what of it? If the effect is interesting enough, someone else may well attempt a similar experiment and manage to find the difference we didn't uncover. On the other hand, suppose we "discover" that some independent variable has an effect when it actually does not (that is, the null hypothesis is true). By falsely rejecting the null hypothesis, we will have added an inaccurate "fact" to the store of scientific knowledge and run the risk of leading other investigators up a blind alley.

THE ROLE OF SAMPLE SIZE

A last point concerns the role of sample size in affecting the interpretations of results. The larger the sample, the smaller the standard error and the smaller the confidence interval around the mean or the proportion. This can have major effects on hypothesis testing.

Suppose that, in the population, a certain independent variable produces a very small difference. As an example, suppose that the population difference between men and women on a certain test of spatial relations is 1 percent. We would probably be unable to reject the null hypothesis (that there is no sex difference on the test) with samples of moderate size. But if the sample size were sufficiently increased, we could reject the null hypothesis. For such a sizable increase in N would lead to a decrease in the standard errors of the sample means, which in turn would lead to an increase in the critical ratio. Someone who read a report of this experiment would now learn that, by using thousands of subjects, we discovered a "significant" difference of 1 percent. A fair reaction to this bit of intelligence would be that the null hypothesis can indeed be rejected, but that the *psychological* significance of this finding is rather slight. The moral is simple. Statistical significance is required before a result can be considered reliable, but this statistical significance does not guarantee that the effect discovered is of psychological significance or of any practical importance.

SUMMARY

1. Statistical methods concern the ways in which investigators describe, gather, organize, and interpret collections of numerical data. A crucial concern of statistical endeavors is to deal with the variability that is encountered in all research.

2. An early step in the process is *scaling,* a procedure for assigning numbers to psychological responses. Scales can be *categorical, ordinal, interval,* or *ratio scales.* These differ in the degree to which they can be subjected to arithmetical operations.

3. There are three main methods for conducting psychological research: by means of an *experiment,* an *observational study,* or a *case study.* In an experiment, the investigator manipulates the *independent variable* to see how it affects the subject's response, the *dependent variable.* In an observational study, the investigator does not manipulate any variables directly but rather observes them as they occur naturally. A case study is an investigation in which one person is studied in depth.

4. An important distinction in psychological research is that between *sample* and *population.* The population is the entire group about which the investigator wants to draw conclusions. The sample is the subset (usually small) of that population that is actually tested. Generalizations from sample to population are only possible if the one is representative of the other. This requires the use of *random samples.* In some cases a special version of the random sample, the *stratified sample,* may be employed.

5. A first step in organizing the data is to arrange them in a *frequency distribution,* often displayed in graphic form, as in a *histogram.* Frequency distributions are characterized by a *central tendency* and by *variability* around this central tendency. The common measure of central tendency is the *mean,* though sometimes another measure, the *median,* may be preferable, as in cases when the distribution is *skewed.* Important measures of variability are the *variance* and the *standard deviation.*

6. One way of comparing two scores drawn from different distributions is to convert both into *percentile ranks.* Another is to transform them into *z-scores,* which express the

distance of a score from its mean in standard deviation units. The percentile rank of a z-score can be computed if the shape of that score's distribution is known. An important example is the *normal distribution*, graphically displayed by the *normal curve*, which describes the distribution of many psychological variables and is basic to much of statistical reasoning.

7. In observational studies, the relation between variables is often expressed in the form of a *correlation*, which may be positive or negative. It is measured by the *correlation coefficient*, a number that can vary from +1.00 to −1.00. While correlations reflect the extent to which two variables vary together, they do not necessarily indicate that one of them causes the other.

8. A major task of any investigator is to explain the variability of some dependent variable, usually measured by the variance. One means for doing so is to see whether that variance is reduced when a certain independent variable is controlled. If so, this independent variable is said to account for some of the variability of the dependent variable.

9. One of the main functions of statistical methods is to help test hypotheses about a population given information about the sample. An important example is the difference between mean scores obtained under two different conditions. Here the investigator has to decide between the *null hypothesis*, which asserts that the difference was obtained by chance, and the *alternative hypothesis*, which asserts that the difference is genuine and exists in the population. The decision is made by dividing the obtained mean difference by the *standard error*, a measure of the variability of that mean difference. If the resulting ratio, called the *critical ratio*, is large enough, the null hypothesis is rejected, the alternative hypothesis is accepted, and the difference is said to be *statistically significant*. A related way of making statistical decisions is by using a *confidence interval*, or margin of error. This is based on the variability of the scores from a sample and determines the interval within which the population mean or proportion probably falls.

GLOSSARY

abnormal psychology *See* psychopathology.

absolute threshold The lowest intensity of some stimulus that produces a response.

accessory structures In sensory processing, the parts of sensory systems that gather external stimulus energies and fashion the proximal stimulus, which the receptors then transduce.

accommodation (1) The process by which the lens is thickened or flattened to focus on an object. (2) In Piaget's theory of development, one of the twin processes that underlies cognitive development. *See* assimilation and accommodation.

accommodative distortion Retrospective alterations of memory to fit a schema. *See also* schema.

acetylcholine A neurotransmitter found in many parts of the nervous system. Among many other functions, it serves as an excitatory transmitter at the synaptic junctions between muscle fibers and motor neurons.

achromatic colors Colors that do not have the property of hue, such as black, white, and the neutral grays.

across-fiber theory The theory that a certain sensory quality is signaled by the pattern of neural activity across a number of different nerve fibers.

action potential A brief change in the electrical potential of an axon, which is the physical basis of the nervous impulse.

activation-synthesis hypothesis A modern account which holds that dreams are a reflection of the brain's aroused state during REM sleep, when the cerebral cortex is active but shut off from sensory input. This helps explain the content and often disjointed form of dreams.

active memory *See* working memory.

active sleep (or REM sleep) A stage of sleep during which the EEG is similar to that of the waking brain; in this stage there are rapid eye movements (REMs) and dreams occur.

actor-observer difference The difference in attributions made by actors who describe their own actions and observers who describe another person's. The former emphasizes external, situational causes; the latter, internal, dispositional factors. *See also* attribution theory, fundamental attribution error, self-serving bias.

acuity The ability to distinguish between separate points projected on the retina. Acuity is greatest in the fovea, where the receptors are closely bunched together.

adaptation The process by which the sensitivity to a particular stimulus declines when it is continually presented.

adaptive value In biological terms, the extent to which an attribute increases the likelihood of viable offspring. Also, the unit of inheritance.

addiction The result of repeated drug use. The consequences are increased tolerance and withdrawal symptoms, which cause addiction to be self-perpetuating.

additive color mixture Mixing colors by stimulating the eye with two sets of wavelengths simultaneously (e.g., by focusing filtered light from two projectors on the same spot). *See also* subtractive color mixture.

adequate stimulus An electrical pulse above the threshold, or critical point, that induces an action potential in a neuron.

adrenaline *See* epinephrine.

adrenal medulla The inner core of the adrenal gland, which regulates the release of epinephrine (adrenaline) and norepinephrine into the bloodstream.

affective disorders *See* mood disorders.

afferent nerves Sensory nerves that carry messages to the brain.

agnosia A serious disturbance in the organization of sensory information produced by lesions in certain cortical association areas. An example is visual agnosia in which the patient can see but often does not recognize what it is that he sees.

agonists Drugs that enhance the activity of a neurotransmitter, often by increasing the amount of transmitter substance available (e.g., by blocking reuptake or by increasing the availability of precursors).

agoraphobia The fear of being alone and outside of the home, especially in a public place; often observed in those with panic disorder.

alarm call Special, genetically programmed cry that impels members of a given species to seek cover. A biological puzzle, since it suggests a form of altruism in which the individual appears to endanger his own survival. *See also* altruism.

algorithm In computer problem solving, a procedure in which all of the operations are specified step-by-step. *See also* heuristics.

all-or-none law A law that describes the fact that once a stimulus exceeds threshold, further increases do not increase the amplitude of the action potential.

alpha blocking The disruption of the alpha rhythm by visual stimulation or by active thought with the eyes closed.

alpha waves Fairly regular EEG waves, between eight to twelve per second, characteristic of a relaxed, waking state, usually with eyes closed.

alternative hypothesis In statistics, the hypothesis that the null hypothesis is false, that an obtained difference is so far from zero that one has to assume that the mean difference in the population is greater than zero and that the experimental condition has some effect. *See also* null hypothesis.

altruism (1) Acting so as to elevate the interests and welfare of others above one's own. (2) As used by sociobiologists, any behavior pattern that benefits individuals who are not one's own offspring (e.g., an alarm call). According to the kin-selection hypothesis, such altruism has biological survival value because the altruist's beneficiaries tend to be close relatives who carry a high proportion of his or her own genes. According to the reciprocal altruism hypothesis, altruism is based on the expectation that today's giver will be tomorrow's taker. *See also* alarm call.

Alzheimer's disease A degenerative brain disorder characterized by increasing memory loss followed by increasing disorientation and culminating in total physical and mental helplessness and death. One of the major sites of the destruction is a pathway of acetylcholine-releasing cells leading from the base of the forebrain to the cortex and hippocampus. *See also* acetylcholine.

ambiguity (in sentence meaning) The case in which a sentence (i.e., one surface structure) has two meanings (i.e., two underlying structures). (For example, "These missionaries are ready to eat" overheard in a conversation between two cannibals.)

American Sign Language (ASL) The manual-visual language system of deaf persons in America.

amphetamines Drugs that increase the availability of norepinephrine, causing increased arousal and excitement. Large doses may lead to frenetic hyperactivity and delusions.

amplitude The height of a wave crest.

anal character According to Freud, a personality type that derives from serious conflicts during the anal stage and is distinguished by three symptomatic traits: compulsive orderliness, stubbornness, and stinginess. *See also* anal stage.

analgesic A pain reliever.

analogical representation A representation that shares some of the physical characteristics of an object; for example, a picture of a mouse is an analogical representation because it looks like the small rodent it represents.

anal stage In psychoanalytic theory, the stage of psychosexual development during which the focus of pleasure is on activities related to elimination.

androgen Any male sex hormone.

angiotensin A substance produced by the kidneys when there is a decrease in the amount of liquid passing through them, activating receptors in the brain that monitor the volume of blood and other fluids in the body.

anomia A difficulty in finding words that is often experienced by people with brain injuries.

anorexia nervosa An eating disorder that primarily afflicts young women and that is characterized by an exaggerated concern with being overweight and by compulsive dieting, sometimes to the point of self-starvation and death. *See also* bulimia and obesity.

A-not-B effect The tendency of infants around nine months of age to search for a hidden object by reaching for place *A,* where it was previously hidden, rather than a new place *B,* where it was hidden most recently while the child was watching.

antagonists Drugs that impede the activity of a neurotransmitter, often by decreasing the amount available (e.g., by speeding reuptake and decreasing availability of precursors).

anterograde amnesia A memory deficit suffered after some brain damage. It is an inability to learn and remember any information imparted after the injury, with little effect on memory for information acquired previously. *See also* retrograde amnesia.

antidepressant drugs Drugs that alleviate depressive symptoms, presumably because they increase the availability of certain neurotransmitters (especially norepinephrine and serotonin) at synaptic junctions. The three major classes are monoamine oxidase (MAO) inhibitors, tricyclics, and selective serotonin reuptake inhibitors.

antidiuretic hormone (ADH) A hormone secreted by one of the parts of the pituitary gland. This hormone instructs the kidneys to reabsorb more of the water that passes through them. *See also* pituitary gland.

antipsychotic drugs Drugs, e.g., Thorazine and Haldol, that alleviate the psychotic patient's symptoms, such as thought disorders and hallucinations. Also known as major tranquilizers.

antisocial personality disorder Also called psychopathy or sociopathy. The term describes persons who get into continual trouble with society, are indifferent to others, are impulsive, and have little concern for the future or remorse about the past.

anxiety An emotional state akin to fear. According to Freud, many mental illnesses center around anxiety and on attempts to ward it off by various unconscious mechanisms.

anxiety disorders *See* generalized anxiety disorder, obsessive-compulsive disorders, phobia, specific phobia.

anxiety hierarchy *See* systematic desensitization.

anxiolytics More commonly known as tranquilizers, these drugs are given to patients suffering from disabling anxiety. Most types work by increasing the activity of the neurotransmitter GABA and are highly addictive.

aphagia Refusal to eat (and in an extreme version, to drink) brought about by a lesion of the lateral hypothalamus.

aphasia A disorder of language produced by lesions in certain association areas of the cortex. A lesion in Broca's area leads to expressive aphasia, one in Wernicke's area to receptive aphasia.

apparent movement The perception of movement produced by stimuli that are stationary but flash on and off at appropriate time intervals.

appetitive stimulus In instrumental conditioning, a stimulus that the animal will do everything to attain and nothing to prevent.

apraxia A serious disturbance in the organization of voluntary action produced by lesions in certain cortical association areas, often in the frontal lobes.

artificial intelligence A field that draws on concepts from both cognitive psychology and computer science to develop artificial systems that display some aspects of human-like intelligence. Examples are computer programs that recognize patterns or solve certain kinds of problems.

assimilation and accommodation In Piaget's theory, the twin processes by means of which cognitive development proceeds. Assimilation is the process whereby the environment is interpreted in terms of the schemas the child has at the time. Accommodation is the way the child changes her schemas as she continues to interact with the environment.

association A linkage between two psychological processes as a result of past experience in which the two have occurred together. A broad term that subsumes conditioning and association of ideas among others.

association areas Regions of the cortex that are not projection areas. They tend to be involved in the integration of sensory information or of motor commands.

attachment The tendency of the young of many species to stay in close proximity to an adult, usually their mother. *See also* imprinting.

attention A collective label for all the processes by which we perceive selectively.

attitude A fairly stable, evaluative disposition that makes a person think, feel, or behave positively or negatively about some person, group, or social issue.

attribution theory A theory about the process by which we try to explain a person's behavior, attributing it to situational factors or to inferred dispositional qualities or both.

attributional style The characteristic manner in which a person explains good or bad fortunes that befall him. A particular attributional style in which bad fortunes are generally attributed to internal, global, and stable causes may create a predisposition that makes a person vulnerable to depression. *See also* depression.

attribution-of-arousal theory An approach that combines the James-Lange emphasis on bodily feedback with a cognitive approach to emotion. Various stimuli can trigger a general state of arousal, which is then interpreted in light of the subject's present situation and shaped into a specific emotional experience.

authoritarian personality A cluster of personal attributes (e.g., submission to persons above and harshness to those below) and social attitudes (e.g., prejudice against minority groups), which is sometimes held to constitute a distinct personality.

authoritative-reciprocal pattern A pattern of child rearing in which parents exercise considerable power but also respond to the child's point of view and reasonable demands. Parents following this pattern set rules of conduct and are fairly demanding, but also encourage the child's independence and self-expression.

autocratic pattern A pattern of child rearing in which the parents control the child strictly, setting stern and usually unexplained rules whose infraction leads to severe, often physical, punishment.

automatization A process whereby components of a skilled activity become subsumed under a higher-order organization and are run off automatically.

autonomic nervous system (ANS) A part of the nervous system that controls the internal organs, usually not under voluntary control.

availability heuristic A rule of thumb often used to make probability estimates, which depends on the frequency with which certain events readily come to mind. This can lead to errors, since very vivid events will be remembered out of proportion to their actual frequency of occurrence.

aversion therapy A form of behavior therapy in which the undesirable response leads to an aversive stimulus (e.g., the patient shocks himself every time he reaches for a cigarette).

aversive stimulus In instrumental conditioning, a stimulus such as an electric shock, which the animal does everything to avoid and nothing to attain.

avoidance learning Instrumental learning in which the response averts an aversive stimulus before it occurs. This poses a problem: What is the reinforcement for this kind of learning? *See also* punishment training, escape learning.

axon Part of a neuron that transmits impulses to other neurons or effectors.

backward pairing A classical conditioning procedure in which the conditioned stimulus (CS) follows the unconditioned stimulus (US). *See also* forward pairing, simultaneous pairing.

Barnum effect Describes the fact that a description of one's personality will often be uncritically accepted as valid if it is stated in sufficiently general terms.

basal ganglia In the extrapyramidal motor system, a set of subcortical structures in the cerebrum that send messages to the spinal cord through the midbrain to modulate various motor functions.

base rate *See* representativeness heuristic.

basilar membrane *See* cochlea.

behavioral-cognitive approach to personality An approach that defines personality differences by the way in which different people act and think about their actions. It tends to emphasize situational determinants and prior learning in trying to explain how such differences come about. *See also* humanistic approach, psychodynamic approach, sociocultural approach, situationism, trait theory.

behaviorism A theoretical outlook that emphasizes the role of environment and of learning, and insists that people must be studied objectively and from the outside.

behavior therapy A general approach to psychological treatment which (1) holds that the disorders to which it addresses itself are produced by maladaptive learning and must be remedied by reeducation, (2) proposes techniques for this reeducation based on principles of learning and conditioning, (3) focuses on the maladaptive behaviors as such rather than on hypothetical unconscious processes of which they may be expressions.

belongingness in learning The fact that the ease with which associations are formed depends upon the items to be associated. This holds for classical conditioning in which some CS-US combinations are more effective than others (e.g., learned taste aversions) and for instrumental conditioning in which some response-reinforcer combinations work more easily than others (e.g., specific defense reactions in avoidance conditioning of species).

between-family differences A term often used in the discussion of the role of environment. It describes environmental differences that apply to entire families, such as differences in socioeconomic status, religion, or child-rearing attitudes. For personality attributes, these seem to be less important than within-family differences. *See also* within-family differences.

between-group heritability The extent to which variation between groups (as in the difference between the mean IQs of U.S. whites and blacks) is attributable to genetic factors. *See also* heritability, within-group heritability.

bidirectional activation models Models of pattern recognition in which elements are activated as well as inhibited from both lower levels (bottom-up processing) and higher levels (top-down processing).

binocular disparity An important cue for depth perception. Each eye obtains a different view of an object, the disparity becoming less pronounced the farther the object is from the observer.

bipolar cells The intermediate neural cells in the eye that are stimulated by the receptors and excite the ganglion cells.

bipolar disorder A mood disorder in which the patient swings from one emotional extreme to another, experiencing both manic and depressive episodes. Formerly called manic-depressive psychosis.

blindsight The ability of a person with a lesion in the visual cortex to reach toward or guess at the orientation of objects projected on the part of the visual field that corresponds to this lesion, even though they report that they can see absolutely nothing in that part of their visual field.

blind spot The region of the eye that contains no visual receptors and therefore cannot produce visual sensations.

blocking effect An effect produced when two conditioned stimuli, *A* and *B,* are both presented together with the unconditioned stimulus (US). If stimulus *A* has previously been associated with the unconditioned stimulus while *B* has not, the formation of an association between stimulus *B* and the US will be impaired (that is, blocked).

bottom-up processes *See* top-down processes.

brightness A perceived dimension of visual stimuli—the extent to which they appear light or dark.

brightness contrast The perceiver's tendency to exaggerate the physical difference in the light intensities of two adjacent regions. As a result, a gray patch looks brighter on a black background, darker on a white background.

brightness ratio The ratio between the light reflected by a region and the light reflected by the area that surrounds it. According to one theory, perceived brightness is determined by this ratio.

Broca's area *See* aphasia.

bulimia An eating disorder characterized by repeated binge-and-purge bouts. In contrast to anorexics, bulimics tend to be of roughly normal weight. *See also* anorexia nervosa, obesity.

bystander effect The phenomenon that underlies many examples of failing to help strangers in distress: The larger the group a person is in (or thinks he is in), the less likely he is to come to a stranger's assistance. One reason is diffusion of responsibility (no one thinks it is *his* responsibility to act).

case study An observational study in which one person is studied intensively.

catatonic schizophrenia A subcategory of schizophrenia. Its main symptoms are peculiar motor patterns, such as periods in which the patient is immobile and maintains strange positions for hours on end.

catecholamines A family of neurotransmitters that have an activating function, including epinephrine, norepinephrine, and dopamine.

categorical scale A scale that divides responses into categories that are not numerically related. *See also* interval scale, nominal scale, ordinal scale, ratio scale.

catharsis An explosive release of hitherto dammed-up emotions that is sometimes believed to have therapeutic effects.

CAT (Computerized Axial Tomography) scan A technique for examining brain structure in living humans by constructing a composite X-ray picture based on views from all different angles.

censorship in dreams *See* Freud's theory of dreams.

central nervous system (CNS) The brain and spinal cord.

central pattern generators (CPGs) Circuits in the nervous system that orchestrate lower level reflexes and other neural activities into larger, organized acts. CPGs instigate certain crucial basic actions, such as, chewing, breathing, locomotion, etc.

central route to persuasion *See* elaboration-likelihood model of persuasion.

central tendency The tendency of scores in a frequency distribution to cluster around a central value. *See also* measure of central tendency and variability.

central trait A trait that is associated with many other attributes of the person who is being judged. Warm and cold are central because they are important in determining overall impressions.

cerebellum Two small hemispheres that form part of the hindbrain and control muscular coordination and equilibrium.

cerebral cortex The outermost layer of the gray matter of the cerebral hemispheres.

cerebral hemispheres Two hemispherical structures that comprise the major part of the forebrain in mammals and serve as the main coordinating center of the nervous system.

childhood amnesia The failure to remember the events of our very early childhood. This is sometimes ascribed to massive change in retrieval cues, sometimes to different ways of encoding memories in early childhood.

chlorpromazine *See* phenothiazines.

choice reaction time A measure of the speed of mental processing in which the subject has to choose between one of several responses depending upon which stimulus is presented.

chromosomes Structures in the nucleus of each cell which contain the genes, the units of hereditary transmission. A human cell has 46 chromosomes, arranged in 23 pairs. One of these pairs consists of the sex chromosomes. In males, one member of the pair is an X-chromosome, the other a Y-chromosome. In females, both members are X-chromosomes. *See also* gene, X-chromosome.

chunking A process of reorganizing (or recoding) materials in memory which permits a number of items to be packed into a larger unit.

circadian rhythm A rhythm that spans about a twenty-four-hour day, such as that of the sleep-waking cycle. Circadian rhythms in humans originate from a clock circuit in the hypothalamus that is set by information from the optic nerve about whether it is day or night.

classical conditioning A form of learning in which a hitherto neutral stimulus, the conditioned stimulus (CS) is paired with an unconditioned stimulus (US) regardless of what the animal does. In effect, what has to be learned is the relation between these two stimuli. *See also* instrumental conditioning.

classical psychoanalysis The method developed by Sigmund Freud which assumes that a patient's ills stem from unconscious defenses against unacceptable urges that date back to early childhood.

client-centered therapy A humanistic psychotherapy developed by Carl Rogers. *See also* humanistic therapies.

closure A factor in visual grouping. The perceptual tendency to fill in gaps in a figure so that it looks closed.

cochlea A coiled structure in the inner ear which contains the basilar membrane whose deformation by sound-produced pressure stimulates the auditory receptors.

cocktail-party effect The effect one experiences in settings such as noisy parties, where one tunes in to the voice of the person one is talking to and filters out the other voices as background noise. This phenomenon is the model for studying selective attention based on listening to speech.

coding The translation of stimulus information into various dimensions of sensation (e.g., intensity and quality) that are actually experienced.

cognitive development Intellectual growth from infancy to adulthood.

cognitive dissonance An inconsistency among some experiences, beliefs, attitudes, or feelings. According to dissonance theory, this sets up an unpleasant state that people try to reduce by reinterpreting some part of their experiences to make them consistent with the others.

cognitive interpretation theory of emotions A theory proposed by Schachter and Singer which asserts that emotions are an interpretation of our own autonomic arousal in the light of the situation to which we attribute it. *See also* attribution theory.

cognitive map *See* cognitive theory.

cognitive neuropsychology A field in which evidence of damage to certain areas of the brain and corresponding behaviors are used to make inferences about underlying psychological functions.

cognitive theory A conception of human and animal learning which holds that both humans and animals acquire items of knowledge (cognitions) such as what is where (cognitive map) or what leads to what (expectancy). This contrasts with theories of instrumental learning such as Thorndike's or Skinner's which assert that learning consists of the strengthening or weakening of particular response tendencies.

cognitive therapy An approach to therapy that tries to change some of the patient's habitual modes of thinking about himself, his situation, and his future. It is related to behavior therapy because it regards such thought patterns as a form of behavior.

collectivism-individualism A dimension used to characterize the differences in the dominant personality patterns of different cultures. Collectivist societies emphasize the needs, demands, and values of the family and immediate community, whereas individualist societies emphasize an individual's private goals and aspirations.

common sense As used in the discussion of artificial intelligence, the term refers to an understanding of what is relevant to a problem and what is not.

complementary colors Two colors that, when additively mixed with each other in the right proportions, produce the sensation of gray.

compulsions *See* obsessive-compulsive disorder.

concept A class or category that subsumes a number of individual instances. An important way of relating concepts is through propositions, which make some assertion that relates a subject (e.g., *chickens*) and a predicate (e.g., *lay eggs*).

concordance The probability that a person who stands in a particular familial relationship to a patient (e.g., an identical twin) has the same disorder as the patient.

concrete operational period In Piaget's theory, the period from ages six or seven to about eleven. At this time, the child has acquired mental operations that allow her to abstract some essential attributes of reality, such as number and substance; but these operations are as yet applicable only to concrete events and cannot be considered entirely in the abstract.

conditioned emotional response (CER) A technique in which a conditioned stimulus evokes fear, which in turn suppresses whatever other activities that the animal is currently engaged in. For example, a rat will no longer press a lever for a food reward after several trials involving a light or tone that precedes an electrical shock.

conditioned reflex *See* conditioned response.

conditioned reinforcer An initially neutral stimulus that acquires reinforcing properties through pairing with another stimulus that is already reinforcing.

conditioned response (CR) A response elicited by some initially neutral stimulus, the conditioned stimulus (CS), as a result of pairings between that CS and an unconditioned stimulus (US). This CR is typically not identical with the unconditioned response though it often is similar to it. *See also* conditioned stimulus, unconditioned response, unconditioned stimulus.

conditioned stimulus (CS) In classical conditioning, the stimulus which comes to elicit a new response by virtue of pairings with the unconditioned stimulus. *See also* conditioned response, unconditioned response, unconditioned stimulus.

cones Visual receptors that respond to greater light intensities and give rise to chromatic (color) sensations.

confidence interval An interval around a sample mean or proportion within which the population mean or proportion is likely to fall. In common practice, the largest value of the interval is 2 standard errors above the mean or proportion, and the smallest value is 2 standard errors below it.

confirmation bias The tendency to seek evidence to confirm one's hypothesis rather than to look for evidence to see whether the hypothesis is false.

conformity The act of going along with what other people think or do. Evidence suggests that there are two main reasons people conform: the desire to be right and the desire to be liked.

conjunction of features In a visual search procedure, a target that is composed of several different features (i.e., a red X as opposed to the feature red or the feature diagonal). Search times required to find these kinds of targets are longer and increase with the number of distractors that are displayed.

conservation of number In Piaget's theory, the understanding that the number of objects in a group remains constant despite their spatial arrangement (e.g., a child at age six realizes that there is the same number of objects in a row of six closely spaced bottles as in a row of six bottles spaced far apart).

conservation of quantity In Piaget's theory, the understanding that the quantity of a substance remains unchanged despite a visible change in appearance (thus in liquid conservation, the realization that the amount of liquid remains the same when poured from a tall, thin beaker into a short, wide jar).

construct validity The extent to which performance on a test fits into a theoretical scheme about the attribute the test tries to measure.

content morphemes Morphemes that carry the main burden of meaning (e.g., *strange*). This is in contrast to function morphemes that add details to the meaning but also serve various grammatical purposes (e.g., the suffixes *s* and *er*, the connecting words *and, or, if,* and so on).

context effects *See* top-down processes.

contiguity The togetherness in time of two events, which is sometimes regarded as the condition that leads to association.

contingency A relation between two events in which one is dependent upon another. If the contingency is greater than zero, then the probability of event *A* will be greater when event *B* is present than when it is absent.

control group A group to which the experimenter's manipulation is not applied.

convergence The movement of the eyes as they swivel toward each other to focus upon an object.

conversion disorders Formerly called conversion hysteria. A condition in which there are physical symptoms that seem to have no physical basis. They instead appear to be linked to psychological factors and are often believed to serve as a means of reducing anxiety. *See also* hysteria.

conversion hysteria *See* conversion disorders.

corpus callosum A bundle of fibers that connects the two cerebral hemispheres.

correct negative See payoff matrix.

correlation The tendency of two variables to vary together. If one goes up as the other goes up, the correlation is positive; if one goes up as the other goes down, the correlation is negative.

correlation coefficient A number, referred to as *r,* that expresses both the size and the direction of a correlation, varying from +1.00 (perfect positive correlation) through 0.00 (absence of any correlation) to −1.00 (perfect negative correlation).

counterconditioning A procedure for weakening a classically conditioned CR by connecting the stimuli that presently evoke it to a new response that is incompatible with the CR.

criterion groups Groups whose test performance sets the validity criterion for certain tests (e.g., the Minnesota Multiphasic Personality Inventory, MMPI, which uses several psychiatric criterion groups to define most of its subscales).

critical period A period in the development of an organism when it is particularly sensitive to certain environmental influences. Outside of this period, the same environmental influences have little effect (e.g., the period during which a duckling can be imprinted). After embryonic development, this phenomenon is rarely all-or-none. As a result, most developmental psychologists prefer the term *sensitive period*.

critical ratio A *z*-score used for testing the null hypothesis. It is obtained by dividing an obtained mean difference by the standard error *(SE)* so that critical ratio = obtained mean difference/*SE*. If this ratio is large enough, the null hypothesis is rejected and the difference is said to be statistically significant. *See also* standard error of the mean.

cross-cultural approach The view that people differ in some regards as a result of the cultural group of which they are a member. *See also* behavioral-cognitive approach, humanistic approach.

cross-cultural method The study of the relation between a culture's beliefs and practices and the typical personality characteristics of its members. *See also* sociocultural approach.

crystallized intelligence The repertoire of information, cognitive skills, and strategies acquired by the application of fluid intelligence to various fields. This is said to increase with age, in some cases into old age. *See also* fluid intelligence.

cultural anthropology A branch of anthropology that compares the similarities and differences among human cultures.

culture fairness of a test The extent to which test performance does not depend upon information or skills provided by one culture but not another.

curare A drug that completely paralyzes the skeletal musculature but does not affect visceral reactions.

cutoff score A score on a test used for selection below which no individual is accepted.

decay A possible factor in forgetting, producing some loss of the stored information through erosion by some as yet unknown physiological process

decibels The logarithmic units used to describe sound intensity (or amplitude).

decision making The process of forming probability estimates of events and utilizing them to choose between different courses of action.

declarative knowledge Knowing "that" (e.g., knowing someone's name) as contrasted with procedural knowledge, which is knowing "how" (e.g., knowing how to ride a bicycle).

deductive reasoning Reasoning in which one tries to determine whether some statement follows logically from certain premises, as in the analysis of syllogisms. This is in contrast with inductive reasoning in which one observes a number of particular instances and tries to determine a general rule that covers them all.

defense mechanism In psychoanalytic theory, a collective term for a number of reactions that try to ward off or lessen anxiety by various unconscious means. *See also* displacement, projection, rationalization, reaction formation, repression.

definition (of a word) A set of necessary and sufficient features shared by all members of a category which are the criteria for membership in that category.

deindividuation A weakened sense of personal identity in which self-awareness is merged in the collective goals of a group.

deinstitutionalization A movement intended to obtain better and less expensive care for schizophrenic patients in their own communities rather than at large, centralized hospitals.

delay of gratification The postponement of immediate satisfaction inorder to achieve a more important reward later on, a process that plays an important role in some behavioral-cognitive approaches to personality.

delusion Systematized false beliefs, often of grandeur or persecution.

dendrites A typically highly branched part of a neuron that receives impulses from receptors or other neurons and conducts them toward the cell body and axon.

dependent variable *See* experiment.

depolarization A drop of the membrane potential of a neuron from its resting potential. The basis of neural excitation.

depression A state of deep and pervasive dejection and hopelessness, accompanied by apathy and a feeling of personal worthlessness.

depth-of-processing approach An approach to memory that stresses the nature of encoding at the time of acquisition. It argues that deeper levels of processing (for example, attending to a word's meaning) lead to better retention and retrieval than shallower levels of processing (for example, attending to the word's sound). Thus maintenance rehearsal leads to much poorer retrieval than elaborative rehearsal. *See also* encoding, elaborative rehearsal, maintenance rehearsal.

descriptive rules *See* prescriptive rules.

deviation IQ A measure of intelligence-test performance based on an individual's standing relative to his own age-mates (e.g., an IQ of 100 is average and IQs of 70 and 130 correspond to percentile ranks of 2 and 98 respectively). *See also* Intelligence Quotient.

diathesis *See* diathesis-stress conception.

diathesis-stress conception The belief that many organic and mental disorders arise from an interaction between a diathesis (a predisposition toward an illness) and some form of precipitating environmental stress.

dichotic listening A procedure by which each ear receives a different message while the listener is asked to attend to only one.

difference threshold The amount by which a given stimulus must be increased or decreased so that the subject can perceive a just-noticeable difference (jnd).

differentiation A progressive change from the general to the particular and from the simpler to the more complex which characterizes embryological development. According to some theorists, the same pattern holds for the development of behavior after birth.

diffusion of responsibility *See* bystander effect.

diminishing returns principle Applied to the perceived value of money, the principle states that the increase in the subjective value produced by every additional dollar decreases the more dollars the person has already. The same principle applies to the subjective value of other gains and losses. It also applies to the psychological magnitude of sensory qualities, as in the case of Weber's law.

directed thinking Thinking that is aimed at the solution of a problem.

direct perception In Gibson's theory, our ability to perceive information about sizes directly, without any intermediate cognitive steps.

discrimination A process of learning to respond to certain stimuli that are reinforced and not to others that are unreinforced.

discriminative stimuli In instrumental conditioning, the external stimuli that signal a particular relationship between the instrumental response and the reinforcer. For example, a green light is a positive discriminative stimulus when it signals to a pigeon that it will get food if it hops on a trea-dle; the reverse is true of a red light, or the negative discriminative stimulus, which indicates that this action will not lead to a food reward.

disinhibition An increase of some reaction tendency by the removal of some inhibiting influence upon it (e.g., the increased strength of a frog's spinal reflexes after decapitation).

disorganized type of schizophrenia A subtype of schizophrenia formerly called hebephrenia in which the predominant symptoms are extreme incoherence of thought and marked inappropriateness of behavior and affect.

displaced aggression *See* displacement.

displacement In psychoanalytic theory, a redirection of an impulse from a channel that is blocked into another, more available outlet (e.g., displaced aggression, as in a child who hits a sibling when punished by her parents).

display A term used by ethologists to describe genetically preprogrammed responses that serve as stimuli for the reaction of others of the same species, and thus serve as the basis of a communication system (e.g., mating rituals).

display rules A culture's rules about what facial signals may or may not be given and in what contexts.

dispositional quality Any underlying attribute that characterizes a given individual and makes her more disposed than others to engage in a particular behavior (e.g., the presence or absence of some ability or some personality trait).

dissociation (1) A term used for symptoms when a patient is impaired in one function but relatively unaffected in another. (2) In post-traumatic stress disorder, the period of numbness immediately after the trauma in which the sufferer feels estranged, socially unresponsive, and oddly unaffected by the traumatizing event.

dissociative disorders Disorders in which a whole set of mental events is stored out of ordinary consciousness. These include dissociative amnesia, fugue states and, very rarely, cases of dissociative identity disorder.

dissociative identity disorder Formerly multiple personality disorder. A dissociative disorder that results in a person developing two or more distinct personalities.

dissonance theory *See* cognitive dissonance.

distal stimulus An object or event outside (e.g., a tree) as contrasted to the proximal stimulus (e.g., the retinal image of the tree), which is the pattern of physical energies that originates from the distal stimulus and impinges on a sense organ.

distance cues The visual clues that allow us to perceive depth and the distance of objects.

distress calls The innate signals through which a human or animal infant indicates its need of aid.

doctrine of specific nerve energies The assertion that qualitative differences in sensory experience are not attributable to the differences in the stimuli that correspond to different sense modalities (e.g., light versus sound) but rather to the fact that these stimuli excite different nervous structures.

dominance hierarchies A social order developed by animals that live in groups by which certain individuals gain status and exert power over others.

door-in-the-face technique A method for achieving compliance in which a certain request is preceded by a much larger one. The refusal of the first request, and the apparent concession on the part of the requester, makes people more likely to agree to the second demand, feeling that they should now make a concession of their own.

dopamine (DA) A neurotransmitter involved in various brain structures, including those that control motor action.

dopamine hypothesis of schizophrenia Asserts that schizophrenics are oversensitive to the neurotransmitter dopamine and are therefore in a state of overarousal. Evidence for this view comes from the fact that the phenothiazines, which alleviate schizophrenic symptoms, block dopamine transmission. *See also* phenothiazines.

double-blind technique A technique for evaluating drug effects independent of the effects produced by the expectations of patients (placebo effects) and of physicians. This is done by assigning patients to a drug group or a placebo group with both patients and staff members in ignorance of who is assigned to which group. *See also* placebo effect.

drive-reduction theory A theory that claims that all built-in rewards are at bottom reductions of some noxious bodily state. The theory has difficulty in explaining motives in which one seeks stimulation, such as sex and curiosity.

drug tolerance The compensatory reaction developed after repeated use of a drug. Addicts must use increasingly larger doses to obtain the same effect that was produced previously.

DSM-III The diagnostic manual of the American Psychiatric Assocaition adopted in 1980. A major distinction between it and its predecessor is that it categorizes mental disorders by their descriptive characteristics rather than by theories about their underlying cause. Thus a number of disorders that were formerly grouped together under the general heading "neurosis" (e.g., phobias, conversion disorders) are now classified under separate headings. *See also* conversion disorders, neurosis, phobia.

DSM-III-R The diagnostic manual of the American Psychiatric Association adopted in 1987, a relatively minor revision of its predecessor, DSM-III.

DSM-IV The current diagnostic manual of the American Psychiatric Association (adopted in 1994), a substantial revision of its predecessor, DSM-III-R.

duplex theory of vision The theory that rods and cones handle different aspects of vision. The rods are the receptors for night vision; they operate at low light intensities and lead to achromatic (colorless) sensations. The cones are used in day vision; they respond at higher illumination levels and are responsible for sensations of color.

eardrum The taut membrane that transmits vibrations caused by sound waves across the middle ear to the inner ear.

effectors Organs of action; in humans, muscles and glands.

efferent nerves Nerves that carry messages to the effectors.

ego In Freud's theory, a set of reactions that try to reconcile the id's blind pleasure strivings with the demands of reality. These lead to the emergence of various skills and capacities that eventually become a system that can look at itself—an "I." *See also* id and superego.

egocentrism In Piaget's theory, a characteristic of preoperational children, an inability to see another person's point of view.

ego psychology An approach to psychology that, in addition to the neo-Freudian concern with cultural and interpersonal factors, stresses the healthy aspects of the self as it tries to cope with reality.

eidetic memory A relatively rare kind of memory characterized by relatively long-lasting and detailed images of scenes that can be scanned as if they were physically present.

elaboration-likelihood model of persuasion A theory that asserts that the factors that make for persuasion depend on the extent to which the arguments of the persuasive message are thought about (elaborated). If they are seriously thought about, the central route to persuasion will be used, and attitude change will depend on the nature of the arguments. If they are not seriously considered, the peripheral route to persuasion will be used, and attitude change will depend on more peripheral factors.

elaborative rehearsal   Rehearsal in which material is actively reorganized and elaborated while in working memory. In contrast to maintenance rehearsal, this confers considerable benefit. *See also* maintenance rehearsal.

Electra complex   *See* Oedipus complex.

electroconvulsive shock treatment (ECT)   A somatic treatment, mostly used for cases of severe depression, in which a brief electric current is passed through the brain to produce a convulsive seizure.

electroencephalogram (EEG)   A record of the summed activity of cortical cells picked up by wires placed on the skull.

embryo   The earliest stage in a developing animal. In humans, up to about eight weeks after conception.

emergency reaction   Intense sympathetic arousal that mobilizes an organism for a crisis.

empathic concern   A feeling of sympathy and concern for the sufferings of another coupled with the desire to relieve this suffering. *See also* vicarious distress.

empathy   A direct emotional response to another person's emotions.

empiricism   A school of thought that holds that all knowledge comes by way of empirical experience, that is, through the senses.

encoding   The form in which some information is stored.

encoding specificity principle   The hypothesis that retrieval is most likely if the context at the time of recall approximates that during the original encoding.

endocrine system   The system of ductless glands whose secretions are released directly into the bloodstream and affect organs elsewhere in the body (e.g., adrenal gland).

endorphin   A drug produced within the brain itself whose effects and chemical composition are similar to such pain-relieving opiates as morphine.

epinephrine (adrenaline)   A neurotransmitter released into the bloodstream by the adrenal medulla whose effects are similar to those of sympathetic activation (e.g., racing heart).

episodic memory   Memory for particular events in one's own life (e.g., I missed the train this morning). *See also* generic memory.

erogenous zones   In psychoanalytic theory, the mouth, anus, and genitals. These regions are particularly sensitive to touch. According to Freud, the various pleasures associated with each of them have a common element, which is sexual.

escape learning   Instrumental learning in which reinforcement consists of the reduction or cessation of an aversive stimulus (e.g., electric shock). *See also* punishment training, avoidance learning.

estrogen   A female sex hormone that dominates the first half of the female cycle through ovulation; in animals, estrus performs this function.

estrus   In mammalian animals, the period in the cycle when the female is sexually receptive (in heat).

ethology   A branch of biology that studies the behavior of animals under natural conditions.

excitation transfer effects   The transfer of autonomic arousal from one situation to another, as when strenuous exercise leads to an increased arousal when presented with aggression-arousing or erotic stimuli.

existential therapy   A humanistic therapy that emphasizes people's free will and tries to help them achieve a personal outlook to give meaning to their lives.

experiment   A study in which the investigator manipulates one (or more than one) variable (the independent variable) to determine its effect on the subject's response (the dependent variable).

expert systems   Computer problem-solving programs with a very narrow scope which only deal with problems in a limited domain of knowledge (e.g., the diagnosis of infectious diseases).

explicit memory   Memory retrieval in which there is awareness of remembering at the time of retrieval. *See also* implicit memory.

expressive aphasia   A disorder in which the patient has difficulty with the production of speech. Expressive aphasia is caused by a cortical lesion that damages one's ability to organize the movements necessary for speech production into a unified sequence.

expressive movements   Movements of the face and body in animals and humans that seem to express emotion. They are usually regarded as built-in social displays.

externality hypothesis   The hypothesis that some and perhaps all obese people are relatively unresponsive to their own internal hunger state but are much more susceptible to signals from without.

extinction   In classical conditioning, the weakening of the tendency of CS to elicit CR by unreinforced presentations of CS. In instrumental conditioning, a decline in the tendency to perform the instrumental response brought about by unreinforced occurrences of that response.

extrapyramidal system   One of the two cerebral motor control systems; it is older in evolutionary terms, and it controls relatively gross movements of the head, limbs, and trunk.

extroversion/introversion   In Eysenck's system, a trait dimension that refers to the main direction of a person's energies; toward the outer world of objects and other people (extroversion) or toward the inner world of one's own thoughts and feelings (introversion).

facial feedback hypothesis   The hypothesis that sensory feedback from the facial muscles will lead to subjective feelings of emotion that correspond to the particular facial pattern. *See* fundamental emotions.

factor analysis   A statistical method for studying the interrelations among various tests, the object of which is to discover what the tests have in common and whether these commonalities can be ascribed to one or several factors that run through all or some of these tests.

false alarm   *See* payoff matrix.

familiarity effect   The fact that increased exposure to a stimulus tends to make that stimulus more likable.

family resemblance structure   Overlap of features among members of a category of meaning such that no members of the category have all of the features but all members have some of them.

family therapy   A general term for a number of therapies that treat the family (or a couple), operating on the assumption that the key to family or marital distress is not necessarily in the pathology of any individual spouse or family member but is rather in the interrelationships within the family or marriage system.

feature detectors   Neurons in the retina or brain that respond to specific features of the stimulus, such as movement, orientation, and so on.

Fechner's law   The assertion that the strength of a sensation is proportional to the logarithm of physical stimulus intensity.

feedback system   A system in which some action produces a consequence that affects (feeds back on) the action. In negative feedback, the consequence stops or reverses the action (e.g., thermostat-controlled furnace). In positive feedback, the consequence strengthens the action (e.g., rocket that homes in on airplanes).

fetus   A later stage in embryonic development. In humans, from about eight weeks until birth.

figure-ground organization   The segregation of the visual field into a part (the figure) that stands out against the rest (the ground).

final common path   The single neural output upon which two groups of nerve fibers converge.

fixation   (1) In problem solving, the result of rigid mental sets that makes it difficult for people to approach a problem in new and different ways. (2) In Freud's theory of personality, the lingering attachment to an earlier stage of pleasure seeking, even after a new stage has been attained.

fixed-action patterns   Term used by ethologists to describe stereotyped, species-specific behaviors triggered by genetically pre-programmed releasing stimuli.

fixed-interval schedule   *See* interval schedule.

fixed-ratio schedule   *See* ratio schedule.

flashbulb memories   Vivid, detailed, and apparently accurate memories said to be produced by unexpected and emotionally important events.

flooding   A form of behavior therapy based on concepts derived from classical conditioning in which the patient exposes himself to whatever he is afraid of, thus extinguishing his fear. *See also* implosion therapy.

flow chart   (1) In computer science, a diagram that shows the step-by-step operation of a computer program. (2) In human cognition, similar diagrams that show the hypothesized flow of information as it is thought to be processed by the human mind.

fluid intelligence   The ability, which is said to decline with age, to deal with essentially new problems. *See also* crystallized intelligence.

forced compliance effect   An individual forced to act or speak publicly in a manner contrary to his own beliefs may change his own views in the direction of the public action. But this will happen only if his reward for the false public pronouncement is relatively small. If the reward is large, there is no dissonance and hence no attitude change. *See also* cognitive dissonance.

forebrain   In mammals, the bulk of the brain. Its foremost region includes the cerebral hemispheres; its rear includes the thalamus and hypothalamus.

forgetting curve   A curve showing the inverse relationship between memory and the retention interval.

forward pairing   A classical conditioning procedure in which the conditioned stimulus (CS) precedes the unconditioned stimulus (US). This contrasts with simultaneous pairing, in which CS and US are presented simultaneously, and backward pairing, in which CS follows US. *See also* classical conditioning, conditioned stimulus, unconditioned stimulus.

framing   A heuristic that affects the subjective desirability of an event by changing the standard of reference for judging the desirability of that event.

fraternal twins   Twins that arise from two different eggs that are (simultaneously) fertilized by different sperm cells. Their genetic similarity is no greater than that between ordinary siblings. *See also* identical twins.

free association   Method used in psychoanalytic therapy in which the patient is to say anything that comes to her mind, no matter how apparently trivial, unrelated, or embarrassing.

free recall   A test of memory that asks for as many items in a list as a subject can recall regardless of order.

frequency distribution   An arrangement in which scores are tabulated by the frequency in which they occur.

Freud's theory of dreams   A theory that holds that at bottom all dreams are attempts to fulfill a wish. The wish fulfillment is in the latent dream, which represents the sleeper's hidden desires. This latent dream is censored and reinterpreted to avoid anxiety. It reemerges in more acceptable form as the manifest dream, the dream the sleeper remembers upon awakening.

frontal lobe   A lobe in each cerebral hemisphere which includes the motor projection area.

function morphemes   *See* content morphemes.

functional fixedness   A set to think of objects in terms of their normal function.

fundamental attribution error   The tendency to attribute behaviors to dispositional qualities while underrating the role of the situation. *See also* actor-observer difference, attribution theory, self-serving bias.

fundamental emotions   According to some theorists, a small set of elemental, built-in emotions revealed by distinctive patterns of facial expression. *See also* facial feedback hypothesis.

galvanic skin response (GSR)   A drop in the electrical resistance of the skin, widely used as an index of autonomic reaction.

ganglion (*plural* ganglia)   Neural control centers that integrate messages from different receptor cells and coordinate the activity of different muscle fibers.

ganglion cells   In the retina, one of the intermediate links between the receptor cells and the brain. The axons of the ganglion cells converge into a bundle of fibers that leave the eyeball as the optic nerve. *See also* bipolar cells.

gender constancy   The recognition that being male or female is for all intents and purposes irrevocable.

gender identity   The inner sense of being male or female. *See also* gender role, sexual orientation.

gender role   The set of external behavior patterns a given culture deems appropriate for each sex. *See also* gender identity, sexual orientation.

gene   The unit of hereditary transmission, located at a particular place in a given chromosome. Both members of each chromosome pair have corresponding locations at which there are genes that carry instructions about the same characteristic (e.g., eye color). If one member of a gene pair is dominant and the other is recessive, the dominant gene will exert its effect regardless of what the recessive gene calls for. The characteristic called for by the recessive gene will only be expressed if the other member of the gene pair is also recessive. *See also* chromosomes.

general intelligence (g)   According to Spearman, a mental attribute that is called upon in any intellectual task a person has to perform.

generalization decrement   In classical conditioning, the weakening of a response to a new stimulus compared to the response elicited by the original CS. The greater the difference between the new stimulus and the original CS, the larger the generalization decrement. In instrumental conditioning, a similar effect occurs when a new discriminating stimulus is presented instead of the original stimulus.

generalization gradient   The curve that shows the relationship between the tendency to respond to a new stimulus and its similarity to the original conditioned stimulus (CS).

generalized anxiety disorder   A mental disorder (formerly called anxiety neurosis) whose primary characteristic is an all-pervasive, "free-floating" anxiety. A member of the diagnostic category "anxiety disorders," which also includes phobias and obsessive-compulsive disorders. *See also* phobia, obsessive-compulsive disorders.

general paresis   A psychosis characterized by progressive decline in cognitive and motor function culminating in death, reflecting a deteriorating brain condition produced by syphilitic infection.

generic memory   Memory for items of knowledge as such (e.g., The capital of France is Paris), independent of the occasion on which they are learned. *See also* episodic memory.

genital stage In psychoanalytic theory, the stage of psychosexual development reached in adult sexuality in which sexual pleasure involves not only one's own gratification but also the social and bodily satisfaction brought to another person.

genotype The genetic blueprint of an organism which may or may not be overtly expressed by its phenotype. *See also* phenotype.

Gestalt An organized whole such as a visual form or a melody.

Gestalt psychology A theoretical approach that emphasizes the role of organized wholes (Gestalten) in perception and other psychological processes.

glove anesthesia A condition sometimes seen in conversion disorders, in which there is an anesthesia of the entire hand with no loss of feeling above the wrist. This symptom makes no organic sense given the anatomical arrangement of the nerve trunks and indicates that the condition has a psychological basis.

glucose A form of sugar which is the major source of energy for most bodily tissues. If plentiful, much of it is converted into glycogen and stored away.

glucose receptors Receptors in the brain (probably the hypothalamus) that detect changes in the way glucose is used as a metabolic fuel.

glycogen A stored form of metabolic energy derived from glucose. To be used, it must first be converted back into glucose.

good continuation A factor in visual grouping. Contours tend to be seen in such a way that their direction is altered as little as possible.

gradient of reinforcement The curve that describes the declining effectiveness of reinforcement, with increasing delay between the response and the reinforcer.

group-factor theory of intelligence A factor-analytic approach to intelligence-test performance which argues that intelligence is the composite of separate abilities (group factors such as verbal ability, spatial ability, etc.) without a sovereign capacity that enters into each. *See also* factor analysis, general intelligence.

group therapy Psychotherapy of several persons at one time.

habituation A decline in the tendency to respond to stimuli that have become familiar. While short-term habituation dissipates in a matter of minutes, long-term habituation may persist for days or weeks.

habituation procedure A widely used method for studying infant perception. After some exposure to a visual stimulus, an infant becomes habituated and stops looking at it. The extent to which a new stimulus leads to renewed interest and resumption of looking is taken as a measure of the extent to which the infant regards this new stimulus as different from the old one to which she became habituated.

hair cells The auditory receptors in the cochlea, lodged between the basilar membrane and other membranes above.

hallucination Perceived experiences that occur in the absence of actual sensory stimulation.

hebephrenia *See* disorganized type of schizophrenia.

heritability As measured by *H,* the heritability ratio, this refers to the relative importance of heredity and environment in determining the variation of a particular trait. More specifically, *H* is the proportion of the variance of the trait in a given population that is attributable to genetic factors.

heritability ratio (H) *See* heritability.

hermaphrodite A person whose reproductive organs are anatomically ambiguous so that they are not exclusively male or female.

hertz (HZ) A measure of frequency in number of cycles per second.

heterosexuality A sexual orientation leading to a choice of sexual partners of the opposite sex.

heuristics In computer problem solving, a procedure that has often worked in the past and is likely, but not certain, to work again. *See also* algorithm.

hierarchical organization Organization in which narrower categories are subsumed under broader ones, which are subsumed under still broader ones, and so on. Often expressed in the form of a tree diagram.

hierarchy of needs According to Maslow and other adherents of the humanistic approach, human needs are arranged in a hierarchy with physiological needs such as hunger at the bottom, safety needs further up, the need for attachment and love still higher, and the desire for esteem yet higher. At the very top of the hierarchy is the striving for self-actualization. By and large, people will only strive for the higher-order needs when the lower ones are fulfilled. *See* self-actualization.

higher-order conditioning In classical conditioning, a procedure by which a new stimulus comes to elicit the conditioned response (CR) by virtue of being paired with an effective conditioned stimulus (CS) (e.g., first pairings of tone and food, then pairings of bell and tone, until finally the bell elicits salivation by itself).

hindbrain The most primitive portion of the brain, which includes the medulla and the cerebellum.

hippocampus A structure in the temporal lobe that constitutes an important part of the limbic system. One of its functions seems to involve memory.

histogram A graphic rendering of a frequency distribution which depicts the distribution by a series of contiguous rectangles. *See also* frequency distribution.

hit *See* payoff matrix.

homeostasis The body's tendency to maintain the conditions of its internal environment by various forms of self-regulation.

homogamy The tendency of like to marry like.

homosexuality A sexual orientation leading to a choice of partners of the same sex.

hue A perceived dimension of visual stimuli whose meaning is close to the term *color* (e.g., red, blue).

humanistic approach to personality Asserts that what is most important about people is how they achieve their selfhood and actualize their potentialities. *See also* behavioral-cognitive approach, cross-cultural approach, psychodynamic approach, situationism, sociocultural approach, trait theory.

humanistic therapies Methods of treatment that emphasize personal growth and self-fulfillment. They try to be relatively nondirective, since their emphasis is on helping the clients achieve the capacity for making their own choices. *See also* nondirective techniques.

hyperphagia Voracious, chronic overeating brought about by a lesion of the ventromedial region of the hypothalamus.

hypnosis A temporary, trancelike state that can be induced in normal persons. During hypnosis, various hypnotic or posthypnotic suggestions sometimes produce effects that resemble some of the symptoms of conversion disorders. *See also* conversion disorders.

hypothalamus A small structure at the base of the brain which plays a vital role in the control of the autonomic nervous system, of the endocrine system, and of the major biological drives.

hysteria An older term for a group of presumably psychogenic disorders that included conversion disorders and dissociative disorders. Since DSM-III, it is no longer used as a diagnostic category, in part because of an erroneous implication that the condition is more prevalent in women (Greek *hystera*—womb). *See also* conversion disorders, dissociative disorders, glove anesthesia.

id In Freud's theory, a term for the most primitive reactions of human personality, consisting of blind strivings for immediate biological satisfaction regardless of cost. *See also* ego and superego.

ideas of reference A characteristic of some mental disorders, notably schizophrenia, in which the patient begins to think that external events are specially related to him personally (e.g., "People walk by and follow me").

identical twins Twins that originate from a single fertilized egg that then splits into two exact replicas that develop into two genetically identical individuals. *See also* fraternal twins.

identification In psychoanalytic theory, a mechanism whereby a child models himself or herself (typically) on the same-sex parent in an effort to become like him or her.

idiot savant *See* savant.

ill-defined problems *See* well-defined problems.

imipramine A tricyclic antidepressant drug.

implicit memory Memory retrieval in which there is no awareness of remembering at the time of retrieval. *See also* explicit memory.

implicit theories of personality Beliefs about the way in which different patterns of behavior of people hang together and why they do so.

implosion therapy A form of behavior therapy related to flooding in which the patient exposes herself to whatever she is afraid of, in its most extreme form, but does so in imagination rather than in real life (e.g., a person afraid of dogs has to imagine herself surrounded by a dozen snarling Dobermans). *See* flooding.

impossible figure A figure that appears acceptable when looked at locally but poses unresolvable visual contradictions when seen as a whole.

impression management According to Goffman, the characteristic of much social interaction in which people maintain a certain image that goes along with social or professional roles.

imprinting A learned attachment that is formed at a particular period in life (the critical, or sensitive, period) and is difficult to reverse (e.g., the duckling's acquired tendency to follow whatever moving stimulus it encounters twelve to twenty-four hours after hatching).

incidental learning Learning without trying to learn (e.g., as in a study in which subjects judge a speaker's vocal quality when she recites a list of words and are later asked to produce as many of the words as they can recall). *See also* intentional learning.

incremental validity The extent to which a test adds to the predictive validity already provided by other measures (e.g., the extent to which a projective technique adds to what is already known through an ordinary interview).

independent variable *See* experiment.

induced movement Perceived movement of an objectively stationary stimulus that is enclosed by a moving framework.

inductive reasoning Reasoning in which one observes a number of particular instances and tries to determine a general rule that covers them all.

information processing A general term for the presumed operations whereby the crude raw materials provided by the senses are refashioned into items of knowledge. Among these operations are perceptual organization, comparison with items stored in memory, and so on.

insightful learning Learning by understanding the relations between components of the problem; often contrasted with "blind trial and error"

and documented by wide and appropriate transfer if tested in a new situation.

instrumental conditioning Also called operant conditioning. A form of learning in which a reinforcer (e.g., food) is given only if the animal performs the instrumental response (e.g., pressing a lever). In effect, what has to be learned is the relationship between the response and the reinforcer. *See* classical conditioning.

insulin A hormone with a crucial role in utilization of nutrients. One of its functions is to help promote the conversion of glucose into glycogen.

Intelligence Quotient (IQ) A ratio measure to indicate whether a child's mental age (MA) is ahead or behind her chronological age (CA); specifically IQ = $100 \times MA/CA$. *See also* deviation IQ, mental age.

intentional learning Learning when informed that there will be a later test of learning. *See also* incidental learning.

interference theory of forgetting The assertion that items are forgotten because they are somehow interfered with by other items learned before or after.

intermittent reinforcement *See* partial reinforcement.

internalization The process whereby moral codes are adopted by the child so that they control his behavior even where there are no external rewards or punishments.

interneurons Neurons that receive impulses and transmit them to other neurons.

interposition A monocular depth cue in which objects that are farther away are blocked from view by any other opaque object obstructing their optical path to the eye.

interval scale A scale in which equal differences between scores can be treated as equal so that the scores can be added or subtracted. *See also* categorical scale, nominal scale, ordinal scale, ratio scale.

interval schedule A reinforcement schedule in which reinforcement is delivered for a first response made after a given interval of time has elapsed. In a fixed-interval schedule, the interval is always the same. In a variable-interval schedule, the interval varies around a specified average.

introversion *See* extroversion/introversion.

invariant Some aspect of the proximal stimulus pattern that remains unchanged despite various transformations of the stimulus.

ions Atoms or molecules that have gained or lost electrons, thus acquiring a positive or negative charge.

iris The smooth circular muscle in the eye that surrounds the pupil and contracts or dilates under reflex control in order to govern the amount of light entering.

isolation A mechanism of defense in which anxiety arousing memories are retained but without the emotion that accompanied them.

James-Lange theory of emotions A theory that asserts that the subjective experience of emotion is the awareness of one's own bodily reactions in the presence of certain arousing stimuli.

just-noticeable difference (jnd) *See* difference threshold.

kinesthesis A general term for sensory information generated by receptors in the muscles, tendons, and joints which informs us of our skeletal movement.

kin-selection hypothesis *See* altruism.

Korsakoff's syndrome A brain disorder characterized by serious memory disturbances. The most common cause is extreme and chronic alcohol use.

latency General term for the interval before some reaction occurs.

latency period In psychoanalytic theory, a stage in psychosexual development in which sexuality lies essentially dormant, roughly from ages five to twelve.

latent dream *See* Freud's theory of dreams.

latent learning Learning that occurs without being manifested by performance.

lateral hypothalamus A region of the hypothalamus which is said to be a "hunger center" and to be in an antagonistic relation to a supposed "satiety center," the ventromedial region of the hypothalamus.

lateral inhibition The tendency of adjacent neural elements of the visual system to inhibit each other; it underlies brightness contrast and the accentuation of contours. *See also* brightness contrast.

lateralization An asymmetry of function of the two cerebral hemispheres. In most right-handers, the left hemisphere is specialized for language functions, while the right hemisphere is better at various visual and spatial tasks.

law of effect A theory that asserts that the tendency of a stimulus to evoke a response is strengthened if the response is followed by reward and is weakened if the response is not followed by reward. Applied to instrumental learning, this theory states that as trials proceed, incorrect bonds will weaken while the correct bond will be strengthened.

learned helplessness A condition created by exposure to inescapable aversive events. This retards or prevents learning in subsequent situations in which escape or avoidance is possible.

learned helplessness theory of depression The theory that depression is analogous to learned helplessness effects produced in the laboratory by exposing subjects to uncontrollable aversive events.

learning curve A curve in which some index of learning (e.g., the number of drops of saliva in Pavlov's classical conditioning experiment) is plotted against trials or sessions.

learning model As defined in the text, a subcategory of the pathology model that (1) views mental disorders as the result of some form of faulty learning, and (2) believes that these should be treated by behavior therapists according to the laws of classical and instrumental conditioning, or by cognitive therapists who try to affect faulty modes of thinking. *See also* behavior therapy, cognitive therapy, medical model, pathology model, psychoanalytic model.

learning set The increased ability to solve various problems, especially in discrimination learning, as a result of previous experience with problems of a similar kind.

lens The portion of the eye that bends light rays and thus projects an image on the retina.

lesions The damage incurred by an area of the brain.

lexical access The process of recognizing and understanding a word, which is presumably achieved by making contact with (accessing) the word in the mental lexicon.

lightness constancy The tendency to perceive the lightness of an object as more or less the same despite the fact that the light reflected from these objects changes with the illumination that falls upon them.

limbic system A set of brain structures including a relatively primitive portion of the cerebral cortex and parts of the thalamus and hypothalamus; it is believed to be involved in the control of emotional behavior and motivation.

line of best fit A line drawn through the points in a scatter diagram; it yields the best prediction of one variable when given the value of the other variable.

lithium carbonate A drug used in the treatment of mania and bipolar disorders.

lobotomy *See* prefrontal lobotomy.

lock-and-key model The theory that neurotransmitter molecules will only affect the postsynaptic membrane if their shape fits into that of certain synaptic receptor molecules.

longitudinal study A developmental study in which the same person is tested at various ages.

long-term habituation *See* habituation.

long-term memory Those parts of the memory system that are currently dormant and inactive, but have enormous storage capacity. *See also* stage theory of memory, working memory.

looming A rapid magnification of a form in the visual field that generally signals impending impact.

luminance ratio The ratio between the light reflected off a figure and that reflected off the background against which the figure is seen. Whatever the illumination, the ratio remains the same.

Mach bands The accentuated edges between two adjacent regions that differ in hue. This sharpening is maximal at the borders where the distance between the two regions is smallest and the contrast most striking.

Magic Number According to Miller, the number (seven plus or minus two) that represents the holding capacity of the working (or short-term) memory system.

Magnetic Resonance Imaging (MRI) A neurodiagnostic technique that relies on nuclear magnetic resonance. An MRI scan passes a high frequency alternating magnetic field through the brain and detects the different resonant frequencies of nuclei. A computer then puts this information together to form a picture of the brain that shows damaged areas.

maintenance rehearsal Rehearsal in which material remains in working memory for a while. In contrast to elaborative rehearsal, this confers little benefit. *See also* elaborative rehearsal.

major depression A unipolar disorder in which a patient suffers depressive mood extremes.

major tranquilizers *See* antipsychotic drugs.

mania Hyperactive state with marked impairment of judgment, usually accompanied by intense euphoria.

manic-depressive psychosis *See* bipolar disorder.

manifest dream *See* Freud's theory of dreams.

marital therapy *See* family therapy.

matching hypothesis The hypothesis that persons of a given level of physical attractiveness will seek out partners of a roughly similar level.

matching to sample A procedure in which an organism has to choose one of two alternative stimuli which is the same as a third sample stimulus.

maturation A programmed growth process based on changes in underlying neural structures that are relatively unaffected by environmental conditions (e.g., flying in sparrows and walking in humans).

maximum-likelihood principle The assertion that we interpret the proximal stimulus pattern as that external stimulus object that most probably produced it.

mean (M) *See* measure of central tendency.

measure of central tendency The summary of an entire distribution of experimental results in a single, central score. There are three commonly used measures: (1) the mode, or the score that occurs most frequently; (2) the median, or the point that divides the distribution into two equal halves; and (3) the mean, or the arithmetic average.

medial forebrain bundle (MFB) A bundle of fibers that runs through the base of the forebrain and parts of the hypothalamus. Electric stimulation of this bundle is usually rewarding.

median *See* measure of central tendency.

medical model As defined in the text, a subcategory of the pathology model that (1) holds that the underlying pathology is organic, and that (2) the treatment should be conducted by physicians. *See also* learning model, pathology model, psychoanalytic model.

medulla The rearmost portion of the brain, just adjacent to the spinal cord. It includes centers that help to control respiration and muscle tone.

memory search An internal process preceding memory retrieval that usually occurs very quickly and without our awareness.

memory span The number of items a person can recall after just one presentation.

memory trace The change in the nervous system left by an experience that is the physical basis of its retention in memory. What this change is, is still unknown.

mental age (MA) A score devised by Binet to represent a child's test performance. It indicates the chronological age at which 50 percent of the children in that age group will perform. If the child's MA is greater than his chronological age (CA), he is ahead of his age mentally; if his MA is lower than his CA, he lags behind.

mental images Analogical memories that reserve some of the characteristic attributes of our senses.

mental representations Internal symbols that stand for something but are not equivalent to it, such as internalized actions, images, or words.

mental retardation Usually defined as an IQ of 70 or below.

mental set The predisposition to perceive (or remember or think of) one thing rather than another.

meta-analysis A statistical technique by means of which the results of many different techniques can be combined. This has been useful in studies on the outcome of psychotherapy.

metacognition A general term for knowledge about knowledge, as in knowing that we do or don't remember something.

midbrain Part of the brain that includes some lower centers for sensory-motor integration (e.g., eye movements).

middle ear An antechamber to the inner ear which amplifies sound-produced vibrations of the eardrum and imparts them to the cochlea. *See also* cochlea.

minimal-sufficiency principle A principle of socialization that states that a child will internalize a certain way of acting if there is just enough pressure to get her to behave in this new way, but not enough so that she feels she was forced to do so.

Minnesota Multiphasic Personality Inventory (MMPI) *See* criterion groups.

miss *See* payoff matrix.

mnemonics Deliberate devices for helping memory. Many of them utilize imagery.

mode *See* measure of central tendency.

monoamine oxidase (MAO) inhibitors *See* antidepressant drugs.

monocular depth cues Various features of the visual stimulus which indicate depth, even when viewed with one eye (e.g., linear perspective and motion parallax).

monogamy A mating pattern in which a reproductive partnership is based on a special, more or less permanent tie between one male and one female.

mood disorders A group of disorders (formerly called affective disorders) whose primary characteristic is a disturbance of mood and which is characterized by two emotional extremes—the energy of mania, the despair or lethargy of depression, or both. *See also* bipolar disorder, depression, mania, unipolar disorder.

morpheme The smallest significant unit of meaning in a language (e.g., the word *boys* has two morphemes, *boy* and *s*).

motherese A whimsical term for the speech pattern that mothers and other adults generally employ when talking to infants.

motion parallax A depth cue provided by the fact that, as an observer moves, the images cast by nearby objects move more rapidly on the retina than the images cast by objects farther away.

motor neurons Neurons whose cell bodies are in the spinal cord or brain and whose axons terminate in individual muscle cells.

motor projection areas *See* projection areas.

multiple intelligences In Gardner's theory, the six essential, independent mental capacities, some of which are outside of the traditional academic notions of intelligence (i.e., linguistic, logical-mathematical, spatial, musical, bodily-kinesthetic, and personal intelligence).

multiple personality disorder *See* dissociative identity disorder.

myelin sheath A tube mainly composed of several elongated segments of fatty tissue that insulates an axon from other axons.

nalaxone A drug that inhibits the effect of morphine and similar opiates, and blocks the pain alleviation ascribed to endorphins.

nativism The view that some important aspects of perception and of other cognitive processes are innate.

natural selection The explanatory principle that underlies Darwin's theory of evolution. Some organisms produce offspring that are able to survive and reproduce while other organisms of the same species do not. Thus organisms with these hereditary attributes will eventually outnumber organisms who lack these attributes.

negative correlation The tendency of one variable to increase when a corresponding second variable decreases.

negative feedback *See* feedback system.

negative symptoms of schizophrenia Symptoms that involve a lack of normal functioning, such as apathy, poverty of speech, and emotional blunting. *See* positive symptoms of schizophrenia.

neo-Freudians A group of theorists who accept the psychoanalytic conception of unconscious conflict but who differ with Freud in (1) describing these conflicts in social terms rather than in terms of particular bodily pleasures or frustrations, and (2) maintaining that many of these conflicts arise from the specific cultural conditions under which the child was reared rather than being biologically ordained.

neophobia   A term used in the study of food selection, where it refers to an animal's tendency to refuse new foods.

nerve impulse   *See* action potential.

network model   Theories of cognitive organization, especially of semantic memory, that assert that items of information are represented by a system of nodes linked through associative connections. *See also* node.

neurodevelopmental disorder   A disorder in which pathological genes produce abnormalities in the brain during fetal development; these abnormalities in turn lead to behavioral and cognitive eccentricities.

neuron   A nerve cell.

neuropsychological assessment   A specialized kind of test used to pinpoint cognitive impairments that may stem from learning disabilities, aging, or brain injuries or diseases.

neurosis   In psychoanalytic theory, a broad term for mental disorders whose primary symptoms are anxiety or what seem to be defenses against anxiety. Since the adoption of DSM-III, the term has been dropped as the broad diagnostic label it once was. Various disorders that were once diagnosed as subcategories of neurosis (e.g., phobia, conversion disorders, dissociative disorders) are now classified as separate disorders.

neuroticism   A trait dimension that refers to emotional instability and maladjustment.

neurotransmitters   Chemicals liberated at the terminal end of an axon which travel across the synapse and have an excitatory or inhibitory effect on an adjacent neuron (e.g., norepinephrine).

node   A point in a network on which a number of connections converge.

nodes of Ranvier   Gaps in the myelin sheath surrounding an axon that allow for a considerable increase in the transmission speed of neural impulses.

nominal scale   A scale in which responses are ordered only into different categories. *See also* categorical scale, interval scale, ordinal scale, and ratio scale.

nondirective techniques   A set of techniques for psychological treatment developed by Carl Rogers. As far as possible, the counselor refrains from offering advice or interpretation but only tries to clarify the patient's own feelings by echoing him or restating what he says.

nonsense syllable   Two consonants with a vowel between that do not form a word. Used to study associations between relatively meaningless items.

noradrenaline   *See* norepinephrine.

norepinephrine (NE)   The neurotransmitter by means of which the sympathetic fibers exert their effect on internal organs. It is also the neurotransmitter of various arousing systems in the brain.

normal curve   A symmetrical, bell-shaped curve that describes the probability of obtaining various combinations of chance events. It describes the frequency distributions of many physical and psychological attributes of humans and animals.

normal distribution   A frequency distribution whose graphic representation has a symmetric, bell-shaped form—the normal curve. Its characteristics are often referred to when investigators test statistical hypotheses and make inferences about the population from a given sample.

norms   In intelligence testing, the scores taken from a large sample of the population against which an individual's test scores are evaluated.

null hypothesis   The hypothesis that an obtained difference is merely a chance fluctuation from a population in which the true mean difference is zero. *See also* alternative hypothesis.

obesity   A condition of marked overweight in animals and humans; it is produced by a large variety of factors including metabolic factors (oversecretion of insulin) and behavioral conditions (overeating, perhaps a nonresponsiveness to one's own internal state).

object permanence   The conviction that an object remains perceptually constant over time and exists even when it is out of sight. According to Piaget, this does not develop until infants are eight months old or more.

observational learning   A mechanism of socialization in which a child observes another person who serves as a model and then proceeds to imitate what that model does.

observational study   A study in which the investigator does not manipulate any of the variables but simply observes their relationship as they occur naturally.

obsessions   *See* obsessive-compulsive disorder.

obsessive-compulsive disorder   A disorder whose symptoms are obsessions (persistent and irrational thoughts or wishes) and compulsions (uncontrollable, repetitive acts), which seem to be defenses against anxiety. A member of a diagnostic category called anxiety disorders, which also includes generalized anxiety disorder and phobias. *See also* generalized anxiety disorder, phobia and specific phobia.

occipital lobe   A lobe in each cerebral hemisphere which includes the visual projection area.

occlusion   The partial concealment of one object by another object in front of it.

Oedipus complex   In psychoanalytic theory, a general term for a whole cluster of impulses and conflicts that occur during the phallic phase, at around age five. In boys, a fantasied form of intense sexual love is directed at the mother, which is soon followed by hate and fear of the father. As the fear mounts, the sexual feelings are pushed underground and the boy identifies with the father. An equivalent process in girls is called the Electra complex.

olfaction   The sense of smell.

olfactory epithelium   The small area at the top of the nasal cavity that contains receptors that react to chemicals suspended in air.

operant   In Skinner's system, an instrumental response. *See also* instrumental conditioning.

operant conditioning   *See* instrumental conditioning.

opponent-process theory of color vision   A theory of color vision that asserts that there are three pairs of color antagonists: red-green, blue-yellow, and white-black. Excitation of one member of a pair automatically inhibits the other member.

opponent-process theory of motivation   A theory that asserts that the nervous system has the general tendency to counteract any deviation from the neutral point of the pain-pleasure dimension. If the original stimulus is maintained, there is an attenuation of the emotional state one is in; if it is withdrawn, the opponent process reveals itself, and the emotional state swings sharply in the opposite direction.

optic nerve   A bundle of fibers, made up of the axons of ganglion cells, that leave the eyeball.

oral character   According to Freud, a personality type based on a fixation at the oral stage of development whose symptomatic attribute is passive dependency. *See also* oral stage.

oral stage   In psychoanalytic theory, the earliest stage of psychosexual development during which the primary source of bodily pleasure is stimulation of the mouth and lips, as in sucking at the breast.

ordinal scale   A scale in which responses are rank-ordered by relative magnitude but in which the intervals between successive ranks are not necessarily equal. *See also* categorical scale, interval scale, nominal scale, and ratio scale.

osmoreceptors   Receptors that help to control water intake by responding to the concentrations of body fluids. *See also* volume receptors.

ossicles   The three small bones in the ear that transmit vibrations from the eardrum to the oval window.

out-group homogeneity effect   A phenomenon related to stereotyping in which a member of a group (the in-group) tends to view members of another group (the out-group) as more alike than members of his or her own.

oval window   The membrane separating the middle ear from the inner ear.

paired-associate method   A procedure in which subjects learn to provide particular response terms to various stimulus items.

panic disorder   A disorder characterized by sudden anxiety attacks in which there are bodily symptoms such as choking, dizziness, trembling, and chest pains, accompanied by feelings of intense apprehension, terror, and a sense of impending doom.

parallel distributed processing (PDP)   Models of cognitive processing in which the relevant symbolic representations do not correspond to any one unit of the network but to the state of the network as a whole.

parallel search   The simultaneous comparison of a target stimulus to several items in memory. *See also* serial search.

paranoid schizophrenia   A subcategory of schizophrenia. Its dominant symptom is a set of delusions that are often elaborately systematized, usually of grandeur or persecution.

paraphrase   The relation between two sentences whose meanings (underlying structures) are the same but whose surface structures differ (e.g., *The boy hit the ball/The ball was hit by the boy*).

parasympathetic system   A division of the autonomic nervous system that serves vegetative functions and conserves bodily energies (e.g., slowing heart rate). Its action is antagonistic to that of the sympathetic system.

parietal lobe   A lobe in each cerebral hemisphere that includes the somatosensory projection area.

Parkinson's disease   A degenerative neurological disorder characterized by various difficulties of movement. Produced by degeneration of dopamine-releasing neurons in a pathway of the brain crucial for motor control.

partial reinforcement   A condition in which a response is reinforced only some of the time.

partial-reinforcement effect   The fact that a response is much harder to extinguish if it was acquired during partial rather than continuous reinforcement.

pathology model   A term adopted in the text to describe a general conception of mental disorders which holds that (1) one can generally distinguish between symptoms and underlying causes, and (2) these causes may be regarded as a form of pathology. *See also* learning model, medical model, psychoanalytic model.

pattern recognition   The process by which the perceptual system matches the form of a figure against a figure stored in memory.

payoff matrix   (1) In a detection experiment, a table that shows the costs and benefits of each of the four possible outcomes: a hit, reporting the stimulus when it is present; a correct negative, reporting it as absent when it is in fact absent; a miss, failing to report it when it is present; and a false alarm, reporting it as present when it is not. (2) In the context of the use of tests for selection an analogous table that shows the costs and benefits of correct and incorrect acceptances and rejections respectively.

peak experience   Profound and deeply felt moments in a person's life, sometimes said to be more common in self-actualized persons than in others. *See* self-actualization.

perceived locus of control   A person's belief about the source of outcomes that befall him. That perceived source (locus) may be internal, the result of something he did, or external, the result of forces outside of his own control.

percentile rank   The percentage of all the scores in a distribution that lie below a given score.

perceptual adaptation   The gradual adjustment to various distortions of the perceptual world, as in wearing prisms that tilt the entire visual world in one direction.

perceptual constancies   Certain constant attributes of a distal object, such as its shape and size, that we are able to perceive despite vagaries of the proximal stimulus.

perceptual hypothesis   The perceiver's assumption about what the stimulus is, which is tested as the perceptual system analyzes the stimulus for appropriate features.

perceptual parsing   The process of grouping various visual elements of a scene appropriately, deciding which elements go together and which do not.

period of formal operations   In Piaget's theory, the period from about age eleven on, when genuinely abstract mental operations can be undertaken (e.g., the ability to entertain hypothetical possibilities).

peripheral route to persuasion   *See* elaboration-likelihood model of persuasion.

periphery   In vision, the area towards the outside of the retina that has a high concentration of rods, is highly sensitive to dim light, and is responsible for colorless sensations.

permissive pattern   A parental style in which parents try not to assert their authority and impose few restrictions or demands on their children.

personal space   The physical region all around us whose intrusion we guard against; this aspect of human behavior has been likened to territoriality in animals.

personality inventories   Paper-and-pencil tests of personality that ask questions about feelings or customary behavior. *See also* projective techniques.

person-by-situation interaction   The fact that the effect of a situational variable may depend on the person. Thus some people may on average be equally fearful, but while one is afraid of meeting people but unafraid of large animals, another may be afraid of large animals but be unafraid of meeting people. *See also* reciprocal interaction, situationism.

persuasive communications   Messages that openly try to convince us to act a certain way or to hold a particular belief.

PET scan (Positron Emission Tomography)   A technique for examining brain structure and function by recording the degree of metabolic activity of different regions of the brain.

phallic stage   In psychoanalytic theory, the stage of psychosexual development during which the child begins to regard his or her genitals as a major source of gratification.

phenothiazines   A group of drugs, including Thorazine, that seem to be effective in alleviating the major symptoms of schizophrenia.

phenotype   The overt appearance and behavior of an organism, regardless of its genetic blueprint. *See also* genotype.

phenylalanine   An amino acid that cannot be transformed due to an enzyme deficiency in those with phenylketonuria (PKU). It is instead converted into a toxic agent that accumulates in an infant's bloodstream and damages the developing nervous system. *See also* phenylketonuria.

phenylketonuria (PKU)   A severe form of mental retardation detemined by a single gene. This disorder can be treated by means of a special diet (if detected early enough), despite the fact that the disorder is genetic. *See also* phenylalanine.

pheromones   Special chemicals secreted by many animals which trigger particular reactions in members of the same species.

phi phenomenon   *See* apparent movement.

phobia   One of the anxiety disorders which is characterized by an intense and, at least on the surface, irrational fear. *See also* generalized anxiety disorder, obsessive-compulsive disorder, specific phobia.

phoneme   The smallest significant unit of sound in a language. In English, it corresponds roughly to a letter of the alphabet (e.g., *apt, tap,* and *pat* are all made up of the same phonemes).

phonology   The rules in a language that govern the sequence in which phonemes can be arranged.

phrase   A sequence of words within a sentence that function as a unit (e.g., *The ball/rolled/down the hill*).

phrase structure   The organization of sentences into phrases. Surface structure is the phrase organization of sentences as they are spoken or written. Underlying structure is the phrase organization that describes the meaning of parts of the sentence, such as doer, action, and done-to.

phrase structure description   The tree diagram that shows the hierarchical structure of a sentence. The descending branches of the tree correspond to smaller and smaller units of sentence structure.

pictorial cues   The monocular depth cues that the eye exploits as an optical consequence of the projection of a three-dimensional world upon a flat surface (such as, interposition, linear perspective, and relative size).

pitch   The psychological dimension of sound corresponding to frequency; as frequency increases, the pitch appears to rise.

pituitary gland   An endocrine gland heavily influenced by the hypothalamus. A master gland because many of its secretions trigger hormone secretions in other glands.

placebo   In medical practice, a term for a chemically inert substance that the patient believes will help him.

placebo effect   A beneficial effect of a treatment administered to a patient who believes it has therapeutic powers even though it has none.

place theory   A theory of pitch proposed by Hermann von Helmholtz which states that different parts of the basilar membrane in the cochlea are responsive to different sound frequencies; the nervous system interprets the excitation from different basilar places as different pitches.

pleasure center   According to some theorists, a special region of the brain that is triggered whenever any motive is satisfied.

pleasure principle   In Freud's theory, the id's sole law, that of obtaining immediate satisfaction regardless of circumstances and whatever the cost.

pluralistic ignorance   A situation in which individuals in a group don't know that there are others in the group who share their feelings.

polyandry   A mating system in which one female monopolizes the reproductive efforts of several males.

polygenic inheritance   Inheritance of an attribute whose expression is controlled not by one but by many gene pairs.

polygyny   A mating system in which one male monopolizes the reproductive efforts of several females.

population   The entire group of subjects (or test trials) about which the investigator wants to draw conclusions. *See also* sample.

positive feedback   *See* feedback system.

positive reinforcement   A reinforcement procedure in which a response is followed by the reduction or cessation of an aversive stimulus.

positive symptoms of schizophrenia   Symptoms that center on what these patients do (or think or perceive) that normals don't, for example, hallucinations, delusions, and bizarre behaviors. *See* negative symptoms of schizophrenia.

postsynaptic membrane   The membrane of the receiving cell across the synaptic gap that contains specialized receptor molecules.

postsynaptic neuron   The cell receiving a neural message.

post-traumatic stress disorder   A disorder sometimes experienced after an especially stressful traumatic event. Symptoms include dissociation, recurrent nightmares, flashbacks, and sleep disturbances.

potentiation   In motivation, the tendency to make some behaviors, perceptions, and feelings more probable than others.

precursor   A substance required for the chemical manufacture of a neurotransmitter.

predicate   *See* concept.

predictive validity   A measure of a test's validity based on the correlation between the test score and some criterion of behavior the test predicted (e.g., a correlation between a scholastic aptitude test and college grades).

prefrontal lobotomy   A somatic treatment for severe mental disorders which surgically cuts the connections between the thalamus and the frontal lobes.

preoperational period   In Piaget's theory, the period from about ages two to six during which children come to represent actions and objects internally but cannot systematically manipulate these representations or relate them to each other; the child is therefore unable to conserve quantity across perceptual transformations and also is unable to take points of view other than her own.

preparedness   A built-in predisposition of an animal to form certain associations rather than others.

preparedness theory of phobias   The theory that phobias grow out of a built-in predisposition (preparedness) to learn to fear certain stimuli (e.g., snakes and spiders) that may have posed serious dangers to our primate ancestors.

prescriptive rules   Rules prescribed by "authorities" about how people *ought* to speak and write that often fail to conform to the facts about natural talking and understanding. This is in contrast to the structural principles of a language which describe (rather than prescribe) the principles according to which native speakers of a language actually arrange their words into sentences. Sentences formed according to these principles are called well-formed or grammatical.

presynaptic neuron   The cell that sends a neural message across the synaptic gap.

primacy effect   (1) In free recall, the recall superiority of the items in the first part of a list compared to those in the middle. (2) In forming an impression of another person, the phenomenon whereby attributes first noted carry a greater weight than attributes noted later on. *See* recency effect.

primary memory   *See* short-term memory, working memory.

prisoner's dilemma A particular arrangement of payoffs in a two-person situation in which each individual has to choose between two alternatives without knowing the other's choice. The payoff structure is so arranged that the optimal strategy for each person depends upon whether he can trust the other or not. If trust is possible, the payoffs for each will be considerably higher than if there is no trust. *See also* social dilemma.

proactive inhibition Disturbance of recall of some material by other material learned previously. *See* retroactive inhibition.

procedural knowledge *See* declarative knowledge.

progesterone A female sex hormone that dominates the latter phase of the female cycle during which the uterus walls thicken to receive the embryo.

projection In psychoanalytic theory, a mechanism of defense in which various forbidden thoughts and impulses are attributed to another person rather than the self, thus warding off some anxiety (e.g., "I hate you" becomes "You hate me").

projection areas Regions of the cortex that serve as receiving stations for sensory information or as dispatching stations for motor commands.

projective techniques Devices for assessing personality by presenting relatively unstructured stimuli that elicit subjective responses of various kinds (e.g., the TAT and the Rorschach inkblot test). Their advocates believe that such tasks allow the person to "project" her own personality into her reactions. *See also* personality inventories.

proposition *See* concept.

prosopagnosia The inability to recognize faces produced by a brain lesion.

prototype The typical example of a category of meaning (e.g., robin is a prototypical bird).

proximal stimulus *See* distal stimulus.

proximity (1) In perception, the closeness of two figures. The closer together they are, the more they will tend to be grouped together perceptually; (2) the nearness of people, which is one of the most important determinants of attraction and liking.

pseudohermaphroditism The condition of individuals with ambiguous genitalia.

psychoanalysis (1) A theory of human personality formulated by Freud whose key assertions include unconscious conflict and psychosexual development. (2) A method of therapy that draws heavily on this theory of personality. Its main aim is to have the patient gain insight into his own, presently unconscious, thoughts and feelings. Therapeutic tools employed toward this end include free association, interpretation, and the appropriate use of the transference relationship between patient and analyst. *See also* free association, transference.

psychoanalytic model As defined in the text, a subcategory of the pathology model which holds that (1) the underlying pathology is a constellation of unconscious conflicts and defenses against anxiety, usually rooted in early childhood, and (2) treatment should be by some form of psychotherapy based on psychoanalytic principles.

psychodynamic approach of personality An approach to personality originally derived from psychoanalytic theory that asserts that personality differences are based on unconscious (dynamic) conflicts within the individual. *See also* behavioral-cognitive approach, humanistic approach, situationism, sociocultural approach, trait theory.

psychogenic disorders Disorders whose origins are psychological rather than organic (e.g., phobias). *See also* somatogenic mental disorders.

psychometric approach to intelligence An attempt to understand the nature of intelligence by studying the pattern of results obtained on intelligence tests.

psychopath *See* antisocial personality disorder.

psychopathology The study of psychological disorder.

psychophysics An approach to sensory experience that relates the characteristics of physical stimuli to attributes of the sensory experience they produce.

psychophysiological disorders In these disorders (formerly called psychosomatic), the primary symptoms involve genuine organic damage whose ultimate cause is psychological (e.g., coronary heart disease).

psychophysiology An approach to sensory experience that concerns the neural consequences of a given stimulus input.

psychosexual development In psychoanalytic theory, the description of the progressive stages in the way the child gains his main source of pleasure as he grows into adulthood, defined by the zone of the body through which this pleasure is derived (oral, anal, genital) and by the object toward which this pleasurable feeling is directed (mother, father, adult sexual partner). *See also* anal stage, genital stage, oral stage, phallic stage.

psychosis A broad category that describes some of the more severe mental disorders in which the patient's thoughts and deeds no longer meet the demands of reality.

psychosocial crises In Erik Erikson's theory, a series of crises through which all persons must pass as they go through their life cycle (e.g., the identity crisis during which adolescents or young adults try to establish the separation between themselves and their parents).

psychotherapy As used here, a collective term for all forms of treatment that use psychological rather than somatic means.

punishment training An instrumental training procedure in which a response is suppressed by having its occurrence followed by an aversive event. *See also* avoidance learning, escape learning.

pyramidal system One of two motor systems that originates in the motor cortex in the brain and sends its tracts directly to the motor neurons that activate the muscles. The pyramidal system is younger in evolutionary terms and supervises the more delicate movements of the body.

quiet sleep Stages 2 to 4 of sleep during which there are no rapid eye movements and during which the EEG shows progressively less cortical arousal. Also known as non-REM sleep.

radical behaviorism An approach usually associated with B. F. Skinner that asserts that the subject matter of psychology is overt behavior, without reference to inferred, internal processes such as wishes, traits, or expectations.

random sample *See* sample.

range A measure of variability given by the highest score minus the lowest.

rationalization In psychoanalytic theory, a mechanism of defense by means of which unacceptable thoughts or impulses are reinterpreted in more acceptable and thus less anxiety-arousing terms (e.g., the jilted lover who convinces himself he never loved her anyway).

ratio scale An interval scale in which there is a true zero point, thus allowing ratio statements (e.g., this sound is twice as loud as the other). *See also* categorical scale, interval scale, nominal scale, ordinal scale.

ratio schedule A reinforcement schedule in which reinforcement is delivered for the first response made after a certain number of responses. In a fixed-ratio schedule, the number of responses required for a reward is always the same. In a variable-ratio schedule, the number of responses required varies irregularly around a specified average.

reaction formation In psychoanalytic theory, a mechanism of defense in which a forbidden impulse is turned into its opposite (e.g., hate toward a sibling becomes exaggerated love).

reaction time The interval between the presentation of a signal and the observer's response to that signal.

reality principle In Freud's theory, the set of rules that govern the ego and that dictate the way in which it tries to satisfy the id by gaining pleasure in accordance with the real world and its demands.

recall A task in which some item must be produced from memory. *See* recognition.

receiver-operating-characteristic curve (ROC curve) A graphical representation of the relationship between stimulus sensitivity and response bias.

recency effect In free recall, the recall superiority of the items at the end of the list compared to those in the middle. *See* primacy effect (in recall).

receptive aphasia A language disorder usually associated with lesions in Wernicke's area in which patients talk rapidly and grammatically but convey little information and do not understand meanings.

receptive field The retinal area in which visual stimulation affects a particular cell's firing rate.

receptor cells A special type of neuron that can respond to various external energies and translate physical stimuli into electrical changes to which other neurons can respond.

receptor molecules The specialized molecules in the postsynaptic membrane that open or close certain ion gates when activated by the correct neurotransmitter.

recessive gene *See* gene.

reciprocal altruism *See* altruism.

reciprocal inhibition The arrangement by which excitation of some neural system is accompanied by inhibition of that system's antagonist (as in antagonistic muscles).

reciprocal interaction The fact that different people seek out different situations.

reciprocity principle A basic rule of many social interactions that decrees that one must repay whatever one has been given.

recoding Changing the form in which some information is stored.

recognition A task in which a stimulus has to be identified as having been previously encountered in some context or not. *See also* recall.

reference The relations between words or sentences and objects or events in the world (e.g., "ball" refers to ball).

reflection The process by which objects give off light from an illuminating source.

reflex A simple, stereotyped reaction in response to some stimulus (e.g., limb flexion in withdrawal from pain).

rehearsal *See* elaborative rehearsal, maintenance rehearsal.

reinforced trial In classical conditioning, a trial on which the CS is accompanied by the US. In instrumental conditioning, a trial in which the instrumental response is followed by reward, cessation of punishment, or other reinforcement.

reinforcement In classical conditioning, the procedure by which the US is made contingent on the CS. In instrumental conditioning, the procedure by which the instrumental response is made contingent upon some sought-after outcome.

relative size A monocular depth cue in which far-off objects produce a smaller retinal image than nearby objects of the same size.

releasing stimulus Term used by ethologists to describe a stimulus which is genetically programmed to elicit a fixed-action pattern (e.g., a long, thin, red-tipped beak which elicits a herring gull chick's begging response). *See also* fixed-action patterns.

reliability coefficient Coefficient used in determining the consistency of mental tests that are derived from test-retest correlations or from correlations between alternative forms of a test.

REM sleep *See* active sleep.

repetition priming An increase in the likelihood that an item is identified, recognized, or recalled by recent exposure to that item, which may occur without explicit awareness.

representational thought In Piaget's theory, thought that is internalized and includes mental representations of prior experiences with objects and events.

representations Cognitions that correspond to (represent) certain events, or relations between events, in the world.

representativeness heuristic A rule of thumb in estimating the probability that an object (or event) belongs to a certain category based on the extent to which it resembles the prototype of that category regardless of the base rate at which it occurs. *See also* prototype.

repression In psychoanalytic theory, a mechanism of defense by means of which thoughts, impulses, or memories that give rise to anxiety are pushed out of consciousness.

resistance In psychoanalysis, a collective term for the patient's failures to associate freely and say whatever enters his head.

response bias A preference for one or another response in a psychophysical experiment, independent of the stimulus situation.

response rate The number of responses per unit time; this measures response strength in operant conditioning.

response suppression The inhibition of a conditioned response by conditioned fear.

resting potential The difference in charge across the membrane in a cell's normal state.

restrained-eating hypothesis The hypothesis that the oversensitivity of obese persons to external cues is caused by the disinhibition of conscious restraints on eating. *See also* externality hypothesis, setpoint hypothesis.

restructuring A reorganization of a problem, often rather sudden, which seems to be a characteristic of creative thought.

retention The survival of the memory trace over some interval of time.

retention intervals In memory experiments, the time between original learning and the time of the test.

retina The structure that contains the visual receptors and several layers of neurons further up along the pathway to the brain.

retinal image The image of an object that is projected on the retina. Its size increases with the size of that object and decreases with its distance from the eye.

retrieval The process of searching for some item in memory and of finding it. If retrieval fails, this may or may not mean that the relevant memory trace is not present; the trace simply may be inaccessible.

retrieval cue   A stimulus that helps to retrieve a memory trace.

retroactive inhibition   Disturbance of recall of some material by other material learned subsequently. *See also* proactive inhibition.

retrograde amnesia   A memory deficit suffered after head injury or concussion in which the patient loses memory of some period prior to the injury. *See also* anterograde amnesia.

reuptake   A mechanism by which a neurotransmitter is drawn back into the presynaptic terminal that released it.

rhodopsin   The visual pigment used in the rods.

ROC curve   *See* receiver-operating-characteristic curve.

rods   Visual receptors that respond to lower light intensities and give rise to achromatic (colorless) sensations.

Rorschach inkblot test   A projective technique that requires the subject to look at inkblots and say what she sees in them.

safety signal   A stimulus that has been contingent on the absence of an electric shock (or another negative reinforcer) in a situation in which such shocks are sometimes delivered. *See also* contingency.

sample   A subset of a population selected by the investigator for study. A random sample is one so constructed that each member of the population has an equal chance to be picked. A stratified sample is one so constructed that every relevant subgroup of the population is randomly sampled in proportion to its size. *See also* population.

saturation   A perceived dimension of visual stimuli that describes the "purity" of a color—the extent to which it is rich in hue (e.g., green rather than olive).

savant   A mentally retarded person who has some remarkable talent that seems out of keeping with his or her low level of general intelligence. Previously called *idiot savant,* a term now abandoned as derogatory.

scaling   A procedure for assigning numbers to a subject's responses. *See also* categorical scale, interval scale, nominal scale, ordinal scale, ratio scale.

scatter diagram   A graphical representation showing the relationship between two variables.

scatter plot   A diagram of correlation data in which each axis represents a single variable.

schedule of reinforcement   A rule that determines the occasions when a response is reinforced. *See also* ratio schedule, interval schedules.

schema   (1) In theories of memory and thinking, a term that refers to a general cognitive structure in terms of which information can be organized. (2) In Piaget's theory of development, a mental pattern.

schizophrenia   A group of severe mental disorders characterized by at least some of the following: marked disturbance of thought, withdrawal, inappropriate or flat emotions, delusions, and hallucinations. *See also* catatonic schizophrenia, disorganized type of schizophrenia, paranoid schizophrenia.

score profile   *See* test profile.

script   A subcase of a schema, which describes a characteristic scenario of behaviors in a particular setting, such as a restaurant script. *See also* schema.

seasonal affective disorder   A mood disorder with a seasonal pattern, with depressions that start in the late fall when the days become shorter and end in the spring when the days lengthen.

secondary memory   *See* long-term memory.

second-order conditioning   *See* higher-order conditioning.

self-actualization   A major concern of Maslow and other adherents of the humanistic approach, it is the realization of one's potentialities so that one becomes what one can become. *See also* hierarchy of needs, peak experience.

self-monitoring   Monitoring one's own behavior so that it fits the situation.

self-perception theory   A theory that asserts that we do not know our own attitudes and feelings directly but must infer them by observing our own behavior and then performing much the same attribution processes that we employ when trying to understand the behavior of others.

self-serving bias   The tendency to deny responsibility for failures but take credit for successes. *See also* attribution theory, fundamental attribution error, actor-observer difference.

semantic feature   The smallest significant unit of meaning within a word (e.g., male, human, and adult are semantic features of the word "man").

semantic memory   The component of generic memory that concerns the meaning of words and concepts.

semantics   The organization of meaning in language.

semicircular canals   Three canals within the inner ear that contain a viscous liquid that moves when the head rotates, providing information about the nature and extent of the movement.

sensation   According to the empiricists, the primitive experiences that the senses give us (e.g., green, bitter).

sensation seeking   The tendency to seek novel experiences, look for thrills and adventure, and be highly susceptible to boredom.

sensitive period   *See* critical period.

sensory adaptation   The decline in sensitivity found in most sensory systems after continuous exposure to the same stimulus.

sensory code   The rule (code) by which the nervous system represents sensory characteristics of the stimulus. An example is firing frequency, which is the general code for increased stimulus intensity.

sensory coding   The process by which the nervous system translates various aspects of the stimulus into dimensions of our sensory experience.

sensory interaction   The fact that a sensory system's response to any given stimulus rarely depends on that stimulus alone and is affected by other impinging stimuli.

sensory modalities   A technical term for the sensory domains: taste, touch, kinesthesis, vision, and hearing.

sensory-motor intelligence   In Piaget's theory, intelligence during the first two years of life which consists mainly of sensations and motor impulses with, at first, little in the way of internalized representations.

sensory process   According to signal detection theorists, the underlying neural activity in the sensory system upon which all psychological judgments are based. *See also* signal-detection theory.

sensory projection areas   *See* projection areas.

Sentence Analyzing Machinery (SAM)   A set of procedures by which listeners comprehend sentences.

serial reproduction   An experiment in which a drawing is presented to one subject, who reproduces it from memory for a second subject, whose reproduction is shown to a third, and so on. Each subject's memory distortions become part of the stimulus for the next subject down the line, amplifying the reconstructive alteration.

serial search   The successive comparison of a target stimulus to different items in memory. *See also* parallel search.

serotonin (5HT)   A neurotransmitter involved in many of the mechanisms of sleep and emotional arousal.

servomechanisms   Industrial devices, such as home furnaces, that operate on negative feedback systems and can maintain themselves in a particular state.

set   *See* mental set.

setpoint   A general term for the level at which negative feedback tries to maintain the system. An example is the setting of a thermostat. *See also* setpoint hypothesis.

setpoint hypothesis   The hypothesis that different persons have different setpoints for weight. *See also* setpoint.

sexual dimorphism   A condition that describes a species in which there is a marked difference in the size and/or form of the two sexes as in the case of deer (antlers) or peacocks (long tail feathers).

sexual orientation   The direction of a person's choice of a sexual partner, which may be heterosexual or homosexual. *See also* gender identity, gender role.

shape constancy   The tendency to perceive the shape of objects as more or less the same despite the fact that the retinal image of these objects changes its shape as we change the angle of orientation from which we view them.

shaping   An instrumental learning procedure through which an animal (or human) is trained to perform a rather difficult response by reinforcing successive approximations to that response.

short-term habituation   *See* habituation.

short-term memory   *See* stage theory of memory.

signal-detection theory   A theory that asserts that observers who are asked to detect the presence or absence of a stimulus try to decide whether an internal sensory experience should be attributed to background noise or to a signal added to background noise. *See also* sensory process.

similarity   In perception, a principle by which we tend to group like figures, especially by color and orientation.

simple reaction time   A measurement of the speed with which a subject can respond to a stimulus.

simulation heuristic   A mental shortcut used in making decisions and evaluating outcomes that refers to imaginary replays of events or situations.

simultaneous color contrast   The effect produced by the fact that any region in the visual field tends to induce its complementary color in adjoining areas; for example, a gray patch will tend to look bluish if surrounded by yellow and yellowish if surrounded by blue.

simultaneous pairing   A classical conditioning procedure in which the conditioned stimulus (CS) and the unconditioned stimulus (US) are presented simultaneously. *See also* backward pairing, forward pairing.

sine waves   Curves that correspond to the plot of the trigonometric sine function.

situational factors   *See* attribution theory.

situationism   The view that human behavior is largely determined by the characteristics of the situation rather than those of the person. *See also* behavioral-cognitive approach, humanistic approach, psychodynamic approach, sociocultural approach, trait theory.

size constancy   The tendency to perceive the size of objects as more or less the same despite the fact that the retinal image of these objects changes in size whenever we change the distance from which we view them.

skeletal musculature   The muscles that control the skeleton, such as those of the arms and legs.

skewed   A term used to describe asymmetrical distributions of experimental results with extreme values at one end.

smooth muscles   The muscles of the internal organs that are controlled by the autonomic nervous system.

social cognition   The way in which we interpret and try to comprehend social events.

social comparison   A process of reducing uncertainty about one's own beliefs and attitudes by comparing them to those of others.

social development   A child's growth in his or her relations with other people.

social dilemma   A problem similar in structure to the prisoner's dilemma but expanded to include any number of individuals, each of whom has to decide whether to cooperate or defect. *See also* prisoner's dilemma.

social exchange theory   A theory that asserts that each partner in a social relationship gives something to the other and expects to get something in return.

social facilitation   The tendency to perform better in the presence of others than when alone. This facilitating effect works primarily for simple and/or well-practiced tasks.

social impact theory   A theory that asserts that the influence others exert on an individual increases with their number, their immediacy, and their strength (e.g., status).

social influence   A general term for interactions in which the influence of other people affects one individual.

socialization   The process whereby the child acquires the patterns of behavior characteristic of his or her society.

social learning theory   A theoretical approach to socialization and personality that is midway between behavior theories, such as Skinner's, and cognitive approaches. It stresses learning by observing others who serve as models for the child's behavior. The effect of the model may be to allow learning by imitation and also may be to show the child whether a response he already knows should or should not be performed.

social loafing   An example of the diffusion of social impact in which individuals working as a group on a common task generate less effort than they would if they had worked alone.

social phobia   A fear of embarrassment or humiliation in front of others that causes people to avoid situations in which they must expose themselves to public scrutiny. *See also* phobia, specific phobia.

sociobiology   A recent theoretical movement in biology that tries to trace social behavior to genetically based predispositions; an approach that has led to some controversy when extended to humans.

sociocultural approach   The view that people differ in at least some regards as a result of the cultural group in which they were raised and of which they are a member. *See also* behavioral-cognitive approach, humanistic approach, psychodynamic approach, trait theory, situationism.

sociopath   *See* antisocial personality disorder.

somatic nervous system   A division of the peripheral nervous system primarily concerned with the control of the skeletal musculature and the transmission of information from the sense organs.

somatic therapies   A collective term for any treatment of mental disorders by means of some organic manipulation. This includes drug administration, any form of surgery, convulsive treatments, etc.

somatoform disorders   The generic term for disorders that take bodily form in the absence of any known physical illness.

somatogenic mental disorders Mental disorders that are produced by an organic cause. This is the case for some disorders (e.g., general paresis) but almost surely not for all (e.g., phobias). *See also* psychogenic disorders.

somatosensory area A cortical area located in the parietal lobe just behind the motor area in the frontal lobe. This region is the projection area for bodily sensations, including touch, pain, and temperature.

sound waves Successive pressure variations in the air which vary in amplitude and wavelength.

source memory The knowledge of the event from which a certain memory derived.

Spearman's theory of general intelligence (g) Spearman's account, based on factor analytic studies, ascribes intelligence-test performance to one underlying factor, general intelligence *(g)*, which is tapped by all subtests, and a large number of specific skills *(s's)* which depend on abilities specific to each subtest. *See also* factor analysis, group-factor theory.

specificity theory An approach to sensory experience which asserts that different sensory qualities are signaled by different neurons. These neurons are somehow labeled with their quality, so that whenever they fire, the nervous system interprets their activation as that particular sensory quality.

specific phobia A fear of certain objects or events, such as a fear of heights or enclosed places.

spectral sensitivity curve A graphical representation of the eye's sensitivity to each of the separate wavelengths that constitute a light stimulus.

split brain A condition in which the corpus callosum and some other fibers are cut so that the two cerebral hemispheres are isolated.

spontaneous recovery An increase in the tendency to perform an extinguished response after a time interval in which neither conditioned stimulus (CS) nor unconditioned stimulus (US) are presented.

spreading activation model A memory model that assumes that elements in a semantic memory network are more readily activated the smaller the distance between them.

stabilized image technique A procedure by which the retina receives a stationary image even though the eye is moving.

stage theory of memory A theoretical approach that asserts that there are several memory stores. One is short-term memory, which holds information for fairly short intervals and has a small capacity; another is long-term memory, which holds information for very long periods and has a vast capacity. According to the theory, information will only enter into long-term memory if it has been in short-term memory for a while.

standard deviation (SD) A measure of the variability of a frequency distribution which is the square root of the variance. If *V* is the variance and *SD* the standard deviation, then $SD = \sqrt{V}$. *See also* variance.

standard error of the mean A measure of the variability of the mean whose value depends both on the standard deviation *(SD)* of the distribution and the number of cases in the sample *(N)*. If *SE* is the standard error, then $SE = SD/\sqrt{N-1}$.

standardization group The group against which an individual's test score is evaluated.

standard score (*z*-score) A score that is expressed as a deviation from the mean in standard deviation units, which allows a comparison of scores drawn from different distributions. If *M* is the mean and *SD* the standard deviation, then $z = (\text{score} - M)/SD$.

stereotypes Simplified schemas by which people try to categorize complex groups. Group stereotypes are often negative, especially when applied to minority groups. *See also* out-group homogeniety effect.

stimulus Anything in the environment that the organism can detect and respond to.

stimulus generalization In classical conditioning, the tendency to respond to stimuli other than the original conditioned stimulus (CS). The greater the similarity between the CS and the new stimulus, the greater this tendency will be. An analogous phenomenon in instrumental conditioning is a response to stimuli other than the original discriminative stimulus.

storage capacity The amount of information that can be kept in memory. The capacity of long-term memory is much larger than that of working (or short-term) memory.

stratified sampling An experimental procedure in which each subgroup of the population is sampled in proportion to its size.

stroboscopic movement *See* apparent movement.

Stroop effect A marked decrease in the speed of naming the colors in which various color names (such as green, red, etc.) are printed when the colors and the names are different. An important example of automatization.

structural principles (of language) *See* prescriptive rules.

subjective contours Perceived contours that do not exist physically. We tend to complete figures that have gaps in them by continuing a contour along its original path.

subroutines In a hierarchical organization, the lower level operations that are controlled by higher level operations.

subtractive color mixture Mixing colors by subtracting one set of wavelengths from another set (as in mixing colors on a palette or superimposing two colored filters). *See also* additive color mixture.

successive approximations *See* shaping.

superego In Freud's theory, a set of reaction patterns within the ego that represent the internalized rules of society and that control the ego by punishing with guilt. *See also* ego, id.

surface structure *See* phrase structure.

symbolic representation A type of mental representation that does not correspond to the physical characteristics of that which it represents. Thus, the word *mouse* does not resemble the small rodent it represents.

symmetrical distribution A distribution of experimental evidence in which deviations in either direction from the mean are equally frequent.

sympathetic system A division of the autonomic nervous system that mobilizes the body's energies for emergencies (e.g., increasing heart rate). Its action is antagonistic to that of the parasympathetic system.

symptoms The outward manifestations of an underlying pathology.

synapse The juncture between the axon of one neuron and the dendrite or cell body of another.

syndrome A pattern of symptoms that tend to go together.

syntax The system by which words are arranged into meaningful phrases and sentences.

systematic desensitization A behavior therapy that tries to remove anxiety connected to various stimuli by a gradual process of counterconditioning to a response incompatible with fear, usually muscular relaxation. The stimuli are usually evoked as mental images according to an anxiety hierarchy whereby the less frightening stimuli are counterconditioned before the more frightening ones.

taste buds The receptor organs for taste.

taxonomy A classification system.

temperament In modern usage, a characteristic level of reactivity and energy, often thought to be based on constitutional factors.

temporal lobe A lobe in each cerebral hemisphere which includes the auditory projection area.

temporal summation The process whereby two or more stimuli that are individually below threshold will elicit a reflex if presented together at different spatial points on the body.

territory A term used by ethologists to describe a region a particular animal stakes out as its own. The territory holder is usually a male, but in some species the territory is held by a mating pair or by a group.

testosterone The principal male sex hormone (androgen) in mammals.

test profile A graphic indication of an individual's performance on several components of a test. This is often useful for guidance or clinical evaluation because it indicates which abilities or traits are relatively high or low in that person.

test-retest method A way of increasing test reliability by administering the same test to the same group of subjects after a certain time lag. *See also* reliability coefficients.

texture gradient A distance cue based on changes in surface texture which depend on the distance of the observer.

thalamus A part of the lower portion of the forebrain which serves as a major relay and integration center for sensory information.

Thematic Apperception Test (TAT) A projective technique in which persons are shown a set of pictures and asked to write a story about each.

theory of mind A set of interrelated concepts we use as we try to make sense of our own mental processes and those of others, including the variability of human beliefs and desires.

Thorazine *See* antipsychotic drugs.

threat displays In animals, signs of aggression that are less costly ways of intimidating the enemy than actual combat.

threshold The value a stimulus must reach to produce a response.

tip-of-the-tongue phenomenon The condition in which one keeps on feeling on the verge of retrieving a word or name but continues to be unsuccessful.

token economy An arrangement for operant behavior modification in hospital settings. Certain responses (e.g., talking to others) are reinforced with tokens which can be exchanged for desirable items.

tolerance *See* opponent-process theory of motivation.

top-down processes Processes in form recognition that begin with higher units and then work down to smaller units (e.g., from phrases to words to letters). This is in contrast with bottom-up processes, which start with smaller component parts and then gradually build up to the higher units on top (e.g., from letters to words to phrases). One demonstration of top-down processing is provided by context effects in which knowledge or expectations affect what one sees.

trace consolidation hypothesis The hypothesis that newly acquired memory traces undergo a gradual change that makes them more and more resistant to any disturbance.

trait *See* trait theory.

trait theory The view that people differ in regard to a number of underlying attributes (traits) that partially determine behavior and that are presumed to be essentially consistent from time to time and situation to situation. It tends toward the view that many such traits are based on genetic predispositions. *See also* behavioral-cognitive approach, humanistic approach, psychodynamic approach, situationism, sociocultural approach.

transduction The process by which a receptor translates some physical stimulus (e.g., light or pressure) to give rise to an action potential in another neuron.

transference In psychoanalysis, the patient's tendency to transfer emotional reactions that were originally directed toward one's own parents (or other crucial figures in one's early life) and redirect them toward the analyst.

transposition The phenomenon whereby visual and auditory patterns (i.e., figures and melodies) remain the same even though the parts of which they are composed are changed.

tree diagram A branched diagram that represents a hierarchical structure.

tricyclics *See* antidepressant drugs.

two-syndrome hypothesis of schizophrenia The hypothesis that schizophrenia is a composite of two different syndromes, Type I and Type II. According to the hypothesis, Type I is produced by a malfunction of transmitters, especially dopamine, and produces primarily positive symptoms, while Type II is caused by cerebral damage and atrophy and leads to negative symptoms.

Type A personality A personality type characterized by extreme impatience, competitiveness, and vehement aggressiveness when thwarted. *See also* Type B personality.

Type B personality In contrast to the Type A personality, Type B is characterized by a more easygoing, less hurried, less competitive, and friendlier behavior pattern. *See also* Type A personality.

unconditioned reflex *See* unconditioned response.

unconditioned response (UR) In classical conditioning, the response that is elicited by the unconditioned stimulus without prior training. *See* conditioned response, conditioned stimulus, unconditioned stimulus.

unconditioned stimulus (US) In classical conditioning, the stimulus that elicits the unconditioned response and the presentation of which acts as reinforcement. *See* conditioned response, conditioned stimulus, unconditioned response.

unconscious inference A process postulated by Helmholtz to explain certain perceptual phenomena such as size constancy. An object is perceived to be in the distance and is therefore unconsciously perceived or inferred to be larger than it appears to be retinally. *See also* size constancy.

underlying pathology model An approach to psychopathology which asserts that various overt signs and symptoms are produced by an underlying cause that may be mental or organic or both. The therapist's objective is to discover and remove the underlying pathology, which will then cause the symptoms to disappear.

underlying structure *See* phrase structure.

unilateral neglect syndrome The result of certain lesions on the right side of the parietal lobe, which disables a patient from perceiving features in the left visual field and causes the patient to ignore the left side of his or her body.

unipolar disorder Mood disorder (usually depression) in which there is no back-and-forth swing between the two emotional extremes.

unreinforced trial In classical conditioning, a trial in which the unconditioned stimulus (US) is omitted.

validity The extent to which a test measures what it is supposed to measure. *See also* construct validity, incremental validity, predictive validity.

validity coefficient   The correlation between test scores, such as those for scholastic aptitude, and some appropriate criterion, such as the grade-point average, which provides information about a test's ability to predict future performance.

variability   The tendency of scores in a frequency distribution to scatter away from the central value. *See also* central tendency, standard deviation, variance.

variable-interval schedule   *See* interval schedule.

variable-ratio schedule   *See* ratio schedule.

variance (V)   A measure of the variability of a frequency distribution. It is computed by finding the difference between each score and the mean, squaring the result, adding all the squared deviations obtained in this manner, and dividing it by the number of cases. If V is the variance, M the mean, and N the number of scores, then $V = \text{sum of } (\text{score} - M)^2/N$.

vasoconstriction   The constriction of the capillaries brought on by activation of the sympathetic division of the autonomic nervous system in response to excessive cold.

vasodilatation   The dilating of the skin's capillaries (brought on by activation of the parasympathetic division of the autonomic nervous system in response to excessive heat) that sends warm blood to the body's surface and results in heat loss by radiation.

ventral tegmental area (VTA)   A region in the midbrain thought to be involved in dopamine releasing pathways.

ventromedial region of the hypothalamus   *See* lateral hypothalamus.

vesicles   The tiny sacs in the presynaptic neuron that contain neurotransmitters.

vestibular senses   A set of receptors that provide information about the orientation and movements of the head, located in the semicircular canals and the vestibular sacs of the inner ear.

vicarious distress   The distress produced by witnessing the suffering of another. This is a less reliable motive for helping that person than empathic concern. *See also* empathic concern.

vicarious reinforcement   According to social learning theorists, a form of reinforcement said to occur when someone watches a model being rewarded or punished.

visible spectrum   The range of wavelengths to which our visual system can respond, extending from about 400 (the wavelength of the color violet) to 750 nanometers (the wavelength of the color reddish orange).

visual cliff   A device for assessing depth perception in young organisms; it consists of a glass surface that extends over an apparently deep side (the cliff) and an apparently shallow side.

visual search task   A test in which subjects have to indicate whether a certain target is present or absent in a briefly presented display.

visual segregation   *See* perceptual parsing.

volume receptors   Receptors that help to control water intake by responding to the total volume of fluids in the body. *See also* osmoreceptors.

wavelength   The distance between the crests of two successive waves that is a major determinant of perceived color.

Weber fraction   In Weber's law, the fraction given by the change in stimulus intensity divided by the standard intensity required to produce a just-noticeable increase.

Weber's law   The observation that the size of the difference threshold is proportional to the intensity of the standard stimulus.

well-defined problems   Problems in which there is a clear-cut way for deciding whether a proposed solution is correct. This is in contrast to ill-defined problems in which it is not clear what a correct solution might be.

Wernicke's area   *See* aphasia.

wish fulfillment in dreams   *See* Freud's theory of dreams.

withdrawal effects   *See* opponent-process theory of motivation.

withdrawal symptoms   A consequence of drug addiction that occurs when the drug is withheld; these effects are the opposite of those produced by the drug itself.

within-family differences   A term often used in the discussion of the role of environment. It describes differences in the environment of different members of the same family (e.g., different schools). For personality attributes, these seem to be more important than between-family differences. *See also* between-family differences.

within-group heritability   The extent to which variation within groups (e.g., among U.S. whites) is attributable to genetic factors. *See also* between-group heritability, heritability.

working memory   Also called active memory. A part of the memory system that is currently activated, but has relatively little cognitive capacity..

X-chromosome   One of the two sex chromosomes that contains the genetic commands which determine whether a given animal will be male or female. In mammalian females, both members of the pair of chromosomes are X-chromosomes; in mammalian males, there is one X-chromosome and one Y-chromosome.

Y-chromosome   *See* X-chromosome.

Young-Helmholtz theory   An explanation of the psychological properties of color that states that each of the three receptor types (short-wave, medium-wave, and long-wave) gives rise to the experience of one basic color (blue, green, or red).

z-score   *See* standard score.

zygote   The fertilized ovum resulting from the union of a sperm and an egg cell in sexual reproduction.

REFERENCES

ABRAHAM, K. 1927. The influence of oral eroticism on character formation. In Abraham, K., *Selected papers,* pp. 393–406. London: Hogarth Press.

ABRAMS, M. H. 1953. *The mirror and the lamp: Romantic theory and the critical tradition.* New York: Oxford University Press.

ABRAMSON, L. Y.; METALSKY, G. I.; AND ALLOY, L. B. 1989. Hopelessness depression: A theory-based subtype of depression. *Psychological Review* 96:358–72.

ABRAMSON, L. Y., AND SACKHEIM, H. A. 1977. A paradox in depression: Uncontrollability and self-blame. *Psychological Bulletin* 84: 835–51.

ABRAMSON, L. Y.; SELIGMAN, M. E. P.; AND TEASDALE, J. D. 1978. Learned helplessness in humans: Critique and reformulation. *Journal of Abnormal Psychology* 87:49–74.

ACSF INVESTIGATORS. 1992. AIDS and sexual behaviour in France. *Nature* 360: 407–409.

ADAMSON, E. 1984. *Art as healing.* London: Coventure Ltd.

ADOLPH, E. F. 1947. Urges to eat and drink in rats. *American Journal of Physiology* 151:110–25.

AINSWORTH, M. D. S., AND BELL, S. M. 1970. Attachment, exploration, and separation: Illustrated by the behavior of one-year-olds in a strange situation. *Child Development* 41:49–67.

AINSWORTH, M. D. S.; BLEHAR, M. C.; WATERS, E.; AND WALL, S. 1978. *Patterns of attachment.* Hillsdale, N. J.: Erlbaum.

ALBA, J. W., AND HASHER, W. 1983. Is memory schematic? *Psychological Bulletin* 93:203–31.

ALEXANDER, B. K., AND HADAWAY, B. F. 1982. Opiate addiction: The case for an adaptive orientation. *Psychological Bulletin* 92:367–81.

ALLARD, F.; GRAHAM, S.; AND PAARSALU, M. E. 1980. Perception in sport: Basketball. *Journal of Sport Psychology* 2:14–21.

ALLDERIDGE. P. 1979. Hospitals, mad houses, and asylums: Cycles in the care of the insane. *British Journal of Psychiatry* 134:321–24.

ALLEN, L. S.; HINES, M.; SHYRNE, J. E.; AND GORSKI, R. A. 1989. Two sexually dimorphic cell groups in the human brain. *Journal of Neuroscience* 9: 497–506.

ALLEN, V. L. 1975. Social support for non-conformity. In L. Berkowitz (Ed.), *Advances in experimental social psychology,* vol. 8. New York: Academic Press.

ALLEN, V. L., AND LEVINE, J. M. 1971. Social support and conformity: The role of independent assessment. *Journal of Experimental Social Psychology* 7:48–58.

ALLOY, L. B.; HARTLAGE, S.; AND ABRAMSON, L. Y. 1988. Testing the cognitive-diathesis stress theories of depression: Issues of research design, conceptualization, and assessment. In Alloy, L. B. (Ed.), *Cognitive processes in depression.* New York: Guilford.

ALLPORT, F. 1920. The influence of the group upon association and thought. *Journal of Experimental Psychology* 3:159–82.

ALLPORT, G. W. 1937. *Personality: A psychological interpretation.* New York: Henry Holt.

ALLPORT, G. W., AND ODBERT, H. S. 1936. Trait-names: A psychological study. *Psychological Monographs* 47(Whole No. 211).

ALTMAN, I. 1973. Reciprocity of interpersonal exchange. *Journal for Theory of Social Behavior* 3: 249–61.

AMERICAN PSYCHIATRIC ASSOCIATION. 1968. *Diagnostic and statistical manual for mental disorders,* 2nd ed. Washington, D.C.: American Psychiatric Association.

AMERICAN PSYCHIATRIC ASSOCIATION. 1987. *Diagnostic and statistical manual for mental disorders,* 3rd. ed., Revised (DSM-III-R). Washington, D.C.: American Psychiatric Association.

AMERICAN PSYCHIATRIC ASSOCIATION. 1993. Practice guidelines for major depressive disorder in adults. *American Journal of Psychiatry* 150 (Supplement):1–26.

AMERICAN PSYCHIATRIC ASSOCIATION. 1994. *Diagnostic and statistical manual for mental disorders,* 4th ed. Washington, D.C.: American Psychiatric Association.

AMOORE, J. E.; JOHNSON, J. W., Jr.; AND RUBIN, M. 1964. The sterochemical theory of odor. *Scientific American* 210:42–49.

ANASTASI, A. 1958. *Differential psychology,* 3rd ed. New York: Macmillan.

ANASTASI, A. 1971. More on hereditability: Addendum to the Hebb and Jensen interchange. *American Psychologist* 26:1036–37.

ANASTASI, A. 1984. The K-ABC in historical perspective. *Journal of Special Education* 18:357–66.

ANASTASI, A. 1985. Review of Kaufman's Assessment Battery for Children. *Ninth Mental Measurements Yearbook,* vol. 1, pp. 769–71.

ANDERSON, J. R. 1990. *Cognitive psychology and its implications,* 3rd ed. San Francisco: Freeman.

ANDERSON, R. C., AND PICHERT, J. 1978. Recall of previously unrecallable information following a shift in perspective. *Journal of Verbal Learning and Verbal Behavior* 17:1–12.

ANDREASEN, N. C., AND BLACK, D. W. 1991. *Introductory Textbook of Psychiatry.* Washington, D.C.: American Psychiatric Press, Inc.

ANDREASEN, N. C.; NASRALLAH, H. A.; DUNN, V.; OLSEN, S. C.; GROVE, W. M.; EHRHARDT, J. C.; COFFMAN, J. A.; AND CROSSETT, I. H. W. 1986. Structural abnormalities in the frontal system in schizophrenia: A magnetic resonance imaging study. *Archives of General Psychiatry* 43:136–44.

ANDRES, R. 1980. Influence of obesity on longevity in the aged. In Borek, C.; Fenoglio, C. M.; and King, D. W. (Eds.), *Aging, cancer, and cell membranes,* pp. 230–46. New York: Thieme-Stratton.

ANDREWS, G., AND HARVEY, R. 1981. Does psychotherapy benefit neurotic patients? A reanalysis of the Smith, Glass, and Miller data. *Archives of General Psychiatry* 38:1203–1208.

ANSTIS, S. M. 1975. What does visual perception tell us about visual coding? In Gazzaniga, M. S., and Blakemore, C. (Eds.), *Handbook of psychobiology.* New York: Academic Press.

APPEL, L. F.; COOPER, R. G.; MCCARRELL, N.; SIMS-KNIGHT, J.; YUSSEN, S. R.; AND FLAVELL, J. H. 1972. The development of the distinction between perceiving and memorizing. *Child Development* 43:1365–81.

ARANOFF, M. 1976. *Word-formation in generative grammar* (Linguistic Inquiry Monograph 1). Cambridge, Mass.: MIT Press.

ARBIB, M. A. 1972. *The metaphorical brain.* New York: Wiley.

ARENDT, H. 1965. *Eichmann in Jerusalem: A report on the banality of evil.* New York: Viking Press.

ARIETI, S. 1959. Schizophrenia: The manifest symptomatology, the psychodynamic and formal mechanisms. In Arieti, S. (Ed.), *American handbook of psychiatry,* vol. 1, pp. 455–84. New York: Basic Books.

ARMSTRONG, S. L.; GLEITMAN, L. R.; AND GLEITMAN, H. 1983. What some concepts might not be. *Cognition* 13:263–308.

ARNOLD, M. B. 1970. Perennial problems in the field of emotion. In Arnold, M. B. (Ed.), *Feelings and emotion: The Loyola symposium.* New York: Academic Press.

ARONFREED, J. 1968. *Conduct and conscience.* New York: Academic Press.

ARONFREED, J. 1969. The problem of imitation. In Lipsett, L. P., and Reese, H. W. (Eds.), *Advances in child development and behavior,* vol. 4. New York: Academic Press.

ARONSON, E. 1969. The theory of cognitive dissonance: A current perspective. In Berkowitz, L. (Ed.), *Advances in experimental social psychology,* vol. 4, pp. 1–34. New York: Academic Press.

ARONSON, E., AND MILLS, J. 1959. The effect of severity of initiation on liking for a group. *Journal of Abnormal and Social Psychology* 59:177–81.

ARONSON, E.; TURNER, J. A.; AND CARLSMITH, J. M. 1963. Communicator credibility and communication discrepancy as determinants of opinion change. *Journal of Abnormal and Social Psychology* 67:31–36.

ASCH, S. E. 1946. Forming impressions of personality. *Journal of Abnormal and Social Psychology* 41:258–90.

ASCH, S. E. 1952. *Social psychology.* New York: Prentice-Hall.

ASCH, S. E. 1955. Opinions and social pressure. *Scientific American* 193:31–35.

ASCH, S. E. 1956. Studies of independence and conformity: A minority of one against a unanimous majority. *Psychological Monographs* 70 (9, Whole No. 416).

ASCH, S. E., AND GLEITMAN, H. 1953. Yielding to social pressure as a function of public or private commitment. Unpublished manuscript.

ASHER, E. J. 1935. The inadequacy of current intelligence tests for testing Kentucky Mountain children. *Journal of Genetic Psychology* 46:480–86.

ASLIN, R. N. 1987. Visual and auditory development in infancy. In Osofsky, J. D. (Ed.), *Handbook of infant development,* 2nd ed., pp. 5–97. New York: Wiley.

ASTON-JONES, G. 1985. Behavioral functions of locus coeruleus derived from cellular attributes. *Physiological Psychology* 13:118–26.

ATKINSON, D.; MORTEN, G.; AND SUE, D. W. 1983. *Counseling American minorities.* Dubuque, Iowa: W. C. Brown.

ATKINSON, J. W., AND MCCLELLAND, D. C. 1948. The projective expression of needs. II. The effect of different intensities of the hunger drive on thematic apperception. *Journal of Experimental Psychology* 38:643–58.

ATKINSON, R. C., AND SHIFFRIN, R. M. 1968. Human memory: A proposed system and its control. In Spence, K. W., and Spence, J. T. (Eds.), *The psychology of learning and motivation,* vol. 2, pp. 89–105. New York: Academic Press.

ATTNEAVE, F. 1971. Multistability in perception. *Scientific American* 225:62–71.

AUSTIN, J. L. 1962. *How to do things with words.* Oxford: Clarendon Press.

AUSTIN, J. L. 1970. Other minds. In Austin, J. L. *Philosophical papers,* 2nd ed. Oxford: Oxford University Press.

AX, A. F. 1953. The physiological differentiation of fear and anger in humans. *Psychosomatic Medicine* 15:433–42.

BABIGIAN, H. M. 1975. Schizophrenia: Epidemiology. In Freedman, A. M.; Kaplan, H. I.; and Sadock, B. J. (Eds.), *Comprehensive textbook of psychiatry—II,* vol. 1, pp. 860–66. Baltimore: Williams & Wilkins.

BADDELEY, A. D. 1976. *The psychology of human memory.* New York: Basic Books.

BADDELEY, A. D. 1986. *Working memory.* Oxford: Clarendon Press.

BADDELEY, A. D. 1990. *Human memory: Theory and practice.* Needham Heights, Mass.: Allyn and Bacon.

BAHRICK, H. P. 1984. Semantic memory content in permastore:50 years of memory for Spanish learned in school. *Journal of Experimental Psychology: General* 113:1–29.

BAILEY, J. M., AND PILLARD, R. C. 1991. A genetic study of male sexual orientation. *Archives of General Psychiatry* 48: 1089–96.

BAILEY, J. M.; PILLARD, R. C.; NEALE, M. C.; AND AGYEI, Y. 1993. Heritable factors influence sexual orientation in women. *Archives of General Psychiatry* 50: 217–23.

BAILLARGEON, R. 1987. Object permanence in $3\frac{1}{2}$- and $4\frac{1}{2}$-month-old infants. *Developmental Psychology* 23:655–664.

BAILLARGEON, R.; SPELKE, E. S.; AND WASSERMAN, S. 1985. Object permanence in five-month-old infants. *Cognition* 20: 191-208.

BALDWIN, D. A. 1991. Infants' contribution to the achievement of joint reference. *Child Development* 62:875–90.

BALL, W., AND TRONICK, E. 1971. Infant responses to impending collision: optical and real. *Science* 171:818–20.

BALTES, P. B.; REESE, H. W.; AND LIPSITT, L. P. 1980. Life-span developmental psychology. In Rosenzweig, M. R., and Porter, L. W. (Eds.), *Annual Review of Psychology* 31:65–110.

BANDURA, A., AND WALTERS, R. H. 1963. *Social learning and personality development.* New York: Holt, Rinehart & Winston.

BARD AND RIOCH, 1937. Quoted in Gallistel, R. C., 1980. *The organization of action.* Hillsdale, N.J.: Erlbaum.

BAREFOOT, J. C.; DODGE, K. A.; PETERSON, B. L.; DAHLSTROM, W. G.; AND WILLIAMS, R. B. 1989. The Cook-Medley Hostility Scale: Item content and ability to predict survival. *Psychosomatic Medicine* 51:46–57.

BARGLOW, P.; VAUGHN, B. E.; AND MOLITOR, N. 1987. Effects of maternal absence due to employment on the quality of infant-mother attachment in a low-risk sample. *Child Development* 58(4): 945–54

BARLOW, D. H. 1988. *Anxiety and its disorders.* New York: Guilford Press.

BARLOW, H. B., AND HILL, R. M. 1963. Evidence for a physiological explanation of the waterfall illusion and figural after-effects. *Nature* 200:1345–47.

BARLUND, D. C. 1975. *Public and private self in Japan and the United States.* Tokyo: Simul Press.

BARNETT, S. A. 1963. *The rat: A study in behavior.* Chicago: Aldine.

BARRY, H., III; CHILD, I. L.; AND BACON, M. K. 1959. Relation of child training to subsistence economy. *American Anthropologist* 61:51–63.

BARTOL, C. R., AND COSTELLO, N. 1976. Extraversion as a function of temporal duration of electric shock: An exploratory study. *Perceptual and Motor Skills* 42:1174.

BASS, B. M. 1981. *Stogdill's handbook of leadership: Theory, research, and managerial applications,* rev. ed. New York: Free Press.

BASS, B. M. 1990. *Bass and Stogdill's handbook of leadership: Theory, research, and managerial applications,* 3rd ed. New York: Free Press.

BASS, E., AND DAVIS, L. 1988. *The courage to heal.* New York: Harper and Row.

BATES, E. 1976. *Language and context: The acquisition of pragmatics.* New York: Academic Press.

BATES, E., AND MACWHINNEY, B. 1982. Functionalist approaches to grammar. In Wanner, E., and Gleitman, L. (Eds.), *Language acquisition: State of the art.* New York: Cambridge University Press.

BATESON, P. P. G. 1984. The neural basis of imprinting. In Marler, P., and Terrace, H. S. (Eds.), *The biological basis of learning,* pp. 325–39. Dahlem-Konferenzen. Berlin: Springer.

BAUM, W. M. 1970. Extinction of avoidance response following response prevention. *Psychological Bulletin* 74:276–84.

BAUMRIND, D. 1967. Child care practices anteceding three patterns of preschool behavior. *Genetic Psychology Monographs* 75: 43–88.

BAUMRIND, D. 1971. Current patterns of parental authority. *Genetic Psychology Monographs* 1.

BAUMRIND, D. 1977. *Socialization determinants of personal agency.* Paper presented at the biennial meetings of the Society for Research in Child Development, New Orleans. (Cited in Maccoby, E. E. 1980. *Social development.* New York: Harcourt Brace Jovanovich.)

BAUMRIND, D. 1986. Sex differences in moral reasoning: Response to Walker's (1984) conclusion that there are none. *Child Development* 57:511–21.

BECK, A. T. 1967. *Depression: Causes and treatment.* Philadelphia: University of Pennsylvania Press.

BECK, A. T. 1976. *Cognitive therapy and the emotional disorders.* New York: International Universities Press.

BECK, A. T. 1985. Cognitive therapy. In Kaplan, H. I., and Sadock, J. (Eds.), *Comprehensive textbook of psychiatry,* 4th ed. Baltimore: Williams & Wilkins.

BECK, A. T.; RUSH, A. J.; SHAW, B. F.; AND EMERY, G. 1979. *Cognitive therapy of depression.* New York: Guilford Press.

BECK, J. 1966. Effect of orientation and of shape similarity on perceptual grouping. *Perception and Psychophysics* 1:300–302.

BECK, J. 1982. Textural segmentation. In Beck, J. (Ed.), *Organization and representation in perception,* pp. 285–318. Hillsdale, N.J.: Erlbaum.

BÉKÉSY, G. VON. 1957. The ear. *Scientific American* 197:66–78.

BELL, A. P.; WEINBERG, M. S.; AND HAMMERSMITH, S. K. 1981. *Sexual preference: Its development in men and women.* Bloomington, Ind.: Indiana University Press.

BELL, R. Q. 1968. A reinterpretation of the direction of effects in studies of socialization. *Psychological Review* 75:81–95.

BELL, R. Q., AND HARPER, L. V. 1977. *Child effects on adults.* Hillsdale, N.J.: Erlbaum.

BELLI, R. F. 1989. Influences of misleading postevent information: Misinformation interference and acceptance. *Journal of Experimental Psychology: General* 118:72–85.

BELLUGI, U. 1971. Simplification in children's language. In Huxley, R., and Ingram, E., (Eds.), *Language acquisition: Models and methods.* New York: Academic Press.

BELOFF, H. 1957. The structure and origin of the anal character. *Genetic Psychology Monographs* 55:141–72.

BELSKY, J. 1988. The "effects" of infant day care reconsidered. Infant Day Care, *Early Childhood Research Quarterly* (Special Issue) 3: 235–72.

BELSKY, J., AND BRAUNGART, J. M. 1991. Are insecure-avoidant infants with extensive day-care experience less stressed by and more independent in the Strange Situation? *Child Development* 62: 567–75.

BEM, D. J. 1972. Self-perception theory. In Berkowitz, L. (Ed.), *Advances in experimental social psychology,* vol. 6, pp. 2–62. New York: Academic Press.

BEM, S. L. 1989. Genital knowledge and gender constancy in preschool children. *Child Development* 60: 649–62.

BENBOW, C. P. 1988. Sex differences in mathematical reasoning ability in intellectually talented preadolescents: Their nature, effects, and possible causes. *Behavior and Brain Sciences* 11:169–232.

BENBOW, C. P., AND STANLEY, J. C. 1983. Sex differences in mathematical reasoning: More facts. *Science* 222:1029–31.

BENEDICT, R. 1934. *Patterns of culture.* New York: Houghton Mifflin.

BENTLEY, E. 1983. *The life of the drama.* New York: Atheneum.

BERGIN, A. E. 1971. The evaluation of therapeutic outcomes. In Bergin, A. E. and Garfield, S. L. (Eds.), *Handbook of psychotherapy and behavior change: An empirical analysis.* New York: Wiley.

BERMANT, G., AND DAVIDSON, J. M. 1974. *Biological bases of sexual behavior.* New York: Harper & Row.

BERNARD, V. W.; OTTENBERG, P.; AND REDL, F. 1965. Dehumanization: A composite psychological defense in relation to modern war. In Schwebel, M. (Ed.), *Behavioral science and human survival,* pp. 64–82. Palo Alto, Calif.: Science and Behavior Books.

BERNSTEIN, I. L. 1978. Learned taste aversions in children receiving chemotherapy. *Science* 200:1302–1303.

BERSCHEID, E. 1985. Interpersonal attraction. In Lindzey, G., and Aronson, E. (Eds.), *Handbook of social psychology,* vol. 2, pp. 413–84. New York: Academic Press.

BERSCHEID, E.; DION, K.; WALSTER, E.; AND WALSTER, G. W. 1971. Physical attractiveness and dating choice: A test of the matching hypothesis. *Journal of Experimental Social Psychology* 7: 173–89.

BERSCHEID, E., AND WALSTER, E. 1974. Physical attractiveness. In Berkowitz, L. (Ed.), *Advances in experimental social psychology,* vol. 7. New York: Academic Press.

BERSCHEID, E., AND WALSTER, E. H. 1978. *Interpersonal attraction,* 2nd ed. Reading, Mass.: Addison-Wesley.

BEST, D. L.; WILLIAMS, J. E.; CLOUD, J. M.; DAVIS, S. W.; ROBERTSON, L. S.; EDWARDS, J. R.; GILES, E.; AND FOWLES, J. 1977. Development of sex-trait stereotypes among young children in the United States, England, and Ireland. *Child Development* 48:1375–84.

BEUTLER, L. E., AND CLARKIN, J. 1990. *Systematic treatment selection: Toward targeted treatment interventions.* New York: Brunner-Maazel.

BICKERTON, D. 1984. The language bioprogram hypothesis. *Behavioral and Brain Sciences* 7:173–221.

BIGELOW, A. 1987. Early words of blind children. *Journal of Child Language* 14(1):1–22.

BJORK, R. A. 1970. Positive forgetting: The noninterference of items intentionally forgotten. *Journal of Verbal Learning and Verbal Behavior* 9:255–68.

BLACK, D. W., AND NOYES, R. 1990. Comorbidity in obsessive-compulsive disorder, pp. 305–16. In Maser, J. D., and Cloninger, C. D. (Eds.), *Comorbidity in anxiety and mood disorders.* Washington, D.C.: American Psychiatric Press.

BLEULER, E. 1911. *Dementia praecox, or the group of schizophrenias.* English translation by Zinkin, J., and Lewis, N. D. C. New York: International Universities Press, 1950.

BLISS, E. L. 1980. Multiple personalities: Report of fourteen cases with implications for schizophrenia and hysteria. *Archives of General Psychiatry* 37:1388–97.

BLOCK, J. 1971. *Lives through time.* Berkeley, Calif.: Bancroft Books.

BLOCK, J. 1977. Advancing the psychology of personality: Paradigmatic shift or improving the quality of research. In Magnusson, D., and Endler, N. S. (Eds.), *Personality at the crossroads,* pp. 37–64. New York: Wiley.

BLOCK, N.J., AND DWORKIN, G. 1976. *The IQ controversy: Critical readings.* New York: Pantheon.

BLOOM, F. E. 1983. The endorphins: A growing family of pharmacologically pertinent peptides. *Annual Review of Pharmacology and Toxicology* 23:151–70.

BLOOM, F. E. 1993. Advancing a neurodevelopmental origin for shizophrenia. *Archives of General Psychiatry* 50:224–27.

BLOOM, F. E.; LAZERSON, A.; AND HOFSTADTER, L. 1988. *Brain, mind, and behavior.* New York: Freeman.

BLOOM, L. 1970. *Language development: Form and function in emerging grammars.* Cambridge, Mass.: MIT Press.

BLOOMFIELD, L. 1933. *Language.* NY: Henry Holt.

BLUM, J. E.; JARVIK, L. F.; AND CLARK, E. T. 1970. Rate of change on selective tests of intelligence: A twenty-year longitudinal study. *Journal of Gerontology* 25:171–76.

BLURTON-JONES, N., AND KONNER, M. J. 1976. !Kung knowledge of animal behavior. In Lee, B., and DeVore, I. (Eds.), *Kalahari hunter-gatherers.* Cambridge, Mass: Harvard University Press.

BODNAR, R. J.; KELLY, D. D.; BRUTUS, M.; AND GLUSMAN, M. 1980. Stress-induced analgesia: Neural and hormonal determinants. *Neuroscience and biobehavioral reviews* 4:87–100.

BOGEN, J. E. 1969. The other side of the brain II: An appositional mind. *Bulletin of the Los Angeles Neurological Societies* 34:135–62.

BOGEN, J. E.; FISHER, E. D.; AND VOGEL, P. J. 1965. Cerebral commissurotomy: A second case report. *Journal of the American Medical Association* 194:1328–29.

BOLLES, R. C. 1970. Species-specific defense reactions and avoidance learning. *Psychological Review* 77:32–48.

BOLLES, R. C., AND BEECHER, M. D., Eds. 1988. *Evolution and learning.* Hillsdale, N.J.: Erlbaum.

BOLLES, R. C., AND FANSELOW, M. S. 1982. Endorphins and behavior. *Annual Review of Psychology* 33:87–102.

BOND, M. H. 1979. Dimensions of personality used in perceiving peers: Cross-cultural comparisons of Hong Kong, Japanese, American, and Filipino university students. *International Journal of Psychology* 14:47–56.

BOOTH, D. A. 1980. Acquired behavior controlling energy and output. In Stunkard, A. J. (Ed.), *Obesity*, pp. 101–43. Philadelphia: Saunders.

BORNSTEIN, M. H. 1985. Perceptual development. In Bornstein, M. H., and Lamb, M. E. (Eds.), *Developmental psychology: An advanced textbook*, pp. 81–132. Hillsdale, N.J.: Erlbaum.

BOTTGER, P. C. 1984. Expertise and air time as bases of actual and perceived influence in problem-solving groups. *Journal of Applied Psychology* 69: 214–22

BOTVIN, G. J., AND MURRAY, F. B. 1975. The efficacy of peer modelling and social conflict in the acquisition of conservation. *Child Development* 46:796–97.

BOUCHARD, T. J., JR.; LYKKEN, D. T.; MCGUE, M.; SEGAL, N. L.; AND TELLEGEN, A. 1990. Sources of human psychological differences: The Minnesota study of twins reared apart. *Science* 250:223–50.

BOUCHARD, T. J., JR., AND MCGUE, M. 1981. Familial studies of intelligence: A review. *Science* 212:1055–59.

BOWER, G. H.; BLACK, J. B.; AND TURNER, T. J. 1979. Scripts in memory for text. *Cognitive Psychology* 11:177–220.

BOWER, T. G. R. 1966. Slant perception and shape constancy in infants. *Science* 151:832–34.

BOWERS, K. S. 1984. On being unconsciously influenced and informed. In Bowers, K. S., and Meichenbaum, D. (Eds.), *The unconscious reconsidered*. New York: Wiley.

BOWLBY, J. 1969. *Attachment and loss: Vol. 1. Attachment*. New York: Basic Books.

BOWLBY, J. 1973. *Separation and loss*. New York: Basic Books.

BOWMAKER, J. K., AND DARTNALL, H. J. A. 1980. Visual pigments and rods and cones in a human retina. *Journal of Physiology* 298:501–11.

BRABECK, M. 1983. Moral judgement: Theory and research on differences between males and females. *Developmental Review* 3:274–91.

BRADY, I. 1983. Special section. Speaking in the name of the real: Freeman and Mead on Samoa. *American Anthropologist* 85:908–47.

BRAIN, L. 1965. *Speech disorders: Aphasia, apraxia, and agnosia*. London: Butterworth.

BRAINE, M. D. S. 1963. The ontogeny of English phrase structure: The first phase. *Language* 39:3–13.

BRAINE, M. D. S. 1976. Children's first word combinations. *Monographs of the Society for Research in Child Development* 41(1, Serial No. 164).

BREGER, L.; HUNTER, I.; AND LANE, R. W. 1971. The effect of stress on dreams. *Psychological Issues* 7(3, Monograph 27):1–213.

BREGGIN, P. R. 1979. *Electroshock: Its brain-disabling effects*. New York: Springer.

BRELAND, K., AND BRELAND, M. 1951. A field of applied animal psychology. *American Psychologist* 6:202–204.

BRETHERTON, I. 1988. How to do things with one word: The ontogenesis of intentional message-making in children. In Smith, M. D., and Locke, J. L., (Eds.), *The emergent lexicon: the child's development of a linguistic vocabulary*, pp. 255–57. New York: Academic Press.

BRICKMAN, J. C., AND D'AMATO, B. 1975. Exposure effects in a free-choice situation. *Journal of Personality and Social Psychology* 32:415–20.

BROADBENT, D. E. 1958. *Perception and communication*. London: Pergamon Press.

BRODY, N. 1988. *Personality*. New York: Academic Press.

BRONSON, W. C. 1966. Central orientations. A study of behavior organization from childhood to adolescence. *Child Development* 37: 125–55.

BRONSON, W. C. 1967. Adult derivatives of emotional expressiveness and reactivity control: Developmental continuities from childhood to adulthood. *Child Development* 38:801–17.

BROWN, A. L.; BRANSFORD, J. D.; FERRARA, R. A.; AND CAMPIONE, J. C. 1983. Learning, remembering, and understanding. In Mussen, P. (Ed.),

Carmichael's manual of child psychology: Vol. 3. Cognitive development (Markman, E. M., and Flavell, J. H., volume editors). New York: Wiley.

BROWN, R. 1957. Linguistic determinism and parts of speech. *Journal of Abnormal and Social Psychology* 55:1–5.

BROWN, R. 1958. *Words and things*. New York: Free Press, Macmillan.

BROWN, R. 1965. *Social psychology*. New York: Free Press, Macmillan.

BROWN, R. 1973. *A first language: The early stage*. Cambridge, Mass.: Harvard University Press.

BROWN, R., AND BELLUGI, U. 1964. Three processes in the child's acquisition of syntax. *Harvard Educational Review* 34: 133–51.

BROWN, R.; CAZDEN, C.; AND BELLUGI-KLIMA, U. 1969. The child's grammar from 1 to 11. In Hill, J. P. (Ed.), *Minnesota Symposium on Child Psychology*, vol. 2, pp. 28–73. Minneapolis: University of Minnesota Press.

BROWN, R., AND HANLON, C. 1970. Derivational complexity and order of acquisition in child speech. In Hayes, J. R. (Ed.), *Cognition and the development of language*, pp. 11–53. New York: Wiley.

BROWN, R., AND KULIK, J. 1977. Flashbulb memories. *Cognition* 5:73–99.

BROWN, R., AND MCNEILL, D. 1966. The tip of the tongue phenomenon. *Journal of Verbal Learning and Verbal Behavior* 5:325–27.

BRUCH, H. 1973. *Eating disorders*. New York: Basic Books.

BRUCH, H. 1978. *The golden cage*. Cambridge, Mass.: Harvard University Press.

BRUNER, J. S. 1974/1975. From communication to language—a psychological perspective. *Cognition* 3:255–78.

BRUNER, J. S., AND TAGIURI, R. 1954. The perception of people. In Lindzey, G. (Ed.), *Handbook of social psychology*, vol. 2. Reading, Mass.: Addison-Wesley.

BRYAN, W. L., AND HARTER, N. 1897. Studies in the physiology and psychology of telegraphic language. *Psychological Review* 4:27–53.

BRYAN, W. L., AND HARTER, N. 1899. Studies on the telegraphic language: The acquisition of a hierarchy of habits. *Psychological Review* 6:345–75.

BRYDE, J. F. 1972. *Indian students and guidance*. Boston: Houghton Mifflin.

BUCHANAN, B. G., AND SHORTLIFFE, E. H. (Eds.). 1985. *Rule-based expert systems: The MYCIN experiments of the Stanford Heuristics Programming Project*. Reading, Mass: Addison-Wesley.

BUGELSKI, B. R., AND ALAMPAY, D. A. 1961. The role of frequency in developing perceptual sets. *Canadian Journal of Psychology* 15:205–11.

BULLOCK, W. A., AND GILLILAND, K. 1993. Eysenck's arousal theory of introversion-extraversion: A covergent measures investigation. *Journal of Personality andSocial Psychology* 64:113–23.

BURCKHARDT, J. 1860. *The civilization of the Renaissance in Italy*. Oxford: Phaidon Press, 1945.

BURGESS, E. W., AND WALLIN, P. 1943. Homogamy in social characteristics. *American Journal of Sociology* 49:109–24.

BURNETT, S. A.; LANE, D. M.; AND DRATT, L. M. 1979. Spatial differences and sex differences in quantitative ability. *Intelligence* 3:345–54.

BURNS, J. M. 1978. *Leadership*. New York: Harper and Row.

BURTON, R. V. 1963. Generality of honesty reconsidered. *Psychological Review* 70:481–99.

BURTON, R. V., AND WHITING, J. W. M. 1961. The absent father and cross-sex identity. *Merrill-Palmer Quarterly* 7:85–95.

BURY, J. B. 1932. *The idea of progress*. New York: Macmillan.

BUSS, A. H., AND PLOMIN, R. 1984. *Temperament: Early developing personality traits*. Hillsdale, N.J.: Erlbaum.

BUSS, D. M. 1989. Sex differences in human mate preferences: Evolutionary hypotheses tested in 37 cultures. *Behavioral and Brain Sciences* 12:1–50.

BUSS, D. M. 1992. Mate preference mechanisms: Consequences for partner choice and intrasexual competition. In Barkow, J. H.; Cosmides, L.; and Tooby, J. *The adapted mind*, pp. 249–66. New York: Oxford University Press.

BUSS, D. M., AND BARNES, M. F. 1986. Preferences in human mate selection. *Journal of Personality and Social Psychology* 50:559–70.

BUSS, D. M., AND CRAIK, K. H. 1983. Dispositional analysis of everyday conduct. *Journal of Personality* 51:393–412.

BUTCHER, J. N.; DAHLSTROM, W. G.; GRAHAM, J. R.; TELLEGEN, A. M.; AND KAEMMER, B. 1989. *MMPI-2: Manual for administration and scoring.* Minneapolis, Minn.: University of Minnesota Press.

BUTTERWORTH, G., AND COCHRAN, E. 1980. Towards a mechanism of joint visual attention in human infancy. *International Journal of Behavioral Development* 3:253–72.

BUTTERWORTH, G., AND JARRETT, N. 1991. What minds have in common is space: Spatial mechanisms serving joint visual attention in infancy. Special issue: Perspectives on the child's theory of mind. *British Journal of Developmental Psychology* 9:55–72.

CAIN, W. S. 1988. Olfaction. In Atkinson, R. C.; Herrnstein, R. J.; Lindzey, G.; and Luce, R. D. (Eds.), *Stevens' handbook of experimental psychology: Vol. 1. Perception and motivation,* rev. ed., pp. 409–59. New York: Wiley.

CAMMALLERI, J. A.; HENDRICK, H. W.; PITTMAN, W. C., JR.; BOUT, H. D.; AND PRATHER, D. C. 1973. Effects of different styles of leadership on group accuracy. *Journal of Applied Psychology* 57: 32–37.

CAMPBELL, J. B., AND HAWLEY, C. W. 1982. Study habits and Eysenck's theory of extraversion-introversion. *Journal of Research in Personality* 16:139–46.

CAMPBELL, J. D.; TESSER, A., AND FAIREY, P. J. 1986. Conformity and attention to the stimulus: Some temporal and contextual dynamics. *Journal of Personality and Social Psychology* 51:315–24.

CAMPOS, J. J.; BARRETT, K. C.; LAMB, M. E.; GOLDSMITH, H. H.; AND STERNBERG, C. 1983. Socioemotional development. In Mussen, P. E. (Ed.), *Carmichael's manual of child psychology: Vol. 2. Infancy and developmental psychobiology* (Haith, M. M., and Campos, J. J., volume editor), pp. 783–916. New York: Wiley.

CANNON, T. D. 1991. Genetic and prenatal sources of structural brain abnormalities in schizophrenia. In Mednick, S. A.; Cannon, T. D.; Barr, C. E.; and Lyon, M. (Eds.), *Fetal neural development and adult schizophrenia.* Cambridge: Cambridge University Press.

CANNON, T. D.; MEDNICK, S. A.; AND PARNAS, J. 1990. Antecedents of predominantly negative- and predominantly positive-symptom schizophrenia in a high-risk population. *Archives of General Psychiatry* 47:622–32.

CANNON, W. B. 1927. The James-Lange theory of emotions: A critical examination and an alternative theory. *American Journal of Psychology* 39:106–24.

CANNON, W. B. 1929. *Bodily changes in pain, hunger, fear and rage,* rev. ed. New York: Appleton-Century.

CANNON, W. B. 1932 and 1960 (revised and enlarged). *The wisdom of the body.* New York: Norton.

CANTOR, N., AND MISCHEL, W. 1979. Prototypes in person perception. In L. Berkowitz (Ed.), *Advances in experimental social psychology,* vol. 12. New York: Academic Press.

CAREY, S. 1978. The child as word learner. In Halle, M.; Bresnan, J.; and Miller, G. A. (Eds.), *Linguistic theory and psychological reality.* Cambridge, Mass.: MIT Press.

CAREY, S. 1982. Semantic development: State of the art. In Wanner, E., and Gleitman, L. R. (Eds.), *Language acquisition: State of the art.* New York: Cambridge University Press.

CARLSON, N. R. 1986. *Physiology of behavior,* 3rd ed. Boston: Allyn and Bacon.

CARLSON, N. R. 1991. *Physiology of behavior.* Boston: Allyn and Bacon.

CARLYLE, T. 1841. *On heroes, hero-worship, and the heroic in history.* Berkeley: University of California Press, 1992.

CARON, A. J.; CARON, R. F.; AND CARLSON, V. R. 1979. Infant perception of the invariant shape of objects varying in slant. *Child Development* 50:716–21.

CARROLL, L. 1865. *Alice in Wonderland.* Abridged by Frank, J. and illustrated by Torrey, M. M. New York: Random House, 1969.

CARTWRIGHT, R. D. 1977. *Night life: Explorations in dreaming.* Englewood Cliffs, N.J.: Prentice-Hall.

CASE, R. 1978. Intellectual development from birth to adulthood: A neo-Piagetian interpretation. In Siegler, R. S. (Ed.), *Children's thinking: What develops?,* pp. 37–72. Hillsdale, N.J.: Erlbaum.

CASE, R. 1985. *Intellectual development: Birth to adulthood.* New York: Academic Press.

CASPI, A., AND HERBENER, E. 1990. Continuity and change: Assortative marriage and the consistency of personality in adulthood. *Journal of Personality and Social Psychology* 58: 250–58.

CASSIDY, K. E. W. 1993. The development of the child's theory of mind. Unpublished doctoral dissertation. Philadelphia: University of Pennsylvania.

CATEL, J. 1953. Ein Beitrag zur Frage von Hirnenentwicklung under Menschwerdung. *KlinischeWeisschriften* 31:473–75.

CATTELL, R. B. 1957. *Personality and motivation structure and measurement.* New York: Harcourt, Brace and World.

CATTELL, R. B. 1963. Theory of fluid and crystallized intelligence: A critical experiment. Journal of Educational Psychology 54: 1–22.

CATTELL, R. B. 1966. *The scientific analysis of personality.* Chicago: Aldine.

CECI, S. J., AND LIKER, J. 1986. Academic and nonacademic intelligence: An experimental separation. In Sternberg, R. J., and Wagner, R. K. (Eds.), *Practical intelligence: Nature and origins of competence in everyday life,* pp. 119–42. New York: Cambridge University Press.

CHAIKEN, S. 1987. The heuristic model of persuasion. In Zanna, M. P.; Olson, J. M.; and Herman, C. P. (Eds.), *Social influence: The Ontario symposium,* vol. 5, pp. 3–40. Hillsdale, N.J.: Erlbaum.

CHAMBERS, D., AND REISBERG, D. 1985. Can mental images be ambiguous? *Journal of Experimental Psychology: Human Perception and Performance* 11:317–28.

CHAPMAN, L. J., AND CHAPMAN, J. P. 1973. *Disordered thought in schizophrenia.* New York: Appleton-Century-Crofts.

CHARNESS, N. 1981. Search in chess: Age and skill differences. *Journal of General Psychology: General* 110:21–38.

CHASE, W. G., AND SIMON, H. A. 1973a. Perception in chess. *Cognitive Psychology* 4:55–81.

CHASE, W. G., AND SIMON, H. A. 1973b. The mind's eye in chess. In Chase, W. G., *Visual information processing.* New York: Academic Press.

CHENEY, D. L., AND SEYFARTH, R. M. 1980. Vocal recognition in free-ranging vervet monkeys. *Animal Behavior* 28:362–67.

CHENEY, D. L., AND SEYFARTH, R. M. 1982. Recognition of individuals within and between groups of free-ranging vervet monkeys. *American Zoologist* 22:519–29.

CHENEY, D. L., AND SEYFARTH, R. M. 1990. *How monkeys see the world.* Chicago: University of Chicago Press.

CHENEY, D. L., AND SEYFARTH, R. M. 1992. The representation of social relations by monkeys. *Cognition* 37:167–96.

CHERRY, E. C. 1953. Some experiments upon the recognition of speech, with one and with two ears. *Journal of the Acoustical Society of America* 25:975–79.

CHEVRIER, J., AND DELORME, A. 1983. Depth perception in Pandora's box and size illusion: Evolution with age. *Perception* 12:177–85.

CHI, M. T. H. 1978. Knowledge structures and memory development. In Siegler, R. S. (Ed.), *Children's thinking: What develops?,* pp. 73–96. Hillsdale, N.J.: Erlbaum.

CHI, M. T. H. 1985. Changing conceptions of sources of memory development. *Human Development* 28:50–56.

CHOMSKY, C. 1984. From hand to mouth: A study of speech and language through touch (manuscript, Harvard University).

CHOMSKY, N. 1959. Review of B. F. Skinner. *Verbal learning, Language* 35:26–58.

CHOMSKY, N. 1965. *Aspects of the theory of syntax.* Cambridge, Mass.: MIT Press.

CHOMSKY, N. 1975. *Reflections on language.* New York: Pantheon.

CHOMSKY, N. 1980. *Rules and representations.* New York: Columbia University Press.

CHOMSKY, N. 1986. *Barriers.* Cambridge Mass.: MIT Press.

CIALDINI, R. B. 1984. *Influence: How and why people agree to do things.* New York: Quill.

CIALDINI, R. B.; PETTY, R. E.; AND CACIOPPO, J. T. 1981. Attitude and attitude change. In Rosenzweig, M. R., and Porter, L. W. (Eds.), *Annual Review of Psychology* 32:357–404.

CIALDINI, R. R.; VINCENT, J. E.; LEWIS, S. K.; CATALAN, J.; WHEELER, D.; AND DARBY, L. 1975. Reciprocal concession procedure for inducing compliance: The door-in-the-face technique. *Journal of Personality and Social Psychology* 31:206–15.

CLARK, D. M. 1986. A cognitive approach to panic. *Behavior Research and Therapy* 24:461–70.

CLARK, E. V. 1993. *The lexicon in acquisition.* New York: Cambridge University Press.

CLARK, H. H. 1978. Inferring what is meant. In Levelt, W., and Flores d'Arcais, G. (Eds.), *Studies in the perception of language.* Chichester: Wiley.

CLARK, H. H. 1979. Responding to indirect speech acts. *Cognitive Psychology* 11: 430–77.

CLARK, H. H., AND CLARK, E. V. 1977. *Psychology and language: An introduction to psycholinguistics.* New York: Harcourt Brace Jovanovich.

CLARKE, A. C. 1952. An examination of the operation of residual propinquity as a factor in mate selection. *American Sociological Review* 27:17–22.

CLARKE-STEWART, A. 1978. And daddy makes three: The father's impact on mother and young child. *Child Development* 49: 466–78.

CLARKE-STEWART, A. 1989. Infant day care: Malignant or maligned. *American Psychologist* 44: 266–73.

CLECKLEY, J. 1976. *The mask of sanity,* 5th ed. St. Louis: Mosby.

CLEMENTE, C. D., AND CHASE, M. H. 1973. Neurological substrates of aggressive behavior. *Annual Review of Physiology* 35:329–56.

COBB, S. 1941. *Foundations of neuropsychiatry.* Baltimore: Williams and Wilkins.

COFFMAN, C. E. 1985. Review of Kaufman's Assessment Battery for Children. *Ninth Mental Measurements Yearbook,* vol. 1. pp. 771–73.

COHEN, N. J., AND SQUIRE, L. R. 1980. Preserved learning and retention of pattern-analyzing skill in amnesia: Dissociation of knowing how and knowing what. *Science* 210:207–10.

COHEN, Y. A. 1953. A study of interpersonal relations in a Jamaican community. Unpublished doctoral dissertation, Yale University.

COLBY, A., AND KOHLBERG, L. 1986. *The measurement of moral judgment.* New York: Cambridge University Press.

COLBY, A.; KOHLBERG, L.; GIBBS, J.; AND LIEBERMAN, M. 1983. A longitudinal study of moral judgment. *Monographs of the Society for Research in Child Development* 48 (1, Serial No. 200).

COLE, M. 1975. An ethnographic psychology of cognition. In Brislin, R. W.; Bochner, S.; and Lonner, W. J. (Eds.), *Cross-cultural perspectives on learning.* New York: Wiley.

COLE, M., AND COLE, S. R. 1993. *The development of children,* 2nd ed. New York: Scientific American Books.

COLE, M.; GAY, J.; GLICK, J. A.; AND SHARP, D. W. 1971. *The cultural context of learning and thinking.* New York: Basic Books.

COLEMAN, J. C. 1972. *Abnormal psychology and modern life,* 4th ed. Glenview, Ill.: Scott, Foresman.

COLLIER, G. 1985. *Emotional expression.* Hillsdale, N.J.: Erlbaum.

COLLINS, A. M., AND QUILLIAN, M. R. 1969. Retrieval time from semantic memory. *Journal of Verbal Learning and Verbal Behavior* 8:240–47.

COLLIS, G. 1975. The integration of gaze and vocal behavior in the mother-infant dyad. Paper presented at Third International Child Language Symposium, London.

COLWILL, R. M., AND RESCORLA, R. A. 1985. Postconditioning devaluation of a reinforcer affects instrumental responding. *Journal of Experimental Psychology: Animal Behavior Processes* 11:120–32.

COMRIE, B. 1987. Introduction. In Comrie, B. (Ed.), *The world's major languages.* New York: Oxford University Press.

CONEL, J. L. 1939. *The postnatal development of the human cortex,* vol. 1. Cambridge, Mass.: Harvard University Press.

CONEL, J. L. 1947. *The postnatal development of the human cortex,* vol. 3. Cambridge, Mass.: Harvard University Press.

CONEL, J. L. 1955. *The postnatal development of the human cortex,* vol. 5. Cambridge, Mass.: Harvard University Press.

CONRAD, C. 1972. Cognitive economy in semantic memory. *Journal of Experimental Psychology* 92:149–54.

CONWAY, M. A.; COHEN, G.; AND STANHOPE, N. 1991. On the very long-term retention of knowledge acquired through formal education: Twelve years of cognitive psychology. *Journal of Experimental Psychology (General)* 120:395–409.

COOK, M., AND BIRCH, R. 1984. Infant perception of the shapes of tilted plane forms. *Infant Behavior and Development* 7:389–402.

COOLEY, C. H. 1902. *Human nature and the social order.* New York: Scribner's.

COOPER, J., AND FAZIO, R. H. 1984. A new look at dissonance theory. In Berkowitz, L. (Ed.), *Advances in experimental social psychology,* vol. 17. New York: Academic Press.

COREN, S., AND WARD, L. M. 1989. *Sensation and perception,* 3rd ed. San Diego, Calif.: Harcourt Brace Jovanovich.

CORKIN, S. 1965. Tactually-guided maze-learning in man: Effects of unilateral cortical excisions and bilateral hippocampal lesions. *Neuropsychologia* 3:339–51.

CORKIN, S. 1984. Lasting consequences of bilateral medial temporal lobectomy: Clinical course and experimental findings in H. M. *Semin. Neurology* 4:249–59.

CORNSWEET, T. M. 1970. *Visual perception.* New York: Academic Press.

COSTA, E. 1985. Benzodiazepine-GABA interactions: A model to investigate the neurobiology of anxiety. In Tuma, A. H., and Maser, J. D. (Eds.), *Anxiety and the anxiety disorders.* Hillsdale, N.J.: Erlbaum.

COSTA, P. T., JR.; MCCRAE, R. R.; AND ARENBERG, D. 1980. Enduring dispositions in adult males. *Journal of Personality and Social Psychology* 38:793–800.

COUVILLON, P., AND BITTERMAN, M. E. 1980. Some phenomena of associative conditioning in honeybees. *Journal of comparative and physiological psychology* 94:878–85.

COWEY, A., AND STOERIG, P. 1992. Reflections on blindsight. In Milner, A. D., and Rugg, M. D. (Eds.), *The neuropsychology of consciousness,* pp. 11–38. San Diego, Calif.: Academic Press.

COWLES, J. T. 1937. Food-tokens as incentives for learning by chimpanzees. *Comparative Psychology Monographs* 14 (5, Serial No. 71).

CRAIK, F. I. M., AND WATKINS, M. J. 1973. The role of rehearsal in short-term memory. *Journal of Verbal Learning and Verbal Behavior* 12:599–607.

CRONBACH, L. J. 1970a. *Essentials of psychology testing,* 3rd ed. New York: Harper & Row.

CRONBACH, L. J. 1970b. Test validation. In Thorndike, R. L. (Ed.), *Educational measurement.* Washington, D.C.: American Council on Education.

CRONBACH, L. J. 1975. Beyond the two disciplines of scientific psychology. *American Psychologist* 30:116–27.

CRONBACH, L. J., AND MEEHL, P. E. 1955. Construct validity in psychological tests. *Psychological Bulletin* 52:281–302.

CROOK, C. 1987. Taste and olfaction. In Salapateck, P., and Cohen, L. (Eds.), *Handbook of infant perception: From perception to cognition,* vol. 2, pp. 237–64. Orlando, Fla.: Academic Press.

CROW, T. J. 1980. Molecular pathology of schizophrenia: More than one disease process? *British Medical Journal* 280:66–68.

CROW, T. J. 1982. Two dimensions of pathology in schizophrenia: Dopaminergic and non-dopaminergic. *Psychopharmacology Bulletin* 18:22–29.

CROW, T. J. 1985. The two-syndrome concept: Origins and current status. *Schizophrenia Bulletin* 11:471–86.

CROWDER, R. G. 1976. *Principles of learning and memory.* Hillsdale, N.J.: Erlbaum.

CROWDER, R. G. 1982. The demise of short-term memory. *Acta Psychologica* 50:291–323.

CRUTCHFIELD, R. S. 1955. Conformity and character. *American Psychologist* 10:191–99.

CUNNINGHAM, M. R. 1986. Measuring the physical in physical attraction: Quasi-experiments on the sociobiology of female beauty. *Journal of Personality and Social Psychology* 50:925–35.

CURTISS, S. 1977. *Genie: A linguistic study of a modern-day "wild child."* New York: Academic Press.

CUTLER, A. 1994. Segmentation problems, rhythmic solutions. In Gleitman, L. R., and Landau, B. (Eds.), Lexical acquisition, (Special Issue) *Lingua* 92:81–104.

CUTTING, J. 1986. Outcome in schizophrenia: Overview. In Kerr, T. A., and Snaith, R. P. (Eds.), *Contemporary issues in schizophrenia*, pp. 436–40. Washington, DC: American Psychiatric Press.

DALE, A. J. D. 1975. Organic brain syndromes associated with infections. In Freedman, A. M.; Kaplan, H. I.; and Sadock, B. J. (Eds.), *Comprehensive textbook of psychiatry—II*, vol. 1, pp. 1121–30. Baltimore: Williams & Wilkins.

DARLEY, J. M., AND BATSON, C. D. 1973. "From Jerusalem to Jericho": A study of situational and dispositional variables in helping behavior. *Journal of Personality and Social Psychology* 27:100–108.

DARLEY, J., AND LATANÉ, B. 1968. Bystander intervention in emergencies: Diffusion of responsibility. *Journal of Personality and Social Psychology* 10:202–14.

DARWIN, C. 1872a. *The origin of species.* New York: Macmillan, 6th ed., 1962.

DARWIN, C. 1872b. *The expression of the emotions in man and animals.* London: Appleton.

DASSER, V. 1988. A social concept in Java monkeys. *Animal Behaviour* 36(1): 225–30.

DAVIDSON, A. R., AND JACCARD, J. J. 1979. Variables that moderate the attitude-behavior relation: Results of a longitudinal survey. *Journal of Personality and Social Psychology* 37:1364–76.

DAVIDSON, J. M. 1969. Hormonal control of sexual behavior in adult rats. In Rasp, G. (Ed.), *Advances in bioscience,* vol. 1, pp. 119–69. New York: Pergamon.

DAVIDSON, J. M. 1986. Androgen replacement therapy in a wider context: Clinical and basic aspects. In Dennerstein and Fraser (Eds.), *Hormones and behavior,* pp. 433–40. Amsterdam: International Society of Psychosomatic Obstetrics and Gynecology, Elsevier.

DAVIES, K. G., AND WEEKS, R. D. 1993. Temporal lobectomy for intractable epilepsy: Experience with 58 cases over 21 years. *British Journal of Neurosurgery* 7:23–33.

DAVIS, D. E. 1964. The physiological analysis of aggressive behavior. In Etkin, W. (Ed.), *Social behavior and organization among vertebrates.* Chicago: University of Chicago Press.

DAVIS, J. M. 1974. A two-factor theory of schizophrenia. *Journal of Psychiatric Research* 11:25–30.

DAVIS, J. M. 1985a. Antipsychotic drugs. In Kaplan, H. I., and Sadock, J. (Eds.), *Comprehensive textbook of psychiatry,* 4th ed., pp. 1481–1513. Baltimore: Williams & Wilkins.

DAVIS, J. M. 1985b. Antidepressant drugs. In Kaplan, H. I., and Sadock, J. (Eds.), *Comprehensive textbook of psychiatry,* 4th ed., pp. 1513–37, Baltimore: Williams & Wilkins.

DAVIS, K. 1947. Final note on a case of extreme social isolation. *American Journal of Sociology* 52:432–37.

DAWES, R. W. 1980. Social Dilemmas. *Annual Review of Psychology* 31:169–93.

DAY, R. H., AND MCKENZIE, B. E. 1981. Infant perception of the invariant size of approaching and receding objects. *Developmental Psychology* 17:670–77.

DAY, R. H.; STUART, G. W.; AND DICKINSON, R. G. 1980. Size constancy does not fail below half a degree. *Perception and Psychophysics* 28:263–65.

DECASPER, A. J., AND FIFER, W. P. 1980. Of human bonding: Newborns prefer their mothers' voices. *Science* 208:1174–76.

DE GROOT, A. D. 1965. *Thought and choice in chess.* The Hague: Mouton.

DEMBROSKI, T. M.; MACDOUGALL, J. M.; COSTA, P. T.; AND GRANDITS, G. A. 1989. Components of hostility as predictors of sudden death and myocardial infarction in the Multiple Risk Factor Intervention Trial. *Psychosomatic Medicine* 51:514–22.

DEMENT, W. C., AND KLEITMAN, N. 1957. The relation of eye movements during sleep to dream activity: An objective method for the study of dreaming. *Journal of Experimental Psychology* 53:339–46.

DEMENT, W. C., AND WOLPERT, E. A. 1958. The relationship of eye-movements, body motility, and external stimuli to dream content. *Journal of Experimental Psychology* 55:543–53.

DENNETT, D. C. 1978. *Brainstorms: Philosophical essays on mind and psychology.* Montgomery, Vt.: Bradford Books.

DENNETT, D. C. 1991. *Consciousness explained.* Boston: Little, Brown.

DENNIS, W. 1940. Does culture appreciably affect patterns of infant behavior? *Journal of Social Psychology* 12:305–17.

DENNIS, W. 1973. *Children of the creche.* New York: Appleton-Century-Crofts.

DESCARTES, R. 1662. *Trait de l'homme.* Haldane, E. S, and Ross, G. R. T (trans.). Cambridge, Eng.: Cambridge University Press.

DESIMONE, R.; ALBRIGHT, T. D.; GROSS, C. G.; AND BRUCE, C. 1984. Stimulus-selective properties of inferior temporal neurons in the macaque. *The Journal of Neuroscience* 4:2051–62.

DEUTSCH, J. A.; PUERTO, A.; AND WANG, M. L. 1978. The stomach signals satiety. *Science* 201:165–67.

DE VALOIS, R. L. 1965. Behavioral and electrophysiological studies of primate vision. In Neff, W. D. (Ed.), *Contributions of sensory physiology,* vol. 1. New York: Academic Press.

DE VALOIS, R. L., AND DE VALOIS, K. K. 1975. Neural coding of color. In Carterette, E. C., and Friedman, M. P. (Eds.), *Handbook of perception,* vol. 5, pp. 117–62. New York: Academic Press.

DE VILLIERS, J. G., AND DE VILLIERS, P. A. 1973. Development of the use of word order in comprehension. *Journal of Psycholinguistic Research* 2:331–41.

DI VESTA, F. J.; INGERSOLL,G.; AND SUNSHINE, P. 1971. A factor analysis of imagery tests. *Journal of Verbal Learning and Verbal Behavior* 10:471–79.

DIAMOND, R., AND ROZIN, P. 1984. Activation of existing memories in the amnesic syndrome. *Journal of Abnormal Psychology* 93:98–105.

DICKINSON, A. 1987. Animal conditioning and learning theory. In Eysenck, H. J., and Martin, I. (Eds.), *Theoretical Foundations of Behavior Theory.* New York: Plenum.

DICKS, H. V. 1972. *Licensed mass murder: A sociopsychological study of some S. S. killers.* New York: Basic Books.

DIENER, E. 1979. Deindividuation: The absence of self-awareness and self-regulation in group members. In Paulus, P. (Ed.), *The psychology of group influence,* pp. 209–42. Hillsdale, N.J.: Erlbaum.

DIENER, F; FRASER, S. C.; BEAMAN, A. L.; AND KELEM, Z. R. T. 1976. Effects of deindividuation variables on stealing among Halloween trick-or-treaters. *Journal of Personality and Social Psychology* 5:143–55.

DILGER, W. C. 1962. The behavior of lovebirds. *Scientific American* 206:88–98.

DOLGER, H., AND SEEMAN, B. 1985. *How to live with diabetes,* 5th ed. New York: Norton.

DOMJAN, M. 1980. Ingestional aversion learning: Unique and general processes. *Advances in the Study of Behavior* 11:275–336.

DOMJAN, M. 1983. Biological constraints on instrumental and classical conditioning: Implications for general process theory. In Bower, G. H. (Ed.), *The psychology of learning and motivation,* vol. 17. New York: Academic Press.

DORNBUSCH, S. M.; RITTER, P. L.; LEIDERMAN, P. H.; AND ROBERTS, D. F. 1987. The relation of parenting style to adolescent school performance. Schools and development, *Child Development* (Special Issue) 58: 1244–57.

DOUVAN, E., AND ADELSON, J. 1958. The psychodynamics of social mobility in adolescent boys. *Journal of Abnormal and Social Psychology* 56:31–44.

DRISCOLL, R.; DAVIS, K. E.; AND LIPITZ. 1972. Parental interference and romantic love: The Romeo and Juliet effect. *Journal of Personality and Social Psychology* 24:1–10.

DUDA, R. O., AND SHORTLIFFE, E. H. 1983. Expert systems research. *Science* 220:261–68.

DUNCKER, K. 1929. Über induzierte Bewegung. *Psychologische Forschung* 12:180–259.

DUNCKER, K. 1945. On problem solving. *Psychological Monographs* (Whole No. 270):1–113.

DURANT, W., AND DURANT, A. 1967. *The story of civilization: Part X. Rousseau and Revolution.* New York: Simon and Schuster.

EAGLE, M. N., AND WOLITSKY, D. L. 1992. Psychoanalytic theories of psychotherapy. In Freedheim, D. K. (Ed.), *History of psychotherapy.* Washington, D.C.: American Psychological Association.

EAGLY, A. H., AND CHAIKIN, S. 1984. Cognitive theories of persuasion. In Berkowitz, L. (Ed.), *Advances in experimental social psychology,* vol. 17. New York: Academic Press.

EBBINGHAUS, H. 1885. *Memory.* New York: Teacher's College, Columbia University, 1913. (Reprint edition, New York: Dover, 1964.)

ECCLES, J. C. 1973. *The understanding of the brain.* New York: McGraw-Hill.

ECCLES, J. C. 1982. The synapse: From electrical to chemical transmission. *Annual Review of Neuroscience* 5:325–39.

EDMONDS, J. M., ed. and trans. 1929. *The characters of Theophrastus.* Cambridge, Mass.: Harvard University Press.

EFRON, R. 1990. *The decline and fall of hemispheric specialization.* Hillsdale, N.J.: Erlbaum.

EGGER, M. D., AND FLYNN, J. P. 1963. Effect of electrical stimulation of the amygdala on hypothalamically elicited behavior in cats. *Journal of Neurophysiology* 26:705–20.

EICH, J. E. 1980. The cue-dependent nature of state-dependent retrieval. *Memory and Cognition* 8:157–73.

EIMAS, P. D.; SIQUELAND, E. R.; JUSCZYK, P.; AND VIGORITO, J. 1971. Speech perception in infants. *Science* 171:303–306.

EKMAN, P. 1971. Universals and cultural differences in facial expression. In Cole, J. K. (Ed.), *Nebraska Symposium on Motivation,* pp. 207–84. Lincoln, Neb.: University of Nebraska Press.

EKMAN, P. 1973. Cross-cultural studies of facial expression. In Ekman, P. (Ed.), *Darwin and facial expression,* pp. 169–222. New York: Academic Press.

EKMAN, P. 1977. Biological and cultural contributions to body and facial movement. In Blacking, J. (Ed.), *The anthropology of the body,* A. S. A. Monograph 15. London: Academic Press.

EKMAN, P. 1980. *The face of man: Expression of universal emotions in a New Guinea village.* New York: Garland STPM Press.

EKMAN, P. 1984. Expression and the nature of emotion. In Elkman, P., and Scherer, K. (Eds.), *Approaches to emotion,* pp. 319–43. Hillsdale, N.J.: Erlbaum.

EKMAN, P. 1985. *Telling lies.* New York: Norton.

EKMAN, P., AND FRIESEN, W. V. 1975. *Unmasking the face.* Englewood Cliffs, N.J.: Prentice-Hall.

EKMAN, P., AND FRIESEN, W. V. 1986. A new pan-cultural facial expression of emotion. *Motivation and Emotion* 10:159–68.

EKMAN, P.; FRIESEN, W. V.; AND O'SULLIVAN, M. 1988. Smiles when lying. *Journal of Personality and Social Psychology* 54: 414–20.

EKMAN, P., AND OSTER, H. 1979. Facial expression of emotion. *Annual Review of Psychology* 30:527–54.

EKSTRAND, B. R. 1972. To sleep, perchance to dream (about why we forget) In Duncan, C. P.; Sechrest, L.; and Melton, A. W. (Eds.), *Human memory: Festschrift for Benton J. Underwood,* pp. 59–82. New York: Appleton-Century-Crofts.

EKSTRAND, B. R.; BARRETT, T. R.; WEST, J. M.; AND MAIER, W. G. 1977. The effect of sleep on human memory. In Drucker-Colin, R., and McGaugh, J. L. (Eds.), *Neurobiology of sleep and memory.* New York: Academic Press.

ELDER, G. H., JR. 1980. Adolescence in historical perspective. In Adelson, J. (Ed.), *Handbook of adolescent psychology.* New York: Wiley.

ELKIN, I.; SHEA, M. T.; WATKINS, J. T.; IMBER, S. D.; SOTSKY, S. M.; COLLINS, J. S.; GLASS, D. R.; PILKONIS, P. A.; LEBER, W. R.; DOCHERTY, J. P.; FEISTER, S. J.; AND PARLOFF, M. B. 1989. National Institute of Mental Health treatment of depression collaborative research program: General effectiveness of treatments. *Archives of General Psychiatry* 46:971–82.

ELLENBERGER, H. F. 1970. *The discovery of the unconscious.* New York: Basic Books.

ELLIS, A. 1962. *Reason and emotion in psychotherapy.* Secaucus, N.J.: Lyle Stuart.

ELMS, A. C., AND MILGRAM, S. 1966. Personality characteristics associated with obedience and defiance toward authoritative command. *Journal of Experimental Research in Personality* 1:282–89.

EMMELKAMP, P. M. G. 1986. Behavior therapy with adults. In Garfied, S. L., and Bergin, A. E. (Eds.), *Handbook of psychotherapy and behavior change,* 3rd ed. New York: Wiley.

EMMERICH, W. 1966. Continuity and stability in early social development, II. Teacher ratings. *Child Development* 37:17–27.

ENDLER, N. S., AND HUNT, J. M. 1969. Generalization of contributions from sources of variance in the S-R inventories of anxiousness. *Journal of Personality* 37:1–24.

EPSTEIN, S. 1979. The stability of behavior: I. On predicting most of the people much of the time. *Journal of Personality and Social Psychology* 37:1097–1126.

EPSTEIN, S. 1980. The stability of behavior. II. Implications for psychological reasearch. *American Psychologist* 35:790–806.

ERDELYI, M. H. 1985. *Psychoanalysis: Freud's cognitive psychology.* New York: Freeman.

ERDELYI, M. H., AND GOLDBERG, B. 1979. Let's not sweep repression under the rug. In Kihlstrom, J. F., and Evans, F. J. (Eds.), *Functional disorders of memory,* pp. 355–402. Hillsdale, N.J.: Erlbaum.

ERIKSEN, C. W., AND PIERCE, J. 1968. Defense mechanisms. In Borgatta, E. F., and Lambert, W. W. (Eds.), *Handbook of personality theory and research,* pp. 1007–40. Chicago: Rand McNally.

ERIKSON, E. H. 1963. *Childhood and society.* New York: Norton.

ERICKSON, E. H. 1974. *Dimensions of a new identity: The Jefferson lectures in the humanities.* New York: Norton.

ERON, L. D. 1950. A normative study of the thematic apperception test. *Psychological Monographs* 64 (Whole No. 315).

ERVIN, S. 1964. Imitation and structural change in children's language. In Lenneberg, E. H. (Ed.), *New directions in the study of language.* Cambridge, Mass.: MIT Press.

ESSOCK-VITALE, S. M., AND MCGUIRE, M. T. 1985. Women's lives viewed from an evolutionary perspective: II. Patterns of helping. *Ethology and Sociobiology* 6:155–73.

ESTES, W. K., AND SKINNER, B. F. 1941. Some quantitative properties of anxiety. *Journal of Experimental Psychology* 29:390–400

EXNER, J. E. 1974. The Rorschach system. New York: Grune and Stratton.

EXNER, J. E. 1978. *A comprehensive system: Current research and advanced interpretation,* vol. 2. New York: Wiley Interscience.

EXNER, J. E., AND CLARK, B. 1978. The Rorschach. In Wolman, B. B. *Clinical diagnosis of mental disorders.* New York: Plenum.

EYFERTH, K. 1961. Leistungen verschiedener Gruppen von Besatzungskindern im Hamburg-Wechsler Intelligenz Test für Kinder (HAWIK). *Archiv für die gesamte Psychologie* 113:222–41.

EYSENCK, H. J. 1961. The effects of psychotherapy. In Eysenck, H. J. (Ed.), *Handbook of abnormal psychology,* pp. 697–725. New York: Basic Books.

EYSENCK, H. J., AND EYSENCK, S. B. G. 1983. Recent advances: The cross-cultural study of personality. In Butcher, J. N., and Spielberger, C. D. (Eds.), *Advances in personality assessment,* vol. 2, pp. 41–72. Hillsdale, N.J.: Erlbaum.

EYSENCK, H. J. VERSUS KAMIN, L. 1981. *The intelligence controversy.* New York: Wiley.

EYSENCK, H. J., AND RACHMAN, S. 1965. *The causes and cures of neurosis.* San Diego, Calif.: Robert E. Knapp.

FALLON, A. E., AND ROZIN, P. 1985. Sex differences in perceptions of desirable body shape. *Journal of Abnormal Psychology* 94:102–105.

FANCHER, R. E. 1987. *The intelligence men: Makers of the IQ controversy.* New York: Norton.

FANT, L. G. 1972. *Ameslan: An introduction to American Sign Language.* Silver Springs, Md.: National Association of the Deaf.

FARAH, M. 1990. *Visual agnosia.* Cambridge, Mass.: MIT Press.

FEDER, H. H. 1984. Hormones and sexual behavior. *Annual Review of Psychology* 35:165–200.

FEINGOLD, A. 1988. Matching for attractiveness in romantic partners and same-sex friends: A meta-analysis and theoretical critique. *Psychological Bulletin* 104: 226–32.

FELDMAN, H.; GOLDIN-MEADOW, S.; AND GLEITMAN, L. R. 1978. Beyond Herodotus: The creation of language by linguistically deprived deaf children. In Lock, A. (Ed.), *Action, gesture, and symbol: The emergence of language.* London: Academic Press.

FERNALD, A. 1992. Human maternal vocalizations to infants as biologically relevant signals: An evolutionary perspective. In Barkow, J. H.; Cosmides, L.; and Tooby J. (Eds.), *The adapted mind: Evolutionary psychology and the generation of culture.* New York: Oxford University Press.

FERSTER, C. B., AND SKINNER, B. F. 1957. *Schedules of reinforcement.* New York: Appleton-Century-Crofts.

FERSTER, D. 1981. A comparison of binocular depth mechanisms in areas 17 and 18 of the cat visual cortex. *Journal of Physiology* 311:623–55.

FESTINGER, L. 1954. A theory of social comparison processes. *Human Relations* 7:117–40.

FESTINGER, L. 1957. *A theory of cognitive dissonance.* Evanston, Ill.: Row, Peterson.

FESTINGER, L., AND CARLSMITH, J. M. 1959. Cognitive consequences of forced compliance. *Journal of Abnormal and Social Psychology* 58:203–10.

FESTINGER, L.; PEPITONE, A.; AND NEWCOMB, T. 1952. Some consequences of deindividuation in a group. *Journal of Abnormal and Social Psychology* 47:387–89.

FESTINGER, L.; RIECKEN, H.; AND SCHACHTER, S. 1956. *When prophecy fails.* Minneapolis: University of Minnesota Press.

FIEDLER, F. E. 1978. Recent developments in research on the contingency model. In Berkowitz, L. (Ed.), *Group processes.* New York: Academic Press.

FIGLEY, C. R. 1978. Symptoms of delayed combat stress among a college sample of Vietnam veterans. *Military Medicine* 143:107–10.

FINKE, R. A.; PINKER, S.; AND FARAH, M. J. 1989. Reinterpreting visual patterns in imagery. *Cognitive Science* 13:51–78.

FISHER, S., AND GREENBERG, R. P. 1977. *The scientific credibility of Freud's theory and therapy.* New York: Basic Books.

FITZGERALD, F. T. 1981. The problem of obesity. *Annual Review of Medicine* 32:221–31.

FLANAGAN, J. C. 1947. Scientific development of the use of human resources: Progress in the Army Air Forces. *Science* 105:57–60.

FLAVELL, J. H. 1970. Developmental studies of mediated memory. In Reese, H. W., and Lipsitt, L. P. (Eds.), *Advances in child development and behavior,* vol. 5. New York: Academic Press.

FLAVELL, J. H. 1977. *Cognitive development.* Englewood Cliffs, N.J.: Prentice-Hall.

FLAVELL, J. H. 1985. *Cognitive development. 2nd ed.* Englewood Cliffs, N.J.: Prentice-Hall.

FLAVELL, J. H.; BEACH, D. H.; AND CHINSKY, J. M. 1966. Spontaneous verbal rehearsal in a memory task as a function of age. *Child Development* 37:283–99.

FLAVELL, J. H.; FLAVELL, E. R.; AND GREEN, F. L. 1983. Development of the appearance-reality distinction. *Cognitive Psychology* 15:95–120.

FLAVELL, J. H.; SHIPSTEAD, S. G.; AND CROFT, K. 1978. Young children's knowledge about visual perception: Hiding objects from others. *Child Development* 49:1208–11.

FLAVELL, J. H., AND WELLMAN, H. M. 1977. Metamemory. In Kail, R. V., Jr., and Hagen, J. W. (Eds.), *Perspectives on the development of memory and cognition,* pp. 3–34. Hillsdale, N.J.: Erlbaum.

FLODERUS-MYRHED, B.; PEDERSEN, N.; AND RASMUSON, L. 1980. Assessment of heritability for personality, based on a short form of the Eysenck Personality Inventory: A study of 12,898 twin pairs. *Behavior Genetics* 10:153–62.

FLYNN, J.; VANEGAS, H.; FOOTE, W.; AND EDWARDS, S. 1970. Neural mechanisms involved in a cat's attack on a rat. In Whalen, R. F.; Thompson, M.; Verzeano, M.; and Weinberger, N. (Eds.), *The neural control of behavior.* New York: Academic Press.

FLYNN, J. R. 1980. *Race, IQ and Jensen.* London: Routledge and Kegan Paul.

FOCH, T. T., AND McCLEARN, G. E. 1980. Genetics, body weight, and obesity. In Stunkard, A. J. (Ed.), *Obesity,* pp. 48–71. Philadelphia: Saunders.

FODOR, J. A. 1972. Some reflections on L. S. Vygotsky's *Thought and language. Cognition* 1:83–95.

FODOR, J. A. 1983. *The modularity of mind.* Cambridge, Mass.: MIT Press, Bradford Books.

FODOR, J. A. 1988. *Psychosemantics.* Cambridge, Mass.: MIT Press.

FODOR, J. A. 1992. A theory of the child's theory of mind. *Cognition* 44:283–96.

FORD, C. S., AND BEACH, F. A. 1951. *Patterns of sexual behavior.* New York: Harper & Row.

FORSTER, E. M. 1927. *Aspects of the novel.* New York: Harcourt, Brace, and World.

FOUCAULT, M. 1965. *Madness and civilization.* New York: Random House.

FOUTS, R. S. 1972. Use of guidance in teaching sign language to a chimpanzee *(Pantroglodytes). Journal of Comparative and Physiological Psychology* 80:515–22.

FOUTS, R. S.; HIRSCH, A. D.; AND FOUTS, D. H. 1982. Cultural transmission of a human language in a chimpanzee mother-infant relationship. In Fitzgerald, H. E.; Mullins, J. A.; and Gage, P. (Eds.), *Child nurturance: Vol. 3, Studies of development in nonhuman primates,* pp. 159–69. New York: Plenum.

FRANKEL, F. H. 1993. Adult reconstruction of childhood events in the multiple personality disorder literature. *American Journal of Psychiatry* 150:954–58.

FREEDMAN, J. L., AND FRASER, S. C. 1966. Compliance without pressure: The foot-in-the-door technique. *Journal of Personality and Social Psychology* 4:195–202.

FREEMAN, D. 1983. *Margaret Mead and Samoa: The making and unmaking of an anthropological myth.* Canberra: Australian National University Press.

FREEMAN, D. 1986. Rejoinder to Patience and Smith. *American Anthropologist* 88:161–67.

FREGE, G. (1892/1952). On sense and reference, In Geach, P., and Black, M. (Eds.), *Philosophical writings of Gottlob Frege.* Oxford: Oxford University Press.

FREMOUW, W. J.; DE PERCZEL, M.; AND ELLIS, T. E. 1990. *Suicide risk: Assessment and response guidelines.* Elmsford, N.Y.: Pergamon.

FREUD, A. 1946. The ego and the mechanisms of defense. London: Hogarth Press.

FREUD, S. 1900. The interpretation of dreams. In Strachey, J., trans. and ed., *The complete psychological works,* vols. 4–5. New York: Norton, 1976.

FREUD, S. 1901. The psychopathology of everyday life. Translated by Tyson, A. New York: Norton, 1971.

FREUD, S. 1905. Three essays on the theory of sexuality. In Strachey, J., trans. and ed., *The complete psychological works,* vol. 7. New York: Norton, 1976.

FREUD, S. 1908. Character and anal eroticism. In Rieff, P. (Ed.), *Collected papers of Sigmund Freud: Character and culture.* New York: Collier Books, 1963.

FREUD, S. 1911. Psychoanalytic notes upon an autobiographical account of a case of paranoia (dementia paranoides). In Strachey, J., trans. and ed., *The complete psychological works,* vol. 12. New York: Norton, 1976.

FREUD, S. 1917. *A general introduction to psychoanalysis.* Translated by Riviere, J. New York: Washington Square Press, 1952.

FREUD, S. 1923. *The ego and the id.* Translated by Riviere, J. New York: Norton, 1962.

FREUD, S. 1926. *Inhibitions, symptoms, and anxiety.* Translated and revised by Strachey, J. New York: Norton, 1959.

FREUD, S. 1930. *Civilization and its discontents.* Translated by Strachey, J. New York: Norton, 1961.

FREUD, S., AND BREUER, J. 1895. Studies on hysteria. In Strachey, J., trans. and ed., *The complete psychological works,* vol. 2. New York: Norton, 1976.

FRIDLUND, A. J. 1990. Evolution and facial action in reflex, social motive, and paralanguage. In Ackles, P. K.; Jennings, J. R.; and Coles, M. G. H. (Eds.), *Advances in psychophysiology,* vol. 4. Greenwich, Conn.: JAI Press.

FRIDLUND, A. J.; EKMAN, P.; AND OSTER, H. 1983. Facial expression of emotion: Review of literature, 1970–1983. In Siegman, A. (Ed.), *Nonverbal behavior and communication.* Hillsdale, N.J.: Erlbaum.

FRIEDMAN, M., AND ROSENMAN, R. H. 1974. *Type A behavior.* New York: Knopf.

FRIEDMAN, M. I., AND STRICKER, E. M. 1976. The physiological psychology of hunger: a physiological perspective. *Psychological Review* 83:409–31.

FRIEDMAN, M. J. 1990. Interrelationships between biological mechanisms and pharmacotherapy of posttraumatic stress disorder, pp. 205-25. In Wolf, M. E., and Mosnaim, A. D. (Eds.), Posttraumatic stress disorder: Etiology, phenomenology, and treatment. Washington, D.C.: American Psychiatric Press.

FROMKIN, V.; KRASHEN, S.; CURTISS, S.; RIGLER, D.; AND RIGLER, M. 1974. The development of language in Genie: A case of language acquisition beyond the "critical period." *Brain and Language* 1:81–107.

FUNKENSTEIN, D. H. 1956. Norepinephrine-like and epinephrine-like substances in relation to human behavior. *Journal of Mental Diseases* 124:58–68.

GALLISTEL, C. R. 1980. *The organization of action.* Hillsdale, N.J.: Erlbaum.

GALLISTEL, C. R. 1990. *The organization of learning.* Cambridge, Mass.: MIT Press (Bradford).

GALTON, F. 1869. *Hereditary genius: An inquiry into its laws and consequences.* London: Macmillan.

GALTON, F. 1883. *Inquiries into human faculty and its development.* London: Macmillan.

GANAWAY, G. K. 1989. Historical versus narrative truth: Clarifying the role of exogenous trauma in the etiology of MPD and its variants. *Dissociation* 2:205–20.

GARCIA, J.; ERVIN, F. R.; AND KOELLING, R. A. 1966. Learning with prolonged delay of reinforcement. *Psychonomic Science* 5:121–22.

GARCIA, J., AND KOELLING, R. A. 1966. The relation of cue to consequence in avoidance learning. *Psychonomic Science* 4:123–24.

GARDNER, H. 1983. *Frames of mind: The theory of multiple intelligences.* New York: Basic Books.

GARDNER, R. A., AND GARDNER, B. T. 1969. Teaching sign language to a chimpanzee. *Science* 165:664–72.

GARDNER, R. A., AND GARDNER, B. T. 1975. Early signs of language in child and chimpanzee. *Science* 187:752–53.

GARFIELD, S. L. 1992. Major issues in psychotherapy research. In Freedheim, D. K. (Ed.), *History of Psychotherapy.* Washington, D.C.: American Psychological Association.

GARFINKEL, P. E., AND GARNER, D. M. 1982. *Anorexia Nervosa.* New York: Bruner/Mazel.

GARRIGAN, J. L. 1987. Post-traumatic stress disorder in military disaster workers. In *The human response to the Gander military air disaster: A summary report* (Division of Neuropsychiatry Report No. 88–12). Washington, D.C.: Walter Reed Army Institute of Research.

GAZZANIGA, M. S. 1967. The split brain in man. *Scientific American* 217:24–29.

GAZZANIGA, M. S. 1970. *The bisected brain.* New York: Appleton-Century-Crofts.

GEERTZ, C. 1983. Local knowledge. In *Further essays in interpretative anthropology.* New York: Basic Books.

GEFFEN, G.; BRADSHAW, J. L.; AND WALLACE, G. 1971. Interhemispheric effects on reaction time to verbal and nonverbal visual stimuli. *Journal of Experimental Psychology* 87:415–22.

GELMAN, R. 1972. Logical capacity of very young children: Number invariance rules. *Child Development* 43:75–90.

GELMAN, R. 1978. Cognitive development. *Annual Review of Psychology* 29:297–332.

GELMAN, R. 1982. Basic numerical abilities. In Sternberg, R. J. (Ed.), *Advances in the psychology of human intelligence,* vol. 1, pp. 181–205. Hillsdale, N.J.: Erlbaum.

GELMAN, R., AND BAILLARGEON, R. 1983. A review of some Piagetian concepts. In Mussen, P. (Ed.), *Carmichael's manual of child psychology: Vol 3: Cognitive development* (Markman, E. M., and Flavell, J. H., volume editors), pp. 167–230. New York: Wiley.

GELMAN, R., AND GALLISTEL, C. R. 1978. *The child's understanding of number.* Cambridge, Mass.: Harvard University Press.

GERARD, H. B.; WILHELMY, R. A.; AND CONOLLEY, E. S. 1968. Conformity and group size. *Journal of Personality and Social Psychology* 8:79–82.

GERGEN, K. 1973. Social psychology as history. *Journal of Personality and Social Psychology* 26:309–20.

GERKEN, L.; LANDAU, B.; AND REMEZ, R. 1990. Function morphemes in young children's speech perception and production. *Developmental Psychology* 26(2):204–16.

GERSHON, E. S.; NURNBERGER, J. I., JR.; BERRETTINI, W. H.; AND GOLDIN, L. R. 1985. Affective disorders: Genetics. In Kaplan, H. I., and Sadock, J. (Eds.), *Modern synopsis of comprehensive textbook of psychiatry,* 4th ed. Baltimore: Williams & Wilkins.

GESCHWIND, N. 1970. The organization of language and the brain. *Science* 170:940–44.

GESCHWIND, N. 1972. Language and the brain. *Scientific American* 226:76–83.

GIBBONS, R. D.; HEDEKER, D.; ELKIN, I.; WATERNAUX, C.; KRAEMER, H. C.; GREENHOUSE, J. B.; SHEA, M. T.; IMBER, S. D.; SOTSKY, S. M.; WATKINS, J. T. 1993. Some conceptual and statistical issues in analysis of longitudinal psychiatric data. Application to the NIMH treatment of depression Collaborative Research Program dataset. *Archives of General Psychiatry* 50:739–50.

GIBSON, J. J. 1950. *The perception of the visual world.* Boston: Houghton Mifflin.

GIBSON, J. J. 1966. *The senses considered as perceptual systems.* Boston: Houghton Mifflin.

GIBSON, J. J. 1979. *The ecological approach to visual perception.* Boston: Houghton Mifflin.

GILLIGAN, C. 1982. *In a different voice: Psychological theory and women's development.* Cambridge, Mass.: Harvard University Press.

GILLIGAN, C. 1986. Profile of Carol Gilligan. In Scarr, S.; Weinberg, R. A.; and Levine, A. 1986. *Understanding development,* pp. 488–91. New York: Harcourt Brace Jovanovich.

GINZBERG, L. 1909. *The legends of the Jews,* vol. 1. Translated by Szold, H. Philadelphia: Jewish Publication Society of America.

GLANZER, M., AND CUNITZ, A. 1966. Two storage mechanisms in free recall. *Journal of Verbal Learning and Verbal Behavior* 5:531–60.

GLEITMAN, H. 1963. Place-learning. *Scientific American* 209:116–22.

GLEITMAN, H. 1971. Forgetting of long-term memories in animals. In Honig, W. K., and James, P. H. R. (Eds.), *Animal memory,* pp. 2–46. New York: Academic Press.

GLEITMAN, H. 1985. Some trends in the study of cognition. In Koch, S., and Leary, D. E. (Eds.), *A century of psychology as science,* pp. 420–36. New York: McGraw-Hill.

GLEITMAN, L. R. 1981. Maturational determinants of language growth. *Cognition* 10:103–14.

GLEITMAN, L. R. 1986. Biological dispositions to learn language. In Demopolous, W., and Marras, A. (Eds.), *Language learning and concept acquisition*. Norwood, N.J.: Ablex.

GLEITMAN, L. R. 1990. Structural sources of verb learning. *Language Acquisition* 1:1–54.

GLEITMAN, L. R.; GLEITMAN, H.; AND SHIPLEY, E. F. 1972. The emergence of the child as grammarian. *Cognition* 1(2):137–64.

GLEITMAN, L. R., AND LANDAU, B. (Eds.), Lexical Acquisition, *Lingua* (Special Issue) 92, 1994.

GLICK, J. 1975. Cognitive development in cross-cultural perspective. In Horowitz, F. G. (Ed.), *Review of child development research,* vol. 4. Chicago: University of Chicago Press.

GLUCKSBERG, S. 1962. The influence of strength of drive on functional fixedness and perceptual recognition. *Journal of Experimental Psychology* 63:36–41.

GODDEN, D. R., AND BADDELEY, A. D. 1975. Context-dependent memory in two natural environments: On land and underwater. *British Journal of Psychology* 66:325–31.

GOLD, R. 1978. On the meaning of nonconservation. In Lesgold, A. M.; Pellegrino, J. W.; Fokkema, S. D.; and Glaser, R. (Eds.), *Cognitive psychology and instruction.* New York: Plenum.

GOLDBERG, L. R. 1982. From ace to zombie: Some explorations in the language of personality. In Spielberger, C., and Butcher, J. N. (Eds.), *Advances in personality assessment,* vol. 1, Hillsdale, N.J.: Erlbaum.

GOLDBERG, L. R. 1990. An alternative "description of personality": The Big-Five factor structure. *Journal of Personality and Social Psychology* 59:1216–29.

GOLDBERG, L. R. 1993. The structure of phenotypic personality traits. *American Psychologist* 48:26–34.

GOLDEN, T. 1990. Ill, possibly violent, and no place to go. *New York Times,* Monday, April 2, 1990, pp. A1 and B4.

GOLDFARB, W. 1955. Emotional and intellectual consequences of psychological deprivation in infancy: A reevaluation. In Hock, P. H., and Zubin, J. (Eds.), *Psychopathology of childhood.* New York: Grune and Stratton.

GOLDIN-MEADOW, S. 1982. Fragile and resilient properties of language learning. In Wanner, E., and Gleitman, L. R. (Eds.), *Language acquisition: State of the art.* New York: Cambridge University Press.

GOLDIN-MEADOW, S., AND MYLANDER, C. 1983. Gestural communication in deaf children: The non-effects of parental input. *Science* 221:372–74.

GOLDSTEIN, E. B. 1984. *Sensation and perception,* 2nd ed. Belmont, Calif.: Wadsworth.

GOLDSTEIN, E. B. 1989. *Sensation and perception,* 3rd ed. Belmont, Calif.: Wadsworth.

GOLDSTEIN, J. M., AND TSUANG, M. T. 1990. Gender and schizophrenia: An introduction and synthesis of findings. *Schizophrenia Bulletin* 16:179–83.

GOMBRICH, E. H. 1961. *Art and illusion.* Princeton, N.J.: Bollingen Series, Princeton University Press.

GORDON H. 1923. Mental and scholastic tests among retarded children. *Educational Pamphlet,* no. 44. London: Board of Education.

GOREN, C. C.; SARTY, M.; AND WU, P. Y. K. 1975. Visual following and pattern discrimination of face-like stimuli by newborn infants. *Pediatrics* 56: 544–49.

GOTTESMAN, I. I.; MCGUFFIN, P.; AND FARMER, A. 1987. Clinical genetics as clues to the "real" genetics of schizophrenia (a decade of modest gains while playing for time). *Schizophrenia Bulletin* 13:23–47.

GOTTESMAN, I. I., AND SHIELDS, J. 1972. *Schizophrenia and genetics: A twin study vantage point.* New York: Academic Press.

GOTTESMAN, I. I., AND SHIELDS, J. 1982. *Schizophrenia: The epigenetic puzzle.* New York: Cambridge University Press.

GOTTLIEB, G. 1961. Developmental age as a baseline for determination of the critical period for imprinting. *Journal of Comparative and Physiological Psychology* 54:422–27.

GOUGH, H. G. 1975. *California psychological inventory: Manual,* rev. ed. Palo Alto, Calif.: Consulting Psychologists Press (original edition, 1957).

GOULD, S. J. 1977. *Ontogeny and phylogeny.* Cambridge, Mass.: Harvard University Press.

GRAF, P., AND MANDLER, G. 1984. Activation makes words more accessible, but not necessarily more retrievable. *Journal of Verbal Learning and Verbal Behavior* 23:553–68.

GRAF, P.; MANDLER, G.; AND SQUIRE, L. R. 1984. The information that amnesic patients don't forget. *Journal of Experimental Psychology: Learning, Memory, and Cognition* 10:164–78.

GRAHAM, C. H., AND HSIA, Y. 1954. Luminosity curves for normal and dichromatic subjects including a case of unilateral color blindness. *Science* 120:780.

GRAY, S. 1977. Social aspects of body image: Perception of normalcy of weight and affect of college undergraduates. *Perceptual and Motor Skills* 45:1035–40.

GREEN, D. M. 1976. *An introduction to hearing.* New York: Academic Press.

GREEN, D. M., AND SWETS, J. A. 1966. *Signal detection theory and psychophysics.* New York: Wiley.

GREEN, G. D., AND CLUNIS, D. M. 1988. Married lesbians. Lesbianism: Affirming Nontraditional Roles, *Women and Therapy* (Special Issue) 8: 41–49.

GREEN, P., AND PRESTON, M. 1981. Reinforcement of vocal correlates of auditory hallucinations by auditory feedback: A case study. *British Journal of Psychiatry* 139:204–208.

GREEN, R. 1969. Age-intelligence relationships between ages sixteen and sixty-four: A rising trend. *Developmental Psychology* 1:618–27.

GREEN, R. 1979. Childhood cross-gender behavior and subsequent sexual preference. *American Journal of Psychiatry* 136:106–108.

GREEN, S. K.; BUCHANAN, D. R.; AND HEUER, S. K. 1984. Winners, losers, and choosers: a field investigation of dating initiation. *Personality and Social Psychology Bulletin* 10:502–11.

GREENE, R. L. 1991. *The MMPI-2/MMPI: An interpretative manual.* Needham Heights, Mass.: Allyn and Bacon.

GREENFIELD, P. M. 1966. On culture and conservation. In Bruner, R. R.; Olver, R. R.; and Greenfield, P. M. (Eds.), *Studies in cognitive growth.* New York: Wiley.

GREENFIELD, P. M. 1976. Cross-cultural research and Piagetian theory: Paradox and progress. In Riegel, K., and Meacham, J. (Eds.), *The developing individual in a changing world,* vol. 1. The Hague: Mouton.

GREVEN, P. J., Jr. 1970. *Four generations: Population, land, and family in colonial Andover, Massachusetts.* Ithaca: N.Y.: Cornell University Press.

GROSSMAN, H. J. (Ed.). 1983. *Manual on terminology and classification in mental retardation,* rev. ed. Washington, D. C.: American Association for Mental Deficiency.

GROVES, P. M., AND REBEC, G. V. 1988. *Introduction to biological psychology,* 3rd ed. Dubuque, Iowa: W. C. Brown.

GRÜNBAUM, A. 1984. *The foundations of psychoanalysis: A philosophical inquiry.* Berkeley, Calif.: University of California Press.

GUTTMAN, N., AND KALISH, H. I. 1956. Discriminability and stimulus generalization. *Journal of Experimental Psychology* 51: 79–88.

GUYTON, A. C. 1981. *Textbook of medical physiology.* Philadelphia: Saunders.

HABER, R. N. 1969. Eidetic images. *Scientific American* 220: 36–44.

HALL, C. S. 1953. A cognitive theory of dream symbols. *Journal of General Psychology* 48:169–86.

HALL, C. S. 1966. *The meaning of dreams.* New York: McGraw-Hill.

HALPERN, D. 1992. *Sex differences in cognitive abilities,* 2nd ed. Hillsdale, N.J.: Erlbaum.

HALVERSON, H. M. 1931. An experimental study of prehension infants by means of systematic cinema records. *Genetic Psychology Monographs* 47:47–63.

HAMER, D.; HU, S.; MAGNUSON, V.; AND HU, N. 1993a. A linkage between DNA markers on the X-chromosome and male sexual orientation. *Science* 261(5119):321–27.

HAMER, D.; HU, S.; MAGNUSON, V.; AND HU, N. 1993b. Genetics and male sexual orientation (Response) *Science* 261(5126): 1259.

HAMILTON, D. L., AND ROSE, T. L. 1980. Illusory correlation and the maintenance of stereotypic beliefs. *Journal of Personality and Social Psychology* 39:832–45.

HAMILTON, W. D. 1964. The genetical evolution of social behavior. *Journal of Theoretical Biology* 7:1–51.

HANSEN, J. T., AND SCHULDT, W. J. 1984. Marital self-disclosure and marital satisfaction. *Journal of Marriage and the Family* 46: 923–26.

HARE, R. D. 1965. Temporal gradients of fear arousal in psychopaths. *Journal of Abnormal Psychology* 70:422–45.

HARE, R. D. 1978. A research scale for the assessment of psychopathy in criminal populations. *Personality and Individual Differences* 1: 111-19.

HAREVEN, T. K. 1978. The last stage: Historical adulthood and old age. In Erikson, E. H. (Ed.), *Adulthood*, pp. 201–16. New York: Norton.

HARKINS, S., AND GREEN, R. G. 1975. Discriminability and criterion differences between extraverts and introverts during vigilance. *Journal of Research in Personality* 9:335–40.

HARLOW, H. F. 1950. Learning and satiation of response in intrinsically motivated complex puzzle performance in monkeys. *Journal of Comparative and Physiological Psychology* 43:289–94.

HARLOW, H. F. 1958. The nature of love. *American Psychologist* 13:673–85.

HARLOW, H. F. 1962. The heterosexual affectional system in monkeys. *American Psychologist* 17:1–9.

HARRIS, G. W., AND MICHAEL, R. P. 1964. The activation of sexual behavior by hypothalamic implants of estrogen. *Journal of Physiology* 171:275–301.

HARTMANN, H. 1964. *Essays on ego psychology: Selected problems in psychoanalytic theory.* New York: International Universities Press.

HARTSHORNE, H., AND MAY, M. A. 1928. *Studies in the nature of character,* vol. 1. New York: Macmillan.

HARVEY, L. O., JR., AND LEIBOWITZ, H. 1967. Effects of exposure duration, cue reduction, and temporary monocularity on size matching at short distances. *Journal of the Optical Society of America* 57:249–53.

HASE, H. D., AND GOLDBERG, L. R. 1967. Comparative validities of different strategies of constructing personality inventory scales. *Psychological Bulletin* 67:231–48.

HATFIELD, E. 1988. Passionate and companionate love. In Sternberg, R. J., and Barnes, M. L. (Eds.), *The psychology of love.* New Haven, Conn.: Yale University Press.

HATHAWAY, S. R., AND MCKINLEY, J. C. 1940. A multiphasic personality schedule (Minnesota): I. Construction of the schedule. *Journal of Psychology* 10:249–54.

HAY, P.; SACHDEV, P.; CUMMING, S.; SMITH, J. S.; LEE, T.; KITCHENER, P.; AND MATHESON, J. 1993. Treatment of obsessive-compulsive disorder by psychosurgery. *Acta Psychiatrica Scandinavica* 87:197–207.

HAYES, C. 1952. *The ape in our house.* London: Gollacz.

HAYNES, S. G.; FEINLEIB, M.; AND KANNEL, W. B. 1980. The relationship of psychosocial factors to coronary heart disease in the Framingham study: Eight years incidence in coronary heart disease. *American Journal of Epidemiology* 3:37–85.

HEALY, A. F., AND MILLER, G. A. 1970. The verb as the main determinant of sentence meaning. *Psychonomic Science* 20:372.

HEARST, E. 1972. Psychology across the chessboard. In *Readings in Psychology Today,* 2nd ed. Albany, N.Y.: Delmar Publishers, CRM Books.

HEDIGER, H. 1968. *The psychology and behavior of animals in zoos and circuses.* New York: Dover.

HEIDER, F. 1958. *The psychology of interpersonal relationships.* New York: Wiley.

HELLEKSON, C. J.; KLINE, J. A.; AND ROSENTHAL, N. E. 1986. Phototherapy for seasonal affective disorder in Alaska. *American Journal of Psychiatry* 143:1035–37.

HELMHOLTZ, H. 1909. *Wissenschaftliche Abhandlungen, II,* pp. 764–843.

HENLE, M. 1962. On the relation between logic and thinking. *Psychological Review* 69:366–78.

HENRY, J. P., AND CASSEL, J. C. 1969. Psychosocial factors in essential hypertension. *American Journal of Epidemiology* 90:171.

HENRY, W. E. 1973. *The analysis of fantasy.* Huntington, N.Y.: Robert E. Krieger.

HERING, E. 1920. *Outlines of a theory of the light sense,* pp. 150–51. Edited by Hurvich, L. M., and Jameson, D. Cambridge, Mass.: Harvard University Press.

HERDT, G. 1990. Developmental discontinuities and sexual orientation across cultures. In McWhirter, D. P.; Sanders, S. A.; and Reinisch, J. M. (Eds.), *Homosexuality/heterosexuality: Concepts of sexual orientation.* New York: Oxford University Press.

HERMAN, C. P., AND MACK, D. 1975. Restrained and unrestrained eating. *Journal of Personality* 43:647–60.

HERMAN, C. P., AND POLIVY, J. 1980. Restrained eating. In Stunkard, A. J. (Ed.), *Obesity,* pp. 208–25. Philadelphia: Saunders.

HESS, E. H. 1958. "Imprinting" in animals. *Scientific American* 198:82.

HESS, E. H. 1959. Imprinting. *Science* 130:133-41.

HESS, E. H. 1973. *Imprinting: Early experience and the developmental psychobiology of attachment.* New York: Van Nostrand.

HESS, R. D. 1970. Social class and ethnic influences on socialization. In Mussen, P. H. (Ed.), *Carmichael's manual of child psychology,* 3rd ed., vol. 2, pp. 457–558. New York: Wiley.

HILGARD, E. R. 1977. *Divided consciousness: Multiple controls in human thought and action.* New York: Wiley.

HILGARD, E. R. 1986. *Divided consciousness: Multiple controls in human thought and action,* rev. ed. New York: Wiley.

HILL, A. L. 1978. Savants: Mentally retarded individuals with specific skills. In N. R. Ellis (Ed.), *International Review of Research in Mental Retardation,* vol. 9. New York: Academic Press.

HILL, C. T.; RUBIN, L.; AND PEPLAU, L. A. 1976. Breakups before marriage: The end of 103 affairs. *Journal of Social Issues* 32:147–68.

HINELINE, P. N., AND RACHLIN, H. 1969. Escape and avoidance of shock by pigeons pecking a key. *Journal of the Experimental Analysis of Behavior* 12:533–38.

HINTZMAN, D. L. 1990. Human learning and memory: Connections and dissociations. *Annual Review of Psychology* 41:109–39.

HIRSCHFELD, R. M., AND CROSS, C. K. 1981. Epidemiology of affective disorders. *Archives of General Psychiatry* 39:3546

HIRSCHFELD, R. M., AND GOODWIN, F. K. 1988. Mood disorders. In Talbott, J. A.; Hales, R. E.; and Yudofsky, S. C. (Eds.), *The American Psychiatric Press textbook of psychiatry,* vol. 7. Washington, D.C.: American Psychiatric Press.

HIRSH-PASEK, K.; GOLINKOFF, R.; FLETCHER; DEGASPE-BEAUBIEN; AND CAULEY. 1985. In the beginning: one-word speakers comprehend word order. Paper presented at Boston Child Language Conference, October, 1985.

HIRTH, D. H., AND MCCULLOUGH, D. R. 1977. Evolution of alarm signals in ungulates with special reference to white-tailed deer. *American Naturalist* 111:31–42.

HOBBES, T. 1651. *Leviathan.* Baltimore: Penguin Books, 1968.

HOBSON, J. A. 1988. *The dreaming brain.* New York: Basic Books.

HOBSON, J. A., AND MCCARLEY, R. W. 1977. The brain as a dream-state generator: An activation-synthesis hypothesis of the dream porcess. *American Journal of Psychiatry* 134:1335–68.

HOCHBERG, J. E. 1970. Attention, organization and consciousness. In Mostofsky, D. I. (Ed.), *Attention: Contemporary theory and analysis,* pp. 99–124. New York: Appleton-Century-Crofts.

HOCHBERG, J. E. 1978a. *Perception,* 2nd ed. Englewood Cliffs, N.J.: Prentice-Hall.

HOCHBERG, J. E. 1978b. Art and perception. In Carterette, E. C., and Friedman, M. P. (Eds.), *Handbook of perception,* vol. 10, pp. 225–55. New York: Academic Press.

HOCHBERG, J. E. 1980. Pictorial functions and perceptual structures. In Hagen, M. A. (Ed.), *The perception of pictures,* vol. 2, pp. 47–93. New York: Academic Press.

HOCHBERG, J. 1981. On cognition in perception: Perceptual coupling and unconscious inference. *Cognition* 10:127–34.

HOCHBERG, J. 1988. Visual perception. In Atkinson, R. C.; Herrnstein, R. J.; Lindzey, G.; and Luce, R. D. (Eds.), *Stevens' handbook of experimental psychology: Vol. 1. Perception and motivation,* rev. ed., pp. 195–276. New York: Wiley.

HODGKIN, A. L., AND HUXLEY, A. F. 1939. Action potentials recorded from inside nerve fiber. *Nature* 144: 710–11.

HODGKINSON, S.; MULLAN, M. J.; AND GURLING, H. M. 1990. The role of genetic factors in the etiology of the affective disorders. *Behavior Genetics* 20:235–50.

HOEBEL, B. G., AND TEITELBAUM, P. 1976. Weight regulation in normal and hyperphagic rats. *Journal of Physiological and Comparative Psychology* 61: 189–93.

HOFFMAN, H. S. 1978. Experimental analysis of imprinting and its behavioral effects. *The Psychology of Learning and Motivation* 12:137.

HOFFMAN, H. S., AND FLESHLER, M. 1964. An apparatus for the measurement of the startle response in the rat. *American Journal of Psychology* 77:307–308.

HOFFMAN, M. L. 1970. Moral development. In Mussen, P. H., (Ed.), *Carmichael's manual of child psychology,* 3rd. ed., vol. 2, pp. 457–558. New York: Wiley.

HOFFMAN, M. L. 1977a. Empathy, its development and prosocial implications. In Keasey, C. B. (Ed.), *Nebraska Symposium on Motivation* 25:169–217.

HOFFMAN, M. L. 1977b. Sex differences in empathy and related behaviors. *Psychological Bulletin* 84:712–22.

HOFFMAN, M. L. 1979. Development of moral thought, feeling, and behavior. *American Psychologist* 34:295–318.

HOFFMAN, M. L. 1984. Empathy, its limitations, and its role in a comprehensive moral theory. In Kurtines, W. M., and Gewirtz, L. (Eds.), *Morality, moral behavior, and moral development,* pp. 283–302. New York: Wiley.

HOLDING, D. H. 1985. *The psychology of chess skill.* Hillsdale, N.J.: Erlbaum.

HOLDING, D. H., AND REYNOLDS, R. I. 1982. Recall or evaluation of chess positions as determinants of chess skill. *Memory and Cognition* 10:237–42.

HOLLANDER, E., AND McCARLEY, A. 1992. Yohimbine treatment of sexual side effects induced by serotonin reuptake blockers. *Journal of Clinical Psychiatry* 53:197–99.

HOLLANDER, E. P. 1985. Leadership and power. In Lindzey, G., and Aronson, E. (Eds.), *Handbook of social psychology,* 3rd ed., vol. 2. New York: Random House.

HOLLISTER, L. E., AND CSERNANSKY, J. G. 1990. *Clinical pharmacology of psychotherapeutic drugs,* 3rd. ed. New York: Churchill-Livingstone.

HOLMES, D. 1990. The evidence for repression: An examinmation of sixty years of research. In Singer, J. (Ed.), *Repression and dissociation: Implications for personality theory, psychopathology, and health,* pp. 85–102. Chicago: University of Chicago Press.

HOLT, R. R. 1978. *Methods in clinical psychology: Vol. 1. Projective assessment.* New York: Plenum.

HOLTZMAN, P. S.; Kringlen, E.; Malthysse, S.; Flanagan, S. D.; Lipton, R. B.; Cramer, G.; Levin, S.; Lange, K.; and Levy, D. L. 1988. A single dominant gene can account for eye tracking dysfunctions and schizophrenia in offspring of discordant twins. *Archives of General Psychiatry* 45:641–47.

HOLWAY, A. F., AND BORING, E. G. 1947. Determinants of apparent visual size with distance variant. *American Journal of Psychology* 54:21–37.

HOOK, S. 1955. *The hero in history.* Boston: Beacon Press.

HORN, J. L., AND CATTELL, R. B. 1967. Age differences in fluid and crystallized intelligence. *Acta Psychologica* 26:107–29.

HORN, J. M. 1983. The Texas Adoption Project: Adopted children and their biological and adoptive parents. *Child Development* 54:268–75.

HORN, J. M.; LOEHLIN, J. C.; AND WILLERMAN, L. 1979. Intellectual resemblance among adoptive and biological relatives: The Texas Adoption Project. *Behavior Genetics* 13:459–71.

HORN, J. M.; LOEHLIN, J. C.; AND WILLERMAN, L. 1982. Aspects of the inheritance of intellectual abilities. *Behavior Genetics* 12:479–516.

HORNE, J. A. 1988. *Why we sleep: The functions of sleep in humans and other mammals.* New York: Oxford University Press.

HORNE, R. L., AND PICARD, R. S. 1979. Psychosocial risk factors for lung cancer. *Psychosomatic Medicine* 41:503–14.

HORNEY, K. 1937. *The neurotic personality of our time.* New York: Norton.

HORNEY, K. 1945. *Our inner conflicts.* New York: Norton.

HORNEY, K. 1950. *New ways in psychoanalysis.* New York: Norton.

HOVLAND, C. I., AND WEISS, W. 1952. The influence of source credibility on communication effectiveness. *Public Opinion Quarterly* 15:635–50.

HOWARD, D. V. 1983. *Cognitive psychology.* New York: Macmillan.

HOWE, M. L., AND COURAGE, M. L. 1993. On resolving the enigma of infantile amnesia. *Psychological Bulletin* 113:305–27.

HRDY, S. B. 1988. The primate origins of sexuality. In Smith, M. S.; Hamilton, W. D.; Margulis, L.; Hrdy, S. B.; Raven, P. H.; and Hefner, P. J. (Eds.), *The evolution of sex.* San Francisco: Harper & Row.

HRDY, S. B., AND WILLIAMS, G. C. 1983. Behavioral biology and the double standard. In Wasser, S. K., (Ed.), *The social behavior of female vertebrates,* pp. 3-17. New York: Academic Press.

HUBEL, D. H. 1963. The visual cortex of the brain. *Scientific American* 209:54–62.

HUBEL, D. H., AND WIESEL, T. N. 1959. Receptive fields of single neurons in the cat's visual cortex. *Journal of Physiology* 148: 574–91.

HUBEL, D. H., AND WIESEL, T. N. 1970. Stereoscopic vision in the macaque monkey. Nature 225:41–42.

HULL, C. L. 1943. *Principles of behavior.* New York: Appleton-Century-Crofts.

HUMPHREY, G. 1951. *Thinking: An introduction to its experimental psychology.* New York: Wiley.

HUMPHREYS, L. G. 1939. The effect of random alternation of reinforcement on the acquisition and extinction of conditioned eyelid reactions. *Journal of Experimental Psychology* 25:141–58.

HUNT, E. 1985a. The correlates of intelligence. In D. K. Detterman (Ed.), *Current topics in human intelligence,* vol. 1. Norwood, N.J.: Ablex.

HUNT, J. M. 1961. *Intelligence and experience.* New York: Ronald Press.

HUNT, P., AND HILLERY, J. M. 1973. Social facilitation in a coaction setting: An examination of the effects over learning trials. *Journal of Experimental Social Psychology* 9:563–71.

HURVICH, L. M. 1981. *Color vision.* Sunderland, Mass.: Sinauer Assoc.

HURVICH, L. M., AND JAMESON, D. 1957. An opponent-process theory of color vision. *Psychological Review* 64:384–404.

HUSTON, A. C. 1983. Sex-typing. In Mussen, P. (Ed.), *Carmichael's manual of child psychology: Vol. 4. Socialization, personality, and social development,* pp. 387–468. (Hetherington, E. M., volume editor). New York: Wiley.

HUSTON, T. L.; RUGGIERO, M.; CONNER, R.; AND GEIS, G. 1981. Bystander intervention into crime: A study based on naturally occurring episodes. *Social Psychology Quarterly* 44:14–23.

HUTTENLOCHER, J.; SMILEY, P.; AND CHARNEY, R. 1983. Emergence of action categories in the child: Evidence from verb meanings. *Psychological Review* 90:72–93.

HUTTENLOCHER, P. R. 1979. Synaptic density in human frontal cortex—developmental changes and effects of aging. *Brain Research* 163:195–205.

HYDE, D. M. 1959. An investigation of Piaget's theories of the development of the concept of number. Unpublished doctoral dissertation. University of London. (Quoted in Flavell, J. H., *The developmental psychology of Jean Piaget,* p. 383. New York: Van Nostrand Reinhold).

HYDE, J. S. 1981. How large are cognitive gender differences? A meta-analysis using w^2 and d. *American Psychologist* 36:892–901.

HYDE, J. S., AND LYNN, M. C. 1988. Gender differences in verbal ability: A meta-analysis. *Psychological Bulletin* 104:53–69.

ILYIN, N. A., AND ILYIN, V. N. 1930. Temperature effects on the color of the Siamese cat. *Journal of Heredity* 21:309–18.

INBAU, F. E., AND REID, J. E. 1953. *Truth and deception: The polygraph ("lie detector") technique.* Baltimore: Williams & Wilkins.

INGLIS, J. 1969. Electrode placement and the effect of ECT on mood and memory in depression. *Canadian Psychiatric Association Journal* 14:463–471.

INHELDER, B., AND PIAGET, J. 1958. *The growth of logical thinking from childhood to adolescence.* New York: Basic Books.

INSEL, T. R. 1990. New pharmacologic approaches to obsessive compulsive disorder. *Journal of Clinical Psychiatry* (Supplement) 51:47–51.

IZARD, C. E. 1971. *The face of emotion.* New York: Appleton-Century-Crofts.

IZARD, C. E. 1977. *Human emotions.* New York: Plenum.

IZARD, C. E. 1991. *The psychology of emotions.* New York: Plenum.

IZZETT, R. 1971. Authoritarianism and attitudes toward the Vietnam War as reflected in behavioral and self-report measures. *Journal of Personality and Social Psychology* 17:145–48.

JACOBS, A. 1955. Formation of new associations to words selected on the basis of reaction-time-GSR combinations. *Journal of Abnormal and Social Psychology* 51:371–77.

JACOBSEN, F. M. 1992. Fluoxetine-induced sexual dysfunction and an open trial of yohimbine. *Journal of Clinical Psychiatry* 53:119–22.

JACOBY, L. L., AND DALLAS, M. 1981. On the relationship between autobiographical memory and perceptual learning. *Journal of Experimental Psychology: General* 3:306–40.

JACOBY, L. L.; KELLEY, C.; BROWN, J.; AND JASECHKO, J. 1989. Becoming famous overnight: Limits on the ability to avoid unconscious influences of the past. *Journal of Personality and Social Psychology: General* 56:326–38.

JACOBY, L. L., AND WITHERSPOON, D. 1982. Remembering without awareness. *Canadian Journal of Psychology* 36:300–24.

JAHODA, G. 1979. A cross-cultural perspective on experimental social psychology. *Personality and Social Psychology Bulletin* 5: 142-48.

JAMES, W. 1890. *Principles of psychology.* New York: Henry Holt.

JAMESON, D., AND HURVICH, L. M.. 1975. From contrast to assimilation: In art and in the eye. *Leonardo* 8:125–31.

JANICAK, P. G.; DAVIS, J. M.; GIBBONS, R. D.; ERICKSEN, S.; CHANG, S.; AND GALLAGHER, P. 1985. Efficacy of ECT: A meta-analysis. *American Journal of Psychiatry* 142:297–302.

JENCKS, C.; SMITH, M.; ACLAND, H.; BANE, M. J.; COHEN, D.; GINTIS, H.; HEYNS, B.; AND MICHELSON, S. 1972. *Inequality: A reassessment of the effect of family and schooling in America.* New York: Basic Books.

JENKINS, J. G., AND DALLENBACH, K. M. 1924. Oblivescence during sleep and waking. *American Journal of Psychology* 35:605–12.

JENNINGS, E. E. 1972. *An anatomy of leadership: Princes, heroes, and supermen.* New York: McGraw-Hill.

JENSEN, A. R. 1965. Scoring the Stroop test. *Acta Psychologica* 24:398–408.

JENSEN, A. R. 1969. How much can we boost I. Q. and scholastic achievement? *Harvard Educational Review* 39:1–123.

JENSEN, A. R. 1973. *Educability and group differences.* New York: Harper & Row.

JENSEN, A. R. 1985. The nature of the black–white difference on various psychometric tests: Spearman's hypothesis. *Behavioral and Brain Sciences* 8:193–263.

JOHN, O. P. 1990. The "Big Five" taxonomy: Dimensions of personality in the natural language and in questionnaires, pp. 676–1000. In Pervin, L. A. (Ed.), *Handbook of personality: Theory and research.* New York: Guilford Press.

JOHNSON, A. M.; WADSWORTH, J.; WELLINGS, K.; BRADSHAW, S.; AND FIELD, J. 1992. Sexual lifestyles and HIV risk. *Nature* 360: 410–12.

JOHNSON, J., AND NEWPORT, E. 1989. Critical period efforts in second-language learning: The influence of maturational state on the acquisition of English as a second language. *Cognitive Psychology* 21:60–99.

JOHNSON, M. H., AND MORTON, J. 1991. *Biology and cognitive development: The case of face recognition.* London: Blackwell.

JOHNSON, R. E. 1979. *Juvenile delinquency and its origins.* New York: Cambridge University Press.

JOHNSON, S. 1765. Shakespeare criticism. In Danziger, M. K. (Ed.), *Samuel Johnson on literature.* New York: Ungar, 1979.

JONES, E. 1954. *Hamlet and Oedipus.* New York: Doubleday.

JONES, E. E., AND NISBETT, R. E. 1972. The actor and the observer: Divergent perceptions of the cause of behavior. In Jones, E. E.; Karouse, D. E.; Kelley, H. H.; Nisbett, R. E.; Valins, S.; and Weiner, B. (Eds.), *Attribution: Perceiving the causes of behavior.* Morristown, N.J.: General Learning Press.

JONES, H. E., AND KAPLAN, O. J. 1945. Psychological aspects of mental disorders in later life. In Kaplan, O. J. (Ed.), *Mental disorders in later life,* pp. 69–115. Stanford, Calif.: Stanford University Press.

JONES, R. E. 1983. Street people and psychiatry: An introduction. *Hospital Community Psychiatry* 34:807–11.

JORGENSEN, B. W., AND CERVONE, J. C. 1978. Affect enhancement in the pseudo recognition task. *Personality and Social Psychology Bulletin* 4:285–88.

JOSHI, A. K. 1983. Varieties of cooperative responses in question-answer systems. In Keifer, F. (Ed.), *Questions and answers,* pp. 229–40. Amsterdam: D. Reidel Publishing Co.

JOSHI, A. K. 1991. Natural language processing. *Science* 253:1242–49.

JOSSELSON, R. 1980. Ego development in adolescence. In Adelson, J. (Ed.), *Handbook of adolescent psychology,* pp. 188–211. New York: Wiley.

JOURARD, S. M. 1964. *The transparent self.* New York: Van Nostrand.

JOUVET, M. 1967. The stages of sleep. *Scientific American* 216:62–72.

JULESZ, B. 1978. Perceptual limits of texture discrimination and their implications to figure-ground separation. In Leeuwenberg, E. and Buffart, H. (Eds.), *Formal theories of perception,* pp. 205–16. New York: Wiley.

JULIEN, R. M. 1985. *A primer of drug action,* 4th ed. New York: Freeman.

JUSCZYK, P. 1985. On characterizing the development of speech perception. In Mehler, J., and Fox, R. (Eds.), *Neonate cognition: Beyond the blooming buzzing confusion.* Hillsdale, N.J.: Erlbaum.

KAGAN, J. 1976. Emergent themes in human development. *American Scientist* 64:186–96.

KAGAN, J., AND MOSS, H. A. 1962. *Birth to maturity: The Fels study of psychological development.* New York: Wiley.

KAHN, R. S.; DAVIDSON, M.; SIEVER, L.; GABRIEL, S.; APTER, S.; AND DAVIS, K. L. 1993. Serotonin and treatment response to clozapine in schizophrenic patients. *American Journal of Psychiatry* 150:1337–42.

KAHNEMAN, D., AND TVERSKY, A. 1972. Subjective probability: A judgment of representativeness. *Cognitive Psychology* 3:430–54.

KAHNEMAN, D., AND TVERSKY, A. 1973. On the psychology of prediction. *Psychological Review* 80:237–51.

KALAT, J. W. 1984. *Biological psychology,* 2nd ed. Belmont, Calif.: Wadsworth.

KAMNISKY, H. 1984. Moral development in historical perspective. In Kurtines, W. M., and Gewirtz, J. L. (Eds.), *Morality, moral behavior, and moral development.* New York: Wiley.

KAMIN, L. J. 1965. Temporal and intensity characteristics of the conditioned stimulus. In Prokasy, W. F. (Ed.), *Classical conditioning.* New York: Appleton-Century-Crofts.

KAMIN, L. J. 1969. Predictability, surprise, attention and conditioning. In Campbell, B. A., and Church, R. M. (Eds.), *Punishment and aversive behavior,* pp. 279–96. New York: Appleton-Century-Crofts.

KAMIN, L. J. 1974. *The science and politics of I. Q.* New York: Wiley.

KANDEL, D. 1978. Similarity in real-life adolescent friendship pairs. *Journal of Personality and Social Psychology* 36:306–12.

KANIZSA, G. 1976. Subjective contours. *Scientific American* 234:48–52.

KATZ, B. 1952. The nerve impulse. *Scientific American* 187:55–64.

KATZ, J. J. 1972. *Semantic theory.* New York: Harper & Row.

KATZ, J. J., AND FODOR, J. A. 1963. The structure of a semantic theory. *Language* 39:170-210.

KATZ, N.; BAKER, E.; AND MACNAMARA, J. 1974. What's in a name? A study of how children learn common and proper names. *Child Development* 45:469–73.

KAUFMAN, A. S.; KAMPHAUS; R. W.; AND KAUFMAN, N. L. 1985. The Kaufman Assessment Battery for Children (K-ABC). In Newmark, C. S. (Ed.), *Major psychological assessment instruments*. Boston: Allyn and Bacon.

KEELE, S. W. 1982. Learning and control of coordinated motor patterns: The programming perspective. In Kelso, J. A. S. (Ed.), *Human motor behavior;* pp. 143–60. Hillsdale, N.J.: Erlbaum.

KEESEY, R. E., AND POWLEY, T. L. 1986. The regulation of body weight. *Annual Review of Psychology* 37:109–34.

KEETON, W. T. 1972 and 1980. *Biological science,* 2nd and 3rd eds. New York: Norton.

KEETON, W. T., AND GOULD, J. L. 1986 and 1993. *Biological science,* 4th ed. New York: Norton.

KEIL, F. C. 1979. *Semantic and conceptual development: An ontological perspective.* Cambridge, Mass.: Harvard University Press.

KELLER, H. 1985. *Teacher: Anne Sullivan Macy.* Westport, Conn.: Greenwood Press.

KELLEY, H. H. 1967. Attribution theory in social psychology. In Levine, D. (Ed.), *Nebraska Symposium on Motivation,* pp. 192–238. Lincoln, Neb.: University of Nebraska Press.

KELLEY, H. H., AND MICHELA, J. L. 1980. Attribution theory and research. *Annual Review of Psychology* 31:457–501.

KELLEY, H., AND THIBAUT, J. W. 1978. *Interpersonal relations: A theory of interdependence.* New York: Wiley-Interscience.

KELLEY, S., AND MIRER, T. W. 1974. The simple act of voting. *American Political Science Review* 68:572–91.

KELLMAN, P. J., AND SHIPLEY, T. F. 1991. A theory of visual interpolation in object perception. *Cognitive Psychology* 23:141–221.

KELLMAN, P. J., AND SPELKE, E. S. 1983. Perception of partially occluded objects in infancy. *Cognitive Psychology* 15:483–524.

KELLMAN, P. J.; SPELKE, E. S.; AND SHORT, K. R. 1986. Infant perception of object unity from translatory motion in depth and vertical translation. *Child Development* 57:72–86.

KELLY, M. H., AND MARTIN, S. 1994. Domain-general abilities applied to domain-specific tasks: Sensitivity to probabilities in perception, cognition, and language. In Gleitman, L. R., and Landau, B. (Eds.) Lexical acquisition, *Lingua* (Special Issue) 92:108–40.

KEMLER-NELSON, D.; JUSCZYK; P.; AND CASSIDY, K. 1989. How the prosodic cues of motherese might assist language learning. *Journal of Child Language,* pp. 55–68.

KENDLER, K. S., AND GRUENBERG, A. M. 1984. An independent analysis of the Danish adoption study of schizophrenia: VI. The relationship between psychiatric disorders as defined by DSM-III in the relatives and adoptees. *Archives of General Psychiatry* 41:555–64.

KENNY, D., AND ZACCARO, S. J. 1983. An estimate of variance due to traits in leadership. *Journal of Applied Psychology* 68: 678–85.

KERR, M. E., AND BOWEN, M. 1988. *Family evaluation.* New York: Norton.

KESSEL, E. L. 1955. The mating activities of balloon flies. *Systematic Zoology* 4:97–104.

KETY, S. S. 1983. Mental illness in the biological and adoptive relatives of schizophrenic adoptees: Findings relevant to genetic and environmental factors in etiology. *Journal of American Psychiatry* 140:720–27.

KIHLSTROM, J. F. 1987. The cognitive unconscious. *Science* 237:1445–52.

KIHLSTROM, J. F. 1990. The psychological unconscious. In Pervin, L. A. (Ed.), *Handbook of Personality: Theory and Research,* pp. 445–64. New York: Guilford Press.

KIHLSTROM, J. F. 1992. Dissociation and dissociations: A comment on consciousness and cognition. *Consciousness and Cognition: An International Journal* 1:47–53.

KIHLSTROM, J. F. 1993. The recovery of memory in the laboratory and the clinic. Paper presented at the 1993 conventions of the Rocky Mountain and the Western Psychological Associations. Phoenix, Arizona.

KIHLSTROM, J. F., AND CANTOR, N. 1984. Mental representations of the self. In Berkowitz, L. (Ed.), *Advances in experimental social psychology,* vol. 17, pp. 1–47. New York: Academic Press.

KILHAM, W., AND MANN, L. 1974. Level of destructive obedience as a function of transmitter and executant roles in the Milgram obedience paradigm. *Journal of Personality and Social Psychology* 29:696–702.

KIMBLE, G. A. 1961. *Hilgard and Marquis' conditioning and learning.* New York: Appleton-Century-Crofts.

KING, H. E. 1961. Psychological effects of excitation in the limbic system. In Sheer, D. E. (Ed.), *Electrical stimulation of the brain.* Austin: University of Texas Press.

KINSEY, A. C.; POMEROY, W. B.; AND MARTIN, C. E. 1948. *Sexual behavior in the human male.* Philadelphia: Saunders.

KINSEY, A.; POMEROY, W.; MARTIN, C.; AND GEBHARD, P. 1953. *Sexual behavior in the human female.* Philadelphia: Saunders.

KITCHER, P. 1985. *Vaulting ambition: Sociobiology and the quest for human nature.* Cambridge, Mass: M. I. T. Press.

KITCHER, P. 1987. Précis of *Vaulting ambition: Sociobiology and the quest for human nature* (and open peer commentary). *Behavioral and Brain Sciences* 10:61–100.

KLEINMAN, A., AND GOOD, B. 1990. *Culture and depression.* Berkeley: University of California Press.

KLEINMUNTZ, B. 1982. *Personality and psychological assessment.* New York: St. Martin's Press.

KLEITMAN, N. 1960. Patterns of dreaming. *Scientific American* 203:82–88.

KLERMAN, G. L. 1990. The psychiatric patient's right to effective treatment: Implications of Osheroff v. Chestnut Lodge. *American Journal of Psychiatry* 147:409–18.

KLERMAN, G. L.; WEISSMAN, M. M.; ROUNSAVILLE, B. J.; AND CHEVRON, E. S. 1984. *Interpersonal psychotherapy of depression.* New York: Basic Books.

KLIMA, E.; AND BELLUGI, U.; WITH BATTISON, R.; BOYES-BRAEM, P.; FISCHER, S.; FRISHBERG, N.; LANE, H.; LENTZ, E. M.; NEWKIRK, D.; NEWPORT, E.; PEDERSEN, C.; AND SIPLE, P. 1979. *The signs of language.* Cambridge, Mass.: Harvard University Press.

KLINEBERG, O. 1940. *Social psychology.* New York: Henry Holt.

KLOPFER, B.; AINSWORTH, M.; KLOPFER, W. G.; AND HOLT, R. R. 1954. *Developments in the Rorschach technique.* Yonkers, N.Y.: World Book.

KLOPFER, P. H. 1974. *An introduction to animal behavior: Ethology's first century.* Englewood Cliffs, N.J.: Prentice-Hall.

KLUFT, R. P. 1987. An update on multiple-personality disorder. *Journal of Hospital and Community Psychiatry* 38:363–73.

KOHLBERG, L. 1963. Development of children's orientations toward a moral order. *Vita Humana* 6:11–36.

KOHLBERG, L. 1966. A cognitive developmental analysis of children's sex-role concepts and attitudes. In Maccoby, E. E. (Ed.), *The development of sex differences,* pp. 82–171. Stanford, Calif.: Stanford University Press.

KOHLBERG, L. 1969. Stage and sequence: The cognitive developmental approach to socialization. In Goslin, D. A. (Ed.), *Handbook of socialization theory of research,* pp. 347–480. Chicago: Rand McNally.

KOHLBERG, L. AND CANDEE, D. 1984. The relationship of moral judgment to moral action. In Kurtines, W. M., and Gewirtz, L. (Eds.), *Morality, moral behavior, and moral development,* pp. 52–73. New York: Wiley.

KÖHLER, W. 1925. *The mentality of apes.* New York: Harcourt Brace and World.

KÖHLER, W. 1947. *Gestalt psychology.* New York: Liveright.

KOHN, M. L. 1969. *Class and conformity: A study in values.* Chicago: University of Chicago Press.

KOLB, B. AND WHISHAW, I. Q. 1990. *Fundamentals of human neuropsychology,* 3rd ed. New York: Freeman.

KORIAT, A., AND LIEBLICH, I. 1974. What does a person in a TOT state know that a person in a "Don't Know" state doesn't know? *Memory and Cognition* 2:647–55.

KOSSLYN, S. M. 1980. *Image and mind.* Cambridge, Mass.: Harvard University Press.

KOSSLYN, S. M. 1984. *Ghosts in the mind's machine.* New York: Norton.

KOSSLYN, S. M.; BALL, T. M.; AND REISSER, B. J. 1978. Visual images preserve metric spatial information: Evidence from studies of image scanning. *Journal of Experimental Psychology: Human Perception and Performance* 4:1–20.

KOSTLAN, A. 1954. A method for the empirical study of psychodiagnosis. *Journal of Consulting Psychology* 18:83–88.

KOTELCHUK, M. 1976. The infant's relationship to the father: Some experimental evidence. In Lamb, M. (Ed.), *The role of the father in child development.* New York: Wiley.

KRAMER, P. D. 1993. *Listening to prozac.* New York: Viking.

KRANTZ, D. S.; CONTRADA, R. J.; HILL, D. R.; AND FRIEDLER, E. 1988. Environmental stress and behavioral antecedents of coronary heart disease. *Journal of Consulting and Clinical Psychology* 56:333–41.

KREBS, J. R. 1982. Territorial defence in the great tit. *Parus Major L. Ecology* 52:2–22.

KREBS, J. R., AND DAVIES, N. B. 1987. *An introduction to behavioral ecology,* 2nd ed. Boston: Blackwell Scientific Publications.

KRECH, D., AND CRUTCHFIELD, R. 1958. *Elements of psychology.* New York: Knopf.

KUBOVY, M. 1986. *The psychology of perspective and Renaissance art.* New York: Cambridge University Press.

KUHL, P.; WILLIAMS, K.; LACERDA, F.; STEVENS, K.; AND LINDBLOM, B. 1992. Linguistic experience alters phonetic perception in infants by six months of age. *Science* 255:606–608.

KUPFER, D. J.; FOSTER, F. G.; AND REICH, L. 1976. EEG sleep changes as predictors in depression. *American Journal of Psychiatry* 133:622.

KUZNICKI, J. T., AND MCCUTCHEON, N. B. 1979. Cross enhancement of the sour taste of single human taste papillae. *Journal of Experimental Psychology* 198:68–89.

LA BERGE, D. 1975. Acquisition of automatic processing in perceptual and associative learning. In Rabbitt, P. M. A., and Dormic, S. (Eds.), *Attention and performance,* vol. 5. London: Academic Press.

LABOV, W. 1970. The logic of nonstandard English. In Williams, F. (Ed.), *Language and poverty: Perspectives on a theme,* pp. 153–89. Chicago: Markham.

LAKOFF, G., AND JOHNSON, M. 1980. *Metaphors we live by.* Chicago: University of Chicago Press.

LAMB, H. R. 1984. Deinstitutionalization and the homeless mentally ill. *Hospital Community Psychiatry* 35:899–907.

LAMB, M. E. 1977. Father-infant and mother-infant interaction in the first year of life. *Child Development* 48:167–81.

LANDAU, B. 1982. Will the real grandmother please stand up? The psychological reality of dual meaning representations. *Journal of Psycholinguistic Research* 11:47–62.

LANDAU, B. 1994. Where's what and what's where: The language of objects in space. In Gleitman, L. R., and Landau, B. (Eds.), Lexical acquisition, *Lingua* (Special Issue) 92:259–96.

LANDAU, B., AND GLEITMAN, L. R. 1985. *Language and experience: Evidence from the blind child.* Cambridge, Mass.: Harvard University Press.

LANDIS, C., AND HUNT, W. A. 1932. Adrenalin and emotion. *Psychological Review* 39:467–85.

LANGER, E. J., AND RODIN, J. 1976. The effects of choice and enhanced personal responsibility for the aged: A field experiment in an institutional setting. *Journal of Personality and Social Psychology* 34:191–98.

LANGLOIS, J. H., AND DOWNS, A. C. 1980. Mothers, fathers, and peers as socialization agents of sex-typed play behaviors in young children. *Child Development* 51:1237–1347.

LANYON, R. I., AND GOLDSTEIN, L. D. 1971. *Personality assessment.* New York: Wiley.

LANYON, R. I., AND GOLDSTEIN, L. D. 1982. *Personality assessment.* 2nd ed. New York: Wiley.

LAPIERE, R. 1934. Attitudes versus actions. *Social Forces* 13:230–37.

LASH, J. P. 1980. *Helen and Teacher: The story of Helen Keller and Anne Sullivan Macy.* New York: Delacorte Press.

LASHLEY, K. S. 1930. The mechanism of vision:1. A method for rapid analysis of pattern-vision in the rat. *Journal of Genetic Psychology* 37:453–60.

LASKY, J. J.; HOVER, G. L.; SMITH, P. A.; BOSTIAN, D. W.; DUFFENDECK, S. C.; AND NORD, C. L. 1959. Post-hospital adjustment as predicted by psychiatric patients and by their staff. *Journal of Consulting Psychology* 23:213–18.

LASSEN, N. A.; INGVAR, D. H.; AND SKINHOJ, E. 1978. Brain function and blood flow. *Scientific American* 239:62–71.

LATANÉ, B., AND NIDA, S. 1981. Group size and helping. *Psychological Bulletin* 89:308–24.

LATANÉ, B.; NIDA, S. A.; AND WILSON, D. W. 1981. The effects of group size on helping behavior. In Rushton, J. P., and Sorrentino, R. M. (Eds.), *Altruism and helping behavior: Social, personality, and developmental perspectives.* Hillsdale, N.J.: Erlbaum.

LATANÉ, B., AND RODIN, J. 1969. A lady in distress: Inhibiting effects of friends and strangers on bystander intervention. *Journal of Experimental Social Psychology* 5: 189–202.

LAU, R. R., AND RUSSELL, D. 1980. Attributions in the sports pages. *Journal of Personality and Social Psychology* 39:29–38.

LAYZER, D. 1972. Science or superstition: A physical scientist looks at the I. Q. controversy. *Cognition* 1:265–300.

LAZAR, I., AND DARLINGTON, R. 1982. Lasting effects of early education: A report from the Consortium for Longitudinal Studies. *Monographs of the Society for Research in Child Development* 47 (2–3, Serial No. 195).

LAZARUS, A. A. 1971. *Behavior therapy and beyond.* New York: McGraw-Hill.

LAZARUS, A. A. 1981. *The practice of multi-modal therapy.* New York: McGraw-Hill.

LE BON, G. 1895. *The crowd.* New York: Viking Press, 1960.

LEASK, J.; HABER, R. N.; AND HABER, R. B. 1969. Eidetic imagery in children: II. Longitudinal and experimental results. *Psychonomic Monograph Supplements* 3(Whole No. 35):25–48.

LEATON, R. N. 1976. Long-term retention of the habituation of lick suppression and startle response produced by a single auditory stimulus. *Journal of Experimental Psychology: Animal Behavior Processes* 2:248–59.

LEEPER, R. W. 1935. A study of a neglected portion of the field of learning: The development of sensory organization. *Journal of Genetic Psychology* 46:41–75.

LEFF, M. J.; ROATSCH, J. F.; AND BUNNEY, W. E., JR. 1970. Environmental factors preceding the onset of severe depressions. *Psychiatry* 33:298–311.

LEMPERS, J. S.; FLAVELL, E. R.; AND FLAVELL, J. H. 1977. The development in very young children of tacit knowledge concerning visual perception. *Genetic Psychology Monographs* 95:3–53.

LENNEBERG, E. H. 1967. *Biological foundations of language.* New York: Wiley.

LESLIE, A. M. 1992. Pretense, autism, and the theory of mind module. *Current Directions in Psychological Science* 1:18–21.

LETTVIN, J. Y.; MATURAN, H. R.; MCCULLOCH, W. S.; AND PITTS, W. H. 1959. What the frog's eye tells the frog's brain. *Proceedings of the Institute of Radio Engineers* 47:1940–51.

LeVAY, S. 1991. A difference in hypothalamic structure between heterosexual and homosexual men. *Science* 253: 1034–37.

LEVINE, J. D.; GORDON, N. C.; AND FIELDS, H. L. 1979. The role of endorphins in placebo analgesia. In Bonica, J. J.; Liebesking, J. C.; and Albe-Fessard, D. (Eds.), *Advances in pain research and therapy,* vol. 3. New York: Raven.

LEVY, J. 1985. Right brain, left brain: Facts and fiction. *Psychology Today* 19:38–44.

LEWONTIN, R. C. 1976. Race and intelligence. In Block, N. J., and Dworkin, G. (Eds.), *The IQ controversy,* pp. 78–92. New York: Pantheon.

LEWONTIN, R. C.; ROSE, S.; AND KAMIN, L. J. 1984. *Not in our genes: Biology, ideology, and human nature.* New York: Random House.

LEWY, A.; SACK, L.; MILLER, S.; AND HOBAN, T. M. 1987. Antidepressant and circadian-phase shifting effects of light. *Science* 235:352–54.

LIBERMAN, A. M. 1970. The grammars of speech and language. *Cognitive Psychology* 1:301–23.

LICKLEY, J. D. 1919. *The nervous system*. New York: Longman.

LIEBERMAN, P. L. 1975. *On the origins of language*. New York: Macmillan.

LIEBERT, R. M.; POULOS, R. W.; AND STRAUSS, G. D. 1974. *Developmental psychology*. Englewood Cliffs, N. J.: Prentice-Hall.

LIFF, Z. A. 1992. Psychoanalysis and dynamic techniques. In D. K. Freedheim (Ed.), *History of Psychotherapy*. Washington, D.C.: American Psychological Association.

LINDSAY, P. H., AND NORMAN, D. A. 1977. *Human information processing*, 2nd ed. New York: Academic Press.

LIPPERT, W. W., AND SENTER, R. J. 1966. Electrodermal responses in the sociopath. *Psychonomic Science* 4:25–26.

LITTLE, K. B., AND SHNEIDMAN, E. S. 1959. Congruencies among interpretations of psychological test and anamnestic data. *Psychological Monographs* 73 (Whole No. 476).

LOCKE, J. 1690. *An essay concerning human understanding*. Edited by A. D. Woozley. Cleveland: Meridian Books, 1964.

LOEHLIN, J. C.; LINDZEY, G.; AND SPUHLER, J. N. 1975. *Race difference in intelligence*. San Francisco: Freeman.

LOEWI, O. 1960. An autobiographical sketch. *Perspectives in Biological Medicine* 4:2–35.

LOFTUS, E. F. 1975. Leading questions and the eyewitness report. *Cognitive Psychology* 7:560–72.

LOFTUS, E. F. 1993.The reality of repressed memories. *American Psychologist* 48:518–37.

LOFTUS, E. F., AND HOFFMAN, H. G. 1989. Misinformation and memory: The creation of new memories. *Journal of Experimental Psychology: General* 118:100–104.

LOFTUS, E. F., AND LOFTUS, G. R. 1980. On the permanence of stored information in the human brain. *American Psychologist* 35:409–20.

LOFTUS, E. F., AND PALMER, J. C. 1974. Reconstruction of automobile destruction: An example of the interaction between language and memory. *Journal of Verbal Learning and Verbal Behavior* 13:585–89.

LOFTUS, E. F., AND ZANNI, G. 1975. Eyewitness testimony: The influence of the wording of a question. *Bulletin of the Psychonomic Society* 5:86–88.

LOGAN, G. D. 1988. Toward an instance theory of automatization. *Psychological Review* 95:492–527.

LOGUE, A. W. 1979. Taste aversion and the generality of the laws of learning. *Psychological Bulletin* 86:276–96.

LOGUE, A. W. 1986. *The psychology of eating and drinking*. New York: Freeman.

LONDON, P. 1964. *The modes and morals of psychotherapy*. New York: Holt, Rinehart & Winston.

LONDON, P. 1970. The rescuers: Motivational hypotheses about Christians who saved Jews from the Nazis. In Macauley, J., and Berkowitz, L. (Eds.), *Altruism and helping behavior*. New York: Academic Press.

LORD, R. G.; DEVADER, C. L.; AND ALLIGER, G. M. 1986. A meta-analysis of the relationship between personality traits and leadership perceptions: An application of validity generalization procedures. *Journal of Applied Psychology* 7: 401–10.

LORENZ, K. Z. 1966. *On aggression*. London: Methuen.

LUBIN, B.; LARSEN, R. M.; MATARAZZO, J. D.; AND SEEVER, M. 1985. Psychological test usage patterns in five professional settings. *American Psychologist* 40:857–61.

LUBORSKY, L. I.; SINGER, B.; AND LUBORSKY, L. 1975. Comparative studies of psychotherapies. *Archives of General Psychiatry* 20:84–88.

LUCE, R. D., AND RAIFFA, H. 1957. *Games and decisions*. New York: Wiley.

LUCHINS, A. S. 1942. Mechanization in problem-solving: The effect of Einstellung. *Psychological Monographs* 54 (Whole No. 248).

LURIA, A. R. 1966. *Higher cortical functions in man*. New York: Basic Books.

LURIA, A. R. 1971. *International Journal of Psychology* 6: p. 259 ff. (cited in

Scribner, S. & Cole, M. 1973. Cognitive consequences of formal and informal education. *Science* 182:553–59).

LURIA, A. R. 1976. *Cognitive development: Its cultural and social foundations*. Cambridge, Mass.: Harvard University Press.

LYKKEN, D. T. 1979. The detection of deception. *Psychological Bulletin* 86:47–53.

LYKKEN, D. T. 1981. The lie detector and the law. *Criminal Defense* 8:19–27.

MACCOBY, E. E. 1980. *Social development*. New York: Harcourt Brace Jovanovich.

MACCOBY, E. E., AND JACKLIN, C. N. 1974. *The psychology of sex differences*. Stanford, Calif.: Stanford University Press.

MACCOBY, E. E., AND JACKLIN, C. N. 1980. Sex differences in aggression: A rejoinder and reprise. *Child Development* 51:964–80.

MACCOBY, E. E., AND MARTIN, J. A. 1983. Socialization in the context of the family: Parent-child interaction. In Mussen, P. H. (Ed.), *Carmichael's manual of child psychology: Vol. 4. Socialization, personality and social development* (Hetherington, M. E., volume editor), pp. 1–102. New York: Wiley.

MACFARLANE, A. 1975. Olfaction in the development of social preferences in the human neonate. *Parent-infant interaction*. Amsterdam: CIBA Foundation Symposium.

MACNEILAGE, P. 1972. Speech physiology. In Gilbert, J. (Ed.), *Speech and cortical functioning*. New York: Academic Press.

MACNICHOL, E. F., JR. 1964. Three-pigment color vision: *Scientific American* 211:48–56.

MACNICHOL, E. F., JR. 1986. A unifying presentation of photopigment spectra. *Vision Research* 29:543–46.

MAGNUS, O., AND LAMMERS, J. 1956. The amygdaloid-nuclear complex. *Folia Psychiatrica Neurologica et Neurochirurgico Neerlandica* 59:552–82.

MAGNUSSON, D., AND ENDLER, N. S. 1977. Interactional psychology: Present status and future prospects. In Magnusson, D., and Endler, N. S. (Eds.), *Personality at the crossroads*, pp. 3–31. New York: Wiley.

MAGOUN, H. W.; HARRISON, F.; BROBECK, J. R.; AND RANSON, S. W. 1938. Activation of heat loss mechanisms by local heating of the brain. *Journal of Neurophysiology* 1:101–14.

MAHER, B. A. 1966. *Principles of psychopathology*. New York: McGraw-Hill.

MAHONEY, M. J. 1976. *Scientist as subject: The psychological imperative*. Cambridge, Mass.: Ballinger.

MAHONEY, M. J., AND DEMONBREUN, B. G. 1981. Problem-solving bias in scientists. In Tweney, R. D.; Doherty, M. E.; and Mynatt, C. R. (Eds.), *On scientific thinking*, pp. 139–44. New York: Columbia University Press.

MAIER, S. F.; LAUDENSLAGER, M. L.; ANμD RYAN, S. M. 1985. Stressor controllability, immune function, and endogenous opiates. In Bush, F., and Overmier, J. B. (Eds.), *Affect, conditioning, and cognition*. Hillsdale, N.J.: Erlbaum.

MAIER, S. F.; SELIGMAN, M. E. P.; AND SOLOMON, R. L. 1969. Pavlovian fear conditioning and learned helplessness: Effects on escape and avoidance behavior of (a) the CS-US contingency and (b) the independence of the US and voluntary responding. In Campbell, B. A., and Church, R. M. (Eds.), *Punishment and aversive behavior*, pp. 299–342. New York: Appleton-Century-Crofts.

MALINOWSKI, B. 1927. *Sex and repression in savage society*. New York: Meridian, 1955.

MANDLER, G. 1975. *Mind and emotion*. New York: Wiley.

MANDLER, G. 1984. *Mind and body: Psychology of emotion and stress*. New York: Norton.

MANN, F.; BOWSHER, D.; MUMFORD, J.; LIPTON, S.; AND MILES, J. 1973. Treatment of intractable pain by acupuncture. *Lancet* 2:57-60.

MANTELL, D. M., AND PANZARELLA, R. 1976. Obedience and responsibility. *British Journal of Social and Clinical Psychology* 15: 239–45

MARCUS, J.; HANS, S. L.; AUERBACH, J. G.; AND AUERBACH, A. G. 1993. Children at risk for schizophrenia: The Jerusalem Infant Development Study. II. Neurobehavioral deficits at school age. *Archives of General Psychiatry* 50:797–809.

MARKS, D. F. 1983. In defense of imagery questionnaires. *Scandinavian Journal of Psychology* 24:243–46.

MARKS, I. M. 1969. *Fears and phobias.* New York: Academic Press.

MARKUS, H. R., AND KITAYAMA, S. 1991. Culture and the self: Implications for cognition, emotion, and motivation. *Psychological Review* 98:224–53.

MARLER, P. R. 1970. A comparative approach to vocal learning: Song development in white-crowned sparrows. *Journal of Comparative and Physiological Psychology Monographs* 71(No. 2, Part 2):1–25.

MARMOR, J. 1975. Homosexuality and sexual orientation disturbances. In Freedman, A. M.; Kaplan, H. I.; and Sadock, B. J. (Eds.), *Comprehensive textbook of psychiatry—II,* vol. 2, pp. 1510–19. Baltimore: Williams & Wilkins.

MARSDEN, C. D. 1985. Defects of movement in Parkinson's disease. In Delwaide, P. J., and Agnoli, A. (Eds.), *Clinical neurophysiology in Parkinsonism.* Amsterdam: Elsevier.

MARSHALL, D. A., AND MOULTON, D. G. 1981. Olfactory sensitivity to α—ionine in humans and dogs. *Chemical Senses* 6:53–61.

MARSHALL, G. D., AND ZIMBARDO, P. G. 1979. Affective consequences of inadequately explained physiological arousal. *Journal of Personality and Social Psychology* 37:970–88.

MARSLEN-WILSON, W. D., AND TEUBER, H. L. 1975. Memory for remote events in anterograde amnesia: Recognition of public figures from news photographs. *Neurobiologia* 13:353–64.

MASLACH, C. 1979. Negative emotional biasing of unexplained physiological arousal. *Journal of Personality and Social Psychology* 37:953–69.

MASLOW, A. H. 1954. *Motivation and personality.* New York: Harper & Row.

MASLOW, A. H. 1968. *Toward a psychology of being,* 2nd ed. Princeton, N.J.: Van Nostrand.

MASLOW, A. H. 1970. *Motivation and personality,* 2nd ed. New York: Harper.

MATARAZZO, J. D. 1983. The reliability of psychiatric and psychological diagnosis. *Clinical Psychology Review* 3:103–45.

MATHEWS, K. A. 1982. Psychological perspectives on the type A behavior pattern. *Psychological Bulletin* 91:293–323.

MATSUMOTO, D., AND EKMAN, P. 1989. Japanese and Caucasian Facial Expressions of Emotion. JACFEE.

MATTISON, A., AND MCWHIRTER, D. 1987. Male couples: The beginning years. Intimate Relationships: Some Social Work Perspectives on Love, *Journal of Social Work and Human Sexuality* (Special Issue) 5: 67–78.

MAUGH, T. M. 1981. Biochemical markers identify mental states. *Science* 214:39–41.

MAYER, J. 1955. Regulation of energy intake and body weight: The glucostatic theory and the lipostatic hypothesis. *Annals of the New York Academy of Sciences* 63:15–43.

MAYES, A. R. 1988. *Human organic memory disorders.* New York: Cambridge University Press.

MAYNARD-SMITH, J. 1965. The evolution of alarm calls. *American Naturalist* 100:637–50.

MCBURNEY, D. H.; LEVINE, J. M.; AND CAVANAUGH, P. H. 1977. Psychophysical and social ratings of human body odor. *Personality and Social Psychology Bulletin* 3:135–38.

MCBURNEY, D. H., AND SHICK, T. R. 1971. Taste and water taste of twenty-six compounds for man. *Perception and Psychophysics* 10:249–52.

MCCARTHY, R. A., AND WARRINGTON, E. K. 1990. *Cognitive neuropsychology: A clinical introduction.* New York: Academic Press.

MCCLEARN, G. E., AND DEFRIES, J. C. 1973. *Introduction to behavioral genetics.* San Francisco: Freeman.

MCCLINTOCK, M. K. 1971. Menstrual synchrony and suppression. *Nature* 229:244–45.

MCCLINTOCK, M. K., AND ADLER, N. T. 1978. The role of the female during copulation in wild and domestic Norway rats (*Rattus Norvegicus*). *Behaviour* 67:67–96.

MCCLOSKEY, M.; WIBLE, C. G.; AND COHEN, N. J. 1988. Is there a special flashbulb-memory mechanism? *Journal of Experimental Psychology: General* 117:171–81.

MCCONAGHY, M. J. 1979. Gender constancy and the genital basis of gender: Stages in the development of constancy by gender identity. *Child Development* 50:1223–26.

MCEWEN, B. S.; BIEGON, A.; DAVIS, P. G.; KREY, L. C.; LUINE, V. N.; MCGINNIS, M.; PADEN, C. M.; PARSONS, B.; AND RAINBOW, T. C. 1982. Steroid hormones: Humoral signals which alter brain cell properties and functions. *Recent Progress in Brain Research* 38: 41–83.

MCGEOCH, J. A., AND IRION, A. L. 1952. *The psychology of human learning,* 2nd ed. New York: Longmans, Green, and Co.

MCGHIE, A., AND CHAPMAN, J. 1961. Disorders of attention and perception in early schizophrenia. *British Journal of Medical Psychology* 34:103–16.

MCGRATH, M. J., AND COHEN, D. B. 1978. REM sleep facilitation of adaptive waking behavior: A review of the literature. *Psychological Bulletin* 85:24–57.

MCGUIGAN, F. J. 1966. Covert oral behavior and auditory hallucinations. *Psychophysiology* 3:421–28.

MCGUIRE, W. J. 1985. The nature of attitude and attitude change. In Lindzey, G., and Aronson, E. (Eds.), *Handbook of social psychology,* 3rd ed., vol. 2. New York: Random House.

MCKENZIE, B. E.; TOOTELL, H. E.; AND DAY, R. H. 1980. Development of size constancy during the 1st year of human infancy. *Developmental Psychology* 16:163–74.

MEAD, G. H. 1934. *Mind, self, and society.* Chicago: University of Chicago Press.

MEAD, M. 1935. *Sex and temperament in three primitive societies.* New York: Morrow.

MEAD, M. 1937. *Cooperation and competition among primitive peoples.* New York: McGraw-Hill.

MEAD, M. 1939. *From the South Seas: Studies of adolescence and sex in primitive societies.* New York: Morrow.

MEEHL, P. E. 1959. Some ruminations on the validation of clinical procedures. *Canadian Journal of Psychology* 13:102–28.

MEHLER, J.; JUSCZYK, P.; LAMBERTZ, G.; HALSTED, N.; BERTONCINI, J.; AND AMIEL-TISON, C. 1988. A precursor to language acquisition in young infants. *Cognition* 29:143–78.

MELTZER, H. Y. 1986. Lithium mechanisms in bipolar illness and altered intracellular calcium functions. *Biological Psychiatry* 21:492–510.

MELTZER, H. Y. 1987. Biological studies in schizophrenia. *Schizophrenia Bulletin* 13:77–111.

MELZACK, R. 1973. *The puzzle of pain.* New York: Basic Books.

MENYUK, P. 1977. *Language and maturation.* Cambridge, Mass.: MIT Press.

MENZEL, E. W. 1973. Chimpanzee spatial memory organization. *Science* 182:943–45.

MENZEL, E. W. 1978. Cognitive maps in chimpanzees. In Hulse, S. H.; Fowler, H.; and Honig, W. K. (Eds.), *Cognitive processes in animal behavior,* pp. 375–422. Hillsdale, N.J.: Erlbaum.

MERVIS, C. B., AND CRISAFI, M. 1978. Order acquisition of subordinate, basic, and superordinate level categories. *Child Development* 49:988–98.

METALSKY, G. I.; ABRAMSON, L. Y.; SELIGMAN, M. E. P.; SEMMEL, A.; AND PETERSON, C. 1982. Attributional style and life events in the classroom: Vulnerability and invulnerability to depressive mood reactions. *Journal of Personality and Social Psychology* 43: 612–17.

METALSKY, G. I.; HALBERSTADT, L. J.; AND ABRAMSON, L. Y. 1987. Vulnerability to depressive mood reactions: Toward a more powerful test of the diathesis-stress and causal mediation components of the reformulated theory of depression. *Journal of Personality and Social Psychology* 52:386–93.

MICHAEL, R. P., AND KEVERNE, E. B. 1968. Pheromones in the communication of sexual status in primates. *Nature* 218:746–49.

MILGRAM, S. 1963. Behavioral study of obedience. *Journal of Abnormal and Social Psychology* 67:371–78.

MILGRAM, S. 1965. Some conditions of obedience and disobedience to authority. *Human Relations* 18:57–76.

MILGRAM, S. 1974. *Obedience to authority.* New York: Harper & Row.

MILL, J. S. 1865. *An examination of Sir William Hamilton's philosophy.* London: Longman, Green, Longman, Roberts & Green.

MILLER, A. G. 1986. *The obedience experiments: A case study of controversy in social science.* New York: Praeger.

MILLER, G. A. 1956. The magical number seven plus or minus two: Some limits in our capacity for processing information. *Psychological Review* 63:81–97.

MILLER, G., AND GILDEA, P. 1987. How children learn words. *Scientific American* 257:94–99.

MILLER, G., AND JOHNSON-LAIRD, P. 1976. *Language and perception.* Cambridge, Mass.: Harvard University Press.

MILLER, J. G. 1984. Culture and the development of everyday social explanation. *Journal of Personality and Social Psychology* 46:961–78.

MILLER, N. E.; BAILEY, C. J.; AND STEVENSON, J. A. F. 1950. Decreased "hunger" but increased food intake resulting from hypothalamic lesions. *Science* 112:256–59.

MILNER, B. 1966. Amnesia following operation on the temporal lobes. In Whitty, C. W. M., and Zangwill, O. L. (Eds.), *Amnesia,* pp. 109–33. London: Butterworth.

MILNER, B.; CORKIN, S.; AND TEUBER, H. L. 1968. Further analysis of the hippocampal syndrome: 14-year follow-up study of H. M. *Neuropsychologia* 6:215–34.

MINEKA, S. 1979. The role of fear in theories of avoidance learning, flooding, and extinction. *Psychological Bulletin* 86:985–1010.

MINUCHIN, S. 1974. *Families and family therapy.* Cambridge, Mass.: Harvard University Press.

MISCHEL, W. 1968. *Personality and assessment.* New York: Wiley.

MISCHEL, W. 1970. Sex-typing and socialization. In Mussen, P. H. (Ed.), *Carmichael's manual of child development,* vol. 1. New York: Wiley.

MISCHEL, W. 1973. Towards a cognitive social learning reconceptualization of personality. *Psychological Review* 80:252–83.

MISCHEL, W. 1979. On the interface of cognition and personality: Beyond the person-situation debate. *American Psychologist* 34: 740–54.

MISCHEL, W. 1984. Convergences and challenges in the search for consistency. *American Psychologist* 39:351–64.

MISCHEL, W. 1986. *Introduction to personality,* 4th ed. New York: Holt, Rinehart & Winston.

MISCHEL, W., AND BAKER, N. 1975. Cognitive appraisals and transformations in delay behavior. *Journal of Personality and Social Psychology* 31:254–61.

MISCHEL, W.; EBBESEN, E. B.; AND ZEISS, A. R. 1972. Cognitive and attentional mechanisms in delay of gratification. *Journal of Personality and Social Psychology* 21:204–18.

MISCHEL, W., AND MISCHEL, H. N. 1983. Development of children's knowledge of self-control strategies. *Child Development* 54: 603–19.

MISCHEL, W., AND MOORE, B. 1980. The role of ideation in voluntary delay for symbolically presented awards. *Cognitive Therapy and Research* 4:211–21.

MISCHEL, W.; SHODA, Y.; AND PEAKE, P. K. 1988. The nature of adolescent competencies predicted by preschool delay of gratification. *Journal of Personality and Social Psychology* 54:687–96.

MISELIS, R. R., AND EPSTEIN, A. N. 1970. Feeding induced by 2-deoxy-D-glucose injections into the lateral ventrical of the rat. *The Physiologist* 13:262.

MISHKIN, M., AND APPENZELLER, T. 1987. The anatomy of memory. *Scientific American* 256:80–89.

MITA, T. H.; DERMER, M.; AND KNIGHT, J. 1977. Reversed facial images and the mere exposure hypothesis. *Journal of Personality and Social Psychology* 35:597–601.

MITROFF, I. I. 1974. *The subjective side of science.* Amsterdam: Elsevier.

MONSON, T. C.; HESLEY, J. W.; AND CHERNICK, L. 1982. Specifying when personality traits can and cannot predict behavior: An alternative to abandoning the attempt to predict single-act criteria. *Journal of Personality and Social Psychology* 43:385–99.

MOORE, J. W. 1972. Stimulus control: Studies of auditory generalization in rabbits. In Black, A. H., and Prokasy, W. F. (Eds.), *Classical conditioning II: Current research and theory,* pp. 206–30. New York: Appleton-Century-Crofts.

MORA, G. 1975. Historical and theoretical trends in psychiatry. In Freedman, A. M.; Kaplan, H. I.; and Sadock, B. J. (Eds.), *Comprehensive textbook of psychiatry,* vol. 1, pp. 1–75. Baltimore: Williams & Wilkins.

MORAY, N. 1959. Attention in dichotic listening: Affective cues and the influence of instructions. *Quarterly Journal of Experimental Psychology* 11:56–60.

MORELAND, R. L., AND ZAJONC, R. B. 1982. Exposure effects in person perception: Familiarity, similarity, and attraction. *Journal of Experimental Social Psychology* 18:395–415.

MORGAN, C. D., AND MURRAY, H. A. 1935. A method for investigating fantasies: The thematic apperception test. *Archives of Neurological Psychiatry* 34:289–306.

MORGAN, J., AND TRAVIS, L. 1989. Limits on negative information in language input. *Journal of Child Language* 16(3):531–52.

MORRIS, D. 1967. *The naked ape.* New York: McGraw-Hill.

MORTON, T. U. 1978. Intimacy and reciprocity of exchange: A comparison of spouses and strangers. *Journal of Personality and Social Psychology* 36: 72–81.

MOSCOVITCH, M. 1972. Choice reaction-time study assessing the verbal behavior of the minor hemisphere in normal adults. *Journal of Comparative and Physiological Psychology* 80:66–74.

MOSCOVITCH, M. 1979. Information processing and the cerebral hemispheres. In Gazzaniga, M. S., *Handbook of behavioral neurobiology,* vol. 2, pp. 379–446. New York: Plenum.

MOSKOWITZ, D. W. 1982. Coherence and cross-situational generality in personality: A new analysis of old problems. *Journal of Personality and Social Psychology* 43:754–68.

MULFORD, R. 1986. First words of the blind child. In Smith, M., and Locke, J. (Eds.), *The emergent lexicon: The child's development of a linguistic vocabulary.* New York: Academic Press.

MURDOCK, B. 1962. The serial position effect of free recall. *Journal of Experimental Psychology* 64:482–88.

MURRAY, F. B. 1978. Teaching strategies and conservation training. In Lesgold, A. M.; Pellegrino, J. W.; Fekkeman, D.; and Glaser, R. (Eds.), *Cognitive psychology and instruction,* vol. 1. New York: Plenum.

MUSCETTOLA, G.; POTTER, W. Z.; PICKAR, D.; AND GOODWIN, F. K. 1984. Urinary 3-methoxy-4-hydroxyphenylglycol and major affective disorders. *Archives of General Psychiatry* 41:337–42.

MUUSS, R. E. 1970. Puberty rites in primitive and modern societies. *Adolescence* 5:109–28.

NADEL, L., AND ZOLA-MORGAN, S. 1984. Infantile amnesia: A neurobiological perspective. In Moscovich, M. (Ed.), *Infant memory,* pp. 145–72. New York: Plenum Press.

NAIGLES, L. 1990. Children use syntax to learn verb meanings. *Journal of Child Language* 17:357–74.

NATHAN, P. W. 1978. Acupuncture analgesia. *Trends in Neurosciences* 1:210–23.

NAUTA, W. J. H., AND FEIRTAG, M. 1986. *Fundamental neuroanatomy.* New York: Freeman.

NEIMEYER, G. J. Cognitive complexity and marital satisfaction. *Journal of Social and Clinical Psychology* 2: 258–63.

NEISSER, U. 1967. *Cognitive psychology.* New York: Appleton-Century-Crofts.

NEISSER, U. 1982a. *Memory observed.* San Francisco: Freeman.

NEISSER, U. 1982b. *On the trail of the tape-recorder fallacy.* Paper presented at a symposium on "The influence of hypnosis and related states on memory: Forensic implications" at the meetings of the American Association for the Advancement of Science, Washington, D. C., in January 1982.

NEISSER, U. 1986. Remembering Pearl Harbor: Reply to Thompson and Cowan. *Cognition* 23:285–86.

NEISSER, U. 1989. Domains of memory. In Solomon, P. R.; Goethals, G. R.; Kelley, C. M.; and Stephens, B. R. (Eds.), *Memory: Interdisciplinary approaches,* pp. 67–83. New York: Springer Verlag.

NELSON, K. 1973. Structure and strategy in learning to talk. *Monographs of the Society for Research in Child Development* 38: (1–2, Serial No. 149).

NEMETH, C., AND CHILES, C. 1988. Modeling courage: The role of dissent in fostering independence. *European Journal of Social Psychology* 18: 275–80.

NEUGEBAUER, R. 1979. Medieval and early modern theories of mental illness. *Archives of General Psychiatry* 36:477–84.

NEWELL, A., AND SIMON, H. A. 1972. *Human problem solving.* Englewood Cliffs, N.J.: Prentice-Hall.

NEWMEYER, F. 1983. *Linguistic theory in America,* New York: Academic Press.

NEWPORT, E. L. 1984. Constraints on learning: Studies in the acquisition of American Sign Language. *Papers and Reports on Child Language Development* 23:1–22. Stanford, Calif.: Stanford University Press.

NEWPORT, E. 1990. Maturational constraints on language learning. *Cognitive Science* 14:11–28.

NEWPORT, E. L., AND ASHBROOK, E. F. 1977. The emergence of semantic relations in American Sign Language. *Papers and Reports in Child Language Development* 13.

NICHOLSON, R. A., AND BERMAN, J. S. 1983. Is follow-up necessary in evaluating psychotherapy? *Psychological Bulletin* 93:261–78.

NICOL, S. E., AND GOTTESMAN, I. I. 1983. Clues to the genetics and neurobiology of schizophrenia. *American Scientist* 71:398–404.

NISBETT, R. E. 1972. Eating behavior and obesity in man and animals. *Advances in Psychosomatic Medicine* 7:173–93.

NISBETT, R. E. 1977. Interaction versus main effects as goals of personality research. In Magnusson, D., and Endler, L. (Eds.), *Personality at the crossroads: Current issues in interactional psychology,* pp. 235–41. Hillsdale, N.J.: Erlbaum.

NISBETT, R. E. 1980. The trait construct in lay and professional psychology. In Festinger, L. (Ed.), *Retrospections on social psychology,* pp. 109–30. New York: Oxford University Press.

NISBETT, R. E.; CAPUTO, C.; LEGANT, P.; AND MARACEK, J. 1973. Behavior as seen by the actor and as seen by the observer. *Journal of Personality and Social Psychology* 27:154–64.

NISBETT, R., AND ROSS, L. 1980. *Human inference: Strategies and shortcomings of social judgment.* Englewood Cliffs, N.J.: Prentice-Hall.

NISBETT, R. E., AND WILSON, T. D. 1977. Telling more than we can know: Verbal reports on mental processes. *Psychological Review* 84:231–59.

NOLEN-HOEKSMA, S. 1987. Sex differences in unipolar depression: Evidence and theory. *Psychological Bulletin* 101:259–82.

NORCROSS, J. C. 1991. Prescriptive matching in psychotherapy: Psychoanalysis for simple phobias? *Psychotherapy* 28:439–43.

NORCROSS, J. C., AND FREEDHEIM, D. K. 1992. Into the future: Retrospect and prospect in psychotherapy. In Freedheim, D. K. (Ed.), *History of Psychotherapy.* Washington, D.C.: American Psychological Association.

NORMAN, W. T. 1963. Toward an adequate taxonomy of personality attributes: Replicated factor structure in peer nomination personality ratings. *Journal of Abnormal and Social Psychology* 66:574–83.

O'KEEFE, J., AND NADEL, L. 1978. *The hippocampus as a cognitive map.* Oxford: Clarendon Press.

ODIORNE, J. M. 1957. Color changes. In Brown, M. E. (Ed.), *The physiology of fishes,* vol. 2. New York: Academic Press.

OLDS, J., AND MILNER, P. 1954. Positive reinforcement produced by electrical stimulation of septal areas and other regions of rat brains. *Journal of Comparative and Physiological Psychology* 47:419–27.

OLDS, M. E., AND FOBES, T. 1981. The central basis of motivation: Intracranial self-stimulation. *Annual Review of Psychology* 32:523–74.

OLFSON, M., AND KLERMAN, G. L. 1993. Trends in the prescription of psychotropic medications. The role of physician specialty. *Medical Care* 31:559–64.

OLSON, D. J. 1991. Species differences in spatial memory among Clark's nutcrackers, scrub jays, and pigeons. *Journal of Experimental Psychology: Animal Behavior Processes* 17(4):363–76.

OLTON, D. S. 1978. Characteristics of spatial memory. In Hulse, S. H., Fowler, H., and Honig, W. K. (Eds.), *Cognitive processes in animal behavior,* pp. 341–73. Hillsdale, N.J.: Erlbaum.

OLTON, D. S. 1979. Mazes, maps, and memory. *American Psychologist* 34:583–96.

OLTON, D. S., AND SAMUELSON, R. J. 1976. Remembrance of places passed: Spatial memory in rats. *Journal of Experimental Psychology: Animal Behavior Processes* 2:97–116.

OLWEUS, D. 1980. Familial and temperamental determinants of aggressive behavior in adolescent boys: A causal analysis. *Developmental Psychology* 16:644–66.

ORBELL, J. M.; VAN DE KRAGT, A. J. C.; AND DAWES, R. M. 1988. Explaining discussion-induced cooperation. *Journal of Personality and Social Psychology* 54:811–19.

ORLANSKY, H. 1949. Infant care and personality. *Psychological Bulletin* 46:1–48.

ORNE, M. T. 1951. The mechanisms of hypnotic age regression: An experimental study. *Journal of Abnormal and Social Psychology* 58:277–99.

ORNE, M. T. 1975. Psychotherapy in contemporary America: Its development and context. In Arieti, S. (Ed.), *American handbook of psychiatry,* 2nd ed., vol. 5, pp. 1–33. New York: Basic Books.

ORNE, M. T. 1979. The use and misuse of hypnosis in court. *The International Journal of Clinical and Experimental Hypnosis* 27:311–41.

ORNE, M. T., AND HAMMER, A. G. 1974. Hypnosis. in *Encyclopaedia Brittanica,* 5th ed., pp. 133–40. Chicago: Encyclopaedia Brittannica.

ORNSTEIN, R. 1977. *The psychology of consciousness* 2nd ed. New York: Harcourt Brace Jovanovich.

OSOFSKY, J. D., AND DANZGER, B. 1974. Relationships between neonatal characteristics and mother-infant characteristics. *Developmental Psychology* 10:124–30.

PACKER, C. 1977. Reciprocal altruism in olive baboons. *Nature* 265:441–43.

PAGE, E. B. 1985. Review of Kaufman's Assessment Battery for Children. *Ninth mental measurements yearbook,* vol. 1., pp. 773–77.

PARKE, R. D. 1981. *Fathers.* Cambridge, Mass.: Harvard University Press.

PARKE, R. D., AND SLABY, R. G. 1983. The development of aggression. In Mussen, P. H. (Ed.), *Carmichael's manual of child psychology: Vol. 4. Socialization, personality and social development* (Hetherington, M. E., volume editor), pp. 547–642. New York: Wiley.

PARNAS, J., AND JORGENSEN, A. 1989. Premorbid psychopathology in schizophrenia spectrum. *British Journal of Psychiatry* 155:623–27.

PASCALE-LEONE, J. 1978. Compounds, confounds and models in developmental information processing: A reply to Trabasso and Foellinger. *Journal of Experimental Child Psychology* 26:18–40.

PATIENCE, A., AND SMITH, J. W. 1986. Derek Freeman and Samoa: The making and unmaking of a biobehavioral myth. *American Anthropologist* 88:157–61.

PATTERSON, T.; SPOHN, H. E.; BOGIA, D. P.; AND HAYES, K. 1986. Thought disorder in schizophrenia: Cognitive and neuroscience approaches. *Schizophrenia Bulletin* 12:460–72.

PAUL, G. L. 1967. Insight versus desensitization in psychotherapy two years after termination. *Journal of Consulting Psychology* 31:333–48.

PAUL, J. P. 1984. The bisexual identity: An idea without social recognition. *Journal of Homosexuality* 9: 45–63.

PAUL, J. P. 1985. Bisexuality: Reassessing our paradigms of sexuality. Bisexualities: Theory and Research, *Journal of Homosexuality* (Special Issue) 11:21–34.

PAVLOV, I. 1927. *Conditioned reflexes.* Oxford, England: Oxford University Press.

PAVLOV, I. 1928. *Lectures on conditioned reflexes,* vol 1. New York: International Publishers Co., Inc.

PAYKEL, E. S. 1982. Life events and early environment. In Paykel, E. S. (Ed.), *Handbook of affective disorders.* New York: Guilford.

PENFIELD, W. 1975. *The mystery of the mind.* Princeton, N.J.: Princeton University Press.

PENFIELD, W., AND RASMUSSEN, T. 1950. *The cerebral cortex of man.* New York: Macmillan.

PENFIELD, W., AND ROBERTS, L. 1959. *Speech and brain mechanisms.* Princeton, N.J.: Princeton University Press.

PENROSE, L. S., AND PENROSE, R. 1958. Impossible objects: A special type of visual illusion. *British Journal of Psychology* 49:31–33.

PEPITONE, A. 1976. Toward a normative and comparative biocultural social psychology. *Journal of Personality and Social Psychology* 43:641–53.

PERIN, C. T. 1943. A quantitative investigation of the delay of reinforcement gradient. *Journal of Experimental Psychology* 32:37–51.

PETERSON, C., AND SELIGMAN, M. E. P. 1984. Causal explanations as a risk factor for depression: Theory and evidence. *Psychological Review* 91:341–74.

PETERSON, C.; SEMMEL, A.; VON BAEYER, C.; ABRAMSON, L. Y.; METALSKY, G. I.; AND SELIGMAN, M. E. P. 1982. The Attributional Style Questionnaire. *Cognitive Therapy and Research* 6:287–99.

PETITTO, L. A., AND MARENTETTE, P. F. 1991. Babbling in the manual mode: Evidence for the ontogeny of language. *Science* 251:1493–96.

PETTY, R. E., AND CACIOPPO, J. T. 1985. The elaboration likelihood model of persuasion. In Berkowitz, L. (Ed.), *Advances in experimental social psychology,* vol. 19. New York: Academic Press.

PIAGET, J. 1951. *Play, dreams and imitation in childhood.* New York: Norton.

PIAGET, J. 1952. *The origins of intelligence in children.* New York: International University Press.

PIAGET, J., AND INHELDER, B. 1956. *The child's conception of space.* London: Routledge and Kegan Paul.

PIAGET, J., AND INHELDER, B. 1967. *The child's conception of space.* New York: Norton.

PILLEMER, D. B. 1984. Flashbulb memories of the assassination attempt on President Reagan. *Cognition* 16:63–80.

PINKER, S. 1984. *Language learnability and language development.* Cambridge, Mass: Harvard University Press.

PINKER, S. 1994. *The language instinct.* New York: William Morrow.

PINKER, S., AND PRINCE, A. 1988. On language and connectionism: Analysis of a parallel distributed processing model of language acquisition. *Cognition* 28(1):73–194.

PLUTCHIK, R. 1980. The evolutionary context. In Plutchik, R., and Kellerman, H. (Eds.), *Emotion: Theory, research and experience,* vol. 1. New York: Academic Press.

POGGIO, G. F., AND FISCHER, B. 1978. Binocular interaction and depth sensitivity in striate and prestriate cortex of behaving rhesus monkey. *Journal of Neurophysiology* 40:1392–1405.

POLEY, W. 1974. Dimensionality in the measurement of authoritarian and political attitudes. *Canadian Journal of Behavioral Science* 6:83–94.

PORAC, C., AND PORAC, S. 1981. *Lateral preferences and human behavior.* New York: Springer-Verlag.

PORSOLT, R. D.; LEPICHON, M.; AND JALFRE, M. 1977. Depression: A new animal model sensitive to antidepressant treatments. *Nature* 266:730–32.

PRASADA, S., AND PINKER, S. 1993. Generalizations of regular and irregular morphology. *Language and Cognitive Processes* 8:1–56.

PREMACK, A., AND PREMACK, D. 1972. Teaching language to an ape. *Scientific American* 227: 92–99.

PREMACK, A., AND PREMACK, D. 1983. *The mind of an ape.* New York: Norton.

PREMACK, D. 1976. *Intelligence in ape and man.* Hillsdale, N.J.: Erlbaum.

PREMACK, D. 1978. On the abstractness of human concepts: Why it would be difficult to talk to a pigeon. In Hulse, S. H.; Fowler, H.; and Honig, W. K. (Eds.), *Cognitive processes in animal behavior.* Hillsdale, N.J.: Erlbaum.

PREMACK, D. 1988. 'Does the chimpanzee have a theory of mind' revisited. In Byrne, R. W., and Whiten, A. (Eds.), *Machiavellian intelligence: Social expertise and the evolution of intellect in monkeys, apes, and humans,* pp. 160–79. Oxford: Oxford University.

PREMACK, D., AND WOODRUFF, G. 1978. Does the chimpanzee have a theory of mind? *The Behavioral and Brain Sciences* 4:515–26.

PRICE, R. H., AND BOUFFARD, B. L. 1974. Behavioral appropriateness and situational constraint. *Journal of Personality and Social Psychology* 30:579–86.

PRICE-WILLIAMS, D. R. 1981. Concrete and formal operations. In Munroe, R. H.; Munroe, R. L.; and Whiting, B. B. (Eds.), *Handbook of cross-cultural development,* pp. 403–22. New York: Garland.

PRICE-WILLIAMS, D. R. 1985. Cultural psychology. In Lindzey, G., and Aronson, E. (Eds.), *Handbook of social psychology,* vol. 2, pp. 993–1042. New York: Academic Press.

PRICE-WILLIAMS, D., GORDON, W., AND RAMIREZ, M. 1969. Skill and conservation: A study of pottery-making children. *Developmental Psychology* 1:769.

PRINCE, E. 1981. Toward a taxonomy of given-new information. In P. Cole (Ed.), *Syntax and semantics 9 Pragmatics.* New York: Academic Press.

PRINCE, G. 1978. Putting the other half of the brain to work. *Training: The Magazine of Human Resources Development* 15:57–61.

PRINZHORN, H. 1972. *Artistry of the mentally ill.* New York: Springer-Verlag.

PROVENCE, S., AND LIPTON, R. C. 1962. *Infants in institutions.* New York: International Universities Press.

PUTNAM, F. W.; GUROFF, J. J.; SILBERMAN, E. K.; BARBAN, L.; AND POST, R. M. 1986. The clinical phenomenology of multiple personality disorder: Review of 100 recent cases. *Journal of Clinical Psychiatry* 47:285–93.

PUTNAM, H. 1975. The meaning of "meaning." In Gunderson, K. (Ed.), *Language, mind, and knowledge.* Minneapolis: University of Minnesota Press.

PUTNAM, K. E. 1979. Hypnosis and distortions in eye witness memory. *International Journal of Clinical and Experimental Hypnosis* 27:437–48.

QUAY, H. C. 1965. Psychopathic personality as pathological stimulation seeking. *American Journal of Psychiatry* 122:180–83.

QUAY, L. C. 1971. Language, dialect, reinforcement, and the intelligence test performance of Negro children. *Child Development* 42:5–15.

RACHMAN, S. J., AND TEASDALE, J. 1969. Aversion therapy: An appraisal. In Franks, C. M. (Ed.), *Behavior therapy: Appraisal and status,* pp. 279–320. New York: McGraw-Hill.

RADFORD, A. 1988. *Transformational grammar: A first course* New York: Cambridge University Press.

RADKE-YARROW, M.; ZAHN-WAXLER, C.; AND CHAPMAN, M. 1983. Children's prosocial dispositions and behavior. In Mussen, P. E. (Ed.), *Carmichael's manual of child psychology: Vol. 4. Socialization, personality, and social development* (Hetherington, E. M., volume editor), pp. 469–546. New York: Wiley.

RAPOPORT, A. 1988. Experiments with *N*-person social traps. II. Tragedy of the commons. *Journal of Conflict Resolution* 32:473–99.

RAPPAPORT, Z. H. 1992. Psychosurgery in the modern era: Therapeutic and ethical aspects. *Medicine and Law* 11:449–53.

RAVEN, B. H., AND RUBIN, J. Z. 1976. *Social psychology: People in groups.* New York: Wiley.

RAYNER, K. 1978. Eye movements in reading and information processing. *Psychological Bulletin* 85:618–60.

REBER, A. S. 1985. *The Penguin dictionary of psychology.* New York: Viking Penguin.

REISBERG, D.; BARON, J.; AND KEMLER, D. G. 1980. Overcoming Stroop interference: The effects of practice on distractor potency. *Journal of Experimental Psychology: Human Perception and Performance* 6:140–50.

REISBERG, D., AND LEAK, S. 1987. Visual imagery and memory for appearance: Does Clark Gable or George C. Scott have bushier eyebrows? *Canadian Journal of Psychology* 41:521–26.

REISENZEIN, R. 1983. The Schachter theory of emotions: Two decades later. *Psychological Bulletin* 94:239–64.

REISMAN, J. A., AND EICHEL, E. W. 1990. *Kinsey, sex and fraud*. Lafayette, La.: Huntington House.

RESCORLA, R. A. 1966. Predictability and number of pairings in Pavlovian fear conditioning. *Psychonomic Science* 4:383–84.

RESCORLA, R. A. 1967. Pavlovian conditioning and its proper control procedures. *Psychological Review* 74:71–80.

RESCORLA, R. A. 1980. *Pavlovian second-order conditioning*. Hillsdale, N.J.: Erlbaum.

RESCORLA, R. A. 1988. Behavioral studies of Pavlovian conditioning. *Annual Review of Neuroscience* 11: 329–52.

RESCORLA, R. A., AND HOLLAND, P. C. 1982. Behavioral studies of associative learning in animals. *Annual Reviews of Psychology* 33:265–308.

REVLIN, R., AND LEIRER, V. O. 1980. Understanding quantified categorical expressions. *Memory and Cognition* 8:447–58.

REVUSKY, S. H. 1971. The role of interference in association over a delay. In Honig, W. K., and James, H. R. (Eds.), *Animal memory*. New York: Academic Press.

REVUSKY, S. 1977. Learning as a general process with an emphasis on data from feeding experiments. In Milgram, N. W.; Krames, L.; and Alloway, T. H. (Eds.), *Food aversion learning*, pp. 1–51. New York: Plenum.

REVUSKY, S. 1985. The general process approach to animal learning. In Johnston, T. D., and Petrewicz, A. T. (Eds.), *Issues in the ecological study of learning*. Hillsdale, N.J.: Erlbaum.

REYNOLDS, G. S. 1968. *A primer of operant conditioning*. Glenview, Ill.: Scott, Foresman.

RHEINGOLD, H. L.; HAY, D. F.; AND WEST, M. J. 1976. Sharing in the second year of life. *Child Development* 47:1148–58.

RIPS, L. J.; SHOBEN, E. J.; AND SMITH, E. E. 1973. Semantic distance and the verification of semantic relations. *Journal of Verbal Learning and Verbal Behavior* 12:1–20.

RIPS, L. J.; SMITH, E. E.; AND SHOBEN, E. J. 1978. Semantic composition in sentence verification. *Journal of Verbal Learning and Verbal Behavior* 19:705–21.

ROBBIN, A. A. 1958. A controlled study of the effects of leucotomy. *Journal of Neurology, Neurosurgery and Psychiatry* 21:262–69.

ROBINS, L. N.; HELZER, J. E.; WEISSMAN, M. M.; ORVASCHEL, H.; GRUENBERG, E.; BURKE, J. D.; AND REGIER, D. A. 1984. Lifetime prevalence of specific psychiatric disorders in three sites. *Archives of General Psychiatry* 41:948–58.

ROBINSON, H. B., AND ROBINSON, N. M. 1970. Mental retardation. In Mussen, P. H. (Ed.), *Carmichael's manual of child psychology*, vol. 2, pp. 65–66. New York: Wiley.

ROCK, I. 1977. In defense of unconscious inference. In Epstein, W. W. (Ed.), *Stability and constancy in visual perception: Mechanisms and processes*, pp. 321–74. New York: Wiley.

ROCK, I. 1983. *The logic of perception*. Cambridge, Mass.: MIT Press.

ROCK, I. 1986. The description and analysis of object and event perception. In Boff, K. R.; Kauffman, L.; and Thomas, J. P. (Eds.), *Handbook of perception and human performance: Vol. 2. Cognitive processes and performance*, pp. 1–71. New York: Wiley.

RODIN, J., AND LANGER, E. J. 1977. Long-term effects of a control-relevant intervention with the institutionalized aged. *Journal of Personality and Social Psychology* 35:897–902.

RODMAN, H. R.; GROSS, C. G.; AND ALBRIGHT, T. D. 1989. Afferent basis of visual response properties in area MT of the macaque. I. Effects of striate cortex removal. *Journal of Neuroscience* 9:2033–50.

ROEDER, K. D. 1935. An experimental analysis of the sexual behavior of the praying mantis. *Biological Bulletin* 69:203–20.

ROEDER, L. 1967. *Nerve cells and insect behavior*. Cambridge, Mass.: Harvard University Press.

ROEDIGER, H. L., III. 1980. Memory metaphors in cognitive psychology. *Memory and Cognition* 8: 231–46.

ROEDIGER, H. L., III. 1990. Implicit memory: Retention without remembering. *American Psychologist* 45:1043–56.

ROGERS, C. R. 1942. *Counseling and psychotherapy: New concepts in practice*. Boston: Houghton Mifflin.

ROGERS, C. R. 1951 and 1970. *Client-centered therapy: Its current practice, implications, and theory*, 1st and 2nd eds. Boston: Houghton Mifflin.

ROGERS, C. R. 1961. *On becoming a person: A therapist's view of psychotherapy*. Boston: Houghton Mifflin.

ROGOFF, B.; GAUVAIN, M.; AND ELLIS, S. 1984. Development viewed in its cultural context. In Bornstein, M. H., and Lamb, M. E. (Eds.), *Developmental psychology: An advanced textbook*. Hillsdale, N.J.: Erlbaum.

ROMANES, G. J. 1882. *Animal intelligence*. London: Kegan Paul.

ROPER, T. J. 1983. Learning as a biological phenomenon. In Halliday, T. R., and Slater, P. J. B. (Eds.), *Genes, development and behavior*, vol. 3, pp. 178–212: *Animal behavior*. Oxford: Blackwell.

RORER, L. G. 1990. Personality assessment: A conceptual survey. In Pervin, L. A. (Ed.), *Handbook of personality: Theory and research*, pp. 693–722. New York: Guilford Press.

RORER, L. G., AND WIDIGER, T. A. 1983. Personality structure and assessment. In Rosenzweig, M. R., and Porter, L. W. (Eds.), *Annual Review of Psychology* 34:431–63.

ROSCH, E. H. 1973a. Natural categories. *Cognitive Psychology* 4:328–50.

ROSCH, E. H. 1973b. On the internal structure of perceptual and semantic categories. In Moore, T. E. (Ed.), *Cognitive development and the acquisition of language*. New York: Academic Press.

ROSCH, E. H. 1978. Principles of categorization. In Rosch, E., and Lloyd (Eds.), *Cognition and categorization*. Hillsdale, N.J.: Erlbaum.

ROSCH, E. H., AND MERVIS, C. B. 1975. Family resemblances: Studies in the internal structure of categories. *Cognitive Psychology* 7:573–605.

ROSCH, E. H.; MERVIS, C. B.; GRAY, W. D.; JOHNSON, D. M.; AND BOYES-BRAEM, P. 1976. Basic objects in natural categories. *Cognitive Psychology* 8:382–439.

ROSEN, G. 1966. *Madness in society*. Chicago: University of Chicago Press.

ROSEN, L. N.; TARGUM, S. D.; TERMAN, M.; BRYANT, M. J.; HOFFMAN, H.; KASPER, S. F.; HAMOVIT, J. R.; DOCHERTY, J. P.; WELCH, B.; AND ROSENTHAL, N. E. 1990. Prevalence of seasonal affective disorder at four latitudes. *Psychiatry Research* 31: 131–44.

ROSENFELD, P.; GIACALONE, R. A.; AND TEDESCHI, J. T. 1984. Cognitive dissonance and impression management explanations for effort justification. *Personality and Social Psychology Bulletin* 10: 394–401.

ROSENMAN, R. H.; BRAND, R. J.; JENKINS, C. D.; FRIEDMAN, M.; AND STRAUS, R. 1975. Coronary heart disease in the Western Collaborative Group Study: Final follow-up experience of $8\frac{1}{2}$ years. *Journal of the American Medical Association* 233:872–77.

ROSENSTEIN, M. J.; MILAZZO-SAYRE. L. J.; AND MANDERSCHEID, R. W. 1989. Care of persons with schizophrenia: A statistical profile. *Schizophrenia Bulletin* 15:45–58.

ROSENTHAL, A. M. 1964. *Thirty-eight witnesses*. New York: McGraw-Hill.

ROSENTHAL, D. 1970. *Genetic theory and abnormal behavior*. New York: McGraw-Hill.

ROSENTHAL, D. M. 1993. Higher-order thoughts and the appendage theory of consciousness. *Philosophical Psychology* 6:155–66.

ROSENTHAL, N. E.; SACK, D. A.; GILLIN, J. C.; LEWY, A. J.; GOODWIN, F. K.; DAVENPORT, Y.; MUELLER, P. S.; NEWSOME, D. A.; AND WEHR, T. A. 1984. Seasonal affective disorder: A description of the syndrome and preliminary findings with light therapy. *Archives of General Psychiatry* 41:72–80.

ROSS, J., AND LAWRENCE, K. Q. 1968. Some observations on memory artifice. *Psychonomic Science* 13:107–108.

ROSS, L. 1977. The intuitive psychologist and his shortcomings: Distortions in the attribution process. In Berkowitz, L. (Ed.), *Advances in experimental social psychology*, vol. 10. New York: Academic Press.

ROSS, L.; AMABILE, T. M.; AND STEINMETZ, J. L. 1977. Social roles, social control, and biases in social perception processes. *Journal of Experimental Social Psychology* 35:817–29.

ROSS, L., AND NISBETT, R. E. 1991. *The person and the situation*. New York: McGraw-Hill.

ROZIN, P. 1976a. The evolution of intelligence and access to the cognitive unconscious. In Stellar, E., and Sprague, J. M. (Eds.), *Progress in psychobiology and physiological psychology*, vol. 6. New York: Academic Press.

ROZIN, P. 1976b. The psychobiological approach to human memory. In Rosenzweig, M. R., and Bennett, E. L., *Neural mechanisms of learning and memory*, pp. 3–48. Cambridge, Mass.: MIT Press.

ROZIN, P. 1982. Human food selection: The interaction of biology, culture, and individual experience. In Barker, L. M. (Ed.), *The psychology of human food selection*, pp. 225–54. Westport, Conn.: AVI Publ. Co.

ROZIN, P., AND KALAT, J. W. 1971. Specific hungers and poison avoidance as adaptive specializations of learning. *Psychological Review* 78:459–86.

ROZIN, P., AND KALAT, J. W. 1972. Learning as a situation-specific adaptation. In Seligman, M. E. P., and Hager, J. L. (Eds.), *Biological boundaries of learning*, pp. 66–96. New York: Appleton-Century-Crofts.

ROZIN, P., AND SCHULL, J. 1988. The adaptive-evolutionary point of view in experimental psychology. In Atkinson, R. C.; Herrnstein, R. J.; Lindzey, G.; and Luce, R. D. (Eds.), *Steven's handbook of experimental psychology*, 2nd ed., vol. 1: *Perception and motivation*, pp. 503–46. New York: Wiley.

RUBIN, Z; HILL, C. T.; PEPLAU, L. A.; DUNKEL-SCHETTER, C. 1980. Self-disclosure in dating couples: Sex roles and the ethic of openness. *Journal of Marriage and the Family* 42(2): 305–17.

RUMBAUGH, D. M. (Ed.). 1977. *Language learning by a chimpanzee: The Lana Project*. New York: Academic Press.

RUMELHART, D., AND McCLELLAND, J. 1986. On learning the past tenses of English verbs. In McClelland, J.; Rumelhart, D.; and the PDP Research Group (Eds.), *Parallel distributed processing: Explorations in the microstructure of cognition*, vol. I. Cambridge, Mass: MIT Press.

RUSSEK, M. 1971. Hepatic receptors and the neurophysiological mechanisms controlling feeding behavior. In Ehrenpreis, S. (Ed.), *Neurosciences research*, vol. 4. New York: Academic Press.

RUSSELL, G. V. 1961. Interrelationship within the limbic and centremcephalic systems. In Sheer, D. E. (Ed.), *Electrical stimulation of the brain*, pp. 167-81. Austin, Tex.: University of Texas Press.

RUSSELL, M. J. 1976. Human olfactory communication. *Nature* 260:520–22.

RUSSELL, M. J.; SWITZ, G. M.; AND THOMPSON, K. 1980. Olfactory influence on the human menstrual cycle. *Pharmacology, Biochemistry, and Behavior* 13:737–38.

SABINI, J. 1995. *Social psychology*, 2nd ed. New York: Norton.

SACKS, O. 1985. *The man who mistook his wife for a hat*. New York: Harper & Row.

SADLER, H. H.; DAVISON, L.; CARROLL, C.; AND KOUNTZ, S. L. 1971. The living, genetically unrelated, kidney donor. *Seminars in Psychiatry* 3:86–101.

SADOCK, B. J. 1975. Group psychotherapy. In Freedman, A. M.; Kaplan, H. I.; and Sadock, B. J. (Eds.), *Comprehensive textbook of psychiatry*, vol. 2, pp. 1850–76. Baltimore: Williams & Wilkins.

SAGHIR, M. T., AND ROBINS, E. 1973. *Male and female homosexuality*. Baltimore: Williams & Wilkins.

SAGI, A., AND HOFFMAN, M. L. 1976. Empathic distress in the newborn. *Developmental Psychology* 12:175–76.

SAHLINS, M. 1976. *The use and abuse of biology*. Ann Arbor, Mich.: University of Michigan Press.

SARASON, S. B. 1973. Jewishness, blackness, and the nature nurture controversy. *American Psychologist* 28:926–71.

SARBIN, T. R., AND ALLEN, V. L. 1968. Role theory. In Lindzey, G., and Aronson, E. (Eds.), *The handbook of social psychology*, 2nd ed., vol. 1, pp. 488–567. Reading, Mass.: Addison-Wesley.

SARNOFF, C. 1957. *Medical aspects of flying motivation—a fear-of-flying casebook*. Randolph Air Base, Tex.: U. S. Air Force, Air University, School of Aviation Medicine.

SATINOFF, E. 1964. Behavioral thermoregulation in response to local cooling of the rat brain. *American Journal of Physiology* 206:1389–94.

SATIR, V. 1967. *Conjoint family therapy*, rev. ed. Palo Alto, Calif.: Science and Behavior Books.

SAVAGE-RUMBAUGH, E.; McDONALD, D.; SEVCIK, R.; HOPKINS, W.; AND RUPERT, E. 1986. Spontaneous symbol acquisition and communicative use by pygmie chimpanzees. *Journal of Experimental Psychology: General* 115:211–235.

SAVAGE-RUMBAUGH, E.; RUMBAUGH, D.; SMITH, S.; AND LAWSON, J. 1980. Reference: The linguistic essential. *Science* 210:922–25.

SAVAGE-RUMBAUGH, S. 1987. A new look at ape language: Comprehension of vocal speech and syntax. *Nebraska Symposium on Motivation* 35:201–55.

SAXE, L.; DOUGHERTY, D.; AND CROSS, T. 1985. The validity of polygraph testing: Scientific analysis and public controversy. *American Psychologist* 40:355–66.

SCAIFE, M., AND BRUNER, J. S. 1975. The capacity for joint visual attention in the infant. *Nature* 253(5489): 265–66.

SCARR, S., AND CARTER-SALTZMAN, L. 1979. Twin method: Defense of a critical assumption. *Behavior Genetics* 9:527–42.

SCARR, S., AND CARTER-SALTZMAN, L. 1982. Genetics and intelligence. In Sternberg, R. J. (Ed.), *Handbook of human intelligence*, pp. 792–896. New York: Cambridge University Press.

SCARR, S., AND McCARTNEY, K. 1983. How people make their own environments: A theory of genotype-environment effects. *Child Development* 54:424–35.

SCARR, S., AND WEINBERG, R. A. 1983. The Minnesota adoption studies genetic differences and malleability. *Child Development* 54:260–67.

SCHACHER, S. 1981. Determination and differentiation in the development of the nervous system. In Kandel, E. R., and Schwartz, J. H. (Eds.), *Principles of neural science*. New York: Elsevier North Holland.

SCHACHTEL, E. G. 1947. On memory and childhood amnesia. *Psychiatry* 10:1–26.

SCHACHTER, S. 1964. The interaction of cognitive and physiological determinants of emotional state. In Berkowitz, L. (Ed.), *Advances in Experimental Social Psychology*, pp. 49–80. New York: Academic Press.

SCHACHTER, S., AND SINGER, J. 1962. Cognitive, social and physiological determinants of emotional state. *Psychological Review* 69:379–99.

SCHACHTER, S., AND SINGER, J. E. 1979. Comments on the Maslach and Marshall-Zimbardo experiments. *Journal of Personality and Social Psychology* 37:989–95.

SCHACTER, D. L. 1987. Implicit memory: History and current status. *Journal of Experimental Psychology: Learning, Memory, and Cognition* 13:501–18.

SCHACTER, D. L. 1992. Understanding implicit memory. *American Psychologist* 47:559–69.

SCHAIE, K. 1979. The primary mental abilities in adulthood: An exploration in the development of psychometric intelligence. In Baltes, P. B., and Brim, O. G., Jr. (Eds.), *Life-span development and behavior*, vol. 2. New York: Academic Press.

SCHAIE, K., AND STROTHER, C. 1968. A cross-sequential study of age changes in cognitive behavior. *Psychological Bulletin* 70:671–80.

SCHANK, R. C., AND ABELSON, R. 1977. *Scripts, plans, goals, and understanding*. Hillsdale, N.J.: Erlbaum.

SCHEERER, M. 1963. Problem solving. *Scientific American* 208:118–28.

SCHEERER, M.; GOLDSTEIN, K.; AND BORING, E. G. 1941. A demonstration of insight: The horse-rider puzzle. *American Journal of Psychology* 54:437–38.

SCHIFF, M.; DUYME, M.; DUMARET, A.; AND TOMKIEWICZ, S. 1982. How much *could* we boost scholastic achievement and IQ scores? A direct answer from a French adoption study. *Cognition* 12: 165–96.

SCHIFF, W. 1965. Perception of impending collision. *Psychological Monographs* 79:1–26.

SCHIFFRIN, D. 1988. Conversational analysis. In F. Newmeyer (Ed.), *Linguistics: The Cambridge survey: Vol. IV. The socio-cultural context*. Cambridge: Cambridge University Press.

SCHILDKRAUT, J. J. 1965. The catecholamine hypothesis of affective disorders: A review of supporting evidence. *American Journal of Psychiatry* 122:509–22.

SCHILDKRAUT, J. J.; GREEN, A. I.; AND MOONEY, J. J. 1985. Affective disorders: Biochemical aspects. In Kaplan, H. I.; and Sadock, J. (Eds.), *Comprehensive textbook of psychiatry,* 4th ed. Baltimore: Williams & Wilkins.

SCHNEIDER, D. J. 1973. Implicit personality theory: A review. *Psychological Bulletin* 79:294–309.

SCHOFIELD, W. 1964. *Psychotherapy: The purchase of friendship.* Englewood Cliffs, N.J.: Prentice-Hall.

SCHREIBER, F. R. 1973. *Sybil.* New York: Warner Paperback.

SCHWARTZ, B. 1989. *Psychology of learning and behavior,* 3rd ed. New York: Norton.

SCHWARTZ, B., AND REISBERG, D. 1991. *Psychology of learning and memory.* New York: Norton.

SCHWARTZ, G. E.; WEINBERGER, D. A.; AND SINGER, J. A. 1981. Cardiovascular differentiation of happiness, sadness, anger, and fear following imagery and exercise. *Psychosomatic Medicine* 43:343–64.

SCOTT, J. P., AND FULLER, J. L. 1965. *Genetics and the social behavior of the dog.* Chicago: University of Chicago Press.

SCRIBNER, S., AND COLE, M. 1973. Cognitive consequences of formal and informal education. *Science* 182:553–59.

SEARLE, J. R. 1969. *Speech acts: An essay in the philosophy of language.* New York: Cambridge University Press.

SEARS, R. R.; MACCOBY, E. E.; AND LEVIN, H. 1957. *Patterns of child rearing.* Evanston, Ill.: Row, Peterson.

SEIDENBERG, M. S., AND PETITTO, L. A. 1979. Signing behavior in apes: A critical review. *Cognition* 7:177–215.

SELFRIDGE, O. G. 1959. Pandemonium: A paradigm for learning. In Blake, D. V., and Uttley, A. M. (Eds.), *Proceedings of the Symposium on the Mechanisation of Thought Processes.* London: HM Stationary Office.

SELIGMAN, M. E. P. On the generality of the laws of learning. *Psychological Review* 77: 406–18.

SELIGMAN, M. E. P. 1971. Phobias and preparedness. *Behavior Therapy* 2:307–20.

SELIGMAN, M. E. P. 1975. *Helplessness: On depression, development, and death.* San Francisco: Freeman.

SELIGMAN, M. E. P., AND HAGER, J. L. (Eds.). 1972. *Biological boundaries of learning.* New York: Appleton-Century-Crofts.

SELIGMAN, M. E. P.; KLEIN, D. C.; AND MILLER, W. R. 1976. Depression. In Leitenberg, H. (Ed.), *Handbook of behavior modification and behavior therapy.* Englewood Cliffs, N.J.: Prentice-Hall.

SELIGMAN, M. E. P.; MAIER, S. F.; AND SOLOMON, R. L. 1971. Unpredictable and uncontrollable aversive events. In Brush, F. R. (Ed.), *Aversive conditioning and learning.* New York: Academic Press.

SELLS, P. 1985. *Lectures on contemporary syntactic theories.* Stanford, Calif.: Center for the Study of Language and Information.

SENDAK, M. 1979. *Higglety pigglety pop! or There must be more to life.* New York: Harper & Row.

SHALLICE, T., 1988. *From neuropsychology to mental structure.* Cambridge: Cambridge University Press.

SHALTER, M. D. 1984. Predator-prey behavior and habituation. In Peeke, H. V. S., and Petrinovich, L. (Eds.), *Habituation, sensitization and behavior,* pp. 423–58. New York: Academic Press.

SHAM, P. V. C.; O'CALLAGHAN, E.; TAKEI, N.; MURRAY, G. K.; HARE, E. H.; AND MURRAY, R. M. 1992. Schizophrenia following pre-natal exposure to influenza epidemics between 1939 and 1960. *British Journal of Psychiatry* 160:461–66.

SHANAB, M. E., AND YAHYA, K. A. 1977. A behavioral study of obedience in children. *Journal of Personality and Social Psychology* 35:530–36.

SHAPIRO, A. K. 1971. Placebo effects in medicine, psychotherapy, and psychoanalysis. In Bergin, A. E., and Garfield, S. L. (Eds.), *Handbook of psychotherapy and behavior change,* pp. 439–73. New York: Wiley.

SHAPIRO, C. M.; BORTZ, R.; MITCHELL, D.; BARTELL, P.; AND JOOSTE, P. 1981. Slow wave sleep: A recovery period after exercise. *Science* 214:1253–54.

SHAPIRO, D. A., AND SHAPIRO, D. 1982. Meta-analysis of comparative therapy outcome studies: A replication and refinement. *Psychological Bulletin* 92:581–604.

SHEINGOLD, K., AND TENNEY, Y. J. 1982. Memory for a salient childhood event. In Neisser, U. (Ed.), *Memory observed,* pp. 201–12. San Francisco: Freeman.

SHEKELLE, R. B.; HONEY, S. B.; NEATON, J.; BILLINGS, J.; BORLANI, N.; GERACE, T.; JACOBS, D.; LASSER, N.; AND STANDER, J. 1983. Type A behavior pattern and coronary death in MRFIT. *American Heart Association Cardiovascular Disease Newsletter* 33:34.

SHEKELLE, R. B.; RAYNOR, W. J.; OSTFELD, A. M.; GARRON, D. C.; BIELIAVSKAS, L. A.; LIV, S. C.; MALIZA, C.; AND PAUL, O. 1981. Psychological depression and the 17-year risk of cancer. *Psychosomatic Medicine* 43:117–25.

SHERMAN, P. W. 1977. Nepotism and the evolution of alarm calls. *Science* 197:1246–54.

SHERRICK, C. E., AND CHOLEWIAK, R. W. 1986. Cutaneous sensitivity. In Boff, K. R.; Kaufman, L.; and Thomas, J. P. (Eds.), *Handbook of perception and human performance,* Chapter 12. New York: Wiley.

SHERRINGTON, C. S. 1906. *The integrative action of the nervous system,* 2nd ed. New Haven, Conn.: Yale University Press, 1947.

SHERROD, D. 1989. The influence of gender on same-sex friendships. In Hendrick, C. (Ed.), *Close relationships,* vol. 10, *Review of personality and social psychology.* Newbury Park, Calif.: Sage.

SHERRY, D. F.; JACOBS, L. F.; GAULIN, S. J. C. 1992. Spatial memory and adaptive specialization of the hippocampus. *Trends in Neurosciences* 15(8): 298-303.

SHERRY, D. F.; VACCARINO, A. L.; BUCKENHAM, K.; AND HERZ, R. S. 1989. The hippocampal complex of food storing birds. *Brain, Behavior and Evolution* 34: 308-17.

SHETTLEWORTH, S. J. 1972. Constraints on learning. In Lehrman, D. S.; Hinde, R. A.; and Shaw, E. (Eds.), *Advances in the study of behavior,* vol. 4. New York: Academic Press.

SHETTLEWORTH, S. J. 1983. Memory in food-hoarding birds. *Scientific American* 248:102–10.

SHETTLEWORTH, S. J. 1984. Learning and behavioral ecology. In Krebs, J. R., and Davies, N. B. (Eds.), *Behavioral ecology* 2nd ed., pp. 170–94. Oxford: Blackwell.

SHIPLEY, E. F., AND KUHN, I. F. 1983. A constraint on comparisons: Equally detailed alternatives. *Journal of Experimental Child Psychology* 35:195–222.

SHIPLEY, E. F.; KUHN, I. F.; AND MADDEN, E. C. 1983. Mothers' use of superordinate terms. *Journal of Child Language* 10:571–88.

SHIPLEY, E. F.; SMITH, C. S.; AND GLEITMAN, L. R. 1969. A study in the acquisition of language: Free responses to commands. *Language* 45:322–42.

SHIRLEY, M. M. 1961. *The first two years: A study of twenty-five babies.* Minneapolis: University of Minnesota Press.

SHORTER, E. 1992. *From paralysis to fatigue: A history of psychosomatic illness in the modern era.* New York: Macmillan Free Press.

SHORTLIFFE, E. H.; AXLINE, S. G.; BUCHANAN, B. G.; MERIGAN, T. C.; AND COHEN, N. S. 1973. An artificial intelligence program to advise physicians regarding antimicrobial therapy. *Computers and Biomedical Research* 6:544–60.

SHUEY, A. 1966. *The testing of Negro intelligence.* New York: Social Science Press.

SHWEDER, R. A. 1975. How relevant is an individual difference theory of personality? *Journal of Personality* 43:455–85.

SHWEDER, R. A., AND BOURNE, E. J. 1986. Does the concept of the person vary cross-culturally? In Shweder, R. A. (Ed.), *Thinking through cultures,* pp. 113–55. Cambridge, Mass.: Harvard, 1991.

SIEGAL, M. 1991. *Knowing children: Experiments in conversation.* Hillsdale, N.J.: Erlbaum.

SIEGEL, R. K. 1984. Changing patterns of cocaine use: Longitudinal observations, consequences, and treatment. In Grabowski, J. (Ed.), *Cocaine: Pharmacology, effects, and treatment of abuse,* pp. 92–110. NIDA Research Monograph 50.

SIEGLER, M., AND OSMOND, H. 1974. *Models of madness, models of medicine.* New York: Harper & Row.

SIEGLER, R. S. 1983. Information processing approaches to child development. In Mussen, P. H., *Handbook of child psychology: Vol. 1. History, theory, and methods* (Kessen, W., volume editor). New York: Wiley.

SIEGLER, R. S. 1989. Mechanisms of cognitive development. In Rosenzweig, M. R., and Porter, L. W. (Eds.), *Annual Review of Psychology* 40:353–79.

SIEVER, L. J.; DAVIS, K. L.; AND GORMAN, L. K. 1991. Pathogenesis of mood disorders. In Davis, K.; Klar, H.; and Coyle, J. T. (Eds.), *Foundations of psychiatry*. Philadelphia: Saunders.

SILK, J. B. 1986. Social behavior in evolutionary perspective. In Smuts, B. B.; Cheney, D. L.; Seyfarth, R. M.; Wrangham, R. W.; and Struhsaker, T. T. (Eds.), *Primate societies*. Chicago: University of Chicago Press.

SIMNER, M. L. 1971. Newborn's response to the cry of another infant. *Developmental Psychology* 5:136–50.

SIMON, R. J., AND AARONSON, D. E. 1988. *The insanity defense: A critical assessment of law and policy in the post-Hinckley era*. New York: Praeger.

SIMPSON, E. L. 1974. Moral development research: A case of scientific cultural bias. *Human Development* 17: 81–106.

SIMS, E. A. 1986. Energy balance in human beings: The problems of plentitude. *Vitamins and hormones: Research and applications* 43:1–101.

SINHA, D. 1983. Human assessment in the Indian context. In Irvine, S. H., and Berry, J. W. (Eds.), *Human assessment and cultural factors*, pp.17–34. New York: Plenum.

SIZEMORE, C. C., AND HUBER, R. J. 1988. The twenty-two faces of Eve. *Individual Psychology: Journal of Adlerian Theory, Research and Practice* 44:53–62.

SKEELS, H. 1966. Adult status of children with contrasting early life experiences. *Monograph of the Society for Research in Child Development* 31 (No. 3).

SKINNER, B. F. 1938. *The behavior of organisms*. New York: Appleton-Century-Crofts.

SKODAK, M., AND SKEELS, H. M. 1945. A follow-up study of children in adoptive homes. *Journal of Genetic Psychology* 66:21–58.

SKODAK, M., AND SKEELS, H. M. 1947. A follow-up study of the development of one-hundred adopted children in Iowa. *American Psychologist* 2:278.

SKODAK, M., AND SKEELS, H. M. 1949. A final follow-up study of children in adoptive homes. *Journal of Genetic Psychology* 75: 85–125.

SLATER, E., AND GLITHERO, E. 1965. A follow-up of patients diagnosed as suffering from hysteria. *Journal of Psychosomatic Research* 9:9–13.

SLOANE, R. B.; STAPLES, F. R.; CRISTOL, A. H.; YORKSTON, N.J.; AND WHIPPLE, K. 1975. *Psychotherapy vs. behavior therapy*. Cambridge, Mass.: Harvard University Press.

SMEDSLUND, J. 1961. The acquisition of conservation of substance and weight in children. *Scandinavia Journal of Psychology* 2:11–20.

SMELSER, N. J. 1963. *Theory of collective behavior*. New York: Free Press, Macmillan.

SMITH, C. 1985. Sleep states and learning: A review of the animal literature. *Neuroscience and Biobehavioral Reviews* 9:157–68.

SMITH, C., AND LLOYD, B. 1978. Maternal behavior and perceived sex of infant: Revisited. *Child Development* 49:1263–65.

SMITH, D. G. 1981. The association between rank and reproductive success of male rhesus monkeys. *American Journal of Primatology* 1:83–90.

SMITH, E. E., AND MEDIN, D. L. 1981. *Categories and concepts*. Cambridge, Mass.: Harvard University Press.

SMITH, M. 1983. Hypnotic memory enhancement of witnesses: Does it work? *Psychological Bulletin* 94:387–407.

SMITH, M. B. 1950. The phenomenological approach in personality theory: Some critical remarks. *Journal of Abnormal and Social Psychology* 45:516–22.

SMITH, M. L.; GLASS, G. V.; AND MILLER, R. L. 1980. *The benefits of psychotherapy*. Baltimore: Johns Hopkins Press.

SMITH, S. M. 1979. Remembering in and out of context. *Journal of Experimental Psychology: Human Learning and Memory* 5: 460–71.

SNOW, C., AND HOEFNAGEL-HOHLE, M. 1978. The critical period for language acquisition: Evidence from second language learning. *Child Development* 49:1114–28.

SNYDER, M. 1987. *Public appearances/private realities*. New York: Freeman.

SNYDER, M., AND CUNNINGHAM, M. R. 1975. To comply or not comply: Testing the self-perception explanation of the "foot-in-the-door" phenomenon. *Journal of Personality and Social Psychology* 31:64-67.

SNYDER, M., AND ICKES, W. 1985. Personality and social behavior. In Lindzey, G., and Aronson, E. (Eds.), *Handbook of Social Psychology*, 3rd ed., vol. 2. New York: Random House.

SNYDER, S. H. 1976. The dopamine hypothesis of schizophrenia. *American Journal of Psychiatry* 133:197–202.

SNYDER, S. H., AND CHILDERS, S. R. 1979. Opiate receptors and opioid peptides. *Annual Review of Neuroscience* 2:35–64.

SOLOMON, R. L. 1980. The opponent-process theory of acquired motivation: The costs of pleasure and the benefits of pain. *American Psychologist* 35:691–712.

SOLOMON, R. L., AND CORBIT, J. D. 1974. An opponent-process theory of motivation: I. Temporal dynamics of affect. *Psychological Review* 81:119–45.

SOLOMON, R. L., AND WYNNE, L. C. 1953. Traumatic avoidance learning: Acquisition in normal dogs. *Psychological Monographs* 67 (Whole No. 354).

SPERBER, D., AND WILSON, D. 1986. *Relevance: Communication and cognition*. Oxford: Blackwell.

SPERLING, G. 1960. The information available in brief visual presentations. *Psychological Monographs* 74 (Whole No. 11).

SPERRY, R. W. 1974. Lateral specialization in the surgically separated hemispheres. In Schmitt, F. O., and Worden, F. G. (Eds.), *The Neuroscience Third Study Program*. Cambridge, Mass.: MIT Press.

SPERRY, R. W. 1982. Some effects of disconnecting the cerebral hemispheres. *Science* 217:1223–26.

SPIES, G. 1965. Food versus intracranial self-stimulation reinforcement in food deprived rats. *Journal of Comparative and Physiological Psychology* 60:153–57.

SPOONER, A., AND KELLOGG, W. N. 1947. The backward conditioning curve. *American Journal of Psychology* 60:321–34.

SPRINGER, S. P., AND DEUTSCH, G. 1981. *Left brain, right brain*. San Francisco: Freeman.

SQUIRE L. R. 1977. ECT and memory loss. *American Journal of Psychiatry* 134:997–1001.

SQUIRE, L. R. 1986. Mechanisms of memory. *Science* 232:1612–19.

SQUIRE, L. R. 1987. *Memory and brain*. New York: Oxford University.

SQUIRE, L. R., AND COHEN, N. J. 1979. Memory and amnesia: Resistance to disruption develops for years after learning. *Behavioral Biology and Neurology* 25:115–25.

SQUIRE, L. R., AND COHEN, N. J. 1982. Remote memory, retrograde amnesia, and the neuropsychology of memory. In Cermak, L. S. (Ed.), *Human memory and amnesia*, pp. 275–304. Hillsdale, N.J.: Erlbaum.

SQUIRE, L. R., AND ZOUZOUNIS, J. A. 1986. ECT and memory: Brief pulse versus sine wave. *American Journal of Psychiatry* 143: 596–601.

STARK, L., AND ELLIS, S. 1981. Scanpaths revisited: Cognitive models direct active looking. In Fisher, D.; Monty, R.; and Senders, I. (Eds.), *Eye movements: Cognition and visual perception*, pp. 193–226. Hillsdale, N.J.: Erlbaum.

STEELE, C. M., AND LIU, T. J. 1983. Dissonance processes as self-affirmation. *Journal of Personality and Social Psychology* 45:5–19.

STEINBERG, L; ELMAN, J. D.; AND MOUNTS, N. S. 1989. Authoritative parenting, psychosocial maturity, and academic success among adolescents. *Child Development* 60(6): 1424-36

STELLAR, E. 1954. The physiology of motivation. *Psychological Review* 61:5–22.

STERNBERG, R. J. 1985. General intellectual ability. In Sternberg, R. *Human abilities: An information processing approach*. New York: Freeman.

STERNBERG, R. J. 1990. *Metaphors of mind*. New York: Cambridge University Press.

STERNBERG, R. J., AND DAVIDSON, J. E. 1983. Insight in the gifted. *Educational Psychologist* 18:51–57.

STERNBERG, R. J., AND WAGNER, R. K. 1993. The egocentric view of intelligence and job performance is wrong. *Current Directions in Psychological Science* 2:1–5.

STEVENS, A., AND COUPE, P. 1978. Distortions in judged spatial relations. *Cognitive Psychology* 10:422–37.

STOKOE, W. C., JR. 1960. Sign language structure: An outline of the visual communication systems. *Studies in Linguistics Occasional Papers* 8.

STOLLER, R. J. 1968. *Sex and gender: On the development of masculinity and femininity.* New York: Science House.

STOLLER, R. J., AND HERDT, G. H. 1985. Theories of origins of male homosexuality: A cross-cultural look. *Archives of General Psychiatry* 42: 399–404.

STONE, A. 1975. *Mental health and law: A system in transition.* (DHEW Publication No. 75176). Washington, D.C.: U.S. Government Printing Office.

STORMS, M. D. 1973. Videotape and the attribution process: Reversing actors' and observers' points of view. *Journal of Personality and Social Psychology* 27:165–75.

STRICKER, E. M., AND ZIGMOND, M. J. 1976. Recovery of function after damage to catecholamine-containing neurons: A neurochemical model for the lateral hypothalamic syndrome. In Sprague, J. M., and Epstein, A. N. (Eds.), *Progress in psychobiology and physiological psychology,* vol. 6, pp. 121–88. New York: Academic Press.

STROOP, J. R. 1935. Studies of interference in serial verbal reactions. *Journal of Experimental Psychology* 18:643–62.

STUART, R. B., AND MITCHELL, C. 1980. Self-help groups in the control of body weight. In Stunkard, A. J. (Ed.), *Obesity,* pp. 354–55. Philadelphia: Saunders.

STUNKARD, A. J. 1975. Obesity. In Freedman, A. M.; Kaplan, H. I.; and Sadock, B. J. (Eds.), *Comprehensive textbook of psychiatry—II,* vol. 2, pp. 1648–54. Baltimore: Williams & Wilkins.

STUNKARD, A. 1980. Psychoanalysis and psychotherapy. In Stunkard, A. J. (Ed.), *Obesity,* pp. 355–68. Philadelphia: Saunders.

STYRON, W. 1990. *Darkness visible: A memoir of madness.* New York: Random House.

SUE, D. W., AND KIRK, B. A. 1973. Psychological characteristics of Chinese-American college students. *Journal of Counseling Psychology* 19:142–48.

SULS, J. M., AND MILLER, R. L. (Eds.). 1977. *Social comparison processes: Theoretical and empirical perspectives.* New York: Washington Hemisphere Publishing Co.

SUPALLA, I., AND NEWPORT, E. L. 1978. How many seats in a chair? The derivation of nouns and verbs in American Sign Language. In Siple, P. (Ed.), *Understanding language through sign language research.* New York: Academic Press.

SUPALLA, T. 1986. The classifier system in American Sign Language. In Craig, C. (Ed.), *Noun classes and categorization: Typological studies in language,* vol. 7. Amsterdam: John Benjamins.

SYMONS, D. 1979. *The evolution of human sexuality.* New York: Oxford University Press.

SYMONS, D. 1993. The stuff that dreams aren't made of: Why wake-state and dream-state sensory experiences differ. *Cognition* 47:181–217.

TAKAHASHI, Y. 1979. Growth hormone secretion related to the sleep waking rhythm. In Drucker-Colín, R.; Shkurovich, M.; and Sterman, M. B. (Eds.), *The functions of sleep.* New York: Academic Press.

TANNER, J. M. 1970. Physical growth. In Mussen, P. H. (Ed.), *Carmichael's manual of child psychology,* 3rd ed., pp. 77–105. New York: Wiley.

TAYLOR, S. E., AND FISKE, S. T. 1975. Point of view and perceptions of causality. *Journal of Personality and Social Psychology* 32:439–45.

TEITELBAUM, P. 1955. Sensory control of hypothalamic hyperphagia. *Journal of Comparative and Physiological Psychology* 48: 156–63.

TEITELBAUM, P. 1961. Disturbances in feeding and drinking behavior after hypothalamic lesions. In Jones, M. R. (Ed.), *Nebraska Symposium on Motivation,* pp. 39–65. Lincoln, Neb.: University of Nebraska Press.

TEITELBAUM, P., AND EPSTEIN, A. N. 1962. The lateral hypothalamic syndrome: Recovery of feeding and drinking after lateral hypothalamic lesions. *Psychological Review* 69:74–90.

TEITELBAUM, P., AND STELLAR, E. 1954. Recovery from failure to eat produced by hypothalamic lesions. *Science* 120:894–95.

TERRACE, H. S.; PETITTO, L. A.; SANDERS, D. L.; AND BEVER, T. G. 1979. Can an ape create a sentence? *Science* 206:891–902.

TERVOORT, B. T. 1961. Esoteric symbolism in the communication behavior of young deaf children. *American Annals of the Deaf* 106:436–80.

TESSER, A.; CAMPBELL, J.; AND SMITH, M. 1984. Friendship choice and performance: Self-evaluation maintenance in children. *Journal of Personality and Social Psychology* 46:561–74.

THIGPEN, C. H., AND CLECKLEY, H. M. 1957. *The three faces of Eve.* New York: McGraw-Hill.

THOMAS, A.; CHESS, S.; AND BIRCH, H. G. 1970. The origin of personality. *Scientific American* 223:102–109.

THOMPSON, C. P., AND COWAN, T. 1986. Flashbulb memories: A nicer recollection of a Neisser recollection. *Cognition* 22:199–200.

THOMPSON, R. F. 1973. *Introduction to biopsychology.* San Francisco: Albion Publishing Co.

THORNDIKE, E. L. 1898. Animal intelligence: An experimental study of the associative processes in animals. *Psychological Monographs* 2 (Whole No. 8).

THORNDIKE, E. L. 1899. The associative processes in animals. *Biological lectures from the Marine Biological Laboratory at Woods Hole.* Boston: Atheneum.

THORNDIKE, E. L. 1911. *Animal intelligence: Experimental studies.* New York: Macmillan.

THORNDIKE, E. L. 1924. The measurement of intelligence: Present status. *Psychological Review* 31:219–52.

TIETJEN, A. M., AND WALKER, L. J. 1985. Moral reasoning and leadership among men in a Papua New Guinea society. *Developmental Psychology* 21: 982–89.

TINBERGEN, N. 1951. *The study of instinct.* Oxford, England: Clarendon.

TOCQUEVILLE, A. 1835. *Democracy in America.* Mayer, J. P., and Lerner, M. (Eds.). George Lawrence (trans.) New York: Harper and Row, 1966.

TOLMAN, E. C. 1932. *Purposive behavior in animals and men.* New York: Appleton-Century-Crofts.

TOLMAN, E. C. 1948. Cognitive maps in rats and men. *Psychological Review* 55:189–208.

TOLMAN, E. C., AND GLEITMAN, H. 1949. Studies in learning and motivation: I. Equal reinforcements in both end-boxes, followed by shock in one end-box. *Journal of Experimental Psychology* 39:810–19.

TOLMAN, E. C., AND HONZIK, C. H. 1930. Introduction and removal of reward, and maze performance in rats. *University of California Publications in Psychology* 4:257–75.

TOLSTOY, L. 1868. *War and peace,* second epilogue. Henry Gifford (Ed.), Louise Maude and Aylmer Maude (trans.). New York: Oxford University Press, 1922.

TOMASELLO, M., AND FERRAR, M. 1986. Joint attention and early language. *Child Development* 57:1454–63.

TOMKINS, S. S. 1963. *Affect, imagery, consciousness,* vol. 2: *The negative affects.* New York: Springer.

TORGERSEN, S. 1986. Genetic factors in moderately severe and mild affective disorders. *Archives of General Psychiatry* 43:222–26.

TORREY, E. F. 1983. *Surviving schizophrenia: A family manual.* New York: Harper and Row.

TORREY, E. F. 1987. Prevalence studies in schizophrenia. *British Journal of Psychiatry* 150: 598–608.

TREISMAN, A. M. 1964. Verbal cues, language, and meaning in selective attention. *American Journal of Psychology* 77:206–19.

TREISMAN, A. M. 1986a. Properties, parts, and objects. In Boff, K. R.; Kaufman, L.; and Thomas, J. P. (Eds.), *Handbook of perception and human performance,* vol. II (Chapter 35). New York: Wiley.

TREISMAN, A. M. 1986b. Features and objects in visual processing. *Scientific American* 255:114–25.

TREISMAN, A. M. 1988. Features and objects: The Fourteenth Barlett Memorial Lecture. *Quarterly Journal of Experimental Psychology* 40A:201–37.

TREISMAN, A. M., AND GELADE, G. 1980. A feature-integration theory of attention. *Cognitive Psychology* 12:97–136.

TREISMAN, A. M., AND SCHMIDT, H. 1982. Illusory conjunction in the perception of objects. *Cognitive Psychology* 14:107–41.

TREISMAN, A. M., AND SOUTHER, J. 1985. Search assymetry: A diagnostic for preattentive processing of separable features. *Journal of Experimental Psychology: General* 114:285–310.

TRIANDIS, H. C. 1989. Cross-cultural studies of individualism and collectivism. *Nebraska Symposium on Motivation* 37:41–134. Lincoln, Neb.: University of Nebraska Press.

TRIANDIS, H. C.; BONTEMBO, R.; VILLAREAL, M. J.; ASAI, M.; AND LUCA, N. 1988. Individualism and collectivism: Cross-cultural perspectives on self-group relationships. *Journal of Personality and Social Psychology* 54:323–38.

TRIVERS, R. L. 1971. The evolution of reciprocal altruism. *Quarterly Review of Biology* 46:35–57.

TRIVERS, R. L. 1972. Parental investment and sexual selection. In Campbell, B. (Ed.), *Sexual selection and the descent of man,* pp. 139–79. Chicago: Aldine.

TSUANG, M. T.; GILBERTSON, M. W.; AND FARAONE, S. V. 1991. The genetics of schizophrenia. *Schizophrenia Research* 4:157–71.

TULVING, E., AND OSLER, S. 1968. Effectiveness of retrieval cues in memory for words. *Journal of Experimental Psychology* 77: 593–601.

TULVING, E., AND PEARLSTONE, Z. 1966. Availability versus accessability of information in memory for words. *Journal of Verbal Learning and Verbal Behavior* 5:381–91.

TULVING, E.; SCHACTER, D. L.; AND STARK, H. A. 1982. Priming effects in word-fragment completion are independent of recognition memory. *Journal of Experimental Psychology: Learning, Memory, and Cognition* 8:336–42.

TULVING, E., AND THOMSON, D. M. 1973. Encoding specificity and retrieval processes in episodic memory. *Psychological Review* 80: 352–73.

TURING, A. M. 1950. Computing machinery and intelligence. *Mind* 59:433–60.

TVERSKY, A., AND KAHNEMAN, D. 1973. Availability: A heuristic for judging frequency and probability. *Cognitive Psychology* 5: 207–32.

TVERSKY, A., AND KAHNEMAN, D. 1974. Judgment under uncertainty: Heuristics and biases. *Science* 125:1124–31.

TVERSKY, B., AND TUCHIN, M. 1989. A reconciliation of the evidence on eyewitness testimony: Comments on McCloskey and Zaragoza (1985). *Journal of Experimental Psychology: General* 118:86–91.

TYLER, L. E. 1965. *The psychology of human differences.* New York: Appleton-Century-Crofts.

UNDERWOOD, B. J. 1957. Interference and forgetting. *Psychological Review* 64:49–60.

U. S. PUBLIC HEALTH SERVICE, DIVISION OF CHRONIC DISEASES. 1966. *Obesity and health* (Public Health Service Publication No. 1485). Washington, D.C.: U. S. Government Printing Office.

URWIN, C. 1983. Dialogue and cognitive functioning in the early language development of three blind children. In Mills, A. E. (Ed.), *Language acquisition in the blind child.* London: Croom Helm.

VAILLANT, G. E. 1971. Theoretical hierarchy of adaptive ego mechanisms. *Archives of General Psychiatry* 24: 107–18.

VAILLANT, G. E. 1974. Natural history of male psychological health. II. Some antecedents of health adult adjustment. *Archives of General Psychiatry* 31:15–22.

VAILLANT, G. E. 1976. Natural history of male psychological health. V: Relation of choice of ego mechanisms of defense to adult adjustment. *Archives of General Psychiatry* 33:535–45.

VAILLANT, G. E. 1977. *Adaptation to life.* Boston: Little, Brown & Co.

VALENSTEIN, E. S. 1986. *Great and desperate cures.* New York: Basic Books.

VALENTA, J. G., AND RIGBY, M. K. 1968. Discrimination of the odor of stressed rats. *Science* 161:599–601.

VAN CANTFORT, E., AND RIMPAU, J. 1982. Sign language studies with children and chimpanzees. *Sign Language Studies* 34:15–72.

VANDELL, D. L.; HENDERSON, V. K.; AND WILSON, K. S. 1988. A longitudinal study of children with day care experiences of varying quality. *Child Development* 59:1286–92.

VANDENBOS, G. R.; CUMMINGS, N. A.; AND DELEON, P. H. 1992. A century of psychotherapy: Economic and environmental influences. In Freedheim, D. K. (Ed.), *History of psychotherapy.* Washington, D.C.: American Psychological Association.

VAN HOOFF, J. A. R. A. M. 1972. A comparative approach to the phylogeny of laughter and smiling. In Hinde, R. A. (Ed.), *Non-verbal communication.* New York: Cambridge University Press.

VAN KAMMEN, D. P., AND KELLEY, M. 1991. Dopamine and norepinephrine activity in schizophrenia: An integrated perspective. *Schizophrenia Research* 4:173–91.

VAULTIN, R. G., AND BERKELEY, M. A. 1977. Responses of single cells in cat visual cortex to prolonged stimulus movement: Neural correlates of visual aftereffects. *Journal of Neurophysiology* 40: 1051–65.

VERY, P. S. 1967. Differential factor structure in mathematical ability. *Genetic Psychology Monographs* 75:169–208.

VISCOTT, D. S. 1979. A musical idiot savant: A psychodynamic study, and some speculations on the creative process. *Psychiatry* 33: 494–515.

VISINTAINER, M.; VOLPICELLI, J. R.; AND SELIGMAN, M. E. P. 1982. Tumor rejection in rats after inescapable or escapable shock. *Science* 216:437–39.

VOLPICELLI, J. 1989. Psychoactive substance use disorders. In Rosenhan, D. L., and Seligman, M. E. P. *Abnormal psychology,* 2nd ed. New York: Norton.

WABER, D. P. 1977. Sex differences in mental abilities, hemispheric lateralization, and rate of physical growth at adolescence. *Developmental Psychology* 13:29–38.

WABER, D. P. 1979. Cognitive abilities and sex-related variations in the maturation of cerebral cortical functions. In Wittig, M. A., and Petersen, A. C. (Eds.), *Sex-related differences in cognitive functioning,* pp. 161–89. New York: Academic Press.

WACHTEL, P. L. 1977. *Psychoanalysis and behavior therapy: Toward an integration.* New York: Basic Books.

WACHTEL, P. L. 1982. What can dynamic therapies contribute to behavior therapy? *Behavior Therapy* 13:594–609.

WADDINGTON, J. L.; TORREY, E. F.; CROW, T. J.; AND HIRSCH, S. R. 1991. Schizophrenia, neurodevelopment, and disease. *Archives of General Psychiatry* 48:271–73.

WAGNER, A. R. 1979. Habituation and memory. In Dickinson, A., and Boakes, R. A. (Eds.), *Mechanisms of learning and memory: A memorial to Jerzy Konorski,* pp. 53–82. Hillsdale, N.J.: Erlbaum.

WAGNER, D. A. 1974. The development of short-term and incidental memory: A cross-cultural study. *Child Development* 45: 389–96.

WAGNER, D. A. 1978. Memories of Morocco: The influence of age, schooling, and environment on memory. *Cognitive Psychology* 10:1–28.

WAGNER, R. K. 1987. Tacit knowledge in everyday intelligent behavior. *Journal of Personality and Social Psychology* 52:1236–47.

WAGNER, R. K., AND STERNBERG, R. J. 1987. Tacit knowledge in managerial success. *Journal of Business and Psychology* 1:301–12.

WAID, W. M., AND ORNE, M. T. 1982. The physiological detection of deception. *American Scientist* 70:402–409.

WAKEFIELD, J. C. 1992. The concept of mental disorder: On the boundary between biological facts and social values. *American Psychologist* 47(3):373–88.

WALD, G. 1950. Eye and camera. *Scientific American* 183: 32–41.

WALDFOGEL, S. 1948. The frequency and affective character of childhood memories. *Psychological Monographs,* vol. 62 (Whole No. 291).

WALKER, L. J. 1984. Sex differences in the development of moral reasoning: A critical review. *Child Development* 55:677–91.

WALKER, L. J. 1989. Sex differences in the development of moral reasoning: A reply to Baumrind. *Child Development* 57:522–26.

WALLÉN, K. 1989. Mate selection: Economics and affection. Peer commentary to aritcle by Buss, D. M. Sex differences in human mate preferences: Evolutionary hypotheses tested in 37 cultures. *Behavioral and Brain Sciences* 12:3738.

WALSTER, E.; ARONSON, E.; ABRAHAMS, D.; AND ROTTMAN, L. 1966. The importance of physical attractiveness in dating behavior. *Journal of Personality and Social Psychology* 4:508–16.

WALTERS, J. R., AND SEYFARTH, R. M. 1986. Conflict and cooperation. In Smuts, B. B.; Cheney, D. L.; Seyfarth, R. M.; Wrangham, R. W.; and Struhsaker, T. T. (Eds.), *Primate societies.* Chicago: University of Chicago Press.

WARRINGTON, E. K., AND WEISKRANTZ, L. 1978. Further analysis of the prior learning effect in amnesic patients. *Neuropsychologia* 16:169–76.

WASON, P. C. 1960. On the failure to eliminate hypotheses in a conceptual task. *Quarterly Journal of Experimental Psychology* 12: 129–40.

WASON, P. C. 1968. On the failure to eliminate hypotheses—A second look. In Wason, P. C., and Johnson-Laird, P. N. (Eds.), *Thinking and reasoning.* Harmondsworth, England: Penguin Books.

WASON, P. C., AND JOHNSON-LAIRD, P. N. 1972. *Psychology of reasoning.* London: B. T. Batsford, Ltd.

WATERS, E.; WIPPMAN, J.; AND SROUFE, L. A. 1979. Attachment, positive affect, and competence in the peer group: Two studies in construct validation. *Child Development* 50:821–29.

WATSON, C. G., AND BURANEN, C. 1979. The frequency of conversion reaction. *Journal of Abnormal Psychology* 88:209–11.

WATSON, J. B. 1925. *Behaviorism.* New York: Norton.

WATSON, J. S. 1967. Memory and "contingency analysis" in infant learning. *Merrill-Palmer Quarterly* 13:55–76.

WAUGH, N. C., AND NORMAN, D. A. 1965. Primary memory. *Psychological Review* 72:89–104.

WEBB, W. B. 1974. Sleep as an adaptive process. *Perceptual and Motor Skills* 38:1023–27.

WEBB, W. B. 1979. Theories of sleep functions and some clinical implications. In Drucker-Colin, R.; Shkurovich, M.; and Sterman, M. B. (Eds.), *The functions of sleep,* pp. 19-36. New York: Academic Press.

WEBB, W. B. 1982. Some theories about sleep and their clinical implications. *Psychiatric Annals* 11:415–22.

WECHSLER, D. 1958. *The measurement and appraisal of adult intelligence,* 4th ed. Baltimore: Williams & Wilkins.

WEHR, T. A., AND GOODWIN, F. K. 1981. Biological rhythms and psychiatry. In Arieti, S., and Brodie, H. K. H. (Eds.), *American Handbook of Psychiatry,* vol. 7, pp. 46–74. New York: Basic Books.

WEINER, R. D. 1984a. Does electroconvulsive therapy cause brain damage? (with peer commentary). *The Behavioral and Brain Sciences* 7:1–54.

WEINER, R. D. 1984b. Convulsive therapy:50 years later. *American Journal of Psychiatry* 141:1078–79.

WEINER, R. D. 1985. Convulsive therapies. In Kaplan, H. I., and Sadock, J. (Eds.), *Comprehensive textbook of psychiatry,* 4th ed. Baltimore: Williams & Wilkins.

WEINGARTNER, H., AND PARKER, E. S. (Eds.). 1984. *Memory consolidation: Psychobiology of cognition.* Hillsdale, N.J.: Erlbaum.

WEINRICH, J. D. 1987. *Sexual landscapes.* New York: Scribner's.

WEINSTOCK, S. 1954. Resistance to extinction of a running response following partial reinforcement under widely spaced trials. *Journal of Comparative and Physiological Psychology* 47:318–22.

WEISBERG, R. W., AND ALBA, J. W., 1981. An examination of the alleged role of "fixation" in the solution of several "insight" problems. *Journal of Experimental Psychology: General* 110:169–92.

WEISKRANTZ, L., AND WARRINGTON, E. K. 1979. Conditioning in amnesic patients. *Neuropsychologia* 18:177–84.

WEISS, B., AND LATIES, V. G. 1961. Behavioral thermoregulation. *Science* 133: 1338–44.

WEISSMAN, M. 1985. The epidemiology of anxiety disorders: Rates, risks, and familial patterns. In Tuma, A. H., and Maser, J. D. (Eds.), *Anxiety and the anxiety disorders,* pp. 275–96. Hillsdale, N.J.: Erlbaum.

WEISSMAN, M., AND BOYD, J. H. 1985. Affective disorders: Epidemiology. In Kaplan, H. I., and Sadock, J. (Eds.), *Modern synopsis of comprehensive textbook of psychiatry,* 4th ed. Baltimore: Williams & Wilkins.

WEISSTEIN, N., AND WONG, E. 1986. Figure-ground organization and the spatial and temporal responses of the visual system. In Schwab, E. C., and Nusbaum, H. C. (Eds.), *Pattern recognition by humans and machines,* vol. 2. New York: Academic Press.

WEISZ, J. R.; ROTHBAUM, F. M.; AND BLACKBURN, T. C. 1984. Standing out and standing in: The psychology of control in American and Japan. *American Psychologist* 39:955–69.

WELCH, C. A.; WEINER, R. D.; WEIR, D.; CAHILL, J. F.; ROGERS, H. J.; DAVIDSON, J.; MILLER, R. D.; AND MANDEL, M. R. 1982. Efficacy of ECT in the treatment of depression: Wave form and electrode placement considerations. *Psychopharmacological Bulletin* 18:31–34.

WELLMAN, H. M. 1990. *The child's theory of mind.* Cambridge, Mass.: MIT Press.

WELLMAN, H. M., AND BARTSCH, K. 1988. Young children's reasoning about beliefs. *Cognition* 30:239–77.

WELLMAN, H. M.; RITTER, K.; AND FLAVELL, J. H. 1975. Deliberate memory behavior in the delayed reactions of very young children. *Developmental Psychology* 11:780–87.

WENDER, P. H.; KETY, S. S.; ROSENTHAL, D.; SCHULSINGER, F.; AND ORTMANN, J. 1986. Psychiatric disorders in the biological relatives of adopted individuals with affective disorders. *Archives of General Psychiatry* 43:923–29.

WERKER, J. 1991. The ontogeny of speech perception. In Mattingly, I. G., and Studdert-Kennedy, M. (Eds.), *Modularity and the motor theory of speech perception: Proceedings of a conference to honor Alvin M. Liberman,* pp. 91–109. Hillsdale, N. J.: Erlbaum.

WERKER, J., AND TEES, R. 1984. Cross-language speech perception: Evidence for perceptual reorganization during the first year of life. *Infant Behavior and Development* 7:49–63.

WERTHEIMER, MAX. 1912. Experimentelle Studien über das Gesehen von Bewegung. *Zeitschrift frPsychologie* 61:161–265.

WERTHEIMER, MAX. 1923. Untersuchungen zur Lehre von der Gestalt, II. *Psychologische Forschung* 4:301–50.

WERTHEIMER, MICHAEL. 1961. Psychomotor coordination of auditory and visual space at birth. *Science* 134:1692.

WEST, S. G.; WHITNEY, G.; AND SCHNEDLER, R. 1975. Helping a motorist in distress: The effects of sex, race, and neighborhood. *Journal of Personality and Social Psychology,* 31:691–98.

WESTERMEYER, J. 1987. Public health and chronic mental illness. *American Journal of Public Health* 77:667–68.

WETZEL, M., AND STUART, D. G. 1976. Ensemble characteristics of cat locomotion and its neural control. *Progress in Neurobiology* 7:1–98.

WHEELER, L.; REIS, H.; AND BOND, M. H. 1989. Collectivism-individualism in everyday social life: The middle kingdom and the melting pot. *Journal of Personality and Social Psychology* 57:79–86.

WHEELER, L. R. 1942. A comparative study of the intelligence of East Tennessee mountain children. *Journal of Educational Psychology* 33:321–34.

WHITE, G. L. 1980. Physical attractiveness and courtship progress. *Journal of Personality and Social Psychology* 39:660–68.

WHITE, S. H., AND PILLEMER, D. B. 1979. Childhood amnesia and the development of a functionally accessible memory system. In Kihlstrom, J. F., and Evans, F. J. (Eds.), *Functional disorders of memory.* Hillsdale, N.J.: Erlbaum.

WHITING, J. W. M., AND WHITING, B. B. 1975. *Children of six cultures: A psychocultural analysis.* Cambridge, Mass.: Harvard University Press.

WHITLOW, J. W., JR., AND WAGNER, A. R. 1984. Memory and habituation. In Peeke, H. V. S., and Petrinovich, L. (Eds.), *Habituation, sensitization, and behavior*, pp. 103–53. New York: Academic Press.

WICKELGREN, W. A. 1974. *How to solve problems.* San Francisco: Freeman.

WICKER, A. W. 1969. Attitudes versus action: The relationship of verbal and overt behavioral responses to attitude objects. *Journal of Social Issues* 25:41–78.

WIENS, A. N., AND MENUSTIK, C. E. 1983. Treatment outcome and patient characteristics in an aversion therapy program for alcoholism. *American Psychologist* 38:1089–96.

WIESENTHAL, D. L.; ENDLER, N. S.; COWARD, T. R.; AND EDWARDS, J. 1976. Reversibility of relative competence as a determinant of conformity across different perceptual tasks. *Representative Research in Social Psychology* 7:319–42.

WILCOXIN, H. C.; DRAGOIN, W. B.; AND KRAL, P. A. 1971. Illness-induced aversions in rat and quail: Relative salience of visual and gustatory cues. *Science* 171: 826–28.

WILLIAMS, C. D. 1959. The elimination of tantrum behavior by extinction procedures. *Journal of Abnormal and Social Psychology* 59:269.

WILLIAMS, G. C. 1966. *Adaptation and natural selection.* Princeton, N.J.: Princeton University Press.

WILLIAMS, H. L.; TEPAS, D. I.; AND MORLOCK, H. C. 1962. Evoked responses to clicks and electroencephalographic stages of sleep in man. *Science* 138:685–86.

WILLIAMS, M. D., AND HOLLAN, J. D. 1982. The process of retrieval from very long-term memory. *Cognitive Science* 5:87–119.

WILLIAMS, R. B. 1987. Psychological factors in coronary artery disease: Epidemiological evidence. *Circulation* 76 (suppl I) 117–23.

WILLIAMS, W. L. 1986. *The spirit and the flesh: Sexual diversity in American Indian culture.* Boston: Beacon Press.

WILSON, D. H.; REEVES, A. G.; GAZZANIGA, M. S.; AND CULVER, C. 1977. Cerebral commissurotomy for the control of intractable seizures. *Neurology* 27:708–15.

WILSON, E. O. 1975. *Sociobiology.* Cambridge, Mass.: Harvard University Press.

WILSON, E. O. 1978. *On human nature.* Cambridge, Mass; Harvard University Press.

WILSON, G. 1985. *The psychology of the performing arts.* London and Sydney: Croom Helm.

WILSON, G. T. 1980. Behavior modification and the treatment of obesity. In Stunkard, A. J. (Ed.), *Obesity*, pp. 325–44. Philadelphia: Saunders.

WILTSCHKO, R.; NORH, D.; AND WILTSCHKO, W. 1981. Pigeons with a deficient sun compass use the magnetic compass. *Science* 214:34–45.

WIMMER, H., AND PERNER, J. 1983. Beliefs about beliefs: Representation and constraining function of wrong beliefs in young children's understanding of deception. *Cognition* 13:103–28.

WINCHESTER, A. M. 1977. *Genetics*, 5th ed. Boston: Houghton Mifflin.

WINCH, R. F., AND MORE, D. M. 1956. Does TAT add information to interviews? Statistical analysis of the increment. *Journal of Clinical Psychology* 12:316–21.

WINSLOW, J. T., AND INSEL, T. R. 1990. Neurobiology of obsessive-compulsive disorder: A possible role for serotonin. *Journal of Clinical Psychiatry* 51(Supplement): 27–31.

WINTER, R. 1976. *The smell book: Scents, sex, and society.* Philadelphia: Lippincott.

WISHNER, J. 1960. Reanalysis of "impressions of personality." *Psychological Review* 67:96–112.

WITTGENSTEIN, L. 1953. *Philosophical investigations.* Trans. by Anscombe, G. E. M. Oxford, England: Blackwell.

WOLF, M. E., AND MOSNAIM, A. D. 1990. *Post-traumatic stress disorder: Etiology, phenomenology, and treatment.* Washington, D.C.: American Psychiatric Press.

WOLLEN, K. A.; WEBER, A.; AND LOWRY, D. 1972. Bizarreness versus interaction of mental images as determinants of learning. *Cognitive Psychology* 3:518–23.

WOLPE, J. 1958. *Psychotherapy by reciprocal inhibition.* Stanford, Calif.: Stanford University Press.

WOLPERT, E. A., AND TROSMAN, H. 1958. Studies in psychophysiology of dreams: I. Experimental evocation of sequential dream episodes. *Archives of Neurology and Psychiatry* 79:603–606.

WOOD, A. J., AND GOODWIN, G. M. 1987. A review of the biochemical and neuropharmacological actions of lithium. *Psychological Medicine* 17: 579–600.

WOODRUFF, G., AND PREMACK, D. 1979. Intentional communication in the chimpanzee: The development of deception. *Cognition* 7: 333–62.

WOODWORTH, R. S. 1938. *Experimental Psychology.* New York: Henry Holt and Co.

WYERS, E. J.; PEEKE, H. V. S.; AND HERZ, M. J. 1973. Behavioral habituation in invertebrates. In Peeke, H. V. S., and Herz, M. J. (Eds.), *Habituation: Vol. 1. Behavioral studies.* New York: Academic Press.

YAGER, D. D., AND HOY, R. R. 1986. The Cyclopean ear: A new sense for the Praying Mantis. *Science* 231:727–29.

YAGER, D. D., AND MAY, M. L. 1990. Ultrasound-triggered, flight-gated evasive maneuvers in the Praying Mantis *Parasphendale agrionina. Journal of Experimental Biology* 152:41–58.

YANDO, R.; SEITZ, V.; AND ZIGLER, E. 1978. I*mitation: A developmental perspective.* Hillsdale, N.J.: Erlbaum.

YANG, K., AND BOND, M. H. 1990. Exploring implicit personality theories with indigenous or imported constructs: The Chinese case. *Journal of Personality and Social Psychology* 58:1087–95.

YARBUS, A. L. 1967. Eye movements and vision. Trans. by Riggs, L. A. New York: Plenum Press.

YARROW, L. J. 1961. Maternal deprivation: Toward an empirical and conceptual reevaluation. *Psychological Bulletin* 58:459–90.

YERKES, R. M., AND MORGULIS, S. 1909. Method of Pavlov in animal psychology. *Psychological Bulletin* 6:264.

YONAS, A. 1981. Infants' response to optical information for collision. In Aslin, R. N.; Alberts, J. R.; and Petersen, M. R. (Eds.), *Development of perception*, pp. 313–34. New York: Academic Press.

YUSSEN, S. R., AND LEVY, V. M. 1975. Developmental changes in predicting one's own span of memory. *Journal of Experimental Child Psychology* 19: 502–508.

ZAJONC, R. B. 1965. Social facilitation. *Science* 149:269–74.

ZAJONC, R. B. 1968. Attitudinal effects of mere exposure. *Journal of Personality and Social Psychology Monograph Supplement* 9:1–27.

ZAJONC, R. B. 1980. Copresence. In Paulus, P. (Ed.), *The psychology of group influence.* Hillsdale, N.J.: Erlbaum.

ZARAGOZA, M. S., AND McCLOSKEY, M. 1989. Misleading postevent information and the memory impairment hypothesis: Comment on Belli and reply to Tversky and Tuchin. *Journal of Experimental Psychology: General* 118:92–99.

ZEIGLER, H. P., AND LEIBOWITZ, H. 1957. Apparent visual size as a function of distance for children and adults. *American Journal of Psychology* 70:106–109.

ZENTALL, T., AND HOGAN, D. 1974. Abstract concept learning in the pigeon. *Journal of Experimental Psychology* 102:393–98.

ZIEGLER, F. J.; IMBODEN, J. B.; AND RODGERS, D. A. 1963. Contemporary conversion reactions: III. Diagnostic considerations. *Journal of the American Medical Association* 186:307–11.

ZIGLER, E., AND BERMAN, W. 1983. Discerning the future of early childhood intervention. *American Psychologist* 38:894–906.

ZIGLER, E., AND CHILD, I. L. 1969. Socialization. In Lindzey, G., and Aronson, E. (Eds.), *The handbook of social psychology*, vol. 3, pp. 450–589. Reading, Mass.: Addison-Wesley.

ZIGLER, E. F.; LAMB, M. E.; AND CHILD, I. L. 1982. *Socialization and personality development,* 2nd ed. New York: Oxford University Press.

ZILBOORG, G., AND HENRY, G. W. 1941. *A history of medical psychology.* New York: Norton.

ZIMBARDO, P. G. 1969. The human choice: Individuation, reason, and order versus deindividuation, impulse and chaos. In Arnold, W. J. and Levine, E. (Eds.), *Nebraska Symposium on Motivation,* pp. 237–308. Lincoln, Neb.: University of Nebraska Press.

ZOHAR, J.; INSEL, T.; ZOHAR-KADOUCH, R. C.; HILL, J. L.; AND MURPHY, D. 1988. Serotonergic responsivity in obsessive-compulsive disorder. Effects of chronic clomipramine treatment. *Archives of General Psychiatry* 45:167–72.

ZORILLA, L.T. E., AND CANNON, T. D. 1995. Structural brain abnormalities in schizophrenia: Distribution, etiology, and implications. In Mednick, S. A. (Ed.), *Neural development in schizophrenia: Theory and research.* New York: Plenum Press.

ZUBIN, J.; ERON, L. D.; AND SHUMER, F. 1965. *An experimental approach to projective techniques.* New York: Wiley.

ZUCKERMAN, M. 1979. *Sensation seeking: Beyond the optimum level of arousal.* Hillsdale, N.J.: Erlbaum.

ZUCKERMAN, M. 1983. A biological theory of sensation seeking. In Zuckerman, M. (Ed.), *Biological bases of sensation seeking, impulsivity, and anxiety.* Hillsdale, N.J.: Erlbaum.

ZUCKERMAN, M. 1987. All parents are environmentalists until they have their second child. Peer commentary on Plomin, R., and Daniels, D. Why are children from the same family so different from one another? *Behavioral and Brain Sciences* 10:38–39.

ZUCKERMAN, M.; BALLENGER, J. C.; JIMERSON, D. C.; MURPHY, D. L.; AND POST, R. M. 1983. A correlational test in humans of the biological models of sensation seeking and anxiety. In Zuckerman, M. (Ed.), *Biological bases of sensation seeking, impulsivity, and anxiety,* pp. 229–48. Hillsdale, N.J.: Erlbaum.

ZUGER, B. 1984. Early effeminate behavior in boys. *Journal of Nervous and Mental Disease* 172:90–96.

ACKNOWLEDGMENTS AND COPYRIGHTS

FIGURES

Chapter 1: **1.1** Courtesy of Kaiser Porcelain Ltd. **1.2A,B,C** Bugelski, B. R., and Alampay, D. A., The role of frequency in developing perceptual sets, *Canadian Journal of Psychology* 15 (1961): 205-11. Adapted by permission of the Canadian Psychological Association. **1.3A** Courtesy of Richard D. Walk. **1.3B** Courtesy of William Vandivert. **1.4A** Photograph by Ed Reschke/Peter Arnold, Inc. **1.4B** Photograph by David Gillison/Peter Arnold, Inc. **1.4C** Photograph by Fred Bavendam/Peter Arnold, Inc. **1.5A** Photograph by George H. Harrison/Grant Heilman. **1.5B** Photograph by Peter Hendrie/ The Image Bank.

Chapter 2: **2.1** Photograph by Cabisco/Visuals Unlimited. **2.2B** Photograph by Dr. John Mazziotta, UCLA School of Medicine/Science Photo Library/Photo Researchers. **2.4B** Photograph by Manfred Kage/Peter Arnold, Inc. **2.5C** © Guigoz/Dr. A. Privat/Petit Format/Science Source/ Photo Researchers. **2.9** Eccles, J. C., *The Understanding of the Brain*. New York: McGraw-Hill, 1973. Adapted by permission of McGraw-Hill, Inc. **2.14** Lewis, E. R., Everhart, T. E., and Seevi, Y. Y., Studying neural organization in aplysia with the scanning electron microscope, *Science* 165 (12 September 1969): 1140-43. Copyright 1969 by the American Association for the Advancement of Science. Reprinted by permission of the publisher and the author. **2.15** Bloom, F. E., Lazerson, A., and Hofstadter, L., *Brain, Mind and Behavior*. New York: Freeman, 1988. Adapted by permission of WNET/Thirteen. **2.16** *Physiological Psychology*, 2nd ed., by Mark Rosenzweig and Arnold Leiman. Copyright © 1989 by Random House. Reprinted by permission of McGraw-Hill. **2.18** Roeder, K., *Nerve Cells and Insect Behavior*. Cambridge, Mass.: Harvard University Press, 1972, p. 198. Adapted by permission of Harvard University Press. **2.19** Bloom, F. E., Lazerson, A., and Hofstadter, L., *Brain, Mind and Behavior*. New York: Freeman, 1988. Adapted by permission of WNET/Thirteen. **2.20** Lickley, J. D., *The Nervous System*. Essex, England: Longman, 1919. Reprinted by permission of the publisher. **2.21A** Photograph by Biophoto Associates/Photo Researchers. **2.21B** Keeton, W. T., *Biological Science*, 3rd ed. New York: W. W. Norton & Company, Inc., 1980. Copyright © 1980, 1979, 1972, 1967 by W. W. Norton & Company, Inc. Used with permission. **2.24** Bloom, F. E., Lazerson, A., and Hofstadter, L., *Brain, Mind and Behavior*. New York: Freeman, 1988. Adapted by permission of WNET/Thirteen. **2.25** Adapted with permission of Macmillan Publishing Co., Inc., from *The Cerebral Cortex of Man* by Wilder Penfield and Theodore Rasmussen. Copyright © 1950 by Macmillan Publishing Co., Inc., renewed 1978 by Theodore Rasmussen. **2.26** Cobb, S., *Foundations of Neuropsychiatry*. Baltimore, Md.: William & Wilkins, 1941. © 1941, the Williams & Wilkins Co., Baltimore. Adapted by permission of the publisher. **2.27** Photograph by Simon Fraser/Science Photo Library/Photo Researchers. **2.28** NIH/SPL/Photo Researchers. **2.29** Photograph by Dr. John Mazziotta et al./Photo Researchers. **2.30** Photograph © Paul Shambroom. **2.31** From *Higher Cortical Functions in Man* by Aleksandr Romanovich Luria. Copyright © 1966, 1979 Consultants Bureau Enterprises, Inc., and Basic Books, Inc. Reprinted by permission of Basic Books, Inc., New York. **2.32** Photograph by M. Sakka, courtesy Musée de l'Homme et Musée Depuytren, Paris. **2.35** Gazzaniga, M. S., The split brain in man, *Scientific American* 217 (August 1967): 25. Copyright © 1967 by Scientific American, Inc. All rights reserved. Drawing by Maura Conron.

Chapter 3: **3.3** Keeton, W. T., and Gould, J. L., *Biological Science*, 4th edition. New York: W. W. Norton & Company, Inc., 1986. Copyright © 1986, 1980, 1979, 1972, 1967 by W. W. Norton & Company, Inc. **3.4** Weiss, B., and Laties, V. G., Behavioral thermoregulation, *Science* 133 (28 April 1961): 1338-44, Fig 1. Copyright 1961 by the American Association for the Advancement of Science. Reproduced by permission of the AAAS and the author. **3.6B** Courtesy Neal E. Miller, Rockefeller University. **3.7** Adapted from Bouchard, C., Tremblay, A., Desprès, J.-P., Nadeau, A., Lupien, P. L., Thèriault, G., Dussault, J., Moorjani, S., Pinault, S. M., and Fournier, G., The response to long-term overfeeding in identical twins, *New England Journal of Medicine* 322 (1990): 1477-82. Reprinted by permission of the New England Journal of Medicine. **3.8** Herman, H. C., and Mack, D., Restrained and unrestrained eating, *Journal of Personality* 43 (1975): 647-60. Adapted by permission of Duke University Press. **3.9** Andres, R., Influence of obesity on longevity in the aged, in Borek, C., Fenoglio, C. M., and King, D. W. (Eds.), *Aging, Cancer, and Cell Membranes*, pp. 230-46. New York: Thieme-Stratton, 1980. **3.10** Reprinted by permission of Hawthorne Properties (Elsevier-Dutton Publishing Co., Inc.) from *Bodily Changes in Pain, Hunger, Fear and Rage* by W. B. Cannon. Copyright © 1929 by Appleton-Century Co.; 1957 by W. B. Cannon. **3.11** © Walter Chandoha, 1994. **3.12A** Photograph by Mary Shuford. **3.12B** Inbau, F. E., and Reid, J. E., *The Polygraph ("Lie Detector") Technique*, 2nd ed. Baltimore, Md.: Williams & Wilkins, 1977. © Professor Fred E. Inbau. **3.13** Adapted from Keeton, W. T., and Gould, J. L., *Biological Science*, 4th ed. New York: W. W. Norton, 1986. Copyright © 1986, 1980, 1979, 1972, 1967 by W.W. Norton & Company, Inc. Used with permission. **3.14** Adapted from Bloom, F. E., Lazerson, A., and Hofstadter, L., *Brain, Mind, and Behavior*. New York: Freeman, 1988. Adapted by permission of WNET/Thirteen. **3.15A** Blakemore, C., *Mechanics of the Mind*, p. 42. New York: Cambridge University Press, 1977. Reprinted by permission of the publisher. **3.15B** Photograph © Pierre Boulat/Woodfin Camp & Associates. **3.18** Courtesy of William C. Dement. **3.19** Adapted from Kleitman, N., Patterns of dreaming, *Scientific American* 203 (November 1960): 82-88. Copyright © 1960 by Scientific American, Inc. All rights reserved. **3.20** Carlson, N. R., *Psychology of Behavior*, 4th ed., p. 295. Boston: Allyn & Bacon, 1991; graph courtesy of S. T. Inoueye. **3.21** Photograph courtesy of the University of Wisconsin Primate Laboratory. **3.22** Courtesy of Dr. M. E. Olds.

Chapter 4: **4.1** Hoffman, H. S., and Fleshler, M., An apparatus for measurement of the startle response in the rat, *American Journal of Psychology* 77 (1964): 307-308. Copyright © 1964 by the Board of Trustees of the University of Illinois. Used with permission of the University of Illinois Press. **4.11** Photograph by Susan M. Hogue. **4.13** From *A Primer of Operant Conditioning* by G. S. Reynolds. Copyright © 1968 by Scott, Foresman & Co. Reprinted by permission. **4.14A** Photograph courtesy of Animal Behavior Enterprises, Inc. **4.14B** Photograph by Gerald Davis/Contact Press Images. **4.15** Courtesy Yerkes Regional Primate Research Center of Emory University. **4.17** Ferster, C. B., and Skinner, B. F., *Schedules of Reinforcement*, pp. 56, 399. Englewood Cliffs, N.J.: Prentice-Hall, Inc., 1957. Adapted by permission of the author. **4.21** Spooner, A., and Kellogg, W. N., The backward conditioning curve, *American Journal of Psychology* 60 (1947): 321-34. Copyright © 1947 by Board of Trustees of the University of Illinois. Used with permission of the publisher,

The University of Illinois Press. **4.22** Rescorla, R. A., Predictability and number of pairings in Pavlovian fear conditioning, *Psychonomic Science* 4 (1966): 383-84. **4.24** Colwill, R. M., and Rescorla, R. A., Postconditioning devaluation of a reinforcer affects instrumental responding, *Journal of Experimental Psychology: Animal Behavior Processes* 11 (1985): 120-32. Copyright 1985 by the American Psychological Association. Updated by permission of the American Psychological Association and the authors. **4.26** Maier, S. F., Seligman, M. E. P., and Solomon, R. L., Pavlovian fear conditioning and learned helplessness: Effects on escape and avoidance behavior of (a) the CS-US contingency and (b) the independence of the US and voluntary responding, in Campbell, B. A., and Church, R. M. (Eds.), *Punishment and Aversive Behavior*, © 1969, p. 328. Adapted by permission of Prentice-Hall, Inc., Englewood Cliffs, N.J. **4.28** Olton, D. S., and Samuelson, R. J., Remembrance of places passed: Spatial memory in rats, *Journal of Experimental Psychology: Animal Behavior Processes* 2 (1976): 97-116. Copyright 1976 by the American Psychological Association. Reprinted by permission. **4.32** Figure adapted from *Why Chimps Can Read* by A. J. Premack. Copyright © 1976 by Ann J. Premack. Reprinted by permission of HarperCollins Publishers. Drawing by Maura Conron. **4.33** Premack, D., and Woodruff, G., Chimpanzee problem-solving: A test for comprehension, *Science* 202 (3 November 1978): 533-34. Copyright 1978 by the American Association for the Advancement of Science.

Chapter 5: 5.1 Drawing by Maura Conron. **5.2** *The School of Athens* by Raphael, 1505; Stanza della Segnatura, Vatican; courtesy Scala/Art Resource, New York. **5.3A** Krech, D., and Crutchfield, R., *Elements of Psychology*. New York: Knopf, Inc., 1958. Adapted by permission of Hilda Krech. **5.3B** Adapted from *Biological Psychology*, 2nd ed., by James W. Kalat. © 1984 by Wadsworth, Inc. **5.4** Adapted from Carlson, N. R., *Physiology of Behavior*, 3rd ed. Boston: Allyn and Bacon, 1986. Reproduced by permission of the publisher. **5.5** Gibson, James J., *The Senses Considered as Perceptual Systems*, p. 80, Fig. 5.4. Boston: Houghton Mifflin Company, 1966. Reprinted by permission of the publisher. **5.6, 5.7A, 5.8A** Lindsay, P. H., and Norman, D. A., *Human Information Processing*, 2nd edition, pp. 126, 133, and 136. New York: Academic Press, 1977. Adapted by permission of the author and Harcourt Brace Jovanovich. **5.7B, 5.8B, 5.10** Coren, S., and Ward, L. M., *Sensation and Perception*, 3rd ed. San Diego: Harcourt Brace Jovanovich, 1989. Adapted by permission of the author and publisher. **5.9** Wald, G., Eye and camera, *Scientific American* 183 (August 1950): 33. Copyright © 1950 by Scientific American, Inc. All rights reserved. **5.11** Cornsweet, T. M., *Visual Perception*. New York: Academic Press, 1970. Adapted by permission of the author and Harcourt Brace Jovanovich. **5.13** Hering, E., *Outlines of a Theory of the Light Sense*, 1920 (translated by Hurvich, L. M., and Jameson, D., 1964), pp. 150-51. Cambridge, Mass.: Harvard University Press, 1964. Adapted by permission of Harvard University Press. **5.17** Hurvich, L. M., *Color Vision*. Sunderland, Mass.: Sinauer Associates, 1981. Reproduced by permission of Sinauer Associates. **5.19 and 5.20** Courtesy of Munsell Color, 2441 N. Calvert Street, Baltimore, Md., 21218. **5.23** Detail and full use of Georges Seurat's *The Channel of Gravelines (Petit Fort Philippe)*, 1890, oil on canvas. © 1994 Indianapolis Museum of Art, gift of Mrs. James W. Fesler in memory of Daniel W. and Elizabeth C. Marmon. **5.29** DeValois, R. L., and DeValois, K. K., *Neural Coding of Color*, in Carterette, E. C., and Friedman, M. P., (Eds.), *Handbook of Perception*, vol. 5. New York: Academic Press, 1975. Adapted by permission of the publisher. **5.31** Hubel, D. H., The visual cortex of the brain, *Scientific American* 209 (November 1963): 54-58. Copyright © 1963 by Scientific American, Inc. All rights reserved. **5.32** Drawing by Maura Conron.

Chapter 6: 6.1 Julian Hochberg, *Perception*, 2nd ed., 1978, p 56. Adapted by permission of Prentice-Hall, Inc., Englewood Cliffs, N.J. **6.2** Photograph by Roberta Intrater. **6.5A** Photograph by Geoff Dore/© Tony Stone Worldwide. **6.5B** Photograph © G. R. Roberts. **6.6** Figures 40 and 41 from *The Perception of the Visual World* by James J. Gibson. Copyright © 1978, 1950 by Houghton Mifflin Company. Used with permission. **6.7** Coren, S., and Ward, L. M., *Sensation and Perception*, 3rd ed. San Diego: Harcourt Brace Jovanovich. Adapted by permission of the author and Harcourt Brace Jovanovich. Drawing by Maura Conron. **6.9** Duncker, K., Uber induzierte Bewegung, *Psychologische Forschung* 12 (1929): 180-259. Adapted by permission of Springer-Verlag, Inc., Heidelberg. **6.10** Landau, B., Where's what and what's where: The language of objects in space. In Gleitman, L. R., and Landau, B. (Eds.), Lexical acquisition. *Lingua (Special Issue)* 92 (1994): 259-96. Drawing by Maura Conron. **6.13A** Photograph by Jeffery Grosscup. **6.16** Salvador Dali's *The Trojan War*; courtesy Esquire. **6.18** Beck, J., Effect of orientation and shape similarity on perceptual grouping, *Perception and Psychophysics* 1 (1966): 300-302. Reprinted by permission of the Psychonomic Society, Inc. **6.20** Köhler, W., *Gestalt Psychology*. New York: Liveright Publishing Company, 1947. Adapted by permission of the publisher. **6.21A** Photograph by Larry Downing/Woodfin Camp & Associates.

6.21B Photograph © Michael Fogden/Oxford Scientific Films. **6.23** Kanizsa, G., Subjective Contours, *Scientific American* 234 (1976): 48-52. Copyright 1976 by Scientific American, Inc. All rights reserved. **6.25** Boring, E. G., A new ambiguous figure, *American Journal of Psychology* 42 (1930): 444-45; and Leeper, R. W., A study of a neglected portion of the field of learning: The development of sensory organization. *Journal of Genetic Psychology* 46 (1935): 41-75. Reproduced by permission of Lucy D. Boring. **6.26** Selfridge, O. G., Pattern recognition and modern computers, in *Proceedings of Western Joint Computer Conference*, Los Angeles, Calif., 1955. **6.27** *Pintos* by Bev Doolittle, © 1979, The Greenwich Workshop, Inc. Reproduced with the permission of The Greenwich Workshop, Inc. **6.28** Penrose, L. S., and Penrose, R., Impossible objects: A special type of visual illusion, *British Journal of Psychology* 49 (1958): 31-33. Reprinted by permission of the British Psychological Society. **6.29 and 6.30** Yarbus, A. L., *Eye Movements and Vision*, pp. 179-85. Translated by Riggs, R. A. New York: Plenum Press, 1967. Copyright 1967 by Plenum Press. Reprinted by permission of the publisher. **6.32 and 6.33** Photographs by Jeffrey Grosscup. **6.34** Gibson, James J., *The Perception of the Visual World*. Copyright 1978, 1950 by Houghton Mifflin Company. Used with permission. **6.35** Drawing by Maura Conron. **6.36** Courtesy of The Metropolitan Museum of Art. **6.37** *The Annunciation* by Crivelli; courtesy The National Gallery, London. **6.38** *La Cathédrale de Rouen* by Claude Monet (1893), courtesy Le Musée d'Orsay; © photograph R.M.N. **6.39** Pablo Picasso, *Violin and Grapes*. Céret and Sorgues (spring-early fall 1912), oil on canvas, 20 x 24"; collection, The Museum of Modern Art, New York. Mrs. David M. Levy Bequest. **6.40** Giorgio de Chirico, *The Enigma of a Day*, 1914, oil on canvas, 185.5 x 139.7 cm; The Museum of Modern Art, New York, James Thrall Soby Bequest. Photograph © 1994 The Museum of Modern Art, New York.

Chapter 7: 7.1 Adapted from Waugh, N. C., and Norman, D. A., Primary memory, *Psychological Review* 72 (1965): 89-104. Copyright 1965 by the American Psychological Association. **7.2 and 7.4** Adapted from Murdock, B., The serial position effect of free recall, *Journal of Experimental Psychology* 64 (1962): 482-88. Copyright 1962 by the American Psychological Association. Reprinted by permission of the American Psychological Association and the author. **7.3** Glanzer, M., and Cunitz, A., Two storage mechanisms in free recall, *Journal of Verbal Learning and Verbal Behavior* 5 (1966): 351-60. Adapted by permission of the author and Academic Press, Inc. **7.5** Adapted from Bower, G. H., Analysis of a mnemonic device, *American Scientist* 58 (1970): 496-510. Reprinted by permission of *American Scientist*, journal of Sigma Xi, The Scientific Research Society. Drawing by Maura Conron. **7.6** Godden, D. R., and Baddeley, A. D., Context-dependent memory in two natural environments: On land and underwater, *British Journal of Psychology* 66 (1975): 325-31. Used by permission of the British Psychological Society and the author. **7.9** Adapted from Bahrick, H. P., Semantic memory content in permastore: Fifty years of memory for Spanish learned in school, *Journal of Experimental Psychology: General* 113 (1984): 1-35. Copyright 1984 by the American Psychological Association. Used by permission of the American Psychological Association and the author. **7.10** Orne, M. T., The mechanisms of hypnotic age regression: An experimental study, *Journal of Abnormal and Social Psychology* 58 (1951): 277-99. Copyright 1951 by the American Psychological Association. **7.12A** From *Fundamentals of Human Neuropsychology*, 2nd ed., by B. Kolb and I. Q. Whishaw, Figure 20-5, p. 485. San Francisco: W.H. Freeman and Company. Copyright © 1980, 1985. **7.12B** Milner, B., Corkin, S., and Teuber, H. L., Further analysis of the hippocampal amnesic syndrome: Fourteen-year follow-up of H. M., *Psychologia* 6 (1968): 215-34.

Chapter 8: 8.1 Illustration by Marjorie Torrey; from Lewis Carroll's *Alice in Wonderland*, illustrated by Marjorie Torrey. Copyright © 1955 by Random House, Inc. Reprinted by permission of Random House, Inc. **8.2** Adapted from Kosslyn, S. M., Ball, T. M., and Reisser, V. J., Visual images preserve metric spatial information: Evidence from studies of image scanning, *Journal of Experimental Psychology: Human Perception and Performance* 4 (1978): 47-60. Copyright 1978 by the American Psychological Association. Drawing by Maura Conron. **8.10** Adapted from Duncker, K., On problem solving, *Psychological Monographs*, Whole No. 270 (1945): 1-113. **8.13** Adapted from Hearst, E., Psychology across the chessboard, in *Readings in Psychology Today*, 2nd ed., p. 24. Del Mar, Calif.: CRM Books, 1972. Reprinted by permission of McGraw-Hill, Inc. **8.18** Scheerer, M., Goldstein, K., and Boring, E. G., A demonstration of insight: The horse-rider puzzle, *American Journal of Psychology* 54 (1941): 437-38. Copyright © 1941 by Board of Trustees of the University of Illinois. Used with permission of the University of Illinois Press. **8.19** Photographs by Jeffrey Grosscup. **8.20** Drawing by Maura Conron. **8.21** Wickelgren, W. A., *How to Solve Problems*. San Francisco: Freeman, 1974. Reproduced by permission of W. H. Freeman. **8.22** Engraving by Walter H. Ruff; courtesy The Granger Collection. **8.23** Reproduced from Lewis

Carroll's *Alice in Wonderland*, original illustrations by John Tenniel; in color for this edition by Martina Selway. Secaucus, N.J.: Castle Books.

Chapter 9: **9.3** Reproduced from Lewis Carroll's *Alice in Wonderland*, original illustrations by John Tenniel; in color for this edition by Martina Selway. Secaucus, N.J.: Castle Books. **9.4** Courtesy Sharon Armstrong. **9.5A** Photograph by Philip Morse, University of Wisconsin. **9.5B** Eimas, P. D., Siqueland, E. R., Jusczyk, P., and Vigorito, J., Speech perception in infants, *Science* 171 (1971): 303-306. Copyright 1971 by the American Association for the Advancement of Science. **9.6** Drawing by Maura Conron. **9.7** Courtesy of Roberta Golinkoff. **9.9** Reproduced from *Higglety Pigglety Pop! or There Must Be More to Life* by Maurice Sendak, New York: HarperCollins. Copyright M. Sendak. **9.10** Brown, R., Cazden, C., and Bellugi-Klima, U., The child's grammar from 1 to 3, in Hill, J. P. (Ed.), *Minnesota Symposium on Child Psychology* by The University of Minnesota Press, Minneapolis. Copyright © 1969 by the University of Minnesota. **9.12** Photographs courtesy AP/Wide World Photos. **9.13** Frishberg, N., Arbitrariness and iconicity: Historical change in American Sign Language, *Language* 51 (1975): 696-719. **9.14** Drawings courtesy Noel Yovovich. **9.15** Drawings courtesy Robert Thacker. **9.17** Marler, P. R., A comparative approach to vocal learning: Song development in white crowned sparrows, *Journal of Comparative and Physiological Psychology Monograph* 71 (May 1970): (No. 2, Part 2), pp. 1-25. Copyright 1970 by the American Psychological Association. Reprinted by permission of the author. **9.18** Adapted from Johnson, J., and Newport, E., Critical period effects in second language learning: The influence of maturational state on the acquisition of English as a second language, *Cognitive Psychology* 21 (1989): 60-99. Copyright 1989 by Academic Press, Inc. Reprinted by permission of the publisher and authors. **9.19** Photographs courtesy David Premack.

Chapter 10: **10.1A** Adapted from Keeton, W. T., and Gould, J. L., *Biological Science*, 4th ed. New York: W. W. Norton & Company, 1986. Copyright © 1986, 1980, 1979, 1972, 1967 by W. W. Norton & Company, Inc. Used with permission. **10.1B** Photograph courtesy of John Sparks, BBC (Natural History). **10.2** Photograph © M. P. Kahl/DRK. **10.3** Barnett, S. A., 1963. *The Rat: A Study in Behavior*. Chicago: The University of Chicago Press. Reprinted by permission of the University of Chicago Press. **10.4** Photograph by Hans Reinhard, © Bruce Coleman, Inc., 1988. **10.5A** Photograph by Rod Williams, © Bruce Coleman, Inc., 1991. **10.5B** Photograph © Ferrero. **10.6A** Courtesy of L. T. Nash, Arizona State University. **10.6B** Courtesy of Bruce Coleman. **10.7A** © Allan D. Cruikshank, 1978/Photo Researchers. **10.7B** © J. Messerschmidt/Bruce Coleman. **10.8** Photograph by P. Craig-Cooper, Nature Photographers, Ltd. **10.9** © 1987 Garry D. McMichael/Photo Researchers. **10.10A** Photograph by Philip Green. **10.10B** Photograph by Bob and Clara Calhoun/Bruce Coleman. **10.10C** Photograph by Jeff Foott/Bruce Coleman. **10.11** Peter H. Klopfer, *An Introduction to Animal Behavior: Ethology's First Century*, 2nd ed., © 1974, p. 208. Adapted by permission of Prentice-Hall, Inc., Englewood Cliffs, N.J. **10.12** Photograph © Rudie H. Kuiter, Oxford Scientific Films. **10.13** Bermant, G., and Davidson, J. M., *Biological Bases of Sexual Behavior*. New York: Harper & Row, 1974. In turn adapted from data of Davidson, J. M., Rodgers, C. H., Smith, E. R., and Bloch, G. J., Relative thresholds of behavioral and somatic responses to estrogen, *Physiology and Behavior* 3 (1968): 227-29. Copyright 1968, Pergamon Press, PLC. **10.14A** Photograph by Francisco J. Erize/Bruce Coleman. **10.14B** Photograph © Jim Clare, Partridge Films Ltd./Oxford Scientific Films. **10.15A** John Shaw/Bruce Coleman. **10.15B** Courtesy of Ian Wyllie, Monks Wood Experiment Station. **10.16A** Lorenz, K., Die angeborenen Formen möglicher Erfahrung. *Zeitschrift Für Tierpsychologie* 5 (1943): 276. Adapted by permission of Paul Parey Verlagsbuchhandlung, Hamburg and Berlin. **10.16B** © Walt Disney Productions. **10.17** © Paul Ekman, 1971. **10.18B** Photograph © Tommy Thompson, 1992; courtesy of Florida School for the Deaf and Blind, St. Augustine, Florida. **10.19** Ekman, P., and Friesen, W. V., *Unmasking the Face*. Englewood Cliffs, N.J.: Prentice-Hall, 1975. Reprinted by permission of the author. **10.21** Wayne Lankinen/Bruce Coleman. **10.22** Georg D. Lepp/Bio-Tec Images.

Chapter 11: **11.1** Asch, S. E., Studies of independence and conformity: A minority of one against a unanimous majority, *Psychological Monographs* 70 (9, Whole No. 416), 1956. Copyright 1956 by the American Psychological Association. **11.3, 11.4, 11.5** Drawings by Maura Conron.

Chapter 12: **12.1** Drawing by Maura Conron. **12.4** Leonardo da Vinci's *La Jaconde* (Mona Lisa), Louvre, Paris; photograph courtesy of Service Photographique de la Reunion des Musées Nationaux. **12.5 and 12.6** Copyright 1965 by Stanley Milgram. From the film *Obedience*, distributed by the Pennsylvania State University, PCR.

Chapter 13: **13.1** Reproduced from Keeton, W. T., and Gould, J. L., *Biological Science*, 5th ed. New York: W. W. Norton, 1993. Copyright © 1993, 1986, 1980, 1979, 1972, 1967 by W. W. Norton & Company, Inc. Used with permission. **13.2** Liebert, R. M., Poulos, R. W., and Strauss, G. D., *Developmental Psychology*, Fig. III-10, p.81. Englewood Cliffs, N.J.: Prentice-Hall, Inc., 1974. Originally adapted from H. M. Halverston, printed by The Journal Press, 1931. Photographs by Kathy Hirsh-Pasek. **13.3** Tanner, J. M., Physical growth, in *Carmichael's Manual of Child Psychology*, 3rd ed., vol. 1, Mussen, P. H., ed., Fig. 6, p. 85. New York: John Wiley & Sons, 1970. Copyright 1970 by John Wiley & Sons. **13.4** Conel, J. L., *The Postnatal Development of the Human Cortex*, vols. 1, 3, 5. Cambridge, Mass.: Harvard University Press, 1939, 1947, 1955. **13.5** Shirley, M. M., *The First Two Years: A Study of Twenty-five Babies*, vol. II. University of Minnesota Press, Minneapolis. © 1933, 1961, University of Minnesota Press. **13.6** Photographs by Doug Goodman 1986/Monkmeyer. **13.7 and 13.9** Photographs by Chris Massey. **13.8** Photograph by Ed Boswell. **13.10** Piaget, J., and Inhelder, B., *The Child's Conception of Space*. Humanities Press International Inc., Atlantic Highlands, N.J., 1967. Adapted by permission of the publisher and Routledge & Kegan Paul Ltd. Drawing by Maura Conron. **13.11** Drawing by Maura Conron. **13.12** Photographs courtesy of Phillip Kellman. **13.13** Kellman, P. J., and Spelke, E. S., Perception of partially occluded objects in infancy, *Cognitive Psychology* 15 (1983): 483-524. Copyright 1983 by the American Psychological Association. Adapted by permission of the author. **13.14** Adapted from Baillargeon, R., Object permanence in 3½- and 4½-month-old infants, *Developmental Psychology* 23 (1987): 655-64. Used by permission of the author. **13.15** Johnson, M. H., and Morton, J., *Biology and Cognitive Development: The Case of Face Recognition*. Cambridge, Mass.: Blackwell Publishers, 1991. **13.16** Photographs courtesy of Hilary Schmidt. **13.17** Photographs courtesy of Kimberly Cassidy. **13.18A** Photograph by Pat Lynch/Photo Researchers. **13.18B** Photograph by Ray Ellis/Photo Researchers. **13.18C** Photograph by Chris Massey. **13.19** Case, R., 1978. Intellectual development from birth to adulthood: A neo-Piagetian interpretation, in Siegler, R., (Ed.), *Children's Thinking: What Develops*. Hillsdale, N.J.: Lawrence Erlbaum Associates, Inc. Reproduced by permission of Lawrence Erlbaum Associates, Inc.

Chapter 14: **14.1** Photograph by Martin Rogers/Stock, Boston. **14.2** Photograph by Suzanne Szasz. **14.4** Ainsworth, M., Blehar, M., Waters, E., and Wall, S., 1978. *Patterns of Attachment*, p. 34. Hillsdale, N.J.: Lawrence Erlbaum Associates, Inc. Reproduced by permission of Lawrence Erlbaum Associates, Inc. Drawing by Maura Conron. **14.5** Photographs courtesy Kathy Hirsh-Pasek. **14.6** Photograph by Michael Heron/Woodfin Camp. **14.7** Kohlberg, L., Development of children's orientation towards a moral order in sequence in the development of moral thought, *Vita Humana* 6 (1963): 11-36. Adapted by permission of S. Karger AG, Basel. **14.11** Tanner, J. M., Physical growth, in Mussen, P. H., (Ed.), *Carmichael's Manual of Child Psychology*, 3rd ed., vol. 1, Fig. 6, p. 85. New York: John Wiley & Sons, 1970. Reprinted by permission of the publisher. **14.12A** Photograph © Blair Seitz, 1986/Photo Researchers. **14.12B** Photograph by A. Bernhaut/Photo Researchers. **14.13A** T. Lowell/Black Star. **14.13B** © Spencer Grant/The Picture Cube. **14.13C** © Jeff Greenberg/The Picture Cube.

Chapter 15: **15.1** Reprinted with permission of Macmillan Publishing Co., Inc. from *Differential Psychology*, 3rd ed., p. 57, by Ann Anastasi. Copyright © 1958 by Macmillan Publishing Co., Inc. **15.3** Courtesy H. Douglas Pratt. **15.6** Test item from Horn Art Aptitude Inventory, 1953. Courtesy Stoelting Co., Chicago. **15.7** Sample item from the Bennett Test of Mechanical Comprehension. Copyright © 1967, 1968 by The Psychological Corporation. Reproduced by permission. All rights reserved. **15.8** Adapted by permission from the *Wechsler Adult Intelligence Scale—Revised*. Copyright © 1955, 1981 by The Psychological Corporation. All rights reserved. **15.9** SAT questions selected from *10 SAT's*, College Entrance Examinations Board (1983). Reprinted by permission of Educational Testing Service, the copyright owner of the test questions. **15.10** From the Raven Standard Progressive Matrices, by permission of J. C. Raven Limited. **15.11** Jones, H. E., and Kaplan, O. J., Psychological aspects of mental disorders in later life, in Kaplan, O. J. (Ed.), *Mental Disorders in Later Life*, 72. Stanford, Calif.: Stanford University Press, 1945. Adapted by permission of Stanford University Press. **15.12** Selfe, S. *Nadia: A Case of Extraordinary Drawing Ability in an Autistic Child*. New York: Academic Press, 1977. Reproduced by permission of Academic Press and Lorna Selfe. **15.13** Courtesy Photofest. **15.15** Based on Winchester, A. M., *Genetics*, 5th ed. Boston: Houghton Mifflin, 1977. **15.17** Drawing by Maura Conron.

Chapter 16: **16.1** Lanyon, R. I., and Goodstein, L. D., *Personality Assessment*, p. 79. New York: John Wiley & Sons, Inc., 1971. Adapted by permission of John

Wiley & Sons, Inc. **16.4** Eysnck, H. J., and Rachman, S., *The causes and cures of neurosis*, p. 16. San Diego, Calif.: Robert R. Knapp, 1965. **16.5A** Wilfong Photographic/Leo de Wys, Inc. **16.5B,C** Photographs by H. Reinhard/Bruce Coleman.

Chapter 17: **17.3** "Hierarchy of Needs" from *Motivation and Personality* by Abraham H. Maslow. Copyright 1954 by Harper & Row, Publishers, Inc. Copyright © 1970 by Abraham H. Maslow. Reprinted by permission of HarperCollins Publishers.

Chapter 18: **18.1** Negative #31568. Courtesy Department of Library Services, The American Museum of Natural History. **18.2** William Hogarth's *The Madhouse, 1735/1763*; courtesy The Bettmann Archive. **18.3** © Stock Montage, Inc. **18.5** Photograph by Bill Bridges/Globe Photos. **18.7** Nicol, S. E., and Gottesman, I. I., Clues to the genetics and neurobiology of schizophrenia, *American Scientist*, 71 (1983): 398-404. Reprinted by permission of *American Scientist*, journal of Sigma Xi, The Scientific Research Society. **18.9** Rosenthal, N. E., Sack, D. A., Gillin, J. C., Lewy, A. J., Goodwin, F. K., Davenport, Y., Mueller, P. S., Newsome, D. A., and Wehr, T. A., Seasonal affective disorder: A description of the syndrome and preliminary findings with light therapy. *Archives of General Psychiatry* 41 (1984): 72-80. Copyright 1984, American Medical Association. **18.10** Stone, A., Mental health and law: A system in transition, U.S. Department of Health, Education and Welfare, #75176, p. 7, 1975. **18.11** Hare, R. D., Temporal gradient of fear arousal in psychopaths, *Journal of Abnormal Psychology* 70 (1965): 442-45. Copyright 1965 by the American Psychological Association. Reprinted by permission of the author.

Chapter 19: **19.1A** Courtesy Historical Pictures Service. **19.1B** Courtesy National Library of Medicine. **19.1C** Culver Pictures. **19.5** Photograph by James D. Wilson/Woodfin Camp. **19.7** Gibbons R. D., Hedeker, D., Elkin, I., Waternaux, C., Kraemer, H. C., Greenhouse, J. B., Shea, M. T., Imber, S. D., Sotsky, S. M., Watkins, J. T., Some conceptual and statistical issues in analysis of longitudinal psychiatric data. Application to the NIMH treatment of Depression Collaborative Research Program dataset. *Archives of General Psychiatry*, 50 (1993), 739-50.

TABLES

14.1 Adapted from Kohlberg, L., Classification of moral judgment into levels and stages of development, in Sizer, Theodore R., *Religion and Public Education*, pp. 171-73. Copyright © 1967 Houghton Mifflin Company. Used with permission. **14.2** Erikson, E. H., *Childhood and Society*. New York: W. W. Norton & Company, Inc., 1963. Adapted by permission. **15.2** Grossman, H. J. (Ed.), *Manual on Terminology and Classification in Mental Retardation*, revised edition. Washington, D.C.: American Association on Mental Deficiency, 1983. Used with permission. **15.3** Data on twins, siblings, and children reared with biological parents from Bouchard, T. J., Jr., and McGue, M., Familial studies of intelligence: A review. *Science* 212 (1981): 1055-59. Data on adopted children from Horn, J. M., Loehlin, J. C., and Willerman, L., Intellectual resemblance among adoptive and biological relatives: The Texas Adoption Project. *Behavior Genetics* 13 (1979): 459-71. **16.2** Norman, W. T., Toward an adequate taxonomy of personality attributes: Replicated factor structure in peer nomination personality ratings, *Journal of Abnormal and Social Psychology* 66 (1963): 577. Copyright 1963 by the American Psychological Association. Adapted by permission of the author. **16.3** Adapted from Snyder, M., *Public Appearances/Private Realities*. New York: W .H. Freeman & Co., 1987.

UNNUMBERED PHOTOS AND ART

5 *Top* Stock Montage. *Bottom* The Warder Collection. *(Part Opener I)* Detail of *The Battle of the Melvian Bridge*, Stanze di Raffaello, Vatican Palace, Vatican State; courtesy Scala/Art Resource. **10** Courtesy National Library of Medicine. **17** *Top* Photograph by David M. Phillips/Visuals Unlimited. *Bottom* Courtesy National Library of Medicine. **23** *Left* Photograph by B. Malkin/Anthro-Photo. *Right* Photograph © 1992, Comstock. **41** *Left* The Science Museum/Science & Society Picture Library. *Right* Photograph by Leonard

Lessin/Peter Arnold, Inc. **46** Gift of Mrs. George von Lengerke Meyer. Courtesy Museum of Fine Arts, Boston. **49** Photograph by Jane Burton, © 1987, Bruce Coleman, Inc. **52** Photofest. **54** Pieter Bruegel The Elder, *Peasant Wedding Feast*; courtesy Kunsthistorisches Museum, Vienna. **58** *Left The Venus of Willendorf*; courtesy Naturhistorisches Museum, Vienna. *Center* Peter Paul Rubens, *The Three Graces*; © Museo del Prado, Madrid. *Right* Photograph by Mark Cardwell, Reuters/Bettmann. **59** Photograph by Jane Carter. **60** Courtesy National Library of Medicine. **68** Photograph by Grant Leduc/Monkmeyer. **70** Photographs by Takahisa Hirano/Nature Production. **71** Salvador Dali, *The Grand Paranoic*, 1936, oil on panel, 62 x 62 cm.; collection Museum Boymans-van-Beuningen, Rotterdam. **72** *Jacob's Ladder*, from the Lambeth Bible; courtesy the Archbishop of Canterbury and the Trustees of Lambeth Palace Library. **74** *Left* Georg Gerster/Comstock. *Center* Guy Sauvage, Agence Vandystadt/Photo Researchers. *Right* Photofest. **82** Photograph by Bette Splendens/Oxford Scientific Films. **84** The Bettmann Archive. **89** The Granger Collection. **91** Photograph by Nina Leen/Life Magazine, © Time Warner. **94** Photograph © Hank Morgan. **98** Photograph by Erika Stone. **99** Courtesy Psychology Department, University of California, Berkeley. **107** Courtesy of Animal Behavior Enterprises, Inc. **108** Photographs by Lincoln P. Brower. **111** Photograph by Susan Bradnam. **112** *Top* Photograph by Stephen Dalton/NHPA. *Center* Photograph by Joe MacDonald/Bruce Coleman, Inc. *Bottom* Photograph by Stephen Dalton/Photo Researchers, Inc. **114** The Warder Collection. *(Part Opener II)* Detail from Edgar Degas, *Portrait of E. Duranty*, 1879. The Burrell Collection, Glasgow Museums. **124** Courtesy National Portrait Gallery, London. **125** Detail from *The Bermuda Group* by John Smibert; courtesy Yale University Art Gallery; gift of Isaac Lothrop of Plymouth, Mass. **127** Culver Pictures, Inc., New York. **128** Photographs courtesy National Library of Medicine. **132** Photograph by Ed Reschke. **137** Photograph © RDR Productions, 1981; Rex Features USA. **138** Courtesy Nobel Stiftelsen. **139** Courtesy Dr. David D. Yager and Michael L. May; © The Company of Biologists Limited. **140** Courtesy National Library of Medicine. **148** Photographs by Fritz Goro/Life Magazine, © Time Warner, Inc. **160** Claude Monet, *Terrace at Sainte-Adresse*, oil on canvas, 38⅝ x 51⅛"; reproduced with permission of the Metropolitan Museum of Art, New York; purchased with special contributions and purchase funds given or bequeathed by friends of the Museum, 1967. **162** Courtesy E. J. Gibson. **167** Courtesy Omikron. **180** Photograph © Jeff M. Dunn. **192** Photograph by Kathy Hirsh-Pasek. **193** The Kobal Collection. **197** Detail of *Netherlandish Proverbs* by Pieter Brueghel, 1559; courtesy of Gemaldegalerie, Staatliche Museen Preuischer Kulturbesitz, Berlin. **198** Paul Cezanne, *The Cardplayers*; courtesy The Metropolitan Museum of Art, bequest of Stephen C. Clark, 1960. **201** Photofest. **207** Photograph by Suzanne Szasz. **209** *Top* Marc Chagall, *I and the Village*, 1911, oil on canvas, 63⅝ x 59⅝" (192.1 x 151.4 cm); collection, The Museum of Modern Art, New York, Mrs. Simon Guggenheim Fund. *Bottom* Photographs courtesy of The Bettmann Archive. **211** Salvador Dali, *The Persistence of Memory*, 1931, oil on canvas, 9½ x 13"; Collection, The Museum of Modern Art, New York; given anonymously. **217** *Top* Mamie Eisenhower (UPI/Bettmann); Jonas Salk (Bettmann); Adlai Stevenson (Bettmann); Nikita Khrushchev (Bettmann); Mohammed Ali (The Everett Collection/ABC); Golda Meir (Bettmann); Anwar El-Sadat (William Karel/Sygma); Betty Ford (Tony Korody/Sygma); Patty Hearst (UPI/Bettmann); Robert Bork (Michael Evans/Sygma); Walter Mondale (Bill Nation/Portland State University); Bjorn Borg (AP/Wide World). *Bottom* Marslan-Wilson, W. D., and Teuber, H. L., Memory for remote events in anterograde amnesia: Recognition of public figures from news photographs, *Neuropsychologia* 13 (1975):353-64. **224** Rembrandt's *Aristotle with a Bust of Homer*, oil on canvas, 56½ x 53¾"; courtesy The Metropolitan Museum of Art, purchased with special funds and gifts of friends of the Museum, 1961. **225** Pablo Picasso, *Portrait of Ambroise Vollard*, 1909, Pushkin Museum, Moscow; courtesy Scala/Art Resource. **240** Courtesy of Lifesmith Classic Fractals. Copyright © 1993, Lifesmith Classic Fractals, Northridge, Calif. **246** From a British National Theatre production of *Galileo* by Bertolt Brecht; photograph by Zoe Dominic. **250** *Figure 14*, Alfredo Castañeda, 1982. Courtesy Mary-Anne Martin/Fine Art, New York. **252** Photograph by John Gaps III/AP Wide World. **258** Pieter Brueghel the Elder, *Trumbau zu Babel (Tower of Babel)*; courtesy Kunsthistorisches Museum, Vienna. **259** Photograph by Leonard McCombe/Life Magazine, © Time Warner, Inc. **260** William Blake, *Adam Naming the Beasts*, courtesy The Stirling Maxwell Collection, Pollok House, Glasgow Museums & Art Galleries. **261** Henri Rousseau, *The Sleeping Gypsy*, 1897, oil on canvas, 51" x 6'7"; collection, The Museum of Modern Art, New York. Gift of Mrs. Simon Guggenheim. **265** By permission. From *Webster's Ninth New Collegiate Dictionary*. © 1990 by Merriam-Webster Inc., publisher of the Merriam-Webster® dictionaries. **266** Reproduced from Lewis Carroll's *Alice in Wonderland*, original illustrations by John Tenniel; in color for this edition by Martina Selway. Secaucus, N.J.: Castle Books. **267** *Left* Photograph by Kenneth W. Fink/Bruce Coleman. *Center* Photograph by Laura Riley/Bruce Coleman. *Right* Photograph by Des & Jen Bartlett/Bruce

NAME INDEX

Müller, Johannes, 131
Mumford, J., 65
Murray, F. B., 407
Murray, Henry, 500
Muscettola, G., 587
Muuss, R. E., 447
Mylander, C., 282

Nadel, L., 114, 208
Naigles, L., 274
Napoleon I, Emperor of France, 372, 550
Nathan, P. W., 65
Nauta, W. J. H., 14
Nebuchadnezzar, King of Babylon, 565–66
Neimeyer, G. J., 364
Neisser, U., 167, 208, 210, 214, 215
Nelson, K., 272
Nemeth, C., 367
Neugebauer, R., 567
Newcomb, T., 375
Newell, Allen, 241
Newmeyer, F., 263
Newport, E. L., 280, 286
Newton, Isaac, 239, 551
Nicholson, R. A., 627
Nida, S. A., 358
Nisbett, R. E., 57, 252, 340, 341, 508, 510, 512
Nohr, D., 139
Nolen-Hoeksema, S., 589
Norcross, J. C., 628
Norman, W. T., 193, 504
Noyes, R., 592

Odbert, H. S., 504
Odiorne, J. M., 62
O'Keefe, J., 114
Olds, James, 76, 77
Olfson, M., 608, 610
Olson, D. J., 111
Olton, D. S., 113
Olweus, D., 430
Orbell, J. M., 379
Orlansky, H., 428, 540
Orne, M. T., 63, 213, 214, 626
Ornstein, R., 40
Osler, S., 202
Osmond, H., 572
Osofsky, J. D., 430
Oster, H., 316
Ottenberg, P., 371

Paarsalu, M. E., 235
Packer, C., 322
Palmer, J. C., 213
Panzarella, R., 370
Parke, R. D., 422, 437, 438
Parker, E. S., 218
Parnas, J., 581
Pascale-Leone, J., 408
Patience, A., 554
Patterson, T., 579
Paul, G. L., 628
Paul, J. P., 441n
Pavlov, Ivan Petrovich, 83–86, 89, 93, 99, 101, 117, 126n, 406, 618
Paykel, E. S., 590
Peake, P. K., 519
Pearlstone, Z., 201
Pedersen, N., 514
Peek, H. V. S., 82
Penfield, Wilder, 1, 31, 32
Penrose, L. S., 177
Penrose, R., 177

Pepitone, A., 375, 379
Peplau, L. A., 361
Perczel, M. de, 585
Pericles, 442
Perin, C. T., 95
Permer, J., 404
Peterson, C., 517, 589
Petitto, L., 271, 289
Petty, R. E., 333, 334
Philip, Prince, 2
Piaget, Jean, 391–411, 427, 445, 532
Picard, R. S., 106
Picasso, Pablo, 186–87
Pichert, J., 211
Pierce, J., 542
Pillard, R. C., 443
Pillemer, D. B., 208, 210
Pinel, Philippe, 568
Pinker, S., 227, 276, 277, 289
Plato, 4
Plomin, R., 513, 514
Plutchik, R., 348
Poggio, G. F., 167
Poincaré, Jules Henri, 239
Poley, W., 368
Polivy, J., 57
Pomeroy, W. B., 441
Porac, C., 38
Porsolt, R. D., 588
Powley, T. L., 57
Prasada, S., 276
Premack, A., 115
Premack, David, 115, 116, 287, 288, 319, 320, 403
Preston, M., 577
Price, R. H., 510
Price-Williams, D. R., 379, 407, 411
Prince, E., 261
Prince, G., 40
Provence, S., 424
Puerto, A., 53
Putnam, F. W., 597
Putnam, K. E., 214, 264

Quay, L. C., 486, 603
Quetelet, Adolphe, 458–59, 460
Quillian, M. R., 231

Rachlin, H., 110
Rachman, S. J., 620
Radford, A., 263
Radke-Yarrow, M., 431
Raiffa, H., 376
Ramirez, M., 407
Ramu, 279
Rapoport, A., 379
Rappaport, Z. H., 614
Rasmuson, L., 514
Rasmussen, T., 32
Raven, B. H., 380
Rayner, K., 178
Reber, A. S., 363
Redl, F., 371
Reese, H. W., 445
Reeves, A. G., 38
Reich, L., 586
Reis, H., 355
Reisberg, D., 211, 225, 227, 236
Reisenzein, R., 348
Reiser, B. J., 226
Reisman, J. A., 441
Remez, R., 272
Renoir, Pierre Auguste, 58

Rescorla, Robert A., 82n, 100, 101–2, 103, 104, 273
Revlin, R., 245
Revusky, S. H., 110
Reynolds, R. I., 235
Rheingold, H. L., 431
Riecken, H., 330
Rigby, M. K., 134
Rimpau, J., 289
Rioch, 30
Rips, L. J., 231
Ritter, K., 409
Roatsch, J. F., 590
Robbin, A. A., 614
Roberts, L., 1
Robins, E., 442
Robins, L. N., 594
Robins, L. R., 603
Robinson, H. B., 469
Robinson, N. M., 469
Rock, I., 182
Rodgers, D. A., 596
Rodin, Auguste, 223
Rodin, J., 517
Rodman, H. R., 251
Roeder, K. D., 27
Roediger, H. L., III, 193, 204
Rogers, Carl, 550, 552, 622, 625–26, 632
Rogoff, B., 407
Romanes, G. J., 89
Roosevelt, Eleanor, 549, 550
Roper, T. J., 107, 111
Rorer, L. G., 501, 509
Rorschach, Hermann, 499–501
Rosch, Eleanor H., 231, 266, 267, 277
Rose, S., 323
Rose, T. L., 339
Rosen, G., 567
Rosen, L. N., 586
Rosenfeld, P., 335
Rosenman, R. H., 599
Rosenstein, M. J., 609
Rosenthal, A. M., 356
Rosenthal, D., 580
Rosenthal, D. M., 250
Rosenthal, N. E., 586
Ross, J., 200
Ross, L., 340, 341, 508
Rothbaum, F. M., 556, 558
Rousseau, Jean Jacques, 551
Rozin, Paul, 58, 107, 110, 116, 206, 216, 219, A19n
Rubens, Peter Paul, 58
Rubin, J. Z., 380
Rubin, L., 361
Rubin, Z., 355
Rumbaugh, D. M., 287
Rush, Benjamin, 607, 630
Russek, M., 54
Russell, D., 343
Russell, M. J., 135
Ryan, S. M., 106

Sabini, John, 557–58
Sackheim, H. A., 589
Sacks, O., 35
Sadler, H. H., 359
Sadock, B. J., 625
Saghir, M. T., 442
Sagi, A., 431
Sahlins, M., 323
Salinger, J. D., 448
Samuelson, R. J., 113

SUBJECT INDEX

abnormal psychology, *see* psychopathology
absolute threshold, 127
abstract concepts, in animals, 115–16
access, learning and, 116–17
accommodation, in cognitive development, 393, 407
accommodation, in vision, 141
accomodative distortions, 213
acetylcholine (ACh), 20, 22, 23
achievement test, 458
achromatic colors, 145–46
achromatic sensations, 143
acquisition phase of memory, 191
action, 5
    without awareness, 252
    directed, 45–46
    disorders of, 35
action potential, 15–16, 21
activation, 66–67
activation-synthesis hypothesis, 72
active (REM) sleep, 68, 69, 71
actor-observer difference in attribution, 341–42
acuity, of vision, 142
acupuncture, 65
adaptation, 133
    in vision, 150, 154
adaptive evolutionary perspective, 107
adaptive value of genes, 297
addiction, to drugs, 74–75
additive color mixture, 148–50
ADH (antidiuretic hormone), 51
adolescence, 445–49
    competence in, 519
    emotional turbulence in, 448, 534–35
    growth spurt in, 446
    identity seeking in, 448–49
    as transition period, 447–48
adoption studies:
    on intelligence, 484, 485
    on schizophrenia, 580–81
adrenal gland, 24, 61
adrenaline (epinephrine), 25, 61, 62
    emotional experience and, 347
adulthood, 449–51
    old age transition in, 450–51
    stages of development in, 445–46, 449–51
affective disorders, *see* mood disorders
afferent nerves, 12, 17, 27
aftereffect of visual movement, 154
afterimages, negative, 150
age:
    intelligence and, 466–67, 470–71
    mental (MA), 466
aggression:
    appeasement display and, 303

biological sources of, 297, 299–305, 554
bluffs or threat displays and, 302, 316
in boys vs. men, 509
crowd behavior and, 375
displaced, 531
dominance hierarchies and, 303
limiting of, 302–3
ritualized fighting and, 302–3
sex differences in, 300, 437, 438
between species, 300
within species, 300–305
territoriality and, 301, 304–5
use of term, 300
agnosia, 35
agonist drugs, 23
agoraphobia, 594, 618
alarm calls, 321
alcohol, 74–75
Alcoholics Anonymous, 624
alcoholism, 569, 603, 620
    amnesia and, 216
algorithms, 241–42
all-or-none law, 16
alpha males, 303
alpha waves, 67
alternative hypothesis, A22
altruism, 355–59, 546
    in animals, 320–22
    bystander effect in, 356–58
    costs of helping in, 358–59
    genuine, 359
    in humans, 322–24
    reciprocal, 322
    selfish benefits of unselfishness in, 359
    self-sacrifice and, 320–24
ambiguity:
    in altruism, 356
    context effects and, 174–75
    in language, 2, 263
    in modern art, 187–88
    in reversible figures, 2, 170
American Sign Language (ASL), 280, 281, 287
amnesia, 216–18, 252, 595
    anterograde, 216–18
    childhood, 207–8
    dissociative, 595
    retrograde, 218
amoebas, asexual reproduction in, 306
amphetamines, 23–24, 75, 76
amplitude, of sound waves, 135–36
anal character, 533, 539–40
analogies:
    problem solving and, 242
    thought and, 223–29

anal stage, 532
androgens, 309, 310, 554
angina, 599
animal behavior:
    aggression in, 299–305
    bluffs and ritualized fighting in, 302–3
    defense reactions in, 300
    displays in, 298, 302–3, 307–8, 316, 320–22
    dominance hierarchies in, 303
    insightful, 114–17
    parent-child bonding in, 313–15
    personal space in, 327
    predation in, 300
    self-sacrifice and altruism in, 320–22
    sexual, 305–15
    social cognition and, 318–20
    species-specific, 107–13, 297–98, 307–8
    territoriality in, 301
animals:
    abstract concepts in, 115–16
    camouflage of, 172
    cognition in, 100, 103–5, 113–17
    learning in humans vs., 107–13
    olfaction in, 134
    sensory equipment in, 138–39
    vision in, 153–54
animism, 9
anonymity, deindividuation and, 376
anorexia nervosa, 59, 110
ANS, *see* autonomic nervous system
antagonist drugs, 23
antagonists phenomena, 150
anterograde amnesia, 216–18
anthropology, cultural, 539, 553
antidepressants, 587, 588, 610, 613, 614, 629, 630
antidiuretic hormone (ADH), 51
antipsychotic drugs, 24, 608–10, 613, 630
antisocial personality disorder, *see* sociopathy
anxiety, 102, 630
    basic, 544–45
    castration, 534
    free-floating, 420
    and internalization of right and wrong, 430–31
    in psychosexual development, 534
    repression and, 530–31, 542–43
    separation, 421
anxiety disorders, 590–95, 611
    behavior therapy for, 618–21
    generalized, 592–93, 611
    obsessive-compulsive disorders, 573, 592, 614, 618, 620
    panic disorders, 593–94
    phobias, 88, 98, 573, 591, 618–21
anxiolytics, 611, 613, 630

pheromones in, 134–35
see also displays; language; language learning
companionate love, 364
compatibility principle, 202
compensatory education programs, 478
competencies, 516
complementary hues, 149–50
negative afterimages and, 150
compliance, social influence and, 365
compulsions, 592
computers:
artificial intelligence and, 240–43
mind as, 167
concepts:
abstract, in animals, 115–16
in abstract thought, 229
conceptual frameworks and remembering, 210–16
conceptual mental maps and knowledge, 228–29
concordance, in identical twins, 580, 581
concrete operations period, 392, 396–97
conditioned emotional response (CER), 88
conditioned reflexes, 83–85
conditioned reinforcement, 95–97
conditioned responses (CR), 86, 89
acquisition of, 85–86
defined, 85
extinction of, 86, 93, 97
muscular relaxation as, 620
reconditioning of, 97
shaping of, 94–95
conditioned stimuli (CS), 85–87, 92, 95, 99, 110, 111
belongingness and, 107–10
contingency of US and, 101–2
defined, 85
fear and, 88
learned taste aversions and, 109–10
temporal relations between US and, 100–101
conditioning:
of dogs, by Pavlov, 83–84, 86
generalized anxiety disorders and, 593
psychophysiological disorders and, 106
similarities in, among species, 112
see also behavior theory; behavior therapy; classical conditioning; instrumental conditioning
conduction, 12
within vs. between neurons, 18
cones, 142, 143
sensitivity curves for, 151
confidence intervals, A24–A25
confirmation bias, 245–47
conflict, *see* aggression; unconscious conflict
conformity, 365–67
causes of, 366
majorities and minorities in, 366–67
conjunction of features, 179
consciousness:
cognition and, 249
nonconscious and, 250–53
use of, 252–53
conservation of number and quantity, 394–95, 402, 406–7
consistency of behavior, 506–12
construct validity, 463
content morphemes, 262, 275
context effects, 174–75
contiguity, in classical conditioning, 100, 101–2, 109–10
contingency:
in classical conditioning, 101–2
in instrumental conditioning, 104–7
contours, 153

contrast:
brightness, 144–45
color, 150
lateral inhibition and, 144–45
control, 517
control groups, 611, A4
convergent evolution, 112
conversation, principles of, 260
conversion disorders, 570, 598
convulsive treatments, 614–15
coping, 545–47
cornea, 141
coronary heart disease, 599
corpus callosum, 38
correction, language learning and, 270
correct negatives, in signal-detection experiments, 129
correlation, 460–61
correlation coefficient (*r*), 460–61, A16–A17
correlation matrices, 473
correlations, A14–A18
interpretation and misinterpretation of, A17–A18
positive and negative, A14–A15, A18
variance and, A20–A21
courtship and mating rituals, 3, 307–8
of dancing flies, 307–8
of praying mantis, 26–27
creative thinking, 239–40
creativity, in language use, 258–59
credibility, persuasive communications and, 333–34
critical periods:
for imprinting, 421
for language learning, 279, 285–87
critical ratios, A22, A24
Cro-Magnons, 493
cross-cultural method, 554
crowd behavior, 4, 375–79
deindividuation and, 375–76
panic and, 4, 376–79
violence and, 375
crystallized intelligence, 470
cultural anthropology, 539, 553
culture, cultural differences, 526–27, 544–45
adolescence and, 447–48
cognitive development and, 406, 411–13
depression and, 589
emotional expression and, 317–18
family and, 540
gender roles and, 435–36, 437, 438–39, 553, 554
homosexuality and, 441–42
intelligence and, 476–77
mental tests and, 486
moral reasoning and, 434–35
old age and, 450–51
personality and, 552–60
physical attractiveness and, 58, 362–63
psychotherapy and, 626
social behavior and, 322–24
socialization and, 426–27
cupboard theory of attachment, 418–19
curare, 23
curiosity, 73
cutoff scores, 464

dancing flies, courtship and mating rituals of, 307–8
data, research:
collection of, A1, A4–A5
description of, A2–A3
interpretation of, A2, A18–A27
organization of, A1–A14

day-care centers, 423–24
deafness, language learning and, 280–82
death, 449–50
decay, of memory trace, 206
deception, in primates, 320
decibels, 136
decision making, 247–49
availability heuristic in, 248–49
cognitive shortcuts for estimating probabilities in, 247–49
representativeness heuristic in, 247–48
declarative knowledge, 219
deductive reasoning, 244–45, 247, 249
deer, alarm calls of, 321
defense mechanisms, 531–32
displacement, 531
evidence of, 542–43
isolation, 532
projection, 531
psychodynamic approach to personality and, 545–47
rationalization, 531
reaction formation, 531
repression, 528, 530–31, 534, 542–43, 546
defense reactions, 300
deferred imitation, 393
deficiency needs, 548
definitional theory of word meaning, 265–67
dehumanization of victims, 371
deindividuation, 375–76
deinstitutionalization policy, 608–10
delayed reinforcement, 95–96
delay of gratification, 518–19
delay of reward principle, 95–96
delusions, in schizophrenia, 24, 577
demonic possession, insanity as, 566–67
dendrites, 13, 21
depressant drugs, 74
depression, 583, 584–85
attributional style and, 517–18, 589
Beck's cognitive theory of, 588
convulsive treatments for, 614
drug therapies for, 587, 588, 610–11, 614, 629, 630
learned helplessness and, 105–6, 588
MMPI and, 496, 497
psychosurgery for, 614
sex differences in, 589–90
suicide and, 585
deprivation, *see* social deprivation
depth cues, 160–63
binocular, 160–61
monocular, 161–62
pictorial, 185
depth perception, 160–64
in infants, 2–3
through motion, 163
descriptive rules of language, 259
desensitization, systematic, 619–20
development, 5, 384–415
in adolescence, 445–49
in adulthood, 445–46, 449–51
characteristics of, 386
as differentiation, 386
in embryo, 386–87, 389
as growth, 386–89
human, slow rate of, 388–89
as maturation, 406
motor, 386, 389–90, 391–93
as orderly progression, 389–90
physical, 386–89
as progressive change, 386
psychosexual, 532–35, 539–40

higher-order relationships, in chimpanzees' thinking, 116
hindbrain, 28–29, 66
hippocampus, 217
histograms, A7–A8
hits, in signal-detection experiments, 129
homeostasis, 47–58, 75–76
    feeding and, 51–58
    temperature control and, 48–50
    water balance and, 51–52
"homework" assignments, 621, 622–23
homogamy, 361
homosexuality, 441–45
    causes of, 441–45
    evolution and, 443–44
    incidence of, 441–42
hormones:
    adrenaline (epinephrine), 25, 61, 62, 347
    aggression and, 301
    androgens, 309, 310, 554
    antidiuretic (ADH), 51
    behavior and, 309–10
    endocrine system and, 24–25
    estrogen, 309, 589
    estrus and, 309
    growth and, 69
    progesterone, 589
    testosterone, 301, 309
hospitals, mental, 567–68, 608, 613
hostility, 600
hues, 145–46
    complementary, 149–50
hue systems, 152
humanistic approach to personality, 495, 547–52
    empirical and conceptual difficulties in, 550
    evaluation of, 550–52
    major features of, 547–50
    positive view of human motivation in, 548–49
    protest movement in, 551–52
    self-actualization in, 549–50
    self in, 549–50
humanistic therapies, 618, 621–22, 625–26
human nature:
    Hobbes's views on, 296, 297–98, 324, 526
    humanistic view of, 547–50
    as viewed in psychoanalytic theory, 526–27, 543–44
humor, 546
humors, 506
hunger, see feeding
hyperphagia, 55
hypertension, emotional stress and, 600
hypnosis:
    dissociative disorders and, 597
    hysteria and, 527
    memory and, 213–14
hypochondriasis, 598
hypothalamus, 29–30, 77
    feeding control and, 53, 55
    homosexuality and, 443
    hormone receptors in, 309
    lateral and ventromedial regions of, 55
    in temperature control, 50
hypotheses:
    defined, 245
    perceptual, 176
hypothesis testing, A21–A25
    confidence intervals in, A24–A25
    confirmation bias in, 245–47
    conservative nature of, A26
    about means, A22–A25
    probabilistic nature of, A26
    about single scores, A21–A22

hysteria, 527–28, 570, 573, 617
    hypnosis and, 527–28
    symptoms of, 527
hysterical neurosis (conversion disorder), 570, 598

id, 529
ideas of reference, 577
identical twins, personality traits shared by, 514
identification, gender roles and, 439–40, 534
identity, adolescents' search for, 448–49
idiot (retarded) savants, 475–76
ignorance, pluralistic, 356
illusory conjunctions, 168
illusory correlations, 338–39
imagery:
    eidetic, 225–26
    mental, 225–29
    mnemonics through, 199–200
    spatial problem solving and, 227–29
image scanning, 226–27
imitation:
    in sensory-motor period, 393
    in social learning, 426–28, 440
Immigration Act (1924), 478
immune system, learned helplessness and, 106–7
impatience, 600
implicit memory, 192, 203–5, 218–19
implicit theories of personality, 338
impossible figures, 176–77
Impressionism, 185–86
impressions, 337–39
    as cognitive constructions, 337–39
    as patterns, 337
imprinting, 420–21
    sensitive period for, 421
inclusive fitness, 444
incremental validity, 502
incubation, in creative thinking, 240
individualism, 555–58
induced movement, 164
inductive reasoning, 245–47, 249
infants:
    babyness cues in, 315, 316
    beliefs in, 404
    depth perception in, 2–3
    empathy in, 431–32
    face recognition in, 399–400
    habituation in, 271–72
    imitation in, 393
    language learning in, 269–77
    manual differentiation in, 386
    motor development in, 386, 388–89, 392–93
    object perception in, 397–99
    object permanence in, 392, 393
    parent-child bond and, 313–15
    perception in, 2–3
    reared in institutions, 424
    reflexes in, 389
    response capacities of, 389
    response control in, 104
    sensory development in, 389, 392–93
    size constancy in, 183
    smiling by, 4, 315, 419, 422
    space perception in, 397–99
    temperamental differences in, 429
    see also attachment, mother-child; children; cognitive development; newborns
inferential statistics, A18–A27
    implications of, A26–A27
information processing:
    artificial intelligence and, 240–43
    cognitive development and, 408–11

form perception and, 166–67
    intelligence and, 470–71
in-groups, 556
inhibition, of neuron excitation, 19, 21
inhibitions, social, 431
initiation rites, 447
injury, feigning of, 320
inner ears, 136
    vestibules of, 131
insanity:
    use of term, 566n
    see also psychopathology
insight, 623
    in animal behavior, 114–17
    emotional, 623
insight therapy, see psychoanalysis, psychoanalytic theory
instincts, 529n
    Hobbes's and Freud's views on, 526–27
    social behavior and, 297–98
instrumental (operant) conditioning, 89–100, 618
    act-outcome relations in, 110
    arbitrariness vs. belongingness in, 107–10
    aversive stimuli in, 81, 97–99
    and biological constraints on learning, 107–10
    cats in puzzle box in, 90
    classical conditioning vs., 89, 91–93
    cognitive learning and, 99–100, 103–7
    conditioned reinforcement in, 95–97
    contingency in, 104–7
    delay of reinforcement in, 95–96
    evolution theory and, 89–90
    generalization and discrimination in, 81
    and law of effect, 90–91, 95
    major phenomena of, 92–99
    partial reinforcement effect in, 96, 97
    reinforcement schedules in, 96–97
    shaping of responses in, 94–95
    Skinner box in, 92
    socialization and, 427–28
    Thorndike's research and, 89–90
insurance companies, psychotherapy and, 628–29
intellectual aptitudes, sexual differences in, 437–38
intelligence, 456–91
    age and, 466–67, 470–71
    artificial, 240–43
    culture and, 476–77
    definitions of, 464–65
    early social deprivation and, 425
    fluid vs. crystallized, 470
    general (g), 473
    as general cognitive capacity, 466
    group-factor theories of, 473
    multiple, 475–76
    nature of, 471–77
    practical, 474
    psychometric approach to, 471–73
    sensory-motor, 391–93
    and structure of mental abilities, 472–73
intelligence quotient (IQ), 466–67
    between-group differences in, 485–89
    black-white differences in, 479, 485–89
    correlation of, among family members, 481–84
    environmental contributions to, 478–79, 481–85, 486–89
    genetic factors in, 478–84, 486–89
    mental retardation and, 468–69
intelligence tests, 458, 464–71
    for adults, 467–68
    age and, 466–67, 470–71
    for children, 465–67
    cultural bias in, 486

in diagnosis and classification of mental retardation, 468–73
group administration of, 468
new developments in, 468
performance vs. verbal, 467
and psychometric approach to study of intelligence, 471–73
interaction, social, *see* social interaction
interference theory of forgetting, 206–7
internal environment, regulation of, *see* homeostasis
internalization, of moral values, 430–31
interneurons, 12, 14, 17
interpersonal learning, 623, 628
interposition, as depth cue, 161
interval scales, A2–A3
introversion, 505, 514
irises (in eyes), 141–42
isolation, 279, 532

James-Lange theory, 345–46
justice, moral reasoning and, 433–34
justification of effort, 334–35
just-noticeable difference (jnd), 128

Kaufman Assessment Battery for Children
(K-ABC), 468
killer cells, 106
kinesthesis, 131
kin selection, altruism and, 321
knowledge:
empiricist-nativist debate on origins of, 124–28
procedural and declarative, 219
sensory processes and, 124–27
spatial, 227–29
Korsakoff's syndrome, 216, 252

language, 257–91
ambiguity in, 2, 263
in aphasics, 36, 285
creative use of, 258–59
to describe personality attributes, 504
as human capacity, 257, 289
interpersonal aspects of, 258, 260–61
and interpersonal nature of beliefs, 328–31
linguistic hierarchy in, 261, 264–69
major properties of, 258–61
manual systems of, 280–82
meaningfulness of, 258, 260
meaning of words in, 264–68
morphemes and words in, 262–63, 272–74
phonemes in, 262, 264, 271–72
phrases and sentences in, 264, 268–69
as reference, 258, 260
standard vs. black English, 486
structure of, 258, 259–60, 261–63
language areas of brain, 36, 285
language learning, 269–90
by aphasics, 285
with changed endowments, 285–89
by children deprived of access to some meanings, 282–83
by chimpanzees, 287–89
critical period for, 279, 285–87
deafness and, 280–82
development of, 269–77
environment and, 278–85
by Helen Keller, 283–85
by isolated children, 279
later stages of, 275–77
without models, 281–82
normal course of, 269–77
one-word speakers and, 272–74, 281
orderly progression of, 390

over- and undergeneralizations in, 273
phoneme discrimination in, 271–72
propositional thought in, 274, 282
second, 286–87
sign language and, 280–82
as skill, 270
social origins of, 270–71
two-word (telegraphic) speakers and, 274–75, 281
by wild children, 278
word meaning in, 272–74, 282–83
languages, similarities between, 257–61
latency of response, 90
latency period, 534
latent learning, 103
lateral hypothalamic region, 55
lateral inhibition, 144–45
lateralization of brain, 37–40
law of effect, 90–91, 95
leadership, 371–74
learned helplessness, 105–7, 588
biological consequences of, 106
learned taste aversions, 109–10
learning, 81–119, 515
abstract concepts in, 115–16
access in, 116–17
adaptive specializations of, 111
by animals vs. humans, 107–13
associations in, 83, 126
in behavior theory, 81–82
behavior therapy and, 618–19
children's capacity for, 388
cognitive theory of, 99–117
form perception and, 181–82
habituation and, 82–83
imprinting and, 420–21
interpersonal, 623
latent, 103
observational, 426–27
skill development and, 233–34
social, 426–27, 440; *see also* socialization
specific, cognitive development and, 407
see also classical conditioning; cognitive development; instrumental conditioning; language
learning; social development
learning curves, 86, 90, 233–34
learning model of psychopathology, 572
left-handers, 37–38
left hemisphere of brain, 32
lateralization and, 37–40
and sexual differences in maturation, 438
legal aspects of psychotherapy, 629–30
lenses (in eyes), 141
lesions, cortical:
amnesia and, 217
in association areas, 33–36
lateralization and, 37
lesions, hypothalamic, 55
lie detection, hypothesis testing and, A21–A22
lie detector tests, 62–63
light:
as stimulus, 141
visible spectrum of, 141, 145–47
limbic system, 29, 30, 63, 113–14
linear perspective, 126, 161, 184–85
line of best fit, 460, A15
linguistic hierarchy and meaning, 264–69
meaning of words in, 264–68
organizing words into meaningful sentences in,
268–69
listening:
context effects in, 175
selective, 179–80
see also hearing

lithium, 610–11
liver, 53
lobes of brain, 29, 32–33
loci, method of, 200
lock-and-key model of synaptic transmission, 22
locomotion, development of, 388–89
see also motor development
logic, 244–54
deductive reasoning and, 244–45, 247
inductive reasoning and, 245–47
longitudinal studies, 470, 545–46
long-term memory, 191
forgetting from, 205–10
retrieval from, 201–5
storage capacity of, 194
transfer from short-term memory into, 195–96
varieties of, 230–31
looming, 163
loudness, wave amplitude and, 135–36
love:
biological basis of, 305–15
companionate, 364
romantic, 363–64
see also attachment, mother-child; male-female
bond

madness:
use of term, 566*n*
see also psychopathology
magic number, 194
Magnetic Resonance Imaging (MRI), 34–35, 579
maintenance dose, 613
maintenance rehearsal, 197–98
majority, conformity and, 366–67
male-female bond:
biological basis of, 305–15
courtship and mating rituals in, 307–8, 310–13
evolution and mating systems in, 310–13
physical attractiveness and, 361–63
physical proximity and, 360
reproduction and timing in, 309–10
sexual choice in, 306–8
similarity and, 361
see also sexual behavior
mammals:
parent-child bonding in, 313–14
temperature regulation in, 48–50
mania, 584, 611, 630
manic-depressive psychosis (bipolar disorder), 573,
583, 586, 610–11
manual skills, development of, 386
manual systems of language, 280–82
many-on-many social interactions, 353, 374–79
many-on-one social interactions, 353, 364–71
MAO (monoamine oxidase) inhibitors, 610
marital therapy, 625
matching hypothesis, 362
matching to sample, 115
mathematical aptitude, sex differences in, 437–39
maturation:
cognitive development as, 406
sexual differences in rate of, 438
mean, statistical (*M*), 459, A8–A9
defined, A8
standard error of, A24
mechanistic world view, 10, 17
median, statistical, A8, A9
medical model of psychopathology, 568–69, 572
medulla, 28
melancholic personality, 506
melatonin, 586
memory, 191–221, 253
as active process, 197–98

persuasive communications, attitudes and, 333–34
PET scans (Positron Emission Tomography), 34, 579
phalaropes, sexual choice in, 308
phenothiazines, 579
phenotype, 479–80
phenylalanine, 480
phenylketonuria (PKU), 480
pheromones, 134
phi phenomenon (stroboscopic movement), 164
phlegmatic personality, 506
phobias, 88, 98, 573, 591
  avoidance learning in, 98
  behavior therapy for, 618–21
  classical conditioning and, 98, 591
phonemes, 262, 264
  infants' discrimination of, 271–72
photographic memory (eidetic imagery), 225–26
phrases, 263, 264
  structure of, 268–69
physical attractiveness, 361–63
  culture and, 58, 362–63
  matching for, 362
physical development, 386–89
  in adolescence, 446
  in embryo, 386–87, 389
physical proximity, 360
physiological arousal, personality and, 514–15
pictorial depth cues, 185
piloerection, 62
pitch, 135, 137–38
  place theory of, 137–38
pituitary gland, 24, 25
placebo effects, 611–13, 630
place theory of pitch, 137–38
pleasure, pain vs., 75–76
"pleasure center," 76
pleasure principle, 529
pluralistic ignorance, 356
Pointillist art, 149
polarization, of cell membranes, 15
polygenic inheritance, 481
polygraph tests, 62–63
polygyny, 312
population, samples and, A5–A6, A24–A25, A26, A27
population growth, 296
positive feedback systems, 46–47
positive reinforcers, 93
positive symptoms of schizophrenia, 580
post-traumatic stress disorder, 594–95, 611
potentiation, 45
praying mantis, 26–27, 139
predation, 300
  altruism and, 320–22
predicates of sentences, 268
predictive validity, of personality tests, 498
prefrontal lobotomy, 614
preoperational period, 392, 393–96
  conservation of quantity and number in, 394–95
  egocentrism in, 395–96, 403
preparedness, 108
prescriptionism, 628
prescriptive rules of grammar, 259
pressure sensations, 131
primacy effect, 195, 196
primates:
  aggression in, 437
  dominance hierarchies in, 303
  rate of growth in, 388
  social cognition in, 318–20
  see also specific primates

primitive features, 167–68
prisoner's dilemma, 376–78
proactive inhibition, 207
probabilities, decision making and, 247–49
problems, well-defined vs. ill-defined, 242–43
problem solving, 231–43
  algorithms and heuristics in, 241–42
  chunking in, 233–36
  by computers, 240–43
  creative thinking in, 239–40
  fixation in, 236–37
  hierarchical organization in, 232–36
  masters vs. beginners in, 234–35
  mental set and, 236–38, 240
  motivation in, 237–38
  obstacles to, 236–38
  perceptual, 175–77
  restructuring in, 239–41
  skill development in, 233–34
  solutions to, 242
  spatial thinking in, 227–29
procedural knowledge, 219
processing information, 240–43, 408–11, 470–71
progesterone, 589
Progressive Matrices Test, 468
prohibitions, internalization of, 431
projection, 531
projection areas, 31–33
projective techniques, 499–502
  incremental validity and, 502
  Rorschach inkblots, 499–500, 501–2
  TAT, 500–502
  validity of, 501–2
proportions, standard error of, A25
propositional thought, 229–30
  in chimpanzees, 288
  language learning and, 274, 279, 282
propositions in sentence meaning, 268–69
prosopagnosias, 35, 155
Protestant Reformation, 557
prototype theory of word meaning, 266–68
proximal stimuli, 125, 159, 164, 180
proximity:
  attraction and, 360
  in perceptual grouping, 171
Prozac, 610
psychoanalysis, psychoanalytic theory, 526–44
  classical, 616–17
  contributions of, 543–44
  cultural absolutism and, 539
  defense mechanisms in, 531–32, 542–43
  dream interpretation in, 535–36, 541–42
  emotional insight in, 623
  evaluation of, 627
  after Freud, 538–39, 617–18
  human nature as viewed in, 526–27, 543–44
  id, ego, and superego in, 529–30
  methodological issues in, 537–38
  modern versions of, 617–18
  origins of, 526–28
  psychosexual development in, 532–35, 540
  recovery of unconscious memories in, 616–17
  reexamination of, 537–44
  repression in, 528, 530–31, 534, 542–43
  sex typing and, 439–40
  somatoform disorders and, 598
  unconscious conflict and, 528–37, 543–44
psychoanalytic model of psychopathology, 572
psychodynamic approach to personality, 494–95, 525–47
  adult personality differences in, 544–47
  coping and the unconscious in, 545–47

coping patterns and mental health in, 545–47
  patterns of neurotic conflict in, 544–45
psychodynamic therapy, 617
psychogenic disorders, 570
psychogenic symptoms, 527
psychological intensity, 127–28
psychological studies:
  selection of subjects for, A5–A7
  types of, A4–A5
psychometric approach to intelligence, 471–73
psychopathology, 564–605
  anxiety disorders, 590–95, 611
  conversion disorders, 570, 598
  definition of, 565
  demonological approach to, 566–67
  diathesis-stress conception and, 574–75, 590
  as disease, 567–71
  dissociative disorders, 595–96
  early mental hospitals and, 567–68
  and historical conceptions of madness, 565–71
  mood disorders, 583–87
  as psychological illness, 569–70
  schizophrenia, 575–83
  scope of, 603
  sociopathy, 601–3
  symptoms of, 572–73
  underlying pathology model of, 571–75
  witchcraft and, 566–67
  see also anxiety disorders; mood disorders; schiz-
    ophrenia; treatment of psychopathology
psychopathy, *see* sociopathy
psychophysics, 127–31
  object of, 127
  sensory intensity and, 127
  signal detection theory and, 129–30
psychophysiological disorders, 64, 597–600
  coronary heart disease, 599–600
  diathesis-stress concept and, 600
psychosexual development, 532–35, 539–40
  Electra complex and, 535
  obstacles to smooth progression in, 533–34
  Oedipus complex and, 533–34, 540
psychosis, 573
psychosurgery, 614
psychotherapy, 572, 615–26
  accountability for, 628–30
  behavior therapy, 618–21, 622–23
  classical psychoanalysis, 616–17
  client-centered, 622
  cognitive, 620–21, 622
  common factors in, 628
  common themes in, 622–23
  cultural competence in, 626
  evaluation of, 626–30
  and expansion of therapeutic goals, 623–26
  group therapy, 624–25
  humanistic, 618, 621–22
  legal aspects of, 629–30
  marital and family therapy, 625
  modern versions of psychoanalysis, 618
  psychodynamic, 617
  repressed memories and, 215
  specific factors in, 628
  as step-by-step process, 623
punishment, in conditioning, 97–98
puzzle boxes, 90

quantity, conservation of, 394–95, 406
quiet sleep, 68

racial-ethnic groups, intelligence and, 486
rage, emergency reaction and, 61–63
rapid eye movement (REM) sleep, 68, 69, 71